C ntral Asi

a Lonely Planet travel survival kit

John King
John Noble
Andrew Humphreys

Central Asia

1st edition

Published by
   Lonely Planet Publications
   Head Office: PO Box 617, Hawthorn, Vic 3122, Australia
   Branches: 155 Filbert St, Suite 251, Oakland, CA 94607, USA
                  10 Barley Mow Passage, Chiswick, London W4 4PH, UK
                  71 bis rue du Cardinal Lemoine, 75005 Paris, France

Printed by
   Colorcraft Ltd, Hong Kong

Photographs by
   Andrew Humphreys   Mark Hannafin
   John King   John Noble

   Front cover: Herders in Tölök River Valley, Kyrgyzstan (John King)
   Title page & Manas illustration: by Theodor Herzen, reproduced with permission of the artist from
      Manas: the Epic Vision of Theodor Herzen

First Published
   June 1996

**Although the authors and publisher have tried to make the information as
accurate as possible, they accept no responsibility for any loss, injury or
inconvenience sustained by any person using this book.**

National Library of Australia Cataloguing in Publication Data

King, John (John S.).
   Central Asia

   Includes index.
   ISBN 0 86442 358 6.

   1. Asia, Central – Guidebooks. I. Humphreys, Andrew, 1965-.
   II. Noble, John, 1951 Oct.11- . III. Title. (Series:
   Lonely Planet travel survival kit)

915.804

John King (JK)

John King grew up in the USA, destined for the academic life (in past incarnations he was a university physics teacher and an environmental consultant), but in a rash moment in 1984 he headed off to China. Since then he has squeaked out a living as a travel writer, encouraged by his wife, Julia Wilkinson, who is also one. Together they and their son Kit split their time at 'home' between south-west England and remoter parts of Hong Kong. John has spent four months in former Soviet Central Asia, eight months in Pakistan and 13 months in China at various times. He is also the author of LP's *Karakoram Highway*, co-author of *Russia, Ukraine & Belarus* (formerly *USSR*), *Pakistan* and *Czech & Slovak Republics* travel survival kits and of the *Prague city guide*, and has helped update *West Asia on a Shoestring*.

For this project John concentrated on Kyrgyzstan, eastern Uzbekistan, Xinjiang and the Karakoram Highway.

John Noble (JN)

John Noble comes from the valley of the River Ribble in northern England. After a decade of itinerant journalism covering everything from weddings by the Ribble to coal mines in Sumatra, he turned to guidebook writing and in 1989 found himself taking on, with John King, Lonely Planet's *USSR* guide. Just when that gargantuan project had finally, irrevocably been handed over to the printers 2½ years later, the country it was about decided to abolish itself. John took a long, deep breath in less unstable parts of the world, and then, hooked into an abiding love-hate relationship with the old Russian empire, came back to write Lonely Planet's *Baltic States* guide, followed by parts of *Russia, Ukraine & Belarus* and this book. He now lives in southern Spain, along with his wife, travel writer Susan Forsyth, and their children Isabella and Jack, where he is working on Lonely Planet's new Spain guide.

John's main turf in this project was Kazakstan, western Uzbekistan and northern Turkmenistan. He also wrote about the Aral Sea and the Semey polygon in the Environment section of the Facts about the Region chapter.

Andrew Humphreys (AH)

Born in England, Andrew stayed around just long enough to complete his studies in architecture before relocating to Egypt. He spent three years in the dust and fumes, documenting Islamic monuments and working for the country's largest English-language magazine, *Cairo Today*. In 1991, he took a circuitous sweep via Jamaica to land in newly-independent Estonia where he began working for the *Tallinn City Paper*, moving on to co-found *The Baltic Outlook*.

Whilst living in Estonia, Andrew updated the Baltic chapters of LP's *Scandinavian & Baltic Europe on a shoestring*, which earned him the dubious privilege of being despatched to Siberia to work on the mammoth *Russia, Ukraine & Belarus*. Central Asia sees him complete his 'post-Soviet trilogy' of LP titles and Andrew has now returned to the Middle East . There he slurps his *borsch* on the beach with the Russian community of Tel Aviv while updating Lonely Planet's guide to Israel.

Andrew concentrated his efforts on this project in southern Turkmenistan, south-east Uzbekistan and war-weary Tajikistan. He also prepared the Arts section.

Acknowledgments

The authors could not have researched and written this book without the help they received from many people throughout Central Asia and at home. Likewise, all those involved in producing this book greatly appreciate the contribution of travellers who put so much effort into writing and telling us of their experiences. These people are fully acknowledged at the back of the book on pages 537-9.

From the Publisher

This book was edited and proofed at the Lonely Planet office in Melbourne by Katie Cody, Anne Mulvaney, Rowan McKinnon, Jane Fitzpatrick and Brigitte Barta. Nicola Daly and Sally Steward produced the Language guide. Indexing was by Rowan McKinnon and Katie Cody. Matt King designed the book and produced many new illustrations with additional help in layout from Tamsin Wilson and Michelle Stamp. Maps were drawn by Jacqui Saunders, Chris Love and Anthony Phelan. Fonts and technical assistance came from Dan Levin. The cover was designed by Simon Bracken and the back cover map was drawn by David Kemp.

Warning & Request

Things change – prices go up, schedules change, good places go bad and bad places go bankrupt – nothing stays the same. So if you find things better or worse, recently opened or long since closed, please write and tell us and help make the next edition better.

Your letters will be used to help update future editions and, where possible, important changes will also be included in a Stop Press section in reprints.

We greatly appreciate all information that is sent to us by travellers. Back at Lonely Planet we employ a hard-working readers' letters team, headed by Julie Young, to sort through the many letters we receive. The best ones will be rewarded with a free copy of the next edition or another Lonely Planet guide if you prefer. We give away lots of books, but, unfortunately, not every letter/postcard receives one.

Contents

Map Legend

BOUNDARIES

.... International Boundary
.... Regional Boundary
.... Disputed Boundary

ROUTES

.... Freeway
.... Highway
.... Major Road
.... Unsealed Road or Track
.... City Road
.... City Street
.... Railway
.... Underground Railway
.... Walking Track
.... Bus Route
.... Ferry Route
.... Cable Car or Chairlift

AREA FEATURES

.... Parks
.... Built-Up Area
.... Pedestrian Mall
.... Market
.... Cemetery
.... Non-Christian Cemetery
.... Beach or Desert
.... Glacier, Ice Cap
.... Mountain Range

HYDROGRAPHIC FEATURES

.... Coastline
.... River, Creek
.... Rapids, Waterfalls
.... Lake, Intermittent Lake
.... Canal
.... Swamp

SYMBOLS

✪ CAPITAL	National Capital
◉ Capital	Regional Capital
⬤ CITY	Major City
● City	City
● Town	Town
● Village	Village

.... Place to Stay, Place to Eat
.... Cafe, Pub or Bar
.... Post Office, Telephone
.... Tourist Information, Bank
.... Transport, Underground Station
.... Museum, Parking
.... Youth Hostel, Camping Ground
.... Church, Cathedral
.... Mosque, Synagogue
.... Buddhist Temple, Hindu Temple
.... Hospital, Police Station

.... Embassy, Petrol Station
.... Airport, Airfield
.... Swimming Pool, Gardens
.... Shopping Centre, Zoo
.... Winery or Vineyard, Picnic Site
.... One Way Street, Route Number
.... Stately Home, Monument
.... Castle, Tomb
.... Cave, Hut or Chalet
.... Mountain or Hill, Lookout
.... Lighthouse, Shipwreck
.... Pass, Spring or Sanatorium
.... Beach, Surf Beach
.... Archaeological Site or Ruins
.... Ancient or City Wall
.... Cliff or Escarpment, Tunnel
.... Railway Station

Note: not all symbols displayed above appear in this book

.....STOP PRESS.....STOP PRESS.....STOP PRESS.....STOP

As this book was going to print, we heard that from 1 January 1996 Uzbekistan was seriously tightening up its visa policies. This has been confirmed by several travel agencies in the UK and Australia, and in fact the Uzbekistan Embassy in London will now only issue visas for a stay that has been fully pre-booked and arranged through the state company for tourism, Uzbektourism, or one of its licensees. They further insist that visitors must be met by a representative of the licensed local agency, so it won't work to pre-book, get the visa and then default on the hotel pre-payment. Prospects are also uncertain for private homestays in the country. If this turns out to be a uniform, strictly enforced policy, you might in future only be able to stay in Uzbektourism's grossly overpriced hotels, and budget travel to many of the Silk Road's finest old sites could come to an untimely end. Stay tuned.

.....STOP PRESS.....STOP PRESS.....STOP PRESS.....STOP

Introduction

The region known loosely as Central Asia or 'Turkestan' is a vast arena of desert, steppe and knotted mountain ranges stretching from the Caspian Sea in the west to Mongolia in the east, from the Siberian forests in the north to the Hindu Kush and the Tibetan plateau in the south. It spans five former Soviet republics and parts of western China. Until just a few years ago it was as inaccessible and unfamiliar to the outside world as Antarctica, thanks in part to its isolation within the former Soviet Union and communist China. Even now, most westerners – if they know where it is at all – think of it as a desert wasteland populated by illiterate nomads. Nothing could be further from the truth.

For more than 2000 years Central Asia has been a meeting ground between Europe and Asia, the locus of ancient east-west trade routes collectively called the Silk Road, and at various points in history a cradle of scholarship, culture and power. It was the board on which the 19th and 20th centuries' greatest geopolitical chess match, the 'Great Game' between imperial Britain and imperial Russia, was played. And it's as geographically diverse as it is historically rich. Along with ferocious deserts it takes in fertile valleys full of shoulder-high pasture, and some of the highest mountain peaks on the planet. The nomadic population has largely been brought to a standstill in thousands of small towns and a score of Russianised oasis-cities whose people are, if not worldly, at least intensely interested in the outside world.

Though the people of Central Asia have had fairly distinct cultural identities for centuries, the separate countries that this book is mostly about – Uzbekistan, Kyrgyzstan, Tajikistan, Turkmenistan and vast Kazakstan – were more or less invented in the 1920s and 1930s as republics of the Soviet Union, and only became sovereign states upon the collapse of that union. Despite serious post-partum blues, Central Asia is again at a

geopolitical pivot-point – a hot political prize, a repository of immense natural wealth, and a reservoir of potential converts to Islam, pan-Turkism or the free market – up for grabs in the midst of Russia, China, the Middle East and south Asia. This former blank on the map is being 'discovered' again by scholars, aid workers, missionaries of every sort, and travellers.

There is of course much that's *not* romantic about the region. What we think of as Central Asia is in many ways a Soviet creation – a set of gerrymandered republics with invented alphabets, designated cultural heroes and oversimplified histories. In the name of Soviet ideals, its people have for two generations been severed from their past and taught to pity their ancestors' ways, which are displayed in condescending museums of history and applied arts, empty architectural monuments and slick music-and-dance troupes. Now they are struggling to cope with the sudden death of those Soviet ideals and the failure of the economic and political life-support system that gave them all a minimal share of the pie.

In this vacuum poverty, unemployment and crime are on the rise, and one state (Tajikistan) has been shattered by civil war. The natural desolation of desert and steppe now seems overlaid with human desolation: impoverished towns and broken-down housing blocks, corrupt and suffocating bureaucracy, ethnic unease and ecological disaster zones like the dying Aral Sea and the Semey nuclear 'polygon'. Everyone wants a new 'tsar' – a strong leader, a revived union, a heroic past, Islam or the free market – to put things right again, and to help with the recovery of their stolen cultural identities.

Not surprisingly, travel here can be a struggle, especially for independent travellers. Getting visas can be like pulling teeth. Hotels tend to be shoddy and overpriced, food cheap but unvarying, transport unpredictable. Outside the cities little English is spoken. Greedy officials are everywhere with their obscure, mutable and sometimes fictional 'regulations'. The widespread use of alcohol can turn the friendliest daytime scene ugly after dark. While it's easy to see the sights safely in a group or with a guide, if you're travelling independently and on the cheap, your relative wealth by local standards creates a steady element of risk.

So why come? In spite of the difficulties, the region's story-book history, its present ferment, and the sense of mutual rediscovery between Central Asians and the rest of the world, make it a gripping place to travel. The ancient pace and Silk Road flavour are still there if you look, especially outside the cities. Open markets in every town seem lifted from the days of Timur, the 14th century despot-turned-cultural-icon whose capital, Samarkand, has become a symbol of Central Asia's past and future potential. The region's backdrop, especially the snowcapped mountains, offers the physically adventurous a wide range of possibilities. While the word 'Islam' makes many westerners nervous, here it's more likely to represent extraordinary, and overwhelming, hospitality than any kind of threat.

Uzbekistan, with the longest settled past, has the most interesting historical and architectural heritage, but is the most like the old USSR and the most difficult for independent travellers. Kyrgyzstan and Kazakstan are the most welcoming, though their attractions are mainly human or geophysical. Turkmenistan is the least familiar and least connected to the outside world. Tajikistan remains the most tantalising because it is presently the most dangerous and therefore least accessible.

As a practical matter, it's easy to burn out (and spend your budget) on the standard hotels-and-monuments route. Combat this by making local friends and getting invited home. You'll understand and remember Central Asia best through individual contacts and insights (and you may also discover how pliant rules and prices can be). This is partly a matter of luck – or of booking up front with overseas 'homestay' agencies – but partly a matter of attitude. Central Asians are softies for a handshake and a *salam aleykhum* (the traditional Islamic greeting, 'Peace be with you'), and Russians for a smile and a few words of pidgin Russian. Most of them are keen to learn about you, to tell you their stories and to help you discover Central Asia.

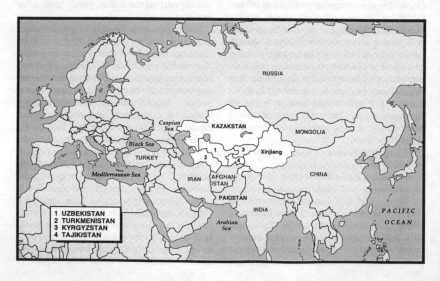

Facts about the Region

HISTORY

Central Asia is perhaps the best place on earth to explore the reality of the phrase 'the sweep of history'. Populations, conquerors, cultures and ideas have swept colourfully across the region's steppes, deserts and mountains for thousands of years. The notion of the Silk Road stresses Central Asia's important linking role as the territory through which the great civilisations of the East and the West made contact and carried on cultural exchange. But Central Asia was, and is, more than just a middle ground, and its cultural history is far more than the sum of the influences brought from the East and the West.

Scholar and writer, Stuart Legg, dubbed Central Asia – together with Mongolia and Siberia – the 'Heartland' and wrote a book with the same title. Here in the heart of the largest landmass on earth, vast steppes provided the one natural resource, grass, required to build one of this planet's most formidable and successful forms of statehood, the nomadic empire. The grass fed horses by the millions, and mounted archers – a Heartland invention – remained the unstoppable acme of open-ground warfare for over 2.5 millennia. The Heartland was a hotbed of social energies and explosions of conquest which reached the farthest corners of Eurasia.

How the settled civilisations on the periphery of the Eurasian continent interacted with successive waves of mounted nomadic hordes is the main theme of the story of Central Asia.

Prehistory & Early History

In the Middle Paleolithic period, from 100,000 to 35,000 years ago, people in Central Asia were isolated from Europe and elsewhere by ice sheets, seas and swamps. The *Homo sapiens neanderthalensis* remains found at Aman-kutan cave near Samarkand date roughly to 100,000 to 40,000 years ago, and are the earliest known human remains in Central Asia.

Cultural continuity begins in the late 3rd millennium BC with the Indo-Iranians, speakers of an unrecorded Indo-European dialect related distantly to English. The Indo-Iranians are believed to have passed through Central Asia on their way from their Indo-European homeland in southern Russia. From Central Asia, groups headed south-east for India and south-west for Iran. These peoples herded cattle, went to battle in chariots, and probably buried their dead nobles in mound-tombs, or *kurgans*. The Tajiks are linguistic descendants of these ancient migrants.

Central Asia's recorded history begins in the 6th century BC, when the large Achaemenid Empire of Iran held three satrapies beyond the Amu-Darya river: Sogdiana, Khorezm and Saka. These territories changed hands and fluctuated in relative importance countless times over the next 2500 years, but their outlines remained principally the same and helped shape the destiny of Asia.

Sogdiana was the land between the Amu-Darya and Syr-Darya, called Transoxiana by the Romans and Mawarannhr by the Arabs. Here Bukhara and Samarkand later flourished. Khorezm lay on the lower reaches of the Amu-Darya south of the Aral Sea, where one day the khans of Khorezm would lord it from the walled city of Khiva until well into the 20th century. Saka (called Semireche by the Russians), extending indefinitely over the steppes beyond the Syr-Darya and including the Tian Shan range, was the home of nomadic warriors until the Heartland way of life ended in the late 19th century.

Alexander the Great

In 330 BC this former pupil of Aristotle, from Macedonia, led his army to a key victory over the last Achaemenid emperor, Darius III, in Mesopotamia. With the defeat

Alexander the Great

right-hand general, Cleitus. He tried to adopt the dress and autocratic court ritual of an Oriental despot. His Greek and Macedonian followers refused to prostrate themselves before him, however.

When he died in Babylon in 323, Alexander had no named heir. But his legacy included nothing less than the West's perennial romance with exploration and expansion.

Chang Ch'ien

The aftermath of Alexander's short-lived Macedonian Empire in Central Asia saw an increase in East-West cultural exchange and a chain reaction of nomadic migrations. The Hellenistic successor states disseminated the aesthetic values of the classical world deep into Asia, while trade brought such goods as the walnut to Europe. Meanwhile, the grassy plains of the Heartland had been the scene of fomentation amongst the nomad tribes.

Along the border of Mongolia and China, the expansion of the warlike Hsiung-nu confederacy (probably the forebears of the Huns) uprooted the Yüeh-chih of western China (the Yüeh-chih ruler was slain and his skull made into a drinking cup). The Yüeh-chih were sent packing westward along the Ili river into Saka, whose displaced inhabitants in turn bore down upon the Sogdians to the south.

The Hsiung-nu were also irritating more important powers than the Yüeh-chih. Though protected behind its gradually expanding Great Wall since about 250 BC, China eagerly sought tranquillity on its barbarian frontier. In 138 BC the Chinese emperor sent a brave solitary volunteer emissary, Chang Ch'ien, to persuade the Yüeh-chih king to form an alliance against the Hsiung-nu.

Chang Ch'ien's 13 year voyage is the first great traveller's saga of Central Asia. Taken prisoner by the Hsiung-nu immediately after departure, he spent 10 years in captivity, then escaped and wandered west over the Pamir to the Ferghana Valley. There the fertile land yielded the pleasures of the vine, knowledge of which Chang Ch'ien brought back to

of the Persian nemesis, Alexander (356-323 BC) warmed up to conquest. By 329 he had reached modern Kabul. Crossing the Hindu Kush, he pressed northward across the Oxus (Amu-Darya) and proceeded via Marakanda (Samarkand) towards the Jaxartes (Syr-Darya), which he crossed in order to crush Scythian defenders. Perhaps in celebration he founded the city of Alexandria Eschate (Farthest Alexandria) near the site of modern Khojand.

Alexander met the most stubborn resistance of his career in the Sogdians, who in concert with the Massagetes, a Saka tribe, revolted and held the mountainous parts of their homeland until 328.

The rebels' fall was a poignant one: attacked and defeated at their last redoubt, the 'Rock of Sogdiana' (whose location today is a mystery), they yielded the beautiful Bactrian princess Roxana into captivity, and marriage to Alexander. The Macedonian generalissimo's sojourn in Central Asia was marked by a growing megalomania. It was at Marakanda that Alexander murdered his

China. Other discoveries were in store – the Heavenly Horses, untiring tiger-striped steeds which sweated blood and captured the imagination of Chinese militarists and poets for centuries to come; booming trade in Hellenistic Bactria, which featured standardised coinage in the likeness of the king; and reports of a rich, distant land called India.

The Yüeh-chih had settled down in Bactria to a peaceable life of trade and agriculture, and no longer had an axe to grind with the Hsiung-nu. But Chang Ch'ien's mission was still a great success of Chinese diplomacy and exploration. The stage had been set for major East-West contact.

The Silk Road

No one knows for sure when the miraculously fine, light, soft, strong, shimmering, sensuous fabric spun from the cocoon of the *Bombyx* caterpillar first reached the West from China. In the 4th century BC, Aristotle described a fibre that may have been Chinese silk. Some people give credit for history's first great industrial espionage coup to a Chinese princess who was departing to marry a Khotanese king: the legend goes that she hid live worms and cocoons from customs agents so she would be able to wear silk in her distant home. But even after the secret of sericulture arrived in the Mediterranean world, the Chinese consistently exercised the advantage of centuries-acquired know-how. Chinese silk was by far the best. Writing a short while after the time of Christ, Pliny the Elder was scandalised by the luxurious, transparent cloths which allowed Roman women to be 'dressed and yet nude'. He also fell wide of the mark in describing silk's origin and processing. The Chinese, had they known, would no doubt have been pleased.

Parthia, on the Iranian plateau, was the most voracious foreign consumer of Chinese silk at the close of the 2nd century BC. In about 105, Parthia and China exchanged embassies and inaugurated official bilateral trade along the caravan route that lay between them. With this the Silk Road was born, in fact if not in name.

It was said to take 200 days to traverse the route, though geographically the Silk Road was a complex and shifting proposition. It was no single road, but rather a web of caravan tracks that threaded through some of the highest mountains and bleakest deserts on earth. Though the road map expanded over the centuries, the network had its main eastern terminus at the Chinese captial Ch'ang-an (modern Xian); west of there, the route divided at Dunhuang, one branch skirting the dreaded Taklamakan desert to the north through Turfan, Kucha and Aksu, while the other headed south via Khotan and Yarkand. The two forks met again in Kashgar, whence the trail headed up to any of a series of passes confronting the traveller who attempted to cross the Pamir and Tian Shan (one pass again in use today is the Torugart on the border with Kyrgyzstan).

Beyond the mountains, the Ferghana Valley fed westward through Kokand, Samarkand and Bukhara, past Merv and on to Iran, the Levant and Constantinople. Goods reached transshipment points on the Black and Mediterranean seas, where caravans took on cargo for the march back eastward over the same tracks. In the middle of the network, major branches headed south over the Karakoram range to India and north via the Ili river across the Saka steppes.

Goods heading west and goods heading east did not fall into discrete bundles. In fact there was no 'through traffic'; caravanners were mostly short and medium-distance haulers who marketed and took on freight along a given beat according to their needs and inclinations. At any given time any portion of the network might be beset by war, robbers or natural disaster. As with motion in an anthill, trends are visible when one steps back. In general, the eastern end was enriched by the importation of gold, silver, ivory, jade and other precious stones, wool, Mediterranean coloured glass (an industrial mystery originally as inscrutable to the Chinese as silk was in the West), grapes and wine, spices and – an early Parthian craze –

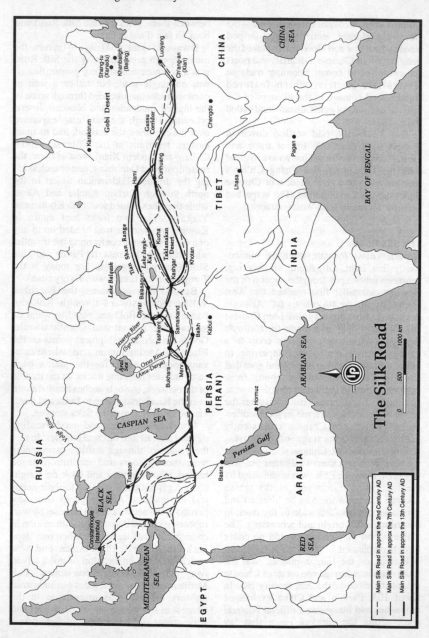

The Silk Road

- - - Main Silk Road in approx the 2nd Century AD
——— Main Silk Road in approx the 7th Century AD
——— Main Silk Road in approx the 13th Century AD

0   500   1000 km

acrobats and ostriches. Goods enriching the western end were silk, porcelain, spices, gems and perfumes. And in the middle lay Central Asia, a great clearinghouse which provided its native beasts – horses and two-humped camels – to keep the goods flowing in both directions.

The Silk Road gave rise to unprecedented trade, but its true glory and unique status in human history were the result of the interchange of ideas, technologies and religions that occurred among the very different cultures that used it. Religion alone presents an astounding picture of diversity and tolerance that would be the envy of any modern democratic state. Manichaeism, Zoroastrianism, Buddhism, Nestorian Christianity, Judaism, Confucianism, Taoism and the shamanism of grassland nomads coexisted and in some cases mingled, until the coming of Islam.

The Kushans
The peaceable, put-upon Yüeh-chih finally came into their own in the 1st century BC when their descendants, the Kushan Dynasty, converted to Buddhism. The Kushan Empire controlled northern India, Afghanistan and Sogdiana from its core in the Gandhara region of north-west Pakistan. At its height in the first three centuries after

Christ, it was one of the four great powers of the world, along with Rome, China and Parthia.

Vigorous trade on the Silk Road helped spread Kushan culture. The rich Kushan coinage is concrete testimony to this classic Silk Road power's lively religious ferment: the coins bear images of Greek, Roman, Buddhist, Iranian and Hindu deities. The art of the empire fused Iranian imperial imagery, Buddhist iconography and Roman realism. It was carried out from Gandhara over the mountainous maze of deepest Asia to the farthest corners of Transoxiana, Tibet and the Tarim basin. Indian, Tibetan and Chinese art were permanently affected.

Sassanids to Samanids
For a thousand years after the birth of Christ, Central Asia was the scene of pendulum-like shifts of power between the nomadic hordes of the Heartland and the sedentary civilisations of Eurasia's periphery. Both sought to profit from Central Asia's long-distance trade routes. With the push and pull of a piston gathering steam, the continent's two major lifestyles played an extended overture to the Mongol conquest. Meanwhile the Turks, namesake of today's Turkestan, appeared on the scene at this time.

The Way of the Pilgrim
Travelling through Chinese Turkestan with insufficient documents along a string of tenuously Han-controlled frontier outposts, the lone traveller is repeatedly asked by officials to return to the safety of China proper. At the jumping-off place, a sympathetic local governor burns his orders to seize the man and tells him to make a run for it. At a loose end, the traveller meets a self-styled local guide with a plan to get him across the border. With no choice but to trust the man, he follows the guide, who backs out en route and leaves him stranded in the middle of a dreadful stretch of desert.

Sound like a recent travel story? Guess again. This scenario took place in 630 AD, when a tall, handsome, 28-year-old Buddhist monk named Hsüan-tsang (602-664) set out from China for the holy places of India, the homeland of his faith. In his day, the available Chinese copies of Buddhist sacred texts were corrupt and inaccurate. In visiting India, his most pious wish was to procure good copies of the *sutras* to take back to China.

In the 16 years of his pilgrimage, Hsüan-tsang bracketed his grand tour of Indian sacred sites with extensive travels through Central Asia. Turfan, Kucha, the Bedel pass, Lake Issyk-Kul, the Chu valley (near present-day Bishkek), Tashkent, Samarkand, Balkh and Khotan were all blessed by the footsteps of the pilgrim, whom Buddhists devotedly call Tripitaka. ∎

The Silk Road's first flower faded by about 200 AD, as the Chinese, Roman, Parthian and Kushan empires went into decline. Sogdiana came under the control of the Sassanid empire of Iran. As the climate along the middle section of the Silk Road became drier, the Heartland nomads increasingly sought wealth by plundering, taxing and conquering their settled neighbours. The Sassanids lost their Inner Asian possessions in the 4th century to the Huns, who ruled a vast area of Central Asia at the same time that Attila was scourging Europe.

The Huns were followed south across the Syr-Darya by the Western Turks (the western branch of the empire of the so-called Kök Turks or Blue Turks), who in 559 made an alliance with the Sassanids and ousted the Huns. The Western Turks, who had arrived in the area from their ancestral homeland in southern Siberia, nominally controlled the reconquered region. The mixing of the Western Turks' nomadic ruling class with the sedentary Sogdian elite over the next few centuries produced a remarkable creole group in the cities. The populations thus invigorated by tolerant interchange would need every ounce of courage they could muster to weather the coming centuries of turmoil.

When the Western Turks faded in the late 7th century, an altogether new and formidable kind of power was waiting to fill the void – the religious army. The new faith was Islam. Bursting out of Arabia just a few years after the Prophet Muhammad's death, the Muslim armies rolled through Persia in 642 but met stiff resistance from the Turks of Transoxiana. The power struggle in between the Amu-Darya and Syr-Darya rivers briefly placed the Türgesh Turks in control, while Arab armies spread east and south, to occupy Kashgar and northern India by 714.

China, meanwhile, had revived under the Tang Dynasty. The Tang presence in 8th century Central Asia was a classic image of great-power expansionism, with colonial governors and over-extended expeditionary forces policing the dynasty's interests outside its borders, deep into Sogdiana,

Lost Battle, Lost Secrets

The Chinese lost big to the Arabs at the Battle of Talas in 751. But to add insult to injury, some of the Chinese rounded up after the battle were no ordinary prisoners: they were expert at the crafts of paper and silk making. Soon China's best-kept secrets of producing high-quality silk cloth were giving the Arabs' silk makers in Persia a commercial advantage all over Europe. It was the first mortal blow to the Silk Road. Paper, meanwhile, arrived in the Mediterranean from Talas at a moment that couldn't have been better if planned: just in time to help the Muslims develop and disseminate their vibrant culture. ■

Kashmir and even Bactria. Provided the Chinese and the Arabs avoided confrontation, the resulting security on the trade routes meant more wealth and prosperity for everybody.

But one Chinese viceroy wanted more than his share, and murdered the khan of the Tashkent Turks to get it. It was perhaps the most costly incident of skulduggery in Chinese history. The enraged Turks were joined by the opportunistic Arabs and Tibetans; in 751 they squeezed the Chinese forces into the valley of the Talas river (in present-day Kazakstan and Kyrgyzstan) and sent them flying back across the Tian Shan. Many soldiers and colonists were taken prisoner. From the south the Tibetan Empire moved quickly to exert its control over vast areas of the Tarim basin.

From the north, the Uyghur Turks swept down to make their debut as saviours of the Tang throne. As a direct result of their political alliance with Tang China, the Uyghurs began to live the settled and literate life which later bore the first flowering of Turkic culture.

After Talas, the Arab's Central Asian territories receded rapidly in the wake of local rebellions. By the 9th century, Transoxiana had given rise to the peaceable and affluent Samanid Dynasty. It generously encouraged the development of Persian culture while remaining strictly allied with the Sunni Caliph of Baghdad. It was under the Samanids that Bukhara grew into a world centre of Muslim culture and garnered the epithet 'Pillar of Islam'. Some of the Islamic world's best scholars were nurtured in its 113 medressas, including the physician Abu Ali ibn-Sina (Avicenna), the mathematician and encyclopaedist al-Beruni (who is said to have predicted the existence of the New World five centuries before Columbus reached it), and many poets and writers.

Qarakhanids to Karakitay
By the early 10th century, internal strife at court had weakened the Samanid Dynasty and opened the door for two Turkic usurpers to divide up the empire: the Ghaznavids in Khorasan south of the Amu-Darya, and the Qarakhanids in Transoxiana and the steppe region beyond the Syr-Darya. The Qarakhanids are credited with finally converting the populace of Central Asia to Islam. They held sway from three mighty capitals: Balasagun (now Burana in Kyrgyzstan) in the centre of their domain, Talas (now Zhambyl in Kazakstan) in the west, and Kashgar in the east. Bukhara continued to shine, and Qarakhanid Kashgar was the home of rich culture and science.

One luminary of the 11th century was the scholar Mahmud al-Kashgari. He drew a remarkably accurate map of the world with his hometown, Barskoön on Lake Issyk-Kul, at the centre. He also compiled a comparative dictionary of the Turkic languages which remains a vital resource for linguists.

The Qarakhanids and Ghaznavids coveted each other's lands. In the mid-11th century, while they were busy invading each other, they were caught off guard by a third Turkic horde, the Seljuqs, who annihilated both after pledging false allegiance to the Ghaznavids. In the Seljuqs' heyday their sultan had himself invested as emperor by the caliph of Baghdad. The empire was vast. On the east it bordered the lands of the Buddhist Karakitay, who had swept into Balasagun and Kashgar from China; to the west it extended all the way to the Mediterranean and Red seas.

(When the Seljuqs appeared on the scene as vassals of the Ghaznavid Sultan Mahmud, they were asked how many troops they would be able to field as auxiliaries in the war with the Qarakhanids. One can only imagine the scene of restrained terror around the sultan's throne when the Seljuqs announced the result of their head-count: no fewer than 200,000 men! It is doubtful whether Sultan Mahmud had a single good

The Legends of Prester John
As beleaguered European Crusaders hunkered down in Palestine and Syria facing the prospect of a war about as winnable as the Vietnam War, they took heart from rumours of a far-flung ally. The talk was of Prester (or Presbyter, meaning Priest) John, a powerful Christian king in the East who was preparing to smash his way through Persia and Armenia and join ranks with the Europeans against the Muslims.

Prester John never existed, but stories about him were varied and durable – passed along by Saracen-bashers from the mid-11th to the late 14th centuries.

The Buddhist Karakitay have a footnote place in world folklore for their probable role in forming this legend. They surely were enemies of the Muslim powers of their day. The legend very likely rested on the simple facts that the Karakitay rulers had crushed the Seljuq Turk empire and had a favourable attitude towards Nestorian Christianity. The Karakitay rulers bore a title which in Hebrew and Syriac may have been transliterated to sound like the Latin name *Johannes*, or John. Later the Mongols, the scourge of Islam, were also reported to be lenient on Nestorian Christians. Wishful thinking and millennial fervour smoothed over the gaps in truth and cemented the legend of the priest-king Prester John. ■

night's sleep for the brief remainder of his life.)

An incurable symptom of Heartland dynasties through the ages was their near inability to survive the inevitable disputes of succession. The Seljuqs lasted a century before their weakened line succumbed to the Karakitay and to the Seljuqs' own rearguard vassals, the Khorezmshahs. From their capital at Gurganj (present-day Konye-Urgench), the Khorezmshahs burst full-force into the tottering Karakitay. They emerged as rulers of all Transoxiana and much of the Muslim world as well.

And so Central Asia might have continued in a perennial state of forgettable wars. As it is, the Khorezmshahs are still remembered primarily as the unlucky stooge left holding the red cape when the angry bull was released.

Mongol Terror, Mongol Peace

Jenghiz Khan felt he had all the justification in the world to ransack Central Asia. In 1218 a Khorezmian governor in Otrar (now in Kazakstan) received a delegation from Jenghiz to inaugurate trade relations. Scared by distant reports of the new Mongol menace, the governor assassinated them in cold blood. Up until that moment Jenghiz, the intelligent khan of the Mongols who had been lately victorious over Chung-tu (now Beijing), had been carefully weighing the alternative strategies for expanding his power: commerce versus conquest. Then came the crude Otrar blunder – and the rest is history.

In early 1219 Jenghiz placed himself at the head of an estimated 200,000 men and began to ride west from his Altay mountain stronghold. By the next year his armies had sacked

Jenghiz Khan & the Mongol Horde

The reign of Jenghiz Khan (1167-1227) is all the more remarkable for the fact that he started with nothing. The story (as preserved in the Mongolian *Secret History*) goes that the boy Temujin was born with noble blood in a clan down on its luck. His fatherless childhood was an unending series of hardships as he hid and fled from rival tribe leaders bent on extinguishing his line. This experience bred a certain hardness of heart in Temujin: he killed his half-brother in cold blood when still in his teens.

With a combination of skill, luck and chutzpah perhaps unmatched by anyone before or since, Temujin managed to bring together a group of loyal tribes around his stamping-ground, the Orkhon river region. By the age of 39 he was elected supreme khan, having taken the name Jenghiz (Mongolian for 'ocean') and it seems the ruler had no intention of stopping until his Heartland energy had inundated the world, like the oceans towards which his ambitions were expanding.

His war/state machine was a confederation of both Mongol and Turkic tribes, and hence the group he controlled is correctly called Mongol Tatars (the Western term *Tartar* comes from *Tatar* via association with *Tartaros,* the Greek name for Hell, from whence the barbarians were said to have sprung). Once things got rolling, ethnic Mongols actually made up a very small percentage of the fighting force outside Mongolia, mainly occupying command positions.

When Jenghiz Khan's realm disintegrated a generation after his death, it was the beginning of the end for the Heartland, and the steppe was gradually eclipsed as a factor in world history. This was partly because the Mongol conquerors implanted the techniques necessary for victory among the peoples they conquered. The settled states of the Eurasian periphery, adopting and adapting horse warfare, began to raise armies that could challenge the steppe invaders. Over the centuries, these states combined technological and military superiority in a new way. Eventually their expanding empires devoured the steppe. Grass, after centuries of enjoying special geopolitical status, became just a plant again.

Social historians point to Mongol roots in medieval chivalry. The horseback military culture of the Mongol elite was adapted and changed by their vassal rulers in Europe, acquiring the air of refined gallantry and romance associated with knights of old. ■

Khojand and Otrar (the murderous governor was dispatched with savage cruelty in Jenghiz's presence), and Bukhara soon followed.

It was in that brilliant city, as soldiers raped and looted and horses trampled Islamic holy books in the streets, that the unschooled Jenghiz ascended to the pulpit in the chief mosque and preached to the congregation. His message: 'I am God's punishment for your sins'. Such shocking psychological warfare is perhaps unrivalled in history. This was no heavy metal rock video, but the real thing.

Bukhara was burned to the ground, and the Mongol hosts swept on to conquer and plunder Samarkand, Merv, Termez, Kabul, Balkh and, eventually under Jenghiz's generals and heirs, most of Eurasia.

Methods were bloody, brutal, meticulously destructive and, according to historians, each conceived with a definite goal in mind. For instance, in massacring populations (a common practice only when cities resisted), Mongol officers were instructed to spare artisans, architects, clerks and other professionals; these were appointed to run the empire as they knew how. And the Mongol armies were employed with an understanding of grand strategy which not a single opposing general could even remotely match. The condescending western belief that the uncivilised, almost subhuman Tartars conquered the civilised world by force of overwhelming numbers may have contributed to the persistent schism between East and West.

It is difficult to deny that Central Asian settled civilisation took a serious blow, from which it only began to recover 600 years later under Russian colonisation. The Mongols' ravages were largely to blame, while other circumstances also caused damage. Jenghiz's descendants controlling Persia favoured Shia Islam over Sunni Islam, a development which over the centuries isolated Central Asia from the currents of the rest of the Sunni Muslim world.

But there was stability, law and order under the *Pax Mongolica*. Like their numer-

Jenghiz Khan, the Mongolian warrior-ruler, mobilised a huge army of cavalry and devastated the empire that is now Uzbekistan.

ous nomadic predecessors, it was a cherished wish of the Mongols to sit astride flourishing trade routes. Jenghiz Khan perceived that his large empire would not survive him without swift, reliable communications. To achieve these ends he laid down a thorough network of guard and post stations, employed express mail riders who could cover over 200 miles a day, and gave tax breaks to traders. In 20th century terms, the streets were safe and the trains ran on time. The resulting modest flurry of trade on the Silk Road was the background to many famous medieval travellers' journeys, including the greatest of them all, Marco Polo's.

On Jenghiz Khan's death in 1227, his empire was divided among his sons. By tradition the most distant lands, stretching as far as Ukraine and Moscow and including western and most of northern Kazakstan, would have gone to the eldest son, Jochi, had Jochi not died before his father. They went instead to Jochi's sons, Batu and Orda, and came to be known collectively as the Golden Horde. The second son, Chaghatai, got the

The Travelling Polos

In the 1250s Venice was predominant in the Mediterranean and looking for new commercial routes. The Venetian brothers Nicolo and Maffeo Polo set out to do some itinerant trading. Sailing from Constantinople with a cargo of precious stones, they made their way to the Crimea. Choice business deals followed and took them gradually up the Volga (they stayed a year at the Mongol khan's encampment), eastward across the steppes, south to Bukhara (for a three year stay), then across Central Asia to Karakorum (now in Mongolia), the seat of Kublai Khan, grandson of Jenghiz.

Kublai welcomed the Europeans warmly and questioned them at length about life and statecraft in Europe. Such was the style of hospitality on the steppe that the khan couldn't bear to let them go (modern travellers know similar treatment!). The Polos remained at Kublai's court for some four years.

In the end Kublai made them ambassadors to the Pope in Rome. Always searching for worthy doctrines from settled civilisations, Kublai requested that the Pope send him 100 of his most learned priests. They were to argue the merits of their faith over others, and if they succeeded, Kublai and his whole empire would convert to Christianity. It took the Polos three difficult years to get home; when they arrived, no one believed their stories.

Marco Polo, the teller of the world's most famous travel tale, was not born when his father Nicolo and uncle Maffeo set out on their journey. When they returned he was a motherless teenager. After a couple of years the elder Polos set off once more for Kublai's court, this time with Marco along.

The Pope had supplied only two monks, and they stayed behind in Armenia when the going got tough. It is tempting to conjecture how the fate of Eurasia might have been different if the requested 100 doctors of religion had shown up at Karakorum and converted the entire Mongol Empire. But it is more probable that they would have been politely detained and made into imperial bureaucrats. The Mongols liked to use the services of foreigners whenever possible.

The Polos made their way from Hormuz on the Persian coast, to Balkh, and on through the Hindu Kush and Pamir (stopping by Lake Karakul, now in Tajikistan, on the way), then on past Kashgar, Yarkand and the southern route around the Taklamakan desert, reaching China via Dunhuang and the Gansu Corridor. They found the khan dividing his time between Khanbaligh (now Beijing) and his nearby summer capital of Shang-tu (Xanadu of the Coleridge poem).

Marco was exceptionally intelligent and observant, and Kublai took a great liking to him. He was soon made a trusted advisor and representative of the ageing khan. The three Polos spent about 16 years in China; Marco travelled far afield and brought the khan news of his far-flung and exotic empire, little of which he had seen.

The Polos were only allowed to go home when they agreed to to escort a Mongol princess on her way to be married in Persia. To avoid long hardship the party took the sea route from the east coast of China around India and up the Gulf. Back in Venice, *still* no one believed the Polos' tales.

Many years later during a war with Genoa, Marco Polo was captured in a naval battle. While in prison he dictated the story of his travels. The resulting book has become the most-read travel account ever written. Hounded all his life by accusations that the exotic world he described was fictitious, Marco Polo was even asked to recant on his deathbed. His answer: 'I have not told the half of what I saw.' ■

next most distant portion, including most of Kazakstan, Uzbekistan and western Xinjiang; this came to be known as the Chaghatai khanate. The share of the third son, Ogedei, seems to have eventually been divided between the Chaghatai khanate and the Mongol heartland inherited by the youngest son, Tolui. Tolui's portion formed the

basis for his son Kublai Khan's Yüan dynasty in China.

Unlike the Golden Horde in Europe and the Yüan Dynasty, the Chaghatai khans tried to preserve their nomadic lifestyle, complete with the khan's roving tent encampment as 'capital city'. But as the rulers spent more and more time in contact with the Muslim collaborators who administered their realm, the Chaghatai line inevitably began to settle down. They even made motions towards conversion to Islam. It was in a fight over this issue, in the mid-1300s, that the khanate split in two, with the Muslim Chaghatais holding Transoxiana and the conservative branch retaining the Tian Shan, Kashgaria (the region around Kashgar at the west end of the Taklamakan desert) and the vast steppes north and east of the Syr-Darya – an area collectively known as Moghulistan.

Timur & the Timurids

One clear sign of the perennial viability and vitality of the steppe-based, nomadic-military form of government was that it appeared like crab grass at any crack in the status quo. The fracturing of the Mongol Empire immediately led to resurgence of the Turkic peoples. From one minor tribe near Samarkand arose a tyrant's tyrant, Timur ('the Lame', or Tamerlane). After assembling an army and wresting Transoxiana from Chaghatai rule, Timur went on a spectacular nine year rampage which ended in 1395 with modern-day Iran, Iraq, Syria, eastern Turkey and the Caucasus at his feet. He also despoiled northern India (the founder of India's Moghul Dynasty, Babur, was his grandson).

All over his realm, Timur plundered riches and captured artisans and poured them into his capital at Samarkand. The city grew, in stark contrast to his conquered lands, into a lavish showcase of treasure and pomp. The postcard skyline of today's Samarkand dates to Timur's reign, as do many fine works of painting and literature. Foreign guests of Timur's, including the Spanish envoy Ruy Gonzales de Clavijo, took home stories of enchantment and barbarity which for centuries fed the West's dream of remote Samarkand.

Timur claimed indirect kinship with Jenghiz Khan, and his exploits certainly show that he was a pretender to Jenghiz's destiny. But it seems he had none of his forerunner's good sense and gift for statecraft. History is strange: both conquerors

Business Bypass
The last chapter of the Silk Road's dominant role more or less ended with Timur's line. The coup de grâce to that once-glorious artery was the opening of sea trading routes between Europe and Asia. These had begun with a famous wrong-way attempt, the groping Asia-bound voyage of one of Marco Polo's most admiring readers – Christopher Columbus. ■

savagely slaughtered hundreds of thousands of innocent people, yet one is remembered as a great ruler and the other not. The argument goes that Timur's bloodbaths were insufficiently linked to specific political or military aims. On the other hand, Timur is considered the more cultured and religious of the two men. At any rate, Timur died an old man at Otrar in 1405, having just set out in full force to conquer China.

Important effects of Timur's reign can still be traced. For instance, when he pounded the army of the Golden Horde in southern Russia, Timur created a disequilibrium in the bloated Mongol empire which led to the seizure of power by its vassals, the petty and fragmented Russian princes. This was the pre-dawn of the Russian state. Like the mammals after the dinosaurs, Russia had small beginnings.

For a scant century after Timur's death his descendants ruled on separately in small kingdoms and duchies. From 1409 until 1449, Samarkand was governed by the conqueror's mild, scholarly grandson, Ulughbek. Gifted in mathematics and astronomy, he built a large celestial observatory and attracted scientists who gave the city lustre as a centre of learning for years to come (in the end, Ulughbek was the victim of a cultural and religious backlash, and beheaded as part of a plot that involved his own son Abdul Latif).

The Timurids were generous patrons of art and literature. In addition to Persian, a Turkic court language came into use, called

Chaghatai, which survived for centuries as a Central Asian lingua franca.

Uzbeks & Kazaks

Modern Uzbekistan and Kazakstan, the two principal powers of post-Soviet Central Asia, eye each other warily across the rift dividing their two traditional lifestyles: sedentary agriculture (Uzbeks) and nomadic pastoralism (Kazaks). Yet these two nations now jockeying for influence in Central Asia are closely akin, and parted ways with a family killing.

The family in question was the dynasty of the Uzbek khans. These rulers, one strand of the modern Uzbek people, had a pedigree reaching back to a grandson of Jenghiz Khan and an original territory in southern Siberia. In the 14th century they converted to Islam, gathered strength, and started moving south. Under Abylqayyr (or Abu al-Khayr) Khan they reached the north bank of the Syr-Darya, across which lay the declining Timurid rulers in Transoxiana. But Abylqayyr had enemies within his own family. The two factions met in battle in 1468, and Abylqayyr was killed and his army defeated.

After this setback, Abylqayyr's grandson Muhammad Shaybani brought the Uzbek khans to power once more. He invaded Transoxiana and established Uzbek control over the territory between the Syr-Darya and Amu-Darya – the same land which Alexander and Ptolemy had known as Transoxiana, and which is now Uzbekistan. Abylqayyr's rebellious kinsmen became the forefathers of the Kazak khans.

The Uzbeks gradually adopted the sedentary agricultural life best suited to the fertile river valleys they occupied. Settled life involved cities, which entailed administration, literacy, learning and – wrapped up with all of these – Islam. The Shaybanid Dynasty, which ruled until the end of the 16th century, attempted to excel the Timurids in religious devotion and to carry on their commitment to artistic patronage. But the Silk Road had disappeared, usurped by spice ships, and Central Asia's economy had entered full

decline. As prosperity fell, so did the region's importance as centre of the Islamic world. The Astrakhanid khans and Iranian Safavids held sway over the benighted remains of Transoxiana until the mid-18th century.

The Kazaks, meanwhile, stayed home on the range and flourished as nomadic herders. Their experience of urban civilisation and organised Islam remained slight compared to their Uzbek cousins. By the 16th century the Kazaks had solidly filled a power vacuum on the old Saka steppes between the Ural and Irtysh rivers and established what was to be the world's last nomadic empire. In their heyday in the late 15th and 16th centuries the Kazaks controlled a vast region of grassland with as many horse soldiers as Jenghiz Khan and the Seljuqs had commanded.

Inevitably the political 'cell division' of the nomads produced three distinct Kazak groups or hordes, each centred in a separate area on the steppe (the word *horde,* which conjures up images of immense swarms of people, comes through French from the Turkic word *orda,* meaning the yurt or pavilion where a khan held his court). The Great Horde roamed the steppes of the Jeti-suu region (Russian: Semireche) north of the Tian Shan; the Middle Horde occupied the grasslands extending east from the Aral Sea; and the Little Horde nomadised west of there as far as the Ural river.

In good times, such as the reigns of Qasym Khan and his son Haq Nazar in the 16th century, the Kazak hordes were a unified nation acting under the firm control of a single khan. Unity brought military might and expansion; the Kazaks menaced the dying Chaghatai khanate of the Tian Shan and Kashgaria, invaded Transoxiana, and even entered Samarkand as conquerors. But during the years when the power of the principal khans waned and the individual hordes split apart, the Kazaks suffered badly at the hands of another steppe power whose star was briefly on the rise.

The Zhungarian Empire

The Oyrats were a western Mongol tribe who had been converted to Tibetan Buddhism.

✿ o o ✿ o o ✿ o o ✿ o o ✿ o o ✿

Epic Echoes of the Oyrats
The Oyrat people were mostly exterminated when Manchu forces shattered the Zhungarian Empire in 1758. But their memory has been preserved by the Kazaks and by their mountain-dwelling relatives the Kyrgyz, who both suffered under the Oyrats' ruthless predations. The medium was epic poetry. Probably first the Kazaks, then the Kyrgyz, began to weave their heroic songs into reflections of their fierce and seemingly endless struggle against the Mongols. With the name of the ageless foes transformed along the way to Kalmak, the Kyrgyz epic poems of the *Manas* cycle have preserved the general national anxiety (though few actual historical details) from a time when the Oyrat Mongols of the Zhungarian Empire seemed poised to crush all resisters.

Descendants of the Oyrats continue to live in China and in the Altay Republic in Russia. ■

✿ o o ✿ o o ✿ o o ✿ o o ✿ o o ✿

Their day in the sun came when they subjugated eastern Kazakstan, the Tian Shan, Kashgaria and western Mongolia to form the Zhungarian (or Dzungarian) Empire (1635-1758). During this time the Oyrats exploited the weaknesses of their neighbors well, and sent alarms sounding through the courts of Manchu (Qing) China and Russia. Russia's frontier settlers were forced to pay heavy tribute, China lost large amounts of territory, east Turkestan and Tibet were invaded, and the Kazak hordes – with their boundless pasturage beyond the mountain gap known as the Zhungarian Gate – were cruelly and repeatedly pummelled.

All this continued until the death of the Zhungarian emperor Galdan Tseren, when – surprise – a struggle for the succession caught the inheritors off guard. Alert for an opportunity to make an economical strike, in 1758 the exasperated Manchu Chinese emperor took a large force and fell upon the Oyrat armies. The Zhungarian state was liquidated and Oyrat men, women and children were massacred to a fraction of their former population.

Central Asia after the fall of the Zhungarian Empire was an anarchic place, for the most part lulled by the uneasy peace of exhaustion. The Manchu court was weak and could expend little effort on policing the huge territory which it had garnered. The Chaghatai khans of the Tian Shan and Kashgaria were powerless figureheads. Their mountain provinces were claimed by hard-bitten Kyrgyz strongmen, and their cities were governed by an Uzbek Dynasty of priest-kings called the Khojas. On the steppes, the Kazak khans were reeling from the Zhungarian years. Gradually over the mid-1700s, the Kazaks had accepted Russian protection – first the Little Horde, then the Middle Horde, then part of the Great Horde. But the protection did little to improve the Kazaks' fate at the hands of the Oyrats.

The Russians had by this time established a line of fortified outposts on the northern fringe of the Kazak Steppe. However, it appears that there was no clear conception in St Petersburg of exactly where the Russian Empire's frontier lay. Slow on the uptake, Russia at this stage had little interest in the immense territory it now abutted.

The Khanates of Kokand, Khiva & Bukhara

In the fertile land now called Uzbekistan, the military regime of an Iranian interloper named Nadir Shah collapsed in 1747, leaving a political void which was rapidly occupied by a trio of Uzbek khanates.

The three dynasties were the Kungrats, enthroned at Khiva (in the territory of old Khorezm), the Manghits at Bukhara and the Mins at Kokand. They were all rivals of one another. The khans of Khiva and Kokand and the emirs of Bukhara seemed able to will the outside world out of existence as, like a box of kittens, they stroked and clawed each other. Boundaries were impossible to fix as the rivals shuffled their provinces in endless wars.

Unruly nomadic tribes produced constant unsettling pressure on their periphery. Bukhara and Khiva vainly claimed nominal control over the nomadic Turkmen, who prowled the Karakum desert and provided the khanates with slaves from Persia. Kokand expanded into the Tian Shan mountains and the Syr-Darya basin in the early 19th century, but there it encountered cagey Kyrgyz and Kazak tribes who proved to be more than a handful. Farther afield, various provinces of all three khanates were disputed with Persia, Afghanistan or Chinese Kashgar.

The khans ruled absolutely as feudal despots. And yes, they had large harems. Some of them were capable rulers; some, such as the last Emir of Bukhara, were depraved and despised tyrants. The social sphere was dominated by the mosque. In the centuries since Transoxiana had waned as the centre of Islam, the mullahs had slipped into hypocrisy and greed. The level of education and literacy was low, and the *ulama* or intellectual class seems to have encouraged superstition and ignorance in the people.

It was no dark age, however. Trade was vigorous. This was especially true in Bukhara, where exports of cotton, cloth, silk, karakul wool and other goods gave it a whopping trade surplus with Russia. Commerce brought in new ideas, with resulting attempts to develop irrigation and even to reform civil administrations. European travellers in the 19th century mentioned the splendour of the Islamic architecture in these exotic capitals.

In none of the three khanates was there any sense among the people that they belonged to a distinct *nation* – whether of Bukhara, Khiva or Kokand. In all three, *sarts* (town dwellers) occupied the towns and farms, while tribes who practiced nomadism and semi-nomadism roamed the uncultivated countryside. Sarts included both Turkic-speaking Uzbeks and Persian-speaking Tajiks. These two groups had almost identical lifestyles and customs, apart from language.

In many respects, the three khanates closely resembled the feudal city-states of late medieval Europe. But it is anybody's guess how they and the Kazak and Kyrgyz nomads might have developed had they been left alone.

The Coming of the Russians

'Russia has two faces, an Asiatic face which looks always towards Europe, and a European face which looks always towards Asia'
Benjamin Disraeli

By the turn of the 19th century Russia's vista to the south was of anachronistic, unstable neighbours. Flush with the new currents of imperialism sweeping Europe, the empire found itself embarking willy-nilly upon a century of rapid expansion into its own 'heart of darkness'.

The reasons were complex. The main ingredients were the search for a secure – and preferably natural – southern border, nagging fears of British expansion from India, and the derring-do of the tsar's officers. And probably, glimmering in the back of every patriotic Russian's mind, there was a vague notion of the 'manifest destiny' of the frontier.

The first people to feel the impact were the

Cossacks

The Cossacks, fearsome cavaliers with legendary prowess in war, were instrumental in the Russian Empire's subjugation of Central Asia. By origin they are part social class, part profession and part ethnic group. Back in the 16th century, the Cossacks were Russian serfs who had escaped from their estates and settled on the wild frontier. There they formed legendary bands of semi-nomadic warriors.

The Cossacks were pressed into service as mercenaries in the empire's expansion. In the 19th century, their rugged lifestyle and fighting mettle made them a perfect choice for relocation onto the newly acquired Kazak Steppe. It was Cossack farms which broke up the Kazaks' migration routes and led to riots – which then had to be put down by Cossacks. ■

Kazaks. Their agreements in the mid-18th century to accept Russian 'protection' had apparently been understood by St Petersburg as agreements to annexation. A few decades later Russia began at last to turn its attention to controlling and using its 'new possessions'. Tatars and Cossacks were sent to settle and farm the land. Angered, the Kazaks revolted. As a consequence, the khans of the three hordes were one by one stripped of their autonomy, and their lands were made into bona fide Russian colonies. In 1848, as the USA was gaining land stretching from Texas to California, Russia abolished the Great Horde. Theirs was the last line of rulers in the world directly descended – by both blood and throne – from Jenghiz Khan.

The Kyrgyz were close relatives of the Kazaks, but with no khans and no state. At the turn of the 19th century they were already cornered in the Tian Shan mountains when the long arm of Kokand began to encircle them. As Russia approached from the north, each of the splintered Kyrgyz chiefs acted in his own interests to buy security for his tribe. Kokand took taxes and military conscripts, and promised agreeable Kyrgyz leaders a piece of the pie. Russia exacted assurances of support in the coming confrontation with Kokand, and offered protection. Mostly the Kyrgyz waffled, perhaps wisely. In lieu of unity they opted to continue their age-old feuds and mutual cattle raids.

By the 1860s Russia had received a disappointing rebuke in the Crimean War. Checked in the west, the empire began to focus on eastward expansion. Job one was to stabilise the frontier areas occupied by the nomads – to woo the Kyrgyz and Kazaks into submission. This happened piecemeal, almost tribe by tribe.

Kokand, the nomads' other major suitor, was thus the first of the three Uzbek khanates to be swamped. In 1864 the Kokand city of Turkistan was taken by the Orenburg Corps from the north. That same year, Aulie-Ata (now Zhambyl) fell to a Russian force from Verny (now Almaty) in the east. The Kokand fortress of Pishpek (now Bishkek) had been

Cossacks, from the Turkic word *kazak* meaning 'adventurer' or 'free man', were known as outstanding warriors and hunters.

wiped out two years before by a combined Kyrgyz and Russian siege. Chimkent (now Shymkent) fell in 1864, followed by Tashkent.

The assault on Tashkent in May and June 1865 was as dramatic a moment as any in the conquest. General Mikhail Grigorevich Chernyayev, against explicit orders from St Petersburg, marched a tiny regiment to the outskirts of the medieval walled city and cut off the water supply. But while waiting for thirst to set in, his men were raided by the Kokand army, four times greater in number. The counter-attackers were beaten off, and at dawn on June 14 Chernyayev hurled his men through the gates of Tashkent. The Russians were outnumbered by more than 20 to one; their chaplain led one charge armed only with a cross. Yet the city surrendered after two days of bloody street fighting.

The capture of Tashkent from Kokand closed the gap between two fortified lines on Russia's southern frontier.

For his shrewd disobedience, Chernyayev earned a diamond-encrusted sword from the tsar, and his dismissal. From his vanquished foes he got the nom de guerre 'Lion of Tashkent'.

Bukhara was understandably worried by the news. At about the time General Konstantin Petrovich Kaufman was inaugurated as military governor general of the Russians' new Turkestan Province, the Bukhara mullahs issued a fatwah declaring holy war on Russia. In April 1868 the emir and his army clashed with Kaufman and a small body of Russian troops near Samarkand. It was an overwhelming defeat for Bukhara: everyone was put to flight, including the emir. The very next day Kaufman was presented with the keys to the city of Samarkand.

By late June 1868, after quashing a popular uprising in Samarkand, Kaufman at last brought the Bukharan government to the table for a filling meal of humble pie. The peace treaty ceded three provinces outright to the empire, while the rest of the Bukhara emirate was made a protectorate. The emir also had to pay a hefty war indemnity and allow free access to local markets for Russian businesses.

Khiva, remote and ringed by deserts, held out a little longer. Four forces converging from Tashkent, Orenburg, Mangyshlak and the Caspian port of Krasnovodsk finally pinched the khanate in 1873. In its place remained a protectorate with status similar to Bukhara's. In the meantime Kokand had been losing provinces right and left to the mushrooming Russian Turkestan. The rump Kokand khanate, stripped of all its territories, was finally abolished and annexed in 1877.

The last and fiercest people to hold out against the tsarist juggernaut were the Tekke, the largest Turkmen tribe. Of all nomad groups, the Tekke had managed to stay the most independent of the khanates, in this case Khiva. Some Turkmen tribes had asked to be made subjects of Russia as early as 1865 – for convenient help in their struggle against the Khivan yoke. But none were in a mood to have their tethers permanently shortened as Russia expanded into their territory. To add rancour to the pot, the Russians were anguished by the Tekkes' dealings in slaves, particularly Christian ones.

Much blood was spilled in the subjugation of the Tekke. The Russians were trounced in 1879 at Teke-Turkmen, but returned with a huge force under General Mikhail Dmitrievich Skobelev in 1881. The siege and capture of Geok-Tepe, the Tekkes' last stronghold, resulted in staggering casualties among the defenders.

With resistance ended, the Russians proceeded along the hazily defined Persian frontier area, occupying Merv in 1884 and the Pandjeh oasis on the Afghan border in 1885. It was the southernmost point they reached.

During this conquest, the government in St Petersburg had agonised over every advance. In the field, however, their hawkish generals took key cities without asking for permission. It all seems to have gone according to the precepts of General Skobelev, who is quoted as having said, 'I hold it as a principle that in Asia the duration of peace is in direct proportion to the slaughter you inflict upon the enemy. The harder you hit them the longer they will be quiet afterwards'.

When it was over, Russia found it had bought a huge new territory – half the size of the USA, geographically and ethnically diverse, and economically rich – fairly cheaply in terms of money and lives, and in just 20 years. But while the dysfunctional grabbing-binge was going on upstairs in Central Asia, down in India the other great empire of the 19th century had found it difficult to get any rest. And some disturbing noises from India had caused due alarm up in Russia.

The Great Game

What do two expanding empires do when their fuzzy frontiers draw near each other? They scramble for control of what's between them.

The British called it the Great Game; in Russia it was the Tournament of Shadows. Its backdrop was the first cold war between East and West. All the ingredients were there: spies and counter-spies, demilitarised zones, puppet states and doom-saying governments whipping up smokescreens for their own shady business. All that was lacking was the atom bomb and a Russian leader banging his shoe on the table. Diplomatic jargon acquired the phrase 'sphere of influence' during this era.

The story of the Great Game would be dull as dishwater except that its centre arena was the Roof of the World (a common term for the Pamir range). The history of Central Asia from the beginning of the 19th century onward must be seen in the context of the Great Game, for this was the main reason for Russian interest in the region.

Kashgaria Stage: Yakub Beg The Great Game era is perhaps unique in history for the way it made the British Empire abase itself to local tyrants in exchange for elusive 'favours'. Yakub Beg is a case in point.

In the mid-1800s Uyghurs and Dungans (Chinese Muslims) rose up and wrested the Ili river region and Zhungaria (now in north-west Xinjiang) from the feeble rule of the Chinese Manchu Dynasty. In 1863 Kokand sent its own pretender out to vie for Kashgar. The mission's military officer was one Yakub Beg, a Tajik of low birth and high aspirations. He dumped the would-be puppet ruler he was accompanying and manoeuvred himself into power. By 1867 he had emerged as supreme potentate of Kashgaria, the Ili river region and Zhungaria – a region known as Alty Shaar, or 'the Six Cities'.

Soon Yakub Beg found himself officially recognised by Great Britain and Turkey. The Russians went for economic ties, and swiftly sent trading caravans to Kashgar. Spies and shadowy traders from Britain lined up to whisper sweet nothings in Yakub Beg's ear. Through it all, his strategy was to play the Russians and British off against each other.

But Yakub Beg's diplomatic overtures to Russia were spurned, since St Petersburg still had friendly relations with the Manchu regime he had usurped. In 1871 Russia decided to stabilise its frontier. Troops crossed the 'Chinese' border and captured the rebellious Ili region, including its centre, Kulja (Yining).

Yakub Beg died mysteriously in 1877, and his regime toppled in the succession struggle. The moment the outcome was inevitable, Britain changed course and lavishly financed the Chinese recapture of Kashgaria. The crackdown was savage.

The fortunes of the locals reached low ebb when Russia evacuated its troops from the Ili region. Fearing Chinese reprisals, tens of thousands of Uyghurs, Dungans and Kazaks fled in 1882 as the Russians pulled out (these refugees were the ancestors of the Dungan and Uyghur communities of modern Kazakstan and Kyrgyzstan). The Chinese organised their recaptured territories into Xinjiang Province, the 'New Dominions'.

Ground gained by Russia: zero. Ground gained by Britain: zero.

Pamir Stage The Russian occupation of Merv in 1884 immediately raised blood pressures in Britain and India. Merv was a crossroads leading to Herat – an easy gateway to Afghanistan which in turn offered entry into British India. Her Majesty's government finally lost its cool when the Russians went south to control Pandjeh. But the storm had been brewing long before 1884.

In 1839 Britain installed a hand-picked ruler of Afghanistan, which resulted in an uprising, a death march from Kabul by the British garrison, and a vengeful 'First Afghan War'. By the end of it, Britain's puppet-ruler was murdered and his predecessor was back on the throne. This failure to either control or befriend the headstrong Afghans was repeated in an equally ill-fated 1878 invasion (the Russians likewise failed from 1979 to 1988).

By 1848 the British had defeated the Sikhs and taken Punjab and the Peshawar valley. With a grip now on the 'Northern Areas' Britain began a kind of cat-and-mouse game with Russia across the vaguely mapped Pamir and Hindu Kush. Agents posing as scholars, explorers, merchants – even Muslim preachers and Buddhist pilgrims – crisscrossed the mountains, mapping them, spying on each other, courting local rulers, staking claims like dogs in a vacant lot.

In 1882 Russia established a consulate in Kashgar. A British agency at Gilgit (now in Pakistan), which had opened briefly in 1877, was urgently reopened when the Mir of Hunza entertained a party of Russians in 1888. Britain set up its own Kashgar office in 1890.

Also in 1890, Francis Younghusband (later to head a British incursion into Tibet) was sent to do some politicking with Chinese officials in Kashgar. On his way back through the Pamir he found the range full of Russian troops, and was told to get out or face arrest.

This electrified the British. They raised hell with the Russian government and invaded Hunza the following year; at the same time Russian troops skirmished in north-east Afghanistan. After a burst of diplomatic manoeuvring, Anglo-Russian boundary agreements in 1895 and 1907 gave Russia most of the Pamir and established the Wakhan Corridor, the awkward tongue of Afghan territory that stretches across to meet Xinjiang.

The Pamir settlement merely shifted the focus of the Great Game back towards Kashgar, where the two powers went on conniving. Their consulates in Kashgar became 'listening posts' which buzzed with intelligence and rumours. Local ears were employed, and travellers passing through the consulates' doors were apt to be debriefed exhaustively about what they had seen en route.

The Great Game was over. The Great Lesson for the people of the region was: 'No great power has our interests at heart'. The lesson has powerful implications today.

Colonisation of Turkestan & Semireche
In 1861, the outbreak of the US Civil War

Renaissance Boy of the Steppes
Shoqan Ualikhanov (1835-65) was one of the most remarkable personalities of Russian Central Asia. A grandson of the last khan of the Kazak Middle Horde, Shoqan (the Russian spelling of his name is Chokan Valikhanov) was educated in the prestigious Orenburg Cadet Corps and rose to become an army captain. He served as an intelligence agent among the Kazaks and Kyrgyz, befriended the exiled Dostoevsky and the explorer Nikolai Przhevalsky, and drew and painted with great skill.

He earned his place in history as a member of military-political-scientific expeditions through Semireche and Kashgaria. His notebooks from these journeys are crammed with observations on geography, botany, zoology, ethnography, history, folklore, archaeology, linguistics, literature and politics. Shoqan was also the first person to take down a fragment of the *Manas* epic from the mouth of a Kyrgyz oral bard.

His main claim to fame, though, was his daring infiltration of Kashgar in 1858 and 1859. Arriving by caravan disguised as the son of a Kokand merchant, the 23-year-old officer began his observations with a laconic note in his diary:

In Kashgar, and in the Six Cities in general, there is a custom that all foreigners upon arrival must enter into marriage ...The wedding is conducted in due form, and all that is required of the groom is that he consummate the union with the bride. So as not to depart from common procedure, and at the insistence of our new friends, we too were obliged to submit to this custom ...

Shoqan stayed under cover for five months, befriending Kashgarians of all sorts and gathering political intelligence. The job was not without risk, however. Only a year before, the second European to enter Kashgar since Marco Polo had been unmasked and beheaded. Shoqan escaped that fate.

Leaving Kashgar, Shoqan made his way to St Petersburg. There he lived for a year and a half, writing, reporting to the government on his adventures, and meeting the literati. His liberal ended Russia's imports of American cotton. To keep the growing textile industry in high gear, the natural place to turn to for cotton was Central Asia. Other sectors of Russian industry were equally interested in the new colonies as sources of cheap raw materials and labour, and as huge markets. Russia's government and captains of industry wisely saw that their own goods could not compete in Europe against products from the more industrialised West. But in Central Asia they had a captive, virgin market. Gradually, Russian Turkestan was put in line with the economic needs of the empire.

The Trans-Caspian Railway was begun at Krasnovodsk in 1880 and reached Samarkand in 1888. The Orenburg-Tashkent line was completed in 1905.

In the late 1800s, Europeans began to flood the tsar's new lands – a million in Kazakstan alone. The immigrants were mostly freed Russian and Ukrainian serfs who wanted land of their own. Central Asia also offered a chance for enterprising Russians to climb socially. The first mayor of Pishpek left Russia as a gunsmith, married well in the provinces, got civil appointments, and ended his life owning a mansion and a sprawling garden estate.

The middle class brought with them straight streets, gas lights, telephones, cinemas, amateur theatre guilds, charity drives, parks and hotels. All these were contained in enclaves set apart from the original towns (the central district of Karakol, on Lake Issyk-Kul in Kyrgyzstan, is probably the best-preserved relic of this colonial environment).

Through their lace curtains the Russians looked out on the Central Asian masses with a fairly indulgent attitude. The Muslim fabric of life was left alone, as were the mullahs, as long as they were submissive. Some Russian politicos even maintained that Islam would

sentiments began to run him up against authority during the Russian conquest era of the 1860s. Those were his fellow Muslims, and his fellow Turkestanis, being carved up by the Russian army he was serving. He is said to have had an argument with General Chernyayev himself, in which he condemned unnecessary violence by Russian storm troops.

His early death in April 1865 is wrapped in mystery. Some say his final illness was tuberculosis; others claim it was syphilis contracted at Kashgar. He died in a simple Kazak *aul* or nomadic encampment. His last letters to his commander, the Governor General of Semireche, continued to contain valuable briefings on the political situation in the hinterlands.

Yet in spite of his intelligence work and his illness, the young Kazak kept his priorities straight to the bitter end. One of the last letters the governor general received ended: 'PS Your Excellency would render a great favour if he would send me a few boxes of Havana cigars...'

Shoqan Ualikhanov's reputation suffered relatively little distortion as the Soviets turned him into a national hero for the Kazaks – explorer, scholar, democrat. He is now universally revered in his homeland. ■

surely wither and die in the face of enlightened western society.

Development, both social and economic, was initially a low priority. When it came, it took the form of small industrial enterprises, irrigation systems and a modest programme of primary education.

In culture it was the Kazaks, as usual, who were the first to be influenced by Russia. A small, Europeanised, educated class began for the first time to think of the Kazak people as a nation. In part, their ideas came from a new sense of their own illustrious past, which they read about in the works of Russian ethnographers and historians. Their own brilliant but short-lived scholar, Shoqan Ualikhanov, was a key figure in Kazak consciousness-raising. Nineteenth century Kazak politics were also shaped by contact with the Tatars, a Turkic people of Russia with a strong early sense of nationality.

The Uzbeks were also affected by the 19th century cultural renaissance of the Tatars. The Jadidists, adherents of educational reform, made small gains in modernising Uzbek schools. The Pan-Turkic movement found fertile ground among educated Uzbeks around the turn of the century, and took root.

The 1916 Uprising

Resentment against the Russians ran deep and occasionally boiled over. Andijan was the scene of a holy war from 1897 to 1898 which rocked the Russians out of complacency. After the insurrection was put down, steps were taken to Russify urban Muslims – the ones most under the influence of the mullahs and most likely to organise against the regime.

The outbreak of WWI in 1914 had disastrous consequences in Central Asia. In Semireche, massive herds of Kazak and Kyrgyz cattle were requisitioned for the war effort, while Syr-Darya, Ferghana and Samarkand provinces had to provide cotton and food. Then, in 1916, as Russia's hopes in the war plummeted, the tsar demanded men. Local people in the colonies were to be conscripted as non-combatants in labour battalions. To add insult to injury, the action was not called 'mobilisation' but 'requisition', a term usually used for cattle and materiel.

Exasperated Central Asians just said no. Starting in Tashkent, an uprising swept eastwards over the summer of 1916. It gained in violence, and attracted harsher reprisal, the farther east it went. Kazak and Kyrgyz nomads were indeed a force to be reckoned with. Colonisation of their ancestral grasslands had squeezed them into smaller and smaller areas. In some cases the nomads were forced by the tsarist administration to rent back their own land! Taxed into destitution, they had nothing to lose in fighting.

Accounts of what exactly happened vary. It appears that the Kazaks and Kyrgyz began their uprising under strict discipline, but things quickly got out of hand. Purposeful attacks on Russian militias and official facilities gave way to massive rioting, raiding and looting. Innocent colonists were massacred, their villages burned, and women and children carried off.

The resulting bloody crackdown is a milestone tragedy in Kyrgyz and Kazak history. Russian troops and vigilantes gave up all pretence of a 'civilising influence' as whole Kyrgyz and Kazak villages were brutally slaughtered or set to flight. Manhunts for suspected perpetrators continued all winter, long after an estimated 50,000 Kyrgyz and Kazak families had fled towards China. The refugees who didn't starve or freeze on the way were shown little mercy in China.

But not all unrest amongst Muslims was directed against Russia. The Young Bukharans and Young Khivans agitated for social self-reform, modelling themselves on the Young Turks movement which had begun transforming Turkey in 1908. Though small in number, these groups attracted serious opposition and even repression from the ruling Muslim elite – a measure of their importance.

Revolution & Civil War

For a short time after the Revolution of 1917, which toppled the tsar, there was a real feeling of hope in some Central Asian minds. The society which the West, out of ignorance and mystification, had labelled backward and inflexible had actually been making preparations for impressive progress. The Bolsheviks made sure, however, that we will never know how Central Asia might have remade itself.

The Kokand Government In 1917 an independent state was launched in Kokand by young nationalists under the watchful eye of a cabal of Russian cotton barons. This new government intended to put into practice the philosophy of the Jadid movement – to build a strong, autonomous Pan-Turkic polity in Central Asia by modernising the religious establishment, westernising, and educating the people.

Kokand, its khanate long gone, was politically far ahead of Bukhara and Khiva, where the ruling elite still wallowed in feudal intrigues. The Bolsheviks seized power in Russia in November 1917, and within five months of its inception the Kokand government was smashed by the Red Army's newly formed Trans-Caspian Front. Over 5000 Kokanders were massacred after the city was captured. Central Asians' illusions about peacefully coexisting with Bolshevik Russia were shattered as well.

Bolshevik Conquest Like most Central Asians, Emir Alim Khan of Bukhara hated the Bolsheviks. In response to their first ultimatum to submit, he slaughtered the Red emissaries who brought it and declared a holy war. A truce from spring 1918 to spring 1919 gave the Bolsheviks and the emir time to build up their offensive strategies. The emir conspired with White (ie anti-Bolshevik) Russians and British political agents, while the Reds concentrated on strengthening Party cells within the city.

The end came swiftly after the arrival in Tashkent of the Red Army commander Mikhail Frunze. Khiva went out with barely a whimper, quietly transforming into the Khorezm People's Republic in February

1920. In September Frunze's fresh, disciplined army captured Bukhara after a four day fight. The emir fled to Afghanistan, taking with him his company of dancing boys but abandoning his harem. These women were 'liberated' by Bolshevik soldiers.

Tashkent and much of Semireche, had fallen to the Bolsheviks soon after the October Revolution. Then in December 1918 a counter-revolution broke out, apparently organised from within Tashkent jail by a shadowy White Russian agent named Paul Nazaroff. Several districts and cities fell back into the hands of the Whites. The bells of the cathedral church in Tashkent were rung in joy – but for the last time. The Bolsheviks defeated the insurrection, snatched back their power, and kept it.

Nazaroff, freed from jail, was forced to hide and flee for his life across the Tian Shan to Xinjiang, always one step ahead of the dreaded secret police.

Enver Pasha From the start the Bolsheviks ensured themselves the universal hatred of the people. Worse even than the tsar's bleed-the-colonies-for-the-war policies, the revolutionaries levied grievous requisitions of food, livestock, cotton and land. Turkestanis were even subjected to forced farm labour. Trade and agricultural output in the once-thriving colonies plummeted. The ensuing famines claimed at least 900,000 lives, some say many more.

Meanwhile, a dashing, courageous Ottoman Turkish soldier named Enver Pasha was making his way towards Central Asia. A Young Turk, Enver had served as the Ottoman Empire's minister of war during WWI but was forced to flee his homeland after the empire's defeat in 1918. He wound up in Moscow. There he bent Lenin's ear and convinced the Soviet leader that he was just the person to bring him Central Asia and British India on a platter. In exchange, Lenin was to help him win control of what was left of the Turkish Empire.

Enver left Moscow for Bukhara in November 1921, ostensibly to make ready an army for his benefactor. In reality he had already decided to jilt Lenin and look after his own dream: to conquer and rule a Pan-Turkic state with Central Asia as its core.

In Bukhara he made secret contact with leaders of the *basmachi* – local bands of Turkic and Tajik freedom fighters (the Russians had given them the name, with its overtones of banditry and murder, and it has unfortunately stuck). The basmachi guerrillas, with their grass-roots base and intimate knowledge of the mountain geography, had already proved to be worthy foes of the infant Red Army. But to make great and lasting gains they needed a leader to unify them. It was love at first sight between Enver and the basmachi. He gave his Bolshevik hosts the slip and rode east from Bukhara. In the countryside, exulting like a bridegroom, he gathered swarms of recruits.

Enver Pasha could never be accused of underestimating himself. As support and material aid began to pour in from the exiled Emir of Bukhara and his host the Emir of Afghanistan, Enver styled himself 'Commander in Chief of All the Armies of Islam', a relative by marriage of the caliph, and Representative of the Prophet. The people flocked to his campaign as to a holy war.

Initial successes were stunning. Enver's small army took Dushanbe in February 1922. By the spring they had captured much of the former emirate of Bukhara. The egotistical Enver refused to negotiate with the Bolsheviks until they evacuated Central Asia.

Enraged, the Bolsheviks sent 100,000 additional troops in to crush him. Moscow also played an important political card: it permitted the Islamic courts to reconvene, gave residents of the Ferghana Valley a massive tax cut, and returned confiscated land. Support for the basmachi faltered.

Enver also discovered the downside of his fanatical host of irregulars: they simply dissolved back into the countryside as things started to go against their leader. With his rural support drying up, and with the Emir of Afghanistan turning a cold shoulder, he still refused to surrender. He and a small band of

his closest officers set out for the Pamir east of Dushanbe, never to emerge again.

On 4 August 1922, less than nine months after his portentous arrival at Bukhara, Enver Pasha met his end like a hero. Accounts of the final moments differ. The most popular holds that he galloped headlong with sabre drawn at the head of a suicidal charge against the machine-gun fire of a Bolshevik ambush. In any case the few survivors of the raid scattered, and immediately began feeding the legend of their fallen leader. Had he succeeded in his grandiose vision, Enver Pasha would have been the first Turkic conqueror of all Turkestan since Timur. The fact that he made the attempt is ample fuel for myth.

The basmachi fought on, scattered and dwindling, until the early 1930s. They are now the subject of intensive investigation by post-Soviet historians, the first generation able to commemorate the basmachi without fear of repression.

Xinjiang after 1911

With the fall of the Qing Dynasty in 1911, Xinjiang came under the rule of a succession of warlords, over whom the governments in China proper had very little influence. The first of these warlord-rulers was Yang Zhengxin, who ruled from 1911 until his assassination in 1928 at a banquet in Ürümqi. Yang had managed to maintain a somewhat unhappy peace, and his policy of isolationism had preserved the region from ideas unleashed by the Chinese revolution of 1911. Yang was followed by a second tyrannical overlord, Ma Zhongyin. A Chinese Muslim with extraordinary charisma and military skill, Ma gathered throngs of Muslim followers and fought a bloody war of liberation. He was finally forced to flee in 1933 by a clandestine incursion into Xinjiang by the Soviet army. Ma was replaced by a still more oppressive leader named Sheng Shizai. The latter remained in power almost until the end of WWII, when he too was forced out. Sheng had initially followed a pro-Communist policy, then suddenly embarked on an anti-Communist purge.

The only real attempt to establish an independent state was in the 1940s, when a Kazak named Osman leading a rebellion of Uyghurs, Kazaks and Mongols took control of south-western Xinjiang and established an independent Turkestan Republic in January 1945. The Chinese Nationalist government convinced the Muslims to abolish their new republic in return for a pledge of real autonomy. The promise wasn't kept, but Nationalist preoccupation with the civil war left them with little time to re-establish control over the region. They eventually appointed a Muslim named Burhan as governor in 1948, unaware that he was actually a Communist supporter.

At the same time a Muslim league opposed to Chinese rule was formed in Xinjiang, but in August 1949 a number of its most prominent leaders died in a mysterious plane crash on their way to Beijing to hold talks with the new Communist leaders. Muslim opposition to Chinese rule collapsed, though the Kazak Osman continued to fight until he was captured and executed by the Chinese Communists in 1951.

After 1949 the Chinese government was faced with two problems: proximity to the USSR (considered the paramount threat), and volatile relations with the region's Muslim inhabitants.

The Soviet Era

'The Communist Party is the mind, honour and conscience of our era'

Vladimir Ilych Lenin

In Soviet history books it was typical to weave in pertinent quotations from Lenin (actually it was punishable to leave them out). Heading the sections below are a few of the most oft-repeated – the 'greatest hits' – concerning Central Asia. Even to those not conversant in doublespeak, they provide a sample of the smug, pedantic verbal effluvium which caked everything in Soviet Central Asia for over 70 years.

Forced Collectivisation 'With the help of the proletariat from advanced countries, backward countries can proceed to the Soviet system and, via a definite stage of development, to communism, sidestepping the capitalist stage of development '(Lenin).

Forced collectivisation was the 'definite stage of development' implicit in time-warping the entire population of Central Asia from feudalism to Communism. This occurred during the USSR's grand First Five Year Plan (1928-32). The intent of collectivisation was first to eliminate private property and second, in the case of the nomadic Kazaks and Kyrgyz, to put an end to their wandering lifestyle.

The effect was disastrous. When the orders came down, most people simply slaughtered their herds and ate what they could rather than give them up. This led to famine in subsequent years, and widespread disease. Resisters were executed and imprisoned. Literally millions of people died. Evidence exists that during this period Stalin had a personal hand in tinkering with meagre food supplies in order to induce famines. His aims seem to have been to subjugate the people's will and to depopulate Kazakstan, which was good real estate for Russian expansion.

The basmachi, in twilight for some time, renewed their guerrilla activities briefly as collectivisation took its toll. It was their final struggle.

Political Repression 'Social revolution ... unites civil war by the proletariat against the bourgeoisie in advanced countries with ... democratic and revolutionary, and particularly national-liberation, movements in undeveloped, backward and oppressed countries' (Lenin). '[We must] awaken in the masses an aspiration towards independent political thought and towards independent political action – even in places where there is almost no proletariat' (Lenin).

Undeveloped Central Asia had no shortage of bright, sincere people willing to work for national liberation and democracy. After the tsar fell they jostled for sunshine in their various parties, movements and factions.

Even after they were swallowed up into the Soviet state, some members of these groups had high profiles in regional affairs. Such a group was Alash Orda, which was formed by Kazaks and Kyrgyz in 1917. Alash Orda even held the reins of a short-lived autonomous government.

By the late 1920s, the former nationalists and democrats – indeed the entire intelligentsia – were causing Stalin serious problems. From their posts in the Communist administration they had front-row seats at the Great Leader's horror show, including collectivisation. Many of them began to reason, and to doubt. Stalin, reading these signs all over the USSR, foresaw that brains could be just as dangerous as guns. Throughout the 1930s he proceeded to have all possible dissenters eliminated. Alash Orda members were among the first to die, in 1927 and 1928.

Thus began the systematic murder – the Purges – of untold tens of thousands of Central Asians. Arrests were usually made late at night. Confined prisoners were rarely tried; if any charges at all were brought, they ran along the lines of 'having bourgeois-nationalist or Pan-Turkic attitudes'. Mass executions and burials were common. Sometimes entire sitting governments were disposed of in this way.

Construction of Nationalities 'Now that national privileges have been eliminated, and the equality of nationalities has been brought to life, and the right of national minorities to free national development has been ensured by the very nature of the Soviet system, the task of the Party regarding the working masses of these national groups consists in helping them fully to utilise this right of free development which has been ensured for them' (Tenth Session of the Russian Communist Party).

The solution to the 'nationality question' in Central Asia remains the most graphically visible effect of Soviet rule: it drew the lines on the map.

Before the Revolution the peoples of Central Asia had no concept of a firm national border. They had plotted their iden-

---

Brave New World
As the Purges went on and Stalin's paranoia about people's 'unwholesome backgrounds' grew, the system was at a loss to replace those who had been purged. It seemed that ultimately no one with a mother or a father could escape suspicions of anti-revolutionary allegiances. And so it was that state orphanages became a major reservoir from which the Party fished its new recruits. The Party became mother, father, family and conscience for these protégés. Uzbek President Islam Karimov was an orphanage boy. ■

---

tities by a tangle of criteria: religion, tribe, location, way of life, even social status. The Soviets, however, believed that such a populace was fertile soil for Pan-Islamism and Pan-Turkism. These philosophies were threats to the regime.

So, starting about 1924, nations were invented: Kazak, Kyrgyz, Tajik, Turkmen, Uzbek. Each was given its own distinct ethnic profile, language, history and territory. Where an existing language or history did not exist or was not suitably distinct from others, these were supplied and disseminated. The Muslim religion was cut away from each national heritage, relegated to the status of an outmoded and oppressive cult, and severely suppressed throughout the Soviet period.

Ultimately, each nation became the namesake for a constituent Soviet Socialist Republic (SSR). Uzbek and Turkmen SSRs were proclaimed in 1924, the Tajik SSR in 1929, and the Kazak and Kyrgyz SSRs in 1936.

Some say that Stalin personally directed the drawing of the boundary lines. If he didn't he should have rewarded the mapmaker handsomely. Each of the republics (referred to as 'Central Asia & Kazakstan' in the strict usage of the Soviets, because Kazakstan's boundary extends into the traditionally defined territory of Europe) was shaped to contain numerous pockets of the different nationalities, each with long-standing claims to the land. Everyone had to admit that only a strong central government could keep order on such a map. The present face of Central Asia is a product of this 'divide and rule' technique.

WWII 'The Great Patriotic War Against Fascist Germany' galvanised the whole USSR. It is widely acknowledged that the USSR could not have driven back Hitler's invasion without the unified mentality and productive strength which Stalin's totalitarian regime had begun to build.

In the course of the war Central Asia was drawn further into the fold. Economically the region lost ground from 1941 to 1945 but soon gained it back and surged forward. A sizeable boost came in the form of industrial enterprises arriving ready-to-assemble in train cars: evacuated from the war-threatened parts of the USSR, they were relocated to the remote safety of Central Asia. They stayed there after the war and kept on producing.

Other wartime evacuees – people – have made a lasting imprint on the face of Central Asia. These are the Koreans, Volga Germans, Chechens and others whom Stalin suspected might aid the enemy. They were deported from the borderlands and shuffled en masse. They now form sizeable minority communities in all the former Soviet Central Asian republics.

For many wartime draftees, WWII presented an opportunity to escape the oppressive Stalinist state. One Central Asian scholar claims that over half of the 1.5 million Central Asians mobilised in the war deserted. Large numbers of them, as well as POWs, actually turned their coats and fought for the Germans against the Soviets.

Agriculture The tsarist pattern for the Central Asian economy had been overwhelmingly agricultural; so it was with the Soviets. Cotton was singled out for intensive production. Virtually all land that could be – and even much land which shouldn't have been – was planted in cotton. The labour-intensive 'cotton bowl' covered Uzbekistan as well as sizeable chunks of the other four republics.

Into the cotton bowl poured the diverted waters of the Syr-Darya and Amu-Darya, while downstream the Aral Sea was left to dry up. Over the cotton-scape was spread a whole list of noxious agricultural chemicals, which have wound up polluting waters, blowing around in dust storms, and causing serious health problems for residents of the area. For further detail, see the Environment section in this chapter.

Another noxious effect of cotton monoculture was the 'cotton affair' of the Brezhnev years. A huge ring of corrupt officials habitually over-reported cotton production, swindling Moscow out of billions of roubles. When the lid finally blew off, 2600 participants were arrested and over 50,000 were kicked out of office. Brezhnev's own son-in-law was one of the fallen. For more on this, see The Great Cotton Flim-Flam in the introduction to the Uzbekistan chapter.

In 1954 the Soviet leader Nikita Khrushchev launched the Virgin Lands campaign. The purpose was to jolt agricultural production, especially of wheat, to new levels. The method was to put Kazakstan's enormous steppes under the plough and resettle huge numbers of Russians to work the farms. Massive, futuristic irrigation schemes were drawn up to water the formerly arid grassland – from as far away as the Ob river in Siberia. The initial gains in productivity soon dwindled as the fragile exposed soil of the steppe literally blew away in the wind. The Russians, however, remained.

Advantages of the Soviet Era In spite of their heavy-handedness the Soviets made profound improvements in Central Asia. Overall standards of living were raised considerably with the help of health care and a vast new infrastructure. Central Asia was provided with plants, mines, farms, ranches and services employing millions of people (never mind that no single republic was given the means for a free-standing economy, and that most operations were coordinated through Moscow).

Education reached all social levels. Pure and applied sciences were nurtured. Literacy was made almost universal, and the languages of all nationalities were given standard literary forms. The Kyrgyz language was even given an alphabet for the first time.

Artistic expression was encouraged within the confines of Communist ideology. The Central Asian republics now boast active communities of professional artists who were trained, sometimes lavishly, by the Soviet state. And through the arts, the republics were allowed to develop their distinctive national traditions and identities (again, within bounds).

To the extent that the Central Asian republics were prepared at all when independence came, they were prepared by the Soviet era.

'Ethnic' Violence

Mikhail Gorbachev's debut at the helm of the USSR in 1985 led to the linked policies of *glasnost* and *perestroyka* – openness and restructuring. In Central Asia, as throughout the USSR, these devolved into explosion and disintegration.

Almaty, 1986
   Kazaks riot in response to the replacement of the Kazak Communist Party chief, Dinmukhamed Qonaev, with a Russian.
Andijan, 1989
   Jews are chased and burned out of the area in what observers call a pogrom.
Tashkent & Ferghana Valley, 1989
   Meskhetian Turks, a tiny minority, are attacked by Uzbeks; 150 deaths are reported; 15,000 Meskhetians are made refugees.
Osh region, 1990
   Kyrgyz and Uzbeks face off in a month of carnage and destruction. Estimates of deaths start at 200; thousands of homes are destroyed. During the bloodiest days in Özgön, police and security forces are strangely absent.

Moscow was quick to suggest that these episodes of violence were outbreaks of nationalism, ethnic tensions, or even a resur-

gence of Islamic fundamentalism. But some facts were ignored. There was often no police or army intervention during the worst atrocities (yet at times helicopters were seen hovering overhead). Rioters sometimes arrived at the scene in bus or truck convoys. Agitators frequently had modern communications equipment.

It is now widely accepted that some people in the foundering hard-line part of the Communist regime were doing what they could to harness social discontent for their own ends. Made desperate by their crumbling rule, the conservative camp sought to reassert Moscow's relevance as peacekeeper in a classic divide-and-rule play.

Social discontent there surely was: living standards were poor, competition was strong for scarce housing and water, and unemployment was high. Interestingly, 'ethnic' rioting virtually ceased after the collapse of the USSR.

Post-Soviet Central Asia

By the spring of 1991 the parliaments of all five republics had declared their sovereignty. However, when the failure of the August coup against Gorbachev heralded the end of the Union, none of the republics was well prepared for the reality of independence.

On December 8 the presidents of Russia, Ukraine and Belarus met near Brest (Belarus) to form the Commonwealth of Independent States (CIS). Feeling left out, the Central Asian presidents convened and demanded admission. On December 21, the heads of 11 of the former Soviet states (all except the three Baltic states and Georgia) met in Almaty and refounded the CIS. Gorbachev resigned three days later.

Independence has put the Central Asian republics' similarities and differences under a strong light. All are grappling with huge population shifts as minorities – especially Slavs and Germans – emigrate. All are weathering pressing economic crises while nursing economic beefs with each other. All are experiencing rising nationalism and a resurgence of Islam, and are attempting to modernise and westernise while maintaining their national character. All are feeling pressure from an unhappy Russia seeking to reassert its interests. All are opening themselves more or less to new spheres of influence from Turkey, Iran, China and the industrialised West. And in of the republics there are a lot of ordinary people who complain that things were fine until 'that idiot Gorbachev ruined everything with perestroyka'.

But there are differences. Kyrgyzstan is the odd one out politically: its president, Askar Akayev, is the only one to have professed aspirations to swift democratisation and free market reform, while his neighbours are unabashedly authoritarian. Turkmenistan is the only republic which seems to have bright economic possibilities – sitting pretty on enormous reserves of oil and gas. Tajikistan is the only one experiencing civil war, while the others are all in dread that they will be next to succumb to the political meltdown and recolonisation by Russia.

Even the term 'Central Asia' does not unify the republics: some residents of huge Kazakstan live about as far away from Vienna as they do from their own capital, and Kazaks are a minority in the country.

Xinjiang China's leaders may be wishing by now that they had back their old reliable bugaboo, the USSR. The formation of three new independent states along its north-west border poses little military threat (though Kazakstan has been called 'Upper Volta with nukes').

What makes China nervous is that the post-Soviet example of freedom may encourage the resentful Uyghur population of Xinjiang to rebel. The Kashgar area and the Pakistan border were closed from 1990 to 1992 in response to riots by the 'minority' population.

GEOGRAPHY

The Central Asia of this book includes Kazakstan, which in Soviet parlance (still lingering even in the West) was considered a thing apart. It is true that Kazakstan's enormous territory actually extends westward across the Ural river, the traditional boundary between Europe and Asia, and that parts of the north have been settled by Russians for centuries. But it's a lot easier just to say 'Central Asia'. We're pretty sure nobody in Kazakstan minds this.

Kazakstan, Kyrgyzstan, Tajikistan, Turkmenistan and Uzbekistan together occupy 5.8 million sq km; including Xinjiang, Central Asia's area is 7.5 million sq km, the size of the Australian continent.

A quick spin around the territory covered in this book would start on the eastern shores of the Caspian Sea, dip south-east along the low crest of the Kopet Dag mountains between Turkmenistan and Iran, follow the Amu-Darya river and then its headstream the Pyanj up into the high Pamir, glide eastward along the Kunlun range as it skirts the southern rim of the Tarim basin, round the eastern nose of the Tian Shan range, traverse the Zhungarian basin, skip north-westward over the Altay mountains to float down the Irtysh river, and then turn west to plod along Kazakstan's flat, farmed, wooded border with Russia, ending in the basin of the Ural river and the Caspian Sea.

The sort of blank which is drawn in the minds of many people by the words 'Central Asia' is not entirely unfounded. The overwhelming majority of the territory is flat steppe (arid grassland) and desert. These areas include the Kazak Steppe, the Betpak Dala (Misfortune) Steppe, the Kyzylkum (Red Sands) desert, the Karakum (Black Sands) desert and the Taklamakan (Go-In-and-You-Won't-Come-Out) desert. Xinjiang's landscape includes two large basins, the Zhungarian and the Tarim – the latter is the largest inland basin in the world.

Central Asia's high ground is dominated by the Pamir, a range of rounded, 5000 to 7000 metre mountains which stretch 800 km across Tajikistan. With very broad, flat valleys nearly as high as the lower peaks, the Pamir might be better described as a plateau. The valleys are treeless, grassy (*pamir* roughly means 'pasture' in local dialects) and often swampy with meandering rivers. The Pamir have been called 'The Roof of the

World'; the roof of the Pamir, Tajikistan's 7495 metre Pik Kommunizma, is the highest point in Central Asia and was the highest in the USSR.

The compact, balled-up mass of mountains presided over by Pik Kommunizma is often called the Pamir Knot. It's the hub from which other major ranges extend like radiating ropes: the Himalayas and Karakoram to the south-east, the Hindu Kush to the south-west, the Kunlun to the east and the Tian Shan to the north-east. These young mountains all arose (or more correctly, are arising still) from the shock waves created by the Indian subcontinent smashing into the Asian crustal plate over 100 million years ago.

The Tian Shan range, extending over 1500 km from south-west Kyrgyzstan to beyond Hami in eastern Xinjiang, forms the backbone of eastern Central Asia. The jagged, ice-clad 4000 to 7000 metre crests are grooved by canyons which shelter dense evergreen forests and lush summer pastures or *jailoo*. The summit of the range is 7439 metre Pik Pobedy on the Kyrgyzstan-Xinjiang border.

The Caspian Sea is called either the world's biggest lake or the world's biggest inland sea. The Caspian Depression in which it lies dips to 132 metres below sea level. Lake Balqash, a vast, marsh-bordered arc of half-saline water on the Kazak Steppe, is hardly deeper than a puddle, while mountain-ringed Lake Issyk-Kul in Kyrgyzstan is the fourth deepest lake in the world. Other glacially fed lakes dot the mountains, including Song-Köl in Kyrgyzstan and Kara Kul, first described by Marco Polo, in Tajikistan (another Kara Kul lies nearby in the Muztagh Ata/Kongur area of Xinjiang). Down in the Tarim basin, the salt lake Lop Nor and the surrounding Lop desert are the site of China's nuclear weapons testing ground.

What little water flows out of Central Asia goes all the way to the Arctic Ocean, via the Irtysh river. Most of Central Asia's rainfall drains internally. The Ili river waters Lake Balqash; the Ural makes a short dash across part of Kazakstan to the Caspian Sea. Numerous rivers rise as cold streams in the mountains only to lose themselves on the arid steppes and sands below. The region's two mightiest rivers, the Syr-Darya and Amu-Darya, used to replenish the Aral Sea. Now most of their waters have been diverted onto km of cotton fields, and the Aral Sea is virtually disappearing. High in the mountains, these rivers make the big wheels turn in hydroelectric plants, such as the impressive Toktogul dam on Kyrgyzstan's Naryn river (the Syr-Darya's headstream).

CLIMATE

Central Asian temperatures are wildly variable, with 20°C to 30°C drops at night, dramatic differences between the deserts and mountains, and seasonal transitions full of false starts. Rain is minimal except at higher altitudes; what there is falls mainly in March to April and October to November and turns everything to mud.

The finest times in the lowlands are May to early June (also good for wildflowers) and September to early October (also good for fruit in the markets). Midsummer is for mad dogs, with daytime averages of 30°C to 35°C in foothill cities like Dushanbe, Bishkek and Almaty, and 40°C or more in Tashkent, Samarkand, Bukhara and Ashghabat. The hottest city in Central Asia is Termez in southern Uzbekistan, with summer days over 50°C.

By November, it turns fairly cold everywhere, in fits and starts. January to February days are typically -5°C to 10°C, sometimes much colder. Winter snow stays on the ground in the north and east, and snow and cold are severe in the mountainous interiors of Kyrgyzstan and Tajikistan.

Kazakstan

Like the rest of the region, Kazakstan has hot summers and very cold winters. During the hottest months, July and August, the average daily maximums are 36°C in Almaty and 38°C in Semey, although hot days are never very numerous.

From November through March, frosty mornings are typical in Almaty and afternoon temperatures remain below freezing

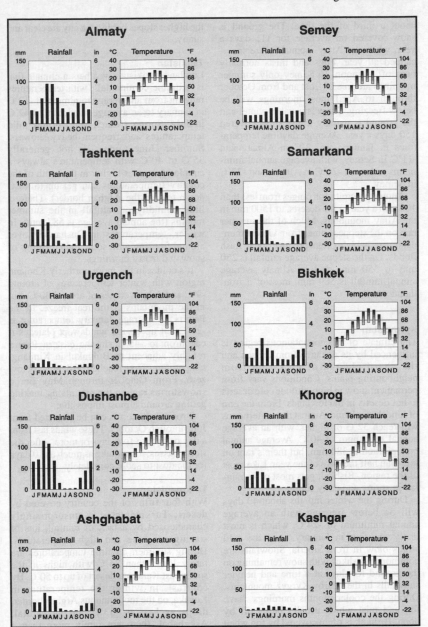

about a third of the time. The ground is snow-covered on average for 111 days a year, while the Altay mountains are snow-capped all year. Fogs and mists normally burn off by noon. In Semey only summer mornings are free of frost and from October through to April most mornings will be below freezing. Snow is usual in winter and the ground is usually thinly snow-covered 150 days a year. Average daytime temperatures in January are -2°C in Almaty and -11°C in Semey, with average annual minimums as low as -26°C in Almaty and -37°C in Semey.

Annual precipitation ranges from less than 100 mm a year in the deserts, to 1500 mm in the Altay mountains. Much of the summer rain on the steppes comes from violent thunderstorms which often produce local flash floods. On the steppe average rainfall is 250 mm to 350 mm, and in Almaty average annual rainfall is 589 mm, most of it from thunderstorms.

Kyrgyzstan

The climate of this mountainous region is influenced by its distance from the sea and the sharp change of elevation from neighbouring plains. Conditions vary from permanent snow in high-altitude cold deserts to hot deserts in the lowlands. From the end of June through mid-August most afternoons will reach 32°C or higher, with an average annual maximum of 40°C. Average annual precipitation is 380 mm, but there's rain on less than half the days of the year. Like most of the region, Bishkek gets most of its rainfall in spring and early summer.

During the winter months about 40 days will be below freezing with an average annual minimum of -24°C, which is most likely to occur in January when the cold winds blow in from Siberia. Snowfalls are common in Bishkek with snow remaining on the ground for days at a time and heavier snowfalls in the nearby Kyrgyz mountains. During the cooler months mornings have fog and mist which usually burns off by noon. Bishkek is often covered by fog when the higher slopes behind the city are clear and sunny.

Tajikistan

Lowland Tajikistan weathers a climate that is 'extreme continental', with temperatures ranging from an average minimum of -12°C in January to an average maximum of 42°C in July. Spring (March-May) brings mild temperatures and frequent heavy showers. Summer (June-August) is hot, generally 35°C to 40°C with temperatures always a couple of degrees higher in the south of the country (temperatures can get up to 48°C down toward the Afghan border). There is little humidity or rainfall in the summer months (the annual average is 587 mm). In winter, temperatures in Dushanbe hover around freezing with some light dustings of snow and frosty mornings.

It's colder in the more northerly Khojand region with winter temperatures of around -9°C and July averages of around 30°C, but in the mountains is the real freeze. In the Pamirs an average January temperature is -20°C but up on the windswept plateaus it can drop to -45°C. In the eastern Pamir, roughly adjacent to Bulunkul in Xinjiang, temperatures have reached 60 degrees below zero. From October through May fierce snowstorms rage in the mountains, making getting around almost impossible.

Strong dust storms can be expected from June through October. These winds last from a day or two, to five days or more. After the storm passes, it may take as much as 10 days for the dust to settle completely.

Turkmenistan

With four-fifths of the country covered by desert, Turkmenistan is unsurprisingly characterised by a lack of rainfall, lots of searing sunshine and high temperatures. During summer, daytime temperatures are rarely lower than 35°C with highs in the south-east Karakum desert of up to 50°C. By contrast, in winter the temperature in Kushka, on the mountainous Afghan border, drops as low as -33°C. In the capital, Ashghabat, there are rarely more than a couple of days when it drops below freezing and by April the heat is already uncomfortable.

Humidity is very low and rainfall meagre. Any rain that falls does so around March, although summer rains do occur up in the mountains. Precipitation ranges from about 80 mm a year in the north-west desert to 300 mm in the mountains.

Uzbekistan

Large areas of Uzbekistan are desert. The difference between the seasons is obvious: summer is long, hot and extremely dry; spring is mild and rainy; autumn has light frosts and rains; and winter, although short, is unstable with snow and temperatures below freezing.

From the middle of June through August average afternoon temperatures will hit 32°C or higher. The average annual maximum temperature is 40°C in June. Light winter rain and summer drought are the characteristic pattern in Samarkand, but no month gets measurable rainfall for half or more of its days. Annual rainfall in the Samarkand area is 315 mm with most rain falling in March to April.

From December through February mornings are generally frosty and snow flurries are common. However, the ground rarely remains snow-covered for more than a few days at a time. The average annual minimum is -14°C and is most likely to occur in January during a cold snap. During the winter months strong winds blowing down from the nearby mountains raise temperatures and lower humidity, resulting in the virtual disappearance of any snow cover. The shepherds of these mountains have a saying that 'two days of these snow-eating winds is better than two weeks of sunshine'.

Western Xinjiang & Northern Pakistan

The hottest months throughout this region are June, July and August, and the coldest are January and February. In Kashgar the average annual maximum is 37°C, and most likely to occur in July or August. The average

minimum will be around -18°C, usually in January. The wettest months are during the monsoon, from mid-July to mid-September, though this only affects the Karokoram Highway as far as north as Gilgit and Hunza, which experience random summer storms (and are also drizzly through the winter and early spring). In Kashgar, not all the thunderstorms of summer bring rain, and what rain does fall does not always reach the ground. When it does, flash floods can sweep through the otherwise dry stream beds.

The driest months are June and September through November in Pakistan, and anytime in Xinjiang, which has no measurable rainfall on 93% of the year's days. From Kashgar to Gilgit, winter is long and cold (often well below freezing), and snow is common in the mountains. Snow usually closes the Khunjerab pass from November through April.

FLORA & FAUNA

Though environmental pressures are as bad in Central Asia as anywhere, there's a reasonably good chance you will see some memorable beasts and plants. At the very least there are the millions of rooks that inhabit the cities and towns and the *Cannabis indica* that grows thick and wild by the roadsides. But there's more, and it goes from wild to very wild.

Many of the region's approximately two dozen nature reserves and protected areas (*zapovednik* or *zakaznik*) and two national parks (*gosudarstvenny prirodny park*, founded for a mixture of preservation and recreation) are accessible for tourists. Moreover it's not unheard of to look out a train or bus window on the open steppe and see a rushing herd of antelope.

The mountains of Kyrgyzstan, Kazakstan, Tajikistan, Xinjiang and (to a lesser extent) Uzbekistan are the setting for high, grassy meadows worthy of *The Sound of Music*. In summertime the wildflowers (including wild irises and edelweiss) are a riot of colour. Trout lurk in the rushing streams. Marmots and pikas provide food for eagles and lammergeiers; the elusive snow leopard preys on

The Grey Wolf lives in packs and is thought to mate for life.

the ibex, with which it shares a preference for crags and rocky slopes. Forests of Tian Shan spruce, larch and juniper provide cover for lynx, wolf, wild boar and brown bear.

Higher up on the tundra-like grasslands, Marco Polo sheep roam in herds, and flamingoes can be seen near lowland lakes and swamps. The Kyrgyz of the Pamir valleys, between 3000 and 4000 metres high, keep herds of domestic yaks. High-altitude herders and mountain climbers pass around stories of yeti sightings.

Lower down in the mountains of southern Kyrgyzstan, Uzbekistan, Tajikistan and Turkmenistan are ancient forests of wild walnut trees. Turkmenistan also has pistachio forests.

The steppes – what's left of them after massive cultivation projects – are covered with grasses and low shrubs such as saxaul. Where they rise to meet foothills, the steppes bear vast fields of wild poppies (including some opium poppies) and tulips. *Chiy,* a common grass with whitish, cane-like reeds, is used by nomads to make decorative screens for their yurts. The nomads sometimes keep Bactrian or two-humped camels in addition to horses and sheep.

Roe deer, wolves, foxes and badgers have their homes on the steppe, as do the saiga, a species of antelope. The ring-necked pheasant, widely introduced in North America and elsewhere, is native to the Central Asian steppe, as are partridges, black grouse, bustards, and the falcons and hawks that prey on them. The ubiquitous tortoise and hedgehog are often the first wild acquaintances made by children.

Rivers and lakeshores in the flatlands are a different world, with dense thickets of elm, poplar, reeds and shrubs. Wild boar, jackal and deer make their homes in these jungle belts – the Amu-Darya is the habitat of a variety of pink deer. The last Turan (or Caspian) tiger was killled in the Amu-Darya delta in 1972.

Geese, ducks and numerous species of wading birds migrate through the marshes. A carp-like eating fish called the *sazan* is the most popular catch. The Sevan trout from

Wildlife at Gunpoint

Controlled hunting was practiced under the Soviet system and still is, but economic strains have unfortunately turned many hunters into poachers. More troubling still, some game wardens have been bribed or have even been known to act as hunting guides in protected areas for rich Western trophy-seekers. Foreign practitioners of falconry have found Central Asia to be an exciting new source of hunting birds – even (or perhaps especially) extremely rare species. Local falconers are often willing first links in the smuggling chain.

The survival pressure felt by these people, like all ordinary people in Central Asia, cannot be overemphasised. The best response to a doubtful offer – someone besides an accredited hunting guide offering to take you hunting, someone selling a snow leopard pelt in a bazar – is 'no'. Illegal treatment of wildlife still carries punishments – of more than conscience. ∎

Armenia which were stocked in Lake Issyk-Kul in the 1960s have unfortunately done very well. They've eaten most of the other fish and grown to gargantuan sizes unheard of in Armenia.

In the Karakum, Kyzylkum and Taklamakan, as in all deserts, there is more than meets the eye. The goitred gazelle (also called jeiran, djeran or jeran) haunts the deserts of western Uzbekistan and Turkmenistan. Gophers, sand rats and jerboas (small jumping rodents with long hind legs) are abundant wherever it's possible to make a hole in the ground. They provide food for foxes, lizards and various kinds of snakes. Turkmenistan is noted for its big poisonous snakes, including vipers and cobras.

Turkmenistan's wildlife has a Middle Eastern streak, understandable when you consider that parts of the country are as close to Baghdad as they are to Tashkent. Leopards and porcupines inhabit the parched hills. The *varan* or 'sand crocodile' is actually a type of large lizard of the region.

GOVERNMENT

Former Soviet Central Asia now consists of five independent republics with their own ambitions and opportunities, but also with a common legacy. The Central Asian republics as such never enjoyed any pre-Soviet political independence and democratic rule. Thus democracy, as Europeans and Americans know it, is a recent and even alien notion, and it shows.

Authoritarian Habits

In recent years, most Central Asian leaders have expressed at least some admiration for South-East Asian models of development which link authoritarian rule and economic development. And all the Central Asian governments are authoritarian to some degree, running the gamut from pure *ancien regime* style autocracy (Turkmenistan), to a tightly controlled mixture of neo-communism and spurious nationalism (Uzbekistan and Tajikistan), to a more enlightened 'channelised transition' to democracy and a market

economy (Kazakstan). Even the liberal-minded Kyrgyzstan is showing signs of tightening up.

In most of the republics the old Communist Party apparatus remains more or less in place under new names – People's Democratic Party (Uzbekistan), Democratic Party (Turkmenistan), People's Unity Party or Socialist Party (Kazakstan), and even the good old Communist Party (Tajikistan). The Central Asian presidents have been either elected by the obligatory 99.9% vote (Uzbekistan and Turkmenistan), furnished with strong executive power (Kazakstan and Kyrgyzstan), or installed in an armed coup (Tajikistan).

The respective parliaments are either dissolved (Tajikistan), operating with curtailed powers under recent constitution revisions (Kazakstan), or filled with the docile comrades and fellow clan members of those in power (Uzbekistan and Turkmenistan); only Kyrgyzstan's has baulked at attempts to increase presidential powers. Political opposition is completely marginalised (Turkmenistan), brought to heel or banned (Uzbekistan), exiled and violent (Tajikistan), or tolerated but closely watched (Kazakstan and Kyrgyzstan).

That old habits die slowly is not surprising after three generations of Soviet rule, and three of tsarist paternalism before that. They appear to be dying more slowly in Central Asia than anywhere else in the former USSR, and there seems little fertile soil for real democracy, so far.

To begin with, the Central Asian republics are pure Soviet inventions; until the late 1920s and 1930s there was no such thing as Uzbekistan, Tajikistan etc. Soviet geographers and ethnologues created new republics and nationalities, assigning borders as artificial as those of, say, Mali or Libya. This yielded a highly volatile ethnic patchwork, made more so by Stalin's ethnic deportation policies.

Furthermore, the absence of clear historical identities and precedents of independence (such as in the Baltic and Transcaucasian states) means there was no strong nationalist or intellectual movement that was capable of articulating alternatives to centralised rule. Militant Islam has begun to fill this void since the Soviet invasion of Afghanistan in 1979, with open or clandestine backing from the Arab Gulf States, Egypt, Iran and Afghanistan. Finally, Central Asians gained their independence essentially as a *fait accompli* rather than as the culmination of a long struggle.

Consequently the old Soviet nomenclature were essentially the only group with the experience and the means to rule after 1991, and there is scant sign that this will change soon. Despite lip service to the concepts of 'democracy' and 'market economy' – largely to please the USA and the European Union – most Central Asian governments are wary of quick political and economic liberalisation. With the Tajik civil war and Russian economic chaos in mind, they argue that rapid change will only open the door to Islamic fundamentalism and ethnic strife, and that a strong hand is the only answer.

At the same time they are ready to play the Islamic and nationalist cards to legitimise themselves in the eyes of their own disoriented subjects. One can only wait and see where this double standard will lead.

Commonwealth of Independent States

With all this in mind, it is no surprise that the Central Asian states were among the founding members and most fervent supporters of the Commonwealth of Independent States, or CIS (Russian: Sodruzhestvo Nezavisimykh Gosudarstv, or SNG), to which all five belong. Seen as a plain tool of Russian neocolonialism by some and as a guarantor of regional security by others, the CIS was founded in late 1991 with its administrative centre in the Belarussian capital of Minsk. With the belated entry of Georgia in 1993, the CIS now includes all the former Soviet republics except the Baltic states.

The CIS is *not* a successor state to the USSR, and in fact is not a state at all but a community of independent states which has taken over some of the international functions of the old USSR. Its original aims were the creation of a common economic zone and a common currency (quite unlikely these days), the setting up of a joint peacekeeping force, and the retention of unitary control over strategic armed forces and nuclear arms in what Russia likes to call its 'near abroad'. The CIS is the formal manifestation of what is, in any case, a huge Russian finger in the Central Asian pie, thanks to the legacy of Soviet interdependence and the rule of Russified Soviet elites in the republican capitals.

The defence aspect is especially important to the Central Asian republics, which have inherited vulnerable borders (Turkmenistan, Tajikistan and Kyrgyzstan), a nuclear arsenal (Kazakstan) and an ongoing civil war next door in Afghanistan. Furthermore, the individual republican armies either still depend heavily on Russian personnel and supplies (Kazakstan and Uzbekistan), are simply Russian expeditionary forces (Tajikistan) or have been abolished and replaced by collective assistance in case of emergency (Kyrgyzstan and Turkmenistan).

Besides the CIS, all the Central Asian republics are also members of the United Nations, the Conference on Security & Cooperation in Europe, the International Monetary Fund, the Economic Cooperation Organisation, the World Bank, the European Development Bank, the Nonaligned Movement, the Organisation of the Islamic Conference and the Asian Development Bank.

Administrative Structures

All the Central Asian republics have maintained the general administrative structures that were in place under the Soviets. The major administrative divisions are national; provincial or regional, corresponding to the Russian oblasts (*velayat* in Turkmen, *oblys* in Kazak, *duban* in Kyrgyz, *viloyat* in Uzbek); extra-municipal, corresponding to the Russian *rayon* (*tuman* in Uzbek, *audan* in Kazak); and municipal, corresponding to the Russian *gorod* or city (*shakhar* in Uzbek, *qala* in Kazak).

The individual traveller is likely to encounter various reincarnations of all-too-familiar Soviet police authorities, in particular the Interior Ministry's branch for keeping track of foreigners, the Office of Visas & Registration, or OVIR (Russian Otdel Vis i Registratsii); the state police or *militisia*; and the traffic police or GAI (DAN in Uzbekistan, MAI in Kyrgyzstan).

ECONOMY

The Central Asian economies remain heavily dependent on that of Russia, itself in a state of profound shock. All partook of the same over-specialisation, over-dependencies and inefficiencies of the centralised Soviet system, and all are paying the morning-after price now that the system has collapsed. But by and large, all are slowly picking themselves up and reinventing their economies.

The Legacy of Russian & Soviet Colonialism

The Russian annexation of Central Asia in the 19th century was not just a geo-strategic move in the Great Game, but an economic move. The Kazak Steppe and Central Asia promised not only indirect access to warm seas and to the rich Persian and Indian markets, but a demographic safety valve and, with their warm climate and traditional irrigated agriculture, an ideal supplier of cotton.

In the 1850s the booming Russian textile industry got much of its raw cotton from the USA, but experienced shortages and steep price rises when the American Civil War broke out. Because imports from British India and Egypt were politically taboo, the alternative was domestic plantations. So, while the grasslands of Kazakstan became a peasant settlement colony, the rest of Central Asia was harnessed to cotton. This criminal waste of its most fertile lands displaced food production, marginalised traditional practices, introduced heavy herbicide use, and created the spectre of crop disease that could in a stroke obliterate vast areas economically. Subsequently Central Asia was

Cotton

Cotton seeds are sown in late April to early May and cultivated all summer. Chemicals are poured on to kill bugs and weeds, make the outer casings fall easily off the bolls (the 'buds') and encourage long fibres. The side-effects of these chemicals on humans, especially cotton pickers, are generally not well known.

The harvest is September through October; many university students and others are still press-ganged to help with it, at least in Uzbekistan. Machines are sometimes used on bigger farms, but they pick young and old bolls indiscriminately; bolls harvested too soon have short fibres and produce inferior thread. In labour-rich regions like the Ferghana Valley the cotton is nearly all harvested by hand. A field can be harvested three or four times as the flowers grow higher and higher.

A boll weighs about five grams. A worker typically picks 12,000 to 20,000 bolls – 60 to 100 kg – in a single day. A hectare of land in the Ferghana Valley yields about 3100 to 3200 kg of cotton bolls in a season. The total harvest for the Ferghana Valley in 1994 was about 400 million kg; for all of Uzbekistan it was about 10 times this. ∎

MARK HANNAFIN

physically grafted onto the Russian economy with the completion of the Trans-Caspian (1899) and Tashkent-Orenburg (1906) railways.

Despite rhetoric about the 'liberation of the peoples of the East', Soviet economic policy in the 1930s only made matters worse. The closing of borders and Stalin's genocidal collectivisation programmes struck the final blow to nomadic animal breeding.

In an attempt to make the USSR economically self-sufficient, each republic (and Soviet satellite country) was 'encouraged' to specialise in a limited range of crops, raw materials and/or industrial products. Uzbekistan alone soon supplied no less than 64% of Soviet cotton, making the USSR the world's second largest cotton producer after the USA. Some 34% of the USSR's wheat, 55% of its wool and 12% of its meat came from Kazakstan.

Northern Kazakstan's development was the most diversified, with mining, machinery and chemical industries. The pattern for the other Central Asian republics was similar, although their positions were more marginal. The development of remote, mountainous Tajikistan proved too costly, leaving it the poorest republic in the USSR.

Most raw materials were shipped to other parts of the USSR for processing – eg 90% of Central Asian cotton went to Russian and Ukrainian mills. Conversely, Central Asia depended for the bulk of its food, machinery, fuels and consumer goods on Russia and Ukraine, mostly at below-market internal rates. Three-quarters of Central Asia's skilled labourers and factory and farming managers were settlers from Russia and the Ukraine.

While Russian and Soviet development did bring modernisation and progress in some fields, on the whole Central Asia got less than its share of the heralded social advantages of the Soviet system. In the last years of the USSR, official reports revealed that while Central Asia proper (without Kazakstan) was home to some 16% of the USSR's population, it held about 64% of its poor. Rates of child mortality and life expec-

tancy were far less appealing than in other Soviet republics.

The newly independent Central Asian republics have been harshly affected by the price liberalisation in Russia from 1992, and plagued by the same shortages, collapse of infrastructure and plunging production that hit Russia after the end of the USSR. All are now suffering severe shortages, rampant inflation and an exodus of Russian and Ukrainian engineers, technicians and skilled workers.

The deepest economic trauma is in the countryside, but even many urbanites are just squeaking by. Factory workers and professionals in Bishkek (for example) earn perhaps US$35 to US$50 a month, and factory managers up to US$80. Many Tashkenters make do with less than US$5 a week for food and clear as little as US$25 to US$35 a month. Persistent images across the region are abandoned or near-empty shops and knots of idle men and boys. Many of those quaint-looking hawkers are selling off their belongings to make ends meet, and longing for pre-Gorbachev days. Most heartrending are the pensioners, especially the Slavic ones whose children have fled Central Asia and whose pensions are now worthless. Watery-eyed *babushkas* sit quietly along the pavements, trying not to look like beggars.

On top of this, central planning, sloppy management and overzealous production quotas have left an ecological disaster zone, of which the most infamous example is the shrinking, toxic Aral Sea.

Rebirth of the Silk Road?

This economic inheritance will not be easily altered, and any transition to a market economy will be slow and painful. A major constraint is fear that privatisation or redistribution of land and other commodities will stir up ethnic and clan tensions. Some of the present ruling elite with major interests in cotton plantations also oppose reform. But the economic potential is considerable, particularly in trade and transport, raw materials, agriculture and an entrepreneurial young labour force.

Trade & Transport Sitting strategically between East Asia, the Indian subcontinent and the Arabian peninsula, Central Asia has a potential role as an economic transit zone, rather like the Silk Road days of old.

Centrally-located Uzbekistan, with its historically resonant cities like Bukhara, Samarkand and the Ferghana Valley, stands to benefit particularly; Tashkent after all is closer to Kashgar and Tehran than to Moscow or Kiev.

Developing this potential as a new Silk Road requires a stable financial system. To this end, and to reduce their dependence on the Russian rouble, Kazakstan, Uzbekistan, Kyrgyzstan and Turkmenistan introduced their own currencies in 1993, and in 1995 Tajikistan introduced its own *rubl*.

Another essential for economic rebirth and freedom from Russia is transport links with neighbouring countries. A major Central Asian handicap is the lack of access to the sea. Hence Iran is an obvious partner, with its access to the Persian Gulf and the Indian Ocean. If peace ever comes to Afghanistan, this could be another outlet to the Indian Ocean, via Pakistan.

In 1969 Turkey, Iran and Pakistan founded the Economic Cooperation Organisation (ECO) in the hope of integrating their transport systems. After a slow start it was opened in 1992 to Azerbaijan, Afghanistan and the five Central Asian republics. One of the enlarged ECO's first acts was a decision to complete a railway link between the Iranian city of Mashhad and the Turkmen capital, Ashghabat, thus offering Turkmen gas access to Persian Gulf ports. Although the ECO's viability remains questionable for financial and political reasons, it offers hope for Central Asia.

Raw Materials The region is a mother lode of energy and raw materials, notably oil and gas but also a range of minerals including coal, copper, silver, gold, iron ore, chromium, bauxite and uranium, while mountainous Kyrgyzstan and Tajikistan offer hydroelectric power. The best endowed republic is Kazakstan, whose Caspian Sea oil reserves rank third after those of the Persian Gulf and Siberia. Kazakstan also has major natural gas reserves. Uzbekistan and Turkmenistan have natural gas; the latter sits on the world's fourth largest reserves.

These riches are becoming the stake in a new economic Great Game, and western energy and mining firms are already striking high-stakes deals, such as Chevron US's multi-billion-dollar agreement with Kazakstan for exploitation of its Caspian oil fields. Such moves also offer another opportunity to loosen the bonds to Russia, to which most pipelines (and roads and railway lines) still go.

Agriculture Despite its overspecialisation in cotton, Central Asia is a major producer of agricultural goods. Agriculture accounts for one quarter to a third of the gross national product of all republics, and employs one third to one half of their workforces. The dominant areas are the grain producing Virgin Lands (see the Environment section later in this chapter) of northern Kazakstan and the cotton belt centred around the Ferghana Valley, but other important sectors are cereals, fruit and vegetables, and animal husbandry (mostly sheep, cattle and horses).

But reform and diversification will prove more difficult in agriculture than in most other fields. Dependence on 'white gold' (cotton), for example, will not be easily kicked. In 1993, 80% of Uzbekistan's export revenues came from cotton, and plantations and associated industry still employ more than a quarter of its workforce. Land reform in favour of small and medium sized farms is a way out, but raises other problems, including the resistance to change of apparatchik landowners, and more importantly the threat of land-related ethnic strife.

Some farmers have already discovered a more lucrative crop – marijuana – and its cultivation is on the rise. But, as with coca in Latin America, the big profits are unlikely to trickle down to the Uzbek, Tajik or Kyrgyz peasants who break their backs over it. In February 1995 the International Narcotics

Control Board said the Central Asian states were a major source of production and transit for drugs on the world market.

New Business Central Asia has a young, fairly skilled and entrepreneurial population capable of starting small manufacturing enterprises to fill out the present lack of industrial diversity, but obstacles abound. As in Soviet days, initiative is often punished, but now through heavy taxation and regulation of new businesses, and obstruction by middle-level apparatchiks. In Kyrgyzstan, banks won't give businesses free access to the money in their own accounts, so they cannot pay their overheads, services are shut off, and so on. As one manager told us, 'first came Socialism, then Communism, now Stupidism'.

So far the main visible form of capitalism in Central Asia is the 'kiosk economy': small-time dealers buying goods (mostly cigarettes, sweets, alcohol, cheap Chinese, Iranian and Russian clothes and furnishings) and reselling them at a higher price. Longer-term projects are frustrated by banks willing to make only the shortest of short-term loans. Another manifestation is 'petrol hookers' – the ubiquitous roadside fuel dealers who have winkled supplies from wholesalers over the border in Russia and elsewhere, and undersell the (usually sold-out) state outlets. Meanwhile, shortages are endemic because of the interruption, at a thousand different points, of the old Soviet interdependencies, with raw materials now going to the highest bidder on world markets instead of to captive markets within the USSR.

ENVIRONMENT

Central Asia is home to a unique range of ecosystems and an extraordinary variety of flora and fauna. But as with many places in the former USSR, its amazing landscapes also served as testing grounds for some of the worst cases of Soviet megalomania. Land and water mismanagement and destruction of natural habitat were part of a conscious effort to tame nature, or 'harness it like a white mare' as the propaganda had it. The

results are almost beyond belief and on a staggering scale.

Even casual students of the region are familiar with some of the most infamous catastrophes of Soviet environmental meddling: the gradual disappearance of the Aral Sea, the excessive levels of radiation around the Semey (Semipalatinsk) Nuclear Testing site, and the consequences of Khrushchev's Virgin Lands programme (which, according to Soviet theoreticians, should have allowed the USSR to overtake the USA in grain production).

Environmental Organisations

Following are some reliable contacts on environmental issues in Central Asia.

Kazakstan
    ISAR, Almaty; e-mail isarata@glas.apc.org
    Ekosys Fund, Almaty (☎ & fax (3272) 48-00-30, 47-60-28)
Tajikistan
    Yurii Skochilov, School of Ecological Education, 12/8 Akhmadi Donish, 734024 Dushanbe; ☎ (3772) 27-09-63, 25-34-03, fax 21-04-04, e-mail umeda@ glas.apc.org
Turkmenistan
    Andre Zatoka, CASDIN, Dashkhovuz Ecological Club, PO Box 4, 746300 Dashkhovuz; ☎ (36022) 283-55, email zatoka@glas.apc.org
Uzbekistan
    Oleg Ivanovich Tsaruk, EKOLOG, 11A/10 Gaydar, 700105 Tashkent; ☎ (3712) 46-72-11, email tashkent@glas.apc.org
Kyrgyzstan
    Emil Shukurov, Ecological Movement Alaine, 265 Chuy prospekt, 720071 Bishkek; ☎ (3312) 25-53-66, 25-53-70, email emil@aleyne. bishkek.su

The Aral Sea

One of the most amazing things about the Aral Sea disaster is that it was no accident. The Soviet planners who fatally tapped the rivers that fed the Aral Sea, to irrigate new cotton fields, *expected* the sea to dry up. They also wanted to bring water to Central Asia by a huge canal from Siberia – not to replenish the Aral Sea but to expand cotton production still further. They either didn't understand that drying up the world's fourth largest lake would wreck a whole region's

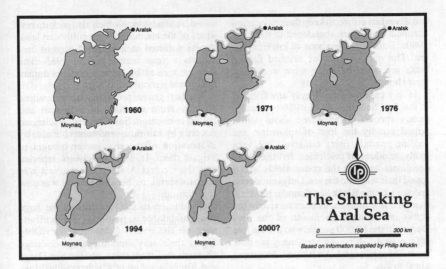

The Shrinking Aral Sea

1960   1971   1976

1994   2000?

0   150   300 km

Based on information supplied by Philip Micklin

climate and ecology, and cause untold suffering to its people, or didn't care.

The Aral Sea – or rather seas, since it split into two in 1987 – straddles the border between western Uzbekistan and southern Kazakstan. It's fed, in the years they actually reach it, by the Syr-Darya and Amu-Darya rivers, flowing down from the Tian Shan and Pamir. Back in the 1950s these rivers brought an average 55 cubic km of water a year to the Aral Sea, which stretched 400 km from end to end and 280 km from side to side, covering 66,900 sq km. The sea had by all accounts lovely clear water, pristine beaches, plenty of fish to support a big fishing industry in the ports of Moynaq and Aralsk, and even passenger ferries crossing it from north to south. The extensive deltas of the Syr-Darya and Amu-Darya were ecologically unique networks of rivers, lakes, reedbeds, marshes and forests supporting very diverse flora and fauna.

Then the USSR's central planners decided to boost cotton production in Uzbekistan, Turkmenistan and Kazakstan, to feed a leap forward in the Soviet textile industry. Although by 1960 the Amu-Darya and Syr-Darya already supported an estimated 50,000 sq km of irrigation – mainly for cotton – the Aral Sea had survived that sort of 'take' without shrinking. But the new cotton fields, many of them on poorer desert soils and fed by long, unlined canals open to the sun, drank much more water than the old ones. The irrigated area grew by only about 20% between 1960 and 1980 but the annual water take from the rivers doubled from 45 to 90 cubic km. The biggest canal, the Karakum canal reaching from the Amu-Darya far across southern Turkmenistan, takes 14 cubic km a year – nearly a quarter of the Aral Sea's old supply. By the 1980s the annual flow into the Aral Sea was less than one-tenth of the 1950s supply.

Production of cotton rose, but the Aral Sea, unavoidably, sank. Between 1966 and 1993 its level fell by more than 16 metres and its eastern and southern shores receded by up to 80 km. Its volume shrank by 75%, and its area by about half. In 1987 the Aral divided into a smaller northern sea and a larger southern one, each fed, sometimes, by one of the rivers.

The two main fishing ports, Aralsk (Kazakstan) in the north and Moynaq (Uzbekistan) in the south, had been left high and dry when efforts to keep their navigation channels open were abandoned in the early 1980s. Both are now about 40 km from the sea. The rusting hulks of beached fishing boats are scattered along what were once their shores.

In any case there are hardly any fish left in the Aral Sea: the last of its 20-odd indigenous species disappeared about 1985, wiped out by the loss of spawning and feeding grounds, rising salt levels and, very likely, residues of pesticides, fertilisers and defoliants used on the cotton fields which found their way into the sea. Only introduced species like the Black Sea flounder remain – though a few indigenous ones survive in the deltas and around the mouth of the Syr-Darya. Of the 60,000 people who used to live off the Aral fishing industry, many are now gone: Moynaq and Aralsk are becoming ghost towns.

In 1992 the little channel still connecting the northern and southern seas was blocked by a small dyke to prevent further water loss from the northern sea, which is now rising again. It's forecast that the northern sea will reach a state of equilibrium, with an area of 3500 sq km, by about 2025. But if recent rates of depletion continue, the southern sea is expected to split again by 2005 into western and eastern parts. The eastern part will receive the Amu-Darya and is expected eventually to stabilise at about 7000 sq km, but the western part will go on shrinking.

The Aral Sea's shrinkage has devastated the land around it, and a visit to anywhere near the sea is a ride into a nightmare of blighted towns, blighted land and blighted people. Locals talk of a new Aq Kum (White desert) forming an unholy trinity with the Kyzylkum (Red desert) and Karakum (Black desert). The climate around the lake has changed: the air is drier, winters are a few degrees colder and a month longer, summers are hotter. The average number of rainless days has risen from 30 to 35 in the 1950s to 120 to 150 now. The dried-up lake bed is extremely salty which makes revegetation difficult. Salt, sand and dust from the exposed bed is blown hundreds of km in big salt-dust-sandstorms which also pick up residues of the chemicals from cultivated land. Aralsk suffered an average 65 days of dust storms a year from 1966 to 1985. The damage caused by these storms to human health and agriculture is huge.

Further grave problems have resulted directly from methods of irrigation and cotton cultivation. Soils have been salinised not only by salt-dust-sandstorms but also by evaporation of the river water brought to irrigate them. In 1994 *Newsweek* reported that the Central Asian cotton harvest was actually shrinking because the soil was now so salinised.

In addition to salt, residues of the huge doses of defoliants, pesticides and fertilisers used on the cotton fields have inevitably found their way into irrigation drainage channels and from there into the Syr-Darya and Amu-Darya, all of which provide drinking water. DDT pesticide was widely used till about 1982 and is still present in high concentrations in soils. Defoliants are used to make cotton harvesting easier but one variety, Butifos, used till about 1990, was so toxic that according to some reports it killed thousands of people. Much food grown in the Aral basin contains residues of these chemicals and is lacking in vitamins. Raw sewage too is dumped in the rivers.

In human terms, the worst affected areas are those to the Aral sea's south – as far as northern Turkmenistan – and east (the areas north and west of the Aral Sea are very sparsely populated). The catalogue of health problems is awful: salt and dust are blamed for increased respiratory illnesses and cancers of the throat and oesophagus; poor drinking water has been implicated in high rates of typhoid, paratyphoid, hepatitis and dysentery; the area has the highest mortality and infant mortality rates in the former USSR, and in parts of Karakalpakstan (far west Uzbekistan) more than one baby in 10 dies (compared to one in 100 or more in Britain or the USA). Karakalpakstan also has high rates of birth deformities and in Nukus, the Karakalpak capital, virtually all pregnant women are anaemic, which leads to many premature births. In Aralsk, tuberculosis is common.

Of the 173 animal species that used to live around the Aral Sea, only 38 survive. Especially devastating has been the degradation of the big Amu-Darya and Syr-Darya deltas, with their very diverse flora and fauna. The deltas have supported irrigated agriculture for many centuries, along with hunting, fishing, and harvesting of reeds for building and paper-making. But the drastically reduced river flow has dried up most of the deltas' vast marshes, reed beds and lakes, and, with the polluted nature of the remaining water, has decimated the once abundant water bird population. The deltas' dense *toghay* forests, unique to the valleys of these desert rivers, on which many animals depended, have shrunk to one-fifth of their old size. Salination has brought lower yields for irrigated agriculture in the deltas, and worse pastures for animals.

Barsakelmes island in the Aral Sea, a nature reserve protecting the saiga antelope and the rare Asiatic wild ass, has reportedly become an unviable habitat because it is now so arid.

Nor can matters have been helped one jot by the use of Vozrozhdenia island as a Soviet biological warfare testing site: locals have blamed Vozrozhdenia for mass deaths of saiga on the Ustyurt plateau south-west of the Aral in the 1980s, and suspicions remain over human illnesses in and near Moynaq. Ironically, the island's name in pious Russian means 'rebirth'.

Long-Term Solutions To restore the Aral would require that irrigation from the Amu-Darya and Syr-Darya cease for three years, or at least a slashing of the irrigated area from over 70,000 to 40,000 sq km, combined with a big improvement in irrigation techniques reducing water use per sq km by one-third. In other words, a complete restructuring of the economies of Uzbekistan (which has over half the Aral basin's irrigated land) and Turkmenistan (also heavily dependent on cotton). No one is seriously thinking of this.

The Aral crisis became apparent to Soviet scientists in the 1970s, and finally in 1988 a gradual increase in water flow to the sea was ordered, to be achieved by more efficient irrigation and an end to the expansion of irrigation. Before the collapse of the USSR some steps were taken to improve human conditions in the Aral area with the building of new water mains, hospitals and desalination plants. But the crack-up of the old empire led to a breakdown of planning and, worse, fears of conflict over rights to the waters of the Syr-Darya and Amu-Darya between the Central Asian republics– two of which, Kyrgyzstan and Tajikistan, hold the rivers' upper reaches while the other three, downriver, are economically dependent on the rivers.

Early promises of cooperation and money from the Central Asian leaders bore little fruit and in 1995 President Karimov of Uzbekistan was still regurgitating the old idea of diverting water from Siberian rivers. International schemes organised by the World Bank, USAID and the European Union seem to offer more hope. The three-year first phase of the World Bank scheme, with a projected budget of US$250 million, aims to clean up water supplies, improve sanitation and public health, restore some economic viability and biodiversity to the Amu-Darya delta, and stabilise the Aral's northern sea.

Longer-term efforts may focus on building dykes around parts of the sea that can be maintained, rehabilitating the blighted region around the sea and stabilising its fragile environment, improving water management and building up local institutions to manage these projects. Whether the will exists among Central Asia's politicians to

The authors would like to extend sincere thanks to Philip Micklin, Professor of Geography at the Western Michigan University, USA, for generous help with information on the Aral Sea. ∎

introduce less water-intensive irrigation methods, or even less thirsty crops than cotton, remains to be seen.

Nuclear Tests

When the USSR decided it had to test nuclear bombs, it chose – as nuclear powers always do – places a long way from where the decision makers lived and which looked, at that safe distance, 'empty' on the map. Several testing sites were used around the USSR during the Cold War, but the main ones were the Novaya Zemlya islands in the Arctic Ocean and, busiest of all, a tract of steppe between the big north-eastern Kazakstan cities of Semey (better known by its old Russian name, Semipalatinsk) and Pavlodar.

Between 1949 and 1989 about 470 nuclear bombs were exploded at the Polygon, as the Semey testing ground was known. Around 150 of the bombs were exploded above or at ground level, the others underground after above-ground testing was banned by international treaty in 1963. The region around the Polygon certainly wasn't uninhabited: the very first bomb test drenched several villages with fallout after a 'late change of wind direction'. The nerve centre of the Polygon was the town of Kurchatov, on the Irtysh river about 150 km north-west of Semey. Kurchatov is named after the scientist considered the father of the Soviet bomb, but locally it's better known as Konechnaya – Russian for 'the end'. Because of the secrecy surrounding the tests, no one was told what danger they might be in, even when some were given health tests. Over the years, evacuations of people living close to the test sites were rare, and temporary. No one was ever evacuated from Semey or other cities.

The end for the Polygon came about as a result of the biggest environmental protest movement the USSR ever saw, – the Nevada-Semey (formerly Nevada-Semipalatinsk) Movement, named after the chief US and USSR nuclear testing grounds. Nevada-Semey was founded in February 1989 on the initiative of Olzhas Suley-menov, a leading Kazak poet and politician, in the wake of two particular tests which created big shock waves and a radioactive cloud over northern Kazakstan. Within a few days more than a million signatures had been collected on Kazakstan's streets calling for an end to bomb tests by the two superpowers and the closure of the sites.

Support from anti-nuclear movements in the USA, Germany, Japan and other countries followed. Such pressure forced the Kazakstan Communist Party to call for closure of the Polygon and no further tests took place there after October 1989.

In 1991, fears arose that the Soviet military were planning new tests at the Polygon, but in the wake of the abortive August coup in Moscow, Kazakstan's President Nursultan Nazarbaev finally closed the Polygon, and announced compensation for the victims. The following year the area around the site was declared an ecological disaster zone, agriculture was banned, and foreign experts invited to help the clean up.

Precise data on the damage to people and the environment by 40 years of radioactive contamination of land, rain, food and water are hard to get. But the Nevada-Semey movement says the effects are spread over a large area with a population of four million people, covering all or part of the Semey, Pavlodar, Qaraghandy and east Kazakstan regions of Kazakstan and the Altay territory of Russia.

Health problems include high numbers of children born blind, mute, deaf or physically or mentally handicapped (in the Abralinsky district 125 of the 3200 children are handicapped); high child mortality (in some areas 38 children out of 1000 die, about four times the British or American average); high rates of fatal cancer and early senility; and 'radiation AIDS', with radiation-impaired immune systems giving in to diseases like tuberculosis, brucellosis and pneumonia.

According to Nevada-Semey, over 900,000 people are entitled to compensation. It's not clear whether all these have specific health conditions caused by the nuclear tests, but in 1992 alone 170,000 people visited health centres in the Semey region for assessments.

If your curiosity stretches that far, it's not too difficult to visit the Polygon; see the Around Semey section in the Kazakstan chapter.

Apart from the legacy of the Polygon, independent Kazakstan also inherited 1400 nuclear warheads from the USSR. From early on it declared its intention to be a non-nuclear state, but President Nazarbaev used the issue as a bargaining chip with Russia and the USA, and quite when and how the warheads are to be got rid of is still not clear.

The Nevada-Semey Movement, meanwhile, today concentrates on reviving the earth, nature and humanity in the affected areas of Kazakstan and on stopping nuclear testing worldwide.

Meanwhile the Chinese still explode their nuclear toys at Lop Nor, in the Taklamakan desert, normally in June and in late October, when the prevailing winds blow towards Central Asia. The Chinese government claims the test will cease once they have signed the nuclear test-ban treaty. Its neighbours, the Central Asian Republics, are vociferous in their demands to end the explosions.

Nevada-Semey is also, in a small way, into tourism. It has about 17 branches around Kazakstan, a few in other countries, and its head office (☎ (7-3272) 63-48-17, fax (7-3272) 50-71-87) is at Vinogradov köshesi 85, Almaty, Kazakstan.

The 'Virgin Lands' Campaign

In 1954 under Khrushchev, the government undertook to expand arable land on a massive scale by irrigating the steppes and deserts of Kazakstan and Uzbekistan. The water was to come via canals from the Amu-Darya and Syr-Darya, and certain Siberian rivers would be tapped or even reversed.

The Siberian part was dropped but the rest went ahead with great fanfare. Most early labour was by volunteers from all over the country, some of whom stayed. Uzbekistan was soon producing 70% of the USSR's cotton and Kazakstan a big share of its wheat, but only under glasnost did the downside become clear. In some areas of the Kazak Steppe, for example, soil has become degraded or is so over-fertilised that local rivers and lands are seriously polluted. By some measures, the problems of erosion, aridity and salinity are on a larger scale than those associated with the Aral Sea.

Conservation & Biodiversity

Threats to biodiversity come from, among other causes, overgrazing, poaching and general unsustainable agriculture, augmented by heavy pesticide and chemical use.

Central Asia covers only 17% of the former USSR's territory, but contains over 50% of its measurable variety in fauna and flora. The existing system of national parks and nature reserves, one of the rare positive legacies of the USSR, is nevertheless antiquated and inadequate. In Kyrgyzstan, for example, just 2% of the country's area is dedicated to land conservation, of which most is only semi-protected and commercially managed, eg as hunting reserves. In Kazakstan, only 2.5% of the land area is protected, and although an additional three national parks and 14 nature reserves have been proposed, this would only add an extra 1%, well below the minimum 10% recommended by the World Conservation Union.

Nature reserves (zapovedniki) and protected areas (zakazniki) throughout Central Asia suffer from a lack of government funding. Staff are few and management tends to be incompetent or toothless. In Tajikistan, civil strife has halted all initiatives; nature reserves have been theatres of battle, with disastrous consequences for their fauna and flora. Other protected areas have suffered repeated logging by the army and by a local populace desperate to survive long and harsh winters.

Kyrgyzstan, annual refuge for thousands of migrating birds, enjoys a unique position among researchers. The mountain goose, among other rare species, nests on the shores of its mountain lakes, but the population has shrunk over the years to less than 15 pairs counted worldwide. Again, lack of funds has prevented local scientists studying the causes of this decline. Many species of reptiles and birds, including the white stork, suffer from general degradation of marshlands and destruction of their nesting sites.

In 1985 the Kyrgyz 'Red Book' – the regional edition of *Krasnaya Kniga SSSR* (The USSR Red Book), bible of endangered species in the former USSR – stated that 15% of mammals and 10% of birds in Kyrgyzstan were threatened with extinction. Since then the situation has further deteriorated.

In many former Central Asian republics, poaching has always been a problem, despite feeble official attempts at control. Now it's on the rise, both as a food source and for trophies to sell for hard currency, and goes almost totally unchallenged. Encouraged by stories of fanatic western hunter-tourists knocking off Marco Polo sheep and snow leopards, local people have joined the trade. Tourist demand for such trophies is still thankfully low.

Overgrazing

Overgrazing is a major problem affecting all the Central Asian republics. The steady rise in livestock grazing has unhinged delicate ecosystems and accelerated desertification and soil erosion. From 1941 to 1991 the population of sheep and goats more than doubled to 5.5 million in Turkmenistan and quadrupled to 10 million in Kyrgyzstan, while a third of Kyrgyzstan's available grasslands has disappeared.

Degradation of pasture is a constant feature of Central Asia's landscape. In Kazakstan much of the semi-arid steppe, traditionally used as pasture over the centuries, was put to the plough under the Virgin Lands campaign. Wind erosion in the steppes of north Kazakstan has accelerated soil depletion. Livestock breeders searching farther and further into semi-arid steppes and semi-deserts for pasture, leave behind a tired and useless land.

Soil degradation is also activated by failure to rotate crops and by excessive use of chemicals, and aggravated by irrigation

water mismanagement. Kazakstan, a major exporter of wheat, and Uzbekistan and Tajikistan, the former USSR's main suppliers of cotton, have suffered the most. In Kazakstan, 40% of rangeland is considered to be overused, and will need 10 to 50 years to be restored to its original fertility.

In Kyrgyzstan an estimated 70% of pastureland suffers erosion above acceptable levels. In Tajikistan the productivity of summer pastures in the mountains has dropped by 50% over the last 25 years.

Chemical Contamination

Cotton is to blame for many of Central Asia's ills. Its present cultivation demands high levels of pesticides and fertilisers, which are now found throughout the food chain – in the water, in human and animal milk, in vegetables and fruit, and in the soil itself.

In Kyrgyzstan, soils are seriously contaminated with DDT, especially in the Osh region where 94% of soils contain DDT. Agricultural chemicals have been found in over 10% of food samples in Kyrgyzstan; and in Uzbekistan almost 20% of food samples did not meet government standards. In Tajikistan, according to the head of the Institute of Maternity & Infancy in Dushanbe, 95% of expectant mothers coming from Tajik villages are unwell or gravely ill, which many researchers blame on pesticide-induced effects on the immune system. See The Aral Sea in this section to read about the appalling situation in Karakalpakstan.

Industrial Pollution

Industrial development is also the cause of severe pollution in Central Asia, with Kazakstan, the third largest industrial power in the CIS, suffering particularly badly. Many cities are over-polluted even by Soviet standards, the worst culprit being power stations running on low-grade coal. Metallurgical factories located in major cities (Öskemen, Shymkent, Jeskazgan and Balqash) are all outdated and highly polluting. Almost two-thirds of the facilities inspected in 1990 had emissions above the state's permissable levels. Other Kazakstan towns with air pollution well above government thresholds were the metallurgical industry town of Leninogor, and the capital, Almaty, with excessive levels of carbon monoxide from heavy traffic, the use of very low octane fuel and the absence of catalytic converters. Lake Balqash has been polluted by copper smelters set up on its shores in the 1930s; bird and other lake life is now practically extinct.

Uzbekistan, also heavily industrialised during the Soviet period, has a concentration of polluting industries in the Ferghana Valley (Ferghana ranked as one of the 30 most polluted Soviet towns in 1989) and in Tashkent. Problem areas in Turkmenistan include air pollution in the industrial centre of Charjou, and oil pollution along the shore of the Caspian Sea. At the mouth of the Caspian bay of Kara-Bogaz-Gol is a dam built to isolate it from declining Caspian Sea water levels; but now that the Caspian is rising rapidly, the dam encourages flooding of the flat seashore.

Mining

Following the same pattern as industrial development, mining techniques are inefficient, outdated and environmentally hazardous. Tajikistan and Kyrgyzstan both served as Soviet raw material sources. Uranium for the Soviet nuclear military machine was mined in both countries (the Kyrgyz SSR's uranium sector earned the sobriquet 'Atomic Fortress of the Tian Shan'), and as many as 50 abandoned mine sites in Kyrgyzstan alone may now leak unstablised radioactive tailings or contaminated groundwater into their surroundings; some are along major waterways which drain eventually to the Aral Sea.

Gold in the mountains naturally attracted the interest of Soviet developers. Since independence, foreign companies have followed in their footsteps. Several large mining and refining projects are underway in Kyrgyzstan, many of them Canadian-Kyrgyz joint ventures.

While foreign companies tend to be more attentive to environmental risks than the old Soviet authorities, the big money involved in such projects encourages environmental abuse both by local governments and by foreign companies. With the promise of hard-currency earnings in an otherwise bleak economic landscape, nature is always the victim.

POPULATION & PEOPLE

The total population of the former Soviet Central Asia is about 54 million, with a 2.4% annual growth rate. With China's Xinjiang Autonomous Region, the region's total is some 67 million. Few areas of its size are home to such tangled demographics and daunting transitions.

It's a social rollercoaster in Central Asia: the overall birth rate is down, deaths from all causes are up, economies are plummeting, crime is skyrocketing, life expectancies have dropped and migration (most especially emigration) is on the rise. But in a few years these setbacks to population growth will

---

Central Asia Country Populations (millions, approx)

Kazakstan	17.2
Kyrgyzstan	4.5
Tajikistan	5.8
Turkmenistan	4.2
Uzbekistan	23
Xinjiang	13

Central Asia Ethnic Breakdown (millions, approx)

These are not worldwide population figures, but only for the former USSR Central Asian republics, plus Xinjiang.

Chinese	5.5	(9%)
Kazaks	9	(15%)
Kyrgyz	2.4	(4%)
Russians	12.3	(20%)
Tajiks	3.3	(5%)
Turkmen	2.7	(4%)
Uyghurs	7	(12%)
Uzbeks	18	(30%)

probably look like small blips on a steep upward curve. Central Asia has shown high birth rates and population growth ever since the Russians started taking censuses.

Each republic has inherited an ethnic grab-bag from the Soviet system. Thus you'll find Uzbek towns in Kyrgyzstan, legions of Tajiks in the cities of Uzbekistan, Kazaks grazing their cattle in Kyrgyzstan, Turkmen in Uzbekistan – and Russians and Ukrainians everywhere. In Xinjiang, Uyghurs are joined by hordes of Chinese and some Kazaks and Kyrgyz.

Tajikistan exemplifies how a Central Asian republic can be demographically complex. Its 3.2 million Tajiks constitute only 59% of the country's population, and fewer than half of the world's Tajiks (more Tajiks inhabit Afghanistan than Tajikistan, and large groups also live in Uzbekistan, Kazakstan and Xinjiang). Some 23% of Tajikistan's population are Uzbeks, with whom there is considerable ethnic rivalry. And on an urgent note, Tajikistan's annual birth rate is an astonishing 5% (in Bangladesh it's 2.2%, in the USA 0.9%).

Ethnic Conflicts

Given the complicated mix of nationalities across national boundaries, Central Asia's ethnic situation is surprisingly tranquil, but it was not always so. From the late 1980s until independence in 1991, there were numerous flare-ups: Kazaks against Russians, Uzbeks against Jews and Meskhetian Turks, Kyrgyz and Uzbeks against each other. Moscow described the violence as 'ethnic', ignoring more complicated causes such as land and water rights and housing space. Rifts do exist, though they hardly deserve the status of the media's ominous 'age-old ethnic feuds'. The most noticeable divide – and a largely amicable one – is between the traditionally sedentary peoples, the Uzbeks, Tajiks and Uyghurs, and their formerly nomadic neighbours, the Kazaks, Kyrgyz and Turkmen.

One serious old wound remains which binds Central Asians together – all share bitter memories of subjugation by two Russian empires, reaching its depths during the Stalin years, and extending right up to 1991. The Uyghurs of Xinjiang have similar grievances with China.

Migration

Most emigration from Central Asia consists of minority groups – Russians, Ukrainians, Germans, Koreans – going to their 'homelands', though the individuals may have spent their entire lives in Central Asia. The Jewish population, even the venerable Bukharan Jewish community with roots to the 9th century, is leaving for Israel. Dungans (Chinese Muslims) and Uyghurs, however, are understandably not flocking to Xinjiang. Those minority groups that do stay are beginning to speak up for recognition and rights.

Immigration is relatively low and is mostly intra-regional and intra-CIS – for example, Uzbeks from Kyrgyzstan moving to Uzbekistan. Tens of thousands of Tajik war refugees are marking time in neighbouring republics. Of Turkic groups living in the so-called 'far abroad' (outside the CIS), few members have immigrated to their Central Asian motherlands.

Peoples

Above all it was the Soviets who created Central Asia's national identities, and the process went deeper than the grotesque and arbitrary boundaries visible on today's maps.

Before the Revolution of 1917, Central Asians usually identified themselves 'ethnically' as simply Muslim, or as Turk or Persian, or by their tribe. Later, separate nationalities were 'identified' by Soviet scholars. Central Asia's linguistic continuum was artificially teased apart into five standardised languages (Tajik, an Indo-European language, was the easiest to distinguish), with a host of in-between dialects lost in the process. Similarly, the ethnic continuum was vivisected and its five most distinguishable parts bottled in separate republics. Distinct, carefully crafted 'traditions' were formulated and parcelled out to each of these nationalities.

While it is easy to see the problems this has created, some Kazaks and Kyrgyz at least will admit that they owe their survival as a nation to the Soviet process of nation-building.

The following sections are a summary of who's who. For further information on the customs and history of the main groups, see the respective country chapters.

Kazaks The name *kazak* is said to mean 'free warrior' or 'steppe roamer'. Kazaks trace their roots to the 15th century, when rebellious kinsmen of an Uzbek khan broke away and settled in present-day Kazakstan. They divide themselves into three main divisions, or *zhuz* corresponding to the historical Great, Central and Little Hordes (see the History section in this chapter). 'What zhuz do you belong to?' is a common opening question among Kazaks. They are the most Russified of Central Asians, owing to long historical contact with Russia.

Most Kazaks have Mongolian facial features similar to the Kyrgyz. Most wear western or Russian clothes but you may see women – particularly on special occasions – in long dresses with stand-up collars, or brightly decorated velvet waistcoats and heavy jewellery, and sometimes fur-trimmed headdresses topped with crane plumes. Some men still wear baggy shirts and trousers and sleeveless jackets, wool or cotton robes, and/or a skullcap or a high, tasselled felt hat resembling nothing so much as an elf-hat.

Kazaks adhere rather loosely to Islam. Their earliest contacts with the religion, from the 16th century, took the form of wandering Sufi darvishes or ascetics. The personal focus of Sufism (see Religion in this chapter) was compatible with their nomadic lifestyle.

The 6.6 million Kazaks are a minority – about 40% – in 'their' country, Kazakstan.

Kyrgyz Some Kyrgyz are fond of suggesting that long ago some of their ancestors from Siberia crossed the Bering land bridge to become the forebears of native Americans (there are indeed some resemblances). Many Kyrgyz derive their name from *kyrk kyz*, which means '40 girls' and goes along with legends of 40 original tribal mothers.

The name 'Kyrgyz' is one of the oldest recorded ethnic names in Asia, going back to the 2nd century BC in Chinese sources. At that time the ancestors of the modern Kyrgyz are said to have lived in the upper Yenisey basin in Siberia. They migrated to the mountains of what is now Kyrgyzstan from the 10th to 15th centuries, some fleeing wars and some in the ranks of Mongol armies. Kazaks and Kyrgyz share many customs and have similar languages, and in a sense they are simply the steppe (Kazak) and mountain (Kyrgyz) variants of the same people.

For special events Kyrgyz women's dress is similar to Kazak women's. Older women may wear a large white turban with the number of windings indicating her status. Kyrgyz men wear a white, embroidered, usually tasselled, felt cap called an *ak kalpak*. In winter, older men wear a long sheepskin coat and a round fur-trimmed hat called a *tebbetey*.

Northern Kyrgyz are more Russified and less observant of Muslim doctrine than their cousins in the south (in Jalal-Abad and Osh provinces). Like the Kazaks, they adopted Islam relatively late and limited it to what could fit in their saddlebags.

The Kyrgyz in Kyrgyzstan are a bare majority. There are sizeable Kyrgyz populations in Xinjiang (147,000) and Afghanistan.

Tajiks With their Mediterranean features, and the occasional green-eyed redhead, Tajiks like to recall that their land was once visited by Alexander the Great and his troops, who are known to have taken local brides. Whether that blood is still visible or not, the Tajiks are in fact descended from an ancient Indo-European people, the Aryans, making them relatives of present-day Iranians. Before this century, *taj* was merely a term denoting a Persian speaker (all other Central Asian peoples speak Turkic languages).

Tajiks have been in Tajikistan for thousands of years, making them the oldest of all

Central Asian groups. They often consider themselves to be the most civilised as well, pointing out that many great 'Persian' literary figures in fact hailed from parts closer to Tajikistan. Some Tajik nationalists have even demanded that Uzbekistan 'give back' Samarkand and Bukhara, as these cities were long-time centres of Persian culture.

Traditional Tajik dress for men includes a heavy quilted coat *(tapan)*, tied with a sash which also secures a sheathed dagger, and a black, embroidered cap *(tupi)*. Tajik women could almost be identified in the dark, with their long, psychedelically coloured dresses *(kurta)* with matching head scarves *(rumol)*, and underneath the dress striped trousers *(izor)* and dayglo slippers. Women may also wear embroidered skullcaps.

Most Tajiks are Sunni Muslims, but Pamiri Tajiks of the Gorno-Badakhshan region belong to the Ismaili sect of Shia Islam.

Turkmen Legend has it that all Turkmen are descended from the fabled Oghuz Khan or from the warriors who rallied into tribes around his 24 grandsons. Most historians think they were displaced nomadic horse-breeding tribes who drifted into the oases around the Karakum desert (and into Persia, Syria and Anatolia) from the foothills of the Altay mountains in the wake of the Seljuq Turks.

The hardships of desert-based nomadism forged them into a distinct group long before Soviet nation-building. Interestingly, there was a Turkmen literary language as early as the mid-1700s. Turkmen remain among the least Russified of Central Asians.

Turkmen tend to be tall, and their faces show a mixture of Mongolian and Caucasian features. They are divided into several tribes, dominated by the Tekke. Turkmen males are easily recognisable in their huge sheepskin hats *(telpek)*, either white and fleecy or black with thick ringlets like dreadlocks, worn year round, hot as the summers may be. They wear baggy trousers tucked into knee-length boots, and white shirts under knee-length cotton jackets, traditionally cherry red. Older

men wear a long belted coat. Turkmen women wear heavy, ankle-length, silk dresses, the favourite colours being wine reds and maroons, with colourful trousers underneath.

The Turkmen had the nomad liking for Sufism, and that sect is now strongly represented in Turkmenistan.

Turkmenistan's population is 72% Turkmen, giving it the highest proportion of the titular nationality of any Central Asian republic.

Uzbeks The Uzbek khans, Islamicised descendants of Jenghiz Khan, left their home in southern Siberia in search of conquest, establishing themselves in what is now Uzbekistan by the 15th century. They resisted Russification and have emerged from Soviet rule with a strong sense of identification with their rich heritage. Uzbek neighbourhoods *(mahalla)* are coherent and solid, both physically and socially. Houses are built behind high walls, sometimes with handsome gates. With their high profile in all the former USSR republics, Uzbeks are often

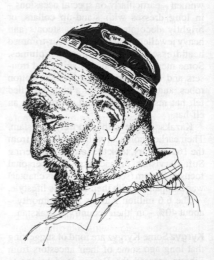

Embroidered skull caps are worn by both Uzbek men and women; those worn by women are the more decorative and colourful.

cast as the regional bogeyman, seeking political hegemony over Central Asia.

Uzbek men usually wear sombre colours, except for the bright-coloured sash which older men use to close their long quilted coats. Nearly all wear the *dopy* or *doppe*, a black, four sided skullcap embroidered in white. In winter, older men wear a telpak. Uzbek women are fond of dresses in sparkly, or in any case brightly coloured, cloth, often as a knee-length gown with trousers of the same material underneath. One or two braids indicates a married woman; more means she's single. Eyebrows that grow together over the bridge of the nose are considered attractive and are often supplemented with pencil for the right effect. Both sexes flash lots of gold teeth.

The most devout and conservative Muslims in Central Asia appear to be the Uzbeks of the Ferghana Valley.

Uyghurs The Uyghurs have a proud heritage stretching over 1100 years to the Uyghur khanate of southern Siberia. Uyghurs were the first Turkic people to settle down, populating Xinjiang during the days of Silk Road trade. Their first writing system, long since discarded, became the basis of Mongolian script. Uyghurs of Xinjiang now write with Arabic letters. Their language is similar to Uzbek.

In Xinjiang, Uyghurs are immediately distinguishable from the occupying Han, or ethnic Chinese. They are larger and have generally darker complexions and more Mediterranean features. The four sided skullcap of the men is also a giveaway, though older Uyghur men may wear a tall black cotton hat with a narrow fringe of fur at the bottom.

Uyghurs make up only 53% of Xinjiang's population. The reason is Sinicisation: China has sought to dilute Uyghur nationalism by flooding the region with Han immigrants. While minorities are exempt from China's one-child family planning regime, noises have been made in Beijing to make the law apply to everybody; the probability of resentment or even revolt in Xinjiang, where

the Uyghur birth rate is high, must surely weigh on the government's mind.

Sizeable Uyghur minorities live in the former USSR Central Asian republics, having moved there after heavy Chinese persecution in the latter 19th century.

Slavs Russians and Ukrainians have settled in Central Asia in several waves, the first in the 19th century with colonisation and the latest in the 1950s during the Virgin Lands campaign. Numerous villages in remoter parts of Central Asia with names like Orlovka or Alexandrovka were founded by the early settlers and are still inhabited by their descendants.

Many Slavs, feeling deeply aggrieved as political and administrative power devolves to 'local' people, have emigrated to Russia and Ukraine. Some have returned, either disillusioned with life in the Motherland or reaffirmed in the knowledge that Central Asia is their home, like it or not.

Other Nationalities The **Han Chinese** are hard to miss in Xinjiang's cities and towns. **Dungans** are Muslim Chinese who first moved across the border in 1882, especially to Kazakstan and Kyrgyzstan, to escape persecution. Few still speak Chinese, though their cuisine remains distinctive. **Koreans** arrived in Central Asia as deportees in WWII. They have preserved little of their traditional culture. They typically farm vegetables and dominate the grocers' stalls of some bazars.

Germans were deported in WWII from their age-old home in the Volga region, or came as settlers (some of them Mennonites) in the late 19th century. Most are now departing en masse to Germany, at a rate of some 150,000 a year. Likewise, **Jews** are making for Israel.

Tatars, a Turkic people from Russia (but descended from the Mongol Golden Horde), began settling in Central Asia with the tsar's encouragement in the mid-1800s. Most look more like Russians than like other Turkic peoples. **Meskhetian Turks** have groups in the Ferghana (the largest concentration), Chu and Ili valleys.

Karakalpaks occupy their own republic in north-west Uzbekistan and have cultural and linguistic ties with Kazaks, Uzbeks and Kyrgyz (see the section on Karakalpakstan in the Uzbekistan chapter). **Kurds** are another WWII-era addition to the pot, with many living in Kazakstan. Estimates of their numbers in Central Asia range from 150,000 to over a million.

EDUCATION

Before the Revolution of 1917, education in Central Asia was largely through the limited, men-only network of Islamic schools and medressas (seminaries). Illiteracy was taken more or less for granted.

As part of the early Bolshevik drive to educate and bring minority nations into the socialist fold, largely state-financed national education, obligatory through secondary school, was provided across the board. The old Arabic alphabet was replaced with a simpler Roman one, and later with a modified Cyrillic script. As a result, male and female literacy shot up during the Soviet years. In Central Asia in 1926, the literacy rate ranged from 2.2% among Tajiks to 7.1% for Kazaks. By 1970 all ethnic groups had achieved literacy rates in excess of 97%, largely in their own languages.

Presently in Central Asia, general education is compulsory to age 14. In 1993 there were 4.9 million students in general (primary and secondary) schools, 220,000 in 440 vocational schools and 322,000 in 53 institutes of higher education. Some 58% of the population over age 25 have full secondary or some post-secondary education, with about 10% receiving higher education. Teacher-student ratios (1:19 according to one source, 1:13 from another) and the number of inhabitants per college or university (two million) are far more favourable than in the rest of the so-called developing world.

But statistics don't tell it all. Many badly paid and disillusioned teachers are moving on to more lucrative 'businesses'. The end of the old Soviet subsidies means the quality

and supporting infrastructure of public schools is deteriorating. Pricey new private schools, accessible only to children of the urban nouveaux riches, are widening the gap between haves and have-nots. Inevitably, some diplomas appear to be awarded less on the basis of merit than on the number of dollars slipped between the exam sheets.

While the Soviet system produced excellent technicians and engineers, the human sciences (eg economics, history, public administration, international relations) were so heavily ideologised that the old textbooks are now worthless. Meanwhile the newly independent republics cannot get their own textbooks into print for lack of funds and even of paper.

The rapid shift from Arabic to Roman and then to Cyrillic as the official script (and recent decisions by several republics to return to Roman) has led to a kind of 'virtual illiteracy', with older people using alphabets incomprehensible to their children and grandchildren.

Free Islamic schools (often financed by Middle Eastern foundations) are multiplying in rural, conservative areas like the Ferghana Valley and southern Tajikistan. While Islamic education is clearly offering Central Asians a return to old values and a new perspective on their own culture, many of these schools are simply conduits for imported fundamentalist ideas.

In Uzbekistan, a university for 5000 in Marghilan and several Saudi-financed medressas of the Wahhabi branch of Sunni Islam were nipped in the bud by 1993 legislation banning private schools, a result of the government's unease about fundamentalism.

Under the Soviet system, women got 'economic equality' – the chance to study and work as hard as men while retaining all the responsibilities of homemakers. Female literacy approached male levels and women assumed positions of responsibility in middle-level administration and academia. But the combination of rising unemployment in post-Soviet economies, and the resurgence of traditional values, which favour early, arranged marriages and large families, has eroded these gains in rural areas. And while some Islamic schools are co-educational, there is still not a woman to be seen in the medressas.

Despite this somewhat gloomy picture, education reforms have included increased emphasis on Central Asian history and literature, the renewed study of Arabic script, and the adoption in 1992 of the American university degree system. The European Union's European Human Rights Foundation (☎ & fax (02) 732.66.53, e-mail ehrf@gn.apc.org) in Brussels is financing a number of education reform projects through non-governmental organisations in Central Asia.

ARTS
Architecture
The most impressive surviving artistic heritage of Central Asia is its architecture, and some of the world's most audacious and beautiful examples of Islamic religious buildings are to be found at Bukhara, Khiva and, especially, Samarkand.

Thanks in the main to the destructive urges of Jenghiz Khan, virtually nothing has survived from the pre-Islamic era or the first centuries of Arab rule. Most of the monumental architecture standing today dates from the time of the Timurids (14th to 15th century), rulers who could be almost as savage as the Mongol warlords but who also had a bent for artistic patronage.

Like a butterfly collector, Timur himself accumulated artists and craftsmen from his conquered territories and brought them to his capital, Samarkand. The methodical collecting was continued by his grandson Ulughbek, and it was this concoction of imported styles from the Arab world, Persia, the Caucasus and India that resulted in a period of building to rival any other of any time, the world over.

The Timurid architectural trademark is the beautiful, often ribbed, azure-blue dome. The colour comes from glazed tiling and in many cases the façades and great arched entrance portals *(pishtak)* are also decorated with intricately patterned tiles, predominantly in blues, turquoises and yellows and

traditionally in abstract geometric or floral designs (in keeping with the Islamic taboo on the representation of living things), but later also incorporating plants and animals. Other than in Central Asia, this kind of glitzy, tiled Islamic architecture is to be found only in relatively inaccessible Iran and parts of Afghanistan.

Central Asia's religious buildings mainly fall into three categories: mosques (sometimes with minarets), mausolea, and medressas and khanakas (Islamic seminaries/monasteries). Some of the most striking examples of all three are in Samarkand.

Next to the city's bazar, the Bibi-Khanym (1399-1404) was Timur's intended masterpiece. A cathedral mosque like an Islamic version of Christendom's gothic cathedral at Chartres, the Bibi-Khanym was designed to be the architectural embodiment of heaven. Unfortunately, it was erected so hastily that it was in ruins almost as soon as it was finished. Only the entrance gate and three domed buildings remain to suggest the colossal dimensions of this folly.

The mosques built from then on were, wisely, more modest in scale but, in many cases, this proved their undoing as the Bolsheviks destroyed almost all of Central Asia's religious buildings except those of architectural or historical value. The new wave of mosques being built today display a varied mixture of influences from the Islamic world, from the grand Ottoman styling of Ashghabat's new central mosque to the blandness of the one in Dushanbe.

Medressas (and khanakas) built, like many Central Asian mosques, one or two storeys high around a central courtyard are distinguishable because of the rows of little doors in the interior façades which lead into cell-like living quarters for students and teachers – or in the case of khanakas, to prayer cells for the ascetic wandering darvishes who stayed there. The Ulughbek (1420) and Sher Dor (1636), the medressas that form two-thirds of the Registan complex, both conform to this standard plan. Their minarets were not used by muezzins for the call to prayer as they would be if attached to a mosque; they're there for decoration – a purpose they serve admirably.

The Islom-Huja or Islam Khoja minaret (1910) – functional at one time – in Khiva is reckoned by Central Asian archaeological specialist Edgar Knobloch to be the last notable architectural achievement of the Islamic era in Central Asia; we'd expand that to say last notable architectural achievement in Central Asia, period.

Fine Art

Rendered in a style which foreshadows that of Persian miniature painting, some splendid friezes were unearthed in the excavations of the Afrasiab palace (6th to 7th century) on the outskirts of Samarkand, depicting a colourful caravan led by elephants. Similar wall frescoes were discovered at Penjikent showing men and women tossed in a sea filled with monsters and fish. This promise of a great artistic heritage for Central Asia failed to develop any further when the Sogdians of Afrasiab and Penjikent fled into the mountains – and into historical obscurity – in the face of the Arab invasion. As a result, representational art in Central Asia was put on hold for the better part of 1300 years.

Islam prohibited the depiction of the living, so traditional arts developed in the form of calligraphy, combining Islamic script with arabesques, and the carving of doors and screens. Examples of this kind of work can be found in museums in Central Asia's capital cities, particularly in Tashkent's Museum of Fine Arts.

'Bukhara' Rugs

Marco Polo commented on the beauty of Central Asian carpets in his journals but it wasn't until centuries later and the arrival of the Great Game players in the bazars of Turkestan that these woven pieces of art began to make their way into the collections and grand homes of Europe. Purchased from traders in Samarkand and Bukhara (hence the name), the handwoven carpets were valued for their quality, the richness of the natural plant dyes used (predominantly a deep wine red) and the beautiful simplicity of their geometric designs – typically a single or double border enclosing a central panel (or field) filled with a simple repeated motif.

The carpets were actually the work of the Turkmen people, scattered throughout northern Afghanistan and northern Iran, and concentrated in what is now Turkmenistan. From the motif (or *gul*), it's possible to identify exactly where a carpet was made as each design is unique to a particular Turkmen tribe. For instance, a stylised anchor means that the carpet was woven by members of the Ersari, a tribe from eastern Turkmenistan beside the Caspian Sea.

For the nomadic Turkmen the only piece of furniture worth having was a carpet or three. Easily transportable, the carpets served not just as floor coverings, they lined the walls of the yurt as well as providing a highly decorative form of insulation. They also acted as a cumbersome form of currency – the result of months of intensive labour, a carpet was naturally an item of great value and often formed the major part of a bride's dowry.

Carpets are still produced in the villages of Turkmenistan, woven by family groups of women who carry the complex patterns in their heads but more commonly now, since the advent of the Soviet era, carpet-making has entered the machine age. The foreign dealers who prowl Ashghabat's Tolkuchka market *(the* premiere carpet showplace) dismissively pass over the factory pieces which tend to be uninspired and coloured with synthetic dyes that are prone to fading. However, the carpets on which an angular Lenin replaces the traditional tribal motifs are absolute masterpieces of kitsch; they can also be a bargain as Turkmen are eager to rid themselves of this aberrant treatment of their national artefact (see the Officials & Paperwork section in the Turkmenistan chapter, on the difficulties of taking a carpet out of the country).

The concrete apartment block may have replaced the yurt but the traditionally-minded Turkmen of today (and that's the majority) still value their carpets dearly and use them both on the floors and the walls – no longer needed for insulation, they now do a fine job of hiding the damp patches. ∎

Painting and two-dimensional art were only revived under the Soviets who introduced European ideas and set up schools to train local artists in the new fashion. Under Soviet tutelage the pictorial art of Central Asia became a curious hybrid of socialist realism and mock traditionalism – Kyrgyz horsemen riding proudly beside a shiny red tractor, smiling Uzbeks at a teahouse with futuristic chimneys thrusting skywards in the background. Unsurprisingly, few Central Asian artists of this era have achieved any recognition outside their own country.

Folk Art

Central Asian folk art developed in tune with a nomadic or semi-nomadic way of life and so the main items that were decorated were clothes, arms, jewellery and, to a lesser extent, weaving, embroidery and rugs – all of which had a practical use as well as value. Wealth had to be portable. For nomad women, it took the form of stupendous jewellery, mostly of silver incorporating semi-precious stones like lapis and carnelian; there was sometimes enough jewellery on marriageable women to make walking difficult. A fantastic collection of Central Asian jewellery in Tashkent's old Antique Jewellery Museum has unfortunately gone into storage with the rearrangement of the city's collections.

Men hung their wealth on their belts (daggers and sabres in silver sheaths) or on their horses (saddles, bridles and blankets). While the saddles and sabres have disappeared, there are still stalls at bazars in Tajikistan and the Ferghana Valley selling nothing but daggers and knives which are definitely not designed for use in the kitchen.

Most Central Asian peoples have traditional rug or carpet styles and some, like the Turkmen, have gone quite commercial in this century. Most 'Bukhara' rugs – so called

Kazak Wall Carpets

Traditionally, a Kazak yurt (kiiz-uy) contained a variety of handmade textile items, including floor carpets made of both wool and felt, embroidered bedspreads, quilts, camel and horse bags, and clothing.

Possibly the most accessible Kazak textile souvenir (with the exception of floor carpets) is a tus-kiiz (тус-киіз) or 'wall carpet' (tus literally means colour and kiiz means felt). These colourful, hand-made textiles, made of both cotton and silk, were traditionally used both for decoration and as a way to keep the yurt warm.

Tus-kiiz vary in size but a typical one measures about 2.3 by 1.3 metres. Smaller ones (1.3 by 1 metres) were usually made for children. Designs vary too, but generally, tus-kiiz are bordered at the top and sides in red material, with a geometrically patterned inner section – usually a circular or diamond design. Many tus-kiiz feature a separately designed inner piece of cloth stitched on to the bottom centre. And while flowers and plant-like designs are common, some feature birds and animals.

When buying a wall carpet, ensure that it is original: older pieces may have been torn or damaged over the years and poorly repaired. Many tus-kiiz bear a name or a date, which also adds to their historical interest. Careful examination may reveal the designer's name and a date intricately embroidered in a circle or along the border.

A date generally represents the year of completion. But if your wall carpet has no date in Roman characters, there are ways of guessing:

- Older pieces usually have a silk background with very simply stitched designs
- Pieces with names or dates stitched in Cyrillic script did not appear until the late 1920s and early 1930s
- Circular patterns with stars began appearing in the mid-1960s

It seems the best wall carpets of all originate in north-east Kazakhstan, near the 'four corners' region of Kazakhstan, Russia, China and Mongolia. The mixed Kazak-Mongolian influences here appear to produce the most intricate and colourful textiles in the whole of Kazakhstan. ■

because they were mostly sold, not made, in Bukhara – are made by Turkmen.

Kyrgyz specialise in felt rugs with coloured panels sewn on *(shyrdak)* or pressed on *(alakiz)*, and wool tapestries. Kazak art also includes multicoloured felt mats *(koshma)*, brightly coloured rugs, wall coverings and bedspreads, traditionally used to decorate the inside of yurts. Uzbeks make silk and cotton wall hangings and coverlets such as the beautiful *suzani* (eg in Tashkent's Museum of Fine Arts).

Literature

The division into Kazak literature, Tajik literature, Uzbek literature and so on, is a modern one; formerly there was simply literature in Turkic and literature in Persian. With most pre-20th century poets, scholars and writers bilingual in Uzbek and Tajik, literature in Central Asia belonged to a shared universality of culture. For example, Abu Abdullah Rudaki, a 10th century Samanid court poet considered the father of Persian literature, stars in the national pantheons of Afghanistan, Iran and Tajikistan and is also revered by Uzbeks by dint of being born in the Bukhara emirate. Omar Khayyam, famed composer of *rubiayyat* poetry, although a native of what is now north-east Iran, also has strong if indistinct ties to Tajikistan and to Samarkand where he spent part of his early life at the court of the Seljuq emir.

A strong factor in the universal nature of Central Asian literature was that it was popularised not in written form but orally by itinerant minstrels in the form of songs, poems and stories. Known as *bakshi* or *dastanchi* in Turkmen and Uzbek, *aqin* in Kazak, *akyn* in Kyrgyz (*manaschi* are a special category of akyn who sang the traditional Kyrgyz *Manas* epos), these story-telling bards earned their living travelling from town to town giving skilled and dramatic recitations of crowd-pleasing verse tales and epics to audiences gathered in bazars and teahouses. Certain bards are folk heroes, regarded as founders of their 'national literatures', even memorialised in

Soviet-era street names. Bardic competitions are still held in some rural areas.

It was only with the advent of Bolshevik rule that literacy became widespread. Unfortunately, at the same time, much of the region's classical heritage never saw print because Moscow feared that it might set a flame to latent nationalist sentiments. Instead writers were encouraged to produce novels and plays in line with official Communist Party themes. While a number of Central Asian poets and novelists found acclaim within the Soviet sphere, such as the Tajik Sadruddin Ayni (1878-1954) and the Uzbek Asqad Mukhtar (1921-), the only native Central Asian author to garner international recognition has been the Kyrgyz Chingiz Aitmatov, who has had novels translated into English and other European languages. His works have also been adapted for the stage and screen, both in the former USSR and abroad.

Music

While during this century the visual arts and literature have succumbed to a stifling Soviet-European influence which they're presently struggling to shrug off, the music of Central Asia remains exotic and untainted, still closely related to the droning melodies of the Middle East and Persia. The instruments used are similar to those found in the Arab world; long-necked lutes, reedy flutes and oboes, tambourines and tablas, small vase-shaped drums.

In the past the development of music was closely connected with the art of the bards (see the Literature section), but these days the traditions are continued by small ensembles of musicians and singers, heavily in demand at weddings and other festivals. In Uzbek and Tajik societies there's a particularly popular form of folk music known as *sozanda*, sung primarily by women accompanied only by percussion instruments like tablas, bells and castanets. Performances can last as much as eight hours, although for the novice ear eight minutes is probably more than enough.

A 1991 recording available from

Smithsonian Folkways called *Bukhara, Musical Crossroads of Asia* (CD catalogue No SF40050) includes songs from a sozanda group as well as from the *shashmaqam*, a more elitist classical canon of songs and instrumental pieces thought to have developed at the court of the Bukhara emirs.

Much more accessible is the folk music of Turkmenistan, which mixes influences from Persia, Azerbaijan and Turkey to create a sound driven by a clattering drumbeat and rounded out with swaying accordians and ferocious strumming of the *dutar*, a two-stringed lute. A five-piece Turkmen ensemble calling itself Ashkhabad has had an international CD release on the Realworld label (CDRW34).

Throughout Central Asia a new hybrid music has developed that mixes traditional melodies and singing styles with keyboards and dance floor-programmed drum machines but the results tend to be very tacky. One Uzbek group that has successfully mixed Central Asian and Middle Eastern folk melodies and poetry with modern pop and dance influences is Yalla; for information on their *Beard of the Camel* and *City of Dreams* albums, contact Imagina Productions in Seattle, USA (fax (206 284-9426, e-mail imagina1@aol.com).

CULTURE
Hospitality

In Islam, a guest – Muslim or not – has a position of honour not very well understood in the West. If someone visits you and you don't have much to offer, as a Christian you'd be urged to share what you had; as a Muslim you're urged to give it all away. Guests are to be treated with absolute selflessness.

For a visitor to a Muslim country, even one as casual about Islam as Kazakstan or Kyrgyzstan, this is a constant source of pleasure, temptation and sometimes embarrassment. More than once we've found ourselves eating a lavish meal with the head of the family while all around, other adults and children look on, unlikely to eat any of it themselves. The majority of Central Asians, especially rural ones, are poor and getting poorer, with little to offer *but* their hospitality, and a casual guest could drain a host's resources and never know it. All you can do is enjoy it, honour their customs as best you can, and take yourself courteously out of the picture before you become a burden.

Consider it a great honour to be invited to someone's house for a meal; to refuse would probably insult them. If for some reason you do want to decline, couch your refusal in gracious and diplomatic terms, allowing the would-be host to save face.

Never arrive empty-handed. Something for the house or for the table will do; if you're stuck for anything else, buy a big bag of the best-looking fruit you can find in the bazar. Better yet would be something for your hosts' children or their parents, preferably brought from your home country (eg sweets, postcards, badges, a picture book). Proffer it when you arrive; you might then be given a gift when you leave, but there seems little point in trying to avoid this by holding onto yours until then! And don't be surprised if you aren't thanked for yours: gifts are taken more as evidence of God's grace than of your generosity.

Pulling out your own food or offering to pay someone for their kindness is likely to humiliate them (though some travellers hosted by very poor people have given a small cash gift to the eldest child, saying that it's 'for sweets').

When you enter a private house, take your shoes off at the door unless told not to. Avoid stepping on any carpet if you have your shoes on. Never put your feet on a table, nor near any food spread on a cloth on the floor. There are other things people do as well – eg Uzbeks enter others' homes with the right foot – but foreigners are forgiven for not knowing everything. For further tips on protocol at meals, see the Home Meals information in the Food section of the Facts for the Visitor chapter.

In China, at least on the tourist trail, generosity is rare. Uyghurs mainly ignore you in

Kashgar. Han Chinese officials, attendants and drivers are generally beastly to everyone.

Dos & Don'ts

Clothing Nowhere is it easier to offend Muslims – and nowhere have more foreigners done so without thinking – than in the matter of dress. To a devout Muslim, clothes that reveal flesh or the shape of the body are like walking around in your underwear in the West – ridiculous on men and scandalous on women. Shorts and singlets are offensive on either sex. Stick with long, loose, non-revealing garments.

This is not true everywhere in Central Asia. Conservative western-style clothes are acceptable in the capital cities and in large towns like Samarkand that see a lot of tourist traffic. But attitudes get more conservative the more remote and rural the locale. Local Russians do get away with dressing as they please, and leeway is generally given to foreigners, but we have heard of stones being thrown at improperly dressed westerners (even in Ashghabat).

This sounds preachy but cannot be emphasised enough. It's not a matter of brownie-points for 'dressing native'. Muslims from everywhere, fundamentalist and liberal, beg to know why so many foreigners refuse this simple courtesy.

Blowing Your Nose in Public Despite the early morning sinus-clearing rituals you may hear in your hotel, most Central Asians are disgusted by the thought of emptying the contents of your nose into a cloth, especially if you then carry it around in your pocket all day. This is especially revolting when done at the table. In Shakhrisabz a western friend blew her nose at length into a restaurant napkin, until finally a man sitting nearby uttered a shout of disgust and spat at her feet.

Some people claim to dislike public spitting too, although most young Uzbek men seem to do it incessantly.

Eating with Your Left Hand Devout Muslims consider the left hand unclean, and handling food with it at the table, especially in a private home, can be off-putting to them. At a minimum, no-one raises food to their lips with the left hand.

Other Customs Never point the sole of your shoe or foot at a Muslim, step over any part of someone's body, or walk in front of someone praying to Mecca.

Men & Women

In bigger cities of the former Soviet republics we found no apparent taboo on unaccompanied local women talking to male visitors in public (as there is in Pakistan and Middle Eastern Islamic countries).

But despite the imposition of Soviet economic 'equality', attitudes in the Central Asian republics remain fairly male-dominated. We found that local men addressed by a woman in a couple would nearly always direct their reply to the man, and we were therefore inclined to do the same. Local women tend not to shake hands or lead in conversations. Because most local women don't drink in public, female visitors may not be offered a shot of the vodka or wine doing the rounds. But these are not taboos as such, and as usual, foreigners tend to be forgiven for what locals might consider gaffes.

In Pakistan, public physical contact between men and women – with fellow travellers or with local people – is a 'touchy' matter. Holding hands in public is acceptable only between members of the same sex (and is not a sign of homosexuality).

Some travellers report unmarried couples being refused shared hotel rooms in Osh, and the same may occasionally be true elsewhere in the Ferghana Valley.

Body Language

Shaking Hands Men at least can establish some rapport in an interaction with a handshake offered straight away, before anything else has happened – even with police officers. In Uzbekistan most younger men seem to shake hands all the time, both in greeting and on departure, so *not* doing it may put them off (older men may simply put the right hand over the heart and incline the head slightly, in a gesture of humility). Between Pakistani men a handshake is as essential to conversation as eye contact is in the West.

A handshake acquires extra warmth if accompanied or followed by a hand over the heart. Don't be offended if someone offers you his wrist; he just considers his hand unclean at the moment, eg if he's been eating with it. Offering a handshake to a local person of the opposite sex may put them in an awkward position; let them make the first move.

If you try to shake hands with someone in China, they may act as if you're trying to kiss them!

Amin A common Muslim gesture at the end of a meal is the *amin*, in which the person brings their cupped hands together and passes them down the face, as if washing. We found this mostly in Uzbekistan and Tajikistan, sometimes done quickly, almost self-consciously.

Sports

In regions with significant nomadic or animal-raising traditions, you may be lucky enough to see traditional horseback games at certain local festivals or on national holidays. The common Central Asian sport in which two large teams of horsemen play a kind of wild, no-holds-barred polo, without sticks and with a beheaded goat carcass instead of a ball, is known in Tajikistan and Pathan areas of Pakistan as *buzkashi*, in Kazakstan as *kökpar*, in Karakalpakstan as *ylaq oyyny* and in Kyrgyzstan as *ulak-tartysh*; Russians call it *kozlodranie*.

In another traditional horseback game, called *kesh-kumay* in Kyrgyzstan ('kiss-the-girl') and *qyz quu* in Kazakstan, a man chases a woman on horseback and tries to kiss her, or gets chased and whipped if he fails. This allegedly began as a formalised alternative to abduction, the traditional nomad way to take a bride. Other events may include races and horseback wrestling.

RELIGION

With the exception of rapidly shrinking communities of Jews (see Bukhara) and Orthodox Christians, small minorities of Roman Catholics, Baptists and Evangelical Lutherans, and a few Buddhists among Koreans of the Ferghana Valley and Kyrgyzstan, nearly everyone from the Caspian Sea to the Taklamakan desert is Muslim, at least in principle. The intensity of faith varies from faint to fanatical, although after the 'militant atheism' of the Soviet

---

Buzkashi

In a region many of whose people are descended from hot-blooded nomads, no one expects cricket to be the national sport. Even so, *buzkashi* is wild beyond belief: a form of rugby on horseback in which the 'ball' is the headless carcass of a sheep.

The game begins with the carcass in the centre of a circle at one end of a field; at the other end is a bunch of wild, adrenaline-crazed horsemen. At a signal they charge for the carcass to collect it, carry it back up the field and around a post with the winning rider being the one who finally drops it back in the circle. All the while there's a frenzied horse-backed tug-of-war going on as each competitor tries to gain possession; smashed noses, wrenched shoulders and shattered thigh bones are all part of the fun.

Not surprisingly, the game is said to date from the days of Jenghiz Khan. The point of the game used to be the honour, and perhaps notoriety, of the victor, but in 1995 at a Navruz festival game at Tajikistan's Hissar fortress, the prize was a new car.

Buzkashi takes place mainly in the cooler months of spring and autumn, at weekends, on feast days or to mark special occasions such as weddings. If you're lucky you'll catch it during Navruz or some local celebration. You can also see it in Pathan areas of Pakistan's North-West Frontier Province. ■

years, few now appear to understand Islam very deeply. Sectarianism is almost nonexistent in the former Soviet republics because, with the exception of the Ismailis of eastern Tajikistan, nearly everyone is of the Sunni branch of Islam (by contrast, sectarian violence is common along parts of the Karakoram Highway in Pakistan).

Islam

History & Schisms In 612 AD, the Prophet Muhammad, then a wealthy Arab of Mecca, began preaching a new religious philosophy, Islam, based on revelations from Allah (Islam's name for God). Islam incorporated elements of Judaism, Christianity and other faiths (eg heaven and hell, a creation story much like the Garden of Eden, myths like Noah's Ark) and treated their prophets simply as forerunners of the Prophet Muhammad. These revelations were eventually to be compiled into Islam's holiest book, the Quran (or Koran).

In 622, Muhammad and his followers were forced to flee to Medina (the Islamic calendar counts its years from this flight or *hejira*). There he built a political base and an army, taking Mecca in 630 and eventually overrunning Arabia. By the end of his life Muhammad ruled a rapidly growing religious and secular dynasty. The militancy of the faith meshed nicely with a latent Arab nationalism, and within a century Islam reached from Spain to Central Asia.

Succession disputes after the Prophet's death soon split the community. When the fourth caliph, the Prophet's son-in-law Ali, was assassinated in 661, his followers and descendants became the founders of the Shia (or Shi'ite) sect. Others accepted as caliph the governor of Syria, a brother-in-law of the Prophet, and this line has become the modern-day orthodox Sunni (or Sunnite) sect. In 680 a chance for reconciliation was lost when Ali's surviving son Hussain and most of his male relatives were killed at Karbala in Iraq by Sunni partisans.

Among Shia doctrines is that of the imam or infallible leader, who continues to unfold the true meaning of the Quran and provides

guidance in daily affairs. Most Shias recognise an hereditary line of 12 imams ending in the 9th century (though imam is still used, loosely, by modern Shias). These Shias are known as Ithnashari (Twelvers). This book refers to them simply as Shias.

An 8th century split among Shias gave rise to the Ismaili or Maulai sect, who disagreed on which son of the sixth imam should succeed him. For Ismaili Shias the line of Imams continues into the present. Ismailis today number several million in pockets of Asia, India, East Africa and the Middle East, and their present leader, Prince Karim Aga Khan, is considered to be imam No 49. Doctrines are more esoteric and practices less regimented than those of Sunnis or Ithnashari Shias.

Today some 85% to 90% of Muslims worldwide are Sunni. About 80% of all Central Asians are Muslim, nearly all of them Sunni (and indeed nearly all of the Hanafi school, one of Sunnism's four main schools of religious law). The main exception is a tightly knit community of Ismailis in the remote mountainous region of Gorno-Badakhshan in eastern Tajikistan (see the Population & People section in the introduction to the Tajikistan chapter). A small but increasingly influential community of another Sunni school, the ascetic, fundamentalist Wahhabi, are found mainly in Uzbekistan's Ferghana Valley; sources differ on their links to Saudi Arabia, where Wahhabism dominates.

Practice The word 'Islam' translates loosely from Arabic as 'the peace that comes from total surrender to God'. The Quran is considered above criticism: the word of God as spoken to his Prophet. This is supplemented by various traditions such as the *hadith*, the collected acts and sayings of the Prophet.

Devout Muslims express their surrender in the 'Five Pillars of Islam': (1) the creed that 'There is only one god, Allah, and Muhammad is his Prophet'; (2) praying five times a day, prostrating towards the holy city of Mecca, in a mosque (for men only) when possible but at least on Fridays, the Muslim holy day; (3) dawn-to-dusk fasting during the month of Ramadan; (4) making the *hajj* (pilgrimage to Mecca) at least once in one's life (many of those who have done so can be identified by their white skull-caps); (5) almsgiving, in the form of the *zakat*, an obligatory 2.5% tithe or alms-tax.

Devout Sunnis pray at prescribed times: before sunrise, just after high noon, in late afternoon, just after sunset and before retiring. For Shias there are three fixed times – before sunrise and twice in the evening – the other two being at one's discretion. Prayers are preceded if possible by washing, at least of hands, face and feet. For Ismailis the style of prayer is a personal matter (eg there is no prostration), the mosque is replaced by a community shrine or meditation room, and women are less excluded.

Just before fixed prayers a *muezzin* calls the Sunni and Shia faithful, traditionally from a minaret, nowadays often through a loudspeaker. The melancholy sounding Arabic *azan* or call to prayer translates roughly as, 'God is most great. There is no God but Allah. Muhammad is God's messenger. Come to prayer, come to security. God is most great'.

In its fullest sense Islam is an entire way of life, with guidelines for doing nearly everything. Among prohibitions – honoured at least by the devout – are those against eating pork and drinking alcohol.

Islam has no ordained priesthood, but members of the *ulama* or class of religious scholars (often called mullahs) are trained in theology, respected as interpreters of scripture, and are sometimes quite influential in conservative rural areas.

Working mosques are closed to women and often to non-Muslim men, though men may occasionally be invited in. When visiting a mosque, always take your shoes off at the door, and make sure your feet or socks are clean (dirty socks, like dirty feet, are an insult to the mosque).

It is polite to refer to the Prophet Muhammad as such, rather than by his name alone.

Islam in Central Asia Islam first appeared in Central Asia with Arab invaders in the 7th and 8th centuries. In the following centuries many conversions were accomplished by teachers from Islam's mystic Sufi tradition who wandered across Asia (see Sufism in the next section).

Tsarist colonisers largely allowed Central Asians to worship as they pleased. Indeed, proselytising by Christian missionaries was forbidden (the intent being to spare local people too much enlightenment). But the Bolsheviks feared religion in general and Islam in particular because of its potential for coherent resistance, both domestic and international.

Three of the Five Pillars of Islam – the fast of Ramadan, the hajj and the alms-tax – were outlawed in the 1920s. Polygamy, the wearing of the veil *(paranjeh)*, and the Arabic script in which the Quran is written were forbidden. Clerical (Christian, Jewish and Buddhist as well as Muslim) land and property were seized. Medressas and other religious schools were closed down. Islam's judicial power was curbed with the dismantling of traditional Sharia courts (based on Quranic law).

From 1932 to 1936 Stalin mounted a concerted antireligious campaign in Central Asia, with mosques closed and destroyed, and mullahs arrested and liquidated as saboteurs or spies. By the early 1940s only 1000 of Central Asia's mosques remained standing, of some 25,000 to 30,000 in 1920. All its 14,500 Islamic schools were shut, and only 2000 of its 47,000 mullahs remained alive. Control of the surviving places of worship and teaching was given to the Union of Atheists, which transformed most of them into museums, dancehalls, warehouses or factories.

During WWII things improved marginally as Moscow sought domestic and international Muslim support for the war effort. In 1943 four Muslim Religious Boards or 'spiritual directorates', each with a *mufti* or spiritual leader, were founded as official administration units for Soviet Muslims, including one – the largest – in Tashkent for all of Central Asia (in 1990

Kazakstan got its own). A few mosques were reopened and a handful of carefully screened religious leaders were allowed to make the hajj in 1947.

But beneath the surface little changed. Any religious activity outside the official mosques was strictly forbidden. By the early 1960s, under Khrushchev's 'back to Lenin' policies, another 1000 mosques were shut. By the beginning of the Gorbachev era, the number of mosques in Central Asia was down to between 150 and 250, and only two medressas were open – Mir-i-Arab in Bukhara and the Islamic Institute in Tashkent.

Following bloody inter-ethnic violence, particularly around the Ferghana Valley in 1989 and 1990, the Soviet authorities fell all over themselves to allow the construction of new mosques. Since the republics' respective declarations of independence, mosques and medressas have sprouted like mushrooms, often with a little help from Saudi or Iranian money. One source suggests a current rate of some 10 mosques a day opening across Central Asia.

But Islam never was a potent force in the former nomadic societies of the Turkmen, Kazaks and Kyrgyz, and still isn't (some researchers suggest that its appeal for nomadic rulers was as much its discipline as its moral precepts). Even in more conservative Uzbekistan and Tajikistan, all those new mosques are as much political as religious statements, with everybody wooing Turkey and Pakistan a way out of Russia's grip. The majority of Central Asians, though interested in Islam as a common denominator, seem quite happy to toast your health with a shot of vodka.

The Central Asian brand of Islam is also riddled with outside influences – just go to any important holy site and notice the kissing and rubbing and circumabulating of venerated objects, the shamanic 'wishing trees' tied with bits of coloured rags, the Mongol-style poles with horse-hair tassel over the graves of revered figures, the Russian-style gravestones, and sometimes candles and flames harking from Zoroastrian times.

And yet the amazing thing is that, after 70 years of concerted Soviet repression, with mainstream Islam in an official hammerlock, so much faith remains intact. Some rural Central Asians in fact take Islam very seriously, enough to create substantial political muscle. The real power in the coalition that seized control of Tajikistan in 1992, and almost won the civil war, was the Islamic Renaissance Party (IRP), with heavy support in the Garm valley. The IRP, though outlawed by the other Central Asian republics, enjoys enormous support in Uzbekistan's Ferghana Valley, the epicentre of what fundamentalism exists is here.

Credit for any continuity from pre-Soviet times goes largely to 'underground Islam', in the form of the clandestine Sufi brotherhoods (and brotherhoods they were, being essentially men-only) who preserved some practice and education – and grew in power and influence in Central Asia as a result (see the following section on Sufism).

For non-Muslim visitors, there is relatively little of the hostility western media associates with Iran's revolutionary version of Shia Islam (which seems to cut little ice with most Central Asians). In the Ferghana Valley you will probably be refused entry to some medressas and mosques, but generally Islam manifests itself in the wholly delightful tendency towards openness and hospitality to strangers.

Ramadan Ramadan is the Muslim month of fasting, meant to be a ritual cleansing of body and mind, with eating, drinking (even water) and smoking forbidden from sunrise to sunset. The devout take meals in the evening and just before sunrise; muezzin calls signal the end of each day's fasting. Children, pregnant women, very old and/or ill people, travellers and non-Muslims are exempt, though they are expected not to eat or drink in front of those who are fasting.

Ismailis don't take part. In Central Asia (with the exception of conservative regions like the Ferghana Valley) and Xinjiang, relatively few people maintain the fast strictly, although Ramadan has become an excuse for a holiday, and some eateries may close early or completely.

In non-Ismaili areas along the Karakoram Highway, on the other hand, Ramadan is taken very seriously, and this is not a cheerful time to travel there – food and drink are hard to find during the day, offices keep odd hours, tempers are short and little serious business gets done. The best places for a non-Muslim to find food along the Karakoram Highway are tourist hotels, bus stands, Ismaili neighbourhoods in Gilgit, or anywhere in Gojal or Hunza (but not the town of Nagar).

Because the Islamic calendar year is shorter than the western calendar year, Ramadan and other holy days occur roughly 10 days earlier each western year. But exact western-calendar dates for Islamic months are not known until the formal sighting of the new moon at the start of each one. Approximate starting dates for Ramadan are 10 January 1997, 31 December 1997, 20 December 1998 and 9 December 1999.

Sufism The original Sufis were simply purists, unhappy with the worldliness of the early caliphates and seeking knowledge of God through direct personal experience, under the guidance of a teacher or master, variously called a *sheikh, pir, eshon, murshid* or *ustad*. There never was a single Sufi movement, but manifestations within all branches of Islam. For many adherents music, dance or poetry about the search for God were routes to trance, revelation and direct union with God. This is the mystical side of Islam, parallel to similar traditions in other faiths.

Sufis were singularly successful as missionaries, perhaps because of their tolerance of other creeds. It was largely Sufis, not Arab armies, who planted Islam firmly in Central Asia and the subcontinent. While abhorred nowadays in the orthodox Islamic states of Iran and Saudi Arabia, Sufism is in a quiet way dominant in Central Asia. Most shrines you'll see are devoted to one Sufi teacher or another.

When Islam was itself threatened by invaders (eg the Crusaders), Sufis assumed the role of defenders of the faith, and Sufism became a mass movement of regimented *tariqas* or brotherhoods, based around certain holy places, often the tombs of the tariqas' founders. Clandestine, anti-Communist tariqas helped Islam weather the Soviet period, and the KGB and its predecessors never seemed able to infiltrate.

The moderate, non-elitist Naqshbandiya was the most important tariqa in Soviet times, and probably still is. Founded in Bukhara in the 14th century (see the Naqshbandis aside under Bukhara), much of its influence in Central Asia may come from the high profile of Naqshbandi fighters in two centuries of revolts against the Russians in the Caucasus.

In 1940 one of the last of these, in Chechnia, was crushed, and in February 1944 the entire Chechen and Ingush populations were deported to Siberia and Kazakstan. When, after Stalin's death, the survivors were permitted to return to their homeland, they left behind several well-organised Sufi groups in Central Asia. A number of well-known basmachi leaders were Naqshbandis.

Another important Sufi sect in Central Asia is the Qadiriya, founded by a teacher from the Caspian region. Others are the Kubra (founded in Khorezm) and Yasauia (founded in Turkistan, in Kazakstan). All these were founded in the 12th century.

Facts for the Visitor

PLANNING

When to Go

Weather It's hard to generalise about such a large region, but to do just that: spring and autumn are the overall best seasons from the standpoint of weather, in particular April to early June and September through October at lower elevations. In April, the desert blooms briefly and the monotonous ochre landscapes of Turkmenistan, Uzbekistan and Kazakstan become a Jackson Pollock canvas of reds, oranges and yellows. Autumn is harvest time, when market tables heave with freshly picked fruit.

Summer is ferociously hot in the lowlands, with sizzling cities, and desert temperatures as high as 40° or more. November is changeable, with snow or cold rain beginning, and mountain passes fill with snow until April or even May. Winters are bitterly cold even in the desert, and food is more of a problem, with many eateries closed for the season. Many domestic flights are also grounded in winter.

On the other hand: March and November, though cool and occasionally wet, see fewer tourist crowds. July through August is the best time to visit the mountains and to trek (earlier and later than that, herders and other summer residents have returned to the lowlands. Northern Kazakstan is comfortable right through the summer.

The best time to travel on the Karakoram Highway is September through October. Mountain roads are in decent condition. Fresh vegetables and fruit are still plentiful. Since most tourists will have gone, hotels may lower their rates. Next-best is May through June. Summer is ferociously hot and dry in Kashgar, pleasantly warm and occasionally stormy in Hunza. Kashgar is unpleasant from mid-October, when the wet and cold weather sets in, to mid-November when winter officially arrives and things become really bleak. From Kashgar to Gilgit, winter is long and cold (often well below freezing), with snow in the mountains.

If you're heading to or from Pakistan, bear in mind that while the Khunjerab pass is officially open from 1 May to 30 November, it tends to close early around mid-November or even sooner because of snow.

See the Climate section of the Facts about the Region chapter for further considerations.

Other Factors Ramadan, the Muslim month of daytime fasting, is a headache for travellers only in Pakistan, and only from Gilgit southwards. People are irritable, offices are closed or their occupants distracted, and food may be hard to find during daylight hours. The dates change each year; see Holidays & Special Events in this chapter.

Border crossings to/from China, especially the Torugart pass, take every opportunity to close, in particular on Chinese holidays and sometimes several days either side of them.

When skirmishing breaks out in Tajikistan, many parts of the country are out-of-bounds.

Maps

Get your big-scale maps before you go. We found Hildebrand's 1:3,500,000 *CIS* to be fairly well updated, and of a useful scale. There are other CIS maps, but most reduce Central Asia to the size of a postcard.

US-published air navigation charts make fine wall hangings but are expensive at US$10 or more per sheet. The 1:1,000,000 ONC series covers all of Central Asia, while coverage by the 1:500,000 TPC series is patchy. These are available from the following mail-order firms:

Edward Stanford Ltd, 12-14 Long Acre, Covent Garden, London WC2E 9LP, UK
   (☎ (071) 836 1321)

GeoCenter ILH, Schockenriedstrasse 44, D-70565
Stuttgart, Germany
(☎ (0711) 788 93 40, fax 788 93 54)
Maplink, 25 East Mason St, Santa Barbara, CA
93101, USA (☎ (805) 965-4402, fax 962-0884)
Michael Chessler Books, PO Box 2436, Evergreen,
CO 80439, USA
(☎ (800) 654-8502, (303) 670-0093)
NOAA Distribution Branch (N/CG33), National
Oceanic & Atmospheric Administration,
Riverdale, MD 20737-1199, USA
(☎ (301) 436-6990)

Arguments & Facts Media in the UK sells a
US$72 paperback *Atlas of Russia and the
Post Soviet Republics* (1994), commissioned
by the business intelligence service Arguments & Facts International, with country
and capital city maps, though even these now
have a few outdated street and place names.
They also sell what they say are unclassified
1:200,000 Soviet military air navigation
maps (probably the only trustworthy Soviet-era maps) for about US$10 each or, for map
freaks, US$950 for all 91 covering Central
Asia! Contact Arguments & Facts Media
Ltd, PO Box 35, Hastings, East Sussex TN34
2UX, UK (☎ (0424) 442741, 444142; fax
442913, 717498).

Local Sources Reliable locally produced
city and regional maps were hard to find at
the time of research. Occasional Soviet-era
city maps, full of errors, languish on the back
shelves of some bookshops. Especially in
Uzbekistan, where Soviet-era street names
were jettisoned en masse, any map older than
about 1994 will drive you crazy (see the title
box or the back of the map for copyright
date).

Especially for trekking, you should avoid
all Soviet-era maps, which were deliberately
distorted (except military ones). The Kyrgyz
Cartographic Agency (see the Bishkek Information section of the Kyrgyzstan chapter)
has useful small maps of major Central Tian
Shan trekking regions for the equivalent of
about US$0.15. They also reprint good
general topographic maps covering all of
Kyrgyzstan plus the Kashgar region at both
1:500,000 (10 sheets) and 1:1,000,000 (five

sheets), for about US$2.50 a sheet. Local
guides claim these trekking maps are clear of
distortions.

What to Bring

Of course, bring as little as you can. You can
usually find batteries (but not as good as
those from home), laundry soap, tooth-brushes, old-style razor blades and shampoo
in big-city department stores, and aspirin in
pharmacies.

An internal-frame or soft pack is most
manageable on buses and trains – though
easy for someone to slash. A 'convertible'
(with a handle, and a flap to hide the straps)
looks respectable when you want.

Clothing With strong social overtones in
Islamic countries, in no other way have westerners managed to offend Asians more than
by the way they dress. To a devout Muslim
(and there are quite a few in Central Asia,
especially in Uzbekistan's Ferghana Valley),
clothes that reveal flesh other than face,
hands and feet, or the shape of the body, look
ridiculous on men, and scandalous on
women. Shorts and singlets are especially
offensive. For women visitors this is not only
an elementary courtesy but may also reduce
hostility or harassment.

This doesn't mean you have to wear a
choir-robe – just long, loose, non-revealing
shirts, trousers or skirts (which are in any
case the most comfortable in summer). In big
cities conservative western dress is common.

It's cheap to have clothes (and sleeping
sheets) made in Pakistani bazaars; you can
even get your western clothes copied.

Shoes Light walking shoes are adequate for
all but long or snowy treks. Sandals are a
relief in warm, dry weather.

Gifts If you intend to stay in (or even just
visit) private homes you should never arrive
empty-handed. Some portable but well-received gifts are international stickers,
badges, pins and key-rings, and sweets, post-cards and flower seeds from home. Drivers
are especially keen on stickers. Placed near

the top of your pack, these may also deflect greedy customs officials from more expensive gadgets.

For special friends, consider a picture book of the nearest big city to your home, a quality fountain pen, or music tapes (1960s and 1970s pop is very big). Family photos always go down well.

Another category of people often deserving of small gifts – western sweets or scented soaps, for example – are the best of the hotel floor-ladies.

Western cigarettes are available in Central Asia, so they don't make as good a gift as they did in Soviet days.

Trekking Equipment If you plan on doing any trekking, bring as much of your own gear and dried food as possible, since equipment – especially sleeping bags – and supplies are hard to find. The easiest stove fuels to obtain in Central Asia are petrol (gasoline) and medicinal spirits.

Miscellaneous A Russian phrasebook (and a dictionary if you have room) will definitely come in handy. Basic Turkish will even be helpful, since all but Tajiks speak languages closely related to Turkish. Lonely Planet publishes a *Russian phrasebook* and a *Central Asia phrasebook* is due for publication at the end of 1996.

Besides the usual items, good ideas for Central Asia include eating utensils, water bottle, sun hat, a light day pack, pen-knife and shower things (flip-flops). Sunglasses, sunscreen and lip salve are especially important if you'll be doing any mountain trekking.

A torch (flashlight) is welcome where the electricity is dodgy or the light bulbs have burned out. A universal sink plug is very handy, as few hotels have plugs. Bottom-end hotels tend not to give you towels, either. Other ideas are a length of cord for a washing-line, nylon or plastic bags, and a small sewing kit.

Bring mosquito repellent, especially if you'll be travelling in the lowland southern border regions of Tajikistan where malaria is a risk (see Health in this chapter).

Seasoned travellers will already have a secure passport-and-money pouch; this is especially important in Central Asia, where everybody wants to get their hands on your money. Half a dozen passport-sized photos will save you trouble in case of paperwork, though it's possible to get them en route. Photocopies of the first few pages of your passport will ease the headaches if you lose it.

Everybody seems to be short of matches. Toilet paper supplies are unpredictable (and lower-end hotels don't supply it), so bring a roll for when you can't find any); the same goes for instant coffee or tea bags if you depend on them. Instant soups are great for long train journeys.

An oversize cup is useful if you're self-catering. You can even boil an egg in one, using a heating coil *(kipyatelnik)* which you can buy in department stores and electrical shops for around US$3 to US$5.

Women should buy tampons before coming to Central Asia, though we spotted them in Tashkent's Almazar Superstore and some Bishkek kiosks, and sample packs are sometimes sold for exorbitant prices in bazars (in a pinch, women Peace Corps volunteers have government-issue stocks!). Chinese department stores, including those in Kashgar, have sanitary towels. Likewise, bring condoms from home.

For a suggested medical kit see the Health section later in this chapter. For photography prerequisites see the Film & Photography section later in this chapter.

HIGHLIGHTS
Here's our pick of the best of Central Asia.

- Open-air bazars everywhere, especially on weekends when people stream in from the countryside: kaleidoscopes of old and young faces, traditional dress and manners, tasty food, a commercial buzz. In any rural area, track down the big weekly market: more than the city ones, these are an essential part of people's lives, not just for stocking up but for catching up, even when they have little money to spend.

- Hiking or trekking in the mountains almost any-where.

For highlights in the individual Central Asian countries see the beginning of each country chapter.

For connoisseurs of the desolate:

- Any decaying industrial city in northern Kazakstan.
- Moynaq, an end-of-the-world place where ill and impoverished inhabitants endure in a Soviet-made environmental cataclysm; rusting hulks of fishing boats lie beached on what were once the shores of the Aral Sea.
- The train ride to Aqtau (Kazakstan), across a desert dotted with salt lakes, decaying settlements and Muslim cemeteries; at the end of the line, a bus ride across town through the ultimate industrial wasteland.

TOURIST OFFICES
Local Tourist Offices
Intourist, the old Soviet travel bureau, gave birth to a litter of Central Asian successors – Yassaui in Kazakstan, Kyrghyzintourist in Kyrgyzstan, Tajik Intourist in Tajikistan, Turkmen-Intour in Turkmenistan, and Uzbektourism in Uzbekistan. But their local offices, and their service bureaus in the top tourist hotels, are on the whole dedicated to hard-currency group and package tourism; the spectrum of help for individuals ranges from modest to none at all (though you'll do better if they think you might buy some of their services).

As to attitude, we found Kyrghyzintourist the most agreeable of the lot. Uzbektourism wins the booby prize – at best uninterested in individual travellers, at worst hostile to them, with few points for public interface beyond the service bureaus; exceptions include the good offices in Ferghana, Urgench and Nukus. Uzbektourism also has a licensing hammerlock on most fledgling tourist agencies inside the country.

You are almost always better off with one of the growing number of private agencies, if you can find one, though their prices tend to be high. We note local offices of both private and state agencies in the Information section for each large town.

China
CITS (Chinese: Lüxingshe), the main state travel bureau, will book hotels, transport, tours and tickets, at high group rates and usually with a service charge. They're generally less than thrilled about helping budget travellers who've come on their own, though CITS in Ürümqi is quite good. CITS in Kashgar rents jeeps and offers some package trips.

Xinjiang Headquarters
    51 Xinhua North Rd, 830002 Ürümqi (☎ (0991) 282-5913, 282-1428; fax 281-0689, 281-8691; telex 79027 CITSXJ CN)
Kashgar
    Chini Bagh Hotel, 93 Seman Rd, 844000 Kashgar (☎ (0998) 223156, fax 223087, telex 79051 CITS CN)
Hong Kong
    Main office, 6th floor, Tower II, South Seas Centre, 75 Mody Rd, Tsimshatsui, Kowloon (☎ 2732-5888)
USA
    Suite 465, 60 East 42nd St, New York, NY 10165 (☎ (212) 867-0271)

China Travel Service (CTS) originally looked after overseas Chinese 'compatriots' with cheaper hotels, lower fares etc; now they're after the non-Chinese market too.

Standards are more modest than at CITS but fees are lower and bookings tend to be cheaper. This is the clear choice for arrangements from Hong Kong. There is also a competent CTS in Ürümqi, at the Overseas Chinese Hotel.

Australia
    757-59 George St, Sydney, NSW 2000 (☎ (02) 211 2633)
Canada
    556 West Broadway, Vancouver, BC V5Z 1E9 (☎ (604) 872-8787)
Hong Kong
    78 Connaught Rd, Central (☎ 2853-3533)
UK
    24 Cambridge Circus, London WC2H 8HD (☎ (0171) 836 9911)
USA
    212 Sutter St, San Francisco, CA 94108 (☎ (415) 398-6627)

China Youth Travel Service (CYTS) offers most of the same services as CITS and CTS, at prices similar to CTS's. They're no longer just for 'youth'. CYTS looks like the best bet for tickets and excursions in Ürümqi.

The Kashgar branch of the China Mountaineering Association (CMA) can arrange trekking and other small group sports trips in the Kashgar region, and can also give on-the-spot help with guides, transport and equipment. They are the clear choice in Kashgar. See Information under Kashgar in the Western Xinjiang & the KKH chapter.

Pakistan

The Pakistan Tourism Development Corporation (PTDC) maintains tourist information centres in several towns, with brochures, advice and sometimes jeeps for hire. The only one on the northern KKH is at Gilgit, in the Chinar Inn on Babar Rd (☎ 2562).

There are PTDC offices in Canada, at Suite 202, 2678 West Broadway, Vancouver, British Columbia V6K 2G3 (☎ (604) 732-4686); and in the UK, at Suite 433, 52-54 High Holborn, London WC1V 6RL (☎ (071) 242 3131).

Tourist Offices Abroad

Any overseas representatives tend to be busy setting up joint ventures, and have little time for enquiring individuals. None, in fact, had any interest in telling us where their overseas offices are. We found only the Uzbektourism office in Russia, at ulitsa Bolshaya Polyanka 41, 109108 Moscow (☎ (7-095) 238-56-32, 238-89-58).

The best sources of information at home tend to be private travel firms specialising in Central Asia or the CIS (see the Travel & Visa Agencies section in the Getting There & Away chapter).

VISAS & EMBASSIES

Visas can be the single biggest headache associated with travel in Central Asia, especially in the former Soviet republics where regulations are still mutating. Up-to-date information is hard to find, and prices for help vary wildly. For every rule there's a loophole, with scores of shifty officials exploiting it. Collecting visas for a multi-country trip can take months.

Note that in most places outside Central Asia you will have trouble getting on a plane without a visa for your destination or letter of support (see the following Visas by Invitation section) if you intend to collect the visa on arrival. Airlines are keen to avoid the costs and fines associated with bringing you back if your papers aren't in order.

Visas for the Central Asian Republics

The steps to obtain a visa, and the attention it gets after you arrive, differ for each republic but their outlines are similar. The following information is general, with individual variations spelled out in the following country-specific sections.

By Invitation The key to getting a visa is 'visa support' or 'sponsorship', which means an invitation, approved by the ministries of Foreign Affairs &/or Interior, from a private individual, company or state organisation in the country you want to visit. After obtaining ministry approval, your sponsor sends the invitation (also known as a letter of support) to you, and when you apply at a consular office for your visa, it's matched with a copy sent directly to them from the Ministry of Foreign Affairs.

The invitation should include: your name, address, citizenship, sex, birth date, birthplace, and passport details; the purpose, proposed itinerary and entry/exit dates of your visit; and the type of visa you will need and where you will apply for it.

Many western visa and specialist travel agencies can obtain invitations through local partner agencies or contacts. Most will also do the aggravating embassy legwork (see Applying for the Visa, later in this section). For some reliable western agencies, see the Travel & Visa Agencies section in the Getting There & Away chapter.

Alternatively you could try dealing directly, by fax or e-mail, with a Central Asian organisation. Though sometimes cheaper than going via an agency at home, this is more cumbersome and problematic. See Travel & Visa Agencies in the Getting There & Away chapter for some trustworthy agencies in Central Asia.

The most expensive way to get sponsored is to arrange your trip through one of the state-run successors to Intourist, the old Soviet travel bureau, and pay in advance for their overpriced accommodation and other services (see the Travel & Visa Agencies section). That bureau becomes your sponsor and, along with a letter of support, you get travel vouchers to present for those services. This route needn't be as outrageously pricey as in USSR days. While some agencies still insist you prebook all accommodation, some can arrange visa support on the basis of more limited bookings.

State Tourist Bureaus in Central Asia

Kazakstan	Yassaui
Kyrgyzstan	Kyrghyzintourist
Tajikistan	Tajik Intourist
Turkmenistan	Turkmen-Intour
Uzbekistan	Uzbektourism

Without an Invitation Some republics have taken the first steps towards scrapping the clumsy, counterproductive invitation system. Kyrgyzstan and Turkmenistan allow at least some of their embassies to grant visas at their own discretion, and Turkmenistan issues visas on arrival at Ashghabat airport – all without the need for invitations. Kazakstan issues an extendable three day visa on arrival at Almaty airport from outside the former USSR, but it's ridiculously expensive at US$100.

Uzbekistan, on the other hand, seems to be trying to make it harder to get visas, except through approved Uzbek agencies and only via cooperating agencies overseas.

Applying for a Visa Visa applications can be made at some or all of the republics'

overseas embassies or consulates, listed in the following sections. Russian embassies in some countries without Central Asian representation will put Central Asian cities on their own visas, or transmit applications to the relevant Central Asian foreign ministries.

In addition to a letter of support and/or travel vouchers, they may want a photocopy of the validity and personal-information pages of your passport, two or three passport-size photos and a completed application form. Some may want more; eg the Kazak embassy in Moscow wants a photocopy of your Russian visa, and Uzbek embassies may ask to see an onward visa.

The visa application asks for the name of every town you want to visit, and these will normally be listed on your visa. For Uzbekistan, Turkmenistan and Tajikistan it's important to list them all. Elsewhere, capital cities and flight destinations might be enough but it's still smarter to ask for every place you might conceivably want to see – no matter what consular officials say. There's no charge for listing extra destinations.

If there's no convenient embassy and you're planning to fly in from outside the former USSR, you may be able to get a visa when you arrive. In Kazakstan and Turkmenistan you simply front up and apply. In Uzbekistan you must bring a letter of support; responsible sponsors and agencies send representatives to meet their invitees and smooth their way through immigration.

Your visa may be stamped or pasted into your passport, or it may be a separate document (as with Russian visas). Errors happen; check the dates and other information carefully before you hit the road, and try to find out what the Russian or other writing says. One couple paid the full fee for an Uzbek visa from the Russian embassy in Kathmandu, and on arrival discovered it was only a three day transit visa, which they couldn't extend.

Getting Central Asian Visas in Central Asia Some (not all) visas are simple and cheap to get after you arrive. It's easy, for example, to get a Kazak visa in Kyrgyzstan or Uzbekistan, or a Kyrgyz visa in Kazakstan, Turkmenistan or Uzbekistan, and not hard to get an Uzbek visa in Kazakstan. Turkmen visas are available on arrival at Ashghabat airport. None appears to need a letter of support.

This could make your *pre-trip* visa search much simpler, if you're willing to take some chances. Indeed, it might be possible (though we have not tried it) to leave home without any visas at all – eg fly to Ashghabat from Istanbul, Tehran or elsewhere outside the former USSR and get a Turkmen visa on arrival, then in Ashghabat get a Kyrgyz visa and fly to Bishkek, get a Kazak visa there and take a bus to Almaty, and so on.

Note that you cannot get a tourist visa at a land border of any Central Asian republic.

Transit Visas & the '72-Hour Rule' Some CIS countries allow a non-CIS visitor with a valid visa for one CIS country to spend up to 72 hours in another at no further cost. But not all CIS visas are honoured in all other CIS countries, and officials contradict one another on which visas are acceptable and for how long. Current '72-hour' agreements that might get you in the door are noted in the Transit information in the following sections on each republic.

Even if you do get in this way, there may be conditions – eg in Uzbekistan you can't go anywhere except Tashkent – and this permission may not be extendable as a tourist visa. While handy, this 'rule' doesn't look like a reliable way to get around.

This 'rule' is not the same as a transit visa, which you can usually apply (and pay) for in advance. You normally don't need a letter of support or prebooked accommodation for a transit visa, though you may have to show an onward ticket or visa.

Visa Extensions Extending an ordinary visa after you get there is tedious, but usually straightforward if you have a sponsor, who must prepare a letter of support in the same way as for the original visa. If your sponsor is a travel agency, or if you have no sponsor and go to an agency for help, you'll have to

pay them, and the relevant ministry will charge its own fee too.

Business Visas A business visa always requires a letter of support. Some travel and visa agencies like them because they can be obtained quickly, but embassies may give business visa applications closer scrutiny than tourist ones. Travellers who hold business visas but don't look like business people may attract more police attention, especially in Uzbekistan.

Exit Visas You don't need a separate visa to exit from any republic, which means that if someone asks for one, they're probably trying to shake you down. The only exit permission we ever heard about is associated with some excursions crossing briefly into another republic, eg from Samarkand to Penjikent. An Uzbek agency arranging such a trip might need to get both entry and exit visas for the adjacent republic, to ensure that your Uzbek visa is not cancelled by this temporary departure.

Border Controls & Visa Checks By agreement with the relevant republics, Russian border troops are still in charge of immigration control between CIS and non-CIS countries. This means thorough visa checks if you fly to Central Asia directly from any non-CIS country (with this in mind, major international carriers may not even let you on board without a visa, letter of support or vouchers), or if you cross any land border between a Central Asian republic and Iran, Afghanistan or China. Border hassles are as much a result of Russian arrogance as local shortcomings.

On the other hand, if you cross a land border between two Central Asian republics, you could be waved right through, and even the border between Russia and Kazakstan is fairly porous. There aren't always arrival checks on flights between Central Asian republics either, though there are usually exit checks.

This is not to recommend visa-less travel, since it's hard to keep a low enough profile for that. You'll usually be asked for your visa when you register at a tourist hotel or buy an air ticket (and sometimes a train or bus ticket). In Uzbekistan you cannot usually check into a hotel without the town itself being listed in your visa. Some travellers have deflected demands to see a visa by saying they're in transit.

Registration This relic of Soviet days allows officials to keep tabs on you once you've arrived. In Uzbekistan you're expected to register in every town where you stay the night. Registration is automatic if you check into a tourist hotel, but not if you're staying in a private home or smaller hotel.

The place to register is the Office of Visas & Registration (OVIR, Russian: Otdel Vis i Registratsii). There's one in every town, sometimes in each city district, functioning as the eyes and ears of the Interior Ministry's administration for policing foreigners. Though it has a local name in each republic (eg OPVR in Kazakstan, IIB in Uzbekistan), everybody still calls it OVIR, and so do we.

Costs Visa-associated costs include consular and ministry fees, payments to agencies at home and in Central Asia for sponsorship and visas, and agency and ministry charges for post-arrival services such as extensions.

At the time of research, typical consular fees for an individual single-entry Central Asian visa were in the range of US$20 to US$60 for two weeks, and more for longer. The visa fee for the Russian embassy in London was US$15 for any duration, but may be more elsewhere. Fast service jacks up the cost. Fees are the same for all applicants from English-speaking countries, except South African passport holders who may be hit with surcharges. Ministries may also add handling and communications charges. For visas on arrival, be prepared to pay in US$ cash.

Agency charges are hard to pin down, partly because their own costs are 'fluid'. People have their hands out everywhere, and petty bribery is sometimes the only way to keep an application moving in Central Asia. At the time of research, typical visa support plus handling charges for a two week visa were about US$50 to US$100 – plus any accommodation (voucher) costs you must pay as a condition of sponsorship.

Per person costs for groups are a fraction of those for individuals, for both consular and agency services. Further cost details, as well as information about China and Pakistan visas, are in the country sections that follow.

Planning Ahead Travel and visa agencies at home prefer to hear from you six weeks to two months before you leave, although they can get visa support more quickly if you pay extra. Individual sponsors may need months to get their invitations approved before they can even be sent to you.

Once you have visa support, even the most helpful Central Asian embassies in the West normally take a week or two to get you a visa, and getting one through a Russian embassy takes longer. Most embassies will speed the process up for an extra fee. Central Asian embassies within the CIS seem to be quicker, eg a day or less at Kyrgyz embassies in other Central Asian republics, a week or less at Kazak embassies.

Try to allow time for delays and screwups. And in the end, despite carefully laid plans, your visa probably still won't be ready until the last minute!

Getting Current Information As with all official mumbo-jumbo in Central Asia, the rules change all the time, so the information here may be out of date by the time you read it. Check with travellers just back from the region, and with one or more CIS-specialist travel or visa agencies (some are listed in the Travel & Visa Agencies section in the Getting There & Away chapter). On the Internet, you can often find useful tips on the rec.travel.asia newsgroup.

Lost or Stolen Passports or Visas The UK embassies in Tashkent and Almaty can issue an emergency passport to Brits or nationals of other unrepresented Commonwealth countries, enough to get you home only. The US embassies in the Central Asian capitals can issue ordinary 10 year passports for US$65.

Replacing a visa is quite another matter. The loss must be reported to the police, and to the local OVIR office (a travel agent or your hotel service bureau might help with this). If you don't have a record of the visa number, you could end up tracking it right back to the issuing embassy. To avoid such a bureaucratic nightmare, it is therefore essential that you carry photocopies of the important pages of your passport, and of your visas.

Kazakstan

First have a look at the preceding section, Visas for Central Asian Republics.

Visa checks are almost nonexistent on flights, trains and buses into Kazakstan from other CIS states (though some have been reported on the Tashkent-Shymkent road). There are always checks on flights arriving in Almaty from outside the former USSR, and at road and rail crossings on the Kazakstan-China frontier (you certainly need a visa in valid Kazakstan to exit the country at Khorgos/Korgas or Dostyq (Russian: Druzhba) /Alashankou. Fines of up to US$250 can be levied for being in Kazakstan without a proper visa.

Your visa normally lists the towns identified in your visa application, but in practice you can go almost anywhere. The only cities we heard of that required explicit visa entries were Petropavl and Qyzylorda. Kurchatov, the command town of the former nuclear testing zone near Semey, and the Baykonur Cosmodrome and its support town Leninsk, are off limits to casual visitors.

Getting a Visa Visas can be obtained from Kazakstan embassies and consulates, from Russian embassies in countries without Kazakstan representation, or – if you fly in from outside the former USSR – on arrival at Almaty airport. In general you must have visa support for any of these, although you

can get an extendable three day visa on arrival at the airport without support – for US$100!

For business and official visits, the inviting organisation must send its invitation to the consular department of the Ministry of Foreign Affairs in Almaty. The ministry then authorises a specific embassy/consulate (or the consular section at Almaty airport) to issue the visa. It may not always be necessary for you to have a copy of the invitation yourself, though it's probably advisable.

The support required for a tourist visa is a letter from an officially licensed Kazakstan tourism firm, or in some cases a foreign travel firm, confirming prebooked services in Kazakstan. The extent of prebooked services required may vary from place to place.

For visits by private invitation, your sponsor must apply to OVIR (known as OPVR in Kazakstan) and may also have to get an approval from his/her workplace. If all goes well at OVIR, in about three weeks your sponsor gets a green *izveshchenie* (Russian for 'notification') which goes to you or your travel/visa agency, to be submitted with your visa application.

At the time of research the fees at Kazakstan embassies or consulates for a single-entry visa for most nationalities were about US$30 for one week, US$50 for two weeks, US$70 for one month, and US$100 for more than one month. For processing in less than one week, fees are 50% higher; for same or next-day processing, fees are doubled. Fees for holders of Japan, Turkey, China and CIS country passports were lower. Fees vary for visas issued through Russian embassies, which may also take longer.

If you plan to cross overland from China to Kazakstan, the only reliable place in China to get a Kazak visa is Beijing. There is no Kazak consulate in Kashgar. Some travellers report that the Kazakstan Airlines office in Ürümqi acts as a consular office and might issue you a Kazakstan visa if you already have a letter of support from a Kazakstan agency, but don't count on it.

There is a small Kazak embassy in Islamabad, where travellers have in the past persuaded them to issue visas without letters of support.

Transit A Russian visa is good for 72 hours in Kazakstan (though travellers have spent as much as a week there with one). So, at the time of writing, are visas for Kyrgyzstan, Tajikistan, Armenia, Belarus and possibly Georgia.

Kazak embassies will issue extendable three day transit visas (not the same as the three day no-support airport visas) in a few working days for about US$15, without sponsorship. Some embassies may want to see a ticket to Kazakstan and/or an onward ticket and/or onward visa. Some people have obtained six day transit visas the same day for US$30 from the Kazak embassy in Beijing.

Multiple Entry Multiple-entry visas cost US$125 for one year or US$250 for two years, and can be obtained from overseas embassies or from OVIR in Almaty. Processing takes about two weeks.

Registration You're *supposed* to register within three days of arrival in every town, which means you can stay up to three days anywhere without doing so. If you don't, you're unlikely to have problems as long as you have a visa valid in Kazakstan to show if necessary when buying tickets or leaving the country. Some tourist hotels register you automatically, some don't.

Embassies & Consulates The Kazak consulate in London was new at research time, and didn't seem to have its visa procedures very well organised.

Australia
    Consulate, Suite 3409, Level 34, Grosvenor Place, 225 George St, Sydney 2000 (☎ (02) 258-6565, fax 258-6999)

Azerbaijan
    Embassy, Baku 370000 (fax (8922) 98-87-08)

Belarus
    Consulate, Minsk 220000 (☎ (0172) 35-59-43, fax 35-84-52)

Belgium
    Embassy, Avenue Vanbever 30, 1180 Brussels (☎ (02) 374-95-62, fax 374-50-91)

China
    Embassy, Beijing (☎ (01) 532-61-82, 532-64-29; fax 532-61-83)

France
    Embassy, 59 rue Pierre Charron, F-75008 Paris (☎ (1) 45.61.52.00, 45.61.52.02; fax 45.61.52.01)

Germany
    Embassy (Consular Section), Lassauxstrasse 1, 53424 Remagen (☎ (02642) 3071/2/3, fax (02642) 938325)

Hungary
    Embassy, Budapest (☎ (01) 275-13-00, 275-13-01; fax 275-20-92)

India
    Embassy, New Delhi (☎ (011) 688-81-88, 688-84-59, 687-23-79; fax 301-86-68)

Iran
    Embassy, Tehran (☎ (021) 801-53-71, 256-59-33, 256-59-34; fax 254-64-00)

Kyrgyzstan
    Embassy, Moskva 161, Bishkek (☎ (3312) 22-45-57, 22-54-63, 22-23-03; fax 22-54-63)

Pakistan
    Embassy, Old Embassy Rd, Islamabad (☎ (051) 262925, fax 262806)

Russia
    Embassy, Chistoprudny bulvar 3A, Moscow 101000 (☎ (095) 208-98-52, 927-18-36; fax 208-08-32, 208-26-50)

Turkey
    Embassy, Ebüzziya Tevfik Sokak 6, TR-06680 Ankara (☎ (312) 441 23 01/2, fax 441 23 03)

UK
    Consulate, 3 Warren Mews, London W1P 5DJ (☎ & fax (0171) 387 1047)

USA & Canada
    Embassy, 3421 Massachusetts Ave NW, Washington, DC 20007 (☎ (202) 333-4507, fax 333-4509)

Ukraine
    Embassy, Kiev 252000 (☎ & fax (044) 290-77-22)

Uzbekistan
    Embassy, Holida Samatova (formerly Frunze) 20, Tashkent (☎ (3712) 33-37-05, 33-59-44; fax 33-60-22)

Kyrgyzstan

First have a look at the preceding section, Visas for Central Asian Republics.

Visa checks are rare on any ground or air approach to Kyrgyzstan from other former USSR states; if you enter overland (eg by bus from Almaty or Tashkent) you may not even notice the border. Checks are possible on flights *from* Kyrgyzstan to other former USSR states, especially Russia. They're 100% certain on flights arriving from outside the former USSR, and at the land border over the Torugart pass to/from China.

Your visa may not list specific towns, and you can go almost anywhere in any case. Most hotels want to see a visa, but none seem interested in town names. But it's not a bad idea to ask for Bishkek when you apply for the visa, and perhaps Osh and Naryn if you're going anywhere near them.

If you're crossing the Torugart pass in either direction, you'll need a Kyrgyz or Russian visa with 'Bishkek' on it. If you're leaving Kyrgyzstan it might help to have a Bishkek registration stamp too; you can't just bop down from Almaty or Tashkent and count on the '72-hour rule' in this case.

There are fines for visa violations, but most officials are fairly casual. If the police find you have no visa or no entry stamp, they'll probably just stamp the date in your passport and bundle you off to Bishkek to get one.

Getting a Visa Many Kyrgyz embassies now issue visas without letters of support. At the time of research the embassy in Washington would give you a one month visa in a week for US$30, in three days for US$60 or immediately for US$100. Those in Almaty and Tashkent quoted US$25, and the one in Moscow US$40, for a visa in a day or two. The embassy in Brussels was giving out its own free letters of support, to be taken to the Russian embassy. In Ankara US$50 gets you 15 days.

If you arrive with only a Russian or Kazak visa, you can stay 72 hours, during which time you *might* be able to get a Kyrgyz visa on your own at OVIR or the Ministry of Foreign Affairs. In practice it's easier to pay a local agency for help. A visa costs anywhere from US$35 to US$150, depending on how long you want to stay, plus whatever cut the agency takes.

Your sponsor or a local agency can also help with extending a visa.

Transit A traveller with a valid Russian or Kazak visa can automatically spend 72 hours in Kyrgyzstan, and a Russian visa might serve you for longer. Some people claim to have gotten in on the basis of an Uzbek visa.

Registration All foreigners staying in the country more than three days are expected to register once with OVIR, preferably in Bishkek. A stamp from Bishkek is good for the whole country, and normally for a month.

Registration is apparently automatic if you check into a tourist hotel. If you're in a local dive or private home it's probably not, and OVIR would like to see a letter from your sponsor or, if you don't have one, a note from your hotel saying how long you've been there.

If OVIR can prove that you've been in the country longer than three days without registering, you could be fined US$60. Some travellers report being fined even though OVIR had no proof.

Registration takes a few minutes and costs about US$3.50 in *som* if you've already got a visa. They don't take the money themselves; you must first stop at a bank (Adil Bank on Chuy is handy in Bishkek), say *'OVIR registratsiya'*, pay them and get a receipt for OVIR. There's obviously no need for travel agency help with this.

Not everyone bothers to register, though OVIR officers have visited travellers in Bishkek hotels. If you're leaving over the Torugart pass, officials there may want to see a Bishkek registration stamp along with your visa.

Embassies & Consulates If you intend to cross into Kyrgyzstan from China over the Torugart pass, note that Beijing is the only place in China where you can get a Kyrgyz visa.

Austria
    Embassy, Naglergasse 25/5, 1010 Vienna
    (☎ (06) 533 90 22, fax 533 09 50)
Belarus
    Embassy, vulitsa Kalvarijaskaja 17, 220000
    Minsk (☎ (0172) 23-61-82, fax 23-58-22)

Belgium & the Netherlands
Embassy, 32 rue du Chatelain (or Kasteleinstraat), 1050 Brussels (☎ (02) 627 19 16, fax 627 19 00)

China
Embassy, Ta Yuan Diplomatic Office Bldg, Chaoyang District, Beijing (☎ 532 6458, 532 4180; fax 532 6459); there is no consulate in Kashgar

Germany
Embassy, Hochkreuzallee 117, 53175 Bonn (☎ (0228) 31 06 94, fax 47 58 63)

India
Embassy, A-9/32 Vasant Vihar, New Delhi 110057 (☎ (011) 688 68 90, fax 688 18 54)

Kazakstan
Embassy, Amangheldy köshesi 68-A, Almaty (☎ 63-33-05, 63-33-09; fax 63-71-90)

Russia
Embassy, ulitsa Bolshaya Ordynka 64, 109017 Moscow (☎ (095) 237-44-81, 237-48-82; fax 237-45-71)

Turkey
Embassy, Boyabat Sokak 11, Gaziosmanpasa, 06700 Ankara (☎ (312) 446 84 08, fax 311 99 21)

Turkmenistan
Embassy, prospekt Saparmurada Turkmenbashi 13 (an office in the Russian embassy compound), Ashghabat 744000 (☎ 46-88-04, 29-25-39)

Ukraine
Embassy, vulitsya Kutuzova 8, 252000 Kiev (☎ (044) 295-53-80, ☎ & fax 295-96-92)

USA & Canada
Embassy, 1511 K Street NW, Suite 707, Washington, DC 20005 (☎ (202) 628-0433, fax 347-3718)

Uzbekistan
Embassy, Mustaqillik maydoni 5, Tashkent (☎ (3712) 39-45-43, fax 39-16-78)

Tajikistan

First have a look at the preceding section, Visas for Central Asian Republics.

Visas are not issued at the airport nor at the borders. In fact we found no Tajik border controls at all on the Termez-Dushanbe train, the Osh-Khojan road and the Khojand-Tashkent road; we were checked only on the Kyrgyz border at Sary Tash.

By contrast there are frequent internal checkpoints, particularly in Gorno-Badakhshan, and if you intend moving outside Dushanbe you must have impeccable documents. As a result of border tensions and the increase in drugs and gun smuggling, the army and militia do not appreciate the presence of foreigners, and if anyone is not completely satisfied with your papers you will probably be deported. At any given time certain areas will be completely out of bounds because of military skirmishing (see the Travel in Tajikistan aside in the Tajikistan chapter).

Getting a Visa At present the only accredited Tajik consular representation outside the former USSR is in Bonn (Germany gave them the building rent-free), and even there they apparently only issue a letter for the Russian embassy. This may also be the case for the other Tajik embassies. The ambassador in Tashkent claims he can issue a visa the same day if you 'fax ahead', otherwise in three or four days, but don't count on this. Fees had not been set nor any formal procedure established when we visited.

If you do arrive in Tajikistan without a visa, the immigration department of the Foreign Ministry (see Dushanbe in the Tajikistan chapter) may give you one. The Tajik consulate in Moscow suggests getting a visa support letter from the tourism company Alfaavruz in Dushanbe (☎ (3772) 35-79-06, 35-94-31).

Every Tajik town that you intend visiting or passing through should be listed on your visa.

Visa Extensions If you need an extension you should probably see Tajik Intourist in Dushanbe. If you speak good Russian and want to try it yourself, go to the Ministry of Foreign Affairs.

Registration There appear to be no registration requirements.

Embassies & Consulates Tajik consular addresses in major cities overseas include:

Germany
Embassy, Hans-Böckler-strasse 3, 53225 Bonn (☎ (0228) 97 29 50, fax 97 29 555)

Kazakstan
Embassy, Yemelev köshesi 70, Almaty (☎ 61-17-60, 61-02-25)

Russia
    Embassy, Skatertny pereulok 19, Moscow
    121069 (☎ (095) 290-02-70, 290-61-02, 290-57-
    36; fax 290-06-09)
Turkmenistan
    Embassy, ulitsa Tellia 6, Ashghabat 744000
    (☎ (3632) 25-13-74)
Uzbekistan
    Embassy, Mustaqillik maydoni 5, Tashkent
    (☎ (3712) 39-40-57)

Turkmenistan

First have a look at the earlier section, Visas
for Central Asian Republics.

Every visitor must get a Turkmen visa,
either from a Turkmen embassy or on arrival,
and travel without one is nearly impossible.
Most hotel receptionists want to see it, as do
train and bus ticket clerks. There may be visa
checks on private vehicles entering from
other Central Asian republics, and on
Caspian Sea ferries from Baku arriving at
Turkmenbashi. While controls appear non-
existent on trains entering Turkmenistan via
Uzbekistan, effective control arises from the
fact that many terminate at Charjou, where
onward passengers must buy a new ticket.
For this you need a visa, but the nearest
places to obtain one are OVIR in Mary and
the Ministry of Foreign Affairs in Ashghabat.

Internal travel is relatively unrestricted.
Exceptions include the chemical-plant town
of Cheleken on the Caspian coast, and Kerki
in the south-east, because of its proximity to
the Afghan border. Saraghs, a few km from
the Iranian border, is also supposedly closed
to foreigners, as are the Kopet Dag mountains along the Iranian border.

If you try to fly out with an expired visa,
you may be sent back to the Ministry of
Foreign Affairs in Ashghabat. Visa checks
are less likely on exit at land borders with
other Central Asian republics, but it does
happen. If you're leaving by train, you might
get through with a lapsed visa on one of the
pokey suburban trains (eg the daily Charjou-
Bukhara service), where checks are very
unlikely.

Getting a Visa Procedures and requirements
seem to vary from one consular office to

another. In Ashghabat we were told that
tourist visas are generally issued for a
maximum of seven days, for US$25. But the
Turkmenistan embassy in Washington
offered 10 days for US$10, 20 days for
US$20, a month for US$30, plus longer visas
all processed in a week. The embassy in
Ankara can apparently issue a visa in a day.
A letter of support is not necessary, but if you
are overseas, this or a note from your own
embassy may speed things up. The application asks for your itinerary, though it's
unlikely you'll be held to it.

Ten day visas are also issued for US$20
on arrival at Ashghabat airport, at the highly
visible visa desk just before immigration. No
letter of support is necessary there either.

If you arrive visa-less by car or train at a
land border crossing, the Turkmenistan
embassy in Washington suggests you apply
for a visa at the nearest *velayat hyakimlik*
(provincial mayor's office), but this sounds
a little dubious. Coming from Azerbaijan on
a Caspian Sea ferry, you should have a visa
already, as immigration is tightly controlled.

Business Business visas can be issued for
stays of six months or longer. The sponsoring
organisation in Turkmenistan gets its invitation certified by the Ministry of Foreign
Affairs and sends it to you. You may have to
show it to buy the air ticket to Ashghabat,
and on arrival at the airport you take a seven
day tourist visa, then get it extended at the
ministry for the period shown on the invitation.

Transit Turkmenistan will not necessarily
honour any other CIS visa for '72-hour' permission, though some travellers report
succeeding with a Russian or Uzbek visa. An
ordinary transit visa can be obtained from an
embassy or on arrival for US$10.

Visa Extensions Visas cannot be extended
without a letter of support from an approved
sponsor in Turkmenistan, though ministry
officials are vague on what constitutes an
approved sponsor. With a letter, a 10 day
extension is US$10 from the immigration

section of the Ministry of Foreign Affairs in Ashghabat (Monday, Thursday or Friday from 9 am to 1 pm). Business visa extensions are US$15. The ministry doesn't seem keen on private invitations.

A week in Turkmenistan is plenty for the average tourist, but if you're determined to spend longer, you might be able to convince the Ministry of Culture (ulitsa Pushkina, Ashghabat 744000, ☎ 25-34-17; fax 51-19-91, 25-69-85) that your interest is genuine, and wangle an invitation from them.

An Ashghabat travel agency which might help is ESCAP-UNEP (see Travel Agencies in the Ashghabat section of the Turkmenistan chapter), though they'd naturally expect you to make your bookings through them too.

Registration There may be a rule that visitors should register with OVIR, but we never heard about it from the Foreign Ministry nor the Department of Tourism, and we were never queried by any hotel or ticket clerk.

Embassies & Consulates Turkmen consular addresses in major cities overseas include:

Afghanistan
     Consulate, Herat; Consulate, Mazar-i-Sharif
Austria
     Embassy, Friedrich-Schmidt-Platz 3/3, 30/39, 1080 Vienna (☎ 1-40 73 190)
France
     Embassy, 13 Rue Picot, F-75116 Paris (☎ (1) 47.55.05.36, fax 47.55.05.68)
Iran
     Embassy, kheyabun-e Maleka 8, Tehran (☎ (021) 761015); Consulate, Mashhad
Russia
     Embassy, Filippovsky pereulok (former pereulok Axakova) 22, 121019 Moscow (☎ (095) 291-66-36, 202-02-78; fax 291-09-35)
Turkey
     Embassy, Rabat Sokak (also called Incirlik Sokak) 22, Gaziosmanpasa, 06700 Ankara (☎ (312) 446 85 63, 446 83 77; fax 446 83 78; Consulate, 2 Tasocegi caddesi, Altan Erbulak Sokak 4, Mecidiyeköy, Istanbul (☎ (212) 272 70 20/1, fax 275 39 93)
USA & Canada
     Embassy, 1511 K Street NW, Suite 412, Washington, DC 20005 (☎ (202) 737-4800, fax 737-1152)

Uzbekistan

First have a look at the preceding section, Visas for Central Asian Republics.

Uzbekistan is the most difficult of the republics for individual tourists to get into and, at the official level, goes on making you feel unwelcome while you're there. Everybody wants to see your papers, all the time, and even when they're in order you may get a hard time. Officials here simply don't comprehend, or don't like, plan-as-you-go travellers.

A foreigner in a bus or train station is certain to be approached by uniformed or plain-clothes police (ask to see *their* IDs too, and don't go anywhere with them). In Tashkent, Termez and elsewhere you may be unable to buy a ticket without the resident OVIR officer's approval.

There are police checkposts at every town and oblast border, and you'll probably be stopped at each one, and you or your driver squeezed for a 'fine'.

Border controls are more thorough than in neighbouring republics (and even internal flights may involve visa checks), though some travellers arriving overland or by air at places other than Tashkent have found none.

Getting a Visa Private travel must be arranged via an invitation from an Uzbek citizen, firm or organisation approved by the Ministry of Foreign Affairs, or through an Uzbek travel agency accredited by Uzbektourism. In turn, Uzbek travel agencies are apparently only permitted to do international business with other agencies, not with individuals.

Some competent Uzbek agencies are identified in the Uzbekistan chapter. Some reliable western agencies through whom you can reach them are listed in the Travel & Visa Agencies section in the Getting There & Away chapter.

Visas are issued by Uzbek embassies or consulates or through Russian embassies where there is no Uzbek representation. Fees for individuals are US$40 for a week, US$50 for 15 days, and US$60 for a month. You may be told to first book your hotels with

Uzbektourism, as in Moscow – though some travellers report paying only a 10% deposit on booked accommodation (Moscow), or booking just one night (Bonn). It's worth applying a month or two before you go, though visas were reportedly being issued in 10 days in Bonn.

It's possible to get an Uzbek visa from elsewhere in Central Asia; the Uzbek embassies in Almaty and Ashghabat can issue one without an invitation in 1½ to two weeks, or 'immediately' if you have a ministry-approved letter of support and the Ministry of Foreign Affairs has informed them. Not all other Uzbek embassies are as agreeable. One traveller wrote that Uzbekistan Airways main offices in some South-East Asian cities such as Bangkok, were acting as temporary Uzbek visa agencies, but we haven't confirmed this.

A less satisfactory alternative is to present a letter of support at Tashkent airport immigration on arrival, and collect your visa there. It's important that your sponsor meet you, since airport immigration is chaotic and some officials there are incompetent, bloody-minded or greedy (for more on this very unpleasant experience, see the Arriving in Tashkent by Air aside in the Getting There & Away chapter).

Experienced agency reps can often wheedle their way right into the arrivals lounge. Know your sponsor's name, address and telephone number before you leave home, since they're best placed to get you out of any jam. They should check in advance that you're in the immigration officer's log-book for your arrival day.

Visas on arrival are only issued at the international terminal; arrivals from CIS countries who want one must make their way to the 24 hour consular office of the Ministry of Foreign Affairs in that terminal. In fact you probably wouldn't have to fly in at all, if you could get out to Tashkent airport from elsewhere without being stopped by the police.

The only way you might conceivably get a visa on arrival without any letter of support is through the joint connivance of the airport Ministry of Foreign Affairs office and Uzbektourism, in which case you will probably have to book every night of your stay in expensive Uzbektourism hotels.

Get your visa inscribed with the names of every place you might want to visit. Being anywhere that's not on your visa is an invitation for a shakedown. Most tourist hotels want to see the town name on your visa before giving you a room. Individual dates for each town are not necessary. If you collect your visa on arrival, be sure all names are copied onto the visa, and not just the habitual Tashkent-Samarkand-Bukhara. Less satisfactory alternatives are a letter in Russian or Uzbek from an accredited local agency, listing the towns, or travel vouchers.

Uzbekistan has signed agreements with France, Germany, the UK and the USA allowing for unrestricted travel by one another's nationals, and some travellers now show up (or are issued in Tashkent) with so-called 'open' visas bearing only 'Republic of Uzbekistan' and no town names. Of course this is a great idea, but few small-time Uzbek officials know about these international agreements, and you may be turned back at every checkpost you try to pass! For the time being, insist on town names. Visa fees don't depend on the number of towns you want to visit.

Transit If you fly into Tashkent with a valid visa for Russia, Kyrgyzstan, Kazakstan, Tajikistan, Armenia or Belarus, you should get 72 hours here at no cost, though probably only in Tashkent. Ordinary transit visas – possibly good for other transit points than Tashkent – are issued by embassies and at Tashkent airport for US$20 for one day, US$25 for two days or US$30 for three days.

If you arrive elsewhere than Tashkent without an acceptable visa, in every town where you're caught you'll have to fork out at least US$20 for a one day transit visa, and possibly US$20 more for one for Tashkent. Your passport may be stamped to indicate you've been hauled in, in case you're thinking of jumping again. The police are keen to move you on, and bribes reportedly don't work in such instances.

But rules are made to be broken: one visa-less traveller bumped out of Urgench went out to the consular office at Tashkent airport, where he was given a tourist visa on the spot.

Visa Extensions To extend a visa, the Ministry of Foreign Affairs needs a further letter of support. Extensions are US$30 for a week, US$40 for 15 days, US$50 for a month, and so on. The consular office at the airport is marginally easier to deal with than the one at the ministry. If you ask Uzbektourism to extend it (eg at the service bureau of one of their hotels) they may insist on priccy hotel bookings too.

A municipal OVIR office or the consular office at the airport will add towns to your visa at no charge.

Registration Foreigners staying in Uzbekistan for even one day are supposed to register in each town where they stay. You're automatically registered if you stay at a tourist hotel. They take your passport for anything from a few minutes to a few days, returning it with a scrap of paper with the hotel's stamp and the dates of your stay.

Save these chits until you're safely out of Uzbekistan for the last time, since somebody (eg OVIR at the Tashkent bus station) is bound to want to see them. In practice a few will do since hardly anybody looks closely at them. Having none at all is asking for trouble. Fines for not being registered start at US$20 for the first five days and you could even be nabbed as you're boarding your flight home.

If you're staying in a private home, your host is supposed to register you, but this can be a time-gobbling nightmare. Some people have a friend in a hotel who'll 'register' you; or you can simply spend one night in a hotel for the registration. To do it by the book, you and your host must go to the city OVIR with your passport, a valid visa and US$20; you get a stamp on your visa.

Embassies & Consulates Uzbek consular addresses in major cities overseas include:

Afghanistan
    Consulate, Mazar-i-Sharif
Austria
    Embassy, Friedrich-Schmidt-Platz 3, 1080 Vienna (☎ (06) 405 09 27, fax 405 09 29)
France
    Embassy, 96 Avenue de Suffren, F-75116 Paris (☎ (1) 43.06.62.98)
Germany
    Embassy, Deutschherrenstrasse 7, 53177 Bonn (☎ (0228) 95 35 715, fax 95 35 799)
India
    Consulate, D-2/5 Vasant Vihar, New Delhi 110057 (☎ (011) 67 37 52, 67 89 91)
Iran
    Consulate, Grand Hotel Ozodi, Suite 1301, Tehran (☎ (021) 8083021)
Israel
    Consulate, 1 Ben-Yehuda St, Tel Aviv 63801 (☎ 510-4684, fax 510-4679)
Kazakstan
    Embassy, Baribaev köshesi 36, Almaty (☎ 61-83-16, fax 61-92-03)
Pakistan
    Consulate, D-66/1 Block 4, Clifton, Karachi (☎ 57-25-66)
Russia
    Embassy, Pogorelsky perculok 12, Moscow 113017 (☎ (095) 230-13-01, 230-00-76; fax 230-00-32; visa enquiries ☎ 230-00-54)
Saudi Arabia
    Consulate, 4412/T As-Sirat St, Khalidiya, Jeddah (☎ 682-52-23)
Turkey
    Embassy, Ahmet Rasim Sokak 14, Chankaya, 06680 Ankara (☎ (312) 439 27 40, fax 440 92 22); Consulate, Cumhuriyet caddesi 39/4, Taksim, Istanbul (☎ (212) 237 19 93, fax 237 33 22)
UAE
    PO Box 23088, King Faisal Rd, Sharjah (☎ 54-37-32, fax 54-33-22)
UK
    Consulate, 73 Wigmore St, London W1H 9DL (☎ (0171) 935 1899, fax 935 9554); this is in the Uzbekistan Airways office
USA & Canada
    Embassy, 1511 K Street NW, Suite 619, Washington, DC 20005 (☎ (202) 638-4266, fax 861-0472)

Russia

The following information is included because many visitors to Central Asia will go by way of Russia. For more details on the Russian paper-chase, see Lonely Planet's *Russia, Ukraine & Belarus*.

All foreigners visiting Russia need visas. At present a Russian visa is a paper document; nothing goes into your passport. It lists cities, but this doesn't matter much in terms of where you can go. Few Russian cities are still off limits to foreigners. Practically speaking, no-one cares where you go.

Getting a Visa Tourist visas are intended for visitors going for non-business purposes. Other possibilities are business, student, 'private', 'on-the-spot' and transit visas. A 'private' visa is as easy to get as a tourist visa except for the hoops your host must jump through to issue you with an approved invitation. 'On-the-spot' visas are basically expensive, fast-track, short-term business visas, issued at Moscow's Sheremetevo-2 or St Petersburg's Pulkovo-2 airports, but you must be met there by a representative of a Russian company, who will 'invite' you to Russia.

Individuals can get their own visas from a Russian embassy or consulate, though long queues are common in the high season and officials rarely answer the telephone. Travel or visa agencies will do the work for an extra fee (see the Travel & Visa Agencies section in the Getting There & Away chapter for some reliable ones).

You'll need a valid passport, three photos, to pay a fee that varies from country to country and according to your citizenship, and confirmation of accommodation. In theory you must book accommodation for every night you'll be there, but in practice you can often get away with booking as little as one night; ask the agency, hotel or hostel through which you book.

Business, tourist, private and student visas all take the same amount of time to process once you have the right documents – normally 10 working days, possibly longer at busy embassies like the one in London. For an extra fee you can get it sooner, even the same day.

Transit If you're passing through by air, a regular transit visa is usually good for 48 hours. For a nonstop Trans-Siberian Railway journey it's valid for 10 days.

Under certain circumstances, travellers who hold visas for Armenia, Belarus, Kazakstan, Kyrgyzstan, Tajikistan or Uzbekistan are entitled to 72 hour transit permission without a Russian transit visa, but you may have trouble convincing some border officials of this. Play it safe and get a transit visa.

Visa Extensions It's a pain to extend a tourist visa and you don't usually get much extra time. You can only do it in Moscow, either through an official hotel or at UVIR, the Department of Visas & Registration (☎ 207-01-13) at ulitsa Pokrovka 42. UVIR will also extend a transit visa, though rarely for more than five days. You may be asked for your outbound ticket.

Registration When you check in to a hotel, you surrender your passport and visa for the night so they can register you with OVIR. All Russian visas *must* be registered with the nearest office of OVIR within three working days of your arrival in Russia. Extending an unregistered visa can be impossible, and leaving the country with one can involve steep fines.

The company or organisation that invited you to Russia is responsible for your registration, and no other company can support your visa. Theoretically, the company or organisation that invited you to Russia is responsible for your registration. On tourist visas their name is on the beginning *V uchrezhdenie*, but if it isn't, or if you can't make it out, you can spend a night at one of the major (expensive) hotels, which will register you for a fee.

Embassies & Consulates Some (not all) Russian consular addresses overseas include:

Australia
  Embassy, 78 Canberra Avenue, Griffith, Canberra, ACT 2603 (☎ (06) 295 9033, 295 9474; fax 295 1847)
  Consulate, 7-9 Fullerton St, Woollahra, NSW 2025 (☎ (02) 327 5065)
Austria
  Embassy, Reisnerstrasse 45-47, 1030 Vienna (☎ (1) 712 1229, 712 3233, 713 1215; fax 712 3388)
Belgium
  Embassy, 66 Avenue de Fre, 1180 Brussels (☎ (2) 374 3406, 374 6886, 374 3106; fax 374 2613, 346 2453)
Canada
  Embassy (Consular Section), 52 Range Road, Ottawa, Ontario K1N 8J5 (☎ (613) 236-6215, 236-7220; fax 238-6158)
  Consulate, 3655 Avenue du Muse, Montreal, Quebec H3G 2E1 (☎ (514) 843-5901, 842-5343; fax 842-2012)
China
  Embassy, 4 Baizhongjie, Beijing 100600 (☎ (10) 532 2051, visa section 532 1267)
  Consulate, 20 Huangpu Lu, Shanghai 200080 (☎ (01) 324 2682)
France
  Embassy (Consular Section), 8 Rue de Prony, 75017 Paris (☎ (1) 44.43.29.00, fax 44.43.29.94)
Germany
  Embassy (Consular Section), Waldstrasse 42, 53177 Bonn (☎ (0228) 31 20 83, fax 38 45 61)
Ireland
  Embassy, 186 Orwell Rd, Rathgar, Dublin (☎ (01) 492-3525, 492-2048; fax 492-3525)
Kazakstan
  Embassy, Zhandosov köshesi 4, Almaty (☎ (3272) 44-64-91, fax 44-82-23, visa enquiries 44-64-44)
Kyrgyzstan
  Embassy, Razzakov (Pervomayskaya) 17 (☎ 22-17-75, fax 22-17-10)
Mongolia
  Embassy, Friendship Street A 6, Ulan Bator (☎ (1) 32 52 07)
Netherlands
  Embassy (Consular Section), Andries Bickerweg 2, 2517 JP The Hague (☎ (070) 346 7940)
New Zealand
  Embassy, 57 Messines Rd, Wellington (☎ (04) 476 6113, fax 476 3843)
South Africa
  Embassy (Consular Section) 135 Bourke Street, Sunnyside (Pretoria) 0002 (☎ (12) 344 4820, fax 343 8636)
Switzerland
  Embassy (Consular Section), Brunnadernrain 53, 30006 Bern (☎ (031) 352 05 67, fax 352 64 60)

Tajikistan
  Embassy, Hotel Oktyabrskaya, prospekt Rudaki 105a, Dushanbe (☎ (3772) 21-10-15)
Turkey
  Embassy, Karyagdi Sokak 5, Cankaya, 06692 Ankara (☎ (312) 440 8217, fax 438 3952)
Turkmenistan
  Embassy, prospekt Saparmurada Turkmenbashi 11, Ashghabat 744004 (☎ (3632) 51-02-62, 25-39-57,(☎ & fax 29-84-66)
UK
  Embassy (Consular Section), 5 Kensington Palace Gardens, London W8 4QS (☎ (0171) 229 8027, fax 229 3215, premium-rate interactive visa message (0891) 171271)
  Consulate, 9 Coates Crescent, Edinburgh E113 7RL (☎ (0131) 225 7098, fax 225 9587)
USA
  Embassy (Consular Section), 1825 Phelps Place NW, Washington, DC 20008 (☎ (202) 939-8907, -8913, -8918; fax 939-8909); information also from consulates in New York (☎ (212) 348-0926; fax 472-4732, 831-9162); San Francisco (☎ (415) 202-9800, 928-6878; fax 929-0306) and Seattle (☎ (206) 728-1910, e-mail consul@consul.seanet.com)
Uzbekistan
  Embassy, Nukus 83, Tashkent 750015 (☎ (3712) 54-36-41, 55-29-48)

China

Everyone needs a visa to enter the People's Republic of China (PRC). Most tourists are issued a single-entry visa, valid for entry within three months of the date of issue, and good for a 30 day stay (see the Getting a Visa in Central Asia section below). With it you can visit any open city or region, and while in China you can extend it, and get travel permits for some restricted areas. You cannot get a visa at the border.

Getting a Visa Visas are readily available from PRC embassies in most western and many other countries. The easiest place is probably Hong Kong, most cheaply from the Visa Office of the PRC Ministry of Foreign Affairs (☎ 2835-3657, 2835-3660), 5th floor, lower block, China Resources Building, 26 Harbour Rd, Wanchai. Fees are HK$100 (single-entry), HK$150 (double-entry) or HK$200 (multiple-entry) – plus a HK$160 surcharge for US passport holders. Visas are issued in two or three working days; 24-hour and same-day service cost more. See the Travel & Visa Agencies section in the Getting There & Away chapter for some reliable Hong Kong travel agencies.

Elsewhere, processing times and fees depend on where you're applying, eg at the time of research, in up to three weeks for £10 or more quickly for £25 in London; on the same day for US$20 in Istanbul; and in two days for US$20, or next day for US$50, in Moscow.

On the visa application you must identify an itinerary and entry/exit dates and points, though nobody will hold you to them once you're in the country. To avoid snags, don't mention Tibet or bicycles – and don't give your occupation as journalist or writer. You'll need one or two passport-sized photos.

Getting a Visa in Central Asia This is possible, although uncertain as rules seem to change frequently. At the PRC embassy in Tashkent you must have a letter (or arrange a telex) of invitation or confirmation of pre-booked services from a Chinese state travel organisation; a 30 day visa will probably take a week and cost about US$20.

They said the same at the embassy in Bishkek, but there two travellers picked up 10 day China transit visas simply by showing Chinese consular staff their valid onward visas for Pakistan (which were examined closely); they needed no letter of support. It may well be possible to do this with onward visas for other countries bordering China.

It appears possible to get an ordinary PRC visa in Almaty without an invitation, and travellers confirm getting a transit visa without one for US$30. The PRC Embassy in Ashghabat will issue a visa in three days for US$10, or sooner for more; an invitation is 'optional', whatever that means. The embassy in Dushanbe doesn't issue visas.

Try to get your visa specifically endorsed for the place where you will cross – Alashankou on the train to/from Kazakstan (Dostyq in Kazak or Druzhba in Russian, on the Kazak side), Korgas (Khorgos) on the road to/from Kazakstan, Tuergate (Torugart) on the road to/from Kyrgyzstan. Though the vast majority of travellers cross without problems, a few have been asked by Chinese border guards at Korgas for such endorsements (though fast talking got them one on the spot).

Visa Extensions You can get at least one 15 day extension at the Foreign Affairs office of any Public Security Bureau (PSB). In Kashgar this office – called the Division of Aliens & Exit-Entry Administration – is on Shengli Lu. Travellers report that a second extension is hard to get.

Travel Permits Besides the open areas you can visit with just a visa, there are others you can go to by applying at the PSB for an Alien's Travel Permit (waiguoren lüxingzhen). An example in the Kashgar area is Karakul Lake.

Embassies & Consulates Chinese consular addresses in major cities overseas include:

Australia
Embassy, 15 Coronation Drive, Yarralumla, ACT 2600 (☎ (06) 273 4780, 273 4781); Consulate, Melbourne (☎ (03) 8220604)
Canada
Embassy, PO Box 8935, 515 St Patrick St, Ottawa, Ontario KIN 5H3 (☎ (613) 234-2706, 234-2682)
Consulate, 240 St George St, Toronto, Ontario M5R 2P4 (☎ (416) 964-7260)
Consulate, 3380 Granville St, Vancouver, BC V6H 3K3 (☎ (604) 736-3910)
France
Embassy, 11 Ave George V, 75008 Paris (☎ (1) 47.23.36.77, 47.36.77.90)
Hong Kong
Visa Office, PRC Ministry of Foreign Affairs, China Resources Building, 26 Harbour Rd, Wanchai (☎ 2835-3657, 2835-3660)
India
Embassy, 50-D Shantipath, Chanakyapuri, New Delhi 110021 (☎ (011) 60 03 28)
Kyrgyzstan
Embassy, Toktogul 196, Bishkek (☎ (3312) 22-24-23)

Kazakstan
> Embassy, Furmanov köshesi 137, Almaty (☎ (3272) 63-49-66, 63-92-91; fax 63-93-72)

Netherlands
> Embassy, Adriaan Goekooplaan 7, 2517 JX The Hague (☎ (070) 355 15 15, 355 92 09)

New Zealand
> Embassy, 2-6 Glenmore St, Kelburn, Wellington (☎ 472 1382, 472 1384)

Pakistan
> Embassy, Diplomatic Enclave, Islamabad (visa office ☎ (051) 821114)

Russia
> Embassy, ulitsa Druzhby 6, 101000 Moscow (☎ (095) 143-15-40; for visa enquiries 143-15-43; fax 938-21-32)

Turkey
> Embassy, Gölgeli Sokak 34, Gaziosmanpasa, Ankara ☎ (312) 436 06 28, 436 14 53
> Consulate, Ortaklar caddesi 14, Gayrettepe, Istanbul

Turkmenistan
> Embassy, ulitsa Sankt Pazina 2, Ashghabat (☎ 47-36-83, 47-46-76)

UK
> Embassy (Consular Section), 31 Portland Place, London W1N 3AG (☎ (0171) 636 5637 or premium-rate info ☎ (0891) 880808)
> Consulate, 49 Denison Rd, Rusholme, Manchester MI4 5RX (☎ (061) 224 7478)

USA
> Embassy, 2300 Connecticut Ave NW, Washington, DC 20008 (☎ (202) 328-2500, 328-2517)
> Consulate, 104 South Michigan Ave, Suite 1200, Chicago, IL 60603 (☎ (312) 346-0287)
> Consulate, 3417 Montrose Blvd, Houston, TX 77006 (☎ (713) 524-4311)
> Consulate, 502 Shatto Place, Suite 300, Los Angeles, CA 90020 (☎ (213) 380-2507)
> Consulate, 520 12th Ave, New York, NY 10036 (☎ (212) 330-7409)
> Consulate, 1450 Laguna St, San Francisco, CA 94115 (☎ (415) 563-4857)

Uzbekistan
> Embassy, Gogol 79, Tashkent (☎ (3712) 33-37-79, 33-80-88), but does not normally issue tourist visas

Pakistan

Everyone from European and English-speaking countries needs a visa to enter Pakistan. With a tourist visa you can normally enter up to six months from the date of issue, and stay for up to three months. You can go almost anywhere except sensitive border areas, and remote or high-elevation

places where you'd need a trekking or mountaineering permit.

Travellers arriving without a visa may get a 15 day transit visa, but policies on this change as fast as the weather, and officials at Sust, the border crossing from China, can be a bit arbitrary. It's sensible to get a visa in advance if you can.

There are many stories of visa hassles, mostly on arrival or departure. If you're staying more than 30 days, register with the police and don't lose the papers. Don't let anything expire; it's just an excuse for impromptu 'fees' you can't verify the validity of. Important-looking cards and documents with seals, stamps, logos and plastic laminations may come in handy to wave in front of officials.

Getting a Visa You can apply at most embassies or consulates of Pakistan. In addition to fee, passport and passport-size photos you may need to show an onward ticket or a receipt for one. This might be deflected by saying you're leaving over the Khunjerab pass to China. Advance hotel bookings are not required.

Visas from the Pakistan High Commission in London cost £24 for UK citizens. The Pakistan embassies in Tashkent and Almaty (and probably those in Ashghabat and Bishkek) can issue single-entry tourist visas for stays of a week or more. Fees depend on nationality, eg in Tashkent at the time of research, the fee was US$20 for Americans and US$34 for Britons. Processing takes about half a week.

The Pakistan embassy in Dushanbe apparently doesn't issue visas.

Visa Extensions Islamabad is the only place to extend a visa. Try first to get a letter from your embassy, or the Ministry of Tourism in Jinnah Market, asking that your stay be extended. Then go to the Visa Section office of the Directorate of Immigration & Passports on Khayaban-i-Suhrawardy in Aabpara, with the fee and photocopies of the front pages of your passport. Get there before about 2 pm. You get a form saying your visa has been extended. At the time of research this was free for US citizens, Rs35 for Australians and New Zealanders, Rs880 for British and Rs1000 for Canadians.

Finally, go to the Foreigners' Registration office, beside the Senior Superintendent of Police (SSP) in the city where your hotel is – in the Civil Courts in Rawalpindi, or Ayub Market in Islamabad – and register (see the following section).

Registration On arrival immigration theoretically gives you a paper called Form C, Temporary Certificate of Registration. If you're staying for 30 days or less on a tourist visa, you just give it back when you leave, in exchange for an exit stamp.

If you stay more than 30 days you're supposed to register. Most large towns have a foreigners' registration office, usually part of the police office. There is no fee. Bring two photos and Form C and they give you a Certificate of Registration and a Residence Permit. You turn these in to the foreigners' registration or police office at the last town where you stay the night, in exchange for an Exit Permit which you show to immigration on departure.

Travellers coming from China may not get Form C at Sust, but somebody may want to see it later, so ask for it. On the KKH you can easily register at Gilgit, Abbottabad, Rawalpindi or Islamabad.

A last-minute recent reader's letter suggests that the whole Form C rigmarole may have been discontinued, but we haven't been able to verify this.

Embassies & Consulates Pakistan consular addresses in major cities overseas include:

Afghanistan
    Embassy, Shar-e-nau, Kabul (☎ 21374)
    Consulate, Herat Rd, Kandahar (☎ 2452)
Australia & New Zealand
    Pakistan High Commission, 59 Franklin St, Manuka, Canberra, ACT 2603 (☎ (06) 290 1676)
    Consulate, 500 George St, 11th floor, Sydney, NSW 2000 (☎ (02) 267 7250)

Canada
    Pakistan High Commission, 151 Slater St, Suite 608, Ottawa K1P 5H3 (☎ (613) 238-7881)
    Consulate, 3421 Peel St, Montreal, Quebec H3A 1W7 (☎ (514) 845-2297)
    Consulate, 4881 Yonge St, Suite 810, Willowdale, Toronto, Ontario M2N 5X3 (☎ (416) 250-1255)
China
    Embassy, 1 Dongzhimenwai Dajie, Sanlitun Compound, Beijing (☎ (01) 532-2504); there is no consulate in Kashgar
Hong Kong
    Consulate, Suite 3806, China Resources Building, 26 Harbour Rd, Wanchai (☎ 2827-0681)
India
    Pakistan High Commission, 2/50-G Shantipath, Chanakyapuri, New Delhi (☎ (011) 60 06 04)
Iran
    Embassy, Kheyabun-e Doktor Fatemi, 1 Kheyabun-e Shahid Sarhang Ahmad E'temad Zade (☎ (021) 934331/2); there are also consulates at Zahedan and Mashhad
Kazakstan
    Embassy, Tölebaev köshesi 25, Almaty (☎ (3272) 33-35-48, 33-15-02)
Russia
    Embassy, Sadovaya-Kudrinskaya ulitsa 17, Moscow (☎ (095) 250-3991, fax 956-00-07)
Turkey
    Embassy, Iran caddesi, Cankaya, Ankara
Turkmenistan
    Embassy, ulitsa Kemine 92, Ashghabat (☎ 51-22-87, 51-23-17)
Tajikistan
    Embassy, prospekt Rudaki 37a, Dushanbe (☎ 21-22-27)
UK
    Pakistan High Commission, 35 Lowndes Square, London SW1X 9JN (☎ (0171) 235 2044)
    Consulate, 45 Cheapside, Bradford BD1 4HP (☎ (0274) 721921)
USA
    Embassy, 2315 Massachusetts Ave NW, Washington, DC 20008 (☎ (202) 939-6200), for Washington area only
    Consulate, 12 East 65th St, New York, NY 10021 (☎ (212) 879-5800)
    Consulate, 10850 Wilshire Blvd, Los Angeles 90024 (☎ (310) 441-5114)
Uzbekistan
    Chilonzor 25, Tashkent (☎ (3712) 77-93-02, 77-10-03)

Afghanistan

The situation in northern Afghanistan is still too volatile to predict how safe it is to travel there or what the visa regulations will be at any given time. At the time of research, anyone with a valid Afghan visa could in principle cross from Uzbekistan at Termez, though we spoke with a travel agent in Termez who had consistently been denied permission to take a coach across to Mazar-i-Sharif. We cannot yet recommend this itinerary!

DOCUMENTS

Besides your passport and visa, there are a number of other documents you may need to pack:

- Customs declaration form filled out when you first enter the CIS: you're unlikely to have to show this when you leave for another CIS country (though you may have to fill in another one when you *enter* another CIS country). You may then have to show it (or them) when you finally leave the CIS, and to any bank where you want to sell back local money. Hang onto them in any case. If they're lost or stolen, a police certificate to this effect may satisfy officials on departure.
- Entry-Exit card filled out when you enter China.
- Currency-exchange and hard-currency purchase receipts: you may need to show these when you sell back local money. The total should be more than the amount you want to sell back.
- Alien Travel Permit *(wàibīn tōngxíng zhèng)*: in China you need one of these to visit certain restricted areas, eg Kara Kul lake; they're available from the police in Kashgar and elsewhere.
- Hotel registration chits: in Uzbekistan, you may need to show these little bits of paper (showing when you stayed at each hotel) to OVIR officials at the stations in order to buy bus or train tickets.
- HIV certification: Uzbekistan's blanket HIV test requirement has proved unfeasible, but travellers are still occasionally asked for proof of a negative test. Long-term visitors (eg more than a month in Kyrgyzstan) still need an HIV certificate, though this too is patchily enforced. China requires a certificate from students and others staying more than a year, but short-term travellers also report being asked for one on entry from Kyrgyzstan and Kazakstan.
- Other health certifications: travellers coming to Kazakstan or Kyrgyzstan directly from other Asian countries or Africa may need to show a cholera vaccination certificate. Anyone required to take medication containing a narcotic drug should have a doctor's certificate.
- Vouchers: if you prepaid accommodation, excursions or transport, these are the only proof that you did so.

Student, youth or other card: flashing these to hotel staff can occasionally get you a useful discount (one traveller waved a diving club card!). They can often be left as a deposit (instead of your passport) when you rent a bicycle in China.

CUSTOMS

Barring the occasional greedy official at a remote posting, few western tourists have major customs problems in Central Asia. When they do, it's usually over the export of 'cultural artefacts' from the former Soviet republics, the import of politically sensitive material into China, or the import of alcohol or firearms into Pakistan.

In the former Soviet republics you're most likely to encounter customs formalities on flying between the republics and on entering and leaving the CIS by air or overland. Some remote overland customs posts between Central Asian countries may want to snoop around your vehicle. Westerners' bags tend to be examined less readily than those of local people, except when it comes to rugs and antiques (see Exporting Antiques in this section).

Customs Declaration

On arrival you fill out a customs declaration, listing all your money and valuables including cameras, electronics and jewellery. Hang onto your declaration and, when you leave, turn it in along with another declaration of what you're taking out. If you lose it, your embassy might help with a letter to Central Customs requesting a replacement. Failing this, arrange to have the absolute minimum of hard-currency cash when you leave, and cross your fingers.

Some border officials seem to think there's still a Soviet Union. When you finally leave after a multi-country Central Asia trip, you may well be asked for the declaration you filled out when you entered your first CIS state. A friend who had been living in Tashkent for five years was asked for his original Uzbekistan declaration when he crossed from Kyrgyzstan to China at the Torugart pass! Moral: save *everything*.

Declaring money on entry to a former

Soviet republic is an awkward matter – total honesty reveals how much cash you're carrying to possibly dishonest officials, while fudging can create problems later. JK opted to carefully hide some of his cash and fib consistently on entry and exit. Count up your money privately before you arrive but, especially in Uzbekistan, be prepared to pull out and display everything you've declared.

Travellers leaving Kazakstan for China by bus through Zharkent and Khorgos have been allowed to take out up to US$500 without showing an entry customs declaration. If you have more than that, be sure you have an entry customs declaration from some CIS country which shows that you arrived with at least the amount you're leaving with.

A few travellers report getting no declaration forms on entering China, and many say none were demanded when they left. On the whole Chinese customs seems relatively quick and straightforward compared to that on the other side.

What You Cannot Bring In

There are no significant limits anywhere on items for personal use, except on guns and drugs. Cameras, video cameras, radios and personal stereos are OK. Large amounts of anything saleable are suspect, and pornography tends to raise alarms. Uzbek officials are also on the lookout for 'anti-Uzbek propaganda' (sound familiar?), and Chinese officials are after printed material, film and tapes 'detrimental to China's politics, economy, culture and ethics' – but don't worry too much about your own reading material. Pakistani officials are mainly looking for booze and guns.

What You Cannot Take Out

The main prohibitions are 'antiques' and local currency. Certain electrical appliances bought in the former USSR are apparently unexportable, though we've never been able to find out which. Everybody's regulations prohibit the export of endangered animals and plants, though few officials would recognise an endangered species if it bit them.

There is little customs control in Tajikistan, except at the border with Kyrgyzstan, where opium is the worry and vehicles and baggage are searched frequently and exhaustively on the Murgab-Osh road.

Chinese officials are mainly concerned that you not leave with lots of Chinese currency (as if anyone would want to), and seldom search westerners.

Inspection in Pakistan is usually cursory for foreigners, but if you have something obvious like furniture you may be asked for sales and exchange receipts. Theoretically you need an export permit to post out purchases over Rs500 or to carry or post out a carpet; the dealer might help with this, or possibly the Pakistan Tourism Development Corporation (PTDC) or your hotel-wallah. Airport security staff may confiscate batteries from cameras, personal stereos, etc.

Exporting Antiques

From the former Soviet republics, you cannot export antiques or anything of 'historical or cultural value' – including art, furnishings, manuscripts, musical instruments, coins, clothing and jewellery – without an export licence and payment of a stiff export duty.

Get a receipt for anything of value that you buy, showing where you got it and how much you paid. If your purchase looks like it has historical value, you should also have a letter saying that it has no such value or that you have permission to take it out anyway. Get this from the vendor, from the Ministry of Culture in the capital, or from a curator at one of the state art museums with enough clout to do it. Without it, your goodies could be seized on departure, possibly even on departure from *another* CIS state. If you wait until you get to the airport you could be out of luck. Some travellers end up abandoning their purchases in order to catch their flights, or handing them over to local friends seeing them off.

In Uzbekistan any book or artwork made before 1945 is considered antique. In Turkmenistan 'cultural artefacts' seems to

embrace almost all handicrafts and traditional-style clothing, no matter how
mundane, cheap or new. AH had to surrender
a pair of socks knitted as a gift by the grand-
mother in a family he visited, because they
were 'traditional'. Airport searches at
Ashghabat are thorough and time-consuming. Rules on the export of carpets from
Turkmenistan are also stringent (see the
Turkmen Carpet aside in the Ashghabat
section of the Turkmenistan chapter).

You're expected to show Chinese officials
any cultural relics, handicrafts, gold and
silver ornaments, and jewellery you bought
there, and receipts for them.

MONEY
Because of continuing inflation in Central
Asia, prices in this book are in US$ equiva-
lents. This doesn't mean you have to pay in
dollars – indeed the local currencies are the
only legal tender, though in practice dollars
and Deutschmarks may be accepted or even
requested for some cash-in-hand transactions. Most people still seem to expect
payment in local money.

The Kazakstan and Uzbekistan banking
systems are moving fast to cope with the
outside world, eg with credit-card transactions, wire transfers and regulated foreign
exchange. By contrast, the Kyrgyzstan
banking system is considered archaic by
some foreign workers, and Tajikistan hasn't
one to speak of at the moment.

Costs
Travelling with a friend, staying in modest
hotels where possible, eating in cheaper restaurants and the occasional street stall, and
travelling by bus or train, you can get around
Central Asia for US$20 to US$40 per day (at
the time of research). This assumes US$12
to US$20 for half a double room, US$3 to
US$8 for food, and ground transport costs of
US$4 to US$12 every three or four days.

You can do a bit better by self-catering in
shops and bazaars, staying in private homes
and the occasional bottom-end place,
sharing larger hotel rooms with more people,
getting around town by local bus instead of

taxi, taking trains instead of buses, riding
overnight trains or buses to save hotel costs,
and spending less time in (expensive) cities.
Don't forget to bargain in the bazaars.

These are average prices, and there are
important imponderables. Sometimes you
will have no choice but a pricey tourist hotel
at US$25 to US$35 or more for half a double;
on the other hand you could spend as little as
US$2 in western Uzbekistan. Food is
cheaper on the street than in a restaurant, and
cheaper in the countryside than in the city.
You can blow your budget with imported
beer (US$1 to US$2 a can) and Mars bars.

Hiring cars and doing excursions jumps
up your costs. Regional ground and air transport costs can depend on the carrier and the
country of origin (eg Tashkent to Almaty by
bus is about US$8, Almaty to Tashkent about
US$21; Almaty to Tashkent by air is about
US$150 with Kazakstan Airlines, US$80
with Uzbekistan Airways). In some places
you may not have to pay foreigners' fare on
trains.

A big transport unknown is the lurching
cost of petrol, with unpredictable price leaps
that depend more on availability than on
inflation; these are naturally passed right on
to travellers.

Geographical variations are significant
too. Turkmenistan and Kyrgyzstan tend to be
cheaper than Uzbekistan, which tends to be
cheaper than Kazakstan. In unstable
Tajikistan, outside of Dushanbe and
Khojand, services are scarce and costs highly
unpredictable. China and Pakistan are
cheapest of all, especially because of cheap
accommodation options.

Don't forget visa costs, which can add a
bundle (see the Visas & Embassies section in
this chapter), and of course long-distance
transport to get you to and from Central Asia
(see the Getting There & Away chapter).

Two-Tier Pricing Foreigners often pay sub-
stantially more than local people for services
in the former Soviet republics and China –
airfares and sometimes train fares, hotel
rooms, even museums and theatres. Ask why
and you'll be told, 'It's not so much for you,

I think', 'You have more money than us' etc. There's little you can do but try as often as possible to get the local rate – speak your best Russian, proffer the local price, don't show your passport unless asked, or have local friends buy your tickets for you (this last option doesn't always work; in Uzbekistan, for example, police often check departing buses and trains).

It's fair, and it's unfair. Before you complain, however, ponder the fact that in Uzbekistan at the time of research, the typical monthly wage for a professional such as a university professor was less than a single tank of black-market petrol or 10 kg of meat.

Carrying Money

At the moment most of former Soviet Central Asia is effectively a cash-only zone. This creates a sickening dilemma: for a long trip you simply must carry huge amounts of hard cash, making you extraordinarily vulnerable to crooks, con artists and greedy officials, many of whom know perfectly well that you've got all that lucre. All you can do is to bury it deeply and in several different places, with only tiny sums in wallets, purses and outside pockets (the exception is at customs, where some travellers have been made to display their entire hoard).

Cash

US$ cash is by far the easiest to exchange, followed by Deutschmarks in the former Soviet republics, or UK£ in western China and Pakistan. Dollars can also be exchanged unofficially when nothing else can, making them good emergency money. Though officially you may not spend foreign currency anywhere, private hotels and homestays nevertheless usually want US$.

Take a mixture of denominations: larger notes (US$50, US$20) are the most readily accepted, but a cache of small ones (US$10, US$5) is handy for when you're stuck with a lousy exchange rate, or need to offer a wee inducement (taxi drivers, for example, often won't go long distances for local money).

High-quality counterfeit US$100 notes

Decoy Money

Though so far cashable only in a few places in Uzbekistan, Kyrgyzstan and Kazakstan, travellers' cheques make excellent decoys when someone is pressing you for a bribe. Keep them handy, and tell your inquisitor you only use these, exchanging them in big cities. Most people haven't the faintest idea what to do with a travellers' cheque and may press you no further. ■

---

have become so common in Russia – and therefore probably in Central Asia – that many banks won't even accept notes of this size. The newest US$50 and US$100 notes have an embedded thread running approximately beneath the words 'This Note Is Legal Tender...', visible when held against the light. Moneychangers may check for it.

Russian, Chinese and Central Asian currencies all attract poor exchange rates outside their own countries. Russian roubles are often refused outright.

Old Money As if carrying huge amounts of cash weren't problem enough, a further headache is that most places in the Central Asian republics will accept only crisp, brand-new banknotes, convinced somehow that anything older is worthless. That means you will have to carry only the most current series US$ banknotes – 1988 for US$5; 1990 for US$100, US$50 and US$10; and 1993 for US$20 and US$1 (though new-looking 1990 notes might be acceptable). Deutschmarks should be 1990 or later. Worn, torn, faded or written-on notes of any date will almost certainly be refused.

Post offices and banks are especially stubborn; even black-market dealers are fussy. Private banks might accept older notes at a deep discount (about 20%). The same anxiety prevails to a lesser extent in Pakistan. You may raise eyebrows at your bank back home, asking for large amounts of US$ cash in small, brand-new notes, but rest assured it is worth the trouble.

Uzbekistan
Detail of ceramic tiles, Tosh-Khovli Palace, Khiva

CENTRAL ASIA

ANDREW HUMPHREYS

Uzbekistan
Detail from the Registan, Samarkand

Taxi drivers and others (and probably banks) often fob off their own ragged foreign notes on tourists as change, so of course *you* should refuse to accept old notes too!

Travellers' Cheques

Travellers' cheques are of limited use in the former Soviet republics. At the time of research, you could get local currency with major-brand cheques denominated in US$ (American Express is the most widely recognised, but others can be cashed) at certain banks in Almaty, Bishkek and Tashkent, as noted under those cities. The US State Department says Vneshekonobank in Turkmenistan accepts travellers' cheques (as well as some credit cards for cash advances) but gives no address; it's probably in Ashghabat. A substantial commission is added if you want to get dollars instead of local money, and not all banks will do this.

Travellers' cheques can be cashed with little problem at Bank of China in Kashgar or Ürümqi. Pakistani banks in more remote places may refuse to accept them early in the day, until someone can be roused to telex the main office for that day's rates.

See the Decoy Money aside earlier for another use for travellers' cheques.

Credit Cards

Major credit cards can be used for payment at certain hotels, restaurants and shops in Almaty; at Uzbektourism hotels in tourist centres of Uzbekistan; and at a very few posh hotels in Ashghabat. They're of no use yet for payment in Kyrgyzstan, Tajikistan or western China, and of little use in Pakistan except at top-end hotels and shops in Rawalpindi and Islamabad. Visa seems the most widely recognised brand but others (American Express, Diners Club, Eurocard, MasterCard) are accepted in some places.

Cash advances are possible – for commissions of 3% to 5% – in Almaty (and a few other Kazakstan towns), Bishkek and Tashkent with a Visa card, and in Almaty with MasterCard. You can get cash with major cards at western banks in Rawalpindi and Islamabad in Pakistan, and at Bank of China

in Kashgar and Ürümqi. All need at least a day or two, charge for an international telex to verify the card, and may have upper limits on how much you can get.

International Transfers

Direct bank-to-bank wire (telegraphic) transfer is also possible through some banks in Almaty, Bishkek and Tashkent, as noted. Commissions of 1% to 4% are typical, and service takes one to five days.

Friends or relatives can wire *emergency* money to American citizens via the nearest US embassy, and British or other citizens may have some luck with their embassies. The process takes several business days. The sender in the USA should contact the State Department ☎ 202-647-5225 (☎ 647-4000 after hours), and you can collect the money in a few days from a designated US embassy. The British Foreign Office number is ☎ 071-270 3000; the Australian Department of Foreign Affairs & Trade is ☎ 06-261 3331.

Currency

Currency abbreviations are our own for this book, chosen in some cases just to avoid confusion. Abbreviations for the former Soviet republics' currencies follow the amount, eg 50 S or 25 t. Those for Russia, China and Pakistan precede it, eg R3, Y10 or Rs75. Russian residents still tend to call everything roubles and kopecks, though of course they aren't.

Kazakstan The *tengge* (T) is divided into 100 *tiyn* (t). There are 1000, 500, 200, 100, 50, 20, 10, 5, 3 and 1 T notes. *Tiyn* come in 50 t coins and a variety of notes that look like Monopoly money.

Kyrgyzstan The *som* (S) is divided into 100 *tyyyn* (t). Notes come in 100, 50, 20, 10, 5 and 1 S, and 50, 10 and 1 t denominations. We saw no coins.

Tajikistan With no appreciable assets with which to back a national currency, Tajikistan long clung to the Russian rouble. But in May 1995 it began issuing its own money, with one Tajik *rubl* (R) initially equal to 100 Russian roubles. Massive inflation may well be the main consequence. Notes come in 1000, 500, 200, 100, 10, 5, 3 and 1 R denominations.

Turkmenistan The *manat* (M) is divided into 100 *tenge* (t). Notes come in 1000, 500, 100, 50, 20, 10, 5 and 1 M denominations. Coins of 50, 20, 10, 5 and 1 t value are fast disappearing.

Uzbekistan The *sum* (S) is divided into 100 *tiyin* (t). There are 500, 100, 50, 25, 10, 5, 3 and 1 S notes. Coins have gone out of use, which makes the *tiyin* itself rather obsolete.

China The *yuan* (Y) is divided into 10 *jiao* or 100 *fen*. But when talking prices in Chinese, yuan is called *kuai (koi* in Uyghur) and jiao is called *mao (mo* in Uyghur); fen is still *fen* (pronounced 'fun'). Notes come in denominations of 100, 50, 10, 5, 2, 1 *yuan*, 5 and 2 *jiao*, and 5, 2 and 1 *fen*, and there are still a few 5, 2 and 1 *fen* coins about. Once there were two kinds of money, *renminbi* (RMB) or 'people's money' for local people, and Foreign Exchange Certificates (FEC) for tourists, but FEC has thankfully been phased out. Travellers sometimes talk about 'RMB' as if it were a unit of money, instead of yuan.

Pakistan The *rupee* (R) is divided into 100 *paisa*. Notes come in denominations down to one rupee and there are one-rupee and half

rupee coins (and a few 25 and 10 paisa coins). Anything other than one rupee is abbreviated in the plural, ie Rs3.

Currency Exchange

Unless otherwise specified, these are approximate bank rates for buying cash, at the time of writing. Inflation will push them all up considerably by the time you read this. Few Central Asian banks or dealers want Russian roubles, and exchange rate information is scarce and almost meaningless.

Changing Money

Nearly all official tourist hotels have branch-bank exchange desks where you can at least swap US$ cash for local money.

Because officially you cannot use foreign currency for anything, many shops, post offices, airline booking offices, airports and railway stations in the former Soviet republics also have their own exchange kiosks – with signs in Russian like ОБМЕН ВАЛЮТЫ *(obmen valyuty,* currency exchange) or ОБМЕННЫЙ ПУНКТ *(obmennyy punkt,* exchange point) – where you can exchange dollars for local money, or sometimes for a voucher that you carry to the purchase point. Some Uzbekistan hotels carry this further – even if you front up with local banknotes you may be asked for an exchange receipt to prove you got them legitimately, or even told to go and change more dollars!

In Uzbekistan, Kazakstan and Kyrgyzstan, some hotel exchange points

Exchange Rates							
Western Currency	Kaz tengge	Kyr som	Taj rubl	Turk manat	Uzb sum	Chi yuan	Pak rupee
US$1	64	11.4	285	2300	34.6	8.3	34.1
UK£1	99.7	17.8	444	3583	53.9	12.9	53.1
A$1	47.9	8.5	214	1722	25.9	6.2	25.6
NZ$1	41.9	7.5	186.6	1505	22.6	5.4	22.4
C$1	47.4	8.4	211	1703	25.6	6.1	25.3
DM1	44.3	7.9	197.2	1592	23.9	5.8	23.7
FFr1	13	2.3	57.8	467	7	1.7	6.9
SFr1	55	9.9	245	1975	29.7	7.1	29.4

now accept other major currencies too, and at least in Uzbekistan, US$ travellers' cheques. Main offices of the National Bank in larger Uzbekistan towns will exchange most major currencies (both cash and travellers' cheques), and give cash advances on Visa cards. Kyrgyzstan and Kazakstan also license private exchanges, which are all over the place in Bishkek – very convenient but usually with poorer rates.

Banks in Turkmenistan and Tajikistan may not even have a currency exchange counter, and the best places to try are tourist hotels. At the time of writing, in most of Tajikistan (except the Khojand area) there was simply a physical scarcity of money. If you do find a supply of *rubls* and the rate's fair, consider changing enough for your whole stay.

Banks frequently do not have small bills, but you should try to avoid large notes in local currency (except to pay your hotel bills), since few people can spare much change.

Swapping between currencies can be a pain, with most former Soviet republics uninterested in the others' money (an exception is Kazakstan and Kyrgyzstan). In Kyrgyzstan, licensed private dealers will swap these.

In China you must go to the Bank of China; in Xinjiang there are branches in Kashgar and Ürümqi. In Pakistan you can exchange at half a dozen domestic banks, the most competent being the National Bank of Pakistan.

Of course you can often change money personally, eg with hotel waiters or receptionists, or with dealers who approach you at markets, stations or your hotel (see the Black Market section below). In the former Soviet republics everybody, but everybody, wants dollars; even your truest friends and hosts will ask you to change a little with them. It can be hard to refuse, although saying you need official exchange receipts at the border in order to sell back local currency usually closes the matter.

Exchange Receipts Whenever you change

money, ask for a receipt *(kvitantsiya* or *spravka* in Russian) showing your name, the date, the amounts in both currencies, the exchange rate and an official signature. Not everyone will give you one (Kyrgyzstan's licensed private dealers never do), but when it's time to resell your local currency you may need enough recent ones to cover what you want to resell (as we did at Uzbekistan's National Bank, for example).

Customs officials also may want to see exchange receipts at crossings to non-CIS countries, and Chinese customs officials always do. In Pakistan these receipts also allow you to spend the rupees you already have for air tickets, without further exchanges.

Try to avoid receipts without the bottom portion that you fill out when reselling. In Uzbekistan we got some like this, which explicitly say they confer no right of re-exchange.

Selling Back Local Currency At any official exchange point you will probably need your customs declaration, plus the originals of enough recent exchange receipts to cover the amount you want to resell. Exchange receipts normally have a resale form at the bottom, which you sign at this time.

At the time of research you had to sell Uzbek *sum* back at a main city office of the National Bank – *not* at the airport, nor the hotels, nor the border. A few kiosks in private Tashkent shops would buy *sum*, but took commissions in the order of 10%! The easiest thing, of course, is to spend it up before you leave, or swap it with travellers going the other way.

You can't officially trade *yuan* in Pakistan nor *rupees* in China. At the China-Pakistan border you're normally given US dollars which you change again on the other side.

Security

Petty crime is a growing problem in all the former Soviet republics (see also Crime under Dangers & Annoyances in this chapter). Don't leave money in any form lying around your hotel room. Carry it securely zipped in one or more money belts or shoulder wallets buried deep in your clothing, with only what you'll immediately need (or would be willing to hand over to a thief or to an official on the take) accessible in an exterior pocket, wallet or purse.

When paying for anything substantial, eg a hotel bill or a pricey souvenir, count out the money beforehand, out of public sight. At exchange kiosks, have your money in hand; don't go fumbling in your money belt in full view of the sleazeballs who tend to frequent these places.

Be careful when paying by credit card that you see how many slips are being made from your card, that you destroy all carbon copies, and that as few people as possible get hold of your card number and expiry date. There are tales of thieves targeting people coming out of banks with fat cash advances, so keep your eyes open.

By contrast, China and Pakistan are generally quite safe for travellers, except in parts of China's biggest cities, and in remote areas off the Karakoram Highway (KKH) south of Gilgit in Pakistan.

Make sure you note the numbers of your cards and travellers' cheques, and the telephone numbers to call if they are lost or stolen – and keep all numbers separate from the cards and cheques!

Black Market

There is a black market for dollars and Deutschmarks in the Central Asian republics, with dealers lurking in bus and train stations, bazars, around post offices and tourist hotels. But you stand to gain very little in return for the risks. Uzbekistan has the biggest differences between official and black rates, but police often prey, not on local dealers, but on their foreign customers, from whom they can then extort a bribe. If you must, at least confine your transactions to trustworthy local friends.

In Turkmenistan a black market for foreign currency only seems to exist in Ashghabat, typically at no better than official rates. In Kyrgyzstan many moneychangers are licensed, hence the open trading found in

Bishkek – though these are mainly for Central Asian currencies, and seem pretty amateurish: one young man offered us a poorer rate than at the bank! In Tajikistan no private individual ever asked us for dollars – probably no-one had any cash to trade.

In Xinjiang (and elsewhere in China), Uyghurs have been changing money for centuries, and you'll be asked to change money until you're sick of it. Many dealers are skilled sleight-of-hand artists. If you have a legal alternative, avoid them; if you must use them, be very careful:

- Trade a round sum, for quick mental calculations.
- Fold it up in a pocket, to avoid fumbling in an open purse or wallet.
- Isolate yourself and the dealer from his friends; never let yourself be at the centre of a group.
- Tell them what you have, but don't pull it out; some claim they want to check it for counterfeit, and may substitute smaller notes.
- Insist on their money first, and take your sweet time counting it. Once you're sure it's right, do *not* let the dealer recount it (a common scam: you find some missing, he adds the missing Y20 or whatever and hands it back, palming Y500 off the bottom); hand over your little wad, and split.

Small Change

In the former Soviet republics, hang onto coins and small notes or you will end up paying over the odds to people who 'haven't any change'. In shops and markets, small change from purchases is often given in sweets, bubble gum, telephone tokens, bus or Metro tokens, stamps, even plastic shopping bags. Hotel exchange kiosks, on the other hand, seem to have nothing but small bills; in Uzbekistan a US$20 note might get you a two cm stack of 5 S notes!

Tipping

Tipping is not common anywhere in Central Asia, western China or Pakistan, although a few top-end restaurants automatically add a 5% to 15% service charge to the bill. Tipping runs counter to many people's Islamic sense of hospitality, and may therefore even offend them. In rural and/or lower-end places you may have yours refused or returned.

Bribery

Bribery clearly can work in Central Asia, especially Uzbekistan, and sometimes in Pakistan; it almost certainly won't in China. But it feeds the already-widespread notion that we all just love throwing our money around, and makes it harder for future travellers. In fact a combination of smiles (even if over gritted teeth) and patient persistence can very often work better – we've seen it happen.

Baksheesh is a way of life in Pakistan. This doesn't just mean a hand-out or bribe, but any gratuity for services rendered. Lower-echelon staff who depart even minutely from normal routine – opening a closed gate, getting a bigwig's signature, fixing a broken tap – may expect something for it, and a bit here and there goes a long way when it's deserved.

Bargaining

Shops have fixed prices but in markets – food, art or souvenirs – bargaining is usually expected. For food, initial asking prices tend to be in a sane proportion to the expected outcome. Sellers will be genuinely surprised if you reply to their '5000' with '1000'; they're more likely expecting 3500, 4000 or 4500 in the end. But press your luck further in places like art and craft markets heavily patronised by tourists.

POST & COMMUNICATIONS
Sending Mail

The postal systems of the former Soviet republics are definitely not for urgent items – due in part to the scarcity of regional flights. In fact, you'll probably get home before your postcards do. An air-mail letter to anywhere outside the CIS, if it arrives at all, may take four to eight weeks or more.

The cost of an air-mail letter under 10 grams to anywhere outside the CIS is US$0.10 to US$0.20, with postcards (if you can find them) at about half that. A two kg parcel of books by surface mail would cost about US$2. Tourist hotels and central post offices are the safest places to post things.

Prestamped envelopes can be bought at some hotels.

From China, air-mail letters and postcards will probably take under 10 days, even from Kashgar. Air-mail letters are US$0.35, postcards US$0.30, and a five kg parcel to the UK by surface mail is about US$18.

Pakistan's service is fairly dependable for letters from Gilgit, Rawalpindi and Islamabad. Air-mail letters are about US$0.25 and postcards US$0.20. Postal staff will usually frank outgoing letters on the spot, eliminating the risk of stamp theft.

Address mail as you would from any country, in your own language, though it will help to write the destination country in the local language too – in Central Asia put the Cyrillic name *before* the address; in China put the Chinese characters after the address; in Pakistan, English is enough.

Receiving Mail

Incoming mail service is so flakey in Central Asia that it's rare for anyone on the move to find anything. Letters can take anything from 10 days to several months to arrive – and then get lost in the shuffle.

A private or company address is best. A hotel address might work, though staff tend to be careless with mail. Central post offices are pretty unreliable for poste restante service. Few western embassies are keen to hold mail, though some (eg the US embassy in Tashkent) will do so for a couple of months for their own nationals.

Mail to former Soviet republics should be addressed in the reverse order from western practice, ie country, postal code, town, street or PO box address, addressee (family name first). If you can write it all a second time in Russian, so much the better. To avoid confusing your own post office, add the country name again at the bottom, in English.

The 'street' address for poste restante is Главпочтамт, до востребования (Glavpochtamt, Do Vostrebovania – Russian for 'main post office, for collection'). These are more likely to end up in the right cubbyhole if the addressee's family name is capitalised and underlined. To check for poste restante mail, bring your passport to the main post office and ask for *do vostrebovania*. Check under your given name too.

For letters within the CIS, the address is best written in Russian. The return address is written below the main address.

China and Pakistan have fairly reliable poste restante services at the main post offices of major towns. The Kashgar post office has even returned unclaimed mail.

Courier Services

If you have something that absolutely must get there, several international courier services have offices in Central Asian cities (as noted for each city). A letter to a western country is about US$40, a 500 gram package around US$60 to US$90, and it takes about a week.

Telephone

Calls to Points Outside the CIS

You can place international calls (as well as local and intercity ones) from the central telephone and telegraph offices in most towns. You tell a clerk the number and prepay in local currency. After a wait of anything from half a minute to several hours, you're called to a booth (they usually shout out the destination and a booth number, in Russian). Early morning and late night calls, and those from capital cities, go through faster.

Hotel operators will also place your calls, but it takes longer and costs more (typically 20%, though the business centre at the Hotel Dostuk in Bishkek slaps on 55%).

You can set up your own calls – theoretically from anywhere in Central Asia – by dialling 062. This gets you a local operator who speaks at least minimal English, who will book the call and ring you back within about half an hour. If you do this from a private telephone, the operator rings afterward with the call length and charges, which are the same as at a telephone office. Doing this from your hotel generates hotel surcharges, however.

In Kazakstan, Almaty has numerous quick-service telephone and fax offices; the best station rate we found, to points outside

the CIS, was US$1.50/min. Calls there are cheaper from 8 pm to 8 am. Calls from Kyrgyzstan, Turkmenistan and Tajikistan to Europe, North America and Australasia range from US$2 to US$4 per minute. In Tajikistan it's almost impossible to make international calls from anywhere outside Dushanbe or Khojand.

Uzbekistan has the lowest per-minute rates – Europe US$0.75, North America US$1.25, Australasia US$1.50, though connections can be lousy. Much better, and much pricier per minute, are satellite-linked business services – eg at Tashkent's Hotel Uzbekistan, where Europe is US$6, Asia US$7, North America US$10, Australasia US$12 (with a three minute minimum) and the Hotel Samarkand, with lower rates and no three minute minimum.

Collect Calls

Americans can call home collect from anywhere in Central Asia by dialling AT&T in Moscow (☎ (095) 155-50-42 for an English-speaking operator). You can also use an AT&T calling card on this number.

There looks to be no other way to make a collect call (Russian: *obratnaya oplata*) from Central Asia. The next-cheapest strategy is a quick call to ask your party to call you back – if possible to one of those satellite-linked services. Most hotel-room telephones in the former Soviet Union are not connected to a switchboard but have direct-dial numbers (on a card in the room, or ask reception).

Calling from Outside the CIS

To call a number in any CIS country, dial your own country's access code, plus 7 (the original USSR country code), plus the city code, plus the number.

Intercity & CIS Calls

Points within the CIS can often be dialled directly from telephone offices, private telephones and sometimes hotels. Dial 8 (the original USSR intercity code); when you hear a new dial tone, dial the city code and the number.

Local Calls Placing a local or trunk call on Central Asia's decomposing telephone systems is usually harder than placing an international one. There are token-operated telephones on the streets of bigger cities (though many seem to be permanently out of order), and in municipal telephone offices. Tokens *(jeton)* are sold at post & telephone offices, and some kiosks, for the equivalent of about US$0.05.

China & Pakistan In China and northern Pakistan, calls can be made from government telephone exchanges, from top-end hotels in Kashgar and Gilgit and, in Pakistan, from PCOs (public call offices, many privately run). The telephone exchanges, usually open 24 hours a day, are quickest. Most large towns now have direct dialling, so international calls can be direct-dialled in, though not necessarily out. In any case late-night outward connections can be surprisingly quick.

Some per minute rates for overseas station calls from China are US$4.50 to Europe and North America and US$4 to Australasia, with no three minute minimum. A three minute overseas call from Pakistan would be about US$6 to US$10.

Telegram

The cheapest way to stay in touch is by short telegram, sent from the central telephone and telegraph offices in most towns, and from some top-end hotels. They usually arrive within a day, almost always within two. A message in English is no problem if it's clearly printed, though you may pay a surcharge.

An English-language telegram from Uzbekistan is about US$0.05 per word to points outside the CIS, or US$0.10 if it's urgent. From Tajikistan it's US$0.10 to US$0.15, from Kyrgyzstan US$0.40, and from Turkmenistan US$0.50 to US$0.75. An overseas telegram is around US$0.50 a word from China, or US$0.08 to US$0.12 a word from Pakistan.

Fax

Faxes can sometimes be sent from post, telephone and telegraph offices, and some top-end hotels. Note that they're charged at telephone rates for the time it takes to transmit them – about one minute per page in China or Pakistan, but up to *five* minutes or more on Central Asia's dicey telephone lines. Moreover there may be a three minute minimum, and you pay for failed attempts too, so the total cost is unpredictable and often huge.

If your fax goes through the first time, Tashkent's telephone and telegraph office charges about US$2 for one page to Europe, US$3.20 to North America, and US$3.80 to Australasia. We found only one public fax in all of Turkmenistan, at Ashghabat's central telephone office, and none in Tajikistan. Per-*page* rates from China are about US$16 to Europe and North America and US$13 to Australasia, plus US$2.50 for each failed connection.

E-Mail

There are now several commercial Internet providers in capital cities of Central Asia, where short-term visitors can send or receive e-mail messages for a fee. We list those under each city. Several sources of information on e-mail to/from the former Soviet republics are on the World-Wide Web at http://solar.rtd.utk.edu/ccsi/emaildir.html.

BOOKS

All books listed here are available in paperback unless noted otherwise.

Lonely Planet

Other Lonely Planet guidebooks with further information on areas covered by this book are *Karakoram Highway*; *Pakistan*, *Trekking in the Karakoram & the Hindukush*; and *China*.

Guidebooks

Maier, Frith, *Trekking in Russia & Central Asia*. This is an unrivalled guide to the former USSR's wild places, by an American who first started exploring them as a student in 1984, and pioneered the

US firm REI's adventure travel programme there. It has 77 pages of Central Asia route descriptions, plus chapters of useful background and planning info. A few maps don't tally with the text. It's published in the USA by The Mountaineers, Seattle (☎ (800) 553-4453 toll-free); in Canada by Douglas & McIntyre, Vancouver; and in Britain by Cordee, Leicester.

Streatfeild-James, Dominic, *Silk Route by Rail*. Here's the first and only dedicated guide to the railway line across China from Beijing, through Xinjiang, to Almaty in Kazakstan, through Uzbekistan and on to Moscow. If you are crazy enough to try it, this book has detailed planning tips, a bit of history, very basic information and maps for major cities en route.

Whittell, Giles, *Central Asia; The Practical Handbook*. This is what Central Asia budget travellers used to have to carry. It's entertaining and adventurous but is now seriously out of date.

Travel

Akchurin, Marat, *Red Odyssey* (hardback). In 1990 Akchurin, a Russian-Tatar poet and journalist, toured the Soviet Muslim republics 'witnessing the violence and misery brought about by the dying Communist system'. Definitely not of the 'historical sketches and sightseeing' school of travel writing, this is gritty stuff – concrete and vomit, blood and bribery.

Dalrymple, William, *In Xanadu: A Quest*. Dalrymple tries to follow in the footsteps of Marco Polo from Jerusalem to Xanadu, Kublai Khan's fabled city on the Mongolian steppe. His trip turns out rather grittier – and far more entertainingly narrated – than Polo's. The man knows his history but merely drops obscure hints; he loves castles and gets a bit tedious about them. But by the time he gets to the Karakoram Highway (this and Kashgar are the deepest he gets into the territory of this guidebook) he's into his stride, observant and wry.

Danziger, Nick, *Danziger's Travels*. An incredible modern-day overland odyssey through Turkey, Iran, Afghanistan, Pakistan, China and Tibet – without much regard for visas, immigration posts, civil wars and the like. He's entitled to sound a bit self-important and melodramatic about it.

Glazebrook, Philip, *Journey to Khiva*, and Moorhouse, Geoffrey, *Apples in the Snow; A Journey to Samarkand*. Two travel writers' Central Asian voyages on what turned out to be the eve of independence, weaving history and contemporary observation around its cities and sites. Moorhouse's book was published in the USA as *On the Other Side; A Journey Through Soviet Central Asia*.

Jamie, Kathleen, *The Golden Peak: Travels in Northern Pakistan*. A finely written, insightful, occasionally drifting book about Pakistan's Northern Areas, by a poet with an eye for the ironies of life for women, Muslims and travellers. Included are glimpses of private lives that male visitors will never see.

Maclean, Sir Fitzroy, *Eastern Approaches*. Maclean, a young British diplomat in Moscow, managed by guile or stealth to snoop into many corners of Central Asia and the Caucasus during the bloody years from 1937 to 1939, usually with the NKVD (a KGB forerunner) hot on his heels. This old but reprinted book recounts these forays, as well as Maclean's celebrated adventures in wartime Yugoslavia. A much more interesting Maclean book – in hardback and now unfortunately out of print – is his detailed and reflective *To the Back of Beyond; An Illustrated Companion to Central Asia and Mongolia*.

Maillart, Ella, *Turkestan Solo*. This is the engaging account of a Swiss woman adventurer's low-budget solo travels in Soviet Central Asia in the early 1930s, including a winter camel ride across the Kyzylkum desert, and a show-trial of basmachi guerrillas in Samarkand's Registan. 'Kini' Maillart was an internationally known sportswoman as well as a traveller and writer. Not long after this trip she joined Peter Fleming in a tempestuous seven month journey across remote western China, out of which came two amazingly different books, her *Forbidden Journey* and Fleming's *News from Tartary*.

Malcolmson, Scott, *Empire's Edge; Travels in South-Eastern Europe, Turkey and Central Asia*. A series of erudite, meditative, sometimes caustic mini-essays, as the author journeys among peoples trying to relocate themselves in the planet's post-imperial cultural fault-lines.

Maslow, Jonathon, *Sacred Horses: The Life of a Turkmen Cowboy*. Fired by a desire to ride a legendary Akhal-Teke horse across the sands of the Karakum desert, naturalist Maslow made two extended visits to Turkmenistan, recounted here. The abrasive Maslow is not always easy to get along with but he has written a very good account of the modern-day Turkmen's struggle to maintain traditions while simultaneously making a few bucks.

Stein, Sir Aurel, *On Alexander's Track to the Indus* (hardback 1929). Stein, a Hungarian-English archaeologist famous for his plundering of central Asian sites between 1900 and the 1940s, retraced the routes of many earlier travellers, including Alexander the Great.

Terzani, Tiziano, *Goodnight Mr Lenin*. This Italian journalist happened to be in the USSR when it collapsed, and decided to stay and take the pulse of Siberia, Central Asia and the Caucasus in those first post-Soviet months. The result is personal and unpolished, full of small factual errors (eg China and Uzbekistan have a common border) and irritating references to girls when he means women, but his interviews and encounters make for a unique and occasionally very perceptive chronicle, sympathetic to the huge problem of creating a new, non-Soviet reality.

Thubron, Colin, *The Lost Heart of Asia*. Thubron has always been just ahead of us with his careful research, first-hand explorations, delicate observations and Baroque prose. But his books make poor travelling companions because they can be more compelling than being there. This one, moreover, is condescending and unrelentingly downbeat.

Teichman, Sir Eric, *Journey to Turkistan*. Beijing to Kashgar by car in 1935, by a British diplomat and friends, at a time when Xinjiang was virtually in Russian hands.

Whittell, Giles, *Extreme Continental: Blowing Hot and Cold Through Central Asia*. Undeterred by the theft of his money, a motorbike that needed more attention than a baby and a host who used him as a punchbag, Whittell in 1991 completed a comprehensive tour across Central Asia, researching his own guidebook. This is the personal version of that trip, against which independent travellers can check off their own experiences, good and bad.

History & Politics

Bailey, F M, *Mission to Tashkent*. One of the best reads of any kind about Central Asia. Bailey, a British intelligence officer sent to the region in the wake of the Revolution of 1917, pulled off a sequence of hair's-breadth escapes from the Bolsheviks, too implausible to be fiction, which he recounts in a disarmingly understated way. At one stage, under an assumed identity, he was even employed as a Bolshevik agent with the job of tracking himself down.

Franck, Irene, and David Brownstone, *The Silk Road: A History* (hardback). Three hundred well-illustrated, well-mapped pages of history of the multi-stranded caravan routes that began crossing Central Asia in the 2nd century BC.

French, Patrick, *Younghusband*. Sir Francis Younghusband is known to Asia scholars (and Peter Hopkirk fans) as the archetypal Great Gamester – crossing China solo, facing down Hunza bandits and Russian spies in the Karakoram, and leading the British invasion of Tibet. He was also a detached and stubborn individual, a dyed-in-the-wool imperialist (some say racist), and at the end of his life a raging mystic. This excellent biography intertwines the lives of

its subject and of its author as he tracks the story down.

Grousset, René, translated by Naomi Walford, *The Empire of the Steppes; A History of Central Asia*. A huge, rich paperback tome published by Rutgers University Press.

Hiro, Dilip, *Between Marx and Muhammad*. An opinionated, somewhat depressing history of Central Asia since the collapse of the Soviet Union, fairly tedious unless you have a serious academic interest in the region – and a good dictionary to hand.

Hopkirk, Kathleen, *Central Asia; A Travellers' Companion*. Handy and very readable historical background on the region (though not half as entertaining as her husband Peter's books), an excellent companion book for those keen to know more about the places they're seeing.

Hopkirk, Peter, *Foreign Devils on the Silk Road*. Tales of turn-of-the-century adventurers and archaeologists who criss-crossed Xinjiang (then called Chenese Turkestan) in search of Buddhist art treasures buried in its desert sands, and hauled them off by the tonne to western museums. Hopkirk steers carefully between calling them heroes (as many of their peers did) and plunderers (as the Chinese continue to do).

Hopkirk, Peter, *The Great Game*. A fast-paced, very readable history of the Great Game – the 19th century cold war between Britain and Russia – as it unfolded across Europe and Asia. It's carried along in Hopkirk's trademark style, in a series of personal stories – all men, all westerners, all resolute and square-jawed, with Victoria Crosses for everybody – real Boys' Own stuff, melodramatic but essentially true.

Hopkirk, Peter, *Setting the East Ablaze*. Takes up where *The Great Game* stops – a gripping cloak-and-dagger history of the murderous early years of Soviet power in Central Asia, and Communist efforts to spread revolution to British India and China. Of the many original books upon which Hopkirk's research is based, the best, now reprinted in paperback, are F M Bailey's *Mission to Tashkent* (reviewed separately) and Paul Nazaroff's *Hunted Through Central Asia*. Another good one is Gustav Krist's *Alone Through the Forbidden Land*.

Keay, John, *The Gilgit Game* (hardback). An account of some of the explorers and oddballs who played in the Great Game across the Pamirs, Hindu Kush and Karakoram in the 1800s.

Knobloch, Edgar, *Beyond the Oxus; Archaeology, Art & Architecture of Central Asia*. An oddly appealing book for a specialist cultural history of Central Asia, perhaps because it's so rich in all the background information, reconstructions, floor-plans and close-ups that nobody in Central Asia seems to know about any more.

Legg, Stuart, *The Heartland*. Takes a holistic and readable look at a very grand subject: the cultural history of all Eurasia. Legg paints an original picture of how the ebb and flow of nomadic grassland empires in inner Asia profoundly affected European and Asian civilisations. It's filled with interesting and well-woven details, and almost begs to be made into a Kenneth-Clarke-esque documentary TV series.

Maclean, Sir Fitzroy, *A Person from England* (hardback, now out of print). Better known for his own colourful exploits in the former USSR (see Travel Books), Maclean here offers well-written historical sketches of 19th century Persia and Central Asia. He has also produced good popular histories of Russia *(Holy Russia)* and of the USSR up to the August 1991 putsch *(All the Russias: the End of An Empire)*.

Marshall, Robert, *Storm From the East*. A good way to get to grips with just who Jenghiz Khan was, which cities his hordes annihilated and when, and what happened to his empire afterwards, based on a BBC television series. The paperback version is not so lavishly illustrated as the hardback.

Rashid, Ahmed, *Islam or Nationalism: The Resurgence of Central Asia*. A specialist journalist's informed and well-written assessment of the region's recent political history and contemporary issues, dense with facts and figures.

Waller, Derek, *The Pundits: British Exploration of Tibet & Central Asia*. An account of the heroic but unsung journeys of Indian scholars and soothsayers trained by the British to be undercover surveyors and spies across the Hindu Kush and Karakoram in the Great Game.

Islam

Ahmed, Akbar, *Living Islam*. Highly recommended, a sensitive introduction to Islam by a Pakistani scholar who has dedicated himself to bridging the mutual ignorance and misunderstanding between the Muslim and non-Muslim worlds, based in part on a BBC television series.

Guillaume, Alfred, *Islam*. Dry as dust but dense with information on history, doctrine and practice.

Ethnography & Arts

Kalter, Johannes, *The Arts and Crafts of Turkestan*. A detailed, beautifully illustrated, historical guide to the nomadic dwellings, clothing, jewellery and other 'applied art' of Central Asia. A similar work for anyone with a serious interest in traditional Turkmen ways and lifestyles is George O'Bannon's *The Turkoman Carpet*.

Manas; the Epic Vision of Theodor Herzen. A dignified coffee-table book of illustrations of the Kyrgyz folk epos, by an artist less well known than his elegant images (which have been pirated by Soviet publishers for years), with text and commentaries by Dan Prior. Bishkek publisher Akcent's American distributor is the Middle East Studies Center, Portland State University, 1950 SW 6th Ave, Portland, OR 97201, USA.

Olcott, Martha Brill, *The Kazakhs*. The ultimate English-language tome on that people, several hundred pages of great detail which could keep you quiet for many a long evening on the steppe.

Flora & Fauna

Sparks, John, *Realms of the Russian Bear*. An elegant, beautifully illustrated work on the flora and fauna of the old Soviet empire, including 80-plus pages on the Tian Shan mountains and Central Asia's steppes, deserts and seas.

Fiction

Aitmatov, Chinghiz. The Kyrgyz writer Chinghiz Aitmatov (born 1928) is among the few Central Asian writers whose stories are even remotely familiar to western readers. One of his earliest and best known books is *Djamila* (1967). Aitmatov lost his father in Stalin's purges and the loss of a father is a recurring theme, eg in the gripping 1978 novella *Piebald Dog Running Along the Shore* (made into a prize-winning Russian film in 1990), the 1970 *White Steamship* and the 1975 *Early Cranes*. In *The Day Lasts Longer Than a Century* (1980) two boys witness the arrest by the NKVD of their father, who never returns. Aimatov's *The Place of the Skull* (1986) confronted previously taboo subjects like drugs and religion and was an early attack on bureaucracy and environmental destruction. Many of his books have been translated into German and French and a few, like *Djamila* and *The Day Lasts Longer Than a Century*, are fairly easy to find in English.

Aldiss, Brian, *Somewhere East of Life* (hardback). This must be one of the few English-language novels ever to employ Ashghabat as a backdrop. At the time he wrote it, the author had yet to visit Turkmenistan, and consequently the Ashghabat visited by the protagonist as he searches for his stolen memory is far more colourful and exotic than the real thing.

Kipling, Rudyard, *Kim*. The master storyteller's classic epic of the Raj during the Great Game.

Malouf, Amin, *Samarkand*. Not much really to do with Samarkand, this is a fictionalised account of the life of the Persian poet and mathematician Omar Khayyam, or rather of his famed book of *rubaiyat*. The ripping good novel follows the manuscript through the ages and through the hands of the Assassins, a 20th century Persian princess and finally onto the Titanic. Indiana Jones meets The Thousand and One Nights.

Bookshops

Zwemmer (☎ (0171) 379-6253) at 28 Denmark St, London WC2H 8NJ, is a bookshop devoted to the former USSR and Eastern Europe, with a fair range of current Central Asia titles. You can send for their catalogue.

Some specialist travel bookshops have a reasonable range on Central Asia. In London these include the Travellers' Bookshop at 25 Cecil Court, WC2N 4EZ; the Travel Bookshop at 13 Blenheim Crescent, W11 2EE; and Edward Stanford at 12-14 Long Acre, WC2E 9LP. In New York, The Complete Traveller (☎ (212) 685-9007) at 199 Madison Avenue, 10016, is good. Chessler Books (☎ (800) 654-8502 toll-free, (303) 670-0093, fax 670-9727), PO Box 399, 26030 Highway 74, Kittredge, CO 80457, USA, has a fat catalogue covering mountaineering, exploration, maps and guidebooks, biographies etc.

You won't find very much in English at any of the bookshops in Central Asia.

NEWSPAPERS & MAGAZINES

The Kazakstan press is theoretically free, though stories unfavourable to the powerful are scarce except in *Karavan*, the weekly Russian-language paper which has broken several scandals. Along with the Kazak and Russian press, there are newspapers and periodicals in several minority languages, including German. Western newspapers and magazines, a few days old and expensive, are available in Almaty but not elsewhere in Kazakstan.

In Kyrgyzstan there are few international English-language papers or magazines to be found (though some two week old *Newsweeks* were spotted at one Bishkek kiosk). The *Kyrgyzstan Chronicle* is an eight page English-language weekly, sold in tourist hotels and some bookshops in Bishkek, with news and features aimed at business people

and Central Asia watchers, and a strong editorial line on rounding up crooks and charlatans.

Foreign journalists crazy enough to set up in what the *Economist* calls Uzbekistan's 'information-free capital, Tashkent' are constantly harassed and intimidated. The officially 'free' Uzbek press is monitored to ensure conformity and is frequently used to denounce foreign journalists critical of the state. Long-term residents say the supply of western newspapers and magazines dried up completely in 1994. Even interesting Russian papers like *Moscow News* and *Argumenty i Fakty* are gone. Our more naïve local friends said this was merely a fuel and distribution problem!

The printed media are very unhealthy in both Tajikistan and Turkmenistan. Neither country has outright censorship, but if a paper is not singing the right tune, essential supplies like newsprint and ink are suddenly hard to find. There is nothing published in English in Tajikistan, nor anything in Turkmenistan apart from one glossy cultural magazine, *Türkmen Medeniyeti*, with a back-page English summary of its not-very-interesting stories.

RADIO & TV

Radio

Bring your shortwave radio if you want to keep up with the outside world. Nothing in English (other than Radio Moscow) seems to be actually beamed *towards* Central Asia, so reception is often poor. Strongest is Radio Australia, followed by Voice of America and BBC World Service. For current schedule information, contact Radio Australia at PO Box 428G, Melbourne, Vic 3001 (☎ (03) 9626 1800, fax 626 1899, e-mail raust@ozemail.com.au); Voice of America at VOA, Washington, DC 20547 (fax (202) 619-0211); and BBC at PO Box 76, Bush House, London WC2B 4PH.

TV

In the popularity stakes the soaps and glitzy cabaret shows of Moscow One and Ostankino, beamed from Russia, win hands down over the dour national channels. At 7.30 pm Moscow time (9.30 or 10.30 pm in Central Asia) most sets are tuned to *Rosa*, a hugely popular Mexican soap opera dubbed into Russian, featuring the misadventures of the eponymous heroine, a former street urchin married to a rich socialite.

Uzbekistan has five channels – one from Russia and two each from Tashkent and Samarkand – but with little of interest other than concerts, and dubbed western films. BBC World Service News, over-dubbed with Uzbek, is on Tashkent-2 late in the evening. Channel 1 has lightweight stuff from Moscow early and late, but hard-hitting current affairs programmes are blanked out during the day.

In Kyrgyzstan, channel 1 is Kyrgyz TV, 2 and 3 are from Moscow, 4 from Turkey, and 5 is the private Pyramid channel, broadcasting alternately from Almaty and Tashkent with news, music videos, and dubbed B-grade movies from overseas. There is nothing in English, though channel 3 has ABC World News at 9 am, overlaid with a Russian voice.

Kazakstan has two state channels. One shows mainly Kazak and Russian-language information programmes (including nightly news) and films; the other broadcasts documentaries and cultural shows in Kazak and Uyghur. Ostankino (Russia) is more popular than either of these. Some cities have independent stations with pirated, badly dubbed American films, local news, talk shows and classified ads.

Turkmenistan TV troops out a turgid procession of folk dancing, traditional music ensembles and paeans to the president. There is a nightly news bulletin delivered in English at about 9 pm.

PHOTOGRAPHY
Customs
There are no significant customs limits on camera equipment and film for personal use.

Film & Processing
Kodak has franchise outlets in some department stores – eg in Bishkek – selling 35 mm

print film, Ektachrome (but not Kodachrome) slide film and video cassettes, but prices are high, so it's wise to bring your own (more than you think you'll need; Central Asia is a photographer's dream). It's safest to get film developed at home too, though most of the Kodak franchises can develop print film (Kodak C41 process) for prices in line with their film prices.

Kashgar department stores have cheap Chinese film and lots of Fujicolor and Konica, though processing there is second-rate and dusty. Western-brand colour print film and processing are available in Kashgar, and on the KKH at Karimabad and Gilgit. Colour slide film (E6 only, eg Fujichrome, Agfachrome, Ektachrome) is available in Pakistan, but it may have to go to Lahore or Karachi for processing. Kodachrome is scarce and cannot be processed in China or Pakistan.

Posting film from anywhere in Central Asia, China or Pakistan is asking for trouble; better to take it home or to a reliable place like Hong Kong for posting or processing.

Equipment
This is a personal matter, but with an SLR camera, a mid-range zoom – eg 35 mm to 135 mm – covers a wide range of situations; a good second lens might be a 28 mm for panoramas and indoors. Strong summer sunlight has a tendency to bleach out shots, so anybody serious about their photography should pack the relevant filters. Similarly, for shooting in the mountains, you get the best results with a UV or skylight filter and a lens shade.

Restrictions & Etiquette
There are few major restrictions on what you can photograph in Central Asia any more, though military installations and border zones are still taboo. Surprisingly, so is the Tashkent Metro (beware the red-capped attendants). Some museums and galleries forbid flash pictures.

A lifetime with the KGB has made many older people uneasy about having their picture taken. Many people are also touchy about you photographing embarrassing subjects like drunks, run-down housing or consumer queues. And you may find people sensitive about you photographing women, especially in rural areas and even among Ismailis; if a husband or brother is nearby it's risky as well. Women photographers may get lucky if they've established some rapport. The Russian for 'may I take a photograph?' is *fotografirovat mozhno?* ('fa-ta-gruh-FEE-ra-vut MOZH-na?').

In China you can't photograph military sites, factories, airports, railway stations or bridges, and often there are people nearby who'll collar you and take your film. You're not supposed to take pictures from aeroplanes but I've never seen a flight attendant swoop down on anybody. Some older Chinese shy away from cameras but nearly everyone loves having their kids photographed.

Prohibited subjects in Pakistan are military sites, airports, major KKH bridges and, above all, women. Pakistani men, on the other hand, are irrepressible in front of a camera, and quick to ask you for a print.

Hazards

Heat To avoid magenta-tinted memories of Central Asia, keep film away from heat. If you line a stuff-sack with a patch cut from an aluminised mylar 'survival blanket', film will stay cool inside through fierce summer days.

Cold & Condensation Camera batteries get sluggish in the cold, eg on mountain treks. Carry the camera inside your coat and keep some spare batteries warm in your pocket. In very cold weather, avoid ruinous moisture on film and inside the camera by putting them in plastic bags *before* going indoors, and leaving them there till they're warm.

Dust Some back roads are a wallow of fine dust that gets into everything. Keep everything bagged up, and carry a squeeze-bulb for blowing dust from inside the camera.

X-Rays One dose of airport x-rays won't harm slow or medium-speed films, but the effects are cumulative and too much will fog your pictures. Lead 'film-safe' pouches help but the best solution is hand inspection. Officials will hate you for asking but most will do it if you persist. Having all your film in one or two clear plastic bags makes it easier.

TIME

The official time in most of Central Asia is Greenwich Mean Time (GMT) plus five hours, but giant Kazakstan straddles GMT plus four, five and six hours. All China officially runs on Beijing time (GMT plus eight hours), though Kashgar also runs unofficially on 'Xinjiang time' (two hours earlier) which means visitors must keep track of both. All Pakistan is at GMT plus five hours.

To complicate matters, Kazakstan and Kyrgyzstan have Daylight Savings Time (DST), setting their clocks forward by one hour from the last Sunday in March until the last Sunday in September. Tajikistan, Turkmenistan, Uzbekistan, China and Pakistan don't have DST.

When it's noon on a summer (winter) day in Tashkent, it's:

- midnight (11 pm) the previous day in San Francisco
- 3 am (2 am) in New York and Toronto
- 8 am (7 am) in London
- 11 am (10 am) in Moscow
- noon (11 am) in extreme western Kazakstan (Aqtau, Oral)
- noon (noon) in all of Tajikistan, Turkmenistan, Uzbekistan and Pakistan
- 1 pm (noon) in all of Kyrgyzstan, and most of western Kazakstan
- 2 pm (1 pm) in eastern Kazakstan (including Almaty)
- 1 pm (1 pm) in Xinjiang – unofficially
- 3 pm (3 pm) in Beijing
- 5 pm (6 pm) in Sydney
- 7 pm (8 pm) in Wellington

Countries outside Central Asia switch to DST on their own schedules, so in early spring and early autumn, expect other one-hour differences to come and go.

Timetables

Amazingly, trains (but not buses or flights)

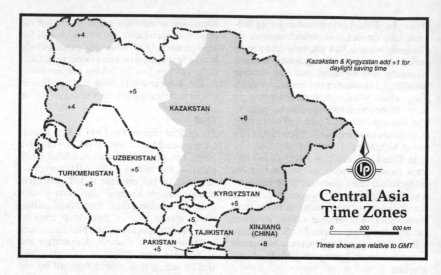

Kazakstan & Kyrgyzstan add +1 for daylight saving time

KAZAKSTAN +6

+4

+5

+4

UZBEKISTAN +5

TURKMENISTAN +5

KYRGYZSTAN +5

+5

TAJIKISTAN XINJIANG (CHINA) +8

PAKISTAN +5

Central Asia Time Zones

0   300   600 km

Times shown are relative to GMT

in Kazakstan and Kyrgyzstan were still running on Moscow time when we were there.

ELECTRICITY

The entire former USSR is the same: nominal 220v at 50 cycles, using European two-pin plugs (round pins, with no earth connection) everywhere. Bring a torch: light bulbs are in short supply.

WEIGHTS & MEASURES

Central Asia is metric. It's also worth knowing that while Russian dictionaries define *choot choot* as 'a little bit', when applied to a shot of vodka it would appear to mean 'up to the rim'.

LAUNDRY

Nearly all hotels have a place where the bed linen and towels are washed; there you're sure to find someone who can do washing and ironing fairly cheaply. In better hotels, just ask your floor-lady, who might do it herself. Figure on about US$0.50 per piece. But don't give her anything you're particularly fond of; a woman friend got a pair of leggings back, hacked off at the knees.

Of course you can do it yourself, but be sure to bring a universal sink plug, since almost no hotel bathrooms have them. Laundry soap is easy to find in department stores or markets of larger towns.

You'll find occasional dry-cleaning shops in the cities, but you take your chances with the quality of the job.

HEALTH

Good health on the road includes pre-departure planning, day-to-day care and readiness for emergencies. With a little forethought you should have nothing worse than the occasional grumpy stomach in Central Asia. Routine care can often be arranged through your hotel or embassy, and foreigners usually get the best available in any area.

Having said this, significant health problems have arisen in all the former Soviet states as a result of the collapse of universal health care, declining stocks of drugs, falling vaccination rates and, in places like Tajikistan, civil strife. It is probably somewhat riskier to your health to travel in Central Asia now than it was in the 1980s.

Summary of Risks Gut infections, in particular hepatitis A and undulant fever (from bacteria in unpasteurised milk products), are a significant risk, but are easily avoidable with good sense concerning food and drink. Hepatitis B is avoidable with good sense about unprotected sex and the use of needles. There are also effective vaccines for hepatitis A and B, as well as for other diseases considered significant in at least some areas – diphtheria, typhoid and, less importantly, cholera, encephalitis, meningitis, tuberculosis, polio and tetanus. A low malaria risk exists in the lowland southern border regions of Tajikistan, and in lower-altitude parts of Pakistan.

Trekkers must of course beware of hypothermia and altitude sickness, and be cautious in tick habitats (high grass and woodlands) to avoid two tick-borne diseases, haemorrhagic fever and Lyme disease, for which there are no vaccines. Rabies is significant, mainly in connection with guard dogs in remote areas. There is a vaccine available.

Travel Health Information

A thorough, well organised and portable guide is *Staying Healthy in Asia, Africa, & Latin America*. If you can't find it write to Moon Publications, 722 Wall St, Chico, CA 95928, USA. *Travel with Children* by Maureen Wheeler (Lonely Planet) is full of basic advice on travel health for young people. *Where There is No Doctor* by David Werner (Hesperian Foundation) is a very detailed reference intended for someone going to work in an undeveloped country, rather than for the average traveller.

Medical Advisory Services for Travellers Abroad (MASTA), a private UK group associated with the London School of Hygiene & Tropical Medicine, has a travellers' health line (☎ 0891-224100) where you can order a basic 'health brief' with information on immunisations, malaria, Foreign Office advisories and health news, for the cost of the (premium-rate) call. They also offer more detailed briefs for long or complex trips, plus mail-order health supplies. Also in the UK, the Malaria Reference Laboratory

has a 24 hour premium-rate helpline at ☎ (0891) 600 350. A network of British Airways Travel Clinics (call ☎ 0171-831 5333 for information) offers low-cost immunisations.

MASTA in Australia, associated with the Tropical Health Program of the University of Queensland, offers similar services to those in the UK. Contact them at ☎ (02) 971 1499 or fax 971 0239. Alternatively, call the Australian Government Health Service (part of the Commonwealth Department of Human Services & Health) or consult a clinic like the Travellers' Medical & Vaccination Centre (☎ (03) 670 3969) at Level 2, 393 Little Bourke St, Melbourne, Victoria.

In the USA you can call the Centers for Disease Control travellers' hotline (☎ (404) 332-4555 or ☎ 332-4559), or the International Medicine Program at Cornell University Medical Center in New York (☎ (212) 746-5454).

Pre-Departure Planning

Health Insurance A policy for theft, loss, flight cancellation and medical treatment overseas is a good idea. If you're a frequent traveller it's possible to get year-round insurance at reasonable rates. For travel in Central Asia, a 'medevac' clause or policy, covering the costs of being flown to another country for treatment, is wise (for some private medevac outfits, see Medical Help, further in this section).

Check the small print. Some policies are not valid outside the country of issue. Some exclude 'dangerous activities', which can include white-water rafting or even trekking. If these are on your agenda, ask about an amendment to permit some of them (at a higher premium). Few medical services in Central Asia will accept your foreign insurance documents for payment; you'll have to pay on the spot, get receipts for everything, save all the paperwork, and claim later.

The UK has reciprocal agreements with all the former Soviet republics except the Baltic states, allowing UK nationals and their dependents (who are normally resident in Britain) *emergency* treatment – such as it is – on the same terms as local people get; you must show your British passport. If you plan to live or work in Central Asia, other agreements may apply instead; contact the UK Department of Health, International Relations Unit, Room 518, Richmond House, 79 Whitehall, London SW1A 2NS, ☎ 071-210 3000, or toll-free ☎ 0800-555777.

Medical Kit A small kit for routine problems might include tweezers, scissors, thermometer (mercury thermometers are prohibited by most airlines), insect repellent, aspirin, antiseptic, plasters (band-aids), a few gauze pads and adhesive tape, moleskin (for foot blisters) and something for diarrhoea (kaolin preparation – eg Pepto-Bismol – or Imodium or Lomotil). For severe diarrhoea, especially in children, a rehydration mixture is a good idea. Water-purification tablets, iodine tincture or a water filter is useful for the rare occasion when there's no boiled or bottled water. Other suggestions are a toothache kit, sunscreen, lip salve and antifungal cream or powder (eg athlete's foot powder).

If you wear corrective lenses, bring a spare pair, and the prescription. If you wear contact lenses, ask your opthalmologist about accessories you might want out in the middle of nowhere.

Doctors don't usually recommend dosing yourself with antibiotics, but a broad-spectrum antibiotic like tetracycline or amoxycillin is useful to carry. Be sure you have no allergies to it. For this and any other prescription drug, bring the prescription too, as proof of what it is. If you're required to take a narcotic drug, carry a doctor's letter to this effect. If you need medication for an ongoing ailment, bring a complete supply with you. Keep medicines in their original, labelled containers and in your hand luggage.

Considering the potential for contamination through dirty needles, some travellers now routinely carry a sterile pack of disposable syringes, available from medical supply shops. SAFA (☎ (0151) 709-6075), 59 Hill Street, Liverpool LP 5SE, UK, specialises in travel medical kits for developing countries or other remote areas. They'll ship anywhere in the world; their international fax order number is ☎ ++44-151-708 7211.

Health Preparations If you're going on a long trip get your teeth checked in advance; there are few good dentists anywhere in Central Asia.

Immunisations No immunisations are required for travellers to Central Asia, but you should consider the kind of protection you would want for off-the-beaten-track travel anywhere in Asia. Most western travellers will have been immunised in childhood against measles, polio and 'DPT' (diphtheria, pertussis and tetanus), and you should get any boosters necessary to bring you up to date with these. Children of any age should be immunised against tuberculosis; in 1994 the World Health Organisation noted large increases in TB deaths in Turkmenistan and Kyrgyzstan.

Following are other options, with our recommendations indicated by an asterisk (*). Plan ahead, since some jabs cannot be given simultaneously, and some take weeks or months for the onset of full protection. They're best recorded on an official-looking International Health Certificate, available from your physician or government health authority – some border officials are especially fond of these.

* Cholera: Though all countries have dropped cholera immunisation as a requirement, there have been recent small outbreaks in Kazakstan, Tajikistan and China. Also, travellers often face bureaucratic problems over it (eg on entering China, or on coming from African or Latin American countries), so it's wise to have it on your certificate anyhow. Protection is limited and lasts only three to six months, and it's contraindicated in pregnancy.

* Diphtheria & tetanus: Diphtheria immunisation is highly recommended for travel anywhere in the former USSR. Many people will have been immunised in childhood, but a further booster is needed every 10 years. A full diphtheria course involves three doses at monthly intervals. Tetanus boosters are highly recommended.

* Hepatitis A (infectious hepatitis): For regular or long-term travellers, there is a hepatitis A vaccine, called Havrix; two initial shots two to four weeks apart give a year's protection, and a booster six to 12 months later extends that to 10 years. An older alternative, gamma globulin, is not a vaccine but a prepared antibody that reduces the chances of infection for about six months, but some doctors feel its effects are far outweighed by common-sense eating habits. You don't need either if you've had the disease before.

Hepatitis B (serum hepatitis): You'd need to plan ahead for this one: you get at least three shots, the second a month after the first, the third two months later; a booster 12 months after that extends the protection.

Japanese B encephalitis: A single injection is good for about three years; it's mainly recommended for China.

Malaria: Malaria drugs are prophylactic pills, not preventative shots, but you should sort them out before you go too; see the later section on malaria.

Meningitis A & C: The US embassy in Almaty recommends immunisation against this, though no other source does. A single injection gives around three years protection.

Polio: A booster of either the oral or injected vaccine is required every 10 years to maintain our immunity from childhood vaccination. Polio is a very serious, easily transmitted disease and is widespread in the region.

Rabies: Three injections of human diploid cell rabies vaccine gives full protection.

* Typhoid: There are single-dose and two-dose vaccines, both giving three years protection, and a four-dose oral vaccine requiring annual boosters. Older people who've had several boosters may not need any more.

* Tick-borne encephalitis: A treatment of three shots gives full protection.

Basic Rules

Many problems can be avoided with common sense – eg get out of the sun when it's blazing hot, carry enough clothes for potential plunges in temperature. Wash your hands frequently – it's easy to contaminate your own food.

Water Play it safe and *don't drink the water*; that includes no brushing your teeth in tap water, even in better hotels, and no ice in your drinks. Tourism officials often say the local tap water is OK to drink; sometimes it is and sometimes it isn't.

Nearly all tourist hotel dining rooms have bottled mineral water, which is safe. Failing that, you might cajole your nearest hotel attendant into boiling some water for you.

Even in the mountains, some streams may be contaminated with giardia, though springs are truly drinkable.

Water Purification The best way to purify water is to boil it for five to 10 minutes. If you can't do that or can't find boiled water, treat it chemically or use a good portable filter.

Iodine treatment kills bacteria, amoebae and giardia and is safe for short-term use unless you're pregnant or have thyroid problems. It's available in tablet form (eg Potable Aqua or Globaline), or you can buy 2% tincture of iodine from a pharmacy; add two drops per litre or quart of clear water. With either, let treated water stand for half an hour before you drink it. Iodine degrades when exposed to air so keep it sealed. Chlorine tablets (eg Puritabs, Steritabs) won't kill amoebae or giardia.

Most commercial water filters – charcoal, ceramic or resin – won't stop all pathogens, particularly the hepatitis A virus. However, combined charcoal and iodine-resin filters will.

Food What you put in your mouth is the most important thing, but don't get paranoid – after all, eating local food is part of being there. An upset stomach is the most common health problem – not surprising, considering the amount of oil used in Central Asian cooking – but it's rarely serious.

In the tourist hotels, restaurant food can be considered safe, but choose café and street food with care. Go for hot, freshly made dishes; avoid salads (usually washed in untreated water); avoid undercooked meat; peel fruit yourself or wash it in water you trust (pesticides are still heavily used), and don't buy any with broken skins. We're told that in a few stalls in Kashgar, noodles are quenched in river water after they've been cooked!

Milk is usually unpasteurised, but pure

cultured products like yoghurt are always hygienic.

A good hepatitis A defence is to carry your own utensils. In Xinjiang, bamboo restaurant chopsticks may be the worst culprit; if you're stuck with nothing else, soaking them in boiling hot tea may at least reduce the risks. You can buy your own chopsticks in department stores.

Nutrition You're likely to find enough edible and fairly healthy food at your hotel and at restaurants, but the mere stress of finding decent eateries and dealing with rude staff can lead you to skip meals and put your health at risk.

Keep your diet balanced. Eggs, beans, lentils and nuts are safe protein sources. Fruit you can peel is always safe and a good vitamin source. Don't forget grains (eg rice) and bread. But it's not always possible to find these things, so a vitamin-mineral supplement is not a bad idea. While well-cooked food is safer, it loses much of its nutritional value.

Everyday Health You should know how to take temperature and pulse readings. Normal body temperature is 37°C (98.6°F). More than 2°C (4°F) higher is a serious fever. Normal adult pulse rate is 60 to 80 per minute (children 80 to 100, and babies 100 to 140). As a rule pulse increases about 20 beats per minute for each 1°C rise in fever.

Breathing rate is another indicator of illness. Adults and older children breathe about 12 to 20 times a minute (up to 30 for young children, and 40 for babies). People with high fever or serious respiratory illness breathe faster than normal.

Medications Ideally, antibiotics should be taken under medical supervision, and never indiscriminately. Overuse weakens the body's natural immunities and can reduce the drug's future effectiveness. Take the prescribed dose at the recommended times – and *don't* discontinue the course early, even if you feel better. However if you experience any serious reaction you should stop taking

the medication immediately, and don't use a drug at all if you're not sure it's the right one. Likewise, be sure you have no penicillin allergy before taking penicillin or its derivatives.

Give children from eight to 12 years old half the adult dose, and younger children one third to one fourth the adult dose.

Problems & Treatment
Do-it-yourself diagnosis and treatment have their own risks, so whenever possible get qualified help. Unfortunately, this is scarce in Central Asia, even in the capital cities. Medical equipment and standards are poor, and many common medications are unavailable. Turkmenistan and Tajikistan in particular don't seem to have even the most basic supplies (except on the black market, where medicines tend to be of poor quality, badly handled, and therefore ineffective or even dangerous).

The best source of western-trained medical help in Central Asia is almost certainly the Tashkent International Clinic (see the Tashkent Information section in the Uzbekistan chapter). Elsewhere, contact your own nearest embassy (these are listed under Information for each capital city). US embassies may be willing to help non-Americans in dire straits. Embassies cannot provide treatment, but they can tell you what, if any, reliable help is available. They cannot take formal responsibility for the quality of service you get, though.

Some public hospitals have agreements for the treatment of foreigners. Doctors and hospitals often expect immediate cash payment for their services. The average pharmacy (Russian: *apteka*) doesn't have much, though there are expensive hard-currency pharmacies in Tashkent.

Medical Emergencies
Ambulance The local number for an ambulance is ☎ 03 everywhere, but this service is not very reliable. You're probably better off hiring a taxi!

Evacuation US embassy medical officers in

several Central Asian capitals agree that in the case of a serious illness, the best place to head is the airport. But if you aren't ambulatory or can't get a scheduled flight when you want it, a charter flight on short notice could cost you up to US$30,000 – hence the obvious value of a medevac clause in your travel insurance.

Following are a few reliable 'air ambulance' services:

Air Ambulance Network, Miami, Florida,
☎ +1-305-447-0458
Air Ambulance of America, Texas, Chicago, Illinois, USA, ☎ +1-512-479-8000
Alpha Aviation, Dallas, Texas, ☎ +1-214-352-4801
Delta Consulting, Moscow, ☎ +7-095-229-6536
National Air Ambulance, Fort Lauderdale, Florida, ☎ +1-305-525-5538
SOS International, Geneva, Switzerland,
☎ +41-22-476161

Mountain Rescue Local mountain-rescue services are listed in the Tashkent and Bishkek sections.

Environmental Hazards

Altitude Sickness Reduced oxygen at high altitudes can cause headaches, dizziness, breathlessness, nausea, insomnia and/or low appetite, especially if you're dehydrated or exerting yourself. You're less likely to suffer if you take it easy for a few days, drink plenty of water, eat well and avoid alcohol and cigarettes.

The symptoms usually go away after a few days but if they don't the only treatment is to descend – even a few hundred metres can help. Continuing breathlessness, severe headache, nausea, lack of appetite or dry cough – sometimes with frothy pink sputum – are cause for concern. Profound tiredness, confusion, lack of coordination and balance are real danger signs. Acute mountain sickness (AMS) can be fatal.

There's no hard-and-fast rule about how high is too high – people have died at 3000 metres, although 3500 to 4500 metres is when it usually starts. It's wise to sleep at an altitude lower than the greatest height reached during the day.

Sunburn In the desert or at high elevations you can get sunburnt very fast, even through cloud. Take Australian advice and slip (on a shirt) – slop (on some sunscreen) – slap (on a hat). Calamine or aloe vera lotion eases the pain of mild sunburn. Severe sunburn also carries the risk of dehydration.

Prickly Heat This is an itchy rash caused by excess perspiration trapped under the skin. It usually strikes people who've just arrived in a hot climate from cooler places. Keep cool, bathe often, use a mild talcum powder; and you'll eventually acclimatise.

Dehydration & Heat Exhaustion You breathe and sweat away body water very fast in the mountains as well as the desert. Dark yellow urine and not much of it are signs you're dehydrated, though you may not feel very thirsty. Dehydration and salt deficiency from sweating a lot can bring on lethargy, headaches, giddiness, rapid pulse and possibly muscle cramps. In severe cases, vomiting or diarrhoea deplete fluid and salt levels further. Drink lots of water, salt your food generously and take the heat in small doses until you've acclimatised.

Heat Stroke This serious, sometimes fatal, condition is a failure of the body's heat-regulating mechanism caused by long periods in extreme heat. Symptoms are general discomfort, little or no sweating and a dangerously high body temperature (39°C to 41°C). When sweating ceases the skin becomes flushed. Severe headaches, poor coordination, sometimes confusion or aggression may also occur, and eventually delirium or convulsions. Hospitalisation is essential but meanwhile get victims out of the sun, remove clothing, cover them with a wet sheet or towel and fan them continuously.

Hypothermia Excess cold is as dangerous as excess heat. Trekkers run a risk of hypothermia, in which the body loses heat faster than it can generate it and the body's core temperature drops. It's surprisingly easy to go from chilly to dangerously cold with a combination of wind, wet clothing (from rain or just sweat), fatigue and hunger, even when the air temperature is well above freezing.

Symptoms are exhaustion, lethargy, dizzy spells, numbness (especially in toes and fingers), shivering, muscle cramps, slurred speech, clumsiness, irrational behaviour and violent bursts of energy. You're more likely to recognise it in someone else than in yourself.

To prevent it, dress in easily donned layers. Silk, wool and some synthetic fibres insulate well even when wet; cotton doesn't. A hat makes a big difference, as lots of heat is lost through the head. A waterproof outer layer is obviously important. Frequent drinks of water and sugary snacks help to generate heat quickly.

To treat hypothermia, take shelter and replace wet clothing with dry. Drink hot liquids (not alcohol) and eat high-calorie, easily digestible snacks. In more advanced cases it may be necessary to put the victim in a sleeping bag and get in with them. Don't rub a victim down or put them near a fire. If possible give them a warm (not hot) bath.

Infectious Diseases

Diarrhoea A change of water, food or climate, even jet-lag, can bring on the runs (Ulughbek's Revenge). But a few dashes to the loo with no other symptoms is nothing to worry about. More serious is diarrhoea due to contaminated food or water.

Dehydration is the main danger, particularly in children. Thirst is not a reliable indicator of dehydration. Weak black tea with sugar, or soft drinks allowed to go flat and diluted with purified water, are good for replacing fluids. In severe cases a rehydrating solution is necessary to replace minerals and salts. If you didn't bring a commercial rehydration mix, add a level teaspoon of salt and eight level teaspoons of sugar to a litre of purified water and sip it slowly all day. An alternative is rice water with some salt. Stick to a bland diet as you recover.

Lomotil or Imodium plugs you up but doesn't cure you. Use it only if absolutely

necessary – eg if you *must* travel. Don't use it if you have a fever or are severely dehydrated.

Giardiasis *Giardia lamblia* is a parasite found in contaminated water. Symptoms of infection – cramped or bloated stomach, nausea, watery foul-smelling diarrhoea and frequent gas – may not appear for weeks, and can come and go for weeks or months more.

There is no preventative drug. Treat it with metronidazole (brand-name Flagyl) or tinidazole (brand-name Fasigyn), adults 400 to 600 mg three times daily for two or three days, preferably under medical supervision. *Don't* take any alcohol while taking these. Avoid Enterovioform and Mexaform, which can have serious side effects. Antibiotics are of no use.

See Water Purification in the preceding section about ways to avoid giardia in the first place.

Dysentery The main symptom of this serious illness, caused by contaminated food or water, is severe diarrhoea, often with traces of blood or mucus. There are two forms, and only a stool test can reliably distinguish the two.

Bacillary or bacterial dysentery (Shigella) shows rapid onset, high fever, headache, vomiting and stomach pains. It generally doesn't last more than a week, but is highly contagious. Treat severe cases with tetracycline – adults 250 mg four times a day for seven to 10 days. This should be given to children only if it's essential. Pregnant women should not take it after the fourth month.

Amoebic dysentery develops more gradually, has no fever or vomiting but is a more serious illness – it will persist until treated and can recur and do long-term damage. Treat it with metronidazole (brand-name Flagyl, adults 800 mg three times daily for five days) or tinidazole (brand-name Fasigyn, adults 600 to 700 mg three times daily for three to six days); don't drink alcohol while taking these. Avoid taking

Enterovioform or Mexaform, which can have serious side effects.

Hepatitis Hepatitis is a general term for inflammation of the liver. There are many causes of this condition: drugs, alcohol and infections are but a few.

Hepatitis A or infectious hepatitis is the most frequent vaccine-preventable infection occurring in unprotected travellers to developing countries. It's spread by contaminated food, water or utensils. Minimal symptoms are fatigue, aches and pains, and loss of appetite; you may also have a fever, chills, headache and in later stages nausea, vomiting, liver pain (under the rib cage), dark urine, light-coloured faeces and jaundiced skin. The whites of your eyes may turn yellow.

You should seek medical advice, though there isn't much you can do but rest, drink lots of fluids, eat lightly and avoid fatty foods. People who've had hepatitis A must forgo alcohol for six months afterward, since the disease attacks the liver. The severity of the disease increases with age of the victim, and some cases have been fatal.

Hepatitis B or serum hepatitis is spread through unprotected sexual contact, the use of dirty needles (eg syringes, suture needles, acupuncture, tattooing and ear or nose piercing needles) or other sharp instruments (eg barber-shop razors), or in infected blood transfusions. Avoid injections and transfusions where you have doubts about sanitation. Symptoms and treatment are much the same as for type A.

Hepatitis A vaccine won't prevent type B, and vice-versa. Boiling syringes etc in water only kills type A.

Hepatitis E is a recently discovered virus, of which little is yet known other than it is food and water-borne like Hepatitis A. Large epidemics can occur in the region, generally causing mild hepatitis.

Hepatitis E was in fact epidemic around Kashgar in 1987 and many eating places were shut down for cleaning. It was allegedly under control a year later, but the need for caution there is obvious. There are no specific vaccines for this type of hepatitis.

Undulant Fever This bacterial infection, normally caught from unpasteurised dairy products (especially from goat's milk) reveals itself by fever, weakness and depression that can start a few weeks after contact and last for months. There is no vaccine.

Cholera Though all countries have dropped cholera immunisation as a requirement, there have been recent minor outbreaks in Kazakstan, Tajikistan and China (outbreaks are generally widely reported, so you can avoid problem areas). The bacteria responsible for this disease are water-borne, so that attention to the rules of eating and drinking should protect the traveller.

The disease is characterised by a sudden onset of acute diarrhoea with 'rice water' stools, vomiting, muscle cramps and extreme weakness. You need medical help – but meanwhile treat for dehydration, which can be extreme. If there is an appreciable delay in getting to hospital, begin taking tetracycline – 250 mg four times daily for adults – but not for pregnant women nor for children aged eight years or less. An alternative drug is Ampicillin. Fluid replacement is by far the most important aspect of treatment.

Diphtheria Said to be eradicated in the USSR in the 1960s, diphtheria is back as a serious health risk throughout the former Soviet republics. This can be a potentially fatal throat infection, caused by the inhalation of infected cough or sneeze droplets, or a less dangerous skin infection, spread by contaminated dust contacting the skin.

There's a higher risk of getting the throat infection in cities and crowded places. Symptoms include fever, sore throat, swollen lymph nodes, coughing and shortness of breath. In later stages, heart, kidney and nervous system damage is possible. The very young are at especially high risk. A vaccine is available, and highly recommended. You can reduce the risk by avoiding indirect contact with strangers, eg sharing bottles or glasses.

Meningitis This bacterial infection of the membranes around the brain is spread by close contact, and can be anything from mild to fatal. It tends to run in epidemics (which you are likely to hear about from official sources) rather than single cases. Symptoms appear three or four days after contact and typically include fever, severe headache and stiff neck, and later convulsions, vomiting and delirium.

Rabies Rabies is a significant risk in Central Asia, spread by infected animals – most commonly dogs, but also cats and other animals, even cattle. Animal herders' guard dogs are a major risk. Rabies not treated before the onset of symptoms (a few days to as much as several years later) is almost always fatal. Avoid it simply by avoiding all animals, domestic or wild.

Any bite or scratch (or even a lick at the site of one) should be cleaned immediately and thoroughly with soap and running water and, if possible, with alcohol solution. If the offending animal cannot be caught alive or the owner identified (a rabid animal usually acts strangely and dies within a week), get medical attention at once. A rabies vaccine is available.

Sexually Transmitted Diseases Abstinence is the only sure preventative against STDs, but use of a condom is very effective. Gonorrhoea and syphilis are the most common; symptoms include sores, blisters or a rash around the genitals and discharge or pain when urinating. Syphilis symptoms eventually disappear but the disease continues and can cause severe problems in later years. Treatment of gonorrhoea or syphilis is by antibiotics.

Hepatitis B (see Hepatitis in the preceding text) is the only vaccine-preventable sexually transmitted disease, though full vaccination takes at least three months.

Infection by the herpes virus is unpleasant but not dangerous. Symptoms include tiny blisters around the genitals or mouth and sometimes fever, aches, fatigue or swollen lymph nodes. Herpes is spread by sexual activity when genital sores are present. There's no cure, though symptoms may be milder after the first appearance.

HIV/AIDS HIV (human immuno-deficiency virus) may develop into AIDS (acquired immune deficiency syndrome). Consistently safe sex using condoms is the most effective preventative; it is impossible to detect the HIV status of an otherwise healthy-looking person without a blood test.

HIV/AIDS can also be spread through infected blood transfusions; something to keep in mind given most developing countries cannot afford to screen all blood used for transfusions. It can also be spread by dirty needles, so vaccinations, acupuncture, tattooing and ear or nose piercing can potentially be as dangerous as drug use if the needle is not clean. If you need an injection, it may be a good idea to buy a new syringe from a pharmacy (or bring your own from home) and ask the doctor to use it.

All the countries covered in this book, except Tajikistan, have reported AIDS cases. Laws in the former Soviet states requiring certification from visitors of a negative HIV test (eg for those staying more than one month in Kyrgyzstan or any length of time in Uzbekistan) have been enforced feebly or not at all. Visitors staying in China longer than six months or in Pakistan longer than a year must give proof of a negative HIV test when they apply for a visa.

Some (but not all) short-term visitors arriving in China have been asked for such a certification. Saying you're in transit seems to get you off the hook, but it's better to avoid the possibility of a test with questionably sterile needles at the border by bringing a certificate!

Insect-Borne Diseases
Malaria This serious disease is spread by mosquitoes infected with a parasite. There is a low risk in the southern border regions of Tajikistan and all year round in Pakistan,

anywhere below about 2000 metres. Symptoms, which may not appear for three to six months or even longer and vary from person to person, may resemble flu at first, and include headaches, fever, nausea, tiredness, chills and sweating which may subside and recur. Untreated malaria is potentially fatal.

The mainstay of malaria prevention is simply to avoid mosquitoes. Malarial mosquitoes appear after sunset and at dawn. Thus wearing long clothes, using a repellent or burning mosquito coils, and sleeping under a mosquito net or in a screened room will reduce the chances of being bitten in the first place. Mosquitoes may be attracted by perfume or aftershave lotion.

It's also very important to take anti-malarial drugs, though none are completely free of side effects and none are 100% effective. They don't prevent the disease but interfere with the parasite's life-cycle. At the time of writing the recommended regimen in the region covered by this book was chloroquine (common brands Nivaquine, Avloclor or Aralen), 300 mg once a week. In Pakistan, if you're going beyond the upper KKH, you may need additional treatment. In any case, malarial parasites mutate into drug-resistant forms almost faster than science can come up with new drugs, and information about what's needed gets old fast, so see your local health authority for a proper update.

Always take malarial tablets at the same time of day, or day of the week, from two weeks before you get to a malarial area to at least four weeks after you've left it. Women who are pregnant (or plan to be soon after the course of treatment) should consult a doctor since some drugs are not safe.

An improvement on chloroquine is mefloquine, but it's not recommended for stays of more than three months in a malarial area. Fansidar has dangerous side effects, though it's used as a treatment for known cases. Others with possible side effects are Maloprim and Amodiaquine.

Tick-Borne Haemorrhagic Fever This severe viral illness is characterised by the sudden onset of intense fever, headache, aching limbs, bleeding gums and sometimes a rash of red dots on the skin, a week or two after being bitten by an infected tick. Though not all ticks are infected, it's a risk for trekkers and campers in Central Asia during the summer months.

There is no vaccine, so you need to know what to do about ticks (*kleshch* in Russian). Search for them during and after walking in scrubland, pasture or forests, where the little blighters hitch rides on anything passing by. If you find one burrowed into your skin, *don't* just pull it off, as that can leave the head in place and increase the risk of infection. Coax it out with Vaseline, alcohol or oil (or the touch of a freshly extinguished match if you don't have those), trying not to touch it even then. If it has been there for some time, a red blotch may appear around the site.

A strong insect repellent may discourage ticks in the first place, and long trousers tucked into your socks will give them less flesh to burrow into.

Lyme Disease This tick-borne bacterial disease causes a form of arthritis. Infected ticks live on horses or deer, usually in rural areas in April through September. Along with a rash around the bite come aching joints, and the disease can have serious long-term effects. There is no vaccine. See Tick-Borne Haemorrhagic Fever for what to do about ticks.

Tick-Borne Encephalitis This tick-transmitted viral disease of moderate to low risk occurs mainly from mid-May to mid-June or July. Symptoms – an enlarged red blotch at the bite site, headache, fever, stiffness, extreme weakness and tiredness, cold sweat and confusion – appear a week or two after being bitten, and it can be fatal if it's not treated fairly quickly. A vaccine is available. See Tick-Borne Haemorrhagic Fever for what to do about ticks.

Japanese B Encephalitis This viral disease carried by infected mosquitoes occurs mainly from June through September, and mainly in China. Flu-like symptoms are accompanied by severe headaches, stiff neck, confusion, and in later stages coma and possibly death. There's no specific treatment, but a vaccine is available. See Malaria for advice about avoiding mosquito bites in the first place.

Snake Bites

Venomous snakes are found in unpopulated rural areas, up to about 3000 metres. You're likely to encounter them on treks and in architectural ruins. To minimise your chances of being bitten, wear boots, socks and long trousers when walking through undergrowth. Don't put your hands into holes and crevices, and be careful when collecting firewood. Snakes tend to strike moving objects so if you encounter one, keep perfectly still until it slithers away.

Most people bitten by venomous snakes don't actually suffer serious effects, and venom rarely acts so fast that you can't get to where it can be treated. Keep the victim calm and still, wrap the bitten limb tightly (as you would for a sprained ankle), and attach a splint to immobilise it. Then seek medical help, if possible with the dead snake for identification (but don't attempt to catch it if there is even a remote possibility of being bitten again).

Tourniquets and cut and suck remedies are now comprehensively discredited. Serious trekkers should consider carrying an anti-venin kit.

Women's Health

Poor diet, lowered resistance from the use of antibiotics, even contraceptive pills can pave the way for vaginal infections in hot climates. Keeping the genital area clean, wearing cotton underwear and skirts or loose-fitting trousers will minimise the risk.

Yeast infections, characterised by a rash, itch and discharge, can be treated with a vinegar or lemon juice douche or with yoghurt. Nystatin suppositories are the usual medical prescription.

Trichomonas is a more serious infection, with discharge and a burning sensation when urinating. Male sexual partners must also be

treated and if a vinegar-water douche is not effective medical attention should be sought. Metronidazole (brand-name Flagyl) is the prescribed drug and you should not drink alcohol while taking it.

TOILETS

Public toilets are scarce as hen's teeth. Those you can find – eg in bus and train stations – charge the equivalent of US$0.10 or so to use their squatters, either flush or pit. Most are fairly awful. Some have someone out front selling sheets of toilet paper. But capitalism may prevail; a few privately run toilets have already appeared, where you pay more and get paper, running water, soap and reasonable hygiene. Carry a small pencil-torch for restaurant toilets which rarely seem to have functioning lights.

Toilet paper appears sporadically for sale in markets and department stores, though you may want to take a roll or two for when it can't be found. Flush systems don't like toilet paper (some people don't even seem to like it in their pit toilets). The waste-basket in the loo is for used paper.

PUBLIC BATHS

Public baths are not just a way to get clean. They also offer the true budget traveller the sublime experience of endless hot water. Most sizeable towns have at least one. Some are grottier than others. Typically there are men's and women's common rooms, where you can spend a couple of hours soaping and rinsing, for less than half a dollar. Some have private rooms with tubs, some have steam rooms. If you're taking a private room, bring your washing too – who's to know?

WOMEN TRAVELLERS

Central Asia can be hard work for the lone woman traveller. Both Russian and Islamic societies traditionally relegate women to secondary status, and here some of the worst elements of both are combined – further aggravated by the often twisted images of western women available in imported B-grade films. Many local men cannot understand why women (in groups of any size, for that matter) would travel without men, and assume they have ulterior sexual motives. Although harassment is not so unrelenting as in some Middle Eastern countries, it tends to be more physical. Macho Uzbekistan tops the list, with Kyrgyzstan by far the least sexist.

Young men subject solo women to rude noises and suggestive language on city streets everywhere. Groping and deliberate bumping is common in bazars and other crowded places, especially in Uzbekistan. Taxi drivers often can't keep their hands to themselves. Gangs of grab-and-run kids are increasingly common in Samarkand, and probably elsewhere. In Tajikistan an aid workers' report referred to threatening incidents in corridors and lifts at Dushanbe hotels.

Even when there is no physical annoyance or threat, one cannot trust any local man completely, nor just wander and be left alone. Even in the company of a male companion, local people may tend to speak only to him.

The soundest advice, unfortunately, is that women should simply avoid travelling alone. And clothes *do* matter: a modest dress code is essential (even if local Russian women don't seem to have one). See Avoiding Offence in the Culture section of the Facts About the Region chapter, for more on the important matter of clothing.

Local women are not immune from hassles either. A Turkmen woman sharing a railway compartment with AH's fianceé confirmed that all this was part of her daily life too. In fact, when this woman realised they were billeted for the journey with two men, it was she who had the attendant rearrange things to form an all-female compartment. That is good advice in general on trains.

Sadly, the opportunities for genuine cross-cultural woman-to-woman interactions are limited outside larger cities, partly because relatively few local women speak any western language, and partly because tradition denies many of them the right to invite their own guests into their homes.

Pakistan, without even the pseudo-liberation of the Soviet years, is still more difficult

for women travellers, though much less so in Ismaili areas (Hunza and Gojal) along the northern KKH. China is by contrast an extraordinarily egalitarian place, where everyone is treated with equal rudeness and sexual hassles are rare.

USEFUL ORGANISATIONS
Technical Assistance Organisations

There are presently thousands of western technical assistance workers all over Central Asia – over 2000 in Tashkent alone – including a few real ideological missionaries (and the occasional religious missionary too). Of course they all have their own jobs to do, but many are happy to chat with visitors and help them to see beneath the surface of life here.

One of the single biggest representations is the US Peace Corps, involved in both English language teaching and business development. Peace Corps volunteers in remoter places may be delighted to talk their own language, see faces from home and offer useful tips, though they also seem to be incredibly busy. In smaller towns they tend to have a high profile, and almost everybody knows where to find them (Peace Corps is *Korpus Mira* in Russian).

Many of these volunteers have moved on to kick-start locally staffed 'networking' organisations to put local people in touch with foreign resources. These outfits are often happy to have visitors, especially those with something to offer, eg a little volunteer time, expertise or useful contacts. Some may also know of volunteer or other work opportunities. We have identified these under individual cities, including Tashkent, Samarkand and Bishkek.

Cultural Exchange

The Britain Russia Centre and the Britain East-West Centre (☎ (0171) 235 2116), 14 Grosvenor Place, London SW1X 7HW, and 4 Bruntsfield Crescent, Edinburgh EH10 4HD, (☎ (0131) 452 8132) encourage non-political contacts between Britons and the peoples of the old Soviet empire, with talks, films and other events.

The Society for Co-operation in Russian & Soviet Studies (☎ (0171) 274 2282, fax 274 3230), 320 Brixton Rd, London SW9 6AB, UK, organises artistic/cultural exchanges and study tours. Both have good libraries, publish small journals, sponsor talks, and offer student memberships.

The Royal Society for Asian Affairs

This small but venerable organisation on London's fashionable Belgrave Square has one of the best specialist libraries anywhere devoted to Asia, or rather westerners' views of Asia, including many out-of-print editions. Membership is steep, however, at about £31 a year. They're at 2 Belgrave Square, London SW1X 8PJ (☎ (0171) 235 5122, fax 259 6771).

Central Asia Political Discussion List (Cenasia)

Internetters can take part in, or just listen in on, informal electronic conversations among a constantly changing group of Central Asia scholars, expatriate workers and others, on topics as varied as politics, semantics and music. Bulletins also pop up all the time for specialist conferences and other events. This isn't your usual 'bulletin board' but a serious discussion forum. There's no charge, of course. To subscribe, send an e-mail message to listserve@vm1.mcgill.ca, with a message containing the words 'subscribe cenasia' and your first and last name.

Other Internet Information Some general Central Asia information sites are available on the Web. These include Welcome to Uzbekistan http://www.uni.uiuc.edu/%7Ekrasavin/sk/Uzbek.html and Welcome to Kazakstan (has links to Kyrgyzstan and Turkmenistan) http://ils.unc.edu/kiree/kazakhstan.html.

The Lonely Planet home page is http://www.lonelyplanet.com.

DANGERS & ANNOYANCES

Travel in Central Asia can be a delight for those who are ready for it, but a nightmare for the unprepared. Side by side with an almost legendary hospitality, you will find legions of beastly, often greedy, officials with a residual Soviet dislike of visitors. Starting before you even go, with the visa chase, don't expect anything to go smoothly. The other thing likely to make you miserable at some point is alcohol, drunk by others or by yourself.

Crime, though minimal by western urban standards, is on the rise everywhere, and visitors are tempting, high-profile targets. Especially in rural areas, the gap between some people's extreme poverty and your own relatively fantastic wealth can be simply

---

How You Can be Contacted

In an emergency the simplest way for someone to reach you from outside Central Asia is by telephone to your hotel, or by telegram which takes one to two days. Of course this depends on someone knowing where you're staying, and on cooperative hotel staff!

Most foreign offices maintain 24 hour emergency operators – eg the British Foreign Office (☎ 071-270 3000), the US State Department Citizens Center (☎ 202-647-5225; 647-4000 in off-hours), the Australian Department of Foreign Affairs & Trade (☎ 06-261 3331) – who can contact your embassy in one of the Central Asian capitals. Embassies prefer that other means have been exhausted before they're contacted.

Obviously they will be better able to track you down if you have let them know what your plans are. The US Embassy in Tashkent is keen for Americans to register their travel plans if they're passing through, though the one in Bishkek is not interested unless you'll be in Kyrgyzstan for three months or more. All of them suggest you carry the telephone numbers of your embassies in the region. ■

Government Travel Advice

The US State Department's Bureau of Consular Affairs, Washington, DC 20520, USA, issues periodically updated Consular Information Sheets that include entry requirements, medical facilities, crime information and other topics. They also have recorded travel information at ☎ 202-647-5225.

If you're on the Internet, you can subscribe to a mailing list for all current State Department travel advisories by sending a message containing the word 'subscribe' to travel-advisories-request@stolaf.edu (St Olaf College, Northfield MN, USA). You can check out current and past sheets or search by keywords via St Olaf's gopher server, gopher.stolaf.edu, in directory Internet Resources/US-State-Department-Travel-Advisories. St Olaf's World Wide Web server's URL is http://www.stolaf.edu/network/travel-advisories.html.

Get British Foreign Office travel advisories from the Travel Advice Unit, Foreign & Commonwealth Office, Room 605 Clive House, Petty France, London SW1H 9HD, UK, (☎ 071-270 4129, fax 270 4228). Regularly updated Foreign Office travel advice is also displayed on BBC2 Ceefax, pp 564 ff.

Australians can ring the Department of Foreign Affairs advice line in Canberra on ☎ 06-261 3305 for advisories on specific countries. Also, any travel agent hooked up to the Apollo, Fantasia or Galileo networks (which covers most if not all of them) can access these advisories directly. ∎

---

too big to bridge enjoyably. In some conservative areas like the Ferghana Valley you may find a few sour faces shown to non-Muslims, especially women. Local and regional transport can be unpredictable, uncomfortable and occasionally unsafe. And, churlish as it sounds, some Central Asian 'hospitality' can be just too much to bear.

This section, all about the headaches, is not meant to put you off but to prepare you for the worst. Patience, tolerance, a thick skin and a good sense of humour are a big help too. Here's hoping you run into none of these problems.

Emergencies

Many kinds of emergencies are covered in other sections of this chapter: see Health for medical emergencies; Money for lost or stolen travellers' cheques, credit cards and money; and Visas for Central Asian republics, under Visas & Embassies, for lost or stolen visas and passports.

Your embassy in the nearest capital city is your best first stop in any emergency, but bear in mind that there are some things they cannot do for you. These include: getting local laws or regulations waived because you are a foreigner; investigating a crime; providing legal advice or representation in civil or criminal cases; getting you out of jail, or even getting you better treatment there than local people get; lending money (the UK embassy can do this in exceptional circumstances) or paying your bills. Nor can your embassy trace you if you haven't left them any information about where you're going.

Standard emergency telephone numbers, with calls free from public telephones in most sizeable towns of the former Soviet Union, include ☎ 01 for the police, ☎ 02 for the fire brigade (or vice-versa) and ☎ 03 for an ambulance. But these all tend to be pretty unreliable, and further hampered by the language barrier. Where we have found alternatives, we identify them under individual towns.

Tajikistan

Civil strife in Tajikistan presents extraordinary dangers for travellers at present, except in the north around Khojand, and in the vicinity of Penjikent. See the Safety in Tajikistan aside, in the Tajikistan chapter introduction.

Alcohol & Assault-by-Hospitality

Whether it's being poured down your throat by a zealous host, or driving others into states of pathological melancholy, brotherly love, anger or violence, alcohol is one of the biggest problems travellers now face in the former Soviet Union. The Islamic injunction against alcohol has had little obvious impact in Central Asia. Some Central Asians drink vodka in moderation, though Russians seem to slam the stuff back with the sole aim of getting blitzed as quickly as possible.

Many foreigners fall victim to what one worn-out expatriate resident calls 'terrorist hospitality'. Initially flattered by the attention and afraid of giving offence by refusing, they end up bullied by would-be hosts into going places they don't want to go, eating things they don't want to eat, and of course washing it down with more vodka than their systems can stand – all administered with toasts to international friendship which boost the moral pressure and magnify their guilt. The host-cum-captor rarely pays any attention to their condition, wishes or alibis. Such overbearing treatment can come not just from the odd garrulous drunk but from the most apparently urbane of dinner hosts. Your only recourse is to refuse politely but firmly, without wavering or falling for the 'just one little drink' line. Friendships based on such treatment can be skipped. For more tips on coping with alcohol over meals, see Vodka in the Food & Drink section of this chapter.

Alcoholism is epidemic in the former USSR, and after dark the streets of most Central Asian towns fill with drunks – ranging from the obnoxious to the downright dangerous. This is especially true in economically depressed areas, where violence hovers just below the surface, and young men may grow abruptly violent, seemingly at random. Take your strolls during the day, and stay inside or travel by taxi after dark.

General Greed

Real knowledge of the world outside (as opposed to the fantasy representations on imported TV soaps) is hard to come by for Central Asians in remoter places, and we are the subject of every kind of exaggerated rumour about our collective wealth. The less scrupulous feel justified in squeezing from us everything they can. A Dushanbe taxi driver who had just overcharged AH told him he had no right to complain when westerners earn at least US$15,000 per month! The official manifestation of this is the two-tier pricing system for hotels, flights and train tickets, though there is some justification for that.

It's important to add that most local people we met couldn't be dishonest if they tried. We ordered plov from a Tashkent stall and to our 'skolko stoit?' the proprietor replied with downcast eyes, '20 sum'. We said nothing but just cleared our throats and looked at him. 'Fifteen,' he muttered; we stayed accusingly silent. 'Okay, nine sum,' he surrendered, 'I'm sorry'.

Crime

With the lifting of the Soviet lid, crime has exploded. 'Democracy' is now OK, and to most people who never thought about it before, that means the freedom to do whatever you want. 'Capitalism' is OK too, and that means the freedom to get money any way you can. With the arrival of large numbers of western visitors, often with conspicuously more in their pockets or on their backs than a rural labourer can earn in several years, the temptations can be immense. The wonder is that there is not more crime against visitors, and it may be Islam that keeps most people honest.

Incidents of mugging, theft and pickpocketing are on the rise in cities and towns of all the former Soviet republics (though it must be said that these have risen from near-zero levels in Soviet days, and don't even approach the levels in many western cities). The best defence is common sense. Don't be paranoid but be careful. Group or package tourists are not at risk, being effectively guests of the state.

Refer to Security, under Money in this chapter, on sensible ways to handle your money. Other tips, especially for individual travellers, include:

- Dress down, and keep expensive jewellery, watches and cameras out of sight; carry only as much cash as you would be willing to surrender to a thief (which is the sensible alternative to resistance in every case).
- Be especially alert in crowded situations such as bazars and bus-station ticket scrums, where pockets and purses may be easily picked.
- Avoid going out at night, or at least go in a large group; avoid parks at night, even if it means going a long way out of your way.
- Do not approach groups of men after dark or even pass close by, and at all costs, stay away from drunks.
- Take officially licensed taxis in preference to private ones (in the major town sections we have tried to indicate how to distinguish one from the other); some people also advise against climbing into any taxi with more than the driver in them, and against sharing it with other passengers.

Western men who speak Russian have on rare occasions been mistaken for Russians by drunken young Central Asians out for an evening of Slav-bashing. If you're physically threatened under these circumstances, you're somewhat less likely to have a punch thrown at you if you make it clear you're a westerner.

Travellers who rent a flat in Tashkent are warned to be sure the doors and windows are secure, and *never* to open the door – day or night – to anyone they do not clearly know, because of the danger of robbery or worse. It's good advice in Bishkek and other big cities too.

Cons are almost as common as crimes. A common one, at least in Bishkek, involves what looks like accidentally dropped money. If you pick it up, someone rushes up saying it's theirs; if you hand it back you may be accused of substituting a smaller note, and unpleasantries can escalate. There are also two-person variants of this scam. Play it safe and let it lie.

If you're the victim of a crime, contact the *militsia* (police), though you may get no help from them at all. Get a report from them if you hope to claim on insurance for anything that was stolen, and contact your own closest embassy for a report in English. If your passport is stolen, the police should also provide a letter to OVIR, essential for replac-ing your visa. See the Money section in this chapter about loss or theft of credit cards or travellers' cheques.

By contrast with the former Soviet Central Asian countries, China and Pakistan are generally quite safe for travellers, except in parts of China's biggest cities, and in the remote areas off the Karakoram Highway south of Gilgit in Pakistan.

Crooked Officials

Unfortunately you cannot rely on the police for much help in Central Asia. A few officers are helpful and honest, and many are just bureaucratic ciphers, but a lot, especially at lower echelons, are venal and corrupt, and there is nobody to protect you from them! This seems especially true in Uzbekistan and Kyrgyzstan, and more so in remoter places. Uzbekistan has police checkposts at most municipal and provincial borders, and it's a near certainty you'll meet a gendarme or two in every bus and train station, wanting to see your papers and know where you're going.

If you are approached by the police, your best bet is to be polite and agreeable; cringing tends to make you more of a target, while an uncooperative attitude will only get their backs up. A forthright, friendly manner – starting right out with a *salam aleykhum* and a handshake for whomever appears to be in charge – may help to defuse a potential shakedown, whether you are male or female. If someone refers to a 'regulation', ask to see it in writing. If you are dealing with lower-level officers, ask to see their *administrator* (chief).

Try to avoid being taken somewhere out of the public eye, eg into an office or into the shadows; it should be just as easy to talk right where you are. The objective of most detentions of westerners is simply to extort money, and by means of intimidation rather than violence. If your money is buried deeply, and you're prepared to pull out a paperback and wait them out, and even to miss the next bus or train, most inquisitors will eventually give up. Make it harder for them by speaking only in your own language.

On the street, you are almost as likely to

be hassled by police as by non-uniformed crooks. Young, bored cops in Bishkek are well known for shaking down foreigners to boost their small earnings, and there are stories of planted drugs. If officers show signs of force or violence, and *provided they are not drunk*, do not be afraid to make a scene – dishonest cops will dislike such exposure. Two plainclothes officers tried to frogmarch JK away from a bus station at Kara Kul on the Bishkek-Osh road, until he started yelling in English.

In fact, just about anybody holding any kind of power seems liable to abuse it. A friend was waiting for her train (again at Tashkent station) with a ticket bought for dollars from the foreigners' window, when a uniformed official asked her to go to his office. There he accused her of being a thief and trying to travel on a local-price ticket (which it patently wasn't) and threatened her with prison. He would let her go, he said, if she paid a $100 fine. But she held out, and in the end, two minutes before the train departed, he gave up the charade and let her go without a fine.

It's unlikely you will ever be actually arrested, unless there are supportable charges against you. If you are arrested, authorities in the former Soviet states are obliged to inform your embassy immediately and allow you to communicate with a consular official without delay.

Crime on the Rails

Robberies on long-distance trains have increased. Try to get a compartment with friends, be careful about who you invite in, never the leave the compartment unattended, and keep the door securely locked at night. The UK Foreign Office advises tying the door closed from the inside with wire or strong cord; paranoid as that may sound, travellers have indeed reported attempts by strangers to enter their compartments at night. Stash your bags in the compartment under the lower bunk, not in the overhead spaces.

Many of the crooks are in uniform. On the Moscow-Urgench train, after customs offi-

cers had taken their pick of passengers' goods at the Uzbek border, a policeman entered the compartment of three British travellers and demanded US$50 from each or he would throw them off the train, though all had valid tickets. They stood their ground and soon whittled him down to a single US$5 note and three packets of cigarettes, though not all officials are this easily bribed.

The Border Crossing from Hell

Despite being the final link in a potential rail journey from Shanghai to Paris, through the Tian Shan and along the Kazak Steppe, a trip on the relatively new Ürümqi-Almaty line is definitely not recommended, simply because of the unpleasant China-Kazakstan border crossing. Border procedures, changing of bogeys (between Chinese and Russian track gauges) and general waiting around takes up to eight hours, during which there is no exit from the train, no water and, except for a desperate 10 minutes between the Chinese and Kazak posts, no toilets.

This, however, is nothing compared to the systematic, humiliating plunder of each train's captive passengers by the laughing Russian and Kazak customs and immigration officials at the Kazak border post at Dostyq (the Kazak translation of the deeply ironic Russian name, Druzhba or 'Friendship'). For more information on this ugly experience, see Crossing by Rail in the Kazakstan chapter.

Like Chinese officials elsewhere, those at Alashankou on the Chinese side are officious and thorough but essentially honest. Travellers report no such hassles on the bus journey in either direction.

Trekking Problems

While most commonly used trekking routes are quite safe, there are reports of bandits in the mountains between Almaty and Lake Issyk-Kul, and there are *guligans* (hooligans) everywhere in rural areas, who are usually just dirt-poor herders. Reliable trekking guides (including those listed in this book) have thought about this already; some take guards or dogs along for protection, while others do careful advance PR along their routes. It's definitely not smart to just strike out into back country on your own in Central Asia.

Drugs

Marijuana grows openly in many parts of Turkmenistan, Kyrgyzstan and Kazakstan, and is seen as an increasingly profitable cash crop. A 1994 UN survey estimated there were several hundred thousand hectares of opium poppies in Kyrgyzstan and Kazakstan. Visitors are subject to the laws of the country they're visiting, and penalties in the Central Asian republics for possession, use and trafficking include fines and jail sentences. Don't risk it.

Nasvai

You may notice some men chewing and copiously spitting, or talking as if their mouth were full of saliva. *Nasvai* or *nasvar* is basically finely crushed tobacco, sometimes cut with spices, ash or lime. As a greenish sludge or as little pellets, it's stuffed under the tongue or inside the cheek, from where the active ingredients leach into the bloodstream, revving up the user's heart rate and self-image. Amateurs who fail to clamp it tightly in place, thus allowing the effluent to leak into the throat, may be consumed with nausea.

Before you try it, bear in mind that nasvai is often cut with opium, and can be quite potent. ■

Domestic Flights

Not everyone is happy with the thought of flying in an ageing Soviet or Chinese-built airplane, and aircraft maintenance is not always up to snuff with the descendants of Aeroflot (the old Soviet mega-airline), nor with the many regional splinter airlines now operating throughout China. Uzbekistan Airways airplanes, however, are maintained by Lufthansa-trained staff. Refer to the Getting Around chapter for more on travel safety in Central Asia.

Other Annoyances

Getting bus and train tickets can be like a rugby scrum, with the occasional added ingredient of organised pickpockets in the churning crowds around the ticket windows. Departures of internal flights as well as ground transport are always subject to delay or cancellation.

Finding a decent meal, especially if you are a vegetarian, is an occasion for celebration. Refer to the Food section in this chapter.

Other common Central Asian irritants include museums, shops – and even some restaurants, for pity's sake – that close for lunch, and sometimes indefinitely for 'repairs'; alcoholic late-night comings, goings and door-banging in hotel corridors; and the brain-numbing volume of restaurant bands.

According to travellers' tales, in some hotels in the religiously conservative Ferghana Valley, eg in Kokand and Jalal-Abad, heterosexual couples were unable to stay in the same room unless their passports showed they were married.

BUSINESS HOURS

All business hours seem mutable in the former Soviet republics. Foreign exchange banks usually open from 9 or 10 am to noon or 1 pm on weekdays, and those in major cities sometimes in the afternoon and evening too. Exchange offices in tourist hotels may keep longer hours, including weekends. Post and telephone offices are typically open from 8 am to 5 pm on weekdays, with the central offices sometimes open on weekends too. Government office hours are usually 9 or 10 am to 5 or 6 pm on weekdays.

Most shops are open Monday to Saturday from 10 or 11 am to 7 or 8 pm, with a one hour lunch break at 1 or 2 pm. Department stores may stay open from 8 am to 8 or 9 pm without a break. Food shops are usually open from 7 or 8 am to 8 pm except for a lunch break; some open on Sundays too. A few shops stay open through the weekend and close Mondays. Bigger bazars open at 6 or 7 am and carry on until 8 pm in summer.

Restaurants typically open from 11 am or noon to 11 pm or midnight, with a break in the afternoon; cafés may open and close earlier.

Museum hours change like quicksilver, as do their weekly days off. Most shut entrance doors 30 minutes or an hour before closing time, and have shorter hours on the day *before* their day off. Some just seem to close without reason and a few stay that way for years.

Public places in the former Soviet republics often display their business days visually, as a stack of seven horizontal bars with the top one representing Monday; blue means open, red means closed.

In Pakistan nearly everything official is closed on Friday, the Muslim day of rest, and often for a half-day on Thursday or Saturday. In Xinjiang the official day of rest is Sunday; a few offices may take a half-day off on Saturday too.

PUBLIC HOLIDAYS & SPECIAL EVENTS
National Holidays
Banks, businesses and government offices are closed on the following dates. Though single dates are listed for most, you may find office workers pushing their chairs back and commencing to eat and drink early on the day before as well.

1 January
  New Year's Day (Kyr, Kaz, Taj, Tur, Uzb, China, plus Kaz 31 December or 2 January)
7 January
  Russian Orthodox Christmas (Kyr)
12 January
  Remembrance Day, anniversary of the 1948 earthquake (Tur)
Late January-Early March
  Spring Festival or Chinese New Year, the biggest holiday of the year for the Chinese, their only three day break. It's calculated on the Chinese lunar calendar so dates change from year to year. Chinese embassies elsewhere are also closed (China)
28 January
  Kazakstan Constitution Day (Kaz)
19 February
  National Flag Day, formerly a celebration of the president's birthday (Tur)

8 March
  International Women's Day (Kaz, Kyr, Taj, Tur, Uzb, China)
21 March (approximately)
  Navrus, major spring festival; see the following Cultural Events section (Kaz, Kyr, Taj, Tur, Uzb, Pak)
23 March
  Pakistan Day, celebrating the 1956 proclamation of Pakistan as a republic (Pak)
1 May
  International Labour Day (Kaz, Kyr, Taj, Tur, Uzb, China, Pak)
4 May
  Youth Day (China)
5 May
  Constitution Day (Kyr)
9 May
  Victory Day, a commemoration of the end of WWII for the USSR in 1945 (Kaz, Kyr, Taj, Tur, Uzb)
18 May
  Day of Revival & Unity (Tur)
29 May
  Armed Forces Day (Kyr)
1 June
  Children's Day (China)
1 July
  Anniversary of the founding of the Communist Party of China (China)
1 July
  Bank holiday, but government offices and businesses remain open (Pak)
1 August
  Anniversary of the founding of the People's Liberation Army (China)
14 August
  Independence Day (Pak)
31 August
  Kyrgyzstan Independence Day (Kyr)
1 September
  Independence Day (Uzb)
6 September
  Defence of Pakistan Day, commemorating the India-Pakistan War of 1965 (Pak)
11 September
  Anniversary of the death of Mohammed Ali Jinnah, regarded as the founder of Pakistan (Pak)
1 October
  National Day, celebrating the founding of the People's Republic of China in 1949 (China)
25 October
  Republic Day (Kaz)
27 October
  Turkmenistan Independence Day (Tur)
9 November
  Iqbal Day, honouring the poet Mohammed Iqbal, who in 1930 first proposed the idea of a Muslim Pakistan (Pak)

8 December
Uzbekistan Constitution Day (Uzb)
16 December
Kazakstan Independence Day (Kaz)
25 December
Birthday of Mohammed Ali Jinnah, regarded as the founder of Pakistan (Pak)
31 December
Bank holiday, but government offices and businesses remain open (Pak)

Navrus

By far the biggest Central Asian holiday is the spring festival of Navrus ('New Days' – Nauryz in Kazak, Novruz in Turkmen, Nooruz in Kyrgyz, Nauroz in Urdu, etc), an Islamic adaptation of pre-Islamic vernal equinox or renewal celebrations, celebrated approximately on the vernal equinox.

In Soviet times this was a private affair, with special foods prepared at home, including a wheat dish called *sumalakh* for women and a dish from young beef, *khalem*, for men. In 1989, in one of several attempts to deflect growing Muslim nationalism, Navruz was adopted by the then-Soviet Central Asian republics as an official two day festival, with traditional games, music and drama festivals, street art and colourful fairs, plus much partying and visiting.

It's celebrated in a low-key way in Pakistan but is not a public holiday. Polo matches may be held in Gilgit; in smaller Northern Areas villages there is visiting, and sometimes music and dancing. It's also celebrated in parts of Afghanistan, Iran, Azerbaijan and India.

Muslim Holy Days

The Islamic calendar is lunar, and shorter than the western solar calendar, beginning 10 to 11 days earlier in each solar year. Modern astronomy notwithstanding, religious officials have formal authority to declare the beginning of each lunar month, based on sightings of the moon's first crescent. Future holy days can be estimated, but are in doubt by a few days until the start of that month, so dates given here are only approximate. They normally run from sunset to the next sunset.

Ramadan and Qurban are observed with

little fanfare in most of Central Asia (where travellers will find plenty of food available in any case), while these and several other holy days are taken quite seriously in Pakistan. The first day of each Eid is a public holiday in Uzbekistan and Pakistan.

10 January (1997), 31 December (1997), 20 December (1998), 9 December (1999)
Ramadan or Ramazan, the month of sunrise-to-sunset fasting (see Religion in the Facts about the Region chapter for more information).
22 February (1997), 31 January (1998), 20 January (1999)
Eid-ul-Fitr (also called Hayit in Uzbekistan, Orozo Ait in Kyrgyzstan, Ruza Eid in Xinjiang, Chhoti Eid or Small Eid in Pakistan), two or three days of celebrations at the end of Ramadan, with family visits, gifts, banquets and donations to the poor.
14 April (1997), 8 April (1998), 28 March (1999)
Eid-ul-Azha (also called Qurban, Qurban Hayit or similar names in Central Asia, Bari Eid or Big Eid in Pakistan), the Feast of Sacrifice. This is also celebrated over several days. Those who can afford it buy and slaughter an animal, sharing the meat with relatives and with the poor. This is also the season for hajj (pilgrimage to Mecca).

Other Events

Every September, Tashkent hosts a festival featuring Asian, African and Latin American films. For three or four days in early August each year, Medeu (outside Almaty) hosts the Voice of Asia rock festival, with bands from all over the CIS and Asia.

One upshot of the post-Soviet urge to establish national identities (and coax in a few more tourist dollars) is a rash of anniversaries, some of them fairly preposterous – eg 1000 years of *Manas*, the Kyrgyz collection of oral epics (though they are not based on any single person or event), 3000 years of Osh (dating from what?), 600 years of Ulughbek and so on. Turkmenistan is said to be planning a National Carpet Day and a National Horse Day, both in March.

On 1 November Pakistan's Northern Areas celebrate their Independence Day, commemorating the local 1947 uprising against the Maharajah of Kashmir after he decided to join India. The major event is a week-long polo tournament in Gilgit, starting on Independence Day. Polo matches are also common in Gilgit in April.

ACTIVITIES

Following is an indication of the possibilities for adventure-travel in the region. Refer to the country chapters for more details on where to go, what to do, and with whom. We list overseas agencies with Central Asia, Xinjiang and KKH-area adventure-travel programmes under Travel & Visa Agencies in the Getting There & Away chapter.

Trekking & Mountaineering

The various arms of the Tian Shan and Pamir ranges present some grand opportunities for both trekking and climbing. Top of the line for altitude junkies are Khan-Tengri, Pobedy and other peaks of the central Tian Shan in eastern Kyrgyzstan and south-east Kazakstan. The ranges below (west of) these summits also offer fine treks of up to two or three weeks. The other prime high-altitude playground is the Pamir in eastern Tajikistan, but turmoil in that country puts much of it out of reach at present.

The Alatau – a northern arm of the Tian Shan – stretches west from Lake Issyk-Kul in Kyrgyzstan towards Tashkent, Shymkent and Zhambyl. There are good trips across the Zailiysky and Küngey Alatau between Almaty and Issyk-Kul. Some of Central Asia's most accessible and beautiful treks are in the Kyrgyz Alatau above Bishkek. In the Talassky Alatau range between Shymkent and Zhambyl is the Aqsu-Zhabaghly nature reserve.

East of Taldy-Qorghan in Kazakstan is the smaller Zhungar Alatau range, with additional opportunities in the Altay mountains of far north-east Kazakstan.

One of Central Asia's better-known trekking areas is the Fan mountains, at the western end of the Alay range (along the Kyrgyzstan-Tajikistan border), far from Tajikistan's civil strife and safely accessible from Samarkand in Uzbekistan.

Turkmenistan's Kopet Dag mountains are mostly out of bounds because they form the sensitive border with Iran, although Sputnik Turkmenistan (see Ashghabat) can organise supervised hiking trips of up to two weeks there.

Bring your own equipment. Though agencies may have bits and pieces, gear is hard to find anywhere in the region. Sleeping bags are especially scarce.

In May 1995 an American trekker died of exposure in the mountains above Almaty after being caught, dressed in shorts and T-shirt, in a sudden spring storm. The best walking season is June through September, but be ready for bad weather at any time.

Banditry is a problem in some areas – eg the Zailiysky and Küngey Alatau between Almaty and Issyk-Kul, and low-traffic areas all over Kyrgyzstan. Trustworthy local knowledge, and preferably a local guide, are essential for trekking in Central Asia. The safest way to go is with a reliable agency. In the country chapters we identify places where you can safely go on your own.

An essential resource for all serious trekkers and climbers is Frith Maier's *Trekking in Russia & Central Asia*. It provides information on seasons, paperwork, safety, equipment, detailed routes and more; see the Books section in this chapter for further details.

Trekking in Xinjiang In the Kashgar-Tashkurgan region the most accessible treks are around Karakul Lake and the lower reaches of Mt Kongur and Muztagh Ata. This is a restricted area, for which you need a travel permit, and for visits of more than a day or so it's wise to make arrangements through a local agency (see the Kashgar section in the Western Xinjiang & the KKH chapter).

Trekking in Northern Pakistan Trekking and climbing in the Karakoram – with some of the world's highest mountains and longest glaciers – is a serious business for participants and government alike. The Pakistan Ministry of Culture, Sports & Tourism has designated open, restricted and closed zones. Treks in open zones are well removed from sensitive areas and need no permits; routes and arrangements, and guides if you want them, are up to you. Restricted zones include sensitive areas and anything above 6000 metres, and travel there requires more planning, is expensive and bound by red tape.

The treks near the KKH noted in this book are all in open zones. The popular big treks – and the messy business of arranging porters and guides – are described in detail in LP's upcoming *Trekking in the Karakoram & Hindukush*, and in less detail in *Pakistan – a travel survival kit*. A booklet setting out regulations, permit procedures, recommended agencies and a more or less current list of 'approved' treks is *Trekking Rules and Regulations*, available from the Deputy Chief for Operations, Tourism Division, College Rd, Sector F-7/2, Islamabad, Pakistan.

Horse & Camel Treks

Some of the agencies that arrange treks can also set up mountain or desert horse treks. ESCAP-UNEP (see Ashghabat) can arrange eight day camel treks from Merv across the Karakum desert to Konye-Urgench, and might also be able to arrange trips with Turkmenistan's famed Akhal-Teke horses.

Skiing

Central Asia's ski season is approximately November or December to March or April, with local variations. The region's best-known downhill area is Shymbulaq (Russian: Chimbulak), day trip distance from Almaty, and February is the best time to be there. Second-best are the Kyrgyz Alatau valleys (especially Ala-Archa) south of Bishkek, and the Chimgan area above Tashkent. Another good base for skiing is Karakol on Lake Issyk-Kul. Summer skiing is sometimes possible at Ala-Archa and above Karakol.

A few travel firms in Kazakstan and Kyrgyzstan offer ski-mountaineering trips in the central Tian Shan in July and August, and in the Alatau ranges between Almaty and Lake Issyk-Kul from February through April.

Nearly every sports-related agency in Central Asia appears to offer heli-skiing (in which old Aeroflot helicopters drop you off on remote high peaks and you ski down), probably because a few ski junkies have come over and spent big bucks on it.

Boating

A good venue for rafting and kayaking at all skill levels is Tashkent, where you can find flat water on the Syr-Darya and Angren rivers, and more exciting stretches on the Ugam, Chatkal and Pskem. The best season is September through October. There is easy rafting and canoeing on the Ili river between Lake Qapshaghay and Lake Balqash, north of Almaty, from mid-April to mid-October. Several agencies in Kazakstan, Kyrgyzstan and Uzbekistan will arrange multi-day descents of remote rivers.

A few Pakistan agencies can provide support for white-water rafting or kayaking. A stretch near the northern KKH that's open for rafting or kayaking is the Hunza river from Aliabad to Gilgit.

Other Activities

Some of the same agencies which arrange treks can also set up mountain bike trips (with their own bikes), and bird-watching and botanical trips. Sputnik Turkmenistan offers hang-gliding. Some Pakistan agencies offer packages for fishing trips, yak or pony treks, jeep safaris and bicycle trips.

ACCOMMODATION
Central Asia

In much of the region there is little alternative to the miserable tourist hotels left over from Soviet days, but in areas with significant tourist, business or technical-assistance traffic, alternatives are springing up.

Places once closed to foreigners, such as hotels and resorts for Party bigwigs, and hostels and *turbaza*s (holiday camps) for the proletariat, have opened their doors to all. High-elevation camps once reserved for guests of state sports organisations have done the same. You can pitch your own tent at these and at most turbazas. You can even sleep in a few old medressas, eg in Bukhara and Khiva.

Best of all, some sensibly priced guest-houses have appeared, along with a growing number of private homes where spare rooms are being turned into money-spinners. These cast a harsh light on the hideously bad deals at most former Soviet hotels; the difference between what US$15 gets you at Tashkent's Hotel Rossiya and at a private home in Samarkand, for example, is staggering.

Changes are uneven across the region. While Kazakstan, Kyrgyzstan and Uzbekistan still abound in Soviet-era fossils, they also have some of the best alternatives. Turkmenistan has little beyond hotels and some homestays. In Tajikistan, Dushanbe and Khojand are stuck in the Soviet era, while much of the civil-war-ravaged interior has nothing at all.

Thankfully, it's no longer essential to book all your accommodation in advance at exorbitant prices, as it was before independence, although Uzbektourism is trying hard to carry on that old Intourist tradition.

Price Categories Rates in this book are, unless otherwise noted, for the most basic double room with attached toilet and shower, without breakfast, for individual travellers without advance bookings. Approximate price categories are: bottom end, US$30 or less; middle, up to US$80; and top end, over US$80.

We do not mention all of a hotel's top-end options. Even the worst often have a few *lyux* (deluxe) suites for about twice the price, sometimes with a bathtub – to which they may try to steer you by saying nothing else is available.

Greed is epidemic in Central Asia, and you can expect prices to jump every year; rates in this book are therefore an indication more of *relative* than absolute values.

Hotels Though some are better than others, you almost never get what you pay for in Soviet-era tourist hotels. Many were in better shape before 1991, but the subsidies have now run out. Doorknobs may come off in

your hand; windows may not open, or not close. Electricity is usually dicey with dim or missing light bulbs. Toilets that leak but don't flush give bathrooms a permanent aroma and some bathrooms have permanent cockroach colonies. Despite the dry climate, hotel room walls are often mouldy. All beds are single, with pillows the size of suitcases. Guests themselves are viewed basically as hard-currency dispensers, ranking somewhere below room cleaners in the pecking order, with non-group guests often effectively invisible.

Some hotels take only prebooked guests, although most now accept walk-ins if there is space, often at higher rates. If they say 'no room' there may be one anyway, though you probably won't get it by demanding it or going to the manager. Instead, take advantage of the Islamic habit of hospitality to strangers, or any residual Slavic instinct for generosity – hang around in the lobby looking desperate; ask kindly looking older ladies (not younger men) behind the counter if they know of anyone with a room to let. Someone may relent, or suggest something better.

Where, you may ask, do ordinary local people stay? Some stay at these very places, at more fitting rates from 50% to 90% below yours. Some stay in municipal hotels that don't want foreign guests – perhaps because they're still unsure what the post-Soviet

---

Floor-Ladies

Each floor in Soviet-style tourist hotels usually has a 'floor-lady' (*dezhurnaya*, Russian for 'woman on duty') to keep an eye on things. Often the most godawful hotel can be redeemed by a big-hearted floor-lady, of which there are still many. They can smile, for one thing. They may also boil up water for hot drinks, find someone to do your washing, find a light bulb or stash your bags while you're off on an excursion. The best of them deserve a small gift such as Western sweets or scented soaps before you leave. ■

about 10% (although Tashkent's Hotel Rossiya takes a pocket-lining 50%).

Group rates for equivalent rooms are usually quite a bit lower, and Uzbektourism hotels claim to give a 20% discount, even to individuals, for booking ahead through an Uzbektourism-approved overseas agency. Waving a student or other card can get worthwhile discounts here and there; a traveller with a diving-club card got 50% off in one smaller place!

Private Guesthouses We note private places wherever we found them. Rates tend to be bottom-end or mid-range – eg in Khiva, US$10 for two at the Hotel Orkanchi or US$30 for two in the Muhammad Amin Khan medressa; and in Bukhara, US$40 for a double at Sasha & Lena's B&B.

Homestays These are happily on the increase, though potential hosts still usually face burdensome OVIR requirements about registration of guests. For your own room and a breakfast of some description (and, if you're lucky, information about the town) you'll probably pay US$10 to US$20 per person per night.

Don't expect hotel-style comforts; toilets, for example, are likely to be squatters. Don't expect anything exotic either – you may well end up in a block of flats, in front of a TV all evening. And you may not get as much privacy as you'd like, as hosts are often hungry to learn all about you and your country.

Potential hosts may buttonhole you as you alight at a station or enter a tourist hotel. You may also hear of contacts from sympathetic hotel staff. Many private travel agencies (noted under each town) can set you up with someone, and these are probably the most reliable and most experienced with foreigners, though prices may be a shade higher. Some agencies in the West specialise in advance-booked homestays; see the Visa & Travel Agencies section of the Getting There & Away chapter for a list of some.

In our experience, older people, women and Russians tend to be the most honest to

---

Late-Night Telephone Calls

Those late-night calls to your room aren't wrong numbers. All hotels with significant numbers of foreigners attract prostitutes. Women guests rarely seem to get unexpected calls (and a friend staying at Almaty's Hotel Zhetysu got one from someone who knew his name), so somebody at the front desk knows what's going on. All you can do is work out how to temporarily disable your telephone. ■

---

rules are, perhaps because they can't bother dealing with foreigners' high expectations. These days, of course, most local people cannot afford to leave home in the first place.

A limited number of elegant Party or government places, eg Samarkand's mayoral guesthouses, and the spas of Lake Issyk-Kul in Kyrgyzstan, are now open to all, though even these are not all bargains. Truly international standard hotels – eg Almaty's Rachat Palace, and several Indian-financed hotels in Uzbekistan – are still scarce in Central Asia.

If you're staying at a bottom-end hotel which doesn't have hot water, ask about the local *banya* (public bath), which does. See Public Baths in this chapter.

Most hotels take your passport and visa for anywhere from half an hour to your entire stay, to do the required registration paperwork, and to keep you from leaving without paying. Don't forget them when you leave – no-one is likely to remind you.

Rates For individual travellers, standard Soviet-era tourist hotels at the time of research were asking anywhere from US$30 to well over US$100 a night for double rooms arguably worth half that. For a minimum of comfort you'll probably have to part with at least US$20 to US$30 in bigger towns; in tattier hotels, and small towns, you could get by for US$10 to US$15 or even less. It's common to be hit with an extra 'booking charge' for the first night, usually deal with. Find out exactly what you're paying for: where the place is, and what kind of transport is available. Verify that you'll have a room of your own, and breakfast, if you want them.

Friends you meet on the road may invite you home and ask nothing for it, but remember that most ordinary people have very limited resources (see Hospitality in the Culture section of the Facts About the Region chapter). And staying with someone who hasn't gone through official channels with OVIR could put them at risk, especially if your own papers aren't in order.

Resident Westerners may also offer you a place to sleep – they're a friendly bunch by and large.

Hostels & Student Accommodation
Cheap dormitory rooms are available at some universities, eg in Almaty and Tashkent, for about US$10 per person. The KIMEP hostel in Almaty has doubles with common toilet and shower for under US$6.

Other Possibilities Turbazas are great bargains, although most are only open in summer. The best ones are mostly in out-of-the-way places (though accessible by road), surrounded by grand scenery. Most have bungalows and places to pitch your own tent. Turbazas near towns and cities are sometimes downright awful – run-down, grotty and depressing.

Another place to check for rock-bottom accommodation in larger towns is the main sports stadium, which may have an athlete's hostel that will accept foreigners.

Some nature reserves – eg Aqsu-Zhabaghly nature reserve in Kazakstan – have sleeping huts for visitors. A reader suggests that some railway stations may still have *komnaty otdykha* (resting rooms) where a bed in a triple, quad or big dormitory, with minimal security, is a few dollars.

Western China & Northern Pakistan
Hotels Hotels are mostly state-run in China, mostly private in Pakistan. Prices aren't always fixed in Pakistan; in the Northern

Areas, westerners may be charged *less* than down-country 'Punjabis'. Mainstream hotels in Pakistan sometimes have cheap rope-beds on the roof, if you ask.

Government Resthouses These include some of the best mid-range bargains on the KKH. Also called Circuit Houses, Inspection Bungalows or Dak Bungalows, most are guesthouses run by government agencies for staff on business but available to tourists (at higher rates) if no-one else is using them. The best are in isolated, idyllic locations and each has a *chowkidar* (caretaker) living nearby who can, by arrangement, prepare at-cost meals from whatever's available.

Homestays The PakistanTourism Development Corporation and the Aga Khan Rural Support Programme have initiated a successful 'Village Guest House' programme, in which tourists can book comfortable rooms and meals in private homes all over the Gilgit and Hunza valleys for about Rs 250 for a double. Contact them in Gilgit at ☎ 2562 or via Pakistan Tours Ltd in Rawalpindi at ☎ 563038.

Camping In Xinjiang you can't safely pitch a tent around larger towns but with a travel permit you can camp at places like Karakul and below Muztagh Ata. In Pakistan, hotels will often let you pitch a tent in their yards or on the roof and charge a small fee to use their toilets.

FOOD
Few westerners are familiar with Central Asian cuisine, and most visitors encounter it only in dismal tourist restaurants or grotty kebab stands. A large repertoire of dishes is common to most of the region, and every locale has its own specialities as well. It's amazing how many good and nutritious ways there are to combine mutton, noodles, onions, peppers and vegetables! The best way to appreciate this, and the region's extraordinary hospitality, is at a meal in a private home.

Local Food

Central Asian food resembles that of the Middle East or the Mediterranean in its use of rice, savoury seasonings, vegetables and legumes, yoghurt and grilled meats. Many dishes may seem familiar from elsewhere – *laghman* (like Chinese noodles), *plov* (similar to Persian rice pilafs), *nan* or flatbreads (found all over Asia), pumpkin-filled *samsa* (the 'samosa' of India), and *paklama* (like Greek baklava). Others are more unusual, like sun-dried tomato dumplings or horsemeat sausage.

The cuisine falls into three overlapping groups. First is the once-nomadic subsistence diet in large areas of Kazakstan, Kyrgyzstan and Turkmenistan – mainly meat (including entrails), milk products and bread. Second is the diet of the Uzbeks and Uyghurs (settled Turks), including pilafs, kebabs, noodles and pasta, stews, elaborate breads and pastries. The third group is Persian, from southern Uzbekistan and Tajikistan to northern Pakistan and on into India, distinguished by subtle seasoning, extensive use of vegetables, and fancy sweets.

Seasoning is usually mild, though sauces and chillies are offered to turn up the heat. Principle spices are black cumin, red and black pepper, barberries, coriander and sesame seeds. Common herbs are fresh coriander (cilantro), dill, parsley, celeriac and basil. Other seasonings include wine vinegar and fermented milk products.

In the heavily Russian-populated cities of northern Kazakstan, and in all the Central Asian capitals, the dominant cuisine is Russian.

Meat Mutton is the ever-present and preferred meat. Fat-tailed sheep are prized for their meat, fat and wool, and fat from the sheep's tail actually costs more than the meat. Most dishes contain hefty portions of it for flavour and consistency, and you will soon find that everything smells of it. You may begin to feel your insides getting plugged up with it (so do locals, and they keep themselves unplugged with lots of tea).

Sheep's head is a 'delicacy' which may be served to honoured guests in some homes.

Beef and horsemeat are also common and, in the countryside, camel and goat. Horsemeat, especially as sausage, is often served at special occasions.

The ubiquitous *shashlyk* – kebabs of fresh or marinated mutton, beef, liver, minced meat or, in restaurants, chicken – is usually served with nan and vinegary onions.

Produce Almost all produce is locally grown, and seasonal. The long growing season means many fruits and vegetables have early, middle and late harvests. In general, though, May is the best time for apricots, strawberries and cherries, June for peaches, and July for grapes and figs. Autumn brings apples, quinces, persimmons, dates, pomegranates and pears. Melons, watermelons and lemons ripen in late summer but are available in the markets as late as January.

Fruits are eaten fresh, cooked, dried or made into preserves, jams and drinks. Central Asians are fond of dried fruits and nuts, particularly apricots and apricot stones, which when cracked open have a pith that tastes like pistachios. The white ones are from around Samarkand and the small brown ones from around Bukhara; they're cooked in ash and the shells cracked by the vendor before they reach the market.

Vegetables include aubergines, peppers, turnips, cucumbers, splendid tomatoes and dozens of pumpkin and squash varieties, plus lesser known items like green radishes and yellow carrots. At any time of year you'll find delicious nuts – walnuts, peanuts, pistachios and almonds – and fine honey from the mountains.

Plov Plov (or *palov* or *palu*) – Central Asian pilaf – consists mainly of rice with fried and boiled meat, onions and carrots, and sometimes raisins, barberries, chickpeas or fruit slices. While Uzbek men usually stay out of the kitchen, they pride themselves on preparing good plov; an *oshpaz* or master chef, can dish up a special plov from a single cauldron for thousands on a special occasion like a wedding. Plov is always the piece de résistance when entertaining guests – hence the mistaken impression that Central Asians can prepare only one dish.

Noodles Long, stout noodles (laghman, or la-mian to Xinjiang Chinese) distinguish Central Asian cuisine from any other. Laghman is served everywhere, especially as the base for a spicy soup (usually called laghman too) with fried mutton, peppers, tomatoes and onions. In Xinjiang, so-mian is roughly the same ingredients on a 'bed' of noodles.

A special holiday dish in Kazakstan and Kyrgyzstan is besbarmak or beshbarmak, large flat noodles topped with lamb and/or horsemeat cooked in vegetable broth. The name means 'five fingers' since it was traditionally eaten with the hand. Uzbeks call it shilpildok, and Russians myasa po-kazakhskiy.

Uyghurs are the undisputed Central Asian masters of the dying art of noodle-making – rolling, stretching, slapping, twirling or folding, and defying the laws of physics with flour, water, salt and oil.

Meat & Dough There are four other variations on the meat and dough theme – steamed, boiled, baked and fried. Manty (steamed dumplings) are a favourite from Mongolia to Turkey. Chuchvara (Tajik: tushbera, Uyghur: chuchureh, Russian: pelmeny) are a smaller boiled cousin of manty, served plain or with vinegar, sour cream, butter or whatever, or in soups. Manty and chuchvara are sometimes fried or deep-fried.

A favourite snack is samsa (Uyghur: samsi, Tajik: sambusa), a version of manty usually baked in a tandoori oven – at their best made with flaky puff pastry, distinguishable by a spiral pattern on top. The deep-fried version is an originally Crimean Tatar speciality called chebureki. One of the most common prepared foods in markets and on the street are piroshki, greasy Russian fried pies filled with potatoes or meat.

A mixture of mutton, fat and onions is the customary filling in all these, but you can also find them filled with potato, pumpkin, chickpeas, curd (tvorog in Russian) or, in spring, greens. As with everything made with sheep's fat, they get gummy if you don't eat them straight from the fire or the pot.

Soups In addition to laghman, other soups you may come across frequently are shorpa (or shurpa or sorpo), a broth with chickpeas, a few vegetables, herbs and a chunk of mutton on the bone; manpar, noodle bits, meat, vegetables and mild seasoning in broth; and kesme, a thick Kyrgyz noodle soup with small bits of potato, vegetable and meat. Russian borshch (beetroot soup has also found its way into Central Asian diets. Lapsha is not a 'national dish', just the Russian word for 'noodle' or generically for noodle soup.

Bread The wide array of breads, leavened and unleavened, is a staple for most of the population, and cheap. Nan (non to Uzbeks and Tajiks), usually baked in tandoor ovens, is served at every meal. Some varieties are prepared with onions, meat or sheep's-tail fat

Unleavened breads and flat cakes are baked on the walls of traditional ovens called tarus.

in the dough; others are topped with nigella (the black, onion-tasting seed of a flower from the fennel family) or anise, poppy or sesame seeds. Flat-bread also serves as an impromptu plate, eg for shashlyk.

You may also find breads made from corn or chickpea flour, and pancakes without yeast are common. *Katlama* is an incredible flaky bread made by repeatedly folding oil or butter into the dough and frying in a skillet or cauldron.

Russians call nan *lepyoshka*. Boring, square, white-flour Russian loaves are *khleb* (but to confuse things, some Central Asians use nan for this too).

Milk Products Central Asia is known for the richness and delicacy of its fermented dairy products, which use cow, sheep, goat, camel or horse milk. The milk itself is probably unpasteurised, but its cultured derivatives are safe.

Soured milk is used to make yoghurt *(katyk)* with the addition of bacterial culture. Katyk can be strained to make *suzma*, like tart cottage or cream cheese, used as a garnish or added to soups. *Ayran* is a salty yoghurt-water mix (the Russian equivalent is called *kefir*; don't confuse this with the Russians' beloved *smetana*, or sour cream). Many doughs and batters incorporate sour milk products, giving them a tangy flavour. Milk-based soups, hot and cold, are common.

The final stage in the 'milk cycle' is *kurtob* or *kurut* – dried suzma (often rolled into marble-size balls), a tasty travel snack or soup additive. The pink ones we saw in the Ferghana Valley have chilli pepper added. Scrape away the outer layer if you're uneasy about who's been handling them.

Tvorog is a Russian speciality, made from soured milk, heated to curdle it. This is hung in cheesecloth overnight to strain off the whey. The closest Central Asian equivalent is suzma. *Qaymok* is pure sweet cream, skimmed from fresh milk that has sat over-night. This wickedly tasty breakfast item, wonderful with honey, is available in many markets in the early morning, but sells out fast, usually by sunrise.

Fish You may find caviar and sea-fish dishes in western Kazakstan, by the Caspian Sea. River fish are not recommended, considering the chemical brew they probably swim around in.

Salads Salads are a refreshing break from heavy main courses. Tomatoes dominate in summer, green radishes in winter. Greens – parsley, fresh coriander, green onions and dill – are served and eaten whole. In state-run restaurants you'll probably be offered a plate of tomatoes or cucumbers, or the ubiquitous Russian *salat stolichnyy*, vegetable and beef bits, potato and egg in sour cream and mayonnaise.

Desserts Raisins, nuts, fresh fruit, confections, bland cookies and a hundred types of halvah are generally served with the tea. Cakes and pastries are a European addition to the end of a meal.

Regional Specialities Each region has its own specialities, or at least its own names for local variants. They're mostly served at home; in restaurants you'd probably have to ask for them since they're rarely on the menu.

Kazakstan Kazaks prepare good *qazy*, smoked horsemeat sausage (though beef is sometimes substituted). Served on special occasions sliced with cold noodles it's called *naryn*. *Karta* (literally 'horse intestines', used as the casing) and *chuchuk* (or *chuzhuk*) are two other kinds of horsemeat sausage. *Kuirdak* is a pleasant beef and potato stew. Kazaks make a sweet plov with dried apricots, raisins and prunes, while *plov Askabak* is made with pumpkin. *Zhuta* is pasta shaped like a Swiss roll with a carrot and pumpkin filling. Kazak apples are famous in Central Asia (Almaty and its old form, Alma Ata, literally mean 'father of apples').

Kyrgyzstan Spicy laghman dishes reign

supreme, partly the result of Dungan influence. Though Kyrgyz cuisine is not particularly subtle, the Kyrgyz we've met would rather burn a hole in their mouth with a spicy side dish than sit through an entire meal of bland meat and potatoes.

Hoshan are fried and steamed dumplings, similar to manty, best right off the fire from markets. Vendors also carry bags of them to sell in bus stations, or to bars, outdoor cafés etc. *Jarkop* is a braised meat and vegetable dish with noodles.

In Dungan areas (eg Karakol or certain suburbs of Bishkek), ask for *ashlyamfu*, made with cold noodles, jelly and eggs. Also try their steamed buns made with *jusai*, a mountain grass of the onion family, and *fyntyozi*, spicy cold rice noodles. *Gyanfan* is rice with a meat and vegetable sauce. Dungans maintain a spirited rivalry with Uyghurs for noodle supremacy.

Tajikistan & Tajik-Speaking Areas of Uzbekistan
In these days of Tajik civil strife and economic chaos, meat often gives way to vegetables. Try chickpea samsas *(nahud sambusa)* or porridge *(nahud shavla)*. Tajiks also prepare many bean and milk soups, while *oshi siyo halav* is a unique herb soup. *Tuhum barak* is a tasty egg-filled ravioli coated with sesame seed oil. *Chakka (yakka* to Tajik speakers around Samarkand and Bukhara) is curd or suzma (see Milk Products above) mixed with herbs, and delicious with flat-bread.

Many dishes of the Tajik-speaking region around Samarkand and Bukhara are similar to Tajik cuisine. In Samarkand's old town we enjoyed a delicious mutton stew with chickpeas called *nakhot* (which means 'chickpea').

Turkmenistan
Surprisingly for a country that is mostly uncultivable desert, some of the more interesting Turkmen dishes are vegetarian. Herb-filled pastries are common in the markets. Cornmeal pancakes and breads are a change of pace from Turkmen *chorek* or flat-bread. Porridges with mung beans *(mashishulye)*, or of cornmeal and pumpkin,

or of rice, milk and katyk, can make a meal. The Turkmen make a tasty meatless plov with dried fruit.

Economic and political stagnation in Turkmenistan has had a major negative impact on its food industry. Restaurants are scarce and the fare is generally miserable.

Uzbekistan & Uyghur Areas
Uzbeks and Uyghurs share many dishes, although Uyghur food in Xinjiang is being impoverished by the substitution of Chinese dishes. Uyghur standbys include kebabs, *pulau* (plov) and manty, though breads and noodles are their speciality.

Uyghurs boast endless varieties of laghman. While the usual topping is some combination of meat, peppers, tomatoes, eggplant, green beans and garlic, a scrambled egg and jusai is a change of pace. They also make manty with figs and quinces.

In Uzbekistan, steamed pumpkin is a light treat. *Moshkichiri* and *moshhurda* are meat and mung bean gruels. *Dimlama* (also called *bosma*) is meat, potatoes, onions and vegetables braised slowly in a little fat and their own juices; the meatless version is *sabzavotli dimlama*. *Hunon* or *honum* is a noodle roll, usually with a meat and potato filling. Uzbeks are fond of stuffed cabbage and grape leaves *(dulma)*, tomatoes, peppers and quinces.

Where to Eat
You can eat in street-side stalls and cafés, cheap canteens, private restaurants and state-run ones and, best of all, in private homes. The only public places that stay open much beyond dusk are expensive restaurants. In smaller towns, restaurants, if they exist at all, can be pretty dire, and hotels may have the only edible food outside private homes.

Hygiene Most cafés and restaurants have a wash-stand somewhere, and even street stalls may have running water (or you could pack a supply of pre-moistened towellettes). Kitchen hygiene is unpredictable except in the best restaurants. For street food, it can't hurt to carry your own cup and utensils. The rule for market food is 'peel it or boil it'.

In restaurants, salt is usually provided in common bowls, and looks dirty because it's unrefined.

Restaurants A few private restaurants in bigger cities offer interesting Central Asian or European dishes and earnest service, though they almost have to be overpriced just to keep up with their own costs. Choice tends to be limited, and they may close altogether outside the summer season. In the capitals you'll also find some international eateries, especially Turkish, Middle Eastern and Chinese, with meal prices from US$5 to as much as US$25.

The fare in state-run places is modestly priced and boring, tending towards Russian meat and potatoes. Tourist standbys include *kotleta po-Kievski* (chicken Kiev); *befstroganov* (beef stroganoff); *tsyplyonok tabaka* (chicken tabak), grilled chicken with a spicy sauce; *lyulya kebab*, beef or mutton meatballs; *bifshteks* (beefsteak), glorified hamburger; and *gulyash*, a dismal miscellany of meat, vegetables and potatoes.

Russians and Russianised locals don't expect good food from restaurants. What they want at midday is a break. What they want in the evening is a night out – lots of booze and gale-force music or a variety show. If you're just looking for a quiet meal, go in the afternoon when there's no music and sometimes a cheaper set menu. But consider checking out an evening variety show just once, just to sample the rich mix of debauchery and bad taste.

Russian is spoken in all but the cheapest rural eateries. *Mozhna pa-yest?*, 'May I eat?', gets the ball rolling. Don't be awed by the *menyu*; they don't have most of it anyhow, just possibly the items with prices typed or pencilled in. Alternatively you could point at what others have. Visits to the kitchen are frowned upon. *Mozhna zakazat?* is 'May I order?'.

A typical menu is divided into *zakuski* (cold appetisers), *pervye* ('first' courses, ie soups and hot appetisers), *vtorye* ('second'

or main courses), and *sladkye* (desserts). Main dishes may be further divided into *firmennye* (house specials), *natsionalnye* ('national', ie local, dishes), *myasnye* (meat), *rybnye* (fish), *iz ptitsy* (poultry), or *ovoshchnye* (vegetable).

Don't misread meat prices on menus – they are usually given as per 100 grams, not per serving (which is usually something more like 400 grams).

Pitfalls Beware the zakuski, which can kill off (a) your appetite and (b) your budget. One way to save money is to order only from the first-course menu.

A few places in Bishkek and elsewhere run a nasty little scam. You sit down at a table set with zakuski, push them aside and order, but though you didn't ask for them and didn't touch them, you find them all on your bill. In general you must pay for what's on your table; if you don't want it, ask on arrival for *chistyy stol*, Russian for 'clean table'. Some top-end places may also have steep door or 'seating' charges.

The bill may be no more than a scrap of paper showing the total. Ask for an itemisation if you have any doubts. You won't make any friends doing this, but cheating foreigners is not uncommon.

Hotels Every tourist hotel has a restaurant, usually modestly priced and dreary; outside the cities a hotel meal will rarely be more than about US$2. Big-city hotels may have a dance floor and nightly loud music or variety shows. In smaller towns the tourist hotel may have the only decent food and the focus of the local social scene. Staff, accustomed to undemanding groups, tend to be confused or annoyed by individual diners.

Larger hotels also have alternatives. A *bufet*, ('bu-FYET'), is not a buffet but a little deli with cheap cold meats, boiled eggs, salads, bread and pastries. To take something back to your room, say *soboy* ('sa-BOY').

One solution to the problem of booked-out hotel restaurants is to pig out with an early or late lunch and go to the bufet or a street stall for an omelette or shashlyk when it's dinnertime. Lunchtime hotel restaurant meals often feature 'national' dishes, and you can fill up on laghman and salad at cold-course prices.

Teahouses The teahouse (*chaykhana* in Turkmen, *chaykana* in Kyrgyz, *choyhona* in Uzbek and Tajik, *shaykhana* in Kazak) is male Central Asia's essential socio-gastro-nomic institution, especially in Uzbekistan. Usually shaded, often beside a pool or stream, it's as much a men's club as an eatery – though women, including foreigners, are tolerated, and local women may be seated at separate places or times. Old and young congregate to eat, or to drink pot after pot of green tea and talk.

Traditional seating is on a bed-like platform (Uzbeks call it a *takhta*, Tajiks a *chorpoy*), covered with a carpet and topped

with a low table. Take your shoes off to sit on the platform, or leave them on and hang your feet over.

Many chaykhana cooks will accept special orders in the morning or the day before. For the equivalent of a few dollars, some places will provide a cauldron, utensils and firewood for those who bring their own ingredients.

Street Stalls & Kiosks Cheap plov, manty, laghman, shashlyk and green tea are available from stalls around markets and bus and train stations; on every other street corner in older parts of most towns; and at lay-bys on major highways. Such stalls seem rare in Turkmenistan, however.

Central Asian 'street food' can be far better than in hotels and mainstream restaurants, though the meat-to-fat ratio is highly

At all times of day men gather in teahouses, where traditional seating is on a carpet-covered platform.

variable. Those in the markets tend to use the freshest ingredients. The food is generally hygienic if it's straight off the fire. Closing time is whenever the food runs out.

There are booze and snack kiosks everywhere (except Turkmenistan again). You can do more good by buying your snacks from the enterprising grannies trying to make ends meet, though their goods are just as susceptible as the kiosks' to tainting or counterfeit.

Cafés & Canteens A *kafe* can be anything from an ice cream parlour to an elegant place with supper music. Most are mini-restaurants with small menus and no entertainment. They tend to open and close earlier than restaurants and be a bit cheaper.

The canteen (Kazak: *askhana*, Kyrgyz: *ashkana*, Uzbek: *oshhona*, Russian: *stolovaya*) is the ordinary citizen's eatery – dreary but cheap, usually self-service, with a limited choice of cutlet or meatballs, sometimes laghman, soup, boiled vegetables, bread, tea and coffee. You can always find a few in market or station areas. Some are decent, some very grotty.

A 'dietetic canteen' *(parkhez taomlar oshhonaci* in Uzbek, *dieteticheskaya stolovaya* in Russian) is not for dieters or health-food freaks, but a place with 'special diets' for special health problems. Dishes tend to be bland and heavy on dairy products, pasta and potatoes.

Home Meals If you're invited home for a meal this can be your best introduction to local customs and traditions as well as to local cuisine.

Don't go expecting a quick bite. Your host is likely to take the occasion very seriously. Uzbeks, for example, say *mehmon otanda ulugh,* 'the guest is greater than the father'. Poorer families may put themselves under financial strain to show you a proper evening, possibly slaughtering a sheep if they have one, and offering you food most of them will not taste. And yet to refuse such an invitation (or to offer to bring food or to help with the cost) would almost certainly be a grave insult.

It's important to arrive with a gift. Something for the table (eg a bunch of fruit from the market) will do, but don't expect to see it again as some consider it bad form to offer guests any food they have themselves brought. You should be offered water for washing, as you may be eating with your hands at some point (shaking the water off your hands is said to be impolite). Remember that more devout Muslims avoid taking food to the mouth with the left hand; in the same vein, accept cups of tea and plates of food only with the right hand. Men (and foreign women guests) may eat separately from women and children of the family.

Wait until you are told where to sit; honoured guests are often seated by Kyrgyz or Kazak hosts opposite the door (so as not to be disturbed by traffic through it, and because that is the warmest seat in a yurt). The meal might begin with a mumbled prayer, followed by tea. The host breaks and distributes bread. Be careful not to place bread upside-down; it's considered bad luck, or irreverent. After breads, nuts or sweets to 'open the appetite', business or entertainment may begin. The eldest person or the guest is expected to tuck in before the others do.

The meal itself is something of a free-for-all. Dozens of dishes may be spread over a low table, or on a cloth on the floor surrounded by pillows. Food is served, and often eaten, from common plates, with hands or big spoons. It will be heaped on your plate by everyone. Pace yourself – eat too slowly and someone may ask if you're ill or unhappy; too eagerly and your plate will be immediately refilled. Praise the cook early and often; your host will worry if you're too quiet. If you're offered sheep's eyeballs or anything else you really can't face, refuse firmly and solemnly, saying something like 'this is not the custom of my people'. If you find a dish you like, make a show of refilling your plate.

If alcohol consumption is modest, the meal may end as it began, with tea and a prayer, but don't count on it (see Vodka in the preceding section). A common Muslim gesture at the end of any meal is the *amin*, in which cupped hands are brought together and passed down the face, as if washing.

For further tips on the protocol of a home visit, see Hospitality under Culture in the Facts About the Region chapter. Invitations from Uyghurs in Xinjiang are unlikely, as they must get prior approval from the Chinese security apparatus, an exercise that deters all but the most carefree individuals.

Home Restaurants Those not lucky enough to get a personal invitation to dinner can still enjoy some fine home-cooked food in certain old-town neighbourhoods of Tashkent and Samarkand (noted in those sections). Private citizens convert their own courtyards into little unofficial restaurants at midday and in the evening, serving a few simple dishes, and sometimes rarities like quail or other wild game.

There are no signs; family members just solicit customers on the street, and the competition can be intense. Most places are reasonably clean, though you might want to bring your own utensils. Bring your own beer or wine, or buy theirs.

Self-Catering

Markets Every sizeable town has a colourful *bazar* (Russian: *rynok*) or farmers' market, with acres of fresh and dried fruit, vegetables, nuts, honey, cheese, bread, meat and eggs. On weekends the collective farmers come in, so everybody else comes too, for the best deals and freshest goods. During the week you'll find a permanent squad of 'middle-persons'. Go early in the morning for the liveliest scene and the best selection.

Korean and Dungan vendors sell spicy vegetable salads, a great antidote for meat-meat-meat (we've eaten them with no ill effects, though some may be jacked up with MSG). Russians flog ready-to-eat pelmeny, pirozhki and yoghurt. Watch for snacks like salted apricot seeds (a Samarkand and Bukhara speciality), roasted chickpeas and puffed wheat and rice. Fresh honey on hot-from-the-oven bread makes a splendid breakfast.

Don't be afraid to haggle (with a smile) – everybody else does. As a foreigner you may be quoted twice the normal price or, on the other hand, given a bit extra. Insist on making your own choices or you may end up with second-rate produce.

State Food Shops Bigger towns have a *gastronom* (a grocery or speciality-food shop) or two, where you can find prepared foods, cured meat, cheese, biscuits and sweets.

Vegetarians

Central Asia is hell for vegetarians; indeed the whole concept of vegetarianism is unfathomable to most locals. We met many travellers who had suspended their principles just to survive, though with persistence and a few food tips this needn't be the only option. Those determined to avoid meat will need to visit a lot of farmers' markets (see the preceding section).

In restaurants, you'll see a lot of tomato and cucumber salads. Zakuski (cold appetisers) may include things like eggs and mushrooms. Hotel buffets are a godsend. Laghman or soup may be ordered without meat but the broth is usually meat-based. In private homes there are always bread, salads, whole greens and herbs on the table, and you should be able to put in a word to your host in advance.

Oddly, many Central Asians don't consider sausage, or even fat, as 'meat'. Potatoes

---

Smoke Vendors

In markets, stations and parks all over Central Asia you'll see gypsy women and children asking for a few coins to wave their pans of burning herbs around you or the premises. The herb is called *isriq* in Uzbek, and the smoke is said to be good medicine against colds and flu (and the evil eye?), and a cheap alternative to scarce medicines. Some people also burn it when they move into a new flat. ∎

to be filed under 'vegetable' in the former Soviet mind, so you must ask for them separately.

For specifically vegetarian fare in Uzbekistan, try asking for *katykli sholghom hurda* (a dish with rice, turnips, carrots, onions and yoghurt), *mosh qovoq* (mung beans and pumpkin porridge), *shir qovoq* (milk soup with rice and pumpkin) or *nutkhurak* (chickpeas).

Vegetarians can scrape by in Kashgar's Chinese restaurants and in some Hunza and Gilgit cafés. Some hotels in Pakistan will stir up a vegetable entree for you, especially if you bring the ingredients.

If you are vegetarian, say so, early and often – when you check into your hotel, when you book a restaurant, when you order. 'I'm a vegetarian' in Russian is *ya vegetarianka* (f) or *ya vegetarianets* (m). 'Without meat' is *etsiz* in Turkmen, *atsiz* in Kazak and Kyrgyz, *gushsiz* in Uyghur, *gushtsiz* in Uzbek, and *bez myasa* in Russian.

Holidays

Ramadan Ramadan is the Muslim month of fasting, when the devout abstain from eating, drinking and smoking from sunrise to sunset. Since the collapse of the USSR, this has become more popular as a holiday in Central Asia, though relatively few maintain the fast strictly. See Religion in the Facts About the Region chapter for more about Ramadan.

Other Holidays A big occasion for eating is Navrus (see the Holiday section earlier in this chapter). Along with plov and other traditional fare, several dishes are served particularly at this time. The traditional Navrus dish, prepared only by women, is *sumalak* – wheat, soaked in water for three days until it sprouts, ground, mixed with oil, flour and sugar, and cooked on a low heat for 24 hours. *Halim* is a porridge of boiled meat and wheat grains, seasoned with black pepper and cinnamon. *Nishalda* – whipped egg-whites, sugar and licorice flavouring – is also popular at Ramadan.

DRINK

Tea *Chay* (*choy* to Uzbeks and Tajiks, *shay* to Kazaks) is drunk with some reverence in Central Asia. An array of customs surrounds it, and an entire branch of Central Asian cuisine – samsas, bread, halvah and various fried foods – is aimed at tea-time.

It's the drink of hospitality, offered first to every guest, usually in a little cup with no handles. From a fresh pot, an Uzbek host will pour tea into one cup, twice returning it to the pot before offering it the third time to the guest as a sign of respect (or taking it himself to prove it's not tainted). A cup filled only a little way up is a compliment, allowing your host to refill it often, and keep its contents warm (if your host pours to the brim, it may be a signal that he'd prefer you didn't stay too long!). Pass and accept tea with the right hand; it's extra polite to put the left hand over the heart as you do this. If your tea is too hot, don't blow on it, but swirl it gently in the cup, without spilling any. If it has grown cold, your host will throw it away before refilling the cup.

Straight green tea is the favourite; locals claim it beats the heat, and unblocks you after too much greasy plov. Black tea is preferred in Samarkand and Urgench, and by most Russians. Turkmen call green tea *gek* and black tea *gara*; to Russians, green tea is

Gorbachev takes Tea

Gorbachev jokes are still in season in the former USSR. In a Central Asian favourite, Gorbachev comes to visit Uzbekistan's supremo, Islam Karimov, looks at cotton fields, factories and Uzbek dance ensembles, and is then guest of honour at a big banquet. As it starts, Karimov pours a cup of tea, returns it to the pot, does it again, and finally pours tea all around; Gorbachev watches.

Back home in Moscow, Raisa asks, 'how was the trip?'. 'Great,' says Gorby, 'but Karimov doesn't treat his guests very well. At dinner he washed his teacup twice and didn't wash mine at all.' ■

zelyonnyy chay, black tea *chyornyy chay*. Western Turkmen brew tea with *chal*, camels' milk and Pamir Tajiks use goats' milk. Kazak tea is taken with milk, salt and butter – the nomadic equivalent of fast food: hot, tasty and high in calories.

In Xinjiang you can get Chinese jasmine tea *(cha)* everywhere. In Pakistan, 'milky tea' *(dudh-chai)* is equal parts water, leaves, sugar and long-life milk brought to a raging boil, and *khawa* is a sweet and delicious green tea made with cardamom or other spices.

Cardamom or star anise from the market will in fact jazz up boring restaurant tea anywhere.

Other Non-Alcoholic Drinks Don't drink the tap water. Cheap bottled water is easy to find; so is boiling water. Streetside machines and special kiosks dispense soda water in summer, but everybody uses the same glasses so bring your own container.

Napitok (Russian for 'beverage') is usually diluted, sweetened fruit juice, served from pitchers at cafés and restaurants for next to nothing, but it is definitely not safe. *Limonad* is not lemonade but an awful-tasting fizzy drink of questionable origin.

All drinks, including bottled water, are hugely overpriced in hotel and restaurant bars in the former USSR. Brand-name soft drinks on sale in Tajikistan look anaemic and taste flat – hardly surprising when the label reads 'manufactured in Moscow, 1992'.

Ayran is a popular liquid-yoghurt drink, sometimes slightly salty; the Russian equivalent is *kefir*. In Xinjiang, little 200-ml sealed bottles of yoghurt drink are available everywhere.

Restaurant coffee, usually made in large vats with second-rate ingredients, bears no resemblance to what westerners think of as coffee. Tins of cheap imported instant coffee can be found in shops in Uzbekistan and less frequently in Kyrgyzstan and Kazakstan. If you're a serious coffee or black-tea drinker, bring your own, plus a mug and/or thermos; hot water is easy to drum up from a bufet or the floor-lady.

Vodka Despite their Muslim heritage, most Central Asians drink, at least with guests. If you don't enjoy hard booze and heavy drinking, make your excuses early. 'Weak stomach' won't work, for everyone appears to believe that vodka is excellent for killing every sort of microbe. However, many Central Asians know from personal experience about the dysentery medication metronidazole (brand name Flagyl, or *trikhopol* in Russian) and the results of mixing it with alcohol, so this makes a good excuse. Religious beliefs are a possibility if you're prepared for a theological discussion. Oddly enough, claiming to be an alcoholic sometimes works, though you have to be pretty consistent about it.

In a private home or at a restaurant with local friends, a male guest may be expected to offer the first toast. You'll be expected to offer one eventually in any case. Like the Russians who introduced them to vodka, Central Asians take their toasts seriously – small speeches encapsulating their hopes for their guests' wellbeing. Even some of our local friends who don't drink much say it's impolite to refuse the initial 'bottoms up', and/or abstain from at least a symbolic sip at each toast.

But there's usually heavy pressure to drain your glass every time – so as not to give offence, it is implied – and the pressure only increases as everybody gets loaded. If you're joining in, take a bite of bread or a long drink of water before or after each shot, to minimise the sledge-hammer effects.

It's the rare host who understands westerners well enough to give you a way out of such 'terrorist hospitality'. But if your restraint causes offence, this friendship was probably not meant to be. For more on alcohol-related problems see Dangers & Annoyances in the Facts for the Visitor chapter.

Other Alcohol You may now stop at any number of tatty kiosks all over Central Asia and choose from a vast array of industrial-strength spirits and 'champagne'. Beware of imitations and counterfeits, usually awful and sometimes lethal. Check the labels, certifications and seals.

You'll also find European beers (*pivo*) for around US$1 to US$2 a can, dubious Russian beer, and sometimes cheap, decent Chinese beer.

If you order a bottle of restaurant vodka, check the seal; waiters sometimes dilute it and keep a share. Most hotel restaurants have a bufet window somewhere back by the kitchen, where attendants buy the drinks, by the bottle or the carafe, that they resell to diners. For takeaway beer, booze, mineral water or soft drinks, put on your I-know-what-I'm-doing face, walk back and buy your own there – for noticeably less than they charge you at the table.

In Kashgar, Chinese beer, wine, brandy and spirits are available in Chinese restaurants and department stores, although Uyghurs rarely drink in public. Pakistan is officially dry, but in Hunza some people still brew *mel*, a coarse grape wine, and a powerful mulberry brandy they call *araq*, the so-called 'Hunza water'. Non-Muslim foreigners can drink in special lounges at top-end hotels in Rawalpindi and Islamabad.

Kumys & Other Attractions Kumys (properly *kymys* in Kyrgyz, *qymyz* in Kazak) is fermented mare's milk, a mildly alcoholic drink appreciated by Kazaks and Kyrgyz, even those who no longer spend much time in the saddle (non-alcoholic varieties are also made). It's available only in spring and summer, when mares are foaling. The best kumys comes from the herders themselves; the stuff available in the cities is sometimes diluted with cow's milk or water. Drinking too much of it may give you diarrhoea.

Kazaks and Kyrgyz also like a thick, yeasty, slightly fizzy concoction called *bozo*, made from boiled, fermented millet or other grains. Turkmen, Kazak and Karakalpak nomads like *shubat*, fermented camel milk.

ENTERTAINMENT

Theatre, opera and ballet struggle on in Central Asia, though local troupes tend to perform at home in winter and then go on the road in summer. National folk-dance and song troupes are popular, and some better-known ones are mentioned in the country chapters. But in the popularity stakes they're all losing ground to the cinema, which pulls in the crowds with second-rate American films and some foreign pornography, mostly dubbed in Russian.

Kökpar and other horseback sports (see Sports under the Culture section in the Facts About the Region chapter) are thumping good spectacles if you can get to see them. And the Russians have their circuses with prancing horses with acrobats on their backs, snarling lions and tigers, heart-stopping high-wire artists and clowns that are hilarious in spite of the language barrier. Larger towns have their own arenas.

Restaurants still serve as a mainstay of nightlife, with diners passing over their bifshteks for another slammer of vodka and a lurch around the floor to a jackhammer Casio-beat. A few western-style disco-cum-nightclubs have appeared but the western-style cover charges tend to limit the clientele to the nouveaux riches. In Tajikistan, Dushanbe citizens' self-imposed dusk curfew keeps the auditoriums empty.

THINGS TO BUY

Two of the best things to buy in Central Asia are clothing and carpets, but the markets are enjoyable even if you're just looking, with everything from Russian champagne to cow's heads, plus acres of seasonal produce and preserved foods. The best bargains, often at a fraction of the cost in hotel gift shops and cute tourist bazars, are outside heavily touristed areas entirely, eg in small-town bazars. Another surprising souvenir source right under your nose is the local TsUM (department store).

For any shop licensed to accept credit cards, figure on a hefty service charge when you pay the bill back home. See the Customs section in this chapter about buying antiques or items that look antique.

Carpets & Hangings

World-famous 'Bukhara' carpets and rugs

come mostly from Turkmenistan (or Eastern Europe! Check the label). Local Turkmenistan markets (usually weekly affairs) are the places to find them. For more on Bukhara rugs see the 'Bukhara' Rugs aside in the Arts section in the Facts about the Region chapter.

The most distinctive souvenirs from Kazakstan and Kyrgyzstan are colourful wool carpets, felt rugs and cotton and/or silk quilts, which traditionally served as insulation and adornment for the nomadic yurts. An attractive and accessible buy is a Kazak wall carpet is the *(tus-kiiz)* (see the Kazak Wall Carpets aside in the Arts section in the Facts about the Region chapter). In Kyrgyzstan look for *shyr-daks*, heavy rugs made from multiple layers of home-pounded felt in varying colours, with patterns created by cutting away the upper layers to reveal different-coloured lower ones.

Tajiks and Uzbeks make colourful cotton wall hangings. Good examples are the Uzbek *suzana* (silk-on-cotton dowry needlework) and *adras* (silk-and-cotton bedspreads).

Cloth & Clothing

In Uzbekistan's Ferghana Valley, many farmers raise silkworms (see the Silk Production aside in the Uzbekistan chapter). Home-grown silk cloth – especially in the loud patterns favoured by Uzbek women – is for sale everywhere in Uzbekistan. In small-town bazars, moderate-quality silk and high-quality cotton can be the same price. In Chelek, outside Samarkand, silk was about US$1 a metre (and US$1.30 at the TsUM department store in Samarkand).

Traditional clothing (described in the Population & People section in the Facts About the Region chapter) is easy to find in local bazars. For Uzbek or Tajik quilted coats, caps and other gear, the lowest prices and biggest variety are in Uzbekistan cities like

Samarkand and, especially, Bukhara. For a plain quilted coat, a stall-keeper in Chelek opened with the *sum* equivalent of about US$12.

The most beautiful of Central Asian clothing is that of the Turkmen. At certain markets in Turkmenistan you can pick up finely embroidered men's ceremonial knee-length jackets and skullcaps and women's lustrous dresses and brightly patterned scarves.

Pottery

There are two centres for pottery in Uzbekistan. Work from Gizhduvan near Bukhara tends to come in greens, yellows and browns, and that from Rishtan in the Ferghana Valley in bright blues and greens. You can arrange visits to pottery workshops and shops through Uzbektourism or private agencies, or snoop around on your own.

Silver

For Central Asia's nomads, wealth had to be portable, and silver fit the bill. Women sometimes wore huge amounts of silver jewellery, often set with semiprecious stones, while men carried things like silver scabbards for daggers or swords. Some poor samples can be found for sale in bigger bazars.

Other

Among items you might find in the bazars are leather drinking vessels (Kyrgyzstan and Kazakstan), wood carvings, and riding tackle such as saddles, saddle cloths and whips.

A high-visibility market item is garishly painted wooden cradles with a hole to pee through. No, Central Asian babies aren't born toilet-trained: swaddled infants are simply fitted out with wood or plastic tubes (the one for boys looks like a little pipe). These are usually on sale too, a source of endless jokes on tourists.

Getting There & Away

This chapter deals with travel into or out of the area consisting of the ex-Soviet Central Asian republics, far western Xinjiang (China) and far northern Pakistan. That makes travel between Kazakstan and Xinjiang, for example, 'getting around', although for some travellers an Ürümqi-Almaty flight may just be part of getting there from home. Most Xinjiang-Central Asia information is here (see also the Getting Around chapter).

The region's main air links to the 'outside' arc through the ex-Soviet republican capitals – Almaty, Bishkek, Tashkent, Ashghabat and Dushanbe (and some smaller cities connected only to Russia) – plus Ürümqi in Xinjiang, and Islamabad in Pakistan. The long-distance rail connections are mostly with Mother Russia – two routes from Moscow via Samara to Tashkent, and two from the Trans-Siberian Railway to Almaty and Tashkent. Another is the relatively new line to Almaty via Ürümqi from China, and yet another is on the drawing board from Iran.

The other main overland links are two roads from China – one accessible year-round via Ürümqi to Almaty, and a warm-weather one via Kashgar, over the Torugart pass into Kyrgyzstan. Kashgar in turn can be reached by road from Ürümqi, or over the Khunjerab pass on Pakistan's amazing Karakoram Highway (KKH).

Finally there is a hybrid journey by air from Turkey to Baku (Azerbaijan), across the Caspian Sea to Turkmenbashi (Turkmenistan) and by train to Ashghabat, Bukhara and beyond.

Travel Insurance

However you go, it's worth taking out travel insurance. Consider covering yourself for the worst possible case – an accident requiring hospitalisation and a flight home. For an extended trip, insurance may seem an extravagance but if you can't afford it, you can't afford a medical emergency overseas either. See the Health section in the Facts for the Visitor chapter for more on insurance.

AIR

Of the many routes in, two handy corridors are via Turkey (thanks to the geopolitics of the future) and via Russia (thanks to the geopolitics of the past). Turkish Airlines seems to have more good deals than anyone else (to Almaty, Ashghabat, Tashkent and Karachi), while Russian and Central Asian carriers have the most connections. Istanbul, Ankara and Moscow have airline offices, travel agencies and embassies. Arrangements are generally cheaper, simpler and more reliable in Turkey. Moscow has four airports and connections can be flaky.

More flights go to Tashkent than to any other city in the region, though arrival in Tashkent is likely to be the low point of any trip (see To/From Uzbekistan in this section). The other Central Asian city well served internationally is Almaty.

Numerous carriers serve the region. Russia has Aeroflot spin-off airlines and a good, new long-haul airline called Transaero. At present only the spin-off airlines, and not Aeroflot itself, serve Central Asia (although many booking offices are still signposted 'Aeroflot', and some planes still bear the Aeroflot logo); but to simplify matters we still refer in this book simply to 'Aeroflot'. The ex-Soviet republics appropriated the Aeroflot planes sitting in their airfields when the USSR collapsed, but now have fleets of their own – Kazakstan, Kyrgyzstan and Turkmenistan Airlines, Tajikistan International Airlines, and Uzbekistan Airways. Xinjiang has China Xinjiang Airlines, devolved from Air China (CAAC). Pakistan has Pakistan International Airlines (PIA).

Other international carriers with scheduled Central Asia connections include Austrian Air, Iran Air, KLM, Lufthansa, Thai

Airways, Turkish Airlines (THY) and USAir. To Pakistan, most international carriers serve Karachi (but only PIA, British Airways and Saudia stop in Islamabad). Azerbaijan Airlines flies to/from Baku, across the Caspian Sea from Turkmenistan.

Airline Safety

Aeroflot, the former Soviet state airline, has been decentralised into literally hundreds of smaller airlines. The International Airline Passengers' Association (IAPA), a Washington-based consumer watchdog, says that collectively these 'baby-flots' now have the worst regional safety record in the world, thanks to poor maintenance, ageing aircraft and gross overloading – and little money to remedy the situation. After several highly publicised disasters, the IAPA in January 1994 advised travellers to avoid *Russian* domestic carriers.

But of course the Central Asian carriers are not Russian domestic airlines, and in fact most have at least lifted their *international* services towards international safety standards. The US Federal Aviation Administration (FAA) at the end of 1994 found Uzbekistan Airways (which has a co-operative agreement with Lufthansa for the maintenance of its international Airbus fleet and the training of flight crew) to be in compliance with international standards. Transaero also has notably higher standards than most. In general, however, the Central Asian carriers' domestic flights are not up to the same standards.

Visa Checks

You can buy air tickets without a visa or letter of support (see Visas & Embassies in the Facts for the Visitor chapter), but in most places outside Central Asia you will have trouble getting on a plane without one – even if embassies and travel agents tell you otherwise. And no wonder: airlines are obliged to fly anyone rejected because of improper papers back home, and in the UK, at least, they're fined £2000 for every such reject. So check-in staff tend to act like immigration officers. If you have made arrangements to

get a visa on arrival, have your letter of support handy at check-in, and preferably a letter from your travel agency too! If you plan to just take your chances on arrival, you may never get there.

Buying Tickets

The information here is particularly vulnerable to change: prices for international travel are volatile, routes are introduced and cancelled, schedules change, special deals come and go, and rules and visa requirements are amended. Airlines and governments seem to take perverse pleasure in making price structures and regulations as complicated as possible.

The airlines' own best fares (usually advance-purchase fares) will give you a point of reference, but they're usually not the lowest. Various types of discounted tickets can save you a lot of money and/or increase the scope of your travel at marginal extra cost. Shop around, and start early – some cheap tickets must be purchased months in advance. Check the travel ads in major newspapers.

Especially in London and some Asian capitals (notably Delhi and Bangkok), you'll find the lowest fares offered by obscure 'bucket shops' taking advantage of last-minute airline discounts and other deals. Many are honest and solvent, but not all. You're safest if an agency is a member of the International Air Transport Association (IATA), or a national association like the American Society of Travel Agents (ASTA) in the USA, the Association of British Travel Agents (ABTA) in the UK or the Australian Federation of Travel Agents (AFTA) in Australia.

If you're told that an incredibly cheap flight is 'fully booked, but we have another costing just a bit more…', try someone else. Don't part with even a deposit until you know the name of the airline (both outward and return), airports of departure and destination and the date and time of the flights, long stopovers and any restrictions. If the agent won't give this information, try another.

Watch for extra charges, eg surcharges (booking fees should not be necessary as agents get commission from the airlines). Ask whether all your money will be refunded if the flight is cancelled or changed to a date which is unacceptable to you. Once you have the ticket, ring the airline yourself to confirm that you're actually booked on the flight.

You may decide to pay a little more for the security of using a better-known agent. Very convenient are those agencies that specialise in finding low fares, like Trailfinders and Campus Travel (UK), Council Travel (USA), Travel CUTS (Canada) and STA (worldwide). Most offer the best deals to students and people aged under 26 but are open to all, and they won't play tricks on you.

Fares to the region tend to be 10% to 20% higher in peak travel season (roughly July to September and December in North America and Europe; December to January in Australia and New Zealand), though fares to Pakistan are not particularly seasonal.

Fares are approximate summer-season, discounted economy fares advertised at the time of writing. None constitutes a recommendation for any airline.

The USA & Canada The Los Angeles *Times*, San Francisco *Examiner*, Chicago *Tribune*, New York *Times*, Toronto *Globe & Mail* and Vancouver *Sun* all have big weekly travel sections with lots of travel-agent ads.

Council Travel and STA are reliable sources of cheap tickets in the USA. Each has offices across the country. Council's headquarters is at 205 East 42nd St, New York 10017 (☎ (212) 661-1450, or toll-free from the USA and Canada (800) 226-8642). STA's main US offices are at 7204½ Melrose Ave, Los Angeles 90046 (☎ (213) 937-5714) and 10 Downing St, New York 10014 (☎ (212) 627-3111, or toll-free (800) 777-0112). Fair Winds Trading Company (☎ (602) 748 1288, fax 748 1347), 5151 East Broadway Boulevard, suite 1610, Tucson, Arizona 85711, offers flight routings to Almaty and Bishkek via Germany and Austria, using Central Asian airlines for the Europe-Central Asia legs.

The best bargain-ticket agency in Canada is Travel CUTS, with around 50 offices located in all major cities. The parent office is at 187 College St, Toronto M5T 1P7 (☎ (416) 9792406).

Among relevant booking offices are Turkish Airlines (☎ (212) 339-9662, or toll-free from the USA and Canada (800) 874-8875) and Lufthansa (☎ (212) 479-8817, or toll-free (800) 645-3880); both have New York-Almaty connections. Aeroflot is at toll-free ☎ (800) 995-5555.

The UK & Europe In the UK, the Saturday *Independent* and Sunday *Times* have good travel sections, including advertisements for scores of bucket shops. Also check out the Travel Classifieds in London's weekly *Time Out* entertainment magazine.

The best-known bargain-ticket agencies are Trailfinders (☎ (0171) 937 5400) at 42-48 Earl's Court Rd, Kensington, London W8 6EJ; Campus Travel (☎ (0171) 730 8111) at 52 Grosvenor Gardens, London SW1W 0AG; and STA (☎ (0171) 938 4711) at Priory House, 6 Wrights Lane, London W8 6TA. All three have branches across London and the UK, and Campus Travel is also in many YHA shops.

A reliable European source of bargain tickets is NBBS Travels (☎ (20) 638 1738), Leidsestraat 53, 1017 NV Amsterdam; they have another office at Rokin 38 in Amsterdam (☎ (20) 624 0989). STA has offices in Paris; the main one is at 49 Rue Pierre Charron (☎ (1) 43 59 23 69).

Among booking offices in the UK are Turkish Airlines (☎ (0171) 499 9249), Uzbekistan Airways (☎ (0171) 935 1899, 935 2810; fax 935 9554, but don't hold your breath) and Tajikistan International Airlines (☎ (0171) 437 5422, fax 734 8014).

Other offices in Europe include Kazakstan Airlines in Vienna (☎ (1) 512-8782, 512-8656); Frankfurt (☎ (69) 235640, 235679); Hanover (☎ (511) 977-2270); and Glattbrugg, Switzerland (☎ (01) 810-8182). Uzbekistan Airways in Frankfurt is at ☎ 271 00 265/6.

Air Travel Glossary

Apex Tickets Apex stands for Advance Purchase Excursion fare. These tickets are usually between 30 and 40% cheaper than the full economy fare, but there are restrictions. You must purchase the ticket at least 21 days in advance (sometimes more) and must be away for a minimum period (normally 14 days) and return within a maximum period (90 or 180 days). Stopovers are not allowed, and if you have to change your dates of travel or destination, there will be extra charges to pay. These tickets are not fully refundable – if you have to cancel your trip, the refund is often considerably less than what you paid for the ticket. Take out travel insurance to cover yourself in case you have to cancel your trip unexpectedly – for example, due to illness.

Baggage Allowance This will be written on your ticket; you are usually allowed one 20-kg item to go in the hold, plus one item of hand luggage. Some airlines which fly transpacific and transatlantic routes allow for two pieces of luggage (there are limits on their dimensions and weight).

Bucket Shops At certain times of the year and/or on certain routes, many airlines fly with empty seats. This isn't profitable and it's more cost-effective for them to fly full, even if that means having to sell a certain number of drastically discounted tickets. They do this by off-loading them onto bucket shops (UK) or consolidators (USA), travel agents who specialise in discounted fares. The agents, in turn, sell them to the public at reduced prices. These tickets are often the cheapest you'll find, but you can't purchase them directly from the airlines. Availability varies widely, so you'll not only have to be flexible in your travel plans, you'll also have to be quick off the mark as soon as an advertisement appears in the press.

Bucket-shop agents advertise in newspapers and magazines and there's a lot of competition – especially in places like Amsterdam and London which are crawling with them – so it's a good idea to telephone first to ascertain availability before rushing from shop to shop. Naturally, they'll advertise the cheapest available tickets, but by the time you get there, these may be sold out and you may be looking at something slightly more expensive.

Bumped Just because you have a confirmed seat doesn't mean you're going to get on the plane – see Overbooking.

Cancellation Penalties If you have to cancel or change an Apex or other discount ticket, there may be heavy penalties involved; insurance can sometimes be taken out against these penalties. Some airlines impose penalties on regular tickets as well, particularly against 'no show' passengers.

Check In Airlines ask you to check in a certain time ahead of the flight departure (usually two hours on international flights). If you fail to check in on time and the flight is overbooked, the airline can cancel your booking and give your seat to somebody else.

Confirmation Having a ticket written out with the flight and date on it doesn't mean you have a seat until the agent has confirmed with the airline that your status is 'OK'. Prior to this confirmation, your status is 'on request'.

Courier Fares Businesses often need to send their urgent documents or freight securely and quickly. They do it through courier companies. These companies hire people to accompany the package through customs and, in return, offer a discount ticket which is sometimes a phenomenal bargain. In effect, what the courier companies do is ship their freight as your luggage on the regular commercial flights. This is a legitimate operation – all freight is completely legal. There are two shortcomings, however: the short turnaround time of the ticket, usually not longer than a month; and the limitation on your luggage allowance. You may be required to surrender all your baggage allowance for the use of the courier company, and be only allowed to take carry-on luggage.

Discounted Tickets There are two types of discounted fares – officially discounted (such as Apex – see Promotional Fares) and unofficially discounted (see Bucket Shops). The latter can save you more than money – you may be able to pay Apex prices without the associated Apex advance booking and other requirements. The lowest prices often impose drawbacks, such as flying with unpopular airlines, inconvenient schedules, or unpleasant routes and connections.

Economy Class Tickets Economy-class tickets are usually not the cheapest way to go, though they do give you maximum flexibility and they are valid for 12 months. If you don't use them, most are fully refundable, as are unused sectors of a multiple ticket.

Full Fares Airlines traditionally offer first class (coded F), business class (coded J) and economy class (coded Y) tickets. These days there are so many promotional and discounted fares available that few passengers pay full fare.

Lost Tickets If you lose your airline ticket, an airline will usually treat it like a travellers' cheque and, after inquiries, issue you with a replacement. Legally, however, an airline is entitled to treat it like cash, so if you lose a ticket, it could be forever. Take good care of your tickets.

MCO An MCO (Miscellaneous Charges Order) is a voucher for a value of a given amount, which resembles an airline ticket and can be used to pay for a specific flight with any IATA (International Air Transport Association) airline. MCOs, which are more flexible than a regular ticket, may satisfy the irritating onward ticket requirement, but some countries are now reluctant to accept them. MCOs are fully refundable if unused.

No Shows No shows are passengers who fail to show up for their flight for whatever reason. Full-fare no shows are sometimes entitled to travel on a later flight. The rest of us are penalised (see Cancellation Penalties).

Open Jaw Tickets These are return tickets which allow you to fly to one place but return from another, and travel between the two 'jaws' by any means of transport at your own expense. If available, this can save you backtracking to your arrival point.

Overbooking Airlines hate to fly with empty seats, and since every flight has some passengers who fail to show up (see No Shows), they often book more passengers than they have seats available. Usually the excess passengers balance those who fail to show up, but occasionally somebody gets bumped. If this happens, guess who it is most likely to be? The passengers who check in late.

Promotional Fares These are officially discounted fares, such as Apex fares, which are available from travel agents or direct from the airline.

Reconfirmation To minimise your chances of being 'bumped' from an onward or return flight due to airline overbooking, reconfirm directly with the airline at least 72 hours before departure, and ask about any adjustments to departure information compared to what's on your ticket. This is essential for any flight out of Central Asia, where overbooking is common and schedules change unpredictably. Airline booking offices will reconfirm for you free of charge; hotel airline desks may slap on fees.

Restrictions Discounted tickets often have various restrictions on them, such as necessity of advance purchase, limitations on the minimum and maximum period you must be away, restrictions on breaking the journey or changing the booking or route etc.

Round-the-World Tickets These tickets have become very popular in the last few years; basically, there are two types – airline tickets and agent tickets. An airline RTW ticket is issued by two or more airlines that have joined together to market a ticket which takes you around the world on their combined routes. It permits you to fly pretty well anywhere you choose using their combined routes as long as you don't backtrack, ie keep moving in approximately the same direction east or west. Other restrictions are that you (usually) must book the first sector in advance and cancellation penalties then apply. There may be restrictions on how many stopovers you are permitted. The RTW tickets are usually valid for 90 days up to a year.

The other type of RTW ticket, the agent ticket, is a combination of cheap fares strung together by an enterprising travel agent. These may be cheaper than airline RTW tickets, but the choice of routes will be limited.

Standby This is a discounted ticket where you only fly if there is a seat free at the last moment. Standby fares are usually only available directly at the airport, but sometimes may also be handled by an airline's city office. To give yourself the best possible chance of getting on the flight you want, get there early and have your name placed on the waiting list. It's first come, first served.

Student Discounts Some airlines offer student-card holders 15% to 25% discounts on their tickets. The same often applies to anyone under the age of 26. These discounts are generally only available on ordinary economy-class fares. You wouldn't get one, for instance, on an Apex or an RTW ticket, since these are already discounted.

Tickets Out An entry requirement for many countries is that you have an onward or return ticket, in other words, a ticket out of the country. If you're not sure what you intend to do next, the easiest solution is to buy the cheapest onward ticket to a neighbouring country or a ticket from a reliable airline which can later be refunded if you do not use it.

Transferred Tickets Airline tickets cannot be transferred from one person to another. Travellers sometimes try to sell the return half of their ticket, but officials can ask you to prove that you are the person named on the ticket. This may not be checked on domestic flights, but on international flights, tickets are usually compared with passports.

Travel Periods Some officially discounted fares, Apex fares in particular, vary with the time of year. There is often a low (off-peak) season and a high (peak) season. Sometimes there's an intermediate or shoulder season as well. At peak times, when everyone wants to fly, both officially and unofficially discounted fares will be higher, or there may simply be no discounted tickets available. Usually the fare depends on your outward flight – if you depart in the high season and return in the low season, you pay the high-season fare. ■

Australia & New Zealand STA Travel and Flight Centres International are major dealers in cheap airfares, each with dozens of offices. STA's headquarters are at 1st floor, 224 Faraday St, Carlton, Victoria 3053, Australia (☎ (03) 9347 6911), and 10 High St, PO Box 4156, Auckland, New Zealand (☎ (09) 399723). Flight Centre International's main offices are at 19 Bourke St, Melbourne, Victoria 3000, Australia (☎ (03) 9650 2899) and 82 Elizabeth St, Sydney, NSW 2000, Australia (☎ (02) 235 3522). Ex-USSR specialist Gateway Travel (☎ (02) 745 3333, fax (02) 745 3237), 48 The Boulevarde, Strathfield, NSW 2135, Australia, can arrange Sydney-Tashkent flights.

Russia Many travel agencies, good and bad, advertise in the *Moscow Times* and *Moscow Tribune* English-language newspapers. Among reliable agencies in Moscow which could help with air bookings are Intourtrans (☎ (095) 927-11-81, 291-83-94; fax 921-19-96), ulitsa Petrovka 15/13; Intourist (☎ (095) 292-22-93 for air tickets), Mokhovaya ulitsa 13; and IRO Travel (☎ (095) 971-40-59, 280-85-62; fax 280-76-86) at the Travellers Guest House, ulitsa Bolshaya Pereyaslavskaya 50, 10th floor. Local branches of two UK business-travel firms are Alpha-Omega Travel (☎ (095) 928-94-59, fax 928-60-39, ☎ & fax 928-99-58), Lubyansky proezd 3, floor 3, No 12; and East-West Travel (☎ 924-06-29, fax 925-04-60), Bolshaya Lubyanka ulitsa 24/15.

Booking offices in Moscow include Kazakstan Airlines (☎ (095) 229-09-93, 210-83-32) and Uzbekistan Airways (☎ (095) 279-75-09, fax 279-08-48).

Turkey Booking offices in Istanbul include Kazakstan Airlines, Aksarai Ataturk Street 138 (☎ (212) 513-5069, 513-1397), and Uzbekistan Airways, Cumhuriyet Caddesi 39/4, Taksim (☎ (212) 237 1993/4, fax 237 3322).

Some flights also link Ankara and Trabzon with Baku. In Ankara, Azerbaijan Airlines is at Cinnah Caddesi 67/7 (☎ (312) 440 7155).

A good agency in Trabzon for booking Baku and other flights (and arranging visas) is Sarptur, at K Maras Caddesi 35 (☎ (462)123 995, fax 122 119), and there are numerous other agencies there too.

China & Hong Kong The Chinese government-run China Travel Service (CTS) can help with flights to Almaty via Ürümqi, or to Tashkent via Beijing. In Hong Kong, CTS's Foreign Passenger Department (☎ 2853-3533) is at 78 Connaught Rd, Central; the Kowloon Branch (☎ 2721-1331) is at 27 Nathan Rd, Tsimshatsui. In Beijing go to China International Travel Service (CITS) at 28 Jianguomenwai Dajie (☎ (1) 515 8570, fax 515 8603).

Booking offices in Beijing include Air China (Xinjiang Air, ☎ (1) 602 4084), Kazakstan Airlines (☎ (1) 500 2266) and Uzbekistan Airways (☎ (1) 500 6442). In Ürümqi, Air China is at ☎ (1) 414668 or 217942; Kazakstan Airlines is at ☎ (1) 336400 or 335688 ext 1057. The Kashgar office of Air China is at ☎ (0998) 22113.

Elsewhere in Asia Uzbekistan Airways has booking offices in Karachi (☎ & fax (21) 53 38 84), New Delhi (☎ (11) 332 7042, 332 0070; fax 332 3676), Bangkok (☎ (2) 216 9555) and Kuala Lumpur (☎ (3) 244 7506, 244 8994, fax 245 0508). Some of these offices may help you to get an Uzbekistan visa too.

To/From Kazakstan

From the USA, the best Almaty return fares we found range from US$1575 from the east coast to US$1810 from the west coast, both with Turkish Airlines, via Istanbul, departing twice a week in summer. Austrian Air flies New York to Almaty with a change in Vienna, and Lufthansa goes three times a week via Frankfurt.

The best fares from Europe to Almaty are probably with Turkish Airlines, via Istanbul and with Kazakstan Airlines from Frankfurt or Vienna. Turkish Airlines flies Istanbul-Almaty three times a week, Kazakstan Airlines has direct weekly flights to/from

Vienna and Zurich (US$600). Lufthansa flies London-Frankfurt-Almaty four times a week, and Kazakstan Airlines goes to/from Frankfurt (US$620) and Hanover (US$530) twice weekly. The German charter operator Luftbrücke flies weekly from Düsseldorf for US$435. KLM flies Amsterdam-Almaty twice a week. Kazakstan Airlines has daily Moscow-Almaty flights (five hours) for US$200, and Transaero goes to Almaty from Moscow for US$250.

The main Asia link with Almaty is to/from Ürümqi in Xinjiang, a 1½ hour flight, twice weekly with both China Xinjiang Airlines (US$125 in Ürümqi) and Kazakstan Airlines (US$150 in Ürümqi); tickets are said to be more expensive bought in Almaty. Austrian Air has a Beijing-Almaty-Vienna flight, PIA flies Islamabad-Almaty weekly, and Kazakstan Airlines flies Delhi-Almaty weekly.

To/From Kyrgyzstan

Bishkek is not yet very well connected. Kyrgyzstan Airlines flies to/from Istanbul twice a week. Its Russia flights include Moscow (four per week for US$198, one way), St Petersburg via Omsk (seasonal, with St Petersburg Airlines, US$270, one way) and Novosibirsk (weekly, with Novosibirsk Airlines, US$158, one way). Transaero goes to Bishkek from Moscow and Kiev.

It's also easy to get to Bishkek by flying into Almaty. No Kazakstan transit visa is necessary if you're going straight to Bishkek (three hours on the road). Lufthansa even runs its own Almaty-Bishkek ground shuttle service.

To/From Tajikistan

Tajikistan International Airlines flies Boeing 707s London-Dushanbe-Delhi every Saturday, and back the next day. Aeroflot has four Moscow-Dushanbe flights weekly for US$280 (one way). There are also irregular charter connections from Dushanbe to Karachi, Delhi, Aleppo and Abu Dhabi, mainly for small-time importers and smugglers. They fly out half empty but return

overloaded with cargo; generally there is space only on flights *out* of Tajikistan; contact Intourist at the Hotel Tajikistan (☎ (3772) 21 6892, fax 21 5236).

To/From Turkmenistan

From the USA, the best Ashghabat return fares we found range from US$1470 from the east coast to US$2313 from the west coast, both with Turkish Airlines, via Istanbul, departing twice a week in summer.

The cheapest flight from the UK is also with Turkish Airlines, from London via Istanbul (overnight) to Ashghabat, four times a week for £502 return. Alternatively you could fly Istanbul-Baku, take the ferry to Turkmenbashi and a 12 hour train ride across the desert to Ashghabat. Turkmenistan Airlines has a weekly direct London-Ashghabat flight, with links to other UK cities. Its daily Istanbul-Ashghabat flight is US$600 return. It also flies several times a day from Moscow (US$295, one way), three times a week from Baku (US$75 one way), twice a week from Yerevan and Kiev, and weekly from St Petersburg and other Russian cities.

Middle Eastern connections with Turkmenistan Airlines include Abu Dhabi three times a week and Damascus once a week. It also flies to/from Karachi (US$420 return) and Mashhad (Iran, US$70 one way) twice a week, and Delhi once a week. PIA flies to/from Karachi on Sunday, and Iran Air to/from Tehran on Tuesday (US$305 return).

To/From Uzbekistan

Tashkent – seven hours from London, 6½ from Frankfurt, 3½ from Moscow, Istanbul, Tel Aviv and Delhi, 5½ from Beijing and 6½ from Bangkok – may have the most centrally located airport on the Eurasian landmass. More regular international flights serve Tashkent than any other Central Asian city, though it's the least friendly of them all for a first-time arrival (see the Arriving in Tashkent By Air aside). You can book and reconfirm Uzbekistan Airways flights from city airline booking offices all over the country.

Arriving in Tashkent by Air

The role of Central Asian air-transport hub has come to Tashkent too suddenly, and its airport administration is struggling to cope with the huge increase in air traffic since independence. There are plans for a new airport 25 km out of the city, but meanwhile the arrivals hall for non-VIPs is a grim, sweaty place, too small to deal with the passenger load off a Yak-40, let alone a jumbo jet (for a 'tour' of the terminal see the Tashkent Getting There & Away section in the Uzbekistan chapter).

Arrival procedures, even without visa hassles, commonly take three or four hours – passport check, Ministry of Foreign Affairs (MFA) visa check, foreign exchange, baggage collection, customs (with no difference in treatment between red and green channels) and OVIR visa check.

The MFA duty officer meets all flights coming from outside the CIS. If you're coming from inside the CIS you may not find one there. If not, and you don't have a visa, ask to be taken upstairs to the ministry office to get one; don't just saunter out without a visa, as you'll just have trouble later.

The so-called '72 hour rule' (see Visas & Embassies in the Facts for the Visitor chapter) is not graciously honoured here. One traveller, arriving from Bishkek with only a Kyrgyz visa (which should have entitled him to at least 72 hours in Tashkent), was detained for five hours and finally had to pay a US$30 bribe just to get out of the airport.

The main problem is incompetence and bad organisation, but it's greedy, bloody-minded or unscrupulous Uzbek officials that have made Tashkent airport infamous. Some are power-tripping, but most are just looking for a few easy dollars, and new arrivals to Central Asia – disoriented, sleep-deprived and jet lagged – are easy pickings.

One woman arrived with an Uzbek visa but was hassled because she had no hotel booking. One man was told to drop his trousers and open his extra money belt so customs could confirm the sum he had declared. There are plenty of outright cons too – 10 sum for a customs form before you've even found the bank, or the weighing of bags on arrival and demands for excess-baggage charges, for example.

If you have arranged to collect a visa on arrival, they may take a very long time to find you in their Big Book. Be prepared to wait them out, or to call your sponsoring agency if a representative has not come to meet you.

Then, at the end of it all, you're released into a sea of grasping taxi drivers. Stay away from the drivers who loiter just outside (and sometimes inside) the arrivals hall; these are the greediest and most unscrupulous. Local people say some are in league with customs officials, who tip them off about passengers carrying lots of cash. Push your way through to the taxi dispatcher (dispecher in Russian) or the buses, in front of the new terminal. During business hours, the small Uzbektourism office at the old terminal is surprisingly helpful.

All these problems are of course worse if you arrive in the middle of the night, when everybody's irritable, and transport is scarce and even more predatory. If possible, avoid this unless you're certain you will be met. That means choosing your flight time – from London, avoid Uzbekistan Airways' Saturday night flight, which arrives at 4.15 am (their others from Europe are okay); from Asia, avoid their evening flight from Bangkok (there is an early morning one) and their Beijing flight. From the Middle East, avoid all flights from Bahrain and Sharjah. Lufthansa's flights from Frankfurt get in at 3.45 am. ∎

From the USA, the best Tashkent return fares we found range from US$1470 from the east coast to US$1710 from the west coast, both with Turkish Airlines. Uzbekistan Airways flies New York-Tashkent via Riga and Amsterdam, Friday in both directions, an 18 hour flight for almost the same fare, but with Turkish you stop over in Istanbul.

Uzbekistan Airways' London-Tashkent-Delhi run (four per week, £700 return) is comfortable, with good service and good food (but the return is no match, with exhausted Delhi passengers sprawled everywhere and poor food from Tashkent). Its other connections to Tashkent include Manchester (once a week), Frankfurt (three a week) and Istanbul (twice a week).

Lufthansa flies twice a week from Frankfurt for £800 return. Transaero and Aeroflot have numerous Moscow-Tashkent connections at US$220 one way. The Uzbekistan Airways' flight is cheaper at about US$170; they also come from St Petersburg four times a week, and about 20 other Russian cities.

Uzbekistan Airways flies from Tel Aviv once or twice a week, Bahrain and Sharjah two or three times a week, and Jeddah weekly. It flies Delhi-Tashkent-London four times a week and Karachi-Tashkent twice a week. PIA has twice-weekly connections from Islamabad and weekly ones from Karachi and Peshawar.

Other Asia connections with Uzbekistan Airways are Beijing (once a week, US$483 return), Bangkok (twice a week, a seven hour flight for US$403 return) and Kuala Lumpur weekly. Thai Airways also flies from Bangkok. Air China flies Ürümqi-Tashkent once a week.

Some regular Uzbekistan Airways and Aeroflot flights from Russia serve Samarkand, Urgench and Bukhara. Aeroflot flies to Samarkand from Moscow three times a week, and from St Petersburg twice a week. There are apparently some direct London-Samarkand charter flights too; ask your travel agent. Aeroflot also flies Moscow-Urgench, Moscow-Bukhara and St Petersburg-Bukhara, each twice a week in summer.

To/From Western Xinjiang

The only way to fly to Kashgar is from Ürümqi with Air China (China Xinjiang Airlines). Flights depart daily in summer and four times a week in winter, for about US$120 (one way). You may have to stay the night in Ürümqi. There are regional Ürümqi connections to Tashkent weekly and to Almaty twice a week with both China Xinjiang Airlines (US$125, one way) and Kazakstan Airlines (US$150, one way).

International connections to Ürümqi include Islamabad (Sunday in both directions, US$270 return) with Air China, and Moscow via Novosibirsk (Friday in both directions, US$690 return) with Air China

and Aeroflot. There are also direct flights to Ürümqi from cities in China, including Beijing, Guangzhou (Canton), Kunming, Chengdu, Qingdao and Zhengzhou.

The convenience of quick China visas makes Hong Kong a useful stop, but it's generally cheaper to fly directly into China. The cheapest routes from Europe and North America are via Beijing or Shanghai, and those from Australasia are via Guangzhou. The lowest fares are with Air China. If you do stop in Hong Kong, an alternative to flying from there is to take an overnight boat, morning hoverferry or fast train to Guangzhou and fly from there.

It may be possible to fly directly from Hong Kong to Ürümqi. Seasonal charter flights come and go; at time of research they were US$440 return, on Saturday in both directions.

To/From Pakistan

Most international carriers serve only Karachi, and it's cheaper to go to Karachi than to Islamabad (eg from west coast USA, US$1550 return compared to US$1800). From Karachi there are five to eight flights daily to Islamabad, including a 'Night Coach' flight that's 25% cheaper. Since domestic tickets cost about 30% less if you buy them in Pakistan, it's cheaper still to buy the connecting ticket after you arrive.

Central Asia connections with Karachi include Ashghabat and Tashkent, each twice a week with Turkmenistan Airlines and once a week with PIA.

Budget flights from New Zealand and Australia connect with PIA at major hubs in South-East Asia, including Bangkok.

Departure

A week's advance booking is good enough for nearly any domestic or international flight out of Central Asia, even in summer, and two or three days is still pretty safe. You must show an onward visa to buy a ticket within Central Asia, even to Moscow.

Departure Tax You'll pay this for most departures from Central Asian republics to points outside the CIS, though the rules vary – eg from Tashkent, US$10 (at check-in when you leave), with no tax for departures to domestic or CIS points; from Bishkek, US$5 plus 5% of the fare (when you buy the ticket) for all domestic, CIS and international departures.

TRAIN

There are three main rail routes into Central Asia from Russia. One comes from Moscow via Samara or Saratov, straight across Kazakstan via Qyzylorda to Tashkent, with branch lines to Bishkek and Almaty. A second route goes round the other side of the Aral Sea via Urgench, Charjou, Bukhara and Samarkand to Tashkent, with a branch line to Dushanbe. The third main route, the Turkestan-Siberia Railway or 'Turksib', links the Trans-Siberian Railway at Novosibirsk with Almaty.

Another line crosses Kazakstan via Qaraghandy (Karaganda). From the Caspian Sea yet another line crosses Turkmenistan. This is the so-called Trans-Caspian route, the first to be pushed into Central Asia by the Russians in the 19th century.

Completed in 1992, after being delayed almost half a century by Russian-Chinese geopolitics, is a line from China via Ürümqi into Kazakstan, joining the Turksib for connections to Almaty or to Siberia.

The 2½ day trip from Moscow to Tashkent and the 1½ day trip from Ürümqi to Almaty don't have quite the romance or the laid-back feel of the Trans-Siberian, but they're usually cheaper and more frequent than flying, and allow Central Asia to unfold gradually. A guidebook devoted entirely to the Moscow-Beijing rail route via Central Asia is Dominic Streatfeild-James' *Silk Route by Rail*.

Rolling Stock

Trains into Central Asia are either Russian or, from the China side, Chinese. With minor exceptions carriages are the same in corresponding classes of each, with washrooms at either end with cold (and sometimes hot) water and a toilet, and a big samovar dispensing boiling water. Smoking is forbidden in the compartments, but permitted at the ends of the cars. Double-glazed and sealed windows, and often heated carriages, are hardly appropriate for crossing summer steppes and desert, but there you are. Carriages tend to be pretty decrepit.

Chinese railway tracks are about 10 cm narrower than the old Soviet ones, and at the Chinese-Kazakstan border the carriages are hoisted up and their 'bogeys' (wheel assemblies) changed.

Services

A normal long-distance train is called a 'fast train' (СКОРЫЙ, *skoryy* in Russian; in Uzbekistan, where Russian has disappeared from timetables, the Uzbek word is ЙЎЛОВЧИ *(yulovchi)*. A *passazhirskiy* (passenger) train stops more often and may have a smaller proportion of more comfortable accommodation. Foreign tourists are usually put on one of these two types. The best of these often have names, eg the *Uzbekistan* between Moscow and Tashkent.

These named trains *(firmennyy poezd* in Russian) tend to have cleaner cars, more polite staff, more convenient arrival/departure hours, sometimes fewer stops, more top-class accommodation and functioning restaurants.

Note that all trains numbered 900 and up are mail trains and therefore *extremely* slow.

Classes

A deluxe sleeping carriage is called *spets-vagon* (Russian for special carriage, abbreviated СВ in Cyrillic; some say this means *spalnyy vagon*, sleeping carriage), *myagkiy* (soft) or 1st class. Closed compartments have carpets and upholstered seats, and convert to comfortable sleeping compartments for two. An ordinary sleeping carriage is called *kupeynyy* or *kupe* (Russian for compartmentalised), *zhyostkiy* (hard) or 2nd class. Closed compartments are usually four-person couchettes. Seats are leather or plastic and also form the lower pair of bunks.

Chinese trains have something in between 1st and 2nd, called soft-sleepers, with carpets, clean loos etc, but four to a compartment. All closed compartments have, thank goodness, a switch that allows you to turn off the piped muzak.

A *platskartnyy* (reserved-place) or 3rd-class carriage – also called hard-sleeper – has open-bunk accommodation. Bunks (not actually hard, just less soft) are partitioned, but not closed off, and more are squeezed into a carriage. *Obshchiy* (general) or 4th class – also called hard-seat – is unreserved bench-type seating.

We found some agents in Central Asia calling kupeynyy class '1st', so you're better off using the Russian terms just to be sure you get what you ask for.

With a reservation, your ticket normally shows the numbers of your carriage *(vagon)* and seat *(mesto)*. Class may be indicated by what looks like a fraction: eg 1/2 means 1st class two berth, 2/4 means 2nd class four berth.

On Board

Experienced passengers bring comfortable 'lounging' clothes for long trips, eg track suits and slippers. Sleeping compartments are mixed-sex; when women show that they want to change or get out of bed, men go out and loiter in the corridor.

Attendants In Russian called *provodnik* (M) or *provodnitsa* (F), and *fuwuren* in Chinese, carriage attendants are responsible for keeping things clean, filling and stoking the samovars, giving you a change of linen every few days and keeping track of you at halts. Chinese attendants wash the windows and keep compartments stocked with thermos jugs of hot water. Especially on the ex-Soviet side they're a force all their own, ranging from bossy, lecherous young men to sturdy, tank-commander women with hearts of gold. It is worth being on good terms with yours if possible, and exceptional service is worth a small gift at the end of the journey.

Food & Drink Take enough food for the whole journey. The food in restaurant cars is awful (less so in Chinese trains), and only

gets worse and less plentiful as the trip wears on. On long trips local travellers bring great bundles of food which they spread out and – as dictated by rail etiquette – offer to one another (you should do the same). This they may supplement with food bought at station halts.

At many stations, hawkers sell (or come aboard selling) fruit, bread, pasties, dried fish, hot potatoes, preserved food, beer, soft drinks etc. Be suspicious of all the preserved stuff because of the risk of food poisoning. You're expected to pay in local currency.

Most carriages have a samovar with boiling water that's safe to drink. If you don't always fancy a mug of boiling tea, bring bottled water.

Alcohol Local travellers generally love speaking with foreigners, and on long train rides, many love drinking with them as well. Turning this down is tricky. If you are uneasy about the booze or its owner, saying *'Ya alkogolik/alkogolichka'*, meaning 'I'm an alcoholic' (m/f), will usually stop them from pressing (for other tips see Vodka under Food in the Facts for the Visitor chapter). In fact, if you're uneasy about your compartment-mates for any reason, you might persuade the attendant to make some rearrangements if you ask at the start. Foreigners are more carefully segregated on Chinese trains.

Stops These are welcome as much for real air as for exercise. Toilets are locked during stops, and that can be a long time at the border. The 'pok, pok' you hear is a maintenance worker testing the bogeys with a little hammer.

Stops are from one to 20 minutes long except at borders; durations are in the timetable posted in each carriage, though these may be out of date. Departure comes without a whistle and the trains slip out almost soundlessly – and the engineer doesn't care whether a foreigner's been left behind. Be careful too about crossing tracks, which could be carrying a slow, three km long freight train just at departure time.

Most restrictions on taking photos at train

stations no longer exist on the former Soviet side, but border crossings are still a no-no.

Rip-Offs Some long-distance trains routinely experience midnight thefts, occasionally robberies and sometimes assaults. See the entry Crime on the Rails under Dangers & Annoyances in the Facts for the Visitor chapter, for suggestions on how to make your compartment hassleproof. And don't wander off and leave your bags unattended at station halts.

'Official' robbery seems to be a bigger problem. Police and customs officials at border crossings (eg at the Kazakstan-Uzbekistan border on the Moscow-Urgench train, and more infamously the China-Kazakstan border on the Ürümqi-Almaty train) routinely try to shake down passengers for a few dollars – the subtle ones by inventing rules that have been transgressed, the dumber ones by simple threats. Keep your wits about you, stand your ground politely but firmly and you can face down most of them.

Buying Tickets

You should book at least a week ahead for international connections, though as little as two days is probably safe for intra-CIS connections, even in summer. There's not much advantage in buying tickets abroad, and it's more expensive.

Foreigners are supposed to pay more than locals, typically 50% to 100% more, though in the ex-Soviet republics this is not always enforced at station ticket windows. A named train is usually more expensive than others on the same route. Fares frequently lurch upward to compensate for inflation, so we don't quote many in this book.

Keep to the place shown on your ticket. 'Helpful' train attendants may offer to upgrade you – eg from kupeynyy to SV – for a few unofficial dollars, but police or ticket masters may later want a few dollars more, a 'fine' for being in the wrong place.

In Kazakstan and Kyrgyzstan, trains were still running on Moscow time at the time of

research. Be sure to check this when buying tickets.

To/From Russia

Most trains bound for Central Asia depart from Moscow's Kazan(sky) Station. Europe dissolves into Asia as you sleep, and morning may bring a vast panorama of the Kazak steppe.

Two fast trains a day go the most direct route to/from Tashkent (No 5/6 and 85/86, about 56 hours), and one to/from Almaty (No 7/8, 78 hours). Other fast-train connections are less frequent, eg daily to/from Bishkek (No 17/18, 75 hours); Samarkand (No 97/98, 82 hours) via Urgench and Bukhara; and Dushanbe (No 23/24, 86 hours) via Qyzylorda, Tashkent, Samarkand and Termez. A daily service to/from Andijan in the Ferghana Valley (No 133/134, 76 hours) runs on alternate days via Namangan and via Marghilan.

A single-ticket Moscow-Dashkhovuz (Tashauz) service was allegedly to start at press time – Moscow-Baku plus a ferry across the Caspian plus the train via Turkmenbashi, Ashghabat, Mary and Charjou. There are other, slower connections but you could grow old and die on them. Trains out of Moscow have even numbers, those returning have odd numbers.

Typical foreigners' fares for a 2nd-class (kupeynyy) berth at the time of research were US$60 Moscow-Bishkek, US$73 Moscow-Tashkent (plus US$20 commission when bought in Tashkent) and US$110 Moscow-Almaty. Tickets bought in Uzbekistan (but not elsewhere in Central Asia) are noticeably more expensive than those bought at the Moscow end.

To/From China

Apart from the long way round on the Turksib and Trans-Siberian trains, there's just one way to get in or out of Central Asia by rail on the China side – the 1359 km journey between Ürümqi and Almaty on the soft-class Genghis Khan Express (No 13/14, respectively to/from Almaty). The trip takes about 36 hours, with two nights on the train in either direction.

In 1990 the Northern Xinjiang Railway was completed by the Chinese from Ürümqi via Kuytun to the then-Soviet border, from where it joined the Turksib at Aktogay, north of Almaty. The crossing, through the so-called 'Zhungarian Gap', an isolated and ancient gateway to China, is about 200 km north of the highway route. On the Kazakstan side the line runs picturesquely between the steppe and the Zhungar Alatau range.

The problem with this trip is the border crossing, and it's not just the 7½ to nine hours of border procedures, bogey changing and general waiting around without water or toilets. We have described the trip in detail under China-Kazakstan By Rail in the Kazakstan chapter, including the systematic plunder of passengers by customs officials at the Kazak border post of Dostyq (Kazak for the Russian name Druzhba, or 'Friendship'). This crossing simply ruins the journey, and we cannot recommend it until things change at the border.

Officials at Alashankou on the Chinese side are thorough but essentially honest. Most of our information is for the Almaty-bound train, although there is no reason to expect an easier time of it the other way. Travellers report no such serious hassles on the bus journey.

Another problem (which applies as well to the bus trip) is visas. It's not impossible to get a China visa in Central Asia, but awkward to get a Kazakstan (or Kyrgyzstan) visa from anywhere closer to the border than Beijing. You're better off bringing one from home.

Tickets (about US$60) are no problem in either Ürümqi or Almaty (see those cities, and China-Kazakstan By Rail in the Kazakstan chapter), or you can book ahead at a much higher price.

From Hong Kong to Ürümqi by rail is 4900 km and takes a minimum of 4½ days, although few in their right minds would do this all at once, considering not only comfort but all there is to see en route.

To/From Iran & Afghanistan

Work has begun on a line to link Mashhad in Iran with Tejen on the Trans-Caspian mainline, which would complete a connection between Tehran and Ashghabat, but that's some way off (and at research time we heard that work had been halted).

Under discussion, should peace ever come to Afghanistan, is a line from Quetta in Pakistan via Herat to Kushka and the Trans-Caspian line.

OVERLAND

Unless you've entered the Paris-Beijing rally, you cannot bring a personal vehicle – car or motorbike – into China. In fact bringing your own vehicle to anywhere in the region covered by this book is fraught with practical problems, the main one being fuel – unpredictable supplies, often adulterated, and wildly fluctuating prices. There are no motoring associations of any kind. Most seriously, in case of an accident in a remote place, you could be very much up the proverbial creek, and not just for spare parts. If you do damage to a person or to property, you must settle on the spot, and you're at risk of robbery or violence.

The state insurance offices, splinters of the old Soviet agency Ingosstrakh, have no overseas offices that we know of, and your own insurance is most unlikely to be valid in Central Asia. You would probably have to arrange insurance anew at each border. The Black Sea & Baltic General Insurance Co (☎ (0171) 709 9202, 709 9292), 65 Fenchurch St, London EC3M 4EY, in the UK, will write policies for cars (but not motorbikes) in the ex-Soviet Central Asia except Kazakstan.

We note here cross-border roads which are, or may be, open to foreigners, eg by bus or hired car.

China to Kazakstan

A year-round road crosses from Ürümqi to Almaty via the border post at Khorgos (Korgas on the Xinjiang side) and Zharkent (formerly Panfilov). A direct Ürümqi-Almaty bus runs six days a week in each direction, taking about 26 hours, with stops for food and bodily functions but not for sleep. The cost is about US$50, and tickets are easy to buy in Ürümqi or Almaty. You could pay less on a succession of local buses but it's tedious (up to two or three days) and inconvenient. All are packed with Uyghurs and Kazaks, who can cross relatively easily for family visits or 'export-import'.

Travellers report no more than the usual customs hassles, cons and delays at Khorgos, as small-time entrepreneurs shuffle through with their Russian samovars and Chinese tea sets – nothing like the mistreatment at the train crossing. See China-Kazakstan By Road in the Kazakstan chapter for more on this crossing.

There are two other China-Kazakstan crossings farther north, at Bakhty (Tacheng on the China side) and Maykapchigay (Jeminay in China), though we have no information about whether they are open to foreigners.

China to Kyrgyzstan

From at least June to September it's possible to cross the dramatic 3752 metre Torugart pass (*Tu'ergate shankou* to the Chinese) on a rough road from Kashgar into Kyrgyzstan. Most travellers so far have taking the expensive option of hiring a vehicle to the pass and arranging to be met by another one on the other side. But a Chinese outfit now shuttles at least one loosely scheduled, questionably maintained bus between Kashgar and Bishkek three or four times a month in summer; the nonstop 1½ day trip (500 km) costs about US$70 from Bishkek but, curiously, US$100 from Kashgar.

Even the most painstaking arrangements can be thwarted, however, by logistical gridlock on the China side (eg your Kyrgyz car may not be allowed down from the pass to the Chinese immigration post, where your Chinese car awaits you) or by unpredictable border closures (eg for holidays).

For more detail on this fine but frustrating trip – including transport and visa tips – see Bishkek to Kashgar via the Torugart Pass in the Kyrgyzstan chapter.

There are now several choices for the 1480 km overland bus trip to Kashgar from Ürümqi, along the northern edge of the Taklamakan desert – a three day run with two fairly primitive overnight stops for about US$25, and two 36 hour nonstop options, with soft seats (US$35) or doubledecker reclining sleepers (US$40 to US$45) – all daily. See the Kashgar or Ürümqi entries later in this book, about buying tickets.

Another warm-weather crossing is now open for commerce, from Kashgar via Irkeshtam to Osh, but so far not for individual tourists. Exodus (see Tour Operators, Travel & Visa Agencies entry in this chapter) has taken groups this way.

China to Tajikistan

In 1995 a road was apparently opened between Xinjiang and Tajikistan, probably only for commerce. It's said to start from near Bulunkul on the China side, but we were unable to learn its exact location. On the Tajikistan side experienced truck drivers knew nothing of it, and we saw no evidence of it from the Pamir Highway. See the Tajikistan chapter introduction about the serious risks of travelling in eastern Tajikistan.

Pakistan to China

The exciting trip on the Karakoram Highway (KKH) over the 4730 metre Khunjerab pass, said to be the world's highest public highway, is covered in detail in the Western Xinjiang & the KKH chapter. There are regular bus and 4WD services during the season when the pass is open – normally May through early November.

Afghanistan to Tajikistan

There are no road crossings open – at least for non-combatants – between Tajikistan and Afghanistan.

Afghanistan to Uzbekistan

The border at Termez is allegedly open to anyone with a valid Afghan or Uzbek visa, but there lies the rub. Afghanistan embassies represent Kabul, while the crossing here is territory controlled by the rebel Uzbek warlord Rashid Dostam. Uzbekistan is said to have a consulate in Mazar-e Sharif, but we have no information on the safety of the crossing, and cannot recommend it.

Iran to Turkmenistan

The Iran-Turkmenistan border is officially closed to foreigners, though some have managed to cross it (and also the Iran-Azerbaijan border). Three buses a week run between Mashhad in north-eastern Iran and Ashghabat, but no matter what anyone tells you, current regulations forbid foreigners to travel on it, even those holding valid visas for either side.

Turkey-Georgia-Azerbaljan-Turkmenistan

This is a nice idea – eg the bus or ferry from Trabzon into Georgia, the train to Baku (Azerbaijan) and the ferry to Turkmenbashi (ex-Krasnovodsk) – but the Caucasus is far too incendiary to make this safe at present. There are also many consular and other official obstacles at the Turkey end. The legal alternative is to fly Ankara-Baku or Trabzon-Baku and take the ferry.

BOAT

The only regular passenger service to Turkmenistan on the Caspian is from Baku, and it's not strictly a passenger service – nor, for that matter, is it very regular. The boats are freighters between Baku and Turkmenbashi (ex-Krasnovodsk), whose schedules depend totally on what's to be taken and when it can be loaded. On average, there are three sailings a week but the exact day of departure is rarely known until shortly beforehand. Each boat takes 300 passengers on the 12 hour voyage; foreigners price is US$75 each.

Anyone arriving in Turkmenbashi must already have a Turkmen visa as immigration is quite tightly controlled. For more information on the crossing, see the Turkmenbashi section in the Turkmenistan chapter.

Ships to/from Astrakhan, Iran, the Black Sea and even the Mediterranean occasion-

ally call at Turkmenbashi, and individual captains may be willing to take on board a passenger or two.

There is no regular Iran-Turkmenistan service, but you can sail to Baku from Bandar-é Anzali in Iran on Sunday or back on Thursday (both depart at 7 pm, arriving next morning at 9 am), year-round. At research time, the one-way fare was US$100 for 3rd class (like airline economy seating), US$130 for 2nd class, US$160 for 1st class and US$200 for 'super' class. For current information call IRISL (Iran's national shipping line) in London on ☎ (0171) 378 7121.

TRAVEL & VISA AGENCIES

In this section we list reliable agencies who can help you with the logistics of travel in Central Asia, Xinjiang and along the Karakoram Highway (KKH) – whether it be visas, a few excursions or an entire trip. These include travel agencies, package tour operators (especially adventure-tourism), homestay agencies and 'visa shops', and many combine these functions. Most are overseas agencies, but we also list some switched-on young Central Asian outfits that have demonstrated they can handle requests from overseas.

Other agencies specialising in cheap flights are listed under Buying Tickets in the Air section of this chapter.

The USA

Recreational Equipment Inc (REI) is known for its interesting, environmentally-aware trekking, climbing and biking packages throughout the ex-USSR; they're at PO Box 1938, Sumner, WA 98390 ☎ (206) 891-2631, or toll-free from the USA and Canada (800) 622-2236, fax (206) 395-4744.

Among rugged offerings from Mountain Travel Sobek are 24 days from Xian via Kashgar and the KKH to Rawalpindi, and three weeks of hiking, rafting, camel riding and sightseeing in Kazakstan, Kyrgyzstan and Uzbekistan; it's at 6420 Fairmount Avenue, El Cerrito, CA 94530 ☎ (510) 527-8100, toll-free (800) 227-2384, fax (510) 525-7710.

InnerAsia Expeditions (☎ (415) 922-0448, toll-free (800) 777-8183, fax (415) 346-5535), 2627 Lombard St, San Francisco, CA 94123, offers expensive, seductive Asian itineraries that it has often pioneered (eg it took the first western groups across the Torugart pass), and their fat brochure is a great dream-book. Other outfitters with Central Asia programmes include Wilderness Travels (☎ (415) 548-0420, toll-free (800) 368-2794, fax (415) 548-0347), 801 Allston Way, Berkeley, CA 94710, and Asian Pacific Adventures, 826 S Sierra Bonita Ave, Los Angeles, CA 90036 (☎ (213) 935-3156, toll-free (800) 825-1680, fax (213) 935-2691).

MIR Corporation arranges custom tours and seminars in the former USSR, plus homestays in Tashkent, Samarkand, Bukhara and Almaty. With a Moscow office and a Tashkent representative, it's also handy for visas. It's at 85 S Washington St, suite 210, Seattle, WA 98104 (☎ (206) 624-7289, toll-free (800) 424-7289, fax 624-7360, e-mail mir@igc.apc.org). For knowledgeable CIS-related arrangements, correspondents recommend Travel Time, 1 Hallidie Plaza, suite 406, San Francisco, CA 94102 (☎ & fax 391-1856, toll-free (800) 956-9327, e-mail traveltime@igc.apc.org), and Aereo Travel, also in San Francisco (☎ toll-free (800) 755-8747).

Two US agencies specialising in off-the-shelf and customised homestays in some ex-Soviet republics are Home & Host, 2445 Park Ave, Minneapolis, MN 55404 (☎ toll-free 800-SOVIETU), and American-International Homestays, PO Box 7178, Boulder, CO 80306 (☎ (303) 642-3088, toll-free (800) 876-2048, fax (303) 642-3365, e-mail ash@igc.apc.org). Both can also arrange long-term rentals, and Home & Host has visa-only options. St Petersburg-based HOFA (Host Families Association; see Russia in this section) has an agent in the USA (☎ (202) 333-9343).

Specialist visa agencies in the USA include Visa Services (☎ (202) 387 0300), 1519 Connecticut Avenue NW, Washington DC 20036; and Zierer, with offices at 703 Market St, suite 802, San Francisco, CA 94103 (☎ (415) 495-5216, toll-free (800) 843-9151) and at 1875 Connecticut Ave NW, Suite 500, Washington DC 20009 (☎ toll-free (800) 421-6706). US-Tech in New York (☎ & fax (718) 776-5898) can arrange Kyrgyzstan visas.

The UK

Regent Holidays, 15 John St, Bristol BS1 2HR, (☎ (0117) 921-1711, fax (0117) 925-4866) is a good China and ex-USSR specialist with lots of experience helping individual travellers. An old USSR hand doing individual and group holidays and study tours is Goodwill Holidays, Manor Chambers, The Green, School Lane, Welwyn, Herts AL6 9EB (☎ (01438) 716421, fax 840228).

Among offerings from Steppes East (☎ (01285) 810267, fax 810693, telex 444102 STEPPE G), Castle Eaton, Swindon, Wiltshire SN6 6JU, are cultural tours in Uzbekistan and treks and riding in the Fan mountains; they can also help with visas. One Europe Travel (☎ (0181) 566 9424, fax 566 8845), Research House, Fraser Rd, Perivale, Middlesex UB6 7AQ, is a Trans-Siberian specialist offering trans-Central Asia rail trips as well, for independent travellers. City accommodation is mostly with families.

FSC (Field Studies Council) Overseas, Montford Bridge, Shrewsbury SY4 1HW (☎ (01743) 850164, fax 850178), an educational charity dedicated to environmental understanding, runs about 50 trips a year to places of special wildlife or botanical interest. It's 1995 programme included a botanical expedition to Kazakstan.

Intourist Travel Ltd, though still owned by Intourist in Moscow, makes the most of its connections to arrange visas, flights and overpriced hotels. It's at 219 Marsh Wall, London E14 9FJ (☎ (0171) 538 8600). Voyages Jules Verne, 10 Glentworth St, London NW1 5PG (☎ (0171) 486 8080, fax 486 8571), offers striking, upmarket journeys, eg on Chairman Mao's deluxe State Train from Xian to Almaty.

Among adventure-travel firms offering general and special-interest tours and treks in Central Asia, Xinjiang or Pakistan are Exodus Expeditions (☎ (0181) 675 5550, fax 673 0779), 9 Weir Rd, London SW12 0LT; Explore Worldwide (☎ (01252) 344161, fax 343170), 1 Frederick St, Aldershot, Hants GU11 1LQ; and Himalayan Kingdoms (☎ (0117) 923 7163, fax 974 4993), 20 The Mall, Clifton, Bristol, BS8 4DR.

Several competent business-oriented firms specialising in the ex-USSR can help with visas, invitations etc, but tend to be expensive for independent travellers. They include Russia House (Barry Martin Travel), 37 Kingly Ct, Kingly St, London W1R 5LE (☎ (0171) 439 1271, fax 434 0813); Alpha Omega Travel (☎ (0113) 286 2121, fax 286 4964), Amadeus House, 6 Lidgett Lane, Garforth, Leeds LS25 1EQ; and East-West Travel (☎ (0171) 938-3211, fax (0171) 938-1077), 15 Kensington High St, London W8 5NP. All three have Moscow offices, Alpha Omega has one in Almaty and East-West has one in Baku.

The St Petersburg-based homestay agency HOFA (Host Families Association; see Russia in this section) has an agent in Britain (☎ (01295) 710648).

Visa agencies in London include Worldwide Visas (☎ (0171) 379 0419, 379 0376; fax 497 2590), 9 Adelaide St, London WC2N 4HZ; Consular Services (☎ (0171) 486 2887), 87 George St, London W1A 2DA; and Action Visas (☎ (0171) 388 4498). All can obtain Central Asia visas, though fees vary, and rise steeply for short-notice requests.

Australia

Two former USSR specialists in Australia who can help with arrangements and visa support are Gateway Travel (☎ (02) 745 3333, fax 745 3237), 48 The Boulevarde, Strathfield, NSW 2135, and Eastern Europe Travel Bureau (☎ (02) 262 1144), Level 5, 75 King St, Sydney. Red Bear Tours (☎ (03) 9824 7183, toll-free (1800) 337 031; fax (03) 9822 3956; e-mail bmccunn@werple.

mira.net.au; or http://www. travelcentre. com.au), 320B Glenferrie Rd, Malvern, Victoria 3144 can also arrange support letters, visas and provide advice and information in person or via their Web site.

The St Petersburg-based homestay agency HOFA (Host Families Association; see Russia in this section) has an agent in Australia at Shop 17, Terrace Shopping Centre, Mooroolbark, Victoria 3138 (☎ (03) 9725-8555, 9727-1177).

France

Allibert, 14 rue de l'Asile Popincourt, 75011 Paris (☎ (1) 48.06.16.61, fax (1) 48.06.47.22), or route de Grenoble, 38530 Chapareillan, France (☎ 76.45.22.26, fax 76.45.27.28) arranges three or four week sightseeing and trekking trips in the Tian Shan and Alatau ranges, plus Torugart and KKH trips. Tourisme chez l'Habitant, 27 rue Rambuteau, Paris (☎ (1) 42.71.47.47, fax (1) 42.71.27.80) is a homestay agency.

Germany

Programmes of Ikarus Tours (☎ (06174) 29020, fax 22952), Fasanenweg 1, Postfach 1220, D-61452 Königstein, include three weeks in Central Asia, Lake Baykal and Mongolia, plus Alatau and Pamir treks. B&B Worldwide, Sickingenstrasse 6, 10553 Berlin (☎ & fax (030) 345 22 10) arranges China and Central Asia homestays.

The Netherlands

Wilderness Expeditions, Kluverskamp 29, 7271 XM Borculo (☎ (545) 271074, 274711, fax 273756), specialises in 'extreme adventure' tourism, including trekking and climbing in the Tian Shan and around Xinjiang's Muztagh Ata, and expeditions in the Taklamakan desert.

Denmark

Kilroy Travels (formerly Scandinavian Student Travel Services) is experienced with youth travel in the ex-USSR. It's at Skindergade 28 A,1., 1159 Copenhagen K (☎ +45 33 78 03 00, fax 33 32 40 66).

Turkey

A competent Istanbul agency that can arrange Uzbekistan visas is Sumpak (☎ (0212) 235-0211), at Recet Pasa Sokak 3, Kat 3, Taksim Meydani. Another reliable agency is Sarptur (☎ 123 995, fax 122 119), at K Maras Caddesi 35 in Trabzon.

Russia

A reliable and well-recommended adventure-travel firm is Pilgrim Tours (Moskovskoe Turisticheskoe Agentstvo Piligrim; ☎ (7-095) 365-45-63, fax (7-095) 369-03-89, e-mail pilgrimtours@glas.apc.org) at 1-y Kirpichny pereulok 17, 105118 Moscow. They offer trekking, mountaineering, skiing, kayaking, biking and other trips all over the former USSR, including Central Asia.

Travel Russia (☎ (7-095) 290-34-39, 291-03-47; fax (7-095) 291-87-83), korpus 2, Trubnikovsky pereulok 21, 121069 Moscow, offers trekking in the Fan mountains and Tian Shan, riding in the Aqsu-Zhabaghly Reserve, rafting the Chatkal river, and some Tian Shan mountaineering. IRO Travel (☎ (7-095) 971-40-59, 280-85-62; fax (7-095) 280-76-86) at the Travellers Guest House, ulitsa Bolshaya Pereyaslavskaya 50, 10th floor, 129041 Moscow, offers an eight day 'Silk Road Adventure Program' including the Moscow-Ürümqi train trip and some interesting stopovers.

Two Moscow offices of UK business-oriented agencies are Alpha-Omega Travel (☎ 928-94-59, fax 928-60-39, ☎ & fax 928-99-58), Lubyansky proezd 3, floor 3, No 12; and East-West Travel (☎ 924-06-29, fax 925-04-60), Bolshaya Lubyanka ulitsa 24/15.

The Russian state travel bureau, Intourist (☎ 292-23-65, 292-12-78; fax 292-25-47), is at Mokhovaya ulitsa 13, and has service desks in many Moscow hotels.

We have good reports of St Petersburg-based HOFA (Host Families Association; ☎ & fax (812) 275-1992, e-mail alexei@hofak.stu.spb.su), which can provide B&B in centrally located flats with English-speaking hosts in Almaty, Bishkek, Tashkent and Samarkand for around US$50 for two people. There are discounts for students, and for stays of a week or more. They may also help with Central Asia visas.

Some visa agencies advertise in the *Moscow Times* and *Moscow Tribune* English-language newspapers.

China & Hong Kong

From Hong Kong there seems to be no good way to make low-budget Central Asia arrangements, other than taking the Ürümqi-Almaty train. Several agencies will happily make top-end hotel bookings in Ürümqi and Kashgar, and one or two will set you up in the ex-Soviet republics in Soviet style, ie with nightly advance bookings in overpriced state-run hotels.

If you do want the train sewn up from Hong Kong, contact China International Travel Service (CITS) at 6th floor, Tower II, South Seas Centre, 75 Mody Rd, Tsimshatsui, Kowloon (☎ 2732-5888). Other Hong Kong agencies go through CITS themselves. Alternatively you can contact the CITS office in Ürümqi directly, at 51 Xinhua North Rd (☎ (0991) 282-5913, 282-1428; fax 281-0689, 281-8691; telex 79027 CITSXJ CN). Their provicial counterpart, the Xinjiang Mountaineering Association (also calling themselves China Xinjiang International Sports Travel), has also replied to requests from outside China; they're at 1 Renmin Lu, Ürümqi 830002 (☎ (0991) 227072, 227882, fax 281 8365, telex 79064 CXMA CN).

CITS Ürümqi has also proved helpful in arranging visa support and transport for travellers planning to cross from Central Asia at Khorgos or the Torugart pass. Another Ürümqi agency that furnished visa support for someone who contacted them from Bishkek is China Golden Bridge Travel Service, 19 Dong Feng Rd (☎ (0991) 226813, 222706; fax 216978), but give them a few weeks.

The Kashgar Mountaineering Association, a branch of the China Mountaineering Association, used to concern itself only with expeditions but now handles trekking and other group sports too (eg white-water boating, mountain biking, and camel and horse safaris). It's at 8 Tiyu Lu (off Jiefang Nan Lu), Kashgar 844000 (☎ (0998) 223680, fax 222957, telex 79123 KSBTH CN).

Central Asia

Competent agencies within Central Asia clearly able to deal with individuals outside Central Asia are listed here. Others that you can deal with once you're there are listed (along with these) under their headquarters' cities.

Asia Travel (☎ (7-3712) 56-29-27, 33-10-55; fax 32-34-40; telex 116108 PTB RU; contact Radi Bakayev), Taras Shevchenko 44, Tashkent 700060, Uzbekistan – adventure travel

Asia Travel International (☎ (7-3662) 35-86-76, ☎ & fax 21-43-03, telex 116584 ATI RU; contact Igor Salikhov), 2nd floor, Hotel Samarkand, Samarkand, Uzbekistan – general tourism

Central Asia Tourism Corporation (☎ (7-3272) 63-90-17, 69-70-55; fax 63-90-20; contact Christina von Knobloch), Bogenbay Batyr 139, apt 6, Almaty 480092, Kazakstan – general tourism

Dostuck Trekking (☎ (7-3312) 42-74-71, fax 41-91-29, telex 251299 INTUR SU; contact Nikolai Shchetnikov, Vosemnadsataya Liniya 42-1, Bishkek 720053, Kyrgyzstan – adventure travel

ITMC Tien-Shan (☎ & fax (7-3312) 42-98-25, e-mail tienshan@asiemm.bishkek.su; contact Vladimir Komissarov), Panfilov 105, Bishkek 720035, Kyrgyzstan – adventure travel

Kan Tengri (☎ (7-3272) 67-78-66, ☎ & fax (7-3272) 67-70-24, fax (7-3272) 63-12-07), Abai prospektisi 48, Almaty 480072, Kazakstan – adventure travel

Orient Star (☎ (7-3662) 33-00-28, fax 31-14-23, telex 116468 AIRUS RU), room 302, Hotel Samarkand, Samarkand – general tourism

Overseas Meyir Travel (☎ (7-3272) 61-36-18, ☎ & fax 61-60-94; contact Christine M'Cartney, Apartment 25, Lenin prospektisi 50, Almaty – general tourism

Salom (☎ (7-36522) 3-72-77, 2-33-98; contact Raisa Gareyeva), building 11, apt 16, Prospekt Navoi, Bukhara, Uzbekistan – general tourism

Yordamchi (☎ (7-3712) 78-21-05, ☎ & fax 78-45-16, telex 116108 PTB RU; contact Nelli Shushlebina), Tashkent, Uzbekistan – general tourism

Pakistan

The following reputable agencies can help with your own plans or sell you packages for KKH trips, general or special-interest tours, and treks. The largest, Adventure Pakistan and Sitara, work mostly as ground agents for overseas companies and may be reluctant to deal with small groups.

Adventure Centre (☎ (0572) 2409; telex BEGSONS PK), PO Box 516, Gilgit, Pakistan

Adventure Pakistan (Travel Walji's Ltd) (☎ (051) 812151, 823963; fax 823109; telex 5769 or 5836 WALJI PK), PO Box 1088, Islamabad, Pakistan

Adventure Tours Pakistan (☎ (051) 852505), PO Box 1780, Islamabad, Pakistan

Karakoram Tours (☎ (051) 829120), 1 Baltoro House, Street 19, F-7/2, Islamabad, Pakistan

Nazir Sabir Expeditions (☎ (051) 853672, telex 5811 NAIBA PK), PO Box 1442, Islamabad, Pakistan

Pakistan Tours Ltd (☎ (051) 564811, 565449), Flashman's Hotel, The Mall, Rawalpindi, Pakistan

Pamir Tours (☎ (0572) 3939, fax 2525), PO Box 545, Gilgit, Pakistan

Sitara Travel Consultants (☎ (051) 564750, 566272; fax 568105), PO Box 63, Rawalpindi, Pakistan

WARNING

The information in this chapter is particularly vulnerable to change: prices for international travel are volatile, routes are introduced and cancelled, schedules change, special deals come and go, and rules and visa requirements are amended. Airlines and governments seem to take a perverse pleasure in making price structures and regulations as complicated as possible. You should check directly with the airline or a travel agent to make sure you understand how a fare (and ticket you may buy) works. In addition, the travel industry is highly competitive and there are many lurks and perks.

The upshot of this is that you should get opinions, quotes and advice from as many airlines and travel agents as possible before you part with your hard-earned cash. The details given in this chapter should be regarded as pointers and are not a substitute for your own careful, up-to-date research.

Getting Around

Flying is the least edifying and arguably the least safe mode of transport in Central Asia, but to some destinations and in some seasons it's the only sensible alternative. Trains are slow and easy-going, but crowded, grotty and increasingly crime-ridden. Buses are the most frequent and convenient way to get between towns cheaply, and the best way to see what remains of the land of the nomads, though long trips can be tedious and cramped, and vehicles are prone to breakdowns. An option in many areas is a car: taxis or private drivers are often willing to take you between cities.

Refer to Visas & Embassies in the Facts for the Visitor chapter for more on what to expect at borders between the Central Asian republics. You're marginally less likely to get hassled on a bus than on a train.

AIR

Flying saves time and takes the tedium out of Central Asia's long distances; from Tashkent, nothing is more than about 1½ hours away. It's the only sensible way to reach some places, eg Dushanbe (very roundabout by train, but a gorgeous flight over the western Tian Shan) and, in winter, much of Kyrgyzstan and Tajikistan. But the Central Asian airlines (and a few smaller carriers) have some way to go before meeting international safety standards; for more on this see Airline Safety in the Getting There & Away chapter.

Domestic and inter-republic services are absolutely no-frills; for long flights consider packing your own lunch, as locals do.

Connections

In Soviet times there were flights between most large towns on most days, but fuel shortages have done away with many, even between capitals. At the time of research there was no Almaty-Bishkek service (though there were flights between Almaty and other places in Kyrgyzstan), and uncertain services between Dushanbe and other capitals; Almaty-Tashkent, Bishkek-Tashkent and Ashghabat-Almaty went just twice a week. Major internal connections are more frequent, eg daily from Tashkent to Samarkand, Bukhara, Nukus and the Ferghana Valley; between Ashghabat, Turkmenbashi and Dashkhovuz; and Dushanbe-Khojand.

Flights between the biggest cities generally stick to their schedules, but those serving smaller towns are often delayed without explanation, and cancellations are common – usually a result of fuel shortages (big-city flights get priority). Printed schedules are unreliable – routes and individual flights are constantly being cancelled or reintroduced. The only sure way to find out what's flying is to ask at an air booking office. In any case, you should confirm any flight 24 hours beforehand.

Travel Jargon in Uzbekistan

Uzbekistan has made everything doubly hard by eliminating Russian words from timetables and signs in most stations and airports. Following are some of the most useful Uzbek terms you'll see in their place.

Airport =	ТАЙЁРГОХ
Railway station =	ТЕМИР ЙЎЛ (or Т/ЙЎЛ) ВОКЗАЛИ (or БЕКАТ)
Bus station =	АВТОБЕКАТ
Departure time =	ЖЎНАШ ВАҚТ
Duration =	ЙЎЛДАГИ ВАҚТ
Arrival time =	КЕЛИШ ВАҚТ
Daily =	ХАР КУНИ
Even days of the month =	ЖУФТ КУНЛАРИ
Odd days of the month =	ТОҚ КУНЛАРИ
Fast train =	ЙЎЛОВЧИ ПОЕЗД
Not running =	ОТМЕНЁН

Buying Tickets

A few western agencies can book intra-CIS flights, officially or otherwise. But as flights and information are more plentiful and prices usually lower from within Central Asia, this is not very useful. Also, flights are frequently cancelled and foreigners tend to get priority in any case.

Tickets for Central Asian airlines can be purchased from old Aeroflot municipal booking offices (some now renamed), from hotels' airline reservation desks (though they may attach fees of US$5 or more), or at the airport right up to departure. You'll need your passport and visa. Many booking offices have a special window for foreigners and/or for international flights. Since foreigners pay more than locals, staff are keen to sell to foreigners and may even find seats on supposedly full flights.

Check your ticket closely – mistakes are common. It might help to have a local friend look it over.

Fares

The ex-Soviet republics, China and Pakistan all have two-tier pricing systems, with for-eigners (except those with diplomatic or student visas) paying two to four times what locals do. All fares given in this book are the most current foreigners' fares at the time of research.

Some Central Asian airlines fly to/from one another's republics, and fares can depend on the one you choose – eg Almaty-Tashkent is US$74 (one way) with Uzbekistan Airways but US$144 (one way) with Kazakstan Airlines; Tashkent-Bishkek is US$83 (one way) with Uzbekistan Airways but US$113 (one way) with Kyrgyzstan Airlines.

The airlines like to point out that regional airfares compare nicely with SV (1st class) train fares, but fail to mention that those are local, not foreigners', airfares they're quoting, and that SV train carriages are rare for regional journeys.

The airfare diagram shows approximate one-way foreigners' fares in US dollars, for some major regional connections.

Excess Baggage

Sometimes there are baggage charges over 20 kg – eg US$0.10 per kg from Tashkent to

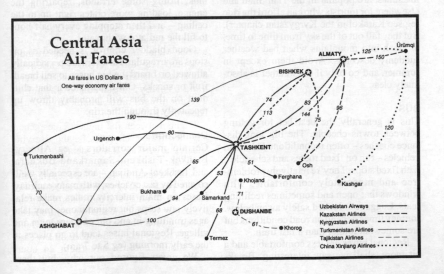

Central Asia Air Fares

All fares in US Dollars
One-way economy air fares

Uzbekistan Airways ———
Kazakstan Airlines — — —
Kyrgyzstan Airlines – – – –
Turkmenistan Airlines –·–·–
Tajikistan Airlines — — —
China Xinjiang Airlines ·······

Almaty, $0.80 per kg from Aqtau to Astra-khan, or 1% of the ticket price per kg at Atyrau – and sometimes not.

Departure Tax

Flights within the CIS are subject to a US$3 departure tax, paid when you buy the ticket. In China, we found the departure tax depended on airline and locale – eg Y45 in the ticket price at Kashgar, Y40 at check-in at Ürümqi, and Y30 at check-in at Guangzhou.

Check-In

Check-in is 40 to 90 minutes before departure and airlines are entitled to bump you if you come later than that. Some airports have special facilities for foreigners, allowing them to board early and miss out on the seating free-for-all (flights are generally single-class, with no assigned seats), especially if the flight is overbooked. To minimise the risk of loss or theft, consider carrying everything on board; many planes have special areas for large carry-ons.

Helicopter Flights

Helicopter flights, in former Aeroflot machines, are popular in the Tian Shan and elsewhere for tourists who can afford the ride (eg see Karakol in the Kyrgyzstan chapter). But they fall out of the sky from time to time, or crash into mountains when bad weather suddenly descends. Avoid them except in summer, and go only if the weather is absolutely clear.

BUS

This is generally the best bet for getting between towns cheaply. The big long-distance coaches – often reconditioned German vehicles – run on fixed routes and schedules, with fixed stops. They're relatively problem-free and moderately comfortable, with windows that open and sometimes reclining seats. Luggage is locked safely away below. Journey times depend on road conditions but are somewhat longer than a fast train.

Regional buses are less comfortable and a bit more, shall we say, interesting. Break-

downs are common. They are also used extensively by small-time traders to shift their goods around the region, and you could gradually become surrounded by boxes, bags, urns and live animals. Runs are occasionally cancelled, resulting in screaming matches as people storm the next available bus.

Private minibuses, which often solicit passengers in front of bus stations, are a bit more expensive, sometimes faster, and usually more hair-raising. They may be called *marshrutnyy* ('marsh-ROOT-ni', Russian for fixed-route) or *arenda* (Russian for for-hire). They generally have fixed fares and routes but no fixed timetable (or no departure at all if there aren't enough passengers to satisfy the driver), but will stop anywhere along the route. They may be clapped-out heaps or spiffy new Toyota vans.

But you're at the mercy of the driver. One of this book's authors rode from Bishkek to Toktogul; out of a 9½ hour trip, it was probably in motion for five or six hours – the first two hours spent cheerfully picking up cargo here and there in Bishkek and loading it all round the passengers, picking up a few friends, getting petrol, fixing a leaky petrol tank, doing some errands, repairing the engine, loading more crates right up to the ceiling – and then stopping every half-hour to fill the radiator with water.

Good bladder control is needed as pit stops are irregular. Hawkers are periodically allowed on board the big buses to sell bread, fruit or snacks. Our experience is that children on the bus will probably throw up repeatedly through the trip.

Connections

Certain major corridors – eg Almaty-Bishkek-Tashkent-Samarkand-Bukhara, and Tashkent-Andijan – are especially well-covered by fast coaches, with many each day. Buses on main intercity routes make relatively few stops but regional ones may take ages trundling in and out of every town and village. Regional buses tend to go places in the early morning (eg 5 to 7 am).

We never figured out why, but there

appear to be no buses between Charjou and any place in Uzbekistan except Urgench, though the border is only about 30 km away. There are some Turkmenistan-Uzbekistan buses farther west around Konye-Urgench and Nukus, however.

Schedules are erratically observed; buses may be cancelled for lack of passengers or petrol. Services thin out in colder weather, especially to/from mountain destinations.

Buying Tickets

Most cities have a main intercity bus station (*avtovokzal*) where you can buy your own ticket. Almost no travel agencies will book buses.

Try to pick buses originating from where you are, enabling you buy tickets as much as a day in advance. Tickets for through buses may not be sold until they arrive, amid anxious scrambles at the ticket window. In a pinch you could try paying the driver directly for a place; one traveller suggested this was also a good way to avoid the police in Uzbekistan bus stations.

In Tashkent, and to a lesser extent in Samarkand, buying a long-distance ticket at the station can be a real headache for a foreigner. You must first satisfy the station's OVIR office that you have a visa for your destination, and at Tashkent they may insist on buying the ticket for you, with your dollars, never mentioning the true price. Long-distance bus stations are in general low-life magnets, rarely pleasant after dark.

Fares

Bus fares are officially two-tier in some ex-Soviet republics – but not Kazakstan – and not in China and Pakistan. Visitors in Uzbekistan pay about three times what local people pay. But you may pay the local price if you buy at some more remote bus stations. Some routes have both 'hard' and 'soft' buses, with fares 15% to 35% higher for the latter. Hard/soft is *zhumsaq/qatty* in Kazak and Karakalpak, *yumshak/gaty* in Turkmen, and *yumshok/kattik* in Uzbek.

Inter-republic fares can depend on which side you start from – eg a ticket from Tashkent to Almaty costs US$8, while Almaty to Tashkent is US$21. Some foreigners' fares (one way) on state-run long-distance coaches to/from Bishkek are: Tashkent US$10, Almaty US$4.50, Naryn US$5 and Karakol US$5.50. Khojand-Osh costs about US$5. A private Bishkek-Osh bus costs about US$20.

TRAIN

Lower-class train travel is the cheapest way to get around, but that also makes it attractive to everybody else, so it's the most crowded way. You can of course sleep or stretch on long journeys, and there is camaraderie if you want it, but you'll always attract lots of attention – everything you do, or pull from your bag, will be of interest to compartment-mates and their friends down the aisle.

It's potluck as far as compartment-mates go (and mixed-sex too), unless you take a whole kupeynyy (2nd class) compartment with friends; SV (1st class) carriages are scarce for trips within Central Asia (see the Getting There & Away chapter about trains, classes and services).

Trains trundle slowly across the countryside, but don't expect much of a view: windows are usually filthy, and covered with steel screens to protect against stone-throwers. They're also sealed, so carriages get stale, smoky and smelly after half a day or so. Food on board is pretty awful, or nonexistent, and food at stops is unpredictable; bring your own (and be prepared to share it with compartment-mates, as is the usual tradition), along with hot-drink ingredients.

Trains are the safest as far as accidents go, but the worst for crime. Foreign passengers have occasionally been mugged for their valuables, and thieves target foreigners on some trains. Read Crime on the Rails, under Dangers & Annoyances in the Facts for the Visitor chapter, for suggestions on how to make your compartment hassle-proof.

As an indication of journey times, Urgench-Tashkent and Tashkent-Almaty are each about 25 hours on a fast train.

Connections

Vast tracts of mountains or desert mean some journeys are a pain by train, eg between north and south in Turkmenistan (Ashghabat-Dashkhovuz goes via Charjou) and Kyrgyzstan (Bishkek-Osh takes almost two days, via Tashkent), and to Dushanbe from anywhere. For these, buses or flights are more sensible. Otherwise there are adequate connections to most destinations of interest, at least every other day. Certain corridors, eg the Turksib (Semey-Almaty), Tashkent-Andijan and Almaty-Tashkent-Samarkand-Bukhara (with a branch to Bishkek), are well-served by fast trains.

Turkmenistan connections are especially awkward. There are no direct lines, for example, between Ashghabat and any other Central Asian capital. To travel from outside Turkmenistan to Mary, Ashghabat or anywhere else in the south of the country (unless it's on the daily Dashkhovuz-Ashghabat run), you must change trains at Charjou. But you don't change at Charjou if you're en route between Bukhara (or places east) and Urgench (or places west) – notably on the Moscow-Samarkand (No 97/98) or any Tashkent-Urgench run.

There are two rail routes to Tajikistan: one to Dushanbe and the other to Khojand, and they don't link up. While Khojand is well-connected to Tashkent, Dushanbe is a long way from anywhere, on the daily Moscow service via Tashkent, Samarkand and Termez.

Many trains to/from Russia (see the Getting There & Away chapter) can be used for getting around Central Asia, and may be faster and in better condition. But any train originating far from where you are is likely to be filthy, crowded and late by the time you board it.

Surprisingly, trains in Kazakstan and Kyrgyzstan were still running on Moscow time when we were there, even for trips entirely within Central Asia. Some suburban trains were running on local time, however.

Buying Tickets

Book at least two days ahead for CIS connections, if you can. You will probably need to show your passport and visa. A few stations have separate windows for advance bookings and for departures within 24 hours; the latter is generally the one with the heaving mob around it (beware of pickpockets).

Many tourist hotels have rail-booking desks, but they have their own mark-up. The region's greediest operator is surely Uzbekistan Railways, which won't allow sales from hotels but only at its own foreigners' booking offices, and slaps a US$20 service charge onto every ticket (transforming a US$12 Tashkent-Samarkand one-way fare, for example, to a US$32 rip-off). Few travel agencies are interested in booking trains.

If you can't get a ticket for a particular train, it's worth turning up anyway. No matter how full ticket clerks insist a train is, there always seem to be spare kupeynyy berths. Ask an attendant. You'll have to pay at least the equivalent price of the ticket, often more, and usually in dollars. Shop around the attendants for the best offer (the money, of course, all goes into his/her pocket). You can also upgrade this way. But police or ticket masters may later make a fuss and demand a further 'fine' of a few dollars.

Fares

Foreigners (except those with student or diplomatic visas) are supposed to pay three or four times the local fare for train tickets. This is hard to avoid at major centres, where you must show your passport when you buy the ticket, but elsewhere the rule may not always be enforced. You might get a local person to buy you a ticket, but then you're a sitting duck for any train official who wants to make a stink about it.

A few sample kupeynyy fares (one way) for trips to/from Tashkent are US$44 Bishkek, US$35 Almaty, US$25 Dushanbe, US$20 Bukhara and US$12 Samarkand (not including Uzbekistan Railways' US$20 surcharge).

CAR

Intercity travel by car is common in some

areas and you can probably organise it just about anywhere. It's quicker and just as comfortable as a bus or train, and can work out little more expensive than a bus. A car is also handy for reaching off-the-beaten-track places.

Taxis and private drivers willing to take long-distance passengers on common routes – eg Almaty-Bishkek or Shymkent-Tashkent – frequently wait at train or bus stations. Some wait for a full load of passengers before setting off. Hotel staff can sometimes help you find a driver.

You'll have to negotiate a price. On main routes in Kazakstan we found typical car prices to be about five times the bus fare, so if you can fill the car up, your share will be about the same as a bus fare.

Main highways between capitals and big cities, eg Almaty-Bishkek-Tashkent-Samarkand-Bukhara, are fast and fairly well maintained. Mountain roads (ie most roads in Kyrgyzstan and Tajikistan) can be blocked with snow in winter and plagued by landslides in spring.

Driving your own car is fraught with problems (see the Getting There & Away chapter), and we don't recommend it. The biggest problem by far is fuel supplies. Fixed-price official stations never seem to have any supplies at all, or have strict limits on how much you can buy.

You'll see petrol trucks dispensing by the roadside; most of these 'cowboy' dealers are honest and reliable, though you must bargain. Black-market petrol in Uzbekistan and Kyrgyzstan when we were there was US$0.35 to US$0.50 per litre, at least 60% higher than the official price. Often you'll see people sitting by the road selling not vegetables but plastic bottles of fuel, often of very poor quality, adulterated with oil or water. There is no lead-free fuel anywhere.

Distances are daunting; Almaty-Tashkent is about 800 km (10 hours) and Tashkent-Khiva 1000 km (14 hours). Tajikistan's roads have almost as many military checkpoints as potholes. In Uzbekistan there are police at every province (oblast) border and at the limits of larger towns – most of them looking

for excuses to hit drivers (local or otherwise) with a 'fine'.

Rental

A car and driver from Uzbektourism is about US$10 to US$12 per hour. Almaty has a Hertz franchise.

HITCHING

Hitching is never entirely safe in any country in the world, and we don't recommend it. Travellers who decide to hitch should understand that they are taking a small but potentially serious risk. People who do choose to hitch will be safer if they travel in pairs and let someone know where they are planning to go. Under specific locales we have called attention to hitching routes we feel are fairly safe.

LOCAL TRANSPORT

Most sizeable towns have public buses, and sometimes trolleybuses; bigger cities also have trams. Tashkent has a metro (underground) system, and Almaty will too, eventually. Transport is still ridiculously cheap by western standards, but usually packed because there's never enough money to keep an adequate fleet on the road; at peak hours it can take several stops for those caught by surprise to even work their way to an exit.

Uzbekistan makes things extra hard by labelling all buses and trolleybuses in Uzbek only. The supply of taxis is usually inadequate except around tourist hotels, but plenty of people will give you lifts.

Public transport in smaller towns tends to melt away soon after dark.

Bus, Trolleybus & Tram

Services are frequent in city centres, but more erratic as you move towards the edges.

Payment methods vary from city to city, but the most common method is to pay the driver cash on exit. In Tashkent and other big cities, you buy tickets (talony) in strips of five or 10 from drivers, or from street kiosks which display them in the window. You then punch them in little machines fixed inside the vehicles. Most passengers are perfectly honest, patiently passing one another's money and tickets up and down to the nearest conductor or punch.

Manoeuvre your way out by asking anyone in the way: '*Vykhodite?*' ('Getting off?'). If you're asked this, but aren't getting off, step aside.

Marshrutnoe Taxi

A marshrutnoe taxi ('marsh-ROOT-na-yuh tahk-SEE') is a minibus running along a fixed route. You can get on at fixed stops but can get off anywhere, eg by saying '*zdes pozhaluysta*' ('Here please'). Routes are hard to figure out and schedules erratic, and it's usually easier to stick to other transport. Fares depend on the distance travelled.

A variant, at least in some Kyrgyzstan towns, is the *marshrutnyy avtobus*, usually a clapped-out old snub-nose bus, like marshrutnoe taxis but devoid of the latter's speed, and slightly more expensive.

Metro

Tashkent has a metro (underground) system, and one is under construction in Almaty (though work is currently stalled). Refer to the Tashkent Getting Around section about using it.

Taxi

There are two kinds of taxis: officially-licensed ones and anything else. In bigger city entries we describe how to tell them apart from their licence plates. Official ones are more trustworthy, and sometimes cheaper – if you can find one. 'Taxi' painted on the door and a roof light are no guarantee

of official license. They may have meters but they're always 'broken' and you'll have to negotiate. Or let a local friend negotiate for you – they'll do better than you will.

Unofficial taxis are anything else you can stop. Some 'gypsy' taxis are also painted and have roof lights, while others are just private cars driven by people trying to cover their huge petrol costs. Stand at the side of the road, and extend your arm and wait, as scores of others around you will probably be doing. When someone stops, negotiate destination and fare through the passenger-side window or through a partially open door. The driver may say *sadytse* (sit down) or beckon you in, but get that fare sorted out first.

A typical fare across Tashkent at the time of research was under US$2; Urgench to Khiva (30 km) was US$5. Fares go up at night, and extra charges are incurred for radio calls (we note telephone numbers for these under individual town entries), eg about US$2 in Bishkek.

Precautions Avoid taxis lurking outside tourist hotels – drivers charge far too much and get uppity when you try to talk them down. Know your route, be familiar with how to get there and how long it should take. Never get into a taxi with more than one person in it, especially after dark; check the back seat of the car for hidden friends too. Keep your fare money in a separate pocket to avoid flashing large wads of cash. Have the taxi stop at the corner nearest your destination, not the specific address if you're staying at a private residence. Trust your instincts – if a driver looks creepy, look for another one.

Kazakstan
Қазақстан

Kazakstan, reaching from the Caspian Sea to China and from Siberia to the Tian Shan range, is more than twice as big as the four other former Soviet Central Asian republics put together. It's also the least densely populated and potentially the richest country in Central Asia, with huge mineral resources attracting serious investment from the West. Though unquestionably Central Asian, and aspiring to political and economic leadership of the region, it's set apart from the other states in several important ways.

In contrast to the deserts, mountains and river valleys of the other states, Kazakstan lies at the heart of the great Eurasian steppe, the band of grassland stretching from Mongolia to Hungary which has served for millennia as the highway and grazing ground of nomadic horseback peoples. The Kazak people remained largely nomadic until well into the 20th century – and as a result have left no ancient cities or ruins. The few historic remains are from non-Kazak cultures.

Because of the fertility of the steppe, and because it's the only Central Asian territory bordering directly on Russia, Kazakstan was colonised far earlier, and to a far greater extent, than the rest of Central Asia, by the tsarist and Soviet empires. They turned much of the steppe into farmland and built grey industrial cities to exploit the mineral resources.

The 'emptiness' and 'remoteness' of the steppe also made Kazakstan a convenient dumping ground for unwanted tsarist or Soviet subjects – from Dostoevsky, Trotsky and Solzhenitsyn to whole peoples disliked or feared by Stalin – as well as a place to hide the USSR's chief nuclear bomb testing zone and its main space launching centre.

Two centuries of colonisation have turned Kazakstan into a volatile ethnic compound, in which Kazaks number less than half and have only in recent years overtaken Rus-

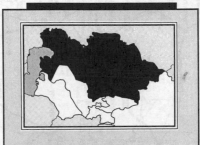

Highlights
- The Zailiysky and Küngey Alatau mountains, fine trekking country but can also be reached on day trips from Almaty.
- Aqsu-Zhabaghly nature reserve, Kazakstan's most accessible reserve, with fine scenery.
- The majestic mausoleum of Qozha Akhmed Yasaui in Turkistan.

sians. Now that the country is back under largely Kazak control, the Russians and other Slavs are leaving in big numbers.

For many travellers Kazakstan is chiefly a staging post for more famous Central Asian destinations. Almaty is one of Central Asia's main international air gateways, and is also linked to Ürümqi in China by bus and train. All trains from Russia to Central Asia cross Kazakstan.

To look at, this country is almost unremittingly bleak, from its treeless steppe to the deserts of the south to its decaying industrial cities. The chief exceptions are the cosmopolitan capital Almaty and, above all, the high mountains along Kazakstan's southern and eastern fringes – the Tian Shan, the Zhungar Alatau and the Altay among them. The real attractions of the country – unless you appreciate long, hypnotic train rides across steppe or desert, or have a yearning to experience post-Soviet urban decay – are in

KAZAKSTAN

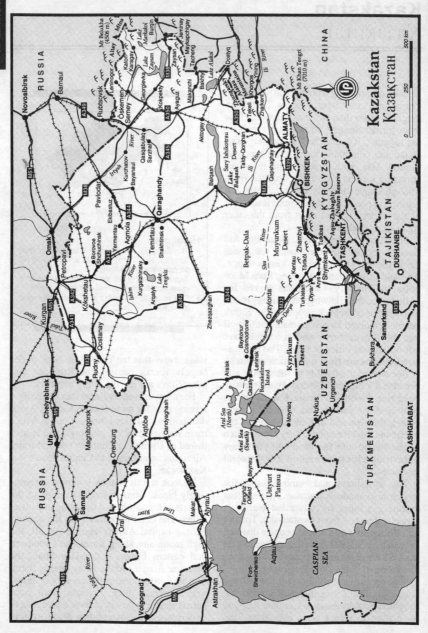

Kazakstan
Қазақстан

these mountains, with their icy peaks, forested valleys, swift rivers and clear lakes. A four or five day trek can take you across two Tian Shan ranges from Almaty to Kyrgyzstan's Lake Issyk-Kul.

You'll meet as many Russians as Kazaks here, and probably a few other nationalities too. The Kazaks, descended from Jenghiz Khan's hordes, present great contrasts. Though mainly rural and still just two or three generations from nomadism – as is shown by their wild horseback sports, the lingering custom of bride-stealing, and the collective farmers who disappear off to the hills with their herds and yurts for months on end – they can also be, in the cities, much more sophisticated and stylish than their Russian counterparts.

History

The early history of Kazakstan is a shadowy procession of nomad empires, mostly moving in from the east and hedged around with much uncertainty, since they left few written records or other traces. The Kazak people did not emerge as a distinct entity until the 15th century. Down the millennia, abiding threads include a great deal of large-scale slaughter, and a contrast between the far south, which was within the ambit of the settled Silk Road civilisations of Transoxiana (modern Uzbekistan), and the rest of Kazakstan which remained a domain of nomadic horseback animal herders until the 20th century. Since the 18th century the involvement of Russia has been paramount.

Early Peoples Around 500 BC southern Kazakstan was inhabited by the Saka, a nomadic people considered part of the vast network of Scythian cultures which stretched across the steppes from the Altay mountains to Ukraine. One southern Saka tribe, the Massagetes, succeeded in repelling Alexander the Great in the 4th century BC. The Saka did leave at least one important relic to posterity – the Golden Man, a fabulously worked golden warrior's costume discovered in a tomb near Almaty, and now

Kazakstan's greatest archaeological treasure.

Around 200 BC eastern Kazakstan was briefly under the control of the Hsiung-nu, a great nomad confederacy from China's northern borders, and probably ancestors of the Huns who later conquered large parts of Europe, Persia and India.

Turks Turkic peoples, again from the region of Mongolia and northern China, began moving into Kazakstan as the Huns were leaving. From about 550 to 750 AD the southern half of Kazakstan was the western extremity of the Kök (Blue) Turk empire which reached across the steppe from Manchuria.

The far south of Kazakstan was within the sphere of the Bukhara-based Samanid Dynasty from the mid-9th century and here the cities of Otyrar and Yasy (now Turkistan) developed on the back of agriculture and Silk Road trade. When the Qarakhanid Turks from the southern Kazak steppe ousted the Samanids in the late 10th century, they took up the Samanids' settled ways (as well as Islam) and left probably Kazakstan's earliest surviving buildings (in and around Zhambyl).

Jenghiz Khan Around 1130 the Qarakhanids were displaced by the Khitans, or Liao, a Buddhist people driven out of Mongolia and northern China. The Central Asian state the Khitans set up – known as the Karakitay Empire – stretched at its height from Transoxiana to Xinjiang but in the early 13th century became prey to rising powers from both west and east. To the west was the Khorezmshah Empire, based in Khorezm, south of the Aral Sea. In 1210 the Khorezmshah Mukhammad II conquered Transoxiana, also gaining control of the southern tip of Kazakstan.

East of the Karakitay was Jenghiz Khan, and to make matters worse a Mongolian named Kuchlug, enemy of Jenghiz Khan since the khan's early days, had set himself up as the Karakitay ruler.

Jenghiz Khan sent an army to crush the

Karakitay in 1218, then in 1219 turned to the Khorezmshah Empire, which had misguidedly rebuffed his relatively peaceable overtures by murdering 450 of his merchants at Otyrar and killing one of his ambassadors at Samarkand. The biggest Mongol army yet – 150,000 or more – sacked Samarkand, Bukhara and Otyrar (after a six month siege), then carried on westwards to Europe and the Middle East. All of Kazakstan, like the rest of Central Asia, became part of the Mongol Empire.

After Jenghiz Khan On Jenghiz Khan's death in 1227, his empire was divided between his sons. The lands most distant from the Mongol heartland – west, north and north-east of the Aral Sea – went to sons of his eldest son Jochi, who had died before his father. This territory, which stretched as far as Ukraine and Moscow and included western and most of northern Kazakstan, came to be known as the Golden Horde. The bulk of Kazakstan went, along with Transoxiana and western Xinjiang, to Jenghiz Khan's second son Chaghatai, and became known as the Chaghatai khanate.

The Chaghatai khanate split in the mid-14th century between Transoxiana, whose rulers adopted that region's settled lifestyle and Islam, and the lands farther north and east, where the Mongols maintained their nomadic ways. Timur, who took over in Transoxiana soon afterwards, wrecked Otyrar and constructed the grand Mausoleum of Qozha Akhmed Yasaui at Turkistan, but otherwise didn't bother much with Kazakstan.

The Kazaks It was from the descendants of the Mongols, and of Turkic and other peoples who survived their coming in Kazakstan, that the Kazaks emerged. The story actually starts with the Uzbeks, a group of Islamicised Mongols taking their name from an early 14th century leader Özbeg (or Uzbek), who were left in control of northern Kazakstan as the Golden Horde disintegrated in the 14th and 15th centuries. The Uzbeks spread southward, mingling with

---

When is a Kazak Not a Kazak?

'Kazak' is a Turkic word meaning free rider, adventurer, outlaw – just what the Kazaks were to the settled Uzbeks south of the Syr-Darya. Confusingly, Russians use the same word to refer to the Cossacks, an entirely different group of free riders, and until the 20th century Russians called the Kazaks 'Kyrgyz', and the Kyrgyz – just to make things straight – 'Kara (Black) Kyrgyz'. When the Russians decided in the 1920s to call the Kazaks 'Kazaks', they distinguished them from the Cossacks by using the Cyrillic letter x (kh) instead of the second k in Kazak. Thus in Soviet times Kazakstan was spelt Kazakhstan. The Kazak spelling of the country name is Қазақстан and in 1995 the government said it would like this to be rendered as Kazakstan in Roman script. ∎

---

other peoples, adopting the Turkic language as they went, and eventually crossing the Syr-Darya to attack the decaying empire of Timur's descendants.

In 1468 an internal feud split the Uzbeks into two groups. Those who ended up south of the Syr-Darya ruled the old Timurid empire from Bukhara as the Shaybanid Dynasty, settled down to agriculture and ultimately gave their name to modern Uzbekistan. Those who stayed north remained nomadic and became the Kazaks.

In the late 15th and 16th centuries the Kazaks established one of the world's last great nomadic empires, stretching across the steppe and desert north, east and west of the Syr-Darya. Under the chiefs Burunduk Khan (ruled 1488-1509), Qasym Khan (1509-18) and Haq Nazar (1538-80) they are said to have been able to bring 200,000 horsemen into the field. They menaced the remnants of the Chaghatai khanate in the Tian Shan and Xinjiang and raided Transoxiana. Haq Nazar's successor, Tevkel Khan, even briefly occupied Samarkand around 1590.

In the north, in 1563, a Kazak leader called Kuchum took over the Siberian khanate, a Golden Horde remnant with its capital deep inside present-day Russia at Sibir (modern Tobolsk). Sibir was captured by the eastward-advancing Russians in 1582, but Kuchum and his descendants harassed the Russian advance until the 1670s.

Those Russians who today claim that northern Kazakstan is 'traditionally part of Russia' seem unaware that, by similar logic, southern Siberia could be considered 'traditionally part of Kazakstan'!

The Hordes & the Great Disaster After Haq Nazar the fissures between the three great hordes of Kazaks deepened, weakening their ability to resist external threats. The hordes – with which Kazaks today still strongly identify – were the Great (or Elder) Horde in the south, the Middle Horde in the centre and north-east, and the Little (or Young or Lesser) Horde in the west. Each was ruled by a khan and was composed of a number of clans whose leaders held the title *aksakal, bi* or *batyr*.

The ruin of the Kazaks came from the Oyrats, a warlike, expansionist Mongolian people who subjugated eastern Kazakstan, the Tian Shan and parts of Xinjiang to form the Zhungarian Empire in the 1630s. The Kazaks were savagely and repeatedly pummelled, particularly between 1690 and 1720. They still remember this as the 'Great Disaster'.

The Russians Arrive Russia's expansion into Siberia also ran up against the Oyrats, against whom the Russians built, between 1716 and 1720, a line of forts along the Kazaks' northern border – Omsk, Pavlodar, Semipalatinsk (now Semey) and Ust-Kamenogorsk (now Öskemen). The Kazaks, evidently considering the Russians the lesser of two evils, sought tsarist protection from the Oyrats, and the khans of all three hordes swore loyalty to the Russian crown between 1731 and 1742. This brought little tangible help to the Kazaks, but the Russians took it as an excuse to stretch their defensive line right across the north of the Kazaks' territory to the Ural river. In the 1750s this line began to move south and Russian, Cossack and Tatar settlers moved in behind it.

Russia chose to interpret the Kazak khans' oaths of allegiance as agreement to annexation, despite the annihilation of the Oyrats by the Manchu Chinese in the 1750s. Spurred by Kazak attacks on Russian forts, and by Kazak revolts against their own leaders which were provoked by the deterioration of life during the Great Disaster, Russia gradually extended its 'protection' of the khanates to their abolition – the Middle Horde in 1822, the Little Horde in 1824 and the Great Horde in 1848. The khanates as political entities were abolished, but the hordes (as social/ethnic entities) remained.

Despite repeated Kazak uprisings, notably

Resistance Heroes

Many street names in Kazak cities commemorate leaders of the mostly hopeless resistance to the Oyrats: Tauke Khan (1680-1718) was the last Kazak leader able to bring the hordes together in one confederacy; Töle Bi, Kazybek Bi and Ayteke Bi were leaders from the three hordes who held a famous meeting at Ordabasy near Shymkent in 1726 to try to forge a united defence; Abylay Khan, Qabanbay Batyr and Bögenbay Batyr were other leaders against the Oyrats. Abylay Khan, of the Middle Horde, was one of those who tried to enlist Russian help by swearing loyalty to Russia in 1740 – you can see his likeness on the 100 *tengge* banknote.

Akhmed Baytursun and Mir Yakub Dulatov were prominent figures in a later Kazak independence struggle, the early 20th century Alash Orda movement. Dulatov was a radical Muslim nationalist and Baytursun a poet and educationalist.

Manshuk Mametova was a Kazak woman who volunteered for front-line service in WWII, and was one of the first Central Asian women to be named a Hero of the USSR. ■

by Abylay Khan's grandson Kenisary Qasimov in the 1840s, Russia steadily tightened its grip. The last bits of Kazakstan to fall were northern outposts of Uzbekistan's Kokand khanate – Aq-Meshit (now Qyzylorda) in 1853 and Zhambyl, Shymkent and Turkistan in 1864. In 1854 the Russians founded a fort in the south-east called Verny, which became Almaty.

Tsarist Rule Revolts were brutally suppressed. By some estimates one million of the four million Kazaks died in revolts and famines before 1870. Movement of peasant settlers into Kazakstan was stimulated by the abolition of serfdom in Russia and Ukraine in 1861. One million came to the north in the 1890s. The tsarist regime also used Kazakstan as a place of exile for dissidents – among them Fyodor Dostoevsky and the Ukrainian nationalist writer and artist Taras Shevchenko.

Russia governed southern Kazakstan as part of its Turkestan region, which also included much of the other modern Central Asian republics. Northern Kazakstan was treated separately and known as the Steppe region.

In 1916, Russian mobilisation of Kazaks as support labour behind the WWI front caused a widespread uprising, led by Abdulghaffar and Amangeldy Imanov. It was brutally put down, with an estimated 150,000 Kazaks killed and perhaps 200,000 fleeing to China.

The Communist Takeover In the chaos following the Russian Revolution of 1917 , a Kazak nationalist party, Alash Orda – which had been formed as an underground movement by aristocratic Kazak intellectuals in 1905 – tried to establish an independent government. Alash Orda's leader was Ali Khan Bukeykhanov, a prince and descendant of Jenghiz Khan, and ultimately a victim of Stalin's 1930s purges. The Alash Orda government had two centres – Semey in the north-east and Zhambeyty in the west. As the Russian civil war raged across Kazakstan, Alash Orda vacillated between support for the Red and White factions, eventually siding with the Bolsheviks who emerged victorious in 1920 – only for Alash members to be purged from the Communist Party of Kazakstan (CPK) and executed or sent to labour camps from 1925 on.

Meanwhile many thousands more Kazaks and Russian peasants had died in the civil war, which devastated the land and economy, and several hundred thousand fled to China and elsewhere. The Kazaks have been a minority in Kazakstan ever since.

Under Communist rule, southern Kazakstan was initially part of the Turkestan Autonomous Soviet Socialist Republic (ASSR), which included most of the rest of Soviet Central Asia. A separate ASSR covered northern Kazakstan – the old tsarist Steppe region – with its capital at Orenburg (now in Russia). From 1924 to 1925 the latter was enlarged by the addition of Kazak-peopled parts of the Turkestan ASSR, and its capital moved to Qyzylorda. The capital was shifted once more, to Almaty, in 1928. Kazakstan was made a full Soviet Socialist Republic (SSR) of the USSR in 1936.

Collectivisation & Colonisation The next disaster to befall the Kazaks was denomadisation, which began in the late 1920s. The world's biggest group of semino-madic people was forced one step up the Marxist evolutionary ladder, to become settled farmers in new collectives. They literally decimated their herds rather than hand them over to state control and, unused to agriculture, died in their hundreds of thousands from famine and disease. Those who opposed collectivisation were sent to labour camps or killed. Many more escaped to China. Kazakstan's population fell by more than two million between 1926 and 1933.

In the 1930s and 1940s more and more people from other parts of the USSR were settled in Kazakstan to work in its new industrial cities, or sent as prisoners to its many labour camps. The latter included whole peoples deported en masse from various parts of the USSR by Stalin around the time of WWII.

'Development' In the 1950s a new wave of around 800,000 migrants arrived when Nikita Khrushchev decided to plough up 250,000 sq km of north Kazakstan steppe to grow wheat in the Virgin Lands scheme, a bid to achieve Soviet grain self-sufficiency. One Leonid Brezhnev, as deputy head and later head of the CPK, did his own cause no harm by making the Virgin Lands appear more of a success than it really was (storms and wind savaged nearly half the new land in the early 1960s); see also the Great Cotton Flim-Flam aside in the Uzbekistan chapter.

Though the labour camps were wound down in the mid-1950s, many survivors stayed on, adding to the country's highly varied ethnic mixture. Yet more Russians, Ukrainians and other Soviet nationalities arrived to mine and process Kazakstan's reserves of coal, iron and oil. By 1959, 43% of Kazakstan's 9.3 million people was Russian, and only 29% was Kazak.

During the Cold War the USSR decided Kazakstan was 'empty' and 'remote' enough to use as its chief nuclear testing ground – almost 500 nuclear bombs were exploded from 1949 to 1989, mainly near Semipalatinsk (now Semey) – and as its space launch centre: all crewed Soviet space shots have blasted off from the Baykonur Cosmodrome on the steppe east of the Aral Sea. See the Environment section in the Facts About the Region chapter for more on nuclear testing in Kazakstan.

Unrest The CPK's first Kazak leader was Zhumabay Shayakhmetov, appointed during WWII but replaced in 1954 because of his lack of enthusiasm for the Virgin Lands campaign. A second Kazak, Dinmukhamed Qonaev (Kunaev to Russians), was in charge from 1964 to 1986. Though he was corrupt, Qonaev's replacement by a non-Kazak, Gennady Kolbin, in 1986 provoked big demonstrations and violent riots by Kazaks in many cities.

In 1989 Kazakstan produced the first great popular protest movement the USSR had seen – the Nevada-Semipalatinsk Movement, named after the US and USSR chief

nuclear testing grounds. Founded in the wake of two tests which sent a radioactive cloud over northern Kazakstan, the movement gathered over a million Kazakstani signatures within a few days, calling for an end to nuclear testing by the two superpowers. This pressure forced the CPK to demand an end to tests in Kazakstan, and there have been none since 1989.

Nazarbaev Nursultan Nazarbaev, a Kazak and former Qonaev protégé, took over from Kolbin in 1989 and has ruled Kazakstan since, with the title of president since 1990. Nazarbaev's approach to government follows the Chinese or South Korean mould – economic liberalism and political authoritarianism. Nazarbaev did not welcome the break-up of the USSR in 1991 – when the CPK renamed itself the Socialist Party – and Kazakstan was the last Soviet republic to declare independence from the USSR. Democracy has been limited, with radical Kazak nationalist groups harassed, and Nazarbaev dissolving a recently elected parliament in 1995 after it obstructed his economic and ethnic policies.

The country is still basically run by former communists but after independence Nazarbaev's market-oriented economic policies won popularity, and aid, from western governments. Privatisation is fairly advanced and major western investments have been won – the biggest being multibillion dollar deals with American and European companies to develop the Tenghiz oilfield and the Karachaganak gas field in western Kazakstan. The Kazakstan economy initially suffered as badly as all other post-Soviet economies and living standards across the country fell, leading to widespread disgruntlement, though Nazarbaev remained popular.

Ethnic Questions Ethnically, Kazakstan has the potential to be a tinderbox but Nazarbaev has so far prevented it from being set alight. Kazaks, thanks mainly to their higher birth rate, are again the biggest group in the country (about 44% of the population).

Russians form about 35% and there are also large groups of Ukrainians, Germans, Uzbeks and Tatars as well as about 100 other nationalities. The government's problem is on two levels – to placate both the Kazaks (who want supremacy) and the Slavs (who see little future in Kazakstan under Kazak rule); and to keep the three Kazak hordes together.

Though Nazarbaev is far from a rabid Kazak nationalist, there has been a clear swing towards Kazaks in awarding senior jobs, and Slavs also complain of discrimination in education – trends which have their origins in the 1986 riots. Many Slavs and Germans have already gone: by some estimates, one in seven Russians and Ukrainians (about one million people) left Kazakstan between 1992 and 1994, and up to 900,000 of the perhaps one million Germans have gone too. Radical Kazak nationalists are happy about this but the losses of the generally more educated Slavs and Germans damage the economy. The Slav population is particularly concentrated in the economically important north, and there have been rumblings of a movement to unify some parts of the north with Russia.

Perhaps as a sop to the Russians but also as recognition of the overwhelming economic and military importance of Russia itself, Nazarbaev has said he favours much closer ties with Russia, even at times mentioning a single parliament and a single currency. In 1995 the two countries signed a common defence agreement.

On the internal Kazak level, the Middle and Little hordes were virtually excluded from national power in the Qonaev years. Though Nazarbaev himself is Great Horde, he has taken some steps to correct this imbalance, no doubt aware that most of Kazakstan's vital mineral resources lie in Middle and Little horde territory. He appointed a Middle Horde prime minister and a Little Horde oil and gas minister in 1994. And his plan, announced in 1994, to transfer the capital from Almaty (in Great Horde territory) to the northern city of Aqmola (Middle Horde territory) has been interpreted partly as an attempt to reduce Great Horde hegemony.

Post-Independence Politics Kazakstan's first multi-party elections, held in 1994, returned a parliament considered favourable to Nazarbaev, but were judged unfair by foreign observers. Complaints included arbitrary barring of some candidates, ballot stuffing and media distortion. Of the 177 seats, 42 were reserved for candidates from Nazarbaev's personal list. Kazaks made up three-quarters of all the candidates, and ended up with 59% of the seats. The parliament turned out to be a thorn in Nazarbaev's side, obstructing his economic reforms – which one deputy called 'shock surgery without anaesthetics' – and refusing to even debate the question of making Russian an official state language alongside Kazak (which had been controversially declared the sole official tongue in 1989).

In 1995, following a court ruling that the elections had been illegal, Nazarbaev dissolved parliament. Soon afterwards, in the manner of Uzbekistan's Islam Karimov and Turkmenistan's Saparmurat Niyazov, he held a referendum on extending his presidential term, without elections, until the year 2000, and won with an overwhelming majority. Elections to a new parliament, under a new constitution, began in December 1995.

Geography

Covering 2.7 million sq km, Kazakstan is the ninth biggest country in the world, about the size of western Europe. Its border with Russia in the north and west is one of the world's longest, at about 5000 km. It borders Turkmenistan, Uzbekistan and Kyrgyzstan in the south, and China in the east. It has a lengthy shoreline (almost 1000 km) on the Caspian Sea, and a shrinking one on the Aral Sea, which it shares with Uzbekistan.

The country is mainly flat except for its alpine south-east and eastern fringes. Southeast Kazakstan lies along the northern edge of the Tian Shan, and Mt Khan Tengri (6995 metres), one of the great Tian Shan peaks, stands on the Kazakstan-Kyrgyzstan border.

Lesser Tian Shan ranges straddling the border west of here, most topping 4000 metres, are the Küngey Alatau, Zailiysky Alatau, Kyrgyz Alatau and Talassky Alatau.

Kazakstan's eastern border, with China, is a series of alternating mountain ranges and gaps through which roads or railways pass. The road route from Almaty to Ürümqi passes between the Tian Shan and the Zhungar Alatau range (which tops 5000 metres); the rail route traverses the so-called Zhungarian Gap, or Gate, at the east end of the Zhungar Alatau. Farther north are the Tarbagatay hills (mostly 2000 to 3000 metres) and, north of the headwaters of the Irtysh river, the Altay mountains (4000 metres-plus) which straddle Russia, Mongolia, Kazakhstan and China.

The only serious elevations elsewhere in the country are the Karatau hills, really a spur of the Tian Shan north-west of Zhambyl and Shymkent, and a band of upland that stretches west from the Tarbagatay hills, occasionally topping 1000 metres as in the Shyngghystau hills south of Semey.

The north of the country is flat, mostly treeless steppe, much of its original grassland now turned over to wheat or other agriculture. Farther south the steppe is increasingly arid, turning into desert or semidesert – often with some scrub vegetation – across much of the southern third of the country.

The Ustyurt plateau, a stony desert, reaches west from the Aral Sea towards the Caspian; south-east of the Aral Sea, Kazakstan shares the Kyzylkum desert with Uzbekistan; the Betpak-Dala clay desert stretches between the Aral Sea and Lake Balqash; south of the Betpak-Dala is the Muyunkum desert, and south of Lake Balqash is the Sary Ishikotrau desert.

The most important rivers are the Syr-Darya, flowing north-west across the south of Kazakstan into the Aral Sea; the Ural, flowing south from Russia's Ural mountains into the Caspian Sea; the Ili flowing out of China into Lake Balqash; the Irtysh which flows across north-east Kazakstan into Siberia; and the Ishim and Tobol which flow

north from northern Kazakstan to join the Irtysh.

Other rivers, such as the Shu (Kyrgyz: Chuy or Chu) flowing north out of Kyrgyzstan and the Sarysu in the centre of the country, peter out into nothing in the deserts.

Lake Balqash in the central east is the fourth largest lake in Asia (17,400 sq km) but very shallow – only 26 metres at its deepest point. Its eastern half is salty, and its western half fresh water.

Government

In the early post-Soviet years Kazakstan looked to be moving towards something approaching western-style democracy. But events in 1995 indicated that President Nazarbaev viewed democracy as an expendable luxury in the pursuit of economic reform and ethnic harmony.

Radical nationalists – whether Kazak or Russian – have never been welcome in Nazarbaev's Kazakstan. The most radical Kazak group, Alash, founded in 1989 with Pan-Turkic, Islamic revivalist and Kazak supremacist policies, was harassed and prevented from registering as a political party. Candidates for Kazakstan's first direct presidential election in 1991 were required to collect 100,000 signatures of support in order to run. It's rumoured that Hasan Qozhakhmetov, leader of another Kazak nationalist party, Zheltoqsan, had his signatures stolen two days before the election. In the event, Nazarbaev was the sole candidate and received 99% of the vote. Zheltoqsan was later merged with other groups to form the 'official' Kazak nationalist party, Azat.

A new constitution in 1993 enshrined the president (the head of state and de facto most powerful figure) and cabinet of ministers (headed by the prime minister) as the supreme executive power, and the Supreme Kenges (parliament) as the legislature. The Supreme Kenges replaced a part-time Supreme Soviet – a hangover from Soviet times elected in 1990. Under the 1993 constitution the president and Kenges were both supposed to have five-year terms and to be elected by universal suffrage.

The first elections to the Supreme Kenges, which began in 1994 produced an assembly that, though initially considered favourable to Nazarbaev, obstructed some of his key goals. The elections were criticised as unfair by foreign observers on various counts (see the History section in this chapter), and when in 1995 Kazakstan's constitutional court ruled that they had been illegal, Nazarbaev dissolved the Kenges, to rule by decree pending new elections. Soon afterwards Nazarbaev held a referendum on extending his presidential term, without elections, until the year 2000, and won an overwhelming 'yes' vote.

A new constitution in August 1995 provided for elections to a new, two-tier Kenges in December 1995.

Party politics is not highly developed and over one-third of the 1994 Supreme Kenges members were independents. Nazarbaev is non-party though he is associated with SNEK, the People's Unity Party, which contains many ex-communists and has vague social harmony, anti-radical-nationalist policies. SNEK won 33 seats in 1994. Other parties include the Socialist Party (the Communist Party under a new name), the People's Congress Party, headed by the former Nevada-Semipalatinsk Movement leader Olzhas Suleymenov, and Lad (Harmony), a Slavic party.

For administrative purposes Kazakstan is divided into 19 regions (Kazak: *oblys*, Russian: *oblast*).

Economy

Resources In terms of natural resources Kazakstan is probably the per-capita richest country on earth. The task is to exploit the resources and spread the wealth around the population. The country has some 60% of the former USSR's mineral resources, extracting big quantities of iron from the Qostanay basin in the north-west and huge amounts of coal from around Qaraghandy and Ekibastuz, plus oil, gas, lead, aluminium, copper, zinc, nickel, uranium, silver, gold,

bismuth, cadmium and thallium – these last three essential in electronics, nuclear engineering and rocketry. In 1989 Kazakstan supplied 25% of the USSR's coal, and 27% of its electricity from power stations near Ekibastuz.

Kazakstan also has 20% of the cultivated land in the former USSR. Much of the north was turned into one big wheat field by the 1950s Virgin Lands campaign in which about 250,000 sq km of steppe were ploughed up to grow grain (see the History section). Despite little success, Kazakstan continues to grow an awful lot of wheat – up to one-third of the former USSR total. In arable areas in the south, fruit, vegetables, tobacco, rice, hemp and cotton are grown. Drier areas are used for seasonal grazing of sheep, cattle, horses and camels, and Kazakstan's sheep produce high quality wool.

Problems & Policy After the break-up of the USSR, Kazakstan suffered the universal former Soviet problems of collapsed trade and distribution systems, runaway inflation, lack of funds to modernise ageing equipment, drying up of state subsidies and a slump in production. In 1993 up to one-third of a bumper wheat harvest was lost because of poor harvesting methods, lack of storage facilities and shortage of transport. Another problem has been that many of the key industrial and agricultural areas are in the heavily Slav-populated north. The loss of qualified and skilled Slavs and Germans through emigration has not been good for the Kazakstan economy.

The government's consistent policy to bring the economy around has been privatisation and price liberalisation, and a big effort to lure foreign investment. In 1993 Kazakstan introduced its own currency, the *tengge*, to free itself from the inflation and banknote shortages of the Russian rouble. Though there's still a long way to go, by 1995 these policies seemed to be bearing some fruit. Annual inflation was down to around 20% (from 2000% in 1993) and unemployment was estimated at 10% (from

30%). Gross domestic product was expected to finally start growing in 1997.

Privatisation The private sector quickly became dominated by seven big companies with diverse interests, from banking and investments to shops and restaurants, and all with close, often family, connections to the government. In 1994 a major scheme was launched to sell off 3500 medium-sized state-owned companies. Privatisation of land and agriculture was slower, with Kazaks worried that it would consolidate Russian colonial dominion and upset historical horde and clan land rights. A majority of Kazaks still live on often poor collective farms.

Foreign Investment & Trade The big headlines were grabbed by deals with western companies to exploit enormous oil and gas reserves in the west of the country. In 1992 the US oil giant Chevron agreed to a 40 year US$20 billion plan to develop the Tenghiz oilfield near the Caspian coast, hailed as the biggest oil find since Alaska and capable of producing about US$4.5 billion worth of high-quality oil a year. Kazakstan is to receive 80% of the earnings from sales. A consortium of US and European companies is exploring for offshore oil in the Caspian Sea, which could hold even more oil than Tenghiz. British Gas, Agip of Italy and Russia's Gazprom are developing the vast gas fields at Karachaganak, which hold three times as much gas as the British North Sea.

The Tenghiz project was initially bedevilled by the problem of getting the oil out of Kazakstan – the only pipeline was through Russia, which imposed restrictive quotas on the amount of Kazak oil allowed to flow through it, and demanded high fees. An extra pipeline is needed and the two possibilities are to go through Russia or to Turkey. Routes to Turkey are fraught with political instability as they must either go through Iran or through the Caucasus, while a new Russian route would leave Russia holding all the aces. High-stakes power games are being played by all the countries concerned.

Russia remains easily Kazakstan's major trading partner, with China now in second place since the opening up of Kazakstan's eastern border. Turkish firms are also very active in Kazakstan.

Population & People

Kazakstan's population is around 17.2 million, which makes it one of the planet's least densely peopled places (6.3 per sq km). Most people are concentrated in the south and north – which are both the most fertile and most industrially developed areas. The biggest cities are Almaty (estimated population 1.5 million), Qaraghandy (600,000), Shymkent (400,000), Semey (340,000), Pavlodar (335,000), Öskemen (330,000) and Zhambyl (310,000). Six other cities each has over 200,000 people.

Composition The total conceals an extraordinary, changing and troublesome ethnic mixture. At the 1989 census, 40% of Kazakstanis include Kazak, 38% Russian, 6% German, 5% Ukrainian, 2% Uzbek and 2% Tatar. Of about 100 other groups, the main ones are Belarussians, Koreans, Greeks, Chechens, Poles, Uyghurs and Jews.

The Slavs and other non-Central-Asian groups reached Kazakstan in several waves, chiefly as: peasant settlers from the 19th century on; industrial workers from the 1930s on; political prisoners from 1930s to 1950s (many of these stayed on if they survived); and entire peoples deported before or during WWII because Stalin feared they would collaborate with the enemy. The latter included Germans from the Volga region, Ukraine and elsewhere; Ingush, Karachay, Balkar, Chechens, Meskheti Turks and Kalmyks from the Caucasus region; Crimean Tatars; and Koreans from areas of Russia bordering Korea. Many died on the way to Kazakstan or soon after arriving. Of the survivors, many Germans and Koreans subsequently moved into technical, professional and managerial jobs. The Caucasus peoples were permitted to return to their homelands in 1957, though many stayed on.

There was also an influx of Virgin Land agricultural workers in the 1950s.

At the same time as these migrants were flooding into Kazakstan, the Kazaks themselves suffered repeated devastating blows from famine, wars, repression and emigration (see the History section). In 1959 there were 2.7 million Kazaks in Kazakstan (just 29% of the population) – only slightly more than estimates for 90 years earlier. Thanks to its relatively high birth rate, the Kazak population has now made a big comeback, and since independence, large-scale emigration by Slavs and Germans has tilted the ethnic balance further in the Kazaks' favour.

The country's total population actually shrank in 1993 and 1994. Exact current figures are hard to determine because data on emigrants are erratic, but by 1995, according to one estimate, Kazaks numbered 44% and Russians 35%. Probably one million Russians and Ukrainians left between 1992 and 1994, and possibly 900,000 Germans in the same period.

Ethnic distribution is very uneven. Kazaks form over 80% only in the Qyzylorda and Atyrau regions. Before the recent wave of Slav emigration, they numbered less than 20% in the Qostanay, Qaraghandy and Petropavl regions in the north. Kazaks are a minority in Almaty.

Large communities of Kazaks, many of them descendants of those who fled Russian and Soviet invasions, famines and repression, remain in nearby countries – an estimated 650,000 in China, 30,000 in northern Afghanistan and 70,000 in Mongolia. There are also some 900,000 Kazaks in Uzbekistan and 700,000 in other former Soviet states. Kazaks outside Kazakstan were invited to settle in Kazakstan after independence in 1991; perhaps 100,000 came.

So far, serious ethnic conflict has been avoided but there is tension – chiefly between Kazaks and Slavs – over issues like language, education and jobs (see the History section).

The Kazaks The Kazaks were nomadic horseback pastoralists till the 1920s and a

Kazak men usually wear western and Russian clothes; traditional dress is baggy shirts and trousers with sleeveless jackets.

majority are still rural. Some maintain a seminomadic existence, moving out with herds, flocks and yurts from their collective farms to summer pastures every year. Nor have they lost their affinity with the horse, as shown by sports like kökpar, the wild, free-for-all ancestor of polo (with a headless goat's carcass instead of a ball), and qyz quu, a boy-girl horse chase – if a boy catches a girl he kisses her, if a girl catches a boy she beats him with her riding whip, all the while both of them riding hell for leather.

Family and ancestry remain crucial to Kazaks. 'If a man cannot name his ancestors for seven generations, he is no Kazak,' it is said. Ancestry determines both a person's *zhus* (horde) and clan, which are still highly important. The best ancestor of all is Jenghiz Khan; right up to the 20th century the Kazak nobility consisted of those who could trace their lineage to him. There are even those today who mutter that, as President Nazarbaev cannot do this, he is not qualified to rule Kazakstan.

Though Kazaks are Muslim (Sunni) they are not, by and large, militantly or strictly so, and Islam is not a major political force. Reasons for this include the Kazaks' location on the fringe of the Muslim world, and their traditionally nomadic lifestyle, unsuited to central religious authority. Many were not converted till the 19th century, and shamanism apparently coexisted with Islam even after conversion. Though the number of functioning mosques in Kazakstan has reportedly grown to over 1000 from just 25 in 1985, many of the most faithful Muslims are from non-Kazak minorities.

Kazak women appear the most confident, and least restricted by tradition or Islam, in Central Asia – again perhaps a function of nomadic traditions. Urban Kazak women often seem more modern and cosmopolitan than their Russian counterparts, and occupy many senior jobs. All this is despite the lingering custom of wife-stealing, whereby a man may simply kidnap a woman he wants to marry (often with some collusion, it should be said), leaving her parents with no option but to negotiate the bride-price.

Arts

The biggest name in Kazak cultural history is Abay Qunanbaev, a 19th century poet and man of letters who launched Kazak as a literary language (see the following Abay aside and the Semey section in this chapter). He also translated Russian works into Kazak. Before Abay, Kazak literature consisted chiefly of long oral poems. Recitals by bards (*aqins*), and contests between them known as *aitys*, are still important and popular.

Orientation

Many Kazakstan cities now have new Kazak names instead of their Soviet-era Russian names. In many cases they are close to the Russian (eg Almaty instead of Alma-Ata, Zhambyl for Dzhambul, Qaraghandy for Karaganda). Less obvious changes include Aqmola for Tselinograd, Aqtau for Shevchenko, Aqtöbe for Aktyubinsk, Atyrau for Gurev, Dostyq for Druzhba, Oral for Uralsk, Öskemen for Ust-Kamenogorsk, and Semey for Semipalatinsk. You'll sometimes find Russian names still in use.

Similarly, many cities have changed their street names from Russian to Kazak. Often

---

Abay

Abay (Ibrahim) Qunanbaev (1845-1904), the Kazaks' greatest early writer, translator, and educator, was decidedly pro-Russian. He wrote: 'Study Russian culture and art – it is the key to life. If you obtain it, your life will become easier ...'

Ironically, the author of those prophetic words suffered a brief period of disfavour, years after he died, early in the Soviet period. The charge: Abay's politics were undeveloped and feudal. But soon the Soviets needed to raise up native fathers for the decimated Kazak nation they were trying to reconstruct. Abay's reputation was at last 'officially licensed' by Moscow, and his Russophile writings were enshrined. ∎

---

the Kazak is similar to the Russian, with a different ending to the name and the substitution of *köshesi* for *ulitsa* (street); *prospektisi*, *prospekti* or *dangghyly* for *prospekt* (avenue); or *alangy* for *ploshchad* (square). It helps to be aware of both names, since not all signs have been changed, and in any case many people are still more familiar with the old names. In this chapter we try to give the names you're most likely to see on signs, noting important alternatives.

Almaty
Алматьч

Population: 1.5 million
First impressions of the capital of Kazakstan reveal much about the country's predicament. To the eye, Almaty's long, straight avenues and uniform architecture bear the unmistakable thumbprint of the USSR. To the ear, the sound of Russian – spoken even by most Kazaks here – reveals the continuing hold of the colonial culture over much of Kazakstan's way of life. Founded in 1854 as a Russian frontier fort when the Kazaks were

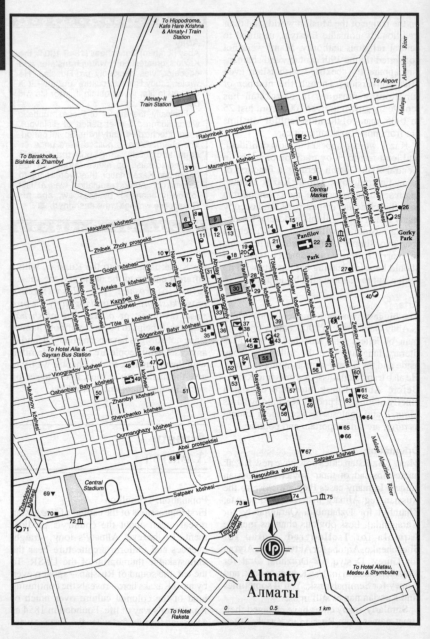

To Hippodrome,
Kafe Hare Krishna
& Almaty-I Train
Station

Almatinka River

To Airport

Malaya Almatinka River

Almaty-II
Train Station

Ralymbek prospektisi

Pushkin köshesi

To Barakholka,
Bishkek & Zhambyl

Mametova köshesi

Central
Market

Barlybaev köshesi
Yemelev köshesi
Tastjiar köshesi
8-Mart köshesi

Magataev köshesi

Zhibek Zholy prospekti

Panfilov
Park

Gorky
Park

Gogol köshesi

Ayteke Bi köshesi

Naurzbay Batyr köshesi
Seyfullin prospektisi
Zheltoqsan köshesi
Ablai Khan dangyly
Panfilov köshesi
Furmanov köshesi
Tölebaev köshesi
Oqsnay köshesi
Ulikhanov köshesi

Kazybek Bi
köshesi

Töle Bi köshesi

Bögenbay Batyr köshesi

Pushkin köshesi
Lenin prospektisi
Zenkov köshesi

Masanchi köshesi

To Hotel Alia &
Sayran Bus Station

Vinogradov köshesi

Qabanbay Batyr köshesi

Mukanov köshesi

Zhambyl köshesi

Bayseitova köshesi

Shevchenko köshesi

Qurmanghazy köshesi

Abai prospektisi

Zhandosov köshesi

Central
Stadium

Satpaev köshesi

Malaya Almatinka River

Satpaev köshesi

Respublika alangy

Im Vrazey köshesi

To Hotel
Raketa

To Hotel Alatau,
Medeu & Shymbulaq

Almaty
Алматы

0   0.5   1 km

PLACES TO STAY

5	Hotel Turkistan
8	Hotel Zhetisu
16	Hotel Otrar
34	Hotel Issik
35	Hotel Ekvator
45	Hotel Almaty
56	Hotel Kazpotrebsoyuza
59	Hotel Dostyk
61	Hotel Kazakstan
65	Gostinitsa N 1
70	Rachat Palace Hotel
73	Hotel Ankara

PLACES TO EAT

3	Kafe Marmara
10	1001 Nights
15	Seyhanlar Kebap Salonu
17	International Business Club
28	Solyanka Cafeteria
36	Shenyan Restaurant
39	Blinnaya
50	Ristorante Adriatico
52	Besiktas Restaurant
53	Restoran Alma-Ata
54	Samal Delicatessen
57	BBQ-USA
60	Tomiris Restaurant
62	Shaggies
67	Kafe Pitstseria
69	Pitstseria-Bar Astana-Momors & Circus

OTHER

1	Sayakhat Bus Station
2	Mosque
4	Pakistan Embassy
6	City Air Terminal (Aerovokzal)
7	Bus Stop from Airport
9	Zanghar (TsUM) Department Store
11	Bus Stop to Airport
12	Kodak Express
13	Central Telephone Office
14	Bukinist
18	Supreme Court
19	Akademkniga
20	US Embassy
21	Arasan Baths
22	Zenkov Cathedral
23	War Memorial
24	Museum of Kazak Musical Instruments
25	Uzbekistan Embassy
26	Main Entrance to Gorky Park
27	Central Concert Hall
29	Kulinaria Brigantina
30	Supreme Kenges Building
31	Kazkontsert Hall
32	Tilek Supermarket
33	Ministry of Foreign Affairs Consular Section
37	Post Office
38	Conservatory
40	Tajikistan Embassy
41	Alem Bank
42	Chinese Embassy
43	Akademkniga
44	Republican Telegraph
46	Nevada-Semey Movement
47	Kyrgyzstan Embassy
48	OVIR
49	St Nicholas Cathedral
51	Dinamo Stadium
55	Opera & Ballet Theatre
58	British, French & German Embassies
63	Kazak Business Centre
64	Arman Cinema
66	KIMEP Main Entrance
68	Capos
71	Russian Embassy
72	State Art Museum
74	Presidential Residence
75	Central State Museum

still nomads, Almaty has always been a very Russian place.

But though neither old nor exotic nor even very Kazak, Almaty is a city on an upswing. As the capital of Central Asia's richest country, it's a honeypot not just to Kazakstanis but to a host of foreigners ranging from Chinese, Uzbek, Russian and Turkish traders to big-time business folk, diplomats and financiers from the West and from East Asia. This exposure to the outside world has, in just a few years, turned a provincial outpost of the USSR into Central Asia's most cosmopolitan city. The goods in shops and markets, the range of good places

to eat, the direct flights from several world capitals, the boom in banks, advertising and other accoutrements of capitalism, the new hotels, the casinos – all these would make Almaty unrecognisable to anyone who had been away since 1990.

That said, there's not much to *do* in the city – which is why, for many travellers, Almaty is little more than a way-station between Bishkek or Tashkent and Ürümqi or Siberia. But for those with time, there are some fine trips into the surrounding region, and Almaty has some experienced travel firms which can also arrange trips farther afield.

The city is clean (except sometimes for its

air) and easy on the eye. The Zailiysky Alatau mountains rise like a wall along its southern fringes and form a superb backdrop when weather and smog permit. There are lots of parks, space and greenery, and many of the monumental Soviet-era buildings are striking if you look at them individually.

Most of the city's architecture is fairly low-rise, thanks to Almaty's earthquake-prone location. All this makes it a pleasant city to walk around, though the central area is very spread out and distances between places are long.

Almaty's people are a typical mix of dozens of nationalities but, untypically for southern Kazakstan, Russians and Ukrainians form the majority, with Kazaks making up about 30%. To these have been added in the past few years several thousand Americans, Europeans, Turks and south and east Asians, all after a foothold in the developing Kazakstan economy. The expat scene is quite lively and if you can tap into it your time here will be more entertaining and informative.

The best times of year here are mid-April to late May, and early September to mid-October, when it's neither too cold nor too hot.

History

Almaty is on the site of a Silk Road oasis called Almatu which was laid waste by the Mongols. The Russians built a frontier post called Verny here in 1854 and settled Cossacks and Siberian peasants around it. The town was twice almost flattened by earthquakes, in 1887 and 1911. In the late 19th and early 20th centuries it was a place of exile, its best known outcast being Leon Trotsky.

Renamed Alma-Ata (a souped-up Soviet version of the original, meaning Father of Apples), it became the capital of Soviet Kazakstan in 1928, and was connected to

---

Capital Transfer

For the capital of such a big country, Almaty is in an odd location – tucked away in a corner of Kazakstan just 25 km from the border of Kyrgyzstan, yet nearly 900 km from the nearest point on Kazakstan's border with Russia.

Almaty only became the capital because the Bolsheviks in the 1920s found its more centrally placed predecessor, Qyzylorda, too hot. In Soviet times Almaty's off-centre location perhaps also reduced the political heat on the USSR's central rulers as they manoeuvred to maintain their grip on Kazakstan; the fact that north-west Kazakstan was nearer to Moscow than to Almaty, and northern Kazakstan closer to Siberia, would always strengthen Moscow's hand against Almaty's and balance any tendencies to independent-mindedness among the republican leadership.

But after independence was thrust upon Kazakstan, President Nazarbaev began to view this quirky political geography somewhat differently. In 1994 he announced, to universal amazement, a plan to transfer Kazakstan's capital by the year 2000 to the northern city of Aqmola (population 300,000), which had grown since the 1950s as the centre of the Virgin Lands grain-growing region. Almaty was overcrowded, Nazarbaev said, while Aqmola was nearer the heart of the Russian rail network and farther from national borders and conflicts in Tajikistan and Afghanistan. Constructing government buildings and embassies would be cheaper in Aqmola, he added, because there was no need to safeguard against earthquakes.

Cynics dismissed the scheme as hare-brained and unaffordable, saying it would never be enacted and speculating on Nazarbaev's motives. Did he aim to secure Kazakstan's hold over its heavily Russian-populated north and its main oil and gas reserves in the west, perhaps reducing the alienation of ethnic Russians into the bargain? Did he want to foster unity among ethnic Kazaks by moving the capital from the territory of the Great Horde, currently dominant among the three main groups of Kazaks, to that of the Middle Horde?

Whether the move will take place and whether, if it does, it will turn out to be a stroke of visionary genius or a divisive disaster, remains to be seen. ■

Siberia by the Turkestan-Siberia Railway or 'Turksib' in 1930, by which time its population was about 50,000. The railway brought big growth and so did WWII, as factories were relocated here from the Nazi-threatened western USSR and many Slavs came to work them. Large numbers of ethnic Koreans, forcibly resettled from the Russian Far East, came at the same time.

Almaty was the scene of the first unrest unleashed in Central Asia by the Gorbachev era of glasnost and perestroika. In December 1986, after Dinmukhamed Qonaev, a Kazak, was replaced as head of the CPK by Gennady Kolbin from Russia, thousands took to the streets in protest. An apparently communist-organised counter-demo of workers armed with metal bars and cables turned the protest into riots, police opened fire and several people were killed, with hundreds injured.

The riots spread to several other cities before being quelled by martial law.

Almaty made more headlines in 1989 as the focus of the successful campaign to stop nuclear testing near Semey, and in 1991 as the venue for a meeting at which the USSR was finally pronounced dead, when all five Central Asian republics (along with Azerbaijan, Armenia and Moldova) joined the CIS, founded by Russia, Ukraine and Belarus. The name Almaty, close to that of the original Silk Road settlement, replaced Alma-Ata soon after.

Orientation

Almaty can be a disorienting place owing to the uniform appearance of many of its long, straight streets. Remember that the mountains are to the south, and that the city slopes

New & Old Street Names in Almaty

Almaty has done away with many Soviet street names and gone over to Kazak rather than Russian on many signs. We use the new Kazak street names wherever possible in this section. Signs may also give the Russian equivalent of the new name, and a few give the Russian only. To confuse things, signs bearing out-of-date names remain on some streets and many local people are still more familiar with the old names than the new. The table shows important streets whose names have been changed. If the name you give doesn't seem to work, try the old one instead.

New Name	Old Name
Abylay Khan dangghyly	Kommunistichesky prospekt
Ayteke Bi köshesi	Oktyabrskaya ulitsa
Baytursunuly köshesi	ulitsa Kosmonavtov
Bögenbay Batyr köshesi	ulitsa Kirova
Kazybek Bi köshesi	Sovietskaya ulitsa
Maqataev köshesi	ulitsa Pastera
Nauryzbay Batyr köshesi	ulitsa Dzerzhinskogo
Qabanbay Batyr köshesi	ulitsa Kalinina
Qonaev köshesi (Russian: ulitsa Kunaeva)	ulitsa Karla Marxa
Raiymbek prospektisi	prospekt 50-letia Oktyabrya
Respublika alangy	Novaya ploshchad
Töle Bi köshesi	Komsomolskaya ulitsa
Ualikhanov köshesi (Russian: ulitsa Valikhanova)	ulitsa Krasina
Zenkov köshesi	Proletarskaya ulitsa
Zhambyl köshesi	ulitsa Dzhambula
Zhandosov köshesi	ulitsa Dzhandosova
Zheltoqsan köshesi	ulitsa Mira (Kazak: Beibitshilik köshesi)
Zhibek Zholy prospekti (Russian: prospekt Shyolkovy Puti)	ulitsa Gorkogo

upward from north (650 metres high) to south (950 metres).

The central area is large, stretching four km from Almaty-II train station in the north to the Respublika alangy ceremonial square in the south, and over two km from 8-Mart köshesi in the east to Seyfullin prospektisi in the west. Blocks are long. The airport is about half an hour's bus ride north of the centre; Almaty-I trainstation is half and hour north; the Sayran long-distance bus station is half an hour west.

In the centre, the main north-south streets are Lenin prospektisi, Qonaev köshesi, Furmanov köshesi and Abylay Khan dangghyly. The main east-west streets are Gogol köshesi in the north of the centre and Abai prospektisi in the south.

Maps A variety of Almaty city maps are sold in hotel kiosks and bookshops, some up-to-date, some not. The most comprehensive we have come across, but in Russian, is *Almaty Biznes-Plan Goroda*, with a good close-up of the city centre and useful addresses and phone numbers.

Information
Foreign Embassies
Embassies in Almaty include:

Afghanistan
    Abai prospektisi 16 (☎ 62-95-19)
Canada
    Vinogradov 34 (☎ 48-01-00)
China
    Furmanov 137 (☎ 63-49-66, 63-92-91;
    fax 63-93-72, 63-92-91)
France
    Furmanov 173 (☎ 50-77-10, 50-62-36;
    fax 50-61-59)
Germany
    Furmanov 173 (☎ 50-61-55, 50-61-56;
    fax 50-62-76)
Hungary
    apartment 29, Tölebaev 162 (☎ 63-64-37,
    fax 50-70-99)
India
    Kazybek Bi, between Nauryzbay Batyr and
    Seyfullin prospektisi (☎ 69-47-46, 67-14-11;
    fax 67-20-70)

Iran
    Qabanbay Batyr 119 (☎ 67-78-46, 67-50-55;
    fax 64-27-54)
Israel
    Zheltoqsan 87 (☎ 50-72-15, 62-48-17;
    fax 62-23-36)
Italy
    Mikrorayon SAMAL-2, No 69, 6th floor
    (☎ 54-17-99, fax 54-19-98)
Japan
    Mikrorayon SAMAL-1D, No 36, apartment 4
    (☎ 53-32-05, 53-32-04; fax 53-31-94)
Kyrgyzstan
    Amangeldy 68A (☎ 63-33-05, 63-33-09)
Mongolia
    Consulate: Kazybek Bi, corner of 8-Mart
    (☎ 60-17-23, 60-17-33)
Pakistan
    Tölebaev 25 (☎ 33-15-02, 33-35-48;
    fax 33-13-00)
Russia
    Zhandosov 4 (☎ 44-66-44 (visas), 44-64-91,
    fax 44-82-23)
Switzerland
    Dom Otdykha Almaty, Gornaya ulitsa 97
    (☎ 63-15-16, fax 53-20-00)
Tajikistan
    Yemelev 70 (☎ 61-17-60, 61-02-25)
Turkey
    Töle Bi 29 (☎ 61-39-32, 61-81-53; fax 50-62-08)
UK
    Furmanov 173 (☎ 50-61-91, 50-61-92;
    fax 50-62-60)
Ukraine
    Hotel Kazakstan, Lenin prospektisi 52
    (☎ 61-90-33, 61-90-34)
USA
    Furmanov 99 (☎ 50-76-21, 50-76-23, 63-28-80,
    63-24-26; fax 63-38-83)
Uzbekistan
    Baribaev 36 (☎ 61-83-16, fax 61-10-55,
    61-92-03)

Visas It's possible to obtain a visa extension, or a new visa, in Almaty through the Ministry of Foreign Affairs or, if the sponsor of your existing visa is a private individual, through OVIR (known as OVPR in Kazakstan), the Interior Ministry's Visa Department. Your sponsor should be able to organise this.

Travel agencies can often help, always for a fee, though it may be a reasonable one: for example the Nevada-Semey Movement quoted us US$16 all-in for a 10 day visa extension, or US$40 for a one month visa extension. Doing it all yourself may be difficult and time-consuming.

The Ministry of Foreign Affairs Consular Section (☎ 63-17-95, 63-25-31, 64-46-24, 63-46-26) is at Zheltoqsan 118, though the entrance is round the corner: take the first entry on the right going east along Töle Bi from Zheltoqsan, and go up a flight of steps. It's open Monday to Friday from 2 to 5 pm.

OVIR, the Passport & Visa Department of the Interior Ministry (Bas Basqarmasynyng Ishki Ister Töl Kuzhat Bölimi, Otdel Pasportnoy i Vyzovoy Raboty Glavnogo Upravlenia Vnutrennykh Del, ☎ 60-77-56), is at Vinogradov 84 just west of Masanchi. Hours are Monday to Friday from 9 am to 6 pm.

The ministries normally take about one week to process applications. If this means you'll be without a valid visa while you're waiting, fines of up to US$250 can in theory be levied, but in practice they usually seem to exercise sensible discretion. Two travellers we met actually fronted up at OVIR with no valid visa or invitation of any kind and talked their way into one week visas on the spot.

Obtaining Foreign Visas

If you haven't already obtained the visas you need for your Central Asian trip, Almaty is one of the best Central Asian capitals for doing so, though the information given here is subject to change. Some travel agencies (see the following section) may be able to speed up visa processes, or obtain otherwise difficult visas, for a fee.

China
Visas (usually for 30 days) are issued after one week. An invitation or confirmation of pre-booked services is not needed. Fees depend on nationality – eg US$25 for Australians, US$60 for Britons. The consular section is open Mondays, Wednesdays and Fridays only, from 9 am to noon, and is usually a real scrum. For information only, go to reception in the main entrance at the front of the building.

Kyrgyzstan
Visas cost US$25 for up to a month and take up to a few days to issue. An invitation is not needed, but if you have one your visa might be issued immediately.

Pakistan
Visas are issued on the third working day from application. The embassy is open for submission of documents Monday to Friday from 10 am to roon, and for collection of documents from 5 to 6 pm.

Uzbekistan
The embassy will issue visas, without invitation, in about 10 days – or immediately if an invitation has been sent to the Foreign Affairs Ministry in Tashkent and the ministry has informed the embassy here. You don't have to leave your passport with the embassy while your application is being processed. Hours are Monday to Friday from 3 to 5 pm.

Money There are exchange kiosks all over the place, including at the main transport terminals. When you can, avoid kiosks on the street or in other very public places, to minimise the risk of theft during or after the transaction.

Alem Bank in the Otrar, Dostyk and Kazakstan hotels, and at Lenin prospektisi 39 (on the corner of Vinogradov köshesi) will cash American Express, Visa or MasterCard travellers' cheques and give cash advances on Visa card or MasterCard (into *tengge*).

Post & Communications Post, telephone and fax services are in different buildings.

Post The main post office is on Baysetova just off Bögenbay Batyr, a block south of the Supreme Kenges (Parliament) building. It's open Monday to Friday from 8 am to 7 pm, and Saturdays and Sundays from 9 am to 5 pm. There are also post offices at the airport and the Hotel Otrar.

The following international courier services are in Almaty:

DHL
Vinogradov 193
(☎ 53-05-11, 50-94-17; fax 63-61-66)
Federal Express
Bögenbay Batyr 134 (☎ 62-14-00)
RSE
apartment 157, Furmanov 127 (☎ 62-44-29)
UPS
ulitsa Belinskogo 260
(☎ 36-55-73, fax 63-12-07)

Telephone & Fax A good place to make long-distance or international telephone calls is the Republican Telegraph (Kazak: Respublikaliq Telegraf, Russian: Respublikansky Telegraf) at Panfilov 129, near the Hotel Almaty. Queues are short, prices reasonable, you can dial direct yourself and you'll often get through straight away. You can also send faxes here, at about three times the telephone rate. Hours are Monday to Thursday 8 am to 8 pm, and Friday and Saturday 8 am to 3 pm .

You can also phone, fax or photocopy at the press centre in the Hotel Otrar (room 101, ground floor) or the business centres in the Hotel Kazakstan (ground floor) and the Hotel Dostyk (4th floor). At the Otrar, phone calls are much more pricey than at the Republican Telegraph, but faxes cost the same.

The Central Telephone Office (with a sign in Russian saying Tsentralny Peregovorny Punkt) is at Zhibek Zholy prospekti 100, a block east of the Zanghar (TsUM) department store. It has long queues.

The Almaty telephone code is 3272.

Travel Agencies General travel agencies useful for air tickets, hotel bookings and the like include:

Overseas Meyir Travel (☎ 61-36-18, fax 61-60-94), apartment 25, Lenin prospektisi 50 (an apartment block at the corner of Qurmanghazy). It has some western staff.
Central Asia Tourism Corporation (☎ 63-90-17, 69-70-55; fax 63-90-20), apartment 6, Bögenbay Batyr 139, also in an apartment block. It has some western staff.
Intourist Southern (☎ 33-00-07, 33-00-37; fax 33-12-34) at the Hotel Otrar.
Alpha Omega Travel (☎ 50-99-44, ☎ & fax 50-95-73), office 22, floor 6, Abai prospektisi 155 (corner of Rozybakiev) is a branch of a British business travel agency specialising in the former USSR. It also offers visa services. See the Getting There & Away chapter for details of its UK and Moscow offices.

Kan Tengri (☎ 67-78-66, ☎ & fax 67-70-24, fax 63-12-07) at Abai prospektisi 48 is one of Central Asia's leading mountain tourism firms, focusing on climbs, trekking, heli-skiing and ski-mountaineering in the Central Tian Shan and the ranges between Almaty and Lake Issyk-Kul. They also offer summer-season bird-watching, and botanical, mountain biking and horse-riding trips. It works with several overseas firms but you can also organise an independent trip with them, often at a few days notice. For treks and climbs they charge around US$50 to US$70 a day per person, from Almaty. They also offer visa support, whether or not you are using their services. The office is in the central stadium: go in the entrance about halfway along the left-hand side of the stadium (approaching from Abai prospektisi), to rooms 10 and 11 on the 3rd floor.

Tour Asia (☎ & fax 49-79-36) at apartment 46, Zharokov 269, offers possibilities from trekking or mountaineering in the Central Tian Shan, Alatau, Altay and Fan mountains, to helicopter trips to the Charyn canyon, Köl-Say lakess or the Central Tian Shan, and possibly even to Baykonur Cosmodrome. A five day guided trek in the Zailiysky Alatau for four people costs around US$500. Tour Asia can also arrange homestays in Almaty, and says it can obtain Uzbekistan visas in three to five days.

In order to raise funds and spread its message the Nevada-Semey Anti-Nuclear Movement (Yadrolyq Apatqa Qarsy Khalyqaralyq Nevada-Semey Qozghalysy, Mezhdunarodnoe Antiyadernoe Dvizhenie Nevada- Semipalatinsk, ☎ 63-48-17, 63-49-02; fax 50-71-87), has turned its hand to tourism services (see also the Environment section in Facts about the Region). Its head office, at Vinogradov 85, can arrange accommodation (including apartment rental) in Almaty with visa support, car rental, guides in Almaty, visa extensions, help in setting up business meetings and media contacts. Ask for Rima Dzimisova, who speaks excellent English. For more on its specific services see relevant headings in this section.

Three individuals worth contacting for reasonably priced activity trips are Karlygash Makatova (a Kazak sportswoman and the in-house travel agent at the Almaty office of USAID); Jorge Romero (a Mexican

Kazakstan

Top Left: Malaya Almatinka River Valley, en route to Shymbulaq, near Almaty
Top Right: Zenkov Cathedral (1904), built entirely of wood and without nails,
  Panfilov Park, Almaty
Bottom: WWII Memorial, Panfilov Park, Almaty

JOHN KING

JOHN NOBLE

Kazakstan
Top: School children visiting the mausoleum of Qozha Akhmed Yasaui, Turkistan
Bottom: Charyn Canyon helipad

living in Almaty); and Tahir (editor of an Almaty zoological journal, tuned in to the ecological scene). All can be contacted at ☎ 36-58-88 (after 10 pm or before 8 am) or ☎ 65-09-54, or at fax 63-79-49 or 63-77-95 ('attention Romero Jorge & Makatova Karlygash, ☎ 36-58-88'). Possibilities include helicopter day trips to the Charyn canyon or Lake Issyk-Kul, car trips to Charyn canyon, day hikes to Bolshoe Almatinskoe lake or waterfalls near Medeu, skiing at Shymbulaq, boating on the Ili river, climbing in the Zailiysky Alatau, riding and trekking. For helicopter, river or climbing trips 1½ to two weeks' notice is normally needed.

Kramds Mountain Company (☎ 53-72-11, 53-68-50; fax 69-67-53, 63-69-73) is another firm worth contacting about adventure trips.

The state tourism company Yassaui has inherited some of the property and work of the old Intourist monopoly and says it can offer all the usual tourism services, but seems a pale shadow of its predecessor. Its Almaty office (☎ 33-00-02, 33-00-26; fax 33-20-56, 33-20-13) is beside the reception desk in the Hotel Otrar.

Useful Organisations The Nevada-Semey Anti-Nuclear Movement, which campaigned successfully for the closure of the Polygon nuclear testing site near Semey, and is now working for regeneration of that region and for a worldwide end to nuclear testing, has its head office in Almaty (see the Travel Agencies section above).

Bookshops If you're going to spend much time in Almaty, it's worth finding a copy of *A-Business*, a 40-odd page directory of useful addresses and telephones. It's published in English and Russian.

Akademkniga at Furmanov 139, next to the Chinese embassy, has a good range of maps of Kazakstan cities, districts and regions, including trekking and river maps. It also sells dictionaries and phrasebooks. Another branch of Akademkniga at Furmanov 91, next to the US embassy, has

some books in English and also dictionaries and phrasebooks. You'll also find some dictionaries, phrasebooks and maybe some second-hand book bargains in Bukinist at Gogol 75.

Media Western newspapers and magazines are sold at the major hotels and the Kulinaria Brigantina shop on Panfilov south of Kazybek Bi. They are expensive.

You can pick up the BBC World Service on 15.070 MHz (short wave), and Voice of America on 1341 KHz (medium wave) at 9 am and 10 pm.

Film There's a Kodak Express shop, offering print film and processing, and various photo supplies including batteries, at Zhibek Zholy prospekti 106 opposite Zanghar (TsUM).

Emergency & Medical Services To call the police, ☎ 02; for the fire brigade, ☎ 01.

Contact your embassy or hotel reception for advice on medical or dental services. There are numerous hospitals and clinics in Almaty but few staff speak foreign languages. The US embassy has its own medical unit. In a serious emergency, for an ambulance call ☎ 62-12-88 or 62-12-80, or if the patient is 16 years or less, ☎ 44-80-01 (night: ☎ 44-45-43). You may need to speak Russian.

At the time of research Almaty tap water had been judged safe to drink by US government contractors.

Toilets There's a public pay-toilet, open from 7 am to 7 pm daily, in the City Air Terminal at the corner of Zhibek Zholy prospekti and Zheltoqsan.

Dangers & Annoyances Crime has increased markedly in Almaty. Many resident foreigners do not walk on the streets after dark. If you do go out at night, try to go with at least one other person, and don't stop if you're approached by strangers. Be especially on your guard near obvious foreigners' haunts such as the US embassy and the major hotels, where foreigners have been targeted by muggers. Don't linger outside these places. Inside hotels, don't open your room door to a stranger.

Prostitution is common at many Almaty hotels: one traveller reported being telephoned in the middle of the night at the Hotel Zhetisu by a prostitute who addressed him by name.

Panfilov Park

This large rectangle of greenery between Gogol and Kazybek Bi makes a pleasant focus for the northern part of the central area. In the middle is the bright **Zenkov cathedral**, designed by A P Zenkov in 1904. This is one of Almaty's few surviving tsarist-era buildings (most of the others were wrecked in the 1911 earthquake). Though at first glance it doesn't look like it, the cathedral is built entirely of wood – and without nails. Used as a museum and concert hall in the Soviet era, then boarded up, it was returned to the Russian Orthodox Church in 1995 and is now a functioning place of worship. Even the bells ring out from time to time.

The park's rather fearsome full title – the Park Named After the 28 Panfilov Guardsmen (28 Gvardiyalyq Panfilovshylar Atyndaghy Park, Park Imeni 28 Gvardeytsev Panfilovtsev) – is explained by an equally fearsome **war memorial** east of the cathedral. This represents the 28 soldiers of an Almaty infantry unit who died fighting off Nazi tanks in a village on the outskirts of Moscow in 1941. Nearby is an eternal flame commemorating the fallen of 1917-20 (the Civil War) and 1941-45 (WWII).

The park is on the routes of trolleybus Nos 1, 2, 8, 12 and 16 along Gogol from anywhere in the central area.

Museum of Kazak Musical Instruments

In a striking 1903 wooden building at the east end of Panfilov Park is the city's most original museum (Qazaqtyng Zhalyq Muzyka Aspaptary Muzey, Muzey Kazakhskikh Narodnykh Muzykalnykh Instrumentov). It has a fine collection of traditional Kazak instruments – wooden harps and horns, bagpipes, the lute-like two

stringed *dombra* and the viola-like three stringed *kobiz*. Get an attendant to show you the buttons which play tapes of the instruments – the wild, rough-hewn music of steppe nomads. The museum is open daily from 10 am to 6 pm except Monday and the last day of the month. Admission is US$0.30.

Arasan Baths

Facing the west end of Panfilov Park is the elaborate Arasan Baths building, a favourite Almaty relaxation spot. There are Russian (Russkaya banya), Turkish (Vostochnaya banya) and Finnish (Finskaya banya) baths, each with separate sections for women and men. The Russian and Finnish ones are always busy – men spend hours there with their salami and vodka. Women swim naked. The main entrance is at the south end of the building and the baths are open daily except Monday. Sessions for all types of bath begin every two hours from 8 am to 8 pm. Cost is US$2 except for the first three sessions of the day (US$1) or the lyux sections (US$4.50). You can hire a dressing gown and towel cheaply, and get an hour's massage for around US$5. There's a café serving *qymyz* (kumys; fermented mare's milk, the traditional nomad's brew) in the building.

Gorky Park

This large leafy expanse (M Gorky Atyndaghy Park, Park Imeni M Gorkogo) at the east end of Gogol, one km from the Hotel Otrar, harbours boating lakes, funfair rides, a zoo, several cafés, shashlyk and beer stands, and a camel for rides. It's busiest on Sundays. Trolleybus Nos 1, 8, 12 and 16 run along Gogol to the main entrance from anywhere in the central area.

Supreme Kenges

Kazakstan's parliament, the Supreme Kenges (Zhongharghy Kengesi), sits in a large Brezhnev-era building fronting Töle Bi, west of Panfilov. The park across the road still flaunts a Lenin statue. A block north of the Kenges, across another park, is the Supreme Court (Zhongharghy Soty, Verkhovny Sud), on Ayteke Bi.

Respublika Alangy

This wide ceremonial square at the high southern end of the city centre, created in Soviet times, is a block up the hill from Abai prospektisi. The huge official residence of the president (Prezidentsining Residentsiasy, Residentsia Prezidenta) overlooks it.

You can reach the square on bus Nos 2, 11 or 100 going up Furmanov from Gogol, or bus Nos 32 or 70 up Zheltoqsan from Gogol.

Central State Museum

One of the city's best museums (Qakaqstan Memlekettik Ortalyq Muzeyi, Tsentralny Gosudarstvenny Muzey Kazakhstana) stands at Furmanov 44, 300 metres up the hill from Respublika alangy. It gives a worthwhile if patchy picture of Kazakstan's history. The downstairs rooms cover geology, archaeology and early history, including a miniature replica of Kazakstan's chief archaeological treasure, the Golden Man.

Upstairs covers the Soviet era, including exhibits on space flight from the Baykonur Cosmodrome, nuclear testing at Semey, and the Aral Sea; and the era of the Kazak khanates and the coming of the Russians. One chief exhibit is a colourfully kitted-out yurt.

The crafts stall in the foyer is worth a look. Also in the foyer are Kazak carpets for sale – but they don't come cheap at around US$250 and upwards.

The museum is open daily except Tuesday from 10 am to 6 pm and entry is US$0.10. Entry is not permitted after 5 pm. Get there by bus Nos 2, 11 or 100 going up Furmanov from Gogol.

State Art Museum

This large, modern museum (Memlekettik Körkemöner Murazhayy, Gosudarstvenny Muzey Iskusstv) is south-west of the central area but worth finding.

The many rooms of paintings and sculpture give a fairly comprehensive view of Kazak art and there are also collections of Russian and West European art. Perhaps most interesting is the one-room section of

---

The Golden Man

The Golden Man (Zolotoy Chelovek in Russian) is a warrior's costume made up of 4000 separate gold pieces – many of them finely worked with animal motifs – found in a Saka tomb near Yessik, about 40 km east of Almaty. It has a 70-cm-high headdress bearing skyward-pointing arrows, a pair of snarling snow leopards and a two-headed winged mythical beast. There's some confusion about its age: the Central State Museum says it's from about the 12th century AD but most other sources put its origin at about the 5th century BC. Its Scythian-style artwork would certainly favour the latter. The original of this treasure is considered too fragile to be pieced together for display. ■

Kazak applied art which has some fine carpets, wall carpets, saddle covers, wood carving and jewellery.

The museum is at Satpaev 30A, near the Rachat Palace Hotel, and is open daily except Monday from 10 am to 7 pm. Entry is US$0.30 and there's a small café on the ground floor.

You can get there by trolleybus No 16 west on Gogol from Gorky Park then south on Zheltoqsan; or take any transport to the circus on Abai prospektisi (such as bus No 92 southbound on Zheltoqsan or trolleybus Nos 5 or 6 southbound on Abylay Khan dangghyly), then walk one block south.

St Nicholas Cathedral

West of the centre, on Baytursynuly at the corner of Qabanbay Batyr, St Nicholas (Nikolsky Sobor) was the main Russian Orthodox church in Almaty before the Zenkov cathedral reopened. Built in 1909, it was later used as a stable for Bolshevik cavalry before reopening about 1980. It's like a corner of old Russia, with icons and candles inside and black-clad old supplicants outside. It's most atmospheric at festival times such as Orthodox Christmas Day (7 January), which begins with a midnight service.

Mosque

A big new mosque is being built on the corner of Pushkin and Mametova and may be working by the time you visit.

Activities

There are decent indoor and outdoor public swimming pools at the Dinamo Stadium at Nauryzbay Batyr 89, on the corner of Shevchenko. It's US$3 for a swim. In winter you can ice-skate here. Joggers can jog at the central stadium on Abai prospektisi or (better) the Spartak Stadium in Gorky Park.

It might be fun to try your hand at the local version of billiards or pool in the hall downstairs in the Restoran Alma-Ata building at Abylay Khan dangghyly 125.

Festivals

The Voice of Asia pop festival held at Medeu enlivens Almaty's summer scene, attracting big-name groups from China, Central Asia, Russia and elsewhere – though few from Kazakhstan. It's usually held in early August and lasts about four days.

Places to Stay – bottom end

Student Hostel There's cheap accommodation, if you have a visa valid for Almaty, in a student hostel near the Hotel Kazakstan. It's *Gostinitsa (Hotel) No 1* (☎ 64-37-39) at KIMEP, the Kazakhstan Institute of Management, Economics & Strategic Research. The address is Abai prospektisi 4 but the entrance is on Ualikhanov, half a block uphill from Abai. The hostel building is on the left inside the gate. Doubles sharing communal toilets and showers cost just US$2.50 per person. There's a canteen and a bufet too. Trolleybus No 4 from Almaty-II station or from any southbound stop on Abylay Khan dangghyly runs along Abai prospektisi.

Hotels The *Hotel Raketa* (☎ 49-24-98) is south-west of the central area but a bargain. For US$4 you get a spic-and-span double, sharing bathroom with one neighbouring room, and the staff are friendly and helpful. It's in a quiet area at the corner of Zharokov and Timiryazev. Bus Nos 32 or 70 south-

bound on Zheltoqsan will get you there, about a half-hour ride from the stop south of Gogol: get off at the Atakent exhibition centre on Timiryazev and walk a couple of minutes west to the Zharokov corner.

The *Hotel Alatau* (☎ 64-48-65, 64-48-64) at Lenin prospektisi 105, about two km south of the Hotel Kazakstan, used to be one of the cheapest with some rooms at US$6 to US$10 a person. It has been closed for renovation by a Turkish company which will probably put prices up. Most buses and trolleybuses heading south on Lenin prospektisi from Abai prospektisi will get you there.

Homestays & Guesthouses Locals offering very cheap *rooms* in their homes hang around outside some hotels. The Hotel Kazakstan seems most favoured: one pair of travellers reported finding here a 'very hospitable' woman who 'made tea and jam sandwiches for us all the time, and gave us breakfast and dinner too. Our room was immaculately clean, the bathroom had hot running water – and the quoted price was US$2 a night! We gave her a bit more'.

Jorge Romero and Karlygash Makatova (see the Travel Agencies section) can provide homestay accommodation for up to five people at US$15 per person in the city centre or US$10 in the suburbs. The travel agency Tour Asia can arrange lodging in private homes for US$20 per person, meals included.

Reception staff at the Hotel Kazakstan have sometimes helped travellers who can't afford their high prices by calling round for somewhere cheaper.

Places to Stay – middle

Hotels The *Hotel Zhetisu* (☎ 39-20-25) at Abylay Khan dangghyly 55 is conveniently located near the City Air Terminal and is also about the nearest hotel to Almaty-II train station (one km by trolleybus Nos 4, 5, 6 or 14). Rooms are clean and OK but while the floor staff are on the whole pleasant, some of the receptionists are astonishingly rude. If they say hello you're doing well, if they smile you're in heaven. Don't be put off – a lot of foreigners stay here. Rooms cost from under US$10 a double with toilet but no bathroom, to US$20 for the cheapest doubles with private bathroom, up to US$65 for lyux doubles. Lately some travellers have reported a first-night registration fee of US$10 per room. The hotel's restaurant seems permanently closed but there's a bufet upstairs.

The *Hotel Kazpotrebsoyuza* (☎ 62-04-09), also called the *Hotel Daulet*, on Ualikhanov just uphill from Zhambyl köshesi is a no-frills hotel but the rooms are good for US$23 and up for a double with bathroom, TV and phone. Trolleybus No 4 from Almaty-II station, or any southbound stop on Abylay Khan dangghyly, runs along Lenin prospektisi two blocks away.

Hotel Alia (☎ 53-94-13) at Auezov 19, outside the central area on the corner of Töle Bi about 2.5 km west of Seyfullin prospektisi, has doubles with private bathroom for about US$25. Take bus No 43 west along Töle Bi from the City Air Terminal.

The *Hotel Turkistan* (☎ 30-18-32, 33-39-03) at Maqataev 49, facing the north side of the central market, is another plain but adequate hotel. Singles/doubles with private bathroom are US$28/34. Trolleybus Nos 1, 2, 8, 12 or 16 along Gogol from anywhere in the central area will take you within two blocks.

The *Hotel Issik (Qonaq Uy Yesik* in Kazak; ☎ 60-02-11) at Bögenbay Batyr 140, just west of Zheltoqsan, has singles/doubles for US$60/70 and up with TV and satellite phones. Some rooms are nice, some tatty. The hotel has a European restaurant and a café. Room prices include breakfast. It's close to the routes of bus Nos 92 and 97 on Zheltoqsan and trolleybus Nos 4, 5, 6 and 14 along Abylay Khan dangghyly. Also close to these routes is the *Hotel Ekvator* at Zheltoqsan 121 near Vinogradov, which was closed for reconstruction when we checked but looked as if it might turn into a nice middle-range place.

At the Railway Stations There's a small *gostinitsa* (hotel) upstairs from the interna-tional hall of Almaty-II train station. Cost is US$20 per person for rooms which are small, with hard beds, but may be acceptable if you arrive late in the day by train. There's one two room suite at the same price. Toilets and showers are separate – the showers were not working when we checked.

At Almaty-I there are reportedly *komnaty otdykha* – dormitories with communal showers and toilets for about US$15 a person. Most rooms have three or four beds but there's one with 20 beds.

Apartments The Nevada-Semey Movement and Alpha Omega Travel (see Travel Agencies) offer comfortable *apartment* rental in Almaty and can arrange visa support and other services. Nevada-Semey charges about US$30 or US$40 a night per person.

Places to Stay – top end
Though top-end hotel space in Almaty is slowly increasing as new hotels are opened, it's best to book a month or more ahead by telephone or fax.

The *Hotel Almaty* (☎ 63-09-43, fax 63-02-02) at Qabanbay Batyr 85, between Abylay Khan dangghyly and Panfilov, is one of the cheaper hotels used by respectable business types. It has comfortable enough singles/doubles at US$60/80 including breakfast, plus a restaurant and a lobby café. You can reach it by trolleybus Nos 4, 5, 6 or 14 which run along Abylay Khan dangghyly from Almaty-II station.

The *Hotel Otrar* (☎ 63-09-43, 33-00-46; fax 33-20-13) at Gogol 73, facing Panfilov Park, was the Intourist flagship in Soviet days. It's still a decent hotel with a good location and comfortable rooms boasting satellite TV for US$80/90, with a good help-yourself breakfast. Trolleybus Nos 1, 2, 8, 12 and 16 along Gogol from anywhere in the central area pass the door.

The *Hotel Kazakstan* (☎ 61-99-06, fax 61-96-00) at Lenin prospektisi 52 is the highest in town, with 20-odd floors. Rooms are standard Soviet tourist-hotel issue – comfortable but some are rather cramped for US$80/115 (though the prices include lunch as well as breakfast). There's a reasonable range of eateries. It's on the routes of trolley-bus No 4, which runs south on Abylay Khan dangghyly from Almaty-II station, and trolleybus No 19 eastbound on Gogol from Pushkin.

The *Hotel Dostyk* (☎ 63-65-55, 63-78-65, 63-92-42; fax 63-68-04, 63-09-04), at Qurmanghazy 36 on the corner of Qonaev, close to the Hotel Kazakstan, was the best in Almaty till the Rachat Palace came along. A former Communist Party hotel, built in the mid-1980s, it's smaller than the Kazakstan and has excellent restaurants. Singles/doubles are US$135/162 including breakfast.

The *Rachat Palace Hotel*, Almaty's first international luxury hotel, opened in 1995. It's a bit outside the central area, at Satpaev 29, about two km west of Respublika alangy. Run by the Austrian Marco Polo group, it has 295 rooms, international direct-dial phones, satellite TV, and two fine and expensive restaurants plus the good Café Vienna coffee shop. There is also a business centre, an indoor swimming pool, Turkish bath, sauna and tennis. Standard rooms are about US$300 a night. It can be reached by the same transport as the state art museum.

Almaty's second international five star hotel will be the Turkish *Hotel Ankara*, being built on Timiryazev just off Respublika alangy.

Places to Eat – bottom end & middle

Cafés & Restaurants In the warmer seasons several of Almaty's cafés and restaurants have tables outside.

City Centre – North For a quick, inexpensive lunch or early dinner head to the *Solyanka* cafeteria at Panfilov 100 on the corner of Kazybek Bi. It's clean and modern, with good Russian and Kazak food and helpful staff, and open from 10 am to 3 pm and 4.30 to 8 pm.

There's good Turkish food towards the north end of Abylay Khan dangghyly at the *Kafe Marmara* (☎ 39-85-62), on the corner of Mametova, a neat little place with friendly

service. Soup, bread and döner kebab with potatoes costs about US$4.50. There's shashlyk, pizza, small salads, tea, beer and expensive soft drinks too. The Marmara is open daily from 11 am to 9 pm.

Another good Turkish restaurant is the *Seyhanlar Kebap Salonu* (☎ 33-56-50) at Qonaev 64, in a courtyard behind the Hotel Otrar. Lentil soup and shish kebab – both excellent – with tea and ayran (liquid yoghurt) costs about US$7. It's open from noon to 9 pm.

Yet another reliable Middle Eastern place is the Lebanese *1001 Nights* (☎ 39-08-51) at Nauryzbay Batyr 37 on the corner of Gogol. It has both a grill-bar (open noon to 11 pm), and a restaurant (noon to midnight) with menus in English. In the grill-bar a portion of grilled chicken is around US$4, pizza US$2.50, and chips or salad US$1.25. In the restaurant, starters include several vegetarian offerings such as hummus and baba-ganouge, as well as soups. Main courses are mainly lamb or chicken dishes at around US$5 to US$8, but there are also steaks and pizza. Portions could be bigger. At night there's dancing to Central Asian music and it can get rowdy. Tax of 13% is added to prices in the restaurant section.

The *International Business Club* (☎ 32-27-01) at Gogol 86, east of Nauryzbay Batyr, has a good restaurant, populated mostly by smartly dressed business people. The food is international: soups and starters are mainly US$3 to US$6, main courses (including steaks, shish kebab and chicken Kiev) US$5 to US$10. Forget the tasty-sounding crepas dessert – it's minuscule. Your bill will have 15% tacked onto the menu prices. Hours are 11 am to midnight daily.

The *Hotel Otrar* restaurant does reasonably priced Russian food – OK for a quick lunch but plagued by gale-force music in the evenings. It does a good help-yourself breakfast.

City Centre – South One of Almaty's best places to eat is the busy but relaxed *Besiktas* restaurant (☎ 63-17-19) at Abylay Khan dangghyly 121 just up the hill from

Qabanbay Batyr. Open 24 hours, it serves a mixture of tasty Turkish and Central Asian fare, with a good stab at pizza too. You pay around US$1.50 for plov, and US$3 for shashlyk or pizza. There are good cakes, pastries and coffee, and salads and beer too.

Restoran Alma-Ata at Abylay Khan dangghyly 125, one block up the hill from the Besiktas, has an echoing and unappealing restaurant hall upstairs, but a more inviting shashlyk place with open-air tables out the front. A block downhill from the Besiktas, the *Restoran Issyk* is OK for pastries and coffee, from 8 am to 2 pm and 3 to 8 pm.

A *blinnaya* at Furmanov 120 south of Bögenbay Batyr has good khachapuri (hot Georgian flat bread with a cheese filling) as well as bliny (pancakes) with meat or sour cream, and tea. Nothing costs more than US$0.50. Hours are Monday to Friday 9 am to 3 pm and 4 to 6 pm, and Saturday 9 am to 3 pm.

The *Hotel Kazakstan*, Lenin prospektisi 52, has the economical *Kafe Kosmos* on the top floor, open from 8 am to 4 pm and 6 to 11 pm, with main dishes around US$3. There's also a reasonable bufet on the 2nd floor.

Shaggies (Shegis), next door to the Hotel Kazakstan, is Almaty's attempt at a western-style fast food joint. It's anyone's guess what the name is supposed to conjure up. The décor is in the correct mood but the hostesses who greet you at the door look embarrassed – probably about the food, which is drab, and not cheap either. A burger, chips and a drink add up to around US$6. Hours are 10.30 am to 10.30 pm daily.

Food at the *Italian Bar-Restaurant* (☎ 62-25-20) on the 2nd floor of the Kazak Business Centre (Qazaq Biznes Ortalyghy) at Lenin prospektisi 85, opposite the Hotel Kazakstan, is nothing great – about US$4.50 for spaghetti or an omelette, and US$2 for a small salad. But it's convenient for a cappuccino or a quick bite if you're in the area. Hours are noon to 4 pm, and 6 to 9.30 pm daily.

The *Kafe Pitstseria* at Furmanov 220, just down the hill from Respublika alangy, does round, thick, crisp pizzas with good toppings for US$3. Just two varieties were on offer – gribnoy (with mushrooms) and myasnoy (with sausage slices). Atmosphere is of the dark and intimate genre – the waitresses seem rather taken aback by lone diners.

Two late arrivals on the scene which sound worth checking out are *BBQ-USA* (☎ 69-63-57, 69-64-28) at Shevchenko 44, on the corner of Tölebaev, and *Capos* off Abai prospektisi just west of Seyfullin prospektisi. BBQ-USA serves steaks, hamburgers, chicken and hot dogs – all with chips and salad – and resident foreigners rate it 'less expensive'. It's open from 11 am to 11 pm and will deliver too. Capos is more of a bar (with American music and satellite TV) but it serves American pizza and barbecue sandwiches too: it's at the end of a short driveway beside Abai prospektisi 32, behind the Yuzhny shop.

Outside the Centre Some of the Almaty's best-value eating is at the small, clean *Kafe Hare Krishna* (☎ 35-14-44) at Seyfullin prospektisi 54/4, which serves good Indian vegetarian meals at around US$3, from 1 to 8 pm (open daily but closed two Mondays a month). It also makes its own cheese from its own cow. The only snag is that it's a long way out – five km north of Raiymbek prospektisi – and a bit hard to find. Take bus Nos 30 or 34, or trolleybus Nos 7 or 8, north on Seyfullin prospektisi from anywhere in the central area. The restaurant is actually about 300 metres off Seyfullin prospektisi but next to the Shugla cinema, which is on the east side of Seyfullin between ulitsa Sormovskaya and ulitsa Budennogo. There's a sign pointing to the restaurant.

There's good pizza at the busy and informal *Pitstseria-Bar Astana-Momors* in the circus building at Abai prospektisi 50. Several varieties are available, from US$1 to US$2.50. Also served are bifshtex with vegetables, mixed salad, cappuccino, espresso, beer and wine. It's open daily except Monday from 11 am to 11 pm and worth the excursion. You can get there by bus No 92 southbound on Zheltoqsan or trolleybus Nos

5 or 6 southbound on Abylay Khan dangghyly.

Self-Catering There are several grocery shops selling fresh fruit and vegetables, and supermarkets selling imported western food (expensive). The best central supermarket is Tilek, on Nauryzbay Batyr between Ayteke Bi and Kazybek Bi. Universam, on the corner of Zhibek Zholy prospekti and Tölebaev, is a big Kazakstani store with groceries on the ground floor. Samal at Abylay Khan dangghyly 96, down the hill from Zhambyl, is a good delicatessen, open 10 am to 10 pm. It has a few tables where you can sit down to enjoy some of its offerings immediately!

Lots of vegetables, fresh and dried fruit, nuts and dairy products – including qymyz and shubat (camel milk, said to be good with tea) – are sold at the large central market, also known as the Köq Bazary or Zelyony Rynok (Green Market). It's at Zhibek Zholy prospekti 53, and open daily except Monday. Goods in the main building tend to be better but more expensive than those outside. Some stalls in and outside the market sell manty, ready-to-eat salads, pizza and other ready-made snacks.

There's a smaller farmer's market by St Nicholas cathedral, west of the centre on Baytursunuly.

Places to Eat – top end

Cafés & Restaurants A popular, good and central place is the Chinese *Shenyan Restaurant* (☎ 69-19-71) at Bögenbay Batyr 136, west of Abylay Khan dangghyly. Main dishes range from US$8 to US$30-plus. Servings are generous. Count on about US$20 per person. The Shenyan is open daily except Sunday from noon to 5 pm and 6 to 11 pm.

The *Tomiris Restaurant* (☎ 61-68-07) at Lenin prospektisi 48, half a block down the hill from the Hotel Kazakstan, is posh and pricey and serves excellent Turkish food, though portions are not enormous. Starters, salads and soups are around US$8, and main courses around US$15 to US$20 – the mixed

grill is a good choice. There's noisy music at night. The Tomiris is open from noon to 4 pm and 6 to 11 pm.

The *Hotel Dostyk*, whose kitchen is overseen by American chefs, has two of the best eateries in Almaty – the ground floor *Café Bastau* (☎ 63-92-42) with French cuisine, and the more formal 2nd floor *Dostyk Restaurant* (☎ 63-67-11) with international fare. A typical full meal in either will come to US$25 or more but there are cheaper offerings such as burgers and pizza for around US$10 in the international restaurant. These are also available in the hotel's 4th floor bar. The international restaurant does a Sunday brunch for about US$20, popular with resident foreigners.

On the ground floor of the Hotel Kazakstan is a *Korean restaurant* of variable quality – usually with a floor show, which may include Korean ethnic dance, in the evenings. Fried rice is about US$10.

The *Ristorante Adriatico* (☎ 67-29-44) at Mechnikov 90 near Zhambyl offers a long menu of good Italian food in clean surroundings with good service, though portions can be small. Starters and pasta are mostly from US$8 to US$15, and main courses US$12 to US$20. There's also a weekend brunch, less expensive than at the Dostyk or Rachat Palace hotels. It's outside the central area, about one km west of Seyfullin prospektisi. Opening hours are 1 to 2.30 pm and 7 to 10.30 pm, and it's advisable to book.

The Rachat Palace Hotel has the good *Café Vienna* on the ground floor with soups, salads, sandwiches and coffees, open from 11 am to midnight, plus two fine restaurants, also on the ground floor: the *Zhambyl Restaurant* with European and local dishes, and the *Grill Room* with Austrian and other European fare.

Entertainment

Nightlife There are a few discos and clubs around Almaty, mainly at weekends. Foreign students and younger expats should be able to fill you in. We found an idiosyncratic mixture of western and CIS rock and an offbeat, student crowd at a regular disco in the Arman Cinema (Kinoteatr Arman) on Lenin prospektisi opposite the end of Abai prospektisi. Hours are Friday, Saturday and Sunday from 10 pm to 1 am; entry is US$1.50 and a beer US$0.75.

The favourite disco among resident foreigners is Dr Bang's in KIMEP, the Kazakstan Institute of Management, Economics & Strategic Research, on Ualikhanov between Abai prospektisi and Satpaev. It's open on Friday and Saturday nights from 9 pm, with a cover charge of US$5. It's officially called Club KIMEP; its common name comes from Dr Bang Chan Young, a Korean-American economist and former top adviser to President Nazarbaev, who founded KIMEP.

Almaty has several casinos including in the Otrar, Dostyk, Kazakstan and Almaty hotels.

Concerts, Opera & Ballet Keep your eye open for posters advertising the good Otyrar Sazy Kazak Folk Orchestra. The two main concert halls are the Central Concert Hall (Ortalyq Kontsert Zaly, Tsentralny Kontsertny Zal) at 8-Mart 35, on the corner of Töle Bi, and the Kazkontsert hall at Abylay Khan dangghyly 83, south of Ayteke Bi. Good, inexpensive classical concerts are also given at the conservatory on Baysetova next to the main post office.

The Opera & Ballet Theatre (Opera zhane Balet Teatry, Teatr Opery i Baleta), Qabanbay Batyr 110 on the corner of Panfilov, has high standards, and tickets as cheap as US$1. It stages a repertory programme of several shows concurrently.

Spectator Sports

Horseraces and occasionally kökpar (see the Buzkashi aside in the Culture section of the Facts about the Region chapter) are held at the Hippodrome (Ippodrom, ☎ 38-09-83), several km north of the centre at ulitsa Lesnaya 10A, on the corner of ulitsa Belinskogo. Take a taxi or bus Nos 8 or 16 north on Furmanov from Töle Bi. Get someone to call ahead and see what's on.

Almaty's soccer team Kayrat plays its home games at the central stadium (Ortalyq Stadion, Tsentralny Stadion) at Abai prospektisi 48. Kazakstani baseball teams play regularly at a field behind the stadium with equipment provided by the San Francisco Little League and the US oil company Chevron, which helped construct the field.

Things to Buy

Markets The central market on Zhibek Zholy prospekti (see Places to Eat) is a sprawling place with a big indoor hall and vendors spread outside too. It's interesting to explore, but watch out for pickpockets. Much of it is devoted to food but there are stalls with clothing and other goods, as well as sad lines of people selling odd shoes, shirts and socks along nearby streets.

There's a big, busy flea-market known as the Barakholka, or Veshchevoy rynok out in the western suburbs. Uzbeks, Chinese, Uyghurs and others converge here selling everything from animals and cars to fur hats and (if you're lucky) carpets. Much of the stuff is cheap imported ware from China and elsewhere, but even if there's nothing you want to buy, it's a revealing Almaty experience. The pet section is among the most interesting. Weekends, especially early Sunday morning, are the busiest times (it's not always open other days). Watch out for pickpockets here, too. Buses going there include No 530 westbound on Raiymbek prospektisi (you can pick it up at Abylay Khan dangghyly).

A curious little market in stamps, coins and lapel pins is held in Gorky Park, just north of the funfair area, on Sundays.

Shops Partly pedestrianised Zhibek Zholy prospekti is the street with the biggest cluster of shops, of which Zanghar, the central department store (commonly known by its Russian name TsUM), near the corner of Abylay Khan dangghyly, is most worth a look. Zanghar has a bit of everything, including a few Kazak crafts and other souvenirs (on the ground floor just inside the Zhibek Zholy entrance), and is an eye-opener on what goods are available to Kazakstanis.

Agai at Ayteke Bi 63, on the corner of Panfilov, sells old Kazak carpets, plus paintings and a variety of souvenirs at reasonable prices. Miras at Baysetova 49, just off Respublika alangy, is a bit hard to find, but worth it for a fine selection of Kazak carpets, textiles, wooden bowls, carvings etc. You can bargain over prices. The craft stall in the Central State Museum is worth a look too.

For fur hats (as well as other fur and leather items), a good shop is Mekha at Kurmanghazy 157, at the corner with Panfilov.

Getting There & Away

Almaty is one of Central Asia's major international and internal transport hubs. It's served by a growing range of flights from European and Asian cities; flights from Moscow (daily) and other Russian cities; trains from Moscow, Siberia, and Ürümqi; and buses from Ürümqi. It has good bus service to Bishkek and south-east Kazakstan cities, and daily trains and several daily buses to Tashkent, but air links with other Central Asian countries are, to date, sparse.

Almaty is also the main hub of internal Kazakstan flights, and linked to most major Kazakstan cities by daily trains. A good way of getting to Tashkent is to go by train to Shymkent, then by bus between Shymkent and Tashkent to avoid the long rail loop between those two places. Look after your belongings on buses or trains to/from Zhambyl, Shymkent or Tashkent – there have been thefts.

Air The airport, about 12 km north-east of the city centre, has separate buildings for non-CIS arrivals and departures either side of the main terminal. The main building has a left-luggage office (saqtau qoymasy, kamera khranenia) in the basement, open round the clock except from 8 to 9 am and 7 to 8 pm. There's a bufet on the ground floor, and a restaurant upstairs.

To/From Non-CIS Countries Flights are by Kazakstan Airlines (Qazaqstan Aue Zholy, Kazair) and a variety of foreign airlines.

Kazakstan Airlines is generally cheaper than foreign airlines. The list of carriers and destinations is in flux but at the time of writing included the following (also see the Getting There & Away chapter):

Kazakstan Airlines
  Ürümqi, Istanbul, Frankfurt and Hanover twice a week; Ulgiy (Mongolia), Delhi and Vienna weekly; Zurich
Air China (Xinjiang Airlines)
  Ürümqi twice a week
Austrian Air
  Beijing and Vienna twice a week
KLM
  Amsterdam twice a week
Luftbrücke (a German charter airline)
  Düsseldorf about weekly
Lufthansa
  Frankfurt four times a week, with connections around Europe and from New York
PIA
  Islamabad weekly
Turkish Airlines
  Istanbul three times a week

To/From Kazakstan & Other CIS Countries These flights are by Kazakstan Airlines and a few other Russian and CIS airlines.

To/from Russia there are daily Moscow flights (five hours) by both Kazakstan Airlines (US$200, one way) and Transaero (US$250 to US$460, one way); three flights a week to St Petersburg; and one or two a week to Barnaul, Krasnoyarsk, Mineralnye Vody, Novosibirsk, Orenburg and Yekaterinburg.

At the time of writing the only flights to other Central Asian locations were to Tashkent twice a week (Thursdays by Uzbekistan Airways for US$83, Saturdays by Kazakstan Airlines for a much dearer US$144); to Ashghabat twice a week (once each by Kazakstan and Turkmenistan Airlines); and at least on paper, to Osh five times weekly and Karakol (Kyrgyzstan) twice weekly. There was no service to Bishkek.

Almaty has flights to/from about 20 other cities in Kazakstan. Schedules are subject to change (including last-minute cancellations) but at the time of research flights went daily once or more to the following destinations: Aqmola, Aqtöbe, Ekibastuz, Kökshetau,

Öskemen, Pavlodar, Qaraghandy, Qostanay, Qyzylorda, Semey, Shymkent and Zhambyl; five or six days a week to Aqtau, Petropavl and Zhezqazgan; and three or four days a week to Atyrau, Balqash, Oral and Zaysan. Foreigners' one-way fares include Zhambyl US$89, Shymkent US$92, Semey US$105 and Aqtau US$155.

Ticket Offices See the Travel Agencies section earlier in this Almaty section for some useful agents for booking air tickets.

You can buy tickets on Kazakstan Airlines and other CIS airlines, including Transaero, at the City Air Terminal (Aerovokzal) at Zheltoqsan 59, on the corner of Zhibek Zholy prospekti. The international windows, where foreigners must go for *all* tickets, are at the right-hand end of the building and are open daily from 9 am to 1 pm and 2 to 7 pm (to 6 pm on weekends). You'll need to show your passport. There are also ticket windows at the airport – worth trying for last-minute tickets.

Last-minute Xinjiang Airlines tickets to Ürümqi are reportedly sold at the airport hotel, but they're cheaper at travel agents.

Airline offices include:

Kazakstan Airlines
  City Air Terminal, Zheltoqsan 59 (☎ 54-15-55, 39-05-94, 62-95-67, 39-64-52, 39-35-00; fax 33-55-06, 23-35-06)
  Airport (☎ 33-89-21, 33-89-25)
KLM
  Intourist Southern, Hotel Otrar (☎ 33-00-07, 33-00-37; fax 33-12-34)
Luftbrücke
  apartment 25, Furmanov 48 (corner of Zhibek Zholy prospekti, ☎ 33-54-71); also at the airport
Lufthansa
  Airport (☎ 34-47-20, 34-44-75; fax 34-40-49, 34-04-04)
PIA
  Airport (☎ 34-42-97)
Transaero
  Intourist Southern, Hotel Otrar (☎ 33-00-07, 33-00-37; fax 33-12-34); also at the airport
Turkish Airlines
  Room 102, Hotel Otrar (☎ 50-62-20, fax 50-62-19)

Bus Long-distance buses use the Sayran bus station on the corner of Töle Bi and Mate Zalki, several km west of the centre. Sayran is called the *novy avtovokzal* (new bus station) or *tsentralny mezhdugorodny avtovokzal* (central inter-city bus station). It has a left-luggage office, open daily from 5 am to 3 am. Nearer destinations are served by the Sayakhat bus station on Raiymbek prospektisi at the north end of Pushkin, just over one km from Panfilov Park. Sayakhat is also called the *stary avtovokzal* (old bus station).

To/From China Buses leave Sayran for Ürümqi (Kazak: Urimshi; Russian: Urumchi) daily except Sunday at 7 am. Schedules may change so check in advance – in any case it's advisable to buy your ticket a day or two ahead, though there may be free seats on the day of departure. You might be asked for your China visa when you buy the ticket (about 26 hours, US$50). A separate bus goes daily to Yining (which you may also find called Ely, Inin, Gulya or Guldzha) for US$30. Tickets are sold at the bus station's international ticket windows, Nos 3 and 4. For more on the Almaty-Ürümqi trip, see China-Kazakstan by Road, later in this chapter.

To/From Kyrgyzstan & Uzbekistan From Sayran, around 30 buses a day, almost round the clock, run to Bishkek (240 km, five hours, US$6). Buses go to Tashkent (806 km, 18 hours, US$21) five times daily – at 1 and 7 am and 2.30, 7 and 10.30 pm.

There are also daily buses to Cholpon-Ata (US$12) and Karakol (US$17) near Lake Issyk-Kul in Kyrgyzstan, via Georgievka near Bishkek. There are no buses taking the rougher and far more scenic easterly road to Issyk-Kul via Kegen, but see the Karkara Valley section later in this chapter for possible ways of getting round this way.

To/From Elsewhere in Kazakstan Services from Sayran include Balqash, Öskemen and Qaraghandy (one bus each daily), Shymkent (a few buses daily; Tashkent buses will normally take you to Shymkent too),

Taldy-Qorghan (a few buses daily), Zhambyl (12 buses daily) and Zharkent (a few buses daily).

From Sayakhat, buses go to Yessik around 30 times daily, Qapshaghay seven times daily, Talgar every few minutes, and Kegen, Saryzhaz (Saryjaz) and Narynqol each once daily.

Train Almaty has two main stations. All main long-distance trains stop at Almaty-I, on the Turksib main line several km north of the centre, but many trains (including those to/from Ürümqi) terminate at Almaty-II, at the end of a spur line much nearer the centre. Almaty-I is at the north end of Seyfullin prospektisi; Almaty-II is at the north end of Abylay Khan dangghyly. Tashkent trains use Almaty-I only. See the Getting Around section for city transport to/from the stations.

At the time of research you needed to show your passport when buying train tickets at Almaty's stations, so there was no avoiding foreigners' fares. A kupeynyy berth to Shymkent costs US$30, Tashkent about US$35, and Moscow about US$110. At Almaty-II, foreigners can avoid queues by using the international ticket window (*khalyqaralyq kassa, mezhdunarodnaya kassa*) in the left-hand end of the station building. You can buy tickets here for trains leaving from Almaty-I too. It's open daily from 9 am to 1 pm and 2 to 8 pm.

Remember that train timetables in Kazakstan are in *Moscow time*. From Almaty-II there are trains at least once a day to Shymkent, Aqmola, Petropavl, Dostyq (Druzhba) and Moscow; and trains every two days to Bishkek, Novosibirsk, Mezhdurechensk, Krasnoyarsk, Yekaterinburg and St Petersburg. From Almaty-I only, there are trains at least daily to Tashkent, Aqtöbe and Novosibirsk, and every two days to Bishkek, Semey, Qostanay, Pavlodar, Omsk, Novokuznetsk and Krasnoyarsk; and three trains weekly to Irkutsk.

For Zhambyl or Shymkent, take a Shymkent or Tashkent train; for Semey you can also take a Novokuznetsk, Mezhdurechensk, Novosibirsk, Krasnoyarsk or Irkutsk train.

Typical journey times include Zhambyl 14 hours, Shymkent 18 hours, Tashkent 24 hours, Semey 20 hours, Novosibirsk 35 hours, and Moscow 77 hours.

To/From China Trains to Ürümqi leave Almaty-II about 8.10 pm (local time) and Almaty-I about 8.45 pm, on Mondays and Saturdays only, but check this yourself. Tickets are sold at the international ticket window at Almaty-II. A kupeynyy berth to Ürümqi is US$60. Tickets go on sale 10 days before departure. At the time of research you had to show your passport and Chinese visa when buying the ticket. See the China-Kazakstan by Rail section later in this chapter for more information.

Car Hiring a car and driver for inter-city travel is common practice in Kazakstan. It's quicker than buses and can be economical. The best place to find drivers – of taxis or personal vehicles – looking for inter-city passengers is outside Sayran bus station. Choose your driver and car with care. The normal fare is four or five times the bus fare, *for the car*, so if the car is full each passenger pays only a little more than the bus fare. Some drivers may ask for more from foreigners but you should be able to bargain them down. Joining a car that already has some passengers should ensure that you pay the local price.

Rental The Nevada-Semey Movement (see the Travel Agencies section) offers car rental for about US$30 to US$40 a day.

Hertz (☎ 62-25-15, fax 63-18-32) is on the 2nd floor of the Kazak Business Centre at Lenin prospektisi 85, opposite the Hotel Kazakstan, open Monday to Friday from 9 am to 6 pm; and (☎ 34-40-30) at the airport, open daily from 9 am to 6 pm. It rents American cars only: the cheapest are US$45 a day plus US$0.40 per km, or US$110 for three days with unlimited mileage.

Getting Around

Almaty has a vast network of bus, trolleybus and tram routes but there are sometimes long gaps between services and they can get very crowded. If you have much baggage or are short of time, it's worth taking a taxi. On buses, trolleybuses and trams, the fare is a flat US$0.15 except on limited-stop 'Express' buses, which are US$0.25. You pay the driver.

To/From the Airport Bus Nos 92 and 97, both sometimes marked 'Express', go every few minutes from outside the main terminal to the City Air Terminal (Aerovokzal) on Zheltoqsan, then on down Zheltoqsan to Abai prospektisi, then west on Abai. It's a 30 minute ride from the airport to the city terminal. Going out to the airport, these buses stop on Zheltoqsan a block south of the city terminal, heading north. They run every few minutes from 6 am to 10 pm. Outside these hours, the occasional bus No 500 runs between the airport and the city terminal.

Lots of taxis wait outside the airport and drivers often approach you inside the building. You have to bargain a price – US$5 to the city centre is standard.

Hertz (see the Car Rental section) runs an airport shuttle service to/from anywhere in the city for US$10 per person, one way.

To/From the Train Stations Trolleybus Nos 4, 5, 6 and 14 run the full length of Abylay Khan dangghyly, north-south through the city centre between Almaty-II train station and Abai prospektisi, passing close to several hotels and other useful places. No 4 continues east along Abai prospektisi and north up Lenin prospektisi, passing near KIMEP and the Kazpotrebsoyuza, Dostyk and Kazakstan hotels on the way.

From Almaty-I train station, trolleybus No 8 runs down Seyfullin prospektisi then east along Gogol to 8-Mart; bus Nos 30 and 34 and trolleybus No 7 go all the way down Seyfullin prospektisi to Qurmanghazy or beyond. While you're making this trek through suburban Almaty, ponder the growth that Almaty has seen since Fitzroy Maclean made it by truck in 1937, when the train station was several km outside the city: 'After a fierce jolting down long dusty roads lined with poplars, we passed through a colony of dilapidated Kazak yurts on the outskirts and immediately found ourselves in the centre of town'.

To/From Sayran Bus Station A taxi is US$1.50 or so. By public transport, it's a long uncomfortable ride – about half an hour to/from the city centre. Bus No 43, heading west on Töle Bi from the corner of Zheltoqsan, goes to Sayran. So do tram Nos 4 and 7 heading west on Shevchenko anywhere between Qonaev and Seyfullin prospektisi. Heading into the city from the bus station, catch any of these outside the station on Töle Bi, going east.

An equally slow alternative is trolleybus No 19, which heads south from Pushkin opposite Sayakhat bus station, then east on Gogol, south on 8-Mart and Lenin prospektisi, and west on Abai prospektisi. Going into the city from the bus station, wait for this on Mate Zalki, across the street from the west side of the station.

To/From Sayakhat Bus Station Bus Nos 92 and 97 (see To/From the Airport) stop on Raiymbek prospektisi in front of Sayakhat. Bus No 32, between Sayakhat and Zhandosov in the south-west of the city, runs the length of Zheltoqsan between Raiymbek prospektisi and Respublika alangy. Trolleybus No 19 (see To/From Sayran Bus Station) is also useful.

Bus, Trolleybus & Tram Routes The following is a summary of useful routes, or sections of routes. All run in the opposite directions too.

Bus Nos 2, 11 & 100
    Furmanov from Gogol to Respublika alangy and beyond
Bus No 29
    south on 8-Mart at Gogol, Bögenbay Batyr, south on Lenin prospektisi
Bus No 30
    Almaty-I station, Seyfullin prospektisi, Qurmanghazy, south on Baytursunuly

Bus No 32

Sayakhat bus station, Raiymbek prospektisi, Zheltoqsan, Respublika alangy, Timiryazev, Zhandosov

Bus No 34

Almaty-I station, Seyfullin prospektisi, west on Abai prospektisi

Bus No 61

Töle Bi from Zheltoqsan to Sayran bus station

Bus No 61

Furmanov from Vinogradov to Respublika alangy and beyond

Bus No 66

Lenin prospektisi at Qurmanghazy, Abai prospektisi, Zhandosov

Bus No 70

Zheltoqsan from Gogol to Respublika alangy, Timiryazev

Bus No 92

airport, Sayakhat bus station, City Air Terminal, Zheltoqsan, west on Abai prospektisi

Bus No 97

airport, Sayakhat bus station, City Air Terminal, Abai prospektisi, south on Baytursunuly

Bus No 99

Abai prospektisi at Lenin prospektisi, Zheltoqsan, Töle Bi

Trolleybus No 1

Gorky Park, Gogol, south on Auezov

Trolleybus No 2

Gogol at 8-Mart, Nauryzbay Batyr, west on Abai prospektisi

Trolleybus No 4

Almaty-II station, Abylay Khan dangghyly, Abai prospektisi, north on Lenin prospektisi

Trolleybus Nos 5 & 6

Almaty-II station, Abylay Khan dangghyly, west on Abai prospektisi

Trolleybus No 7

Almaty-I station, Seyfullin prospektisi to Qurmanghazy

Trolleybus No 8

Almaty-I station, Seyfullin prospektisi, Gogol to 8-Mart

Trolleybus No 9

Pushkin opposite Sayakhat bus station, Gogol, 8-Mart, Bögenbay Batyr, Lenin prospektisi, Qabanbay Batyr, Masanchi, south on Baytursunuly

Trolleybus No 11

Lenin prospektisi at Bögenbay Batyr, Abai prospektisi, south on Baytursunuly

Trolleybus No 12

along Gogol from Gorky Park to Mukanov and beyond

Trolleybus No 14

Almaty-II station, Abylay Khan dangghyly, Abai prospektisi to the central stadium

Trolleybus No 16

Gorky Park, Gogol, Zheltoqsan, Abai prospektisi, Baytursunuly, Satpaev, Zhandosov

Trolleybus No 19

Pushkin opposite Sayakhat bus station, Gogol, 8-Mart, Bögenbay Batyr, Lenin prospektisi, Abai prospektisi, Sayran bus station

Tram No 1

Maqataev at the central market, Baytursunuly, Töle Bi

Tram Nos 4 & 7

Shevchenko from Qonaev to Seyfullin prospektisi, Sayran bus station

Taxi Taxis cost about US$0.20 per km. If you book a taxi (dial ☎ 58 and speak Russian or Kazak), there's usually an extra charge of about US$1. There are a lot of official taxis – marked with chequerboard logos or other obvious signs – but many private cars will also act as taxis (see the Local Transport section in the Getting Around chapter, including tips on personal safety).

Metro Building of a metro system has started but stalled because of lack of funds.

AROUND ALMATY
Medeu & Shymbulaq
Медеу & Шымбулак

These are Almaty's playgrounds in the foothills of the Zailiysky Alatau, both easily visited on a day trip from the city. If you want to get away from crowds come on a weekday.

Medeu is a scattering of buildings around the huge Medeu ice rink, 1700 metres high, about 15 km south-east of central Almaty up the Malaya (Lesser) Almatinka canyon. Shymbulaq (Russian: Chimbulak) at 2300 metres, is one of Central Asia's top skiing centres. Both are starting points for treks in the Zailiysky Alatau, and for good day hikes (see the Travel Agencies section in the Almaty section for information on guided trips).

Medeu is always several degrees cooler than Almaty, and Shymbulaq cooler again. If it's raining in the city, Medeu will probably have snow and zero visibility. Your Almaty hotel might call about conditions and what's open.

The Medeu rink is made for speed skating

and many champion Soviet skaters trained here. It normally functions from about October to May; at weekends it's open to the public and you can hire skates for about US$0.60 an hour. Even when the rink is closed crowds come to relax at the shashlyk and drink stands which sprout at weekends, and to walk in the surrounding valleys and hills.

There are good walks of a few hours east from Medeu up the wooded Komissarovka (also called Kim-Asar) valley towards the 2870 metre Butakovsky pass: take the paved road which leaves the main road between the Hotel Medeu and the ice rink. Pass the Kazaul restaurant and keep going (the paved road becomes a track). A variation is to return by descending north to the waterfalls on the Butakovka river, from which there's a track back to Medeu – a round trip of about 16 km.

What looks like a dam up the main valley past the ice rink (about one km by road or 800-odd steps on foot) is actually there to stop avalanches and mudslides. The road climbs a farther three km from this barrier to the small cluster of buildings which constitutes Shymbulaq. The skiing season here runs from at least November through April

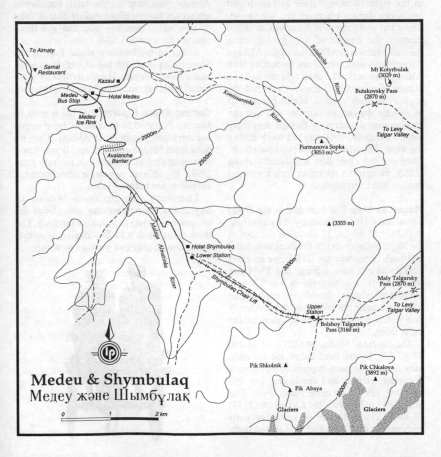

Medeu & Shymbulaq
Медеу және Шымбұлақ

0   1   2 km

but it's usually best in January, February and early March. Like the ice rink at Medeu, the slopes get crowded at weekends. The round building next to the Hotel Shymbulaq has ski equipment and sledges *(sani)* for hire, though the gear is worn and supplies may run out at weekends.

You can take walks from Shymbulaq itself – a track continues some way up the Malaya Almatinka valley – but from the Hotel Shymbulaq, chair lifts will carry you 900 metres up to Bolshoy Talgarsky pass. This is the top of the ski slope, and in summer about two hours hike from some small glaciers, up to the right (warning: there is year-round avalanche danger wherever you see snow). Three km south rises Pik Komsomola (4330 metres), the nearest of a ring of glacier-flanked peaks around the top of the Malaya Almatinka valley, which are favourites with Almaty climbers. The chair lifts run daily in winter from about 10 am to 4 pm, but the higher one may close in March because of avalanche danger. In summer and autumn they run at weekends – though they may close a bit early – but may not work during the week. The alternative is a two hour climb. Price for the chair lifts is officially about US$3, though the operators may try to get double that from foreigners.

Places to Stay The best deal is the *Hotel Shymbulaq* (Biik Taudagy Shymbulaq, ☎ (3272) 33-86-24, 33-26-23) at the foot of the Shymbulaq chair lift. Doubles with toilet and bath or shower are US$9. For an extra US$2 you can have a fridge and TV. Lyux rooms, with a sitting room and TV, are US$16.50 single, double or triple. The rooms are basic but adequate, and in Almaty you would pay three times as much for the same thing.

The big *Hotel Medeu* (☎ (3272) 64-85-68, 64-87-52), by the road below the ice rink, may once have been impressive but is now decaying, gloomy and depressing. For this they ask US$75 or more for doubles. The alternative at Medeu is the *Kazaul* (☎ (3272) 64-88-71), a collection of upmarket yurts with two or four beds each and shared bath-

rooms, open from May to about October. It's up the road to the left, past the Hotel Medeu, and is run by the state tourism company Yassaui. Contact their Almaty office (☎ (3272) 33-00-02, 33-00-26; fax 33-20-56, 33-20-13), in the Hotel Otrar, for rates.

Places to Eat Bring some food with you if you plan to hike or stay up here because there is nowhere here to buy supplies. The *Kazaul* at Medeu has a restaurant open all year, and at weekends you can snack from the shashlyk stands below the ice rink. About 1.5 km down the road from Medeu back towards Almaty (one stop on the bus), the *Samal* restaurant has excellent mainly Kazak food at reasonable prices – you can get three courses for around US$4.

A *bar* in the building at the foot of the Shymbulaq chair lift has shashlyks, coffee and alcoholic drinks. There's a *canteen* in the round building next to the Hotel Shymbulaq.

Getting There & Away Bus No 6 goes to Medeu, every 30 to 40 minutes from opposite the Hotel Kazakstan in Almaty. They go back from Medeu up to at least 10 pm. A taxi should be about US$10 or less, including the US$2 payable at a vehicle checkpoint a couple of km before Medeu.

The only way up from Medeu to Shymbulaq is on foot (an hour from the avalanche barrier) or by taxi or hitching. The road from Medeu to Shymbulaq is sometimes closed after bad weather in winter.

Bolshoe Almatinskoe Lake
Озеро Большое Алматинское

To reach the lake involves a longer day trip from Almaty into the Zailiysky Alatau foothills. Bolshoe Almatinskoe lake is a turquoise lake 1.25 km long, 2500 metres high, and about 32 km south of central Almaty. Like Medeu and Shymbulaq, it's a starting point for treks higher into the mountains. The route up to it, along the Bolshaya (Greater) Almatinka canyon, is scenic, though part of it is slightly disfigured by minor hydroelectric installations. The same warnings about the weather apply as at Medeu and Shymbulaq.

From Almaty, start by taking bus No 63 southbound on Zheltoqsan from beside the City Air Terminal, or bus Nos 18 or 63 from farther south on Zheltoqsan, to the Arman bus station (Avtostantsia Arman) on al-Farabi prospektisi in the south-west of the city. Then take a No 28 (Kokshoky) or No 93 (Alma-Arasan) bus to the small settlement of Kokshoky, a ride of about half an hour (check return times before you go). The Kokshoky bus stop is at a fork where a sign points to Alma-Arasan (four km) in one direction, and Kosmostantsia (23 km) in the other. Bolshoe Almatinskoe lake is about 16 km up the Kosmostantsia road, a climb of 1100 metres.

The forester (lesnik) Viktor Bornikov (☎ (3272) 29-38-55) may be able to rent you horses for a day trip, at about US$10 each including a shashlyk lunch. He lives in a farmstead close to the Kokshoky bus stop. Walking, you can cut six km off the road distance by following the big water pipe straight uphill from the road after some seven km, shortly before the road becomes dirt – altogether about a four hour walk from the bus stop to the lake.

At the north end of the lake are a dam and the small settlement of Ozyorny. Otherwise it's surrounded by unspoiled nature. You can cross the dam and follow the track along the east side of the lake (this is apparently passable by 4WD at least as far as the 3609 metre Ozyorny pass, 10 km south of the lake, in suitable weather).

The main dirt road zigzags on up in a general westward direction from Ozyorny, passing a sprawling, seemingly abandoned observatory complex, on the right after two km, to Kosmostantsia (3330 metres). This untidy collection of buildings beside the Zhusalykezen pass is either a weather station or a space energy research centre, depending on whom you ask.

By car or taxi, the last few km of the climb to the lake may well be impassable after bad weather. A 4WD helps in any case, though locals do it without. Leave Almaty by Furmanov and al-Farabi prospektisi, and

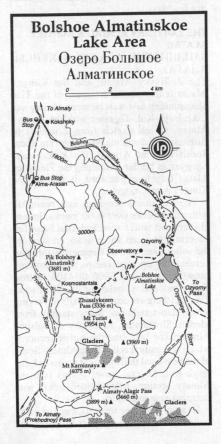

Bolshoe Almatinskoe Lake Area
Озеро Большое Алматинское

To Almaty
Bus Stop ● Kokshoky
Bolshoy
1800m
Bus Stop
Alma-Arasan
3000m
Pik Bolshoy Almatinsky (3681 m)
Observatory ●
Ozyorny
Bolshoe Almatinskoe Lake
To Ozyorny Pass
Kosmostantsia
Zhusalykezen Pass (3336 m)
Mt Turist (3954 m)
Glaciers
▲ (3969 m)
Mt Karniznaya (4075 m)
Almaty-Alagir Pass (3660 m)
(3899 m) ▲
Glaciers
To Almaty (Prokhodnoy) Pass
Almatinka River
Pipeline
2400m
3600m
Prokhodnaya River
Ozyornaya River

turn left at the roundabout after you cross the Bolshaya Almatinka river.

South-East Kazakstan

This is the hub of Kazakstan for most visitors. Here lies the capital, Almaty. There are also good trips to be made from Almaty, notably into the Zailiysky Alatau range along the Kyrgyzstan border, a northern spur of the Tian Shan with plenty of spectacular scenery and good walking and skiing. You can trek right across to Lake Issyk-Kul in Kyrgyzstan in a few days.

THE ZAILIYSKY ALATAU & KÜNGEY ALATAU
ЗАИЛИЙСКИЙ АЛАТАУ & КУНГЕЙ АЛАТАУ

The Zailiysky Alatau, and the Küngey Alatau farther south, are spurs of the Tian Shan running east-west between Almaty and Lake Issyk-Kul. Together with the Kyrgyz Alatau, which stretch from Zhambyl to Bishkek, they form the Northern Tian Shan. South-west of Almaty the Kazakstan-Kyrgyzstan border runs along the Zailiysky Alatau ridgeline; eastward, it follows the Küngey Alatau ridgeline.

The mountains are high and beautiful, with many peaks over 4000 metres, lots of glaciers and wild rivers, and Tian Shan firs covering the steep valley sides. In summer the valleys are used as summer pasture and herders set up yurt camps. The summer snowline is around 3800 to 4100 metres. These mountains make for excellent trekking and there are dozens of trails of varying length and toughness, many starting from Medeu, Shymbulaq, Kokshoky or Bolshoe Almatinskoe lake (see the earlier sections) which are easily reached from Almaty. Some of the best-used trails go right across to Lake Issyk-Kul. Several travel agents (see the Almaty section) offer guided treks, with camping gear available.

Russian-language trekking maps of many routes, including those described here, are available in Almaty; the best place to find them is the Akademkniga bookshop. Most are 1:50,000 and called *Marshrutnaya Turistskaya Karta (Tourist Route Map)*. The *Vysokogornye Perevaly Severnogo Tyan-Shanya (High Mountain Passes of the Northern Tian Shan)* map covers virtually the whole area between Almaty and Lake Issyk-Kul at 1:200,000 and grades all the passes in the region. Passes marked H/K (Unclassified) or 1A are simple, with slopes no steeper than 30° and glaciers, where they exist, are flat and without open crevasses. Grade 1B (1Б) passes may have ice patches or glaciers with hidden crevasses and may require ropes. Passes of grade 2A and above may require special equipment and technical climbing skills. The route descriptions in this section note all grade 1B passes and include none of greater difficulty.

It's feasible to trek unguided if you have suitable experience and equipment, but watch out for two things. One is the possibility of 'bandits' in the hills who rob hikers especially when they are camped at night. To this end guides often take big dogs along to deter robbers. The other hazard is the weather: be equipped for conditions to turn bad suddenly. The trekking season lasts from about mid-May to mid to late September: in July and August the weather should be OK, but outside those months it can often rain or even snow in the mountains when it's warm in Almaty. If you're caught unprepared by a sudden storm, it could be fatal.

You should check closely about what lies in store before embarking on any trek: some routes cross glaciers and tricky passes over 4000 metres high. Don't attempt without a guide anything you're doubtful about. Times given here are for a fairly unstrenuous pace: one or two days can be cut off several routes if you wish.

The Almatinsky nature reserve (Almatinsky Zapovednik), a rugged area of about 750 sq km south of the towns of Talgar and Yessik, east of Almaty, is an important snow leopard habitat. Other inhabitants include the *arkhar* (a big-horned wild sheep) and the goitred gazelle, known locally as the *zheyran*. The reserve also contains Mt Talgar, the highest peak in the Zailiysky Alatau at 4979 metres. The reserve is off limits to those without special permits.

Routes to Lake Issyk-Kul

The two most-used routes run from Bolshoe Almatinskoe lake to Grigorievka on Lake Issyk-Kul, 35 km east of Cholpon-Ata (or Semyonovka, 42 km east of Cholpon-Ata); and from Kokshoky to Chong-Sary-Oy, on Lake Issyk-Kul 15 km west of Cholpon-Ata. The Bolshoe Almatinskoe lake-Grigorievka route and variations described here all pass

through the Chong-Kemin valley, between the main ridges of the Zailiysky Alatau and Küngey Alatau, which is a summer pasture for yurt-dwellers. Jasyl-Köl lake towards the upper (eastern) end of the valley, at 3200 metres, is one of the loveliest spots in these mountains. Routes using the Ozyorny pass (which it's possible to reach by 4WD) tend to be most used.

Bolshoe Almatinskoe Lake to Grigorievka

This route takes four to six days. From Bolshoe Almatinskoe lake (2500 metres), up the Ozyornaya river to the Ozyorny pass

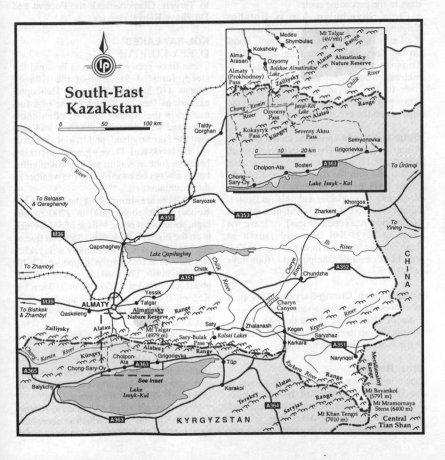

(3609 metres, on the Zailiysky Alatau main ridge). Down the Kol-Almaty river to the Chong-Kemin river (2800 metres). East up the Chong-Kemin valley to Jasyl-Köl lake. Back west down the Chong-Kemin valley to the Aksu river. South up the Aksu river and the Vostochny (Eastern) Aksu glacier to the Severny (Northern) Aksu pass (4062 metres, on the Küngey Alatau main ridge). Eastward down to the Chong Aksu river, then down the Chong Aksu river (eastward, then southward) to Grigorievka.

Variation from Shymbulaq This adds three days to the preceding route.

From Shymbulaq, across Bolshoy Talgarsky pass (3160 metres) and down to the Levy Talgar river (2300 metres). South up the Levy Talgar river then west up the Turistov river to Turistov pass (3930 metres). South-west down the Kyzylsay river to the Ozyornaya river. Up the Ozyornaya river to Ozyorny pass then continue as on the preceding route.

Other Variations Variations on the Bolshoe Almatinskoe lake-Grigorievka route, all with grade 1B passes, enable you to start at Medeu and join the route at Jasyl-Köl lake (three days extra); or leave the route at Vostochny Aksu glacier and finish at Bosteri village close to Lake Issyk-Kul, nine km east of Cholpon-Ata (one day less); or leave the route at Jasyl-Köl lake and finish at Semyonovka, nine km from Lake Issyk-Kul, and 42 km east of Cholpon-Ata (four days extra).

Kokshoky to Chong-Sary-Oy This is a more westerly route of about six days.

From Kokshoky, south through Alma-Arasan and up the Prokhodnaya river valley to the Almaty (Prokhodnoy) pass.

Other Routes

One relatively easy two or three day route is the 35 km circuit from Kokshoky to Alma-Arasan via Bolshoe Almatinskoe lake and the 3660 metre Almaty-Alagir pass.

A harder two or three day route goes from

Kokshoky to Shymbulaq via the Lokomotiv glacier and Lokomotiv pass (grade 1B, 4050 metres), the Tuyuksu glacier and the Malaya Almatinka river.

A longer possibility is the 115 km circuit from Shymbulaq to Turgen, 55 km east of Almaty – about eight days. The route goes by the Bolshoy Talgarsky pass, Levy Talgar river and Popova pass (grade 1B, 4250 metres), then follows the Zhangyryk and Chilik rivers skirting the southern boundary of the Almatinsky nature reserve, then turns north over Druzhnye Rebyata pass (grade 1B, 4070 metres) and down the Turgen river to Turgen. Glaciers flank the Popova and Druzhnye Rebyata passes.

KÖL-SAY LAKES
ОЗЕРА КОЛСАИ

These three pretty green lakes lie amid the steep, forested foothills of the Küngey Alatau, 110 km east of Almaty. Helicopter excursions (see the Travel Agencies information in the Almaty section) often come here, and with camping gear you can also visit the lakes by land, and trek or ride over to Lake Issyk-Kul. There's great trout fishing here too. June to August are the best months, but as always be careful with the weather in the mountains.

The lakes are strung along the Köl-Say (or Kolsai) river, about 1800 to 2200 metres high, south-west of the village of Saty which is on the bigger Chilik river. Saty is a five or six hour bus ride from Almaty's Sayakhat bus station, across barren steppe via Chilik and Zhalanash. The road takes a very round-about route (at least 250 km, or 350 km via Kegen). If there's no bus to Saty, get one to Zhalanash and hitch or catch a truck for the last 33 km to Saty.

You should be able to hire horses and/or a guide in Saty: ask for Serik Sadyrbaev or the forester (lesnik) Azanbekov Sharybek. Herders at the middle lake may also have horses for rent. They may ask no more than US$1 or US$2 a day for a horse.

From Saty it's about 15 km up to Nizhny (Lower) Köl-Say lake, which is accessible by vehicle. The lake is one km long. From here it's a two to three hour, five km walk up the valley to the similarly sized Sredny (Middle) Köl-Say lake, also called Minzhilka (Thousand Horses), whose surrounding meadows are used as pasture. This is a good camping spot. From the middle lake to the smaller Verkhny (Upper) Köl-Say lake is about four km and two hours farther.

The route over to Lake Issyk-Kul starts from the middle lake, crosses the 3200 metre Sary-Bulak pass on the Küngey Alatau ridge (also the Kazakstan-Kyrgyzstan border), and descends to the village of Balbay (also called Sary-Bulak) on Issyk-Kul. By horse, this can be done in one day, on foot in two. From the pass there are fine views north towards the Kazak steppe and south into the Issyk-Kul basin.

CHARYN CANYON
ЧАРЫНСКИЙ КАНЬОН

This 'Kazakstan Colorado', as some tourist brochures style it, isn't quite that, but it's a dramatic enough destination for a helicopter trip from Almaty (US$100 or more per person; see the Travel Agencies section in the Almaty section).

The Charyn river, flowing rapidly down from the Tian Shan, has carved a deep canyon into the otherwise flat and barren steppe 175 km east of Almaty, and time has weathered this into all sorts of weird, wonderful and colourful rock formations. Your helicopter will fly up and down between the canyon walls and land on one of the few flat spots for you to look around.

When we did it (rather late in the year), a high wind suddenly blew in from the steppe after we had landed in the canyon, and made taking off again a very interesting event! Trips usually also visit the Köl-Say lakes and make at least one other stop.

KARKARA VALLEY
КАРКАРА ДОЛИНА

The valley of the Karkara river sweeping down northwards from the Central Tian Shan is an age-old summer pasture for herds from both sides of what's now the Kazakstan-Kyrgyzstan border. The river forms the border for some 40 km before heading north to join the Kegen river, beyond which it becomes the Charyn. In its lower reaches the Karkara valley is up to 40 km wide, a broad green expanse filled with wildflowers and grazing herds in summer.

From Kegen, 190 km east of Almaty (or 250 km of bleak steppe by road), a rough but scenic road heads south up the valley to the settlement of Karkara, then across the border into Kyrgyzstan about 28 km from Kegen. There are said to be Scythian (Saka) burial mounds between Kegen and the border. This is about the most laid-back border you're likely to find in Central Asia. The road then veers westwards towards Tüp and Lake Issyk-Kul.

The Karkara valley's annual Chabana (Cowboy) festival, held around 15 to 20 June, is a bazar and 'rodeo' of local sports such as kökpar and qyz quu, bringing together Kazaks and Kyrgyz in a reminder of the valley's historic role as a meeting place of nomads and Silk Road traders. The location of the festival apparently changes from year to year, and the exact dates depend on weather, work requirements, etc. See the Lake Issyk-Kul section in the Kyrgyzstan chapter for more on the Issyk-Kul region, the Karkara valley and the festival.

The Almaty mountaineering and trekking company Kan Tengri maintains a base camp on the Kazakstan side of the Karkara river, about 35 km south of Kegen, at 2200 metres. Accommodation is in yurts and there are a bar and sauna too. From here climbers go by helicopter to mountain base camps in the Central Tian Shan.

Getting There & Away

Though there are no buses taking this cross-border route, in summer you could take a Kegen, Saryzhaz or Narynqol bus from Almaty's Sayakhat bus station to Kegen, then hitch south from there – though traffic is thin. On the Kyrgyzstan side, the valley is an easy hitch from Tüp or Karakol. A taxi from Karakol would be about US$30 to US$50.

LAKE QAPSHAGHAY, THE ILI RIVER & LAKE BALQASH
СУ КОЙМАСЫ КАПШАҒАЙ, РЕЧКА ИЛИ & БАЛКАШ КӨЛ

Lake Qapshaghay is a 140 km long reservoir formed by a dam on the Ili river near the town of Qapshaghay (Russian: Kapchagay), 60 km north of Almaty. This is a favourite out-of-town retreat for Almaty people, many of whom have dachas there. The lake has cold, fresh waters.

The **Ili river** flows west out of China into the lake, then north-west to Lake Balqash. As it approaches the southern end of Lake Balqash, the Ili enters a delta wetland region of many lakes, marshes and thick, jungle-like vegetation. The river is navigable by kayak all the way from lake to lake (around 460 km), and by raft at least some of the way. See the Travel Agencies section in the Almaty section for day trips on the river.

These trips usually include a visit to the **Tamgaly-Tas petroglyphs**, about 20 km downstream from Lake Qapshaghay. Some of these 1000 or more rock drawings are very old. Many depict deer and hunters but there's also a large image of the Buddha or Shiva (depending who you believe) which probably dates to at least the 8th century when Chinese influence in Central Asia ended.

Lake Balqash is Asia's fourth largest lake at 17,400 sq km, but very shallow – only 26 metres at its deepest point. Its eastern half is salty, its western half fresh water. Pollution from copper smelters set up on its shores in the 1930s has diminished lake life, though it still supports a fishing industry. The town of Balqash on the north side is the only significant settlement here.

Getting There & Away

Qapshaghay is on the route of trains and buses between Almaty and Zharkent, Taldy-Qorghan, Aktogay or Semey. There are also a few buses to Qapshaghay from Almaty's Sayakhat bus station. The few small settlements along the Ili river are linked by road to Qapshaghay and/or to the Almaty-Qaraghandy road. Some, such as Akzhar and Akkol, and Kuygan on Lake Balqash near the Ili's mouth, can be reached by bus from Almaty.

Balqash is served by bus (one daily from Almaty, a 695 km trip for US$16) and plane from Almaty and other cities.

CHINA-KAZAKSTAN BY ROAD

A year-round road crosses between Almaty and Ürümqi (Xinjiang) via the border post at Khorgos (Korgas on the Xinjiang side). A direct Almaty-Ürümqi bus runs six days a week in each direction, taking about 26 hours, with no stops except for food and toilets. The road is 70 km from Yining (Xinjiang), about 100 km from the border and the largest town en route, but the Ürümqi buses don't stop there (and it's pretty dismal in any case).

There are at least three other road crossings between Kazakstan and China, further north of Kohogos, though we were unable to learn whether foreigners can use them. See the China Crossings information in the Northern Kazakstan section.

Zharkent
Жаркент

Zharkent (formerly Panfilov), 340 km by road north-east of Almaty on the northern fringe of the Ili river valley, is the last real town in Kazakstan on the bus route to China. It has a substantial Uyghur population. Its limited attractions include a curious late 19th century mosque with a minaret in the form of a Chinese pagoda, beside a more conventional Central Asian dome; adding to the crosscultural symbolism, the mosque's ground floor windows look Russian.

Be ready for a local scam known as the 'Zharkent Free Trade Zone'. At a checkpost a few km before the town, all non-Kazak passengers – traders or not – must pay a 'fee'. Non-CIS travellers have been asked for US$10 or more, though you might persuade them to accept the CIS rate (around US$1) on the grounds that you're only passing through. There doesn't seem to be any way to avoid this little municipally sanctioned highway robbery.

Khorgos
Хоргос

The Kazak customs and immigration post, a foreign-exchange bank and the tiny, cheap *Khorgos Hotel* are at Khorgos, 40 km east of Zharkent and about four km west of the border. Taxis can go no farther than Khorgos.

Be ready for tedious border formalities; the crossing is usually crammed with Kazak and Uyghur families and traders, who can cross more easily than foreigners but seem to have about 10 times as much baggage. You may also encounter Russian or Kazak officials looking for bribes or goodies, though travellers report few hassles in comparison with the rail crossing (see the China-Kazakstan by Rail section).

In summer, official time throughout China is one hour later than in eastern Kazakstan; in winter it's two hours later. But unofficial 'Xinjiang time' is an hour *earlier* than eastern Kazakstan in summer, and the same as eastern Kazakstan in winter.

Visas

You must already have a valid Chinese or Kazak visa to cross here. No visas are issued at the border, nor are there embassies or consular offices closer than Beijing, Almaty and the other Central Asian capitals. Some travellers report that the Kazakstan Airlines office in Ürümqi acts as a consulate and may be able to issue Kazakstan visas, but don't count on it. See the Visas & Embassies section in the Facts for the Visitor chapter for information on getting visas.

The Journey

Direct buses depart daily except Sunday from Almaty, and daily except Saturday from Ürümqi. The cost is about US$50 in local currency, and tickets are easy to buy at the long-distance bus stations in these cities (see Getting There & Away under each city). You'll probably be asked to show an onward visa. It's advisable to buy your ticket a day or two ahead in summer. Bring some food of your own; if the bus is running late, you may get pretty hungry.

You could pay less on a succession of taxis

and local buses, though it would be a headache. There are daily buses between Almaty and Zharkent (seven to eight hours, US$8), and buses and taxis run from Zharkent to Khorgos.

There are said to be minibuses shuttling between the Kazak and Chinese border posts, and Chinese buses run between the border and Ürümqi (15 hours, about US$10). A bus also goes daily between Almaty and Yining (elsewhere also called Ely, Inin, Gulya or Guldzha) for US$30.

TALDY-QORGHAN & THE ZHUNGAR ALATAU
ТАЛДЫ-ҚОРАН & ЖУНГАР АЛАТАУ

Population: 130,000

Taldy-Qorghan (Russian: Taldy-Kurgan) is a predominantly Kazak town, about 250 km north-east of Almaty and lacking the ethnic tension of some other southern Kazakstan cities. From here you could reach the rarely visited Zhungar Alatau mountains along the Chinese border to the east.

Orientation & Information

The main street is Lenin köshesi and most other streets of any importance intersect this. You'll find money changers in the bazar, which is open daily from 8 or 9 am to 5 pm. The post and telephone offices, both open from 8 am to 6 pm, are near the Rodina cinema, off the square on Lenin köshesi. The Taldy-Qorghan telephone code is 32822.

Things to See & Do

There's a local history and culture museum near the square on Lenin köshesi, and a museum dedicated to the Soviet-era Kazak writer Ilyas Zhansugurov next door.

The town of Tekeli, 45 km east of Taldy-Qorghan, lies in the western foothills of the Zhungar Alatau. This is lovely country in summer, with herds of horses and carpets of wildflowers in some of the valleys reaching back into the mountains from Tekeli. You can, for instance, drive to within 15 km or so of the head of the Kora river valley, which reaches about 80 km up from Tekeli.

The valley head is 3000 metres high and

surrounded by glacier-covered peaks. The trekking map *Po Dzhungarskomu Alatau, Marshrut No 1* (you might pick it up at Akademkniga bookshop in Almaty) details a 12 day trek here, but it shouldn't be undertaken lightly as it crosses several big glaciers and difficult passes.

Places to Stay

The *Hotel Taldy-Kurgan*, close to Taldy-Qorghan's main square on Lenin köshesi, has clean rooms for around US$4 per person (it seems they don't know about foreigners' prices yet). There's another slightly more expensive hotel nearby.

Places to Eat

There's good food at the *Chinese restaurant* in Central Park – US$2 or less for a meal. The *Zhetisu* restaurant on Lenin köshesi is also good but more expensive at around US$7 a meal. The *Bar* on Lenin köshesi near the square has beer, coffee and chocolate, and a live band doing pop covers, nightly except Monday. Food at the *Hotel Taldy-Kurgan* is dire.

Getting There & Away

Taldy-Qorghan is on the main road from Almaty to north-east Kazakstan, but off the Turksib railway. A few daily buses run from Almaty (250 km, six hours, US$6); a car or taxi takes about four hours. There are buses about hourly from here to both Tekeli and Ushtobe, the nearest station on the Turksib railway – both about an hour away for around US$1. Taldy-Qorghan's bus station is at the end of Shevchenko köshesi, off Lenin köshesi.

CHINA-KAZAKSTAN BY RAIL

The 1359 km train journey between Almaty and Ürümqi takes about 35 hours, with two nights aboard in either direction.

From Almaty the route runs north on the Turksib mainline for 565 km to Aktogay, then south-east for 305 km to the Kazakstan-China border at Dostyq. For most of the way there's little life beyond a few wind-blasted

villages and the occasional herder. It runs near the large Lake Alakol for some distance west of Dostyq, with the Zhungar Alatau mountains visible to the south. Just west of the border, at the north end of the Zhungar Alatau, the line crosses a low pass known as the Zhungarian Gate or Zhungarian Gap. East of the border you may catch sight of another shallow lake, Ebinur Hu. From the border to Ürümqi is 489 km.

The border crossing is about 200 km north of the regular highway route (see China-Kazakstan by Road). There is also a road crossing at Dostyq, although it doesn't appear to be open to foreigners.

Dostyq (Druzhba)
Достык (Дружба)

Dostyq, like its widely used Russian name, Druzhba, means 'friendship' – an extraordinary misnomer in view of travellers' experiences.

There is almost nothing here except border facilities and a local train station. Border procedures are roughly as follows: at Dostyq, one to 1½ hours sitting at the local station for local passengers and the addition or removal of the Kazak restaurant car; two hours while the carriages are jacked up and the bogeys (wheel assemblies) changed between Russian and Chinese track gauges; 2½ to 3½ hours with Kazakstan customs and immigration; 10 minutes between Dostyq and the Chinese post at Alashankou; and at Alashankou, one to two hours with Chinese customs and immigration.

That makes 7½ to nine hours, during which there is probably no exit from the train, no running water and – except for the dash between the Kazakstan and China posts – no toilets! This, however, is nothing compared to the unmonitored corruption of customs officials at Dostyq (see the Snouts in the Trough aside on the next page), which fairly well ruins the journey, and poisons an otherwise promising trans-continental route.

Officials at Alashankou on the Chinese side can be maddeningly thorough but are fundamentally honest. Travellers report no

Snouts in the Trough

Grinning and joking amongst themselves, customs officials at Dostyq work their way systematically through everyone's belongings, setting aside items they might accept in return for overlooking the minor irregularities they will almost certainly find on customs forms or in baggage.

They will want to see all consumer goods and may well go through everything you have, occasionally asking with a smirk if they can have this or that (go ahead and say no; they'll take it anyway if they really want it). They will want to see and carefully count all your money; any mismatch with what you have written on your customs form produces the theatrical elevation of an eyebrow and a probable 'fine'. It's potluck whether you get a polite official or an animal, but all of them are on the take, with each day bringing them a new trainload of goods and dollars.

Local people come off worst, especially those who look like they're carrying goods for resale. One of our Uyghur fellow travellers gave up a pile of clothing and Y500 (she failed to report all the money, so officials simply took it). But individual foreigners are shaken down fairly regularly too, mainly for dollars. An American travelling with his son was allegedly detained for hours, stripped to his money belt and forced to contribute half its contents (though this is the worst story of several we heard). Group tourists, as far as we know, have not been harassed in this way.

All you can do is to have your papers in order, be deadly accurate on your customs form, and hang in there. It's clear from watching one savvy Uzbek granny that a friendly but no-nonsense attitude helps, but only so much. Anger gets you nowhere, though officials seem less sure of themselves faced with a western woman than a man.

Lying about your cash probably won't work because they want to see everything, and may even body-search you for it. Implausibly small reported sums will only pique their interest. One trick, however, is to carry mostly travellers' cheques and next to nothing in cash on the train journey (you can exchange cheques in both Ürümqi and Almaty), since officials haven't the first idea what to do with travellers' cheques.

This is all extra excruciating for those heading *into* Kazakstan. Just as you're unwinding at Dostyq station, you may see those same officials stroll by the train again, flushed and cheerful. Finally, just as the train pulls out, toilets are unlocked and everybody breaks out their picnics to celebrate their escape, along come the Kazakstan militsia for their own passport check. After that the trip seems delightful by comparison.

Most of our information is for the Almaty-bound train, although there is no reason to expect an easier time of it going the other way. ■

---

such serious hassles on either side on the bus journey.

In summer, official time throughout China is one hour later than in eastern Kazakstan; in winter it's two hours later. But unofficial 'Xinjiang time' is an hour *earlier* than eastern Kazakstan in summer, and the same as eastern Kazakstan in winter.

Visas

No visas are issued at the border. It's possible to get a China visa in Central Asia, but awkward to get a Kazakstan or other Central Asian visa from anywhere closer to the border than Beijing. You're better off bringing one from home.

Some travellers report that the Kazakstan Airlines office in Ürümqi may be able to issue Kazakstan visas, but don't count on it. See Visas & Embassies in the Facts for the Visitor chapter for more information on visas.

The Journey

The 2nd or soft-class *Genghis Khan Express* (No 13/14) departs on Monday and Saturday in each direction and takes, by the timetable, 36 hours from Almaty or 34½ hours from Ürümqi – more or less, depending on your misadventures at Dostyq.

Buying your own ticket is no problem at either end (see Ürümqi or Almaty). The price at the time of research was about US$60, in local currency. You can book ahead through

Almaty-Ürümqi Timetable

Following is a partial timetable for the Almaty-Ürümqi train journey at the time of research (some smaller stations have been omitted). Times in China are official Beijing time; those in Kazakstan are Moscow and local time (Kazakstan Railways still runs on Moscow time!). These are winter times; as far as we know, the timetable is the same under Kazakstan daylight savings time. Times are for departure except as noted:

Station	Ürümqi to Almaty	Almaty to Ürümqi
China (Beijing time):		
Ürümqi	11.00 pm	arrives 9.30 am
Kuytun	4.20 am	4.15 am
Alashankou	11.00 am	11.30 pm
Kazakstan (Moscow/local time):		
Dostyq (Druzhba)	12.50/3.50 pm	arrives 10.15 am/1.15 pm
Aktogay	7.05/10.05 pm	4.15/7.15 am
Almaty-I	5.15/8.15 am	5.45/8.45 pm
Almaty-II	arrives 5.35/8.35 am	5.10/8.10 pm

a travel agency, for a significantly higher price.

Food There was no restaurant carriage on our trip from Ürümqi to the border; one was added at Dostyq, with grumpy Russian staff selling soft drinks, Chinese beer, manty and gulyash at Almaty prices. They wanted only *tengge* or dollars, and had a tendency to overcharge in dollars and give *tengge* change. You're much better off bringing your own food and sharing with your fellow travellers, as everyone else does.

Southern Kazakstan

Southern Kazakstan, the region from Kyrgyzstan's western border to the Aral Sea, is the most Kazak part of Kazakstan. Kazaks form a higher percentage of the population here than almost anywhere else. The two main cities, Zhambyl and Shymkent, saw some of the worst of the December 1986 riots (after the Kazak Dinmukhamed Qonaev was replaced by a Russian as head of the CPK), and both were under martial law for a year afterwards. Some anti-Russian sentiment remains today.

This is an arid region of deserts and barren steppe, dissected by the Syr-Darya but with only pockets of cultivation. You'll cross it if you travel by land between Tashkent and Almaty, or by rail between Moscow and Tashkent, Almaty or Bishkek. Zhambyl and Shymkent come from the usual shabby Soviet mould: the chief reasons to stop lie elsewhere, in the mountainous Aqsu-Zhabaghly nature reserve on the region's southern fringe, or the great 14th century mausoleum of the Sufi poet and teacher Qozha Akhmed Yasaui at Turkistan.

ZHAMBYL
ЖАМБЫЛ
Population: 310,000
Zhambyl, 516 km west of Almaty and 170 km east of Shymkent, has an ancient pedigree but the modern reality is drab. It's of interest mainly for side trips (see the Around Zhambyl section).

The town's past as the 6th century Silk Road settlement of Taraz (or Talas) was discovered by archaeologists in 1938. In the 11th century it was a capital of the Turkic (and Islamic) Qarakhan state which also ruled Bukhara for a while. Levelled by Jenghiz Khan, it only rose again 600 years later, under the name Aulie-Ata (Holy Father), as a northern frontier fort of the Kokand khanate. It fell to the Russians in

1864. The whole town seems to have been demolished and rebuilt in Soviet times. Its modern name is Soviet coinage too, after the Kazak bard Zhambyl Zhabaev, who was born here. In Soviet times it was spelt Dzhambul.

Two of Zhambyl's three giant fertiliser complexes, which used to turn the town's air foul and dark when the wind was blowing the wrong direction, have switched to other products – partly, it's said, because of economic problems and partly because of environmental pressure. But it's still a far from unpolluted town.

Orientation

The meeting of east-west Töle Bi köshesi with north-south Abay köshesi is the centre of town. West from here a government and ceremonial square, still called ploshchad Lenina by everyone, stretches along Töle Bi. East of Abay is Park Lenina.

Maps The Soviet-era *Dzhambul Turistsky Plan* map is reasonable apart from the out-of-date street names. It shows public transport routes but some of these are out of date too.

PLACES TO STAY

2 Hotel Taraz
7 Hotel Zhambyl & Restoran Vesna

PLACES TO EAT

1   Pitstseria
10 Kafesi
13 Kafe Vostochnaya Kukhnya
14 Tyulman Restaurant

OTHER

3   Gorbolnitsa Bus Stops
4   Russian Orthodox Church
5   Post Office
6   TsUM Department Store
8   Museum
9   Long-Distance Telephone Office
11 Drama Theatre
12 Air Ticket Office
15 Art Exhibition Gallery
16 Qarakhan Mausoleum
17 Dauilbek Mausoleum
18 Mosque
19 Local Bus Station

Zhambyl
Жамбыл

0   300   600 m

New & Old Street Names in Zhambyl

Street signs may be in either Kazak or Russian, and people still think of many streets by their now-discarded Soviet names. Some less obvious name changes are as follows:

New Name	Old Name
Ayteke Bi köshesi	ulitsa 30 let Pobedy
Baluan Shcholaq köshesi	ulitsa Druzhby Narodov
Bayzak Batyr köshesi	ulitsa Voroshilova
Buryl köshesi	ulitsa Kirova
K Zhalairi köshesi	ulitsa Lunacharskogo
Kapal köshesi	ulitsa Karla Marxa
Kazybek Bi köshesi	Sovietskaya ulitsa
Kolbasshy Koykeldi köshesi	ulitsa 50 let Oktyabrya
Kösheney köshesi	ulitsa Furmanova
Sukhe-Bator köshesi	ulitsa Kolkhoznaya
Töle Bi köshesi	Kommunisticheskaya ulitsa
Zhambyl prospekti or Zhambyl dangghyly	ulitsa Trudovaya/prospekt Dzhambula
Zheltoqsan köshesi (north of Töle Bi köshesi)	ulitsa Gorkogo
Zheltoqsan köshesi (south of Töle Bi köshesi)	Parkovaya ulitsa

Information

Money There's an exchange office in the TsUM department store on Töle Bi, and several street exchange kiosks.

Post & Communications The main post office is on Töle Bi just west of Zhambyl prospekti. The long-distance telephone office is at the corner of Töle Bi and Abay. The Zhambyl telephone code is 32622 for five digit numbers, 3262 for six digit numbers.

Travel Agencies The office of the state tourism company Yassaui (or Kazakstan Intourist as it was still calling itself when we were there, ☎ 3-15-59, 3-18-19) in the Hotel Taraz can organise excursions, book flights etc.

Alexandr Zagribelny, a friendly journalist, a leading light in the Zhambyl Green Movement, and an excellent English-speaker, can set up some more unusual trips (see Around Zhambyl). He can also provide a map with all the new Zhambyl street names (in Russian). He lives at K Zhalairi 42/2, postal code 484006 (☎ 5-26-09, or leave a message in Russian with his mother at ☎ 5-24-83).

Qarakhan & Dauitbek Mausolea

Two small mausolea in a wooded park near the town centre, both reconstructed in this century, apparently don't much resemble the originals, but they are worth a look.

The Qarakhan mausoleum (Qarakhan mazarynyng, Mavzoley Qarakhana) marks the grave of an 11th century Qarakhan potentate. It does recycle a few old bricks. It was a museum with some finds from excavations of old Taraz, but there's talk of it becoming a mosque.

Nearby, the Dauitbek mausoleum (Dauitbek mavzoleyi, Mavzoley Davudbeka) was built for a 13th century Mongol viceroy. It's said to have been built lopsided in revenge for the man's infamous cruelty. It appears to be a place of worship now, with a sheet-covered tomb and carpets inside.

Museum & Gallery

Zhambyl's history and art museums closed several years ago, to be combined in a renovated building on ploshchad Lenina. The building looks ready, but hadn't yet opened its doors when we were there. It will apparently contain remains of an 11th century bathhouse and aqueduct unearthed near the present bazar. The museum runs an art gallery (Oblystyq Murazhaydyng Körme Zaly, Vystavochny Zal Oblastnogo Muzeya) just off Abay.

Other Sights

The central Park Lenina is disfigured by a stadium in one corner and some shabby buildings and disused funfair rides. Park Ryskulbekova, a block west along Töle Bi, is prettier. There's a small, almost disguised, mosque near the central bazar, and a new Russian Orthodox church on Töle Bi just west of Zhambyl prospekti.

Places to Stay

Alexandr Zagribelny (see the Information section) offers *apartment* rentals for around US$10 a person.

The *Hotel Zhambyl* (☎ 4-25-52), in the centre at Töle Bi 42 opposite Aytiev, has ordinary but adequate doubles with bathroom and TV for US$36.

The *Hotel Taraz* (☎ 3-34-91) at Zhambyl prospekti 75 near the corner of Sukhe-Bator is a bit newer but a half-hour walk from the centre. Singles/doubles are US$40/50 and up. Bus No 29, trolleybus Nos 9 and 10 and marshrutnoe taxi No 2 all run along Zhambyl köshesi from where it's a one to 1.5 km walk, or a ride on bus No 2 or 16 or any trolleybus, to/from the centre.

Work on a new hotel on Töle Bi opposite Park Lenina seems to have stalled.

Places to Eat

The *Restoran Vesna* in the Hotel Zhambyl is a good bet. It's clean and economical, with good service, and popular but quiet. The menu is a mixture of Kazak and Russian, with a modest meal about US$1.50. The *Hotel Taraz* has a restaurant too.

There's a moderate take-away *Pitstseria* (Pizzeria) on Zhambyl prospekti at the corner of Satpaev, 1.5 km north-east of the Hotel Taraz. Hours are erratic – opening (if at all) any time from 11 am to 2 pm, and closing any time between 8 pm and midnight. A one-person pizza with pickles or

sausage is around US$1. Transport is the same as for the Hotel Taraz.

In Park Lenina is a *kafesi* (café), and you might also try the *Kafe Vostochnaya Kukhnya* at Kazybek Bi 107 or the *Tyulman* restaurant next door.

There are shashlyk and nan stalls, and lots of fruit and vegetables, at the sprawling *ortalyq bazar* (central bazar) on Töle Bi one km east of Park Lenina. Bus Nos 2 and 16 and trolleybus Nos 3, 4 and 5 run along Töle Bi from the park.

Things to Buy

Amid all the food and cheap clothes in the central bazar, you may find the occasional Uzbek selling woven rugs.

Getting There & Away

Watch out for thefts on trains and buses between here and Almaty, Bishkek and Shymkent.

Air Flights go to/from Almaty (US$89) daily. Others are scheduled (but don't always go) to/from Pavlodar and Moscow three times weekly; Novosibirsk twice weekly; and Balqash, Semey, Omsk and Yekaterinburg once a week. The ticket office is on Töle Bi just east of Abay, and is open daily from 9 am to 1 pm and 2 to 7 pm.

Some flights by the German charter airline Luftbrücke to/from Düsseldorf call at Zhambyl.

Bus From the bus station on Zhambyl prospekti, about four km north-east of the centre, buses go to Almaty 12 times daily (516 km, 10 hours, US$12), Bishkek 11 times daily (277 km, US$7), Shymkent seven times daily (170 km, four hours, US$8) and Tashkent eight times daily (295 km, US$14). All Tashkent buses stop at Shymkent too. Buses to Almaty and minibuses to Bishkek also wait outside the train station.

Train The train station is on Baluan Shcholak about four km south of the centre. Trains stop here several times a day to/from the following destinations: Almaty (14 hours), Shymkent (five hours), Bishkek, Tashkent (10 hours), Aqtöbe and Moscow; Semey, Qaraghandy and Aqmola on most days; and Novosibirsk, Krasnoyarsk, Yekaterinburg and Irkutsk several times a week.

Car You can pick up cars to Almaty, Bishkek or Shymkent from the the long-distance bus station on Zhambyl prospekti.

Getting Around

The airport is west of the town off the Shymkent road. A taxi to/from the centre costs US$3 to US$4 and takes about 15 minutes. Bus No 9 to/from the centre is rare.

Direct transport between the bus station and the town centre appears to be non-existent. Least inconvenient seems to be bus No 29 or marshrutnoe taxi No 2, along Zhambyl prospekti to the Gorbolnitsa stop just before Töle Bi, then bus Nos 2 or 16 or any trolleybus, or a walk, east on Töle Bi to the centre.

Trolleybus Nos 4 and 6 from the train station run into the centre along Abay. Heading to the station, catch them on Abay south of Kazybek Bi.

Buses, trolleybuses and even marshrutnoe taxis are often very crowded, with long waits between them. You may find taxis easier for longer trips.

AROUND ZHAMBYL

Alexandr Zagribelny (see Information in the Zhambyl section) can make the Zhambyl area more interesting than most. He can arrange visits to archaeological sites – such as Akyrtas (Stone Troughs), the remains of an ancient palace about 50 km east which was already in ruins when Chinese travellers came across it in the 12th century – or participation in digs, and trips to the Talassky Alatau range spanning the Kazak-Kyrgyz border. Zhambyl is also an access point for rafting on the Chatkal river in Kyrgyzstan, south of the Talassky Alatau.

The Shu river valley, about 200 km east of Zhambyl on the Kyrgyzstan border, must be one of the world's biggest marijuana plantations. The weed, which grows wild in many parts of Central Asia, is said to cover 2500 sq km here. But it would not be smart to wander carelessly in the valley, where many 'entrepreneurs' are armed and touchy.

Aysha-Bibi & Babazhi Katun Mausolea

Near Aysha-Bibi village (formerly Golovachovka), 20 km west of Zhambyl, are the tombs of two Qarakhan women, though little else is known about them. The 12th century mausoleum of Aysha-Bibi – one wall of it – is probably the only authentically old building around Zhambyl. Made of splendid, delicate terracotta bricks in over 50 different motifs, it looks almost weightless. A Muslim shrine for centuries, it was damaged by the removal of bricks in Soviet times but later restored. It now stands in a glass box meant to ward off the corrosive air.

Beside it is a recent reconstruction of the 11th century tomb of one Babazhi Katun, with an interesting pointed, fluted roof.

Getting There & Away Aysha-Bibi village is on the Shymkent road from Zhambyl. A sign points to the mausolea, about one km south, from the main road in the village. Shymkent or Tashkent buses will take you to Aysha-Bibi; there may also be buses from the local station at the back of Zhambyl's central bazar.

AQSU-ZHABAGHLY NATURE RESERVE
АҚСУ-ЖАБАҒЛЫ ҚОРЫҒЫ

This beautiful 750 sq km patch of foothills and mountains in the Talassky Alatau range of the Western Tian Shan is the easiest visited of Kazakstan's nature reserves. Guided hikes or horseback trips, and nights at huts in the reserve, can be arranged at the reserve office in the village of Zhabaghly, 100 km west of Zhambyl and 75 km east of Shymkent.

The reserve (Kazak: Aqsu-Zhabaghly Qoryghy; Russian: Aksu-Zhabagly Zapovednik) stretches towards the Kazak-Kyrgyz border, rising from about 1000 metres to 4000 metres. You stand a chance of seeing bear, ibex and rare birds of prey. You're rather less likely to see a snow leopard, though this is an important habitat for it. The plant life is diverse and scenery ranges from mountain meadows and juniper and pine forests, to glaciers. It might even be possible to arrange a trip up to the Talassky Alatau's highest peak, 4480 metre Mt Manas, just across the border in Kyrgyzstan.

May to September or October are the best months to visit. In Zhabaghly village the reserve office, with a small museum, is on the main street, Lenin köshesi. Horseback trips cost about US$10 a day. To contact the reserve in advance, send a telegram (preferably in Russian and including your phone number) to the director, Amanbek Akaevich, at Kazakstan 487964, Selo Zhabagly, Shymkentskaya Oblast, Tyulkubas Rayon, Zapovednik Aksu-Zhabagly.

Places to Stay
In Zhabaghly village there's a small *hotel* next to the reserve office, but better is B&B at the house of *Zhenia & Lyuda*, just up Lenin köshesi from the post office in the direction of the reserve office. This friendly couple will take you along to the office to arrange your trip into the reserve.

Getting There & Away
To reach Zhabaghly village you must first get to Tulkibas, about 60 km before Shymkent on the railway from Zhambyl and 15 km from Zhabaghly. Most trains between Shymkent and Zhambyl stop at Tulkibas. From Tulkibas bus station, about 500 metres from the train station, there are buses to Zhabaghly for US$0.40 (a taxi is about US$8). Alternatively get a bus to Vannovka on the Shymkent-Zhambyl road, 70 km from Shymkent, then another bus from there to Tulkibas (30 minutes) or Zhabaghly. There were no direct buses from Shymkent to Tulkibas at the time of research.

In Zhabaghly the nature reserve office is at the stop after the post office.

SHYMKENT
ШЫМКЕНТ
Population: 400,000
Shymkent (Russian: Chimkent) is Zhambyl's twin in many ways: it's polluted

(this time by industries based on locally mined lead), has a high Kazak population, and is of interest mainly as a jumping-off point for other places (Turkistan, Otyrar, and the Aqsu-Zhabaghly nature reserve). Shymkent's past, too, reads like Zhambyl's: the Mongols razed a minor Silk Road stop here; the Kokand khanate built a frontier fort in the 19th century, Russia took it in 1864, and the whole place was rebuilt in Soviet times.

Orientation
The main central streets are north-south Kazybek Bi köshesi (formerly ulitsa Sovietskaya) and east-west Turkistan köshesi and Tauke Khan dangghyly (or Tauke Khan köshesi, formerly prospekt Lenina). The bus and train stations are both a short ride by bus south of the centre. The airport is at Kirov, about 12 km north of Shymkent off the Turkistan road.

Street names may appear in Kazak, Russian or both. Old Soviet names are still used by some people but linger on only a few signs.

Information
There are exchange desks in the post office and the Znanie bookshop (both on Kazybek Bi), the Shymkent Sauda Uyi (TsUM) department store on Tauke Khan dangghyly, and the Hotel Shymkent, as well as kiosks in the bazar and elsewhere. Most exchange points are open from 9 am to 6 pm.

The main post office is at Kazybek Bi 24, on the corner of Turkistan. There are long-distance telephone offices at the corner of Turkistan and Kazybek Bi (always open) and on Tauke Khan dangghyly opposite Karl Marx.

The Shymkent telephone code is 3252 for six-digit numbers, 32522 for five-digit numbers.

Znanie bookshop near the south end of Kazybek Bi sells a little book called *Turkistan* with text in English, Russian and Kazak for US$0.25, worth picking up if you're going to Turkistan.

The state tourism firm Yassaui (still

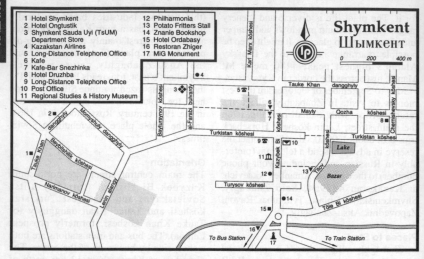

1 Hotel Shymkent
2 Hotel Ongtustik
3 Shymkent Sauda Uyi (TsUM) Department Store
4 Kazakstan Airlines
5 Long-Distance Telephone Office
6 Kafe
7 Kafe-Bar Snezhinka
8 Hotel Druzhba
9 Long-Distance Telephone Office
10 Post Office
11 Regional Studies & History Museum

12 Philharmonia
13 Potato Fritters Stall
14 Znanie Bookshop
15 Hotel Ordabasy
16 Restoran Zhiger
17 MiG Monument

Shymkent
Шымкент

0   200   400 m

To Bus Station   To Train Station

calling itself Kazakstan Intourist here) has a small, underemployed but willing office (☎ 12-45-98, 18-52-52) in the Hotel Shymkent. For around US$20 an hour they'll do guided car trips to Turkistan, Otyrar, Sayram and other old sites in the region, or wine tasting at the grape and apple-growing Michurin state farm east of Shymkent. A typical trip to Turkistan and Otyrar takes about 10 hours.

Regional Studies & History Museum

This museum (Oblystyq Tarikhi-Ölketanu Murazhayy, Oblastnoy Istoriko-Kraevedchesky Muzey) on Kazybek Bi is worth a visit.

There's material on old Otyrar, a yurt, some fine old carpets, jewellery and costumes, and a nature section with a comically grinning stuffed wolf and some info on Aqsu-Zhabaghly nature reserve. In the 20th century section upstairs you can learn all about Shymkent's twin town, Stevenage, in England, and wonder what Kazaks would do with a cricket bat if they were allowed to play with it. The museum is open daily except Monday.

Memorial

The **MiG fighter plane** on the hill facing the Hotel Ordabasy is a monument to WWII pilots who trained at Shymkent.

Places to Stay

The hotel situation is bleak. In summer, try to make sure your room has mosquito netting on the windows.

The *Hotel Ordabasy* (☎ 3-98-42, 3-98-12) at Kazybek Bi 1 is conveniently located but pestered by noise and fumes from buses at the big intersection out the front. It's a standard, fairly shabby Soviet hotel with foreigners' prices of US$26 for singles and a ridiculous US$80 for doubles, both including private bathroom but limited hot water. But some travellers have managed to get rooms for local prices, which are about one-fifth of the above. The hotel used to be called the Voskhod.

The *Hotel Druzhba* (Qonaq Uyi Dostyq in Kazak, ☎ 44-48-01) on Chernishevsky near Mayly Qozha (formerly ulitsa Kregera) is on a more peaceful, leafy back street. It has plain but clean rooms with bathroom for US$21/42 (or US$26/55 upstairs with TV).

The biggest hotel, the *Hotel Shymkent*

Uzbekistan
   Top: Registan Square, Samarkand
Bottom: Detail of dome over Guri Amir, mausoleum of Timur, Samarkand

Uzbekistan

Top Left: Nadir Divanbegi khanaka, Sufi meditation hall and hostel, Bukhara

Top Right: Master instrument maker, Kharatjidin Mukhidinov, at crafts fair, Tashkent

Bottom: Rehearsal in front of Sher Dor medressa by young men playing traditional Uzbek drums, Registan Square, Samarkand

(☎ 3-19-93, 3-98-42), on Tauke Khan dangghyly two km west of the centre, has tatty rooms with bathroom but no hot water for US$35/47. Take bus No 16 from the bus station, or bus Nos 16 or 29 or trolleybus No 1 from Znanie bookshop on Kazybek Bi in the centre, to the Gostinitsa Yuzhnaya stop, a block from the hotel. To the centre, take bus Nos 16 or 29 or trolleybus No 4 from the stop on Tauke Khan dangghyly at the corner of Beybitshilik.

Hotel Ongtustik (Gostinitsa Yuzhnaya in Russian, ☎ 12-80-46) on Tauke Khan dangghyly a block east of the Hotel Shymkent is grotty and decaying but one of the few economical options near the centre. Standard triples with toilet and washbasin cost US$6.75 per bed; lyux doubles with private bath are US$15.

Places to Eat

The *Restoran Zhiger*, across the stream from Hotel Ordabasy, does good Kazak and Russian food at reasonable prices, and the service isn't bad; plov is US$0.40. It's open daily from 10 am to 11 pm.

At the entrance to the park on Kazybek Bi, a collection of outdoor tables with the name *Kafe* is Shymkent's 'hamburger' hangout. What you actually get is a 'gamburger' – a long bread roll with bits of meat and veg inside, not bad for US$0.45 – and coffee. *Kafe-Bar Snezhinka* across the way does plov and soup.

The restaurant in the *Hotel Ordabasy* has a noisy band and drunken prostitutes in the evening: a couple of little salads, beef stroganov and mineral water come to about US$2. The *Hotel Druzhba* has a more pleasant restaurant. The *Hotel Shymkent* has restaurants at either end of the building, neither very special though the laghman is OK, plus a *kokteyl-bar* (cocktail bar) which may have snacks, but probably won't have cocktails.

There's a *stall* selling good potato fritters (pirozhki s kartoshkami) for US$0.05 across Titov from the bazar entrance. There are numerous *shashlyk stands* around town, and plenty of fruit and vegetables in the *bazar*.

Things to Buy

The bazar on Titov is big and bustling and open every day. You could pick up a skullcap here, or a rather less portable wooden chest with colourful stamped tin decoration. The main department store, Shymkent Sauda Uyi – commonly known by its Russian name, TsUM – is on Tauke Khan dangghyly.

Getting There & Away

Between Shymkent and Tashkent, bus is much quicker than train as the latter goes round by Arys, the junction of the Tashkent-Moscow and Almaty-Moscow lines 70 km west of Shymkent.

There have been highway hold-ups on the Shymkent-Tashkent road, and north of the airport turn-off on the Turkistan road. Locals say it's safer to go by bus than by car, and safer in a local car than an expensive foreign one. But you also need to watch for thefts on trains and buses into or out of Shymkent.

Border controls on the crossing to/from Tashkent are erratic.

Air Tickets are sold at the Kazakstan Airlines office on the corner of Tauke Khan dangghyly and al-Farabi bulvardy, open daily from 8 am to noon and 1 to 7 pm, and at a table in the lobby of the Hotel Shymkent. Scheduled flights include Almaty five times daily (US$92); Aqtau, Atyrau, Pavlodar, Qaraghandy and Semey a few times a week; Novosibirsk five days a week; Moscow four times a week (US$180); and Baku (US$155) three times a week.

Bus The bus station is about one km south of the Hotel Ordabasy. Many buses from here are in transit, with tickets not usually sold till the bus has arrived; to reduce anxiety try to pick a bus that starts here. Buses for Tashkent may also wait outside the train station when trains arrive from Almaty or Bishkek.

Scheduled departures from the bus station include Almaty (13 hours, US$16) and Bishkek (11 hours, US$12), each with around 10 departures daily, most in transit; Tashkent (three hours, US$3.50) with 30 daily buses starting here; Turkistan (3½ hours, US$3) with nine daily buses; and Zhambyl (four hours, US$8) with about 11 buses daily, some starting here.

Train Foreigners' fares may not be enforced here which makes the train cheaper than the bus. The train station is at the end of Qabanbay Batyr dangghyly in the south-east of town. Trains go several times a day to/from Turkistan, Aqtöbe, Zhambyl (about five hours), Almaty (18 hours), Bishkek, Tashkent (six hours) and Moscow (60 hours); Semey, Qaraghandy and Aqmola most days; and Novosibirsk, Krasnoyarsk, Yekaterinburg and Irkutsk several times a week.

Car The bus station and the Hotel Ordabasy are the best places to look for cars to Tashkent or Zhambyl.

Getting Around

From the airport, bus No 12 goes occasionally to/from the Kazakstan Airlines ticket office. Going to the airport, catch it as it heads north on al-Farabi bulvardy outside the office. A taxi is about US$5.

Bus No 2 from in front of the Hotel Ordabasy goes to the train station, then the bus station, then back to the Ordabasy. From the same stop, trolleybus No 6 goes to the train station and back, and bus Nos 9 and 16 and marshrutnoe taxi No 14 go to the bus station and back (bus No 16 also serves the Shymkent and Ongtustik hotels). Bus Nos 2

and 6 run from the train station to the bus station.

AROUND SHYMKENT

Sayram

Сайрам

About 12 km east of Shymkent, this was the birthplace of Qozha Akhmed Yasaui (see the Turkistan section). Three small mausoleums and a mosque, all from the 14th century, still stand.

Otyrar

Отырар

About 150 km north-west of Shymkent lie the scanty ruins of Otyrar (also called Farab, Otrar or Utrar), the town that brought Jenghiz Khan to Central Asia. Much of the rest of Asia and Europe, too, might have been spared the Mongols if Otyrar's 13th century governor had not had the Great Khan's merchants murdered here. There's little left but hillocks which were once town walls, and a few bits uncovered by archaeologists. Such desolation, where a busy town once stood, may have its appeal.

Close to the ruins is the intact 11th century Arslan-Bab mausoleum, tomb of an early mentor of Qozha Akhmed Yasaui (see the Turkistan section), and five km away is the village of Shauildir (Russian: Shaulder) is the al-Farabi museum which includes some finds from Otyrar.

The road to Shauildir and Otyrar is from Törtköl, 95 km north of Shymkent on the Turkistan road. Shauildir is 50 km west of Törtköl. The travel agency Yassaui can take you there (see Information in the Shymkent section).

Somewhere east or south-east of Otyrar is Ordabasy, where in 1726 Töle Bi, Kazybek Bi and Ayteke Bi – elders from the three Kazak hordes – met to coordinate defence against the marauding Oyrats. Three mounds and a large *kazan*, or cauldron, for holy water mark the spot. In 1993 President Nazarbaev held a commemorative meeting at this highly symbolic site with presidents Karimov of Uzbekistan and Akaev of Kyrgyzstan. Restoration work is being done by the Shymkent

Desert Flower

Dust to Dust

Otyrar existed from about the 5th century AD, and was home to the celebrated philosopher and mathematician al-Farabi in the 9th century, and reached its peak in the 10th to 13th centuries, when it and Turkistan were the major cities of this part of Kazakstan, thriving on settled agriculture and Silk Road trade.

By the 13th century Otyrar was a northern outpost of the Khorezmshah Empire. Here in 1218 a caravan of about 450 Muslim merchants arrived from Jenghiz Khan to put into practise a recently concluded trade agreement with Khorezmshah Muhammad II. But the governor of Otyrar, Inalchuq, suspected they were spies and had them all killed. Jenghiz Khan sent ambassadors to the Khorezmshah to demand reparations for this but one of these, too, was killed. Thus the biggest Mongol army to date, perhaps 150,000 or more, was assembled to squash the Khorezmshah.

In 1219, while the Great Khan himself was taking care of Samarkand and Bukhara, about 50,000 of his forces, under his sons Chaghatai and Ogedei, laid siege to Otyrar. It took them six months to break through into the citadel where Otyrar's 80,000-strong garrison and most of its civilians had taken refuge. They slaughtered virtually everyone except Inalchuq and his wife, whom Jenghiz Khan wanted taken alive. The couple retreated to the roof of the armoury, so the Mongols demolished the building to capture them. They then took him to Samarkand and killed him by pouring molten silver into his eyes and ears, before demolishing Otyrar.

Otyrar revived as a trading centre in the subsequent Mongol peace, picked itself up again after another demolition job by Timur in the late 14th century, but was finally laid to rest by the Oyrats (Zhungarians) from Mongolia in the 17th and 18th centuries. ■

company Melioservis (☎ (3252) 45-29-61, fax 45-17-46), which may be able to take you there.

TURKISTAN
ТҮРКІСТАН
Population: 70,000

At Turkistan, 165 km north-west of Shymkent past cotton fields and salt marsh at the edge of the Kyzylkum desert, stands Kazakstan's greatest building and its most important site of Muslim pilgrimage. The mausoleum of the first great Turkic Muslim holy man, Qozha Akhmed Yasaui, was built on a grand scale by Timur in the late 14th century. Unfortunately, ongoing restoration work diminishes its splendour. You can still visit, but cranes dwarf its mighty proportions, and when we visited, parts of the interior were awash in rubble. It's advisable not to visit on a Tuesday which, as long as the mausoleum remains at least in part a museum, is the weekly closing day.

Founded perhaps as early as the 5th century AD, and known as Yasy or Shavgar till the 16th, the town was by the 12th century an important trade and religious centre, on a boundary between settled and agricultural societies. It once had 14 mosques. Later it became a northerly outpost of the Kokand khanate, falling to the Russian push of 1864.

It's an almost entirely Kazak town (some of whose people understand little or no Russian), with a thriving bazar.

Orientation & Information

If you come by bus from Shymkent, the mausoleum will loom into view on your left as you enter the town along Tauke Khan dangghyly (formerly prospekt Lenina). Tauke Khan dangghyly continues one km or so past the mausoleum, to a fork where the Qyzylorda road goes straight on and the street to the left leads to the bus station (after about half a km) and the bazar.

The Znanie bookshop in Shymkent sells a useful little book on Turkistan with text in English, Russian and Kazak, for US$0.25.

Qozha Akhmed Yasaui Mausoleum

Qozha Akhmed Yasaui, the revered 12th century Sufi teacher and Turkic mystical poet, was born at Sayram east of Shymkent. He underwent ascetic Sufi training in

Bukhara, but lived much of the rest of his life in Turkistan, dying here about 1166. One legend tells that at the age of 63 he retired to an underground cell for the rest of his life, in mourning for the Prophet Muhammad who had died at the same age. He founded the Yasauia Sufi sect.

Yasaui's original small tomb was already a long-time place of pilgrimage before Timur ordered a far grander mausoleum built here in the 1390s. The building has the biggest intact dome in Central Asia and is all that's left of the old town.

Timur died before it was complete and the front face was left unfinished, flanked by two round towers but still studded with scaffolding, like whiskers. The loveliest parts are the exquisite tiling – mainly blue and turquoise – on the outer rear walls and on the small fluted rear dome which rises over the burial chamber.

The interior was mainly a mess of reconstruction work when we visited (the place was being de-museumised but some visitors were still charged a small fee to enter) but you can still see in the main chamber a vast bronze kazan for holy water, donated by Timur. To either side are 35 smaller rooms on two floors. Yasaui's tomb is in the room behind the main chamber – you can see it through an opening.

To its right of Yasui's tomb is the tomb of Abylqayyr, a 15th century leader of the then-nomadic Uzbeks, who was killed in the 1468 feud which split the Uzbeks and effectively gave birth to the Kazak people. Earlier, Abylqayyr had rescued Samarkand's Timurid sultan Abu Sayid from a usurper, and been rewarded with a noble Timurid wife, Rabigha-Sultan Begim, a replica of whose own tomb stands outside the main mausoleum (the original was torn down for tsarist building material in 1898). Nearby is a bathhouse, in use from the 15th or 16th century until it was made a museum in 1975.

In 1995 the Turkish government, which has already financed much of the restoration work here, pledged a further $35 million, so work can be expected to go on for a few years yet.

Places to Stay

The main hotel, the *Hotel Turkistan* on Tauke Khan dangghyly near the mausoleum, was closed when we visited, for a 'renovation' that had been going on – or rather not going on – for several years. That's no great loss as the six room *Hotel Saule* nearby is much more personal, and cheap. The Saule is round the back of the Nauryz restaurant, diagonally across the park opposite the Hotel Turkistan. Clean little single/doubles with shared bathroom cost US$5.50. There's no hot water.

At the other end of town opposite the bus station, the *Hotel Karavansaray* has about 12 rooms for US$4, singles or doubles. Bathrooms are shared. It's identified only by a small 'Gostinitsa' sign.

Places to Eat

The *Nauryz* restaurant across the park opposite the Hotel Turkistan has greasy laghman (US$1 with tea and bread), and maybe one or two other things if you're lucky. A short distance along the street to the south, a *stolovaya* on the west side offers no worse fare and stays open longer in the evenings.

The *bazar* heaves with produce and does justice to Turkistan's historic role as a market centre. It has *shashlyk stands* too. To find it walk a short distance west past the bus station and turn left. There's a *bufet* in the bus station.

Getting There & Away

Buses come from Shymkent (3½ hours, US$3) seven times daily, and from Tashkent (six hours, US$5) once a day. There were no buses from Qyzylorda when we visited.

The train station, out on the western edge of town, has at least four daily trains to/from Qyzylorda, Töretam (Leninsk), Aralsk, Aqtöbe and Moscow. There are at least three daily trains to Shymkent, Zhambyl and Almaty, one to Bishkek, and two or three to Tashkent. If you have trouble getting tickets, ask for the *dispetcher* or *nachalnik* (manager), whom we found very helpful.

Getting Around

Public transport is infrequent and often jam-packed. Flagging down a car or taxi may be easier for getting to/from the bus station, bazar or train station. Bus Nos 2 and 5 and marshrutnoe taxi No 5 run between the Hotel Turkistan, the bus station and the train station.

QYZYLORDA
КЫЗЫЛОРДА

This town of 155,000 people, 280 km north-west of Turkistan on the Syr-Darya and the road and railway to Aqtöbe, was the capital of Soviet Kazakstan from 1925 to 1928 but was abandoned in favour of Almaty because it was too hot. Like Zhambyl, Shymkent and Turkistan, it was (under the name Aq-Meshit) part of the Kokand khanate's 19th century northern frontier defences, and the first of these to fall to Russia, in 1853. Today it's the capital of the Qyzylorda Oblys which has an 82% Kazak population, the highest of any in the country.

BAYKONUR COSMODROME & LENINSK
БАЙКОНУР КОСМОДРОМ & ЛЕНИНСК

The Baykonur Cosmodrome, amid semi-desert about 250 km north-west of Qyzylorda, has been the launch site for all Soviet and Russian crewed space flights since Yury Gagarin, the first human in space, was lobbed up in 1961. In fact this isn't really Baykonur, which is actually a town 300 km to the north-east, but the USSR told the International Aeronautical Federation that Gagarin's launch-point was Baykonur, and that name has stuck.

The nearest town is the Russian military town of Leninsk, on the Syr-Darya, south of the cosmodrome which it was built to guard and service. The train station just north of Leninsk is called Töretam (Russian: Tyuratam). A space tracking station is visible two or three km north of the station; the launch site is about 30 km farther north.

After the collapse of the USSR, Baykonur and Leninsk became useful cards in Kazakstan's dealings with Russia, which

inherited the Soviet space programme. While Russia insisted that the cosmodrome and its associated military forces were its own, Kazakstan wanted them under joint control. The military construction units, meanwhile, were under Kazakstani control, and their numbers were reportedly run down from around 30,000 to 5000. All this and a shortage of funds led to a number of space projects being suspended, falling living standards at Baykonur and Leninsk, and riots by Kazak soldiers here in 1992 and 1993. Many of the Russians and Ukrainians left. Finally in 1994 Kazakstan agreed to lease Baykonur and Leninsk to Russia for 20 years for about US$120 million a year. A few months later the Kazak Talgat Musabaev and the Russian Yury Malenchenko took off on a symbolic joint visit to the Mir space station.

Baykonur may or may not be open to visitors. It depends who you talk to. One group of travellers we met said they had bumped into a cosmodrome scientist who invited them in to watch a launch. Less likely to work is just fronting up and trying to talk your way in (see the Mission Aborted aside).

Probably your best chance is to look for a travel agent in Almaty who can organise a helicopter trip to Baykonur. We were told in Almaty that tourist visits were currently off the menu but may be permitted in future. The Nevada-Semey Movement and Tour Asia (see the Travel Agencies section in the Almaty section) are two organisations worth asking. But you'd probably be up for US$500 a person.

Cosmodrome staff told us, unhelpfully, that visitors need a permit from the Russian military general staff in Moscow and said foreigners should contact their own embassies in Moscow to start this process.

Places to Stay & Eat

In Leninsk, official foreign visitors are accommodated in a special comfortable *hotel*, to the left as you go down the main street from the town entrance. For ordinary visitors, the large *Hotel Tsentralnaya* (☎ (33622) 6-22-05) on Leninsk's wide central square has decent singles/doubles

Mission Aborted

The US$500 I was quoted for a helicopter trip to the cosmodrome from Almaty was way beyond my budget, so I thought I'd just see what happened when I arrived.

My train pulled into Töretam in the middle of the night. I hopped into a taxi heading into Leninsk, kept quiet at the checkpoint entering the town, one km or so down the road, and was delivered to the Hotel Tsentralnaya by my rather bemused driver. A bleary-eyed receptionist checked me in without turning a hair, and as dawn illuminated a very typical Soviet town outside, I went to bed.

Within an hour, a knock on the door woke me. A leather-jacketed gent checked my passport and left. I went back to sleep. In another hour came another knock. This time my visitor was in uniform, with an arm badge proclaiming *Voenno-Kosmicheskie Sily Baykonur Kosmodrom* (Military Space Forces, Baykonur Cosmodrome). Briskly and firmly but always politely, this officer questioned me about what I was doing in Leninsk. I hoped to visit the cosmodrome, I said. He smiled. How had I got into Leninsk? In a taxi, I answered, to his evident surprise. Did I have an invitation or any friends at the cosmodrome? I showed him the name and St Petersburg phone number of a scientist I had met a few months earlier, who worked at Baykonur from time to time. Then he wrote out a report stating where I'd come from, and when, who I was and what I was wearing, which I agreed to sign.

By now both of us were seeing the funny side of things and we moved on to 'Mikhail' and 'Dzhon' terms. Might I be able to visit the cosmodrome, I asked, thinking Mikhail might turn out to be a pretty good guide. 'Maybe,' he said, as he left to consult his boss, adding that I was not to go away.

Before I had time to fall sleep again, Mikhail was back, motioning me to pack my bags. 'Kosmodrom?' I asked, brightly. 'Nyet, vokzal.' I had to leave town, on the first train, and he was taking me to the station, now. What he did do was stop his jeep by an enormous rocket on a stand by Leninsk's main street and let me take pictures of it.

Back at the station, no train was heading in my direction for seven hours. Mikhail wanted me to wait in the station. 'But I have to eat', I protested. OK, I could go back into Leninsk later to find food, Mikhail agreed, and left me.

A couple of hours later I set off back to Leninsk. In the daylight Leninsk's protecting ring of walls and guard posts was clear to see, as was the extreme bleakness of the surrounding country. I reached the checkpoint but the young soldiers on duty insisted that no, I couldn't enter the town. They phoned a superior who said the same. I stood my ground and eventually the least junior of them said he would accompany me into Leninsk.

Yegor couldn't have been much more than 20 years old and his military greatcoat looked far too big for him. After a few minutes he led me off the street, round to the back of a block of flats and up its shabby stairs, where he knocked on a door. An equally young man let us in. This was Alex, and Alex's father, I learned, was someone not unimportant in the Russian Space Agency. So Yegor was trying to help me get into the cosmodrome.

But Alex's father was away, so our luck was out. Instead, Alex fed me a big breakfast and of course a shot of vodka as we half-watched an aged California soap on TV and the boys told me how life here was going downhill. Alex was studying aerospace technology but didn't seem to think it held much future for him. Leninsk used to be a green town, they said, but now most of the trees were dead. There was no hot water, and little in the shops. Many of the Russians had gone home.

As we left, Alex stuffed my pockets full of souvenir Baykonur stickers and photos, and apples for the journey. 'Next time, we can help,' he said, giving me his phone number.

Yegor decided he now had time to give me a brief tour of the town, which even at midday remained largely asleep. He pointed out the hotel where official foreign visitors, including western astronauts on joint missions, stay, and took me to the bank of the Syr-Darya on the edge of the town. The river was a sad trickle. Passenger vessels used to serve Leninsk, said Yegor, but no more.

So I returned to the station to wait for my train, leaving Yegor and Alex on their sad little island of Russia in the middle of a not very friendly foreign country. If I ever go back there, I'll have friends – if they haven't gone home.

John Noble

with hot water at US$10/16, helpful staff, and a bar serving food at lunchtime and in the evening. A cheaper option might be *Gostinitsa N 1* (Hotel No 1) in the street behind.

Getting There & Away

To Töretam there are at least four daily trains from Aralsk, Aqtöbe and Moscow, two or three from Tashkent, Shymkent, Zhambyl and Almaty, and one from Bishkek.

ARALSK
АРАЛЬСК

Aralsk is about 220 km north-west of Leninsk on the same road and railway. It also used to be on the Aral Sea, and was an important fishing port. Now, the shrinking sea has withdrawn about 30 km from the town, and Aralsk, its lifeline cut, is in danger of becoming a ghost town. Rusting ships lie in the sand, and idle cranes stand over ditches that drain into what was the shipping channel until efforts to keep it open were abandoned in the 1980s. Dust storms from the dried-up sea bed frequently batter the town; polluted water supplies have brought alarming levels of disease to the dwindling population, now probably under 20,000.

Rooms in the *Hotel Aral*, beside what used to be the town's beach, cost around US$1 a person. Local police take an interest in any outsiders curious enough to call here.

For more on the Aral Sea, see the Environment section in the Facts about the Region chapter.

Western Kazakstan

North and west of the Aral Sea stretches more desert and steppe, significantly populated only towards the Russian border, but of crucial importance to Kazakstan because here lie great reserves of oil and natural gas, now being extracted by foreign companies under deals bringing millions of vital dollars into the country. The most important sites are the Tenghiz oilfield, near the eastern shore of the Caspian Sea, and the Karachaganak gas field, west of Aqtöbe (see the Economy section in the introduction to this chapter for more on these projects).

The rail routes from Central Asia to Moscow and the Volga region cross this wilderness but otherwise, if you're not in the oil or gas business, there's little reason to come – unless you happen to have a niggling ambition to swim in the Caspian Sea, or you just like taking slow trains across empty deserts relieved only by roaming camels, salt lakes and pink rock outcrops – in which case the town of Aqtau would suit your purposes nicely.

AQTÖBE
АҚТӨБЕ

Population: 260,000

Aqtöbe (Russian: Aktyubinsk) is the last town in Kazakstan on the main rail line to Moscow, about 100 km from the Russian border in north-west Kazakstan. It's a glum, grey place whose best hope may lie in spin-offs from the huge Karachaganak gas field to its west. You might need to change trains here.

If you have time to waste or food to get, there's a market, backed by some very satanic-looking factories, about 1.5 km east of the train station: walk to the right from the station along Kökkhar köshesi and the market's at the top of the hill. For the local museum, open daily except Tuesday, take the first street left (Frunze) off Kökkhar köshesi, then the first right (Altynsarin) and walk 1½ blocks.

The Aqtöbe telephone code is 3132.

KAZAKSTAN

Places to Stay & Eat

If you have to stay over, the economical answer is the *komnaty otdykha* at the train station. These are big, quite comfortable bedrooms costing just US$3.50/5.50 for single/double occupancy for up to 24 hours. The shared toilets and showers are tolerable. Go through the door marked Медпункт (Medpunkt) by the exit to the platform in the station's main hall, and up to the 3rd floor.

The *Hotel Ilek* (☎ 22-06-64) at Lenin köshesi 44 has ordinary singles/doubles for US$20/40, plus a restaurant open for lunch and dinner, and a bufet on the 3rd floor open from 8 am to 8 pm. From the train station, walk to the right along Kökkhar köshesi: Lenin köshesi is the second street on the left and the hotel is just before the first intersection. The less central *Hotel Aktyubinsk* (☎ 55-41-94) at former Leninsky prospekt 44 may be better.

Getting There & Away

Air There's an air ticket office, marked Кассы Аэрофлота (Kassy Aeroflota) and open daily except Sunday, in the train station. Flights are scheduled to Almaty twice daily, Moscow and Kazan (Russia) five days a week, Atyrau, Aqtau, Kökshetau, Semey, Pavlodar, St Petersburg and Mineralnye Vody (Russia) all one to three days a week. Luftbrücke, at the airport, has charter flights to/from Düsseldorf every week or so (see the Getting There & Away chapter).

Train Trains run to Orenburg, Samara, Oral, Saratov, Moscow (32 to 37 hours), Shymkent, Zhambyl, Töretam (Leninsk), Turkistan, Tashkent (27 to 31 hours) and Almaty (42 hours) several times a day, and to Bishkek (40 hours) once a day. There's also a daily train to Atyrau (14 hours) and Astrakhan (Russia), pulling carriages to Mangghyshlak near Aqtau.

Getting Around

A taxi to/from the airport, south-east of the centre, is US$2. Bus No 8 also links the two.

ATYRAU
АТЫРАУ

Population: 150,000

Atyrau, on the Ural river 15 km upstream from its mouth on the northern shore of the Caspian Sea, is Oil City Kazakstan. Two hundred km to the south-east, on the Caspian's eastern shores, lie the rich, high-quality wells of the Tenghiz oilfield, being exploited by the USA's third biggest oil company, Chevron, in a multi-billion dollar joint venture, called Tengizchevroil, with the Kazakstan government. There are many other oil and gas fields in the Atyrau region, and offshore reserves in the Caspian may hold the greatest potential yet.

Unless the logistical problems of getting the oil out of Kazakstan prove insuperable, Atyrau is likely to see a steady stream of western oil people – and correspondingly inflated hotel prices – until well into the 21st century. The town needs to do something, however, to avoid being submerged by the rising Caspian Sea. Spring floods in recent years have brought the shoreline close to the town and it's feared that much of Atyrau will be under water by the early 21st century if steps are not taken to protect it.

Atyrau was founded in the 17th century by a Russian trader named Gurev, whose name it bore until the 1990s. Caviar was its chief source of wealth until oil was found in Soviet times. Some 80% of the town's population is Kazak, one of the highest levels in the country. Atyrau is 2000 km west of Almaty; the nearest sizeable town is Astrakhan in Russia, 350 km to the west.

Orientation

The Ural river meanders through the town, flowing roughly north-south beneath the central bridge on ulitsa Abaya (street signs are still mostly in Russian here). A short distance west of the bridge, ulitsa Abaya becomes ulitsa Satpaeva. The train station is on the eastern edge of town, about three km from the centre, the bus station is about 1.5 km west of the river on ulitsa Avangard (turn right off ulitsa Satpaeva), and the airport is out to the west.

Information

There are currency exchange points at the airport, in the main hotels and in several banks. The Hotel Chagala has a business centre with phone and fax. If you're prepared for a wait, you can also telephone worldwide from the Central Telephone Office next to the Hotel Aq Zhayyk, open daily except Sunday from 8 am to midnight.

The Atyrau telephone code is 31222.

Things to See

The **regional arts museum** at ulitsa Satpaeva 5, near the corner of ulitsa Avangard, displays costumes as well as art. It's open Wednesday to Sunday, from 9 am to 1 pm and 2 to 6 pm. The **Atyrau history museum** at ulitsa Ordzhonikidze 14, on the west side of the river about half a km north of the bridge, has artefacts and information on the town and region, plus a section on flora and fauna. It's open daily except Sunday, the same hours as the arts museum.

Places to Stay & Eat

The *Hotel Kaspii* (☎ 5-33-07, 2-34-85) at ulitsa Satpaeva 15 (actually down a side street by the Kazakstan Airlines office) is a reasonable little place with just three single rooms at US$20, 12 doubles at US$36, a few more expensive suites, a restaurant and a shop.

The big *Hotel Aq Zhayyk* (☎ 2-20-11) at ploshchad Abaya 4, just east of the main bridge over the Ural river, has singles/doubles for US$55/85; single occupancy of a double is US$43. It's a decent hotel with a restaurant, café and bufet all in good working order.

Top place is the Scandinavian-managed *Hotel Chagala* (☎ 5-40-33, fax 5-40-34) at Smagulov ulitsa 1, the end of the street parallel to the river beside the Hotel Aq Zhayyk. Singles/doubles are US$126/216, for which you can enjoy satellite TV, international direct-dial phones, a swimming pool and gym. The hotel also has the best restaurant in town (international food at US$12/18/24 for breakfast/lunch/dinner), a bar, business

centre, shop, laundry service and free airport transfers.

There's a *food market* a short distance along ulitsa Abaya west of the bridge, and another down the first street to the left after the Kazakstan Airlines office.

Getting There & Away

Air The Kazakstan Airlines ticket office (☎ 2-49-49) on ulitsa Satpaeva, about half a km west of the Ural river bridge, is open daily except Sunday from 8 am to noon and 1 to 7 pm. Flights are scheduled to Moscow daily; Aqtau six days a week; Almaty four days; Aqtöbe and Oral three days; Qaraghandy, Zhambyl, Qostanay, Baku (Azerbaijan), Samara, Krasnodar and Mineralnye Vody (all Russia), and Vienna (Austria) all once or twice a week.

Bus There's bus service to Oral, 500 km to the north.

Train There are daily trains to/from Aqtöbe (14 hours), Mangghyshlak (near Aqtau, 22 hours) and Astrakhan. Services to/from Moscow, Volgograd, Tashkent and Almaty are scheduled every two days, but may be unreliable.

AQTAU
АҚТАУ
Population: 165,000

Stuck between the desert and the Caspian, with all its water derived from desalination plants, and supplied mainly by air because it's hundreds of km from any other town and not linked by any decent roads, Aqtau (Aktau in Russian) is one of the most improbable of all the 'why-on-earth-does-anyone-live-here?' places scattered across the former USSR.

It didn't exist at all till 1963. Then Soviet architects began to lay out a model town of wide, straight streets, dividing residential quarters into numbered *mikrorayony* (microregions) of apartment blocks, uncomplicated by street names. Why, here?

The answer is simple: local uranium deposits. And thanks to its sandy Caspian beaches, the place was also developed as a holiday resort for the Soviet élite. Now the Soviet system is gone, the uranium and tourism industries are in decline, and Aqtau has the feel of a place whose bubble has burst. But the development of the Tenghiz oilfield, 200 km north-east, and the prospect of offshore oil in the Caspian, hold out hopes of a recovery, and are already bringing a steady trickle of westerners.

If you should get here, you'll at least find it a clean town, still fairly well supplied, and with a longer summer than most of the rest of Kazakstan.

In Soviet times Aqtau was named Shevchenko, after the 19th century Ukrainian poet and artist Taras Shevchenko, who was exiled to Kazakstan for his nationalist views.

The population is a mixture, mainly of Russians, Kazaks and Caucasus peoples.

Orientation
The only street with a name seems to be prospekt Lenina, a broad avenue running parallel to the coast about half a km inland. Other Aqtau locations are identified by their mikrorayon and *dom* (building) numbers. Prospekt Lenina slopes down from north to south.

The Hotel Aktau, at a fork towards its south end, is one recognisable landmark. A war memorial with an eternal flame, 1.7 km north, is another. Landmarks on the seafront road parallel to prospekt Lenina are an MiG fighter plane on a pedestal, at the end of the street leading from the war memorial on prospekt Lenina, and a statue of Taras Shevchenko, one km south.

The airport is 30 km north of the town.

Information
There's an Alem Bank currency exchange in the TsUM department store on prospekt Lenina, almost opposite the Hotel Aktau. One post and telephone office is beside the Hotel Aktau; a bigger one is 2.3 km north on prospekt Lenina.

The Aqtau telephone code is 3292 for six digit numbers, 32922 for five digit numbers.

Things to See & Do
Apart from wandering around and taking in the bizarre atmosphere, the main thing, in summer, is the long **beach** and the seafront walk. One of the best bits of beach is roughly in front of the MiG. The water's still just about warm enough for a swim in September.

The **Regional History & Local Studies Museum** (Oblystyq Tarikhi-Ölketanu Muzeyi, Oblastnoy Istoriko-Kraevedchesky Muzey) is worth a visit. It's on prospekt Lenina, 1.7 km north of the Hotel Aktau. Enter through the blue gate. Hours are Tuesday to Saturday from 9 am to noon and 1 to 5 pm.

A possible out-of-town trip is to **Fort-Shevchenko**, a small town 90 km north up the coast, which originated in the 19th century as a Russian bridgehead, called Fort Alexandrovsk, on the east side of the Caspian Sea. Buses are scheduled to Fort-

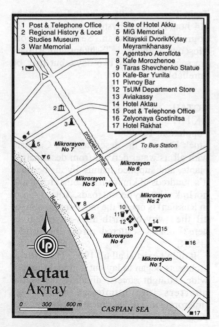

1 Post & Telephone Office	4 Site of Hotel Akku
2 Regional History & Local Studies Museum	5 MiG Memorial
3 War Memorial	6 Kitayskii Dvorik/Kytay Meyramkhanasy
	7 Agentstvo Aeroflota
	8 Kafe Morozhenoe
	9 Taras Shevchenko Statue
	10 Kafe-Bar Yunita
	11 Pivnoy Bar
	12 TsUM Department Store
	13 Aviakassy
	14 Hotel Aktau
	15 Post & Telephone Office
	16 Zelyonaya Gostinitsa
	17 Hotel Rakhat

prospekt Lenina

To Bus Station

Mikrorayon No 7

Mikrorayon No 6

Mikrorayon No 5

Mikrorayon No 2

Mikrorayon No 4

Mikrorayon No 1

Beach

Aqtau
Ақтау

0   300   600 m

CASPIAN SEA

Grain Train

The train to Aqtau can be an unearthly experience, and not just because of the moon-like quality of the desert on the way. If you come all the way from Aqtöbe, the two-day trip is long enough to relax your grip on time: the slow rhythmical progress of the train through an empty landscape, the intermittent lengthy stops nowhere in particular, the surprising numbers of other passengers shuffling on and off the train at odd hours of the clock, all combine to make day and night merge into one. You get a constantly evolving range of compartment companions, too – half of them carting huge boxes and bundles of goods to trade somewhere along the line or in Aqtau, whose isolation means good prices for scarce goods brought in from outside.

Somewhere along the route, during hours of darkness, I was happily stretched out along a bottom bunk when my compartment door opened, on went the light, and in piled five tough-looking men with several huge bundles which left no floor space and little seat space. Not bothering to conceal my annoyance, I climbed grumpily to a top bunk and turned my back on them. They talked a guttural language I'd never heard before.

After a while, curiosity won me round. I saw they had a leader (in a check cloth jacket), and a No 2 (leather jacket); the three younger men (thin plastic jackets), were patently tired and hungry. I asked what was in their bundles.

'Material,' uttered No 2, without elaboration.

'Ah...and where are you from?'

'Grozny.'

At this time Grozny, capital of the breakaway Muslim republic of Chechnya in the Russian Caucasus, had not yet been flattened by Russian bombs and tanks. But the Chechens already had a frightening reputation for violent gangsterism and feuding. They had, too, fought a ferocious holy war against the Christian Russians in the 19th century. People I definitely did not want to upset.

'Ah, Chechnya!' I smiled, as if they'd said 'Paris'. I then kept very quiet for a long time, hoping fervently that my earlier rudeness hadn't offended them.

I needn't have worried. Eventually No 2 pulled out some bread and apples, dividing them among his party. Before they started to eat, No 1 stood up and looked at me.

'Bread, Christian?' he said.

On all long train rides in the former USSR, a lot of drinking goes on among some of the men. I was relieved that the Chechens were abstainers. So, I thought, was my one constant companion all the way from Aqtöbe, a likeable Kazak from Aqtau. Then, still several hours out of Aqtau (about 8 am, I guess), he reached under his seat and pulled out a crate of bottles labelled 'Grain Alcohol, Product of the USA – 95% alc/vol'.

Had I ever tried this, he asked? No, I said, wasn't it for cooking, or medicinal purposes?

For answer he poured half a tumbler and offered it to me. I declined, whereupon he downed it himself, in one. Followed soon by a couple more. I watched anxiously, but all it made him do was grin stupidly, turn my radio up loud, then fall noisily asleep.

John Noble

Shevchenko from Aqtau bus station four times daily.

Places to Stay

The *Hotel Aktau* (☎ 51-47-07) at the fork in prospekt Lenina is about the easiest place to find and is a standard Soviet hotel with standard Soviet rooms. 'Superior' (*vysshaya*) category singles/doubles, with bathroom, are US$16/23. There are several categories of cheaper rooms from US$7/11.50 upwards, plus lyux rooms they'll automatically try to put you in. The hotel had an original angle on post-Soviet plumbing when we stayed – plenty of hot water, but no cold.

The *Zelyonaya Gostinitsa* (Green Hotel, ☎ 51-73-04) is favoured by some western business people. It's set back among other buildings on prospekt Lenina, 500 metres south down the left-hand fork from the Hotel Aktau. Doubles are US$43 to US$71.

The *Hotel Rakhat* (☎ 51-17-55), on the shore south of the centre, has been renovated and has very comfortable, though not very big, singles/doubles for US$70/90. It's also known as the *Vengerskaya Gostinitsa* (Hungarian Hotel). To get there take the left-hand fork south from the Hotel Aktau, then turn right after about 700 metres, then first left, and then first right.

The 120 room Turkish-built *Hotel Akku*, facing the sea opposite the MiG, will be the top place in town when it is built.

Places to Eat

The *Kafe/Bar Yunita*, in the round-roofed building next to the TsUM department store, is a pleasant little place with good dishes like tsiplyata tabaka (chicken in a spicy Georgian sauce) or zharkoe (meat and vegetable hotpot) for US$1 to US$2. It's open from 1 am to 4 pm and 7 pm to 2 am. Next door is a *pivnoy bar* serving large mugs of beer.

Kitayskii Dvorik/Kytay Meyramkhanasy, on the seafront road just south of the MiG, has fine Chinese décor and acceptable Russian food at around US$4 for a meal. It's open for lunch and dinner.

The *Hotel Aktau* has a bufet with drinks and snacks, and an intermittently open restaurant.

There's a reasonable café in the *TsUM* department store, and excellent ice cream at the *Kafe Morozhenoe* on the seafront road just north of the Taras Shevchenko statue, open daily from 11 am to 7 pm. The *Hotel Rakhat* has a bar with food.

Getting There & Away

Air Tickets for most places are sold at the Agentstvo Aeroflota, on prospekt Lenina 750 metres north of the Hotel Aktau, open daily from 8 am to 1 pm and 2 to 9 pm. For a few destinations such as Mineralnye Vody or Siberia, you must go to the *aviakassy* (air ticket office) in the north end of the building opposite the Hotel Aktau.

Flights are scheduled to Almaty, Atyrau and Oral six times a week; Aqtöbe and Aqmola four times; Moscow twice; Astrakhan and Vladikavkaz (Russia) daily; Baku (Azerbaijan) four days a week; and Rostov-on-Don and Mineralnye Vody (both Russia) and Istanbul all twice a week.

Train The station for Aqtau is Mangghyshlak (also called Mangghystau), about 12 km east of the town. Daily trains run to/from Atyrau, 400 km north as the crow flies, but 800 km and about 24 hours by rail. These trains also pull carriages to/from Aqtöbe which is about 1400 km and two days away, including 14 hours in a siding at Atyrau if you're Aqtöbe-bound (seven hours if you're Aqtau-bound): the consolation is that this entire trip only costs US$9 in 2nd-class (local price).

Getting Around

There are occasional buses and marshrutnoe taxis from the town bus station to the airport. A taxi is about US$3. On the way you pass a Muslim cemetery whose crenellated skyline of miniature domes and towers looks from a distance like some town out of an Arabian fairy tale.

Bus No 101 runs between Mangghyshlak train station and Aqtau bus station (avtovokzal or avtostantsia), a ride of about 30 minutes across a wilderness of pipelines and cables on the eastern side of Aqtau. The bus station is about one km inland and two or three km north of the Hotel Aktau, to which it's connected by bus No 3, which covers much of prospekt Lenina along the way. Several other buses run up and down prospekt Lenina.

Northern Kazakstan

Until the 19th century, the flat steppe of northern Kazakstan was largely untouched except by Kazak nomads and their herds, a few Russian forts in places like Semey, Pavlodar and Öskemen, and a smattering of Russian settlements behind the line of forts. As Russia's grip stretched southwards over Kazakstan, settlers from the west came in increasing numbers to farm the steppe – a million or more had settled in the north by

1900 – displacing the Kazaks from their pastures. The Kazaks' resistance was largely futile and many thousands died in rebellions or famines.

An even bigger transformation came in Soviet times. The nomadic Kazaks were forced into collective farms, with hundreds of thousands starving in the ensuing famine. New industrial cities like Qaraghandy, Ekibastuz and Qostanay sprouted to process coal, iron ore and other minerals, and in the 1950s vast areas of steppe were turned over to wheat in Nikita Khrushchev's Virgin Lands scheme, engendering yet more cities such as Aqmola. A huge influx of Russians, Ukrainians and others came to work the new projects.

The region was useful to Moscow for more sinister reasons, too. A network of Gulag labour camps was set up here, and many of those deported from other parts of the USSR around the time of WWII were sent here. In the 1950s most of the camps were closed and most of the deportees were allowed to go home, but many of the survivors stayed, including a large German population, only now shrinking as its members disappear off to Germany. Moscow also chose northern Kazakstan as its chief nuclear testing ground, detonating 470 nuclear bombs between 1949 and 1989 near Semey, and causing untold health and environmental damage in an area inhabited by four million people.

The legacy of the Soviet era is a high Russian and Ukrainian population (Kazaks number less than 20% in several regions) and a lot of decaying, dirty industry. Many of the Slavs, disgruntled by economic decline and seeing little future in a Kazakstan dominated by Kazaks, are leaving like the Germans. Most of the cities are bleak, impoverished places, usually with unreconstructed Russian (and Soviet) street names.

The region is crossed by the railways linking Central Asia with Siberia – the Turksib line from Almaty to Novosibirsk and another line up the middle of Kazakstan to Yekaterinburg, but there's a limited amount to stop for unless you *have* to come here. The

two most interesting cities are Aqmola, the friendly Virgin Lands capital and supposedly the future capital of Kazakstan, and Semey, which has famous literary connections, some history and a kind of morbid fascination stemming from the Polygon nuclear testing site. Mountain lovers could head for the beautiful Altay mountains in the far east of the region – an untrammelled contrast to the endless, treeless steppe elsewhere.

The better months up here are May to September. Winter can be fierce, with howling blizzards and temperatures dropping to -35°C in January or February.

SEMEY
СЕМЕЙ
Population: 340,000

Semey is better known to the world as Semipalatinsk – the Russian equivalent of its name, used during the 40 years the Soviet military was exploding nuclear bombs at the Polygon, on the steppe 150 km south-west of Semey. Semey residents say they knew when tests were going on because the ground would shake – often on Sunday mornings. An unprecedented wave of popular protest in Kazakstan, the Nevada-Semipalatinsk Movement (now the Nevada-Semey Movement), was largely instrumental in halting the tests in 1989. See also the Environment section in the Facts about the Region chapter for more information.

Despite the terrible health and environmental legacy of the tests, Semey is one of Kazakstan's more interesting cities. Set in the territory of the Middle Horde, who are noted for their eloquence and intellect, the city and its surrounding region have bred several major Kazak writers and teachers, among them the national poet Abay Qunanbaev (1845-1904). In 1917 Semey was a capital of the short-lived Alash Orda independent Kazakstan government.

Its Russian past is interesting, too: it began life in the 18th century as a Russian fort, remnants of which can still be seen, and in the 19th century the great Russian writer Fyodor Dostoevsky spent five years of exile here.

Semey is 850 km north of Almaty and 550 km south of Novosibirsk in Russia. It's the most northerly major stop in Kazakstan on the Turksib railway which joins those two cities. Like most other Kazakstan cities, it's Russian-looking and shabby but, thanks to its longer pedigree, less gloom-engendering than some of the already-decaying Soviet creations elsewhere on the steppes.

Ironically, the nuclear testing programme helped maintain the intellectual traditions of the place by bringing in top scientists and teachers. Semey's people – a fairly even and seemingly harmonious ethnic mixture –

seem to be making a determined effort to regenerate their economy.

Orientation

Semey is dissected from north-east to south-west by its main street, Shakarim Qudayberdiev prospektisi, and from south-east to north-west by the Irtysh river. The older part of the city and nearly everything of use or interest is on the north-east side of the Irtysh. The train station is just off the north-east end of Shakarim Qudayberdiev prospektisi, about three km from the centre. Street names are now mostly in Kazak

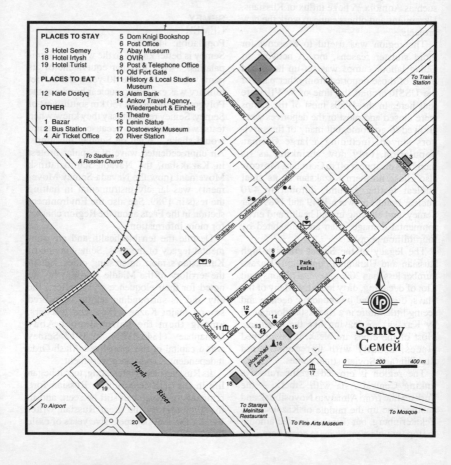

PLACES TO STAY

3 Hotel Semey
18 Hotel Irtysh
19 Hotel Turist

PLACES TO EAT

12 Kafe Dostyq

OTHER

1 Bazar
2 Bus Station
4 Air Ticket Office
5 Dom Knigi Bookshop
6 Post Office
7 Abay Museum
8 OVIR
9 Post & Telephone Office
10 Old Fort Gate
11 History & Local Studies Museum
13 Alem Bank
14 Ankov Travel Agency, Wiedergeburt & Einheit
15 Theatre
16 Lenin Statue
17 Dostoevsky Museum
20 River Station

Semey
Семей

except, it seems, for the square opposite the Hotel Irtysh which everyone still calls ploshchad Lenina.

Information
Money You can change money in the hotels and at Alem Bank at ploshchad Lenina 3, open Monday to Friday from 8 am to 5 pm. There are also moneychangers in the bazar, but beware of rip-offs.

Post & Communications The main post office is at the corner of Dulatov köshesi and Bauyrzhan Momyshuly köshesi, open Monday to Friday from 8 am to 8 pm, and Saturday and Sunday from 9 am to 6 pm. The long-distance telephone office is combined with another post office on Shakarim Qudayberdiev prospektisi.

The Semey telephone code is 3222.

Travel Agencies For help with trips out of town, you might try Ankov (☎ 66-23-22, 66-24-37) at ploshchad Lenina 5, Bogas-Inturservis (☎ 54-12-24, fax 44-67-83) in the Hotel Irtysh, or the excursion bureau (*byuro puteshestviy i exkursiy*) at the Hotel Turist.

Useful Organisations If you're interested in contacting some of the local Germans, down to about 20,000 in the city and 40,000 in the Semey oblys by 1994, try the organisations Wiedergeburt and Einheit, both at ploshchad Lenina 5, which help emigrating Germans with paperwork and language.

The OVIR (officially OPVR in Kazakstan) office is in rooms 119 and 120 of the building on the corner of Bauyrzhan Momyshuly köshesi and Karl Marx köshesi. It's open Monday, Wednesday and Friday from 9 am to 1 pm, and Thursdays from 9 am to 6 pm.

The leader of the local branch of the Nevada-Semey Movement is Razia Mamatova (☎ 44-88-80).

Dostoevsky Museum
This well set-out museum (Muzey F M Dostoevskogo) is just off ploshchad Lenina and incorporates the house where the writer lived from 1857 to 1859. There are exhibits covering both his life and work. It has a lot of pictures and photos and is worth a visit even if you can't understand its mainly Russian texts.

The two main parts of the museum are a display on Dostoevsky's life and works (with sections devoted to his childhood in Moscow, residence in St Petersburg, periods in Omsk and Semey, and creative life from 1860 to 1881), and the rooms where he lived, maintained in the style of his day. Don't bother getting an extra ticket for the *vystavka*, an exhibition from the museum's archives, unless you have a special interest.

The museum is open daily except Monday from 9 am to 6 pm. Guided tours are available in Russian and Kazak only.

Dostoevsky in Exile
In 1849, at the age of 28, Dostoevsky was sentenced to death with several others for attending meetings of the Petrashevsky Circle, a group of utopian socialist intelligentsia who gathered on Friday nights in a St Petersburg house. The group was lined up before a firing squad – only to be told at the last moment that their sentences had been commuted to exile in Siberia.

Dostoevsky spent the next five years in a convict prison at Omsk – an experience which produced his first major novel, *The House of the Dead*. This was followed by five years enforced military service in the garrison at Semey, which was then starting to prosper mildly as a trading town but was still as remote and inhospitable a place as the tsarist authorities could think of for dissidents.

It was in Semey that Dostoevsky met and made friends with the extraordinary Shoqan Ualikhanov, a prince of the Middle Horde, explorer, artist, intellectual, and officer and spy in the Russian army, whose statue stands outside the museum. See the Renaissance Boy of the Steppes aside, in the History section of the Facts about the Region chapter, for more on Shoqan. ∎

Abay Museum

This big new complex which looks like a mosque, at the corner of Dulatov köshesi and Internatsional köshesi, was due to be unveiled in 1995 for the 150th anniversary of Abay Qunanbaev's birth. It will cover all things to do with his life, with a section on wider Kazak culture too.

Abay, who was born in the Shyngghystau hills south of Semey (see Around Semey) and spent much of his life there and in the city, is the No 1 Kazak cultural guru – a 19th century humanist poet and teacher who valued Kazak traditions as well as aspects of the progress that came with the Russians. His translations of Russian and other foreign literature into Kazak, and his public readings of them, as well as his own work, were the beginning of Kazak as a literary language and helped broaden Kazaks' horizons. Other Kazak bards took up and passed on the stories he read so that, for example, Dumas' *Three Musketeers* became widely known. See the Abay aside in the Arts section in this chapter.

Many literary successors also came from the Shyngghystan hills – notably the bard Shakarim Qudayberdiev, Abay's nephew, and Mukhtar Auezov, playwright and author of the epic Kazak novel *Abay Zholy* (The Path of Abay). This book, a tale of 19th century steppe life based on Abay and other historical figures, has been translated into many languages and helped perpetuate the memory of Abay among Kazaks.

History & Local Studies Museum

This museum (Oblystyq Tarikhi Ölke-tanu Murazhayy, Oblastnoy Istoriko-Kraevedchesky Muzey) at Lenin köshesi 5 has an English-speaking guide on duty on weekends. Otherwise it's only moderately interesting if you can't understand Russian or Kazak. It has material on the growth of Semey, a small display on nuclear testing and the Nevada-Semey Movement, and a few old Kazak artefacts. An intriguing array of ancient stone heads stands outside the door. It's open daily except Monday from 10 am to 2 pm and 3 to 6 pm.

Fine Arts Museum

Located in an apartment block behind the statue of Abay in a small park on Abai köshesi, about 500 metres from the Hotel Irtysh, the fine arts museum (Muzey Izobrazitelnykh Iskusstv) has some good work by Kazak, Russian and west European painters, with an art shop next door. There's also an art gallery, with sometimes good visiting exhibitions, on Bauyrzhan Momyshuly köshesi.

Old Semey

The original fort was founded in 1718, a few km away along the Irtysh river, as Russia's expansion across Siberia ran up against the warlike Mongolia-based Oyrat (Zhungarian) Empire.

Semey shifted to its present site in the 1770s: one of the fort gates built then still stands on Abai köshesi north-west of Shakarim Qudayberdiev prospektisi just before the railway bridge. Also still standing (and working), down the third street on the left after the railway, is a pretty Russian church with a blue tower and dome, which stood at the centre of the fort. In the streets north-east of here, towards the bus station and bazar, are many old one storey wooden houses.

The streets south-east of Shakarim Qudayberdiev prospektisi were redeveloped in Soviet times but a few reminders of their past remain – notably the Dostoevsky museum (incorporating the house he lived in), and a disused 19th century mosque (a Russian-style building with a minaret sticking out of the top) – on Pavlov köshesi four blocks farther east. The mosque was used as an exhibition hall in Soviet times but was boarded up when we checked.

Irtysh River

The walk along the north-east bank of the Irtysh is pleasant. The bridge about 700 metres south-east of the Hotel Irtysh leads to an island which in summer is the favourite local spot for sunbathing, sitting round campfires and watching members of the opposite sex. Drunken gangs are said to prowl there after dark, however.

Places to Stay

The best hotel is the *Hotel Irtysh* (☎ 93-33-15, 93-33-45) at Abai köshesi 97 facing ploshchad Lenina. Adequate singles/doubles with private bathroom, TV, fridge and balcony are US$22/35.

The *Hotel Turist* (☎ 44-75-07), just off Shakarim Qudayberdiev prospektisi on the south-west bank of the river, is more dilapidated than the Hotel Irtysh and the staff are less helpful. Rooms with private bath are US$16 per person. The ageing *Hotel Semey* facing the park on Qabanbay Batyr köshesi is cheaper but was 'full' when we checked. Rooms share shower and toilet with others on the corridor.

Places to Eat

The restaurant of the *Hotel Irtysh*, open from 11 am to 4 pm and 6 to 11 pm, is reliable. A decent three course meal and a beer is around US$4. The band is awful but they don't play every night. The hotel also has *bufety* serving hot food, salads and drinks on floors two and four.

Just off ploshchad Lenina, in the back of the nine storey building next to the red industrial school, is *Dokka Pitstsa*, doing respectable pizzas for US$1.50 (two will fill you up) and selling tasty loaves of bread for US$0.50.

The *Restoran Kayrat* in the Hotel Semey building is reasonable – three courses and a drink will cost you around US$3. It's open from lunchtime till midnight. The *Hotel Turist* has a restaurant too.

Kafe Dostyk on Lenin köshesi has music in the evenings and may be booked up with banquets. Prices are similar to the Hotel Irtysh restaurant.

The *Staraya Melnitsa* (Old Windmill) – actually a modern wooden building 600 metres south-east along the riverbank from the end of Internatsional köshesi – is expensive and its food very average. You pay around US$8 for zakuski followed by meatballs and noodles.

We didn't manage to locate the *Kafe Morozhenoe*, but it sounds good, with reportedly excellent manty (three for US$0.75), good fish dishes, reasonably priced caviar, decent imported beers, and friendly service. Despite its name, which means 'Ice Cream Café', they say it has no ice cream.

The *bazar*, off Qabanbay Batyr köshesi three blocks north-west of Shakarim Qudayberdiev prospektisi, has fruit and vegetables.

Entertainment

Kazak, Russian, Ukrainian or German dance performances are staged several times a month in the orange Culture Centre building facing the park in front of the Hotel Semey. The Semey philharmonic orchestra occasionally plays in the theatre on ploshchad Lenina. You may also find good concerts in the Children's Culture Place, the dome-topped building on Abai köshesi near the Hotel Irtysh.

Yelimay Semey is one of Kazakstan's top soccer teams and its home games are advertised on posters around town. The season runs from about April to September. To find the stadium, follow Abai köshesi north-west from Shakarim Qudayberdiev prospektisi, take the first street on the right after you go under the railway, and head for the floodlight pylons.

Getting There & Away

Air Tickets are sold at the 'Aeroflot' ticket office at Shakarim Qudayberdiev prospektisi 38, open daily from 8 am to 1 pm and 2 to 5 or 6 pm. Flights go to/from Almaty daily and are scheduled (unreliably) to other cities such as Aqmola, Öskemen, Pavlodar, Qaraghandy and Zhambyl a few days a week. Luftbrücke (☎ 66-64-05) has charter flights to Düsseldorf about every two weeks.

Bus From the bus station off Naymanbaev köshesi, 400 metres north-west of Shakarim Qudayberdiev prospektisi, several daily buses run to Pavlodar (seven hours) and Öskemen (six hours), and one to Barnaul in Russia (11 hours).

Train Semey is on the Turksib railway and has fairly good service south to Almaty and beyond, and north into Russia. Northbound there are three or four trains a day to Barnaul (nine hours) and Novosibirsk (16 hours), one a day to Krasnoyarsk, and a train to Irkutsk every three days. Southbound, three or four trains go daily to Almaty (21 hours), one or two daily to Tashkent, and one most days to Bishkek.

If you're heading for China, you can connect with the Almaty-Ürümqi trains at Aktogay, 12 hours south of Semey. At the time of writing these trains leave Aktogay for Ürümqi at 7.15 am (4.15 am Moscow time), on Sunday and Tuesday only.

Since most trains from Semey are in transit, getting tickets at short notice can be a pain. You may have most luck, if you're prepared to pay foreigners' prices (eg US$24 for a kupeynyy to Novosibirsk), at the station's international ticket window (*kassa dlya mezhdunarodnykh perevozok*).

Getting Around

Bus Nos 11, 22, 33 and 44 run from the train station to the centre along Shakarim Qudayberdiev prospektisi. Bus No 22 turns right along Qabanbay Batyr to the bazar; the others continue across the Irtysh, with bus No 33 going all the way to the airport. For the Hotel Irtysh get off when you see the river bridge ahead, and walk back to Abai; for the Hotel Turist get off after the bridge. A taxi from the train station to the centre is about US$2.

From the theatre on ploshchad Lenina, bus Nos 2 and 35 run to the bazar and bus No 50 to the bus station. None is very frequent. Buses run from about 6 am to 8 pm.

AROUND SEMEY
The Polygon
Полигон

The Polygon is an area of about 15,000 sq km, around 150 km south-west of Semey. Between 1949 and 1989 some 470 nuclear bombs were detonated here, 150 of them (all before 1963) above or at ground level. Today there's little overt evidence of the testing

apart from the 'Atomic lake' (Atomnoe Ozero), a huge circular water-filled hole in the ground, blasted out to create a reservoir in 1965. One bomb installed but not exploded by the Soviet military in 1991 was reportedly being dismantled in 1994.

The nerve-centre of the test zone was the purpose-built town of Kurchatov, on the Irtysh river 150 km north-west of Semey, named after Igor Kurchatov, leader of the team that developed the Soviet bomb. Today the town is still known locally as Konechnaya (Russian for 'The End'), or even just 'K'. At the time of research for this book it was closed to visitors except for officially invited delegations. Some foreign scientists were said to be there working on medical and biological research.

To visit the Atomic lake you should be able to find a driver outside the Hotel Irtysh in Semey or in the town of Sarzhal, 150 km south-west of Semey. Sarzhal has a hotel with rooms for about US$2 and is reached by one bus a day from Semey. There isn't really much to see apart from the lake and the dominating bleak beauty of the steppe.

See the Environment section in the Facts About the Region chapter for more information on the Polygon and the Nevada-Semipalatinsk Movement which forced its closure.

Shyngghystau Hills
Шыңғыстау

The Shyngghystau (Russian: Chingistau) are a range of low rocky hills – 1200 metres at their highest – 100 to 200 km south of Semey. Apart from its natural beauty, this sparsely peopled area is full of Kazak legends and is famed as the homeland and inspiration of the writers Abay Qunanbaev, Mukhtar Auezov and Shakarim Qudayberdiev (see the Semey section in this chapter). Numerous legendary sites, and memorials, tombs and museums dedicated to these men and their relatives, are dotted around the Shyngghystau. If you had a guide it could be interesting. Regular excursions apparently go from Semey from spring to autumn – check with travel agencies there.

Abay was born in Qasqabulaq on the northern fringe of the hills, reached by one bus a day from Semey. Abay's last home, in Zhidebai, is now a museum, as is Auezov's home in Borli.

ÖSKEMEN
ӨCKEMEH
Population: 330,000

This dire uranium-processing town (Russian: Ust-Kamenogorsk) 180 km east of Semey is a starting point for trips into the Altay mountains in the far eastern corner of Kazakstan. Öskemen, like Semey, was founded as a Russian fort in the early 18th century. It has grown from a small town since the 1940s when Russians and Ukrainians began to arrive to mine and process local minerals. Its telephone code is 3232.

Information
A good contact is Boris Vasilevich Shcherbakov (☎ 65-76-29 home, 66-49-00 work) at the Ekobiotsentr, Dom Yunatov, ulitsa Ushanova 64/221. He's an ornithologist – with a collection of parrots! – who with a bit of notice can organise trips to the Altay's Lake Markakol area and maybe the Mt Belukha area, for reasonable fees. Also possibly helpful for Altay trips are the travel agencies Öskemen Turist (☎ 66-57-00, contact Viktor Nikolaevich Yasak), Sputnik (☎ 42-56-11, 42-14-39) at ulitsa Bespalova 45, and Altay Tour (☎ 42-80-22, 44-92-44) at prospekt Lenina 79/3-34.

Places to Stay
The *Hotel Ust-Kamenogorsk* is at ulitsa Proletarskaya 158.

Getting There & Away
From Semey, both road and railway take circuitous routes to Öskemen. There might be flights but otherwise the bus is best – there are several a day (290 km, six hours). By rail from Semey you can choose between an overnight train which loops into Russia and takes 10 hours, and a morning train which makes a much longer southern detour and

takes 20 hours. From Almaty there are daily planes and buses (24 hours, US$28).

ALTAY MOUNTAINS
АЛТАЙ
The far eastern corner of Kazakstan borders Russia and China, and Mongolia is only 50 km away. The Altay mountains spread across all four countries. Only a small portion of them is in Kazakstan but it's a beautiful portion, with alpine steppe and meadows, forested valleys, rocky, snow-covered peaks and wooden villages. The highest peak in all the Altay, the 4506 metre Mt Belukha, rises on the Kazakstan-Russia border. According to Asian legends, the Belukha area is the location of Shambhala, a paradisal realm that will reveal itself after humanity destroys itself. Others believe Shambhala is a state of heightened energy and awareness induced by supernatural phenomena or inner means – or perhaps simply by experiencing the beauty of Belukha!

Lake Markakol, 40 km long and 1400 metres high in the remote Southern Altay range, south of Belukha and the Bukhtarma river valley, is noted for the purity of its waters and the beautiful and pristine alpine country around it, especially to its east. The area is a nature reserve, with its base at Urunkhayka at the east end of the lake.

Getting There & Away
See the Öskemen section for contacts who may be able to help arrange an Altay visit. The Almaty travel agency Tour Asia offers Altay trekking trips in summer.

Under your own steam, it's a 300 km, all-day bus ride from Öskemen to Katon-Karagay in the Bukhtarma valley, which has a small hotel and *stolovaya* (canteen). From Katon-Karagay there should be onward buses to the village of Berel, 80 km farther up the Bukhtarma, from where a road heads about 80 km north up to the tiny village of Kokkol, about 15 km south-east of Mt Belukha. From Kokkol it's possible to trek round either side of the Belukha massif, but only if you're thoroughly prepared, suitably experienced and preferably accompanied, as there are glaciers and 3000-metre-plus passes which may require crampons, ropes and ice screws.

Another place you could head for from Katon-Karagay is Rakhmanovskie Klyuchi (Rakhmanov Springs), with a turbaza for accommodation, in a valley 30 km up a different track north from Berel.

CROSSING TO CHINA AT BAKHTY & MAYKAPCHIGAY

Two road crossings from Kazakstan to China are at Bakhty (opposite Tacheng in China; called Shaueshen in Kazak and Chuguchak in Russian); and at Maykapchigay, opposite Jeminay, between Zaysan (Kazakstan) and Burqin (China). Take soundings before you try to cross at these points to find out if they are open to non-CIS or non-Chinese passport holders. The Chinese may be the most difficult to convince, unless you happen to have your Chinese visa endorsed for one of the crossings (state this when you apply for the visa, but don't get your hopes up).

Neither of these crossings is reached by regular bus from major cities in Kazakstan, though it should be possible to reach them by a combination of bus as far as you can get, then taxi. There are daily buses from Semey to Zaysan (12 hours), 64 km from Maykapchigay, and to Makanchi (13 hours overnight), 66 km from Bakhty. There may be local buses onward to the border points.

PAVLODAR
ПАВЛОДАР

Pavlodar is 320 km north-west across the steppe from Semey, on the Irtysh river and 110 km from the Russian border. The Russian city of Omsk is 400 km north-west. Founded as a Russian fort in the early 18th century, Pavlodar was developed as an industrial town in Soviet times, with drab Soviet architecture and oil refining, chemical and aluminium processing plants, plus a tractor factory. The tractor factory now makes washing machines but the chemical plant on the outskirts continues to pollute the town. Pavlodar was closed to foreigners until 1992.

Things to See & Do

There's an art museum and gallery on ulitsa Toraygirova, and a pleasant embankment on the Irtysh, along which you can also take summer ferry rides. The very busy main bazar is on ulitsa 1 Maya.

Places to Stay & Eat

Hotels include the *Sariarka*, *Kazakstan* and *Irtysh*; there are *Chinese restaurants* on ulitsa Yestaya and ulitsa Tolstogo, and a *stolovaya* in the TsUM department store on ulitsa Dzerzhinskogo.

Getting There & Away

There are daily flights to/from Almaty and service to/from some other Kazakstan cities, plus Omsk, Novosibirsk and Moscow in Russia.

The train and bus stations are both in the north of town on ulitsa Toraygirova. To/from Semey (about seven hours) there's a reportedly comfortable daily private-enterprise *(kommerchesky)* bus from the river station, as well as public buses. Other bus routes include to/from Aqmola and Omsk. Train services include to/from Aqmola (12 hours) and Barnaul in Russia, both daily, Almaty (36 hours) and Moscow (69 hours) both every two days via Aqmola.

Getting Around

Bus No 22 links the airport to the centre, a 15 km ride, and the train station.

AROUND PAVLODAR

About 130 km south-west of Pavlodar is **Ekibastuz** (population: 140,000), probably the dirtiest place in Kazakstan thanks to its vast power stations burning low-grade coal from the local coalfields.

Some 90 km south of Ekibastuz is **Bayanaul national park**, a pretty oasis of rocky hills, caves, trees and lakes amid the steppe. The focus is Lake Zhasybay, 12 km from Bayanaul town, which can be reached by bus from Ekibastuz and possibly Pavlodar.

QARAGHANDY
КАРАГАНДЫ
Population: 600,000

Qaraghandy (Karaganda in Russian), founded only in 1926 but now Kazakstan's second biggest city, is famous for two things: coal and Gulag labour camps. The two are intimately connected, as the big network of camps around Qaraghandy was set up to provide slave labour for the mines. Much of the city itself was built by Gulag labour. The Samarka and Kengir camps near Qaraghandy were the centre of a famous revolt in 1954 – 700 prisoners were killed when tanks moved in to put it down.

When the camps were closed soon afterwards, many surviving inmates stayed on as miners. There are around 30,000 miners (average life expectancy: 49) in the area's 27 mines today. Since WWII the large steel town Temirtau (population: 200,000) has sprung up 25 km to the north.

Qaraghandy is a bleak place on the steppe 800 km north-west of Almaty, surrounded by iron and steel works and mikrorayony of apartment blocks, and beset by the typical problems of a post-Soviet industrial city. About half of its estimated 140,000 German population, many of them labour camp descendants, had left for Germany by 1994.

Orientation & Information

The train and bus stations are next door to each other on the main street, Bukhar Zhirov (formerly Sovietsky prospekt). To the left of the bus station is a visitors' centre run by Yassaui (Kazakstan Intourist).

The bookshop on the corner of Bukhar Zhirov and Mira has a Russian-language Karaganda encyclopaedia which is full of maps. The shop may also have loose city maps.

The Qaraghandy telephone code is 3212.

Things to See & Do

No-one comes here who doesn't have to, but if you're here anyway, have a look at the Central Park at the corner of Bukhar Zhirov and Mira facing the Dvorets Gornyakov (Miners' Culture Palace). The park has play-

grounds, a café and restaurant, and art and sculpture exhibitions. There's a **history museum** on Yurabaev near the Kafe Botagos, open Monday to Friday.

Out of town, well, you can visit a coalmine. The one at **Shakhtinsk**, 40 km west, is an old Intourist standby, but **Kostenko**, 25 km north, might be more interesting – it's the region's most successful mine, employing 400 miners in a 140 km warren of tunnels as deep as 476 metres. The miners have a fine heated swimming pool but that doesn't mean they always get paid.

At **Spassk** village, about 40 km from Qaraghandy, is a cemetery where about 4000 foreigners who died in the camps are buried. The French ambassador laid a wreath in 1994 to 32 French citizens known to lie here.

Places to Stay & Eat

The least expensive central hotel is the *Hotel Karaganda* at Bukhar Zhirov 63. The *Hotel Kazakstan* (☎ 57-70-23) at Bukhar Zhirov 42 is more expensive and has poor service. The *Hotel Chayka* at Krivoguza 36, also near the centre, was once the Communist Party's hotel. It's now owned by the Qaraghandy Coal Authority and is still very plush – though it may lack water and/or electricity and be near-empty. A suite costs around US$80 per person.

All these hotels have restaurants and bars. The Chayka has a café too. Other restaurants worth trying include the *Orbita* next to the TsUM department store, and *Kafe Botagos* on Yurabaev.

You can buy Korean salads at the *bazar*, reached by bus Nos 52 and 70 and trolleybus Nos 2, 3, 6 and 7 from Bukhar Zhirov.

Things to Buy

The Azia shop on Bukhar Zhirov at the corner of Lenin has a good selection of souvenirs.

Getting There & Away

Qaraghandy has daily flights to/from Almaty and a few a week to/from other Kazakstan cities such as Shymkent, Semey and Atyrau. There are buses to/from Almaty (1059 km, about 20 hours, US$26) and Aqmola (four hours). Trains run about three times daily to/from Almaty, at least daily to/from Aqmola, Petropavl and Qostanay, and most days to/from Zhambyl, Shymkent, Tashkent and Yekaterinburg.

Getting Around

Bus No 152 goes from the airport to the train and bus stations – a one hour ride.

AQMOLA
АҚМОЛА

Population: 300,000

Until the 1950s Aqmola, 220 km north-west of Qaraghandy, was a tiny mining town. Then Nikita Khrushchev announced his Virgin Lands scheme to turn 250,000 sq km of Kazakstan steppe into wheat fields. Aqmola became the project's capital and was renamed Tselinograd (Virgin Lands City). An influx of Russians and others from the western USSR came to work here. Despite wind erosion which turned a lot of the new wheat fields back into steppe, Aqmola is still the centre of a very important grain-growing region. After Kazakstan's independence, it got back its old name (which means White Tomb).

Aqmola may yet achieve even greater fame: in 1994 President Nazarbaev named it, to universal scepticism, as Kazakstan's future capital, to replace Almaty by the year 2000. Nazarbaev cited Aqmola's more central and less earthquake-prone location, and better rail links with Russia, among its advantages.

It's a friendly and fairly low-rise town, with some attractive tree-lined streets, but prone to strong steppe winds and harsh winters. The population is around 70% Russian, Ukrainian and German, and 30% Kazak.

Orientation & Information

The main streets are ulitsa Mira, which links the train and bus stations to the central square with its big Lenin statue, and ulitsa Tselinakov.

You can change money at the air ticket office at ulitsa Mira 24, at Turanbank at ulitsa Revolyutsia 61, or at the long-distance telephone office. The main post office is behind the Hotel Ishim at the corner of Oktyabrskaya ulitsa and ulitsa Lenina, with the long-distance telephone office across the street. The Aqmola telephone code is 31722.

There's a Yassaui (Kazakstan Intourist) office (☎ 2-57-53) in the Hotel Ishim.

Things to See

The local history museum at Komsomolskaya ulitsa 107 is particularly proud of its pictures of Khrushchev, who was a frequent visitor to Aqmola and is still popular here. The home of the Soviet-era Kazak writer Saken Seyfullin at the corner of Oktyabrskaya ulitsa and ulitsa Revolyutsia is a museum too. The main park is across Ishim river from the central square.

Places to Stay

The *Hotel Turist* (☎ 6-14-38) on ulitsa Tselinakov is a bargain with rooms for US$10 or less, and a small café and bar. To find it from the train and bus stations, head along ulitsa Mira and turn left on the last intersecting street, Komsomolskaya ulitsa, then right on ulitsa Tselinakov.

The *Hotel Ishim* (☎ 2-50-50) on the central square at ulitsa Mira 8 has decent rooms ranging from about US$25 to US$40 a double, including breakfast. It has a cosy beer bar.

Places to Eat

Politicians, bureaucrats and diplomats worrying about moving from Almaty to Aqmola have one consolation: Aqmola is the pizza capital of the north. The hip place to eat is the seemingly nameless *pizza café* behind a big iron fence at ulitsa Mira 12. Actually the pizza is microwaved and not the best in town, but the beer and Coke are good. Expect to spend about US$2.

The *Pitstsa Restoran*, down an alley beside the drama theatre at Komsomolskaya ulitsa 17, has more microwaved pizza but at least is cheap and friendly. The best place is the *Kipchak* in a big brick building with no street number on Studentsky prospekt – everyone knows it. Service is friendly: offerings include good un-microwaved pizza and beer on tap and you can eat for US$4 to US$5. The *Ganover* restaurant at ulitsa Tselinakov 13 has good food, including pizza, at moderate prices.

In a more traditional vein, the *Tereza* restaurant at ulitsa Mira 20 does good beef stroganov, and draught beer too, though service is poor. Count on about US$2.50 per person.

There's a promising *Chinese restaurant* at Kazakhskaya ulitsa 22. Shashlyk is available in the bazar, and there are several street stands doling out manty.

Getting There & Away

There's an air ticket office at ulitsa Mira 24 and a train ticket office at Komsomolskaya ulitsa 25. Flights go to/from Almaty daily and if you're lucky to/from a few other Kazakstan cities. Buses run to/from Qaraghandy (four hours, US$4) and elsewhere. Trains go to/from Qaraghandy, Almaty (24 hours, kupeynyy US$38 foreigners, US$20 local) and Kökshetau (five hours) at least twice daily; and to/from Petropavl, Qostanay (16 hours) and Moscow (60 hours) at least daily. There's service to/from Pavlodar, Zhambyl, Shymkent, Tashkent and Yekaterinburg on most days.

Getting Around

Bus No 10 runs infrequently between the airport and ulitsa Tselinakov. A taxi is about US$4. From the train and bus stations, bus Nos 9 and 25 and trolleybus Nos 2, 3, 4 and 5 go along ulitsa Mira to the town centre. Taxis are numerous and cost about US$0.25 a km.

AROUND AQMOLA

About 150 km south-west of Aqmola **Kurgalzhino nature reserve** includes both virgin feather-grass steppe and numerous malarious lakes which make it a water bird habitat of major importance. The largest, salty Lake Tenghiz, supports a breeding colony of 30,000 or more greater flamingoes – the

world's most northerly habitat of these graceful birds, which migrate to the Caspian Sea at the end of their breeding season. The reserve is undeveloped for visitors but you can get a bus to the town of Kurgalzhinsky (two to three hours, US$2.50) then look for a driver there.

Around **Yermentau**, 135 km north-east of Aqmola, there are granite cliffs popular with climbers, and some fine scenery. It's two hours by daily trains from Aqmola.

Lake Burabay (see the following section) is another outing from Aqmola.

KÖKSHETAU & LAKE BURABAY
КӨКШЕТАУ & БҰРАБАЙ КӨЛ

Population: 130,000

Kökshetau (Russian: Kokchetav) is another wheat-growing centre, 300 km north of Aqmola. The region is optimistically known as Kazakstan's 'Little Switzerland' owing to a few areas of lakes, trees and hills dotting the otherwise flat and treeless steppe. The best known of these is Lake Burabay (Russian: Borovoe Ozero), 95 km south-east of the town: the scenery's nice and it's popular with locals but hardly a place you'd travel far for.

Places to Stay & Eat

The best hotel in Kökshetau is the *Hotel Novy Kokshetau* on the central square, opposite the large Lenin statue. One long block away, opposite the department store, is the *Hotel Dostyk*. The Novy Kokchetau has a mediocre restaurant and the Dostyk an irregularly open one. The *Argonaut* restaurant in the town centre just off ulitsa Karla Marxa has fairly good, inexpensive food and occasionally live music. The *Vitas*, on a hilltop outside the centre, is good if you fancy music and dancing. It's open in the evenings from Wednesday to Sunday. Get there by taxi.

Lodging at Lake Burabay is reportedly expensive.

Getting There & Away

Flights are scheduled to Kökshetau from Almaty daily, and from a few other places a few times a week. Trains run to/from

Petropavl, Aqmola, Qaraghandy and Almaty (29 hours) daily.

To reach Lake Burabay, get a train to Shchuchinsk on the Aqmola-Kökshetau line, then a bus (30 minutes, US$1) from the bus station beside Shchuchinsk train station. Daily trains run to Shchuchinsk from both Aqmola (four hours) and Kökshetau (1½ hours).

PETROPAVL
ПЕТРОПАВЛ

Population: 240,000

Petropavl (Russian: Petropavlovsk) is Kazakstan's most northerly city, 175 km north of Kökshetau and just 60 km from the Russian border. It's an important rail junction, at the meeting of the north-south line through central Kazakstan with a branch of the Trans-Siberian Railway, and Kazakstan's busiest freight terminal. It's also on the highway linking the Russian cities of Kurgan (270 km west) and Omsk (260 km east).

With a 90% Russian population, Petropavl is as much a part of Siberia as of Kazakstan, and is a centre of ethnic Russian discontent. In 1990 the Russian writer Alexandr Solzhenitsyn proposed that this, and other northerly regions of Kazakstan, be transferred to Russia – a dream which many locals still harbour. Climatically it's certainly Siberian, with harsh winters and mild summers. The surrounding area has many lakes and a fair amount of forest.

Some suspicion of foreigners lingers among the city's officials, perhaps because of the four major defence plants in Petropavl (though they're all virtually closed now, with sad consequences for the local economy), and you at least need to have the place named on your visa if you want to stay here.

Petropavl is older and architecturally more diverse than most northern Kazakstan cities.

Orientation & Information

The main street is east-west ulitsa Lenina, a busy, tree-lined, pedestrian mall for much of its length.

There are many currency exchange kiosks and offices, the biggest at the corner of ulitsa Lenina and ulitsa Kirova. Better rates are offered by moneychangers in the central aisle of the bazar. The main post office, open daily, is opposite the drama theatre on ulitsa Pushkina. The best place for long-distance telephone calls is another post office on the corner of ulitsa Kirova and ulitsa Krasnoarmeyskaya (closed Sunday).

Yassaui (☎ 33-77-40, 33-27-98) is at ulitsa Lenina 70

The Petropavl telephone code is 3152.

Things to See

The **history & local studies museum**, in an attractive red brick building on the corner of ulitsa Lenina and ulitsa Kirova, traces the growth of Petropavl from its origins as a Cossack fort, built to protect Russia's Siberian frontier against the Kazaks. There's also a nature section with the usual stuffed animals.

The **art museum**, in a park near the corner of ulitsa Internatsionalnaya and ulitsa Kuybysheva, is housed in easily the city's most interesting building – an old log construction that used to belong to a rich lumber merchant. Exhibits change quarterly.

Central Park, occupying several blocks in the city centre, has a small zoo, rides, and a café. It's populated by mothers and small children by day, and by teenagers on summer evenings, when there may be live music.

Places to Stay

The best is the *Hotel Kyzyl Zhar* (☎ 36-11-83), an unmissable 11 storey block on the corner of ulitsa Lenina and ulitsa Kuybysheva. Rooms with private bathroom are about US$50. You need an advance reservation, which may even have to be made for you by a Petropavl resident: Yassaui might be able to help.

The *Hotel Voskhod* (☎ 36-43-20), three blocks west along ulitsa Lenina from the Kyzyl Zhar, on the corner of ulitsa Gorkogo, is not as nice. It may or may not accept foreigners and the price has to be negotiated.

Places to Eat

Tutti at the corner of ulitsa Dzhumabaeva and ulitsa Proletarskaya is a little café with good Italian ice cream, good coffee and loud music. The rest of the fare is average – a meal is around US$6.

There's good shashlyk, plus fruit and vegetables, available from stalls in the *bazar* between the Central Park and the train station. Just, on the corner of ulitsa Krasnoarmeyskaya and ulitsa Kamanina, the *Gril-Bar Valday* is a neat, quiet restaurant with a simple menu costing up to US$10 a meal.

Kafe Ishim on the ground floor of the building on the corner of ulitsa Dzhumabaeva and ulitsa Lenina is a pleasant, reasonably priced place with something like a real bar. Avoid the cavernous banquet hall upstairs.

The *Rus* restaurant on the corner of ulitsa Pushkina and ulitsa Krasnoarmeyskaya has good service, moderate food, high prices, and live jazz once in a while.

The most expensive place is the *Bavaria* restaurant at the corner of ulitsa Teatralnaya and ulitsa Karim Sutyusheva. Décor seems to represent the Russian image of a Bavarian beer hall – dark and gaudy, no doubt to the liking of mafia customers. Food and service are good: dinner with a couple of beers will be US$15 to US$20. It doesn't get going till about 9 pm, though.

Service in the Hotel Kyzyl Zhar restaurant is appalling.

Getting There & Away

Air and train tickets are sold at a ticket office on the corner of ulitsa Kirova and ulitsa Lenina.

The only flights at the time of research were to/from Almaty three times a week, but others to/from Semey and Moscow were due to start.

Daily trains go to/from Almaty via Kökshetau, Aqmola and Qaraghandy. There are also several daily trains heading across Siberia – west to Yekaterinburg and Moscow or St Petersburg, east to Omsk and beyond.

Getting Around

The airport is a 20 minute ride from the centre off Surgeevenoe shosse. A taxi is US$5 or so.

The train station is in the south-east of the city on ulitsa Ruzaeva, about a 20 minute walk from the centre or a ride on bus Nos 1 or 2 or trolleybus Nos 2, 19 or 22.

QOSTANAY
КОСТАНАЙ

Population: 250,000

Qostanay (Russian: Kustanay) is another Virgin Lands wheat centre and also an industrial town processing the vast iron-ore deposits of the Qostanay basin, discovered by chance in the 1950s when a pilot flying over the region noticed his compass whirling crazily about for no apparent reason. The town is on the Tobol river in a remote corner of Kazakstan, 700 km north-west of Aqmola and 450 km west of Kökshetau. The nearest big city is Chelyabinsk in Russia, 300 km north-west. Only about 15% of the town population is Kazak, the rest being mainly Russian, Ukrainian and German.

Orientation & Information

The main drag is ulitsa Lenina, with the train station at its west end. Two blocks are pedestrianised. From the bus station, ulitsa Sverdlova runs north to the centre.

The main post office and the long-distance telephone office are both on ulitsa Lenina, either side of the corner of ulitsa Altynsarina. You can change money in either.

The Qostanay telephone code is 3142.

Things to See

Opposite the TsUM department store on ulitsa Lenina, there's a **museum** dedicated to Ibray Altynsarin, a 19th century Kazak educationalist who developed the Kazak Cyrillic alphabet and pioneered public schooling.

There's an **art gallery** and shop next to the theatre on ulitsa Bagamavetova, between ulitsa Lenina and ulitsa Gogolya.

The main entrance to the **Central Park** is on ulitsa Altynsarina, just off ulitsa Lenina.

KAZAKSTAN

If you should happen to be here between December and March, check out the ice castles and carvings along ulitsa Lenina.

Places to Stay & Eat

Hotels are the *Hotel Tselina* (☎ 54-14-13) at the corner of Sovietskaya ulitsa and ulitsa Pushkina, and the *Hotel Aray* around the corner on ulitsa Tarana. Both are a short walk from ulitsa Lenina.

Kafe Kolos on ulitsa Lenina by the Detsky Mir shop does good chicken at reasonable prices. The *pivnoy bar* on ulitsa 5 Aprelya, a block from ulitsa Sverdlova, has good cheap salads and beer on tap. The *President Bar* in the Hotel Tselina has some food, but is expensive.

Getting There & Away

The air ticket office is on ulitsa Sverdlova near the corner of ulitsa Lenina. There are daily flights to/from Almaty, and most days to/from Moscow, plus a few scheduled to/from other cities such as Atyrau.

Qostanay is on a rail route between Moscow (52 hours), Samara and Aqmola (16 hours), with services in both directions every day. Trains go to/from Almaty (40 hours) every two days.

Getting Around

Bus No 20 links the airport to the town centre. A taxi is about US$6. From the train station, any bus or trolleybus will take you to the centre; from the bus station, any trolleybus will take you there.

Uzbekistan
Узбекистан

Uzbekistan (officially Uzbekiston Jumhuriyati), in the ancient cradle between the Amu-Darya and Syr-Darya rivers, is certainly the most historically fascinating of the Central Asian republics. Within it are some of the oldest towns in the world, some of the Silk Road's main centres and most of Central Asia's architectural attractions. Samarkand – capital of the cultured empire of Timur (Tamerlane) – and Bukhara and Khiva are virtual outdoor museums.

Uzbekistan likes to see itself as the most important of the former Soviet Central Asian republics in addition to being the 'spiritual home' of sizeable Uzbek minorities in the other republics (and in Afghanistan), the only republic sharing borders with all the others, and increasingly fulfilling the role of regional gendarme. Uzbeks are the most self-confident of the region's peoples, historically settled, pious and community-minded.

The hell of it is, the republic with arguably the most to discover has the worst attitude towards visitors. Politically the old USSR is alive and well here, and for individuals not under the wing of the state travel conglomerate Uzbektourism, travel tends to be an endless series of petty bureaucratic irritations and not-so-petty official hassles. Fortunately, the farther you get from the capital, Tashkent, the more relaxed, friendly and helpful people become.

History
The land along the upper Amu-Darya, Syr-Darya and their tributaries has always been different from the rest of Central Asia – more settled than nomadic, with patterns of land use and communality that changed little from the time of the Achaemenids (6th century BC) right into the 19th century. An attitude of permanence and proprietorship

Highlights
- Bukhara old town: late breakfasts and lazy afternoons at Labi-hauz plaza, where it's as if the 20th century never arrived, nor the 19th, 18th, 17th ...; the Kalan mosque and Mir-i-Arab medressa, a working ensemble with a live heart; Ismail Samani mausoleum, a 1000 year old confection that changes by the hour; and the mausoleum of Bakhautdin Naqshband, serene hub of underground Islam during the Soviet era.
- Samarkand: the Registan, reduced to a museum piece but admittedly one of the world's most spectacular museum pieces; Shahi-Zinda, a sublime, spirit-filled street of tombs.
- Khiva old town: except for its lifeless central strip, perhaps the best place in Central Asia to let your imagination go; almost fitting the image of a medieval Silk Road town, with few modern buildings to spoil the effect.
- Shakhimardan: from the Ferghana Valley, a peaceful secret door into the Altay mountains, and one of Central Asia's most venerated holy places.

still sets the people of the region apart, and to a large extent the history of Central Asia *is* the history of present-day Uzbekistan.

Ancient Empires The region was part of several very old Persian states, including Bactria, Khorezm and Sogdiana. Into Cyrus the Great's Achaemenid Empire came Alexander the Great in the 4th century BC. He

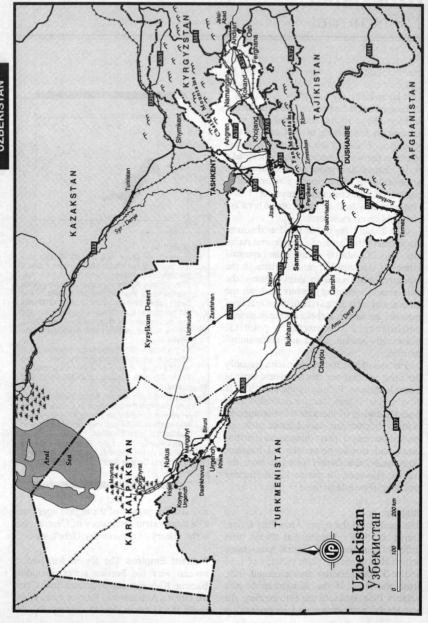

Uzbekistan
Узбекистан

stopped near Samarkand and married Roxana, the daughter of a local chieftain. Under the Kushans, Buddhism took hold and the Silk Road brought peaceful contact with the wider world and facilitated the growth of wealthy, culturally diverse towns. With its decline came a brief return to Persia under the Sassanians.

Then out of the northern steppe in the 6th century AD came the Western Turks – the western branch of the empire of the so-called Kök (Blue) Turks. They soon grew attached to life here and abandoned their wandering ways. The Arabs brought Islam and a written alphabet in the 8th century but found Central Asia too big and restless to govern.

A return to the Persian fold came with the Samanid Dynasty in the 9th and 10th centuries. Its capital, Bukhara, was the centre of an intellectual, religious and commercial renaissance. In the 11th century the Ghaznavids moved into the southern regions. For a time the Turkic Khorezmshahs dominated Central Asia from what is now Konye-Urgench in Turkmenistan, but their fun was cut short, and the region's elegant oases ravaged, by Jenghiz Khan.

Central Asia again became truly 'central' with the rise of Timur, the ruthless warrior and would-be patron of the arts who fashioned a glittering Islamic capital at Samarkand.

The Uzbeks By contrast with the familiar history of the land they live on, little is known of early Uzbek history. At the time the Golden Horde was founded, Shibaqan or Shayban, a grandson of Jenghiz Khan, inherited what is today northern Kazakstan and adjacent parts of Russia. The greatest khan of these Mongol Shaybani tribes (and probably the one under whom they swapped paganism for Islam) was Özbeg or Uzbek (ruled 1313-40). By the end of the 14th century these tribes had begun to name themselves after him.

The Uzbeks began moving south-east, mixing with sedentary Turkic tribes and adopting the Turkic language, reaching the Syr-Darya in the mid-1400s. Following an internal schism (which gave birth to the proto-Kazaks), the Uzbeks pulled themselves together under Muhammad Shaybani and thundered down upon the remnants of Timur's empire. By 1510 all of Transoxiana, 'the land beyond the Oxus' (now Amu-Darya) to the Jaxartes (what the Arabs called Mawarannahr and the Uzbeks Movarounnakhr; now Syr-Darya) belonged to the Uzbeks, as it has since. They ruled at this time from Bukhara, with a separate line in Khorezm, at Khiva.

The greatest (and last) of the Shaybanid khans, responsible for some of Bukhara's finest architecture, was Abdullah II, who ruled from 1538 until his death in 1598. After this, as the Silk Road fell into disuse, the empire unravelled under the Shaybanids' distant cousins, the Astrakhanids. For a time Khorezm and the Astrakhanid lands again became part of Persia, after the warlord Nadir Shah defeated Bukhara and Khiva in 1740.

The Astrakhanid throne was usurped by the first of the Bukhara emirs, Masum Shah Murad, in 1785. By the start of the 19th century the entire region was dominated by three weak, feuding Uzbek city-states – Khiva, Bukhara and a Bukhara breakaway, Kokand.

The Russians Arrive In the early 18th century the khan of Khiva made an offer to Peter the Great of Russia – to become his vassal in return for help against marauding Turkmen and Kazak tribes – stirring the first Russian interest in Central Asia. Peter's appetite had been whetted by Khiva's potential as a staging post for trade with India, by reports of gold along the Amu-Darya, and by a mistaken idea that the Amu-Darya could be made navigable right into the heart of Central Asia (by destroying the 'dams' which he believed forced it to run into the Aral Sea instead of the Caspian Sea). But by the time the Russians got round to marching on Khiva in 1717, the khan no longer wanted Russian protection, and after a show of hospitality he had almost the entire 4000-strong force slaughtered.

Their fingers burnt, the Russians only gradually renewed interest, starting with trade, mainly with Bukhara – buying raw cotton in exchange for textiles and tools. The slave market in Bukhara and Khiva was the excuse for further Russian visits – to free a few unfortunate Russian settlers and travellers. In 1801 the insane Tsar Paul sent 22,000 Cossacks on a madcap mission to drive the British out of India, with orders to free the slaves en route. Fortunately for all but the slaves, Paul was assassinated and the army recalled while struggling across the Kazak steppes in midwinter.

The next try, by Tsar Nicholas I in 1839 to 1840, was really a bid to pre-empt expansion into Central Asia by Britain, which had just taken Afghanistan, although Khiva's Russian slaves were the pretext on which General Perovsky's 5200 men and 10,000 camels set out from Orenburg. In January 1840, a British officer, Captain James Abbott, arrived in Khiva (having travelled from Herat in Afghan disguise) offering to negotiate the slaves' release on the khan's behalf, thus nullifying the Russians' excuse for coming.

Unknown to the khan the Russian force had already turned back, in the face of the worst winter for ages on the steppes. He agreed to send Abbott to the tsar with an offer to release the slaves in return for an end to Russian military expeditions against Khiva. Incredibly, Abbot made it to St Petersburg.

In search of news of Abbott, Lieutenant Richmond Shakespear reached Khiva the following June and convinced the khan to unilaterally release all Russian slaves in Khiva and even give them an armed escort to the nearest Russian outpost, on the eastern Caspian. Russian gratitude was doubtlessly mingled with fury over one of the Great Game's boldest propaganda coups. (For more information see Great Game in the Khiva section later in this chapter.)

But when the Russians finally got themselves together 25 years later, the khanates' towns fell like dominoes – Tashkent in 1865 to General Mikhail Chernyaev, Samarkand and Bukhara in 1868, Khiva in 1873, and Kokand in 1875 to General Konstantin Kaufman.

Soviet Daze Even into the 20th century, most Central Asians identified themselves ethnically as Turks or Persians. The connection between 'Uzbek' and 'Uzbekistan' is very much a Soviet matter. Following the outbreak of the Revolution in 1917 and the infamous sacking of Kokand in 1918, the Bolsheviks proclaimed the Autonomous Soviet Socialist Republic (SSR) of Turkestan. Temporarily forced out by counter-revolutionary troops and *basmachi* guerillas, they returned two years later and the Khiva and Bukhara khanates were forcibly replaced with 'People's Republics'.

Then in October 1924 the whole map was redrawn on ethnic grounds, and the Uzbeks suddenly had a 'homeland', an official identity and a literary language. The Uzbek SSR changed shape and composition over the years as it suited Moscow, hiving off Tajikistan in 1929, acquiring Karakalpakstan from Russia in 1936, getting bits of the Hungry Steppe from Kazakstan in 1956 and 1963 and losing some in 1971.

For rural Uzbeks, the main impacts of Soviet rule were the forced and often bloody collectivisation of the republic's mainstay, agriculture, and the massive shift to cotton cultivation. Life hardly changed in other ways. The Uzbek intelligentsia and much of the republic's political leadership was decimated by Stalin's purges. This and the traditional Central Asian respect for authority meant that by the 1980s *glasnost* and *perestroyka* would hardly trickle down here, and few significant reforms took place.

Towards Independence Uzbekistan's first serious non-Communist popular movement, Birlik (Unity), was formed by Tashkent intellectuals in 1989 over issues that included Uzbek as an official language and the effects of the cotton monoculture. It immediately began gathering support, eventually claiming 1.5 million members, but was barred from contesting the election in February 1990 for the Uzbek Supreme

The Great Cotton Flim-Flam

The feudal boss of the Communist Party of Uzbekistan, Sharaf Rashidov, was at the head of a mammoth, lengthy swindle over cotton harvests in the late 1970s and early 1980s, during the years of Brezhnev (who himself rose to power from a Central Asia base). After spy satellites revealed that many 'cotton fields' were in fact empty, it was discovered that cotton production figures for Uzbekistan had been massively falsified for years, that cotton was being sold off on the black market, and that some 5000 million roubles had been embezzled.

Rashidov was never prosecuted, but some 50,000 lesser officials were dismissed between 1984 and 1988. A well-publicised trial in 1988 convicted one of Rashidov's protectors, Brezhnev's son-in-law Yury Churbanov, of abuses when he was Uzbekistan's Deputy Interior Minister, including amassing several million dollars in bribes. The former chairman of the Uzbek Council of Ministers, Narmakhonmardi Khudayberdiev, was jailed for 11 years for taking bribes.

Another figure in the scandal was the chairman of the Pap Agroindustrial complex, Akhmajon Adylov, who took a page straight out of the Emir of Bukhara's book – running a virtual slave labour plantation with the help of a private army, keeping a bevy of concubines, and torturing those who crossed him.

After the August 1991 coup in Moscow, the Russian Supreme Court dropped the charges against Adylov and the legislature pardoned Khudayberdiev. In August 1993, Russian president Boris Yeltsin pardoned Churbanov, who was halfway through his 12 year sentence. It's a fairly clear indication of how little has changed, that Rashidov (who was born in Karimov's own neighbourhood of Jizak) is now being posthumously 'rehabilitated' in Uzbekistan, and presented as a defender of Uzbek interests against Moscow. ■

Soviet (legislature). The resulting Communist-dominated body elected Islam Karimov, the First Secretary of the Communist Party of Uzbekistan (CPUz), to the new post of executive president.

During the abortive coup in Moscow in August 1991, Karimov was conspicuously quiet, but within days of its failure the Supreme Soviet on 31 August declared Uzbekistan independent. Soon afterward the CPUz reinvented itself as the Popular Democratic Party of Uzbekistan (PDPU), inheriting all of its predecessor's property and control apparatus, most of its ideology, and of course its leader, Karimov.

In December 1991 Uzbekistan held its first direct presidential elections, which Karimov won with 86% of the vote. His only rival was a poet named Muhammad Salih, running for the small, figurehead opposition party Erk (Will or Freedom) party, who got 12%.

The real opposition groups, Birlik and the Islamic Renaissance Party (IRP), and all other parties with a religious platform, had been forbidden to take part.

Uzbekistan Today The following years have seen Karimov's power grow, and dissent shrivel – thanks to travel and publishing restrictions, police harassment, imprisonment on trumped up charges, and a not inconsiderable amount of violence. In June 1992 a Birlik founder, Abdurakhim Pulatov, had his skull fractured by 'unidentified assailants' with iron bars, outside a police station where he had just been interrogated. Other Birlik leaders have been similarly assaulted. The criminal code has been amended to give the police wider powers against 'antigovernment activity'. Hundreds of activists have been arrested, and some jailed.

On 8 December 1992, the day the Uzbek Supreme Soviet adopted a new constitution committed to multi-party democracy and human rights, Pulatov's brother Abdumannov, founder of the Uzbek Human Rights Organisation, was abducted from a conference in the Kyrgyz capital, Bishkek, and charged with sedition. A few weeks later, Birlik was banned, and has now been essentially crushed.

Erk is officially still legal, though members have been hounded from the legislature, bumped out of jobs, detained and interrogated, and their newspaper banned. In May 1993 they simply agreed to stop criticising the regime. The IRP, with powerful support in the Ferghana Valley, has gone underground. Most opposition leaders live in exile in Moscow.

'Multi-party' elections were held in December 1994 for a new, streamlined parliament. The two participating parties were the PDPU and another set up with Karimov's blessing, Vatan Tarikiati or the National Progress Party. In March 1995, voters agreed to extend Karimov's term until 2000. He ran unopposed.

Suppression of dissent is officially called a temporary necessity in a country new to democratic traditions, with a civil war and Islamic fundamentalism right across the border in Tajikistan, but it's hard to see how a democratic framework could grow here. It's no accident that Uzbekistan's newly adopted cultural role model is Timur (whose image has replaced Karl Marx's head in Tashkent's central square).

Geography

Uzbekistan sprawls over 447,400 sq km (about the size of Sweden), third in size after Kazakstan and Turkmenistan but the most populous (and densely populated) of the five former Soviet republics. Well over two-thirds of it – most of the central and western part – is flat, monotonous desert or steppe: the Ustyurt plateau in the far west with its salt marshes and streams that go nowhere, and the vast, barren Kyzylkum (Red Sands) desert in the middle. The only faint relief here is the delta where what remains of the Amu-Darya empties into what remains of the Aral Sea (see the Environment section in the Facts About the Region chapter).

By contrast, eastern Uzbekistan tilts upward towards the mountains of Kyrgyzstan – Tashkent's Chatkal mountains running into the western Tian Shan range, and Samarkand's Fan mountains and a mass of smaller ranges in the south-east flowing into the Pamir Alay.

The life-giving rivers all rise in these mountains. Central Asia's greatest waterway, the broad Amu-Darya, forms much of Uzbekistan's short border with Afghanistan and its long one with Turkmenistan, before a trickle enters the Aral Sea, the rest having been bled off by irrigation. The region's other defining artery, the Syr-Darya, originating in the Ferghana Valley from two rivers rising in Kyrgyzstan, arcs into Kazakstan on its way to the Aral Sea. Arguably the most valuable river is the Zeravshan, nourisher of ancient Bukhara and Samarkand; theoretically the Amu-Darya's biggest tributary, it actually dies in the desert. Most other rivers are either emptied by irrigation or swallowed by the desert.

The bulk of Uzbekistan's population, and its richest farmland, are in gaps in the mountains (especially the Ferghana Valley), on the alluvial plains at their feet, and in the Amu-Darya, Syr-Darya and Zeravshan valleys.

Fully 37% of the country – the worst of it, probably – is occupied by the autonomous Republic of Karakalpakstan (see the Karakalpakstan aside in the Nukus section in this chapter).

Government

Formally speaking, under the terms of its December 1992 constitution Uzbekistan is a secular, democratic presidential republic. The president, who is both supreme executive and head of state, is directly elected for a five year term and may serve at most two consecutive terms. The president appoints the government (the Cabinet of Ministers), subject to approval by the legislature; its chairperson becomes prime minister. The highest legislative body is the Ali Majlis (Supreme Assembly), whose 150 members are also elected for five-year terms. The Ali Majlis can be dissolved by the president with the approval of the Constitutional Court. The country is administratively divided into 12 provinces (viloyati) plus the Republic of Karakalpakstan.

In reality, while Uzbekistan is most certainly

UZBEKISTAN

secular, with a determined separation between religion and state, it's decidedly not 'democratic' in any sense that westerners understand. The man ultimately in charge of everything from municipal gardeners' salaries to gold production quotas is President Islam Karimov – as he was, under a different title, even before independence. Trends towards pluralism evident in other Central Asian republics are absent here (see the preceding History section). The president smiles from roadside billboards, with faintly Soviet epigrams like 'Uzbekistan has a bright future' and 'This beautiful land is for all of us'.

Social control is ensured by the government's grip on the traditional network of urban districts (mahallahs), a concept unique to Uzbeks in Central Asia. The neighbourhood in which an Uzbek is raised is a web of intimate social ties; neighbours attend one another's weddings, celebrations and funerals. Advice on all matters is sought from a revered elder (aksakal), whose authority is conferred by the community. The government has usurped these structures by employing aksakals as district custodians and informants – to the extent that you cannot even sell your flat without their permission.

Economy

Uzbekistan's basically agrarian economy is dominated by two realities. The first is the massive artificial irrigation and fertilisation of arid and semi-arid areas needed to sustain production of its major crop, raw cotton, and the resulting severe ecological and economic strains. The second (true of the other Central Asian republics too) is the crumbling of the old Soviet trade system, leaving the country a producer of far more raw materials than finished goods, despite industrialisation around Tashkent, Samarkand, Bukhara and the Ferghana Valley.

Uzbekistan faces the daunting job of curing its addiction to the cotton market and returning its rich soil to food production. This republic alone provided two-thirds of all the cotton grown in the USSR (plus a startling 60% of its fruit and vegetables). Its present annual output of 1.5 million tonnes makes it the world's second or third largest cotton producer.

Other major agricultural sectors are fruit and rice, especially in the Ferghana Valley, which is also the main centre for silkworm cultivation. The Ferghana Valley was self-sufficient in wheat, fruit and vegetables before the Revolution of 1917, says an Uzbek official there. Presently grain is grown mainly in the higher, less fertile plains, but only enough to meet about 30% of the country's requirements. The dry west is used mostly for animal husbandry – most famously Karakul sheep, with their velvety wool of many colours, in Bukhara province.

Surprisingly, Uzbekistan is the world's eighth largest producer of gold, extracting some 65 metric tonnes annually, most of it from the Murantau mine in the Kyzylkum desert, said to be the world's biggest opencast gold mine. Other natural resources are coal (around Angren), natural gas (around Bukhara), petroleum (reserves in the Ferghana Valley, Bukhara province and Karakalpakstan), uranium and other non-ferrous and rare-earth metals. Though some 12% of the country is forest, timber and lumber are still imported. Most electricity comes from thermal plants, a bit from hydro-electric stations.

But Uzbekistan is still a net importer of electricity, machinery, building materials, food, oil and gas, and with limited hard currency reserves to pay for it. Its main exports are of course raw cotton (over 40% of the value of all agricultural output) and cotton thread, cloth and clothing, plus some non-ferrous metals. Most revenue from gold production is said to go towards purchases of food, fuel and spare parts. Over four-fifths of Uzbekistan's trade is still with CIS countries (although it has refused to sell any more cotton to Russia, accusing it of buying at deflated Soviet-era prices and reselling on the world market).

The economy has been on the slide since independence, thanks to knock-on effects from the chaos in Tajikistan, and to the absence of any significant market reforms in comparison to Kazakstan and Kyrgyzstan. Jolted by a GDP that fell 10% both in 1992 and 1993, the government announced measures to encourage foreign investment, including fewer import restrictions, a privatisation scheme, sales of public assets and a system of public share ownership, but little has happened yet. There has been no attempt to decollectivise agriculture or industry, and only the most hesitant stabs have been made at deregulation. The government's policy to gradually replace Russian workers with Central Asians has created a brain drain. Far from being 'free', farmers' markets are patrolled by police looking for 'speculators'.

President Karimov has decreed a goal of reducing the land area for cotton from 70% to 40%, shifting much of the difference to cereal grains. He also talks of joint-venture mills to capture value-added benefits (eg cloth and clothing have a many times greater value per original tonne of cotton than does the raw material). But the 715 state farms remain collectivised and state-serving, despite talk of cooperative and private farms and joint-stock companies.

To escape the 'rouble zone', Uzbekistan introduced *sum* coupons in November 1993, then a fully fledged (but not hard) *sum* currency in July 1994. But inflation continues, with prices outpacing wages. Though the government has accumulated a sizeable gold reserve in Swiss banks, it has refused to use any of it to stabilise the *sum*.

To the tourist's eye, produce in the bazars – at least in the bigger towns – seems modestly priced, diverse and of good quality. But UN figures portray Uzbekistan as one of the world's most poorly developed countries, with a mean monthly income of around US$50. When we were there, a typical monthly wage for an urban professional such as a university professor was less than a single tank of black market petrol, or 10 kg of meat, or an air ticket from Tashkent to Ferghana. Uzbek friends from the countryside said people there are in even more desperate straits.

Population & People

In 1995 an estimated 23 million people lived in Uzbekistan, of which Uzbeks made up 71%, Russians about 8%, Tajiks 5%, Kazaks 4%, Tatars 3%, Karakalpaks (see the Karakalpakstan aside) 2%, and Kyrgyz and Koreans about 1% each, plus smaller communities of Ukrainians and others. According to unofficial figures there were about 200,000 Arabs living in Kashkadarya province (around Qarshi) in 1990.

Some 40% of Uzbekistan's people are urban and 60% rural; 88% are Muslim (almost all Hanafi Sunni) and 10% Christian. Fully a third of them live in the Ferghana Valley, Central Asia's mostly densely populated region. The biggest towns, with estimated 1995 populations, are Tashkent (2.3 million), Samarkand (404,000), Namangan (360,000), Andijan (310,000), Bukhara (250,000), Ferghana (193,000) and Kokand (176,000).

The population growth rate is among the highest in the world, and in Central Asia second only to Tajikistan's. A typical rural family has nine or 10 children. Over half the population is under 15 years of age.

In the 1920s Stalin dismembered Turkestan and the Bukhara and Khorezm People's Republics and redrew the borders, ostensibly along ethnic lines but very often across them. The most blatant gerrymandering was in the Ferghana Valley (see the Ferghana Valley map) where, for example, majority-Uzbek Khojand ended up in Tajikistan, and majority-Uzbek Osh in Kyrgyzstan.

On the other hand, Samarkand, Bukhara, Qarshi and Termez went to Uzbekistan, although they are Tajik-speaking towns. But most people there call themselves Uzbeks, for the same reasons their parents or grandparents did in the 1920s, for their own protection or convenience. Says a young Tajik in Samarkand (quoted in the *International Herald Tribune*), 'In 1924 they started writing in our passports that we were all Uzbek. And if an old man insisted that, no, he was Tajik ... he ended up very far away from here.' Ethnicity remains a volatile company for tourism', is geared only for this kind of business, with inflated prices, generally second-rate services, no information outlets, and a degree of licensing control over private agencies that borders on strangulation. One friend called it the Ministry for the Prevention of Tourism.

Of course we've found exceptions, including the Uzbektourism offices in Ferghana and Nukus and the occasional open-minded hotel excursion bureau. But for professional, switched-on help and some comprehension of budget travel, you should try one of the growing number of private firms (listed under individual cities).

Dangers & Annoyances

This may not be a police state, but there are more police per square inch in Uzbekistan than anywhere else in Central Asia – on the streets, at provincial and town borders, in bus and train stations, even in the bazars – throwing their weight around, eager (and apparently free) to supplement their small salaries by discovering or inventing 'irregularities' for which they can 'fine' locals and visitors alike. The police of Namangan and Andijan in the Ferghana Valley appear to be the worst of an already bad lot. Group travellers, being paying guests of Uzbektourism, rarely experience any of this.

Assuming your papers *are* in order, there isn't much you can do but politely stand your ground. Try to avoid being taken somewhere out of public view. The objective of most detentions of westerners is simply money, and by means of intimidation rather than violence. If your money is buried deeply, and you're prepared to pull out a paperback and wait them out, your inquisitors will eventually give up.

Of course this may not work if you badly want to buy a ticket for the next bus out or to just move on down the road into the next province. In our experience, a forthright, friendly manner – starting right out with *salam aleykhum* and a handshake for those who appear to be in charge – is the best way

Uzbek men normally wear sombre colours, except for the bright sashes used to close their long, quilted coats.

subject here, so don't bring it up lightly. Many Tajik speakers feel these cities should never have been part of Uzbekistan, and there is still wild-eyed talk of taking them back.

See History in this section for more on the origins of the Uzbek people.

Officials & Paperwork

No control-obsessed state likes individual travellers, who make their plans a day at a time, go wherever they can and ask lots of questions. Uzbekistan would prefer that tourism be just a handy source of hard currency, confined to groups who spend freely and do as they're told. Uzbektourism, the country's big but moribund 'national to defuse a shakedown, whether you are male or female.

In religiously conservative areas, particularly Namangan and Andijan, western women have been sexually harassed (the US Peace Corps finally withdrew all its volunteers from the Uzbekistan parts of the Ferghana Valley after three women volunteers were assaulted).

Orientation
More than the other republics, Uzbekistan has tried to erase Soviet names completely (in perfect imitation of the Soviets themselves). Streets everywhere have been renamed, sometimes several times, since 1991, often with unpronounceable new names. Some names have merely been shifted to other streets. Russian Cyrillic script has been aggressively eliminated too; even the signs on buses and in stations have mostly gone over to Uzbek.

But many people – Russians and Uzbeks alike, including taxi drivers – and available maps still use old names, complete with Russian endings and Russian words for 'street' etc. In towns where these still seem to be the most common, we use them too. In Uzbek, a street is *kuchasi* (Russian *ulitsa*), an avenue *prospekti* (Russian *prospekt*), a boulevard *hiyoboni* (Russian *bulvar*), a square *maydoni* (Russian *ploshchad* or *skver*). In Karakalpakstan the words are different again.

Tashkent
Тошкент

Population: 2.3 million

Like it or not, Tashkent, the Uzbek capital, is Central Asia's hub – its biggest and worldliest city (the fourth biggest population in the old USSR after Moscow, St Petersburg and Kiev), bang in the middle of the Eurasian landmass, and better connected by international flights than any other city in the region.

Uzbekistan is not a user-friendly place, and likes its guests in pre-programmed, obedient pods, and here at the heart of the republic, individual travellers find the air of uptightness and administrative unwelcome palpable. Cheap accommodation is practically non-existent and staff are rarely polite; getting help is like pulling teeth (the *Economist* calls this 'the information-free capital'); and if you're a solo traveller, officials want to see your papers if you so much as ask the time of day.

Most visitors agree Tashkent is still the most 'Soviet' city in Central Asia. It's said that many of the region's anxious Slavs who won't or can't return to the Motherland are moving to the relative cultural security of Tashkent, which is still at least half Russian-speaking (if not Russian).

For a city of its size there isn't a lot to see, beyond museums. There are few signs of Tashkent's 2000 year history, thanks to a huge earthquake in 1966 and the subsequent enthusiasm of Soviet planners. Much of the truly old quarter has been bulldozed. But it's hard to visit Uzbekistan without passing through Tashkent, and there are consular, communications, medical and other facilities you can't find elsewhere in the republic, along with a busy (and pleasantly affordable) cultural life.

History
Tashkent's earliest incarnation may have been as the settlement of Ming-Uruk (Thousand Apricot Trees) in the 2nd or 1st century BC. Known variously since then as Chach, Shash, Shashkent and Binkent, by the time the Arabs took it in 751 it was a major caravan crossroads. It got the name Toshkent or Tashkent ('City of Stone' in Turkic) in about the 11th century.

The Khorezmshahs and Jenghiz Khan stubbed out Tashkent's life in the early 13th century, though it slowly recovered under the Mongols and under Timur (who in 1404 bequeathed the town to his grandson Ulughbek). Despite the general decline of the cities of the Silk Road, the town once again grew prosperous under the Shaybanids in the late 15th and 16th centuries, and most of its surviving 'architectural monuments' date from this period.

The khan of Kokand annexed Tashkent in 1809. In 1865, as the Emir of Bukhara was preparing to snatch it away, the Russians under General Mikhail Chernyayev beat him to it, against the orders of the tsar and despite being outnumbered 15 to one. They found a proud town, enclosed by a 25 km long wall with 11 gates (of which not a trace remains today). Installing General Konstantin Kaufman as governor general, the tsar made Tashkent the capital of his new Turkistan 'satrapy', building a cantonment and town across the Ankhor (or Bozsu) canal from the Uzbek town and filling it with Russian settlers and merchants.

From Tashkent, General Kaufman was to gradually widen the imperial net around the other Central Asian khanates. Tashkent also became the tsarists' (and later the Soviets') main centre for espionage in Asia, during the protracted imperial rivalry with Britain known as the 'Great Game'.

The city's bondage became literally iron-clad with the arrival of the Trans-Caspian Railway in 1889, and Russian workers on the railway were at the front of the Revolution of 1917. With Osipov's treachery and Bolshevik reprisals (see History in the Facts About the Region chapter), this was a bloody place during the Russian Civil War. Peter Hopkirk's thumping good *Setting the East Ablaze* documents the cruelty, duplicity and mayhem at this time, as the Bolsheviks fought to get a grip on the region in the face of local and White-Russian resistance.

Tashkent became the capital of the Turkestan Autonomous SSR, declared in 1918. When this was further split, the capital of the new Uzbek Autonomous SSR was Samarkand until 1930, when this status was restored to Tashkent. The city acquired industrial muscle with construction of the agricultural machinery combine, Tashselmash, in the 1920s, and the whole-sale relocation of factories from western Russia to Central Asia during WWII.

Physically, Tashkent was changed forever on 25 April 1966, when a massive earthquake levelled vast areas of the town and left 300,000 people homeless. Soviet historians made much of the battalions of 'fraternal peoples' and eager urban planners who came from around the Soviet Union to help with reconstruction and give the city its present-day face of shady streets, immense plazas, fountains and acres of bland architecture.

But when Moscow later announced it would give 20% of the newly built apartments to these (mainly Russian) volunteers and invite them to stay, local resentment boiled over in the so-called 'Pakhtakor Incident' of May 1969. At Pakhtakor stadium (by the present-day Yoshlik hotel), brawls erupted between Uzbeks and Russians, and Soviet troops had to be deployed on the streets.

Orientation

Tashkent sits at an elevation of 480 metres at the foot of the Chatkal mountains, a finger of the Tian Shan range reaching across Kyrgyzstan from Chinese Central Asia. Westward yawns the Kyzylkum desert, unbroken for 800 km to Khiva and the Aral Sea. South of the city, the Chirchik river flows down to meet the Syr-Darya.

Before the 1966 earthquake the Ankhor canal separated old (Uzbek) and new (Russian) Tashkent, the former a tangle of alleys around the Chorsu bazar, the latter with shady avenues radiating from what is now Amir Temur maydoni. Uzbeks perhaps still consider Chorsu their 'centre', though it now lies exposed at the edge of the old town, with the Hotel Chorsu planted beside it like a sword. Civil servants and diehard Communists might home in on Mustaqillik maydoni (Independence Square, formerly Lenin Square), the vast parade grounds just east of the canal. But for most tourists the reference point is the Hotel Uzbekistan on Amir Temur maydoni, though hotels and eateries are scattered all over the city.

Tashkent airport is six km south of Amir Temur maydoni. Tashkent train station (also called Main or North station) is 2.5 km south of Amir Temur maydoni at the end of

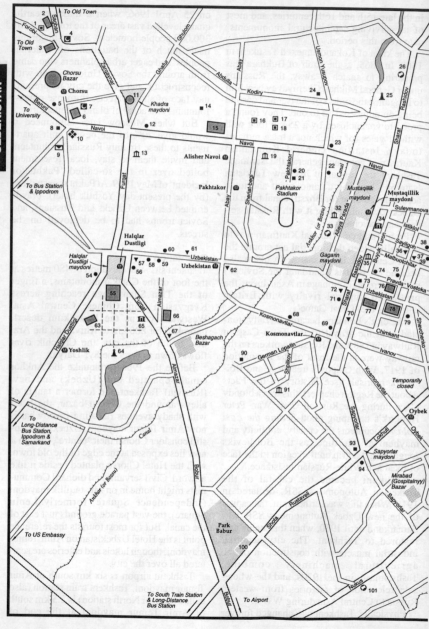

UZBEKISTAN

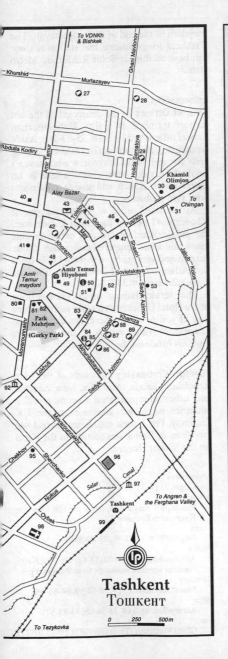

PLACES TO STAY

8	Hotel Chorsu
14	Green Flag Hotel
21	Hotel Yoshlik
24	Hotel Turon
40	Hotel Dustlik
49	Hotel Uzbekistan
51	Hotel Taj Babur
73	Hotel Tashkent & Gastronom
80	'House Market'
90	Hotel Turkestan
93	Hotel Rossiya

PLACES TO EAT

31	Kafe Oleg
36	Zarafshan Restaurant Complex & Diet Café
37	Diet Café
44	Coffee Shop
45	Chayhona
48	Istanbul Restaurant
57	Kafe
61	Restaurant Festival, in Dom Kino Cinema Palace
62	Kooperator Restaurant
67	Arpapoya Kafe
70	Blue Domes Café & Chayhona
72	Vernisaj Kafe, in Union of Artists Hall
82	Canteen
83	Osiyo Kafe (Asia Café)

OTHER

1	Mausoleum of Abu Bakr Kaffal Shoshi
2	Institute of Islam
3	Barak Khan Medressa
4	Telyashayakh Mosque
5	Mustaqillik International Library
6	Kukeldash Medressa
7	Jami (Friday) Mosque
9	Post Office
10	GUM Department Store
11	Circus
12	Khamza Drama Theatre
13	Geology Museum
15	Central Telephone & Telegraph Office
16	Yunus Khan Mausoleum
17	Kaldergach Bi Mausoleum
18	Sheikh Hobandi Tahur Mausoleum
19	Navoi Literary Museum
20	Ilkhom Theatre
22	OVIR (Registration & Visa) Office
23	'Drugstore' Pharmacy
25	Earthquake Memorial
26	German Embassy
27	UK & Swiss Embassies
28	Iranian Embassy
29	Kazak Embassy
30	Bookshop
32	Bakhor Concert Hall & Mukarram Tuzunbayeva Museum

Continued next page

UZBEKISTAN

33	Kyrgyz & Tajik Embassies
34	Romanov Palace
35	Museum of History & Museum of Antiquities
38	Open-Air Art Gallery
39	Gorky Drama Theatre
41	Photo Studio
42	Indian Embassy
43	Main Post Office
46	Mukhtar Ashrafi Conservatory
47	Bookshop
50	Uzbektourism
52	Pharmacy
53	Former German Protestant Church
54	Pakistan International Airlines Booking Office
55	Palace of the Friendship of Peoples
56	Gift Shop
58	Almazar Superstor
59	Bookshop
60	System Educatif Français
63	Abdul Khasim Medressa
64	Navoi Monument
65	Wedding Palace
66	Muqimi Musical Theatre
68	Puppet Theatre
69	Pharmacy
71	Bookshop
74	Asian Business Agency
75	Turkish Airlines Booking Office
76	Navoi Opera & Ballet Theatre
77	TsUM Department Store
78	Ministry of Foreign Affairs
79	Tashkent International Clinic
81	Clock Tower
84	National Bank
85	French Embassy
86	Turkish Embassy
87	Chinese Embassy
88	Afghan Embassy
89	Japanese Embassy
91	Museum of Applied Arts
92	Museum of Fine Arts
94	City Airline Booking Office
95	Asia Travel Agency
96	Railway Booking Office
97	Railway Museum
98	Assumption Cathedral (Uspensky Sobor)
99	Tashkent (Main or North) Train Station
100	Seattle Peace Park
101	Russian Embassy

Movarounnakhr (formerly Proletarskaya), by Tashkent Metro station. South (Uzbek *janubiy*, Russian *yuzhniy*) train station is seven km south-west of Amir Temur maydoni at the end of Shota Rustaveli. The Tashkent long-distance bus station is three km beyond this, at Sobir Rakhimov Metro station.

Information

Tourist Offices In the courtyard of the old airport terminal is a tiny Uzbektourism liaison office (☎ 55-18-36, 55-33-90). Aside from this, Uzbektourism in Tashkent is a big zero for individual travellers who haven't booked services with them. There is no tourist office as such, and no-one to help you with visa problems.

At the head office of Uzbektourism, at Khorezm 47 behind the Hotel Uzbekistan, the public interface consists of a souvenir kiosk and a bad-tempered policeman. Some determined visitors have received help from the Advertising & Information office of Uzbektourism (☎ 33-07-33).

The 'service bureau' on the ground floor of the Hotel Uzbekistan mainly seems to hire cars. If you're a guest there, you can arrange excursions (and visas) at the Tours & Options office on the 3rd floor.

Foreign Embassies Nationals of the Irish Republic, Canada, Australia, New Zealand and other unrepresented Commonwealth countries might get assistance at the UK Embassy. For Uzbek embassies abroad see the Visas & Embassies section in the Facts for the Visitor chapter.

Afghanistan
    Gogol 73 (☎ 33-91-89)
Belarus
    Mustaqillik maydoni 5, down the hall from the Kyrgyzstan Embassy
China
    Gogol 79 (☎ 33-37-79, 33-80-88)
France
    Akhunbabayev 25 (☎ 33-53-82, fax 33-62-10); consular services weekdays from 9 am to 6 pm
Germany
    Sharaf Rashidov 15 (☎ 39-12-59, 34-66-96)
India
    Alexey Tolstoy 5 (☎ 33-56-65, 33-83-57)
Iran
    Ghani Mavlonov (Timiryazeva) 16 (☎ 35-07-77)

Old & New Names in Tashkent

Name changes in Uzbekistan, and Tashkent in particular, seem driven more by bloody-mindedness than the erasure of Soviet memories. Renaming has been widespread and indiscriminate, and many old names have simply been moved to other streets. Many people, including taxi drivers, still use some Soviet-era names.

Many new names are just tongue-defying translations of old ones; eg ploshchad Druzhba Narodov is now Halqlar Dustligi maydoni, which means the same thing, the Friendship of Peoples Square. Some 'changes' listed here aren't really changes, just transliterations from Uzbek instead of from Russian, such as Oybek instead of Aybek. Some streets appear not to have changed yet, eg 1 May (Pervomayskaya or Pervogo Maya).

Uzbek forms are generally used in this guide, but Russian speakers add on various grammatical suffixes, even to Uzbek names. Common variations of this kind are included.

New Name	Old Name
Streets	
Akhunbabayev	Kuybysheva
Alexey Tolstoy	Alexeya Tolstogo
Amir Temur hiyoboni	Engelsa
Buyuk Ipak Yuli	Lunacharskoe shosse
Buyuk Turon	Gazeta Pravda
Chilonzor	Chelanzarskaya
Forobi	Farabi
Ghani Mavlonov	Timiryazeva
Gogol	Gogolya
Halqlar Dustligi	Druzhba Narodov
Holida Samatova	Frunze
Istiklol	Kommunisticheskaya
Khamza	Karla Marxa (east of Amir Temur maydoni)
Kosmonavtlar prospekti	prospekt Kosmonavtov
Lokhuti	Lakhuti
Matbuotchilar	Leningradskaya
Movarounnakhr	Proletarskaya
Mustafa Kemal Ataturk	
(Kemol Otaturk in Uzbek)	Kirova
Nukus	Poltoratskaya
Sadyk Azimov	Zhukovskogo
Sayilgoh	Karla Marxa (west of Amir Temur maydoni)
Sharaf Rashidov prospekti	(prospekt) Lenina
Shota Rustaveli	Usmana Nasira
Suleymanova	Suleymanovoy
Uzbekistan	Uzbekistanskaya
Parks & Squares	
Amir Temur maydoni	Skver Revolyutsii, Markaziy skver
Halqlar Dustligi maydoni	Ploshchad Druzhba Narodov
Park Mehrjon	Gorky Park
Metro Stations	
Amir Temur Hiyoboni	Oktyabrskoy Revolyutsii, Markaziy Hiyoboni
Halqlar Dustligi	Druzhba Narodov
Kosmonavtlar	Prospekt Kosmonavtov
Mashinasozlar	Tashselmash
Minor	Ulugbek
Mirzo Ulughbek	50 Let SSSR
Mustaqillik Maydoni	Ploshchad Lenina
Oybek	Aybek
Pakhtakor	Pakhtakorskaya
Yoshlik	Komsomol

Israel
Lokhuti 16a (☎ 56-57-79, fax 54-39-07); but we never did find it and they don't answer the telephone
Italy
Amir Temur 95 near VDNKh (☎ 35-42-72)
Japan
Sadyk Azimov (Zhukovskogo) (☎ 33-73-46)
Kazakstan
Holida Samatova (ex-Frunze) 20 (☎ 33-59-44, 33-37-05, fax 33-60-22), a five minute walk from Khamid Olimjon Metro station; visas weekdays from 9 am to 5 pm and Saturday mornings
Kyrgyzstan
Mustaqillik maydoni 5 (☎ 39-45-43, 39-18-77), the salmon-and-green building on the west side of the square, left end, one flight up, at an unmarked door left of the stairs; visas weekdays with no waiting, for US$25
Pakistan
Chilonzor 25 (☎ 77-93-02, 77-10-03), 800 metres east of the US Embassy; visa applications Monday and Thursday from 9 am to noon, pick-up on the next application day from 4.30 to 5 pm
Russia
Nukus 83 (☎ 54-36-41, 55-29-48), just left of a yellow-green high-rise (take bus No 2 from Tashkent Metro station)
Switzerland
Murtazayev 6 (☎ 44-25-91)
Tajikistan
Mustaqillik maydoni 5 (☎ 39-47-81, fax 39-86-23), down the hall from the Kyrgyzstan Embassy
Turkey
Gogol 87 (☎ 33-80-37, 33-21-07)
UK
Murtazayev 6, flats 84 & 85 (☎ 34-56-52, 34-76-58; satellite fax 89-15-49); consular services weekdays 9.30 am to 5.30 pm
USA
Chilonzor 82 (☎ 77-14-07, 77-22-31), a five minute walk from Mirzo Ulughbek Metro station (east on Volgograd, then north on Chilonzor); American citizen services walk-in Tuesday and Friday from 2 to 4 pm, or call ahead

Visas Theoretically the Consular Section of the Ministry of Foreign Affairs, Uzbekistan 5, is the place for visa matters. Join the supplicants at the right-hand door, weekdays from 3 to 5 pm (some travellers report success in the morning). You may have better luck if you have Uzbektourism vouchers, or a letter (or live person) from a Tashkent agency with whom you have booked services.

Travellers report that the ministry's 24 hour office (☎ 55-18-36) on the 2nd floor of the new terminal at the airport is marginally more helpful. These are also the people to see if immigration hassles you on arrival at the airport (ask for *konsulsky otdel*, consular office).

The Tours & Options office at Hotel Uzbekistan appears to be a good place for visa help, but only for hotel guests and in connection with excursions booked through the hotel. Other hotels that claim to offer visa help are the Yoshlik and the Chorsu, but only in the guise of 'private' hosts, so they need more time than the Uzbekistan.

A photo studio for passport-size visa photos is on Amir Temur just off the square.

Registration If you're staying at a hotel, police registration is automatic. The OVIR office – the Tashkent Department of Home Affairs, Registration & Visa Office – is on Yusupov, a block east of the Hotel Yoshlik. The nearest bus stop is 'Urda'. The OVIR officer at the long-distance bus station might accost you on arrival, to record the date in your visa and remind you of registration requirements.

Useful Organisations A place to meet young Tashkenters who speak some English is the little Mustaqillik International Library (satellite TV and a modest collection of donated books, periodicals and English-language teaching materials) run by a group calling themselves the Central Asian Free Exchange, at Navoi 48 at the edge of Chorsu bazar, opposite the Hotel Chorsu.

Another place to meet young people is the Language Faculty (*Fakultet zarubezhnoy filologiy* in Russian) at Tashkent State University. Follow '*na ulitsu Beruni*' signs out of Beruni Metro station and ask for Vuzgorodok or University Town.

Money There are hundreds of foreign exchange desks around the city – at tourist hotels, at the airport, bus and train stations, and in every other shop. They use the official rate, though commissions vary. Most accept only US$ cash, though the Hotel

Uzbekistan's 24 hour desk changes US$ travellers' cheques as well as cash in several major currencies.

To exchange any other currencies go to the National Bank's city headquarters (☎ 33-60-70, 33-40-68) at Akhunbabayev 23, open weekdays from 8.30 am to 12.30 pm. The hall for foreign exchange is two flights up the far left-hand stairs. For US$ cash advances from Visa credit cards, go to Room 8 on the ground floor.

Black-market money changers are thick as flies around Alay bazar, the main post office, Tashkent train station and the bus station, but many are just plain crooked.

Credit Cards Visa, American Express and some other cards are accepted at the Uzbekistan, Chorsu, Yoshlik and Sayokhat hotels, and at a swarm of private hard-currency shops.

Reselling Sum on Departure At the time of research, you could only sell *sum* at window 6 in the foreign-exchange hall at the National Bank city headquarters. Sign over your exchange receipts and take the paperwork to window 5 at the left-rear corner of the ground floor.

Post & Communications

Post The main post office (Uzbek: *pochta bulimi*, Russian: *glavpochtamt*, ☎ 33-47-49) is at 1 May 7 at the corner with Alexey Tolstoy. Poste restante is dubious here, although the US Embassy will hold mail for US citizens. DHL (☎ 77-98-02) and UPS (☎ 78-86-25) have services to and from Uzbekistan.

Telephone & Fax For Central Asia's pre-eminent capital, Tashkent's telephone system is awful. The cheapest and slowest place to make intercity and international calls is the central telephone and telegraph office (☎ 44-65-35), the big yellow building at Navoi 28. You can also call from the main post office. Bad lines make sending local faxes dicey and pricey; see Post & Communications in the Facts for the Visitor chapter.

The Hotel Uzbekistan's business centre (☎ 33-62-44; fax 89-11-15, 89-11-22) has quick, clear satellite-linked services – for about eight times the rate at the central telephone and telegraph office.

Tashkent's telephone code is 3712.

Telegrams These can be sent from the central telephone and telegraph office or the main post office.

E-mail Nuron Relcom (☎ 67-86-76, e-mail root@nuron.tashkent.su), Buyuk Ipak Yuli 42, has an e-mail node and fax and telex services. For an initial fee, plus monthly and kilobyte rates, anyone can get an e-mail box and other services. From Pushkin Metro station go under the railway bridge; it's across the road beyond a nine storey blue and white building.

Travel Agencies Several dozen travel agencies have sprouted here since 1991. Most are unprepared for walk-in individual travellers, and few have English-speakers, but the following claim they can arrange excursions, and visas or visa extensions to go with them. All prefer at least a few weeks warning.

Asia Travel (☎ 56-29-27, 33-10-55; fax 32-34-40; telex 116108 PTB RU), Taras Shevchenko 44; competent specialists in trekking, climbing, rafting, cycling and other adventure travel in all the former Soviet republics, from US$40 per person per day for individuals; contact Radi Bakayev

Asian Business Agency (☎ 32-58-78, fax 56-77-79), Buyuk Turon 41, room 803 (the high-rise with the clock); strictly business specialists but their annual briefing booklet for long-term visitors called *Understanding Uzbekistan* (trade, finance, services, culture) is 50% off the US$25 price if you mention Lonely Planet (so they said)

Sayokh Extrem (☎ 35-43-91, fax 33-20-25, telex 116329 ICIT RU); contact Alexander Trofimov or Evgenia Krylova

Yordamchi (☎ 78-21-05, ☎ & fax 78-45-16, telex 116108 PTB RU); can handle detailed advance plans, as well as outbound international flights; contact Nelli Shushlebina

Bookshops Most bookshops are of little interest unless you read Russian or Uzbek;

even the English titles of Soviet days have disappeared. Shops on Sharaf Rashidov opposite the Blue Domes Café, and on the north-west corner by Khamid Olimjon Metro station, do have an interesting miscellany of art books, maps, coins, old postcards and second-rate handicrafts, and the latter has a random stock of city and regional maps.

Cultural Centres Systeme Educatif Français (☎ 45-19-41) isn't precisely a cultural centre but a language school. It's on the 3rd floor of Dom Uchiteley (House of Teachers), Uzbekistan 80 near Halqlar Dustligi Metro station. The United Nations (☎ 56-06-06, 33-09-77) is at Taras Shevchenko 4.

Emergency & Medical Services Local emergency numbers are: police 01 or 001; fire 02; ambulance 03, ☎ 33-26-24/25 or ☎ 33-19-03.

Medical Clinic The Tashkent International Clinic (☎ 56-04-33, emergencies ☎ 31-70-05, switchboard ☎ 56-06-06; fax 77-69-53), in the UN complex at Taras Shevchenko 4, is a joint project of the UN, the US Embassy and the Peace Corps, meant for long-termers but available to visitors in emergencies. Visitors are asked for US$50 per visit plus medication (and they'd probably be grateful for any of your own medicines that you can leave behind). If that sounds expensive, remember that this is one of the few sources of western-quality medical care in Central Asia. They're open weekdays from 8 am to 5 pm, with western-trained personnel on call 24 hours a day. They can also advise you on dental emergencies. Tell the taxi driver *oh on* (OON, Russian for UN).

The US Embassy (and probably others) maintains lists of other medical contacts as well.

Pharmacies Well-stocked but pricey are several hard-currency *dorihona* (Russian: *apteka*), including a Turkish joint venture called 'Drugstore' on Navoi at the corner with Yusupov, and one on 1 May between

Sovietskaya and Khamza. A big *sum* pharmacy is just north of Kosmonavtlar Metro station on Sharaf Rashidov.

Mountain Rescue Uzbekistan's mountain-rescue service (☎ 68-67-95) is in the offices of Uzbekmakhsustour (Uzbekspetstour), around the corner from the Hotel Sayokhat complex, Buyuk Ipak Yuli 115, near Maxim Gorky Metro station. The parent company of the Yordamchi agency (see the Travel Agencies section) apparently runs a private mountain rescue service.

Old Town Walking Tour

What remains of the old town (Uzbek: *eski shakhar*, Russian: *staryy gorod*) starts beside Chorsu bazar and the Hotel Chorsu. A maze of narrow, dusty streets – undoubtedly spared by Soviet planners to show what things would have been like without socialism – is lined with low mud-brick houses and dotted with mosques and old medressas. These few handsome religious buildings date from the 15th and 16th centuries.

If you're lucky enough to be invited into someone's home, you'll discover that the blank outer walls of traditional homes conceal cool, peaceful garden-courtyards.

Kukeldash Medressa This grand 16th century medressa (called Kukaldosh in Uzbek) on a hill opposite the Hotel Chorsu has a domed courtyard at the rear which has been under restoration for years. For a time after independence the building was returned to service as an Islamic school. At the moment there's mainly a lot of construction rubble, though on warm Friday mornings the plaza in front overflows with worshippers.

Behind Kukeldash is the tiny 15th century Jami (Friday) mosque, used in Soviet times as a sheet metal workshop.

Chorsu Bazar It's open every day, but on weekend mornings this huge open market beside Kukeldash is a great place to find crowds of people from the surrounding countryside – many in traditional dress –

along with fresh produce, prepared food, tea and cheap souvenirs.

Tashkent has at least 16 such farmers' markets. See the Things to Buy section for information on these and other big bazars.

Hastimom This is one name for a plain intersection half a km north of Chorsu, at the lower end of Sagban kuchasi, which is the official religious centre of the republic. On the south-west corner the 16th century Barak Khan medressa (Madrasa Barok Hon) houses the Central Asian Muslim Religious Board, whose Grand Mufti is roughly the Islamic equivalent of an archbishop for Uzbekistan, Kyrgyzstan, Tajikistan and Turkmenistan. In *The Lost Heart of Asia*, Colin Thubron describes seeing what is probably the oldest Quran in the world in the library here, though it's off-limits to the general public.

East from here across Zarqaynar kuchasi is the Telyashayakh mosque, also called Hastimom mosque. The big block on the north side is the Institute of Islam, a five year post-medressa academy, the only one allowed in Central Asia in Soviet times (now there are others at Bukhara and Namangan). Just west of this is the little 16th century mausoleum of Abu Bakr Kaffal Shoshi, an Islamic scholar of the Shaybanid period.

All these buildings are normally closed to tourists. Visitors who have made prior arrangements to go inside should be modestly dressed, and women should cover their hair.

Yunus Khan Mausoleum Across Navoi from the Navoi Literary Museum are three 15th century mausolea, restored in the 19th century and now ignored in a forest of office and university buildings. The biggest bears the name of Yunus Khan, grandfather of the Mughal Emperor Babur. Two small ones are eastward inside a fence – Sheikh Hobandi Tahur and the pointy-roofed Kaldergach Bi, the latter now used as a neighbourhood mosque.

Abdul Khasim Medressa The old town has

disappeared from around this medressa, 1.5 km south of Chorsu bazar by the Palace of the Friendship of Peoples, near Halqlar Dustligi Metro station. Presently under snail's-pace restoration, it was meant to become a working medressa again after independence. Perhaps the money ran out; for the time being it's a museum of traditional arts – a ragtag collection of souvenir vendors, artists and the occasional folk ensemble. It's open daily from 9 am to 6 pm.

Getting To & Around the Old Town The easiest way to the old town is by Metro to Chorsu station. Alternatively, from near the Hotel Uzbekistan, tram No 16, trolleybuses Nos 4 and 8 and express bus No 28-3 go west down Navoi to Chorsu bazar. Russian taxi drivers, if they'll go into the old town at all, may get immediately lost.

On foot, you could easily get lost too. Three major streets that head into Chorsu bazar are Forobi (Farabi), Sagban and Zarqaynar. Sagban is said to be the city's oldest street.

Museums & Galleries

What Tashkent lacks in old things it makes up for in big museums about them. A few *sum* admission is charged at all the museums.

Museum of Fine Arts Here on the 1st floor is a fine collection of the art of pre-Russian Turkestan – Zoroastrian artefacts, serene 1000 year old Buddhist statues, Sogdian murals, royal furnishings too splendid to use. All this is worth seeing with a museum guide. Down the hall is 19th and 20th century Uzbek applied art, notably the brilliant silk-on-cotton embroidered hangings called *suzana*. Less impressive is the Russian and Asian art upstairs.

The museum is in the giant cube-shaped building at Movarounnakhr (Proletarskaya) 16. Maybe the Ministry of Culture isn't paying its electricity bills because it's dark and dank inside. Some items have already been moved elsewhere to keep them from rotting in the humidity. The museum (☎ 32-74-36) is open daily from 10 am to 5.30 pm (except to 4.30 pm Monday, and closed Tuesday). They nail you for about US$3 to take photographs, even more for videos.

Behind the museum, over the graves of the Tashkent commissars executed in 1919 by the treacherous Osipov, is a statue of the Uzbek SSR's first president, Yuldash Akhunbabayev.

Museum of Applied Arts In 1898 Alexander Polovtsev, a wealthy tsarist diplomat, retired to a house built for him in traditional style by artisans from Tashkent, Samarkand, Bukhara and Ferghana. After a post-Revolutionary stint as an orphanage, the house was surrounded by ugly museum buildings and opened in 1937 as a showcase for turn-of-the-century applied arts.

Full of bright carved plaster decorations *(ghanch)* and carved wood, the house itself is the main attraction, though there are also exhibits of ceramics, textiles, jewellery, musical instruments and toys, and a good but pricey gift shop. The museum (☎ 56-39-43), on Shpilkov, in what was a Jewish neighbourhood at the turn of the century, is open daily from 10 am to 5 pm. You must fork out a few US dollars cash to shoot photos or videos inside.

Museum of History Tashkent's history museum, in the former Lenin Museum at Sharaf Rashidov 30, is a slick, well-arranged walk through regional prehistory and history, with nothing in English or even Russian except vague introductory panels on 'The Rise of Class Society' etc. Those in any doubt about the seamless continuity from Soviet times should check out the two storey mural in the lobby, dense with Central Asian historical motifs. At the centre, just above the Quran and haloed by the Uzbek flag, beams the president, Islam Karimov.

One highlight in the museum is a small, peaceful Buddha figure from a Kushan temple excavated at Fayoz-Tepe near Termez, but conspicuously absent is a famous big Buddha from Kuva in the Ferghana Valley. The museum is open daily, except Monday, from 10 am to 6 pm.

Museum of Antiquities Also missing is the striking collection of Central Asian jewellery, Crimean Tatar filigree and gold ingots which used to be in the Museum of Antiquities, once housed in the **Romanov Palace** just to the north of the Museum of History.

The vaguely comical St Petersburg-style palace was built about 1890 for Konstantin Mikhailovich Romanov, a kinky uncle of Tsar Nicholas II, exiled here to avoid embarrassing the royal family. Requisitioned since 1991 as a state reception hall, it's now permanently closed to the public.

Mukarram Tuzunbayeva Museum In a courtyard behind the Bakhor concert hall on Mustaqillik maydoni is a tiny museum dedicated to the first Uzbek woman to dance professionally in public. There are displays with photos, costumes, information about the Bakhor troupe, and a gift shop. It's open daily, except Sunday, from 9.30 am to 5 pm.

Navoi Literary Museum Besides memorabilia of 15th century poet Alisher Navoi and other Central Asian literati, this small museum has replica manuscripts, Persian calligraphy, and 15th and 16th century miniatures. Open daily, except Monday, it's on Navoi, a block east of Alisher Navoi Metro station.

Geology Museum This surprisingly grand museum, full of beautiful minerals, a dinosaur skeleton, natural history dioramas and a giant three-dimensional map of Central Asia, is open weekdays from 9 am to 5 pm.

Railway Museum Railway freaks might like this collection of locomotives and coaches, on a siding near the main train station and Tashkent Metro station.

Union of Artists Hall The Central Exhibition Hall of the Uzbekistan Union of Artists features an art gallery, occasional sponsored art exhibitions, an 'antiques' shop and, in the basement, the Vernisaj Kafe. It's on Sharaf

Rashidov, diagonally opposite the Hotel Tashkent; enter on the north side.

Navoi Opera & Ballet Theatre

Not only is this a venue for some of the cheapest classical opera outside the Covent Garden piazza, it's also the only Soviet building in Tashkent with any personality. The interior is itself a museum, its Soviet brashness hidden behind a veneer of regional artistic styles – a different one in each room – executed by the best artisans of the day, under the direction of the architect who did Lenin's tomb in Moscow. There is a separate ticket office, inside the main door, just for guided tours of the place.

The theatre (☎ 33-35-28) is across Buyuk Turon kuchasi from the Hotel Tashkent. See the Entertainment section for programmes at this and other theatres in the city.

Squares, Parks & Memorials

Amir Temur Maydoni The glowering bust of Marx has been replaced by a suitably patriotic statue of Timur, due to be dignified with a bronzing when there's enough money in the municipal budget. Nearby is a loud, mafia-ridden nightclub.

Mustaqillik Maydoni Yawning Independence Square – still Lenin Square to most Russians – is the place for parades. Its giant Lenin statue, once the biggest in the USSR, was replaced on Uzbekistan's first birthday with a boring brass globe. The salmon-and-green building on the west side was Tashkent's first Soviet administration building (1930); it now has the city library, some embassies and government offices, and the Bakhor concert hall. The president's office and most ministries are just to the south, around Gagarin maydoni.

Earthquake Memorial The New Soviet Men & Women who rebuilt Tashkent are remembered in stone here. Russian newlyweds still come here to have their photos taken. It's three long blocks north on Sharaf Rashidov from Mustaqillik Maydoni Metro station, barely worth going that far for.

VDNKh Ride down memory lane with some old-fashioned fun and propaganda, at the Uzbek Exhibition of Economic Achievements (properly VDNKhU, Vystavka Dostizheniy Narodnogo Khozyaystva Uzbekistana). Munch a sausage, take a ride in the flash new amusement park, or try the rotating café atop the 375 metre radio-TV tower. From the corner of 1 May and Pushkin, or from opposite Alay bazar, take express bus No 72-3or almost anything else north to the VDNKh (*veh-deh-neh-KHA*) stop.

Seattle Peace Park In the days of *glasnost*, Americans from Seattle – one of Tashkent's sister cities – built a little park out on Shota Rustaveli. The photo displays and sculptures are looking a bit threadbare now. Take bus No 67-3 from Movarounnakhr (Proletarskaya), or tram No 13 from TsUM (Tsentralnaya Univermag, the central department store), near the Navoi Theatre, to the Park Babur (formerly Park Kirova) stop.

Palace of the Friendship of Peoples

This testament to Soviet gigantism contains – naturally – an enormous concert hall. Out the front is a bit of Soviet mythologising, a memorial to a blacksmith named Sham Akhmudov and his wife who adopted 15 war orphans (thousands were sent to Tashkent during WWII), all of whom are said to still live in the province.

Up behind the palace, meanwhile, is a vast promenade and a post-Soviet (but decidedly Soviet-scale) monument to Alisher Navoi, Uzbekistan's newly chosen cultural hero, with the eerie feeling of a Lenin shrine. East of the promenade is the city's biggest Wedding Palace.

Churches

Near Mirabad (Gospitalnyy) bazar is one of Tashkent's four Orthodox churches, the Assumption Cathedral (Uspensky Sobor), which is bright blue with copper domes. Around it you can find perestroyka's losers, elderly Russians whose pensions collapsed along with the Soviet Union, reducing them to beggars.

Looking quite out of place is a former German Protestant church, now used as a recital hall, on Sadyk Azimov (Zhukovskogo) near Sovietskaya.

Organised Tours

The Hotel Uzbekistan can organise a fairly boring four hour Uzbektourism city tour for about US$55 per person, as well as other excursions for US$5 per hour for a guide plus US$9 per hour for a car and driver.

Festivals

In May of even-numbered years, the city hosts a festival of Asian, African and Latin American films.

Places to Stay

Homestays These are hard to find in Tashkent. One travel agency told us they're 'forbidden', while another (Yordamchi) said it was no problem.

Rental Accommodation Through a gate opposite the clock tower on Movarounnakhr (Proletarskaya) is a courtyard where people gather informally to swap information on flats for sale. Some may be willing to rent one to visitors for a few days or weeks. When we were there, you could find a sparsely furnished place for about US$30 per week; US$60 a week might get you TV, a telephone or other luxuries.

This is also a good place to get ripped off; deal with the Russian grandmothers, not the Uzbek spivs. Travellers who sublet flats should never open the door to anyone they do not clearly know, day or night, because of the danger of robbery or worse. See Visas & Embassies in the Facts for the Visitor chapter about registration.

Bottom End Cheapest is a bed in a *student dorm* at Tashkent State University, especially at the Language Faculty (Fakultet zarubezhnoy filologiy, in Russian). Follow 'na ulitsu Beruni' signs out of Beruni Metro station and ask for 'Vuz-gorodok' (University Town). Students say you get an official registration chit just as you would at a hotel, but we couldn't verify this. There's an Uzbek canteen in the basement of the Language Faculty.

The *Green Flag Hotel* (☎ 44-10-60) – Yashil Bayroq in Uzbek, Zelyony Flag in Russian – is full of Afghan and Pakistani traders flogging trousers and woollens from Peshawar. Rooms with toilet and shower are about US$6 per person. It looks to be men-only, and in any case is *not* recommended for women. It's up a track to the left of the central telephone and telegraph building (on Navoi opposite Alisher Navoi Metro station), in the third building on the left. The address is Ts(entralnyy)-14, *dom* 14-Б.

Last resort in this category is the *Hotel Rossiya* (☎ 56-29-63) at Sapyorlar maydoni 2, at the east end of Shota Rustaveli, an awkward location for transport (take westbound tram No 28 from TsUM on Uzbekistan). Noisy singles/doubles with TV, toilet, cold shower and no security start at US$15/20, plus a cheeky 50% extra 'booking fee' the first night. The 'foreigners administrator' has the manners of Jenghiz Khan, and service is slack except in the cavernous restaurant.

The decaying *Hotel Dustlik* (☎ 34-73-58) at Navoi 8, on the corner with Amir Temur, is shy of foreigners but you might still talk your way into a cheap room. Renovation is on the cards.

Middle Best mid-range value for money is the city-owned *Hotel Turon* (☎ 41-07-05), formerly the Leningrad, at Abdulla Kodiry 1, with polite service, a good, clean restaurant, and plain rooms with toilet and shower (but dicey hot water) at US$18/32 and up. Take bus No 18 north from Pakhtakor Metro station, or tram No 23 or 27 west on Navoi from Amir Temur maydoni.

Uzbektourism's *Hotel Yoshlik* (☎ 41-44-10, fax 41-44-04) is popular with Pakistani and Indian traders. It's at Pakhtakor 5, a five minute walk east of both Pakhtakor and Navoi Metro stations. A sign modestly refers to the 'Foreign Economic Industrial

Complex Yoshlik', but it's crumbling inside. Plain rooms with toilet, hot shower and TV are US$30/40, and 25% less from November through March. Disable your telephone to stop the late-night prostitute calls. The restaurant is grim; decline the US$5 hotel breakfast and go instead to the 5th floor bufet or the cheap stalls around the Metro station.

Uzbektourism also runs the *Hotel Chorsu* (☎ 42-76-00, fax 42-87-00), the three sided tower at Akhunbabayev maydoni 1 by Chorsu bazar. This was to be Tashkent's flagship hotel, but it has succumbed to mediocrity; travellers say the bottom-end rooms (singles/doubles/triples for US$35/50/60, less in the off-season) are bug-ridden and 'awful'.

The *Hotel Tashkent* (☎ 33-27-35), very central at Sharaf Rashidov 50 (or Buyuk Turon 56), opposite the Opera Theatre, is only for pre-booked guests, who get plain rooms with shower, toilet, fridge, TV and balcony for US$20/30. Visa credit cards are accepted. There is a good snack and coffee shop at the north end.

A private, business-oriented hotel that has opened since we were there is the *Tsorbi* (☎ 67-43-82, fax 68 94-60) near the Metro in the western part of the city. Air-con suites with TV, international telephone, shower and toilet are US$54.

Top End Most tourists end up at Uzbektourism's giant *Hotel Uzbekistan* (☎ 33-27-73, fax 33-51-20), at Khamza 45 facing Amir Temur maydoni. For walk-in guests, air-con rooms with tiny fridge, TV and telephone are US$73/106 and up from April through October, less the rest of the year – and a bit less if you pay by credit card (Visa, MasterCard or American Express). Were the rooms half this price, few would object to the bugs, rusty water and self-detaching sinks. Avoid the front rooms, or listen to the nearby clock tower 'chime' every 15 minutes all night.

The ground-floor restaurant has all-you-can-eat breakfasts when groups are staying, and there are three upstairs bar/bufets with cheap salads, omelettes etc. This is the only

tourist hotel with restricted access. If you're not a guest, saying 'business centre' or 'restaurant' may get you in; otherwise you must get a *propusk* (pass) from the tiny window at the left end of the building.

Behind the Hotel Uzbekistan looms the potentially five-star *Hotel Taj Babur*, finished but unopened when we were there. This and sibling hotels in Samarkand and Bukhara were awaiting a World Bank-assisted bail-out after Uzbekistan defaulted on some US$22 million in loans from the Indian banks who financed them.

Uzbektourism operates another big top-end place, the *Hotel Sayokhat* complex (☎ 67-53-74, fax 68-67-72) at Buyuk Ipak Yuli 115, well east of the centre near Maxim Gorky Metro station, and lately under renovation.

Finally there is the *Hotel Turkestan*, the place against which all others in Central Asia must be measured: elegant and secluded (at the far end of German Lopatin kuchasi, a five minute walk from Kosmonavtlar Metro station), with clean, comfortable rooms (at about US$50 per person) and a small, inexpensive restaurant with European and Asian dishes, and polite service. Alas, you cannot stay there unless you're a guest of the Communist – sorry, Popular Democratic – Party of Uzbekistan. This only goes to show what's been possible all along, and highlights the republic's miserable attitude towards tourists.

Places to Eat

Fast Food *Choyhonas* (teahouses) abound in parks, bazars and transport stations, dishing up shashlyk, plov, laghman and tea. Hygiene is variable; look for high turnover and service right off the fire. There are several around Park Mehrjon (Gorky Park) near the Hotel Uzbekistan. Better yet, cross to the cheap-and-cheerful stalls lining Sayilgoh (Karl Marx) kuchasi. Because of its vaguely carnival atmosphere, expats call this 'the Arbat', though it's a pale imitation of its Moscow namesake.

Cafés & Snacks The friendly *Halqlar*

Dustligi Qakhvahonasi (Friendship of Peoples Coffeehouse), has salads, hamburgers, roast chicken, good laghman and manty for under US$1, plus pastries, coffee, Coke and beer. It's on the corner of Uzbekistan and Furqat, by Halqlar Dustligi Metro station, and stays open only until 6 pm.

The outdoor *Osiyo Kafe* (Asia Café) on 1 May south of Khamza has soups, laghman and so-so Turkish pizzas *(s myasa* or *bez myasom*, with or without meat), and lots of Uzbek wide-boys with dark glasses and cellular phones. Fill up for US$1.50. It's open from noon to 8 pm, daily except Sunday.

The pleasant *Arpapoya Kafe* on Beshagach maydoni, across the canal from the Muqimi Theatre, serves shashlyk, light meals, coffee and sweets.

In the park between Sharaf Rashidov and Buyuk Turon, the *Blue Domes Cafe* (Kafe Golubye kupola) has good shashlyk, samsa and plov in clean surroundings. It's self-serve at lunch and has waiters in the evening. Next door is a choyhona.

On Atatürk south of Sayilgoh, the immense *Zarafshan* complex has several restaurants and bars, dealing more in atmosphere than decent food. But upstairs at the north end is a clean *parkhez taomlar oshhonaci* or 'diet café' with plain, cheap Uzbek and Russian fare. Another one is just across Atatürk. See the Food section in Facts for the Visitor for more information about diet cafés.

Hotels Service at the Hotel Uzbekistan's ground-floor *restaurant* lurches from civil to barbaric. The food includes US$5 all-you-can-eat breakfasts when there are groups here, fairly good Uzbek dishes at lunch for under US$2, and the usual overpriced *kotlets* and boiled cabbage for dinner. Avoid the extremely overpriced club on the top floor.

At the north end of the Hotel Tashkent is a good *coffee shop* with pastries and ice cream.

Restaurants In the basement of the Union of Artists Hall, opposite the Hotel Tashkent, the *Vernisaj Kafe* (☎ 56-34-07) offers interestingly prepared meat dishes and soups, quiet live music and red velvet décor. A modest lunch without booze is about US$3. It's open from 10 am to 10 pm, daily except Sunday.

Kafe Oleg (☎ 33-45-22) serves good Uzbek and European specialities (eat well for US$10, but is best known for its cold Carlsberg on tap! From Khamid Olimjon Metro station, it's at the bottom of the steps on the left (south) side of Pushkin, on Jakub Kolos kuchasi underneath. It's open from 1 to 10.30 pm, daily except Sunday. Try to call ahead, as this small place sometimes gets block-booked. Check your bill.

East of Halqlar Dustligi Metro station at Uzbekistan 98 is the Dom Kino cinema palace. Around the left side in the *Restaurant Festival* (☎ 45-81-23) you can fill up on good European dishes for US$5 to US$10, though it's easy to drop much more if you fall for their huge zakuski (starters) menu.

The *Kooperator Restaurant* (☎ 45-73-72), right by Uzbekistan Metro station, offers cordial service and decent Turkish and European food from noon to 11 pm every day, with a loud band in the evening. In the sunless *Istanbul Restaurant* (☎ 33-73-67), across Pushkin from the Hotel Uzbekistan, you'll find so-so but very pricey local and European (but not Turkish) food, sometimes a belly dancer with a snake, and unexpected extra charges. It's open daily from 11 am to 11 pm.

Some expatriates claim *Restaurant Europe*, 600 metres east of the US Embassy on Chilonzor (closest Metro station Mirzo Ulughbek), is the best place in town. From an international menu, you can dine grandly for about US$10 per person.

Korean Restaurants Uzbek Koreans say there is no Korean fast-food here, though there are some good, pricey restaurants, offering a hybrid Korean-Uzbek menu.

Possibilities include the *Seoul Restaurant* (☎ 53-57-86) on the south side of Shota Rustaveli, two tram stops beyond Babur Park, and *Sam Yang* (☎ 74-45-71) at Chilonzor 11 (take the westbound trolleybus

No 11 from Mirzo Ulughbek Metro station). For a full meal figure at least US$30 per person at either place.

Home-Restaurants Anyone who has been invited into an Uzbek home knows that ordinary restaurant food is a pale imitation of what Uzbeks cook for themselves. One place to taste Uzbek home cooking is in one of the unofficial *restaurants* that people open in their homes in parts of the old town – just tables in the dirt-floored courtyard, where you're served one or two simple dishes from the same pots that feed their families, plus tea or beer.

One such neighbourhood in Tashkent is a few minutes from Tinchlik Metro station. From the station, walk to the closest traffic signal on the main street, Beruni prospekti, and turn right into Abid Sadykov kuchasi. Most of the house-restaurants are between five and 10 minutes walk along (or just off) this street.

There are no signs or shop-fronts. Family members solicit customers for the midday and evening (after 7 pm) meals. Try for a home, not one of the little cafés that seem to be run by post-adolescent kids. Most places are fairly clean, but it's OK to peek into the kitchen. Anything more than about US$1 per dish (in *sum*) is probably too much. Gentle bargaining is OK.

Lunch is best, as it's easy to get hassled or lost here in the dark. Local friends say the best of the lot is at the far end of Abid Sadykov on the right, by a water channel; but get there before noon, as it's popular and can run out of food by 1 pm.

Self-Catering There are farmers' markets all over town; see the Things to Buy section for some near the centre. In season, an informal melon bazar springs up near the Navoi Literary Museum. There is a well-stocked gastronom at the south end of the Hotel Tashkent, and others around the city.

Are you craving cornflakes, chocolate pudding, English tea? Tashkent has a real supermarket, an Uzbek-Turkish joint venture called Almazar Superstor, complete with bar-codes and shopping trolleys, stocked with reasonably priced British dry goods, canned foods and more. Payment is in *sum*. It's on Uzbekistan just east of Halqlar Dustligi Metro station, and is open from 9 am to 6 pm, daily except Sunday.

Entertainment

Folk Music & Dance Uzbeks delight in singing, although the style – a reedy sound from the front of the mouth, not the chest – is strange to western ears. And for a foreigner who doesn't know the words or traditions, the attraction can soon wear off.

Less authentic but more accessible than traditional performances are the rousing instrumentals and lush choreography of the state-supported company, Bakhor (Spring). They have their own concert hall at Alleya Parada 5, at the north end of the long salmon-and-green building on Mustaqillik maydoni. The box office is open from 9.30 am to 5 pm (or you can book a pricier ticket through Uzbektourism), but they're away on tour from June through September.

Theatre & Concert Halls Tashkent has a full cultural life – some of it, like drama, of interest mainly to Uzbek and Russian speakers. But one of Asia's best cultural bargains is surely the Navoi Opera & Ballet Theatre, at Atatürk 28 opposite the Hotel Tashkent, where you can enjoy quality classical western opera almost any night (except June through August) for about US$2 in *sum*. The box office (☎ 33-90-81), in one of the columns out front, is open daily from 10 am to 3 pm and 4 to 6 pm. Even if you don't like opera, the theatre interior makes a visit worthwhile, and the box office will arrange a tour, for about US$1 per person, for any group of three or four who ask.

Other theatres include:

Gorky Drama Theatre (☎ 33-81-65), Sayilgoh 28 (Amir Temur Hiyobon Metro): classical western drama, with performances weekdays at 5 pm (large stage) or 5.30 pm (small stage)

Ilkhom Theatre (☎ 41-22-52), Pakhtakor 5 (Pakhtakor Metro): modern theatre and occasional jazz concerts, with performances at 6 pm

Khamza Drama Theatre (☎ 44-35-42), Navoi 34: Uzbek and classical western drama in Uzbek

Muqimi Musical Theatre (☎ 45-36-45), Almazar 187 (Halqlar Dustligi Metro): traditional Uzbek operettas

Mukhtar Ashrafi Conservatory, Pushkin 31: chamber concerts, Uzbek and western vocal and instrumental recitals, with announcements posted outside

Musical Comedy Theatre, Volgograd (Mirzo Ulughbek Metro): operettas

Palace of Friendship of Peoples, Halqlar Dustligi maydoni

Puppet Theatre (☎ 56-73-95), Kosmonavtlar prospekti 1 (Kosmonavtlar Metro): performances at 11 am and 1 pm

Nightlife The standard night out for Uzbeks and Russians is a long, boozy dinner. Some expatriate westerners gather for vodka and the floor show in the pricey club at the top of the Hotel Uzbekistan, but we've seen visitors overcharged and roughed up there, so we cannot recommend it.

Sayilgoh (Karl Marx) kuchasi, west of the Timur statue, is a dog-eared local version of Moscow's Arbat, with artists, buskers, cheap outdoor eateries, and cheerful young Uzbeks after your dollars. It's seedy and fun, though unaccompanied women may find some of these characters unpleasant after dark.

There's said to be an outdoor disco in Ulughbek Park (by Mirzo Ulughbek Metro station) on Wednesday, Saturday and Sunday evenings.

Circus There's no local circus company, but you can sometimes catch visiting troupes at the arena on Khadra maydoni.

Things to Buy

Handicrafts The Museum of Applied Arts, on Shpilkov south of Kosmonavtlar Metro station, has a good but expensive shop with some genuinely old items (how about a silk cloak for US$120, or a samovar for US$3000?), and overpriced carpets. The museum is open daily from 10 am to 5 pm.

The shop in the Museum of Fine Arts is said to sell good Turkmen rugs on commission occasionally. The museum, at Movarounnakhr (Proletarskaya) 16, is open

daily from 10 am to 5.30 pm (except to 4.30 pm Monday, and closed Tuesday).

The former Abdul Khasim medressa, behind the Palace of Friendship near Halqlar Dustligi Metro station, is currently a 'museum of traditional arts', with some attractive souvenirs by local artisans. It's open daily from 9 am to 6 pm. You could also try the 'antiques' shop in the Union of Artists hall, diagonally across Sharaf Rashidov from the Hotel Tashkent.

There is a good general gift shop (for locals, not tourists) on Furqat by Halqlar Dustligi Metro station.

Silk They haven't got the atmosphere of the bazars, but for the best prices and a surprisingly good selection of silk by the metre, try the big department stores (*univermag*) – one across Uzbekistan from the Hotel Tashkent, the other south across the road from the Hotel Chorsu.

Art Galleries In the Exhibition Hall of the Uzbek Artists' Union, opposite the Hotel Tashkent, is the Union's own Hamar Gallery; enter on the north side. For kitsch street-level art, try the little open-air gallery on Sayilgoh (Karl Marx).

Open-Air Markets In warm weather, a big goods bazar sprawls by the Ippodrom (Hippodrome) every morning except Monday, but it's biggest by far on Sunday, with small-time *biznesmen* selling cheap goods of every kind. The Ippodrom is two km south-west from Sobir Rakhimov Metro station, along Halqlar Dustligi prospekti on bus No 108 or tram No 17.

Tezykovka is the local name for a vast Sunday 'flea market' near the airport. Once a place for hobbyists, bookworms and talkers, it's now a sombre sea of junk – 'anything from nails to nukes' as one resident put it – some of it probably stolen. Take bus No 2 from Tashkent Metro station to the 'GAI' stop and walk south on Starodubtsev, or bus No 25 south on Movarounnakhr near the Hotel Uzbekistan to the 'Pervomaysky

Rynok' stop and cross under the railway tracks.

Watch your purse or wallet; gangs of pickpockets are said to work these bazars.

Farmers' Markets Tashkent has at least 16 open-air farmers' markets or bazars (Uzbek: *dekhqon bozori*, Russian: *rynok*). The best for produce in season, say locals, are:

Alay (Russian Alaysky), four blocks north of the Hotel Uzbekistan on Amir Temur hiyobon; being closest to the tourist zone, this one also has money changers, pickpockets and other lowlife
Chorsu, the central bazar for the old town, at Chorsu Metro station
Farhad (Russian: Farkhadsky), six stops west from Khamza Metro station on tram No 9
Mirabad (Russian: Gospitalnyy), four blocks west of Tashkent Metro station on tram No 8, 9 or 24

Also worth a look is the modest 'Beshagach' bazar (Uzbeks write it Besh-Yoghoch, 'Five Karagach Trees'), in an isolated section of the old town near the Palace of the Friendship of Peoples (Halqlar Dustligi Metro station). On nearby Beshagach maydoni is the pleasant Arpapoya Kafe.

Supermarket Western toiletries – including shampoo, toilet paper and tampons – are available at the joint-venture Almazar Superstor on Uzbekistan, by the second block of flats east of Halqlar Dustligi Metro station. It's open from 9 am to 6 pm, daily except Sunday.

Getting There & Away

Air Tashkent airport is Central Asia's main international airport. If you're arriving here for the first time see the Air section of the Getting There & Away chapter, for important information and warnings.

Airport Orientation Following is a walkthrough of Tashkent airport at the time of research, though things are sure to change as it frantically adjusts to being a major international hub.

The old terminal is currently for arrivals, departures and baggage claim (although for-

eigners arriving here are shuttled to immigration at the new terminal, then back to collect their bags), and for CIS departures. Uzbektourism's airport office (☎ 55-18-36, 55-33-90) is inside the right-hand door, on an inside courtyard.

The new terminal is for international arrivals, departures and baggage claim, and CIS arrivals (CIS baggage claim could be in either terminal). On the ground floor is the claustrophobic arrivals hall, a foreign exchange bank, a duty-free shop and medical services. Upstairs is the international departures hall, including VIP lounge, an information window, a cashier for last-minute international tickets from Uzbekistan Airways, a restaurant and some shops.

Up a further (circular) stairway is the Foreign Affairs Consular Section office (☎ 55-18-36), offices of other international airlines using the airport, a transit lounge and another restaurant.

Connections From Tashkent, Uzbekistan Airways flies daily to Samarkand (one hour), Bukhara (1½ hours), Urgench (2¼ hours) and Ferghana (one hour). Other daily or almost-daily connections are to Andijan, Namangan and Kokand in the Ferghana Valley; Qarshi and Termez in the south; and Nukus on the Aral Sea.

Regional connections include Ashghabat daily, and Almaty, Bishkek, Chimkent, Charjou and Turkmenbashi (Krasnovodsk) two or three times a week. A Kyrgyzstan Airlines Yak-40 also goes to/from Bishkek once a week. CIS flights include Moscow (daily), and St Petersburg and other Russian centres several times a week.

Direct international connections to/from at least 18 other cities are detailed in the Getting There & Away chapter.

Buying Tickets Outbound Uzbekistan Airways tickets are best bought a few days in advance, at the city booking office (☎ 066 or ☎ 56-38-37), Shota Rustaveli 9 opposite the Hotel Rossiya. Take tram No 28 west from the TsUM department store, or tram No 7, 8 or 10 south on Sharaf Rashidov by the

UZBEKISTAN

UZBEKISTAN

Hotel Tashkent. Some credit cards are accepted. Information for English speakers is at window No 25.

Uzbektourism hotels will book flights for a US$5 fee. You can also buy last-minute international tickets at a window on the departures level of the new terminal. Airport staff say the international dispatcher's office (just to the right of passport control on the departures level) might help if you have an open ticket and want to leave the same day.

City offices of other airlines serving Tashkent are:

THY (Turkish Airlines), Mustafa Kemal Atatürk 24
    (☎ 56-46-54, 56-15-63)
PIA (Pakistan International Airlines), Halqlar
    Dustligi 4 (☎ 54-92-15)

These also have offices at the airport, along with Lufthansa (☎ 54-85-69), Ariana Afghan, Iran Air and Transaero, a Russian carrier.

Bus The Tashkent long-distance bus station is 200 metres north-west from Sobir Rakhimov Metro station, through a complex of stalls and hawkers (don't confuse it with the regional bus stand beside the Metro station).

Bus Connections Major destinations and departure frequencies include Samarkand (hourly until 5 pm), Bukhara (five a day), Urgench/Khiva and Termez (each one a day), Chimkent (every 25 minutes until 6.30 pm), Bishkek and Almaty (each at least five a day). For Ashghabat, change at Bukhara.

Buying Tickets You can buy tickets up to 10 days before departure, but only with clearance from the 24 hour passport (OVIR) office, upstairs at the left end. Show them your passport, visa and hotel registration receipts and get a chit to show the cashier. Change money at window No 5. An OVIR gopher might buy your ticket for you, but then you'll never know the real price.

There is *no fee* for this, though if your visa has expired you're asking for a 'fine'. Even

travellers whose papers were in order have been shaken down here; one who came on the final day of his visa was told he should have bought the ticket the day before, and only avoided forking over US$100 when a Russian-speaking friend raised a fuss. If you have trouble, offer to discuss it with Uzbektourism and Foreign Affairs; they should speak enough English to get the point.

You could ask one of the station's money changers to buy a ticket for you, or go to one of the private minibuses in front of the station, but the police usually check tickets and papers on all buses. We had few hassles of this kind outside Tashkent.

Beware of 'crowds' that form around the window where you buy your ticket – these are often gangs of young pickpockets.

Train Tashkent station, right by Tashkent Metro station, is mainly for destinations north and east of the city (eg the Ferghana Valley, Bishkek and Almaty), and for Moscow. South station is for those to the south and west (eg Samarkand, Bukhara, Urgench, Termez and Dushanbe); take tram No 7 or 28 from near the Hotel Tashkent, or tram No 24 from Tashkent Metro station.

Train Connections Fast trains originate here every day for Samarkand and Bukhara; four times a day to Andijan via Kokand and Marghilan in the Ferghana Valley (and on to Jalal-Abad in Kyrgyzstan on some days); and at least twice a week to Bishkek (16 hours), to Almaty (24 hours), and to Termez and Dushanbe. Three or four trains a day make the 56 hour odyssey to/from Moscow; train No 5 departing at 8.10 am includes two-berth cabins.

Some fares at the time of research were US$10 to Samarkand, US$15 to Bukhara, US$25 to Khiva and US$90 to Moscow – *plus* US$20 commission.

Buying Tickets Uzbekistan Railways decided to keep more hard-currency takings by selling tickets only at their own booking office near Tashkent station (though there are signs they may put booking desks back in the hotels).

First go to the 24 hour passport (OVIR) office at Tashkent station (out onto the platform and down to the left) with your passport, Uzbek visa and hotel registration receipts. Go there no matter which station your train leaves from. They give you a chit for the railway booking office, or they might call ahead for you.

It's a five minute walk from there (turn right from the station, left at the corner and across the canal) to the booking office (ТЕМУР ЙЎЛ КАССАЛАРИ) at Movarounnakhr (Proletarskaya) 51, opposite the old Railway Workers' Palace of Culture. The foreigners' hall at the right end is open daily from 8 am to noon and 1 to 5 pm. You pay in US\$ cash, including a cheeky US\$20 commission for each ticket of any size. They'll sell you 2nd class (kupeynyy) unless you ask for something else. They like you to buy them at least five days ahead.

Getting Around

To/From the Airport Tedious they are, but buses are the cheapest way to and from the airport. Coming *from* the airport, they're also an alternative to greedy, sometimes crooked taxi drivers. Unfortunately they don't run late at night.

Bus No 25 and the infrequent express bus No 67-3 take 25 minutes to/from the clock tower on Movarounnakhr (Proletarskaya) near the Hotel Uzbekistan. The No 14 trolleybus takes 30 to 40 minutes to/from Navoi Metro station, near the Hotel Yoshlik. Express bus No 11-3 runs between the airport and the Hotel Chorsu.

The six km, 20 minute taxi ride to/from the Hotel Uzbekistan should be about US\$2, but drivers at the airport seem to have formed a cartel and won't accept less than about US\$10 from foreigners.

Metro The Tashkent Metropolitan opened as the VI Lenin Tashkent Metropolitan in 1978,

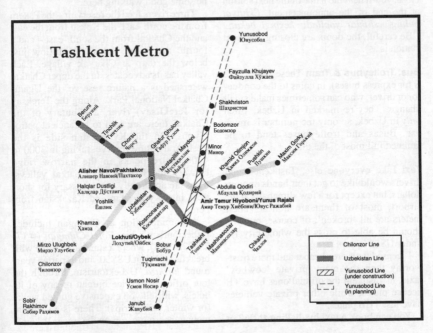

and still bears brave, incongruous Soviet-era murals and reliefs. Despite the queues and the jam-packed stations, this is the easiest way to get around. During the day you'll never wait more than five minutes for a train, and the stations are all squeaky clean.

There are two lines (the red-mapped Chilanzor and blue-mapped Uzbekistan lines), with a crowded pedestrian interchange between them at Pakhtakor and Alisher Navoi stations. A new line (the green-mapped Yunusabad line) is under construction. Plastic tokens, good for a one-way journey between any two stations, are 1 S. The system runs from 6 am to about 1 am daily.

Despite the use of Uzbek for signs and announcements, the system is easy to use, and well enough signposted that you hardly need a map. The most important signs are КИРИШ (entrance), ЧИҚИШ (exit), and ЎТИШ (interchange).

If you listen as the train doors are about to close, you'll hear the name of the next station at the end of the announcement, *Ekhtiyot buling, eshiklar yopiladi; keyingi bekat...* ('Be careful, the doors are closing; the next station is...').

Bus, Trolleybus & Tram These cost 1 S (2 S for express buses), in coins to the conductor or driver, who can sometimes make small change. They're marked in Uzbek, often *only* in Uzbek, so only the number is much use. Buses and trolleybuses tend to be jammed full most of the time.

Taxi Like everyone else, Tashkent's taxi drivers would like to get their hands on your dollars, but except for a few slimeballs at the airport, most of them are honest. Their meters are all 'broken', of course, but you should be able to cross the whole city for under US$2 in *sum*.

Licensed taxis are cheaper and more trustworthy than the many private 'cowboy' taxis. In Tashkent the official ones have TH licence plates, while other private vehicles have just ТНБ plates.

You can book a taxi by dialling ☎ 062 or ☎ 34-51-60, though you'll have to pay a surcharge on the fare.

Car There are no car-rental agencies here, but you can hire a car and driver from the service bureau at the Hotel Uzbekistan for US$10 per hour and up. A cheaper alternative is to hire a taxi for about half that.

AROUND TASHKENT

What opportunities there are for outdoor recreation near Tashkent are in the Chatkal mountains, an outrider of the Tian Shan, east of the city.

Chimgan
УЙМГАН

This recreation zone on the south shore of the Charvak reservoir, 80 km (2½ hours by bus) up the Chirchik river valley, is popular for winter sports (though it runs a poor second to those near Bishkek and Almaty). But it's open year round, and there is said to be some good walking here.

Three rivers feed the reservoir – the Pskem from the north-east, the Koksu from the east and the Chatkal from the south-east – and a fourth, the Ugam, joins the outflow just below the dam at Charvak village. Each valley has its advocates. In the upper Chatkal watershed is a nature reserve, the Ugam-Chatkal National Park. Along the Tereksay (or Tereklisay) river, a tributary of the Chatkal, there are said to be ancient petroglyphs. On the Kyrgyzstan side is the Besh-Aral nature reserve, taking in 3000 to 4000 metre peaks in the narrow ridge between the Koksu and Chatkal valleys. Visas are apparently not necessary for short treks into Kyrgyzstan and Kazakstan from here.

Accommodation at Chimgan includes Uzbektourism's big *Hotel Chimgan* (☎ (7-274222) 444), where a standard double with breakfast is about US$50, and a spartan year-round *turbaza*. Uzbektourism, through the tour office or service bureau of any of its hotels, will sell you expensive guided walks (or winter skiing trips). There is a seasonal mountaineering camp on the upper Pskem.

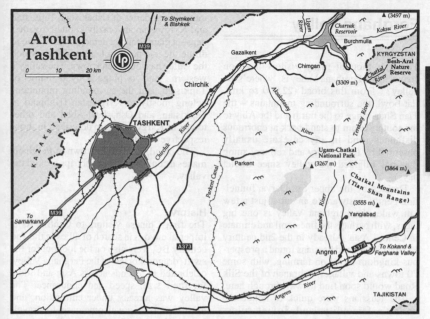

You can get to Chimgan on your own by bus, or as far as Charvak village and the dam by train.

Angren River Valley

Another river, the Angren (or Akhangaran), drops out of the Tian Shan south-east of Tashkent. The canyon of the upper Angren is the most dramatic and least accessible part of Tashkent's natural surroundings.

The coal town of Angren is about 100 km (3½ hours by bus) up the valley from Tashkent. Nearby is a 12th century mausoleum. Thirteen km north up a side canyon is the grotty Yangiabad turbaza (better to stay at Angren's modest hotel or bring your own tent, say locals), from where there are fine walks past cliffs and waterfalls towards the Ugam-Chatkal National Park, and a week-long trek over to Chimgan.

Crawling over the 2267 metre Kamchik pass at the top of the Angren valley is a warm-weather road, too steep for buses, into

the Ferghana Valley – the only way to get there by land from Tashkent without going through Tajikistan. See Getting There & Away in the Ferghana Valley section.

White-Water Boating

Several rivers in this region offer the chance for rafting and kayaking. The Angren and Syr-Darya are for beginners. More experienced boaters will appreciate the Ugam and the Chatkal rivers, while the most challenging is said to be the upper Pskem. The white-water season is September through October.

Ferghana Valley

The first thought many visitors have on arrival in the Ferghana Valley is, 'where's the valley?'. From this broad (22,000 sq km), flat bowl, the surrounding mountains – the Tian Shan range to the north and the Alay to the south – seem to stand back at enormous distances (and in any case are usually obscured by the foundry and refinery smog that has blighted the valley since Soviet days).

Drained by the upper Syr-Darya, funnelling gently westward to an outlet just a few km wide, the Ferghana Valley is one big oasis, with perhaps the finest soil and climate in Central Asia. Already in the 2nd century BC the Greeks and Persians found a prosperous kingdom based on farming, with some 70 towns and villages. A branch of the Silk Road would soon find its way through here.

The Russians were quick to notice the valley's fecundity, and Soviet rulers enslaved it to an obsessive raw-cotton monoculture that will only slowly be dismantled and allow Uzbekistan an economic equilibrium of its own. But there is also abundant seasonal fruit, and this is the centre of Central Asian silk production (see the Silk Production in Uzbekistan aside in Marghilan, this section).

With seven million people – a third of Uzbekistan's population – the valley is the most densely settled area in Central Asia, and thoroughly Uzbek – 85% overall, and higher in the smaller towns. Unlike Samarkand or Bukhara, it has few architectural monuments and no tradition of religious or secular scholarship, and on the whole its towns are architecturally uninspiring. But it has always wielded a large share of Uzbekistan's political and religious influence. For the visitor its main assets are a conservative but hospitable people, several kaleidoscopic bazars, and the proximity of the mountains.

Although this is a kind of Uzbek heartland in terms of language, population and tradition, it's not all part of Uzbekistan. The mutual boundaries of Uzbekistan, Tajikistan and Kyrgyzstan are crazily knotted together here – a giant Stalinist demographic fiddle to dilute the independent tendencies for which the valley has long been known. The valley's western 'gate' is plugged by a thumb of Tajikistan, and the surrounding mountains belong mostly to Kyrgyzstan (Khojand in Tajikistan, and Osh, Jalal-Abad and other towns in Kyrgyzstan, are described in those respective chapters).

The bland, Russian-era town of Ferghana makes a convenient base for trips around the valley.

History

The first Chinese visitors to Central Asia, imperial envoys in search of allies in the 2nd century BC, were also on the lookout for the swift 'dragon-horses' of the Ferghana Valley, celebrated in legends across Asia and India for their size, speed and endurance. The valley was already under cultivation, and must have been a welcome oasis for travellers coming from the deserts in the east.

Temple remains at Kuva and elsewhere suggest the valley was Buddhist-ruled before the arrival of the Arabs in the 8th century. The valley's best-known son is probably Zahiruddin Babur, founder of India's Moghul Dynasty in the 16th century.

About 1709, valley tribes elected one Shahrukh Bey as their leader, and the so-called Kokand khanate split from its Bukhara parent. The bickering of the Khiva, Bukhara and Kokand city-states would thereafter dominate Central Asia until the mid-19th century. At its height the Kokand khanate's claims extended west to Tashkent, north to Shymkent (Chimkent) and east as far as Kashgar. The last Kokand ruler was a Russian puppet named Khudoyar Khan.

Kokand, Andijan and Osh were taken by the tsar's troops in 1876 with little effort, and the khanate was dissolved. Uncomfortable in the valley's medieval towns, the first military governor, General Mikhail Skobelev (soon to achieve infamy for the massacre of the Turkmen at Geok-Tepe) founded the New

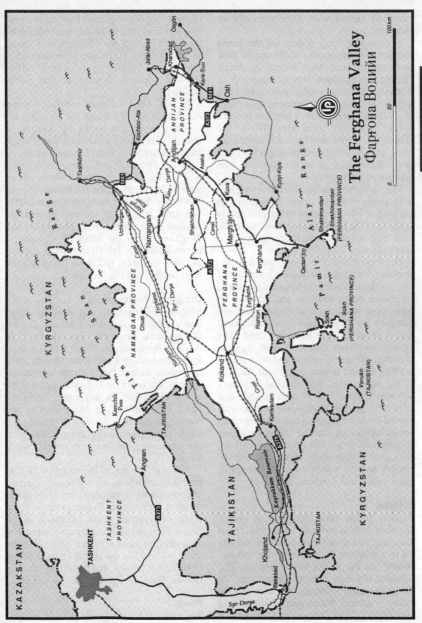

Margilan cantonment, later renamed as Ferghana.

In trying to keep a grip on the tsar's domains, the Bolsheviks made one of their worst moves here. After a rival, moderate Islamic government was proclaimed in Kokand, Tashkent revolutionaries in 1918 sacked the town and slaughtered thousands of civilians. Central Asia's previously somnolent Muslims were electrified, the basmachi rebellion was ignited in town after town, and any trust Muslims might have had in the Revolution or in the Russians was permanently destroyed.

The valley's legendary fertility brought it to its knees in Soviet times. Less than 300 km long, it was harnessed to provide nearly a quarter of the USSR's raw cotton, and aside from fruit and silkworms little else is raised here even now.

The frustrations of this lopsided, seasonal economy, coupled with Stalin's invention of 'us-and-them' republican boundaries, stirred up intense ethnic tensions, and glasnost let these loose in the form of bloody violence that gave the valley a bad name in the final Soviet years and left hundreds dead. The ugliest incidents included riots against Meskheti Turks in Ferghana and other towns in 1989, an anti-Jewish pogrom in Andijan in the same year, and mutual butchery between Uzbeks and Kyrgyz at Osh and Özgön (Uzgen) in 1990. Abundant circumstantial evidence suggests that in many cases Soviet authorities allowed originally minor disturbances to get out of hand – military units were mysteriously withdrawn, provocateurs arrived equipped with transport, maps, radios and weapons, and so on.

Religion

Muslims in this rural, conservative corner take their faith as seriously as any in Central Asia, and the end of Soviet rule has naturally led to a religious revival (or to an 'Islamic hotbed', as the media like to put it). The outlawed IRP enjoys strong support here. To the government's unease, the east end of valley – around Namangan, Andijan and over the border in Osh and Jalal-Abad – is

also proving fertile ground for fundamentalism, especially the Wahhabi brand offered by the Saudi-backed Ahle Sunnah movement. In March 1992, 70 people were arrested in Namangan following fundamentalist-inspired attempts to seize several public buildings.

In Jalal-Abad we made our first Central Asian sightings of *paranji*, the tent-like, all-covering garments worn by women in conservative Muslim communities, though locals insisted they were Iranian visitors.

In the 18th and 19th centuries, Kokand was Central Asia's second Islamic centre after Bukhara, its khans the bitter rivals of Bukhara's. Worship, forbidden in the 1920s, was later grudgingly allowed at a single mosque each in Kokand, Marghilan and Ferghana. After the 1989/90 violence, a nervous Moscow fell all over itself approving new mosques, and since independence their number has mushroomed.

Dangers & Annoyances

Visitors to Namangan and Andijan report heavy-handed police and a general distrust of outsiders, especially non-Muslims. In Andijan three women Peace Corps volunteers were assaulted, and others shaken down by police, before Peace Corps operations were moved out of the Uzbekistan part of the valley altogether. In any case, Andijan's bazar has nothing on Marghilan's, and Namangan has little to offer. If you do go, stash your greenbacks deep (travellers' cheques make good decoys, as nobody wants them).

Although the rest of the valley is as hospitable as anywhere in Uzbekistan, standard of dress remains a major source of misunderstanding everywhere. Except perhaps in the centre of Ferghana town, too much tourist flesh will be an insult and a provocation. For your safety as much as others' peace of mind, dress modestly, ie no shorts or tight-fitting clothes for either sex, and preferably no short sleeves. Bare legs are decidedly a bad idea.

Food

The valley is known for its cuisine, but you

won't find it in restaurants. The way to taste a Ferghana plov is to be invited to someone's home. Uzbek men here are proud of their cooking skills. The best choyhonas include special rooms where guests can cook their own meals with ingredients from the nearest bazar. Hotel restaurants mainly limit themselves to dreary Russian fare and imitation laghman.

Vegetarians and self-caterers will do fairly well at the valley's well-stocked bazars. The most colourful bazar is Marghilan's, on Thursday and Sunday. The biggest and perhaps most thoroughly Uzbek one is in Andijan.

Getting There & Away
Overland to/from Tashkent There are two main routes into the valley from the west. The only one that stays within Uzbekistan is a serpentine road via Angren over the 2267 metre Kamchik pass. It's too dicey for big buses but is normally open to minivans and cars from mid-April to mid-November – though you might hire a taxi between Kokand and Angren anytime the road isn't snowbound.

It takes about 3½ to four hours from Tashkent to Kokand this way.

The other, longer route goes via Khojand in Tajikistan. When we were there, this was far enough from Tajikistan's civil strife to be quite safe, but check before you go. Unless you try to get off in Tajikistan without a Tajik visa, or are laden with goods, you should have few official hassles on this route. If the Tajik 'troubles' heat up, buses to/from Tashkent and Samarkand may be curtailed or there may be stiffer checks at the Uzbek-Tajik border crossings.

Overland to/from Kyrgyzstan Osh is 115 km east of Ferghana town, with frequent bus connections. From Osh, via Jalal-Abad, a dramatic, two-lane mountain road snakes for 650 km to Bishkek (with a change of bus at Toktogul). See the Bishkek-Osh Road section in the Kyrgyzstan chapter for more information.

A less travelled, less comfortable road climbs from Jalal-Abad, east via the gold-mining town of Kazarman to Naryn, from where you can get to the Torugart pass into China. Jalal-Abad to Naryn takes at least two days. See the Naryn to Jalal-Abad section in the Kyrgyzstan chapter.

Even if you miss the border post, you'll notice when you have crossed the border. The Kyrgyz part of the Ferghana Valley has fewer services and poorer food, but lower prices and cooler air, than the Uzbek part.

Train Daily fast trains connect Tashkent with Khojand, Kokand, Marghilan and Andijan (there is no station at Ferghana). To get to/from Bishkek you must go via Tashkent, a dreary 1½ day trip originating in Jalal-Abad every other day.

Trains seem to cross the short strip of Tajikistan more or less independently of civil strife in that country. A weekly fast train goes to/from Moscow, 3½ days away.

Air Tashkent is linked to Kokand, Ferghana and Andijan by daily flights, and Moscow to Ferghana and Andijan once weekly.

Getting Around
A car with driver is US$10 to US$12 per hour from Uzbektourism in Ferghana.

KOKAND
ҚЎҚОН
Population: 176,000
This was the capital of the Kokand khanate in the 18th and 19th centuries, and the valley's true 'hotbed' in those days – second only to Bukhara as a religious centre in Central Asia, with at least 35 medressas and hundreds of mosques. But if you walk the streets today, you'll find only a polite, subdued Uzbek town, its old centre hedged by colonial avenues, bearing little resemblance to Bukhara.

Nationalists fed up with empty revolutionary promises met here in January 1918 and declared a rival administration, the 'Muslim Provincial Government of Autonomous Turkestan'. Jenghiz Khan would have admired the response by the Tashkent Soviet, who immediately had the town sacked, most of its holy buildings desecrated or destroyed, and somewhere between 5000 and 14,000 Kokandis slaughtered. What little physical evidence of Kokand's former stature remained was either left to decay, or mummified as 'architectural monuments'.

Many of the mosques and medressas that did survive are coming back to life now, and non-Muslim visitors, especially women, are no longer welcome in some.

There's a hotel here, but you can do the town justice on a day trip from Ferghana (1½ hours away by bus).

Orientation

The khan's palace is now just another amusement in the central Muqimi Park (called 'Russian Park' by locals). The remnants of pre-Russian Kokand are roughly between the park, the train station to the south-west, and the main bazar (and adjacent main bus station) to the south-east. Off Khamza and Akbar Islamov kuchasi are old-town lanes good for a wander, plus most of the town's surviving religious buildings. The centre of 'tourist' Kokand is Abdulla Nabiev maySdoni, a 15 minute walk west of the park. The airport is about 10 km south of town.

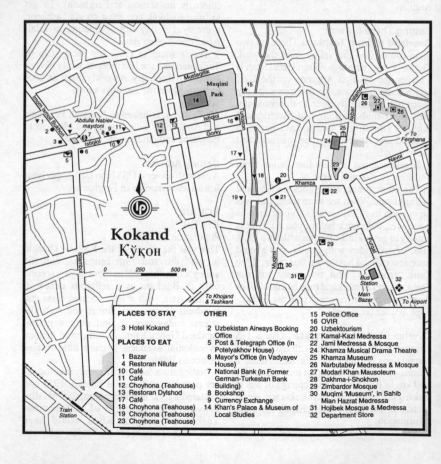

PLACES TO STAY	OTHER	15 Police Office
3 Hotel Kokand	2 Uzbekistan Airways Booking Office	16 OVIR
		20 Uzbektourism
PLACES TO EAT	5 Post & Telegraph Office (in Potelyakhov House)	21 Kamal-Kazi Medressa
1 Bazar	6 Mayor's Office (in Vadyayev House)	22 Jami Medressa & Mosque
4 Restoran Nilufar		24 Khamza Musical Drama Theatre
10 Café	7 National Bank (in Former German-Turkestan Bank Building)	25 Khamza Museum
11 Café		26 Narbutabey Medressa & Mosque
12 Choyhona (Teahouse)	8 Bookshop	27 Modari Khan Mausoleum
13 Restoran Dylshod	9 Currency Exchange	28 Dakhma-i-Shokhon
17 Café	14 Khan's Palace & Museum of Local Studies	29 Zimbardor Mosque
18 Choyhona (Teahouse)		30 Muqimi 'Museum', in Sahib Mian Hazrat Medressa
19 Choyhona (Teahouse)		31 Hojibek Mosque & Medressa
23 Choyhona (Teahouse)		32 Department Store

UZBEKISTAN

UZBEKISTAN

Information

On Abdulla Nabiev maydoni are the main post and telegraph office and the National Bank (open weekdays from 8.30 to 11 am). A private currency exchange office is on Istiqlol just east of the square. On the east side of the park on Turkiston are OVIR and a police office. A small Uzbektourism office is on Khamza, south of the park.

Khan's Palace

The palace of the final khan, Khudoyar, now shares space in a pleasure park with a dance pavilion and a mothballed Yak-40. It's easy to see this as a Soviet insult to the memory of Kokand's glory, but the khan seems to have managed that pretty well on his own.

His bloated palace, with seven courtyards and 113 rooms, was completed in 1873 – just three years before the tsar's troops arrived, blew up its fortifications and abolished his job. He fled, not from the Russians but from his own subjects (who were probably encouraged to ransack the palace); indeed he fled *to* the Russians at Orenburg, and a comfortable exile (he was later killed by bandits as he returned through Afghanistan from a pilgrimage to Mecca).

The palace's surviving two courtyards and 19 rooms, now under restoration, house a staid Museum of Local Studies, with jewellery and musical instruments in the throne room, Uzbek furniture in the waiting room, and Oriental porcelain in the khan's well-used bedroom. It's open daily, except Sunday and Monday, from 9 am to 5 pm.

Narbutabey Medressa & Around

The Bolsheviks closed the 1799 **Narbutabey medressa** but it's now open again with about 80 students, one of two in town (the other is the 1818 Jami medressa on Khamza kuchasi); visitors are not welcome at either medressa. To win wartime support from Muslim subjects, Stalin had the adjacent **mosque** reopened, the only one for all of Kokand at the time.

The first right turn beyond the medressa takes you into a **graveyard** with several prominent mausolea associated with another khan, Umar. To the right inside the graveyard is the bright sky-blue cupola of the unrestored **Modari Khan mausoleum**, built in 1825 for the khan's mother. To the left is the 1830s **Dakhma-i-Shokhon** (Grave of Kings), the tomb of the khan and other family members, with an elegant wooden portal carved with Quranic verses and/or Umar's poetry.

Nasrullah Khan, the Emir of Bukhara, is said to have kidnapped Umar's independent-minded wife, a poetess named Nodira, and demanded that she marry him. When she refused, Nasrullah had her beheaded, along with her children and her brothers-in-law. Originally buried behind Modari Khan, she was adopted by the Soviets as a model Uzbek woman and moved to a prominent place beneath a white **stone tablet**, beyond Dakhma-i-Shokhon.

Russian Buildings

Around Abdulla Nabiev maydoni (named for a prominent Kokand Bolshevik) is a knot of sturdy brick buildings, built by the Russians in turn-of-the-century 'mixed style', with sculptured façades and copper cupolas. They include the former headquarters of the German-Turkestan Bank (and still a bank), Potelyakhov House (1907, now the main post and telegraph office) and Vadyayev House (1911, now the mayor's office).

Sahib Mian Hazrat Medressa

From the uninteresting Kamal-Kazi medressa on Khamza, walk five minutes down Muqimi kuchasi to No 77, the truncated remnants of a big medressa called Sahib Mian Hazrat (1861). Most of it was appropriated in Soviet times for a factory, but in a couple of surviving cells the Uzbek poet and 'democrat' Muhammedamin Muqimi (1850-1903) is said to have spent his last days. For about US$0.25 in *sum* the earnest caretaker will give you a tedious tour of every inch, plus a few photos of pre-WWI Kokand. Muqimi's childhood home is apparently nearby too.

Khamza Museum

This could just as well be dedicated to Lenin – a fatuous shrine to a Soviet-imposed 'national hero', the poet Khamza Khakimzade Niyazi (who was born in Kokand) – full of manuscripts and Socialist-realism (and the odd photo of old Kokand), and staffed by guides who shadow you like the KGB. Kokand's main bazar was blasted away to make room for this Soviet-gigantic building and the twin Khamza Musical Drama Theatre – both now crumbling. The museum, on Akbar Islamov, is open daily, except Monday, from 9 am to 5 pm.

Places to Stay

The decrepit *Hotel Kokand* (☎ 3-74-83) on Abdulla Nabiev maydoni doesn't make Uzbektourism's top 10, but it does have hot water, clean linen and earnest service. Singles/doubles with bath and toilet are overpriced at US$16/22, and a few singles with shared bathroom are US$8. It was facing privatisation (and probable price hikes) when we were there. Get there from the bus station on south-bound marshrutnoe taxi No 1 or 8, or bus No 3, 8 or 14. From the train station take almost anything northbound on Istambul.

Places to Eat

The biggest place in town, with decent Russian and Uzbek dishes inside and shashlyk and plov outside, is *Restoran Dylshod* on the west side of Muqimi Park. Opposite the Hotel Kokand, the gloomy *Restoran Nilufar* has scrawny chicken tabak and other just-edible Russian items. Fill up at either for about US$1.50. Despite flies grazing on the tables and a front hall smelling of urine, the glum place by the *Hotel Kokand* will do early breakfast.

There are choyhonas dotted all over the place, some of them serving food, though hygiene is dubious. A pleasant *choyhona* is in the little park near the Khamza Museum. Vegetarians and self-caterers can go to the big *bazar* by the bus station, or a small one near the hotel.

Getting There & Away

Air The only regular connection is to/from Tashkent, six times a week for about US$53. The Uzbekistan Airways booking office is beside the Hotel Kokand.

Train There are four fast trains a day to Tashkent from here. Every other day one passes through from Jalal-Abad to Bishkek.

Bus & Taxi The bus station, by the main bazar on Furqat, is to be phased out in favour of a new one out on the Tashkent road. Ferghana and Marghilan are 90 km (two hours) away by bus, with departures about every half hour. Buses go hourly to Andijan and Namangan, four times a day to Tashkent (via Khojand) and twice a day to Samarkand. Taxi drivers may want the equivalent of US$70 for four passengers to Tashkent via the Kamchik pass, or about half that to go up to the pass and back.

On the road to Ferghana, watch for the original of many stone gates erected, in venerable Soviet style, to celebrate the first year of Uzbekistan's independence.

Getting Around

Bus No 14 links the airport, train station and bus station, but apparently only to meet incoming and departing flights. Bus No 4 runs back and forth past the Hotel Kokand, Khan's Palace, Jami medressa and the bus station and bazar. Bus Nos 16 and 23 go north from the bus station to the area around Narbutabey medressa.

FERGHANA

ФАРГОНА

Population: 193,000

This is among the valley's least ancient and least Uzbek towns. It began in 1877 as Novy Margelan (New Marghilan), a colonial annex to nearby Marghilan. For a short time it was called Sim (meaning 'wire', possibly in honour of the arrival of the telephone here), then Skobelev. The name Ferghana (say 'FAIR-gha-na') dates from the 1920s.

With streets shaded by maples and dotted with sky-blue buildings, it should be a nice

Uzbekistan
Tilla-Kari (Gold Covered) medressa, Registan Square, Samarkand

Top: Stranded fishing boat, Moynaq, Uzbekistan
Bottom: Main road of Arslanbob, an Uzbek village in the Babash-Ata mountains
near Jalal-Abad, Ferghana Valley, Kyrgyzstan

place to hang out, but it's vaguely gloomy – perhaps because, like a mini-Tashkent, it's still the state's administrative and military base in the valley, as it was all through tsarist and Soviet times. It's also where most of the valley's industry is concentrated. Nevertheless it's the most convenient and comfortable town from which to look around the valley.

Orientation

The streets radiate from what's left of the old tsarist fort, 10 metres of mud-brick wall within an army compound (off limits to vis-

itors) behind the city and provincial administration buildings.

Ferghana doesn't quite have its own long-distance transport system. It's served by two bus stations, the regional Ferghana station behind the bazar and the long-distance station at Yermazar, out on the road to Marghilan. The nearest train station is at Marghilan (though it's far easier to book the train here).

Information

Tourist Offices Uzbektourism, on the 2nd

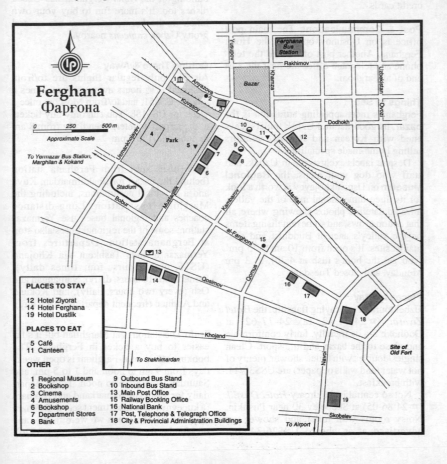

Ferghana
Фарғона

0   250   500 m
Approximate Scale

To Yermazar Bus Station,
Marghilan & Kokand

Park

Stadium

Site of
Old Fort

To Shakhimardan

To Airport

PLACES TO STAY
12 Hotel Ziyorat
14 Hotel Ferghana
19 Hotel Dustlik

PLACES TO EAT
5 Café
11 Canteen

OTHER
1 Regional Museum
2 Bookshop
3 Cinema
4 Amusements
6 Bookshop
7 Department Stores
8 Bank
9 Outbound Bus Stand
10 Inbound Bus Stand
13 Main Post Office
15 Railway Booking Office
16 National Bank
17 Post, Telephone & Telegraph Office
18 City & Provincial Administration Buildings

floor of the Hotel Ziyorat, can arrange transport and valley excursions, preferably for cash. Egitaly Usmanov, the assistant manager and chief English-speaking guide, makes a serious effort to go beyond the tourist sites; he can, for example, arrange informal home visits, trips to the mountains or, in May and June, to a silkworm 'nursery'.

Money Change US$ cash to *sum* at the Hotel Ziyorat, the Hotel Dustlik or the National Bank (open weekdays from 9 am to noon) at al-Farghoni 69. At the time of research nobody was accepting travellers' cheques or credit cards.

Post & Communications The main post office is on Qosimov opposite the Hotel Ferghana. Another post office and the telephone and telegraph office are near the east end of al-Farghoni.

Things to See
Ferghana's most appealing attraction is the **bazar**, its good-natured Uzbek traders leavened with Korean and Russian vendors selling home-made specialities.

Despite labels exclusively in Uzbek, and staff who dog your steps, the **Regional Museum** on Usmankhojayev is worth a look for its three-dimensional map of the valley, infrared satellite photos showing where all that cotton grows, and some tantalising items on the valley's ancient Buddhist and shamanist sites. It's open from 10 am to '5 pm' (you get the bum's rush at 4.30), to 3 pm Monday, and closed Tuesday.

Places to Stay
Uzbektourism's decaying flagship, the *Hotel Ziyorat* (☎ 24-77-42, fax 24-77-62) at Dodhokh 2-a, is friendly, fairly comfortable and close to the bazar and transport. Clean singles/doubles with toilet, shower, plenty of hot water (and walls of paper) are US$30/44, with breakfast.

Not so central is the dreary *Hotel Dustlik* (☎ 24-86-05) at Skobelev 30 near Pushkin. Noisy rooms with toilet and shower are advertised at an absurd US$26/34, but

Ferghana Uzbektourism's chief told us that individuals could stay there for US$12 per person, with breakfast.

The drab, city-run *Hotel Ferghana* (☎ 24-94-56) at Qosimov 29 has rooms with toilet and shower from about US$4/7. Foreigners stay in the middle building of three.

Places to Eat
The *Hotel Ziyorat's* clean, charmless restaurant offers a small, unvarying selection of Russian and pseudo-international food at modest prices. The restaurant in the east building of the *Hotel Ferghana* has Uzbek dishes too. It's more fun to buy your own lunch in the *bazar*, and there are several grotty Uzbek *canteens* nearby.

Getting There & Away
Air The only regular flights are to/from Tashkent (1½ hours away) several times a day for US$51, and to/from Moscow once a week for US$188. You can only buy tickets at the airport counter, open daily from 8 am to noon and 1 to 7 pm.

Bus Buses start from Ferghana station (behind the bazar) for Shakhimardan, Kuva and a few local destinations, including the Marghilan bus station. Long-distance coaches and regional buses use Yermazar station; some of the regional buses also stop at Ferghana station. Departures from Yermazar include Tashkent via Khojand (US$6, eight hours, four times daily), Samarkand (10 hours, daily), Namangan and Osh (every two hours, daily), and Kokand and Andijan (frequent departures each day).

Train The station is at Marghilan but it's far easier to buy a ticket in Ferghana. The booking office on al-Farghoni is open weekdays from 9 am to noon and 1 to 5 pm, and Saturday from 8 am to noon. Trains depart daily for Tashkent, Samarkand and Bukhara (a kupeynyy or compartment seat to Bukhara was about US$6 when we were there), and on Monday for Moscow (kupeynyy US$26).

Getting Around

The airport is a 25 minute trip on bus No 22; bus No 3 takes longer. Yermazar bus station is 10 minutes away on bus No 21, marked ЕРМОЗОР - МАРКАЗ (Yermazar-Centre). All these, and other local buses, depart from Marifat kuchasi near the bazar, returning to adjacent Kuvasoy kuchasi. There are also marshrutnoe taxis to Yermazar from Ferghana station.

The easiest option for getting to the train station in Marghilan is by taxi (locals estimate about US$2.50 in *sum*). There are said to be 'Ferghana-Marghilan' buses from Ferghana station but we never saw any. If you arrive by train, take a taxi to Ferghana, or one to Yermazar station (we paid about US$1) and bus No 21 on to Ferghana bazar.

In general, to home in on Ferghana bazar, ask for *markaz* (centre).

MARGHILAN
МАРГИЛОН
Population: 145,000

Often treated as if it were an appendage of Ferghana, Marghilan in fact came first by a couple of millennia, having been around

(originally as Marginan) since at least the 1st century BC.

It's probably the valley's pre-eminent market town. Marghilan's merchant clans, key players in Central Asia's commerce, are said to be a law unto themselves. In the closing decades of Soviet rule, this was the heart of Uzbekistan's black-market economy. Not surprisingly the main (and only real) attraction here is the bazar.

Marghilan has long been known in Central Asia for its silks. The biggest silk factory and mill in the former Soviet Union are here, dependent for their success on widespread household cultivation of silkworms.

Things to See

On Thursday and Sunday especially, Marghilan's **central bazar** is a time capsule, full of weatherbeaten Uzbeks in traditional clothing exchanging solemn greetings and gossip, with hardly a Russian or a tourist in sight. In summer and autumn the stalls groan under fruit of all kinds, and the air smells of spices.

Half a km east of the bazar is a **mosque** under devoted reconstruction, with two new

Silk Production in Uzbekistan

Although silk thread production and clothmaking have been largely automated, the raising of silkworms is still almost entirely a 'cottage industry', with most worms raised in individual farmers' homes, as they have been since perhaps the 4th century.

Out of its stock from previous years' husbandry, the Uzbekistan government distributes an average of 20 g of young silkworm grubs to any farmer willing to 'raise' them in late April and early May. Each farmer prepares special rooms with large bedding boxes. The worms' entire diet consists of chopped up mulberry leaves culled from trees along lowland roads and canals. The farmers use the leftover branches as fuel, and the stripped mulberry trees regrow their branches the following year.

The initial 20 g of grubs takes up about a sq metre of space and consumes about three kg of leaves a day. But each week, after a sleep cycle of a few days, the worms wake up and eat more than before. At the end of just a month, each of those originally microscopic creatures has grown to the size of a little finger, and together they occupy two or three rooms and devour some 300 kg of leaves each day! Then abruptly they stop eating altogether and spend a week or so rolling themselves up into a cocoon of silk fibres. The farmers (exhausted from trying to gather 300 kg of leaves each day) sell the cocoons back to government silk factories – typically 80 to 120 kg of cocoons at about US$1 to US$2 per kg.

Some worms, called 'seed-worms', are set aside and allowed to hatch as moths, which will lay eggs and produce the next generation of grubs. The rest are killed inside their cocoons by steaming (otherwise they would break out and ruin the silk filaments), and each cocoon is boiled and carefully unwound. A typical three or four cm cocoon yields about one km of filament (800 to 1200 metres)! Several filaments are twisted together to make industrial thread, which is used to make clothing.

Uzbekistan as a whole produces about 30,000 metric tonnes of cocoons a year. The biggest silk factory in the former Soviet Union is at Marghilan. Uzbektourism in Ferghana can arrange overpriced individual and group tours of the factory. ■

minarets out the front. Modestly dressed male visitors may be welcomed into the courtyard and proudly shown the oldest part, an unrestored prayer room dating back, they say, to 1452. It seems to have been too small to catch the Bolsheviks' attention.

Places to Stay

The *Hotel Marghilan* opposite the bazar says 'no foreigners' (by order of Uzbektourism) but two determined travellers phoned the police, who made the hotel take them in. A room is about US$5. It's simpler and more pleasant to come here on a day trip from Ferghana.

Getting There & Away

The trip from Ferghana is simplest in a taxi, for the equivalent of about US$2 (ask for the bazar). A cheaper alternative is the slow, claustrophobic bus from Ferghana station, half an hour via Yermazar bus station and the

Marghilan train station. It's marked simply ФАРГОНА - МАРГИЛОН.

The bazar is right across the intersection from Marghilan's bus station. From the train station it's a half hour trek north on Mustaqillik (formerly ulitsa Karla Marxa), or five minutes by almost any marshrutnoe taxi.

See the Ferghana section for information on long-distance train and bus connections.

RISHTON

This mainly Tajik town near the border with Kyrgyzstan, 50 km west of Ferghana, is known for its potters and pots. But unless you speak Tajik, or shell out for Uzbektourism's half-day excursion to selected studios and workshops (US$60 per person), it's difficult to see how you could find them on your own. Local buses go to Rishton from Ferghana and Marghilan stations.

KUVA

In 1979 the remains of a large Buddhist temple, dating from the 4th to 7th century and destroyed by the Arabs, were excavated at Kuva, about 35 km north-east of Ferghana. Everything loose, including a large Buddha statue, was carted off to the Tashkent History Museum's warehouse. There is virtually nothing left to see now except the adjacent brickworks and a cement plant, but if you insist, take the Kuva bus from Ferghana station (several departures each morning) and ask for *tepa* (high place). Don't fall for Uzbektourism's excursion.

SHAKHIMARDAN
ШОХИМАРДОН

One of the odder results of Stalin's diabolical gerrymandering around the Ferghana Valley is the existence of several tiny 'offshore islands' of one republic entirely surrounded by another. There are about 12 of them through Kyrgyzstan, and one of these is the Uzbek enclave of Shakhimardan, 55 km south of Ferghana.

Shakhimardan's main appeal for visitors is that it's nestled in a 1500 metre high alpine valley, a fine place to clear your lungs and take an easy look at the Alay mountains. Even at the height of summer the air is clean and cool, and above the village is a cheap turbaza within easy reach of trails that hardly anyone seems to use. (Another equally scenic but less accessible Uzbek 'island' is Sokh, 60 km west of Shakhimardan.)

Its main attraction for Muslims is that it's said to be the resting place of Ali, son-in-law of the Prophet Muhammad and fourth Caliph, whose descendants Shia Muslims regard as the true heirs of the Caliphate (at least seven places in the Middle and Far East make the same claim). *Shakh-i-mardan* is Persian for 'King of Men', a reference to Ali. For centuries pilgrims came to pray at the simple Hazrat Ali mosque and mausoleum on a ledge above the village (*hazrat* is an honorific title meaning majestic or holy).

In an effort to suppress this traffic, successive Soviet administrations have tried to reinvent Shakhimardan. The mosque and mausoleum were burned to the ground in the early 1920s – by basmachi rebels trying to flush out 48 Red Army soldiers who had taken refuge there, according to Soviet historians; but by the Bolsheviks, according to local Uzbeks. In any case, the pilgrims stopped coming.

The village was later renamed Khamzaabad, in honour of one of the Bolsheviks' adopted martyrs, the secular Kokandi poet and playwright Khamza Khakimzade Niyazi. Khamza encouraged women to join his first-ever Uzbek theatre company and come out from behind their veils – for which, intoned the Soviets, he was stoned to death by Muslim fundamentalists here in 1929. The real story is undoubtedly more complex.

In the 1960s a Khamza mausoleum was built nearby and, to add true insult to injury, a huge, grotesquely ugly memorial statue to the 48 Red Army soldiers was erected directly beside the ruined shrine to Ali. In 1989, the centenary of Khamza's birth, a Khamza Museum was added, and the hillside below was cleared for a vast Khamza memorial park, complete with a little ersatz Parthenon and a covered escalator up to the complex.

Following Uzbekistan's independence, local donations were used to build a simple replacement for the Ali shrine, and pilgrims once again mingle with holiday-makers during the high season, April through September.

Orientation & Information

From the long-distance bus stand it's a 1.5 km walk up to the village centre, where the valley splits. Up the right-hand canyon, 2.5 km by road or a steep 1.5 km on foot, is Turbaza Shakhimardan. Up the left-hand canyon, past dozens of workers' holiday camps, is Kul-i-Kubbon (Sky-Blue lake).

Sky-Blue Lake

At the end of the road, 4.5 km from the village up the left-hand canyon, is a cable car (or a further steep two or three km walk) to pretty, icy Kul-i-Kubbon, created centuries ago by a landslide. The shore of this alpine lake, at 1740 metres, is crowded in the high season and apparently deserted (but very cold) after that. The path around the lake has collapsed in places.

A boat trip to the head of the lake is 20 S return. From its outlet flows a clear river called Kuk-Sub (Green Water).

Khamza Museum

This dreary building behind Hazrat Ali is mostly full of Soviet-style propaganda – happy Uzbeks organising collective farms etc – but there are some photos of pre-Bolshevik Shakhimardan and the original Hazrat Ali mausoleum. The museum is open daily except Tuesday from 9 am to 1 pm and 2 to 5 pm.

Treks

Turbaza Shakhimardan crawls with Uzbek holiday-makers during high season, enjoying volleyball, videos, excessive food and drink, clean air, and the views. You may be the only guest interested in actually trekking into the hills.

Beyond the turbaza, about 15 km from the village and above 2000 metres, is an ex-military training camp, now an international mountaineering camp (alpinistskiy lager or alplager) and trekking base called Dugoba. Most treks from here cross into Kyrgyzstan, but as this is more or less the only access there's no need for a Kyrgyz visa.

Experienced, well-supplied trekkers could go on their own. Ferghana Uzbektourism can take you on anything from a day trek to a week or more trekking. Guide, equipment (except sleeping bags) and three meals a day will cost about US$40 per person per day for a group of three or four, plus US$45 each way for transport from Ferghana. Agencies in Tashkent and Samarkand may also do trips up here. Trekking season is roughly May through October.

Places to Stay & Eat

The village has lots of choyhonas and food stalls but no hotel. The main place to stay is Turbaza Shakhimardan, with 360 beds in very basic two-bed 'cottages' with common shower and toilets, for US$12 per person per day, including three plain meals. It's jammed in the high season but they can always squeeze in one or two walk-in visitors.

The Dugoba alplager features spartan doubles with common toilet and shower, sauna, and a snack-bar with basic food during trekking season.

Getting There & Away

Buses depart on the scenic trip to Shakhimardan from Ferghana station at least 10 times a day in the high season, or two or three times between 6 and 8 am the rest of the year, for the sum equivalent of about US$0.70. There's no regular transport beyond Shakhimardan village. Do-it-yourselfers may get hassled crossing in and out of the Kyrgyz zone by amateur, self-appointed 'guards' looking for a wee donation. Stand your ground: citizens of Uzbekistan cross freely and so should you if you have an Uzbek visa, especially with Shakhimardan on it.

Uzbektourism's excursion is grossly overpriced at US$111 per person, but for under US$100 you could just hire a car from them for the day.

ANDIJAN
АНДИЖОН

Population: 310,000

Andijan dates to at least the 9th century, but its claim to historical fame is as the birthplace of Zahiruddin Babur (see the Zahiruddin Babur aside) in the 15th century, when it was the capital of the Ferghana state and its main Silk Road trading centre.

It fell to the tsar in 1876, but was the scene of an abortive anti-Russian uprising in 1898. In 1902 an earthquake did what the Bolsheviks might have felt compelled to do two decades later – destroying the town and killing over 4000 people.

Andijan province, the most densely settled part of the valley, is today Uzbekistan's main oil-producing region, and the town is its dour capital. Andijan is said to have the most traditional bazar in the valley, but travellers and expatriate workers say it also has, with Namangan, the most unpleasant police in Uzbekistan. Visitors, especially at the bus station, are prime targets for a shakedown from these idle and underpaid police.

Orientation & Information

Museums, medressa, bank, bookshop, department store, post and telegraph office and a municipal hotel are clustered around the main bazar, about three km north of the bus and train stations (which are a two or three minute walk from one another). Uzbektourism has a small office (☎ 6-10-22) in its own Hotel Zolotaya Dolina (Golden valley), almost two km south of the bus and train stations, which means neither is much use unless you're in a group or have your own transport.

Things to See

The **bazar** is not the biggest in the valley but it's certainly colourful in the early morning. Across Oltinkul is the handsome 19th century **Jami medressa & mosque**, said to be the only building to survive the 1902 earthquake. A factory appears to have been

Andijan
Андижон
0   200   400 m
Approximate Scale
To Train & Bus Stations (2.5 km), Hotel Zolotaya Dolina & Uzbektourism (4 km) & Ferghana

---

Zahiruddin Babur

Born in 1483 to Ferghana's ruler, Umar Sheikh Mirzo, Zahiruddin Babur inherited his father's kingdom before he was even a teenager, but his early career was less than brilliant. At 17 the young king (a descendant of Timur on his father's side and Jenghiz Khan on his mother's) took Samarkand, but was then abruptly driven right out of Ferghana and into the political wilderness by the Uzbek Shaybanids. He found new turf in Afghanistan, where he ruled Kabul for two decades. Then in 1526 he marched into Delhi to found the line of Persian-speaking emperors of northern India known as the Moghuls (a corruption of 'Mongol', local parlance for anybody from Central Asia). He died four years later in Delhi. ■

---

dropped squarely upon most of it. What's left is now a working medressa again. Beside it is a **regional museum** with the usual historical exhibits and stuffed animals, open daily, except Sunday, from 9 am to 5 pm (to 3 pm on Saturday).

The marginally more interesting **Babur Literary Museum**, in the lane behind the bazar, occupies the site of the royal apartments where Babur lived and studied as a boy within Ark-Ichy, the town's long-gone citadel. The museum, though visually pleasant, is more like a slicked-up shrine, with books, paintings and hyperbolic text about Babur and his literary friends. It's open daily, except Monday, from 9 am to 4 pm.

Places to Stay & Eat

Best bet to stay the night, and see the bazar at its liveliest early in the morning, is the friendly *Hotel Andijan* (☎ 5-78-07), 250 metres down Fitrat (ex-Oktyabrskaya) at No 241. Spartan rooms are about US$5 in *sum*. The hotel *restaurant* serves basic Uzbek food, *choyhonas* on Fitrat have shashlyk and laghman, and of course the *bazar* has abundant fruit, vegetables, nuts and honey.

Uzbektourism's run-down *Hotel Zolotaya*

Dolina (☎ 6-87-08) at Mashrab 19 has fairly clean singles/doubles with toilet and shower, absurdly overpriced at US$20/30 (20 times higher than local price), a decent bufet and a dreary restaurant.

Getting There & Away

The easiest way to get between Andijan and other points in the valley is by bus. There are buses to Andijan about every 45 minutes for about US$1 from Ferghana's Yermazar station (a 2½ hour trip), as well as frequent connections all day to/from Kokand, Namangan and Osh, and Jalal-Abad every two to three hours. Buses come from Tashkent twice a day for about US$6.

From Andijan-I train station, not Andijan II, there are daily fast trains to/from Tashkent, Samarkand and Bukhara, and trains five days a week to/from Moscow.

You can fly here from Tashkent (a one hour flight) several times a day, or from Moscow once a week. There are also summer connections with Almaty (daily) and Termez (weekly). Outbound tickets are only sold at the airport.

Getting Around

The airport is five km from the bazar by bus Nos 1-A or 8; from the Zolotaya Dolina take bus No 6 or marshrutnoe taxi No 4. Bus No 2 connects the Zolotaya Dolina, the bus station and the bazar, and bus No 8 and trolleybus No 2 run directly between the Zolotaya Dolina and the bazar.

OSH & JALAL-ABAD

See the Kyrgyzstan chapter for information.

KHOJAND

See the Tajikistan chapter for information.

South-East Uzbekistan

SAMARKAND
САМАРҚАНД
Population: 404,000

No name is so evocative of the pungent smell of the Silk Road as Samarkand. For most people it's as mythical as Atlantis, fixed in the western popular imagination by poets and playwrights, sealed there by James Elroy Flecker with his 1913 poem *The Golden Journey to Samarkand*, and recycled in his play *Hassan*, which concludes with the over-famous lines,

> We travel not for trafficking alone,
> By hotter winds our fiery hearts are fanned.
> For lust of knowing what should not be known
> We take the Golden Road to Samarkand.

The reality is harsher, but not much. From the airplane your eye locks onto the domes and minarets, and on the ground the sublime, larger-than-life monuments of Timur, the technicolour bazar and the city's long, rich history do work some kind of magic. Outside the centre, though, this is a sprawling Soviet-style city with few redeeming features. Ahead of spring and autumn storms it's engulfed by choking sandstorms.

Most of Samarkand's high-profile attractions are the work of Timur, his grandson Ulughbek and the Uzbek Shaybanids. You can visit them all, plus some ancient excavations, in two or three days. If you're short on time, at least see the Registan, Guri Amir, Bibi-Khanym mosque, Shahi-Zinda and the bazar.

Note that the people of Samarkand, Bukhara and south-eastern Uzbekistan don't speak Uzbek but an Uzbek-laced Tajik (Farsi) – and there are a few Samarkandis who still think Stalin should have made the whole area part of Tajikistan.

History

Samarkand (Marakanda to the Greeks), one of Central Asia's oldest settlements, was

UZBEKISTAN

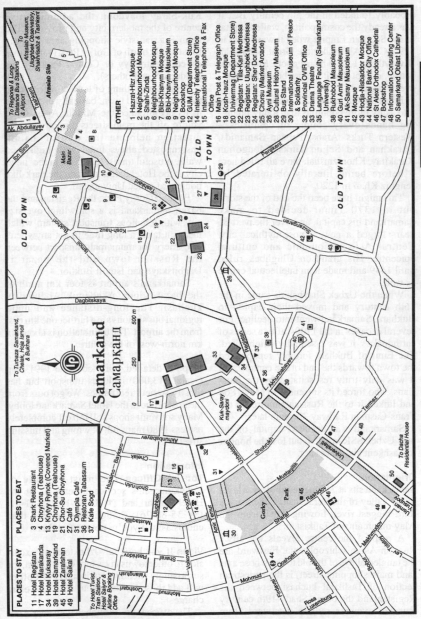

Samarkand
Самарканд

PLACES TO STAY

11 Hotel Registan
17 Hotel Marakanda
34 Hotel Kuksaray
39 Hotel Samarkand
45 Hotel Zarafshan
49 Hotel Saikal

PLACES TO EAT

3   Shark Restaurant
4   Choyhona (Teahouse)
13 Krytky Rynok (Covered Market)
19 Choyhona (Teahouse)
21 Chor-Su Choyhona
27 Café
31 Olympia Café
36 Restoran Tabassum
37 Kafe Sogd

OTHER

1   Hazrat-Hizr Mosque
2   Neighbourhood Mosque
5   Shahi-Zinda
6   Neighbourhood Mosque
7   Bibi-Khanym Mosque
8   Bibi-Khanym Mausoleum
9   Neighbourhood Mosque
10 Bookshop
12 GUM (Department Store)
14 Intercity Telephone Office
15 International Telephone & Fax Office
16 Main Post & Telegraph Office
18 Kosh-hauz Mosque
20 Univermag (Department Store)
22 Registan: Tilla-Kari Medressa
23 Registan: Ulughbek Medressa
24 Registan: Sher Dor Medressa
25 Chorsu (Market Arcade)
26 Ayni Museum
28 Cultural History Museum
29 Bus Stand
30 International Museum of Peace & Solidarity
32 Provincial OVIR Office
33 Drama Theatre
35 Language Faculty (Samarkand University)
38 Rukhobod Mausoleum
40 Guri Amir Mausoleum
41 Ak-Saray Mausoleum
42 Mosque
43 Hodja-Nisbaddor Mosque
44 National Bank City Office
46 St Alexi Orthodox Cathedral
47 Bookshop
48 Information Consulting Center
50 Samarkand Oblast Library

probably founded in the 5th century BC. It was already the cosmopolitan, walled capital of the Sogdian Empire when it was taken in 329 BC by Alexander the Great, who said, 'Everything I have heard about Marakanda is true, except that it's more beautiful than I ever imagined'.

From the 6th to the 13th centuries it grew into a city more populous than today, changing hands every couple of centuries – Western Turks, Arabs, Persian Samanids, Qarakhan and Seljuq Turks, Mongolian Karakitay, Khorezmshah have all ruled here – before being literally obliterated by Jenghiz Khan in 1220.

This might have been the end of the story, but in 1370 Timur decided to make Samarkand his capital, and over the next 35 years forged a new, almost-mythical city, Central Asia's economic and cultural epicentre. His grandson Ulughbek ruled until 1449 and made it an intellectual centre as well.

When the Uzbek Shaybanids came in the 16th century and moved their capital to Bukhara, Samarkand went into decline. For several decades in the 1700s, after a series of earthquakes, it was essentially uninhabited. The Emir of Bukhara forcibly repopulated the town towards the end of the century, but it was only truly resuscitated by the Russians, who forced its surrender in May 1868 and linked it to the Russian Empire by the Trans-Caspian Railway 20 years later.

Samarkand was declared capital of the new Uzbek SSR in 1924, but lost the honour to Tashkent six years later.

Orientation

Samarkand sits at 710 metres above sea level in the valley of the Zeravshan, Uzbekistan's third biggest river, flowing down from the Alay mountains of Tajikistan.

A map of the centre reveals the city's Russian-Asian schizophrenia. Eastward are the tangled alleys of the old town, whose axis (and main shopping street) is the pedestrian section of Tashkent kuchasi between the Registan and the bazar. Shady 19th century Russian avenues radiate westward from

Kuk-Saray maydoni, the administrative centre of the modern city and province. The main Russian-style shopping area is along Mustaqillik north of Gorky Park (sometimes called Tsentralnyy or Central Park by bus conductors and others).

Almost everything of tourist interest is in the sun-dried old town, basically unchanged in its layout since the Middle Ages. Once you're off the main streets a good sense of direction helps in the web of mainly unsignposted alleys lined with high mud walls. A useful tourist landmark in the 'new' city is the Hotel Samarkand on the park-like boulevard called Universiteti.

Beyond Gorky Park, the Registan and the bazar, Samarkand is a sprawling, oversize city with a tedious transport system which means it takes a long time to get anywhere. The artery for municipal transport between the Russian town and the bazar is Dagbitskaya and Ismoil Bukhori.

Samarkand's airport is four km north of the bazar, along Akademik Abdullayev kuchasi. The long-distance and main regional bus stations are a farther one km east from the airport. The train station is about six km north-west of the centre.

Maps A detailed, fairly accurate 1991 map (scale 1:13,000) includes transport but has mostly Soviet street names. We got ours from the post office in the Hotel Samarkand lobby. Many souvenir shops still fob off completely useless 1980 maps full of wrong and missing streets.

Information
Tourist Offices The most capable of Uzbektourism's service bureaus is at the Hotel Samarkand (☎ 35-88-12, 35-71-51; fax 35-88-26), though they're less than enthusiastic if you're not a guest there.

Visas If you book an Uzbektourism excursion to other towns in eastern Uzbekistan, the surprisingly friendly provincial OVIR office will add those towns to your visa at no extra charge.

The office is on Akhunbabayev near Amir

Temur, marked by a sign ИИБ ВИЗАЛАР БЕРИШ КАЙД ЭТИШ БЎЛИМИ. Or you can let the hotel service bureau arrange it for a few dollars.

Registration If you're not staying in a tourist hotel, you are required to stop in at OVIR to register.

Useful Organisations The Information Consulting Center (АХБОРОТ МАСЛАҲАТ МАРКФЗИ) is a networking centre for local people and overseas non-governmental agencies, but visitors willing to stop and chat are welcome. For a fee they might also let you use their e-mail connection. Its in the Physics Faculty building just east off Universiteti, and open daily except Sunday from 9 am to 1 pm and 2 to 5 pm.

A place you might find young Samarkandis keen to try out their English, French or German, and perhaps act as unofficial guides, is the Language Preparation Centre (Tsentr Yazykovoy Podgotovki) in room 52, two flights up at the University's Language Faculty, across the roundabout from the Hotel Samarkand. An informal English-language club operates from an office at the Samarkand Oblast Library, at the other end of Universiteti at No 21.

Money Hotel Samarkand has twin exchange desks, open from 8 am to 8 pm. The National Bank desk on the left accepts US$ travellers' cheques and cash; the Central Bank desk on the right accepts only US$ cash, but in most major currencies. The National Bank city office on Firdavsi changes cash and travellers' cheques in all major currencies and can arrange cash advances (at least from Visa cards), but they're only open from about 9 am to noon. All exchanges are to *sum* only.

Old & New Names in Samarkand

We use official Uzbek forms where possible, minus Russian endings, for street and other names, although Russian cabbies and others may not. An Uzbek street is *kuchasi* (Russian *ulitsa*), a boulevard *hiyoboni* (Russian *bulvar*), a square *maydoni* (Russian *ploshchad*).

New Name	Old Name
Akademik Abdullayev	Magistralnaya
Amir Temur	Frunze
Beruni	Oktyabrskaya
Bobur	Narimanova
Firdavsi	Shaumyana
Husaino Baykaro	Vozrozhdeniya
Ibn Sino	Titova (east of Dagbitskaya)
Ismoil Bukhori	Kayruanskaya
Makhmudov	Kosmodemyanskoy
Mohmud Qoshqari	Engelsa
Mustaqillik	Lenina
Pochta	Pochtovaya
Registan	Registanskaya
Rudaki	Titova (west of Dagbitskaya)
Sharaf Rashidov	Sovietskaya
Shohrukh	Kommunisticheskaya
Tashkent	Tashkentskaya
Ulughbek	Karla Marxa
Universiteti (hiyoboni) (bulvar)	Maxima Gorkogo
Uzbekistan	Uzbekistanskaya
Yalangtush	Respublikanskaya

Post & Communications The unhelpful main post and telegraph office is on Pochta behind the small farmers' market, Krytyy Rynok. The Hotel Samarkand's tiny stamp desk and drop-box seems to open mainly when tour groups are around.

The Hotel Samarkand has a 24 hour, direct-dial satellite telephone link with connections as clear as if they were next door, for US$5 per minute (to Europe) to US$7 per minute (to Australia). With no three minute minimum this may actually be the cheapest place to make a *short* overseas call. The small international telephone & fax office on Shohrukh at the corner with Pochta (not the intercity office next door) has cheaper rates but dicier connections, and you pay even if the connection is lost.

Overseas faxes feed slowly and can therefore get hideously expensive. The telephone and fax office on Shohrukh has a per-page rate, independent of feed rate and bad lines, and though it's steep (US$30 a page), you'd probably pay less here than at the Hotel Samarkand.

Samarkand's telephone code is 3662.

Travel Agencies Two competent agencies have offices in the Hotel Samarkand – Asia Travel International (☎ 35-86-76, ☎ & fax 21-43-03, telex 116584 ATI RU) on the 2nd floor (no sign), and Orient Star (☎ 33-00-28, fax 31-14-23, telex 116468 AIRUS RU) in room 302. Both can set up conventional tourism or adventure travel in Uzbekistan, Kyrgyzstan and Kazakstan, plus local car rental, Uzbek homestays and international flights. Although they are both group-oriented and not cheap, they are willing to do individual bookings. They prefer a few weeks warning.

Travellers recommend a young outfit called Sitora (☎ 33-09-44, 33-37-25; contact Jamshid Nasrullayev), which offers places in city flats, suburban dachas or rural camps for around US$15 per person per day, and can help with other arrangements, including visas.

Bookshops The only things we found in English in any bookshop were a few English-language teaching workbooks at a bookshop on Universiteti near Termez kuchasi. Another on Tashkent kuchasi has Russian computer magazines and occasionally city maps.

Cultural Centres Alliance Française (which mainly offers French tuition) is in the Samarkand Oblast Library at Universiteti 21.

Dangers & Annoyances Like other Central Asian cities, Samarkand has grown less safe since the break up of the USSR, and it's no fun on the streets here after dark. The streets around the centre fill with young men looking for something to do, and women travellers report gangs of grab-and-run kids. Later come the drunks. Things can get rowdy and unpleasant even *inside* lower-end hotels in the evening. The old town around the bazar is unsafe for foreigners at night, and easy to get lost in.

You *can* go out, eg to restaurants, but call ahead for their hours, and sort out your transport beforehand.

Less serious, but annoying, is the rise in petty crime. Know in advance the price of things you buy or order. Keep an eye on your bags. And don't count on the police for much help with disputes or petty crime.

The Registan

This ensemble of majestic, tilting medressas – a near-overload of majolica, azure mosaics and vast, well-proportioned spaces – is the centrepiece of the city, and one of the most awesome single sights in Central Asia. It was medieval Samarkand's commercial centre and the plaza was probably a wall-to-wall bazar. Heavy Soviet-era restoration included digging down three metres to its original level, exposing the buildings' full height. The Uzbek government is gradually restoring the second-rate Soviet job.

Ulughbek medressa on the west side is the oldest, finished in 1420 under Ulughbek (who is said to have taught mathematics there; other subjects included theology, astronomy and philosophy). Beneath the little corner domes were lecture halls, and at the rear a large mosque. About 100 students lived in two storeys of dormitory cells, some of which are still visible.

The other buildings are imitations by the Shaybanid Emir Yalangtush. The entrance portal of the Sher Dor (Tiger) medressa, opposite Ulughbek's and finished in 1636, is decorated with roaring tigers, flouting Islamic prohibitions against the depiction of live animals. In between is the Tilla-Kari (Gold-Covered) medressa, completed in 1660, with a pleasant, garden-like mosque courtyard.

The hexagonal building in the square's north-east corner is a 19th century *chorsu* or market arcade.

The complex is a 10 minute walk from the Hotel Samarkand, and entry is 30 S. Many inner rooms now serve as art and souvenir shops, and the Sher Dor's courtyard is favoured for lavish official banquets. On some summer evenings, there's a tacky son et lumière in the square.

A decorated mosaic Minaret from the Registan, once Samarkand's commercial centre.

Bibi-Khanym Mosque

The gigantic congregational mosque north-east of the Registan, powerful and shapely even in ruins, was finished shortly before Timur's death, and must have been the jewel of his empire. It's a victim of its own grandeur; once one of the Islamic world's biggest mosques (the main gate alone was 35 metres high), it pushed construction techniques to the limit. Slowly crumbling over the years, it finally collapsed in an earthquake in 1897.

Legend says that Bibi-Khanym, Timur's Chinese wife, ordered the mosque built as a surprise while he was away. The architect fell madly in love with her and refused to finish the job unless he could give her a kiss. The smooch left a mark and Timur, on seeing it, executed the architect and decreed that women should henceforth wear veils so as not to tempt other men.

Restoration of the main gate is underway (apparently with UNESCO patronage) and parts of the courtyard are closed off. Are they really going to try and *rebuild* this magnificent ruin?

If you wander through the south gate, a caretaker may ask for a few *sum* – a scam, but probably worth it for a look at the enormous marble Quran stand in the open courtyard, and to get a feel for the scale of this place. Local lore has it that any woman who crawls under the stand will have lots of children.

Across Tashkent kuchasi is what appears to be Bibi-Khanym's own compact, 14th century mausoleum, also under restoration.

Shahi-Zinda

The most moving of Samarkand's sights is this street of tombs east of Bibi-Khanym. The name, which means Tomb of the Living King, refers to its original, innermost and holiest shrine – a complex of cool, quiet rooms around what is probably the grave of Qusam ibn-Abbas, a cousin of the Prophet Muhammad who is said to have brought Islam to this area. This is among the oldest standing buildings in the city. It's also an important place of pilgrimage, so enter with respect and dress conservatively.

Except for this and a few other early tombs at the end, the rest belong to Timur's and Ulughbek's family and favourites. Vaguely disfigured by donation boxes, they nevertheless feature some of the city's finest majolica tilework, largely unrenovated. The most beautiful is probably that of Timur's niece, second on the left after the entry stairs (which climb over the ancient city wall from the outside).

The site is open daily from 8 am to 6 or 7 pm except national holidays and entry is 30 S. You'll only have it more or less to yourself if you go very early or at lunchtime.

Guri Amir Mausoleum & Around

Guri Amir is Tajik for Tomb of the emir. Timur, two sons and two grandsons, including Ulughbek, lie beneath this surprisingly modest mausoleum topped by a fluted azure dome, at the edge of the old town behind the Hotel Samarkand. One reason it looks small is that a medressa that used to be in front is now gone, except for the gate.

Timur had built a simple crypt for himself at Shakhrisabz, and apparently had this one built in 1404 for some of his sons or grandsons. But the story goes that when he died unexpectedly of pneumonia in Kazakstan (in the course of planning an expedition against the Chinese) in the winter of 1405, the passes back to Shakhrisabz were snowed in and he was interred here instead.

The simple inner room was originally decorated in gold (a 1970 restoration used some 2.5 kg of the stuff). As with other Muslim mausolea, the stones are just markers; the actual crypts are in a chamber beneath. In the centre is Timur's stone, once a single block of dark-green jade. In 1740 the warlord Nadir Shah carried it off to Persia, where it was accidentally broken in two – from which time Nadir Shah is said to have had a run of very bad luck, including the near-death of his son. At the urging of his religious advisers he returned the stone to Samarkand, and of course his son recovered.

The plain marble marker to the left of Timur's is that of Ulughbek, and to the right is that of Mersaid Baraka, one of Timur's

teachers. In front lies Muhammad Sultan, Timur's grandson by his son Jehangir. The stones behind Timur's mark the graves of his sons Shah Rukh (Shohrukh in Uzbek/Tajik; father of Ulughbek) and Miran Shah. Behind these lies Sheikh Umar, the most revered of Timur's teachers; the pole with the horsehair tassel further identifies him as a Muslim 'saint'. Two other sons, Jehangir and Umar Sheikh, are buried at Shakhrisabz.

The Soviet anthropologist Mikhail Gerasimov opened the crypts in 1941 and, among other things, confirmed that Timur was tall (1.7 metres) and lame in the right leg and right arm (from injuries suffered when he was 25) – and that Ulughbek died from being beheaded. According to every tour guide's favourite anecdote, he found on Timur's grave an inscription to the effect that 'whoever opens this will be defeated by an enemy more fearsome than I'. The next day, 22 June, Hitler attacked the Soviet Union.

In front of the gate are the remains of an earlier medressa, and to the right are the foundations of an even older *khanaka* (Uzbek: *hanako*, a Sufi contemplation hall and hostel for wandering mendicants). The complex, under restoration when we visited, is open daily from 8 am to 8 pm and entry costs 15 S.

Just behind Guri Amir is the derelict little Ak-Saray mausoleum (1470), said to have beautiful frescoes inside. From Guri Amir you can walk north through a patch of the old town, emerging near the weedy, crumbling Rukhobod mausoleum, dated 1380 and possibly the city's oldest surviving 'monument'.

Main Bazar

Around and behind Bibi-Khanym is the best live show in town, the kinetic, colourful main farmers' market, called Siab Market on maps. It's a Tower of Babel, full of the dresses and shawls, hats and turbans of every nationality, and great for photographers, souvenir hunters and vegetarians, especially in the early morning and on weekends. There's an extension on the other side of Tashkent kuchasi too.

The bazar is a 25 minute walk from the

Hotel Samarkand, or take bus No 10 or marshrutnoe taxi Nos 17, 18, 19 or 23.

Ancient Samarkand

At a 2.2 sq km site called Afrasiab (Uzbek/ Tajik Afrasiob, after a real or mythical Sogdian king), north-east of the bazar, are excavations of Marakanda – early Samarkand. The dry, dusty excavations have by now been more or less abandoned to the elements. The Afrasiab Museum beside them has a site plan, chronological maps and models but nothing in English, and renovations have temporarily truncated everything in mid-history – overall a disappointment unless you have a guide. The only real attraction, in a ground-floor room, is fragments of some striking 7th century frescoes depicting hunting, an ambassadorial procession and visits by local rulers.

The museum, 1.5 km beyond the bazar on the Tashkent road, is open daily, except Thursday and the last day of the month, from 9 am to 5 pm. Bus No 26 from the bazar, and marshrutnoe taxi Nos 17 and 45 from the Hotel Samarkand and the bazar, stop there.

In *The Lost Heart of Asia*, Colin Thubron describes stumbling upon what the caretaker claimed was the tomb of the Old Testament prophet Daniel, whose remains, legend has it, were brought from Mecca by Timur. Though we never found it, Thubron places the tomb by the Siab river which forms the north-east boundary of the site.

Ulughbek Observatory

Ulughbek was probably more famous as an astronomer than as a ruler. About one km beyond the Afrasiab Museum are the remains of an immense (30 metre tall) astrolabe for observing star positions, part of a three storey observatory he built in the 1420s. All that remains is the instrument's curved track, unearthed in 1908. Next door is a little museum, open from 9 am to 6 pm daily, about Uzbek astronomers. Entry is 30 S. Transport is the same as for Afrasiab.

Other Mosques

The fine Hodja-Nisbaddor mosque, a small 19th century summer mosque with open porch, tall carved columns and brightly

Ulughbek

Ulughbek, Timur's favourite grandson (son of Shah Rukh), became viceroy in Samarkand and ultimately ruler of Timur's Central Asian territories. But he broke the family pattern of savage grandeur with his intelligence, his breadth of knowledge and his love of science, especially astronomy.

In 1420 he opened the doors of Samarkand's greatest Islamic 'university', the Ulughbek medressa, on what is now Registan Square. Using a huge, specially constructed marble astrolabe he charted star positions, discovered some 200 previously unknown stars, and did his own amazingly accurate calculations of the length of the year. Nowadays his reputation as an astronomer dominates his achievements as a Timurid sultan, although the West didn't learn of him until after his death.

This cultured man was to prove the exception to the rule, however, as small-mindedness and puritanism closed in. The Islamic clergy resented his preference for science over scripture as a source of truth, and their resulting loss of influence. His own son, Abdul Latif, arranged his murder by decapitation in 1449, and the observatory was razed to the ground, although his work was saved and published to posthumous acclaim in the West.

It was only in 1908 that a stubborn Russian teacher and amateur archaeologist named Vladimir Vyatkin excavated what he calculated to be the site of the observatory, and found the astrolabe's massive semicircular track, untouched. Vyatkin remained in Samarkand through the Revolution, became the city's Director of Antiquities and after his death was buried beside the observatory. ∎

restored ceiling, is on Suzangaran kuchasi. Don't confuse it with the smaller, less interesting mosque a block nearer the Registan.

Beside a scummy pool on Kosh-hauz behind the Registan is the peaceful, run-down Kosh-hauz mosque (a sign says, improbably, 1319). Across the intersection from the bazar is the neglected 19th century Hazrat-Hizr mosque.

Museums

Afrasiab Museum See Ancient Samarkand in this section.

International Museum of Peace & Solidarity This remarkable collection of disarmament and environmental memorabilia is a world away from the stodgy state museums. Started in 1986 by a serious Esperanto and English speaker named Anatoly Ionesov, it's crammed floor-to-ceiling with 15,000 exhibits from over 100 countries – peace posters, buttons, flags, books, children's art, bits of decommissioned missiles, plus gifts and endorsements from the famous and the obscure around the world.

Ionesov will proudly walk you past each item, and tell you about other projects, including his Children's Peace & Disarmament Festival, held annually here on 23 October (just before United Nations Disarmament Week), when kids turn in their toy weapons and learn alternative pastimes.

On Amir Temur kuchasi, go through the main entrance to Gorky Park and bear right to a two storey arcade building beyond the roller coaster; the museum is upstairs. It's usually open daily except Sunday from 9 am to 4 or 5 pm – or you can call Ionesov at his nearby home (☎ 33-17-53). He'll charge you nothing but will appreciate a genuine donation.

The museum's mailing address is PO Box 76, Samarkand 703000.

State Museum of the Cultural History of Uzbekistan In the crumbling edifice east of the Registan are earnest exhibits on regional archaeology, Samarkand history, folk art (including a mock-up yurt) and some modern art. A semi-permanent exhibit of paintings of old Samarkand and Bukhara has a lingering aroma of Socialist propaganda but is still a good aid for the imagination. Admission is only a few *sum*, though foreigners pay five times more than local people.

Ayni Museum On Registan kuchasi behind a bust of the 20th century Tajik poet Sadriddin Ayni is a little museum about him, but we never found it open. They're probably busy replacing old Soviet propaganda with new versions.

Churches

A refuge of sorts for Samarkand's beleaguered Slavs is the sturdy 1912 St Alexi Orthodox Cathedral on Rashidov, under slow restoration.

Festivals

During Navrus (see Holidays & Festivals in the Facts for the Visitor chapter) there is a parade and a giant fair, with food, music, dancing and lots of colour, around the old Cholpan-Ata Restaurant, east of town on the road to Shakhrisabz. Samarkand hosts the Children's Peace & Disarmament Festival every 23 October (see the International Museum of Peace & Solidarity in this section).

Places to Stay

Homestays The agencies listed under Samarkand Information can put you in touch with people ready to give travellers bed and breakfast, typically for about US$20, or US$25 with an evening meal too. One of these that has now gone independent is the competent *Zarina's Bed & Breakfast* (☎ 35-41-53, fax 31-06-41) at Obi-Rakhmat kuchasi 2, off the Tashkent road, east of the Afrasiab site. Some travellers have received help from sympathetic counter staff at the Hotel Samarkand.

If you're staying in a home far from the centre, keep in mind that public transport fades away in the evening.

Bottom End The *Hotel Zarafshan* (☎ 33-33-72) has noise, vagrants, dubious security and a few bugs, but it's cheap for the location, at Sharaf Rashidov 65 on the edge of Gorky Park. A basic double with toilet and shower (hot water in the morning and evening) is about US$10 in *sum*; big corner suites with balcony are US$13. The restaurant is miserable but the park has cheap snacks. Trolleybus No 1 runs along Universiteti to/from the Registan.

Failing this, it's just three blocks to the truly awful *Hotel Registan* (☎ 33-52-25) at Ulughbek 36, once the *Leningrad* but none the better for privatisation. Travellers report a wide spectrum of quoted prices for the noisy, smelly triples with dicey common toilet and shower – for us it was US$2 per bed; a few suites with toilet are US$5. Nocturnal visitors of every kind are also reported. The restaurant is grand, the food disappointing, but a small bufet has some Uzbek dishes. There is good shopping and plenty of transport to the centre.

At the *Hotel Turist* (☎ 24-07-04), a tired 15-storey tower with damp rooms and elevators that stop where they like, a single/double with toilet and shower is US$30/40. It's way out at Gagarin 85, a 25 minute ride on bus Nos 3, 10, 21 or 27 or trolleybus No 14. Its Uzbek/Tajik name is Sayokh, not to be confused with Saiyor (see the mid-range listings).

At the bottom in every respect are the slapped-up rooms of *Turbaza Samarkand* (☎ 35-41-94). Doubles with common shower and toilet are about US$1 per bed, quads even less. Staff are spaced-out, security is dubious and the place looks creepy for women. The location – well out on the Bukhara road at Dagbitskaya 33 – couldn't be worse for both food and access (bus No 27 to the Hotel Samarkand, bus No 7 or 8 to the bazar, neither very often).

Middle Samarkand is Uzbekistan's favourite place for conventions and other big bashes, and when there's one in town, all but the genuinely bottom-end hotels fill right up.

Good deals never last, but the little *Hotel Saikal* (☎ 33-18-14) at Universiteti 17 opposite the Navoi statue was the best in this range when we visited. One of two city *hokimyat* (mayoral) guesthouses, its spotless singles/doubles with bath and toilet were US$39/60; two double-bed suites only at US$45 show what a bad joke the Hotel Samarkand is. It's a 20 minute walk from the Registan, or take trolleybus No 1 or 2. Booking ahead is essential in summer.

Uzbektourism's *Hotel Samarkand* (☎ 35-88-12) has a choice location at Universiteti 1, an eager service bureau and fairly clean, comfortable rooms. But at US$50 for a double with toilet (US$32 November through March), the pre-Ulughbek plumbing and unpredictable hot water are a drag. Breakfast for individuals is stingy compared to that laid on for groups, unless you make a fuss or make a friend there.

West of the centre at Ulughbek 148a is the three storey *Hotel Saiyor* (☎ 21-49-16). Old, plain, clean singles/doubles with toilet (and plenty of hot water) are US$23/40, good value in this range, and every room has a little balcony. Service is nonexistent in the lobby but unnervingly eager upstairs. Though far away, it's well-connected to the centre (express bus No 21, bus No 2, trolleybus No 1 and marshrutnoe taxis). Across the road is a big department store.

The five storey *Hotel Boghishamol* across the intersection from the Saiyor at Mirsharopov 15 doesn't take foreigners.

Top End The *Dacha Residential House* (☎ 35-14-76, telex 116366 SAMRA RU) is the other hokimyat guesthouse – a peaceful, rather stately place with three hectares of trees and gardens kept lush by its own water system, behind a gate at Usman Yusupov 33.

The *Hotel Marakanda* has rented a wing in the joint-venture building, where doubles with bath are US$45 with breakfast. From November through March rates drop by 40%. It's mainly for groups but you might get in if they like your face. It may shut down when the 16 storey Hotel Marakanda and *biznes tsentr* (business centre), currently under construction on the north side of Kuk-Saray maydoni, is completed.

On another prime parcel of land beside Kuk-Saray maydoni is the completed *Hotel Kuksaray* which was still unopened when we were there. This and two other potentially five star places in Tashkent and Bukhara were awaiting a bail-out after Uzbekistan defaulted on its Indian bank loans.

Places to Eat

There seem to be more eateries open at midday than in the evening, perhaps because most sensible Samarkandis stay home and lock their doors after dark (see Samarkand Dangers & Annoyances).

Fast Food The *Olympia Café* (also called Enterprice Olympia) is a cheap, fairly clean burger-and-sometimes-pizza joint with adequate offerings, on Shohrukh opposite Gorky Park. It is open daily except Sunday from 8 am to 4 or 5 pm. Gorky Park is rimmed with *shashlyk stands* and other *snack shops* with bottom-end prices and poor hygiene.

Hotels The *Hotel Samarkand's* restaurant has erratic service but adequate Uzbek and western food, if you can get past the men at the door attempting to filter out all but tour groups. The evening café across the lobby tends to serve the same food, with a smile. The cheap ground-floor *sum* bar runs out of beer early, after which you can throw away US$ cash at the dollar bar in the basement (though their beer is actually *cold*).

The *Saiyor's* restaurant is adequate (and apparently dishes up a good breakfast) but it's a thuggish, very overpriced scene in the evening. The friendly *café* in the office block next door serves good Russian standards.

The dining rooms at the *Hotel Saikal* and *Dacha Residential House* will apparently prepare whatever you want using local ingredients, if you order ahead.

Take your chances at the fly sanctuary posing as a restaurant at the *Hotel Zarafshan*, and woe betide you if there's an Uzbek tour group in the hotel (they are 'guests', you are

nobody). The menu is hit-or-miss, the prices mercurial, and it's a struggle to get served at breakfast.

Restaurants The quiet *Shark Restaurant* across Tashkent kuchasi from the bazar has good service and decent Uzbek dishes at reasonable prices (eat well for about US$1.50). They don't serve fish here: the *sharq* in the name is Uzbek for 'east'.

Another best-bet is the popular outdoor *Yulduz Choyhona*, beside Ulughbek Observatory on the Tashkent road (take the No 26 bus from the bazar, or marshrutnoe taxi No 17 or 45 from the Hotel Samarkand or the bazar). Fill up on well-prepared shashlyk, laghman, shorpa or other standards, along with tea and excellent bread, for about US$2. It's packed out at lunchtime.

A busy place in the centre is the big choyhona called *Chor-Su* at the south end of Tashkent kuchasi. A smaller *choyhona* is nearby, just west of the univermag. Less interesting is the *café* at the rear of the Museum of the Cultural History of Uzbekistan.

The *Kafe Sogd* opposite the Hotel Kuksaray serves adequate but overpriced soup, shashlyk and salads. There's no menu, no prices and a tendency for sleight-of-hand (we asked in clear Russian for four shashlyks and a salad, and got six shashlyks and three salads). A sizeable lunch without drinks is under US$4. The sign says it's open daily from 11 am to 9 pm, but don't count on it.

The *Restoran Tabassum* just north of the Hotel Samarkand looks like one of those oversize places surviving on the who-cares-what-we-eat banquet trade. They served us a 'roast chicken' that barely had the feathers singed off, and then tried to charge us double. Give it a miss.

Home-Restaurants In summer in the old town between the bazar and Ismoil Bukhori, you can track down a simple home-cooked meal in one of the unlicensed *restaurants* in the courtyards of private homes. There are said to be over 50 of them, though we found only a few on an October evening. Family members quietly solicit customers; go with the women or kids, not the brash young men. If you're uneasy about hygiene, ask to have a look first. In Russian, 'can we have a look in the kitchen?' is *'mozhno posmotret v kukhne?'*. Agree on the price in advance. We enjoyed a steaming common plate of mutton stew, salad, bread and tea for US$1 each, in *sum*. Bargaining might be appropriate if you're asked for more than about US$2 or US$3.

The old town around the bazar is creepy after dark, unsafe for men as well as women, and easy to get lost in. A midday meal there is much more sensible.

Self-Catering The bazar has bread, boiled eggs, tomatoes, fruit and more, and there's a smaller bazar – the *krytyy rynok* or covered market – on Ulughbek near the main post office.

Entertainment

We suggest skipping Samarkand's nightlife, which consists mainly of eating and drinking too much until very late. Enjoy the old town and bazar early in the morning instead.

Things to Buy

A major shopping district is the pedestrianised Tashkent kuchasi near the bazar, heavy on Uzbek cloth (including silk), clothing and housewares, and some souvenirs. The main Russian-style shopping area is pedestrian Mustaqillik north of Gorky Park, with the GUM department store plus food, toiletry and electrical goods shops. Smaller department stores are at the south end of Tashkent kuchasi and opposite the Hotel Saiyor on Mirsharopov.

Down the middle of Gorky Park a kiosk mini-bazar takes shape every day, offering imported clothing, tapes, snacks, cheap beer and useful items like soap and toilet paper. The craftier vendors probably graduate to the tinselly *savdo dukoni* (commercial shops) scattered around town, good for anything from imported coffee to kitchen appliances, at wildly variable prices.

We cannot confirm the information, but expatriate friends recommend an outfit called Afghan-Uzbek Joint Venture for carpets, most of them pure silk, and pricey. They have their own factory, and a small showroom in the Registan (☎ 35-07-36, 35-88-16; contact Ewat Badghissi Abdulwahet).

Silk prices in hotel kiosks are not too much higher than in the bazar, but the selection is poorer.

Getting There & Away

Air There are apparently some direct London-Samarkand charter flights; ask your travel agent. All scheduled flights from Samarkand are to points within the former USSR.

Uzbekistan Airways flies to Tashkent daily. Aeroflot goes to Ashghabat twice a week and Moscow three times a week. Foreigners' fares include Tashkent (US$53), Ashghabat (US$100), Moscow Domodedovo (US$170) and Moscow Vnukovo (US$185).

Tickets are best bought a few days in advance. Hotel service bureaus charge an extra US$5 or so to send someone over to the city booking office, on Gagarin south of the Hotel Turist. You can do it yourself on bus No 10 outbound on Universiteti near the Hotel Samarkand, or north-bound on Sharaf Rashidov near the Hotel Zarafshan; ask for *aerovokzal*. They'll also reconfirm flights at no charge. Check your tickets – mistakes are common.

See the To/From the Airport section in the Getting Around chapter.

Bus Tashkent is five hours away by bus across a flat, dry landscape that tsarist Russians nicknamed the Hungry Steppe, now fouled with factories and ugly buildings. There are hourly departures and tickets (about US$4) are available as little as a few hours in advance. Other major destinations are Bukhara (six hours, six times daily), Urgench (twice each evening), and Termez, Dushanbe and major Ferghana Valley towns (daily). For Bishkek, change at Tashkent.

Buy tickets at one of the little booths outside the long-distance station (take the bus No 10 past the Turist, Zarafshan and

Samarkand hotels), it's not clear who uses the huge, empty station building. You may encounter a policemen or two, but if your visa is in order you get none of the hassle typical of Tashkent. Travellers report gangs of pickpockets here, who board a bus or minivan, distract you with some kind of fuss, and dip into your pockets or slash your bag.

Just beyond the long-distance bus station entrance is a smaller regional bus station, mainly for points north (eg Hoja Ismoil). There is also a bus stand on Penjikent kuchasi east of the Registan, mainly for points south and east (eg Jumabazar and Penjikent).

Train Fast trains leave here for Moscow on Monday, Wednesday and Friday about 7 am. One fast train departs for Tashkent on Tuesday, Thursday and Saturday at 10.40 am, and many others pass through to Tashkent. A fast Tashkent-Bukhara train passes here daily at 2.45 pm, and others depart three times a week to Dushanbe and once a week to Almaty. Two daily trains stop en route between Tashkent and Termez.

Buy tickets at the depressing train station in the north-west outskirts. If you need help, the OVIR office upstairs is actually friendly. Go to the end of the line on bus No 1, trolleybus No 1 or marshrutnoe taxi No 17 near the Hotel Saiyor; bus Nos 3 or 10 or marshrutnoe taxi No 22 near the Turist; or any of these plus express bus 10- 3 near the Samarkand and Zarafshan.

Getting Around

To/From the Airport The No 10 bus goes from the long-distance bus station and the airport, to the bazar, Hotel Samarkand, Hotel Zarafshan, Hotel Turist and the train station, and back, about every 20 minutes (but express bus No 10-3 doesn't stop near the Turist). Any marshrutnoe taxi at the airport goes to the Hotel Samarkand. A taxi from the airport to the Samarkand should be the *sum* equivalent of about US$2.

Bus, Trolleybus & Marshrutnoe Taxi

Buses and trolleybuses run from about 6 am

until dusk. Pay cash to the conductor, or to the driver when you get off – 30 t when we were there (50 t for express buses). Marshrutnoe taxis (about 2 S) disappear by 8 or 9 pm.

Taxi There are unlicensed and licensed taxis. The former have number plates with the letters CH, like other private cars. The latter, with CHA plates, tend to be more reliable and hardly more expensive – you should be able to go from the Hotel Samarkand to the Ulughbek Observatory for US$0.50, or across town for under US$1. Rates jump after 8 pm when buses and marshrutnoe taxis start thinning out, and taxis themselves are scarce by 10.30 or 11 pm.

Don't expect Russian taxi drivers to know their way around the old town, nor to know all the post-Soviet street names (see the table under Orientation). If you're alone, be suspicious of any taxi that already contains more than just the driver.

Horse-Cart A horse-drawn taxi plies Tashkent kuchasi between the Registan and Bibi-Khanym for a few *sum*.

AROUND SAMARKAND
Hoja Ismoil
ХӮЖА ИСМОИЛ

In Hoja Ismoil, a village 30 km north of Samarkand, is one of Islam's holier spots, the very modest mausoleum of Ismail al-Bukhari (Uzbek/Tajik Ismoil Bukhori, 810-87). He was one of the greatest Muslim scholars of the *hadith*, the collected acts and sayings of the Prophet Muhammad. His main work is regarded by Sunni Muslims as second only to the Quran as a source of religious law. Following his refusal to give special tutoring to Bukhara's governor and his children, he was forced into exile here.

This is definitely not a tourist spot – just a courtyard, a mosque and a smaller courtyard around the tomb – but a place of pilgrimage. On weekdays the loudest sound is that of boys chanting prayers in the mosque; on Friday and Sunday the pilgrims and the curious crowd in.

It's essential to dress conservatively, respect the calm and reverent atmosphere, and ask before you take photos. Take your shoes off before you step onto any carpet.

Getting There & Away Hoja Ismoil village is 30 km north of Samarkand, off the road to Chelak. Buses from the regional bus station (beside the long-distance bus station) to Oqqurghon stop at Hoja Ismoil, and there are said to be buses to Chelak from the bus stand on Penjikent kuchasi. A taxi should be under US$15 for the return trip plus a short wait.

With a day's notice the Hotel Samarkand service bureau can arrange a three hour excursion for up to four people in a car for US$21. They may tell you non-Muslims are not especially welcome, perhaps to encourage you to go with one of their guides. There are no visa problems because this is within Samarkand province.

Jumabazar
Жумонозор

Local people say there is a big Sunday bazar at Jumabazar village, about 25 km south-east of Samarkand. Others say the *really* big bazar is 15 km farther on at the town of Urgut.

Buses for Urgut, via Jumabazar, leave from Penjikent kuchasi in Samarkand, just east of the Registan, around 5 am on Sunday. Both towns are in Samarkand province so all you need is a Samarkand visa, says OVIR.

Penjikent
Пенджикент

On a high, valley terrace on the banks of the Zeravshan river, 1.5 km from the modern town of Penjikent, are the ruins of ancient Penjikent or Bunjikath, a major Sogdian town founded in the 5th century and abandoned in the 8th century when the Arabs came. The ancient city has not been built upon since. The foundations of houses, a citadel with a couple of Zoroastrian temples, and the city bazar are visible in the excavated ruins, but the best of the frescoes (some of them 15 metres long), sculptures, pottery and manuscripts have been taken off to the Tashkent History Museum and St Petersburg's Hermitage. An annotated map at the site describes what all the furrows and mounds once were.

Some lesser finds are on display at the Rudaki Museum in modern Penjikent. The museum's name arises from the claim that Penjikent was the birthplace of Abu Abdullah Rudaki, the Samanid court poet considered by many to be the father of Persian poetry.

Places to Stay There is no good reason to stay overnight, but if you absolutely must, the prefab-concrete *Hotel Penjikent*, in the town centre at ulitsa Mirnaya 22, is overpriced at US$40 per person.

Getting There & Away Penjikent is 70 km east of Samarkand, just across the border into Tajikistan. It's listed here because the only sensible way to get there is from Samarkand. You'll almost certainly need a Tajik visa (or at least Penjikent or Dushanbe written on your Uzbek visa). This apparently cannot be arranged in Samarkand, but only at the Tajik Embassy in Tashkent.

The Hotel Samarkand service bureau will arrange a half day car trip to the excavations and museum for US$42 for up to four people (or three people and a guide), but they won't get the visa for you. Alternatively you could take a taxi from Penjikent kuchasi or Suzangaran kuchasi in Samarkand, sticking with the more trustworthy licensed taxis, the ones with the letters CHA (not just CH) on their number plates. Ask for *'drevniy gorod'* (ancient city), and don't pay until you get back.

If you're coming from Khojand in Tajikistan, there's a daily bus to/from Penjikent, a fantastically scenic route through the Turkestan range, climbing in places to 3500 metres. In fact Penjikent-Khojand would make an exciting alternative route from Samarkand to Tashkent for anyone with a couple of days to spare (the Khojand-Tashkent connections are good).

In summer, when the passes are clear of

snow, there are also buses between Penjikent and Dushanbe, 255 km to the south.

Fan Mountains

Another Tajik attraction accessible from Samarkand is Fansky Gory (Fan mountains), collective name for the parallel Turkestan and Zeravshan ranges that cut the Ferghana Valley part of Tajikistan off from the rest. These are a favoured place for trekking and climbing, being only a couple of hours from both Samarkand and Dushanbe. Several western adventure-travel outfits do regular trips there (see the introduction to the Northern Tajikistan section in the Tajikistan chapter).

SHAKHRISABZ
ШАХРИСАБЗ
Population: 60,000

Shakhrisabz is a small, un-Russified town south of Samarkand, across the hills in Kashka-Darya province. The town seems nothing special – until you start bumping into the ruins dotted around its back streets, and the megalomaniac ghosts of a wholly different place materialise. This is Timur's home town, and once upon a time it probably put Samarkand itself in the shade. It's worth a visit just to check out the great man's roots.

Timur was born on 9 April 1336 into the Barlas clan of local aristocrats, at the village of Hoja Ilghar, 13 km to the south. Ancient even then, Shakhrisabz – called Kesh at the time – was a kind of family seat. As he rose to power Timur gave it its present name – Tajik for 'Green Town' – and turned it into an extended family monument. Most of its current attractions were put here by Timur (including a tomb intended for himself) or his grandson Ulughbek.

The town was trashed in the 16th century by the Emir of Bukhara, Abdullah Khan II, in a quest for the Shaybanid throne. He is said to have been subsequently overcome with remorse for his stupidity. Nowadays its easy-going older generation is being displaced on the streets by post-Soviet, post-adolescent males sporting identical baggy trousers and twirling keychains.

Though less than two hours from Samarkand, this is not in Samarkand province, and you must have a visa that says Shakhrisabz. Without one you're certain to be hassled at the provincial border and again at the town limits, and quite possibly turned back. The Hotel Samarkand service bureau will get you a visa in a day for about US$6.

The road from Samarkand to Shakhrisabz and on to the border at Termez was once the main route for Soviet soldiers and hardware going into Afghanistan.

Orientation & Information

The town's main road is Ipak Yuli, Uzbek for 'Silk Road' (Russian: Sholkoviy Put). The long-distance bus station is at the south end of town, about 400 metres beyond the Kok-Gumbaz mosque. The train station is several km south of the centre, and a small airport is beyond that. There is a post office in the centre of town.

There is no charge to enter any of the town's monuments.

Ak-Saray Palace

Timur's summer palace, called Ak-Saray (Uzbek/Tajik: Oq-Saroy, meaning White Palace), has as much grandeur per sq cm as anything in Samarkand. There's actually nothing left of it except bits of the gigantic, 40 metre high entrance, covered with gorgeous, filigree-like blue, white and gold mosaics. It was probably Timur's most ambitious project, 24 years in the making, following a successful campaign in Khorezm and the 'import' of many of its finest artisans. It's staggering to try and imagine what the rest of it was like, in size and glory. It's just north of the centre.

Kok-Gumbaz Mosque & Dorut Tilyovat

This big Friday mosque was completed by Ulughbek in 1437 in honour of his father Shah Rukh (Timur's son). The name means Blue Dome, though the luminous outer tiles are long gone and it's full of pigeons now. It appears to be under snail's-pace restoration.

Behind it was the original burial complex of Timur's forebears; the sign says Dorut

Tilyovat (House of Meditation). On the left as you enter the complex is the **mausoleum of Sheikh Shamseddin Kulyal**, spiritual tutor to Timur and his father, Amir Taragay (who may also be buried here), completed by Timur in 1374. Inside are some fine carved columns, but the walls, coarsely restored in Soviet times, are already rotting.

On the right is the **Gumbazi Seyidan** (Dome of the Seyyids), which Ulughbek finished in 1438 as a mausoleum for his own descendants (though it's not clear whether any are buried in it). The shortest of its four grave-markers, called Tosh (Blue Stone), has

a deep, smooth depression on top, worn by centuries of supplicating hands.

Khazrati-Imam Ensemble

A few streets east of Kok-Gumbaz are a few melancholy remnants of a 70 by 50 metre mausoleum complex called Dorussiadat or Dorussaodat (Seat of Power & Might) which Timur finished in 1392 and which may have overshadowed even the Ak-Saray Palace.

The main survivor is the tall, crumbling **Tomb of Jehangir**, Timur's eldest and favourite son, who died at 22. It's also the resting place for another son, Umar Sheikh (Timur's other sons, Shah Rukh and Miran Shah, are with him at Guri Amir in Samarkand). It's a mess inside, though restoration looks imminent.

You may find someone to unlock the tomb at the adjacent **Khazrati Imam mosque**. The mosque itself dates only from the late 19th century, although the plane trees in its peaceful courtyard are probably much older. The name refers to a revered 8th century imam, or religious leader from Iraq, and the story goes that Abdullah Khan II spared the mausoleum because he was told the imam was buried there. The legend (and the name) have stuck, though there is no evidence that the Khazrati Imam ever came here.

Shakhrisabz
Шахрисабз

To Taxi Stand & Samarkand

Gagarin

Pushkin

Abay

Ipek Yuli

Namatmon

Gorky

Bazar

Akhun babayev

Shamseddin Kulol

Houvzi Matbon

To Long-Distance Bus Station, Train Station & Airport

1	Ak-Saray Palace
2	Malik-Adjar Khanaka
3	Hotel Shakhrisabz
4	Department Store
5	Hoja Mirkamida (or Abdushukur Okhoylik) Mosque
6	Caravanserai
7	Old Bathhouse
8	Shakhrisabz Restaurant
9	Post Office
10	Cinema
11	Chorsu
12	Ak-Saray Kafe
13	Department Store
14	Kok-Gumbaz Mosque
15	Mausoleum of Sheikh Shamseddin Kulyal
16	Gumbazi Seyidan Mausoleum
17	Khazrati Imam Mosque
18	Tomb of Jehangir
19	Crypt of Timur

Crypt of Timur

In an alley behind the mausoleum (and within the perimeter of the long-gone Dorussiadat) is a bunker with a green door leading to an underground room. The room, plain except for Quranic quotations on the arches, is nearly filled by a single stone casket. On the casket are biographical inscriptions about Timur, from which it was inferred (when the room was discovered in 1963) that this crypt was intended for him. Inside are two unidentified corpses.

Unfortunately the only way to see the crypt is to take an Uzbektourism guided city tour from the Hotel Shakhrisabz, at about US$35 per person.

Malik-Adjar Khanaka

A small complex west of the Hotel Shakhrisabz was once a khanaka, a Sufi meditation hall and hostel for wandering mendicants. Its mosque, built in 1904 and for a time a local museum and archives, has lately become a mosque again.

Other Sights

In the centre of town is a 17th century bath-house, in use right up until 1983, now under interminable restoration. Next door is a 1914 mosque which maps call Hoja Mirkamida, converted into a choyhona in the 1980s and recently reinstated as a mosque. Locals call it Abdushukur Okhoylik and say a mosque was first built here in 1705.

Across the street is a 16th century caravanserai, now restored as a shopping complex. The round, five domed building in front of the bazar is a chorsu, possibly a copy of one here as early as the 15th century.

Places to Stay & Eat

Quiet, fairly clean singles/doubles with toilet and shower at Uzbektourism's *Hotel Shakhrisabz* (☎ 3-33-01, 3-38-66) are US$25/42 with breakfast. Credit cards are accepted and there is a foreign exchange desk. It's at Ipak Yuli 26. The hotel has a pricey restaurant, several bufets, and a café with Uzbek/Tajik dishes.

For US$1 you can fill up with decent local food and gallons of tea in the choyhonas on the main road. Flyblown but best of the lot, and friendliest towards women visitors, is the *Ak-Saray Kafe*. In the *bazar* you may find women dishing out a wonderful hot soup of noodles, vegetables and yoghurt.

Things to Buy

The local Khujum Arts Factory produces Uzbek dresses, carpets and embroidery. Uzbektourism will take you there or to a cap, silk, pottery or wine factory. All but the carpets and wine are easy to find in the bazar or the department stores too.

Getting There & Away

Shakhrisabz is about 90 km from Samarkand across the arid foothills of the Zeravshan range, over the 1788 metre Takhtakaracha (or Aman-kutan) pass. By car this takes 1½ to two hours. The pass is intermittently closed by snow from January through March, forcing a three hour detour around the mountains.

Taxis go from Suzangaran kuchasi in Samarkand for about US$30 per carload for the round trip and a wait. Drivers from Shakhrisabz will know more and may be keener to bargain, as they're trying to get home. Licensed Shakhrisabz taxis have number plates with the letters КФА, and their vehicles are usually yellow. Private drivers have КФand will probably charge you more. Figure on several police checkpoints en route.

You can find taxis in Shakhrisabz by the bus station, the bazar or the post office, or at a stand about 10 minutes walk north of the centre. In this case look for Samarkand taxis (CHA or CH plates), as Shakhrisabz drivers may demand a round-trip fare.

Buses depart Samarkand's main bus station at 8.10 am and 12.50 pm for about US$2.50, but may take the long way around the hills. You could be asked for your Shakhrisabz visa when you buy a ticket.

The Hotel Samarkand offers an unguided day trip (with four to five hours in Shakhrisabz) for US$80 for up to four people per car. Their minibuses are a better deal if you can round up a dozen friends.

Getting Around

Bus No 10 and marshrutnoe taxi No 10 run between the hotel and the bus station.

BUKHARA
БУХОРО

Population: 255,000

After Samarkand's luminous mosaics, Bukhara's universal brown is a bit of a letdown. But with buildings spanning 1000 years of history, and a thoroughly lived-in old centre that probably hasn't changed much in two centuries, this is one of the best places in Central Asia for a glimpse of pre-Russian Turkestan.

Most of the centre is an architectural preserve, full of former medressas, a massive, decaying royal fortress and the remnants of a once-vast market complex. The government is pumping money into restoration, ahead of what is being called the town's 2500th birthday in 1997. Although the centre has become a bit too clean and quiet ('Ye Olde Bukhara' as one traveller put it), the 20th century has still been kept more or less at bay.

Until a century ago Bukhara was watered by a network of canals and some 200 stone pools called *hauz* where people gathered and gossiped, drank and washed. As the water wasn't changed often, Bukhara was famous for plagues; the average 19th century Bukhari is said to have died by the age of 32. The Bolsheviks modernised the system and drained the pools, except a few for irrigation and as 'architectural monuments'.

Storks, considered good omens, roosted here for a thousand years, and many buildings and trees are still crowned with their huge nests. But with the loss of the hauz that bred bugs and frogs, the storks have disappeared and the nests are empty. Among improbable birds still to be seen are seagulls.

Bukhara is a much friendlier and safer place than either Tashkent or Samarkand. Women travellers report minimal hassles and those exploring on their own during the day may be invited in for tea by local women.

As in Samarkand, most people speak Tajik but tend to call themselves Uzbeks. There are a few self-declared Tajiks, and a dwindling minority of Russians, Tatars and Bukharan Jews.

You'll need at least two days to look around. Try to allow time to lose yourself in the old town; it's easy to overdose on the 140-odd protected buildings and miss the whole for its many parts. If you're short on time, at least see Labi-hauz, the covered markets, the Kalan minaret and mosque, the mausoleum of Ismail Samani and the marvellously tacky summer palace of the last emirs.

History

When the Arabs arrived in 709 they found an already prosperous trading centre. Although they succeeded in Islamicising much of what they controlled, they faced almost continuous revolts and soon lost their enthusiasm for the place.

It was as capital of the Samanid state in the 9th and 10th centuries that Bukhara – *Bukhoro-i-sharif* (Noble Bukhara), the 'Pillar of Islam' – blossomed as Central Asia's religious and cultural heart, and simultaneously brightened with the Persian love of the arts. Among those nurtured here were the philosopher-scientist ibn Sina and the poets Firdausi and Rudaki – figures with the stature in the Persian Islamic world that, for example, Newton or Shakespeare enjoy in the West. It was said that 'while elsewhere light radiates from heaven onto the land, in holy Bukhara it radiates upward to illuminate heaven'.

After two centuries under the smaller Qarakhan and Karakitay dynasties, Bukhara succumbed in 1220 to Jenghiz Khan – and in 1370 fell under the shadow of Timur's Samarkand.

A second lease of life came in the 16th century when the Uzbek Shaybanids made it the capital of what came to be known as the Bukhara khanate, which (along with its smaller Shaybanid cousin, the Khiva

UZBEKISTAN

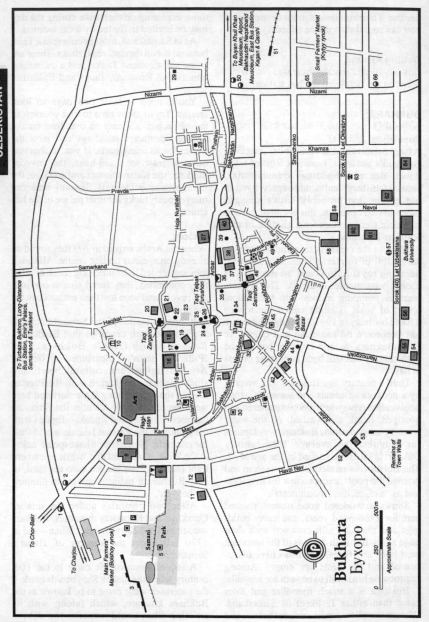

To Bagir Khuli Khan
Mausoleum, Airport,
Bakhauddin Naqshband
Mausoleum, East Bus Station,
Kagan & Qarshi

Small Farmers' Market
(Kolipy rynok)

Nizami

Khamza

Shevchenko

Navoi

Tsentralnaya

Arabon

Kukluk
Bazar

Gazzoli

Havzi Nav

Remains of
Town Walls

Bukhara
University

Bukhara
Бухоро

To Turbaza Bukhoro, Long-Distance
Bus Station, Tourist Palace,
Samarkand & Tashkent

Nizami

Pushkin

Bakhauddin Naqshband

Pravda

Hoja Nurabad

Samarkand

Haqiqat

Taqi
Zargaron

Taqi Telpak
Furushon

Taqi
Sarrafon

Hoja Rushnoi

Anbar

Nawzobokh

Bakhauddin Naqshband

Arbon

Arbon

Eshon

Jahangitov

Sorok (40) Let Uzbekistana

Sorok (40) Let Oktyabrya

Gazzoli

Islamov

Regi-
stan

Marx

Karl

Samani

To Chor-Bakr

To Chaljou

Main Farmers'
Market (Bolshoy rynok)

Park

Approximate Scale

0   250   500m

Ark

UZBEKISTAN

khanate) eventually embraced most of present-day Central Asia and parts of Iran and Afghanistan. The old town's present appearance owes most to that period, especially to the greatest of the Shaybanid khans, Abdullah II (ruled 1583-98).

The centre of Shaybanid Bukhara was a vast marketplace with dozens of specialist bazars and caravanserais, over 100 medressas (with 10,000 students) and more than 300 mosques.

Under the Astrakhanid Dynasty, the Silk Road's decline slowly pushed Bukhara out of the mainstream. Then in 1753 Muhammad Rahim, the local deputy of a Persian ruler, proclaimed himself emir, founding the

Manghit Dynasty which was to rule until the Bolsheviks came. In a parody of its ancient glory, Bukhara had a final fling as a decadent, feudal city-state, one of three (with Khiva and Kokand) that by this time dominated Central Asia and spent their time picking fights with one another.

The worst of the depraved Bukhara emirs was probably Nasrullah Khan – also called 'the Butcher' behind his back – who ascended the throne in 1826 by killing off his brothers and 28 other relatives. He made himself a household word in Victorian England after he executed two British officers (see the Stoddart & Conolly aside on the following page).

PLACES TO STAY

29	Sasha & Lena's B&B
49	Mubinjon Tajiev's House
55	Hotel Gulistan
60	Hotel Bukhoro
61	Hotel Fohira
62	Hotel Varaksha
64	Hotel Zarafshan

PLACES TO EAT

| 7 | Teahouse |

OTHER

1	Marshrutnoe Taxi to Chor-Bakr
2	'Bolshoy Rynok' Bus Stand
3	Remains of Town Walls & Talli-Pach Gate
4	Chashma-Ayub 'Mausoleum'
5	Ismail Samani Mausoleum
6	Ayni Uzbek Theatre of Drama & Musical Comedy
8	Bolo-hauz Mosque & Minaret
9	Water Tower
10	Zindon
11	Abdullah Khan Medressa
12	Modari Khan Medressa
13	Hoja Zaynuddin Mosque
14	Medressa
15	Women's Baths
16	Kalan Mosque
17	Kalan Minaret
18	Mir-i-Arab Medressa
19	Amir Alim Khan Medressa
20	Ulughbek Medressa
21	Abdul Aziz Khan Medressa
22	Site of Hindu Caravanserai
23	Tim Abdullah Khan (Market)

24	Site of Former Raja Begi Caravanserai
25	Spice Shop
26	Men's Baths (Under Reconstruction)
27	Kukeldash Medressa
28	Char Minar
30	Mausoleum of Imam Muhammad Gazzoli
31	Medressa
32	Gaukushan Medressa
33	Museum of Art
34	Site of Former Caucasus Caravanserai
35	Maghoki-Attar Mosque
36	Post Office
37	Nadir Divanbegi Khanaka
38	Labi-hauz
39	Hoja Nasruddin Statue
40	Nadir Divanbegi Medressa
41	Ruined Mosque
42	Baths
43	Hoja Gazian Medressa
44	Fayzulla Khujayev House (National House)
45	Turki Jangi Mausoleum
46	Baths (Under Reconstruction)
47	Bookshop
48	Jewish Community Centre & Synagogue
50	'Vokzal' Bus Stop
51	Old Train Station
52	Medressa
53	Mosque
54	Namozgokh Mosque
56	OVIR
57	National Bank
58	Bukhara PDPU Central Committee Offices
59	Provincial PDPU Central Committee Offices
63	Telephone & Telegraph Office
65	'Krytyy Rynok' Bus Stop
66	'Gorgaz' Bus Stop

Stoddart & Conolly

On 24 June 1842 Colonel Charles Stoddart and Captain Arthur Conolly were marched out from a dungeon cell before a huge crowd in front of the Ark, the emir's fortified citadel, made to dig their own graves and, to the sound of drums and reed pipes from atop the fortress walls, beheaded.

Colonel Stoddart had arrived three years earlier on a mission to reassure Emir Nasrullah Khan about Britain's invasion of Afghanistan. But his superiors, underestimating the emir's vanity and megalomania, had sent him with no gifts, and with a letter not from Queen Victoria (whom Nasrullah regarded as an equal sovereign) but from the Governor-General of India. To compound matters Stoddart violated local protocol by riding, rather than walking, up to the Ark. The piqued Nasrullah had him thrown into jail, where he was to spend much of his time at the bottom of the so-called 'bug pit', in the company of assorted rodents and scaly creatures.

Captain Conolly arrived in 1841 to try and secure Stoddart's release. But the emir, believing him to be part of a British plot with the khans of Khiva and Kokand, tossed Conolly in jail too. After the disastrous British retreat from Kabul the emir, convinced that Britain was a second-rate power and having got no reply to an earlier letter to Queen Victoria, had both men executed.

Despite general revulsion back in England, the British government chose to let the matter drop. Outraged friends and relatives raised enough money to send their own emissary, an oddball clergyman named Joseph Wolff, to Bukhara to verify the news. According to Peter Hopkirk in *The Great Game*, Wolff himself only escaped death because the emir considered him so hilarious, dressed up in full clerical regalia. ∎

In 1868, Russian troops under General Kaufman occupied Samarkand (which at the time was within Emir Muzaffar Khan's domains). Soon afterward Bukhara surrendered, and was made a protectorate of the tsar, with the emirs still nominally in charge. The Russians did insist that the Bukharis discontinue their thriving slave-trade. The Trans-Caspian Railway arrived in 1888, but at Emir Abdallahad Khan's request the train station was built a respectful 15 km away at Kagan, then called New Bukhara.

In 1918, as the Russian Revolution took hold in Central Asia, a party of emissaries and a military escort arrived from Tashkent (by then under Bolshevik control) to persuade Emir Alim Khan to surrender peacefully. The wily despot stalled long enough to allow his agents to stir up an anti-Russian mob which slaughtered nearly the whole delegation, and the emir's own army sent a larger Russian detachment packing, back towards Tashkent.

But the humiliated Bolsheviks had their revenge. Following an orchestrated 'uprising' in Charjou by local revolutionaries calling themselves the Young Bukharans,

and an equally premeditated request for help, Red Army troops from Khiva and Tashkent under General Mikhail Frunze converged on Bukhara on 2 September 1920, stormed the Ark and captured the Bukhara. Alim Khan fled with his entourage into the mountains and, in the following year, via Dushanbe into Afghanistan (where he died in Kabul in the 1940s). Local people are said to have swarmed into the Ark to free children kept as his playthings.

Around this time a group of Bukhara women, members of a movement known as Khujum, achieved Soviet martyrdom when they gathered in front of the Ark and burned their veils – symbol of purity for Muslims and of religious tyranny for the Bolsheviks. Whether this was a spontaneous demonstration or a Bolshevik put-up, afterwards most of the women are said to have been killed by their humiliated husbands or brothers.

Bukhara won a short 'independence' as the Bukhara People's Republic, but after showing rather too much interest in Pan-Turkism it was absorbed in 1924 into the newly created Uzbek SSR.

Much of the town's old aristocracy –

judges, merchants etc – had fled in the early post-Revolution years to Dushanbe, Afghanistan and Iran.

Orientation

An oasis in the enveloping Kyzylkum desert, Bukhara sits 250 km downstream of Samarkand on the Zeravshan river. The bulk of the modern town lies south of the historical centre. In between old and new, violating the otherwise low skyline, is a knot of tourist hotels and Party buildings.

The heart of Shakhristan, the old town, is the pool and square called Labi-hauz, a 10 minute walk north-west of the Hotel Bukhoro; the landmark Kalan minaret is five minutes farther, the Ark five more. Farther west are Samani Park and the main farmers' market or *bolshoy rynok*.

The long-distance bus station is five km north of the centre by bus or taxi, and the airport is four km east of the centre. The nearest functioning train station is 15 km south-east at Kagan.

Many Soviet and/or Russian names hadn't changed when we were there, among them Karl Marx (the road passing before the Ark), Sorok Let Uzbekistana ('40 Year Anniversary of Uzbekistan', between the Gulistan and Zarafshan hotels) and Sorok Let Oktyabrya ('40 Year Anniversary of October', by the Hotel Bukhoro). Samarkand is also known as Gijduvan.

Information

Tourist Office There aren't any, other than the hotel service bureaus with their hyperbolic Uzbektourism brochures.

Visas See Travel Agencies in this section.

Registration If you're not staying in a tourist hotel, OVIR is in the four storey building east of the Hotel Gulistan on Sorok Let Uzbekistana.

Money The National Bank on Sorok Let Uzbekistana 10 changes US$ travellers' cheques. The exchange desk at the Hotel Bukhoro will change US$ and DM cash.

Post & Communications The best place to mail anything is probably back in Tashkent, although the Hotel Bukhoro has a desk with stamps and a postal drop-box, and there is a small post office near Labi-hauz.

Bukhara's telephone system is totally flakey, and there's no good place from which to make an international call. You can try from the Hotel Bukhoro, but you'll do as well and pay a lot less at the 24 hour telephone and telegraph office a block east of the hotel (middle door).

Bukhara's telephone code is 36522.

Travel Agencies Salom (☎ 3-72-77, 2-33-98, contact Raisa Gareyeva) offers help with

Street Names in Bukhara	
New Name	Old Name
Arabon	Sovietskaya
Bakhautdin Naqshband	Lenina
Eshoni Pir	Tolstogo
Haqikat	Frunze
Havzi Nav	Ordzhonikidze
Hoja Nurabad	Kommunarov or Kommunarlar
Jubar	Oktyabrskaya
Namozgokh	Kirova
Nizami	Ulyanova
Samani Park	Kirov Par

UZBEKISTAN

Uzbek visas, homestays, transport and off-the-beaten-track excursions, from a switched-on former Intourist guide sympathetic to budget requirements. A similar outfit is Bukhara-Visa (☎ 6-00-85, contact Mila Akhmedova). Sasha at Sasha & Lena's B&B can also help with transport, onward bookings etc.

Business Hours & Tourist Season Museums are open daily from 9 am to 5 pm, except to 3 pm Tuesday, closed Wednesday and closed for lunch. Some hotels drop their rates outside the tourist season, which here is April through October.

Baths There are at least four public baths near the centre. Two old ones now under reconstruction (which may turn them into tourist traps) are a men's bath *(erkaklar hammomi)* just north of Taqi-Telpak Furushon and a bath just south of Taqi-Sarrafon. An operating women's bath *(ayollar hammomi)*, with common room *(hammomi kunjak)* only, is behind Kalan minaret. A bath on Jubar, south-west of Taqi-Sarrafon, has private rooms *(hammomi*

numur) and both men's and women's common rooms.

A common room is typically less than US$0.20 (in *sum)* for as long as you want to stay. A private room, with tub, shower and endless hot water, is about US$0.50 for an hour – pure heaven. Bring your own towel, soap, flip-flops, laundry etc. They're all closed on Sunday.

Labi-hauz
Labi-hauz, a plaza built around a pool in 1620 (the name is Tajik for 'around the pool'), is the most peaceful and interesting spot in town – shaded by mulberry trees as old as the pool and peopled with street-sellers, crazies, old men hunched over chessboards or gossiping over tea, and anyone else with nowhere else to go. Pray that municipal officials don't decide to pretty it up.

On the east side is a statue of **Hoja Nasruddin**, a semi-mythical 'wise fool' who appears in Sufi teaching-tales around the world.

To the east, the **Nadir Divanbegi medressa** was built as a caravanserai, but the khan thought it was a medressa so they

---

Hoja Nasruddin
Hoja Nasruddin was a mullah and a Sufi, with a sense of humour which he put to use in his teaching, if only to loosen his students up. Hundreds of tales about him are the theological equivalent of a running joke. Following is a good example:

One day the Hoja borrowed a pot from his neighbour. When he returned it the neighbour noticed a little pot nestled inside and called his attention to it. The Hoja exclaimed that the pot must have fallen pregnant and that this was its baby. Since the pot was the neighbour's, so was the baby! The neighbour went home, pleased.

Some time later, the Hoja came to borrow the neighbour's *kazan* (a large steel pan for making plov and other dishes). The neighbour was happy to lend it, thinking that this larger mother would surely produce an even bigger baby.

Time passed, and the kazan wasn't returned. Finally the neighbour enquired with the Hoja.
'Oh my!,' the Hoja exclaimed, 'I was going to tell you, it's so very sad!"
'What?' asked the neighbour.
'I'm sorry to say your kazan has died, so I cannot return it to you!'
'What? Kazans are made of metal, they don't die.'
'Ah,' said the Hoja, 'but you were quite happy to learn that a pot could become pregnant and give birth, so it's only fitting that you also accept the consequences of a kazan's mortality!' ■

hurried up and made it one in 1630. On the west side of the square, and built at the same time, is the **Nadir Divanbegi khanaka**. Both are named for Abdul Aziz Khan's treasury minister, who financed them in the 17th century.

North across the street, the **Kukeldash medressa**, built by Abdullah II, was at the time the biggest Islamic school in Central Asia.

South of Labi-hauz is what's left of the old town's unique **Jewish quarter** (see the Jews of Bukhara aside). Down the lane opposite the west end of the pool is a relatively recent Jewish community centre, and around the corner a much older synagogue.

Covered Bazars

From Shaybanid times, the area west and north from Labi-hauz was a vast warren of market lanes, arcades and crossroad mini-bazars whose multidomed roofs were designed to draw in cool air. Three remaining domed bazars, heavily renovated in Soviet times – Taqi-Sarrafon (Moneychangers), Taqi-Telpak Furushon (Cap-Makers) and Taqi-Zargaron (Jewellers) – were among dozens of specialised bazars in the town. They are returning tentatively to life, with games of backgammon-like *shishbesh* being played in the shade, and new shops to lure new consumers.

Local people call the covered markets by the following numbers: – Sarrafon No 1, Telpak Furushon No 2 and Zargaron No 3.

Taqi-Sarrafon Area Just to the north, in what was the old herb and spice bazar, is Central Asia's oldest surviving mosque, the Maghoki-Attar (meaning 'pit of the herbalists'), a lovely mishmash of 12th century façade and 16th century reconstruction. This is probably also the town's holiest spot: under it 1930s archaeologists found bits of a 5th century Zoroastrian temple wrecked by the Arabs, and an earlier Buddhist temple. Until the 16th century Bukhara's Jews are said to have used the mosque in the evenings as a synagogue.

The Jews of Bukhara

There have been Jews in Bukhara since perhaps the 12th or 13th century, evolving into a unique, non-Hebrew-speaking branch of the Diaspora. They have become major players in Bukharan commerce in spite of deep-rooted, institutionalised discrimination. A century ago there were at least seven synagogues here, reduced after 1920 to this one (now there is said to be another as well).

Since the collapse of the Soviet Union, Jews have dwindled from roughly 7% of the town's population to 2% (about 5000) at the last count, and even that is probably a big overestimate. Recent emigration to Israel and North America is a result of both Jews' new freedom to emigrate and others' freedom to act out prejudices. Some predict there will be no Jews here by the end of the century. ■

Only the top of the mosque was visible when the digging began; the present plaza surrounding it is the 12th century level of the town. A section of the excavations has been left deliberately exposed inside. Also here is an exhibition of beautiful Bukhara carpets and prayer mats.

West of this bazar is the site of a caravan-serai for traders from the Caucasus, destroyed by the Bolsheviks and replaced with a small park.

Taqi-Telpak Furushon Area On the north side is a men's bathhouse, still working a few years ago and now being rebuilt. The late 16th century covered arcade beyond it is called Tim Abdullah Khan (a *tim* was a general market, a kind of proto-department store, which it is again).

Two more caravanserai wrecked by the Bolsheviks were on the site of a fountain west of the path, and one for Hindu traders was north of Tim Abdullah Khan. A construction site beyond the fountain was to become a new, Saudi-financed medressa however the government, nervous about

Islamic fundamentalism, has clamped down on such projects.

Taqi-Zargaron Area A few steps east of the bazar, on the north side of Hoja Nurabad, is Central Asia's oldest medressa, and a model for many others – the elegant, blue-tiled Ulughbek medressa (1417), one of three built by Ulughbek (the others are at Gijduvan, 45 km away on the road to Samarkand, and in Samarkand's Registan complex). For a time after Uzbekistan's independence this was again a working medressa, closed to visitors, but the government has since shut it down.

The Abdul Aziz Khan medressa opposite was begun in 1652 by the Astrakhanid ruler of the same name, but left unfinished when he was booted out by the first of the Manghit emirs. This and the Divanbegi medressa (built by his treasury minister) are the only ones in town to flout the Sunni Muslim prohibition against the depiction of living beings (Adul Aziz Khan was a Shia).

Inside, the former lecture hall on the left – now a shop – still has original frescoes, including one in Chinese style. Inside on the right is a little winter mosque. A single two storey students' cell is open in the courtyard.

Kalan Minaret

When it was built by the Qarakhan ruler Arslan Khan in 1127, the Kalan minaret was probably the tallest building in Central Asia (*kalon* means 'great' in Tajik). It's an incredible piece of work, 47 metres tall with 10 metre deep foundations (including reeds stacked underneath in an early form of earthquake-proofing), which in 850 years has never needed any but cosmetic repairs. Jenghiz Khan was so dumbfounded by it that he ordered it spared. It was also used as a beacon and watchtower, and the Manghit emirs threw criminals off it until forbidden to do so by the Russians.

Its 14 ornamental bands, all different, include the first use of the glazed blue tiles that were to saturate Central Asia under Timur. Up and down the south and east sides are faintly lighter patches, marking the restoration of damage by Frunze's artillery in 1920. Its 105 inner stairs are closed to tourists, but special arrangements may be possible.

A legend says that Arslan Khan killed an iman after a quarrel. That night in a dream the imam told him, 'You have killed me; now oblige me by laying my head on a spot where nobody can tread', and the tower was built over his grave.

Kalan Minaret Area

At the foot of the minaret, on the site of an earlier mosque destroyed by Jenghiz Khan, is the 16th century congregational **Kalan mosque**, big enough for 10,000 people. Used in Soviet times as a warehouse, it was reopened as a place of worship in 1991. The roof, which looks flat, actually consists of 288 small domes. Tourists are only allowed into the central courtyard, where early in this century Emir Alim Khan added his own little prayer pavilion.

Opposite, its luminous blue domes in sharp contrast to the surrounding brown, is the **Mir-i-Arab medressa** – a working seminary from the 16th century until 1920, but reopened by Stalin in 1944 in an effort to curry Muslim support for the war effort. It was Central Asia's only functioning medressa in Soviet times (but is no longer). Presently 250 young men, mostly from Uzbekistan, enrol for five years, normally from the age of 17 or 18, to study Arabic, the Quran and Islamic law. In fact most classes are now held in the Kalan mosque, with Mir-i-Arab serving mainly as dormitories.

The medressa is named for a 16th century Naqshbandi sheikh from Yemen who had a strong influence on the Shaybanid ruler Ubaidullah Khan and financed the original complex. Both khan and teacher are buried beneath the northern dome. The tall pole with a horse-hair tassel at the north end of the tomb is a traditional marker for the graves of very revered figures in Islam. The hand symbolises the 'five pillars of Islam' (see the Religion section of the Facts About the Region chapter).

Note the door high above street level,

Kyrgyzstan
Top: View south from the road in the Tölök River Valley, the main route to
  Lake Song-Köl
Bottom: Children in the Tölök River Valley

Kyrgyzstan
Top: View along road about 10 km west of the Torugart Pass
Middle: Outer Kyrgyzstan security checkpost, in front of the Tian Shan range
Bottom: Morning queue of trucks at the Torugart checkpost

pre-dating the Soviet excavation of much of the old centre down to 16th century levels.

Behind Mir-i-Arab is the small **Amir Alim Khan medressa**, built this century, and now used as a children's library.

The Ark

This royal town-within-a-town is Bukhara's oldest structure, occupied from the 5th century right up until 1920, when it was bombed by the Red Army. Bits of it may go back two millennia, though the present crumbling walls are probably less than 300 years old. It's about 75% ruins inside now, except for some remaining royal quarters, now housing a multi-branched museum.

At the top of the entrance ramp is the 17th century **Juma (Friday) mosque**, its porch supported by tall columns of sycamore. Inside is a little museum of 19th and 20th century manuscripts and writing tools.

Turn right into a corridor with courtyards off both sides. First on the left is the former living quarters of the emir's *kushbegi* or prime minister, now housing a seldom-shown exhibit on WWII and the Soviet period (including a little mechanical diorama depicting the celebrated post-Revolutionary burning of the veils).

Second on the left is the oldest surviving part of the Ark, the vast **Reception & Coronation Court**, whose roof fell in during the 1920 bombardment. The last coronation to take place here was Alim Khan's in 1910. The submerged chamber on the right wall was the treasury, and behind the room was the harem.

To the right of the corridor were the open-air royal stables and the *noghorahona*, a room for drums and musical instruments used during public spectacles. Now there are shops and a tedious natural history exhibit.

Around the *salamhona* or Protocol Court at the end of the corridor are what remain of the royal apartments. These apparently fell into such disrepair that the last two emirs preferred full-time residence at the summer palace (see Around Bukhara). Now there are several museums, including ho-hum pre-

Shaybanid history on the ground floor, and coins and bits of applied art on the top floor.

Most interesting is in between – Bukhara's history from the Shaybanids through the tsars. Among items to look for are the huge snakeskin 'Whip of Rustam' that once hung above the Ark's entrance; a nine kg royal robe, padded to make the emir look big; and a surprisingly negative, Soviet-style exhibit on Islam. One on Bukhara's slave trade has conspicuously shrunk since we first visited in Soviet times, with the more 'feudal' items (eg people selling their children, often to the royal court as sexual toys) now covered or missing. Also gone are grisly displays on public executions.

Entry to the Ark is about 25 S, and an English-language guided tour is US$1 – not a bad deal since there are no English labels on anything.

Around the Ark

Out in front of the fortress is medieval Bukhara's main square, the **Registan** (meaning 'sandy place'), a favourite venue for executions, including those of the British officers Stoddart and Conolly (see the Stoddart & Conolly aside in the Bukhara History section). A quick look around the northern walls reveals how far gone the whole structure is in comparison with the restored front.

Behind the Ark is **Zindon**, the emir's jail, now a museum. Cheerful attractions include a torture chamber and several dungeons, including the gruesome 'bug pit' where Stoddart and Conolly languished. Nowadays the real stinking mess is not in the pits but outside, in a street full of mud and toilet smells.

Beside a pool opposite the Ark's gate is the **Bolo-hauz mosque**, the emirs' official place of worship, built in 1718 and probably very beautiful at the time. The brightly painted porch, supported by 20 columns of walnut, elm and poplar, was added in 1917, as was the stubby minaret nearby. It's now a mosque again. Beside it is a now-disused water tower, built by the Russians in 1927 as part of their new water system.

Ismail Samani Mausoleum & Around

In Samani Park is the town's oldest monument (completed about 905) and one of the most elegant structures in Central Asia, the **mausoleum of Ismail Samani** (the Samanid Dynasty's founder), his father and grandson. Its delicate baked terracotta brickwork – which gradually changes 'personality' through the day as the shadows shift – disguises walls almost two metres thick, helping it survive without restoration (except of the dome) for almost 11 centuries. The bricks pre-date the art of majolica tiles. Though dating from early Islamic times, the building bears Zoroastrian symbols such as the circle in nested squares – symbolising eternity – above the door. Jenghiz Khan overlooked it because it was partly buried in the dust of ages.

Behind the park is one of the few remaining, eroded sections (a total of two km out of an original 12) of the Shaybanid **town walls**, and a reconstructed gate called Talli-Pach. Another big section is about half a km west of the Hotel Gulistan.

At the edge of the main farmers' market is the peculiar **Chashma-Ayub 'mausoleum'**, built in the 12th century over a spring. Its middle domes were added in the 14th century, the front one in the 16th, and no-one was buried in it until even later. The name means 'Spring of Job'; legend says Job struck his staff on the ground here and a spring appeared. Inside you can drink from the spring and check out a little exhibit on the town's ancient waterworks.

Buyan Khuli Khan & Saifuddin Bukharzi Mausolea

One of Bukhara's oldest, prettiest and saddest 'monuments' is far off the tourist track, in the middle of factories and railway sidings east of the centre. It can only have survived the Soviet era through low-key patronage by some sympathetic non-Russian official.

The tiny, 14th century Buyan Khuli Khan mausoleum (now also used as a mosque) may be the tomb of a Karakitay ruler. On a trip to London, a sharp-eyed Uzbektourism guide discovered that the mausoleum's original gravestone, and large sections of its exterior tiles, had somehow found their way into the Victoria and Albert Museum. Some unrestored tilework, beautiful and delicate, remains over the portal.

Nearby is the Saifuddin Bukharzi mausoleum, resting place of a revered early 16th century teacher. The grave has been moved out in front (the horsehair tassel and sign-of-the-hand indicate a 'saint' on a level with Mir-i-Arab) and the mausoleum converted to another mosque.

Turki Jangi Mausoleum

Deep in the old town is a tiny mausoleum favoured as a place for getting one's prayers answered. It's the resting place of a holy man known as Turki Jangi, his two sons, several grandsons and numerous other relations. Its importance is signalled by the hundreds of other graves around it – allegedly in stacks 30 metres deep! The caretaker told us Turki Jangi was a disciple of Bakhautdin (see the Around Bukhara section), making him 14th century or later. The central chamber is under slow, devoted restoration. It's on Namozgokh about half a km south of Taqi-Telpak Furushon.

Char Minar

This photogenic little building, the gatehouse of a long-gone medressa built in 1807, bears more relation to Indian styles than to anything Bukharan. The name (Chor Minor in Tajik, meaning 'Four Minarets') is wrong on both counts – they aren't minarets but just ornamentation, and there are now just three after one collapsed in March 1995 (and another is in danger of toppling). It served for a time as a neighbourhood mosque, but is now just a hang-out for obnoxious kids. It's in a maze of alleys between Pushkin and Hoja Nurabad; everybody in the neighbourhood knows it by name.

Other Medressas & Mosques

West of Taqi-Sarrafon is the **Gaukushan medressa**, now full of handicraft shops and workshops, and a summer choyhona. Across the canal is a little brother of the Kalan minaret.

South-east of Samani park are two massive facing medressas, one named for the great Shaybanid ruler **Abdullah Khan** and one for his mother (**Modari Khan**, 'mother of the khan'), that would rival the Ulughbek and Abdul Aziz pair if they were cleaned up.

Another neglected giant is the handsome 16th century **Namozgokh mosque**, behind the Hotel Gulistan.

Fayzulla Khujayev House

Uzbektourism calls it 'National House' and the sign says 'The Daily Life of a Bukhara Merchant', but neighbours know it by its most infamous occupant, Fayzulla Khujayev, who plotted with the Bolsheviks to dump Emir Alim Khan. He was rewarded with the presidency of the Bukhara People's Republic, chairmanship of the Council of People's Commissars of the Uzbek SSR, and finally liquidation by Stalin.

The house was built in 1891 by his father Ubaidullah, a wealthy merchant. There are said to be about 20 such merchants' houses left in Bukhara, out of hundreds at the turn of the century. How these survived the anti-bourgeois fury of 1920 is a matter of wonder. Some may have been camouflaged with layers of adobe mud, but most were probably under the wing of Uzbek Communist officials who hadn't completely lost touch with their traditions, or were willing to be bribed. After the Revolution this house served as a Marxist school and then a museum in praise of Khujayev.

Since 1994 the state has let a few former museum employees live here and gradually restore the elegant frescoes, ghanch, lattice-work and ceiling beams (of carved, unpainted elm, Bukhara style), paying for the work with guided tours, special functions and a handicrafts shop. It's a bit contrived, but a very pleasant experience and a long step ahead of the usual sterile tours, for less than US$1 in *sum*. They say 'come anytime', but an advance booking is appreciated. They speak only Russian so bring a translator.

See the Places to Stay – bottom end section, for a similar house where you can stay the night.

Museum of Art

The Museum of Art is in the former headquarters of the Russian Central Asian Bank (1912), just west of Taqi-Sarrafon.

Places to Stay

Homestays The Salom and Bukhara travel agencies can arrange B&B in *private homes*, typically for about US$20. You may also be approached by locals at the tourist spots.

Bottom End Bukhara has at least one local-style B&B, *Mubinjon Tajiev's* 1765 house full of old furnishings, bang in the middle of the old town. There are about 10 dorm beds – mattresses on the floor – for US$10 each (much of which, he says, goes to further restoration), with common toilet and hot shower. Plain, local-style meals by arrangement start at about US$2.50, and hygiene is OK. Crafty Mubinjon speaks no English but makes himself understood. The house (☎ 4-20-05) is at Eshoni Pir 4, in a cul-de-sac about 200 metres south of Labi-hauz.

Perhaps too good to be true are the rates at the municipal *Hotel Zarafshan* (☎ 3-41-73) at Sorok Let Uzbekistana 7. Huge threadbare but clean single/double suites with bath and TV cost US$6/7 year-round (other travellers report rooms cost more). There's a plain, clean restaurant and several snack bars. Uzbektourism literature ignores the place – a good reason to check it out.

The biggest drawback of the *Hotel Gulistan* (☎ 3-38-10) is the location, one km west of the other hotels at Sorok Let Uzbekistana 19. Transport there is poor too. Basic rooms with toilet and shower are US$22/26 in season and US$16/22 the rest of the year. Food may be hard to find except in summer or when a group is staying.

The *Varaksha* (☎ 3-84-94), at Navoi 5, is probably the worst hotel in town. The sheets may be clean and there's hot water for a few hours, but it's disintegrating – broken doors (and dubious security), dangling fixtures and an omnipresent urine smell. The most basic single/double, with toilet and a shower that may or may not work, is an absurd US$22/26 in season, US$17/22 out of season.

If you're on a true starvation budget, you could stay in a damp, rubbishy cell in the *Kukeldash medressa* for almost nothing, in summer only. But other than the amazing location and the price ('three *sum* last summer' is all the shifty director would say), there is nothing to recommend it – cold water, no shower, no toilet other than the foul public toilet nearby. It may be unsafe for women. Enter on the left side and ask at the office in the middle.

In a seedy, very un-rustic patch near the long-distance bus station is the tired-looking *Turbaza Bukhoro* (☎ 4-77-25), with cheap four-bed bungalows and space for pitching tents, open in summer only.

There is also a *student hostel* at the Bukhara University, on Navoi just south of the university headquarters. Readers have written about a budget *B&B* run by a private firm called Marvarid-95 (☎ 3-15-56, contact Jurayev Bakhriddin) at Deputatskaya 103, but we haven't checked it out.

Middle In contrast to Mubinjon's very Asian B&B, *Sasha & Lena's B&B* (☎ 3-38-90) is a spanking-clean, Europeanised place with sauna, hot tub, air--con and satellite TV. Nine dorm beds with shared toilet and bath (and 'continental' breakfast) are US$20 per person in season, US$15 out of season; dinners by arrangement are about US$5. It's at Molodyozhnaya 13, a 10 minute walk east of Labi-hauz. Sasha, a former Intourist guide, can arrange transport, tickets, onward bookings and other help. This is popular with Central Asia's expatriates and gets booked out early, so it's essential to call ahead.

The *Hotel Bukhoro* (☎ 3-22-76, 3-11-04; fax 3-57-50), the place with the 'Uzbektourism' sign at Sorok Let Oktyabrya 6, has quiet rooms with bath for US$43/50 in season and US$30/34 out of season (major credit cards accepted). It's also got the same dodgy water supply and Stone Age elevators it was known for in Cold War days – now with imaginative post-Soviet solutions: staff

blame the lack of hot water on municipal water works, and the elevators bear a permanent, illuminated *remont* (under repair) sign.

The city and provincial party headquarters across the street have merely exchanged 'Communist Party' for Karimov's 'People's Democratic Party'.

Top End Behind the Bukhoro is the potentially deluxe *Hotel Fohira*, frozen in near-completion until the Indian banks who financed it get their loans repaid.

Places to Eat

Bukhara offers little in the way of 'dining' other than home-cooking at the B&Bs and mediocre food at the hotels. The *Hotel Bukhoro's* food is Russian stodge, though the service is polite and the prices aren't bad (about US$2 for an evening meal).

During the day, dine al fresco at *Labi-hauz* with grey-beards, local families and the occasional foreign tourist. Tea and pastries appear by 7.30 am and shashlyk, samsas and laghman are dished up until sunset (pay separately for each). Hygiene is dubious but prices are low and the setting is unmatched.

For vegetarians and other self-caterers there are farmers' markets. The main one by Samani park, known as the *bolshoy rynok*, always seems full of bullying policemen. Better vibes are at the smaller *krytyy rynok* near the Hotel Bukhoro, and the Sunday-only *Kukluk bazar* in the old town, south of Labi-hauz.

Things to Buy

For carpets and old things, the shopping tends to be better here than in other tourist centres of Uzbekistan, and the shopkeepers more honest (though no less interested in your dollars). Some shops to check out are in the Abdul Aziz Khan medressa, the Maghoki-Attar mosque and Taqi-Telpak Furushon. Just north out of Taqi-Telpak Furushon, an engaging and knowledgeable spice merchant named Mirfaiz will lure you with exotic aromas. The Gaukushan medressa is full of handicraft workshops (lots of engraved copper and brass utensils).

Although certain carpet designs originate here, the best 'Bukhara' rugs are made in Turkmenistan (as they have been ever since those regions were part of the Bukhara khanate). See the 'Bukhara' Rugs aside in the Arts section of the Facts about the Country chapter.

Remember to get a receipt showing the price and shop location, and if necessary a letter saying that what you bought has no historical value (see Customs in the Facts for the Visitor chapter).

Traditional Uzbek men's padded coats are US$25 in the Hotel Bukhoro gift shop, and the *sum* equivalent of about US$4 in the bazars!

Getting There & Away

Air There are regular flights from Bukhara to just three destinations – Tashkent (1½ hours away), at least four times a day in summer on Uzbekistan Airways Yak-40s, and Moscow and St Petersburg, each twice a week in summer. Bookings and tickets can be arranged through the Hotel Bukhoro service bureau or at the airport's 'international sector' office, to the right (south) of the main building.

Bus As at most bus stations in Uzbekistan, the police appear as soon as a foreigner does, but there are few of Tashkent bus station's registration hassles.

There are five daily departures to Tashkent (12 hours away), and it's fairly easy to buy a ticket at the last moment. Six buses a day go to Samarkand (6½ hours away). On both, watch for the unrestored gateway of a 12th century caravanserai called Rabati-Malik on the north side of the road about 80 km before Samarkand. A single bus leaves each day for Urgench about 2.30 pm, arriving around midnight. One leaves about 2 pm for the 16 hour trip to Andijan via Khojand, Kokand and Namangan.

For Qarshi (and Termez connections) as well as Shakhrisabz, go to the *sharq avtovokzal* (east station), on the road to Kagan. Of five daily departures to Qarshi (four hours), the 3 pm bus arrives with the best connection to the 11 pm overnight train to Termez.

No direct buses seem to go anywhere in Turkmenistan, only trains to Charjou. We heard about Charjou buses from the main bazar, but found none.

Train Every day a fast train starts from here for Samarkand (5½ hours away) and Tashkent (12 hours away), and another for Nukus (about 20 hours away); one also passes each way between Nukus and Tashkent. On Monday a fast train starts here for Almaty. On odd-numbered days a fast train stops en route from Samarkand to Urgench and Moscow.

There is a train to Charjou in Turkmenistan (75 km or 3 to 4 hours away) but travellers report headaches getting anyone to sell them a ticket; try asking at the police post.

Getting Around

To/From the Airport The 10 minute taxi trip to/from the centre is about US$3 in *sum*. Bus No 10 to/from the Vokzal, Krytyy Rynok or Gorgaz stops takes 15 to 20 minutes. Marshrutnoe taxi No 56 passes the Bukhoro and Varaksha hotels.

To/From the Train Station Take the Kagan-Bukhara (КОГОН-БУХОРО) bus, or a marshrutnoe taxi, from the train station to the Vokzal stop (near Bukhara's disused train station), or a Bukhara-Kagan bus the other way.

To/From the Bus Station Bus No 7 goes from Navoi, near the Hotel Bukhoro to the long-distance bus station.

AROUND BUKHARA

Emir's Palace

For a look at the kitsch lifestyle of the last emir, Alim Khan, go out to Makhosa – Sitorai Mokhi Hosa, meaning 'Palace of Moon-like Stars' (or Moon & Stars) – his summer palace (now a museum) three km north of the centre.

The present buildings were a joint effort

for Alim Khan by Russian architects (outside) and local artisans (inside). A 50 watt Russian generator provided the first electricity the emirate had ever seen. The palace is a fascinating mix of taste and tastelessness – such as a fine collection of Asian porcelain displayed in a room with heart-shaped windows. Next door is the former harem, and beside a pool where the women frolicked is a wooden pavilion from which – says every tour guide – the emir tossed an apple to his chosen bedmate. The harem has a small museum devoted to the traditional silk-on-cotton dowry needlework called *suzana*.

The original complex was built by his father, Abdallahad Khan, who just wanted a cool place to go in the summer. The story goes that he had a sheep slaughtered and the raw meat left in various suburban spots, and it was here that it rotted most slowly.

Getting There & Away Bus Nos 9 and 13 go from the Krytyy Rynok or Vokzal stop near the Hotel Bukhoro, and bus No 12 goes from the main bazar infrequently. The palace is at the end of the line. Taxis can be hard to find coming back.

Mausoleum of Bakhautdin Naqshband

Just east of Bukhara in the village of Kasri Orifon is one of Sufism's more important shrines, the birthplace and the tomb of Bakhautdin (or Bakha ud-Din) Naqshband, the 14th century founder of the most influential of many ancient Sufi orders in Central Asia (see the Naqshbandis aside), and Bukhara's unofficial 'patron saint'.

The huge main dome of the complex covers a 16th century khanaka. Beside it is a precariously leaning minaret and a courtyard with two old mosques, lovingly restored since independence. The tomb itself is a simple two metre high block in the courtyard. Tradition says that three anticlockwise circumambulations of it will bestow blessings/ bring good luck/ grant one's wish/ etc. Beside it, beneath a mulberry tree, you may find a mullah saying prayers for pilgrims with special requests.

The Naqshbandis

Bakhautdin Naqshband was (meaning no disrespect) a kind of Islamic Gandhi, who emphasised the importance of work in a full spiritual life (a *naqshband* was a carver of wooden stamps for printing fabrics). The Naqshbandi are a clandestine, decentralised but non-fanatical, non-ascetic Sufi brotherhood (quite literally, since at least in Central Asia they apparently have little interest in women adepts) who share certain practices such as the *zikr*, a recitation or contemplation of the names of God, sacred verses etc, sometimes combined with techniques of posture and breath control.

Naqshbandi groups exist all over the world, including almost all Muslim areas of the former Soviet Union. Naqshbandi fighters were at the centre of the 19th century struggle against the Russians in the Caucasus, and several of the most famous *basmachi* guerillas were Naqshbandis.

Re-emerging Central Asian Islam has a strong Sufi flavour because it was mainly within such societies that it survived Soviet persecution. The KGB seems never to have managed to plant spies among them. ■

The atmosphere here is amazingly serene compared to the other side of the walls. This is not a tourist attraction but a very sacred place for Muslims. Please dress conservatively, keep a respectful silence and be discreet with cameras.

Outside the courtyard is a small kitchen where wealthier visitors can have a sheep slaughtered and cooked, and the meat distributed to the poor. Nearby is the so-called 'Wishing Tree', the dead trunk of an ancient mulberry tree linked by legends to Bakhautdin himself, and one of those places where Islamic and pre-Islamic traditions mingle. Good luck (in particular for barren women) is said to come from crawling under it three times.

Also here are a small museum and a restaurant, and outside the complex are choyhonas and hostels for pilgrims. The entire village is a place of pilgrimage; in fact the usual first pilgrim stop is the tomb of

Bakhautdin's mother, just north of the complex.

Getting There & Away From Bukhara to Kasri Orifon is about 12 km, past mulberry trees, vineyards and cotton fields. On your own, take an eastbound No 16 bus from the Vokzal stand. A taxi would be perhaps US$5 in *sum* for the round trip plus a wait. Tourist hotel service bureaus can arrange guided excursions.

Chor-Bakr

This haunting 16th century necropolis or 'town' of mausolea 10 km west of Bukhara was built in Shaybanid times, but nobody seems quite sure for whom. The locally preferred story is that it was for Abu-Bakr, devoted friend of the Prophet Muhammad and later first caliph, and his family. Second choice is that it was built by and for a local dynasty called the Jubari Sheikhs.

Two massive structures, a Friday mosque on the left and a former khanaka on the right, dominate the complex. A third structure in the middle is said to have collapsed in the 1980s, according to Colin Thubron in the *The Lost Heart of Asia*. All around are small broken-down mausolea and simple graves built later to capitalise on the site's good vibes. There's little sign of recent restoration (save one small building apparently used by local people for 40 day intensive retreats), but this and the near-absence of visitors are part of its appeal.

For a donation of US$0.50 or so in *sum*, the caretaker may let you climb the (restored) circular staircase to the (restored) roof of the khanaka, for a bird's-eye view.

Getting There & Away The complex is in a tiny village once called Sumitan, now Chor-Bakr. From the main bazar, take a bus labelled СВЕРДЛОВ ШАХ БЕКАТИ (Sverdlov region) and ask for Chor-Bakr (about 10 minutes away), from where the complex is easily visible. There is also said to be a marshrutnoe taxi from the bazar directly to Chor-Bakr.

Kagan

This was the original Russian cantonment and train station of New Bukhara, placed far from old Bukhara to humour Emir Abdallahad Khan, who regarded trains as an evil influence. He apparently had a change of heart, and built a spur line (now disused) into the middle of Bukhara.

It's decidedly not worth a special trip, but if you're waiting for a train, have a look at its assortment of sturdy turn-of-the-century buildings, including an Orthodox church and an office of the Russian Central Asian Bank. Most startling is a huge white palace in a pastiche of Greek, Arab and European styles beside the road to Bukhara, completed in 1903. One source says Abdallahad built it – at a cost of some 300,000 gold roubles – for Tsar Nicholas II (who never came). It was later used for visits by the Russian Governor-General, and then as a Palace of Culture for railway workers.

Getting There & Away See the Bukhara – Getting Around section for information on how to get to Kagan.

Other Things to See & Do

About 40 km south-east of Bukhara is a nature reserve and breeding station founded in 1977 for the Persian gazelle or (*jeiran*), nearly wiped out by hunters. Other endangered creatures here include cheetahs (once prized for hunting the same gazelles) and the little Przhevalsky's Horse. Uzbektourism (via the Hotel Bukhoro service desk) can arrange a half day excursion.

Another Uzbektourism diversion is a half day excursion into the **Kyzylkum desert**, complete with camel rides and tea in a yurt, although you can also get a pretty good look at the desert from the bus to/from Khiva.

Afshona, birthplace of ibn-Sina (Avicenna), is strictly for pilgrims and scholars, with little to see but an Avicenna museum. Excavations of a 6th century Sogdian fortress, a Zoroastrian temple and other ruins at **Varaksha** will thrill only specialists, as will other digs at **Parkent**. You can also visit

Bukhara's **Karakul fleece factory**, one of Central Asia's biggest, and a Karakul sheep collective farm.

QARSHI
ҚАРШИ
Population: 126,000

At least 1000 years old, Qarshi has little to show for it; the couple of blue domes in the old town date only to earlier this century. It grew as a stopover on the caravan route from Samarkand to Afghanistan and India, and fell within the sphere of influence of Bukhara until the 1920s when the emirate capitulated to the Bolsheviks. The present town, administrative centre of Kashkadarya province, is a stop on the Tashkent-Dushanbe railway line, but there's little reason to get off.

Orientation & Information
The main axis is ulitsa Uzbekistan which runs from the train station, east for two km and pivoting north for eight km until it leaves town and becomes the Samarkand road. Qarshi has two centres. The sombre administrative centre is around the junction of prospekt Karla Marxa and ulitsa Uzbekistan, one km north of the pivot, marked by a modernist clock tower. The more humane old town (Russian *staryy gorod*) is five km farther north. The main bus station is on ulitsa Guzarskaya, which connects with ulitsa Uzbekistan about one km east of the railway station.

Things to See & Do
The **regional museum** is at ulitsa Kalinina 309 in the old town, and next door is the **Hoja Abdulaziz medressa** (1912). Nearby, on ulitsa Akhunbabaeva is the fractionally older **Medressa of Bekmir** (1905). Across ulitsa Uzbekistan is the **bazar** and a 17th century **bathhouse**.

Places to Stay
At the *Hotel Qarshi* the rates seem negotiable; we paid US$14 for a deluxe double. At the time of our visit the perverse plumbing delivered only scalding hot water, with cold

water only for an hour each morning and an hour in the evening, when the hot goes off. The Qarshi is on prospekt Karla Marxa, 800 metres west of the clock tower.

The other option is the *Hotel Tong* (☎ 5-19-03), about two km north of the clock tower at ulitsa Uzbekistan 245 (bus Nos 1 and 8 stop outside, the third stop after the clock tower). The rooms are more comfortable and cleaner than the Qarshi's, but US$25 for a double.

Places to Eat
A serviceable *choyhona* is 150 metres east of the train station on the south side of ulitsa Uzbekistan, with excellent plov as well as laghman, shashlyk and shots of vodka. It's open daily until 10 pm. The restaurant *Sado* is an upmarket, private venture with an extensive but firmly meat-based menu of dishes around the US$1.50 mark. Open until 11 pm, it's just off ulitsa Uzbekistan, 150 metres south of the clock tower, down an alley beside a shop marked 'Guzalyaik Salony'.

Getting There & Away
Daily trains go north to Tashkent and Andijan via Samarkand (US$6), and to Kanibadam in northern Tajikistan. Heading south are two overnight trains plus a daily to Termez, plus two daily services to Dushanbe via Termez. Train No 23/24, the Moscow-Dushanbe service, also stops here.

From the bus station there are daily services to Bukhara and Tashkent, two to Termez and three to Samarkand, three hours away.

Getting Around
Bus Nos 1 and 8 go from the train station north along ulitsa Uzbekistan past the clock tower and the Hotel Tong, to the bazar. Bus No 1 continues to the bus station (*avtostantsia*) on the northern edge of town, where incoming Samarkand and Tashkent buses sometimes kick out their passengers. From the central bus station bus No 12 and marshrutnoe taxi No 12 also go north up ulitsa Uzbekistan to the avtostantsia.

UZBEKISTAN

TERMEZ
ТЕРМИЗ
Population: 62,000

Blanched in equal measure by a searing sun and seven decades of stodgy Sovietism, modern-day Termez bears few traces of its colourful, cosmopolitan history. In recent times the town distinguished itself as a major launch pad for the 1979 Soviet invasion of Afghanistan. However, set in attractive landscapes on the fringes of town are some ancient monuments and sites attesting to more glorious times.

Founded on the north bank of the Oxus (Amu-Darya) river by the Bactrians, Termez was a city of Hellenic culture with inhabitants who spoke Persian, Scythian and Greek, while in the bazars a panoply of merchants bought and sold using coins carrying the images of Hindu deities. Under the Arabs the city became a major Muslim religious centre, while at the same time the secular element remained so vibrant that the noise from Termez, so the story goes, could be heard in Balkh, 70 km south of the river. Termez continued to flourish under the Timurids but was destroyed at the end of the 17th century.

The present town was begun in 1897 as a Russian fort and garrison. For most of this century Termez was solely a military post on the wild Afghan frontier; when diplomat-adventurer Fitzroy Maclean passed through in the 1930s, the jungle of reeds on the banks of the nearby Oxus was reputed to harbour tigers.

Considerably tamer now, Termez still has a military role (smack in the middle of town, behind the old fortress walls, the Russians maintain a large armoured vehicle base) but it also has a buoyant civil economy based on cotton and fruit grown on the fertile river plains.

The town centre – most of it less than 30 years old – is well looked after and the central park, next to ploschad Termezy, with its canals and fountains is really pleasant. The monuments, just out of town, are not particularly spectacular and don't compare with those elsewhere in Uzbekistan, but their

setting on the rugged Afghan borderlands goes some way toward compensating.

The actual border crossing is about 10 km south of the town centre where the 'Friendship Bridge' straddles the Amu-Darya. In theory anyone with a valid Afghan visa should be able to cross here. For those who just want to say they've 'seen' Afghanistan, there's a viewing platform beside the bridge from where you can make out the Afghan town of Khairoton on the opposite shore.

Orientation
Termez is surprisingly large and, with no

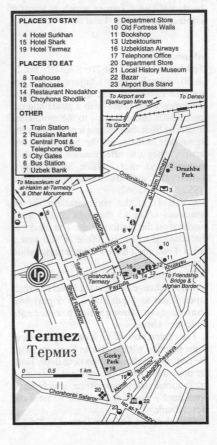

PLACES TO STAY
4 Hotel Surkhan
15 Hotel Shark
19 Hotel Termez

PLACES TO EAT
8 Teahouse
12 Teahouses
14 Restaurant Nosdakhor
18 Choyhona Shodlik

OTHER
1 Train Station
2 Russian Market
3 Central Post & Telephone Office
5 City Gates
6 Bus Station
7 Uzbek Bank
9 Department Store
10 Old Fortress Walls
11 Bookshop
13 Uzbektourism
16 Uzbekistan Airways
17 Telephone Office
20 Department Store
21 Local History Museum
22 Bazar
23 Airport Bus Stand

Termez
Термиз

clustered central district, visitors may find themselves frequently resorting to flagging down taxis to get around. The main thoroughfare is broad al-Hakim Termezy kuchasi, with the train station at its north end and ploshchad Termezy and an adjacent park just off it, three km to the south.

On the south side of the park, on Fayzulla Khujayev, are a few places to eat, the local tourist office, a telephone office and the Hotel Shark. The other main traveller-friendly part of town is a farther two km south around the junction of Sharaf Rashidov and Pedagogicheskaya, where you'll find the bazar and museum. Nearby is the decent Hotel Termez which is also the terminus for bus Nos 4 and 6.

Information

Uzbektourism (☎ 2-64-20, 2-47-02; fax 2-58-50) is at Fayzulla Khujayev 17. They organise excursions taking in all the local monuments (six hours with a guide and car for US$40), and day trips to the mountains or nearby Sherabad, where a cave holds the Stone Age remains of the region's oldest settlers. They also offer various tours of six to nine days that include Shahkrisabz, Samarkand and Bukhara, priced from US$220 to US$362.

OVIR is at the train station, in an unmarked office to the right of the main entrance on the platform side. The clerks in the booking hall may refuse to sell you a ticket if you don't have a Termez registration stamp on your visa.

The Uzbek Bank at al-Hakim Termezy 7a and the exchange office at the Hotel Surkhan (open 9 am to 1 pm and 2 to 6 pm) will change cash, though neither accepts travellers' cheques.

The central post office is on Ordjonikidze, at the junction with al-Hakim Termezy, with the central telephone office next door. Both are open daily from 7 am to 8 pm. A smaller international telephone office which stays open until 1 am is at Gagarina 32 near the Hotel Shark.

The telephone code for Termez is 32622.

Local History Museum

This museum on Pedagogicheskaya was closed at the time of writing because the building had been declared structurally unsafe. But anyone interested in its small collection of Stone Age tools and weapons, ancient ceramics and coins and architectural fragments can arrange a private visit through Uzbektourism, or just by turning up and hammering on the back door.

Zurmala Tower

A baked-mud stump in the middle of a baked-mud field, the Zurmala tower isn't much to look at but it's one of the most ancient remaining examples of monumental architecture in Central Asia. Although it looks like it may have been a minaret the structure predates Islam and is, in fact, a massive stupa from the 2nd century BC when Buddhism was the prevailing local religion. Any decoration it might have had is long gone and the tower isn't worth closer investigation than the view from the road, off to the right about four km out of Termez heading for Sherabad.

Mausoleum of al-Hakim at-Termezy

About one km after the Zurmala Tower, a side road swings off to the left and winds through the barely discernible ruins of the original Arab town of Termez, beyond which is a memorial ensemble built around the grave of al-Hakim at-Termezy. Born in 748, at-Termezy successfully mixed mysticism with science and was revered as one of the great Islamic philosopher-mathematicians. He was also a Sufi sheik who reputedly healed people by reading passages from the Quran and communicated with Allah every Friday at 10 pm, on the dot. According to the script on the wall of his mausoleum, he lived until he was 120, only dying then at the hands of an assassin who struck during morning prayers.

His mausoleum was constructed on the banks of the Amu-Darya in 1091, the adjacent mosque being added in the following century. Out of bounds during the Soviet era because of proximity to the Afghan border, it's only in the last few years that the complex has been open to visitors. Now at-Termezy's white marble cenotaph attracts daily crowds of pilgrims who make a day of it, picnicking in the grounds after prayer.

Supported by money from the Islamic world, there are plans to enlarge the complex to include a library for all the existing ancient copies of at-Termezy's writings, presently scattered among institutions such as the national libraries of Britain and France and theological centres of the Middle East.

Fayoz-Tepe

Back on the main Sherabad road, one km north of the at-Termezy mausoleum turn-off, is another left turn, to a deeply rutted track seemingly headed for a hilltop radar tracking station; in fact it leads to the excavations of Fayoz-Tepe, a 2nd century Buddhist monastery.

Before the Arab conquest, Buddhism was the region's prevailing faith. The remains here take the form of one to two metre high mud walls very clearly defining a central courtyard and surrounding rooms. During the excavations in 1968 Russian archaeologists also unearthed jewellery and coins bearing the image of the Buddha but, as usual, these were packed off to the Hermitage in then-Leningrad. Watch out for snakes, particularly in the shade of bushes.

A km away to the west, the sandy hill riddled with black tunnel entrances is Kara Tepe, a Buddhist cave monastery. This cannot be visited as it lies over the wrong side of the border with Afghanistan – the boundary between the two countries is marked by the three metre high chain-link fence running through the poppy fields.

Kyrk Kyz

Kyrk Kyz (or 'The 40 Maidens', as the place is locally known) was the country seat of a 10th century Samanid noble who feuded with a neighbouring landowner and was slain along with all his soldiers. Fearing for the grieving and now defenceless wives and mothers in the village, the nobleman's

daughter offered them the protection of her family's fortified country palace.

After some weeks within the sheltering walls they grew bold and decided to avenge their husbands and sons by slitting the throats of their murderers. One evening the palaces gates swung open and the women, dressed in men's clothing, crept out on their mission. But brave intentions were insufficient preparation, and every one of them was captured or killed, and the fortress fell into ruin.

At least that's the story. The only verifiable bit is that the fortress fell into ruins. Today it looks like a collapsed mud pie. Sitting in the middle of good farmland the most amazing thing about the ruin is that no farmer in the past thousand years has flattened it and used the land for agriculture.

Kyrk Kyz is about six km east of the Termez-Sherabad road on the territory of the Namouna *kolkhoz* (collective farm).

Sultan Saadat Ensemble

This badly neglected ensemble is a drab group of small mausolea enclosed by a high wall. The biggest two (dating from the 11th and 12th centuries) are joined by a vaulted gateway. A few traces of blue tiling remain on the façade but all other decoration is gone, although the right-hand chamber has some attractive interior brickwork. The other mausolea date from the Timurid period but lack any of that period's architectural splendour.

The ensemble is on the Namouna kolkhoz, less than two km from the airport.

Djarkurgan Minaret

Looking like a brocaded brick-chimney, the minaret in the village of Djarkurgan is a close relative of the Kalan minaret in Bukhara. It was built in 1108 and originally stood much higher than its present 25 metres but the top part has disappeared. At one time there would also have been a mosque attached but no traces of that remain. Instead, the land around the minaret is now actually somebody's back garden and you have to back through the vegetable patch while trying to squeeze the monument into camera frame. Foreigners are very much a rarity in Djarkurgan, and while you gawp at the minaret a crowd of children will gather equally fascinated by you.

Djarkurgan is 20 km north-east of Termez. A taxi there and back (a 90 minute round trip with, say, 30 minutes at the minaret) should cost under US$10. Alternatively, there are several buses a day between Termez and Djarkurgan.

Places to Stay

Termez's flagship *Hotel Surkhan* (☎ 4-65-45), a squat concrete block on al-Hakim Termezy, is seedy and badly looked after by surly staff. But it's about the best comfort-wise that Termez has to offer. Singles/doubles are US$26/34. Rooms at the run-down, grotty *Hotel Termez* (☎ 3-17-53, formerly the Intourist) at Akmal Ikromov 21 do at least have attached toilet and hot shower, and reception staff are friendly. Doubles are US$3 per person. Worst of the lot is the *Hotel Shark* at Khujayev 15 – we'll be surprised if it escapes a demolition order before this book sees print.

Places to Eat

An indifferent restaurant attached to the *Hotel Surkhan* only ever had shashlyk when we visited, and for that they sent out to a street vendor. The other formal dining option is *Restaurant Nosdakhor* behind the Shark Hotel – reportedly the best in town, though it never opened while we were there.

Our best plov in Termez was at *Choyhona Shodlik* on Sharaf Rashidov, at the south-west corner of Gorky Park. Plov tends to be ready around 11 am and gone by 2 pm.

Getting There & Away

There are Tashkent-Termez flights (US$68, three hours, twice daily) and a flight to Moscow (US$188, weekly). Uzbekistan Airways (☎ 3-19-11) is in a white cottage on the edge of the park some hundred metres behind the Hotel Shark, and open daily from 8 am to noon and 1 to 8 pm.

There are two trains daily to Tashkent (US$18 kupeynyy) plus one each to Andijan

and Kanibadam in northern Tajikistan. Every morning at 4.10 am the No 23 pulls in for 10 minutes on its way to Moscow (US$76). All of these services go via Samarkand (US$13, 11½ hours). Three trains a day go to Dushanbe (US$7.50, 6½ hours).

Bus services on the whole are local, though there are services to Qarshi and Samarkand (daily) and even as far as Tashkent (US$8.50, 16½ hours). There is also a bus departing each morning for Dushanbe.

There are no buses or trains across the border into Afghanistan.

Getting Around

Buses, unnumbered but marked аэропорт, leave regularly for the airport from the plaza at the southern end of Sharaf Rashidov. From the train station bus No 4 passes the Surkhon and Shark hotels to terminate beside the museum, a few hundred metres from the Hotel Termez. Bus No 6 follows a similar route but originates at the bus station.

Western Uzbekistan

URGENCH
УРГАНЧ
Population: 130,000

Urgench (Uzbek: Urganch) is a dry, bare Soviet town 450 km north-west of Bukhara across the Kyzylkum desert, in the delta of the Amu-Darya river. It's the capital of Horazm province, wedged between the Amu-Darya and the Turkmen border. Urgench is mainly of use to travellers as the transport hub for Khiva, 35 km south-west, and somewhere to stay if you can't move right on to Khiva.

When the Amu-Darya changed course in the 16th century, the people of Konye-Urgench (Old Urgench), 150 km downriver in present-day Turkmenistan, were left without water and started a new town here. There's virtually nothing to see in Urgench itself, but if you've time to spare after Khiva you might fancy some ruined cities in the

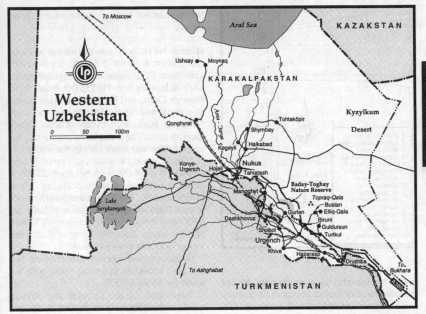

Western Uzbekistan

0   50   100m

To Moscow

Aral Sea

KAZAKSTAN

Ushsay ● Moynaq

KARAKALPAKSTAN

Qonghyrat ●

Kyzylkum
Desert

Tohtaköpir ●

Shymbay ●

Kegeyli ●

Halkabad ●

Konye-Urgench ● Hojeli ●

Nukus ●
Tahiatash

Baday-Toghay
Nature Reserve

Topraq-Qala
◇ Bustan
● Elliq-Qala
● Biruni
Guldursun
Turtkul

Lake
Sarykamysh

Mangghyt ●

Dashkhovuz ●

Gurlen ●

Shobot ●
Urgench ●

Khiva ●

Hazarasp ●
● Druzhba

To Ashghabat

To Bukhara

TURKMENISTAN

---

vicinity or the Baday-Toghay nature reserve north of town (see the Around Urgench section).

Orientation

The town's axis is al-Horazmi (formerly Kommunisticheskaya), with the clock tower at its intersection with al-Beruni marking the centre of things. The train and bus stations are 1.5 km south of the centre down al-Horazmi, the airport three km north, and most hotels around the middle. Street numbering along al-Horazmi is haywire.

Information

Uzbektourism (☎ 6-34-05, 6-64-55; fax 6-76-30) is on al-Horazmi just south of the canal, but more useful are its excursion bureaus in the Horazm and Jayhun hotels. Ask for *otdel exkursii* (excursion department, ☎ 6-08-09) on the second floor of the Jayhun.

You can change money at the Horazm or Jayhun hotels, or at the bazar if you're game. There's an exchange kiosk at the train station, too, but you'll be lucky to find it open.

The post, telephone and telegraph office is the building with the clock tower near the central roundabout.

The Urgench telephone code is 36222.

The travel agency Gulnara (☎ 6-46-58, 4-05-26) at former ulitsa Nekrasova 191 offers airport and station pick-ups, accommodation in Urgench or at the Hotel Orkanchi in Khiva, and trips to Khiva or outlying sites as far away as the Aral Sea. Ask for Gulya or Svetlana, who speak some English.

Things to See

There's a statue of Mahmud al-Horazmi, a local 9th century mathematician who invented algebra, in the park in front of the Hotel Urgench. A block and a half south

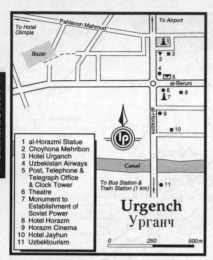

Urgench
Урганч

KEY:
1 al-Horazmi Statue
2 Choyhona Mehribon
3 Hotel Urganch
4 Uzbekistan Airways
5 Post, Telephone &
   Telegraph Office
   & Clock Tower
6 Theatre
7 Monument to
   Establishment of
   Soviet Power
8 Hotel Horazm
9 Horazm Cinema
10 Hotel Jayhun
11 Uzbektourism

down al-Horazmi is a monument to the establishment of Soviet power in the region.

The bazar (mainly food) is about 600 metres west of al-Horazmi. Follow the small street that starts almost opposite the Choyhona Mehribon: the bazar actually begins as street stalls along this street.

Places to Stay
Bottom End For a cheap room try your luck at the central *Hotel Urganch* (☎ 6-20-22), al-Horazmi 22. Sometimes they'll take foreigners, sometimes they won't. You may be luckier if you arrive before 9 pm. Singles/doubles with private bathroom are US$2/4 and up – they're adequate but don't be surprised by cockroaches.

The *Hotel Olimpia* (☎ 3-01-85, 3-39-46), about two km west of the centre, has shabby, gloomy rooms for US$10/15 with private shower and toilet. It's at Sportivnaya 18, just south of Pahlavon Mahmud, near the Olimpia Stadium. Bus No 19 from the train station stops outside the door; a taxi from the town centre is about US$0.50.

One traveller spent the night in a carriage at the train station, used by locals, for US$0.50 (after the police had fined him and he claimed he had no money for a hotel room).

Middle Best is Uzbektourism's *Hotel Horazm* (☎ 6-56-66, 6-54-08; fax 6-61-80) at al-Beruni 2. Simple, clean singles/doubles with balconies are US$35/50 from April through October, US$25/40 at other times. Slightly lower 'individual tourist' rates are for those booked in by an official Uzbek tourism firm. The hotel has a restaurant, bar and a coffee and book stall in the lobby.

Uzbektourism's swanky, newish *Hotel Jayhun* (☎ 6-08-09, 6-66-68; fax 6-23-29) is almost empty and already decaying. It's at al-Horazmi 28, 300 metres south of the clock tower. Bare rooms with private bath are US$30/40 from April to October, US$20/26 at other times. Like the Horazm it also has lower 'individual tourist rates'.

Gulnara travel agency can provide bed and a big breakfast in a clean *house* with hot water for about US$20.

Some staff at the Horazm and Jayhun hotels may offer help in finding a cheaper bed if you can't afford their prices.

Places to Eat
The only restaurants are in the *Urganch*, *Horazm* and *Jayhun* hotels, and the Horazm's is best. The Jayhun's only seems to open when groups are in: at other times try the ground-floor bar. The others have bars with snacks too.

The *Choyhona Mehribon*, between the Hotel Urganch and al-Horazmi, has a small garden and takes ages to make tea.

The *bazar* has fresh fruit and vegetables, and shashlyk stalls.

Getting There & Away
The same police who will probably check your visa in Urgench train or bus station also keep a watch on tourists in Khiva, so you have a chance to strike up a lasting relationship. In fact, these guys could be worse as they have been known to buy train tickets for travellers they have fined.

Air The only flights are to/from Tashkent

(US$80, three daily), and Moscow (US$180, twice weekly). The Uzbekistan Airways office is on al-Horazmi a few steps north of the clock tower.

Gulnara travel agency offers plane or helicopter trips to ancient sites around Urgench or to Moynaq, the former Aral Sea fishing port. The cost for a typical single-destination trip is around US$250 per plane (holding eight passengers) or helicopter (holding three).

Bus Bus schedules are flakey so try to check yours in advance. The bus station is on al-Horazmi just north of the train station. Scheduled departures include Tashkent (16 hours, daily) via Bukhara and Samarkand; Samarkand (12 hours, twice daily) via Bukhara; Bukhara (seven hours, daily); Shakhrisabz via Bukhara (daily); Nukus (twice daily); Charjou in Turkmenistan (Chorjuy in Uzbek, twice daily); and Dashkhovuz in Turkmenistan (Dashkhovuz may appear on Uzbek signs as Toshhovuz, Toshauz, Tashavuz or Tashauz; eight daily).

The Bukhara route sticks to Uzbekistan and passes no towns between Bukhara and Druzhba, 80 km from Urgench. Take food and drink for the ride, which is across the scrub-covered edge of the Kyzylkum desert. There are occasional glimpses of the Amu-Darya, which forms a stretch of the border with Turkmenistan and broadens into a wide reservoir east of Druzhba.

If you find no direct bus to Nukus, you could get one to Hojeli (Uzbek Hujayli), a dreary 4½ hours away crisscrossing the Turkmen border (though without passport checks when we did it) – and then a local bus or taxi for the last 15 km.

Train If you're coming by train from Kazakstan or Russia, be prepared for confiscations and/or fines/bribes by Uzbek customs and border police as you enter Uzbekistan. Keep valuables such as cameras and cash out of sight. You may be able to argue them down from absurd initial demands.

It can be hard to get tickets on trains from

Urgench. Book ahead if you can – if not, your best chance may be to pay a provodnik. Trains leave for Tashkent (25 hours), Samarkand (16 hours), Bukhara (Kagan, 11 hours). Daily Tashkent-Qonghyrat (Uzbek: Qunghirot, Russian: Kungrad) and Tashkent-Nukus trains stop here (though they may not have better than 3rd-class carriages), as do the daily Moscow-Kagan-Samarkand and weekly Almaty-Tashkent-Nukus trains. All go via Charjou and Dashkhovuz. There are also daily Urgench-Qonghyrat and Ashghabat-Dashkhovuz services.

Getting Around

Bus No 3 runs between the train station and the airport, stopping on al-Horazmi near the hotels en route. Bus Nos 2 and 19 also go between the station and the central roundabout. All supposedly run from 7 am to 11 pm.

Taxis cost about US$0.25 a km, though you may not get a short ride for less than US$0.50.

AROUND URGENCH

The Amu-Darya delta, stretching from south-east of Urgench to the Aral Sea, has been inhabited for millennia and was an important oasis long before Urgench or even Khiva were important. The historical name of the delta area, which includes parts of modern-day northern Turkmenistan, was Khorezm (see the Konye-Urgench section in the Turkmenistan chapter for more on old Khorezm).

The ruins of many Khorezmian towns and forts, some well over 2000 years old, still stand east and north of Urgench. None are major sights, nor have remains at all comparable with Khiva, but they may give you some fun. Place names in this section are given in Karakalpak, the official language of the region in which they lie.

Biruni (Uzbek: Beruni), formerly Shabbaz, 25 km north-east of Urgench, is named for the 10th century mathematician and encyclopaedist al-Beruni, who spent time here (and some say was born here).

Another medieval resident was Abu Ali ibn-Sina.

Another possible trip is to the Baday-Toghay nature reserve, an area of jungle-like *toghay* forest with some unusual wildlife. Uzbektourism in Urgench also offers trips into the Karakum desert.

There are apparently hotels in Turtkul, Biruni and Bustan.

Ruins Around Bustan

The isolated ruins of Topraq-Qala, Qavat-Qala and Ayaz-Qala lie on the fringes of the Kyzylkum desert, 10 to 20 km north of Bustan, which is 50 km north-east of Urgench. **Topraq-Qala** is the westernmost and probably most impressive site, thought to have been a fort and temple complex of the rulers of the Khorezm borders in the 3rd and 4th centuries, with high walls and rooms carved out of the rock on a hilltop. Fragments of sculptures and colourful frescoes found here are kept in the Nukus museum.

Qavat-Qala, east of Topraq-Qala, was an important oasis until Jenghiz Khan's arrival. There are substantial remains of fortress walls and towers.

Ayaz-Qala, east of Qavat-Qala, has an impressive mud-walled hilltop fortress from the 6th and 7th centuries.

There are more ruins in the town of **Elliq-Qala** (Fifty Cities), three km north-east of Bustan, and a museum in Bustan.

Ruins Around Turtkul

At **Guldursun**, 20 km south of Bustan on the road to Turtkul, are the high mud walls of a fortress dating from about the 4th century BC to the 4th century AD. Nearby are two ruins both called **Qyrqqyz-Qala**. You'd have to be very dedicated to reach **Qoy Qyrylghan Qala**, a circular fort, temple and, it's thought, observatory complex dating from the same period. It had two rings of circular walls, and Uzbekistan's oldest known inscriptions were found here. Maps show it about 80 km east of Turtkul, in the desert.

Baday-Toghay Nature Reserve

This is a strip of toghay forest about 30 km long and a few km wide on the east bank of the Amu-Darya, beginning 30 km north of Urgench. Toghay is a very dense, jungle-like forest of trees, shrubs and prickly salt-resistant plants and creepers, unique to Central Asia's desert river valleys. Only about one-fifth of the Amu-Darya's and Syr-Darya's toghay has survived the drying-up of the deltas in recent decades. Fauna of the reserve still apparently include the Karakal desert cat and Bukhara deer (both endangered species), jackals, wild boar, foxes and badgers. But the last Turan or Caspian tiger, which also used to inhabit the toghay, was killed in 1972 in the Kegeyli area north of Nukus.

By the Amu-Darya on one edge of the reserve is **Janpyq-Qala**, an impressive fortress inhabited from as early as the 1st century AD to the 14th. At the centre are remains of a colonnaded citadel.

Getting There & Away

Unfortunately all these places lie in Karakalpakstan, outside Horazm province, so Nukus Uzbektourism is better informed and keener to show them than Urgench Uzbektourism. You could arrange a guide from Nukus, or settle for Gulnara or Urgench Uzbektourism for some sites. Urgench Uzbektourism charges US$12 an hour for a car and driver, and US$4 an hour for a guide.

If you go without a guide, the best bet is a taxi, as bus services to these places are rare or nonexistent. A taxi should cost about US$10 to US$15 per 100 km.

KHIVA
ХИВА
Population: 40,000

Khiva's name, redolent of slave caravans, barbaric cruelty and terrible journeys across deserts and steppes infested with wild tribesmen, struck fear into all but the boldest 19th century hearts. Nowadays it's a mere 35 km south-west of Urgench, past cotton bushes and fruit trees.

Khiva (Uzbek Hiva) is an odd place. Its historic heart, unlike those of other Central

Asian cities, is preserved in its entirety – but so well preserved that the life has almost been squeezed out of it. As a result of a Soviet conservation programme in the 1970s and 80s, it's now a squeaky-clean official 'city-museum'. Even among its densely packed mosques, tombs, palaces, alleys and at least 16 medressas, you need imagination to get a sense of its mystique, bustle and squalor. Remind yourself that in its heyday everything tended to be weedy, crowded and filthy. However, streets just a block or two away but still within the walled inner city, the Ichon-Qala, remain lived in and fairly dishevelled.

You can see Khiva in a day trip from Urgench, but you'll take it in better by staying longer. Morning and evening are the best times, and there are two decent places to stay. If your time is limited, don't miss the Kalta Minor minaret, Kukhna Ark, Juma mosque and minaret, Tosh-Khovli palace, Islom-Huja medressa and minaret, and Pahlavon Mahmud mausoleum. A few historic buildings are functioning mosques or shrines, but most are museums. Some of the lesser museums are very missable.

Entry to the Ichon-Qala, where virtually everything of interest is clustered, is US$3 for tourists at its main West Gate, but at the North, East and South gates there is no charge! There are inconsistently applied additional charges of about US$0.15 to US$0.30 – bargainable, in some cases – for a few buildings inside. Attendants may offer to open locked rooms for a small tip, while others may show you round for free.

A visual surprise here, after Samarkand's blue and Bukhara's brown, is the use of turquoise tiles. Khivan art also displays an unusual fondness for plant motifs, which came into favour following a Persian invasion in the 18th century.

History

Agriculture and human settlement go back four, perhaps six, millennia in Khorezm, the large, fertile Amu-Darya river delta isolated in the midst of broad deserts. So Khiva, on the southern fringe of the delta, *may* be very old. Legend has that it was founded when Shem, son of Noah, discovered a well here; his people called it Heivak, from which the name Khiva is said to be derived.

Khiva certainly existed by the 8th century, as a minor fort and trading post on a Silk Road branch to the Caspian Sea and the Volga. But while Khorezm was at its zenith, on and off from the 10th to the 14th centuries, its capital was at old Urgench (present-day Konye-Urgench in Turkmenistan), and Khiva remained a bit player.

See the Konye-Urgench section in the Turkmenistan chapter for more on old Khorezm.

The Khanate It wasn't until well after Konye-Urgench had been finished off by Timur that Khiva's time came. When the Uzbek Shaybanids moved into the decaying Timurid Empire in the early 16th century, one branch founded a state in Khorezm, independent of the more powerful branch in Bukhara. They made Khiva their capital in 1592.

The town ran a busy slave market which was to shape the destiny of the khanate, as the Khiva state was known, for more than three centuries. Most slaves were brought by Turkmen tribesmen from the Karakum desert or Kazak tribes of the steppes, who raided those unlucky enough to live or travel nearby. To keep both of these away from its own door, Khiva eventually resorted to an alliance with the Turkmen against the Kazaks, granting them land and money in return.

Russian Interest Awakens Khiva had earlier offered to submit to Peter the Great of Russia in return for help against marauding tribes. In a belated response, a force of about 4000 led by Prince Alexandr Bekovich, arrived in Khiva in 1717.

Unfortunately, the khan had by that time lost interest in being a vassal of the tsar. He came out to meet them, suggesting they disperse to outlying villages where they could be more comfortably accommodated. This done, the Khivans annihilated the invaders, leaving just a handful to make their way back with the news. He sent Bekovich's head to his Central Asian rival, the Emir of Bukhara, and kept the rest of him on display.

In 1740 Khiva was wrecked by a less gullible invader, Nadir Shah of Persia, and Khorezm became for a while a northern outpost of the Persian Empire. By the end of the 18th century it was rebuilt and taking a small share in the growing trade between Russia and the Bukhara and Kokand khanates. Its slave market, the biggest in Central Asia, continued unabated, augmented now by Russians captured as they

pushed their borders southwards and eastwards.

The 'Great Game' In the early 19th century Russia sent two more armies, ostensibly to free Russian slaves, though neither got anywhere near Khiva. In 1801, 22,000 Cossacks got as far as the Kazak steppes, turning back when Tsar Paul was assassinated.

The second effort, in 1839 to 1840 by order of Tsar Nicholas I, came in response to British activity in Afghanistan. Learning of this, the British sent a single man, Captain James Abbott, to Khiva with an offer to

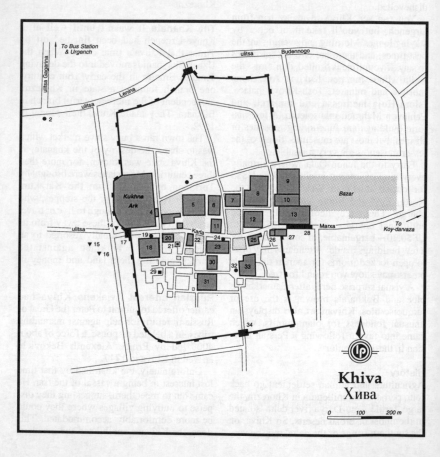

Khiva
Хива

0   100   200 m

negotiate the slaves' release with the approaching Russians on Khan Alloquli's behalf, which would eliminate the Russian excuse for being there.

Again the Russians were turned back, this time by the worst winter for ages, though no-one in Khiva yet knew this. Abbott, though initially treated with suspicion, persuaded Alloquli to send him to St Petersburg with a proposal to release the slaves in return for an end to military expeditions against Khiva and the freeing of Khivan hostages held at Orenburg. Surviving attack and capture, Abbott made it all the way to St Petersburg, only to have his thunder stolen by a fellow officer sent from Herat to find out what had happened to him.

Lieutenant Richmond Shakespear reached Khiva in June 1840. He got along better with Alloquli than Abbott had, and even the news of the Russians' retreat did him no harm since the khan feared they might try again. Shakespear persuaded him to release all the Russian slaves in Khiva and even to give them an armed escort to Fort Alexandrovsk (present-day Fort Shev-chenko in Kazakstan), a Russian outpost on the eastern Caspian. He delivered the 416 freed slaves to Russia, amid astonishment and rejoicing, obtained the release of 600 Khivans, and was personally thanked by a no doubt inwardly seething Tsar Nicholas in St Petersburg (see The Russians Arrive in the History section at the beginning of this chapter).

Russian Conquest When the Russians finally got round to sending a properly organised expedition against Khiva, it was no contest. In 1873 General Konstantin Kaufman's 13,000-strong forces advanced on Khiva from the north, west and east. After some initial guerrilla resistance, mainly by Yomud Turkmen tribesmen, Khan Muhammad Rakhim II surrendered unconditionally. To give his men a bit of action, Kaufman then indulged in a massacre of the Yomud. The khan became a vassal of the tsar and his silver throne was packed off to Russia. Khiva was not permitted an army of its own, while the Russians set up a big garrison at nearby Petro-Alexandrovsk (modern Turtkul).

The enfeebled khanate struggled on until 1920 when the Bolshevik general Mikhail Frunze installed the 'Khorezm People's Republic' in its place. This, like a similar republic in Bukhara, was theoretically independent of the USSR. But its leaders swung

PLACES TO STAY		8	Tosh-Khovli Palace
		9	Alloquli Khan Caravanserai
18	Hotel Khiva		(Department Store)
	(Muhammad Amin Khan Medressa)	10	Alloquli Khan Bazar
29	Hotel Orkanchi	11	Matpana Bay Medressa
		12	Kutlimurodinok Medressa
PLACES TO EAT		13	Alloquli Khan Medressa
		17	West Gate
14	Choyhona	19	Kalta Minor Minaret
15	Café	21	Sayid Alauddin Mausoleum
16	Koop Chovyhona	22	Qozi-Kalon Medressa
20	Restoran Khiva		(Music Museum)
	(Matniyaz Divanbeg Medressa)	23	Juma Mosque
		24	Juma Minaret
OTHER		25	Abdulla Khan Medressa
		26	Aq Mosque
1	North Gate	27	Anusha Khan Baths
2	Navoi Cinema	28	East Gate
3	Toilets	30	Pahlavon Mahmud Mausoleum
4	Zindon	31	Sherghozi Khan Medressa
5	Muhammad Rakhim Khan Medressa	32	Islom-Huja Minaret
6	Arabhana Medressa	33	Islom-Huja Medressa
7	Dost Alyam Medressa	34	South Gate

UZBEKISTAN

Life Under the Khans

Richmond Shakespear, who rescued Khiva's Russian slaves in 1840, left behind far more slaves than he freed, mainly Persians and Kurds. The Russian envoy Captain Nikolai Muraviev, who had travelled here in 1819, estimated there were 30,000 of these, against 3000 Russians. Most of Khiva's slaves were men. Shakespear noted that nearly all the Russians were in good health, an able Russian male slave being worth four good camels.

The khans ruled Khiva by terror, with torture and summary execution among their weapons. The Hungarian traveller Arminius Vambéry in 1863 saw eight old men lying on the ground having their eyes gouged out, their tormenter wiping his knife clean on their beards as he proceeded. Muraviev reported that impalement was a favourite method of execution, with victims taking up to two days to die (you can see pictures of other methods in the Zindon prison at the city's Kukhna Ark). He also noted that people caught smoking or drinking alcohol, which the khan of the day had foresworn, had their mouths slit open to their ears, leaving them with a permanent silly grin.

The khans extorted huge taxes from their people thanks to their ownership of the state's entire irrigation system. Nevertheless Muraviev observed that the villages outside the city were prosperous, and that Khiva's richer citizens had gardens and palaces outside the city walls. His visit came at a time when trade through Khiva was on an upswing, engendering a boom in fine buildings and decorative arts like carving, painting and tilework – especially in the 1830s and 1840s under Khan Alloquli who was responsible for the lovely Tosh-Khovli Palace and the nearby caravanserai and Alloquli Khan Medressa.

The number of medressas in Khiva is testament to its past importance as a centre of Muslim theology. But this didn't stop it being an isolated place ignorant of its own weakness, with horizons that didn't stretch far beyond the rival Uzbek khanate of Bukhara. James Abbott in 1840 recorded Alloquli's boast that he had all of 20 guns, and the belief of many Khivans that the British were a sub-tribe of the Russians. The khans resolutely opposed modernisation and secular education, and even after the Russian annexation, Khan Muhammad Rakhim II refused to allow electricity, schools or telephones. The clergy were a conservative lot who later engineered the murder of the modernising grand vizier, Islom Huja.

Khiva's renown and infamy, far out of proportion to its real significance, were a product of its remoteness, the extreme cruelty and backwardness of its regime, and the very real dangers to outsiders who ventured there: if they survived the surrounding deserts and their marauding tribesmen, their lives were subject to the khans' caprice when they finally arrived. ■

---

away from socialism towards Pan-Turkism, and in 1924 their republic was absorbed into the new Uzbek SSR.

Orientation & Information

The old city, the Ichon-Qala, still surrounded by its centuries-old walls, is in the southern part of a much bigger Soviet town. Transport from Urgench will probably take you straight to the Ichon-Qala's main entrance, the West Gate. Most sights are around its main axis, ulitsa Karla Marxa, running between the West and East gates.

Khiva's dusty bus station is on the Urgench road on the northern edge of town. From an intersection just to its south, ulitsa Gagarina runs 1.5 km south to the Navoi cinema at the corner with ulitsa Lenina. About 150 metres east on Lenina is the north-west corner of Ichon-Qala. The West Gate is 400 metres south and the North Gate 200 metres east.

The Khiva map with a colour picture of the Islom-Huja minaret, commonly sold at the West Gate, has the street plan printed upside down, leaving all the key numbers and street names in the wrong places. Most street names are still Russian – or if they have changed, they aren't on signs or in anyone's minds.

The Khiva telephone code is 36237.

Ichon-Qala Gates & Walls

The main entrance to the Ichon-Qala is the

twin-turreted brick West Gate (Ota-darvoza, literally 'Father Gate'), a 1970s reconstruction – the original was wrecked in 1920. The picturesque 2.5 km long mud walls date from the 18th century, rebuilt after being wrecked by the Persians. The north-west sector, which greets approaching tourists, has been fully restored in recent decades; other stretches are in a more tumble-down state. The walls also have North, East and South gates, respectively Buhoro-darvoza (Bukhara Gate), Polvon-darvoza (Strongman's Gate) and Tosh-darvoza (Stone Gate), as well as about 40 bastions.

Muhammad Amin Khan Medressa & Kalta Minor

The first building on your right inside the West Gate is the Muhammad Amin Khan medressa (Mukhammad Aminhon madrasasi), built in the 1850s and serving since Soviet times as the Hotel Khiva (see Places to Stay). It's a nice enough building, with two storeys of cells around a broad courtyard, and certainly an exotic setting to lay your head, but it's not one of Khiva's major architectural highlights.

Outside stands the fat, turquoise-tiled Kalta Minor minaret, built at the same time and looking like it was originally meant to be far taller, which would have made it much higher than Bukhara's Kalan minaret. Stories say it was stopped either because the architect or the khan died – or perhaps it was all a bluff aimed at Bukhara.

Kukhna Ark

Opposite Muhammad Amin Khan stands the Kukhna Ark – the Khiva rulers' own fortress and residence, first built in the 12th century by one Oq Shihbobo, then expanded by the khans in the 17th century. The khans' harem, mint, stables, arsenal, barracks, mosque and jail were all here. Only parts have been restored.

The squat protuberance by the entrance, on the east side of the building, is the Zindon (Khans' Jail), with a display of chains, manacles and weapons, and pictures of people being chucked off minarets, stuffed into sacks full of wild cats, etc.

Inside the Ark, the first passage to the right takes you into the 19th century Summer mosque, open-air and beautiful with superb blue and white plant-motif tiling and a red, orange and gold roof. Beside it is the old mint, now a museum that includes money printed on silk.

Ahead from the Ark entrance is another restored building that some say was the harem, but which its present guardians maintain was the throne room, where khans dispensed judgement (if not justice). The circular area on the ground was for the royal yurt, which the no-longer-nomadic khans still liked to use. It's said that if a victim was ordered through the right-hand door behind this, it meant death; the left door meant freedom and the middle door, jail.

To the right of the throne room, a door in the wall gives onto a flight of steps up to the Oq Shihbobo bastion, the original part of the Kukhna Ark, set right against the Ichon-Qala's massive west wall. At the top is an open-air pavilion with good views over the Ark and Ichon-Qala.

Muhammad Rakhim Khan Medressa

Facing the Kukhna Ark, across an open space that was once a busy palace square (and place of execution), this 19th century medressa (Mukhammad Rakhimhon madrasasi) is named after Khan Muhammad Rakhim II. A hotch-potch of a museum within is partly dedicated to this khan, who surrendered to Russia in 1873 but had, after all, kept Khiva independent a few years longer than Bukhara. The khan was also a poet under the pen name Feruz. There's more fine blue tilework. Khiva's token camel stands burping and farting outside the medressa's south wall, waiting for tourists to ride it or pose with it.

Sayid Alauddin Mausoleum & Music Museum

Back on the south side of Karla Marxa, beside the medressa housing Restoran Khiva, is the small, plain Sayid Alauddin mausoleum (Said Alavuddin maqbarasi) dating to 1310, when Khiva was under the Golden Horde of the Mongol Empire. You may find people praying in front of the 19th century tiled sarcophagus.

To the east is a Music Museum in the 1905 Qozi-Kalon medressa.

Juma Mosque & Minaret

East of the Music Museum, the large Juma mosque is interesting for the 218 wooden columns supporting its roof – a structural concept thought to be derived from ancient Arabian mosques. The few finely decorated columns are from the original 10th century mosque, though the present building dates from the 18th century. From inside, you can climb the 81 very dark steps of the Juma minaret.

Near the Juma Mosque

Opposite the Juma mosque is the 1905 **Matpana Bay medressa** (Abdullahon madrassi), containing a museum devoted to nature, history, religion and the medressa itself. Behind this are the 17th century **Arabhana medressa** and the 19th century **Dost Alyam medressa**.

East of the Juma mosque, the 1855 **Abdulla Khan medressa** holds a missable nature museum. The little **Aq mosque** dates from 1657, the same year as the **Anusha Khan baths** (Anushahon hammomi) by the entrance to the long tunnel of the East Gate. The baths have supposedly been in continuous use since they were built, but they were firmly closed when we checked.

Alloquli Khan Medressa, Bazar & Caravanserai

The street leading north opposite the Aq mosque contains some of Khiva's most interesting buildings, most of them created by Khan Alloquli in the 1830s and 1840s – a testament to the wealth that Russian trade brought Khiva during his reign. First come the tall **Alloquli Khan medressa** (Alloqulihon madrasasi, 1835) and the earlier **Kutlimurodinok medressa** (1809), facing each other across the street, with

matching tiled façades. Down a few steps under a small dome in the Kutlimurodinok's courtyard is an old drinking-water tank (don't try the water!).

North of the Alloquli Khan medressa and built in the same year are the **Alloqulihon bazar and caravanserai** (Alloquli Khan Saroy-bozori va Karvon-saroyi). The entrance to both is through tall wooden gates, beside the medressa, which are closed from early to late afternoon. The bazar is a domed market arcade, still catering to traders, which opens on to Khiva's modern bazar, outside the Ichon-Qala walls, at its east end. The caravanserai, entered from the bazar arcade, was a travellers' inn with a large courtyard where traders could also sell their wares. Today the caravanserai houses Khiva's department store. Both the arcade and store have some quite attractive cheap pottery.

Tosh-Khovli Palace

Tosh-Khovli (Stone House), facing the caravanserai, contains Khiva's most sumptuous interior decoration, including ceramic tiles, carved stone and wood, and ghanch. Built by Alloquli Khan between 1832 and 1841 as a more splendid alternative to the Kukhna Ark, it's said to have over 150 rooms off nine courtyards, with high ceilings designed to catch any breeze. Alloquli was a man in a hurry – the Tosh-Khovli's first architect was executed for failing to complete the job in two years.

Only parts of the building are open. The biggest courtyard, immediately inside the entrance in the five recesses on the south side, is the **Harem**. it is bedecked with gorgeous geometrical-motif tiles. The five recesses on its south side have beautiful bright patterned ceilings, held up by carved wooden pillars. The rooms off the harem's south-west corner hold craft exhibits. To see the other two main courtyards you'll probably have to ask the door attendants and pay a small fee. The **Ishrot-Khovli** was a ceremonial and banqueting hall with, like the Kukhna Ark, circles for yurts. The **Arz-Khovli** was a court of judgement, with one exit door kept exclusively for people condemned to death.

East Gate & Modern Bazar

The East Gate is a long, vaulted 19th century passage with several sets of immense carved doors. The slave market was held around here, and niches in the passage walls once held slaves for sale. Outside are a small working mosque and the long modern bazar (mostly food) on the left.

Islom-Huja Medressa & Minaret

From the East Gate, go back to the Abdulla Khan medressa and take the lane to the south beside it, to the Islom-Huja medressa and minaret – Khiva's newest Islamic monuments, both built in 1910. The minaret, with bands of turquoise and red tiling, looks rather like an uncommonly lovely lighthouse. At 45 metres tall, it's Khiva's highest. You can climb its 118 steps for fine views across the Karakum desert.

The medressa holds Khiva's best museum, of Khorezm handicrafts through the ages – fine wood carving, metalwork, jewellery, books, Uzbek and Turkmen carpets, pottery, stone carved with Arabic script (which was in use in Khorezm from the 8th to the 20th centuries), and large pots called *hum* for storing food underground.

Islom Huja himself was an early 20th century grand vizier and, by Khivan standards, a liberal: he founded a European-style school, brought long-distance telegraph to the city, and built a hospital. For his popularity, the khan and clergy had him assassinated.

Pahlavon Mahmud Mausoleum & Sherghozi Khan Medressa

Along the street west from the Islom-Huja minaret, this is Khiva's most revered mausoleum and, with its lovely courtyard and stately tilework, one of the town's most beautiful spots. Pahlavon Mahmud was a poet, philosopher and legendary wrestler who became Khiva's patron saint. His 1326 tomb was rebuilt in the 19th century and then requisitioned in 1913 by the khan of the day as the family mausoleum.

The beautiful Persian-style chamber under the turquoise dome at the north end of the courtyard holds the tomb of Khan Muhammad Rakhim II who ruled from 1865 to 1910. Leave your shoes at the entrance. Pahlavon Mahmud's tomb, to the left off the first chamber, has some of Khiva's loveliest tiling on the sarcophagus and the walls. Pilgrims press coins and notes through the grille that shields the tomb; you may feel you are expected to make a donation too. Tombs of other khans stand unmarked east and west of the main building, outside the courtyard.

The 18th century Sherghozi Khan medressa (Shergozihon medrasasi) across the street holds a museum of ancient medicine. The khan it's named after was killed by the slaves he forced to build it.

Dishon-Qala

The Dishon-Qala was old Khiva's outer town, outside the Ichon-Qala walls. Most of it is buried beneath the modern town now, but part of the Dishon-Qala's own wall remains, 300 metres south of the South Gate. One or two Dishon-Qala gates survive too, among them the 19th century Koy-darvaza at the far east end of ulitsa Karla Marxa (1.25 km outside the Ichon-Qala).

Organised Tours

Uzbektourism's standard Khiva tour for individuals takes just three hours from Urgench, at a cost of US$48 for car and guide, plus US$5 per person in entrance fees and US$2.50 per person to take pictures (US$10 for video). They'll do you a longer trip at an extra US$16 an hour.

Places to Stay

There are two 'hotels' in the Ichon-Qala, though the word isn't quite apt for either.

The Uzbektourism-run *Hotel Khiva* (☎ 5-27-75, 5-49-45) is in fact the 19th century Muhammad Amin Khan medressa, inside the West Gate. It's been used as a hotel since Soviet times, but foreigners weren't allowed to stay there until after the USSR collapsed. The US$15-per-person rooms are old students' cells, big enough for two beds, bits of furniture, plus shower and toilet – though often no water. They're clean enough but airless if you want to keep mosquitoes out. The manager can provide a much better meal – a big plov and tea for about US$2.50 – than you'll get in the subterranean choyhona in the courtyard.

The family run *Hotel Orkanchi* (☎ 5-22-30) at Pahlavon Mahmud 10, behind the Hotel Khiva, is a private house with several big clean guestrooms, with beds or mattresses on the floor (or balcony) for US$10 a person, with three good meals for a further US$10. Until bathrooms are completed, toilets and shower are in the garden.

It may be possible to find even cheaper

Karakalpakstan

The Republic of Karakalpakstan is Uzbekistan's biggest 'province', its 165,000 sq km occupying the whole western end of the country, from east of Urgench to half way up the Aral Sea and 200 km across the desolate Ustyurt plateau west of the Aral Sea. Much of the fertile but environmentally blighted Amu-Darya delta lies in Karakalpakstan, and is home to most of the republic's population.

Karakalpakstan gets its name from the Karakalpak people whose homeland it is – though they number only about 400,000 of its 1.2 million population. It's also home to about 400,000 Uzbeks and 300,000 Kazaks. The Karakalpaks are a formerly nomadic and fishing people, first mentioned in the 16th century and now struggling to recapture a national identity after being collectivised or urbanised in Soviet times. (In her book, *Turkestan Solo*, Ella Maillart gives a glimpse of Karakalpakstan in the early years of Soviet rule, when she travelled through by river boat and camel – see Books in the Facts for the Visitor chapter.)

The name Karakalpak means 'Black Hat People' but such has been their cultural decline that the Karakalpaks have had to set up a research project to find out just what this black hat was. Since the break-up of the USSR, there have been rumblings of nationalist discontent against Uzbek rule.

The Karakalpak language – now the official language of the republic – is Turkic, close to Kazak and less so to Uzbek. Its alphabet, written in modified Cyrillic since Soviet times, was due to switch over in 1996 to a modified Roman alphabet.

Karakalpakstan was part of the khanate of Khiva in the 19th century. Under Soviet rule, it was governed as part of Kazakstan, then of the Russian Federation, before being passed to Uzbekistan in 1936. It became the nominally 'sovereign' Republic of Karakalpakstan, within Uzbekistan, after the break-up of the Soviet Union.

Life can never have been very easy here, though the Amu-Darya delta has supported irrigation-based agriculture for probably 4000 years, and Khorezm (the historical name for the delta area) has at times attained considerable importance and prosperity. The Persians thought it significant enough to conquer and turn into one of their satrapies as long ago as the 6th century BC, and briefly in the 13th century AD the then capital of Khorezm, old Urgench (present-day Konye-Urgench, in Turkmenistan), was the centre of the Muslim world. There are many ruins of ancient Khorezmian towns and forts in Karakalpakstan, including at Hojeli (near Nukus) and in distant south-eastern Karakalpakstan (see the Around Urgench section).

Karakalpakstan was probably at its most prosperous in the 1960s and 70s when the fruits of expanded irrigation from the Amu-Darya were coming on stream, and before the disastrous effects of that same expansion were felt. But the republic has borne the brunt of the environmental, economic and health problems that have taken hold since then, and today the age-old oasis of rivers, lakes, reed beds, marshes, forests and farmland that constitute the Amu-Darya delta is being steadily dried up and poisoned. It's really one of the saddest places on the planet.

Cotton, rice and melons are Karakalpakstan's main products. Tahiatash, 20 km south-east of Nukus on the Amu-Darya, has a big hydroelectric station supplying the whole of Karakalpakstan plus Horazm province of Uzbekistan and the Dashkhovuz region of Turkmenistan.

One thing you'll see a lot of is camels, used less as a means of transport than for their milk (known as *shubat*), meat and hides. ■

accommodation in other local *homes* – try asking staff at the Islom-Huja medressa.

Places to Eat

The best food is at the *Orkanchi* and *Khiva* hotels, but you probably need to be a guest. A semblance of a meal can be had in the underground choyhona in the Hotel Khiva. A better option is the cluster of eateries outside the Ichon-Qala's West Gate, including the *Koop Chovyhona* across from the gate with reasonable, moderately priced food and poolside tables, a stand-up *café* nearby and a *choyhona* just outside the gate. These close by late afternoon. The *Restoran Khiva* in the Matniyaz Divanbeg medressa, just east of the Hotel Khiva, always looks empty of both customers and staff.

The *bazar* has fresh fruit and vegetables and a couple of *shashlyk stands*.

Getting There & Away

The easiest way between Urgench and Khiva is the 45 minute trip by marshrutnoe taxi or taxi. Marshrutnoe taxis shuttle between the street outside Urgench's bus station and the West Gate from 8 am to 8 pm, leaving when they're full, for US$0.35 to US$0.50 (depending on the driver).

A taxi is US$5. In Khiva you'll find them outside the West Gate or at the east end of the bazar outside the East Gate.

Buses run between Urgench and Khiva bus stations about three times an hour from 7 am to 6.40 pm, but since Khiva's bus station is a good two km from the Ichon-Qala, this is not so convenient. The only other useful service from Khiva is a couple of daily buses to Dashkhovuz in Turkmenistan (which may appear on signs here as Toshhovuz, Tashavuz, Toshauz or Tashauz).

Getting Around

Bus and marshrutnoe taxi Nos 1 and 2 go the length of Gagarina between Lenina and the intersection near the bus station. Bus and marshrutnoe taxi No 1 will take you to the North Gate (No 2 heads away from the Ichon-Qala at Lenina).

A taxi between the Ichon-Qala and the bus station is about US$0.50.

NUKUS
НУКУС (НӨКИС)
Population: 180,000

If desolation attracts you, welcome to the capital of Uzbekistan's Karakalpakstan Republic, Nukus (Nökis in the local language, Karakalpak). Developed from a small settlement since 1932, Nukus might have been a bright and hopeful place two or three decades ago. Today it tries to present itself as the proud capital of newly 'sovereign'

1	Bazar
2	Bank
3	Airline Booking Office
4	Government Buildings
5	Hotel Nukus
6	OVIR
7	Art & Local Studies Museums
8	Post, Telephone & Telegraph Office
9	Kafe Nukus
10	Theatre
11	Berdakh Statue
12	Hotel Tashkent
13	Trolleybus Stop
14	Karakalpakstan Academy of Sciences

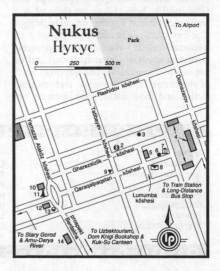

Karakalpakstan (see the Karakalpakstan aside earlier), but it's actually drab, impoverished, unhealthy and forlorn, its broad avenues and big public buildings now looking like jokes in poor taste. The economy of the town, a long way from anywhere at the back end of Uzbekistan, has suffered badly since the collapse of the USSR.

But worse, Nukus has felt – like the rest of poor Karakalpakstan – the full force of the health and environmental disaster from irrigated agriculture in the Amu-Darya basin, in particular the depletion of the Aral Sea (see the Environment section in the Facts about the Region chapter). In this dust-storm-prone wasteland of chemical-doused food and water, virtually all pregnant women are anaemic, leading to many premature births. There are high rates of birth deformities, infant mortality, and diseases like cancer, typhoid, hepatitis and immune depression, along with woefully inadequate medical provision. Furtive drinking seems to be one of the few solaces people have.

Orientation
'Street' in Karakalpak is *köshesi*. The main central streets are Qaraqalpaqstan and Gharezsizlik, both ending on the east at a square surrounded by government buildings. The city centre is bounded on the west by Yernazar Alaköz (which becomes prospekt Berdakha south of Qaraqalpaqstan) and on the east by Dosnazarov. The airport is north of the centre on Dosnazarov, and the train station and most useful long-distance bus

stop about three km from the centre at Dosnazarov's south end.

Russian street names have been replaced by Karakalpak ones on most signs, but Russian ones are still more familiar to many people.

Information
Uzbektourism (☎ 7-09-14, 4-43-81; fax 7-14-07, 7-77-69 Attention Uzbektourism) is at prospekt Berdakha 48, one km south of the Hotel Tashkent. The friendly staff are quite keen to interest foreigners in Karakalpakstan and will set up an excursion to just about anywhere.

OVIR is at the east end of Qaraqalpaqstan by the museum.

You can change money at the Hotel Tashkent, Uzbektourism, the airline booking office, the bank on Gharezsizlik, or at the airport. Street money changers will approach you outside the bazar.

The post, telephone and telegraph office is on Qaraqalpaqstan opposite the Hotel Nukus. The Nukus telephone code is 36122.

The Dom Knigi bookshop on prospekt Berdakha is poverty-stricken but worth a look just in case.

Museums
The Art Museum (Mamleketlik Körkemöner Muzeyi) and Local Studies Museum (Mamleketlik Ulke Tanyu Muzeyi) are in the same building at the east end of Qaraqalpaqstan. Open daily except Sunday from 9 am to 1 pm and 2 to 5 pm, they're well worth a look. The entry fee of US$0.05

Street Names in Nukus

New Name	Old Name
(prospekt) Berdakha	Turtkulsky (prospekt)
Dosnazarov	Kalinina
Gharezsizlik	Kuybysheva
Qaraqalpaqstan	Karla Marxa
Rashidov	Lenina
Yernazar Alaköz	Oktyabrskaya

includes a free, if not very informative, guided tour in English!

There are interesting displays on the fauna and flora of the Karakalpakstan region, including the Karakai desert cat, goitred gazelle (local name: geran), saiga antelope, wild boar (kaban), cheetah (gepard), Bukhara deer, Turan (or Caspian) tiger. The Turan tiger was wiped out in the 1970s. There are also displays on the Aral Sea and local health problems, on archaeology and early history, and of traditional jewellery, costumes, musical instruments and yurt decorations. Art is upstairs.

Other Sights

A **statue of Berdakh**, the Karakalpaks' 19th century cultural guru, poet and thinker, stands outside the theatre opposite the Hotel Tashkent. The building with the big boiled egg on top and a statue of Ulughbek out the front, on prospekt Berdakha just south of the Hotel Tashkent, is the **Karakalpakstan Academy of Sciences**.

The **Amu-Darya river** curves round the west side of town, three km from the centre. To see it, head west on Qaraqalpaqstan. The area on the right after you cross a wide canal (not the river) is pre-1932 Nukus – **Stary Gorod** (Old Town) in Russian. A pontoon bridge crosses the Amu-Darya, providing a short cut for drivers to Hojeli. You can judge the river's former breadth from the trees and buildings now set far back from its banks.

Festival

Karakalpaks apparently still play the wild Central Asian polo-like game – with a goat carcass instead of a ball, and teams of dozens of riders – which they call *ylaq oyyny*. This and other traditional sports like wrestling, ram-fighting and cock-fighting are included in Nukus' Pakhta-Bairam harvest festival in December.

Places to Stay

There are two hotels and neither knew about foreigners' prices when we were there. The towering *Hotel Tashkent* at the corner of prospekt Berdakha and Qaraqalpaqstan has

bare but reasonable singles/doubles with private bathroom for US$1.75/3.50. The older *Hotel Nukus* on Lumumba between Qaraqalpaqstan and Gharezsizlik charges US$1/2 for shabbier rooms, with bath.

Places to Eat

The *Hotel Tashkent's* restaurant block has more reliable service in its downstairs canteen than the upstairs restaurant. The food upstairs is better, if the cook hasn't 'gone home' and you aren't molested by drunks. The ground-floor *bar* has decent coffee and the odd snack. The *Hotel Nukus* has a basement bar with tough shashlyks and rock videos, and a sporadically open restaurant.

There's better food at the Korean *Kuk-Su* canteen on prospekt Berdakha about 2.5 km south of the Hotel Tashkent. A decent bowl of noodles, vegetables and meat, with bread and tea, costs US$0.35. From the Hotel Tashkent, take a Ж Д Вокзал or Т Ж Вокзал trolleybus south on prospekt Berdakha for about seven stops, getting off before Berdakha climbs onto a bridge. The Kuk-Su has a blue door on the west side of the street; enter at the side. It's open till 6 pm.

Kafe Nukus on Qaraqalpaqstan at the corner with Tatibayev is another possibility. There's a sizeable bazar half a km north of the Hotel Tashkent along Yernazar Aläköz.

Getting There & Away

Air The only flights are to/from Tashkent (US$84, three or four daily) and Moscow (twice weekly). The airline booking office, marked Aviatsii Nukusskoe Gorodskoe Agentstvo, is set back from Gharezsizlik köshesi, opposite the Hotel Nukus.

Bus Buses to Tashkent, Urgench and Moynaq go from the yard in front of the train station *(avtovokzal)* at the south end of Dosnazarov – *not* from the bus station, seven km away at the north end of town (but bus No 15 runs between the two if you get confused). Buses leave for Urgench and Moynaq (three to four hours, twice daily) and Tashkent (US$14, 20 hours, daily) via Bukhara and

Samarkand. If Urgench buses are not running, try changing at Hojeli, 15 km west of Nukus. Our Hojeli-Urgench bus took 4½ hours, nipping into Turkmenistan (though there were no border checks). There may also be buses to Konye-Urgench from the train station – or, again, you can change at Hojeli.

Train Nukus is on a branch line with only two services – a daily train to/from Tashkent and a weekly train to/from Almaty. Both go via Hojeli, Dashkhovuz and Urgench, and the Almaty train goes via Tashkent. Nukus is about four hours from Urgench.

Taxi Given the vagaries of public transport, taxis may have advantages for some long trips. A taxi to Konye-Urgench and back should be about US$10 for foreigners. To Moynaq and back, figure US$25 to US$50. If you can't find a willing taxi on the street, try outside the train station or the Hotel Tashkent.

Getting Around
Bus No 3 runs between the airport and the bazar. A taxi between the airport and the centre is under US$1.

To reach the centre from the train station, take any trolleybus from the west end of the station yard (to the left as you exit the station). From the centre to the station, take a Ж Д Вокзал or Т Ж Вокзал trolleybus south on prospekt Berdakha by the Hotel Tashkent.

HOJELI
ХОЖЕЛИ
Population: 55,000
Hojeli (Uzbek: Hujayli, Russian: Khodzheyli), 15 km west of Nukus, is Karakalpakstan's second city. It's a local transport hub and otherwise a mundane place, apart from the remains of ancient Mizdahkan, on a hill a couple of km southwest of town beside the road to Konye-Urgench. Mizdahkan was a big Khorezm trading centre, inhabited from the 4th century BC until Timur's coming. Even

then it remained a holy site, and tombs and mosques continued to be built there right up to the 20th century. Karakalpak cultural festivals are sometimes held here.

The hill is littered with ruined and intact mausolea, mosques and medressas from the 11th to 20th centuries, of which the most impressive is the restored mausoleum (Mahbarasy) of Nazlymhan Sulyu, dating from the 12th to 14th centuries. On the next hill towards Konye-Urgench are the remains of a 4th to 3rd century BC fortress called Gyaur-Qala.

Getting There & Away
Nukus, Urgench and Konye-Urgench buses use a new station on the edge of town, going to Nukus every 20 minutes until 5.50 pm, and to Konye-Urgench every 45 minutes until 2.15 pm. They can be fearfully crowded, and taxis at the station non-existent. More taxis are at the old bus station (*staryy avtovokzal* in Russian), reached by bus No 4 from the new station, or at the train station, a five minute walk off the bus No 4 route. A taxi to/from Nukus is about US$2.

Hojeli is on the Charjou-Urgench-Dashkhovuz-Moscow railway. All trains serving Urgench (except those terminating at Dashkhovuz) also pass Hojeli.

MOYNAQ
МОЙНАҚ
Population: 2000
Moynaq (Uzbek: Muynoq, Russian: Muynak), 210 km north of Nukus, encapsulates more visibly than anywhere the absurd tragedy of the Aral Sea. Once one of the sea's two major fishing ports, it now stands at least 40 km from the water. The waters started receding in the 1970s. Now what remains of Moynaq's fishing fleet lies rusting on the sand, beside depressions marking the town's last futile efforts in the early 1980s to keep channels open to the shore.

Moynaq's shrunken populace suffers the full force of the Aral Sea disaster, with hotter summers, colder winters, debilitating sand-salt-dust storms, and a gamut of health problems (see the Environment section in the

UZBEKISTAN

Facts About the Region chapter). In 1993 it was reported that 70% of Moynaq residents had 'pre-cancerous conditions'. The fish cannery which was the foundation of its livelihood struggled on after the sea left, with fish delivered by Soviet central planning from the Caspian, Baltic and Atlantic, but it's now on its last legs.

Orientation

Moynaq used to be on an isthmus connecting the Ush Say (Tiger's Tail) peninsula to the shore. You can appreciate this on the approach to the town, where the road is raised above the surrounding land. The former shore is about three km north.

The bus station is at the south end of the long main street. The former Aral Sea shore is about three km north. The airfield turn-off is to the right, soon after the bus station as you enter town from the south; an old 'CCCP' propeller biplane stands outside.

Things to See

Poignant reminders of Moynaq's tragedy are everywhere: the sign at the entrance to the town has a fish on it; a fishing boat stands as a kind of monument on a makeshift pedestal at the bus station.

The **beached ships** are near the Niftibaza (a gas storage facility). Locals, seemingly embarrassed about them, might tell you they have been taken away for scrap, but plenty are still there. Head up the main street for about three km from the bus station and turn right just before the Kinoteatr Berdakh cinema, then fork left just after an electricity substation. About one km along this track you'll see the ships poking up from the sands

to your left – a couple of dozen in all. It's all rather unearthly.

Back beside the Kinoteatr Berdakh, a track leads up to the right to a **war memorial** at the top of low cliffs. The Aral Sea used to lap these cliffs. Now you can look a long way out over its dried-up bed, with not a drop of water in sight.

Past the memorial the track continues three km or so to a group of desolate buildings that were once **beach installations**. The wind through the bushes sounds eerily like waves on a shore.

Places to Stay

If you're stuck, there's the *Hotel Muynak*, a two storey building set back to the right of the main street a short distance past the Kinoteatr Berdakh. A room (with toilets outside) is US$0.50 per person. The boys who run it say food can be provided if you ask.

Getting There & Away

In theory you should be able to visit Moynaq from Nukus in a day by bus, but buses are unreliable. Theoretically they run between the two towns (US$2.50, three to four hours, twice daily), departing both towns at 9 am and 3 pm.

A taxi is easier; a day trip from Nukus will probably cost about US$40. The drive is across cotton fields at first, then a desiccated landscape that probably used to be marshland. At Qonghyrat, about half way, is a bazar where you can pick up shashlyks and bread.

The Urgench travel firm Gulnara (see the Urgench section) offers helicopter or plane charters for about US$250 per aircraft.

Kyrgyzstan
Кыргызстан

What Kyrgyzstan lacks in settled history it makes up for in a wealth of nomadic traditions, including laid-back hospitality and a healthy distrust of authority. What it lacks in development it makes up for in determination. What it lacks in historical architecture it more than makes up for in Central Asia's finest mountain 'architecture' – the highest and most dramatic parts of the central Tian Shan and Pamir Alay ranges. Most travellers vote this the most appealing, accessible and welcoming of the former Soviet Central Asian republics.

In Soviet times, because it also appealed as a site for military development, most of the country was closed to foreigners. The Tian Shan abounds in uranium and other valuable metals, and secret mining towns grew at the heads of remote valleys – eg Mayluu-Suu above the Ferghana Valley, Ming-Kush in the interior, Kaji-Say at Lake Issyk-Kul – their imported Russian workers well-provisioned and well-paid. Issyk-Kul itself was the perfect place for naval weapons development, from a top-secret research complex at its eastern end. But independent Kyrgyzstan has closed most of the mines and institutes (and begun to grapple with the environmental health problems they created), and Kyrgyz are gradually replacing the departing Russians.

The collapse of the USSR has left this tiny, under-equipped republic out on a limb, seemingly without the resources to survive on its own. So far it is getting by on pluck, a liberal agenda surprisingly free of self-interest, and goodwill from western donor countries. It is doing more than any other Central Asian republic to encourage and simplify tourism, at least partly because this is one of the few things it has to sell to the outside world.

It has some way to go – away from Bishkek, Issyk-Kul and a few parts of the

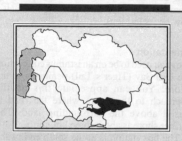

Highlights

- The rugged Ala-Archa valley near Bishkek: some of Central Asia's most accessible alpine grandeur.
- Lake Issyk-Kul and the tree-shaded town of Karakol, a perfect base for getting into the high Tian Shan.
- Osh bazar, one of the best and most eclectic in Central Asia.

high Tian Shan, Kyrgyzstan is not yet very tourist-friendly, and lacks the resources to deal with wretched or nonexistent hotels, limited transport, overpriced fuel, unpoliced roads, and growing crime, driven by alcohol and desperate poverty. It's a great temptation to hop off the bus in the middle of nowhere and hike into the hills but, except in a few places (which we note), this cannot yet be recommended.

But there is still enough to keep you here for weeks, whether or not you're a trekker, and competent agencies to offer help if you want it. One traveller wrote, 'This is the republic the Russians should have fought hardest to hold onto ... in June the mountain valleys are choked with forget-me-nots, gentians, red clover, poppies, wild primroses and the rare black columbine. Kyrgyz horsemen still ride with élan and wear photogenic hats'.

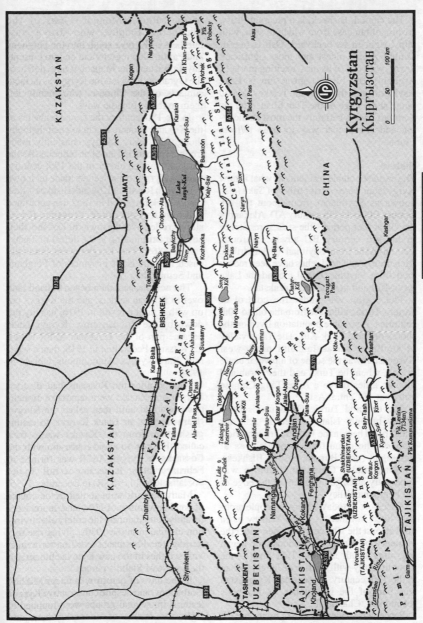

The capital, Bishkek, is a pleasant, leafy, cosmopolitan base from which to start, with 'alps' right in its backyard. Osh is one of Central Asia's oldest and most significant towns, with one of its most exciting markets. Arguably the biggest attraction is Lake Issyk-Kul and the adjacent Terskey Alatau range at the edge of the Tian Shan. And the Torugart pass is certainly the most challenging and spectacular way to cross to/from China.

History

The earliest notable residents of what is now Kyrgyzstan were warrior tribes of Saka (also known as Scythians), from about the 6th century BC to the 5th century AD. Alexander the Great met perhaps the stiffest resistance in his 4th century BC advance through Central Asia from Scythian (Saka) tribes. Rich bronze and gold relics have been recovered from Scythian burial mounds at Lake Issyk-Kul and in southern Kazakstan.

The region was under the control of various Turkic alliances from the 6th to 10th centuries. A sizeable population lived on the shores of Lake Issyk-Kul. The Talas valley in southern Kazakstan and north-west Kyrgyzstan was the scene of a pivotal battle in 751, when the Turks and their Arab and Tibetan allies drove a large Tang Chinese army out of Central Asia.

The cultured Turkic Qarakhanids (who finally brought Islam to Central Asia for good) ruled here in the 10th to 12th centuries. One of their multiple capitals was at Balasagun (now Burana, east of Bishkek). Another major Qarakhanid centre was apparently at Özgön (Uzgen) at the edge of the Ferghana Valley.

Ancestors of today's Kyrgyz people probably lived in Siberia's upper Yenisey basin until at least the 10th century, when under the influence of Mongol incursions they began migrating south into the Tian Shan – the more urgently with the rise of Jenghiz Khan in the 13th century. Present-day Kyrgyzstan was part of the inheritance of Jenghiz's second son, Chaghatai.

Peace was shattered in 1685 by the arrival of the ruthless Mongol Oyrats of the Zhungarian Empire, who drove vast numbers of Kyrgyz south into the Ferghana and Pamir Alay regions and on into present-day Tajikistan. The Manchu (Qing) defeat of the Oyrats in 1758 left the Kyrgyz as de facto subjects of the Chinese, who mainly left them to their nomadic ways.

In the 18th century the feudal tentacles of the Kokand khanate began to encircle them, though the feisty Kyrgyz constantly made trouble from their Tian Shan redoubts. As the Russians moved closer in the 19th century, various Kyrgyz tribal leaders made their own peace with Russia or Kokand. Bishkek – then the Pishpek fort – fell in 1862 to a combined Russian-Kyrgyz force. Russian forces slowly rolled over the towns of Kokand, their advance culminating in the defeat of Tashkent in 1865. The Kyrgyz were gradually eased into the tsar's provinces of Ferghana and Semireche.

The new masters then began to hand land over to Russian settlers, and the Kyrgyz put up with it until a revolt in 1916, heavily put down by the Russian army. Kyrgyz lands became part of the Turkestan ASSR within the Russian Federation in 1918, then a separate Kara-Kyrgyz Autonomous Oblast in 1924.

Finally, after the Russians had decided Kyrgyz and Kazaks were separate nationalities (they had until then called the Kyrgyz 'Kara-Kyrgyz' or Black Kyrgyz, to distinguish them from the Kazaks whom they called 'Kyrgyz' to avoid confusion with the Cossacks) a Kyrgyz ASSR was formed in February 1926. It became a full Soviet Socialist Republic (SSR) in December 1936.

Many nomads were settled in the course of land reforms in 1920s, and more were forcibly settled during the cruel collectivisation campaign in the 1930s, giving rise to a reinvigorated basmachi rebellion for a time. Vast swathes of the new Kyrgyz élite died in the course of Stalin's purges.

In the days of perestroyka under Mikhail Gorbachev, and despite conservative Kyrgyz leadership, several groups were founded to fight the issues of unemployment and homelessness, some activists going so far as to seize vacant land and build houses on it. One group, Ashar (Mutual Help), soon widened its scope as an opposition movement.

Land and housing were in fact at the root of Central Asia's most infamous 'ethnic' violence, between Kyrgyz and Uzbeks around Osh and Özgön (Uzgen) in 1990 – a majority-Uzbek area stuck onto Kyrgyzstan in the 1930s (see the Osh Introduction) – during which at least 300 people were killed.

Elections were held in traditional Soviet rubber-stamp style to the Kyrgyz Supreme Soviet (legislature) in February 1990, with the Kyrgyz Communist Party (KCP) walking away with nearly all the seats. KCP First Secretary Absamat Masaliev was made chairman but, discredited by the Osh violence, failed to get the nod the following October for the new post of president. After multiple ballots a compromise candidate, Askar Akaev, a physicist and president of the Kyrgyz Academy of Sciences, was elected.

Akaev has since gone on to establish himself as a stubborn reformer, restructuring the executive apparatus to suit his liberal political and economic attitudes, and instituting reforms considered the most radical in the Central Asian republics, making the other republics nervous in the process. He faced down an attempt to depose him at the time of the putsch in Moscow in August 1991, came out strongly against the coup and resigned from the KCP, which was soon afterward dissolved.

On 31 August 1991, the Kyrgyz Supreme Soviet reluctantly voted to declare Kyrgyzstan's independence. Six weeks later Akaev was reelected president, running unopposed. Though he was at first reluctant to take part in CIS peacekeeping efforts in Tajikistan, he joined up after armed groups were alleged to have crossed from there into Kyrgyzstan in January 1993. While that conflict may set nerves jangling in Bishkek, Islamic fundamentalism is not officially seen as a serious threat here, as it is in Uzbekistan.

On 5 May 1993 a brand-new Kyrgyzstan constitution and revamped government structure became law, dispensing with the last structural vestiges of the Soviet era. Akaev and his economic programme got a solid popular vote of confidence in a referendum (called by him) in January 1994. In September 1994 the parliament failed to obtain a quorum when only about one-quarter of the deputies came to work; this eventually led to the creation of a smaller, two-chamber legislature. All new members were elected to the legislature in February 1995.

Geography

Kyrgyzstan occupies an area of 198,500 sq km, a bit larger than Austria plus Hungary, about 94% of which is mountains. The country's average elevation is 2750 metres. About 40% of it is over 3000 metres high, with three-quarters under permanent snow and glaciers.

The dominant feature is the Tian Shan range in the south-east. Its crest, the dramatic Kakshaal-Too or Kokshal-Too range, forms a stunning natural border with China, culminating at Pik Pobedy (7439 metres), Kyrgyzstan's highest point and the second-highest peak in the former USSR. The Ferghana range across the middle of the country and the Pamir Alay in the south hold the Ferghana Valley in a scissor-grip.

Not all Kyrgyzs share outsiders' fascination with their mountains, however. One acquaintance at Kara-Köl said, 'we are afraid of these mountains', which can punish with extremes of weather, rockfalls, avalanches and dangerous roads.

In a vast indentation on the fringes of the Tian Shan, Lake Issyk-Kul, almost 700 metres deep, never freezes. One of the country's lacustrine jewels is tiny Song-Köl lake in a smaller pocket to the south-west. Kyrgyzstan's only significant lowland features are the Chuy and Talas valleys, adjacent to Kazakstan. Its main rivers are the Naryn, flowing almost the full length of the country into the Syr-Darya in the Ferghana Valley, and the Chuy along the Kazakstan border.

The mountains effectively isolate the country's northern and southern population

KYRGYZSTAN

centres, in the Chuy and Ferghana valleys, from one another, especially in winter. A major road links them over two 3000-metre-plus passes, but a train journey between them means going round via Tashkent. There has been talk of building a trans-Kyrgyzstan railway.

Government

Under the terms of the May 1993 constitution, legislative power belongs to the parliament, the Jogorku Kenesh or Supreme Council. In its revamped form it consists of two chambers, a 35-seat standing Legislative Assembly elected nationally and a 70-seat People's Assembly based on regional representation. All members are elected to five year terms. The south is represented by 48 deputies compared to the north's 57, guaranteeing the north control of central decision-making.

The president, who is head of state, is also directly elected for a five year term. He appoints the prime minister, who forms the Cabinet of Ministers.

For administrative purposes the country is divided into six oblasts or *duban*s (provinces) – Chuy, Issyk-Kul, Osh, Naryn, Talas and Jalal-Abad – plus Bishkek city.

Economy

Agriculture – mainly farming livestock raising – has traditionally accounted for about one-third of the country's production and employs about one-third of work-age people. (Kyrgyz are outnumbered almost three to one by their livestock). Only about 7% of the land is arable (and most of it needs irrigation) for grains, vegetables, fruit, cotton and tobacco (and some 600,000 hectares of walnut groves). There is a large silk factory at Osh, and lots of apiaries in the mountains. The government has gone a long way towards privatisation of agriculture (6% of the land is now privately farmed) but has seen a simultaneous drop in productivity. It's hoped that the introduction of inheritable leaseholds and the further breakup of collective farms and grazing lands may provide a

sense of proprietorship and give the agricultural sector a boost.

Industry (mainly mining, hydroelectric power generation, agricultural machinery, food processing, electronics and textiles) accounts for about one-fourth of production, employing 27% of workers. By 1994 industry was about 40% privatised, but experienced even worse drops in productivity than agriculture did.

Kyrgyzstan has some important mineral resources, including coal, gold, uranium and other strategic metals. It has few gas or oil reserves of its own, depending heavily on imports and suffering for it after the Soviet collapse. Its mountain rivers offer vast hydro-power potential, though so far this only fills about one-fourth of its requirements, and expanded development will inevitably collide with environmental considerations. Uranium mining in Soviet times has left a fearsome legacy of untended tailings, contaminated water supplies and health problems that are only just becoming understood.

Tightly integrated into the old Soviet system, Kyrgyzstan hung onto the rouble a little too long, and the Russian economic collapse plunged it into trouble. Despite the fastest privatisation program and the most liberal attitudes in Central Asia, it still has the shakiest economy. Its GDP in 1994 was less than Sudan's in 1991. Of all CIS countries, it had the lowest inflation rate but its economy remained the fifth most depressed, and the first four (Tajikistan, Georgia, Azerbaijan and Armenia) all had civil wars of some kind going on. Unemployment in 1995 was estimated at 35%, and the average monthly wage was about US$18. The banking system remains fairly primitive, offering only short-term loans suitable to a 'kiosk economy'.

The sudden introduction of the Kyrgyz *som* in May 1993 plunged Kyrgyzstan into a crisis with Uzbekistan and Kazakstan, still then in the 'rouble zone'. In July 1994, however, all three cemented a closer economic union, perhaps the first step in some kind of Central Asian common market.

Population & People

Kyrgyzstan has 4.5 million people, of whom (in 1993) about 57% were ethnic Kyrgyz, 21% Slav (Russian and Ukrainian, mainly managers, professionals and their families), 13% Uzbeks (mainly in commerce), 1% ethnic Germans, and the rest composed of Dungans (Muslim Chinese), Koreans, Tatars and others.

Since 1989 there has been a major exodus of Slavs and Germans – eg a drop of 15% in the Slav population and at least 50% of Germans between 1989 and mid-1993 – amid dire forecasts of its economic effects. Among the leavers was one of Akaev's closest allies, the Russian First Deputy Prime Minister, German Kuznetsov.

The country's largest cities are Bishkek (670,000), Osh (250,000), Jalal-Abad, Tokmak and Karakol. About two-thirds of the population lives in rural areas.

The geographically isolated southern provinces of Osh and Jalal-Abad are more typical of the conservative, Islamicised Ferghana Valley than of the industrialised, Russified north. Ancient but still-important tribal affiliations reinforce these differences further. In a recent survey, 63.5% of Kyrgyz people thought that north-south contradictions were the main destabilising factor within society.

Kyrgyz (with Kazaks) in general, while probably the most Russified of Central Asian people, were never as deeply 'Leninised', judging by the casual ease with which they have turned away from the Soviet era. There has been none of the wholesale, hypocritical race to cleanse all Soviet terminology that afflicts Uzbekistan.

Islam has always sat lightly on the Kyrgyz people too. One consequence is a high profile for women here. According to Tiziano Terzani in *Goodnight, Mister Lenin*, the Russians in the 19th century *encouraged* the Kyrgyz to be good Muslims in the hopes that they would thereby be more manageable subjects.

For more on the Kyrgyz people refer to the History and Population & People sections in the Facts about the Region chapter.

Kyrgyz Graveyards

Kyrgyz graveyards are frequently located right beside main roads. One local friend told me: 'Death is the only point at which a Kyrgyz stops being a nomad and must stay in a "house".' At least from the afterlife a Kyrgyz should be able to watch the traffic go by. ∎

Arts

Manas Central Asian literature has traditionally been popularised in the form of songs, poems and stories by itinerant minstrels, called *akyn* in Kyrgyz (for more on this oral tradition, see the Arts section in the Facts about the Region chapter). Among better-known 20th century Kyrgyz akyns are Togolok Moldo (real name Bayymbet Abdyrakhmanov), Sayakbay Karalayev and Sagymbay Orozbakov.

But the Kyrgyz have also come to be associated with something rather more complex – an entire cycle of oral legends, 20 times longer than the *Odyssey* and 2½ times the length of the *Mahabarata*, about a hero-of-heroes called Manas (see the following Manas aside).

Akyns who can recite or improvise from these are in a class by themselves, called *manaschi*.

There were originally lots of epics, about various khans or leaders of the so-called Nogay people, who may or may not be related to a tribe by that name that apparently lives near the Aral Sea. The epics have gradually coalesced as bards improvised, attributing everybody's exploits to one person.

Manas in fact predates the Kyrgyz, in the same sense that Achilles or Agamemnon predates the Greeks. The stories are part of a wider, older tradition, but have come to be associated with the Kyrgyz people and culture partly because Soviet scholars 'gave' Manas to them in efforts to create separate cultures for the various Central Asian peoples.

Manas – the Kyrgyz National Epic

Imagine a heroic world of powerful warriors, magic steeds, and the wars they wage. Imagine the wars being fought on a vast landscape of mountains, plains, and an inland sea. Imagine the inhabitants affording glimpses of their daily life – moments both tough and tender, opulent and rustic – as they migrate, make war, and fight for survival. Imagine this world brought to life in poetry on the lips of epic bards.

The *Manas* epics have been called the 'Iliad of the steppes'. But the Kyrgyz didn't get their tradition from the Greeks. Heroic epic has existed among many different peoples, whenever the right cultural, social, and even economic factors coincided. *Manas,* which is the product and high point of a widespread Central Asian oral culture, is acclaimed as one of the finest epic traditions.

The super-hero of the poems is the khan Manas. The narrative revolves around his exploits in carving out a homeland for his people in the face of hostile hordes. The 'good guys' are Muslims and the 'bad guys' are infidels. Manas is of course big, strong, brave, and a born leader. Manas *is,* to an important extent, the Kyrgyz people's self-image.

This is how a 20th century manaschi sends Manas's swarming armies off on a warring campaign, and how the bantamweight Kyrgyz propagate their endearing, larger-than-life national élan through the archaic medium of epic:

> Not a space there was between flag and standard;
> the earth's surface could not be seen!
> Not a space there was between banner and standard;
> the range of the Altay could not be seen!
> Points of lances gleamed; men's heads bobbed;
> the earth swayed on the point of collapse.
> Flags on golden standards fluttered,
> and a ground-splitting din was heard...
> The army, marching with a terrible noise,
> was greater than the eyes could take in –
> eyes were bowed with all the looking!
> Black plains, grey hills,
> the face of the earth was beaten down!
> Coats of mail all a-glitter,
> racers and chargers bursting forth neighing...
> the enormous warrior host
> set a-moving with a crack!

Unfortunately, visitors to Kyrgyzstan are lucky indeed to hear a manaschi in performance. There are few left. These latter-day bards wear sequined costumes and recite short, memorised snippets of the great songs in auditoriums. Traditionally the illiterate bards would belt out their epics in yurts, to enthralled audiences for whom the shifting, artful improvisations on time-worn themes were radio, television, rap music, and myth rolled into one: that tradition is dead.

The end of the oral tradition was inevitable with the advent of literacy. Yet interest in *Manas* is on the rise. Books, operas, movies, comic books, and television serials based on *Manas* have appeared.

Manas mania received an exponential boost when the Kyrgyz government and UNESCO declared 1995 the 'International Year of *Manas*' and, pulling a number out of a hat, the '1000th

Modern Literature Kyrgyzstan has two well-known living authors – Chinghiz Aitmatov (born 1928) and Kazat Akmatov (born 1942).

Aitmatov is better known, having not only been published in Kyrgyz and Russian but translated into English, German and French. Among his novels – which are also revealing looks at Kyrgyz life and culture – are *Jamila* (1967), *The White Steamship* (1970), *Early Cranes* (1975), *Piebald Dog Running Along the Shore* (1978), *A Day Lasts Longer Than*

Anniversary of the *Manas* Epos'. A grand festival was held. Visiting heads of state were fêted, and President Askar Akaev held forth from the world's first (and probably last) three storey yurt.

When a small, poor country spends US$8 million (by some estimates) on celebrating an epic poem, one can be pretty sure it's not just because the government are a lot of bookworms. Manas is a figure for the Kyrgyz to hang their dreams on. Some Kyrgyz consider him to be 'just a little lower than God'. Legend has even assigned Manas a tomb, located near Talas, where Muslim pilgrims come to pray.

Churned out from the death throes of the Soviet empire, Kyrgyzstan is now charting its course into the 21st century with the aid of an epic poem. One of the most popular episodes, dear to the hearts of all Kyrgyz, is the Great Campaign in which Manas's armies conquer all of China ... Stay tuned.

Only one good English translation of a representative group of *Manas* poems exists: *The Manas of Wilhelm Radloff*, edited and translated by Arthur T Hatto (Wiesbaden, 1990). This is a scholarly edition which is well worth the search. *Manas: The Epic Vision of Theodor Herzen*, edited and translated by Daniel Prior (Bishkek, 1995) is an album that tells the *Manas* story in pictures and words. Its overseas distributor is the Middle East Studies Center, Portland State University, 1950 SW 6th Ave, Portland, OR 97201 (contact: Marta Colburn). ■

a Century (1980) and *The Place of the Skull* (1986).

Among Akmatov's works (according to Tiziano Terzani in *Goodnight, Mister Lenin*) are a play called *The Night of the Divorce*, about a corrupt Party official, and a novel

called *Time*, about the repression of ethical values in the Stalin era. Both were instantly banned. Oddly, he eventually became chief of ideology for the Kyrgyz SSR. He was instrumental in the founding of the national-rebirth Movement for Democracy in 1989.

KYRGYZSTAN

Orientation

The Kyrgyz language has not been so bluntly imposed on non-speakers in Kyrgyzstan as has Uzbek in Uzbekistan. In larger towns in the north at least, streets and squares are labelled in both Kyrgyz and Russian. In some smaller towns, the old Russian signs are still up and Russian forms persist (in Osh and other towns in the south you'll hear Uzbek terms as well). Many Soviet-era names have been retained.

We try to use the most current names, but in each town we use the grammatical forms (Kyrgyz, Russian or Uzbek) that seem to be in common use.

A Kyrgyz street is *köchösü* (Russian: *ulitsa*), an avenue *prospektisi* (Russian: *prospekt*), a boulevard *bulvary* (Russian: *bulvar*), a square *ayanty* (Russian *ploshchad*).

Bishkek
Бишкек

Population: 670,000

In 1825, by a Silk Road settlement on a tributary of the Chuy (or Chu; Kazak: Shu) river, the Uzbek Khan of Kokand built a little clay fort, one of several along caravan routes through the Tian Shan mountains. In 1862 the Russians captured and wrecked it, and set up a garrison of their own. The town of Pishpek was founded 16 years later, swelled by Russian peasants lured by land grants and the Chuy valley's black earth.

In 1926 the town, re-baptised Frunze, became capital of the new Kyrgyz ASSR. The name never sat well; Mikhail Vasilievich Frunze (who was born here) was the Russian Civil War commander who helped keep tsarist Central Asia in Bolshevik hands and hounded the basmachi rebellion into the mountains.

In 1991 the city became Bishkek, the Kyrgyz form of its old Kazak name. A *pishpek* or *bishkek* is a churn for kumys. Numerous legends – some quaint, some rude – explain how a town came to be named for a wooden plunger. Dan Prior, in his *Bishkek Handbook* (see the Information section), concludes disappointingly that this was simply the closest familiar sound to its old Sogdian name, Peshagakh, meaning 'place below the mountains'.

With the 4800 metre, permanently snow-capped rampart of the Kyrgyz Alatau range looming over it, the Sogdian name fits. Bishkek, now the capital and industrial centre of independent Kyrgyzstan, is a relaxed and handsome place with wide streets, Ukrainian-style backstreet houses and mainly good-natured people of many races (only about one-third of them Kyrgyz). Boosters boast of more trees per person here than in any other Central Asian city. But when the wind is blowing in the wrong direction, smog from the heating plant east of the centre and factories in the northern outskirts can eat your throat away.

Bishkek wears its recent history without embarrassment. Lenin is still here in his overcoat, gesturing at the mountains from the vast central square. A larger-than-life Frunze still sits on a bronze horse facing the railway station, though his name has been removed. You can still visit the museum built over Frunze's birthplace, if you can keep a straight face.

There's nothing else old here, and little even predating WWII. Even old people now seem sadly marginalised, with some to be seen selling their belongings to make ends meet, and a few begging.

This is mainly a jumping-off point for the Tian Shan mountains and Lake Issyk-Kul, and for the overland crossing to China via the Torugart pass. The city can catch heavy weather, with snow here when it's raining elsewhere, even in October.

Orientation

Bishkek sits 800 metres abve sea level on the northern hem of the Kyrgyz Alatau (or Ala-Too, say 'Ala-TOE') mountains, an arm of the Tian Shan. The Ala-Archa and Alamedin (properly Alamüdün in Kyrgyz) rivers run out of the mountains, north through the city in concrete channels to the Grand Chuy

Canal, north of the centre, and on to the Chuy river, 15 km to the north-east. The Chuy river also forms the Kazak border.

Nineteenth century military planners laid out an orderly, compass-oriented town. Jibek Jolu prospektisi (Silk Road Ave), just north of the centre, was old Pishpek's main street. Now the municipal axes are Chuy prospektisi and park-like Erkindik prospektisi. At the centre yawns Ala-Too Square, flanked by Panfilov and Dubovy Parks.

Bishkek's Manas airport is 30 km north-west of the centre, and the west or long-distance bus station is four km out in the same direction. The east or regional bus station is east along Jibek Jolu. The railway station is at the south end of Erkindik prospektisi by the Hotel Ala-Too.

The best view of the city and the mountains is probably from either the square in front of the Hotel Dostuk, or the Ferris wheel in Panfilov Park!

Maps Rip-off newsagents and souvenir shops buy up city maps cheaply and sell them at absurd prices. The Kyrgyz Cartographic Agency sells good Bishkek and Kyrgyzstan maps, trekking maps (in Russian) and USSR topographic maps of Kyrgyzstan and adjacent areas.

The building is set back behind a bus stop on the north side of Kiev, west of Togolok Moldo. The salesroom, room 510 on the 5th floor, is open weekdays from 7.30 am to noon and 1 to 4.30 pm.

Information
The Bishkek Handbook Check hotels and shops for this thorough, literate look at Bishkek history, sights and practicalities, by Bishkek resident and Kyrgyzophile Dan Prior. We saw it in the Akademkniga and Nuska bookshops on Erkindik and in the lobby kiosk at the Ministry of Foreign

KYRGYZSTAN

Old & New Names in Bishkek
Most of Bishkek's streets, squares and stations are labelled in both Kyrgyz and Russian. We use new names and Kyrgyz forms here, but as a practical matter these may not be familiar to everyone – even Kyrgyz forms of otherwise unchanged names (eg Soviet for Sovietskaya, Kiev for Kievskaya, Moskva for Moskovskaya) – and you may need to refer to the following list when asking directions.

New Name	Old Name
Streets	
Isanov (Prospekt)	40 Let Oktyabrya
Jibek Jolu (prospektisi)	50 Let Kirgizskoy SSR
Abdy Suerkulov	50 Let Komsomola Kirgizii
Erkindik (prospektisi)	(Prospekt) Dzerzhinskogo
Chokmorov	Engelsa
Kiev	Kievskaya
Abdymomunov	Kirova
Tynystanov	Krasnooktyabrskaya
Chuy prospektisi	Leninsky prospekt
Jash Gvardiya prospektisi	Molodoy Gvardii
Moskva	Moskovskaya
Razzakov	Pervomayskaya or Birinchi May
Sulman Ibraimov	Pravdy
Soviet	Sovietskaya
Parks & Squares	
Dubovy Park	Ploshchad Dzerzhinskogo
Ala-Too Square	Ploshchad Lenina

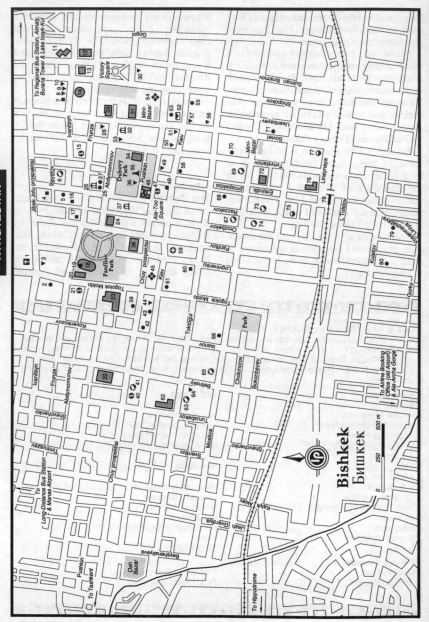

Bishkek
Бишкек

Affairs (Razzakov at the corner with Abdymomunov), for about US$8 in *som*.

Tourist Offices Kyrgyzintourist (☎ 22-63-42, fax 22-39-42, telex 245144 INTUR KH), in the Hotel Ala-Too at Erkindik 1, has no more information than any other travel agency, though they're competent at making arrangements (see Travel Agencies in this section). They're open weekdays to 5 pm (4

pm on Fridays). They also have an airport office.

Foreign Embassies For Kyrgyz embassies overseas, see the Visas & Embassies section in the Facts for the Visitor chapter. The nearest UK Embassy is in Almaty. A Pakistan embassy had just opened in the Hotel Dostuk at press time, with plans to be issuing visas by the end of 1995; they also expected to move, so you may have to ask the Ministry

KYRGYZSTAN

PLACES TO STAY

4	Hotel
7	Hotel Ak-Say
11	Gostinichny Komplex Ilbirs
12	Hotel Dostuk
16	Hotel Sary-Chelek
17	Bishkek International School of Management & Business
19	Hotel Spartak, in Spartak Stadium
29	Hotel Kirghizstan
60	Hotel Polyot
72	Hotel Bishkek
76	Hotel Ala-Too

PLACES TO EAT

3	Mini-Bazar
8	Gril Bar
9	Kafe Ak-Kuu
10	Dostuk Mini-Restoran
13	Naryn Restaurant
22	Flamingo Restaurant (in Philharmonia Hall)
28	Kafe Fenix
30	Ak-Bata Café
33	Kafe Begaim
36	Aksakaldar Chaykanasi
44	Chaykana Jalal-Abad
49	Restaurant Son-Kul
50	Kafe Almair
51	Kafe Ersay
56	Kafe Altyn-Kush
57	Café
64	Primavera Restaurant

OTHER

1	Orthodox Church
2	Pamir IMC
5	Kyrghyz Concept
6	USA Embassy
14	Circus
15	Gosudarstvenny Bank
18	Spartak Stadium
20	Ministry of Tourism & Sport
21	AKB Bank
22	Philharmonia Hall
23	Palace of Sport
24	State Academic Drama Theatre
25	Ministry of Foreign Affairs
26	Frunze House-Museum
27	Ministry of Culture
31	State Opera & Ballet Theatre
32	State Museum of Fine Arts
34	Russian Drama Theatre
35	Bust of Felix Dzerzhinsky
37	State Historical Museum
38	'White House'
39	Imfiko
40	Promstroybank
41	Indian Embassy
42	Photo Salon, at Dom Byta Store
43	Kyrgyz Cartographic Agency
45	Prestige Department Store
46	Tsentr Interbilim, in Dom Druzhby
47	Adil Bank
48	Akademkniga Bookshop
52	Main Post Office
53	Central Telephone Office
54	TsUM Department Store
55	OVIR (Office of Visas & Registration)
58	Nuska Bookshop
59	Kyrgyz Republic Hospital
61	Bilim Bookshop
62	Maksat Bank
63	Chinese Embassy
65	Kazak Embassy
66	Log House
67	Iranian Embassy
68	Memorial to Urkuya Saliyeva
69	Turkish Embassy
70	Sputnik Travel Agency
71	Bukinist Bookshop
73	Russian Embassy
74	German Embassy
75	Kashgar Bus Office
77	Railway Ticket Office (Advance Bookings)
78	Railway Station
79	Dostuck Trekking Agency
80	ITMC Tien Shan Travel Agency

of Foreign Affairs or another embassy for their new address and telephone.

China
    Toktogul 196 (☎ 22-24-23); visas Monday, Wednesday and Friday from 9 to 11.30 am
Germany
    Razzakov 28 (☎ 22-48-11)
India
    Chuy 164, next to Promstroybank (☎ 21-08-62)
Iran
    Razzakov 36 (☎ 22-69-64)
Kazakstan
    Moskva 161 (☎ 22-45-57)
Pakistan
    Hotel Dostuk
Russia
    Razzakov 17 (☎ 22-17-75); visa business Monday and Thursday from 3 to 5 pm, Wednesday 9 to 11 am
Turkey
    Moskva 89 (☎ 22-78-82)
USA
    Erkindik 66 (☎ 22-26-93, 22-27-77, after hours 22-53-58), weekdays from 2 to 5 pm best for consular services; eventually they plan to move out near the old airport

Visas The place to get a visa is the Consular Department (☎ 22-05-45, 22-05-52) of the Ministry of Foreign Affairs, on Razzakov at the corner with Abdymomunov. You may get farther faster with the help of one of the travel agencies listed in this section.

OVIR, the Office of Visas & Registration (☎ 269-06-27, 269-05-98), at Kiev 58 near Shopokov (left-hand door, room 3 on the ground floor), is the place to register or to have your visa extended. They're open weekdays from 9 am to 12.30 pm and 2 to 5 pm. Little English is spoken.

Customs If you've bought anything that looks remotely antique, and didn't get a certificate from the shop saying it's not, you can get one from the Foreign Department (☎ 22-59-54, 22-19-27) of the Ministry of Culture, at Abdymomunov 205.

Useful Organisations A cheerful Kyrgyz-run information and contact point, Tsentr Interbilim (☎ & fax 22-85-77, e-mail root@world.bishkek.su) links local interest groups and foreign organisations. They may also be able to help visitors interested in teaching English or doing volunteer work in Kyrgyzstan. Their postal address is PO Box 2024, Bishkek 720000.

They're on the ground floor of 'Dom Druzhby' (House of Friendship), properly the Kyrgyz Assembly of Peoples. This building, at Pushkin 78-2 by Ala-Too Square, is a centre for advocacy and self-help groups – for mothers, the elderly, Jews, Russians, Koreans, Dungans, etc – and non-governmental organisations.

Money There are exchange desks in most hotels and many shops. Banks doing foreign exchange from US$ cash include Adil Bank at Chuy 114 and the state-run Promstroybank at Chuy 168.

Banks that can change US$ travellers' cheques (into *som* for a commission of about 3%, or possibly into dollars for more) include Promstroybank, AKB (☎ 21-94-73) at Togolok Moldo 94 opposite the stadium, and Maksat (☎ 24-45-11) at Toktogul 187. AKB and Maksat can also arrange telegraphic transfers from some overseas banks. Hours vary but all are open weekdays, at least from 10 am to noon.

Licensed private money-changers in numerous tiny shop-fronts have slightly better rates (for US$ cash only) but give no exchange receipts.

Post & Communications The main post and telephone offices face Soviet, south of Chuy. The post office is open weekdays from 7 to 11 am and 1 to 7 pm, Saturday and Sunday from 9 am to 5 pm. There is a separate mailroom for international letters and parcels – enter the first door on the left (north) side of the post office, turn left and go through another door, cross to the far right corner and go through a third door.

Western priority mail services in Bishkek include DHL (☎ 29-29-34), UPS (☎ 28-53-71, 28-73-14) and TNT (☎ 25-09-85).

The telephone office also provides international fax service. Bishkek's telephone code is 3312.

E-mail At the private business Imfiko (☎ 26-44-16, fax 26-49-43, e-mail root@cct.bishkek.su) at Chuy 219 you can send one-off messages for about US$1.50 per page, or open an e-mail box for US$15 plus US$8/month plus kilobyte charges. There's no sign; enter on the left side, go down the left-hand corridor and try the first door on the left.

Another public-access site (at root@nlkr.info.bishkek.su), operated at the National Library by a non-governmental organisation called Irex (☎ 22-86-90), apparently offers free access and instruction. Kyrghyz Concept (see the Travel Agencies section following) also provides e-mail services.

Travel Agencies The following agencies are starting to figure out what budget-minded individual travellers want and how much they can get for it. For details on help and transport to the Torugart pass, see the Torugart Pass section in this chapter.

Ak-Kuu (☎ 47-22-62, fax 22-54-21), Soviet 3-Г; Boris 'No Problem' Borkeyev speaks little English but can set up budget walking, horseback and ski excursions and, he says, local and long-distance transport, train and air tickets; he also has a little guest house with the same name

Dostuck Trekking (☎ 42-74-71, fax 41-91-29, telex 251299 INTUR KH), in an unmarked house at Vosemnadsataya Liniya 42-1 (Bishkek 720053), over the railway station footbridge; OK for local excursions at about US$50 per day per person and up from Bishkek, though prices are sometimes elusive

ITMC Tien-Shan (☎ & fax 42-98-25, e-mail tienshan@asiemm.bishkek.su), Panfilov 105 (Bishkek 720035), south of the railway tracks; not cheap but competent adventure-travel operator offering package and piece-wise help, including visas, guides, some equipment; also known as Tien-Shan Mountaineering, and not to be confused with their former partners at Tien-Shan Travel

Kyrghyz Concept (☎ 26-58-22, fax 62-07-46, e-mail janar@el.bishkek.su), Razzakov (Pervomayskaya) 100, with overpriced guides, tours and transport

Kyrgyzintourist (☎ 22-63-42, fax 22-39-42, telex 245144 INTUR KH), in the Hotel Ala-Too at Erkindik 1, rents cars and arranges stodgy excursions at about US$50 per person per day for groups, but prices rise steeply for individuals; for a fee they'll help with visas, train tickets and homestays in Naryn

Pamir International Mountaineering Camp (Pamir IMC; ☎ 21-15-23, fax 21-14-72), Togolok Moldo 60, room 406 (Bishkek 720033), contact Bekbolot Koshoyev

Sputnik (☎ 22-57-90, fax 22-47-29, telex 245130 BMT KH), Tynystanov 195, the old Soviet youth-travel bureau still hasn't a clue about individual travellers or what they want to do, other than day trips to Ala-Archa and cheap overnights at Cholpon-Ata on Lake Issyk-Kul

Tien Shan Raft (☎ 28-41-42, fax 23-41-83), Musa Jalil 104 (Bishkek 720051), river raft and kayak rentals and trips around Kyrgyzstan; contact Alexander Kandaurov

Tien-Shan Travel (☎ 27-28-85, fax 27-05-76), Shcherbakov 127 (Bishkek 720042), out-of-work cartographers with expedition gear and a menu of set group tours into the mountains, but short on business sense and unaccustomed to walk-in clients

Western expatriates here recommend a Kyrgyz named Ishen Obolbekov (☎ 26-55-97, 21-35-60), the well-tutored son of a Lake Issyk-Kul shepherd, for excellent horseback trips of two days to two weeks into the Tian Shan.

Two competent non-Bishkek agencies accustomed to serving tourists in Bishkek are Karakol, in Karakol (see the Issyk-Kul section), and Alptreksport in Osh (see the Bishkek to Osh and the Kyrgyz Ferghana Valley section).

Other Bishkek agencies we heard of but did not contact are Ak-Shol (☎ 24-83-04), Bilim (☎ 29-17-58, fax 29-17-46), Karavan Tours (☎ & fax 21-46-80) and Speleotrek (☎ 22-04-78, fax 21-28-45).

Emergency & Medical Services Dial ☎ 02 for the police, ☎ 03 for a municipal ambulance.

The Kyrgyz Republic Hospital (outpatients ☎ 22-89-60, 24-hour duty officer for emergencies and hospital ambulance ☎ 26-17-27 or 22-89-92) at Kiev 110 has an agreement with the US Embassy to provide medical services to foreigners.

Mountain Rescue The ITMC Tien-Shan agency (see the Travel Agencies section) has established a private mountain rescue service, to replace several that folded along with the USSR.

Dangers & Annoyances Bishkek smiles during the day but is neither safe nor well lit after dark. Both locals and foreigners have been roughed up, sometimes by young cops on the take (one man working for a British firm said he'd been robbed three times by uniformed police). If you're out after dark, stick to main streets and avoid the parks; better yet, call a taxi (see the Getting Around section).

If you're approached by plainclothes police at the bus station, stay friendly but *don't budge*; you can answer their questions just as well where you are. Always ask for their identification too; if they don't show it, demand to see a uniformed officer. Two Americans were approached by men claiming to be *militsia*; after showing proper identification they were grabbed by the wrists, taken to a small room in the station and grilled for several hours by men who never showed them any identification.

Osh Bazar is said to be infested with pickpockets and thieves who slash bags. Keep your valuables out of sight, not in your shopping bag. Don't wave your money pouch around if you must fish in it for money, and stay sharp in close crowds.

A common and unpleasant scam here involves what looks like accidentally dropped money. If you pick it up, someone rushes up saying it's his; if you hand it back you may be accused of substituting a smaller note, a crowd (of his cronies) can gather and unpleasantries can escalate. Let it lie, and move on!

Media The *Kyrgyzstan Chronicle*, an English-language newspaper with Kyrgyzstan news and features of interest to expatriate residents, can be picked up at tourist hotel newsstands.

Film & Photography There are Kodak franchises, with print film and fast processing, at TsUM and at the north-east corner of Soviet and Moskva. Passport-size photos can be done at the photo salon in the Dom Byta store, Chuy 150 at the corner with Isanov.

Ala-Too Square

This sea of concrete ceased to be Lenin Square in 1991. Lenin remains on his plinth, but his days are probably numbered.

The brutal block behind him, once the Lenin Museum, has become the **State Historical Museum**, with two yurts, a small archaeology exhibit and a beguiling display of Kyrgyz carpets, embroidery and other applied crafts on the ground floor. The original, stupendously posh shrine to Lenin and the Revolution in Kyrgyzstan was still in place upstairs when we visited, and is definitely worth seeing. The museum is open daily except Mondays from 9 am to 1 pm and 2 to 6 pm.

The grand façades across Chuy prospektisi from Lenin are just that – façades, about 10 metres deep, erected in Soviet times in front of the venerable but unsuitably drab Ilbirs knitwear factory.

The unmarked marble palace full of chandeliered offices just west of the square, the **'White House'**, is the seat of the Kyrgyzstan government, including the President's office and the republic's parliament. Behind this is **Panfilov Park**, whose rusting rides and arcades make it the centre of Bishkek for kids.

The conspicuously older structure east of Ala-Too Square at Pushkin 68 was the headquarters of the Central Committee of the Kyrgyz ASSR, declared in 1926. Occupied until a few years ago by drab history and zoology museums, it's now the **Dom Druzhby** community centre (see the Useful Organisations section).

Beyond this is **Dubovy (Oak) Park**, full of strollers on warm Sundays, and some neglected modern sculpture. The century-old oaks here and along **Erkindik prospektisi** (Freedom Avenue) make Bishkek perhaps the greenest city in Central Asia. Where Erkindik enters the park, a smouldering bust of Felix Dzerzhinsky, founder of the Soviet secret police, dares you to pass. His name has been removed; despite Kyrgyzstan's laid-back attitude to recent history, this name, like Lenin's, disappeared quickly in 1991.

A statue of a woman on the west side of Erkindik is dedicated to Urkuya Saliyeva, a Kyrgyz social reformer from Osh in the conservative Ferghana Valley, and founder of one of Kyrgyzstan's first collective farms. She and her family were murdered, an act Soviet propagandists tried to pin on basmachi guerrillas.

State Museum of Fine Arts
This museum, also called the Museum of Applied Art, at Soviet 196 near Abdymomunov (Kirova), features Kyrghyz embroidery, jewellery, utensils and eye-popping felt rugs, works by local artists, and a startling collection of reproduction Egyptian and classical statuary. It's open daily except Monday from 9 am to 5 pm (from 10 am Friday).

Frunze House-Museum
Is this thatched cottage really where the little Frunze played with his toy soldiers, or just the Soviet way with history? In any case the meticulous two storey museum engulfing it – showcasing Frunze as military and family man, plus the requisite posters, weapons, flags and statues – has itself become a piece of history. It's at the corner of Frunze and Razzakov, and is open daily except Monday from 9 am to 5 pm (to 4 pm on weekends), free of charge.

Victory Square
A weedy plaza with an immense yurt-shaped memorial, erected on the 40th anniversary of the end of WWII, sprawls across an entire city block near the Hotel Dostuk. On cold evenings you may see a knot of young men passing the bottle and warming themselves at its eternal flame.

Pishpek Fort
According to Dan Prior, nothing remains of

Mikhail Vasilievich Frunze
Frunze was born in what was then Pishpek in 1885. After an early adulthood full of revolutionary excitement in Moscow, and numerous arrests, he eventually commanded the Red Guards who occupied the Moscow Kremlin in October 1917. He was a major player in the Russian Civil War, directing the defeat of the White forces of Admiral Kolchak in Siberia and the route of General Wrangel in the Caucasus. It was Frunze who led the Bolshevik forces that seized Khiva and Bukhara in 1920, and pushed the basmachi rebels out of the Ferghana Valley.

Replacing Trotsky as War Commissar, Frunze introduced compulsory peacetime military service, and moulded the Red Army into a potent tool of the Revolution. After Lenin's death, he survived several mysterious auto accidents, but died in 1925 during an officially ordered stomach operation, a victim of Stalin's paranoia. ■

---

the original clay fort but a weedy hill in a dismal neighbourhood north-east of the centre. The Alamedin river, which once flowed past it, is confined to a culvert nearby.

Russian Remnants
Among poignant reminders that there is still a Russian community here are the pretty, blue-steepled Orthodox church on Jibek Jolu near Togolok Moldo, and an incongruous, well-preserved Russian style log house on Moskva west of Togolok Moldo. Gosudarstvenny (Government) Bank at the corner of Erkindik and Frunze was the Bolsheviks' first capital construction project here (built in 1926). It was designed by one A P Zenkov, best known for the far lovelier wooden cathedral (1904) in Almaty.

Places to Stay – bottom end
Homestays Dostuck, Ak-Kuu and probably other travel agencies listed in the Bishkek Information section can arrange bed and breakfast in private homes, typically for under US$20 per person per night.

Hotels & Hostels Cheapest, and not the worst, is a sports hostel, the *Hotel Spartak* (☎ 26-14-22), inside the stadium in Panfilov Park. Ultra-basic dormitory beds were just US$1 when we visited. The water is cold, nobody speaks English, and the nearest food beyond the bufet downstairs is at a mini-bazar on Jibek Jolu. The address is Togolok Moldo 17; enter through the gate on Frunze.

In the same league is *Gostinichny Komplex Ilbirs* (Ilbirs Hotel Complex), the folded-looking building just north of the Hotel Dostuk. Go to the back (east) side, facing Gogol; inside, the first door on the right is the visitors' office (☎ 23-13-04). A bed in a bare-bones room, with common toilet and no showers, is US$2 the first night and US$1.50 thereafter.

The best bottom-end value near the town centre is the hotel of the *Bishkek International School of Management & Business* or Shkola Biznesa (☎ 22-04-14), behind the park at Panfilov 237. Clean doubles, with two rooms sharing toilet and shower (hot water most of the time) are US$11 per person. A small café serves overpriced beer and reasonably priced Kyrgyz dishes and basic breakfast. It appears tourists aren't automatically registered with OVIR if they stay here (see the Kyrgyzstan information in the Visas & Embassies section of the Facts for the Visitor chapter).

In summer only, the *Hotel Ak-Kuu* (☎ 47-22-62), Soviet 3-Г, has four spartan doubles with shared toilet, shower and sauna for about US$5 per room. Food is whatever owner Boris Barkeyev can order in, and there's a small food shop nearby. It's 4.5 km south on Soviet via bus No 4 or trolleybus Nos 3, 6 or 10; enter from the cross street, Abdy Suerkulov (formerly 50 Let Komsomola Kirgizii).

Failing all else, a dismal truckers' hostel, the *Hotel Ak-Say* (☎ 26-14-65) at Ivanitsyn 117 behind the circus, is US$5 per bed. It might be a good place to drum up a ride, though.

A cheapo we have heard about but didn't locate is the *Hotel Saltanat* (☎ 21-34-25) on the 5th floor at Belinsky 22a.

Places to Stay – middle
Kyrgyzintourist runs the *Hotel Ala-Too* (☎ 22-56-43, fax 22-63-42) at Erkindik 1. Plain singles/doubles with toilet and (usually) hot shower are, despite the adjacent railway station, fairly quiet (except for the bar scene at 2 am and occasional station announcements around 5.30 am) but a bit pricey at US$25/45 and up. Skip the US$5 breakfast fee and buy your own in the restaurant for half that. If reception says 'no rooms', Kyrgyzintourist on the ground floor might conjure up one. The hotel and adjacent railway station square are a magnet for lowlife at night.

The *Hotel Polyot* (Pilot) at the corner of Toktogul and Logvinenko, a renovated military hostel, has clean, no-frills doubles for about US$30 – but is apparently only for guests of local firms.

Rooms with TV, bath and a few bugs at the city-run *Hotel Bishkek* (☎ 22-02-20, fax 62-03-65), Erkindik 21, are US$37/47 and up (plus a 20% 'booking charge' on the first night), with breakfast. This is the mid-range place visiting engineers and business types settle for.

The huge *Hotel Kirghizstan* at Soviet 181 is under renovation. Staff at an unsignposted hotel at Bayetov 99 say it's 'not for tourists'.

Behind the park at Orozbekov 87, the glum *Hotel Sary-Chelek* (☎ 22-14-67) has plain doubles with bath for US$37, and a damp café-bar. Equally uncheerful is the *Sayakat* (☎ 44-55-09), with beds for US$19, at Dushanbinskaya 8-A, an awkward location well south of the centre (take bus No 34 on Kiev, bus No 8 on Togolok Moldo or trolleybus No 5 from the long-distance bus station).

Nine km out of town is a concrete hulk whose lower four floors are the state-owned *Hotel Issyk-Kul* (☎ 44-81-60), and also serve as the Presidential guest house. In an unorthodox bit of free-marketism the top four floors are run as the competing *Hotel New Issyk-Kul* (☎ 44-88-55, fax 44-88-58) by a local Korean firm. The state has singles for US$40, the Koreans singles/doubles for

US$50/63, with breakfast. Two reception desks face one another in the lobby. It's at Prospekt Mira 301, half an hour south on Belinsky by bus No 26 or minibus Nos 125 and 126 – no fun, and much too far to be convenient.

Places to Stay – top end

Top of Bishkek's line is the *Hotel Dostuk* (☎ 28-42-78, fax 28-44-66) at Frunze 429-Б near Victory Square, with two restaurants, international telecommunications, and comfortable rooms with all the trimmings for US$79/137. The last we heard, they were not accepting credit cards.

Since we were there the gleaming white, apparently Turkish-financed *Ak-Keme Pinara Hotel* (☎ 44-07-84, 62-02-78) has opened in the pines near the old airport – or at least its restaurant has, with a French-trained chef.

Places to Eat

Cafés & Chaykanas A best-bet for budgeteers is *Kafe Fenix* (☎ 26-43-55), with tasty chicken dishes, soup and salads, and fast, cheerful service from 10 am to 8.30 pm daily – eat well for under US$2. It's downstairs beside the Handelshaus gift shop on Soviet near Frunze. A similar 'chicken-house' is the *Kafe Altyn-Kush* at Soviet 137 near Toktogul.

Another cheap *Gril Bar* is beside the Hotel Ak-Say on Ivanitsyn. Next door the friendly, spartan *Kafe Ak-Kuu* serves salads and Kyrgyz dishes, and round the corner on Shopokov is the dreary *Dostuk Mini-Restoran*.

In the apartment block south of the WWII memorial, the *Ak-Bata Café* dresses up its meat and veg with exotic names and interesting sauces, accompanied by too much disco music – fill up for US$3 to US$4. Other café-bars come and go, with laghman, manty or other meaty items for under US$1. One such place is *Kafe Ersay* at Kiev 49 near the post office.

On Pushkin in Dubovy Park, the *Aksakaldar Chaykanasi* (☎ 26-36-40) serves unexceptional Kyrgyz dishes, sit-down or chaykana style. It's open from 8 am to 6 pm, and uncrowded at lunch. At the outdoor chaykana *Jalal-Abad*, at the corner of Kiev and Togolok Moldo, prices are bottom-end and hygiene acceptable if you stick to hot soups, laghman and tea. Next door is a coffee bar in what almost looks like a small mosque.

For a break from laghman, try *Flash Pizza & Burger* (☎ 28-53-94, 28-42-18), with good one-person pizzas for about US$2, plus hamburgers, hot dogs and fries; they also do take-away. They're open daily from 11 am to 4 pm and 5 to 11 pm at Chuy 36, two stops east by any bus from TsUM, to the 'Vostok-Pyat' stop.

The pizza at the *Kafe Almair* is not so authentic (sausage and cold tomato sauce on flat-bread) but the atmosphere is relaxed; that's all you get except for coffee, beer and ice cream. It's on Tynystanov near Kiev.

Kafe Begaim is an ordinary cafeteria, popular and fairly clean, dishing up Russian standards like pelmeny (dumplings), chops, boiled vegetables and soups. Lunch isn't more than US$1, and you could make a cheap breakfast out of their eggs, blinys and coffee. It's on Abdymomunov (Kirova) behind the Fine Arts Museum and is open from 7 am to 2 pm and 3 to 7 pm.

Hotels Service at the *Ala-Too's* restaurant is polite but the food is middling – and overpriced unless you stick to starters like laghman and salad. Eat before 8 pm to beat the loud music.

Food at the *Dostuk* is seriously overpriced, though for a US culture-fix you might like the US$10 burger and beer at the ground-floor *Arizona Restaurant*. At the upstairs restaurant a cockroach strolled out of a friend's salad but she still had to pay for it. The Dostuk's breakfast buffet (7 to 10 am) has succumbed to naked greed, jacking up the price overnight from US$3 to US$14.

Restaurants Upstairs at *Restaurant Son-Köl* (☎ 22-84-14, 22-78-24), Chuy 110 at Erkindik, you can fill up on European food in Russian style – ie all evening with thunderous music – for US$5 plus drinks, if you send those expensive little zakuski back at the outset. On the top floor (if you find it open) are cheaper, blander Kyrgyz dishes. Theoretical hours are 10 am to 11 pm.

The *Flamingo Restaurant* (☎ 21-96-43, 25-72-62) on the east side of the Philharmonia hall offers polite service and oily but tasty Chinese food (by Chinese cooks) and western dishes for about US$10 per person without drinks, with Kyrgyz music in the evenings. It's open daily from 11 am to 11 pm.

One we did not try is the *Seyil* (☎ 26-21-81), serving up Kyrgyz dishes at Erkindik 37. Locals claim the small, popular *Primavera* (☎ 21-17-26), on Belinsky near Toktogul, has good Kyrgyz and European dishes.

Despite the many ethnic Koreans here, there are no cheap Korean restaurants. You might just get by for US$10 at *Restaurant Mi-Na* (☎ 43-24-46), but drinks will jack the bill up. It's in a five storey building by Alamedin Bazar, a long way north-east at Alma-Atinskaya 115 (take east-bound bus No 17 or 37 from TsUM, return by south-bound bus No 48). Expats say the Korean-run portion of the Hotel Issyk-Kul also has a good *Korean restaurant* (☎ 44-89-75) on the 7th floor, open from 8 am to 11 pm.

The *Naryn Restaurant* (☎ 26-56-26), the cavernous place that looks like a theatre and is near the Hotel Dostuk, is geared for lavish banquets, not tourists popping in for a bite.

Restaurants we heard of, but did not check out, include *Tean-Shan* (Chinese; ☎ 24-78-52, 24-71-90) at the corner of Turusbekov and Moscow; *Nooruz* (Turkish and European; ☎ 22-17-44), Moscow 73; and *Mira* (Turkish; ☎ 22-53-30) at the corner of Logvinenko and Moscow. Some cafés we didn't check out are *Bumerang* at the corner of Chapayev and Ayni; *U Mazaya* (rabbit and chicken), Soviet 199; and *Doka-Pizza*, Chuy 168a near Promstroybank.

Self-Catering The mini-bazar on Moskva near Soviet is a great place for do-it-

---

---

yourselfers to pick up dinner around 5 to 6 pm (bring your own bags and containers) – hot bread, manty and piroshki – plus vegies, fruit, beer and sweets. Bishkek also has three farmers' markets (see the Things to Buy section), with abundant fresh vegetables and fruit, including cheap strawberries and raspberries. The snack bar on the ground floor of TsUM has tasty raisin muffins most mornings. Check out the Prestige department store, on Kiev near Togolok Moldo, for occasional supplies of imported foods.

Entertainment

Traditional Music Kyrgyz musical troupes sometimes perform at the Philharmonia (☎ 21-22-62), Chuy 269 at the corner with Belinsky, but you may need a local person to identify these from the playbills. A matinée performance by the Kyrgyz troupe Kambarkan cost the equivalent of about US$0.30.

There are said to be occasional traditional get-togethers at Dom Druzhby (see the Useful Organisations section) at Pushkin 78-2, by Ala-Too Square. Kyrgyzintourist can arrange Kyrgyz, Dungan, Korean and Uyghur folk music performances, but only for groups.

Traditional Games Once upon a time on summer Sundays you might see traditional Kyrgyz horseback games including *udarysh* (horseback wrestling), *ulak-tartysh* (a kind of no-rules polo played with a dead goat) and *kesh-kumay* or 'kiss-the-girl' (in which a man chases a woman on horseback and tries to kiss her, or gets chased and whipped if he fails). The usual venue was the Ippodrom (Hippodrome), south-west of the centre: take trolleybus No 8 on Moskva. But lately the best you can expect around Bishkek are exhibition games in Ala-Too Square during the Navrus festival and on Kyrgyz Independence Day.

Theatre & Concert Halls The Philharmonia (☎ 21-22-62), at the corner of Chuy and Belinsky, features western and Kyrgyz orchestral works and the occasional Kyrgyz song-and-dance troupe. In front of the hall is a statue of the legendary hero Manas slaying a dragon, flanked by his wife Kanykey and his old adviser Bakay, and a statue gallery of modern Kyrgyz akyn.

At the State Opera & Ballet Theatre (☎ 26-48-63), at Soviet 167 opposite the Fine Arts Museum, classical western as well as local productions play to half-empty halls. The State Academic Drama Theatre by Panfilov Park presents Kyrgyz-language works; the Russian Drama Theatre is on Tynystanov in Dubovy Park.

Circus The 'big top' is on Frunze east of Soviet.

Things to Buy

Department Stores The main shopping district, on Soviet between Chuy and Bokonbayev, includes a surprisingly well-stocked TsUM complete with photo shop, photocopying and other services.

Bookshops Bishkek's bookshops have little of interest in English. Akademkniga, at Erkindik 42, also sells minerals, silver, pre-Soviet coins and postcards – or how about a Kim Il Sung bath-mat? Nuska is another bookshop across Erkindik from Akademkniga. The Bukinist shop on Soviet near Moskva includes a joint-venture stationery shop, and a bookshop to the left of it has a photocopier and imported batteries.

Free Markets On warm days the streets are lined with people selling everything from radio parts to Brazilian oranges, but mostly imported booze and cigarettes. An informal mini-bazar has sprung up along Chuy by TsUM. The best place for self-caterers is

A traditonal polo-like game is played on horseback with a headless goat's carcass instead of a ball.

another mini-bazar on Moskva at the corner with Soviet.

The city has three daily farmers' markets, all fairly distant from the centre – Osh bazar three km to the west (bus No 14 on Chuy, bus No 24 on Kiev or bus No 48 from the Hotel Ala-Too), smaller Alamedin bazar to the north-east (bus No 17 or 37 from TsUM, return by south-bound bus No 48) and Ortosay bazar to the south (trolleybus No 12 on Soviet). All are open daily but biggest on weekends. Osh bazar, though not very colourful, offers a glimpse of Kyrgyz and Uzbeks from the conservative south of the republic. Outside the gates is a separate clothes market, and nearby is a store with a wider variety of cheap Kyrgyz souvenirs than TsUM has.

A huge 'flea market' of imported consumer goods and junk, nicknamed Tolchok (meaning 'jostling crowd'), comes to life at 8 am on Saturday and Sunday, about seven km north of the centre. Special 'Tolchok' (Толчок) buses run along Soviet all Saturday and Sunday, from the corner by TsUM. Watch your wallet or bag.

Carpets Carpets and the brightly coloured Kyrgyz felt-appliqué floor coverings called *shyrdaks* are sometimes sold for reasonable commission prices in the lobby of the Museum of Fine Arts (Soviet 196). Overpriced, inferior ones can also be found at Alamedin bazar, and a few at Osh bazar. The best shyrdaks – with clean-cut shapes, deep colours and double stitching – are said to be found in and around Naryn.

Handicrafts Souvenirs in the Museum of Fine Arts shop tend to be pricey. A good place for cheap Kyrgyz knick-knacks, surprisingly, is TsUM. You may find Kyrgyz men's hats – the familiar white felt kalpak or the fur-trimmed *tebbetey* – for sale here or in the bazars.

Getting There & Away

Air Kyrgyzintourist won't book air tickets for individuals. You must go to the booking office at the old, now-defunct airport, 4.5 km

south of town; take the No 153 airport bus or trolleybus No 5 or 14 on Belinsky, to the end of the line. The 'International Sector' (☎ 42-29-22) at right rear is open weekdays from 8 am to 7 pm, weekends to 5 pm. So far, the nearest booking offices for non-CIS airlines are in Almaty.

Kyrgyzstan Airlines flies several times a day to Osh and Jalal-Abad and every few days to other domestic points – spectacular trips by Yak-40, between the mountain tops and the clouds. Regional and CIS connections include Tashkent twice a week, Moscow four times a week, various Siberian destinations once or twice a week, and St Petersburg seasonally. Azerbaijan Airlines flies to/from Baku twice a week. Some Kyrgyzstan Airlines foreigners' fares at the time of research were US$73 to Osh, US$105 to Tashkent and US$250 to Moscow.

The only scheduled link outside the CIS is weekly to Istanbul with Kyrgyzstan Airlines, though there were rumours that Lufthansa was about to start a Frankfurt-Bishkek flight. But it's only three hours by road to Almaty, which has many international flights, and a Kazakstan visa is apparently not necessary if you're going straight to/from the Almaty airport. Lufthansa runs its own Almaty-Bishkek ground shuttle service. Kyrghyz Concept (see Travel Agencies in the Information section) runs a car shuttle to meet international flights at Almaty for an extortionate US$50 plus US$10 per person plus US$5 per bag (you could take a public bus for what they charge just for your bag).

Bus The west (or new) bus station is the place for long-distance buses; get there via bus No 7 on Chuy, bus No 35 from the train station, or trolleybus No 5 on Belinsky. Don't trust the schedule board at the station.

Buses depart hourly to Balykchy and throughout the morning to Karakol (8½ hours) on Lake Issyk-Kul, though the private mini-vans out on the road are quicker and more comfortable. Three buses go to Naryn (nine hours) each morning.

For Osh and the Ferghana Valley you must

change at Toktogul (nine hours); a single bus goes there daily at 7.15 am, along with private vans out on the road. Alternatively, ropey private buses to Osh announce themselves at the train station, departing when they're full or at the end of the day, for about US$20 in *som*. The overnight trip takes 10 to 15 hours depending on road and vehicle – we saw some old wheezers disabled on the Tör-Ashuu pass.

Comfortable Mercedes buses go from west station to Tashkent (via Kazakstan, though no Kazak visa is needed if you don't get off) four times a day for about US$10, taking as little as 10 hours. Buses go directly to Almaty (4½ hours) every hour or two all day, plus hourly all night with a change at Zhambyl.

The east bus station is for regional points east as far as Balykchy. For Ala-Archa (see the Around Bishkek section), go to Osh bazar.

Kashgar Bus A Chinese-run outfit shuttles at least one bus to and fro between Bishkek and Kashgar via the Torugart pass, roughly three or four times a month in summer. When we were there the price for the 1½-day trip to Kashgar was about US$70 per person; you must see to your own visas. The office (☎ 22-36-70) is in a house at Razzakov 7, not far from the railway station, and is open from 9 am to 5 pm.

Train You can try for your own ticket at the station or at the advance booking office (two blocks east at the corner of Lineynaya and Soviet, open daily from 7 am to noon and 1 to 5 pm), or pay Kyrgyzintourist a few dollars to buy it for you. Avoid the touts infesting the station.

Trains start here three times a week for Tashkent (16 hours) and the Ferghana Valley (16 hours farther to Jalal-Abad; change at Kokand for Ferghana). Three trains a week also go to Almaty (16 hours) and Krasnoyarsk in Siberia, and there's a daily express to Moscow (72 hours). Incredibly, we found schedules still using Moscow time,

two hours earlier than Bishkek time, though this seems likely to change.

Car Private cars and taxis to Osh scout for passengers at the railway station, long-distance bus station and Osh bazar – for about US$25 in *som* per person when we were there. Look for OШ number plates, but choose your car and driver with care!

Getting Around

To/From the Airport Minibuses marked MAHAC run between Manas airport and the long-distance bus station, leaving when they're full; catch bus No 35 or 48 between the bus station and the Ala-Too and Bishkek hotels. Allow an hour from hotel to airport.

Alternatively, express bus No 153 runs every 30 minutes all day between Manas airport and the airline booking office (old airport) via the long-distance bus station, but the closest it gets to the centre is the Philharmonia.

A taxi between the airport and the centre should be about US$10 with baggage, more at night or on weekends. See Getting There & Away about getting to Almaty airport.

Bus Municipal buses are about US$0.10 in *som*, payable as you disembark at the *front*. At rush hour these are so crammed that you must plan your escape several stops ahead. Old school-bus shaped marshrutnoe (jitney) buses ply some routes for a slightly higher fare.

Car Most agencies listed in the Travel Agencies section can arrange a car and driver for about US$100 per day plus petrol costs, though the latter depends on the vehicle and on the daily lurches of the fuel market.

Taxi These are scarce; try the railway station, long-distance bus station or Hotel Dostuk. You should be able to cross town (eg Osh bazar to TsUM) for about US$2, perhaps more at night. Official taxis, with ФИА or БИА number plates, are cheapest and most reliable. You can book a taxi 24 hours a day at ☎ 002, for a surcharge of about US$2.

KYRGYZSTAN

AROUND BISHKEK

Rolling out of the Kyrgyz Alatau, the Ala-Archa, Alamedin and dozens of parallel streams have created a phalanx of high canyons, good for everything from picnics to mountaineering. Some highlights are noted here. Dan Prior's *Bishkek Handbook* (see the Bishkek Information section), with exceptional detail on these canyons plus historical sites in the Chuy valley, is essential reading for those who want to linger.

There are plenty of possible do-it-yourself summer treks, but bring your own food and gear, and be prepared for cold weather and storms even in summer. There is limited public transport, though travel agencies listed in the Bishkek Information section can provide transport and arrange guided trips. Winter excursions are best arranged through an agency, who should know about avalanche and other risks. A recommended reference for treks here is Frith Maier's *Trekking in Russia & Central Asia*.

Ala-Archa Canyon

In this very grand, rugged but accessible gorge south of Bishkek, you can sit by a waterfall all day, hike to a glacier (and ski on it, even in summer) or trek into the region's highest peaks. Most of the canyon is part of a state nature park, and foreigners must pay an entrance fee of US$5 per car plus US$2 per person in summer, US$1 at other times.

Orientation The park gate is 30 km from central Bishkek. Some 12 km beyond the gate, at 2150 metres, the sealed road ends at a shabby base camp or *alplager* with a weather station and a simple hotel (a bigger complex burned down a few years ago). In summer it has recreational facilities, baths and sauna. Beyond this point the only transport is by foot or 4WD.

The Kyrgyz Cartographic Agency (see the Bishkek Information section) sells a good 1:50,000 topographic map of the entire park, called *Prirodnyy Park Ala-Archa*.

Walks & Treks There are dozens of possibilities, but three main options. The gentlest walk runs 300 metres back down-valley from the alplager, then across a footbridge and south-west up the Adygene valley. Along this way is a climbers' cemetery in a larch grove, a pretty and poignant scene. The track continues for about seven km to 3300 metres, below Adygene glacier.

The most popular trek goes straight up the main canyon on a poor jeep track, about 18 km to the Upper Ala-Archa Mountain Ski Base. From there in July and August a two km long ski lift climbs between glaciers to a 3900 metre ridge (other lifts also run during the winter ski season, December through April).

Most demanding and dramatic is Ak-Say canyon, with access via Ak-Say glacier to the area's highest peaks. A trail climbs steeply to the east immediately above the alplager, continuing high above the stream. It's four to five hours up and three to four hours back, just for a view of the glacier. In a grassy meadow en route you may see marmots, chukars, eagles, even ibex. There is a coarse shelter half an hour above the alplager, a stone hut at the base of the icefall at 3350 metres (with a backpackers' tent city in summer) and a steel hut beside the glacier at 4150 metres (this one accessible only with some glacier walking). Serious climbing routes continue up to 4500 metres and beyond.

The trekking season around Ala-Archa is May through September or October.

Places to Stay & Eat The best way to enjoy Ala-Archa is by bringing your own tent and sleeping bag. The only year-round accommodation is a wooden hotel in the alplager, with a dozen spartan doubles with common toilet and no shower for US$2.50 per person. There may be some food available in summer, but it would be wise to bring your own and cook it in the kitchen. In summer there are more spaces at the alplager.

Getting There & Away Bishkek travel agencies can arrange day and longer trips with guides and gear. Alternatively you could just hire a car out and back, or even try the ropey local buses.

Bus From Osh bazar in Bishkek, catch clapped-out arenda bus No 160 or 169 as far as Kashka-Suu village, seven km from the park gate, and hitch from there. There is also said to be a No 177 bus from Osh bazar right to the gate, at least in summer. Ask *'vorota zapovednika?'* ('nature park gate?') when you board. No public buses go beyond the gate, and you may not always find one there to take you back to Bishkek.

Also from Bishkek, on Moskva westbound No 11 buses go about 12 km south to the end of the line near the city limits, from where you can hire a taxi or hitch (ask for 'alplager', not just 'Ala-Archa').

Car From the Hotel Issyk-Kul it's about 2.5 km south to the No 11 bus terminus. Seven km further, turn left towards Ala-Archa, but look off to the right for a view of the Great Wall of China – a wood and plaster mock-up for an Italian-Kyrgyz TV film about Jenghiz Khan. From here it's 11 km to the park gate. If you hire a car to drop you off, be sure your return arrangements are understood!

Other Canyons

Several valleys east of Ala-Archa have good walks and fewer visitors. In next-door **Alamedin canyon**, 40 km from Bishkek, the main destination for local people is an old sanatorium called **Tyoplye Klyuchi** (Hot Springs) run by the Ministry of Power, with cheap accommodation and food. Though unprotected by a national park, the scenery above and beyond this is as grand and walkable as Ala-Archa's, but there are no other facilities.

On your own, take arenda bus No 145 from Alamedin bazar in Bishkek, get off at Koy-Tash village and hitch the 14 km to the gate. Buses are said to depart frequently throughout the day in summer.

Another thermal-spring complex and guesthouse is about 45 km eat of Bishkek in **Issyk-Ata canyon**. A single afternoon bus goes there from Bishkek's east bus station, returning the next morning.

Kyrgyzintourist takes hiking or horse-back-riding groups to a lake and waterfalls in **Kegeti canyon**, 70 km east of Bishkek.

Burana Tower

Beyond Kegeti at the mouth of the Shamshin valley, 80 km from Bishkek, is a sterile but thorough Soviet restoration of the so-called Burana Tower, an 11th century monument that looks like the stump of a huge minaret. A mound nearby is all that's left of the ancient citadel which Dan Prior records as Balasaghun, founded by the Sogdians and later a capital of the Qarakhans, which was excavated in the 1970s by Russian archaeologists. The Shamshin valley itself has yielded a rich hoard of Scythian treasure, including a heavy gold burial mask, all either spirited away to St Petersburg or in storage in the Bishkek History Museum.

To get to Burana on your own, take a bus from Bishkek's east bus station to Tokmak, from where it's about 15 km by taxi.

Chong-Tash

Along a 16 km dirt road linking Kashka-Suu village in Ala-Archa valley with Koy-Tash village in Alamedin valley is a historical spot well worth visiting if you're in a car. About nine km from Kashka-Suu turn south to a small local sanitorium, situated at what was, until at least the 1950s, a KGB 'facility'.

On one night in 1937, the entire Soviet Kyrgyz government – nearly 140 people in all – were rounded up, brought here and shot dead, and their bodies dumped in a disused brick kiln on the site. Apparently almost no-one alive by the 1980s knew of this, by which time the site had been converted to a ski resort. But a watchman at the time of the murders, sworn to secrecy, told his daughter on his deathbed, and she waited until perestroyka to tell police.

In 1991 the bodies were moved to a mass grave across the road, with a simple memorial apparently paid for by the Kyrgyz author Chinghiz Aitmatov (whose father may have been one of the victims). The remains of the kiln are inside a fence nearby.

Lake Issyk-Kul & the Central Tian Shan
Ысык-Көл & Центральньч Тянь-шань

Lake Issyk-Kul is basically a huge dent, filled with water, in the Alatau ranges that form the northern arm of the Tian Shan. The name (we use the more familiar spelling of what is properly Ysyk-Köl from the Kyrgyz) means 'warm lake'. A combination of extreme depth, thermal activity and mild salinity means the lake never freezes; its moderating effect on the climate, plus abundant rainfall, have made it something of an oasis down through the centuries.

Tsarist military officers and explorers put the lake on Russian maps. Immigrants flooded in to found low-rise, laid-back, rough-and-ready towns. Health spas lined its shores in Soviet days, with guests from all over the USSR, and in the mid-1980s it was hard to get a seat on a bus or a room in a hotel in summer. Although spa tourism has crashed thanks to the former USSR's general economic collapse and Kyrgyzstan's official disdain for the rouble, you can still find a few comfortable old places open.

The part of the Central Tian Shan range accessible from the lake comprises perhaps the finest trekking territory in Central Asia. Issyk-Kul's main town is no longer the spa centre of Cholpon-Ata but the provincial headquarters town of Karakol at the east end of the lake, at the feet of the mountains.

Give yourself at least four or five days to take in this region. A week is better, more if you'll be hiking.

History

The Kyrgyz people migrated in the 10th to 15th centuries from the Yenisey river basin in Siberia, and in all probability arrived by way of Issyk-Kul. This high basin would be a natural stopover for any caravan or conquering army as well. It appears to have been a centre of Scythian civilisation, and legend has it that Timur used it for a summer headquarters (see the Karkara Valley section).

The first Russian, Ukrainian and Belarussian settlers came to the east end of the lake in 1868. Karakol town was founded in the next year, followed in the 1870s by Tüp, Teploklyuchenka, Ananyevo, Pokrovka (now Kyzyl-Suu) and a string of others, many of whose Cossack names have stuck. Large numbers of Dungans and Uyghurs arrived at Issyk-Kul in the 1870s and 1880s following the suppression of Muslim uprisings in China's Shaanxi, Gansu and Xinjiang provinces. Local Kyrgyz and Kazaks were still at that time mostly nomadic.

The Issyk-Kul region (and in fact most of Kyrgyzstan beyond Bishkek) was off-limits to foreigners in Soviet times. Locals mention vast, officially sanctioned plantations of opium poppies and cannabis around the lake, though most of these had disappeared under international pressure by the early 1970s (Kyrgyzstan narcotics squads still swoop on isolated plots in the mountains).

More importantly, Issyk-Kul was used by the Soviet Navy to test high-precision torpedoes, far from prying western eyes. An entire polygon or military research complex grew around Koy-Sary, on the Mikhaylovka inlet near Karakol. In 1991 Russian President Boris Yeltsin asked that it be continued but Kyrgyzstan's President Askar Akaev shut down the whole thing, ordering it converted to peaceful pursuits. Little conversion has taken place, though the old facilities have been closed down. Akaev did agree to try and limit western access, but with little success; local tour operators now routinely take visitors camping in the area. Jokes about the 'Kyrgyz Navy' refer to a fleet of some 40 ageing naval cutters, now mothballed at Koy-Sary or decommissioned and hauling goods and tourists up and down the lake.

Geography

Issyk-Kul, 170 km long and 70 km across, is said to be the world's second-largest (in area) alpine lake, after Lake Titicaca in South America. It sits 1600 metres above sea level and presently about 695 metres deep at its deepest, folded between the Küngey Alatau to the north and the Terskey Alatau to the south. Both ranges rise straightaway to over 4000 metres.

The north side is shallow, with flat, sandy shores, while the south side is steep, stoney and deep. The land around the west end is dry and barren, while the east end is well-watered by air masses that collect moisture from the lake and then rise into the mountains. Most of the population and agriculture, and all the decent roads, are along the north shore. Old poplars and apricot trees line the roads around much of the lake, with an increasing number of gaps where desperate locals have recently felled trees for firewood.

Scores of streams enter the lake along its 600 km shoreline, but there is no outflow – at least there has been none for some centuries – and consequently the lake is slightly salty. This plus the physics of deep water, and some underground thermal activity, mean that it never freezes, though in January it drops to 4° or 5°C. In June it's still only about 15° to 16°C. The warmest it gets – 18° to 20°C (and even warmer in the shallows on the north side where most lakeshore spas are) – is from July through October.

Some people say the lake level has periodically risen and fallen over the centuries, inundating ancient shoreline settlements. There has been some fluctuation but the geological evidence points to a long-term drop – eg some two metres in the last 500 years. Nobody is sure why, although the interruption of inflowing streams for irrigation may play a part. Artefacts have been recovered from under shallow water at the east end, but this appears to be the result of seismic events. Mikhaylovka inlet near Karakol was apparently created by an earthquake, and the remains of a partly submerged village can be seen there.

Flora & Fauna

Trout as big as 35 kg have allegedly been caught in Issyk-Kul (introduced from Lake Sevan in Armenia decades ago, they have flourished without natural predators), and trout and carp are caught commercially by a small fleet based at Balykchy.

Mountain wildlife includes big cats, ibex and other mountain goats, Marco Polo sheep, bear, wild boar, marmots, badgers, weasels and otters; raptors from sparrow hawks to vultures and eagles, as well as wild geese, ducks, egrets and other waders, pheasant, partridge and wild turkey. A serious poaching problem exists, thanks to western hunters yearning to bag a snow leopard.

The provincial government has shown a refreshing interest in the lake's unique ecosystem. Limits have been set on near-shore fertiliser use, waste disposal, car traffic and camping, and on motorboats on the lake. A squad of 'eco-police' (Special Environmental Police, ☎ (31922) 4-11-43 in Karakol) attempt to enforce the rules, funded by fines for transgressors and a tax levied on visitors.

People

Slavs and Kyrgyz live in roughly equal numbers in the lake's major towns. Though Slavs we met tended to resent the gradual loss of official authority to Kyrgyz, there is little or no obvious racial tension here. There are low-profile Uyghur and Dungan communities (eg 3% and 1% repectively in Karakol), and a few Koreans.

When to Go

Around the north and east shores, springtime buds appear in April-May, though nights can still be below freezing. Mid-May to mid-June is pleasant but sometimes stormy, and streams are in flood. August is the hottest month (days 25° to 30°C). Overall, the lake is best for scenery and weather in September, with some rain and occasional freezing nights in October. Snow appears from mid-November through March. December through January are the coldest months (daytime temperatures range from -3° to -8°C and nights from -15°C, and even colder temperatures on the south shore).

Of course in the mountains the 'warm' season is shorter. The best time is July-August, although camping and trekking are pleasant from early June through mid-

October. Avalanche danger is greatest in March through April and from September to mid-October. Winter brings ferocious cold in the mountains.

You can get sunburned easily in the warm months, even at the elevation of the lake.

Except for year-round operations as noted, most sanatoria open from June through October.

Orientation

There are no decent town maps available anywhere. For useful trekking maps, stop first at the Kyrgyz Cartographic Agency in Bishkek (see the Bishkek Information section).

Information

Tourist Offices Tourism in the Issyk-Kul region is mostly in the hands of enterprising local officials and 'providers', who have pulled together the Karakol Tourism Association (see the Karakol Information section).

Independent of the moribund state tourism machinery, they aim to be a clearinghouse for reliable information and help, at fair prices and in keeping with the preservation of the region's delicate ecosystem.

Visas Issyk-Kul remains a special military zone, and the higher reaches of the central Tian Shan are in a still-sensitive border zone. Police and other officials may want to see a Kyrgyzstan visa and registration stamp (see the Visas & Embassies section in the Facts for the Visitor chapter). You're unlikely to get any help here with visas or extensions; better to arrive with your papers in order.

Money There's a foreign-exchange bank in Karakol, and moneychangers lurk around bus stations and elsewhere in larger towns.

Dangers & Annoyances A few trekkers across the Alatau to/from Almaty (see the Zailiysky Alatau & Küngey Alatau section,

in the Kazakstan chapter) have been robbed, and there is some risk on any low-traffic, long-distance trekking route here. The 'bandits' are usually dirt-poor chaban (cowboys; Russian: skotovod)). There are also a few 'state bandits' – collective-farm managers who invent fees for crossing or camping on their land.

The well-travelled and popular routes around Altyn Arashan and Ala-Köl (see Trekking Around Issyk-Kul in this section) are safe for do-it-yourselfers. Elsewhere it's probably best to go with a guide who knows the place.

Places to Stay

Locals and Bishkek expats say the pleasantest, cheapest (and still safe) way to bunk down at Issyk-Kul in summer is in a private home. Locals approach visitors at bus stations, offering rooms, flats or entire homes (with the owner and family in another part or nearby). Most are totally honest, especially

the older women. Prices are cheap, from US$3 to US$10 per person per day, usually including a meal or two. You could even go round knocking on doors yourself. Cholpon-Ata also has several apartment bureaux.

Issyk-Kul's health resorts now seem a dying breed, although they still fill up with Bishkekers and local tourists in the hot months. Of at least 115 shoreline sanatoria before 1991, only a handful (mostly around Cholpon-Ata) remain open; best known is the immense *Issyk-Kul Sanatorium* near Cholpon-Ata. All prefer long-term (two or three week) guests, but they can't afford to be fussy now. Room rates usually include three small meals, plus the use of whatever pools or beaches they have. Prices tend to be excessive, especially for foreigners, but they are very seasonal, and bargaining is in order.

Among other survivors are four gently decaying spas *away* from the shore, built around natural hot springs – at Kurort Jergalan, Teploklyuchenka, Jeti-Öghüz and

KYRGYZSTAN

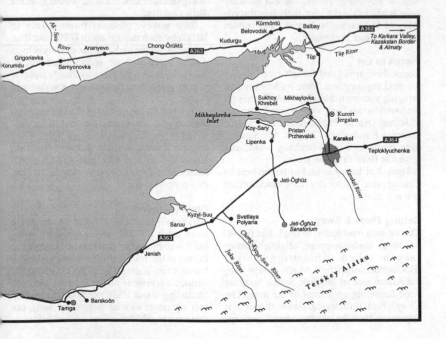

Tamga – where the attractions include cheap beds, hot mineral baths and brisk walks in the hills.

With the exception of one in Karakol, ordinary hotels are pretty plain, many without even hot water (in which case ask about the local banya, where there's likely to be plenty). A *turbaza* is a tourist complex, open in summer with spartan cabins, plain food, sports, a video hall, bar etc, and usually access on foot into the mountains. A *dom otdykha* (rest house) is a similar place for older folks – essentially a sanatorium without the in-house medical staff – for US$15 to US$20 per person per night. There were once many of these, but only a few are still in business now.

If you're camping, some sanatoria may let you pitch your tent on their grounds or beach, and use their facilities for a small fee. Camping in the open is apparently pretty safe, but regulations prohibit cars and camping within 200 metres of the shore, as well as anywhere around the old military zone at Mikhaylovka inlet, including the villages of Mikhaylovka, Lipenka and certain parts of Pristan Przhevalsk.

Places to Eat

Karakol bazar is good for self-catering and for trekking supplies. Some readers suggest bringing your own dried foods along, though we found bazars fairly well-stocked even out of season (April). Public eateries are scarce except in Karakol and Cholpon-Ata. Sanatorium meals tend to be healthily small, and served at fixed times only.

Issyk-Kul honey is said to be the best in Central Asia, and locally made blackcurrant jam is a treat.

Getting There & Away

The western road access to Issyk-Kul is a 40 km long, landslide-prone, slightly sinister canyon called 'Shoestring Gorge' (Boömskoe ushchelie), which climbs into the Alatau east of Tokmak, with a howling wind funneling up it most of the time. The Chuy river thundering down through it appears to drain the lake but doesn't (perhaps

it once did, when the lake was higher). The canyon has several police checkpoints (it's on the main Bishkek-Naryn road), and at one just west of Balykchy an 'eco-tax' is collected from each inbound vehicle from outside Issyk-Kul and Naryn provinces – 50 S per car, 100 S per bus or truck, but US$5/10 or more for those owned by foreigners.

There are scheduled bus services from Bishkek's long-distance bus station, as well as arenda buses and fast minibuses that wait in front of the station in the morning. Karakol, for example, takes six hours for about US$7. Minibus drivers may be willing to take newcomers to specific destinations in Karakol for an extra US$0.50 or so. You can also hire a staggeringly overpriced car through Kyrghyzintourist in Bishkek.

Karakol is closer to Almaty (330 km) than it is to Bishkek (about 400 km) but there are no scheduled buses on the beautiful but steep and twisting route round the east end of the Küngey Alatau to/from Almaty. For ideas on doing this area a bit at a time, see the Karkara Valley section.

Two pokey, pleasant trains climb to Balykchy each day for about US$2, but then you must get through and out of Balykchy, a dismal place with no redeeming features. Balykchy is also the place to change buses if you're going directly between Karakol and Naryn.

You can fly to/from Issyk-Kul too, though these flights are among the first to be cancelled when fuel supplies get tight. They include Karakol-Almaty, Karakol-Bishkek, Karakol-Osh and Cholpon-Ata-Osh. All routes have flights twice weekly in 20 seat, two-prop Yak-40s.

Getting Around

Balykchy-Karakol is 216 km on the north shore road; it's 220 km via the south shore but this route takes much longer. Hiring a car or taxi at the lake is pricier than in Bishkek because fuel is dearer here. We note rates for various excursions at the time of research (including about US$6 per hour charged by tour operators to wait around for you), but these are highly dependent on fuel prices.

Transport in larger towns may include a few clapped-out buses, taxis or even horse-drawn carts. You can hire boats at Cholpon-Ata and Pristan Przhevalsk.

BALYKCHY
БАЛЫКЧЫ

There is no good reason to stop in this depressing industrial town (with probably more leftover Lenin statues per square km than anywhere else in Central Asia) except to change buses between Karakol and Naryn, or to change from train to bus en route between Bishkek and Karakol.

The old Soviet name was Rybache (derived from *ryba*, fish), and it was called Issyk-Kul for a spell after independence. You may find either name on old maps.

Orientation & Information

Ulitsa Frunze is the through road. The bus station is about one km north-east of the train station. To get there from the train station, walk east on Ozyornaya ulitsa, take the first left, then left again (north-west) on ulitsa Frunze. Balykchy's telephone code is 232.

Places to Stay & Eat

The only obvious choice is the ticky-tacky *Hotel Ak-Kuu* (☎ 2-55-59), also called the 'Chinese hotel' (Russian *Kitayskaya gostinitsa*), amongst apartment blocks north of the centre, three or four km from the train station. Plain singles/doubles with toilet (but no shower at lower prices) are US$12/24 and up, but there is a US$1 sauna. There's a small bufet but no restaurant, and nothing in the neighbourhood. From the train station, go east on ulitsa Ozyornaya, take the first left, then go right on ulitsa Frunze for about 1.5 km to ulitsa Gagarin (a boulevard). Go left there for three blocks to ulitsa 40-let Kirgizii, turn right and take the first left for 1½ blocks to the hotel. Both train stations have dubious snack shops.

Getting There & Away

Bus Numerous minibuses go daily to/from Bishkek's long-distance bus station for about US$3. Scheduled buses run about every half-

hour to either Bishkek or Karakol for about US$1, and twice a day to Naryn.

Train To/from Bishkek is a 4½ hour trip for about US$2. Trains depart daily from Bishkek at 6.35 am and 3.40 pm, from Balykchy at 6.30 am and 3.05 pm (local time), though schedules are subject to change.

CHOLPON-ATA & AROUND
ЧОЛПОН-АТА

Cholpon-Ata is no longer worth a stop for its sanatoria, but it does have some very old rock inscriptions, and a boatyard where you can hire a boat for a day trip on the lake. East of the centre is a huge hippodrome where Kyrgyzstan's best horses raced in Issyk-Kul's better days.

Orientation & Information

The town has two reference points – one the bus station and adjacent main bazar, and the other a mini-bazar about two km eastward on the main road. At a crook in the main road right between them is what looks like the town centre. Cholpon-Ata's telephone code is 243. The small airstrip is 1.5 km west of the bus station, then about one km up the hill away from the lake.

Boatyard

About 600 metres west of the bus station is a turn-off south to a bulge of shoreline. One km down this road is a tiny boatyard, Cholpon-Ata's 'yacht club' and town pier, with a handful of sailboats and launches under repair or restoration. From here you can hire a former naval cutter or a sailboat that sleeps four, at US$2 for the first hour and US$1.50 per hour after that. Nearby you can hire sailboats or aqualungs. South of the yard is a small, clean beach with shallow, warm water.

Petroglyphs

Above the town is a huge field of stones, many with pictures scratched or picked into their south-facing surfaces. They apparently date from about 500 BC to the 1st century

AD, and were probably made by Scythian (Saka) people, predating the arrival of the Kyrgyz in the area. Most are of long-horned ibex, along with some wolves, deer and hunters, and some rocks appear to be arranged in patterns. The stones with petroglyphs are those with green inventory numbers painted on them (which unfortunately takes away a bit of the mystique).

Take the road opposite the boatyard turnoff north for 2.2 km, keeping to the asphalted part, to a section of black iron fence. The stones are behind this.

Places to Stay & Eat

There are *kvartirnoe byuro* (apartment bureaux) at the main bazar and the minibazar (the latter with a shifty-looking exchange desk) where you can rent a flat, although you may have no trouble running into eager flat-owners on the street.

There is one tired *hotel* in the centre, above the *Kafe Jyldyz*, though we found

neither open. A boring state-run restaurant next door, the *Restaurant Cholpon-Ata*, has seen better days. About 300 metres westward are a *stolovaya* (canteen) and a *teahouse*. *Stands* along the main road sell apples, dried fish or beer.

For a few dollars in *som* you can pitch your tent in the claustrophobic *boatyard* or sleep on a rusty old clanger too old to go to sea. Staff there can also fix you up with a house in town, with meals. An unmarked house near the yard is said to run a good *café* in summer.

Beyond the boatyard are two dom otdykha, the *Ala-Too* and *Energetik* (neither of them looking very 'energetik'), probably about US$10 to US$15 per person in summer.

Sanatoria Along the shore on both sides of Cholpon-Ata is Issyk-Kul's largest concentration of old sanatoria. By far the most famous is the year-round *Issyk-Kul Sanato-*

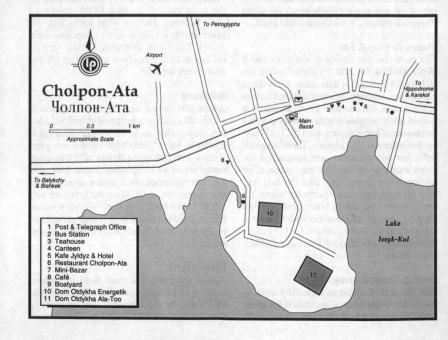

1	Post & Telegraph Office
2	Bus Station
3	Teahouse
4	Canteen
5	Kafe Jyldyz & Hotel
6	Restaurant Cholpon-Ata
7	Mini-Bazar
8	Café
9	Boatyard
10	Dom Otdykha Energetik
11	Dom Otdykha Ala-Too

Cholpon-Ata
Чолпон-Ата

0   0.5   1 km
Approximate Scale

To Petroglyphs
Airport
To Balykchy & Bishkek
To Hippodrome & Karakol
Main Bazar
Lake Issyk-Kul

rium (☎ 4-48-70, 9-53-89), a Soviet monstrosity so big that from the road it obscures half the lake, and nicknamed 'Avrora' (Aurora) after the cruiser of Revolutionary fame in St Petersburg. Rates for a single/double range from US$30/50 out of season (December to April) to US$65/110 and up per person at peak season (July through August), plus a US$5 booking charge – for which you also get three modest meals and the chance to wander idly around 47 hectares of woods, sculpted gardens and a private beach. It's 20 km east of Cholpon-Ata between the hamlets of Bosteri and Korumdu.

Other, cheaper giants include the *Pansiyonat Stroitel* just east of the centre of Cholpon-Ata, and the year-round *Kirgizskoe Vzamorie* at Bosteri, both probably US$20 to US$30 per person in summer.

Getting There & Away

Most bus connections are on through buses between Karakol and Balykchy or Bishkek. When we visited, there were two flights a week to/from Osh, for about US$90.

SEMYONOVKA & ANANYEVO
СЕМЁНОВКА & АНАНЬЕВО

Semyonovka, 42 km east of Cholpon-Ata, is little but a bus stand and a few shops, but above here is the best local access to treks across the Alatau to/from Almaty (see The Zailiysky Alatau & Küngey Alatau, and Köl-Say Lakes, in the Kazakstan chapter). A road runs for about 15 km into the mountains, becoming a jeep track after that. Up this road there was once a good trekking base, the *Turbaza Kyrchyn*, where you could get help and hire a guide, but for now at least, it's closed.

At Ananyevo, 10 km further east, is the Issyk-Kul state nature reserve (Issyk-Kulskiy gosudarstvennyy zapovednik), founded in 1948 and home to pheasants and shore birds. It's three km south of the main road. Ananyevo's other attraction is some cheap, peaceful accommodation.

Places to Stay & Eat

There's a small family-style turbaza in the middle of the reserve, but a better deal is in the adjacent townlet, called Turgorodok, where the reserve's staff live. Two private houses (☎ (31942) 6-27-66 from Bishkek or ☎ (243) 6-27-66 from Karakol) have been converted to secure accommodation for independent travellers. A bed (one of 10 in plain doubles with common toilet and hot shower) and three square meals is about US$10; there's also a sauna for an extra charge. Lyudmila Mirozhnichenko, the friendly *khozyayka* (landlady), can also arrange excursions, transport and horse trips into the hills, though she speaks little English. Take the road south towards the nature reserve, turn right one km along, then left after 200 metres, and call at the third house on the right.

There is a small bazar on the corner of the main road and the road to the reserve, a café in the bazar and a restaurant just outside.

Getting There & Away

Bishkek-Karakol buses call at the bazar. There is also one direct Ananyevo-Bishkek bus each morning, plus arenda buses.

AROUND BELOVODSK
ОКОЛО БЕЛОВОДСКА

Large mounds on both sides of the road just west of the village of **Belovodsk** (50 km east of Ananyevo or 15 km west of Tüp) are said to be unexcavated Scythian (Saka) burial chambers. Other mounds excavated near Barskoön, across the lake, yielded bronze vessels and jewellery (now in museums in St Petersburg). There are more in the Karkara valley just across the Kazak border. One near the town of Yessik in Kazakstan yielded a fabulous golden warrior's costume, now Kazakstan's greatest archaeological treasure (see the Golden Man aside in the Almaty section of the Kazakstan chapter).

At Belovodsk is a turn-off south to the hamlet of **Svetyy Mys**, which at least one Soviet archaeologist insisted was the site of a 4th or 5th century Armenian Christian

KYRGYZSTAN

monastery. The story goes that its inhabitants were driven out by surrounding tribes, but not before hiding a huge cache of gold that has never been found. From the hills above, the village roads can be seen to trace something approximating an Orthodox cross.

From **Balbay** village (also called Sary-Bulak) it's about five hours walk north across the Kazakstan border to the pretty Köl-Say lakes, east of Almaty (see the Köl-Say Lakes section in the Kazakstan chapter).

KARAKOL
КАРАКОЛ
Population: 80,000

Karakol (or Kara-Kol; Przhevalsk in Soviet times) is a peaceful, low-rise town with back streets full of Russian gingerbread cottages, shaded by rows of huge white poplars. Around the town are apple orchards for which the area is famous. This is the administrative centre of Issyk-Kul province, and the best base for exploring the lakeshore, the Terskey Alatau and the central Tian Shan. It also has a very good Sunday market.

It's not quite paradise for those who live here – the economic stresses of independence and the decline in spa tourism have led to considerable hardship, thinned out available goods and services, and returned a kind of frontier atmosphere to this old boundary post – but hardly anybody talks about leaving. For better or worse, Karakol looks like headquarters for a new wave of tourism, from overseas.

The name means something like 'black hand/wrist', possibly a reference to the hands of immigrant Russian peasants, black from the valley's rich soil. Karakol is not to be confused with dismal Kara-Köl on the Bishkek-Osh road.

History
After a military garrison was established at nearby Teploklyuchenka in 1864, and it dawned on everybody what a fine spot it was – mild climate, rich soil, a lake full of fish and mountains full of hot springs – the garrison commander was told to scout out a place for a full-size town. Karakol was founded on 1 July 1869, with streets laid out in a European-style checkerboard, and the garrison was relocated here. The town's early population had a high proportion of military officers, merchants, professionals and explorers.

It was called Przhevalsk in Soviet times, after the explorer Nikolai Przhevalsky, whose last expedition ended here, and who is buried on the lakeshore nearby (see the Przhevalsk aside in the Around Karakol section). It didn't escape a trashing by the Bolsheviks: its elegant Orthodox church lost its domes and became a club; only one small church on the outskirts was allowed to remain open. Of nine mosques (founded by Tatars, Dungans and various Kyrgyz clans), all but the Dungan one were wrecked.

Orientation
Karakol has a central square, but the real centre is a small plaza and shop complex nearby, nicknamed *gostinny dvor* (the Russian equivalent of a caravanserai or merchants' inn, after its namesake in St Petersburg), built in the 1870s. The long-distance bus station is about two km to the north, and the small airport is right at the north-eastern edge of town.

Russian street names are still in common use in spite of many official changes to Kyrgyz names, and we use the Russian ones here.

Information
Tourist Offices The Karakol Tourism Association (☎ & fax 2-37-98, e-mail info@ tour.karakol.su, director Yuri Morgachev) is not a state tourism bureau but a fledgling cooperative effort by Karakol's municipal tourism department and local agencies to provide reliable information on services and destinations for individuals as well as group tourists. They're on the ground floor of the city administration building at Kalinina 120 (postal code 722360) on the corner with Gagarina.

Registration & Permits OVIR is on

Leninskogo Komsomola, at the corner with Kommunisticheskaya.

To go up into the Tian Shan past Inylchek town, eg towards Inylchek glacier or Khan-Tengri (see the Central Tian Shan section), you need a permit *(propusk)* from the permit station (Kontrolno-propusknoy punkt, KPP) of the Russian border detachment (Rossiya pogranichnye voyska) stationed at the Army base here (at the site of Karakol's original garrison).

It takes less time than it does to say their name, but you must have a letter with the stamp of a recognised travel agency in Karakol, Bishkek or Almaty, a list of everyone in your party, and your itinerary. A local agency can arrange it easily. Go to the base gate, on a No 1 bus from the centre.

Money A bank with a foreign exchange office is on Toktogula near Kalinina, and there's talk of opening an exchange desk in the Hotel Karakol.

Post & Communications The post and telegraph office is on Kalinina opposite the square. Karakol's telephone code is 31922.

The KRD Tien Shan agency, operating

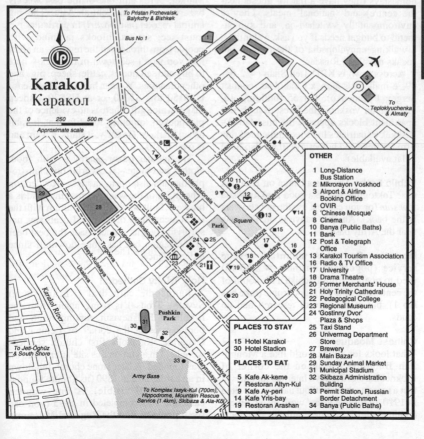

Karakol
Каракол

0   250   500 m
Approximate scale

To Pristan Przhevalsk,
Balykchy & Bishkek

Bus No 1

To Teploklyuchenka
& Almaty

To Jeti-Öghüz
& South Shore

Karakol River

Pushkin
Park

Park

Square

Army Base

To Kompleks Issyk-Kul (700m),
Hippodrome, Mountain Rescue
Service (1 4km), Skibaza & Ala-Köl

OTHER
1 Long-Distance
   Bus Station
2 Mikrorayon Voskhod
3 Airport & Airline
   Booking Office
4 OVIR
6 'Chinese Mosque'
7 Banya (Public Baths)
8 Cinema
10 Banya (Public Baths)
11 Bank
12 Post & Telegraph
   Office
13 Karakol Tourism Association
16 Radio & TV Office
17 University
18 Drama Theatre
20 Former Merchants' House
21 Holy Trinity Cathedral
22 Pedagogical College
23 Regional Museum
24 'Gostinny Dvor'
   Plaza & Shops
25 Taxi Stand
26 Univermag Department
   Store
27 Brewery
28 Main Bazar
29 Sunday Animal Market
31 Municipal Stadium
32 Skibaza Administration
   Building
33 Permit Station, Russian
   Border Detachment
34 Banya (Public Baths)

PLACES TO STAY
15 Hotel Karakol
30 Hotel Stadion

PLACES TO EAT
5 Kafe Ak-keme
7 Restoran Altyn-Kul
9 Kafe Ay-peri
14 Kafe Yris-bay
19 Restoran Arashan

under the name GlobalX (☎ & fax 2-64-89, e-mail psi@glob_x.karakol.su), offers limited e-mail services (see also the Travel Agencies section).

Travel Agencies There are two outfits in town. The veteran of the two is Karakol (contact Valentin or Galina Derevyanko), with offices in summer at the Hotel Karakol (☎ 2-79-79) and year-round at home (☎ 2-23-68, fax 2-30-36), Novorossiskaya 8, Karakol 722360. In addition to group tours they'll do on-the-spot arrangements for individuals, including treks, horse treks and other sports, transport and equipment rental, homestays (they have a flat for guests near the centre) and 'national' meals. They're environmentally switched-on, and sympathetic to budget needs if you ask. Valentin is a walking encyclopedia of the region, but speaks mostly in Russian.

Across town is KRD Tien Shan (☎ 2-64-89, e-mail psi@glob_x.karakol.su, contact Sergey Pyshnenko), flat 55, building 10, mikrorayon Voskhod (the forest of high-rise apartment blocks opposite the bus station). Bishkek expatriates have recommended this firm for treks and homestays (they also have a flat available).

Public Baths There is a banya on Kalinina near Toktogula, where a good soak is just a few *som* (or you can just use the hot showers at the back). Another banya is on Telmana near the Army base.

Mountain Rescue A mountain rescue service (pogornaya sluzhba; ☎ 2-30-15) used to operate from Fuchika 119, south of the centre opposite the hippodrome (take bus No 1), but at the time of research had no funds.

Chinese Mosque

What looks for all the world like a Mongolian Buddhist datsan on the corner of Libknekhta and Tretievo Internatsionala is in fact a mosque, built without nails, completed in 1910 after three years' work by a Chinese architect and 20 Chinese artisans, for local

Dungans. It was closed by the Bolsheviks from 1933 to 1943, but since then has again been a place of worship. The 40 year old architect is said to have landed in hot water back in China over it, though the reasons are tangled with legends. It may be related to a discovery allegedly made by a visiting Buddhist monk in 1995, who was aghast to find previously unnoticed Chinese characters in the building saying something like 'this is a Buddhist temple'! A right royal flap was still going on about it when we left.

Sunday Market

This is no match for Kashgar's Sunday Market, but is still one of the best weekly bazars we saw in Central Asia. The big animal market *(mal bazari)* in particular is a must-see: several blocks jammed with people from throughout the region – an array like you won't see down in Bishkek – here to buy and sell horses, cattle, sheep, pigs and other creatures. You can buy a good horse for US$150 to US$300, or at US$20 a sheep makes a nice gift. There is no evidence of the pickpockets or other low-life that inhabit urban markets. Go early: it starts at 5 am and is over by 10 am.

The regular **bazar** nearby – with food, clothes and more – is cheerful but claustrophobic; it's also open, and less crowded, on other days of the week. Across the road is a brewery, built before the Revolution with the latest technology of the day. Locals say, not surprisingly, that it once made the best beer in the region but has gone downhill since independence.

Holy Trinity Cathedral

A handsome cathedral (Khram imeni Svyatoy Troitsa) is rising again from the rubble of Bolshevism, among birch and poplar trees at the corner of Lenina and Gagarina. Karakol's first church services were held in a yurt on this site after the town was founded. A later stone church fell down in an earthquake in 1890 (its granite foundations are still visible). A fine wooden cathedral was completed in 1895 (you can see a photo of it in the Regional Museum).

But the Bolsheviks closed it in the 1930s, destroyed its five onion-domes and turned it into a club. Serious reconstruction only began in 1961, proceeding at a snail's pace as available money and materials permit. Services are again being held, since its formal reconsecration in 1991. Listen for its chimes on Sunday morning.

Other Colonial Buildings

The colonial-era part of town sprawls southwest from the cathedral and the Hotel Karakol – lots of single storey 'gingerbread' houses, mostly plain but some (eg those built by wealthier officers, scientists etc) quite pretty, and a few (those of Russian merchants and industrialists) of two storeys. Among decaying former merchants' houses are the Pedagogical College on Gagarina opposite the cathedral, the radio and TV office on Kalinina a block south of the Hotel Karakol, and another old merchant's home at the corner of Krasnoarmeyskaya and Lenina.

Regional Museum

Karakol's modest regional museum (Karakolskiy istoriko-kraevedchesky muzey) is in a sturdy colonial brick building, once the home of a wealthy landowner, on Dzerzhinskogo near Toktogula. It's of interest for exhibits on the petroglyphs around the lake, a few Scythian bronze artefacts, a Soviet history of the Kyrgyz union with Russia, some Kyrgyz applied art (including leather bottles for milk), and photographs of old Karakol – all of it better with a guide, since nothing is in English. It's allegedly open daily from 8 am to 5 pm, but don't count on it.

One exhibit features Nikolai Andreevich Nestorov, a Bolshevik hero who later took up life here as a trapper and naturalist (and built the tiny museum at Altyn Arashan). Strangely enough, he died in Karakol on the day we were at the museum.

Pushkin Park

This leafy park by the stadium, four blocks south of the centre, includes the collective grave of a squad of Red Army soldiers killed in the pursuit of basmachi rebels.

Hippodrome

About three km south of the centre (on bus No 1) is Central Asia's very first hippodrome, still in use (though fewer and fewer people have the resources to keep racehorses).

Places to Stay

Cheapest by far (and best value for the price) is the *Hotel Stadion*, a spartan hostel on the west side of the municipal stadium, a 10 minute walk south of the centre. Nobody here has heard of foreigners' prices; beds are about US$2.50 in doubles or US$1 in five-bed dorms – all with common shower (US$0.50 extra) and toilet, and a sauna for US$3.50.

Next best is a *homestay*, which can be arranged by the travel agencies listed in the Information section.

The *Hotel Karakol* (☎ 2-14-55) at Kalinina 22 has plain but clean singles/doubles/triples with toilet and bathtub (but probably no hot water) for about US$6/9/11 and up. It's a 15 minute walk from the bus station, or pick up a marshrutnyy bus marked ЦЕНТР.

One of the best little top-end hotels we found in Central Asia is the so-called 'government hotel', a former Party compound called *Komplex Issyk-Kul*, 2.5 km south of the centre at Fuchika 38 (take bus No 1). Plain, carpeted dorm-style doubles/triples are US$11/9 per person, and the more deluxe building of the two (☎ 2-07-11) has plush singles and doubles for US$11, US$14 or US$18 per person, and one suite for US$55. Also in the leafy grounds are a dining room, a sauna and a hot pool done in marble.

The mountain rescue service has a small *hostel* reserved for visiting climbers, but you can apparently pitch a tent there for a few *som*, if you can find it open. It's at Fuchika 119, three km south of the centre opposite the hippodrome (take bus No 1).

A nice alternative for longer stays, but in an awkward position from the centre of

KYRGYZSTAN

Karakol, are the cheerful *dachas* clustered on the lakeshore between Pristan Przhevalsk and Mikhaylovka. Locals suggest just asking around there; you could get yourself a little basic *chalet* for a few dollars per night per person.

There is a small bazar nearby, but you should bring your own food supplies. Local buses – marked ДАЧИ– run frequently to/from the centre.

Places to Eat

The restaurant at the *Hotel Karakol* has a limited choice of local and Russian standards, but is adequate and cheap (fill up for US$1.50). Try their tasty 'Kyrgyz style *pelmeny*', little dumplings in spicy broth. They say they can whip up vegetarian dishes and Kyrgyz specialities by arrangement.

Just down Pervomayskaya from the hotel is the plain, privately run *Kafe Yris-bay*, in the basement through a door on the left side of the building. It has a small selection of cheap but good Kyrgyz dishes (at about US$0.50 per dish). Resident expatriates say the Kyrgyz and European dishes are good at the *Kafe Ak-keme*, on Leninskogo Komsomol near Lyuxemburg.

Many eateries are only open in summer; places we heard about include a good and not-too-pricey *restaurant* in the Drama Theatre; the *Restoran Arashan* and bar on Pervomayskaya near Lomonosova; the *Restoran Altyn-Kul* opposite the 'Chinese mosque', with outside tables; and the private *Kafe Ay-peri* opposite the banya on Kalinina.

Dungan Food This is more or less traditional Chinese cuisine, adapted to local ingredients. There don't seem to be any Dungan restaurants, but in summer Dungans hawk very tasty snacks and small dishes from roadside stands, eg around Przhevalskogo west of Tretievo Internatsionala. The best Dungan food is of course in Dungan homes, where a slap-up meal may have eight to 10 courses (Dungan weddings can have up to 30 courses!). The Karakol agency can arrange a good Dungan feast.

Self-Catering Along with vegetables and fruit, the well-stocked bazar also features lots of Russian and Dungan home produce, including a yoghurt drink called *kefir* by Russians and *ayran* by Kyrgyz, sausage, honey (Karakol honey is renowned in the region) and bread. This is also a good place to stock up before trekking.

Things to Buy

There are two modest shops in the gostinny dvor with somewhat overpriced Kyrgyz handicrafts of middling quality.

Getting There & Away

Kyrgyzstan Airlines has flights to Karakol-Almaty (US$20, 50 minutes, Monday and Friday) and Karakol-Bishkek (US$75, 1¼ hours) and Karakol-Osh (US$91, 1¾ hours) on Tuesday and Saturday. Ticket sales and the booking office are at the airport.

Most local buses (eg to Pristan Przhevalsk or Teploklyuchenka) go from the centre, around the gostinny dvor. Buses to anywhere farther away (eg Jeti-Öghüz, Tüp or beyond) go from the bus station.

Buses to Bishkek's west station (US$7, seven to eight hours) go about hourly from 6.30 am to 1.30 pm via the north shore of the lake, and at 8 and 10 am via the south shore. Out in front of the station are faster arenda minibuses (eg six hours to Bishkek), and private cars looking for passengers. To catch the train, buses go to Balykchy every hour or two from 6.45 am to 4.30 pm, and via the south road about hourly all day long. There are others all day to destinations around the lake. For Naryn, change at Balykchy; for Osh, change at Bishkek.

Almaty buses via the Karkara valley are for hire only, and run in summer only. There is said to be one daily Karakol-Almaty bus in summer around the west end of the mountains, not stopping at Bishkek.

Unofficial taxis are relatively easy to hire in the centre for trips around the region, but agree on a price beforehand.

Getting Around

Municipal bus connections are pretty flakey

because of fuel and money shortages, and routes come and go (mostly go). When we were there, the only remaining scheduled local route was north-south bus No 1 (see the Karakol map) linking the centre, bazar, army base, Komplex Issyk-Kul and mountain rescue. A marshrutnyy bus, marked Центр (centre) or АВТОВОКЗАЛ (bus station) trundles back and forth between the bus station and the centre whenever it can coax in more than about 10 passengers.

AROUND KARAKOL
Przhevalsky Memorial, Grave & Museum
Thanks perhaps to the efforts of Soviet historiographers, and to the fact that he died here, the Russian explorer Nikolai Przhevalsky (see the Przhevalsky aside) is something of a local icon, an increasingly poignant reminder of what the Russians accomplished in this part of the world. His grave, a memorial park and museum are seven km from the centre of Karakol on the Mikhaylovka inlet, and a visit with a Russian guide still has the flavour of a pilgrimage.

Przhevalsky died in 1888, and a huge monument and tiny chapel were erected by his grave six years later. The museum and garden are Soviet creations opened in 1957, displacing the rest of a village graveyard. The grounds, reverently tended by Russian staff, are always open, though you may have to shout for the caretaker.

The museum, a branch of the one in Karakol, features a huge map of Przhevalsky's explorations in Central Asia and a gallery of exhibits on his life and travels, plus a roll-call of other Imperial Russian explorers. Captions are in Russian. There is usually a guide on duty, but not always English-speaking.

The grave and monument overlook the Mikhaylovka inlet, though it's a rather different scene than that beloved by Przhevalsky. The shore has receded hundreds of metres since 1888, and the area – called Pristan Przhevalsk or just Pristan – is a clutter of cranes, docks and warehouses, all once part of the old Soviet top-secret 'polygon' for torpedo research.

To get there on your own, take bus No 37, marked ДАЧИ (dachas) from the centre of Karakol, or a taxi (budget about US$10 for the return trip plus US$6 per hour to wait).

Pristan Przhevalsk
Пристань Пржевалск
'Pristan' (meaning pier in Russian) is a strip of lakeshore several km long which includes a sea of dachas to the north east, a beach to the west, and in between various factories, warehouses and workers' homes. The beach is a jumping local scene in summer, with swimming, pedal-boats, boats for hire, carts for hire, food, and occasional live music. The beach and dachas are not in the restricted military zone.

From Karakol centre to the beach, take any of the buses marked ПЛЯЖ (Beach), which run all day.

Sukhoy Khrebet
Сухой Хребет
This means Dry Hills, and refers to the headland on the north side of Mikhaylovka inlet. Though parts may be within the restricted zone, locals insist they go there all the time for picnics with a grand view of the lake.

It's a 1½ hour journey from the Karakol bus station to Sukhoy Khrebet village on any bus marked МАЯК (Mayak).

Kurort Jergalan
Курорт Джергалан
Kurort Jergalan (Jergalan Spa; ☎ 2-02-75, 2-02-32) is a quiet summer-only sanatorium nestled in 80 hectares of woods and weeds on the banks of the Jergalan river, two km from the lake and 13 km north of Karakol (it's not to be confused with the mining town of Jergalan or Jyrghölöng, 60 km east of Karakol!). Stay in barracks-like dormitories (or there are a few cabins) and enjoy hot baths, mud baths or massage, for about US$15 per person per day – or come just for the baths, about US$2. They might let you pitch a tent by the river. Take any northbound bus from Karakol centre (eg to Tüp, Cholpon-Ata or Balykchy), or a taxi.

KYRGYZSTAN

KYRGYZSTAN

Przhevalsky

While neglected by missionaries and social do-gooders of the 19th century, Central Asia attracted strong interest from the consummate breed of that day – explorers. Typical expeditions included cartographers, zoologists, botanists, geologists, ethnographers and interpreters, accompanied by scores of pack camels, mountain ponies, shepherds, flocks and guides. When they returned, the explorers donned white tie in London or St Petersburg, gave lantern lectures and accepted awards from their respective geographical societies.

On the Russian side, the Golden Age of Central Asian exploration was presided over by Nikolai Mikhailovich Przhevalsky. Born in Smolensk on 12 April 1839, his passion from an early age was travel. His father was an Army officer and young Nikolai, under heavy pressure to be one too, apparently decided that an Army career would give him the best chance to hit the road, though he never enjoyed the military life.

To prove to both the Russian Geographical Society and his senior officers that he would be a good explorer, he persuaded the Society to sponsor his first expedition, to the Ussuri river region in the Russian Far East in 1867-69. The results impressed everyone, the Society agreed to help finance future trips, and the Army gave him the time he needed, insisting only that on his return from each trip he be debriefed first before saying anything to the Society.

Przhevalsky's Faustian bargain got him his freedom to travel in return for being, in effect, an Army agent. He never married, going on instead to become a Major General and the most honoured of all the tsarist explorers. He focused on Central Asia, launching four major expeditions in 15 years:

- Mongolia, China and Tibet (1870-73)
- Tian Shan, Lop Nor, Taklamakan desert and northern Xinjiang (1876-77)
- Mongolia, China and Tibet (1879-80)
- Mongolia, China, Tibet, Taklamakan desert and Tian Shan (1883-85).

Those starting in Mongolia were devoted to finding a route into Tibet. He finally made it to Lhasa once, and had an audience with the then Dalai Lama.

He was thwarted and threatened at many points in Mongolia, China and Tibet by local people who had no interest in letting foreigners come and look around. On the one non-Tibet trip, he discovered the tiny steppeland horse that now bears his name – Przhevalsky's Horse (and in fact is now gone from its old habitats, surviving only in zoos around the world).

On the last of these trips he arrived via the Bedel pass at Karakol. In 1888 he was at Bishkek (then Pishpek) outfitting for his next, grandest, expedition. For sport, he went out to hunt tiger by the Chuy river. There, he unwisely drank the water, came down with typhus and was bundled off to Lake Issyk-Kul for rest and treatment. From here he wrote to the tsar asking to be buried beside the lake, dressed in his explorer's clothes. He died at the military hospital on 20 October 1888. ■

Skibaza & Ala-Köl
Скибазы и Ала-Көл

About seven km on a steep, snakey road south up the valley of the Kashka-Suu, a tributary of the Karakol river, is a skibaza. A small hotel there is open in winter (usually mid-October to mid-March), and you can rent alpine ski gear, ride a three km lift and shush down from 3000 to 2000 metres. Jeep-buses leave from beside the municipal stadium from the skibaza's administration building, at 7 am and 1 pm, returning at 11 am and 4 pm.

About 13 km above the skibaza is a make-shift base (a fenced patch for tents, a radio shack, field hospital and caravan, and a generator to run a small lift), from which experts can ski on the Terim-Tör glacier in summer.

From May to mid-October you can make a strenuous three-hour climb from the upper base to a crystal-clear lake called Ala-Köl at 3530 metres. It can be reached more easily

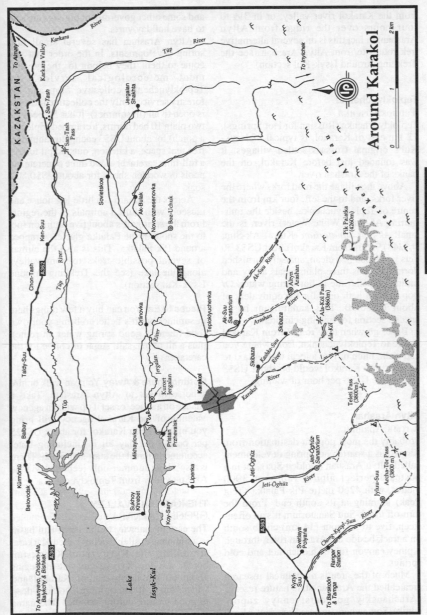

Around Karakol

KYRGYZSTAN

from the Karakol river valley, or in 3½ to four hours over the ridge from Altyn Arashan; in fact this is on several alternative trek routes to/from Altyn Arashan (see the Trekking Around Issyk-Kul section).

Teploklyuchenka
Теплоключенка

Teploklyuchenka (Russian for Hot Springs), 12 km east of Karakol, is typical of Issyk-Kul's original Cossack-settled villages. It was founded just before Karakol, on the banks of the Arashan river.

Above the village the road forks where the river forks, and to the left, four km from the centre of Teploklyuchenka, beside the murmuring Ak-Suu (White Water) river, is the small *Ak-Suu Sanatorium* (Kurort Ak-Suu; ☎ (248) 91561 from Karakol). Just US$3.50 gets you a bed in a clean, sparsely furnished dormitory plus three plain meals a day and unlimited bath time in hot-spring water. Or pop in for a bath only for the equivalent of about US$0.20. This sanatorium has a special section for treating children.

Buses go when they're full from Karakol centre to Teploklyuchenka, from where you can walk, hitch or hire a local taxi. A taxi to the spa from Karakol would be about US$8 return plus US$6 per hour of waiting.

Altyn Arashan
Алтын Арашан

Probably the most popular destination from Karakol is a spartan hot spring development called Altyn Arashan (Golden Spa), set in a postcard-perfect alpine valley at 3000 metres, with 4260 metre Pik Palatka (Tent Peak) looming at its south end. From the turn-off to Ak-Suu Sanatorium it's an often-steep, five to six hour (14 km) climb south on a track beside the Arashan river, through a piney canyon full of hidden hot and cold springs.

Much of the area is a botanical research area called the Arashan state nature reserve (Arashanskiy gosudarstvennyy zapovednik). Somewhere up here President Akaev

and some other government bigwigs are said to have holiday yurts.

Altyn Arashan has several small hot-spring developments. In the order that you come to them, they belong to the government meteorological service, the Teploklyuchenka collective farm and the forestry service. Only the collective farm site is open to all (in summer). It has 30 beds (in two plain 10 bed dorms, a cramped triple and a porch) for about US$3 each, plus abundant free tent space, a kitchen, outside pit toilets, a full-time caretaker – and three concrete hot pools in wooden sheds for about US$0.50 a soak.

Across the stream is a little log house and museum with stuffed animals of the region. From the springs it's about five hours on foot to the snout of the Palatka glacier, wrapped around Pik Palatka. This is also the climax of several possible treks to/from valleys along the lake (see the Trekking Around Issyk-Kul section).

Places to Eat You can buy a few things here in summer but it's better to bring your own food (there is good spring water en route), plus a bit of tea, salt, sugar or coffee for the caretaker.

Getting There & Away You can walk or hire a horse to get to Altyn Arashan. Take a chance on a space, or set it up with an agency. Valentin of the Karakol agency will bring you up here from Karakol for about US$25 per person per day all in, including hotel accommodation at the start and finish. There is also a long summer-only jeep track via the Ak-Suu valley from Teploklyuchenka.

THE KARKARA VALLEY
ӨРӨӨН КАРКАРА

The eastern gateway to the Issyk-Kul basin is an immense, silent valley called Karkara, straddling the Kyrgyzstan-Kazakstan border. On the Kyrgyzstan side it begins about 60 km north-east of Karakol and widens out to 40 km or more, shoulder-deep in good pasture during summer. The name means Black Crane, for the graceful migratory birds that stop here (and at Chatyr-Köl near the Torugart pass) in June and again in August-September, en route between South Africa and Siberia. In contrast to the windy Boömskoe ushchelie at the lake's west end, this is a lovely way in and out, but the road is poorer and far less used.

Every herder in the Karakol region (and in the Kegen region on the Kazakstan side) brings animals up here in summer to fatten, and the warm-weather population is an easygoing mix of Kyrgyz and Kazak chaban and their families. The valley is dotted with yurts at that time, and people are disarmingly friendly, as yet untouched by tourism. The Karkara (or Karkyra) river – which forms the Kyrgyzstan-Kazakhstan border through part of the valley – and its tributaries are said to yield abundant fish.

Every summer, around 15-20 June, all these good vibes come together in the form of the Chabana festival, a good-natured, strictly non-touristic gathering of cowboys and herders, with traditional horseback games and a big bazar. The border seems especially nonexistent at this time. The location apparently shifts around the valley (and from one side of the border to the other) from year to year, and the exact time is only fixed at the last moment, depending on work requirements and weather. (This is not to be confused with an entirely different event called the Karkara Fair, a commercial and trade fair held in either Kegen or Almaty.)

The ancients liked Karkara too. In his *A Day Lasts Longer Than a Century* the Kyrgyz writer Aitmatov has the ancient Kyrgyz peoples arriving from the Yenisey via Karkara.

Some people suggest that Timur made Karkara his summer headquarters for several years, and point to a house-size pile of round stones in the south-west part of the valley. These, they say, were Timur's way of estimating his losses in eastern campaigns – each departing soldier put a rock on the pile, each returnee removed one, and those that remained represented the dead. The name of the site, San-Tash, means 'Counting Stones'. The whole idea was recently given a push by

a slick television advertisement by a Russian bank, showing Timur kneeling reverently beside the stones.

Skeptics and amateur historians point to an adjacent, stone-lined pit which appears to be the remnant of a burial chamber, and suggest that the football-size stones were just used to cover the chamber, and were removed by archaeologists or grave-robbers. Either way, the site has a dreamy, magical feel.

Places to Stay & Eat

Save for a few collective farm settlements, there are almost no buildings to be seen out here, certainly no such thing as a hotel or restaurant. Bring your own tent and food if you plan to stay the night, although you may well be invited into someone's yurt. Visitors are welcome – especially those who have brought along a few supplies; tea and salt are especially well received, and cigarettes and vodka also make good gifts. These might also be traded for fresh milk, *ayran* (yoghurt), *kurut* (hard cheese) or *sary-may* (butter) – or even for the rental of a horse!

Getting There & Away

From Karakol the Karkara valley is about 90 km via Tüp or 70 much prettier km via Novovoznesenkovka, but the road deteriorates about 40 km outside Karakol in either case. The Kyrgyz border post is at the west end of the valley.

On the Tüp route a round trip by taxi would probably be about US$40 to US$50 for the vehicle plus US$6 an hour to wait. Ask for '*pamyatnik San-Tash*', just opposite a small collective farm settlement, 4.7 km from the Kyrgyz border post or 19 km from the Kazakstan border. There are regular daily buses to Tüp, and apparently some to settlements beyond the stones. It's also an easy hitch in summer, and the cheerful Kyrgyz border guards might even flag down a car for you.

The Novovoznesenkovka route passes through the wettest and lushest part of th Issyk-Kul region, then past a former Soviet Army altitude training base and over the low

San-Tash pass (closed by snow in winter) into a western arm of the Karkara valley.

There are daily buses from Karakol as far as Sovietskoe or the mining town of Jyrghölöng (Russians call it Jergalan *shakhta* or mine), from where you might hitch. The border is about 90 km from Karakol on this route.

This would make a fine horseback trip from Karakol. Three km above Novovoznesenkovka is a small sanatorium called Boz-Uchuk, with a hot spring. From Karkara you could also trek east or south into the Terskey Alatau. A sealed road climbs to Inylchek in the high Tan Shan from Ak-Bulak, and Jyrghölöng is one base for serious Tian Shan treks. The Almaty trekking outfit Kan Tengri maintains a base camp on the Kazakstan side of the Karkara river.

From the Kazakstan side, you can get a Kegen, Saryzhaz or Narynqol bus from Almaty and get off at Kegen. The Kazak border post is there but it's apparently a difficult 25 to 30 km hitch south to the border itself.

JETI-ÖGHÜZ
ЖЕТИ-ОГУЗ

About 25 km west of Karakol, at the mouth of the Jeti-Öghüz canyon, is an extraordinary formation of red sandstone cliffs that has become a kind of tourism trademark for Lake Issyk-Kul.

Non-Kyrgyz Meets Manas

In 1856 the explorer Shoqan Ualikhanov (see the aside called Renaissance Boy of the Steppes in the History section of the Facts about the Region chapter) sat down with a Kyrgyz bard at a campsite on the San-Tash pass, and listened to a recitation of part of the *Manas* epic. He was probably the first non-Kyrgyz ever to hear such a performance. As this book went to press an internationally-funded project was underway to erect a little monument to the event, on the San-Tash pass. ∎

A village of the same name is just off the main round-the-lake road. Beyond it the earth erupts in red patches, and soon there appears a great splintered hill called Razbitoye Serdtse or Broken Heart. (Legend says two suitors spilled their blood in a fight for a beautiful woman; both died, and this rock is her broken heart.)

Beyond this on the west side of the road is the massive wall of Jeti-Öghüz. The name means Seven Bulls, and of course there is a story here too – of seven calves growing big and strong in the valley's rich pastures. Erosion has meant that the bulls have multiplied. They are best viewed from a ridge to the east above the road. From that same ridge you can look east into Ushchelie Drakonov, the Valley of Dragons.

Below the wall of Seven Bulls is one of Issyk-Kul's surviving spas, the ageing *Jeti-Öghüz Sanatorium*, built in 1932 with a complex of several plain hotels, a hot pool, a restaurant and some woodland walks. It's open to all, but in summer only. Russian President Boris Yeltsin and Kyrgyzstan's President Askar Akaev had their first meeting here, in 1991.

From here you can walk up the park-like lower canyon of the Jeti-Öghüz river to popular summer picnic spots. Some five km up, the valley opens out almost flat at Dolina Svetov, the Valley of Flowers; it's a kaleidoscope of colours as summer passes and has poppies in May. There are also said to be pre-Islamic petroglyphs up here, similar to those at Cholpon-Ata.

Jeti-Öghüz canyon is one of several alternatives for treks to/from Altyn Arashan and Ala-Köl (see the Trekking Around Issyk-Kul section).

Getting There & Away

Arenda buses run from Karakol bus station to Jeti-Öghüz village, from where it's about six km to the spa (there are said to be shuttle buses and overpriced taxis along here in summer). A taxi from Karakol centre to the spa would be about US$12 return plus US$6 per hour of waiting.

KYZYL-SUU
КЫЗЫЛ-СУУ

The town of Kyzyl-Suu (Pokrovka in Soviet times) is of no interest, though it's home to a joint Russian-Kyrgyz institute of glaciology. But this is the turn-off for the Chong-Kyzyl-Suu river valley, including a primitive hot-spring development – all of which can form part of a trek to/from Altyn Arashan and Ala-Köl (see the Trekking Around Issyk-Kul section).

A few km west of Kyzyl-Suu is the valley of the Juku river, the last leg of Nikolai Przhevalsky's final expedition (see the Przhevalsky aside in the Around Karakol section), and once such a popular smugglers' route – for Issyk-Kul opium, among other things – that there used to be a customs post at the top of the valley. Przhevalsky's route is now paralleled by a 4WD track from Saruu village up and then west to the Barskoön valley.

Places to Stay & Eat

In a stadium half a km east of the river bridge where the main road crosses the Chong-Kyzyl-Suu river is the very cheap and spartan *Gostinitsa Stadion* (Stadium Hotel). A café and restaurant, and a small bazar, are by the main bus stand, 1.2 km west of the river bridge on the main road.

Getting There & Away

The hot spring is about 10 km on a rough road above Kyzyl-Suu or eight km above the next-door village of Svetlaya Polyana. There are buses to both places from Karakol bus station, 40 km away, and a local taxi might take you up to the spring if you're not a walker. From the Kyzyl-Suu bus stand it's 1.2 km east to the Chong-Kyzyl-Suu river (or just ask the driver for *reka*, river); ulitsa Yumatovoy up the west side of the river becomes the valley road. There is a forest ranger station *(kardon)* at the lower end of the valley. The Jyluu-Suu hot-spring site, about 20 km above the village, consists of a plain building with one hot pool, open to all at no charge, and a disused hostel.

BARSKOÖN
БАРСКООН

Barskoön village was an army staging point in the days of Soviet-Chinese border skirmishes, and the small adjacent settlement of Tamga is built around a former military sanatorium, now open year-round to all. Barskoön is all Kyrgyz, with more horses than cars; Tamga is mainly Russian.

The only reasons to come are to soak at the spa's hot pool or mud baths, or to head up the huge Barskoön valley, 20 km to Barskoön waterfall (Russian: *vodopad*) or on into the mountains. Locals camp, socialise and booze it up at the waterfall, gathering their courage to drive the snakey road on up

KYRGYZSTAN

Mahmud al-Kashgari

Mahmud al-Kashgari (also called al-Barskhani) was born in the 11th century at what was then the settlement of Barskhan. He is best known as the author of the first-ever comparative dictionary of Turkic languages, *Divan Lughat at-Turk* (A Glossary of Turkish Dialects), written in Baghdad during 1072-74 and including specimens of pre-Islamic Turkic poetry. He travelled widely to collect his information, and is thought to have drawn the map shown here, his version of the known world, with Barskhan/Barskoön at the centre! His tomb is at Upal, south of Kashgar on the road to Pakistan. ■

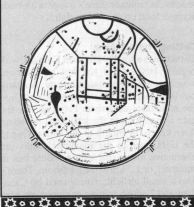

the valley. One Russian book we found makes an obscure reference to Tibetan Buddhist text carved into rocks in the gorge.

The area's most illustrious resident was the 11th century scholar Mahmud al-Kashgari.

Places to Stay & Eat

Tamga's tidy, quiet *sanatorium* is still managed, rather loosely, by the military, but everyone is welcome. To register at the sanatorium itself – about US$5 per person for a room with shower and toilet – go through the gate to a door marked УПРАВЛЕНИЕ (administration) in the second building on the left. However, we found all the officers drunk on the day we visited, and foreigners have been asked for high US$ payments here.

A better option is to enquire at the *bar-café* in the first building on the left inside the gate, or just around the blocks of flats behind the administration building. Even the babushkas in the bazar outside the gate may be able to help – you're sure to find someone with a cheap room. East of Tamga the lakeshore road loops round a pretty inlet, above which is a bankrupt turbaza, though locals say you might find a caretaker who'll let you stay for a few *som*.

The sanatorium canteen serves small meals at fixed times. The bar-café has only snacks. In summer there's a *café* with basic Kyrgyz food up at the waterfall.

Getting There & Away

Barskoön is about 90 km from Karakol, with regular buses from Karakol bus station, which stop at the sanatorium gate. An early bus from Karakol lets you head straight into the mountains on arrival. From outside the gate a road runs to the left (east) for about three km to the mouth of the valley. One to the right goes to the municipal baths (an alternative to the spa, with a shuttle bus in summer), or 1.5 km to the lakeshore. There's also a small airfield, mainly used by Canadian and Turkish mining engineers up here to look around for gold.

TREKKING AROUND ISSYK-KUL

Even if you're not a mountaineer, if you're fit you can get a fine taste of the Tian Shan in the ranges that enclose Lake Issyk-Kul. Several crossings of the Küngey Alatau, north of the lake, are described in the Zailiyskiy Alatau & Küngey Alatau and Köl-Say Lakes sections, both in the Kazakstan chapter.

The finest, safest and most accessible treks are south from around Karakol, into the Terskey Alatau. Of numerous possibilities that climb to passes below 4000 metres, the best of them take in the alpine lake called Ala-Köl above Karakol, and the hot springs called Altyn Arashan above Teploklyuchenka. These are described in the Around Karakol section, and the trailheads at Jeti-Öghüz and Kyzyl-Suu are described under separate headings. Favoured routes include:

From Teploklyuchenka (1800 metres) up the Arashan river valley to Altyn Arashan (3000 metres) and back: minimum one or two nights; a longer variant is to go up via the Ak-Suu river valley

From Karakol via the Karakol river valley (or more strenuously up the Kasha-Suu valley) to Ala-Köl, crossing the 3860 metre Ala-Köl pass east to Altyn Arashan, then down to Teploklyuchenka: minimum two or three nights

From Jeti-Öghüz up the Jeti-Öghüz river valley, crossing east over the 3800 metre Teleti pass to Ala-Köl, then to Altyn Arashan and Teploklyuchenka: minimum four or five nights

From Kyzyl-Suu (Pokrovka) up the Chong-Kyzyl-Suu river valley to Jyluu-Suu hot springs or on to a tent-site below the 3800 metre Archa-Tör pass, crossing east to the Jeti-Öghüz valley, then to Ala-Köl, Altyn Arashan and Teploklyuchenka: minimum six to eight nights

There are also longer, more technical variations on these that climb as high as 4200 metres and cross some small glaciers, but these should not be attempted without a knowledgeable guide and some experience with glacier walking.

When to Go

The season for the treks noted here is normally late June to early October. For Altyn Arashan only, you might go as early as May or as late as the end of October, but nights drop below freezing then. Local people say Altyn Arashan is loveliest in June and in September.

Books & Maps

These routes are indicated on the Around Karakol map, but they should never be attempted without either a local guide or reliable and detailed route maps. The only good maps we have seen for these routes – part of an old Russian series called Gornyy Turizm (Mountain Tourism) – are the 1:150,000 *Lednikam Terskey Ala-Too* and the 1:150,000 *Po Tsentralnomu Tyan-Shan*, for sale at the Kyrgyz Cartographic Agency in Bishkek (see the Bishkek Information section).

The best general book to take along if you're planning to trek here is Frith Maier's comprehensive *Trekking in Russia & Central Asia*, though it does not include these routes.

Dangers & Annoyances

These routes are apparently free of the occasional robbers reported on the Küngey Alatau treks. Weather is perhaps the biggest danger, with unexpected chilling storms, especially in May through June and September through October. Streams are in flood in late May and early June (if you go then, plan your crossings for early morning when levels are lowest). See the Health section in the Facts for the Visitor chapter for information about hypothermia, cold, sunburn, altitude sickness and ticks.

Getting There & Away

For access to trailheads, refer to the Karakol, Around Karakol (Teploklyuchenka), Jeti-Öghüz and Kyzyl-Suu sections. Reliable Kyrgyzstan agencies who can arrange treks in this area include Dostuck Trekking and ITMC Tien-Shan (Tien-Shan Mountaineering) in Bishkek; Karakol and KRD Tien Shan in Karakol; and Kan Tengri and Tour Asia in Almaty (see the Travel Agencies sections for those towns).

THE CENTRAL TIAN SHAN
ЦЕНТРАЛЬНЫЙ ТЯНЬ-ШАНЬ

This highest and mightiest part of the Tian Shan system – the name means Celestial Mountains – is at the eastern end of Kyrgyzstan, along its borders with China and the very south-east tip of Kazakstan. It's an immense knot of ranges, with dozens of summits over 5000 metres, culminating in Pik Pobedy (Victory Peak, 7439 metres, second-highest in the former USSR) on the Kyrgyzstan-China border, and Khan-Tengri (Prince of Spirits, 6995 metres), possibly the most beautiful and demanding peak in the Tian Shan, on the Kazakstan-Kyrgyzstan border.

The first foreigner to bring back information about the central Tian Shan was the Chinese explorer Hsüan-tsang, who crossed the Bedel pass in the 7th century, early in his 16-year odyssey to India and back (see the Way of the Pilgrim aside in the History section in the Facts about the Region chapter). His journey nearly ended here; in the seven days it took to cross the pass, half his 14-person party froze to death.

The first European to penetrate this high region was the Russian explorer Pyotr Semyonov in 1856 (for his efforts the tsar awarded him the honorary name Tian-Shansky). In 1902-1903 the Austrian explorer Gottfried Merzbacher first approached the foot of the elegant, Matterhorn-like Khan-Tengri, but it was only climbed in 1931, by a Ukrainian team.

Of the Tian Shan's thousands of glaciers, the grandest is 60-km-long Inylchek (or Engilchek), rumbling westward from both sides of Khan-Tengri, embracing an entire rampart of giant peaks and tributary glaciers. Across its entire northern arm where it joins the southern one, a huge, iceberg-filled lake – Lake Merzbacher – forms at 3300 metres every summer, and sometime in early August bursts its ice-banks and explodes into the Inylchek river below.

Along with the eastern Pamir, the central Tian Shan is Central Asia's premier territory for serious trekking and mountaineering. Several Central Asian adventure-travel firms will bring you by helicopter, 4WD and/or foot right up to these peaks. Even intrepid, fit do-it-yourselfers can get a look at Inylchek glacier (see the Getting There & Away section).

Among popular ascents on the Kyrgyzstan side, from the south arm of Inylchek glacier, are Khan-Tengri, massive Pik Pobedy and 6181 metre Aqtau. Khan-Tengri can also be climbed from the north side. Other ascents on the Kazakstan side include 6400 metre Mramornaya Stena (Marble Wall) on the Kazakstan-China border, and 5791 metre Bayankol, north of Khan-Tengri.

When to Go
July through August is the warm season at these elevations.

Books & Maps
You're best off bringing maps from home (see the Maps section in the Facts for the Visitor chapter). The only good place in Kyrgyzstan for maps is the Kyrgyz Cartographic Agency in Bishkek (see the Bishkek Information section), where you'll find selected topographic and trekking maps – all supposedly cleared of the deliberate distortions that infected Soviet-era maps. A map of trekking routes that approach Khan-Tengri from the Kazak and Kyrgyz sides is the 1:200,000 *K Verkhvyam Sary-Dzhaza*.

The best book to take along is Frith Maier's comprehensive *Trekking in Russia & Central Asia*, with several maps and basic route descriptions in this region.

Dangers & Annoyances
This is not a place to pop into for a few days with your summer sleeping bag – you need to be properly equipped against the cold, which is severe at night, even in summer, and to give yourself plenty of time to acclimatise to the altitude. Refer to these topics in the Health section in the Facts for the Visitor chapter.

Helicopters do fall out of the sky from time to time, or crash into mountainsides when bad weather unexpectedly descends;

ride them only in absolutely clear summer weather.

Permits
This remains a sensitive border zone, and to go anywhere beyond Inylchek town – even just to have a look at the glacier – you'll need a permit from the Russian border detachment at the Army base in Karakol (see the Karakol Information section). You must have a letter with the stamp of a recognised travel agency in Karakol, Bishkek or Almaty, a list of everyone in your party, and your itinerary.

Places to Stay & Eat
There are several *basecamps* in the Inylchek valley – Maida Adyr below the snout of the glacier, with wagons and tents, mess hall and sauna; and tent-towns at several locations up on the glacier, owned and run by ITMC Tien-Shan (Tien-Shan Mountaineering) in Bishkek and Kan Tengri in Almaty, among others.

Kan Tengri also maintains a *yurt camp* at 2200 metres at the edge of the Karkara valley. All these are intended for trekkers and climbers but anybody with the urge to see this cathedral of peaks can make arrangements with those firms, and pay a visit.

Getting There & Away
Firms organising climbs and treks in the central Tian Shan include Dostuck Trekking, ITMC Tien-Shan (Tien-Shan Mountaineering) and Tien-Shan Travel in Bishkek; Karakol in Karakol; and Kan Tengri and Tour Asia in Almaty (see the Travel Agencies sections for those towns).

Access to the region around Khan-Tengri is by road, by air or on foot. It's a four-hour (150 km) trip on a roller-coastering, all-weather road from Karakol via Inylchek town, a mining centre (and probably a major listening-post in Soviet days) at about 2500 metres and 50 km below the snout of the Inylchek glacier. Do-it-yourselfers could even hire a 4WD or other reliable vehicle for a very long day trip from Karakol, for about US$60 (for the vehicle, not per person) return plus US$6 per hour of waiting if you hire a taxi. Local mountaineers on the cheap hang out at the intersection outside Karakol airport, the conventional place to catch a ride to Inylchek for around US$10 (in *som*).

If you've got the dosh, take a mind-boggling helicopter flight over the Tian Shan to Maida Adyr basecamp – with Kan Tengri from their Karkara valley basecamp, or with other agencies from Karakol. Once upon a time it was possible to hitch a lift on a helicopter taking climbers or mining engineers up from Karakol, for perhaps US$40. Fuel costs have curtailed these flights, but there's no harm in asking at Karakol airport (helicopter is *vertolyot* in Russian).

To Khan-Tengri's north face you can trek from Narynqol (Kazakstan), Jergalan shakhta or Karakol (Kyrgyzstan).

Bishkek to Kashgar via the Torugart Pass

Kyrgyzstan's primo trip for non-trekkers – and the most exciting overland route in or out of Central Asia – is the 700 km journey between Bishkek and Kashgar via the 3752 metre Torugart pass (Chinese: Tu'ergate shankou).

It's not for everyone, being long, sometimes cold and uncomfortable, plagued by uncertainties and officials with their hands out, and not necessarily cheap, but it's the sort of absorbing and grandly beautiful trip you're glad you made once you've made it.

A major, and indeed probably the original, branch of the Silk Road crossed the Tian Shan between Kashgar and the Ferghana Valley, probably near Kök-Art, 85 km southwest of Torugart. The Chinese emissary Chang Ch'ien went that way in 138 BC on an astonishing 13 year search for allies, and for the Heavenly Horses of Ferghana, on behalf of the Han Emperor (see the History section in the Facts about the Region chapter). You can't go that way now, but you can come pretty close on the Torugart.

This section is mainly about the Bishkek-Kashgar route and all there is to see on the way. It includes the stretch of Xinjiang from the border to Kashgar because that's an essential part of this trip and because almost no-one would care to go there for any other reason.

From a purely physical standpoint the whole journey could be done in a sturdy, well-equipped 4WD in under 15 hours, but the country along the way reveals too much about the region's history, geography, people and wildlife to rush through it (and contains formidable official obstacles to slow you down even more). The actual trip, via Balykchy and Naryn, takes a minimum of two or three days.

The Torugart pass is open to all now, but ranks of officials on both sides still make it hard, occasionally impossible, for individual budget travellers. The only way to take (most of) the uncertainty out of the trip is to spend money on it – crossing with the help of accredited and experienced local agencies on both sides. The prospects for success also look marginally better if you cross from Kyrgyzstan into China rather than the other way. If you have time but no money, and are simply trying to get in or out of China, it's easier and surer to cross to/from Kazakstan.

When to Go

The Torugart pass is normally snow-free from May through September. It's apparently kept open all year, but is icy and dangerous in winter, and as soon as there is significant snow, officials tend to turn back anything without snow-tyres or tracks. Nights at higher elevations are still bitterly cold in April, and again by September. The Naryn-Torugart road is problematic from mid-November to early March. The Bishkek-Naryn road may sometimes be blocked with snow at the Dolon pass in winter.

Avoid trying to cross the Torugart pass on any day that might conceivably be construed as a holiday on either side, as it could be closed. Some travellers have been told, incorrectly, that it's closed on weekends too. Try to arrive at the border as early in the day

KYRGYZSTAN

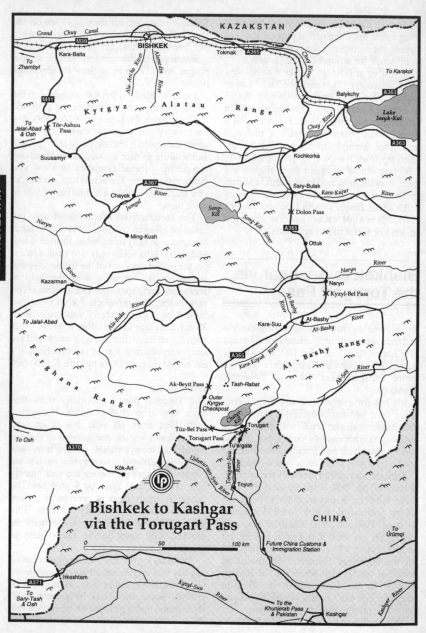

**Bishkek to Kashgar
via the Torugart Pass**

0   50   100 km

as possible, and don't be surprised if nothing is going on at lunchtime.

Visas & Other Requirements

You cannot get visas at the border, and you'll be turned back on either side if you don't have an onward visa (in fact you can't even *leave* Kyrgyzstan here without a proper Kyrgyzstan visa and OVIR registration). It's possible to get a China visa in all the former Soviet Central Asia capitals except Dushanbe; see Getting a China Visa in Central Asia in the Visas & Embassies section in the Facts for the Visitor chapter. Booking onward transport tends to make this easier. In China, you can get a Kyrgyzstan visa only in Beijing.

For entering China, even a China visa isn't enough. At research time, border officials were insisting on written confirmation of onward transport, and detaining visitors until this transport arrived from Kashgar. The best thing to have is a telex from an accredited Chinese tour agency, who will come and meet you. We know of one group that was turned back even with all the right papers, because their transport never turned up or wasn't allowed up to the actual border.

We don't know if the reverse is true – ie whether anyone cares about onward transport into Kyrgyzstan – but it looks unlikely. We even heard of friendly Chinese border officials flagging down vehicles and ordering drivers to take foreigners to the Kyrgyzstan side!

You need an endorsement on your China visa from the Kashgar Public Security Bureau (police) in order to leave China over the Torugart pass, but you're better off leaving this to the agency who will take you there. When we enquired, the PSB man simply told us the Torugart pass was closed to tourists! When we pointed out that we had just arrived that way he switched to 'closed for exit', although the PSB's own wall map shows it's open. We met people who had gone that way with no hassles, but none without the help of a Kashgar agency. If you want to try it on your own, it's probably best not to involve the PSB any sooner than you

have to, as someone could ruin your plans, eg by stamping your visa to say you can't leave there.

In any case the official situation is very fluid, and you should get current advice in Bishkek or Kashgar before you go.

What to Bring

Besides your visas and papers, and winter clothes, gifts are useful to loosen up drivers and guards – cigarettes, western candy bars and dashboard stickers go over well, and may also do in lieu of money as petty bribes. Tea, salt and sugar come in handy to trade with herders at Song-Köl for milk, cheese or yoghurt. Vodka will make you lots of friends in the high pastures, but you're better off keeping that out of your driver's hands.

Time

In summer (roughly April through September) China (ie Beijing) time is two hours later than Kyrgyzstan time, and in winter three hours later.

Money

There is a bank in Naryn, but you can't sell back *som* there. You'll find only private and black-market traders at the Kyrgyzstan customs station. There is a small Bank of China office (open weekdays only) on the China side.

Dangers & Annoyances

Torugart may be one of Asia's most unpredictable border posts, with reliable information scarce, many decisions taken seemingly at random, and plenty of bloody-minded and/or greedy officials to satisfy. The pass may be unexpectedly closed by one side or the other for holidays, road repair or heaven knows what else, and nobody (even ambassadors) knows the score for sure. The three-point border – two customs stations 12 km apart and a security station in between – makes for further confusion, especially in trying to connect with onward transport. The whole place is fairly wild and woolly, and the Kyrgyzstan side doesn't look like a brilliant place for an unaccompanied woman. Be

KYRGYZSTAN

stubborn, expect the unexpected, and don't count on getting across until you have!

Places to Stay & Eat

Accommodation is spartan and scarce in Naryn; Bishkek agencies often make their own arrangements, eg for yurt camping or homestays. Consider skipping Naryn and camping out in the sublime Tash-Rabat valley (but bring everything, including something for the caretakers). Some agencies will arrange this, using their own tents. There are grotty dorms and private wagons at the Kyrgyzstan border post. The China side has a little hotel but you're encouraged to move on.

Getting There & Away

The 500 km trip between Bishkek and the border is best done in two days, though it's possible in a single shot in a reliable vehicle. There are plenty of people in Bishkek ready to take you, and we found a wide range of experience and prices.

Agencies Agencies may also have packages with excursions (eg to Issyk-Kul) and longer stays, as well as round trips to the border and back. Some, but not all, can make arrangements with a cooperating agency on the other side for onward transport. Try to make arrangements at least two or three weeks in advance, especially if you're setting up onward transport too.

Be suspicious of bargain-basement costs – this is not a trip to cut corners on. Ask for a breakdown, since some firms fail to mention all costs. At the time of research you could expect to spend, at a minimum, around US$100 per day for the vehicle, plus petrol (about US$50 in a small car, US$100 in a 4WD minibus), plus oil (about US$5), plus food, accommodation and any excursions. Transport costs are unpredictable because of the wildly fluctuating price of petrol. Prices are no different for a one-way or return trip since the vehicle has to return anyway.

Be clear whether the quote includes the state transport duty (gosposhlina), a per-vehicle customs tax paid when you exit Kyrgyzstan. When we were there this was the som equivalent of US$77 for the vehicle, not per person. It's not charged on vehicles entering Kyrgyzstan.

Ask whether you will be taken across to the Chinese customs station; only drivers with a Foreign Ministry special permit (see the Foreign Ministry Permit for Drivers aside) can go that far. Your driver should have previous experience with Torugart – both getting there and getting across if that's what's planned – eg minimising customs rip-offs, jumping truck queues, handling greedy officials, and of course repairing the vehicle. Those with a Foreign Ministry permit usually do.

And ask to see what you'll get there in! This is a high-elevation road with steep grades, and even the sturdiest vehicles tend to have trouble. Little 2WD cars use less fuel but are dangerously lightweight and uncontrollable on rainy roads, snow or ice, while a 4WD will get you out of all sorts of trouble. Check the tyres too. There is almost no reliable petrol, oil or parts along the way, so the vehicle must carry everything for the round trip, including several hundred litres of fuel in jerry-cans.

In Bishkek we found Kyrgyzintourist offering the best, most reliable deal to the border. Some travellers report them unenthusiastic about setting up onward transport in China, though they can do it, with CITS. ITMC Tien-Shan was pricier but also reliable, and both have drivers with Foreign Ministry permits. Sputnik offered us the clapped-out car of a person who had probably never been to Torugart before!

On the China side, both CITS and the Kashgar Mountaineering Association (KMA) are competent at transport; CITS seems to have more clout for getting right up to the security post at the border. These and several other Chinese agencies (see the Travel & Visa Agencies section in the Getting There & Away chapter) also have agreements with Kyrgyzstan agencies for onward transport. All quoted about US$100 per vehicle for a 4WD Kashgar-Torugart trip.

Foreign Ministry Permit for Drivers
On the Kyrgyzstan side certain drivers have permits from the Kyrgyzstan Ministry of Foreign Affairs, allowing them to drive across the border as far as the main Chinese customs station. There's no guarantee that Chinese officials will let them do so, but it will make your trip easier if your driver has a permit. Drivers without them have sometimes even been turned back at the *outer* Kyrgyzstan checkpoint, 60 km from the border, or had to bribe their way onward. In any case the permit is probably a sign that the driver has some experience with the Torugart pass.

Ask if your driver has one. It's hard to find anyone with one outside Bishkek. They are sometimes, confusingly, called 'open visas'. There is no Chinese equivalent; in China drivers can only go as far as the border, period. ■

The Bishkek-Kashgar trip can also be arranged in advance from overseas, but it's expensive and unnecessary.

Bus At the time of research a Chinese-run company had begun running a single old bus (with a Russian driver) back and forth between Bishkek and Kashgar via Torugart, roughly three or four times a month in summer, on no fixed timetable. They don't help with visas; that's up to you. The nonstop 1½ day trip was about US$70 from Bishkek but US$100 from Kashgar.

See the Getting There & Away section Bishkek or Kashgar for information about buying tickets.

We heard rumours of Kyrgyz buses to/from Kashgar for locals on 'shopping holidays', but could find out nothing more, and never saw any.

Doing It Yourself You can take cheap scheduled or arenda buses from Bishkek to Naryn (three daily) or At-Bashy (one daily), but no further. From there, 'cowboy' taxis will take you to the border for US$100 or more, though they may be turned back or shaken down at the outer checkpost. At the border these same sharks may open with US$200 or more to take you to Bishkek (and may lead you to think that's for the vehicle, then later tell you it's per person), and there seems to be a kind of cartel. One traveller was asked for US$600!

Jeep drivers hanging out at China customs were asking about the same as CITS was

charging, to go to Kashgar. We could find no information about local buses on this route, although there must be some for Kyrgyz who live in the area.

In between, you can take your chances hitching on trucks. The problem, if you're entering China, is what to do at the border, where you may be turned back if you have no confirmation of onward transport. Note also that no trucks from either side go beyond the Chinese customs station; all cargo is transferred there, and you would have to find a new ride. Truck drivers were settling for US$100 or less for Torugart-Bishkek and US$20 for Torugart-Kashgar.

In the end, doing it yourself could cost almost as much as pre-booking transport!

BISHKEK TO NARYN
The route begins as you would for Lake Issyk-Kul, winding up **Dolon pass** or **'Shoestring Gorge'** (Boömskoe ushchelie) towards Balykchy. A shortcut past the azure **Orto-Tokoy reservoir** is full of twists and heaves but saves an hour by cutting off the Balykchy corner.

The village of **Kochkorka**, 185 km from Bishkek, has a small hotel for US$3 per bed (a state guest house *might* be available at US$12). About 38 km onward is small **Sary-Bulak**, where you can buy laghman and snacks by the roadside. Five km south of Sary-Bulak is the turn-off to **Lake Song-Köl** (see the following section).

It's about 11 km on to the 3038 metre summit of the **Dolon pass**, the highest point on the Bishkek-Naryn road, and a further 19 km to a dirt track that apparently climbs the Song-Köl river valley to the lake. About 16 km on is **Ottuk**, a tidy Kyrgyz settlement in the green valley of the Ottuk river, and 24 km further is a fork in the road, both branches of which take you about 10 km into Naryn.

Altogether Bishkek-Naryn, without a stop at Song-Köl, is about 310 km (six to 6½ hours).

Lake Song-Köl
Соң-Көл

Alpine Lake Song-Köl (or Son-Kul, or Song-Kyol), at 3530 metres, is one of the loveliest spots in central Kyrgyzstan. All round it are lush pastures favoured by herders from the Kochkorka valley and farther, who spend June, July and August here with their animals. Visitors are welcome, and this is a sublime place to camp and watch the sun come up. The lake is jumping with fish, and you might be able to trade tea, salt, sugar, cigarettes or vodka with the herders for milk, *kurut* (hard cheese) or full-bodied kymys.

The lake and shore are part of the Song-Köl zoological reserve. Among animals under its protection are a diminishing number of wolves.

Getting There & Away It's 50 paved km from the Bishkek-Naryn road to the lake: 6 km to Keng-Suu (or Tölök) village, 21 km to end of the narrow, fertile valley of the Tölök river, and then a slow 23 km (about 1½ hours) up and into the basin. This upper road is normally open only from late May to late October. The valley has little traffic and few or no regular buses. A car hired from Naryn would be at least US$100 plus petrol for a day trip. Song-Köl is also a popular camping excursion from Bishkek.

There are at least three other unpaved and less convenient 4WD tracks to the lake – from west of the lake at Chayek, from the Naryn-Kazarman road, and another from the Bishkek-Naryn road.

NARYN
НАРЫН

Population: 45,000

Naryn is at about the right place for an overnight stop on the Bishkek-Torugart road, but it's a dismal place. A Russian border detachment and a Kyrgyz army unit are based here, and the streets are full of officers and soldiers to-ing and fro-ing. Nearly everyone else is Kyrgyz, most are desperately poor, and many are unemployed. The biggest problem for visitors is multiple drunks, some of them aggressive, and this is no place to be out on the streets after dark.

Naryn's one real claim to fame is that the best quality shyrdaks (traditional, brightly coloured felt-appliqué rugs) in Kyrgyzstan are said to be made here.

Orientation & Information

Naryn is spread along the Naryn river for 15 km, but is just a km or two wide. The road from Bishkek forks north of town, each fork leading to one end of town. A trolleybus line runs along the main street, ulitsa Lenina, for its entire length.

If there's a centre it's probably the municipal *akimyat* or administration building on Lenina. Travellers' landmarks are a small bazar half a km west of this on ulitsa Orozbaka (formerly Krasnoarmeyskaya), and the bus station, 1.2 km east on Lenina. Naryn's small airport is about 11.5 km east of the centre (5.5 km beyond the end of the trolleybus line).

The post and telephone office is half a block east of the town centre on ulitsa Kyrgyzskaya. Naryn's telephone code is 33522. A bank, with a foreign exchange desk, is 300 metres further east, and OVIR is another block east on ulitsa Togolok Moldo.

Things to See & Do

There's little to see except the town's garish new **mosque**, 2.5 km west of the centre – apparently built with Saudi money, and finished in 1993.

One of central Kyrgyzstan's few sources of hot water south of Lake Issyk-Kul appears to be several private **baths** in private courtyards near the riverbank, west of the centre. Hot/cold water and sauna are about US$0.50 per person, and they might do up meals with enough advance warning. Take any trolley-bus for 10-15 minutes to the Gorodok stop, and ask for the banya.

There is also a public banya just up the road from the Hotel Jyldyz.

Places to Stay

Our bottom-end choice is the very spartan but warm and hospitable *Hotel Jyldyz* (☎ 2-48-92) on Orozbaka (Krasnoarmeyskaya), half a block west of the bazar – a converted playschool with 25 beds in four barren rooms, some with washstands, with no hot water and no shower, and a pit toilet in the garden. In summer it's about US$1.50 per person (US$2 in winter to cover heating bills) plus US$2 for delicious supper and breakfast by arrangement with owners Manas and Roza Beksulmanov (they speak no English). Ask for *detskiy sad* (kindergarten) in the *staryy shveynaya fabrika* (old sewing factory).

The best an independent traveller can hope for in Naryn is the 'government hotel', *Pravitelstvennaya Gostinitsa Kerme-Too*

(☎ 2-26-21), with 25 beds in eight plain rooms with common toilet and shower, for about US$8 each and up. There's no hot water, sometimes no water at all, and food is only by advance arrangement and payment. It's three km east of the centre on trolleybus No 2, in a gap between housing blocks.

In summer, Kyrgyzintourist guests can stay in a rubbish-blown yurt camp with pit toilets and a small restaurant, behind the government hotel near the river. But at US$50 per night, forget it! However Kyrgyzintourist (Bishkek) can also arrange homestays in Naryn for around US$10 per person, including meals.

Stay away from the *Hotel Ala-Too* on Lenina, unless it has changed profoundly since we were there. We found the staff in the bar, reeling drunk at 3 pm, and the place filthy and dysfunctional.

Camping However appealing it may be, you can't camp in the surrounding hills. The town is in a restricted military area (because of the base, not the border) and you're sure to get a visit from Russian border troops, who'll move you right down to the Hotel Ala-Too. You can, however, camp further

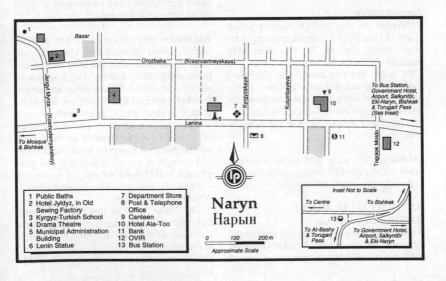

1 Public Baths
2 Hotel Jyldyz, in Old Sewing Factory
3 Kyrgyz-Turkish School
4 Drama Theatre
5 Municipal Administration Building
6 Lenin Statue
7 Department Store
8 Post & Telephone Office
9 Canteen
10 Hotel Ala-Too
11 Bank
12 OVIR
13 Bus Station

Bazar
Orozbaka (Krasnoarmeyskaya)
Jangyl Myrza (Kosmodemyanskoy)
Kyrgyzskaya
Kulumbayeva
Lenina
Topolok Moldo

To Bus Station, Government Hotel, Airport, Salkyntör, Eki-Naryn, Bishkek & Torugart Pass (See Inset)

To Mosque & Bishkek

Naryn
Нарын

0 100 200 m
Approximate Scale

Inset Not to Scale
To Centre   To Bishkek
To At-Bashy & Torugart Pass
To Government Hotel, Airport, Salkyntör & Eki-Naryn

KYRGYZSTAN

east at Salkyntör or, if you have your own transport, at Eki-Naryn (see the Around Naryn section).

Places to Eat

The best food we had in Naryn was at the *Hotel Jyldyz*. There is an adequate canteen (Kyrgyz: *ashkana*, Russian: stolovaya) at the back of the Hotel Ala-Too (thankfully under separate management). There are also two *canteens* in the bazar.

Getting There & Away

Scheduled buses make the tedious trip to/from Bishkek's west station for about US$5, stopping everywhere in between. Faster (a five-hour trip) are minibuses or cars that leave from in front of Bishkek and Naryn bus stations, for a few dollars more. There are also flights but, like the buses, they're subject to frequent cancellation because of insufficient fuel or not enough passengers.

To get to At-Bashy, Tash-Rabat or Torugart, talk to Ulan, son of the Hotel Jyldyz owners, or take your chances with other predatory drivers around the bus station. One daily Bishkek-Naryn bus continues to At-Bashy.

Around Naryn

Salkyntör At this former Pioneer youth camp 17 km east of the centre, a plain guesthouse inside the gate is open from May through October with 12 places for around US$3 each, but you must bring your own food. Or you can trek past the camp into a pretty canyon and pitch a tent. Hitch east for 10.5 km beyond the end of the No 2 trolley-bus line, to a turn-off with a big rainbow arch.

Eki-Naryn We were told about a scenic, piney valley called Eki-Naryn, 30 km east of Salkyntor, but didn't check it out.

NARYN TO JALAL-ABAD
НАРЫН-ДЖАЛАЛ-АБАД

If you're planning to go directly between the Ferghana Valley and the Bishkek-Torugart road, it's possible to cut right across central Kyrgyzstan between Jalal-Abad and Naryn instead of going round via Bishkek. But the gruelling trip over the Ferghana range has few rewards other than getting there (and the rugged scenery en route), and it probably won't save you much money or time either.

The route goes via Kazarman, a gold-mining town in the middle of nowhere where you change buses. The old snub-nose buses on this trip don't look like they could climb a curb, let alone a mountain, and stop everywhere, and don't even start unless they have enough passengers. In a sturdy 4WD you might do it in one long day; by public transport, figure on two or more, depending on weather and road conditions. Don't try it until the snow has melted off the passes. There are stops for food, but you'd be wise to bring your own.

Naryn to Kazarman From the west side of the Naryn bus station a bus departs for Kazarman every Tuesday and Friday about 8 am (about US$8), but only if there are enough passengers. The return trip departs Kazarman on Wednesday and Saturday. It's a nine to 10-hour trip (about 350 km) to Kazarman, a more or less flat 6½ hours along the Naryn river valley plus a climb along little-used dirt roads.

Kazarman This village of 15,000, at 1230 metres, serves the open-cast Makhmal gold mine about an hour to the east, and an ore processing plant nearby. Gold seems to attract trouble, and Kazarman has an uncomfortable, untamed feel. There are said to be some Canadian mining engineers here.

There are two hotels – a two storey white building (shy of foreigners) on the square where Naryn-Kazarman buses terminate, and a single storey white building (the government hotel, *pravitelstvennaya gostinitsa*) just east of the bazar, where Kazarman-Jalal-Abad buses terminate.

The bazar is a 20 minute walk south through back streets from the square. There don't appear to be any restaurants, but there is a teahouse.

Kazarman also has an airport, with US$15

flights to/from Jalal-Abad that are frequently cancelled for lack of passengers.

Kazarman to Jalal-Abad There are no scheduled buses, only when-and-if-it-fills-up buses and cars for about US$15, and taxis offering the trip for about US$50. They'll go only if the weather is good.

The slightly unnerving 6½ hour trip (about 150 km) climbs a narrow dirt track over a 3100 metre pass in the Ferghana range, and finishes at Jalal-Abad bazar. From the scenery on the Ferghana side you can see why the Ferghana Valley is Central Asia's breadbasket.

NARYN TO TORUGART
НАРЫН-ТОРУГАРТ

It's about 130 km from Naryn to the outer checkpost and a further 60 km to the main customs station at Torugart, a total of about 4½ hours driving if you make no stops. But there are two very worthwhile stops, at Koshoy Korgon and Tash-Rabat (see the following sections).

From Naryn it's 24 km to the low **Kyzyl-Bel pass**, with a stupendous view south and west, right down along the crest of the At-Bashy range (highest point 4786 metres). The road runs along the foot of this range and around the far end of it to Torugart. About 13 and 20 km from the pass are two turn-offs to the village of **At-Bashy**, of no interest except as the closest point to the border accessible by regular bus.

West of At-Bashy is a yawning, red-walled notch on the north side of the valley; the road crosses a stream draining everything through this notch and down to the Naryn river. Low bluffs west of the stream partly conceal a bizarre landscape of perfectly rounded, sandy hills. By the roadside is a splendid Kyrgyz graveyard.

About 14.5 km west of the second At-Bashy access road is a turn-off to Kara-Suu village and the ruins of **Koshoy Korgon**.

Some 40 km west of At-Bashy the road turns to gravel, but for a startling three km before it does so, it becomes as wide and smooth as a four-lane superhighway – a mil-

itary airstrip, apparently never used. About 19.5 km off the end of the airstrip (about 99 km from Naryn or 90 km from the main Torugart customs station) is a completely unmarked turn-off south to **Tash-Rabat**.

About 28 km west of this turn-off is the low **Ak-Beyit pass** at the end of the At-Bashy range. Then it's four km to the **outer checkpost**, and another fine view – to the crestline, on the border itself.

Koshoy Korgon
Кошой Коргон

In a field behind the village of Kara-Suu are the surprising ruins of a small citadel, occupied during the 10th to 12th or early 13th century, and probably Qarakhanid. The rapidly eroding walls are now perhaps five metres high, though a local farmer claimed (with mysterious authority) that they were originally 13 metres high and four metres thick. They form a big square, perhaps 300 metres long per side.

A more appealing local legend is that the Kyrgyz superhero Manas built the citadel and a mausoleum here for his fallen friend Koshoy.

Kara-Suu village was founded in 1919 by Kyrgyz refugees from Bolshevik oppression in the Chuy valley near Bishkek.

Places to Stay & Eat At-Bashy is off the Naryn-Torugart road, six km by an easterly access road, four km by a westerly one, and truly the far end of Kyrgyzstan. But there is a small hotel, the *Koshoy* (with a room for perhaps a dollar or two?); from the bus station go west for one km, turn right by a cinema, and it's 200 metres along on the right. There are grotty cafés at the bus station and beside the hotel, and a small bazar, about 600 metres west of the bus station.

Getting There & Away There is one scheduled early-morning bus between At-Bashy and Bishkek each day, for about US$5. On your own you could hire an At-Bashy taxi out to Koshoy Korgon and back for perhaps US$15.

About 14.5 km west of the western access

road to At-Bashy on the Naryn-Torugart road, turn south to Kara-Suu village. Take the first left turn in the village, go out past all the houses and look to the right for the ruins.

Tash-Rabat
Таш-Рабат

At a completely unmarked turn-off 55 to 60 km from At-Bashy or 32 km from the outer Kyrgyz checkpost, a sometimes washed-out dirt track heads into a surprisingly level and very lovely valley in the At-Bashy range. It's the perfect shelter, with lush corduroy hillsides, small farmsteads and the occasional yurt encampment. Indeed it must have been attracting well-to-do travellers for centuries, for about 15 km in is a solitary fortified caravanserai, looking rather like a little mausoleum.

Local sources say it dates from the 15th century, though a clumsy total restoration was completed in 1984. For a donation of US$0.50 or US$1 in *som* to the caretakers in the adjacent house, you can have a look inside. A few fragments of the original interior are visible in the main chamber; leading off this are many other chambers, including a well and a dungeon. An opening in the far right corner leads to what the caretakers say is a tunnel, explored generations ago as far as about 200 metres, and perhaps once leading to a lookout point to the south.

From here you can climb to a broad ridge overlooking Chatyr-Köl lake, but watch out: you're about 3500 metres high, and a short walk could set your head pounding. Chatyr-Köl is four or five hours away on horseback, longer on foot, but it's just a big, flat puddle, surrounded by a boggy plain. Neither Tash-Rabat nor Chatyr-Köl are in a restricted border zone, so no permits are needed.

Places to Stay You can't stay in the caravansai, and the house is private, but the valley is a fine place to camp and very peaceful if you happen to have it to yourself. If you do want to camp, bring all your own supplies – plus tea, cigarettes or vodka for the lonely caretakers (who might also take some in trade for the hire of a horse for the day).

Getting There & Away A day trip by car from Naryn to Tash-Rabat would be perhaps US$70.

THE TORUGART PASS
ПЕРЕВАЛ ТОРУГАРТ

South from the outer checkpost the road rapidly degenerates. About 26 km on, at the 3574 metre **Tüz-Bel pass**, it turns east and skirts Chatyr-Köl. The same black cranes that pause on their journey at the Karkara valley east of Issyk-Kul also stop here, and along with its broad, marshy shoreline the lake comprises the Chatyr-Köl zoological preserve. An old Soviet-era double electrified fence runs near the road, still patrolled by Russians but supposedly no longer charged up. As the road climbs, the surrounding mountains seem to shrink.

Fifty km from the outer checkpost and seven km from the Kyrgyzstan customs & immigration station, a big red and yellow sign says 'Narzan'; 50 metres off the road in a field of bubbling mud is a gushing cold spring, fizzy and tasty.

Customs & Immigration

The Torugart customs & immigration facilities straddle the pass. From the Kyrgyzstan customs & immigration station it's 6.8 km to the summit. There the Chinese have built a miniature red-brick Arc de Triomphe, with a few Russian or Kyrgyz soldiers hanging out on the Kyrgyz side, and a small house with Chinese guards on the other side. Below this, about five km away, is the main Chinese customs & immigration station. The wind seems to howl here all the time.

Most of the traffic through the pass is trucks carrying scrap metal and animal hides from Kyrgyzstan; or porcelain, thermoses, beer and clothing from China. The trucks accumulate in huge tailbacks at both sides, for half a km or more in the mornings.

Kyrgyzstan Side The customs & immigration facilities are open from about 10 am to 5 pm. Besides the various customs sheds, inspection pits and immigration offices, there is a spartan state 'hotel' – slapped-up barracks and a canteen, where a bed (in a triple, quad or dorm, with common pit toilet) plus basic dinner and breakfast is about US$2.50 in *som*. Politely decline to leave your passport with them overnight; OVIR will find and register you by morning in any case.

Below this are several dozen enclosed wooden wagons, each of them a little private 'guesthouse' where you can take simple meals and sleep on cotton mattresses on the floor (family in one end, three or four guests in the other) for US$2 for a bed and US$1.50 each for meals and tea. We saw no obvious toilets or running water around these, and the grounds are pretty foul.

Summit In the border zone, roughly between the two customs & immigration stations, permitted vehicles are allowed, but apparently no pedestrians other than guards (although some travellers are said to have walked it). Once upon a time a shuttle bus covered part of this zone but this has apparently been cancelled.

China Side The customs & immigration facilities (labelled Tu'ergate on the map) are open from noon to 5 pm, Beijing time. Everything is in a chaotic line, muddy or dusty depending on the weather. Queues of trucks stretch in *both* directions here, awaiting reloading. There is a bank (closed on weekends and holidays), a simple noodle shop and a small guesthouse, though travellers in either direction are discouraged from staying. All this is to be relocated to modern facilities 100 km down the road to Kashgar in the near future.

Procedures Following is what we did on our way from Kyrgyzstan into China. Travellers coming the other way reported roughly the same in reverse, minus the delays at the arch.

Kyrgyzstan immigration takes your passport (they want to see Kyrgyzstan visa, OVIR registration, China visa and something that looks like proof of onward transportation in China). Meanwhile, off you

go to quarantine, where you might be asked for a cholera certificate (a ridiculous scam, considering you're *leaving*), and then customs.

There you (and your driver if he's switched-on enough) go into a small room with several of the jackals from customs. They showed no interest in our hotel or foreign exchange receipts, but were happy to see a customs form from our initial CIS entry, and checked off everything reported there; they may want to see your money too. Your best defence against a possible shakedown is probably to speak only English and play dumb. You may also have to pay a per-vehicle gosposhlina, a government levy for crossing the border zone. Then back you go to wait for your passport to be returned and your vehicle to be waved through.

At the arch on the border the toy soldiers on the China side will exhaustively check your passport, China visa, confirmation letter/telex and the inside of your vehicle, with possibly a look at your bags. And here is the moment of truth: if they cannot locate your onward transportation, you may be delayed a long, cold time or sent back. Kyrgyz drivers with a Foreign Ministry permit should be allowed all the way down the other side, but this may not cut much ice at the arch.

Then with luck it's down to China customs & immigration. Immigration is a tiny brick building with a scrum of Uyghurs, Kyrgyz and Chinese around the two windows. The sheer surprise of seeing a westerner may open a path to a window for you, but watch your pockets. Show your passport, China visa and letter/telex, fill out an entry form (no charge) and get your entry stamp. Some travellers report huge delays, with their passports disappearing for hours because everybody was occupied with trucks and truckers, or with lunch.

At quarantine, there was no check of health documents at all when we crossed, but be prepared with your vaccination papers.

If you're not in a group you may have to hang around the customs building (with a fenced courtyard out front) until you find

KYRGYZSTAN

someone not occupied with trucks. Foreigners' bags get only a cursory look; indeed you may have to insist that the official pay attention and write onto the form everything that someone might want to see when you *leave* China. Uyghurs and Kyrgyz get a far more thorough treatment.

TORUGART TO KASHGAR
ТОРУГАРТ-КАШГАР

It's surprising how the climate and landscape change when you cross the pass. The China side is abruptly drier, more desolate and treeless. There is little physical development on the China side other than adobe Kyrgyz settlements, but the traffic, heavy with Japanese 4WDs and minibuses, lends a vague air of prosperity. The road runs through Kyzylsu Kyrgyz Autonomous Country.

The 100 km of road closest to the border, south through crumbling, red-walled canyons, is a miserable washboard surface, spine-shattering to travel along and choked with dust. At 45 km is a gate at the hamlet of **Toyun**, where passports are checked and numbers scribbled in a book. One couple reported staying the night here, in a soldiers' hostel for about US$3 per bed.

About 10 km further on, the Torugart-Suu canyon from the border post enters the equally immense Ushmurvan-Suu canyon from the north-west, flowing down to Kashgar. It's 41 km from here to a river bridge, and a further seven km to the spanking new **China customs & immigration station**, and a petrol station. From here to Kashgar it's 60 km of paved road.

The whole Torugart-Kashgar trip is 160 km, a 3½ to four hour 4WD trip.

Bishkek to Osh & the Kyrgyz Ferghana Valley

From the standpoint of landscape, the Bishkek-Osh road is a sequence of superlatives, taking over two 3000 metre-plus passes, through the yawning Suuasmyr

valley, around the immense Toktogul reservoir, down the deep Naryn river gorge and into the broad Ferghana Valley.

It's not to be taken lightly, however. The road is rough (and buses do little to cushion the spinal impact), and hair-raising with the wrong driver. The Bishkek-Toktogul stretch is blocked occasionally by rockfalls, and in winter frequently by avalanches. Even in summer the passes are icy cold – no place to be stranded with a disabled bus. Snow fills the passes from October or November until February or March; the road is kept open but is dangerous then. Scheduled buses thin out by October and stop over winter, although cars continue to push through. There are frequent police checkpoints (this is a major artery for drugs smuggled from Afghanistan into Russia).

No regular buses go all the way; you must normally change at Toktogul, sometimes at Kara-Köl. Smaller arenda minibuses have an easier time of it than big buses, and you may find a few outside Bishkek's long-distance bus station that go all the way to Jalal-Abad or even Osh.

Bishkek to Toktogul

Even before you climb out of the Chuy valley from Kara-Balta, the craggy Kyrgyz Alatau range rises like a wall. The road climbs through a crumbling canyon towards the highest point of the journey, the 3586 metre **Tör-Ashuu pass** (Russian: Tyuz-Ashuu) at the suture between the Talas Alatau and Kyrgyz Alatau ranges. But instead of climbing over, it burrows through near the top, in a dripping tunnel that opens onto an eagle's-eye view of the Suusamyr basin.

About 4½ hours out of Bishkek a road shoots off straight as an arrow across the basin towards Suusamyr, Chayek and eventually the Bishkek-Naryn road, and after another 1¼ hours another branches right, over the Otmek pass towards Zhambyl in Kazakstan. In another half-hour you have climbed again, to the 3184 metre summit of **Ala-Bel pass** over the Suusamyr-Too mountains. Lower, broader and longer than the

Tör-Ashuu pass, it is nevertheless colder, and said to be the bigger wintertime spoiler.

The beautiful valley down the south side of the pass, though partly in the Chychkan state zoological reserve, is defaced by three ranks of crackling high-voltage lines, running up from the dam at the head of the **Toktogul reservoir** (Russian: Toktogulskoe vodokhranilishche) which now spreads out below. Most buses terminate at Toktogul on the lake's north side.

Bishkek-Toktogul is an eight-hour (about 300 km) trip by minibus.

Toktogul
Токтогул
Population: approx 70,000
This town is named for a well-known Kyrgyz akyn who was born here in 1884 (died 1933). It has nothing to recommend it, but is the usual bus change-over point between Bishkek and Osh, and you'll probably have to spend the night and push off again at sunrise. At night it sounds like it has more stray dogs than people.

From the bus station entrance, walk right (west) and immediately left (south) along a boulevard for about 400 metres. Just off to the right is the grotty town hotel *Ketmen-Töbö*, with beds for US$2 per person in doubles or triples, and filthy toilets one floor down – or a ridiculously huge apartment for US$3.50! They hadn't yet heard of foreigners' prices. Hot water is unlikely. The hotel has an overpriced bufet with survival rations.

If you have your own transportation, a possible alternative is what looks like a trucker's hostel and restaurant, 1¼ hours south on the other side of the reservoir.

Getting There & Away Around 6 am a single bus departs for Bishkek for US$6, and another for Jalal-Abad for US$3. Others go to Osh at 5.40 and 7.30 am for US$3, and to Kara-Köl at noon for US$2. We missed the bus but got a ride in a jeep looking for passengers at the station. There are also arenda buses out on the highway, a block north of the station.

Toktogul to Kara-Köl
The two to 2½ hour journey is mainly occupied with getting around the vast, flat reservoir. We spotted, but did not visit, what looks like a hotel and restaurant, big and yellow, 1¼ hours south from Toktogul where the road leaves the lake.

Kara-Köl
Кара-Көл
Population: approx 22,000
Scribbled in English on a wall in the outskirts of town is a greeting: 'wellcome to fucking Kara-Kul'. Just about everybody here works for the hydroelectric station Toktogulsky Gidroelektrostantsia or GES. The sole reason to alight is to ask for a tour of the dam. JK was roughed up by plainclothes police at the Kara-Köl bus station as he was leaving at dawn, so give the place a wide miss unless you're very interested in dams.

Kara-Köl (Russian: Kara-Kul) is not to be confused with the town Karakol on Lake Issyk-Kul.

Information & Orientation Ask to be dropped, not at the bus station but about two km west by a tiny 'Gostinitsa Turist' sign. This is also close to the dam administration offices.

The Kaskad The dam is part of the Nizhnenarynskiy kaskad (Lower Naryn river cascade), a series of five dams down the lower gorge of the Naryn river. This cascade, topmost in the series, was completed in 1976 after 14 years' work. More and bigger ones are under construction or in planning. Their power is distributed into the grid Kyrgyzstan shares with Uzbekistan and Kazakstan. Hydroelectric power is in fact one of the few things other than tourism that Kyrgyzstan has to sell to the outside world.

You can't see the Toktogul dam (behind a ridge to the west of the hotel) from town or from the road, and you can't just trek over to it – you won't get in without a pass. You might succeed in getting this and a guided tour by asking at kaskad headquarters, a two storey yellow brick building just off the

KYRGYZSTAN

highway near the hotel. Go upstairs to the director's office, where we found one English-speaking staff member.

The massive dam, wedged in the canyon, is a pretty awesome feat of Soviet engineering: 210 metres high, 150 metres wide at the top, and holding back a 19 billion cubic metre lake. Photographs are not allowed of the Toktogul dam.

Places to Stay There's only one place to stay, the quiet *Hotel Turist*, where mouldy triples with bathtub and hot water are about US$2 per person, dorm-style. The dining room does a dreary set meal for about US$0.50, but book ahead or you may find it shut. It's out on the western edge of town, near the kaskad headquarters but over two km from the bus station, which is out on the other side of town.

Getting There & Away Buses for US$4.50 to Jalal-Abad or Osh depart around 6.30 am (ask at the hotel for the exact times), and the bus station is a long, cold, dark walk from the hotel. You're better off flagging the bus down from near the kaskad headquarters,

though you can't be sure of a seat. For Bishkek, change at Toktogul.

Kara-Köl to Jalal-Abad

The gorge of the lower Naryn river is surely one of Central Asia's more impressive passages, with sheer walls and towering pillars of red sandstone, and a little road clinging to the side – but keep your gaze upwards. Looking down you will see that there is no longer any river at all, just a depressing series of narrow, utterly still lakes behind the dams of the Nizhnenarynskiy kaskad. At lower elevations the gorge bristles with pylons. Sit on the 'west' side of the bus for the best views of this ruination.

About 5½ hours from Toktogul is the coal-mining town of Tashkömür (Russian: Tash-Kumyr), strung for miles along the west side of the river below one of the dams. There is said to be a hotel here.

Then out of the mountains you shoot, into the Ferghana Valley, with endless flat fields, mostly of cotton, beyond the roadside borders of poplar and mulberry trees. Near Kochkor-Ata the road briefly enters Uzbekistan. You won't miss it: glowering Uzbek police come aboard to search the bus,

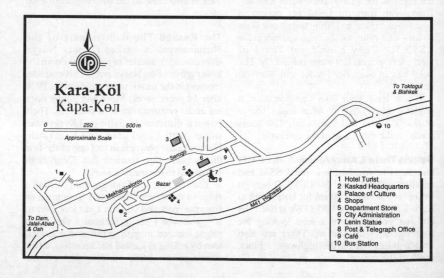

Kara-Köl
Кара-Көл

0   250   500 m
Approximate Scale

To Toktogul & Bishkek

M41 Highway

To Dam, Jalal-Abad & Osh

1 Hotel Turist
2 Kaskad Headquarters
3 Palace of Culture
4 Shops
5 Department Store
6 City Administration
7 Lenin Statue
8 Post & Telegraph Office
9 Café
10 Bus Station

and the atmosphere is heavier than at any Kyrgyz checkpoint.

Only the unnatural boundaries laid down in Soviet days isolate the outer rim of the Ferghana Valley from the rest of it. See also the Ferghana Valley section of the Uzbekistan chapter.

JALAL-ABAD
ЖАЛАЛ-АБАД

Jalal-Abad (Russian: Dzhalalabad) is mainly a resort town. If you're not just changing buses here, head up the hill for a soak at the sanatorium. A turbaza at Arslanbob (see the Around Jalal-Abad section) makes a fine longer digression into the mountains.

If you're coming from the north of Kyrgyzstan, the religiously conservative and politically retrograde atmosphere of the Ferghana Valley may come as a surprise. Here we caught our first sight in Central Asia of the top-to-toe veil *(paranjeh)* worn by fundamentalist Muslim women. Jalal-Abad also feels like it's stuck in a Soviet time-warp.

Like Osh and other border towns, the town is bilingual with both Kyrgyz and Uzbek spoken.

Orientation & Information

The main street is east-west Lenin köchösü (or ulitsa Lenina), and the town centre is a little square at the intersection with Toktogul köchösü. Here and there you'll see little English signs to the airport, train station etc.

The post and telephone office is on Erkindik köchösü near the Hotel Mölmöl. Jalal-Abad's telephone code is 33231.

Things to See & Do

Rise above it all on a three km walk (or five minute ride) up a tree-lined road to the peaceful, threadbare Kurort Jalal-Abad (Russian for Jalal-Abad Sanatorium), with fine views of the almond-grove-blanketed countryside and the Babash-Ata mountains to the north. Head to the rear of the grounds, staying to the right; near a small laghman café are the baths, open to the public, with mud and

mineral water baths for US$1, massage for US$1, sauna for US$0.75, and all the mineral water you can drink.

A taxi from the centre is about US$0.20 (ask for 'kurort'), and there are usually a few hanging around the gate. There is also a yellow bus for sanatorium workers, which leaves from east of the Hotel Mölmöl at about 8.30 am (but doesn't return until midday).

Places to Stay

The old Hotel Jalalabad has been renamed the *Hotel Mölmöl*, but remains unchanged in all other respects from Soviet days, with breathtakingly rude staff, second-hand sheets, broken toilets, no hot water, and a grotty, flyblown restaurant serving cold gulyash. Singles/doubles with toilet and what might charitably be called a shower are US$3.50/6.50 and up. Other travellers report that couples were not allowed to share a room without solid proof of being married.

The sanatorium has a government guesthouse, near the baths. Four suites, each with two double rooms, TV, two bathrooms and a fridge, are rather pricey at US$40. Sanatorium workers apparently rent out their flats here for around US$10 per night.

Places to Eat

The *Islam Sydyk Restaurant* has cheap, tasty Kyrgyz dishes on its 'first-course' menu, including soups (manpar, kesme or shorpa) and the little dumplings called chuchvara, as well as pricier salads and European offerings. It's open daily from 8 am to midnight. Go for lunch and have soup and dumplings for US$1.50; after 6 pm the scene is set for a Russian-style blow-out – shattering music, flashing lights, the works. It's on Lenin, a block west of the square; the building has '1917-1977' on the side.

The privatised *Restaurant Ala-Too* opposite the Hotel Mölmöl has decent soups and Russian standards at lunch, but it's a fly sanctuary, with blow-you-away music in the evening.

Travellers later told us about the good *Bizniz Klub Jergal*, serving Dungan, Kyrgyz

KYRGYZSTAN

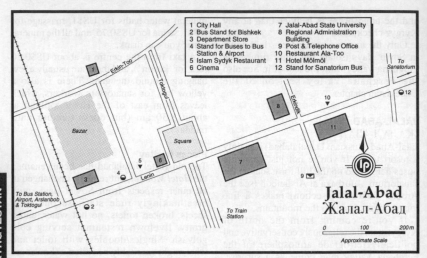

1 City Hall	7	Jalal-Abad State University
2 Bus Stand for Bishkek	8	Regional Administration
3 Department Store		Building
4 Stand for Buses to Bus	9	Post & Telephone Office
Station & Airport	10	Restaurant Ala-Too
5 Islam Sydyk Restaurant	11	Hotel Mölmöl
6 Cinema	12	Stand for Sanatorium Bus

Jalal-Abad
Жалал-Абад

and Russian fare to subdued live music in a clean setting – somewhere on Toktogul just north of Lenin. It's only open for lunch.

Getting There & Away

Air Marshrutnoe taxi No 1 from the centre and taxi No 5 from the bus station go to the airport, north-west of the centre. A taxi is about US$15. On paper, there are flights to/from Bishkek twice a day; buy tickets at the airport only.

Bus The bus station is west of the centre; buses clearly marked АВТОВОКЗАЛ (avtovokzal) run frequently along Lenin near the bazar. Scheduled buses depart for Kara-Köl at 8.20 am, and Toktogul at 6 and 10.20 am. Osh buses leave every half hour or so until 6 pm (US$1). Uzbekistan connections include Marghilan via Andijan at 1.10 pm (US$5). For Tashkent, change at Khanabad (formerly Sovietabad) en route to Osh, or probably at Andijan or Namangan.

At a stand on Lenin opposite the bazar you may find arenda buses going all the way to Bishkek, especially in the evening. Here or at the bazar (someone also suggested the airport) you may find the occasional bus to

Naryn via Kazarman (see the Bishkek to Kashgar via the Torugart Pass section of this chapter).

Train The train station is on Toktogul by any bus or a 10 minute walk south from Lenin (we also saw horse-drawn carts there). A slow passenger train (No 187) to Bishkek starts here every other day, a 30 hour roundabout trip via Tashkent, Zhambyl and Shymkent for US$10 local price for a platskartnyy (hard sleeper) ticket. On the same train Tashkent takes 14 hours, for US$5. There are departures all day to/from Andijan on the Uzbekistan side for about US$1.25. A daily fast train also starts here for Moscow.

Around Jalal-Abad

Better than looking at the mountains from Jalal-Abad is to go up into them. An adventurous do-it-yourself trip goes up to **Arslanbob**, a totally Uzbek village of about 12,000 with a summer turbaza.

The rundown but rustic *Turbaza Arslanbob* (☎ 107, 140 or 177 from Jalal-Abad) swarms all summer with CIS holidaymakers here for the mountain air, grand setting, abundant fruit, and the area's famous walnuts, and – for those who can tear themselves away from the pool, video salon and cinema club – some fine walking and climbing in the Babash-Ata mountains. 'Instructors' lead reasonably priced day-hikes or treks to waterfalls, caves or Ketmen-Köl lake, or into the adjacent valley and to the smaller but similar *Turbaza Kyzyl-Ungur*. Alpinists can take on 4427 metre Babash-Ata (or Weber) Peak.

Prospects of a space at Arslanbob are good even without a booking. The place has over 500 beds, for about US$5 each per night, in bungalows scattered around 29 hectares of grounds, with common showers and toilets; or you could pitch your own tent. A huge dining hall and a teahouse serve Uzbek dishes. There are also several *pansiyonaty* down at the lower end of the village, intended for the very sedentary.

Don't go up outside the season (June through September), when there's nowhere to stay, shops are empty and it's c-o-l-d. Arslanbob is over 3000 metres and even in summer it's considerably cooler than Jalal-Abad.

The only English speaker is the village's schoolmaster, and even Russian is scarce. This is a fairly conservative village, so don't go up in shorts and singlets!

American *biznesmen* are said to have their eyes on the area's vast walnut groves, and not for the nuts.

Getting There & Away From Jalal-Abad, take a bus to Bazar Korgon (40 minutes, departs hourly). Change there for an Arslanbob bus and take it to the end of the line (2½ hours, hourly until 6 pm). The Kyrgyz version of the name, Арстанбап (Arstanbap), is used on buses and timetables. You can also get there on any bus marked Бургөндү (Burghöndü). It's a 1.5 km uphill walk to the turbaza gate. A day trip would be possible by car but not by bus.

OSH
ОШ (Kyrgyz), ҮШ (Uzbek)
Population: 250,000
Osh is Kyrgyzstan's second biggest city, and administrative centre of the huge, populous province that engulfs the Ferghana Valley on the Kyrgyzstan side. It suffers a kind of demographic schizophrenia, being a major centre of Kyrgyzstan but with a dominantly Uzbek population more in tune with Uzbekistan and the rest of the Ferghana Valley, but isolated from it by one of the world's more absurd international borders. The resulting tension has had Osh on a communal knife-edge ever since Stalin drew the line, as Uzbek-Kyrgyz violence in 1990 emphatically showed.

There is almost nothing of architectural interest here, and yet this is one of Central Asia's most interesting cities because of its long history – it's one of the region's genuinely ancient towns, with a history dating back at least to the 5th century BC – its position as an important crossroads for Silk Road trade, its broad mixture of peoples, and its huge market.

It's still a very Soviet place; while other cities scrubbed Lenin's name from their street maps after the collapse of the USSR, Osh merely shifted it politely one block away!

Osh is also the anchor-point of not only the Pamir Highway into Tajikistan but, branching off this, the main road access to the Pamir Alay on the Kyrgyzstan-Tajikistan border, and in the other direction a commercial crossing to/from Kashgar in China.

The city is a common travellers' base for trekking and mountaineering in the spectacular Pamir range.

History
The standard refrain from anyone you ask is that 'Osh is older than Rome'. Legends credit all sorts of people with its founding, from King Solomon (Suleyman) to Alexander the Great. Certainly it must have been a major hub on the Silk Road from its earliest days. The Mongols smashed it in the 13th century but in the following centuries it bounced back, more prosperous than ever.

Its late fame, however, is of a different kind. 'Osh' has become a byword for ethnic conflict in the festering, gerrymandered closeness of the Ferghana Valley. In fact the worst of 'Osh' took place 55 km away in Özgön (Uzgen), during three nights of savage Uzbek-Kyrgyz violence in June-July 1990, during which at least 300 people (some unofficial estimates run to over 1000) died a variety of ugly deaths while Soviet military and police authorities stood oddly by.

When post-Soviet Kyrgyzstan adopted its own currency, Uzbekistan accused it of trying to sabotage Central Asian unity and imposed a blockade on exports of oil and gas to Kyrgyzstan; Osh, caught in the middle, felt the temperature rise again. While the

majority Uzbeks dominate local business, Kyrgyzstan has forced upon them an almost totally Kyrgyz (and apparently widely corrupt) municipal administration, by which they feel constantly 'plundered'.

Rumours abound of weapons stockpiled for future conflicts. But considering the likelihood that most people around Osh and Özgön – Kyrgyz and Uzbek alike – have friends or family members who were murdered in 1990, the wonder is how many Kyrgyz and Uzbeks remain close friends (or married couples) and how determined most of them are to get along.

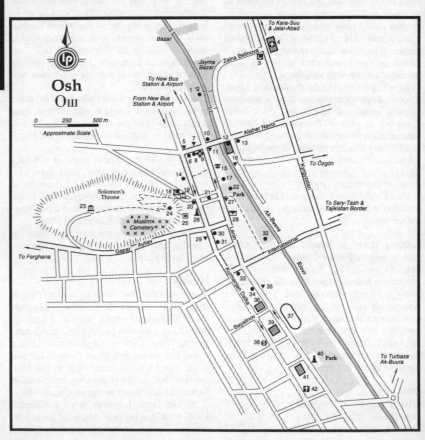

Orientation

Osh sprawls across the valley of the Ak-Buura river, flowing out of the Pamir Alay mountains. The city's most prominent landmark is 'Solomon's Throne', a craggy mountain that squeezes right up to the river from the west.

Along the west bank run two parallel main roads – one-way-south Kurmanjan Datka kuchasi and one-way-north Lenin kuchasi. To confuse matters, Lenin kuchasi used to be ulitsa Sverdlova, while Kurmanjan Datka kuchasi used to be ulitsa Lenina! Be careful with older maps, which may still immortalise Lenin one block over. From the Hotel Osh to the bazar is a 20 to 25 minute walk.

Osh's old bus station (*starry avtovokzal*) is on Alisher Navoi kuchasi just east of the river, while the new one (*novyy avtovokzal*) is about eight km north of Navoi on Lenin or Kurmanjan Datka. The airport is about 20 minutes by bus beyond the new bus station. The nearest train station is at Kara-Suu, halfway to Jalal-Abad.

Information

Useful Organisations You might find keen students of English or other languages to act as unofficial guides to the city, at Osh University's Languages Faculty, on Kurmanjan Datka north of Internatsional.

Money A branch of the state bank (Gosbank) is on Kurmanjan Datka, a block south of the Hotel Osh, although it's easier to change money at the hotel. The only alternative seems to be the moneychangers who hang around in front of the food section of the bazar.

Post & Communications International calls can be made from the main telephone and telegraph office, on Lenin kuchasi south of Navoi, but possibly more easily (and of course more expensively) from the Hotel Osh. The main post office is two blocks south of the telephone office. Osh's telephone code is 33222.

Travel Agencies Alptreksport (☎ 2-30-01, ☎ & fax 7-79-06, contact Yury or Sasha Lavrushin), run by veterans of the Soviet sports agency Sovintersport's Pamir International Mountaineering Camp (IMC), does

KYRGYZSTAN

PLACES TO STAY		13	Taxi Stand
6	Hotel Alay	14	Regional Library
36	Hotel Osh	15	Telephone & Telegraph Office
		17	Bobur Uzbek Musical Drama Theatre
PLACES TO EAT		18	Rabat Abdulla Khan Mosque
		19	Historical-Cultural Museum
1	Food Section of Bazar	20	Silver Dome
5	Teahouse	21	University Administration Building
7	Cholpon Restaurant	22	Yak-40
11	Canteen, in Basement of Commercial	23	Historical-Cultural Museum (Branch)
	Centre	24	Dom Babura (Babur's House)
16	Teahouse	25	Mausoleum
27	Teahouse & Chynar Restaurant	26	War Memorial
29	Teahouse	28	Post Office
35	Restaurant Ak-Buura	30	Bookshop
		31	Languages Faculty
OTHER		32	Circus Tent & Children's Park
		33	Polyclinic
2	Money Changers	34	Bookshop
3	Mosque	37	Stadium
4	Municipal Hospital	38	Bank
8	Airline Booking Office	39	Kyrgyz Drama Theatre
9	Department Store	40	Lenin Statue
10	Cinema	41	Regional Administration Building
12	Old Bus Station	42	Orthodox Church

KYRGYZSTAN

Old & New Street Names in Osh

We use here the Uzbek word for street, *kuchasi*, rather than the Kyrgyz *köchösü*. You will also still hear the Russian word *ulitsa* occasionally with pre-independence street names.

Following are some important name changes around the city centre, along with a few that are just conversions to local form.

New Name	Old Name
Lenin kuchasi	ulitsa Sverdlova
Kurmanjan Datka kuchasi	ulitsa Lenina
Alisher Navoi kuchasi	ulitsa Telmana
Internatsional kuchasi	Internatsionalnaya ulitsa
Gapar Aytiev kuchasi	Pionerskaya ulitsa
Bayalinov kuchasi	ulitsa 25 let Oktyabrya

---

mainly mountaineering, trekking and caving trips for about US$35 to US$40 per person per day from Bishkek or Osh. They prefer advance bookings but can accommodate drop-ins. Yury speaks English. Their address is Gogol kuchasi 3, Osh 714018.

The manager of Turbaza Ak-Buura, Jenishbek Ajimamatov, is also a representative for the Osh Provincial Committee for Tourism & Excursions (Turist), and can arrange transport, excursions and other services. His office (☎ 2-20-36) is at Golubev kuchasi 82, Osh 714017.

Emergency & Medical Services The municipal hospital is at the intersection of Zaina Betinova kuchasi and Kyrgyzstan kuchasi, north-east of the bazar. There's a polyclinic on Internatsional between Kurmanjan Datka and Lenin.

Dangers & Annoyances Public transport shuts down soon after dark, and Osh is probably not very safe for wandering foreigners after that. Don't get stranded.

Bazar

The thunderous daily Jayma bazar is one of Central Asia's best open markets, teeming with Uzbeks, Kyrgyz and Tajiks dealing in everything from traditional hats and knives to pirate cassettes, horseshoes (forged at smithies in the bazar) to Chinese tea-sets,

plus abundant seasonal fruit and vegetables. It stretches for about a km along the west side of the river, and crosses it in several places. It's most kinetic on Sundays, and almost deserted on Mondays.

Solomon's Throne

Solomon's Throne (Uzbek: Takhti-Suleyman; Russian: Suleyman-gora, Suleyman Hill), a jagged, barren rock that seems to loom above the city wherever you go, has been a Muslim place of pilgrimage of some importance for centuries, supposedly because the Prophet Muhammad once prayed here. From certain perspectives it looks like a reclining pregnant woman, and it's especially favoured by women who have been unable to bear children.

In 1497, 14-year-old Zahiruddin Babur, newly crowned king of Ferghana (and later to found India's Moghul Dynasty) built himself a little shelter and private mosque on the rock's high eastern promontory. In later years this came to be something of an attraction in its own right. It collapsed in an earthquake in 1853 and was rebuilt. Then in the 1960s it was destroyed by a mysterious explosion; most local people are convinced it was a Soviet attempt to halt the persistent pilgrim traffic and put a chill on 'superstition', ie Islam, after failing to persuade Uzbek authorities to do so. After independence it was rebuilt again.

JOHN KING

ANDREW HUMPHREYS

JOHN KING

Tajikistan
Top Left: Tajik man, Barakat market, Dushanbe
Top Right: Tajik man, Hissar Fortress, near Dushanbe
Bottom: Excavations of Sogdian city of Bunjikath, near Penjkent

ANDREW HUMPHREYS

Turkmenistan
A woman proudly displays her rugs for sale

Local people call it **Dom Babura**, Babur's House. If you speak Russian, the friendly Uzbek caretaker will tell you more, and he's always grateful for a few *som* for 'upkeep'. The steep 25 minute climb begins at a little gateway behind a futuristic silver dome (a small shop) on Kurmanjan Datka. The promontory offers long views but little to see except for a vast **Muslim cemetery** at the foot of the hill.

Carry on around the south side for another 15 minutes to see Central Asia's most ridiculous **museum**. With typical Soviet subtlety, a hole was blasted in the side of this sacred mountain into one of its many caves, and a grotesque sheet-metal front stuck on – a carbuncle now visible from great distances. Inside is a series of badly lit, unintelligible exhibits of potsherds, old masonry, rocks, bugs and mangy stuffed animals; upstairs is a huge, forlorn yurt. It's open daily except Monday and Tuesday, from 9 am to noon and 1 to 5 pm. Admission is about one *som*.

This is a branch of the Historical-Cultural Museum in Osh. In fact the archaeological bits would probably be worth seeing with a guide. But it's a surprise and a pity that this very old and important Silk Road city doesn't have a better museum of archaeology and history than this.

Back down at the bottom of the hill is the main **Historical-Cultural Museum**, open weekdays from 9 am to 1 pm and 2 to 5 pm with a small display of old and new applied art, including textiles, clothing and jewellery. Just beyond it is the little **Rabat Abdul Khan Mosque**, dating from the 17th or 18th century but rebuilt in the 1980s. It's a working mosque (ie male visitors only, and by permission only; shoes off at the entrance). A small **mausoleum** is to the south along the base of the hill.

Other Sights

There isn't much, other than a long riverbank **park** stretching from Navoi to Internatsional. A central feature is an old Yak-40, now a video salon, looking poised to leap over the river.

Places to Stay

The best Osh has to offer is the *Hotel Osh* (☎ 2-47-17, 2-48-57), also called the Hotel Intourist, at Bayalinov 1 between Kurmanjan Datka and Lenin. Basic clean rooms with toilet and bath start at US$16 per person – not bad except that, even in November, they had no heat or hot water and only faltering electricity. The floor-ladies are angels but everyone else seems foul-tempered. When we were there the restaurant (open from noon) had ear-splitting music and no customers beyond a few pinstriped thugs, though there is a small bufet. Get there on bus or marshrutnoe taxi No 2 from the old bus station, or bus No 13 from the new bus station.

The *Hotel Alay* (☎ 2-17-33) on Navoi is centrally located but depressing – loud, barren, with no hot water and dubious security. Marginally clean rooms without shower or toilet are about US$6 per person. There's a grotty canteen next door and a fair teahouse across the road, and it's a five minute walk to the food section of the bazar.

On the face of it, the year-round *Turbaza Ak-Buura* (☎ 2-20-36) is the city's best bargain – set in 24 hectares of woods, peaceful and cool in summer, with rooms and bungalows with common toilet and shower for US$2 a bed, and a restaurant with Kyrgyz dishes. You can also pitch your own tent. But it has acquired a reputation for sleaze, and travellers report drunks trying to enter lockless doors at night. Take bus or marshrutnoe taxi No 2 south on Kurmanjan Datka until it doubles back and crosses the river; from the traffic roundabout walk up the middle road, Golubev kuchasi (ulitsa Golubeva), for 2½ blocks, carrying on past the gate to reception at the top of the road.

Do not confuse this with the utterly wretched, broken-down *Turbaza Osh*, further out of town (20 minutes from the centre) on the No 2 line.

Nobody mentions the 5% municipal hotel tax until it's time to pay.

Places to Eat

The *bazar* is a good bet; keep an eye open

especially for good prepared foods from Russian and Korean vendors.

There's also good grub at the city's *chayhonas*, though hygiene is always dubious. Resident expatriates say the hot laghman at one on Lenin near the post office, in front of the *Chynar Restaurant*, is the best in town; there's also plov, shashlyk, fat samsas, bread (made on site) and of course endless tea. Pay in advance (and separately for tea). There are several *teahouses* opposite the Hotel Alay too; the one on the corner is popular at lunch, and adequate.

In the basement of the commercial centre with the clock tower and stepped roof at the corner of Lenin and Navoi, we found a little *canteen* run by three Uzbek brothers, with a small, changing menu of delicious, well-prepared Uzbek and Kyrgyz dishes for incredibly tiny prices. There's no sign; from Lenin, walk round to the basement stairs at the rear (south-east) corner, and it's halfway down the corridor on the right. It's open daily except Sunday but only from 11.30 am to 2 pm. Clear your own dishes.

The *Restaurant Ak-Buura* across Lenin from the Hotel Osh offers the standard Russian evening – pretentious atmosphere, loud music and dreary food. Similar places we didn't try include the *Cholpon Restaurant* opposite the Hotel Alay and the *Chynar Restaurant* behind the teahouse on Lenin.

Getting There & Away

Especially in bus stations, don't be confused by the Kyrgyz names for Ferghana Valley towns on the Uzbekistan side – eg Anjiyan for Andijan and Margalan for Marghilan.

Air The main airline booking office (☎ 2-20-87) at the left end of the Hotel Alay, is open from 8 am to 5 pm daily. There's also a branch at the Hotel Osh. But foreigners are told to book or buy their tickets at the international desk at the airport. You'll be charged foreigners' prices of course, but at least there's no scrum, English is spoken, and there are always a few tickets available when the other offices say there aren't.

Flights to/from Osh include Bishkek (US$75, several daily), Almaty (US$96, five weekly), Cholpon-Ata or Karakol (US$91, twice weekly), Moscow (US$203, Tuesday) and Novosibirsk (Saturday). Moscow and some to Bishkek are in big TU-154s; everything else is by 20 seater Yak-40. There are also charter flights, mainly for 'shopping', to Istanbul, Karachi and the United Arab Emirates (try asking at the city booking office), though the return flights are consistently overloaded and dangerous.

Bus & Car The old bus station, near the bazar, is mainly for buses to Özgön (about US$1, every 30 or 40 minutes), Sary-Tash (US$4.50, 7 am daily) and all points in Kyrgyzstan's southern arm. Just about everything else goes to/from the new station, eg Jalal-Abad (US$1, every 20 minutes), Andijan (US$1.50, every 20 minutes), Ferghana (US$2, two hourly), Marghilan (US$2, three daily) and Toktogul (US$6, 7 am daily) for Tashkent, change at Andijan.

The only vehicles going clear to Bishkek are arenda buses (about US$20) and private cars (about US$25), from the airport. Also out at the airport are taxis to Jalal-Abad for about US$15.

If you're trying to get into Tajikistan, try asking around in the bazar about trucks going that way. But read the Safety in Tajikistan aside in the introduction to the Tajikistan chapter first.

Getting Around

Special buses run between the old bus station and the airport about every half-hour until 6 pm every day.

Marshrutnoe taxis tend to have the same numbers as buses on the same routes, and don't cost much more than buses (1½ S when we were there, versus 1 or 1½ S on buses). Useful lines (southbound on Kurmanjan Datka, northbound on Lenin) include No 2 from the old bus station to the Hotel Osh and Turbaza Ak-Buura; No 13 between the centre and the new bus station; and *bus* No 9 between the old and new bus stations. A taxi between the new bus station and the centre is about US$1.50.

Public transport shuts down soon after dark.

ÖZGÖN
ӨЗГӨН (Kyrgyz), ЎЗГАН (Uzbek)

Özgön (Russian: Uzgen), 55 km north-east of Osh, is today best known as the centre of three nights of ferocious Kyrgyz-Uzbek fighting in 1990 (see the introduction to the Osh section). Few outward scars are evident today – though there is a police checkpost on the road from Osh. The town is nominally 85% Uzbek; locals say it was about two-thirds Uyghur in pre-Soviet days, and it seems likely that these account for many of the 'Uzbeks', as they may have called themselves for the sake of convenience in the early days of the Uzbek SSR.

This is claimed to be the site of a series of citadels dating back to the 1st century BC; there is also a story that Özgön began as an encampment for some of Alexander the Great's troops. Some sources say it was one of the multiple Qarakhanid capitals in the 10th and 11th centuries.

All that remains of this history is a quartet of Qarakhanid buildings – three joined mausolea and a stubby minaret (whose top apparently fell down in an earthquake in the 17th century), faced with very fine ornamental brickwork, carved terracotta and inlays of stone. Each mausoleum is unlike the others, though all are in shades of red-brown clay (there were no glazed tiles at this point in Central Asian history). Restoration is ongoing, as money and supplies allow. At the rear of one of the flanking mausolea, a small section has been deliberately left off to reveal older layers of the middle one.

There are some pre-restoration photos of these buildings, as well as artists' renderings of more ancient structures, in Ferghana's Regional Museum (see the Ferghana Valley section of the Uzbekistan chapter).

Getting There & Away
Özgön is an easy half-day trip by bus from Osh's old station, and the closer you get the prettier the landscape becomes – open, rolling, fertile land, past mainly Kyrgyz vil-lages and collective farms, finally to the edge of the broad Kara-Darya or Özgön valley, ringed with big peaks of the Ferghana range.

Turn right out of the bus station. The road curves to the right past 'minarets' at the entrance to the bazar. It's a 10 minute walk to the big administration building on the right (opposite the post office), from where you can see the minaret behind it.

THE KYZYL-SUU VALLEY
The far southern arm of Kyrgyzstan is the exclusive turf of trekkers and mountaineers, consisting as it does mostly of the Pamir Alay range, a jagged, 500 km long suture between the Tian Shan and the Pamir, running from Samarkand to Xinjiang and threaded right up the middle by the Zeravshan river in Tajikistan and the Kyzyl-Suu in southern Kyrgyzstan. Two of Central Asia's earliest and busiest Silk Road branches crossed the Pamir Alay from Kashgar, at Kök-Art and at Irkeshtam.

With civil unrest in Tajikistan closing off other bases and access routes, most trips into the Pamir Alay go from Osh via Sary-Tash

KYRGYZSTAN

and Daraut-Korgon in the Kyzyl-Suu valley. Alptreksport (see the Travel Agencies section for Osh) is one adventure-travel operator with experience in the region. We found no useful agencies on the Tajikistan side, in either Dushanbe or Khorog. This is also the main access for serious mountaineering in Tajikistan's High Pamir – eg to 7495 metre Pik Kommunizma (the highest point in Central Asia, and in the former USSR), 7134 metre Pik Lenina or 7105 metre Pik Korzhenevskaya. Most climbing parties now depart by helicopter from Osh.

Refer to the Pamir Highway section in the Tajikistan chapter for more on low-elevation travel in this region, including the A372 road down the Kyzyl-Suu valley, with its views of Lenina and Kommunizma. But note that this is not a lightweight jaunt. There are Russian border troops stationed at Sary-Tash. From October through May the A372 is often closed by snow, and in summer on the Tajikistan side it runs through the Garm valley region, scene of heavy fighting in the past. Check the current situation before setting out.

Tajikistan

Tajikistan (officially Jomharii Tojikistan) has its own flag, a national airline and a scattering of embassies abroad. Despite this it's a curiously incomplete country, much less than the sum of its parts. The north is in all but name a part of Uzbekistan; the mountainous Pamir region, despite Soviet-era attempts to populate it, remains almost a vacuum; while the capital, Dushanbe, a city not yet three-quarters of a century old, has yet to take on any character – like an apartment awaiting its tenants.

That Tajikistan was easily the most artificial of the five Soviet-fashioned Central Asian republics was tragically illustrated by the way it bloodily fell apart as soon as it was free of direct Moscow rule. In its brief post-Soviet history, the conflict in this remote pocket of the CIS has seen far greater loss of life than in Georgia, Chechenia and elsewhere in the old empire.

Peace has only been imposed by Russia lending its backing to Tajikistan's current ruling clan and in doing so making the country a virtual protectorate. But it's a fragile peace and one unlikely to last.

For the moment a window is open to the determined traveller to explore some of Tajikistan's unparalleled scenery. The Pamirs dwarf anything found outside Nepal and even for non-mountaineers the Pamir Highway provides plenty of high-altitude thrills. Anyone following this road has the added thrill of knowing that few 'foreign devils' have passed this way since Francis Younghusband, the consummate Great Game player, was expelled from the region by the Russians in 1891, marking its closure to the outside world for the next hundred years.

History

Tajik Ancestry In predominantly Turkic Central Asia, the Persian-descended Tajiks are firmly in the minority, yet they can claim to be the region's oldest residents.

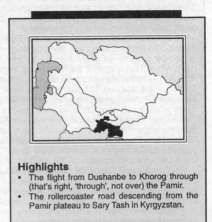

Highlights
- The flight from Dushanbe to Khorog through (that's right, 'through', not over) the Pamir.
- The rollercoaster road descending from the Pamir plateau to Sary Tash in Kyrgyzstan.

Tajik ancestry is a murky area but the lineage seems to begin with the Bactrians and the Sogdians. In the 1st century BC the Bactrians had a large empire covering most of what is now northern Afghanistan, while their contemporaries, the Sogdians, inhabited the Zeravshan valley in present-day western Tajikistan (where some of the few traces of the race remain at a site near Penjikent) until they were displaced in the Arab conquest of Central Asia during the 7th century.

The invaders succeeded in bringing Islam to the region but the Arab domination wasn't secure and out of the melee rose another Persian dynasty, the Samanids. The brief era of the Samanids (819 - 992) gave rise to a frenzy of creative activity.

Bukhara, the dynastic capital, became the Islamic world's centre of learning, nurturing great talents like the philosopher-scientist Abu Ali ibn Sina (also known commonly as Avicenna) and the poet Rudaki – both now claimed as sons by Iran, Afghanistan and Tajikistan.

Safety in Tajikistan

Since 1992, Tajikistan has been embroiled in a bloody civil war which continues to claim lives. There is sporadic fighting along the Afghan border, and unsettled conditions in other parts of the country. At the time of writing it was possible to travel to and within Tajikistan provided you're cautious and take advice on your itinerary.

As a rule of thumb, anywhere near the Tajik-Afghan border is out of bounds and to this effect there's a 25 km exclusion zone along its length. An exception is the Pamir town of Khorog which is usually open to travellers wanting to take the road to the east through Murgab and into Kyrgyzstan. The stretch of the M41 Pamir Highway between Dushanbe and Khorog remained closed in 1995 because of border clashes around Kaliakhum (see Routes & Safety in the Pamirs section of this chapter). The nearby Garm region is also extremely volatile and has seen frequent skirmishes in recent years; travellers considering taking the A372 through the Garm valley towards Kyrgyzstan must make careful enquiries before setting out.

Southern Tajikistan, including the towns of Kulyab and Kurgan-Tyube, is generally safe away from the immediate border areas, which are unpredictable. The more northerly regions around Khojand and Penjikent have always managed to escape the fighting and are safe. Dushanbe, the capital, has also been relatively peaceful since 1993, and should be the first stop in order to gather the most current information on the security situation.

For foreigners in Dushanbe the embassies represent the best source of information – see the Dushanbe section for contact details. There are also many aid organisations based in Dushanbe with operatives throughout Tajikistan, some of which can provide good localised information. The embassies have complete lists of all the agencies and their areas of operation.

Anybody who goes off without first being briefed is asking for trouble. The fighting has never involved foreigners and the last thing any of the factions wants is the adverse publicity that comes from killing one. But if you get caught in the crossfire, artillery shells and shrapnel aren't good at discriminating.

Before setting out for Tajikistan travellers could also consult bodies closer to home: The US State Department issues, through US Embassies or on the Internet (see Dangers & Annoyances in the Facts for the Visitor chapter), Travel Advisories and Consular Information sheets which include travel warnings. But, at least as regards to Tajikistan, they tend to be out-of-date and not a good reflection of the situation. It may be better to try and contact the US Embassy in Tajikistan (☎ (73772) 21-03-56, fax (73772) 21-03-62). In the UK, contact the Travel Advice Unit of the Foreign & Commonwealth Office (FCO; ☎ (0171) 270-41-29, fax (0171) 270-42-28). FCO travel advice is also displayed on BBC2 CEEFAX service, pages 564 onwards. ■

A Blurring of Identity Under the Samanids, the great towns of Central Asia were Persian (the basis of Tajikistan's modern-day claims on Samarkand and Bukhara) but at the end of the 10th century came a succession of Turkic invaders who followed their battle-field successes with cultural conquest. Despite the different ethnicities the two races cohabited peacefully, unified by religion – the Persian-speaking Tajiks absorbed Turk culture and the numerically superior Turks absorbed the Tajik people. Both were subject to the vicissitudes of Central Asia and weathered conquests first by the Mongols then later by Tamerlane. From the 15th century onwards, the Tajiks were under the suzer-

ainty of the emirate of Bukhara, although in the mid-18th century the Afghans moved up to engulf all lands south of the Amu-Darya (Oxus) river along with their resident Tajik population (the Amu-Darya still delineates much of the Afghan-Tajik border today).

The 'Great Game' & the Basmachi As part of the Russian Empire's thrust southwards, St Petersburg made a vassal state of the emirate of Bukhara, which also meant effective control over what now passes for northern and western Tajikistan. But the Pamirs, which account for the whole of modern-day eastern Tajikistan, were quite literally a no-man's-land, falling outside the established borders of the Bukhara emirate and unclaimed by neighbouring Afghanistan and China. Russia was eager to exploit this anomaly in its push to open up possible routes into British India.

The Pamirs became the arena for the strategic duel Kipling was to immortalise as the Great Game, a game in which Russia's players eventually prevailed, securing the region for the tsar.

Following the revolution of 1917, new provisional governments were established in Central Asia and the Tajiks initially found themselves part of two Soviet Socialist Republics (SSRs), though what they wanted was an autonomous Islamic-oriented republic. The following year *basmachi* guerrillas began a campaign to free the region from Bolshevik rule. It took four years for the Bolsheviks to crush this resistance and in the process entire villages were razed, mosques destroyed and great tracts of land laid waste. The surviving guerrillas slipped into

Afghanistan from where they continued for years to make sporadic raids over the border.

Statehood In 1924, when the Soviet Border Commission set about redefining Central Asia, the Tajiks got their own Autonomous SSR (ASSR). Although only a satellite of the Uzbek SSR, this was the first-ever official Tajik state. In 1929 this was upgraded to a full union republic, although (perhaps in reprisal for the basmachi revolt) Samarkand and Bukhara – where over 700,000 Tajiks still lived – remained in Uzbekistan. As recently as 1989 the government of Tajikistan was still trying to persuade the Soviet leadership to 'return' these areas.

The Bolsheviks never fully trusted this troublesome republic and during the 1930s almost all Tajiks in positions of influence within the government were replaced by stooges from Moscow. The industrialisation of Tajikistan was only undertaken following WWII, after the loss of much of European

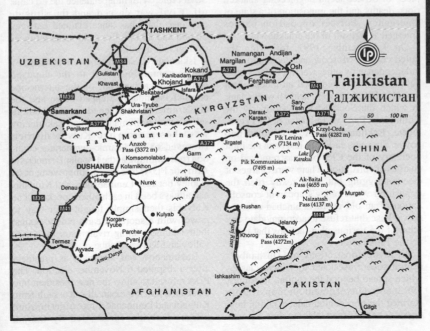

Russia's manufacturing capacity. But living standards remained low and in the late 1980s Tajikistan endured 25% unemployment, plus the lowest level of education and the highest infant-mortality rate in the Soviet Union.

Civil Unrest In the mid-1970s, Tajikistan began to feel the impact of the rise of Islamic forces in neighbouring Afghanistan, particularly in the south around Kurgan-Tyube. This region had been neglected by Dushanbe's ruling Communist elite who were mainly drawn from the prosperous northern province of Leninabad. In 1976 the underground Islamic Renaissance Party (IRP) was founded, gathering popular support as a rallying point for Tajik nationalism. Although in 1979 there had been demonstrations in opposition to the Soviet invasion of Afghanistan, the first serious disturbances were in early 1990 when it was rumoured that Armenian refugees were to be settled in Dushanbe, which was already short on housing. This piece of Soviet social engineering sparked riots, deaths and the imposition of a state of emergency. Further opposition parties emerged as a result of the crackdown.

On 9 September 1991, following the failed coup in Moscow and declarations of independence by other Central Asian states, Tajikistan proclaimed itself an independent republic. Elections were held 10 weeks later in which the Socialist Party (formerly the Communist Party of Tajikistan or CPT) candidate, Rakhmon Nabiev, was voted into power. Six years earlier he had been the First Secretary of the CPT but was removed on charges of corruption. There were charges of election rigging but what really riled the opposition was Nabiev's apparent consolidation of an old guard Leninabad-oriented power base that refuse to accommodate any other of the various clan-factions that make up the Tajik nation.

Sit-in demonstrations on Dushanbe's central square escalated to violent clashes which spread beyond the capital. In August 1992 anti-Government demonstrators stormed the presidential palace, taking hostages. They missed Nabiev but he was captured a few days later at Dushanbe airport trying to flee to Khojand (the post USSR renaming of Leninabad). He was replaced as head of state by Akbarshah Iskandarov who headed a coalition government which included the IRP and secular democratic parties.

But sharing power between regional clans, religious leaders and former Communists proved impossible. Tajikistan descended into civil war.

Civil War During the Soviet era, Moscow and the Party had been the lid on a pressure-cooker of clan-based tensions that had existed long before Russian intervention. Tajikistan's various factions – Leninabaders from the north, Kulyabis from the southern province of Kulyab and their hostile neighbours from Kurgan-Tyube, Garmis from the Garm valley in the east, and Pamiris from the mountainous province of Gorno-Badakhshan – had all been kept in line under Soviet rule. With independence the lid came off. Civil war ensued and the struggle amongst clans has since claimed between 20,000 and 50,000 lives and made refugees of over half a million.

Iskandarov's supporters were attacked by forces remaining loyal to the deposed Nabiev. As a way out of the internecine conflict Iskandarov stepped down and the Government reconvened in Khojand to select a new front man. Imamali Rakhmanov was chosen from the Kulyab district. However, to the Islamic-democratic coalition (now fighting as the Popular Democratic Army or PDA) this was no improvement on Nabiev because Leninabaders and Kulyabis had always been in each others' pockets. The Kulyabis then simply fought their way to power with a scorched earth policy against their Islamic-leaning rivals from the Garm valley and Kurgan-Tyube.

Rakhmanov was sworn in as president after a disputed 6 November election. The PDA refused to allow the new president into Dushanbe and it took an all-out assault from Kulyabi and Leninabad forces to get him into office. Kulyabi forces, led by Sanjak

Safarov, who'd previously spent 23 years in prison for murder, then embarked on an orgy of ethnic cleansing directed at anyone connected with Kurgan-Tyube and the Garm valley – mother and child as equally as political activist and soldier.

Precarious Peace Although the civil war was over by 1993, the fighting still hasn't stopped. The November 1992 elections did nothing to resolve the conflict. The opposition in exile refused to take part in the voting. Instead, the PDA and its supporters continued the war from hideaways in the Pamirs and from Afghanistan – echoing the basmachi campaigns 70 years earlier. Rakhmanov is propped up by Russian-dominated CIS forces who have been drawn into the conflict as de facto protectors of the Kulyab regime.

Why the Kremlin moved to intervene in what was a domestic struggle, Boris Yeltsin has made no secret of, 'Everyone must realise,' he said in a 1993 pronouncement 'that this is effectively Russia's border, not Tajikistan's'. There are now 25,000 Russian troops inside the country operating some 50 border posts along the Afghan border. The Russian (and Uzbek) fear is that if Tajikistan falls then Uzbekistan could be next. The Afghan warlord Ahmed Shah Masoud, an ethnic Tajik, has spoken of 'tasting the grapes of Samarkand'. Pictures of this popular Tajik hero can sometimes be seen hanging in shops.

At the time of writing the Tajik rebels, with an estimated 5000 fighters in northern Afghanistan (assisted, say the Russians, by their old enemies the Afghan mujahideen) continue their campaign of cross-border raids, and assassinations of Russian military officers and Tajik government officials. The CIS border force retaliates with bombing raids on Afghan border towns suspected of harbouring Islamic insurgents.

Rakhmanov's government, still dominated by a single regional faction and uninterested in political reform, is unwilling to share power. A clear indication of this

came in late 1994 when they held a second presidential election in which Rakhmanov romped to victory as the only candidate, all opposition parties having been outlawed.

Western diplomats in Dushanbe predict that the situation will get a lot worse before it gets better.

In mid-January 1996 Mufti Fatkhulla Sharipov, a prominent pro-Moscow Muslim spiritual leader, and his entire family were murdered in the capital, Dushanbe, on the first day of the holy month of Ramadan. The government claimed it was a political assassination, aimed at wrecking the peace process. In any case it highlights the hazards of travelling in Tajikistan, and could well trigger a new cycle of clan and political violence in the country.

Geography
At 143,100 sq km, landlocked Tajikistan is Central Asia's smallest republic. More than half of it lies 3000 metres or more above sea level. The central part encompasses the southern reaches of the Tian Shan range while the south-east is raised high up in the Pamirs. Within these ranges are some of Central Asia's highest peaks, including Pik Lenina (7134 metres) and Pik Kommunizma (7495 metres).

The western third of the country is lowland plain, bisected by two narrow ranges – both western extensions of the Tian Shan which cross into Uzbekistan with the Zeravshan valley cradled between them. The mountain peaks with their sun-melted ice-caps are the source of a fibrous network of fast-flowing streams, many of which empty into Tajikistan's two major rivers – the Syr-Darya, rising in the Ferghana Valley, and the Amu-Darya, formed from the confluence of two Pamir rivers, the Vakhsh and the Pyanj.

Together, the Amu-Darya and Pyanj mark most of the country's 1200 km border with Afghanistan. Tajikistan's other borders are much less well-defined: in the east, 430 km of border meanders through Pamir valleys, while to the north and west are the equally random-seeming borders with Kyrgyzstan and Uzbekistan.

TAJIKISTAN

Government

Since November 1992 Tajikistan has been a parliamentary republic with legislative power vested in an elected 230 member Supreme Soviet. The Soviet is fronted by a speaker or chairperson who is head of state, or president – Imamali Rakhmanov at the time of writing. The highest executive body is the Council of Ministers, whose chairperson becomes prime minister. At present this post is held by Abduljalil Samadov, a former economics minister drafted into the government in September 1993 to try and engineer an upturn in the economy.

Rakhmanov and Samadov both belong to the Socialist Party of Tajikistan (formerly the Communist Party of Tajikistan), pretty much the only party in town. The few other existing minor parties are pro-Government. All opposition parties are banned and have gone underground – the Islamic Renaissance Party (IRP), the secular nationalist Democratic Party of Tajikistan (DPT), the Pamiri separatist party Lale Badakhshan (Ruby of Badakhshan) and Rastokhez (Rebirth), a nationalist-religious party.

For administrative purposes the country is divided into three oblasts or provinces: Khojand, Khatlon and the 60,000 sq km autonomous mountain region of Gorno-Badakhshan.

Economy

Independence proved catastrophic for Tajikistan, always the poorest of Soviet republics, and the civil war completely destroyed any hope of economic self-sufficiency.

With the imposition of Soviet rule in the 1920s, most of Tajikistan's available arable land (only about 7% of the country, the rest being mountains) was turned over to intensive cotton farming. Some grain, vegetables and fruit were also grown but in amounts that fell well short of providing for the populace. Tajikistan was heavily reliant on imports from the Soviet Union – not just food, but fuel and many other commodities.

With the disintegration of the Soviet trading system that accompanied the collapse of the USSR, Tajikistan was left badly equipped to fend for itself. The country might have survived with the help of its considerable deposits of gold, silver and other precious minerals, plus the established cotton industry, but the outbreak of fighting brought the country to a standstill.

The main agricultural areas of the southwest were worst hit by the fighting. Where crops weren't actually destroyed they rotted in the fields, as agricultural workers were either fighting, dead or had fled. A country where agriculture normally accounts for 44% of net material production missed two complete harvests. With the down-scaling of hostilities and a return, of sorts, to normality, 1994 saw a harvest, though a large percentage of the crop was lost for lack of labour and machinery. The national budget of tajikistan is still somewhat less than it costs to produce some Hollywood movies and 40% of that is required for the upkeep of the military presence on the Afghan border.

As a result, at the time of writing, Tajikistan is suffering a severe cash crisis. In Dushanbe no state employee has been paid since sometime in 1994 – and with no privatisation to date, the Tajik government is virtually the country's sole employer. In lieu of wages, credit notes are issued, good for use in state stores where there's nothing to be had anyway. All produce goes directly into the bazars where it can be sold for cash to those who have it. Anybody still receiving a salary is often supporting up to 30 relatives, neighbours and friends. The situation is at its most severe in Gorno-Badakhshan where money is so scarce that commerce has reverted to barter.

Presently, the country exists on a drip-feed of credits and loans from Moscow. In return, Tajikistan has been forced to mortgage its future to the Kremlin, giving the Russians half the shares in the Nurek hydroelectric plant, as well as controlling interests in other national industries. The Russians realise that if the Tajiks ever stop shooting each other, one day they might have quite a prosperous country.

Population & People

July 1993 estimates put the population of Tajikistan at 5.8 million. Tajiks made up 65%, Uzbeks 25% and Russians 4%. But these figures are only approximate because the demographics of Tajikistan have been fluctuating wildly since the start of the civil war in 1992. In addition to tens of thousands killed, more than half a million Tajiks are thought to have fled into Afghanistan, while around two-thirds of the country's 600,000 Russians have headed north. Although the worst of the slaughter seems to have abated for the moment, shortages of food, work and civic amenities mean the flood of emigrants hasn't stopped.

Repatriation of refugees is ongoing, although many have decided they would rather remain in Afghanistan, joining the 4.4 million fellow Tajiks that have lived there since being annexed by Kabul in the 18th century. There are similarly large, historical communities of Tajiks in Uzbekistan (where they number around 860,000), Kazakstan (100,000) and China's Xinjiang Autonomous Region (30,000).

It's only in this century that 'Tajik' came to denote a distinct nationality. Previously 'Taj' was just a term for a Persian speaker (all the other Central Asian peoples speak Turkic languages). Despite their predominantly Persian ancestry, there has been so much intermarrying that it's often hard to distinguish Tajiks from their Mongol Turkic neighbours. Pure-blooded Tajiks tend to have thin faces, with wide eyes and a Roman nose, giving them a hawkish appearance.

There are some recognisable ethnic subdivisions amongst the Tajiks. As well as the Pamiri Tajiks (see below), there are dwindling numbers of Yaghnabis, direct descendants of the ancient Sogdians, in the villages of the Zeravshan valley. In *The Lost Heart of Asia*, Colin Thubron describes visiting a Yaghnabi settlement and discovering that Sogdian, a language last widely in use in the 8th century, is still spoken.

Common to all Tajiks is a preference for rural life. Only around a third of their number live in towns and cities, the majority prefer-

ring to settle in *kishlaks*, small villages of wooden, one-family houses usually huddled on the sloping valley sides above a mountain stream or river.

Many older Tajik men continue to dress in the traditional manner of a *chapan* (long, quilted jackets), knee-length boots and a *tupi* (black, white-embroidered caps). Women of all ages favour the psychedelically coloured, gold-threaded long dresses (*kurta*) with head scarves (*rumol*) to match, and underneath the dress, striped trousers (*izor*) with Day-Glo slippers on their feet.

Pamiri Tajiks Centuries of isolation in high-altitude valleys has meant that the Pamiri people of Gorno-Badakhshan speak languages different not only from those of lowland Tajiks but from one another. Each mountain community has its own dialect of Pamiri, a language which although it has the same Persian roots as Tajik, is as different as English is from German. The different Pamiri tongues, named for the settlements where they're spoken (Ishkashimi, Rushani, Vanchi etc), are not necessarily mutually comprehensible.

The mountain peoples are, however, solidly bound by their shared faith: Ismailism (sometimes referred to locally as Suleymanism). Ismailis are a breakaway sect of Shia Islam with no mosques, no clerics and no weekly holy day. One of the few visible manifestations of the religion is the small roadside shrines at which passers-by stop to ask for a blessing. The shrines also act as charity stations; in return for the blessing, the Ismaili customarily leaves some money or bread for anyone in need. The spiritual leader of the Ismailis is the Aga Khan, a Swiss-born businessman and horse-breeder revered by Pamiris as a living god. But he's no remote, abstract deity – it's the Aga Khan's charity that currently provisions Gorno-Badakhshan, keeping certain starvation at bay (see The Pamirs section); Pamiris venerate him as 'Our God who sends us food'.

Not having two potatoes to fry together has done nothing to lessen the hospitality of the Pamiris, whose natural inclination is to share. Invitations to sit, eat and drink are free-flowing, though unlike some other peoples of Central Asia, the Pamiris allow you the choice of refusal.

If the chance arises it is worth accepting an offer to see inside a traditional Pamiri house. They're built as one large room, with raised areas around four sides of a central pit. There are few if any windows; illumination comes through a skylight in the roof. Carpets and mattresses take the place of furniture and also serve as decoration along with panels of hand-coloured photographs – the most prominent of which is often a portrait of the Aga Khan.

Arts

When Tajikistan was hived off from Uzbekistan in 1929, the new nation-state was forced to leave behind all its cultural baggage. A Moscow-drawn border delivered the glories of Bukhara and Samarkand, to which the tajiks had a legitimate claim, into the cultural treasure chest of Uzbekistan.

The new Soviet order set about providing a replacement pantheon of arts, introducing modern drama, opera and ballet and sending stage-struck Tajik aspirants to study in Moscow and Leningrad. The policy paid early dividends and the 1940s are considered a golden era of Tajik theatre. A kind of Soviet fame came to some Tajik novelists and poets, such as Mirzo Tursunzade and Sadriddin Ayni, the latter now remembered more as a deconstructor of national culture because of his campaign to eliminate all Arabic expressions and references to Islam from the Tajik tongue.

Since independence there has been something of a cultural revival in an attempt to foster a sense of national identity. Ancient figures of art and learning from the region's Persian past are being popularised.

The most famous of the lot is the 10th century philosopher-scientist Abu Ali ibn Sina (known in the West as Avicenna), author of two of the most important books in the history of medicine. He was born in Bukhara when it was the seat of the Persian Samanids,

to whom Rudaki (exact place of birth unknown), now celebrated as the father of Persian verse, served as court poet. Tajiks also venerate Firdausi, a poet and composer of the *Shah-nameh* (Book of Kings), the Persian national epic, and Omar Khayyam, of *Rubiayat* fame, both born in present-day Iran but at a time when it was part of an empire that also included the territory now known as Tajikistan.

Critics attribute the success of Tajikistan's most popular living writer of the moment, Taimur Zulfikarov, to his ability to mimic the ancient Persian style of writing and, in doing so, to appeal to nationalist sentiments.

Orientation

Few cartographical changes accompanied the transformation of the Tajikistan Soviet Socialist Republic to the independent Republic of Tajikistan. Dushanbe was once Stalinabad but shed that unfashionable name in the 1950s. Only with the demise of Russian Communism was the guy with the flat cap and pointy beard seen off – at which point Tajikistan's second city, Leninabad, reverted to its ancient name of Khojand, and the eponymous oblast of which it's the capital became Khojand province. Ordjonikidzeabad (25 km east of Dushanbe), named for the Georgian who imposed Bolshevism in the Caucasus, reverted to Kofarnikhon.

Street signs in Dushanbe have begun to sport the Tajik forms *kuchai* (street) and *khiyeboni* (avenue) but, for the moment, the Russian *ulitsa* and *prospekt*, as well as *ploshchad* for square, are still the more common.

Dushanbe
ДУШАНБЕ

Population: 700,000

With a cool backdrop of mountains, lazy tree-lined avenues and pale oriental-fringed buildings, Dushanbe is a good-looking city but personality-wise it's a dead loss. It is a historically isolated, backwater settlement that's just a little bit boring. Except, that is, at night when it's plain scary and not just a little dangerous.

For the visitor who can't or won't pay upwards of US$40 a night for a bed there are discomforts in the form of some terrible accommodation. Food is extremely scarce and there's very little to see or do in the city. The situation is of course far worse for its residents, who in most cases don't have the option of leaving. As a result the legendary Tajik hospitality is not much on display in Dushanbe at present.

Despite being the capital, the city is more like a cul-de-sac than a transport hub. Other than a couple of daily trains in and out via Termez in southern Uzbekistan, the only other connections are badly over-subscribed flights to Khojand (where it is possible to get easily to Tashkent) and to Khorog in the Pamirs where onward transport requires a lot of forward planning or extraordinary luck.

Unless you have some specific agenda, at this moment in time you won't find a trip to Dushanbe particularly rewarding.

History

Although the remains of a 5th century BC settlement have been found here, modern-day Dushanbe has little history beyond this century. As recently as 80 years ago, Dushanbe (then spelt Dushyambe) was a small, poor village known chiefly for its weekly bazar (Dushanbe means Monday in Tajik).

In 1920, the last Emir of Bukhara took refuge in Dushanbe, fleeing from the advancing Bolsheviks. But he was forced to continue his flight early the next year as the Red Army swept remorselessly on to add the Tajik settlement to the expanding Bolshevik empire. The Russian hold was shaken off for a spell when in 1922 Enver Pasha and his basmachi fighters liberated Dushanbe as part of their crusade to carve out a pan-Islamic empire, but on the Turk's death in a gun battle in southern Tajikistan, Bolshevik authority was quickly reasserted.

With the arrival of the railroad in 1929, Dushanbe was made capital of the new Soviet Tajik republic and renamed Stalinabad – a name it bore until the historical reinvention of the Khrushchev era. The region was developed as a cotton and silk processing centre and tens of thousands of people were relocated here, turning the rural village into a large, urban administrative and industrial centre. The city's numbers were further swollen by Tajik emigres from Bukhara and Samarkand, which had been given over to Uzbek rule.

After almost 70 uneventful years of relative peace, if not prosperity, 1990 saw festering nationalistic sentiments explode into rioting, triggered by rumoured plans to

TAJIKISTAN

Safety in Dushanbe

Although at the time of writing Dushanbe was no longer under official curfew, the streets quickly empty at nightfall. The collapse of local economic conditions, with resulting poverty and unemployment, has created widespread desperation, and street crime is a very real problem. The police are completely ineffective and, according to what we were told, they are as likely to rob you as to help.

You are safe enough during the day but do not go out after dark. Foreigners are soft, lucrative targets. Expats carry radios to call for help and even hardened New Yorkers don't venture out without Mace. If you do have to go out at night order a taxi and arrange to be picked up at your hotel. Don't try to flag down a car on the road as it's unlikely that anyone with decent intentions will stop. (On our night of arrival, not knowing any better, we approached a battered old Lada stopped at a traffic light, only to speedily retreat when we saw that the driver was absorbed in trying to jam a cartridge into the revolver in his hands.)

Be careful in your hotel. There are stories of nasty incidents that have occurred in elevators and corridors, specifically in the Hotel Tajikistan. Do not advertise the fact that you are a foreigner, and keep your door locked at all times. ■

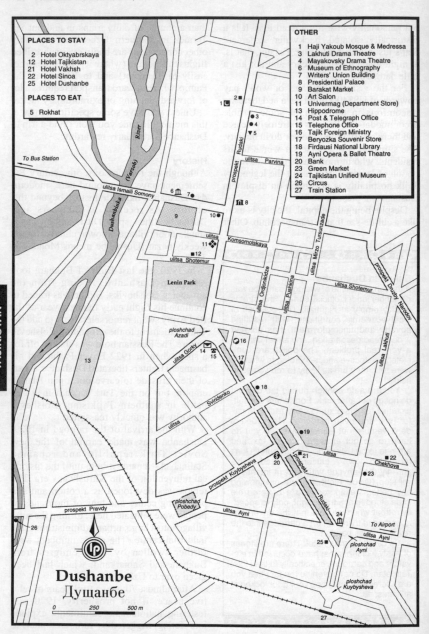

TAJIKISTAN

PLACES TO STAY

2   Hotel Oktyabrskaya
12 Hotel Tajikistan
21 Hotel Vakhsh
22 Hotel Sinoa
25 Hotel Dushanbe

PLACES TO EAT

5   Rokhat

OTHER

1   Haji Yakoub Mosque & Medressa
3   Lakhuti Drama Theatre
4   Mayakovsky Drama Theatre
6   Museum of Ethnography
7   Writers' Union Building
8   Presidential Palace
9   Barakat Market
10 Art Salon
11 Univermag (Department Store)
13 Hippodrome
14 Post & Telegraph Office
15 Telephone Office
16 Tajik Foreign Ministry
17 Beryozka Souvenir Store
18 Firdausi National Library
19 Ayni Opera & Ballet Theatre
20 Bank
23 Green Market
24 Tajikistan Unified Museum
26 Circus
27 Train Station

To Bus Station

River (Varzob)

Dushanbinka

ulitsa Ismaili Somony

ulitsa Parvina

prospekt Rudaki

ulitsa Komsomolskaya

ulitsa Shotemur

Lenin Park

ulitsa Mirzo Tursunzade

prospekt Druzby Narodov

ulitsa Shotemur

ulitsa Ordjonikidze

ulitsa Pushkina

ulitsa Lakhuti

ploshchad Azadi

ulitsa Gorky

Sverdenko

ploshchad Pobedy

prospekt Kuybysheva

ulitsa Ayni

prospekt Pravdy

prospekt Rudaki

ulitsa Chekhova

To Airport

ulitsa Ayni

ploshchad Ayni

ploshchad Kuybysheva

Dushanbe
Душанбе

0   250   500 m

house Armenian refugees in Dushanbe. Twenty-two people died in clashes with the militia.

There were further demonstrations in the autumn of 1991 organised by opposition factions dissatisfied with the absence of political change in Tajikistan. The statue of Lenin that stood opposite the parliament building disappeared overnight and guards had to be set to watch over all other Communist-era monuments. Young bearded men and veiled women took to the streets of Dushanbe calling for an Islamic state. In May 1992 these demonstrations escalated into violence and then civil war. The fighting within the capital itself ended in December 1992 following a successful assault by the Kulyabi militia, supporters of the present government.

The city remained as a capital of chaos. It was kept under a dusk-to-dawn curfew with armed gangs controlling the roads in and out and lawless brigands patrolling the streets. Most Russians fled.

Since then the situation has become considerably calmer and now the only soldiers and tanks on the streets belong to the Russian 201st Armoured Division, part of the resident peace-keeping force stationed on the Afghan border.

Orientation

The focus of Dushanbe is the wide, tree-lined prospekt Rudaki which runs from the train station on ploshchad Kuybysheva, 5.5 km north to ploshchad Rudaki. Roughly central on Rudaki is Ploshchad Azadi, surrounded by government buildings, now under the stern gaze of a sorcerer-like Firdausi in place of Lenin. Here, demonstrators camped out in 1992.

Almost everything useful or interesting is within a 15 minute walk of here. The exception is the central bus station, which is some three km distant on ulitsa Profsoyuzov in the western part of twon. The airport is on the opposite side of the city, roughly five km south-east from ploshchad Ayni, along ulitsa Ayni.

Information

Tourist Offices It's been so long since Tajik-Intourist (☎ 21-68-92, fax 21-52-36) had any foreigners to march around that the staff are at a total loss when any turn up. At present their major business is arranging shopping trips to Abu Dhabi, Aleppo and Karachi. With a couple of days warning they can arrange escorted trips to Hissar, Varzob and other local destinations, but probably nothing more ambitious. We were quoted US$30 for a half-day trip to Hissar with a guide, but prices are probably negotiable. Ask for Hafiza, who is fluent in English. Tajik-Intourist is on the 1st floor of the Hotel Tajikistan in room 11.

TAJIKISTAN

Old Names & New Names in Dushanbe

At the time of our visit there were no street maps of Dushanbe available; the place to look in future would be the foyer kiosk at the Hotel Tajikistan. Following are the old (Soviet-era) names and new names of some important streets and squares.

New Name	Old Name
ploshchad Azadi	ploshchad Lenina
prospekt Rudaki	prospekt Lenina
ulitsa Gorky	prospekt Dzerzhinskogo
ulitsa Ismaili Somony	ulitsa Putovskogo
ulitsa Mirzo Tursunzade	ulitsa Krasnykh Partizan
ulitsa Shotemurulitsa	ulitsa Kommunisticheskaya

Foreign Embassies No embassies in Dushanbe can issue visas, even for transit purposes. Exceptions may be made under persuasive circumstances but the embassy in question has to seek special permission from home and the process could take up to a month. The Consulate of Afghanistan may be an exception, but at present there are no crossing points to Afghanistan from Tajikistan open to travellers. The nearest entry to Afghanistan is at Termez in Uzbekistan, but frontier guards there, we were informed, will only recognise documentation that was issued in Tashkent. Brits in need of consular services should contact the UK Embassy in Tashkent.

Afghanistan
    ulitsa Pushkina 25 (☎ 27-60-58, 27-60-61)
China
    ulitsa Parvina 8 (☎ 21-01-39, 21-01-94, fax 21-02-11)
Germany
    ulitsa Proyezd Azizbekova 21, off Mirzo Tursunzade by the Badakhshan Kafe (☎ 21-21-89, 21-21-98)
India
    Hotel Tajikistan, 3rd floor, ulitsa Shotemur 22 (☎ 21-67-24, 21-11-84)
Iran
    prospekt Rudaki 18, behind and to the left of the Tajik Foreign Ministry (☎ 21-13-45)
Pakistan
    prospekt Rudaki 37a (☎ 21-22-27)
Russia
    Hotel Oktyabrskaya, 3rd floor, prospekt Rudaki 105a (☎ 21-10-15)

USA
Hotel Oktyabrskaya, 4th floor, prospekt Rudaki 105a (☎ 21-03-56, fax 21-03-62)

Visas All Tajik visa problems are dealt with at the Tajik Foreign Ministry, which is the big pink building at prospekt Rudaki 12, on ploshchad Azadi. As you face the building, you need to take the small door on the far right of the façade where you'll be given a pass to enter the building proper and told where to go. Nobody there speaks English.

Money There's a bank on prospekt Rudaki opposite the Hotel Vakhsh but it doesn't always have money. The best place to try is reception at the Hotel Tajikistan, or possibly at the Hotel Oktyabrskaya. If you find somewhere with a stash of *rubls*, change what you might need for your whole stay because sources tend to dry up (though of course you won't be able to reconvert any of it to foreign currency; also remember that foreigners must pay for flights in US dollars).

Post & Communications The central post office at prospekt Rudaki 57, on ploshchad Azadi, is open from 8 am to 6 pm. The telephone office is one door south at Rudaki 55. At the time of writing, it was possible to make international and long-distance calls there, but not local ones. The operator for international calls is at ☎ 21-39-42 or 21-08-27. The only working phone we found in Dushanbe for local calls was at reception in the Hotel Tajikistan. Telegrams can be sent from the post office. There is no public fax service. DHL (☎ 21-71-54) is at ulitsa Ayni 14a but even it takes one to three weeks to get mail to/from the USA or Western Europe.

The telephone code for Dushanbe is 3772.

Travel Agencies Alp-Navruz (☎ & fax 24-53-73) and Sinbad Tourism (☎ 27-73-67, fax 27-65-43) at ulitsa Gorky 7 both specialise in mountaineering and trekking tours. Sinbad also offers boating and bicycle tourism.

Bookshops There are two bookshops on prospekt Rudaki, north of Ismaili Somony. One is very poorly stocked, its shelves buoyed up with knitted cardigans and plastic shoes, while the other is Iranian and strong only on things like religious guidance in Farsi. If you're looking for postcards, try the foyer kiosk at the Hotel Tajikistan.

Emergency & Medical Services Dial ☎ 02 for the police, ☎ 03 for an ambulance. Your best bet in case of illness is to call an embassy – the German and US embassies, and possibly some of the others, should have contact details of recommended doctors, medical services and hospitals.

Museums

The two room **Museum of Ethnography** at Ismaili Somony 14, opposite Barakat market, is a very professional showcase of 20th century Tajik art. The collection includes pottery, carpets, cloaks, embroidery, jewellery, musical instruments, woodwork and more. It's open from 10 am to 6 pm, closed Sunday.

The **Tajikistan Unified Museum**, on a commanding site on ploshchad Ayni, includes exhibits on history, natural history and art. Among the more interesting items are exhibits on Islamic Samarkand and Bukhara, including a beautiful 10th century carved-wood *mihrab* (prayer niche) and a great 12 panel painting of the Russians entering Bukhara. The top floor is given over to a quirky collection, from Italian film festival programmes to Olympic wrestling medals. Opening hours seem variable, but in theory they are from 10 am to 5 pm, Monday to Saturday. Admission costs US$0.20.

Mosque & Markets

With its burnished golden dome and crescent-topped minaret, the **Haji Yakoub mosque & medressa** just west of the Hotel Oktyabrskaya is one of the few visible manifestations of Islam in Dushanbe. It was begun in 1990 and financed by contributions from Iran, Pakistan and Saudi Arabia; construction continues with private funds only. The mosque is named after Haji Yakoub, a Tajik religious leader who fled to Afghanistan.

Tajikistan's Persian past is invoked in the façade of the **Writers' Union Building** on Ismaili Somony. It's adorned like a medieval cathedral with saintly, sculpted-stone figures of Sadriddin Ayni, Omar Khayyam and other poets and writers from the Tajik pantheon. Beside it is a striking **monument to Gorky & Ayni**, in the form of giant statues of the two writers seated on a lawn. West beyond the river, Ismaili Somony is flanked by expansive **parks** with uplifting views of the mountains.

While not particularly exotic or Eastern in flavour, the stalls around the large, covered **Barakat market** are the centre of activity in Dushanbe. It's behind the Hotel Tajikistan, south of Ismaili Somony. A second central bazar, the **Green market**, devoted to fruit and vegetables, lies a block north of ploshchad Ayni. Many more makeshift bazars are scattered round the outskirts. They are harrowing affairs composed of lines of people trying to sell whatever they can find at home – a pair of old shoes, some coverless books, a dismantled washing machine motor, anything that somebody might conceivably trade a little cash for.

Places to Stay

For travellers with a budget that stretches, the *Hotel Tajikistan* (☎ 27-43-93), at Shotemur 22, is a concrete oasis of luxury amidst the deprivations of Dushanbe. The rooms are extremely comfortable and the miraculously clean bathrooms have the only hot water on tap in the city (just possibly related to the fact that two floors are permanently occupied by officers of the 201st division). South-facing rooms also benefit from mountain-edged views over the park. Singles/doubles are US$40/60.

Judging by rates of US$72/90, the *Hotel Oktyabrskaya* (☎ 21-12-80) at prospekt Rudaki 105a aspires to be the classiest hotel in town, but the cold marbled walls and guest-free corridors (much of it is occupied by aid agencies and embassies) give it the feel of a morgue. And there's no hot water for your money. For either hotel take a No 1 trolleybus from the train station or bus No 18 from the bus station, to prospekt Rudaki just south of Ismaili Somony.

At one time, the *Hotel Dushanbe* (☎ 23-36-60) on ploshchad Ayni, just 500 metres from the train station, was an excellent cheap alternative to the Tajikistan, but when we were there it was gutted and laid waste after being a temporary home to 5000 refugees. Considering the country's current cash crisis, it's unlikely that any repairs are imminent.

The next-best contender is the *Hotel Vakhsh* (no phone). At the junction of prospekt Rudaki and ulitsa Chekhova, it has a

TAJIKISTAN

great location by the opera house, but the only culture in the hotel grows on the walls of the leprous rooms. It's usually occupied by drunken Russian soldiers on leave from the Afghan border. It's only US$1.20 for a double.

If anything the *Hotel Sinoa* (no phone) at ulitsa Chekhova 13, across from the Green market, is worse, but costs just US$0.20 per person per night.

Places to Eat

The 'troubles' have shut most of Dushanbe's restaurants; people have no money for eating out, ingredients are hard to come by and it's not safe to be on the streets at night. The main options are the restaurants at the hotels *Tajikistan* and *Oktyabrskaya*, where the menu seems limited to a dish of the day – or maybe even a dish of the week. At the Tajikistan we had the choice of a mutton patty or nothing for four nights running. Whatever's available costs roughly US$2.

An interesting place to snack during the day is the *Rokhat* at prospekt Rudaki 84. It's an unusual, Soviet-era attempt at a grand Persian-style teahouse. In addition to tea in pots the size of footballs, this two storey glasshouse serves shashlyk, manty and laghman (approximately US$0.30 each). It's open from 8 am to 6 pm, possibly later in summer. A stall outside has fresh bread.

Plov and shashlyk are available in Lenin Park although they're usually sold out by about 2 pm. Fruit is available at the bazars, while imported cheese, frankfurters, cake and other scarce edibles can be found at the kiosk in the foyer of the Hotel Tajikistan.

Entertainment

There's still life left at the Ayni Opera & Ballet Theatre at prospekt Rudaki 28, a building that has possibly the finest interior in Dushanbe. The Tajik Lakhuti Drama Theatre at prospekt Rudaki 86 and the nearby Russian Mayakovsky Drama Theatre at No 76 also have regular performances (*Romeo and Juliet* was playing at the time of our visit).

Constrained by the city's self-imposed curfew, nightlife is limited to the ground-floor bar of the Hotel Tajikistan where expats sink imported beers at a dollar a go, and keep their heads down when Russian soldiers, on leave from the Afghan border, let off steam loudly and sometimes violently. When the lights go on, we were told, you can still see the bullet holes in the ceiling. Anyone looking to wind down over a cold beer should take it to their room.

Things to Buy

For thick, colourful Pamiri socks, silver jewellery with lapis inlay, assorted handicrafts and even busts of Lenin, try the art salon at prospekt Rudaki 89. There is a gallery above with a permanent exhibition of paintings that are for sale. The *beryozka*, or hard currency shop (the sign says 'Berzeka'), a block south of ploshchad Azadi at Ordjonikidza 2, has a similar assortment of local handicrafts and souvenirs but of poorer quality and they're more expensive. Barakat market is the place to pick up tupi for US$1.50 to US$3, and chapan for around US$8. You'll also find plenty of sequined, gold-stitched trousers and colourful dresses.

The bazar-like Univermag (department store) at prospekt Rudaki 83 is the place for everything from toilet paper to cassettes and Mars bars, while the best place for imported items like wine, cheeses, toothpaste, shampoo and batteries, is the kiosk on the ground floor of the Hotel Tajikistan – the Harrods of Dushanbe. The huddle of kiosks and trailers in front of the airport are also kept well-stocked from the charter flights to Abu Dhabi and Karachi.

Getting There & Away

Air In theory Tajikistan Airlines flies from Dushanbe to Garm, Kulyab, Murgab and quite a few other towns in Tajikistan. In practice almost the only regular services are daily to Khojand (50 minutes, US$71) and Khorog (40 minutes, US$61), and three or four times a week to Moscow (4 hours, US$280). Even these are frequently cancelled and rescheduled, either due to bad weather or fuel shortages. Often you can't buy a ticket until three days before the flight. The separate foreigners' booking office is at the airport, through a door at the left end of the terminal entrance hall; it's open from about 8 am to 4 pm. The Aeroflot office near the Green market on ulitsa Chekhova won't sell tickets to foreigners.

Internationally, Tajikistan International Airlines has a Saturday flight to Delhi and a Sunday one direct to London; its sales desk is on the ground floor of the Hotel Tajikistan. Irregular charter connections go to Abu Dhabi, Aleppo and Karachi, organised by Tajik-Intourist for the benefit of traders and importers, flying out half empty and returning jam-packed. These flights are generally only available out of Tajikistan. Contact Tajik-Intourist (☎ 21-68-92) at room 11 on the 1st floor of the Hotel Tajikistan.

Bus During the summer there is a daily service from Dushanbe to Samarkand via Penjikent, and a daily bus to Termez. Domestic routes are mainly to southern Tajikistan, eg Kurgan-Tyube and Kulyab, and as far down as Pyanj and Ayvadz – but see the travel warning at the beginning of this chapter. Services to the east reach only around 100 km, as far as Komsomolabad.

Train At the time of writing there were few trains in or out of Dushanbe. The main service is the No 23/24 Dushanbe-Moscow (via Termez, Qarshi, Samarkand and Tashkent), departing daily at 9.30 pm and reaching Moscow 85 hours later. A bed in a four-berth compartment all the way is US$84. A 26 hour Dushanbe-Tashkent service departs early each evening, for about US$25 2nd class. The only link to northern Tajikistan is the No 67, departing early each morning for Kanibadam via Termez, Samarkand and Khojand (ie a train between Tajikistan's first and second cities must first travel into southern Uzbekistan, through Turkmenistan and then back into Uzbekistan for the bulk of its journey, re-entering the country just 30 km from Khojand: the Uzbeks, who charge for usage of their rail track, have the Tajiks over a barrel. Most

other services are suburban, heading down into southern Tajikistan.

Getting Around

Dushanbe is served by bus and trolleybus, but a lack of petrol and spare parts keeps half the fleet off the road and masses of people tapping their feet at bus stops. Fares rarely seem to be collected, and the buses are massively overcrowded. The state bus service is supplemented by an entrepreneurial fleet of less crowded private *marshrutnoe avtobusi* charging around US$0.10.

The airport is a quick ride on marshrutnoe avtobus No 8, or bus No 3 or 12, all caught from prospekt Rudaki or ulitsa Ayni. From the train station, trolleybus No 1 heads north up prospekt Rudaki passing close by all the city's hotels. To get to the bus station take bus No 18 or trolleybus no 12 west from in front of the Museum of Ethnography, a 10 minute ride.

Because of the scarcity of petrol, taxis are rare. You may be able to flag one down during the day on prospekt Rudaki, but the only place you are sure to find them is outside the Hotel Tajikistan. The government-fixed rate at the time of writing was about US$0.30 per km but it's rare that a driver will agree to that – settle on a price before your journey. Private cars are too wary to stop for strangers. If you need a taxi after dark call the dispatcher on ☎ 24-66-29.

There are no self-drive car-hire services but Tajik-Intourist can probably organise a car and driver for about US$30 per day.

AROUND DUSHANBE

The main M34 Ura-Tyube road winds north through the valley of the Varzob river and, though there's no one particular place to head for, there are plenty of picturesque locations, including the **Varzob gorge** 56 km out of Dushanbe. There may be buses up to the village of Varzob during the summer, otherwise Tajik-Intourist can arrange a half-day's drive for about US$20. Dramatic but no longer picturesque, the Vakhsh gorge used to be a big favourite with Intourist because of its 300 metre high hydroelectric dam, the world's highest. The dam is 80 km east of Dushanbe near the new town of Nurek (from which it take its name). If you are travelling on your own, take a Dangara bus.

The remains of a Buddhist temple were found at **Adjina-Tepe** near Kurgan-Tyube, 95 km south of Dushanbe, but everything that could be moved – including a large reclining Buddha figure – was shipped off to the Hermitage in St Petersburg, leaving nothing left to see at the site.

Hissar
Гиссар

On a wide mountain-fringed plain, 30 km west of Dushanbe, are the remains of an 18th century fortress, occupied until 1924 by Ibrahim Beg, the local henchman of the Emir of Bukhara. Once a basmachi stronghold, the fortress was destroyed by the Red Army and all that remains is a reconstructed stone gateway in the cleavage of two massive grassy hillocks. A scramble to the top is rewarded with some excellent views. The sparse hillside brush and the shady lee of boulders are favoured hiding places for the fortress's abundant wild tortoises (*sambaka* in Tajik), but watch out for the snakes which snooze in the same places. Local kids are adept at finding the one while avoiding the other.

Beside the fortress are two plain medressas, one dating from the 18th century and the other 19th, and beyond them is the mausoleum of a 16th century Islamic teacher named Makhtumi Azam. The older medressa (facing the fortress gate) contains a small museum with displays of clothing, ceramics and jewellery.

At the foot of the grassy slopes around the fortress is a pleasant teahouse. There are also plans to build a small hotel and restaurant on the site.

Getting There & Away Take bus No 70 which departs frequently from ulitsa Komsomolskaya just south of Barakat market in Dushanbe. The 30 minute ride costs about US$0.10. In the town of Hissar,

walk down the main street past the market and take the right fork at the bus park. About 50 metres along is a stop for the marshrutnoe avtobus which terminates at the small settlement beside the fortress, some six or seven km farther. Ask for 'KREY-past' (fortress).

Northern Tajikistan

Northern Tajikistan squeezes between Uzbekistan and Kyrgyzstan before exploding in a splurge across the mouth of the Ferghana Valley, the Uzbek heartland. This jigsaw of national boundaries is in fact the result of sober thought. Before 1929 Tajikistan was an autonomous republic within the Uzbek ASSR, but because of its sensitive location on the edge of the Islamic world, Stalin wanted to see it upgraded to a full republic. However, there weren't enough Tajiks; full-republic status required at least one million inhabitants. The Soviets simply topped up the numbers by presenting the Tajiks with the Khojand region (renamed Leninabad). There may also be some truth in the theory that this was in partial recompense for the loss of Bukhara and Samarkand – a bum deal if ever there was one.

The only other settlement of any size in northern Tajikistan is Ura-Tyube, of little interest, although Shakhristan, 40 km to the south, has some old Islamic monuments.

Farther south, the twin Turkestan and Zeravshan ranges, western outriders of the Pamirs, sever northern Tajikistan from the bulk of the country's landmass. Collectively known as the Fansky Gory (Fan mountains), these are impassable from October through May. The highest passes, like the Anzob (3372 metres) and Ayni (3378 metres), are securely plugged with snow.

Inaccessibility, however, is a distinct advantage in certain cases; since the collapse of the Soviet Union this region has become one of the world's most productive opium-growing centres. Peasants who can't get the government to pay them for their less addictive crops have turned to farming the bright red poppies in secluded 3000 metre high valleys. Police estimate that up to 25% of the rural workforce is involved in poppy growing. Although the death sentence is in force for drug trafficking, reportedly no-one is much discouraged, their minds high on the fantasy prices to be got for the opium extract.

The Fan mountains are a favoured place for trekking and climbing, being only a couple of hours from both Samarkand and Dushanbe. The UK-based travel companies, Steppes East and Exodus, and REI in the USA, have run trekking expeditions here. For contact details see Travel & Visa Agencies in the Getting There & Away chapter. Alp-Navruz and Sinbad Tourism in Dushanbe are also Fan specialists.

KHOJAND
ХОДЖАНДюХУЧАНД
Population: 164,500

Khojand (pronounced 'HO-jan') is the capital of northern Tajikistan (known administratively as the Khojand province) and the second largest city in the country. It's also one of Tajikistan's oldest towns, founded by Alexander the Great as his easternmost outpost, Alexandreia-Eskhate, more than 2300 years ago. Commanding the entrance to the Ferghana Valley, Khojand enjoyed prosperity and its riches spawned palaces, grand mosques and a citadel before the Mongols steamrollered the city into oblivion in the early 13th century.

A much reduced Khojand arose on the site and unobtrusively weathered the course of Central Asian history on the Ferghana plain: Uzbek khanates, tsarist Russia and eventually the Bolsheviks. But whereas the rest of Ferghana was incorporated into the Uzbek SSR, in 1929 Khojand was scooped out for the newly formed Tajik SSR where it has remained – albeit, not always contentedly.

Majority-Uzbek Khojand has remained aloof from Dushanbe, although its 'good Communist' credentials meant that it always provided Tajikistan's ruling elite. When Nabiev, a Khojand man, was unseated in 1992 and Tajikistan looked like becoming an Islamic republic, Khojand province threat-

ened to secede. Secure behind the Fan mountains, it has managed to completely escape the ravages of the civil war, and has always been safe for travel. It remains the wealthiest part of the country producing two-thirds of all Tajikistan's industrial output with only one-third of the population. As a result it's the most comfortable and relaxed of Tajikistan's cities. Expats from Dushanbe fly up here for weekends away from it all. Though lacking the spectacles of other Central Asian cities, its sedate riverside atmosphere and grassy parks make for a fine place to drop out for a day or two.

See the Uzbekistan chapter for more on the Ferghana Valley.

Orientation & Information
Khojand sprawls either side of the great Syr-Darya river, which here is a little less than half a km wide. The centre of town is on the south bank, along the main artery of ulitsa Lenina, which runs from north of the river, over the bridge and 1.5 km south to ploshchad Pobedy and the market. From Pobedy, the street is renamed ulitsa Zakirova and continues south a farther five km to the train station, the new bus terminal (for buses east along the Ferghana Valley) and the airport. A second, older bus station, for services to Tashkent and south, is on ulitsa Kamoli Khojandy, west of ulitsa Lenina, 600 metres south of the river. The post office and adjacent telephone office are on ulitsa Ordzhonikidze, west off Lenina, 300 metres south of the river. The only place we found to change money was at the reception desk at the Hotel Leninabad.

The telephone code for Khojand is 37922.

Things to See & Do
The city's oldest remains are the formless baked-earth walls of the 10th century **citadel**, which could just as well be the residue of last summer's ditch-digging. A building beside the walls that once housed the local archaeological museum is long-deserted, but the surrounding **park** is well-kept and pleasant.

At the south end of ulitsa Lenina, east of

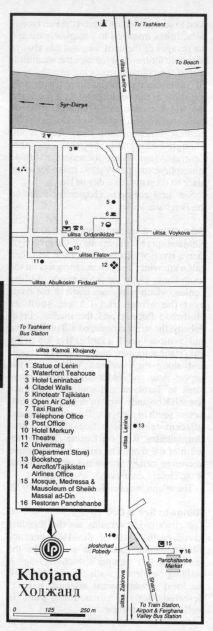

1 Statue of Lenin
2 Waterfront Teahouse
3 Hotel Leninabad
4 Citadel Walls
5 Kinoteatr Tajikistan
6 Open Air Café
7 Taxi Rank
8 Telephone Office
9 Post Office
10 Hotel Merkury
11 Theatre
12 Univermag (Department Store)
13 Bookshop
14 Aeroflot/Tajikistan Airlines Office
15 Mosque, Medressa & Mausoleum of Sheikh Massal ad-Din
16 Restoran Panchshanbe

Khojand
Ходжанд

0   125   250 m

ploshchad Pobedy, is the **Panchshanbe market**, a typical Central Asian bazar that bombards you with sights, smells and sounds, and also presents great temptations to the taste buds. The core of the bazar is an elegant, purpose-built hall (1954) with arched entrance portals that are patterned with brilliant designs.

Opposite the bazar, shielded from the hubbub by a calm white wall, are the **mosque, medressa** and **mausoleum of Sheikh Massal ad-Din**, a modest, relatively modern complex that is quietly busy with chattering young boys clutching Qurans and sage-like old men reclining in the shade. Take a look at the wooden canopy in the courtyard. It's sumptuously decorated like the market arches, but here, unusually, instead of abstract designs, the motifs are recognisable fruits and flowers.

Since the removal of its giant rival in Tashkent, Khojand's **statue of Lenin** is now probably the largest in Central Asia. Considering the town has already ditched its Soviet-era name, surely their monster Communist can't have long to go either. He's on the north bank of the river, 300 metres beyond the bridge.

Places to Stay

Khojand has two accommodation options, both good (a third hotel, the Shark, up by the bazar, was derelict at the time of our visit). The unfashionably named *Hotel Leninabad* (☎ 6-69-27) is superbly placed on the corniche beside the Syr-Darya with great views, but only from its north-facing rooms. The clean, well-tended rooms have hot water in the attached bathrooms. Singles/doubles cost US$8/15.

The *Hotel Merkury* (☎ 6-49-90) couldn't be more different – a two storey villa with painted ceilings, polished banisters, creaky carpeted stairs and possibly the only full-size snooker table in Central Asia. The dozen enormous, very comfortable rooms are priced at an incredible US$10/20 for singles/doubles. The Merkury is at ulitsa Filatov 2, a side street that runs off ulitsa Lenina beside the Univermag.

Places to Eat

The restaurant at the *Hotel Leninabad* is reasonable, if unexciting, with typical meat-and-rice fare for about US$2. The *Hotel Merkury* has no restaurant but there is a kitchen and a cook who will prepare meals for guests on request. Beside the bazar is the large *Restoran Panchshanbe*, closed all the time we were there and not looking half as appealing as the many teahouses, shashlyk grills and vats of plov out front. Nearer the hotels is a small *open-air café* on ulitsa Lenina next to the Kinoteatr Tajikistan, serving shashlyk, soup and gulyash, while on the corniche by the Hotel Leninabad a *waterfront teahouse*, great for green tea and boiled eggs first thing in the morning. The bread is particularly good in Khojand, glazed and sprinkled with sesame seeds.

Getting There & Away

There are daily flights from Khojand to Dushanbe (US$71) and Moscow (US$253), and less frequent services to Orenburg, Novosibirsk and Yekaterinburg in Russia. The Aeroflot/Tajikistan Airlines sales office (☎ 6-02-49) on ploshchad Pobedy at the southern end of ulitsa Lenina is open daily from 9 am to 1 pm and 2 to 8 pm.

By rail, there are daily services to Tashkent (for connections to Moscow) and via Kokand to Andijan. Only one train a day connects Khojand with the rest of Tajikistan, the No 68 to Dushanbe via Samarkand and Termez.

From the old bus station, close to the centre of town, there's a daily 1 pm bus to Tashkent (three hours, US$2.50) and services south via Ura-Tyube to Penjikent and on to Samarkand, Navoiy and Bukhara. Schedules change frequently but there should be at least one service a day. From the new bus station, on the southern outskirts of Khojand, several buses a day go up the Ferghana Valley to Kokand, Ferghana, Andijan and Osh.

Getting Around

To reach the town centre from the airport, train station or Ferghana Valley bus station

take local bus No 2 or 34 and get off opposite Kinoteatr Tajikistan on ulitsa Lenina. It's about a 20 minute journey. You can catch these in the opposite direction at the Univermag stand. Marshrutnoe avtobus No 3 runs the same route. To get to the old bus station on ulitsa Kamoli Khojandy take trolleybus No 2, 5 or 7, also from the Univermag stand.

PENJIKENT
ПЕНДЖИКЕНТ

Right across the border, from Samarkand in Uzbekistan, are the ruins of a major town in one of Central Asia's forgotten civilisations – ancient Penjikent, founded in the fifth century by the Sogdians. See Around Samarkand in the Uzbekistan chapter.

The Pamirs

They're known locally as Bam-i-Dunya (the Roof of the World) and once you're up in the Pamirs it's not hard to see why. A network of high, wide valleys which put you up amongst the peaks, with a dizzying shortage of air and blinding intense sunlight, the Pamirs feel like a land a little bit closer to the heavens. They are the node from which several of the world's highest ranges radiate, including the Karakoram and Himalayas to the south, the Hindu Kush to the west and the Tian Shan straddling the Kyrgyz-Chinese border to the north-east.

Though they don't quite compare with the pinnacles of the Himalayas, the Pamirs do contain three of the four highest mountains in the former Soviet Union, the apex of which is Pik Kommunizma at 7495 metres. Less than an Empire State Building behind is Pik Lenina at 7134 metres. Where the Pamirs cannot be topped, however, is in the sheer prosaic quality of their names: as well as Lenina and Kommunizma (formerly Pik Stalina) there are the Victory and Revolution peaks and, the most romantically impaired of all, an Academy of Sciences range.

For the most part, the Pamirs are too high

The Snow Leopard or Ounce lives in the mountains, moving from altitudes of 1800 metres in winter to 5500 metres in summer.

for human settlement. The part of the country in which most of the mountains are located, the autonomous region of Gorno-Badakhshan, despite accounting for 45% of the country's territory has only 3% of its population. Instead the slopes and valleys are inhabited by hardier creatures, near-mythical animals like the giant Marco Polo sheep, which sports curled horns that would measure almost two metres were they somehow unfurled, and the rarely seen snow leopard. And that's not to mention the similarly elusive 'giant snowman'.

Chance encounters with Yetis aside, most of the Pamir region is reasonably safe excepting the stretch of the M41 highway between Komsomolabad and Rushan (see the Safety in Tajikistan aside at the start of this chapter and the Routes & Safety section below.) There are, however, plenty of other problems and pitfalls as noted in the following sections. Anyone interested in spending time in the mountains should pick up *Trekking in Russia & Central Asia* by Frith Maier

that has many graded itineraries and useful information from trekkers experienced in this region.

Regional Crisis

With no arable land to speak of and no industry, the region of Gorno-Badakhshan has always relied heavily on Dushanbe for its upkeep. But since the Pamiris supported the losing side in Tajikistan's 1992 civil war, the government hasn't been sending much in the way of aid. This is seen by some as a deliberate strategy to weaken the opposition's strength.

At present, the people of the Pamirs are totally reliant on humanitarian aid for their continued survival. Funded primarily by the Aga Khan Foundation, convoys of trucks constantly shuttle between Khorog and the supply depots at Osh (Kyrgyzstan), ferrying in wheat, rice, salt and other staples. Locals supplement this with whatever can be grown in small garden patches. Even so, people generally manage only one substantial meal every three or four days. As well as providing short-term food aid, the Aga Khan Foundation is setting up programmes to create some degree of self-sufficiency, such as dams for electricity and irrigation.

Travel in the Mountains

Travel in the Pamir region is beset with obstacles. The biggest of these is the absolute dearth of transport and food. Also, importantly, outside of the regional capital of Khorog there is no hotel or hostel accommodation. However, there are plenty of isolated farmsteads along the mountain routes which operate as very rough-and-ready guesthouses. What you can expect is some floor space, a pungent sheep-skin blanket and probably a hot bowl of *sher chay*, tea with goats' milk, salt and butter (if you're exceptionally unlucky you might also be served yak-meat soup, a dish which comes close to inducing reflexive vomiting). All drivers in the Pamirs know the whereabouts of such places.

Routes & Safety

The M41, known as the Pamir Highway, runs from Dushanbe to the Ferghana Valley town of Osh in Kyrgyzstan, making a spectacular, rollercoasting sweep around the central Pamirs. Unfortunately, for some time it has not been possible to travel its full length. The stretch of road between Komsomolabad and Rushan passes through one of the most heavily militarised stretches of the Tajik-Afghan border region and as such is a permanent no-go zone for unauthorised traffic. The area around Kalaikhum in particular has seen some of the heaviest skirmishing of recent years and reports in 1995 said that some of the roads in the area had been mined by rebels.

By comparison, the regional capital of Khorog, 239 km south-east of Kalaikhum, is reasonably safe, although in June 1994 it did come under attack from over the border. There are daily flights between Khorog and Dushanbe. Most Pamir travellers fly in here to pick up the Pamir highway, which still has 728 km of quite literally breathtaking high-

altitude passes and plateaus to negotiate before finishing up in Osh.

A second Pamir road, the A372, forks off from the M41 some 150 km north-east of Dushanbe to make a beeline for the Kyrgyz border 200 km away. It rejoins the M41 at Sary-Tash, 200 km south of Osh. Not as exciting as the Pamir Highway, it still winds through passes of over 4000 metres and, in good weather, provides views of Pik Lenina and Pik Kommunizma. From October through May the A372 is intermittently closed by snowfall. In summer it's often rendered unsafe by fighting in the Garm valley region through which it runs – check the current situation before setting out.

Getting Around

Other than the daily Dushanbe-Khorog flight, there's no public transport. The only means of getting around is by private car. But a desperate shortage of fuel and spare parts means there are precious few cars on Pamir roads (making hitching unfeasible). Anyone considering flying to Khorog and somehow carrying on to Osh is strongly advised to firm up arrangements before departing Dushanbe. Try contacting in advance Mosalam Anvarov (☎ (2910) 32-06) in Khorog, who told us that with a couple of days notice he could find a car owner willing to drive to Osh for a negotiable fee.

Provisioning

There's no food to be had in the towns and villages of Gorno-Badakhshan. There are no restaurants, no cafés, no shashlyk stands or plov, no shops or kiosks – nothing. What little food makes it into the region is barely enough to keep the inhabitants from starting on the woodwork. However, local hospitality being what it is, what Pamiris have they'll share. To avoid the acute discomfort of discovering that a family has just slaughtered the last chicken for you, *bring all your own provisions*. When calculating what to bring and how much, be generous, since bad weather, cancelled flights and vehicle breakdowns will probably keep you in the region longer than you expect.

TAJIKISTAN

If you're going to be driving on the Pamir Highway, where many of the passes are well over the 4000 metre mark, read Problems of Climate & Geography in the Facts for the Visitor chapter – especially about the serious risks associated with altitude sickness. It's also essential that you have warm clothing as even in mid-summer, night-time temperatures up on the exposed Pamir plateau can drop as low as -25°C (if you are there in the winter then you're looking at a raw -40°C). To avoid having to adopt a permanent Clint Eastwood squint, take along some sunglasses too.

Visas

At Khorog, *militsia* officers meet all incoming planes and immediately collar obvious foreigners, and no-one makes it off the tarmac if their documentation isn't in perfect order. Similarly, entering Tajikistan from Osh, the border controls, beginning at Sary-Tash and continuing in a six-fold series of hurdles, are fantastically stringent. Whether you have separate Tajik and Kyrgyz visas or an all-in-one 'megavisa', at a minimum you must have specifically listed on them Khorog, Murgab and either Osh or Dushanbe as your goal, depending on your direction of travel. Try to have these places written onto your visa before arriving in Central Asia. In the past Tajik officials in Dushanbe have been very reluctant to help travellers visit Gorno-Badakhshan.

KHOROG
ХОРОГ

Population: 22,000

A small, mountain-valley town, Khorog is the capital of the autonomous Gorno-Badakhshan region. It lies 2000 metres above sea level, strung out irregularly along the slopes either side of the dashing Gunt river. A few km downstream, the Gunt merges with the Pyanj, the river that marks the border with Afghanistan.

The town was only founded in 1932, the result of a Russian drive to populate the southern fringes of Gorno-Badakhshan as a buffer against foreign intervention. Settlers were encouraged to populate the town with the promise of a medal and a free Volga sedan to any mother spawning 16 or more children. Quite what these offspring were supposed to do on maturing is unclear, as Khorog has no industry and no cultivable land. Exacerbated by the civil war and Gorno-Badakhshan's ostracism by Dushanbe, unemployment here presently stands at almost 100%. Almost the only people with work are drivers employed by the Aga Khan Foundation, and for this reason money has disappeared altogether, replaced by barter.

Physically attractive though Khorog is, these factors make it a difficult town for travellers. One person to turn to for help is Mosalam Anvarov (☎ (2910) 32-06), who used to head Khorog's Department of Tourism but is now going it alone. Anvarov is keen to attract parties for three to 10-day trips around the southern Pamir region but he's also someone to talk to about finding transport to Osh. His basic all-inclusive itineraries (he takes care of transport, food and accommodation) involve following the Pamir Highway as far as Jelandy and then looping back on a more southerly road, or going 62 km beyond Jelandy to back-track on a route that hugs the Afghan border. Both trips take in hot springs, mountain lakes and the ruins of pre-Islamic fortresses. Prices seem negotiable. Anvarov is at ulitsa Lenina 1'33/3, kvartel 34, 736000 Khorog; or arrangements can be made through his Moscow partners Balchug (☎ (095) 251-34-33, telex 41-24-92 BALTRSU; ask for Vladimir Treshov).

Khorog has a surprisingly good local history museum with a don't-miss-it collection of kitsch official gifts presented over the years by visiting delegations. The museum is in ulitsa Lenina, virtually the only road in town. A few hundred metres farther on is the post office, at No 40, where it's unlikely you'll be able to put a call through to anywhere but Dushanbe. Opposite the post office is the local university which, believe it or not, is twinned with England's Oxford. There is also a botanical garden on the slopes high above the town. To get there, begin at

Khorog's only traffic lights and take the road north that crosses the river and stick with it for about five km.

Accommodation is provided by the spartan, almost derelict, *Hotel Druzhba* where half the rooms have no toilet or washing facilities. Rates are US$0.50 per person. The Druzhba is by the river, just off ulitsa Lenina. If you're coming from the airstrip it's the first side street on the right after the little silver bust of Lenin.

Flying to/from Khorog
One of the main attractions of Khorog is the flight in from Dushanbe which, depending on your confidence in the pilots of Tajikistan Airlines, will be one of the most exhilarating or terrifying experiences of your life. In Soviet days this was the only route on which Aeroflot paid its pilots danger money. For most of the 45 minute flight the aircraft scoots along mountain valleys, flying in the shadow of the rockface with its wingtips so close you could swear they kick up swirls of snow. It may be reassuring to know that only one flight has failed to make it safely in recent years and that, we were told, was not as a result of pilot error or mechanical failure but because the plane was brought down by rocket fire from Afghanistan.

There are two flights a day each way, though at the first sign of bad weather (which is frequent outside of the summer months) they're grounded. Passengers must then take their chances the next day, tussling for seats with those already booked on that flight. It can happen that, after a run of bad weather, hundreds turn up to fight for the first flight's 40 available seats. As a foreigner paying the hard currency rate (US$61 one-way) you will be given preference.

The mountain-flanked airstrip at Khorog is three km outside town at the western end of ulitsa Lenina. There is no bus service to or from the airstrip.

THE PAMIR HIGHWAY
ПАМИРСКОЕ ШОССЕ
The route from Khorog to Osh on the M41 Pamir Highway is a suspension-wrenching

728 km of badly surfaced road. And that's if it is surfaced at all; large sections have been ripped away by landslides and avalanches, leaving only precarious, deeply rutted tracks of frozen mud. Muscular, high-clearance 4WDs with would-be rally drivers at the wheel have been known to cover the distance in 20 hours, but a more realistic estimate is two full days. This presents the problem of where you're going to spend the night as there are no hotels en route (see the Travel in the Mountains section). Blue km-posts line the way with the distance from Khorog marked on one side and from Osh on the other.

Khorog to Jelandy
The initial stretch out of Khorog contains some of the most attractive scenery of the whole route. As the road relentlessly hauls itself up a succession of switchbacks, climbing 2000 metres in less than 100 km, there are countless spectacular views back along the Gunt valley. At the 120 km-post, at Jelandy, there are mineral springs. The small bathhouse with two murky, sulphurous pools is a favourite stop for truck drivers out of Khorog, a town with no hot water. But while it's fine for the locals, the over-powering whiff of the baths combined with the sudden increase in altitude can leave 'lowlanders' feeling extremely giddy and faint. Jelandy is already close to 4000 metres above sea level and, hot springs or not, from here on it's unwise to indulge in anything too strenuous – no running, no snowball fights.

Jelandy to Murgab
Soon after leaving Jelandy the road climbs to 4272 metres as it crests the Koitezek pass, after which the mountains pull back from the road to create a barren km-wide plain. This is the Pamir plateau; 'the Roof of the World'. The road is raised on a metre-high embankment barely wide enough for oncoming vehicles to pass and quite hazardous for over-tired drivers (a drifting truck in our convoy slid off the crumbling embankment edge and rolled onto the plain).

The plateau town of Murgab, some 310 km

from Khorog, is where many drivers on the highway aim to finish up at the end of the first day. A Soviet-era settlement like Khorog, Murgab is a drab huddle of single-storey white buildings in a forest of telegraph poles. Other than a truck-stop guesthouse, there's nowhere to stay and nowhere to eat. Coming from Khorog, the first Pamir militsia checkpoint is on the outskirts of Murgab; anyone not having the town listed on their visa might have difficulties proceeding any farther.

Beyond Murgab, the highway hugs the Chinese border and in places the twin barbed-wire-topped fences run less than 20 metres from the road. Despite this, there is no crossing between China and Tajikistan; the closest official breach in the Chinese border is at the Torugart pass in Kyrgyzstan.

Murgab to Sary-Tash

Soon after Murgab (around the 371 km-post) the mountains close in as the road climbs towards the Ak-Baital (White Horse) pass, at 4655 metres the highest point of the journey. From there it's a long descent of some 70 km to Lake Karakul, the highest lake in Central Asia. Created by a meteor up on a wind-whipped mountain plateau, Karakul has an eerie, lifeless Twilight Zone air about it, well living up to its name, 'Black lake'. In winter it freezes over and is hidden under snow. Beside the lake is an equally chilly Russian military checkpoint where soldiers have in the past detained foreigners for up to four

hours while officers probe passports and visas for possible defects. All baggage is subjected to a search here. If you've taken any photographs whilst in the Pamirs do not admit to it or you risk having your film confiscated. No sooner are you away from the Russians than the Tajiks bring all traffic to a halt with their own checkpoint.

The actual border between Tajikistan and Kyrgyzstan is some distance farther away at the crest of the Kyzyl Orda pass (4282 metres). There follows a rapid rollercoaster descent down a mountainside, strewn with the skeletons of overly hasty trucks, before the road levels out for the approach to the Kyrgyz border town of Sary-Tash.

Sary-Tash to Osh

At Sary-Tash, after a succession of thorough Kyrgyz border formalities, the A372 branches off the M41 Pamir Highway, making a south-westerly beeline for Dushanbe (see the Routes & Safety section). One hundred km up the A372 is Daraut-Korgon, the gateway to Pik Kommunizma, the Pamir's highest peak. The last 200 km of the highway from Sary-Tash to Osh is, like the initial stretch out of Khorog, stunningly beautiful with the road winding up, down and around verdant green hills and mountains. This all comes as a great relief after the high-altitude desert of the Pamir plateau and provides a very physical full-stop to the journey.

Turkmenistan
Туркменистан

In some ways the most curious of the Central Asian republics, desert-filled Turkmenistan resembles an Arab Gulf state without the money. Its people, the Turkmen, are only a generation or two removed from being in nomadic tribes, roaming by horse the shifting desert sands that have since been found to conceal a fabulous unexploited wealth in oil and gas.

The Turkmen have never formed a real nation and have allowed their cities to become predominantly populated by other peoples, while they place most esteem on a rural life revolving around their famous, traditionally patterned carpets and fleet Akhal-Teke horses, supposedly the ancestor of the Arabian racehorse.

Visitors to Ashghabat, the capital, and other Turkmen towns are often left with the nagging feeling that life goes on elsewhere. There is never much to look at. Rarely does a region with such a rich history have so little to show for it.

The cities that represented 2500 years of civilisation, built by Alexander the Great, the Persians, the Arabs – whose ancient city of Merv is said to have provided the setting for Scheherazade's tales – and even the Russians, have all disappeared save for a few bones. As for landscape, four-fifths of the country is desert – and not a pretty desert at that.

The key to enjoying a visit is the hospitality of the Turkmen. Turkmenistan is as much a culture as a country and the real interest lies in the colourful trappings of Turkmen tradition: the carpets, the clothes, the lifestyle and the ceremonies.

In Ashghabat, try to visit Tolkuchka bazar and the horse races at the ancient hippodrome. Although Turkmen tend to be very reserved with strangers, should you be invited into a Turkmen home, jump at the chance.

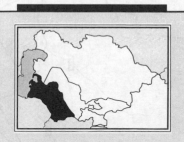

Highlights
* Konye-Urgench: tall, beautiful, ancient buildings strung like a necklace across a dusty plain, survivors of the city they bejewelled before Timur vapourised it.
* Tolkuchka Sunday bazar on the outskirts of Ashghabat, with its colourful Cecil B de Mille cast of thousands.

History
Ancient Armies Though never a goal in itself, the sun-scorched, barren land between the Caspian Sea and the Oxus river (now the Amu-Darya) passed in ancient times from one empire to another as campaigning armies decamped on the way to richer territories. Alexander the Great established a city here on his way to India. Around the time of Christ, the Parthians, Rome's main rivals for power in the east, set up a capital at Nisa, near present-day Ashghabat. In the 11th century the Seljuq Turks appropriated Alexander's old city, Merv, as a base from which to expand their empire into Afghanistan.

Two centuries later, the heart of the Seljuq empire was torn out as Jenghiz Khan stormed down from the steppes and through Trans-Caspia (the region east of the Caspian Sea) on his way to terrorise Europe.

445

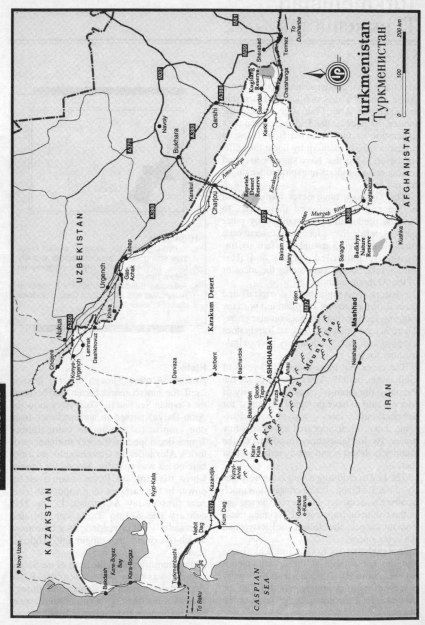

Desert Raiders It's not known precisely when the first Turkmen appeared, but most historians think they drifted here in the wake of the Seljuqs, sometime in the 11th century. A collection of displaced nomadic horse-breeding tribes, possibly from the foothills of the Altay mountains, they found alternative pastures in the oases fringing the Karakum desert and in Persia, Syria and Anatolia (in present-day Turkey). They rode shy of any regional powers and remained largely unaffected by all the dynastic musical chairs.

With the decline in the 16th century of the Timurids, the last of Central Asia's empire-builders, Trans-Caspia became a backwater, punctuated with feudal islands like the khanates of Khiva and Bukhara. From their oasis strongholds the Turkmen preyed on straggling caravans and raided the peaceable settlements of northern Persia to steal hostages for sale in Turkic markets. According to Arminius Vambéry, a 19th century traveller in the region, the Turkmen 'would not hesitate to sell into slavery the Prophet himself, did he fall into their hands'. When not harassing and pillaging their neighbours the Turkmen tribes would fall on one another with equal zest.

Geok-Tepe The Turkmen bit off more than they could chew when they began kidnapping parties of Russians in Trans-Caspia, the vanguard of a rapidly expanding tsarist empire. At one time there were perhaps as many as 3000 Russians enslaved in Bukhara, most former captives of the Turkmen. In 1877 the empire struck back. A series of military actions was launched from the newly founded Caspian port of Krasnovodsk (now Turkmenbashi). The first, against the Turkmen encampment of Kyzyl-Arvat, succeeded in routing the tribesmen but the second, against the earthen fortress of Geok-Tepe, resulted in an ignominious retreat for the Russians.

Desperate to save face and put down the now wildly uncontrollable Turkmen, the tsar gave command of his Trans-Caspian forces to General Mikhail Dmitrievich Skobelev, a

soldier with a bloody career. In 1881, under Skobelev, Russian forces again marched on Geok-Tepe. This time its mud walls were blasted apart with gunpowder and the Russians streamed in to massacre an estimated 7000 Turkmen. In adherence to Skobelev's maxim of 'the harder you hit them, the longer they remain quiet', a further 8000 were cut down as they fled across the desert. With the diplomatically stated aim of 'putting an end to the depredations of the Turcoman tribes,' the Russians went on to seize Ashghabat and Merv. Not surprisingly, they met little further resistance and by 1894 had secured all Trans-Caspia for the tsar.

Tsarist Trans-Caspia During the Trans-Caspian campaign, the Russians' biggest problem had been keeping the army provisioned on its trek through the inhospitable sands of the Karakum. The solution was to build a railway. Work on the Trans-Caspian line began at what was to be the western terminus, Krasnovodsk, in 1881 and, via Ashghabat and Merv, it had reached Charjou and the Amu-Darya by 1886. Two years later trains were steaming into Samarkand and, not long after, Tashkent.

Although the swift annexation of Trans-Caspia had alarmed the British, who suspected Russian designs on Afghanistan and ultimately Imperial India, the outbreak of WWI unexpectedly threw the two Great Game rivals together as allies against two of the central powers, Germany and Turkey. The situation took another twist in 1917 with the Bolshevik coup and the signing of a peace treaty between Russia and Germany. Amidst the chaos a loose grouping of counter-revolutionaries seized power in Ashghabat, only to come under attack from the Bolsheviks, who had a strong Central Asian power base in Tashkent. A small British force, dispatched from northern Persia to back up the provisional Ashghabat government, skirmished with the Bolsheviks at a place called Dushakh.

With the end of WWI the British withdrew and the Bolsheviks took Ashghabat in 1919. For a while the region existed as the Turkmen

TURKMENISTAN

oblast of the Turkestan Autonomous Soviet Socialist Republic (ASSR), before becoming the Turkmen Soviet Socialist Republic (SSR) in 1924.

The Turkmen SSR Inflamed particularly by Soviet attempts to settle the tribes and collectivise farming, Turkmen resistance continued and a guerrilla war raged until 1936. More than a million Turkmen fled into the Karakum desert or into northern Afghanistan rather than give up their nomadic ways. The Turkmen also fell foul of a Moscow-directed campaign against religion. According to Dilip Hiro in *Between Marx and Muhammad*, of 441 mosques in Turkmenistan in 1911, only five remained standing by 1941.

A steady stream of Russian immigrants began arriving in the 1920s to undertake the modernisation of the SSR, and a big part of the plan was cotton. Turkmenistan's arid climate was hardly conducive to bumper harvests, and to supply the vast quantities of water required the authorities began work in the 1950s on a massive irrigation ditch: the Karakum canal. The 1100 km long concrete gully they built runs the length of the republic, bleeding the Amu-Darya to create a fertile band across the south. Cotton production quadrupled, though the consequences for the Aral Sea have been disastrous (see Environment in the Facts about the Region chapter).

Supremely Soviet Turkmenistan was slow to pick up on the political changes in the other Soviet republics during the 1980s. The first challenge to the Communist Party of Turkmenistan (CPT) came in 1989 when a group of intellectuals formed Agzybirlik (Unity), a socially and environmentally progressive party. Agzybirlik also hoped to foster a sense of national awareness amongst the Turkmen, a difficult task in a people completely lacking any historical unity. The party was officially, if reluctantly, registered but in 1990, but when it showed signs of garnering too much support, it was promptly banned.

As a concession to dispossessed Agzybirlik supporters, the CPT adopted Turkmen as the official state language and on 22 August 1990 made a declaration of sovereignty which meant Turkmenistan's laws were put above those of the USSR. On 27 October 1990 Saparmurad Niyazov, unopposed and supposedly with the blessing of more than 98% of voters, was elected to the newly created post of president.

Reluctant Independence Despite all these preliminaries, the collapse of the Soviet Union came as a great shock to the Niyazov government. The underdeveloped economy and the republic's dependence on Moscow for subsidies meant that Turkmenistan wasn't ready to go it alone. But just as the Turkmen hadn't been consulted about joining the Soviet Union, they had no say when it came time to leave. Following the unsuccessful coup attempt in Moscow, Turkmenistan accepted the inevitable and on 27 October 1991 became an independent country.

One Man, One Nation The years since independence have belonged to President Saparmurad Niyazov, authoritarian head of the Democratic Party of Turkmenistan (DPT), the new name judiciously adopted by the old (and in no way altered) CPT.

With his statue on every available pedestal, a clutch of towns and villages renamed after him and enough public portraits to fill the world's galleries, Niyazov is the focus of a personality cult that makes Lenin look shy and retiring. After being re-elected president in October 1992 (99.5% of the votes cast in favour) parliament awarded him the Order of the Hero of the Turkmen People. The following year he adopted the modest title of Turkmenbashi (Head of all Turkmen) and parliament extended his term in office until 2002 (this time with a less-than-credible claim of 99.99% of all votes in favour), sparing him the bother of constitutionally required five-yearly elections.

Niyazov has reinvented himself as the embodiment of Turkmen nationalism – if

Turkmenistan
Ruins of the royal fortress-city Nisa, 10 km west of Ashgabat

Western Xinjang
Left: Uyghur boy, bazar, Kashgar
Top: Dentist's advertisment, Kashgar
Bottom: Tools and utensils for sale, bazar, Kashgar

you don't love Turkmenbashi how can you love your country? It's a policy not without effect and Niyazov genuinely does have popular appeal. One political commentator went so far as to suggest that he might even win an election with more than one candidate. For the moment, however, this is unlikely because all opposition parties are banned, as are opposition newspapers and any newspapers at all published in Moscow.

Of course there is dissent, especially amongst the educated, who are frustrated at the slow pace of economic reform and the failure of oil and gas wealth to make an impact on empty shop shelves. Niyazov's talk of a 'new Kuwait' rings a little hollow when the average state salary is stuck firmly at around US$10 per month. The government's slogan is 'Ten years to prosperity' but critics see this as a ploy to give officials sufficient time to cream off enough revenue to finance comfortable overseas retirements.

Relations with the Kremlin are, if not effusive, at least cordial. Russia still has a large stake in Turkmenistan, and Russian soldiers police the Iran-Turkmenistan border. Meanwhile Niyazov's government is trying to cultivate links with Turkey and Pakistan to counter the potentially domineering influences of Russia and Iran.

Geography

Bounded by the Caspian Sea in the west and the Amu-Darya river to the east, Turkmenistan covers 488,100 sq km, the second largest of the former Soviet Central Asian republics after Kazakstan. It's also very sparsely populated, one major reason being that four-fifths of the country is waterless desert. The Karakum (Black Sands), one of the largest sand deserts in the world, fills the entire central region of the country with great crescent-shaped sand dunes and cracked, baked-clay surfaces.

To the south, the Karakum is fringed by the Kopet Dag (Lots of Mountains), an earthquake prone range that forms a formidable 1500 km natural border with Iran and, farther east, Afghanistan. Smaller ranges on the

north-west edge of the desert mark Turkmenistan's border with Kazakstan. Apart from the Amu-Darya there are precious few water courses to bring life to this arid region. The small Tejen and Murgab rivers run off the eastern end of the Kopet Dag but barely make it down from the mountains before they're swallowed up by desert. The Soviet answer was the ambitious Karakum canal, but even so, less than 2.5 % of Turkmenistan's land is irrigated.

The most densely populated areas are the valleys of the Amu-Darya and Murgab, and the necklace of oases that form the Akhal chain, strung between Kyzyl-Arvat and Mary.

Government

To outside appearances the government of Turkmenistan *is* Saparmurad Niyazov. Since 1990 he has been head of state (president), and since 1992 also head of government (prime minister), and in addition he is the Chairman of the Democratic Party of Turkmenistan (DPT; the former Communist Party of Turkmenistan and the country's only legal political organisation). Despite the egalitarian title of his party, Niyazov is on record as saying he is against 'formal democracy', which he considers would be a burden to the people. The leaders of the main opposition group, Agzybirlik, sit in exile in Moscow.

Under the Turkmen constitution of 1992, the president is elected every five years, but in 1994 parliamentary deputies voted to extend Niyazov's reign until the year 2002.

Behind Niyazov is the Turkmen parliament, or Majilis. Elected in December 1994, this is a 50 member version of the 175 member Supreme Soviet, of Soviet days. All successful candidates stood unopposed and were DPT members.

For administrative purposes the country is divided into five provinces (*velayaty* in Turkmen) – Akhal, Mary, Lebap, Dashkhovuz and Balkan. Their five symbols are set vertically on the maroon strip that decorates Turkmenistan's national flag.

Economy

Turkmenistan was badly prepared to cope alone. Decades of dependence on the centralised Soviet market system left it with virtually no manufacturing capability. Since the 1930s it had been developed as a virtual monoculture, with cotton cultivation the backbone of the economy. This was supplemented by natural gas, one of the country's abundant resources. Both cotton and gas were sold raw to Moscow at rouble prices well below world rates, which ensured no development within the republic. As a virtual colony, Turkmenistan never had any processing facilities of its own and at present doesn't have the industrial resources to produce a box of matches.

At the same time, in the new post-Soviet, hard-currency-only order, Turkmenistan is having trouble getting paid for its raw material exports. In early 1995 it was owed US$1.4 billion by other CIS republics but with little hope of remuneration: cash-strapped Ukraine offered to pay off part of its US$700 million debt with 18 red Volvos.

For the average Turkmen this translates to empty supermarket shelves, with the scant items available often priced well out of reach (eg compare the cost of a loaf of bread at the market, about 50 *manat*, with the average monthly salary of just 3000 *manat*). To counter this, the government uses half of its budget to subsidise many aspects of daily life, keeping the prices of state-store bread, butter, cooking oil, petrol etc artificially low, while domestic gas, electricity and water are free.

However, the long-term prospects are promising. Turkmenistan has considerable oil reserves (an estimated 700 million tonnes), and only the USA, Canada and Russia produce more natural gas. The major obstacle to real wealth is getting the gas to paying markets. At present the only pipeline runs into Russia, but in 1994 Niyazov signed an agreement with Tehran to build a 4400 km long, US$7 billion pipeline across Iran and into Turkey and Europe. For the moment, however, Turkmenistan is having trouble raising sufficient funds even to get the work underway, with international financiers reluctant to offer backing because of Iranian involvement.

Population & People

The population of Turkmenistan stands at around 4.2 million, of which close to three-quarters are ethnic Turkmen. The remainder are mainly Russians and Uzbeks, with the Uzbeks just having the edge in numbers.

Turkmen are more likely to live in rural areas (only about a third live in towns and cities), with outsiders forming most of the urban population. In towns near the borders, such as Turkmenbashi, Charjou and Dashkhovuz (Tashauz), non-Turkmen account for as much as 70% of the population, the numbers swollen by refugees from neighbouring CIS republics. Significant numbers of Turkmen have also drifted across the country's borders; over 300,000 live in Afghanistan, where they fled collectivisation in the 1920s, with similar numbers in northern Iran.

Though heavily muted by almost 70 years of Soviet 'komradship', centuries-old tribal loyalties continue to exist. The largest of the 100 or so Turkmen tribes are the Teke in the Ashghabat region, the Ersari in the southeast and the Yomud in the west, each distinguished by their dialect, style of clothing and jewellery, and the patterns woven into their carpets. Even the most urbane Turkmen retains allegiance to his tribe, while in the more remote regions tribalism dominates to such an extent that Ersari marry only Ersari, Yomud only Yomud and so on.

In Jonathan Maslow's book, *Sacred Horses*, a native of Ashghabat makes the claim that of all Central Asian peoples the Turkmen have kept the most traditional dress. While under threat from shell-suit pants and polyester jackets, there is visible truth to this. With baggy blue pantaloons tucked into clumping knee-high boots, a white shirt under a cherry-red and gold-striped heavy silk jacket *(khalat)*, and topped by the trademark shaggy wool hat *(telpek)*, the Turkmen male cuts an impressive figure. The full dress is rarely worn but many men wear their telpek (commonly black or brown – white being reserved for special occasions) year round, even on the hottest days; as one Turkmen explained it, they'd rather suffer the heat of their own heads than that of the sun.

Women are less showy and wear heavy, ankle-length silk dresses of wine red and maroon, hiding spangled, striped trousers beneath. A woman's hair is always tied back and concealed under a kerchief or scarf. Older women often wear a khalat but, curiously, always thrown over their heads like a shawl.

Arts

In the pantheon of national icons, second only to self-proclaimed hero of the Turkmen, Saparmurad Niyazov, is the poet and thinker Fragi Makhtumkuli. Unlike the President, however, the father of Turkmen literature and poetry, Makhtumkuli (1770-1840) is regarded by his people almost as a saint and his words are held in greater reverence than even those of the Koran.

Born in an area of south-west Turkmenistan which now forms part of Iran, Makhtumkuli was something of a tragic figure. Trapped in a loveless marriage, he lost his two young sons to illness; later in life his whole body of work was not only confiscated by the Persians but, as he stood witness, the camel on which his precious manuscripts were loaded lost its footing and fell into a river to be swept away. Despite his misfortunes, Makhtumkuli was anything but bitter and was actually something of a progressive thinker, speaking out against tribalism, bigamy, and openly critical of both the religious mullahs and the secular khans.

In his writing Makhtumkuli spurned classical forms for home-spun wisdom and a simplicity of language that contributed greatly to his popularity with the travelling bards.

The first English-language translations of Makhtumkuli were published in 1995 and at least one academic has hailed him as a latter day Omar Khayyam. Anyone interested in learning more about Makhtumkuli or sampling his verse should contact Yusuf Azemoun, chairman of the UK-based appreciation society, Friends of Makhtumkuli (152 Lowfiled Rd, Caversham Park Village, Reading RG4 6PQ, UK).

The influence of Makhtumkuli was such that afterwards Turkmen literature became a compendium of mere copyists. Of those who managed to struggle out of the shadow of the great scribe, the most noted are the 19th century writers Kemine, whose satirical rhymes castigated the ruling circles, and Mollanepes, the author of popular lyrical poems. Both are sufficiently recognised to have streets names after them in the capital.

Surprisingly, the Soviet era actually led to a flourishing of the arts in Turkmenistan, broadening the cultural field by introducing drama, opera, ballet and providing training in Moscow and St Petersburg for young talent. The flip side was that the talent then had to constrain itself to producing work that satisfied, if not flattered the authorities. The penalties for not doing so could be considerably worse than just a rejected manuscript. For daring to criticise local officials in her poetry, in 1971 Annasultan Kekilova was locked away in a mental asylum where she remained until her death a short time later.

Today, much of the arts in Turkmenistan suffer, in common with most post-Soviet republics, from a lack of funding, particularly those areas which formerly enjoyed the support of the Russian community. By contrast, institutions that serve to buoy Turkmen national pride are thriving – the Mollanepes Drama theatre in Ashghabat draws a full house for most performances, while across town the newly-opened Carpet Museum is the swishest state-owned building in town.

Officials & Paperwork

Forget booze, drugs or guns. What keeps customs officers at Ashghabat airport alert is the worry that someone might be trying to run a shaggy wool hat or a pair of home-knitted socks past them. In the hands of foreigners these everyday items of Turkmen apparel become 'cultural artefacts' and, as such, cannot be taken out of the country.

Depending on the interpretation of the customs officer, 'cultural artefact' can include anything from a factory-produced scarf to a hand-painted wooden spoon. They will allow each traveller only one or two items of this nature, no more, and each is subject to a seemingly arbitrary duty of between US$5 and US$25. Anything else found during their thorough searches is confiscated. If you have paid a lot of money for something like a Turkmen coat or richly embroidered dress, to save your nerves at the airport take it sometime beforehand to the Ministry of Culture in Ashghabat (☎ 25-34-17; fax 51-19-91, 25-69-85), opposite the US Embassy on ulitsa Pushkina, and get written permission to take it out of the country. In our experience, ministry people are much more pleasant than customs officials.

The regulations on carpets are every bit as stringent. All that are allowed out are new (maximum 10 years old), factory-produced carpets, no bigger than three sq metres. Anyone purchasing a carpet within these parameters should take it for certification to the Museum of Ethnography (☎ 25-45-34) at Makhtumkuli 73, a low white building squeezed between the Univermag (department store) and the US Embassy in Ashghabat. The relevant office is marked 'Etnografik Boliki'. There the carpet will be examined to ensure that the country is not being deprived of a national treasure. If not, the certificate takes 15 minutes and payment of 300 *manat* per sq metre. Without the certificate your carpet will not make it past customs, and even with it, customs will demand an additional duty of 4000 *manat* (US$20) per sq metre.

Dangers & Annoyances
Bus and train travel can be a nightmare. Services are infrequent, always full and station staff can be astoundingly surly or even hostile. Same-day departure windows are absolute scrums; you can be elbow-locked and compressed for hours, only to find everything sold out (by contrast, advance-purchase windows rarely have long queues). Bus timetables change frequently so check well beforehand on the state of play. Turn up early to avoid having to wrestle with someone for the seat you have purchased, and also because buses occasionally leave early.

You need your passport to buy rail tickets, and bus tickets from larger bus stations. Foreigners' prices for trains are four times those for locals.

Orientation
In 1992 the Caspian port of Krasnovodsk was renamed Turkmenbashi and, as part of the same promotion of national identity, Turkmen versions of place names (in a new Turkmen Roman alphabet) are now being popularised at the expense of Russian. In most cases the differences are minor: eg Turkmen Tejen instead of Russian Tedzhen, Turkmen Saraghs instead of Russian Sarakhs.

The only significant difference is that Russian Tashauz (ТАШАВУЗ) has become Turkmen Dashkhovuz (ДАШХОВУЗ), pronounced 'dash-KVAUZ'. Travellers from Uzbekistan may see Uzbek variants including Toshhovuz, Toshauz and Tashavuz as well. In this book we transliterate town names from the Turkmen.

The authorities have made a start on replacing Russian Cyrillic street signs with new ones in Turkmen Roman, or in some cases Turkmen Cyrillic too. But Turkmenistan is not renowned for its speed of change, and in this chapter we have transliterated street names from Russian, the most common language on the signs (thus ulitsa Chekhova rather than kochesi Chekhov).

Ashghabat
АШХАБАД

Population: 450,000
Ashghabat is not the end of the world, but you feel that it surely can't be more than a short bus ride away. On the edge of the

Karakum desert, it has a dustblown, shutter-banging-in-the-wind quality, and on a sun-scorched afternoon all that's missing are vultures wheeling in the burning blue sky.

Turkmenistan's out-of-sight-out-of-mind distance from Moscow, and its proximity to less-than-progressive Iran and Afghanistan, have led to a languorous sort of existence where little ever happens. Belying the seductive imagery of its name – the City of Love (from the Arabic *ashk*, 'to love') – nobody seems very excited about the place. Turkmen traditionally don't care for cities, while Russians are drifting away in the face of economic hardship. Foreign parties are, for the most part, kept at bay by obstructionist bureaucracy, corruption and the existence of more lucrative markets elsewhere in the former USSR.

There are a few pioneers: across a no-man's-land of parched grass in the city centre the United Colours of Benetton face off against the Iranian Martyrs Foundation store and its imported household items. There's also the Florida, a wanna-be McDonald's, which is the place to be for everybody from pre-pubescent glamour babes to paunchy businessmen, and the lunchtime haunt of much of the city's foreign community.

The visitor must work to make a stay worthwhile. There are no great camera-friendly monuments and no shady teahouses from which to watch the world go by. But if you're prepared to jump on a few buses or hire a car, there is some satisfaction to be gained. And make sure to be around on a Sunday to visit Tolkuchka bazar, where you'll find pooled all the colour drained from the city.

History

The first recorded comment on Ashghabat is that they made good wine there (something sadly no longer true), written on a Parthian-era tablet noting a gift of several casks to the emperor. At that time Ashghabat was a small town within the Parthian empire, whose capital was Nisa (now ruins, 10 km west of the modern capital). In the 1st century BC Ashghabat was reduced to dust by an earth-quake, but thanks to trade with Silk Road merchants travelling over the mountains into Persia, it was gradually rebuilt, prospering again under the name of Konjikala. In the 11th century it passed into the hands of the Seljuqs, from whom it was snatched at the beginning of the 13th century and destroyed by the Mongols.

In the wake of the Mongols the region became the prowling ground for Turkmen tribes, who never had much use for towns. Consequently, when the Russians arrived in 1881, fresh from their victory at Geok-Tepe, they found only a small village. The major Trans-Caspian town had been Merv, but the Russians chose to develop Ashghabat as a regional centre, possibly because of its more strategic location on the fringes of British-dominated Persia. By the end of the 19th century Ashghabat was graced with European shops and hotels, an architecturally impressive train station and a bicycle club that held glittering balls for the Russian officers. The city was even on the itinerary of a Thomas Cook tour. The population was overwhelmingly Russian with some Armenians, Persians and Jews; even today, Ashghabat is predominantly non-Turkmen.

At around 1 am on 6 October 1948, the city that 19th century tourists had described as 'beautiful' and 'wonderful' vanished in less than a minute, levelled by an earthquake that rattled the Richter scale at nine. Over 110,000 people died – two-thirds of the population – although the official figure was 14,000; this was the era of Stalin, when Socialist countries didn't suffer disasters. For five years the area was closed to outsiders while the bodies were recovered, the wreckage cleared and a new city begun.

The Ashghabat of today is a completely modern creation. Though almost certainly not as attractive as its predecessor, it is, with luck, a lot more earthquake-proof.

Orientation

Replanned after the quake, Ashghabat is a grid of precisely laid-out streets and avenues with barely a curve amongst them. The main artery is prospekt Makhtumkuli, a seven km

TURKMENISTAN

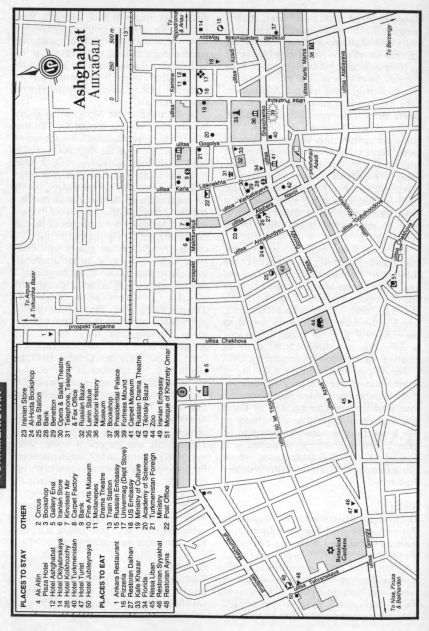

Ashghabat
Ашхабад

0 250 500 m

PLACES TO STAY
4   Ak Altin
    Plaza Hotel
12 Hotel Ashghabat
14 Hotel Oktyabrskaya
26 Hotel Kolkhozchy
40 Hotel Turkmenistan
47 Hotel Turist
50 Hotel Jubileynaya

PLACES TO EAT
1   Ankara Restaurant
16 Pizzeria
27 Restoran Daihan
33 Kafe Khazar
34 Florida
45 Nissa Liban
46 Restoran Syyakhat
48 Restoran Ayna

OTHER
2   Circus
3   Bookshop
5   Gallery Ensi
6   Iranian Store
7   Kinoteatr Mir
8   Carpet Factory
9   Bank
10 Fine Arts Museum
11 Mollanepes
    Drama Theatre
13 Train Station
15 Russian Embassy
17 Univermag (Dept Store)
18 US Embassy
19 Ministry of Culture
20 Academy of Sciences
21 Turkmenistan Foreign
    Ministry
22 Post Office
23 Iranian Store
24 Al-Hoda Bookshop
25 Bus Station
28 Bank
29 Beneton
30 Opera & Ballet Theatre
31 Telephone, Telegraph
    & Fax Office
32 Russian Store
35 Lenin Statue
36 National History
    Museum
37 Bookshop
38 Presidential Palace
39 Fortress Mound
41 Carpet Museum
42 Russian Drama Theatre
43 Tikinsky Bazar
44 Zoo
49 Iranian Embassy
51 Mosque of Khezrety Omar

long, tree-lined avenue running roughly east-west and bisecting the city. Second most important is prospekt Saparmurada Turkmenbashi, running roughly north-south.

The junction of these two streets is an important orientation point; 500 metres north is the train station while 300 metres west, on Makhtumkuli, is the Hotel Ashghabat (at six storeys, one of the city's few high-rise structures; in the next quake the tourists perish first!). While the city has no well-defined centre, most places of interest lie roughly within the sq km south and west of the junction. The busiest street (if any of Ashghabat's streets can be said to be busy) is ulitsa Azadi, roughly parallel to and half a km south of Makhtumkuli. Along it are the two city markets and the bus station, which is a 20 minute walk west of the junction. The airport is five km north of the city.

Maps Maps are difficult to come by, although a government cartography office in the suburbs sells a one metre by 1.5 metre, 1:1,000,000 map of Turkmenistan in English or Russian for US$2, and various 1:200,000 maps of the areas around Turkmenistan's major settlements for about US$0.30 each. The office, Turkmengeod, is on the ground floor at ulitsa Atabayeva 54A. A taxi there should cost the equivalent of about US$0.50.

Once in the building go right, walk to the end of the corridor, and it's the last door on the right.

Information
Tourist Offices Turkmen-Intour (☎ 41-02-24, fax 29-31-69), on the 3rd floor of the Hotel Ashghabat, operates in a Brezhnevian fug of petty officiousness and baffling abrasiveness. We were told that a trip to Anau, Firuza *or* Nisa (none farther than 30 km away) would cost a ludicrous US$126 for a car and driver/guide, while a half-day excursion to Bakharden underground lake would be US$172!

Foreign Embassies & Representations
Many foreign representations in Ashghabat are not full-fledged consular offices and are not set up to issue visas. Even when an embassy does issue visas it can be much more complicated and expensive than elsewhere.

The Russian Embassy, for example, will issue transit visas if proof of onward travel is given, but it takes two weeks and costs US$30 (or 48 hours for an incredible US$150). The Iranian Embassy will issue transit visas but only if proof of onward travel is given, and each case is considered individually with no guarantees.

The pleasant exception is the Chinese

TURKMENISTAN

Street Names in Ashghabat
The following is a list of the new and former (Soviet-era) names of some important streets and squares.

Old name	New name
ulitsa Engelsa	ulitsa Azadi
ulitsa Kalinina	ulitsa Khojov Annadurdyev
ploshchad Karla Marxa	ploshchad Azadi
prospekt Mira	ulitsa Nurmukhameda Andaliba
prospekt Lenina	prospekt Saparmurada Turkmenbashi
ulitsa Pervogo Maya	ulitsa Gorogly
ulitsa Shaumyana	ulitsa Gobshoodova
prospekt Svobody	prospekt Makhtumkuli
ulitsa Timiryazeva	ulitsa Tehranskaya

Embassy, where a visa can be issued in three days for US$10, two days for US$20 or the same day for US$30. An invitation normally required to obtain a Chinese visa is, we were told, optional! Consular hours are generally 9 am to noon on weekdays. Brits in Ashghabat in need of consular services should contact the UK Embassy in Moscow.

Afghanistan
    Hotel Kolkhozchy, ulitsa Azadi 78
    (☎ 25-70-87, 25-74-35)
China
    ulitsa Sankt Pazina 2, at the east end of Makhtumkuli (☎ 47-49-80, 47-46-76)
France
    Hotel Jubileynaya, ulitsa Tehranskaya 6
Germany
    Hotel Ak Altin, prospekt Makhtumkuli
    (☎ 24-49-11, 51-21-44)
India
    ulitsa Nogina (☎ 46-90-30, 41-99-13)
Iran
    ulitsa Tehranskaya 3 (☎ 24-46-11, 24-97-07)
Kyrgyzstan
    prospekt Saparmurada Turkmenbashi 13
    (☎ 46-88-04, 29-25-39)
Pakistan
    ulitsa Kemine 92 (☎ 51-22-87, 51-23-17)
Russia
    prospekt Saparmurada Turkmenbashi 11
    (☎ 51-02-62, 25-39-57, ☎ & fax 29-84-66)
Tajikistan
    prospekt Saparmurada Turkmenbashi 13
    (☎ 25-13-74)
Turkey
    ulitsa Shevchenko 9 (☎ 25-41-18, 51-00-11)
USA
ulitsa Pushkina 1 (☎ 35-00-45, 35-00-46)

Visas The Turkmenistan Foreign Ministry is at Makhtumkuli 83, with the immigration and visa department through a separate door just to the left of the main entrance. It's open for visa extensions and enquiries Monday, Thursday and Friday between 9 am and 1 pm.

Money The most convenient place to change money is the bureau in the Hotel Ashghabat, theoretically open seven days a week until 8 pm. Often when there's no teller a hovering clutch of black marketeers will change money (only at the official rate). The hotel also has an automatic exchange machine accepting four or five major currencies, including US dollars and Deutschmarks.

There are Savings Bank of Turkmenistan exchange counters at Makhtumkuli 86, on the corner of Shevchenko and Kerbabayeva and at the post office.

Post & Communications The central post office, which from outside looks more like a village grocery store, is at ulitsa 50 Let TSSR 16. It's open weekdays from 8 am to noon and 1 to 7 pm, Saturday to 5 pm and Sunday to noon.

The central telephone and telegraph office (*peregovorny punkt* in Russian, *gepleshik punkty* in Turkmen), 100 metres south of the post office at Karla Libknekhta 33, is open daily from 8 am to 7 pm. Fax and telegram services are in the same building, through the door marked 'exchange'. International calls can also be placed from the reception of the Hotel Ashghabat but they cost a little more.

The telephone code for Ashghabat is 3632.

Travel Agencies ESCAP-UNEP (☎ 25-70-91; fax 25-37-16, 25-73-64), with offices in the Desertification Centre of the Academy of Sciences at ulitsa Gogolya 15, is primarily interested in pushing group packages (some, admittedly, sound fascinating: seven to 10-day itineraries including horse-trekking along the Murgab river, exploring the cave-riddled region of Kugitang or taking a camel caravan across the desert from Mary to Khiva). Vladimir Volovik, head of operations, speaks English, is flexible and extremely helpful. With an encyclopedic knowledge of Turkmen history, he's a good person to help arrange excursions to Anau, Bakharden or farther afield.

Sputnik Turkmenistan (☎ 25-12-79, 41-95-41; fax 29-89-65), at ulitsa Kemine 162, specialises in hiking trips. Its programmes vary from a day's walking to three or four day treks, mostly on or around the lower slopes of the Kopet Dag. A three-day hike with two guides, tents, food and transport is

The Bactrian camel is ideal for long overland journeys because of its capacity to store food and water and to carry great loads.

US$390 for a group. It also offers hang-gliding trips.

Bookshops Ashghabat's bookshops are sparsely stocked with musty, yellowing volumes amongst which the only splashes of colour are a series of booklets following the adventures of the president: *Turkmenbashi Goes to Iran*, *Turkmenbashi Does Pakistan*, that sort of thing. The busiest corner of most bookshops is the counter selling lipsticks, videos, bubblegum and stockings. The exception is al-Hoda, an Iranian-run book-shop at ulitsa Azadi 85 which does a respectable trade in Qurans, prayer beads and cassettes of religious sermons. Other, secular, bookstores are at Azadi 83, Saparmurada Turkmenbashi 29 and, possibly the best (you can at least get postcards and a slim English-language book on Turkmenistan), at Makhtumkuli 167. Opening hours are generally from 10 am to 2 pm and 3 to 7 pm.

Emergency & Medical Services If you are seriously ill contact an embassy. The least lethal medical facilities (this is a country, one visiting medical officer told us, where they have a tendency to operate unnecessarily, amputating broken limbs for example) are at the VIP Hospital (*pravitelstvennaya bolnitsa*; ☎ 29-08-77) at Saparmurada Turkmenbashi 21, just south of the Russian Embassy. For an ambulance call ☎ 29-08-77 (day) or 25-57-16 (evening).

Walking Tour
The world over, new towns are short on beauty and interest, and Ashghabat is not one to buck the trend. Worth a look, though, is the **statue of Lenin** in the park south of ulitsa Azadi, one of the few structures to have survived the 1948 earthquake and the only one of a supposed 56 Lenin monuments in the city to have survived the collapse of Communism. A wonderful mix of Soviet iconoclasm and mock Turkmen nationalism, the statue stands on a large, tiered plinth decoratively tiled with traditional carpet patterns.

South through the park and across ulitsa Shevchenko is a large earthen mound, considered by archaeologists to be the site of the original **fortress** of Ashghabat. Excavations here have unearthed artefacts dating from the Parthian era.

The seat of power in Turkmenistan, the drab **presidential palace** (still topped by a red Soviet star) is half a km south-east on ulitsa Karla Marxa.

More a statement of foreign-policy leanings than a sign of religious awakening, a new Turkish-style, Turkish-financed **mosque** is under construction just south of prospekt Makhtumkuli, 600 metres east of the junction with Saparmurada Turk-menbashi. Similar in appearance to the Blue Mosque in Istanbul, it should be quite spectacular when completed. The more modest, modern **mosque of Khezrety Omar**, off ulitsa Chekhova beside the towering radio mast, is also worth visiting for its wonderfully garish painted ceilings.

Also on the west side of town, at ulitsa Azadi 116, is a small and rather decrepit **zoo**, and a couple of km farther out, beyond the Hotel Turist, the **botanical gardens** (*botanichesky sad*) are a good place to take a picnic.

Museums
The pride of Ashghabat's tiny **National History Museum** (*natsionalnyy muzey istorii e etnografii*) is a collection of artefacts from Nisa. Most amazing are about 18 *rhytons*, horn-shaped vessels of intricately

TURKMENISTAN

458 Ashghabat – Hippodrome

carved ivory used for Zoroastrian rituals and official occasions. There are also three rooms of general Turkmen history with a large model of the remains at Merv. The single storey building housing the museum – another earthquake survivor – is at ulitsa Shevchenko 1, facing into the park.

The **Fine Arts Museum** (*muzey izobrazitelnykh iskusstv*), at Makhtumkuli 84, has some great Soviet-Turkmen paintings: happy peasant scenes where at least one stereotyped-Turk has a chest adorned with Order of Lenin medals, and lurking beyond the yurts and tethered horses is invariably a productively smoking factory chimney. The museum also has a small collection of carpets and traditional costumes and jewellery. Both museums are open daily except Tuesday from 10 am to 6 pm, with admission costing US$1.

In contrast to the untended, geriatric air of these two museums, the recently opened **Carpet Museum** (*muzey kovra*) has a pristine marbled foyer with a gurgling fountain, and a fleet of young, traditionally dressed women to lead tours (in Russian and Turkmen only) along its air-conditioned corridors. While there's a limit to the number of rugs the average visitor can stand, the central exhibit, the world's largest handwoven rug, really is something to see. Ten by 18 metres, it was made in just seven months from 1941 to 1942 to be a backdrop at Moscow's Bolshoy Theatre, but it proved too heavy for the stage rigging and was reluctantly returned. The museum, at the junction of ulitsas Shevchenko and Karla Libknekhta, is open weekdays only, from 10 am to 1 pm and 2 to 6 pm. Admission is a bit pricey at US$2.50. A museum store, open only on request, sells carpet bags, telpeks, bright scarves and other small handicrafts.

More carpets and traditional handicrafts, plus some items not to be seen elsewhere, like patterned carpet saddles for motorbikes, are at **Gallery Ensi** (☎ 24-19-25), a private collection maintained by husband and wife Bairam Kovus and Leyli Haidova. Phone first, preferably in early evening, to arrange a visit (no English is spoken). There's no charge but you could leave a dollar in the box by the door. The gallery is at ulitsa Reutov 8, two minutes walk from the Ak Altin Plaza Hotel.

Hippodrome

The hippodrome itself, built in the 1980s, is nothing to see, but the Turkmen are celebrated riders so horse races here ought to be a spectacle. Races are held every Sunday from 21 March through May, and from late August to mid-November.

Anyone more interested in riding than spectating can get a spell in the saddle by turning up in the morning and making a deal with one of the stable boys. We were told that a crisp US$5 note will get you an hour's riding. The hippodrome is five km east of the centre; take bus No 4 along prospekt Makhtumkuli; a taxi journey should cost the equivalent of about US$0.50.

Tolkuchka Bazar

Tolkuchka (from the Russian *tolkat*, to push), with its teeming cast of colourful thousands, is a Central Asian bazar as staged by Cecil B de Mille. It sprawls across acres of desert on the outskirts of town, with corrals of camels and goats, avenues of redclothed women squatting before silver jewellery, and villages of trucks from which garrulous Uzbeks hawk everything from pistachios to car parts. Whatever you want, it's sold at Tolkuchka. Expect to haggle. The wily old men selling telpeks always pitch an inflated price; if they ask for US$15 they'll probably settle for US$10, although the best telpeks – large, fluffy and white, unmatted and non-goat-smelling – genuinely go for US$15 or more. The women give way less (or offer more honest opening prices). At the time of our visit a fair price for a khalat, the attractive red and yellow-striped robe, was roughly US$15, while sequined skull caps and embroidered scarves were US$2 to US$3.

Above all, Tolkuchka is the place for carpets. Hundreds are laid out in a large sandy compound or draped over racks and walls. Predominantly deep red, most are the size of a double bed or a bit smaller, and the average price is US$200 to US$300. Haggling might shave off US$50.

Tolkuchka is in full swing every Sunday from around 7 am to 1 pm and, on a slightly smaller scale, on Thursday morning. Watch out for pickpockets. The site is about eight km north of Makhtumkuli, past the airport and just beyond the Karakum canal. Tolkuchka buses depart irregularly from Ashghabat bus station, heading north on prospekt Gagarina. A taxi should cost US$2 to US$3.

The canal feeds a reservoir near Tolkuchka called **Kurtly lake** where locals like to bathe and lie on the sandy shores, but it's not particularly clean.

Places to Stay

Bottom End There are a couple of privately run options south of Tikinsky bazar and the bus station, one of which is actually the dormitory of a psychiatric institute (☎ 29-36-72, ask for Mikhail). The institute has several surplus rooms and rents out beds for US$3 a night. The rooms, we're told, are clean and air-conditioned and guests have the use of a well-maintained bathroom, toilet and kitchen. The institute is at ulitsa Gobshoodova 106, about 1.5 km south of Tikinsky bazar.

Travellers have also stayed with the family Dhoranov-Sapar (☎ 25-12-18) at ulitsa Krupskoy 36, who have a spare three-room apartment. They charge US$5 per person per night including a daily meal. The family speaks no English. Ulitsa Krupskoy is five minutes walk south of Tikinsky bazar.

Middle A little out of the centre but recommended is the *Hotel Turist* (☎ 24-41-19, 24-40-17) at ulitsa Gorogly 60. It's a six storey Soviet-era slab with clean, comfortable rooms with attached shower (with hot water) and toilet. Those facing south have good views of the Kopet Dag mountains. Singles/doubles are US$25/60. The Turist is a 45 minute walk from the train station, or take trolleybus No 6 south from the junction of Saparmurada Turkmenbashi and

Makhtumkuli. From the bus station it's a two km walk west along ulitsa Azadi.

Also at that end of town is the *Hotel Jubileynaya* (☎ 24-19-55), at ulitsa Tehranskaya 6, but its shabby twin rooms are grossly overpriced at US$60. The Jubileynaya is a 40 minute walk from the centre; or take bus No 13 or trolleybus No 2 west along Makhtumkuli.

More conveniently located is the *Hotel Kolkhozchy* (☎ 25-30-78), at ulitsa Azadi 78 near the bus station, with doubles from US$60. For reasons unknown the door is locked at 11 pm.

Despite its temptingly central location, avoid the *Hotel Oktyabrskaya* (☎ 25-65-28), the colonial-looking white building on the corner of Saparmurada Turkmenbashi and Makhtumkuli. The rooms have leprous walls and slimy, leaking toilets, and no furniture apart from lumpy beds and yellowing, torn sheets. The experience doesn't come cheap at US$25 for a single.

Top End For those who have someone else to pick up the tab, the *Ak Altin Plaza Hotel* (☎ 51-21-81; fax 51-21-77, 51-21-79), on prospekt Makhtumkuli, is the place to stay. A five storey slab of orange panels and copper-tinted glass, the Turkish-owned Ak Altin has 137 air-conditioned rooms with a health centre, pool, tennis courts and other amenities. Singles/doubles are US$180/216; credit cards are accepted.

If the Ak Altin represents the promise of Turkmenistan's future then the *Hotel Ashghabat* (☎ 29-04-47), two km down the road at Makhtumkuli 74, represents the legacy of the past – a sleazy hangover of Soviet-era hotels with unpleasant staff and dingy rooms full of things that don't work. For anyone still interested, rooms are US$80/120.

Lovers of the bizarre will appreciate Berzengy, Turkmenistan'sLas Vegas. Out in the desert 10 km south of the city, rising up like a mirage, is a strip of a dozen postmodernist hotels (one looks like a spaceship, the façade of another is decorated with a carpet design, a third resembles a sheikh's

TURKMENISTAN

palace) all oozing money and almost all empty. Stranger still, despite their great size none has more than 20 rooms. They're actually government guesthouses built in anticipation of the rush of official visitors to be attracted by gushing oil pipelines. The least funereal are the *Hotel Independent* (☎ 44-33-33, fax 52-00-01) with singles at US$200 and the *Gara Altin* (☎ 44-00-43, fax 51-01-75) which charges US$250 for a standard room. Both offer full business facilities and accept Visa, EuroCard and MasterCard.

Also due to open is *Hotel Turkmenistan*, a large classically styled building currently under renovation (from the amount of marble and brass on view in the foyer, expect it to be in the US$150 to US$200 range). It's at ulitsa Gogolya 19 in the city centre.

The Grand Turkmen Hotel has single rooms for US$120. It is located in the large orange building which dominates ulitsa Shevchenko near the junction with Alishera Navoi.

Places to Eat
Cafés & Snacks Sad to say, the best place for snacking is a western-style fast-food copy, the *Florida*. Not that it's particularly good – the pizza (at US$1.50) is terrible while the kebab and cheese-toast (both US$0.50) and the burgers and fries (US$0.75) are merely edible – but there are depressingly few alternatives. The Florida's one nod to Central Asia is ayran, which tastes like sour milk mixed with liver salts and should be good for hangovers. The Florida, at Shevchenko 8, is open from 8 am to 10 pm.

The *Kafe Khazar* at the junction of Azadi and Gogolya is the nearest thing the city has to a teahouse – a roadside terrace shaded by concrete umbrellas where greasy, unidentifiable meat dishes are served from a hatch. Around the corner *Gelateria Italiana* is more cheerful if you'll settle for coffee and ice cream. In summer pizzas are dished out at *Pizzeria* in the park just off Oktyabrskaya but beware, salt is the local topping of preference.

Anyone staying in the Hotel Turist will benefit from the outdoor cafés and kebab

stalls in the parks that line ulitsa Gorogly between the hotel and ulitsa Chekhova.

Restaurants The best places to eat are all private joint-ventures, like the *Nissa Liban* (also known as the *Diplomatic Club*; ☎ 24-34-32), a classy-looking Lebanese restaurant. Main dishes (mostly meat) are from US$7 to US$10, but some bread and a couple of zakuski (appetisers) at US$2 each make a respectable meal. It's on the ground floor of a nondescript residential building (unmarked except for a blue awning over the entrance) at ulitsa Gorogly 48 and is open from 11 am to 11 pm. Both dollars and *manat* are accepted.

Also recommended is the *Ankara* (☎ 24-97-98), a Turkish-run restaurant on the north edge of town at prospekt Gagarina 11. The menu is confined to kebabs (spicy, lamb, kofta etc) served with salad and rice for US$2, but the side orders include some excellent spicy dips served with beautiful cooked-on-the-premises bread (it's possible to buy extra to take away). A decent meal for two comes to around US$6. The Ankara is open 11 am to midnight. To get there it's about 100 *manat* in a taxi from the city centre, or two stops north on Chekhova from the Makhtumkuli bus stop.

Upstairs from the Florida takeaway is the startlingly grand *Florida* restaurant, flaunting a level of opulence totally at odds with the city. The dishes on the extensive international menu are all around US$10 with soups and salads at US$3 to US$4. A three-course meal came to US$15 with no additional charges for the bread, the constantly replenished iced water, or the service. Visa, EuroCard and MasterCard are accepted.

At the other end of the scale is a clutch of gloomy, Russified restaurants including the *Ayna* on ulitsa Tehranskaya opposite the Hotel Jubileynaya and the *Daihan* at ulitsa Alishera Navoi 52. Both have menus heavy on reconstituted meat – kotlets and bifshteks at US$1.50 to US$2. Slightly better is the *Syyakhat*, adjacent to the Hotel Turist, which attempts to add a little variety; 'Ashghabat cutlet' turned out to be a mutton version of chicken Kiev. Dishes here are US$2.

Easily the worst of the lot is the restaurant at the *Hotel Ashghabat*. The night we ate there, at 7 pm everything on the menu was finished; all they had was cold, shrivelled shashlyk, doused with vinegar and accompanied by greyish, inedible bread. The bill was double our estimate because we hadn't thought to include the uneaten bread, the untouched fruit that decorated the table and the obligatory service charge.

Entertainment

There didn't seem to be much going on at the Russian Drama Theatre on Alishera Navoi at the time of our visit but the Turkmen, or Mollanepes, Drama Theatre at Makhtumkuli 76 and the Turkmen Opera & Ballet Theatre on Azadi seemed in good health. Many plays at the Mollanepes were of Turkmen origin, some, we were told, extremely colourful affairs featuring traditional music. With tickets at just US$0.20 it's worth a gamble. The ballet repertoire was a lot less interesting, performed on the night we attended by some fairly ponderous ballerinas and a male dancer who got the biggest cheer of the night when he leapt onto the stage wearing a pair of transparent tights and very visibly nothing more.

There are few other options – try the Kinoteatr Mir on Makhtumkuli which screens voiced-over US action movies, the pricey disco upstairs at the Florida (US$10 admission and drinks at US$5 and up), or join local expats at the bar of Berzengy's Hotel Gara Altin or International on a Wednesday night.

Things to Buy

The main department store (Univermag) opposite the Hotel Ashghabat has three floors stocked with hardly enough goods to open a kiosk. Fuller shelves are at the Ashpromtorg Tent, an Iranian-run store selling household goods, as well as toothpaste and shampoo, Fuji and Kodak film and Duracell batteries. The main store is at Alishera Navoi 44 with another close by on

Makhtumkuli and a third on the top floor of the Univermag. The Garnizon department store on Karla Libknekhta, next to the Florida, is also empty, but for souvenir hunters it does have a back-room counter of Soviet military flashes and buttons. The cassette stalls on the same street are the places for tapes of Turkmen music, both traditional and modern.

The top floor of the Univermag sells traditional jewellery, handicrafts and clothing, but for the best and cheapest selection, as well as carpets, the place to go is Tolkuchka bazar, every Sunday and Thursday (see Tolkuchka Bazar). There are two other markets in town: the lacklustre central market or 'Russian bazar' on ulitsa Azadi, and the Tikinsky bazar five blocks west which has mountains of sweet melons in season. Neither has the cheerful tenor of Tolkuchka or any other Central Asian bazar.

Getting There & Away

Air Turkmenistan Airlines links Ashghabat with Istanbul daily, Abu Dhabi three times a week, Karachi and Mashhad in north-eastern Iran twice a week and Delhi and Damascus once a week. CIS connections include two or three times a day to Moscow, four times a week to Tashkent, three times a week to Almaty and Baku, twice a week to Yerevan and once a week to Orenburg and Samarkand.

Domestic connections include numerous daily flights to Charjou, Mary, Dashkhovuz and Turkmenbashi, with less frequent flights to Gas-Achak in the far north, Kerki in the far south, and Nebit Dag. The Turkmenistan Airlines booking office (☎ 29-05-73, 29-34-69) is in a bunker under the Hotel Ashghabat, although foreigners may still have to buy tickets from the international department (☎ 29-38-95, 29-39-01) at Pushkina 3.

International airlines serving Ashghabat include THY Turkish Airlines which flies four times a week to/from Istanbul, and Iran Air which flies every Tuesday to Tehran. Iran Air (☎ 51-06-41) and Turkish Airlines (☎ 51-06-66, 51-16-66) are both on the ground floor of the department store building on Makhtumkuli, opposite the Hotel Ashghabat.

Bus There's little in the way of long-distance bus services, eg there are no buses to Turkmenbashi or Charjou. The farthest regular destinations are Nebit Dag (departing around 12.30 pm and taking 9½ hours) and Mary (four a day, taking just under eight hours). A Saraghs bus leaves around midday, taking 7½ hours.

The only bus from Ashghabat to cross any border is the Mashhad service, departing at 8 am three times a week, reaching the north-eastern Iranian city 12 hours later, for US$10, but foreigners are not permitted to make this crossing overland.

Train The following trains depart daily. Westward, there are two overnight trains to Turkmenbashi (12 hours), plus an early morning departure that takes all day. Eastward, two overnight trains depart in the early evening to Charjou (11 to 14 hours), one continuing to Dashkhovuz. Another Dashkhovuz-bound train (No 939 from Turkmenbashi) stops here around 9 am. There's also a daily overnight Ashghabat-Kushka service via Mary, although at the time of writing, Kushka was off-limits to foreigners because of its sensitive location on the Afghan border.

Until the proposed Ashghabat-Moscow service via Baku begins, you need to change at Charjou for trains to Bukhara, Samarkand, Tashkent and Moscow.

At the Ashghabat train station, windows Nos 6 and 7 are for advance booking – highly recommended (see Dangers & Annoyances in the chapter introduction). The foreigners' ticket window is only open limited hours. Don't forget you will need your passport to purchase train tickets.

Getting Around
To/From the Airport The airport is about 5 km north of Makhtumkuli via bus Nos 1, 18 and 22 from ulitsa Chekhova. Arriving in town from the airport, the bus passes under railway tracks and the next major junction is

Makhtumkuli, from where it's two km east to the Hotel Ashghabat; or from the next stop it's a 15 minute walk west to the Hotel Turist.

Public Transport Bus No 13 and trolleybus No 2 run the length of prospekt Makhtumkuli to the Hotel Jubileynaya. Trolleybus No 6 goes down Azadi to the Hotel Turist. You pay for your ride by punching a ticket in one of the punches fixed inside the vehicle. Tickets *(pilet)* are sold at street kiosks beside major stops and cost a few *manat* for 10.

There are two types of taxi – the state-service battered old brown and grey Volga sedans and new privately operated bright yellow Renaults. The Renaults are metered, whereas with the others you just have to trust that the driver isn't overcharging or agree on a price beforehand. When we were there the meter rate was roughly US$0.20 per km. It's possible to order a taxi by calling ☎ 25-34-06 or 25-34-21.

For chauffeured car hire call Gooch (☎ 44-67-28 evenings, or daytime via the Peace Corps, ☎ 25-57-31), a reliable English-speaking driver who charges US$5 per hour. If he's not available he'll fix you up with someone in his extended family.

AROUND ASHGHABAT
Nisa
Несса

Standing a little short of the swelling foot-hills of the Kopet Dag, 10 km west of Ashghabat, is a lone green hillock. On a high grassy plateau at the top is a warren of earthen trenches and pits, like an extensive sand castle, blurred and partly demolished by the incoming tide, as Geoffrey Moorhouse put it in *Apples in the Snow*. It takes some imagination to see it, but these are the sun-baked bones of the royal fortress-city, Nisa, that existed 2300 years ago.

Nisa was founded as the capital of the Parthians, nomads who pushed back Alexander's Greek armies and gained an empire stretching to the Euphrates and to the Indus. In its prime Nisa was reinforced with 43 towers, sheltering the royal palace and a couple of temples, and surrounded by a thriving commercial city. One ruling dynasty replaced another until the 13th century when the Mongols arrived, laid siege to the city and after 15 days razed it.

What remains are only vague dusty imprints and suggestive shapes. The ridges surrounding the plateau were the fortress walls and the steep modern approach road follows the route of the original entrance. The single level of rooms and passages incised in the earth are thought to be from the southern part of the citadel. All the finds from here – pottery, tiles, statuettes – have been carried off, some to Ashghabat's history museum and some to the Hermitage in St Petersburg. There really isn't much to see but the setting is beautiful and justifies a visit.

Getting There & Away Take a bus from Ashghabat to the predominantly Kurdish village of Bagir. The grassy mound of the fortress is hard to miss, to your left as you approach Bagir, and there's a very obvious access road to it. Get off the bus here or walk the half-km back from the village bus stop.

Anau
Анау

Anau is the site of another of Turkmenistan's vanished cities. Inhabited since Neolithic times, it was known as Bagabad to Silk Road travellers. By the 15th century it was a fortified town famous for its mosque, which for size and beauty rivalled many in Bukhara and Samarkand, with two domes, two minarets and, most strikingly, a tiled mosaic above the main entrance depicting two sinuous eight metre dragons facing each other. Bagabad dwindled but the mosque, albeit in a badly reduced state, survived and attracted attention right up until the earthquake of 1948, when it was completely demolished (the 50 *manat* note has a picture of the mosque before the quake).

Only traces in the ground remain, the object of study by archaeologists. The mosque exists as piles of rubble strewn over an earthen mound in the middle of the fields, with little to see but the stump of a brickwork

pier, decorated with fragments of blue tiling. The site is still considered holy by locals and a small, new mosque has been built with bricks from the old one. Amidst the ruins a kiosk-sized shrine is also the venue for some very un-Islamic rituals in which, along with their prayers, women offer up torn strips of cloth and items of babies' clothing, dummies and cheap plastic dolls, in the hope of conceiving a child.

The modern settlement of Anau – after which the mosque is now named – is 20 km east of Ashghabat city centre on the Mary road. A few km after leaving the city limits, bear right at a big green 'Turkmen' hoarding at the centre of a fork in the road. After about one km there's a dusty track to the left beside some buildings; beyond the buildings turn right then immediately left and the ruins of the mosque are a further half km. There's no public transport so you'll have to take a taxi. The whole round trip should take no more than two hours.

Firuza
Фируза

Once a hunting reserve for Persian royalty, Firuza is now a popular mountain escape for the people of Ashghabat, who come streaming up in the summer seeking relief in the slightly cooler temperatures. The settlement is squeezed into the gorge of the Firuzinka stream. Though slightly spoilt by its popularity, this is the closest you'll get to the Kopet Dag mountains, which everywhere else are out of bounds because of the proximity of the Turkmen-Iranian border.

Firuza gorge is 30 km south-west of Ashghabat and there are regular services from the central city bus station.

Bakharden
Бахарден

Buried 60 metres underground in the lower slopes of the Kopet Dag mountains is a hotwater mineral lake – known in Turkmen as Kov-Ata or 'Father of Lakes' – where you can take a swim in the 36°C waters if you don't mind the rotten-egg smell. The lake is at the foot of a steep 250 metre stairway, descending through a damp and pungent chamber that spotlights struggle to penetrate.

There are changing rooms for swimmers at the water's concreted edge but it's a little off-putting that only a faint arc of water nearest the shore is illuminated and the rest of the lake's 70 metre length is in complete darkness. While the water is supposedly good for your health, it's recommended that you don't stay in more than 20 minutes.

Plodding back up towards the pinprick of daylight that is the cave mouth, reflect on the locals who, not too long ago, used to lower themselves into the bat-filled blackness on ropes and swim by the light of burning torches. These days there's an admission fee, which for foreigners is US$5.

Midway on the main road between Ashghabat and Bakharden is the village of **Geok-Tepe** (Green Hill), site of the Turkmen's last stand against the Russians. During the Soviet era the uncommemorated site of the breached earthen fortress where 15,000 Turkmen died was part of a collective farm. Now, beside the telltale ridges and burrows, a mosque, museum and memorial park are under construction with the intention of resurrecting some Turkmen history for sale to tourists.

Getting There & Away For the underground lake *(podzemnoe ozero)* take a bus to Bakharden, 100 km west of Ashghabat. From the capital the buses run four times a day, taking 2½ hours. Westbound trains out of Ashghabat also stop at Bakharden but services are infrequent.

From the bus station at Bakharden the lake is 16 km back towards Ashgabat along the main M37 road, then six km south along a dusty minor road. There's usually a taxi lurking at the bus station, or the ticket clerk, Aman Geldemuradov, will run visitors to the lake for US$2 to US$3. Alternatively, you can ask the bus driver to let you off at the lake (Kov-Ata) turn-off or at Akdepe, a small village two km earlier.

The last Ashghabat bus from Bakharden leaves at 3 pm. A later bus can be flagged down in Akdepe at about 4.30 pm.

Western Turkmenistan & the Caspian

Although the Caspian Sea sparkles turquoise-blue, the flat, pocked, desert shoreline seems composed, not of sand, but of grey dust frosted with salt and looks more like NASA footage of the moon.

Apart from the provincial capital, Turkmenbashi, all the Caspian coastal towns are centred around industrial plants and are very missable. **Bekdash**, the farthest settlement north before Kazakstan, is little more than a large salt-refining plant while **Cheleken**, across the bay from Turkmenbashi, is an extremely unhealthy chemical town.

Inland, Nebit Dag is a modern oil town of negligble interest. **Kyzyl-Arvat**, some 100 km east of that, has a richer history as a 19th century Turkmen fortress but there's now nothing to see there either. What may be worth visiting is the mountain village of **Kara-Kala**, 80 km south of Kyzyl-Arvat in the Kopet Dag range. The scenery is reportedly very attractive, with forests and waterfalls, and the place used to be favoured by Party bosses as a secluded hideaway. However, sitting only 30 km north of the border with Iran, it's almost certain that a visit would require special permission from the Department of Tourism in Ashghabat.

Many western maps show a road running from Turkmenbashi north-east across the Karakum desert to Konye-Urgench, Dashkhovuz and Khiva. In reality, this is an unsurfaced track, negotiable only with a truck or 4WD and there is no regular transportation travelling this route.

TURKMENBASHI
ТУРКМЕНБАШИ
Population: 65,000

Though recently renamed after the leader of Turkmenistan, the port town of Turkmenbashi seems to be one of the least loved places in the country. It's been variously

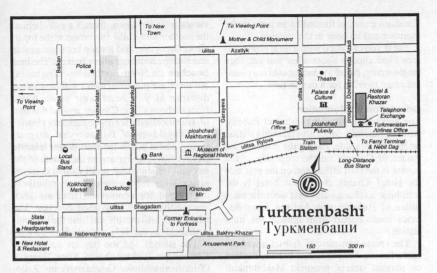

TURKMENISTAN

described as 'miserable', 'joyless' and a 'desolate dust-heap', the opprobrium coming from both English-speaking and Russian writers, of this century and last.

But while the town is dusty and hot, and very little goes on, it's also quite attractive in a sleepy Mediterranean sort of way. Turkmenbashi sits in a hollow enclosed by a crescent of mountains and faces the Caspian Sea. The edges of the town curl up, with buildings tiered on the mountain slopes like spectators in an amphitheatre. An ugly new concrete town and a belching oil refinery are hidden behind a curtain of rocky hills that separates old and new, charming and charmless.

The first settlement here was established when a detachment of Russian troops under Prince Alexandr Bekovich set ashore in 1717 with the intention of marching on Khiva. They chose this spot because it was close to the place where the Oxus (Amu-Darya) had once drained into the Caspian, and the long-dry river bed provided the best road across the desert. But the mission failed, Bekovich lost his head (see History under Khiva in the Uzbekistan chapter) and the Russians didn't come back for over 150 years.

It was 1869 when the next expedition put ashore and built a fortress at Krasnovodsk (Red Water) – a name which stuck until 1993. The fortress became Russia's base of operations in its campaign to break the troublesome khanate of Khiva and subdue the Turkmen tribes, and later became the western railhead of the new Trans-Caspian line, built to consolidate Tsarist gains.

Since then new rail routes have eroded the importance of the Trans-Caspian but Turkmenbashi remains Central Asia's sole port and sea link to European Russia and, via the Volga and Sea of Azov, to the Black Sea and the Mediterranean. These days the main trade is in oil; western Turkmenistan is the site of major reserves and the country's largest refinery is at Turkmenbashi.

But for all the wealth usually associated with oil, the town seems to be getting little from it. The fishing fleet is all but grounded for lack of affordable spare parts and repairs, and all basic foodstuffs, which have to be imported into this completely uncultivable region, are in short supply. At the time of writing sugar, butter, salt, rice and bread were all rationed on a coupon system. Even water, delivered from the Amu-Darya by the

Karakum canal, is limited to an hour in the morning and an hour in the evening.

But if you can cope with a little grime and aren't too choosy about what you eat, then single storey, pastel Turkmenbashi is a pleasant place to relax for a day or two.

Orientation & Information

The hub of the town is ploshchad Pobedy, with the playfully Moorish-style train station on its southern side. Facing the station is the Palace of Culture; on the west side of the square is the post office, and on the east side the Hotel Khazar. Below the hotel is the telephone exchange and next door the sales office of Turkmenistan Airlines. Long-distance buses depart from outside the train station.

The sparse commercial district is a about half a km west of ploshchad Pobedy centred on parallel streets, prospekt Makhtumkuli and ulitsa Turkmenistan. A bank on Makhtumkuli will change money.

Annageldy Annageldyev, head of the local tourist office, Balkansyyhat (☎ 7-38-69, 7-38-70), moved over from directing the oil refinery because of his enthusiasm for the town – though he's concentrating on attracting Turkmen and Russians, and doesn't speak English. He's on the ground floor of the Palace of Culture; inside, turn right and go to the last door on the left.

The telephone code for Turkmenbashi is 43243.

Things to See & Do

The **Museum of Regional History** *(muzey istoriko-kraevedchesky)* is on ulitsa Rylova, a 10 minute walk west of the station, in what used to be the old Russian fort. It was closed when we visited; theoretically it opens daily except Sunday from 9 am to 1 pm and 2 to 6 pm. A block south of the museum, the two things that look like Thunderbird Ones topped by red stars mark the former entrance to the **fortress-town**. A hundred metres on is the gate to the one-time main pier and terminal.

One of the most pleasant things to do is to walk up into the mountains for the beautiful **views** over the town; there's a path behind the mother-and-child monument at the top of ulitsa Garayeva, and a steep but manageable scree-slope route off ulitsa Balkan. The best **beaches** are 50 km north of town (no buses) but there are places to swim within walking distance if you head west down ulitsa Naberezhnaya. The Caspian around this part of Turkmenbashi seems remarkably clean.

Annageldyev of Balkansyyhat suggests taking a boat out to the **Red Water Islands** (Kyzyl-Suv), strung across the mouth of the bay and inhabited by small fishing communities who lead an existence relatively unchanged for centuries. There are also, apparently, some very good beaches. The islands are a 40 minute sail from the harbour; Annageldyev can help to find a boat for hire.

The islands and the bay are part of the Khazar or Turkmenbashi State Reserve (Turkmenbashinsky Gosudarstvenny Zapovednik), set up to protect the region's 280 species of waterfowl and marsh birds, including flamingos and pelicans, plus indigenous colonies of seals and turtles. For anybody interested in seeing the seals or turtles, the reserve headquarters (☎ 7-50-58, 7-42-76) is at ulitsa Naberezhnaya 42a where there's also a small **natural history museum**.

Places to Stay & Eat

At the time of writing the only accommodation was at *Hotel Khazar* (☎ 70-46-33) on ploshchad Pobedy. The large, airy rooms have balconies (nice if you have one facing the square) but antiquated, smelly bathrooms. The price is right at US$1.75/3.20 for a single/double.

The only working *restaurant* in town is next door, and it's truly dreadful, with only one, not necessarily edible, dish available each day. The only recourse is the *kolkhozny market* off ulitsa Shagadam, where you might find fruit and biscuits (and fish if you can find some way of cooking it). The situation might improve with the opening of a Turkish-built hotel and restaurant complex (scheduled for 1995) at the western end of ulitsa Naberezhnaya.

Getting There & Away

Air Flights go twice daily to Ashghabat (US$70) and three times a week to Dashkhovuz. International connections include Moscow (three a week for US$275) and Baku (US$75), and weekly to Tashkent (US$190). The booking office (☎ 7-54-74, 7-58-04) is just off ploshchad Pobedy below the Hotel Khazar, open from 8 am to 6 pm. The airport is tucked away in the mountains that encircle the town.

Bus From the stand in front of the train station, a daily morning bus goes to Nebit Dag. Another, at 7 am, heads north along the Caspian coast, via Bekdash and into Kazakstan, arriving at Novy Uzen in the late afternoon (another goes the other way). Be sure your visas are in order in case of border checks.

Train There are three trains a day, two terminating at Ashghabat (12 hours away) and one continuing to Dashkhovuz via Charjou. A kupeynyy berth to Ashghabat is US$4.50.

Boat It's possible to cross the Caspian from Turkmenbashi to Baku, the Azerbaijani capital. The boats are cargo freighters, with schedules totally dependent on what's to be taken and when it can be loaded, but on average there are three sailings a week. Schedules may firm up if and when the proposed Dashkhovuz-Ashghabat-Baku-Moscow train service comes into operation.

Each boat takes 300 passengers at US$75 for the 12 hour (240 km) voyage. Those arriving in Turkmenbashi this way must have a Turkmen visa already, as immigration is tightly controlled.

The sea terminal (*morskoy vokzal*) and sales office are on the eastern outskirts, just off the Ashghabat highway; you'll need to take a taxi out, for a dollar or two.

Ships to/from Iran, Astrakhan, the Black Sea and even the Mediterranean occasionally stop at Turkmenbashi and captains may be willing to take on a passenger.

Buying Ferry Tickets in Baku

At Baku be careful about asking a local person to buy your ticket, and don't hang around the sea terminal to find someone, as police may be on board and may recognise you, and will use the opportunity to extract a large bribe, eg getting you a 'proper' ticket for some large amount. The usual way to get aboard appears to be a series of small bribes to the customs man, ticket checker etc. The ship leaves not from the sea terminal but north up the coast at the pier where the railway line used to run to connect with the sea voyage. There are shuttle buses from the sea terminal to pier. Crowd control and customs are a madhouse. ■

NEBIT DAG
НЕБИТ ДАГ

Population: 89,000

Nebit Dag isn't so much a small town as a large encampment. Such is the air of impermanence that you feel you might wake up in the morning to find the whole place gone – flimsy, low-rise dwellings dismantled, packed onto the backs of camels and carried away into the desert. One reason for this sensation is that the town is less than 50 years old. The first construction only began after a Professor Gubkin discovered oil here in 1948 (Nebit Dag means 'Oil Mountains'). Since then, the same mountains have also been found to contain small deposits of gold and are under exploration by teams of foreign geologists.

Gold and oil aside, there's little to bring anyone here. As an indicator of civic pride, the muncipal museum is empty, and the tourist office ships visitors straight out to Kara-Kala. The best they could come up with in town was a comical statue of Professor Gubkin on a camel, at the western end of prospekt Makhtumkuli, and an 11 storey apartment block, the town's only high-rise, unoccupied since it was built because of the local fear of earthquakes.

TURKMENISTAN

Orientation & Information

The main axis is prospekt Makhtumkuli, running east-west parallel with the railway. At its mid-point is ploshchad Niyazov, watched over by a forlorn and lonely statue of the president. The train station is one km west and 400 metres south of ploshchad Niyazov. Its forecourt also serves as the long-distance bus terminus.

If you speak Russian or Turkmen you might contact the local branch of the Department of Tourism, Balkansyyhat (☎ 2-20-37) at kvartel 136, house 2, some 100 metres south-east of ploshchad Niyazov.

The telephone code for Nebit Dag is 43243.

Places to Stay & Eat

There are, surprisingly, at least three hotels in town. The *Nebit Dag* (☎ 5-25-20), 1.5 km east of ploshchad Niyazov at kvartel 115, is the shabbiest. The 40 rooms are models of grubby asceticism and guests share a couple of shower blocks and hole-in-the-floor toilets. There is, at least, hot water. A double is US$6.

Rooms at the *Neftyannik* (☎ 3-09-19), at kvartel 225, are gloomy but comfortable and have attached shower and toilet. A plus is the hotel's leafy garden. This is one km north of Makhtumkuli beside a children's hospital (*detskaya bolnitsa*), best reached by car or taxi. A standard double room is US$20, but that may go up with imminent renovations. Near the Neftyannik a large Turkish-financed hotel is under construction, to be finished in perhaps 1996, with an eye on visiting oil executives and probably with executive prices.

Until this hotel opens the only place to eat is a very basic *café/restaurant* on the south side of ploshchad Niyazov which closes at 6 pm. There is a market one block south of Niyazov but there's very little there.

Getting There & Away

There are three trains a day to Turkmenbashi, 3½ hours away, and three to Ashghabat, one of which continues to Charjou and Dashkhovuz. From the forecourt of the train station there's a daily bus for Turkmenbashi at 9 am, taking 2½ hours; tickets only go on sale an hour or two before departure and are fiercely fought for. Nebit Dag also has an airfield with daily flights to/from Ashghabat. The Turkmenistan Airlines booking office is in the train station hall.

Eastern Turkmenistan

With savannah-like plains, cave cities and dinosaur footprints, the eastern region is by far the most interesting part of Turkmenistan. Unfortunately, because of its proximity to Afghanistan and Iran, many of the more worthwhile destinations are out of bounds to the casual traveller. Once off the M37 Ashghabat-Charjou highway, checkpoints are frequent, and wayward foreigners are held until they can be put on a bus heading out of the 'sensitive' zone. They might also be squeezed for a 'fine' (detained at a *militsia* post outside Kerki we haggled ours down from US$100 to US$5).

If you have your heart set on seeing something here, the surest route is through a semi-official channel like one of the Ashghabat tourism firms (see Information in the Ashghabat section). ESCAP-UNEP can organise visits to the Kugitang and Repetek reserves, or you can entrust yourself to a complete, packaged expedition taking in Badkhyz, Kushka and the cave city of Ekedeshik. Sputnik in Ashghabat may also be able to help.

SARAGHS
CEPAXC
Population: about 6000

As a happening town, Saraghs peaked in the 12th century and it's been downhill ever since. It had its beginnings as an oasis on the upper reaches of the Tejen river, inhabited since perhaps the 4th century BC. The town benefited from trade brought by the Arab conquest, and grew into a crowded walled city, dominated by a large citadel.

The fortifications proved useless against

the Mongols, from whom Saraghs never quite recovered.

The telephone code for Saraghs is 234.

Things to See

The Saraghs of today is a small farming village. The only evidence of former glory is the unimposing 11th century **mausoleum of Abu Fazl**, erected over the grave of a Sufi teacher who died in 1023. It's about 2.5 km south of the centre of the village, through a gateway in a long wall, and barely worth the half-hour walk. The great earthen mound beside it is thought to be the remains of the 12th century citadel. From the top, Saraghs' twin Iranian village (also Saraghs, or Sarakhs) is visible a couple of km west.

Places to Stay

The *Saraghs District Hotel* (Saragt rayon mykhmankhansy) is a small, single storey whitewashed building 100 metres north of the bus stand. There's no toilet in the building, just a shack out the back, and washing facilities are limited to buckets of icy water in a kitchen. A bed in a twin room is US$0.50 per person.

Getting There & Away

A new agreement between Turkmenistan and Iran will link Tejen, on the main Trans-Caspian line, via Saraghs with Mashhad in north-eastern Iran, thus completing a connection between Ashghabat and Tehran. Until then, Saraghs languishes in isolation, served by one daily bus each to Ashghabat (six hours away), departing at midday, and to Mary (four hours away), departing at 8 am, both via Tejen. There are no buses south to Badkhyz reserve and Kushka, nor across into Iran (though with your own transport and a valid Iranian visa you should be able to cross into Iran here).

MARY
МАРЫ

Population: 95,000

The industrial centre of Turkmenistan and the country's second largest city, Mary ('ma-RIH') has all the appeal of a cockroach in custard.

The town has its origins in 1884 when the Russians annexed the ancient city of Merv but, unwilling to live at close quarters with the Turkmen, established their own township a short distance away. The new settlement – also initially called Merv – developed rapidly, as both garrison and temporary home for the army of railway workers pushing the Trans-Caspian line across Turkmenistan. With the railway came merchants, hoteliers and even tourists.

Because of its location on one of Turkmenistan's few watercourses, the Murgab river, Mary (as the town was renamed in 1937) developed as a cotton-growing centre. Its continued prominence was assured in 1968 when prospectors discovered huge reserves of gas 20 km west of town, at a site since named Shatlik (Joy). Gas or not, the name seems something of a black joke for a place that on a summer day roasts at 45°C and higher.

Right from the start, Merv was destined never to become a tourist hot spot. In 1886, when Mr Boulangier, a visiting Frenchman, complained of his insect-ridden room he was told to consider himself lucky as the week before the town had suffered a plague of scorpions. By comparison, the modern-day visitor – suffering nothing more than over-priced rooms, a lack of anywhere decent to eat, and possibly, overwhelming boredom – has little to complain about.

But Mary is the closest transport hub to the ruins of ancient Merv, and may be an unavoidable part of your itinerary, in which case aim to arrive early and leave the same day.

Orientation & Information

Mary has few landmarks other than the seven storey Hotel Sanjar on ulitsa Mollanepesa, the town's main thoroughfare, which runs roughly east-west, parallel to the railway. The adjacent train and bus stations are about 200 metres north of the Sanjar.

The central post and telegraph office is one km east of the Sanjar on Mollanepesa, while the central telephone office is 50 metres south of the post office on ulitsa Pervomayskaya. There is a currency-exchange service in the Sanjar, whose foyer seems to have the only working private telephone in town.

Tatyana Lunina (☎ 3-94-22) is an excellent English-speaking guide to the ruins of Merv, though a little expensive at US$40 for three hours of her time (transport extra); try haggling. The local tourist office, Mary-Intourist, was at the airport but is to relocate to the Sanjar.

The telephone code for Mary is 37022.

Things to See & Do

There's a **regional museum** featuring traditional Turkmen life and culture, including displays on weddings and carpet weaving. Surprisingly, no artefacts from the ruins of Merv are on show (although a museum specially devoted to Merv is scheduled to open in 1997 at Bairam Ali). The regional museum

is at ulitsa Komsomolskaya 1, in the park beside the Murgab river. It's closed Monday.

Opposite the park, on the north side of Mollanepesa, is the **Zelyony bazar** (Green market). There is also a Sunday morning market, **Tikinsky bazar**, held four km out of town. Tikinsky is reportedly similar to Ashghabat's Tolkuchka bazar but, so locals claim, with more and cheaper carpets. The simplest way to get there is by taxi, which should cost at most US$1 to US$2.

Places to Stay

The *Hotel Sanjar* (☎ 5-76-44) is well-located just south of the train and bus stations at Mollanepesa 58, but the nondescript rooms are way overpriced at US$40 per person.

A cheaper alternative is the *Hotel Kech* (Кеч; ☎ 3-11-08), a barracks-like establishment with an interesting choice of rooms – the one with the windows that close, or the one with the toilet that flushes, or the one

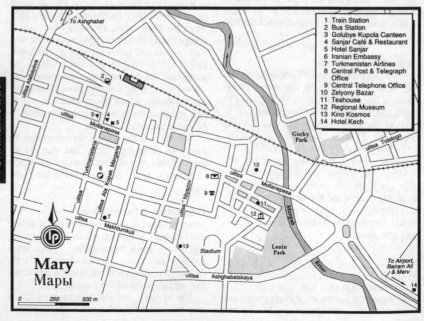

1 Train Station
2 Bus Station
3 Golubye Kupola Canteen
4 Sanjar Café & Restaurant
5 Hotel Sanjar
6 Iranian Embassy
7 Turkmenistan Airlines
8 Central Post & Telegraph Office
9 Central Telephone Office
10 Zelyony Bazar
11 Teahouse
12 Regional Museum
13 Kino Kosmos
14 Hotel Kech

Mary
Мары

0   250   500 m

with the door that locks – at US$20 per double. From the Sanjar, go east on Mollanepesa, across the roundabout and take the first left (little more than a dirt track) after the stomatological clinic – a three or four km walk.

Places to Eat

Next door to the Sanjar is a *café* with a *restaurant* above, but their only virtue is proximity to the hotel. The two daily dishes are the same on both levels but the restaurant has an evening cover charge to pay for the flashing lights and disco band. The café is open from 9 am to 7 pm, and the restaurant from 3 to 5 pm and 7 to 11 pm. The *Golubye Kupola*, the collection of blue domes opposite the Sanjar, also houses a daytime canteen.

Getting There & Away

There are several flights a day to Ashghabat (US$45) and three a week to Dashkhovuz. The Turkmenistan Airlines booking office (☎ 3-27-77) is at ulitsa Makhtumkuli 11; there's also a desk at the airport (☎ 9-22-45, 3-24-72), five km east of town on the Bairam Ali road (take a Bairam Ali bus and ask for 'aeroport'; or a taxi shouldn't cost more than US$1 to US$2).

Four trains a day go to Ashghabat, two leaving in the hour before midnight and two in the hour before midday. The journey is six to seven hours, and a kupeynyy berth is less than US$1. There's a Charjou service plus two other trains that halt at Charjou en route to Dashkhovuz. There's also an overnight train to Kushka.

Mary is well served by buses, with five a day to Ashghabat (five hours away) and three to Charjou (4½ hours). Two daily buses go to Kushka (10 hours), two to Saraghs (4 hours) and one to Kerki (4 hours).

MERV
МЕРВ

Merv, site of one of Central Asia's once-greatest cities, may be a treasure trove for archaeologists and has moved travel writers to muse for pages on the life and death of civilisations, but for the casual visitor it's a bit of a disappointment.

Spread over more than 100 sq km, Merv is actually the site of no less than five walled cities from different periods, each built beside the last. But don't expect an alfresco museum of ancient architecture. What you'll see is a lumpen landscape scarred with ditches and channels, grazed by camels and with every now and again an earthwork mound or a battered sandy-brick structure. Still, Merv does have a certain melancholy attraction, and Sultan Sanjar's mausoleum certainly impresses with its size and solidity. A good guide might bring the site to life.

Unfathomably, photography of some of the monuments is forbidden, so be discreet with your camera.

History

Merv's origins are shrouded in conjecture and romance. As a desert oasis it was definitely a Silk Road staging post. It was possibly settled in the 6th century BC by Zoroastrians (accordingly Merv was to join Bukhara and Samarkand in celebrating 2500 years of existence in 1995, but money earmarked for the festivities went astray and the party had to be postponed).

This was Margiana in Alexander's domain. Under the Persian Sassanians it was a melting pot of religious creeds with Christians, Buddhists and Zoroastrians cohabiting peacefully. However, as a centre of power, culture and civilisation, Merv reached its greatest heights in the 11th and 12th centuries when the Seljuqs made it their capital and (after Baghdad) the greatest city in the Islamic world. Marvishahjahan, or 'Merv, Queen of the World' as it was then known, may even have been the inspiration for the tales of Scheherazade's *Thousand and One Nights*.

Under Sultan Alp Arslan (a man, Colin Thubron tells us, whose moustaches were so long they had to be knotted behind his head), Seljuq Merv became the centre of a dominion that stretched from Afghanistan to Egypt, and a city rich with palaces and treasuries, and with libraries and observatories. The

TURKMENISTAN

Seljuqs dammed the Murgab and dug irrigation ditches to the city's fields, parks and lush gardens.

All of this was completely eradicated in 1221 under the onslaught of the Mongols. In 1218 Jenghiz Khan had demanded a substantial tithe of grain from Merv along with the pick of the city's most beautiful young women. The unfortunate Seljuq response was to slay the tax collectors. It was in retribution that Tuluy, the most brutal of Jenghiz Khan's sons, arrived three years later at the head of an army, accepted the peaceful surrender of a terrified Merv and then proceeded to butcher every last one of the city's inhabitants. Each Mongol fighter had orders to decapitate 300 to 400 civilians. That done, the city was literally torn to pieces and put to the torch.

The effect, comments Geoffrey Moorhouse, was as if Merv had been hit with an atomic bomb; but while the combined death toll of Hiroshima and Nagasaki is estimated

at 225,000, with just swords, knives and axes the Mongols slaughtered perhaps a million. Days later, after they had left, the few survivors crept back into the ruins, only for Tuluy's soldiers to reappear and viciously finish the job.

After this, Merv lay empty for more than a century. Eventually, settlement did return but the domain remained a political no-man's-land, tussled over by Bukhara, Khiva and the Persians. It wasn't until the 18th century that an echo of former glories was heard when a Persian noble, Bairam Ali Khan, rebuilt the old dam and returned a measure of prosperity to the city. That lasted until 1795 when the Emir of Bukhara, covetous of Merv's strategic location as the gateway to Persia, undid the dam and led an army against the city, once again reducing it to dust.

From one-time 'Pearl of the East', a metropolis of artisans, craftsmen and traders, after 1795 Merv was to exist only as an oasis

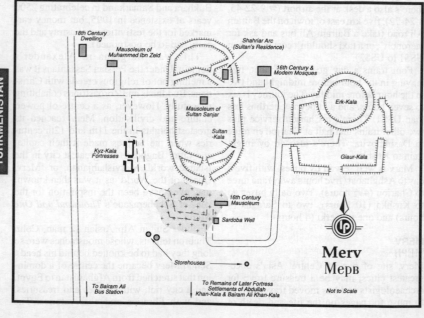

camp for Turkmen tribes, who were in the habit of conducting slave-raids on the villages of northern Persia. Such was the ire the Turkmen roused that it was said, 'If you meet a viper and a Mervi, kill the Mervi first'.

An end to the Persian torment came in 1884 when the Russian army annexed Merv. Choosing not to garrison themselves on the doorstep of the Turkmen, they established their own town some distance away, closer to the shifting Murgab river. They took the name 'Merv' for their new town, leaving the Turkmen settlement to be known as Bairam Ali. In 1937 the Russian town changed its name to Mary, and Merv as a city ceased to exist.

Earliest Remains

The oldest of the five Merv fortresses is **Erk-Kala**, thought to date from the 6th century BC. Today it's a big earthen doughnut about 600 metres across. The ramparts are about 50 metres high, offering a good view of the surrounding savannah-like landscape. From this vantage point it can be seen that Erk-Kala forms part of the northern section of another, larger fortress: **Giaur-Kala**, constructed during the 3rd century BC by the Sassanians. The fortress walls are still solid, with three gaps where the gates once were.

West of the Sassanian fortress is the area developed by the Seljuqs. The 11th century walls of the central citadel, **Sultan-Kala**, are still discernible and in the north-east corner are the remains of the **Shahriar Ark**, possibly the sultan's residence.

Mausoleum of Sultan Sanjar

The best remaining testimony to Seljuq power at Merv is the 38 metre high mausoleum of Sultan Sanjar, at what was the centre of Sultan-Kala. Sanjar, the grandson of Alp Arslan, died in 1157, reputedly of a broken heart when, after escaping from captivity in Khiva, he came home to find that the Khan's soldiers had laid waste to his beloved Merv.

The mausoleum is a simple cube with a barrel-mounted dome on top (it's shown on the reverse of the 100 *manat* note). Origi-

nally it had a magnificent, turquoise-tiled outer dome, said to be visible from a day's ride away, but that is long gone. Interior decoration is sparse, though restoration is being carried out on a blue-and-red frieze that adorns the upper gallery; inside is only Sanjar's simple stone grave. The mausoleum has two doorways; the one on the west side led through to a now absent mosque.

This raises the question of why Sanjar's mausoleum survived when almost nothing else did. The answer lies in the three metre thick walls, strong enough to withstand the destructive urges of a looting army, and the six metre deep conical foundations, designed to allow the structure to ride out any of the earthquakes to which this region is prone.

Mausoleum of Muhammad ibn Zeid

About one km west of Sanjar's tomb, just north of the dusty main road, is another Seljuq monument, the 12th century mausoleum of Muhammad ibn Zeid. The small, unostentatious, earthen-brick building, heavily restored earlier this century, benefits greatly from an attractive setting in a hollow that is ringed by spindly trees, all combining to lend the scene a very Biblical air.

There's confusion as to who is actually buried here. It certainly isn't ibn Zeid, a prominent Shia teacher who died four centuries before this tomb was built and is known to be buried elsewhere. Nearby, the colourful rags tied to the branches of trees are said to be (very un-Islamic) fertility offerings. If a woman conceives in the months following a visit here, to ensure the child's health she must return on the anniversary of the visit and sacrifice a sheep in thanks.

Kyz-Kala

These two crumbling, 7th century fortress-palaces are interesting for their 'petrified stockade' walls, as Colin Thubron describes them, composed of 'vast clay logs up-ended side by side'. They were constructed by the Sassanians in the 7th century and were still in use 600 years later by Seljuq sultans, who used them as function rooms.

TURKMENISTAN

Getting There & Away

The walls of the southernmost of Merv's ruins are less than one km from the bus station at Bairam Ali, but the mausoleum of Sultan Sanjar and much else of interest is a good six or eight km away. While it's possible to spend a day hiking round the site, with summer temperatures in the region of 40°C it's not recommended. It's more convenient to hire a taxi for a couple of hours – from the Bairam Ali bus station or from Mary – to chauffeur you round the sites and take you back again. From Mary we paid US$7.50 for a car and driver for four hours. Buses shuttle between Mary and Bairam Ali every half hour or so and the journey takes approximately 45 minutes

If from Merv you intend heading east by bus, it's better to backtrack to Mary to be sure of getting a seat.

BAIRAM ALI
ВАЙРАМ АЛЫ

This small, drab settlement, 30 km east of Mary, is notable only for the extremely low humidity, supposedly good for the kidneys. Tsar Nicholas II had a palace built here but his R&R plans were interrupted by the Bolshevik Revolution of 1917 and his subsequent execution. The palace is now a sanatorium. Bairam Ali is also the closest settlement to the ruins of ancient Merv. Buses shuttle between Mary and Bairam Ali stations every half hour or so.

TAGTABAZAR
ТАХТА-БАЗАР

About 230 km south of Mary on the road to Kushka is the small village of Tagtabazar, notable for its 7th century cave city, Ekedeshik. Dug into the banks of the Murgab river, the 'city' is a five storey complex of interconnected chambers and passages wide enough to accommodate a camel-drawn cart. The floors are tiled with bricks said to have been scavenged from a bridge built by the armies of Alexander the Great. The cave city was created by Christians as a refuge from the Arab conquest and forcible Islamicisation, although the last storeys were hollowed out almost a thousand years later in the 16th century. In the 1700s and 1800s the caves were a favoured lair of bandits. Today only the upper two storeys are open to visitors, the lower ones being subject to occasional collapse.

Getting There & Away

There is one bus a day to/from Mary but special permission is probably needed to visit Tagtabazar (see the introduction to this Eastern Turkmenistan section).

KUSHKA
ГҮШГЫ

A small outpost on the Afghan border, Kushka was the southernmost town in the former Soviet Union. It was founded as a military garrison in 1887 following an incident in which the Russians provoked the Afghans of Pandjeh into firing on them so that they might seize this little-known oasis, bringing the Tsar's influence that much closer to Herat. The annexation brought Russia within a hair's breadth of war with Britain, who felt its interests in Afghanistan to be under threat. The matter was resolved by the 1887 Joint Afghan Boundary Commission which allowed the Russians their gains in exchange for concessions elsewhere.

Twelve years later Kushka was linked by rail to Mary and in 1901 the town was fortified with seven km of walls, although these failed to keep out the swampland mosquitoes which regularly brought epidemics of malaria.

There have been high-level talks on the possibility of extending the Kushka branch railway line to Herat, just 100 km to the south, and on to Quetta in Pakistan, although while Afghanistan remains in turmoil all plans are on hold. There is a good road from Kushka to Herat, although we have no information about whether you could cross the border, even with a valid visa (check with the Afghan Embassy in Ashghabat).

Visitors to Kushka will need some convincing documentation to avoid being detained and put on the next bus out (see the introduction to this Eastern Turkmenistan section).

BADKHYZ
БАДХЫЗ

Nestled at the south-eastern tip of Turkmenistan, close to the borders of both Afghanistan and Iran, Badkhyz is a region of rolling savannah landscape scored by ravines. Thanks to an impervious rock water table, Badkhyz is carpeted by tulips every spring and has great groves of pistachio trees. The wildlife is no less impressive, with roaming herds of goitred gazelles (known locally as *jieran* or *djeran*) and the rare Asiatic wild asses (Kulan), the preservation of which was a major factor in setting up the Badkhyz nature reserve in 1941.

Anyone interested in Badkhyz should get hold of *The Realms of the Russian Bear* by John Sparks, which has a good, detailed section on the reserve's indigenous flora and fauna. There are no major settlements within the reserve, and no roads through it; you can only get there by special arrangement. Try the Ministry of Nature and Environmental Conservation (☎ (3632) 26-33-54, 29-04-33; fax (3632) 26-96-09) at ulitsa Kemine 192 in Ashghabat, or one of the tourist organisations in the introduction to this Eastern Turkmenistan section.

CHARJOU
ЧАРДЖЕВ

Population: 161,000

Now an unsightly, industrial sprawl, Charjou (pronounced 'char-JO') has actually existed for more than 2000 years. In ancient times, in the shadow of the fortress of Amul, there was a ferry operating here across the Oxus (Amu-Darya) providing a vital Silk Road link between Persian markets and Chinese suppliers. The Oxus also provided an excellent passage north-west to the city-states of Urgench and Khiva, and south-east into Afghanistan. In 14th and 15th century chronicles this caravan crossroads appears as Chahar-Su or 'Four Ways'. It was an Uzbek town from the time there were Uzbeks, under the suzerainty in the 18th and 19th centuries

of the Emir of Bukhara. In 1924 it passed to the Turkmen as a result of the Soviet partitioning of Central Asia.

A large percentage of Charjou's present population are still Uzbeks; the trademark quilted Uzbek coat and black skull-cap are commonly seen on the streets and women here wear calf-length dresses (scandalous in neighbouring Mary). Uzbek-Turkmen intermarriage is not uncommon, their interracial offspring sometimes nicknamed *Charjouski*.

Travellers between Uzbekistan and Turkmenistan will probably land in Charjou at some point because the only major land route passes through here. As a place to kill an hour or two between transport connections, Charjou just about suffices but we can't recommend a longer stay.

Orientation & Information

Charjou's main axis is prospekt Saparmurada Niyazov which runs through town in a north-south dog-leg, roughly parallel with

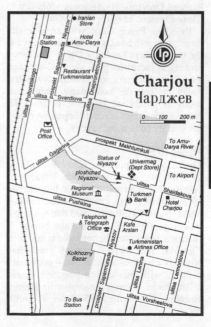

the railway line. The centre of things is ploshchad Niyazov, at one of the kinks in prospekt Niyazov. Most amenities are within a 10 minute walk of this square: the post office 400 metres north-west; the train station 400 metres farther north; and the telephone and telegraph office 300 metres south. Change money at the Turkmen Bank, 100 metres south of the square, daily except Sunday between 9 am and 1 pm. The exception to this convenient clustering is the bus station which is about four km south of the centre, beside a large roundabout on prospekt Niyazov.

The telephone code for Charjou is 37822.

Things to See & Do

There is little to occupy your time in Charjou. There's the obligatory **regional museum** (closed for renovations at the time of our visit), just north of ulitsa Pushkina, and the remains of the old **fortress of Amul**, on the road south out of town – look for the great mound of dried mud that resembles Richard Dreyfuss' living room sculpture in *Close Encounters of the Third Kind*.

Resident Peace Corp volunteers claim there's a usable **beach** on the Amu-Darya at the top of ulitsa Lenina – OK if you fancy looking at industrial plants and oil-streaked mud flats. Although not particularly Central Asian in feel, the **kolkhozny bazar**, just south of ploshchad Niyazov, is good for passing a couple of hours. It's open every day but is at its busiest on Sunday.

Places to Stay

The shabby, unappealing *Hotel Amu-Darya* (☎ 2-24-34), at Saparmurada Niyazov 5 opposite the train station, is the biggest rip-off in Turkmenistan, charging an astounding US$110 to US$130 for a third rate room that would go for US$15 across the border in Bukhara. Hardly any better value is the *Hotel Charjou*, 150 metres east of ploshchad Niyazov on ulitsa Shaidakova – cockroach central, with bus-station-standard shared toilet blocks. Even the receptionist seemed embarrassed by the US$45 for a double room.

Places to Eat

The *restaurant* at the Hotel Amu-Darya is popular only with vodka swilling locals – although thus anaesthetising yourself may be the only way to get the food down. A short distance away on Niyazov, *Restaurant Turkmenistan* is a little better, although, like the Amu-Darya, there's no choice: it was rice with meat and gravy (US$0.50) both times we visited.

The clean *Kafe Arslan* at ulitsa Lenina 37 at leat has a selection of dishes (though all of the meaty variety), plus picture windows onto the street.

But the best food in Charjou – if not in Turkmenistan – is in the *bazar*, at countless stalls selling plov, chicken legs, shashlyk under heaps of onions and herbs, decent bread, fresh honey and, of course, lots of fruit.

Getting There & Away

Charjou is connected by six flights a day to Ashghabat (US$77), with weekly services to Bishkek, Tashkent and Moscow (US$312). The airline booking office is 300 metres south of ploshchad Niyazov, in the second street on the left; it's open daily 9 am to 2 pm and 3 to 8 pm. The airport is about five km out on the eatern edge of town.

Charjou is currently the only town in Turkmenistan with rail connections out of the country. There is a daily train to Bukhara at 12.55 pm (like a chicken shack on wheels) and three to Tashkent (17 hours away) via Bukhara and Samarkand. On Sunday there's a train to Almaty. Daily trains go to Nukus and to Qonghyrat (Kungrad), and No 917 goes to Moscow; all go via Urgench and Dashkhovuz, and there are two other Dashkhovuz services. Two trains go to Ashghabat (a 14 hour trip for US$3.50 kupeynyy) and the No 940 continues to Turkmenbashi.

The train station has a 24 hour left-luggage room off the main concourse.

There are no cross-border buses to/from Uzbekistan, just four a day to Mary, five to Kerki and one to Dashkhovuz.

REPETEK DESERT RESERVE

With recorded air temperatures over 50°C and the surface of the sand sizzling at 70°C, nobody expects the Karakum desert to be inhabited by cuddly creatures, but the animals that do call the rolling ridges of sand home are a particularly repulsive lot. Amongst the thousand-plus indigenous species of insects, spiders, reptiles and rodents are prehistoric-looking monitor lizards which grow to over 1.5 metres but still put on an alarmingly good show at the 100 metre dash. There are also bronze-coloured cobras, large black scorpions and tarantulas lurking in vertical take-off burrows. All are objects of study at the Repetek Desert Research Centre.

The research centre was set up in 1928 to facilitate the study of desert flora and fauna and to investigate ways of developing the barren region, but it also has a visitors' centre with a museum and herbarium.

Visits can be arranged through Turkmen-Intour (☎ (37822) 2-63-74) or the specialist Repetek Tours (☎ (37822) 4-44-70), both in Charjou.

The reserve is 70 km south of Charjou on the Mary road – Mary buses will stop there on request, and one train a day halts at the neighbouring shanty village of Repetek.

GAURDAK
ГОВУРДАК

Gaurdak is the extreme eastern corner of Turkmenistan, squeezed between the Amu-Darya and Uzbekistan. The mountainous landscape is starkly beautiful with gorges, waterfalls and cave complexes forested with stalactites and stalagmites. Right on the Uzbek border is the **Kugitang reserve**, a geological research centre, the pride of which is a rock plateau imprinted with hundreds of dinosaur footprints. It's believed that 150 million years ago, in the Jurassic period, the plateau was the bed of a lagoon which dried up, leaving the wet, footprinted sand to bake in the sun.

Places to Stay

The centre has a lakeside *guesthouse* and they are willing to host visitors and ferry them to the dinosaur plateau, an hour away by 4WD, and to a nine km cave system near Karlouk.

Contact them well in advance at 746680 Turkmenistan, Gaurdak, Kugitang Geological Reserve (746680 Туркменистан, Лебабский Велоят, Шахер Говурдак, Кугитанг Заповедник, Овуинников Александр), attention Alexandr Ovuinnikov (☎ Gaurdak 2-19-19. A price we heard quoted for a stay at Kugitang was US$35 per person per day.

Getting There & Away

Charjou is the only place from which you can fly to Gaurdak (US$47); the flights are once a week but schedules change frequently. Visitors can be collected from Gaurdak airport, or from Charshanga, a stop on the Charjou-Kelif railway line; train No 197 departs Charjou daily at 9.30 pm for Kelif.

ESCAPUNEP in Ashghabat can also arrange visits to Kugitang.

Northern Turkmenistan

DASHKHOVUZ
ДАШХОВУЗ

Population: 125,000

Dashkhovuz (formerly Tashauz) is the only sizeable place in northern Turkmenistan, the focus of the country's portion of the fertile but environmentally blighted Amu-Darya delta. Dashkhovuz and northern Turkmenistan share, with the rest of the delta in Uzbekistan, the full force of the Aral Sea disaster (see the Environment section in the Facts about the Region chapter).

Though founded as a fort in the early 19th century, Dashkhovuz is an entirely Soviet creature of straight streets lined by blocks of flats and desolate empty spaces. With the same lifeless atmosphere as so many other Amu-Darya delta towns, the only reason to come here is to pass on to somewhere else. The Moscow-Urgench-Charjou railway comes through here, and you might also use

TURKMENISTAN

the town as a staging post for Konye-Urgench, northern Turkmenistan's most interesting destination, from Khiva or Urgench in Uzbekistan. See the Western Uzbekistan map in the Uzbekistan chapter.

In Uzbekistan you may find Dashkhovuz spelt Toshhovuz, Tashavuz, Tashauz or Toshauz.

Orientation

The main axis is former ulitsa Karla Marxa, running roughly north-south, with the bazar and bus station near its north end about two km from the town centre. Dashkhovuz street signs, such as they are, are beginning to go over to new Turkmen names, though the old ones are still more familiar to most people.

Places to Stay & Eat

The *Hotel Dashkhovuz* (☎ 2-57-85), fairly central at Andaliba kochesi (formerly Sovietskaya ulitsa) 4, about 600 metres east of former ulitsa Karla Marxa, wants US$20/35 for an air-con single/double. It has a *restaurant*, a Turkmen-Intour office in the lobby with English-speaking staff, and a dinosaur statue across the street. Water supplies may be restricted. There's apparently a dirt-cheap *motel* near the airport.

Getting There & Away

There are several daily flights to/from Ashghabat (US$67), one or two daily to/from Turkmenbashi, four a week to/from Tashkent and three a week to/from Moscow. The air ticket office is in the Hotel Dashkhovuz.

The bus station *(avtostantsia)* is in the north of town on former ulitsa Karla Marxa, just north of the bazar. There are buses to Konye-Urgench every 50 minutes until 5.50 pm, to Urgench every 80 minutes till 5.20 pm, to Nukus (Nokis in Turkmen) and to Khiva twice a day.

The train station is on former Vokzalnaya ulitsa, about 600 metres east of the north end of the former ulitsa Karla Marxa. Trains through here include Moscow-Samarkand (No 98/97) and daily Tashkent-Nukus

service (No 53/54) and Dashkhovuz-Ashghabat services.

Getting Around

Buses and marshrutnoe taxis run up and down Karla Marxa, some continuing to the train station.

KONYE-URGENCH
КӨНЕ-УРГЕНЧ

The ancient state of Khorezm, which encompassed the whole Amu-Darya delta area in northern Turkmenistan and western Uzbekistan, rose to its greatest heights at Konye-Urgench (Old Urgench), 480 km north across the Karakum desert from Ashghabat, and 100 km north-west through cotton fields from Dashkhovuz. Briefly in the early 13th century, old Urgench was the heart of Islam. Then its ruler antagonised Jenghiz Khan and brought down Mongol wrath not just on himself but on large parts of the Muslim and Christian worlds. Old Urgench recovered, only to be flattened again by Timur in the 1370s and 1380s. It didn't come back a second time.

Modern Konye-Urgench is a humdrum place, but its handful of beautiful old buildings (from before, between and after those invasions) make it well worth a day trip if you're in the area – even, border procedures permitting, from the Uzbekistan towns of Nukus, Urgench or Khiva. What's not here is almost as impressive, as evidence of the annihilatory capacity of those medieval conquerors.

History

Khorezm, on a northerly Silk Road branch to the Caspian Sea and Russia, has been an important oasis of civilisation in the Central Asian deserts for thousands of years. The Persians took it into their empire as long ago as the 6th century BC and the Arabs brought Islam in the 8th century AD. Old Urgench (also called Gurganj, Gurgench, Coogentch and even Ourgunge by confused travellers down the centuries) began its upward path when its ruler Mamun succeeded in uniting

Khorezm in 995 AD. At this time the Amu-Darya flowed through the city.

Khorezm fell to the all-conquering Seljuqs, but rose in the 12th century, under a Seljuq dynasty known as the Khorezmshahs, to shape its own far-reaching empire. The Khorezmshahs, with old Urgench as their capital, conquered an area stretching from north of the Syr-Darya river to present-day northern Iran and Afghanistan. With its mosques, medressas, libraries and flourishing bazars, old Urgench became, briefly at the start of the 13th century, the centre of the Muslim world – until Khorezmshah Muhammad II moved his capital to Samarkand when he took that city in 1210.

In 1216 Muhammad II, a man with an inflated sense of his own might who thought of himself as a second Alexander the Great, received from that other empire-builder of the day, Jenghiz Khan, a collection of lavish gifts, along with an offer of trade and a message that Jenghiz Khan regarded Muhammad as his 'most cherished son'. Two years later, 450 merchants travelling from Jenghiz Khan's territory were murdered at Otyrar (or Otrar), a Khorezmshah frontier town east of the Aral Sea. Jenghiz Khan sent three envoys to Samarkand to demand reparation, but Muhammad had one killed and the beards of the other two burnt off.

Within two years Mongol armies had sacked Samarkand, Bukhara, old Urgench and Otyrar and massacred their people. Old Urgench withstood several months of siege but eventually the Mongols smashed the nearby dam on the Amu-Darya and let the river flood through the city. Other great Khorezmshah cities – Merv, Balkh, Herat – went the same way, then the Mongols carried on to the Caucasus and Russia. Muhammad II died, in rags, on an island in the Caspian Sea in 1221. By contrast the tombs of his father Tekesh and grandfather Il-Arslan survive, two of old Urgench's outstanding monuments.

In the following period of peace, Khorezm was ruled as part of the Golden Horde, the huge, wealthy, westernmost of the khanates

into which Jenghiz Khan's empire was divided after his death. Old Urgench, rebuilt, was again Khorezm's capital, and grew into probably Central Asia's major trading city – big, beautiful, crowded and with a new generation of monumental buildings.

Then came Timur, five times. Seeing Khorezm as a rival to his Samarkand, he comprehensively finished off old Urgench in 1388. The city was partly rebuilt but abandoned when the Amu-Darya changed its course in the 16th century (modern Konye-Urgench dates from the construction of a new canal in the 19th century). When a new line of independent Khorezm rulers arose – Uzbek Turks who moved in from the steppes in the early 16th century – they started off at Dev Kesken, out in the desert west of Konye-Urgench, and made Khiva their capital from 1592.

The ruins of Dev Kesken are still there – about 70 km due west of Konye-Urgench according to one map – and Colin Thubron describes a visit in *The Lost Heart of Asia*. The city he found had long outer and inner walls and nothing inside. On the way Thubron came upon a probable abandoned bed of the Amu-Darya, which has changed course several times down the millennia.

Orientation

The road from Dashkhovuz passes the bus station as it enters Konye-Urgench along Gurgench shayoli (formerly ulitsa Kalinina). About half a km west of the bus station is a set of traffic lights where the road from Hojeli and Nukus, marked only as ulitsa Karla Marxa, comes in from the north.

To reach the monuments, go west along Gurgench shayoli from the traffic lights. After about one km, just past the Restoran Gurgench on the right, turn right (north), then first left into G Atabayev kochesi, for the Najm-ed-din Kubra mausoleum and nearby sights. For the southern monuments, head to the west end of Gurgench shayoli (about one km from the Restoran Gurgench intersection), then one km south along the Ashghabat road.

Najm-ed-din Kubra Mausoleum & Around

The sacred Najm-ed-din Kubra mausoleum is the most important of a small cluster of sights near the middle of the town. An intermittently open **museum** (Dash metzhit muzeyi) is housed in the early 20th century Dash mosque, facing G Atabayev kochesi where it turns a right angle into ulitsa Lenina. It includes some finds from old Urgench, and ancient Arabic texts. To one side is the **Matkerim-Ishan mausoleum** (Matkerim Ishanym mazary), also early 20th century.

The path past here leads to the **Najm-ed-din Kubra mausoleum** (Najm-ed-din Kubranyng mazary), on the left, and the **Sultan Ali mausoleum** (Soltanalynyng mazary), facing it across a shady little courtyard. The Najm-ed-din Kubra mausoleum is Konye-Urgench's holiest spot. Najm-ed-din Kubra was a famous 12th to 13th century Khorezm Muslim teacher and poet who founded the Sufic Kubra order, which has followers in Turkmenistan and Karakalpakstan (in Uzbekistan). His tomb is believed to have healing properties and you may find pilgrims praying here. The building has three domes and a fine, unrestored, tiled portal. The tombs inside – one for his body and one for his head, which were separated by the Mongols – are colourful with floral-pattern tiles.

The Sultan Ali mausoleum was begun in 1580. Sultan Ali was a 16th century Uzbek Khorezmshah.

Southern Monuments

These are Konye-Urgench's most striking, dotted like a constellation of stars across an empty expanse straddling the Ashghabat road one km south of the end of Gurgench shayoli. What makes them the more evocative is that across the empty expanse are scattered brick-studded mounds – indicating that this was once a city.

The **Torebeg Khanym mausoleum** (Torebeg Khanymyng mazary), on the west side of the road, is proof of the comeback that old Urgench made in the great Mongol peace which followed the great Mongol destruc-

tion. It was built in the mid-14th century as the family tomb of a Sufi dynasty then ruling Khorezm under the Golden Horde. Torebeg Khanym was wife to Kutlug Temir, one of this dynasty, and a daughter of Khan Uzbek, the leader of the Golden Horde who converted the horde to Islam (and from whom the modern Uzbeks trace their origins).

The mausoleum is one of Central Asia's most perfect buildings (though recently obscured by reconstruction work). Its geometric patterns are in effect a giant calendar signifying humanity's insignificance in the march of time. There are 365 sections, for the days of the year, on the sparkling mosaic on the underside of the dome; 24 pointed arches, for the hours of the day, immediately beneath the dome; 12 bigger arches below for the months of the year; and four big windows for the weeks of the month.

Across the road, past a modern cemetery, stands the **Kutlug Temir minaret** (Kutlug-Temiring minarasy), built by Kutlug Temir in the 1320s and the only surviving part of old Urgench's main mosque. Decorated with bands of brick and a few turquoise tiles, at 67 metres it's the highest minaret in Central Asia – though not quite as tall as it once was, and now leaning noticeably.

Farther along the track is the **Sultan Tekesh mausoleum** (Soltan Tekeshchin mazary). Tekesh was the 12th century Khorezmshah who made Khorezm great with conquests as far south as Khorasan (present-day northern Iran and northern Afghanistan). He built this mausoleum for himself, along with a big medressa and library (which didn't survive) on the same spot. After his death, in 1200, he was buried here by his son Muhammad II. The conical dome, with a curious zigzag brick pattern, is typical of old Khorezm.

Continue along the track to the **Il-Arslan mausoleum** (Ilarslanyng mazary), Konye-Urgench's oldest standing monument. Il-Arslan, who died in 1172, was Tekesh's father. The building is small but well worth a close look. Its 12 faced conical dome is unique, and the floral terracotta moulding on the façade is unusual.

It's a longer walk to the last monument along this track, the main gate of a 14th century **caravanserai** (Kerven Saray). Here you're about 1.5 km from the Torebeg Khanym Mausoleum.

Places to Eat

In town there's the *Restoran Gurgench* on Gurgench shayoli. Near the southern monuments there's *Kafe Chunar*, almost across the road from the Torebeg Khanym mausoleum.

Getting There & Away

Konye-Urgench is about 100 km north-west of Dashkhovuz, 160 km north-west of Urgench and Khiva (Uzbekistan), and 45 km south-west of Nukus (Uzbekistan). You can reach it from any of these places, but make careful enquiries about the situation on the border if you're coming from Uzbekistan. If you're just doing a day trip from Uzbekistan, you may or may not need to show a Turkmenistan visa, but you will need to be sure that your Uzbek visa isn't cancelled as you leave Uzbekistan. One of the authors of this book travelled into Turkmenistan by private car from both Khiva and Nukus, and back again. He also crossed the border in

both directions on a bus trip between Urgench and Nukus. The only time his passport was examined was at the Uzbekistan border post as he was coming from Khiva: his driver explained they were on a day trip and his Uzbek visa wasn't cancelled. Things may have tightened up since then.

Bus Buses run from Dashkhovuz to Konye-Urgench every 50 minutes till 5.50 pm. From Nukus there may be direct buses to Konye-Urgench, but if not they run from Hojeli, 15 km from Nukus on the Konye-Urgench road, every 45 minutes from 9 am to 2.15 pm (but check the time of the last bus back from Konye-Urgench). From Urgench or Khiva, change at Dashkhovuz.

Taxi A taxi from Nukus and back, with a few hours to look round Konye-Urgench, should cost between US$10 and US$20. For a taxi day trip from Khiva or Urgench you're looking at US$50 to US$80.

Tour Uzbektourism can bring a carload from Urgench on a 10 to 12 hour guided trip for around US$200. Turkmen-Intour can bring you from Dashkhovuz.

Western Xinjiang & the Karakoram Highway

Central Asia properly includes 'Chinese Turkestan' too – those parts of what is now China's Xinjiang Autonomous Region sharing the former Soviet Central Asian republics' culture, language and history. Only gradually has the old, hyper-sensitive USSR-China border opened enough for individuals to travel easily over ancient routes between the two regions, and to appreciate how much these still have in common after decades of almost total political separation.

The Tarim basin is a 1500 km long depression covering most of southern Xinjiang and consisting almost entirely of the hostile Taklamakan desert, with a string of oases around the edge. Kashgar is one of these oases, at the western end of the desert in a cul-de-sac formed by the Tian Shan, the Pamir and the Kunlun ranges. Kashgaria is the historical name for the western Tarim basin. Despite its present isolation, Kashgaria was a hub of the Silk Road and has bristled with activity for over 2000 years.

This chapter introduces Kashgaria and how to get to it and through it to the former Soviet Central Asian republics. We also include the practical aspects of Xinjiang's capital, Ürümqi – though heavily Chinese and far from Kashgaria, it's the eastern gateway to the entire region. The other route to Kashgaria is overland via the Khunjerab pass and the Karakoram Highway (KKH) in Pakistan, so we also offer a capsule summary of the KKH as far south as its main hub, Gilgit.

For greater detail about the entire KKH, pick up Lonely Planet's *Karakoram Highway – the high road to China*. For more on the towns of Xinjiang, see LP's *China*.

History

Han Dynasty China had already pioneered its new trade routes (later named the Silk Road) through this region to the west by the

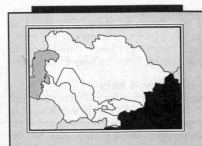

Highlights
- Kashgar's Sunday market: Asia's most mind-boggling bazar, a technicolour sea of people, animals, pony carts and push-carts where you can find anything you want, and a photographer's dream.
- The stupendous and lovely Hunza valley and throne-like Baltit fort, viewed from as high as possible, preferably Hon ridge above the Ultar icefall.

1st century BC. But despite the expenditure of vast resources in policing the region, it eventually succumbed to northern nomadic warrior tribes, Mongols and, later, Turks. Imperial power was not reasserted until the Tang Dynasty in the 7th and 8th centuries.

In the 8th century, Arab armies from Persia visited Kashgar and Gilgit, though it wasn't until later that Islam began to establish itself in this region. Tang armies crossed into what are now Kazakstan, Kyrgyzstan, Tajikistan and the Northern Areas of Pakistan in an attempt to deal with Arab and Tibetan expansion. But they got their fingers burnt at the Battle of Talas in 751 (see the History section in the Facts about the Region chapter) and never returned militarily.

Tang control of Kashgaria came to an end about this time with the arrival of the Uyghur Turks, and the area was ruled by a succession of tribal kingdoms – Uyghur, Qarakhanid and Karakitay – for more than four centuries. It was during Qarakhanid rule in the 11th and 12th centuries that Islam took hold here. Qarakhanid tombs are still standing in Kashgar and nearby Artush.

Kashgaria fell to the Mongols in 1219, and Timur sacked Kashgar in the late 14th century. The area remained under the control of Timur's descendants or various Mongol tribes until a Manchu army marched into Kashgar in 1755.

The Manchus remained for a century, although resentment of their rule often boiled over in local revolts. In 1847 Hunza, then an independent Karakoram state, helped the Chinese quell a revolt in Yarkand. During the 1860s and 1870s a series of Muslim uprisings erupted across western China, and after Russian troops were withdrawn from an occupation of the Ili region in northern Xinjiang, waves of Uyghurs, Chinese Muslims (Dungans) and Kazaks fled into Kazakstan and Kyrgyzstan.

In 1865 a Kokandi officer named Yaqub Beg seized Kashgaria, proclaimed an independent Turkestan and made diplomatic contacts with Britain and Russia (for more

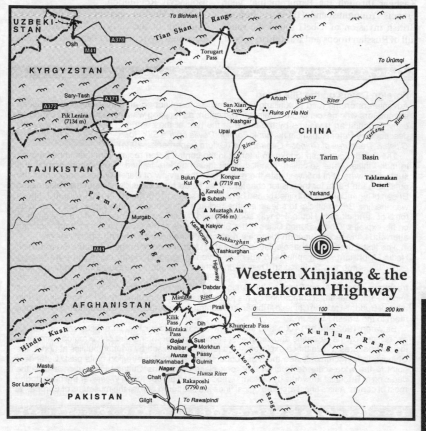

Western Xinjiang & the Karakoram Highway

on this extraordinary episode, see the History section in the Facts about the Region chapter). A few years later, however, a Manchu army returned, Beg committed suicide and Kashgaria was formally incorporated into China's newly created Xinjiang (New Dominions) province.

In 1882, by an agreement extracted from the Manchus, Russia opened a consulate in Kashgar. A British agency at Gilgit, opened briefly in 1877, was urgently reopened after the Mir of Hunza entertained a party of Russians at Baltit in 1888. Britain set up its own Kashgar office in 1890.

On his way back from a mission to Kashgar through the Pamir in that year, Francis Younghusband (later to head a British invasion of Tibet) found the range full of Russian troops and was told to get out.

A year later the British invaded Hunza. After a burst of diplomatic manoeuvring, Anglo-Russian boundary agreements in 1897 and 1907 gave Russia most of the Pamir and established the Wakhan Corridor, the awkward tongue of Afghan territory that stretches across to meet Xinjiang.

The Pamir settlement shifted the focus of the Great Game towards Kashgar, where the two powers went on conniving. But in the chaos following the Chinese Revolution of 1911 the British were no match for Russian economic and political influence in western Xinjiang, despite Russian absence from Kashgar for almost a decade after the 1917 Bolshevik Revolution.

New Muslim uprisings exploded across Xinjiang in the early 1930s. Kashgar was occupied by rebels and declared the capital

---

Foreign Devils on the Silk Road

Adventurers on the road to Xinjiang might well like to reflect on an earlier group of European adventurers who descended on Chinese Turkestan, as Xinjiang was then known, and carted off early Buddhist art treasures by the tonne at the turn of the century. Their exploits are vividly described by Peter Hopkirk in his book *Foreign Devils on the Silk Road – the Search for the Lost Cities & Treasures of Chinese Central Asia* (Oxford Paperbacks, 1984).

The British first began to take an interest in the central Asian region from their imperial base in India. Initially, the so-called 'pundits', local Indian traders trained in basic cartography and surveying, were sent to investigate the region (see the review of Derek Waller's book about the pundits in the Facts for the Visitor chapter). They heard from oasis dwellers in the Taklamakan Desert of legendary ancient cities buried beneath the sands of the desert. In 1864 William Johnson was the first British official to sneak into the region, visiting one of these fabled lost cities in its tomb of sand close to Hotan. He was soon followed by Sir Douglas Forsyth, who made a report on his exploits: 'On the Buried Cities in the Shifting Sands of the Great Desert of Gobi'. Not long afterwards, the race to unearth the treasures beneath the desert's 'shifting sands' was on.

The first European archaeologist/adventurer to descend on the region was the Swede Sven Hedin. A brilliant cartogapher and fluent in seven languages, Hedin made three trailblazing expeditions into the Taklamakan Desert, unearthing a wealth of treasures and writing a two-volume account of his journeys: *Through Asia*. The second explorer, in pursuit of Buddhist art treasures, was Sir Auriel Stein, a Hungarian who took up British citizenship. Stein's expeditions into the Taklamakan, accompanied by his terrier Dash, were to culminate in his removing a gold mine of Buddhist texts in Chinese, Tibetan and central Asian languages from Dunhuang and taking them to the British Museum.

Between 1902 and 1914 Xinjiang saw four German and four French expeditions, as well as expeditions by the Russians and Japanese, all jockeying for their share of the region's archaeological treasures. While these explorers were feted and lionised by adoring publics at home, the Chinese today commonly see them as robbers who stripped the region of its past. Defenders point to the wide-scale destruction that took place during the Cultural Revolution and to the defacing of Buddhist art works by Muslims who stumbled across them. Whatever the case, today most of central Asia's finest archaeological finds are scattered across the museums of Europe. ■

of the Republic of Eastern Turkestan – which lasted only two months. By the mid-1930s an odd coalition of Chinese soldiers, immigrant White Russians and Soviet troops had stamped out these revolts.

The People's Republic of China was declared in 1949, and the Kashgar consulates were shut down. In 1955 the communists declared Xinjiang an autonomous region, though it would never know anything like true autonomy.

In the 1960s a rail link to Ürümqi was completed and massive resettlement tilted northern Xinjiang's population in favour of Chinese, although Uyghurs are still a majority in the Tarim basin. The railway has now been extended to join the old Soviet rail system at the Kazakstan border.

Friction has continued with the Chinese, including riots in Kashgar in the 1970s, an armed uprising by Muslim nationalists in October 1981 that may have left hundreds dead, and another in 1990 in which scores of protesters were said to have been killed by government troops.

The Karakoram Highway China, following its invasion of Tibet in 1950, also occupied parts of what is now Pakistan's Northern Areas. But a China-Pakistan thaw in 1964 led to a formal agreement in 1966 which proposed the building of a two-lane road across the Pamir and the Karakoram from Kashgar to Havelian in Pakistan. The Pakistanis would work northwards and the Chinese southwards from the Khunjerab pass as well as to Kashgar on their own side.

The 1300 km KKH was declared complete (in Pakistan) in 1980. In August 1982 it was formally inaugurated, the Northern Areas were opened to tourism (as far as Passu) and the Khunjerab pass was opened to official traffic and cross-border trade. In May 1986 the Khunjerab and the entire road to Kashgar were opened to tourism. The Chinese finally finished paving the road on their side in 1989.

Maintenance is a huge, endless job. The mountains continually try to reclaim the road, assisted by earthquakes, encroaching glaciers and the Karakoram's typical crumbling slopes. Rockfalls, mud and floods are routine, and travel is inherently unpredictable.

Geography

The road threads its way through a 'knot' of four great mountain ranges: the Pamir, Karakoram, Hindu Kush and Himalaya, all of them part of the vast collision zone between the Asian continent and the Indian subcontinent. Here the ground rises higher, over a greater area, than anywhere else on the planet. The road crosses the eastern limb of the Pamir range, where it might be better described as a plateau, with broad, flat valleys nearly as high as the lower peaks.

The Karakoram – characterised by closely packed jagged high peaks, immense glaciers (the longest outside the sub-polar regions) and lush high valleys – arches for 500 km along the border between China and Pakistan-held Kashmir. Its high backbone is grouped in clusters called *muztagh* (Uyghur for 'ice mountain') from which the biggest glaciers descend. In northern Hunza is the Batura Muztagh, source of the Batura, Passu and Ultar glaciers; south-east is the Hispar Muztagh from which Nagar's glaciers flow. This crest-zone is broken at only one point, by the Hunza river (accompanied by the road) in southern Gojal. The Batura glacier comes right down to the highway at Passu.

People

Xinjiang The overriding majority of people in the Tarim basin are Uyghurs, now mainly farmers; there are also some Kazaks. The summer villages and small camel caravans in the Karakul region, and the settlements along the Torugart-Kashgar road, are mostly Kyrgyz. In evidence near the Pakistan border are Tajiks, most of whom live in Tashkurghan Tajik Autonomous County, south of Kashgar. It's a surprise to encounter occasional Russians, descendants of White Russians who fled after the Bolshevik Revolution of 1917. Han Chinese are still a small minority in the basin, though dominant in government and high-street business.

The official language of Xinjiang is Mandarin Chinese and each tribe has its own tongue, but Xinjiang's lingua franca is Uyghur. Uyghur is written in both Arabic and Roman scripts, the latter introduced for a time in an unpopular Chinese attempt to reduce illiteracy.

Northern Pakistan Tajiks also live in Gojal (upper Hunza), where they are called Wakhi. The Wakhi language is a dialect of Tajik or Persian. The people of Hunza and Nagar have common ancestors, though there is no consensus on their origins; scholarly suggestions have included Kashmir, Baltistan, Persia, Russia and Mongolia. Hunza and Nagar also have a common language, Burushaski, but nobody is sure where that came from either. In lower Nagar and Gilgit, Shina is spoken. Many people speak Urdu and English.

Gojal, Hunza and Nagar once also shared the Shia Islamic faith, but in the last three or four generations Gojal and Hunza have become almost entirely Ismaili. Older shamanistic beliefs also linger.

Gojal and Hunza men and women wear the long shirt and baggy trousers called *shalwar qamiz*. The women's outfits are brightly coloured and many wear embroidered pillbox caps with a *dupatta* or shawl thrown over them. Men wear the distinctive Hunza wool cap, essentially a tube of cloth with the edges rolled up tightly, and in cold weather they may put on a *chogha*, a handsome embroidered woollen cloak with oversized sleeves.

Dangers & Annoyances
The Northern Areas is one of the safest parts of Pakistan, but in 1988 tension between Sunni and Shia Muslims erupted into gun battles at Jalalabad near Gilgit, in which over 100 people died. There have been smaller incidents in the Gilgit area since then. Tense times are the holy days at the end of Ramadan and around the Prophet's birthday. No foreigners have yet been injured, but the KKH has sprouted police checkposts.

When to Go
Peak season for tourists (and peak demand for rooms and transport) is from late June through September. The Khunjerab pass is formally open to travellers from 1 May to 30 November – weather permitting. The only people who know when it will open or close are senior immigration or transportation officials near the border, and they only know a week or so ahead. In the past it has tended to open on time and close early, around the middle of November.

Prices
To minimise the effects of inflation, we quote prices in US$ here, although nearly everything must be paid for in local currency – RMB (yuan) or rupees.

ÜRÜMQI
Population: 950,000
Ürümqi, capital of Xinjiang, started to boom after the railway arrived in the 1960s, bringing throngs of Chinese settlers. The town is now 80% Chinese, a Han island in a sea of Uyghurs (but at least some of the Chinese are of the Muslim Hui minority). There's little reason to linger here if you're on your way into or out of Central Asia.

Orientation
The centre of town for our purposes is the area between two traffic roundabouts – one by the Hongshan department store (Hongshan shanchang) and one by the Hongshan Hotel – where several major arteries intersect. An alternative 'centre' is to the east, near Renmin Square. Hotels are scattered all over the city, though all are accessible on local buses. The train station and long-distance bus station are south-west of the centre, and the airport is 28 km to the north.

Streets tend to change names every few blocks, a headache for visitors. Street names often include a compass direction (north, east, south and west are, respectively, *bei, dong, nan* and *xi*); *lu* means street.

Maps City maps, in English and showing

bus routes, are hawked around stations, the Hongshan department store and the post office, and sold in some hotels. We found China maps in a stall on the ground floor (west end) of the Hongshan department store.

Information

All business hours given here follow Beijing time.

Tourist Offices The pick of the bunch is China Youth Travel Service (CYTS) who are competent at bookings and transport, even at short notice, and fairly cheap. They can organise tickets, provide fairly reliable information and perhaps some maps. The main office is on Jianshi lu just east of the Holiday Inn, and they have branches at the Hongshan and other hotels.

China International Travel Service (CITS) is competent enough too, but expensive – and everyone you ask has a different answer for your questions. The main office (☎ 282 5913, 282 1428; fax 281 0689, 281 8691; telex 79027 CITSXJ CN) is at 51 Xinhua bei lu, just to the left of the Holiday Inn. It's normally open weekdays from 9.30 am to

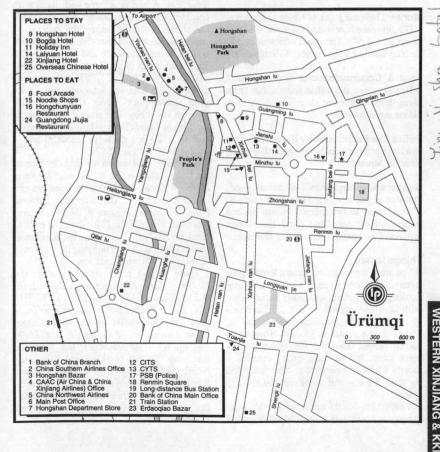

PLACES TO STAY
9 Hongshan Hotel
10 Bogda Hotel
11 Holiday Inn
14 Laiyuan Hotel
22 Xinjiang Hotel
25 Overseas Chinese Hotel

PLACES TO EAT
8 Food Arcade
15 Noodle Shops
16 Hongchunyuan Restaurant
24 Guangdong Jiujia Restaurant

OTHER
1 Bank of China Branch
2 China Southern Airlines Office
3 Hongshan Bazar
4 CAAC (Air China & China Xinjiang Airlines) Office
5 China Northwest Airlines
6 Main Post Office
7 Hongshan Department Store
12 CITS
13 CYTS
17 PSB (Police)
18 Renmin Square
19 Long-distance Bus Station
20 Bank of China Main Office
21 Train Station
23 Erdaoqiao Bazar

Ürümqi

0   300   600 m

WESTERN XINJIANG & KKH

1.30 pm and 4 to 8 pm, with a skeleton staff on weekends from May through October.

There is also a cheap and able office of China Travel Service (CTS) at the Overseas Chinese Hotel. Other agencies such as CICC at the Hongshan have been praised for their ability to come up with train tickets at short notice.

Consulates There are no formal consulates in Ürümqi. The local Kazakstan Airlines office apparently doubles as a consular office and may issue a Kazakstan visa if you already have a visa-support letter – but don't count on it. We couldn't find the office.

Money There are Bank of China branches at CITS, in some hotels, and on Youhao nan lu north of CAAC. The main office is at 343 Jiefang nan lu on the corner of Renmin lu.

Post & Communications The main post office is across the traffic roundabout from Hongshan department store. Ürümqi's telephone code is 0991.

Police The Public Security Bureau (PSB) is in a large government building north-west of Renmin Square.

Dangers & Annoyances Taxi drivers, especially at night, have tried to rip off tourists. If you resort to the incredibly jam-packed public buses, note that there have been reports of pickpocketing and bag slashing.

Things to See
If you have time on your hands, **Erdaoqiao bazar** is said to be Ürümqi's most interesting market, with carpets and other items along with fruit and vegetables. It's 2.5 km south of the Hongshan Hotel on Xinhua nan lu. Closer to the centre is gloomy **Hongshan bazar**, across from the Hongshan department store, full of dark, grotty eateries – mostly Chinese, one after another, all ruled by their TVs – and some vegetables and spices.

Leafy, bird-filled **People's Park** (Renmin gongyuan) occupies a large block bounded on its east side by Hetan nan lu. The best time to go is early in the morning when everyone is out doing their tai chi. Near the north end is a lake where you can hire rowing boats. Stay away on Sundays, when people descend on the place in droves. The pagoda on top of the big hill in **Hongshan Park** (Hongshan gongyuan), just north of People's Park, affords sweeping views over this fairly ugly city.

Places to Stay
The *Hongshan Hotel* (Hongshan binguan; ☎ 281 6018) makes a central and fairly friendly base, and is popular with budget travellers. A bed in a three-bed dorm with communal toilet and showers is about US$5; the showers tend to have long queues. A small double with shower (but unreliable hot water), toilet, telephone and TV is US$18. The hotel is full of small branches of tourist offices (including CYTS), whose staff descend like flies and interview you about your travel plans every time you walk through the lobby. Just around the corner is the *Bogda Hotel* (Bogeda binguan), where a bed in a 20-bed dorm is US$5.50 and a double with bath is US$24.

The only hotel within walking distance of the train station is the bottom-end *Xinjiang Hotel* (Xinjiang fandian) at the southern end of Changjiang lu. The *Overseas Chinese Hotel* (Huaqiao binguan; ☎ 260845) is over three km south of the Hongshan but easy to reach on bus No 7. Prices have escalated over recent years, with staff denying the existence of dormitory accommodation.

Even if you can't afford to stay, the *Holiday Inn* (Xinjiang jiari dajiudian; ☎ 218788, fax 217422, telex 79161 XJGHP CN) at 168 Xinhua bei lu has great coffee, a good breakfast buffet and the wildest disco in western China. Walk-ins pay US$86/96 and up for singles/doubles, but there are discounts for pre-booking and in winter. Nearby is the showy *Laiyuan Hotel* (Laiyuan fandian; ☎ 282 8368), also pricey but definitely not in the same league as the Holiday Inn; doubles with shower, toilet and TV are US$60 and up.

Places to Eat

Fast Food Cheerful Uyghur and Hui (Chinese Muslim) *stalls* compete for your attention with laghman, soups and shashlyk in an arcade under the river bridge west of the Hongshan Hotel. Shop around; not all of them are particularly clean. Fill up for US$1 while you watch them make their own noodles. A few cheap (and not too grotty) *noodle shops* are on the corner a block south of CITS. During the summer the *markets* are packed with delicious fresh and dried fruit.

Hotels The *Hongchunyuan Restaurant*, near PSB, is actually a Chinese-only hotel with two cheap restaurants – one Chinese and one western. From the Overseas Chinese Hotel, walk one block north, turn left and watch on the left for a good Cantonese restaurant called *Guangdong Jiujia*.

The Holiday Inn has several restaurants with high standards and prices to match. *Kashgari's* serves up Muslim dishes, while the *Xi Wang Mu* has everything Chinese from Sichuan to Cantonese dim sum. The excellent breakfast buffet, including free coffee refills, is in the restaurant to the left of the lobby.

Getting There & Away

For long-distance tickets or local excursions, the branch tourist offices in the Hongshan and other hotels are more convenient than going to the stations. All tickets are purchased in RMB.

Air Ürümqi is connected with Beijing and other large cities in China, as well as many smaller places in Xinjiang. China Xinjiang Airlines has flights to/from Kashgar (about US$120, 1½ hours, several times daily). International connections include Almaty (Xinjiang Airlines US$125, Kazakstan Airlines US$150; 1½ hours; Monday and Friday) Tashkent and Islamabad (Air China; weekly), and Moscow via Novosibirsk (Air China and Aeroflot; weekly). There are said to be weekly charter flights on Boeing 737s to/from Hong Kong via Chonqing in summer.

Tickets are usually available, at least to foreigners, as little as a day ahead. Foreigners pay foreigners' prices. The departure tax is included in the ticket price. You can avoid all the commissions by doing it yourself with RMB cash at the CAAC (Air China and China Xinjiang Airlines) office (☎ 481 4668) at Youhao nan lu 62, just north of the Hongshan department store. It's open daily from 9 am to 9 pm, except for lunch. Don't confuse this with the Xian-centred China Northwest Airlines office nearby, or the Guangzhou-centred China Southern Airlines across the road.

Bus Buying long-distance bus tickets is fairly straightforward at the bus station. Even in summer, you should be able to get a Kashgar or Almaty ticket a day or so ahead, and you can book up to four days ahead. Foreigners pay local price.

You can do the 1480 km bus trip to Kashgar in an ordinary coach in three days with two fairly grim overnight stops for about US$25, or in a soft-seat or sleeper bus in 36 hours with only meal stops for US$35 and US$40 to US$45, respectively. All of these depart twice daily. There are also ordinary buses for most other major towns in Xinjiang.

The 1050 km journey to Almaty (see the China-Kazakstan by Road section in the Kazakstan chapter) takes 26 hours with only meal stops. Buses depart daily except Saturday. Ask at window No 8 in the bus station. No visas are issued at the border.

Train The 2nd or soft-class *Genghis Khan Express* (No 13/14) to Almaty (Kazakstan) departs at 11 pm (Beijing time) on Monday and Saturday. The trip takes 35 hours. Tickets were about US$60 from the station at the time of research, but will cost more through CYTS or CITS. In summer you might not be able to get on the next train out unless you go through CYTS or CITS. See China-Kazakstan by Rail in the Kazakstan chapter for details of this not altogether pleasant crossing. No Kazakstan visas are issued at the border.

Ürümqi is well connected to the rest of China by train, with daily eastbound departures for Lanzhou, Zhengzhou, Shanghai, Chengdu, Xian and Beijing.

Getting Around
In addition to the impossibly packed public buses there are now numerous metered taxis.

To/From the Airport Travelling by car at 6 am, the airport is 20 minutes from the centre, but roadworks and rush-hour traffic can push this to 1½ hours. Air China minibuses (marked CAAC) leave from the CAAC office on Youhao nan lu two hours before flight departure, and several of them meet incoming flights and finish at the China Southern Airlines office across the street from CAAC, for about US$0.75 (Y6). From there it's a 15 to 20 minute walk to the Hongshan Hotel.

A taxi from the centre is about US$6, though we found the ones at the airport asked US$7 to US$10; a Chinese friend can help to negotiate the best fare.

To/From the Train Station Bus No 2 from the train station will take you close to the post office (four stops). From there it's a 15 to 20 minute walk to the Hongshan Hotel. A taxi to/from CITS or the Hongshan Hotel is about US$1.20 (Y10).

To/From the Bus Station To get to the Hongshan Hotel from the long-distance bus station, turn right outside the gates and walk 150 metres along Heilongjiang lu to an intersection, across which is the stop for bus No 8. Take this east for four stops and change to bus No 7 or 17 going north for one stop.

KASHGAR
Population: 300,000
Some things haven't changed in Kashgar (Uyghur: Qashghar, Chinese: Kashi or Kashih) since medieval times. Blacksmiths, carpenters and cobblers work by hand in the old town. From surrounding fields come wheat, maize, beans, rice, cotton and fruit in profusion. Id Kah mosque stands over the

town as it has since 1442. After two millennia Kashgar is still just a big market town, with impromptu street-corner negotiations, perpetual bazars, and hotel-room deals with Gilgit traders.

But in most ways the past is decidedly gone – symbolically confirmed by the huge statue of Mao Zedong. The old town walls have been torn down. High-rises have sprouted, department stores multiply. Sleaze, including prostitution, has arrived in the wake of tourism. Shattering vehicle noise and choking fumes now put Kashgar in a league with most other Chinese cities and well above most cities of the former USSR. This, the dust, the Chinese disco music and the moneychangers may soon drive you onward.

The British and Russian consulates, nerve centres of the Great Game for half a century, were closed in 1949 and later reopened as tourist hotels. Both have nearly disappeared under subsequent construction.

The Uyghur population at last count was 74% of the total, and shrinking.

Orientation
Official (Chinese) street names are given here. The main streets out from the centre are Renmin dong lu (East People's Rd) and Renmin xi lu (West People's Rd), and Jiefang bei lu (North Liberation Rd) and Jiefang nan lu (South Liberation Rd). The perimeter road on the north-west is Shengli lu (Victory Rd).

Buses from Pakistan normally go via the Seman Hotel to the Chini Bagh Hotel. If you arrive by air a bus brings you to the China Xinjiang Airlines (CAAC) booking office on Jiefang nan lu. The airport is 12 km north-east of the centre.

Information
Tourist Offices The Kashgar Mountaineering Association (☎ 223680, fax 222957, telex 79123 KSBTH CN, now a joint operation with Walji's, the big Pakistan travel agency, arranges expeditions and sports travel (eg trekking, cycling, rafting and skiing) in Xinjiang and Pakistan. With a few

PLACES TO STAY

2 Chini Bagh Hotel
5 Oasis Hotel
9 West City Hotel
11 Seman Hotel
13 Silk Road Hotel
18 Kashgar Guesthouse
22 Cao Hu Hotel
27 Qian Hai Hotel

PLACES TO EAT

6 Limin & Seman Road
  Restaurants
7 Bakery
8 Bakery
12 John Hu's Café
16 Bakery
20 Bazar
21 Chinese Restaurant
26 Chinese Restaurant
28 Yan Jin Restaurant

OTHER

1 People's Hospital
3 China International Travel
  Service (CITS)
4 Buses to Pakistan
10 Uyghur Hospital
14 Old Town Walls
15 PSB
17 Bicycle Parking
19 Cinema
23 Regional Bus Stand
24 Photo Shop
25 Bank of China
29 City Police Office
30 China Xinjiang Airlines
  (CAAC) Office
31 Kashgar Mountaineering
  Association
32 Tomb of Yusup Hazi Hajip
33 Tomb of Sayyid Ali Asia Khan
34 Stadium

Kashgar

0   250   500 m

To Airport, San Xian Caves, Ürümqi & Torugart Pass

To Abakh Hoja Tomb & Ruins of Ha Noi

Market Road

Sunday Market

Tuman River

East Lake

Rennin dong lu

See Central Kashgar Map

Old Town

Bazar

Bus Station Road

People's Park

Jielang bei lu

Jielang nan lu

To Yarkand & Khotan

Renmin xi lu

Shenqili lu

Seman lu

To Tashkurghan & Pakistan Border

WESTERN XINJIANG & KK

days' notice they can also help independent tourists with guides, transport, permits and equipment. They're at 8 Tiyu lu, off Jiefang nan lu beyond CAAC; they're called Dengshan xiehui in Chinese and Takka chkesh in Uyghur.

China International Travel Service (CITS; ☎ 223156, fax 223087, telex 79051 CITS CN) is up one flight of stairs in its own building inside the Chini Bagh gate. They'll book air tickets or rent you a jeep, but like their Ürümqi counterpart they're not a reliable source of information.

A hustler named John Hu runs a 'service bureau' out of his café (☎ 224186, fax 222861) in the eastern annexe of the Seman Hotel. He can organise bookings, tickets, transport and excursions at competitive rates. But keep your Lhasa plans to yourself.

Travel Permits & Visa Extensions The Division of Aliens and Exit-Entry Administration of the regional Public Security Bureau is in the right-hand door of PSB headquarters on Shengli lu. Aliens' travel permits *(waiguoren lüxingzhen)*, for areas such as Karakul which are not freely open to foreigners, are about US$1.20 (Y10). You can get your Chinese visa extended here too; the price depends on your nationality – eg US$3 for Americans, US$7 for Australians, US$8 for Brits, US$13 for Canadians. The staff speak English.

A few doors south, and also on Jiefang bei lu, are ominous-looking Chinese military compounds. A city police office is on Renmin dong lu, past East lake.

Money The Bank of China on Renmin xi lu, the Seman and Chini Bagh hotels, and Kashgar Guesthouse will change travellers' cheques and cash in major currencies. The bank can also arrange cash advances on major credit cards – in a day or less for amounts below about US$100 – for a 4% commission.

They won't buy back RMB; you can only do that at the Tashkurghan borderpost and only on weekdays. Exchange rates are uniform throughout China.

Moneychanging in Kashgar is an Uyghur business. Dealers loiter outside the hotels, and you'll be asked to change money until you're sick of it. Many of them cheat. For some important warnings about changing money here, see the Black Market information in the Money section of the Facts for the Visitor chapter.

Post & Communications The post office is on Renmin xi lu. Buy stamps downstairs, but hand your overseas letters in to the international and poste restante desk upstairs.

Across the road is the telephone and telegraph office. Through the right-hand door is an 'international' room, open from 9.30 am to 9 pm, where you can make international calls and send faxes and telexes. Some English is spoken here. Kashgar now has international direct-dialling (IDD), so calls go through fairly fast. Kashgar's telephone code is 0998.

Film & Photography There are photo shops with Chinese, Japanese and American brands of print film and some ektachrome, and colour print processing, in the centre of Jiefang bei lu, opposite the Mao statue on Renmin dong lu and at the west end of the Renmin xi lu. You may also find print film in department stores.

Bookshops The Xinhua Bookshop on Jiefang bei lu has everything from English primers to Stalin posters. One flight up, they sell huge maps of the Kashgar region, China and the world, in Chinese or Uyghur.

Hospitals The main Chinese hospital is People's Hospital (Renmin yiyuan) on Jiefang bei lu north of the river. There's a hospital of traditional Uyghur medicine on Seman lu about half a km east of the Seman Hotel.

Sunday Market
Once a week Kashgar's population swells by 100,000 as people stream in to the Sunday market – surely the most mind-boggling

bazar in Asia, and not to be missed. By sunrise the roads east of town are a sea of pedestrians, horses, bikes, motorcycles, donkey carts, trucks and belching tuk-tuks, everyone shouting *'boish-boish!'* (coming through!).

In arenas off the road, men 'test-drive' horses or look into sheep's mouths. A wonderful assortment of people sit by their rugs and blankets, clothing and boots, hardware and junk, tapes and boomboxes – and, of course, hats. In fact the whole town turns into a bazar, with hawkers everywhere.

The grounds are a 10 minute walk from the Kashgar Guesthouse, or 30 or 40 minutes from the Seman Hotel. You can take a bike and park it in the bike-lot on the corner of Market Rd and the ring-road. Donkey-carts are plentiful outside tourist hotels on market day; to minimise hassles, hire an entire cart with friends. Ask for Yenga bazar (New market) or Yekshenba bazar (Sunday market).

There is apparently a 'foreigners' trading market', open every day somewhere on the grounds, where you might make useful contacts for a ride across the border into Kyrgyzstan.

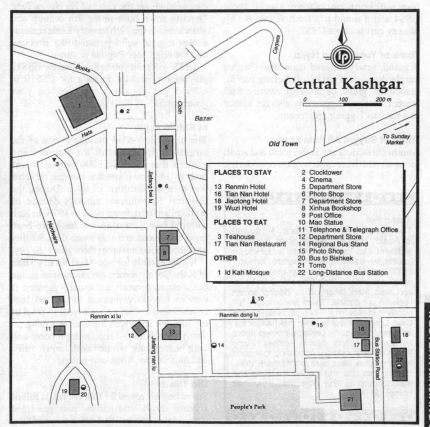

Central Kashgar

0   100   200 m

To Sunday Market

Old Town

Books

Cloth

Bazar

Hats

Jiefang bei lu

Hardware

Renmin xi lu

Jiefang nan lu

Renmin dong lu

Bus Station Road

People's Park

PLACES TO STAY		2	Clocktower
13	Renmin Hotel	4	Cinema
16	Tian Nan Hotel	5	Department Store
18	Jiaotong Hotel	6	Photo Shop
19	Wuzi Hotel	7	Department Store
		8	Xinhua Bookshop
PLACES TO EAT		9	Post Office
		10	Mao Statue
3	Teahouse	11	Telephone & Telegraph Office
17	Tian Nan Restaurant	12	Department Store
		14	Regional Bus Stand
OTHER		15	Photo Shop
		20	Bus to Bishkek
1	Id Kah Mosque	21	Tomb
		22	Long-Distance Bus Station

WESTERN XINJIANG & KK

Abakh Hoja Tomb

Kashgar's best example of Muslim architecture is an elegant mausoleum built in the mid-1600s for the descendants of a Muslim missionary named Muhatum Ajam. With its tiled dome and four minarets, it resembles a brightly coloured, miniature Taj Mahal. Beneath the tiled stones in the main chamber are more than 70 graves, including small ones of children. These include Muhatum Ajam's grandson Abakh Hoja, a local Uyghur aristocrat sometimes called the 'patron saint of Kashgar'. Behind the mausoleum is a vast, run-down graveyard.

The tomb is a half-hour bike ride or a two hour walk north-east of town; a taxi is about US$4 and a round trip from Seman Rd by donkey cart is about US$2.

Tomb of Yusup Hazi Hajip

A grand, newly restored mausoleum with a purple dome on Tiyu lu, off Jiefang nan lu, marks the grave of an 11th century Sufi teacher who was apparently also the author of a famous Uyghur epic poem.

Tomb of Sayyid Ali Asla Khan

Another historical site is this tomb and small mosque, which are quite modest considering

they mark the grave of a ruler of the 11th century Qarakhanid Dynasty. At the end of Renmin dong lu, at the roundabout, go about three-quarters of a km south; the tomb is on the right.

San Xian Caves, Ha Noi & Mor Pagoda

Twenty km north of Kashgar is one of the area's few traces of the flowering of Buddhism, the San Xian (Three Immortals) Caves, three grottoes high on a sandstone cliff, one of which has some peeling frescoes. Unfortunately, the cliff is too sheer to climb, so it's a bit of a disappointment.

At the end of a jarring 35 km drive north-east of town are the ruins of Ha Noi, a Tang Dynasty town built in the 7th century and abandoned in the 12th century. Little remains except a great solid pyramid-like structure and the huge Mor Pagoda or stupa.

CITS will take you to San Xian for US$12 per person, or Mor Pagoda for US$19 to US$33 per person, depending on your group's size.

Id Kah Mosque

The big yellow-tiled mosque is one of the largest in China, with a courtyard and gardens that can hold 8000 people. It was built in 1442 as a smaller mosque on what was then the outskirts of town. During the Cultural Revolution, China's decade of political anarchy from 1966 to 1976, Id Kah suffered heavy damage, but has since been restored. There are also more than 90 tiny neighbourhood mosques throughout the city.

It's acceptable for non-Muslims to go into Id Kah. Local women are rarely seen inside but western women are usually ignored if they're modestly dressed (arms and legs covered and a scarf on the head). In front of the mosque is Id Kah Square, swarming on sunny days with old men in high boots and long black coats, women with brown veils, and quite a few down-and-outers.

Old Town

Sprawling all round Id Kah are roads full of Uyghur shops, and narrow passages lined with adobe houses, that seem trapped in a

---

Xiang Fei

The mausoleum's most celebrated occupant is Abakh Hoja's granddaughter Ikparhan, widow of a Yarkandi prince and better known to Chinese as Xiang Fei (Fragrant Consort). In 1759 she led Uyghurs in an unsuccessful revolt against the Qing Emperor Qian Long, and was then taken off to Beijing as an imperial concubine. There the emperor fell madly in love with her. Two years later, while Qian Long was out of town, his mother the empress dowager – perhaps worried about her son's emotional stability – ordered Xiang Fei to commit suicide. According to legend her body now rests here (some claim, dubiously, that the old sedan chair is the one that bore her home). ∎

time warp. Look for books, hats and regional handicrafts north-west and south-west of the mosque, and dowry chests, brightly painted cradles and hardware of every kind on the road south to the post office. Several streets sport bright new buildings in traditional Uyghur style. Behind a wall of department stores opposite Id Kah is a dusty labyrinth of blacksmiths, farriers, carpenters, jewellers, teashops, bakeries and noodle shops.

At the east end of Seman lu stands a 10-metre-high section of the old town walls, at least 500 years old. Another rank of them are visible from Shengli lu opposite the bazar. Construction around, on and in them makes access impossible, and there's clearly no interest in preserving them.

People's Park
South of the Mao statue is People's Park (Renmin gongyuan), a weedy arboretum with avenues of tall poplars, a little zoo, and Uyghurs playing billiards, chess and *shiang chi* (Chinese chess). East of the park, 200 metres down a back lane, is an old tomb, now quite smashed up and with most of its blue tiles stripped off. According to local people it may have been for an imam (religious leader) in the 19th century.

East Lake
Just outside town along Renmin dong lu is a willow-lined artificial lake, a popular spot for migratory birds and a good place for a picnic or a peaceful walk among the weeds. In the summer you can rent little boats here.

Places to Stay
Bottom End The *Chini Bagh*, *Seman*, and *Tian Nan* hotels have cheap dorm beds (see Middle-range places to stay, below). Kashgar Mountaineering Association (see the Information section) can arrange Uyghur or Chinese homestays in Kashgar, Tajik homestays in Tashkurghan or Kyrgyz home (or yurt) stays at Karakul. Do-it-yourself homestays could land your host in trouble with the PSB. Hotels not currently interested in foreigners include the *Oasis*, *West City*, *Cao Hu*, *Wuzi* and *Jiaotong*; Jiaotong's beds

are about US$3.50 in triples. The *Silk Road Hotel* was closed when we were there.

Middle The well-run Chini Bagh Hotel looks like the best mid-range value. Dorm beds are US$2.50, and noisy doubles/triples/quads with toilet and shower (and hot water most of the time) in the main building are US$20/19/15. Quieter carpeted doubles with TV in the annexe are US$29. A new '3-star' tower was about to open when we were there. Those with a big bankroll and an interest in Kashgar history can stay in VIP quarters in the old British consulate – a suite of two doubles, a single and dining and sitting rooms, which can only be booked a week ahead, is US$95.

The *Seman Hotel* ('si-MAAN'), also called Lao binguan (old hotel), is now a 450-bed complex occupying three buildings and four one-storey blocks (the latter are all that remains of the old Russian consulate). Dorms with two to six beds, with attached bath, are US$2.50 per person; the smaller rooms in blocks Nos 2 and 3 have baths. Doubles range from US$14 to US$48.

The friendly *Tian Nan Hotel* is on Renmin dong lu near the long-distance bus station. Dorm beds are US$1 to US$2, and doubles/triples cost US$15/18. Showers are communal and hot water is unreliable. The *Renmin Hotel* on the corner of Remin dong lu and Jiefang nan lu has noisy doubles with telephone, TV and bath for US$18.

Kashgar is now sprouting gaudy new hotels apparently aimed at Chinese *nouveaux riches*. One that looks like good value is the *Qian Hai* (☎ 223977), down an alley at Renmin xi lu 48, with doubles with telephone, TV and bath at US$19 to US$48, and three clean restaurants.

Chini Bagh offers 20% off for stays of more than three days, plus off-season discounts, and you might persuade other hotels to do the same.

Top End *Kashgar Guesthouse* (☎ 224954, fax 224679), also called Xin binguan (new hotel), is in a quiet compound east of the centre. Doubles with TV, telephone, bath are

US$25, and triples with communal shower are US$18. The drawback is that it's three km out of town, though you can hire a bike or a donkey cart.

Places to Eat

Unless you're a guest in a private home, it's easier to find good, clean Chinese food than good, clean Uyghur food. Most Uyghur eateries are uninterested in western customers, hygiene is awful and your meal is apt to be accompanied by Bananarama or kung-fu videos. 'Muslim Restaurant' on many grotty places just means no pork is used.

Fast Food The pavements along Shengli lu north of Renmin xi lu overflow in the afternoon and evening with Chinese and some Uyghur stalls, some with very dubious hygiene – though you can't go too far wrong dipping your own spoon into hot laghman or jiaozi (dumplings in boiling broth). Also check out the tasty mini-casseroles of noodles, vegetables or meat, called huo guo, which look pretty safe if they're on the boil. You might also find plov, mutton shashlyk or meatballs in broth.

Cafés & Restaurants Everybody says they can make you Mongolian-style hot-pot (shuan yan rou). The best (but not the cheapest) is still at its original purveyor, the *Yan Jin Restaurant* (no English sign), the place on Renmin xi lu with the red doorway. In the middle of your table a brass pot with a gas fire underneath keeps broth nearly boiling. You add herbs and salt and dip in rice noodles, cabbage and meat slivers till they cook, and drink the broth afterward – a great group meal. The cost depends on the ingredients you order.

Two fairly clean Chinese cafés opposite the Seman Hotel – the *Limin* and *Seman Road* – vie with each other to be warm and friendly, an arresting experience in China. Both have big menus featuring spicy dishes, and plentiful tea. Fill up for US$2 to US$3. They also serve chips and an adequate western breakfast. A good restaurant is the *Tian Nan*, around the corner from the hotel

of the same name, open from 8.30 am to 10.30 pm. The sign says 'Han Dining Hall'.

Hotels The *Chini Bagh* and *Seman* hotel and the *Kashgar Guesthouse* have clean, boring Chinese and Uyghur (Muslim) dining halls, open for limited hours, where you can choose from small Chinese menus or eat fixed Uyghur meals.

Self-Catering The best way to eat vegetarian is to self-cater. A small bazar on Shengli lu has fresh fruit and vegetables, hard-boiled eggs (dyed red), steamed yams and fat yellow figs. Early in the morning, small bakeries churn out stout nan bread. Department stores may have dried or preserved fruit, biscuits, sweets, peanut butter, bulk honey and nuts. Dried fruit isn't always clean; soaking it in boiling water reduces (but doesn't eliminate) the risk of illness.

Getting There & Away

Air The only place you can fly to/from is Ürümqi, in a Russian Tu-154 jet (US$95, daily flights in summer, four flights weekly in winter). You should try to book at least a week ahead in summer, at the China Xinjiang Airlines ticket office (CAAC; ☎ 22113) at 49 Jiefang nan lu. There are no discounts. If flights to Ürümqi from elsewhere are cancelled on account of bad weather (as they often are), Ürümqi-Kashgar flights may also be cancelled.

Bus There are buses travelling between Kyrgyzstan, Xinjiang and Pakistan

To Kyrgyzstan A Chinese outfit runs at least one bus back and forth between Kashgar and Bishkek via the Torugart pass, roughly three or four times a month in summer. The terminus is at the Wuzi Hotel (Wuzi binguan), a block south of the post office. Tickets are about US$100 per person in RMB (quite a bit more than from the Bishkek end), from the hotel lobby.

No English is spoken here, but the Chinese characters for 'bus to Bishkek' are:

来巴士去比什饥克

overnight stop – plus whatever you declared to customs on entering China.

If buses have stopped for the season but you're desperate to cross the border, Pakistani traders may have space in a truck or chartered bus. You can also hire a 4WD; see Renting Your Own in this section.

To Ürümqi You can now make the 1480 km trip to Ürümqi in a non-stop, soft-seat coach (Chinese: *haohuache*, Uyghur: *ali mashina*) or sleeper coach (*Chinese: wopoche, Uyghur: qarvatlik mashina*) in 36 hours, for US$35 or US$40 to US$45 respectively. You can also go in an ordinary bus (Chinese: *putongche*, Uyghur: *adetki mashina*) in three days, with two grim overnight stops at Aksu and Korla, for about US$25.

All of these depart from the long-distance bus station twice daily – the regular and soft-seat buses at 1 pm and 6 pm, the sleeper at 9 am and 9 pm. Tickets are on sale up to four days ahead, at the station or more expensively through CITS, and the sleepers sell out quickly. John Hu (see the Information section) also organises occasional minibuses on this run.

Other Destinations Other buses – eg to Tashkurghan every morning except Sunday – use the long-distance bus station (*aptoos biket*). There have been instances of theft at the bus station, especially in the early-morning crush, sometimes with packs cut open, so keep a close watch on your bags.

Renting a 4WD You can hire 4WD Land Cruisers (holding six to eight passengers) and minibuses (holding eight to 12) from the Kashgar Mountaineering Association, CITS or John Hu. At the time of research a Land Cruiser to meet or drop you off at Torugart was about US$200 to US$250. A Land Cruiser to Sust was US$600, a minibus about US$900. Food and lodging are extra, and the driver pays for his own. Book ahead, a week or more in peak season. Try to get an Uyghur driver; most Chinese seem to be lunatics behind the wheel.

There's no fixed schedule; just keep asking. All customs formalities take place at the Torugart pass. You may need a Torugart permit on your Chinese visa, though PSB are apt to tell you that you can't go there at all. You must already have a Kyrgyzstan visa. For more on the Kashgar-Torugart road, as well as the onward journey into Kyrgyzstan, see Bishkek to Kashgar via the Torugart pass, in the Kyrgyzstan chapter.

To Pakistan The terminus for buses to/from Sust in Pakistan is the Chini Bagh Hotel. At the time of writing, a ticket was about US$30 (Y260), from the customs shed in the yard beside the Chini Bagh. From June to September they lay on as many buses as needed, so you needn't book very far ahead. Earlier or later in the season there may not be buses on some days. Landslides can cancel departures even in summer.

The first bus leaves about 11.30 am (Beijing time). The 500 km trip takes two days, with an overnight at Tashkurghan. Bring water and snacks and warm clothes as nights can be cold in any season. Sit on the left side for the best views.

Everything that goes on top of the bus (including mountains of bundles belonging to Pakistani traders) is customs-inspected at Chini Bagh and locked up for the entire journey, so carry whatever you want for the

Hitching You might hitch a lift to Tashkurghan but from there to Pakistan you'll probably have to wait for an empty seat on the bus. We don't know of anyone who has hitched into Kyrgyzstan, but there are plenty of goods trucks making the crossing (see the Bishkek to Kashgar via the Torugart pass section in the Kyrgyzstan chapter).

Getting Around

To/From the Airport A US$1.20 (Y10) CAAC bus leaves from the China Xinjiang Airlines (CAAC) ticket office on Jiefang nan lu 2½ hours before all flight departures, and one meets all incoming flights. A taxi is about US$4.

Bus A regional bus stand at the west end of the field opposite the Mao statue, and another west of the bank, are mainly for buses and tuk-tuks to outlying towns and counties.

Taxis & Tuk-Tuks Taxis hang out at tourist hotels. From the Seman Hotel to the bus station costs about US$2 to US$2.50; to the Sunday market about US$3. Snarling, polluting two-stroke motor tuk-tuks have now appeared too, and although cheaper are no good for longer trips.

Donkey-Carts The traditional Kashgar 'taxis' are getting scarcer. They're not allowed in the centre in the daytime, so routes tend to be roundabout. A few drivers are always outside the tourist hotels, eager to take your money. Some of them cheat foreigners, especially when they have few passengers and no locals on board – prices may go up in mid-journey, rides may end early. If you hire your own, set the price and destination before you go. Don't pay till you get there, and have exact change.

Bicycle Rental A bike is the cheapest and most versatile way to get around Kashgar. One-gear clunkers can be hired by the hour or day at many hotels. A deposit is required; don't leave your passport with them, as some ask you to do.

KASHGAR TO THE KHUNJERAB PASS

To the Chinese the road from Kashgar to the Pakistan border is the China-Pakistan Highway (Zhong-Pa Gong lu, 'China-Pak Big Road'). After 80 km across the flats and a sharp 70 km climb, it runs along a high valley through the eastern Pamir for 250 km to the border. Travelling times given here are for bus travel.

Kashgar to Karakul

As you leave Kashgar the main attraction, rising up from the plain to the west, is the luminous rampart of the Pamir. An hour down the road is **Upal** village (Chinese: Wupaer). About three km off the road here is the small tomb of Mahmud al-Kashgari, an 11th century Uyghur scholar (born at Barsköön in Kyrgyzstan) famous for writing the first comparative dictionary of Turkic languages. Most settlements as far as Karakul are Kyrgyz.

Two hours from Kashgar you enter the canyon of the Ghez river (Uyghur: Ghez Darya), with wine-red sandstone walls at its lower end. **Ghez** itself is just a checkpost; photographing soldiers or buildings here can result in confiscated film. Upstream the road is cut into sheer walls or inches across huge boulder fields. At the top of the canyon, 3½ hours above the plain, is a huge wet plateau ringed with sand dunes.

The corridor from here to the Pakistan border is the **Sarikol valley**, and the mountains on either side are the Taghdumbash (or Sarikol, or Chinese Pamir). Half an hour south, at the foot of Mt Kongur, is the Kyrgyz settlement of **Bulun Kul**, 3700 metres above sea level. It's sometimes a food stop. An hour south of Bulun Kul is **Karakul** – properly Lesser Karakul, as there's a bigger lake of the same name in Tajikistan.

Karakul

Many travellers come to Kashgar hoping to rub shoulders with Kyrgyz nomads in the pastures around Karakul (Chinese: Kalakuli Hu). This is one of the most beautiful places in western China, the deep blue waters (*kara kul* is Uyghur for 'black lake') nestled between two Pamir giants, 7546 metre Muztagh Ata to the south and 7719 metre Mt Kongur to the north-east.

With a tent you could spend days at the lake or on the flanks of Muztagh Ata, and trekking possibilities are good. But this is a restricted area, for which you need a travel permit from the PSB in Kashgar or Tashkurghan – even for a day trip or a day-stop en route to/from Pakistan.

There are several Kyrgyz summer villages in the area (the nearest, on the lake shore, is Subash). You can walk around the lake in half a day; the downstream outflow can be forded at the village nearby. Unless you make arrangements in advance, the only alternative to camping appears to be tacky mock-up yurts in a tour-group site by the lake, where you can also sit on a camel or arrange an excursion on mangy, bad-tempered horses up to high pastures (*jailuu*), about three hours away at the foot of Muztagh Ata.

Go between June and September; at other times the villages and the yurt site are usually closed down. The lake is at 3800 metres and nights are below freezing even in summer; one camper awoke to find snow in the middle of August!

Places to Stay & Eat The yurt site is run by the Aktu County Mountaineering Association. There is also a restaurant at Muztagh Ata basecamp.

Getting There & Away The public Kashgar-Tashkurghan bus will stop at Karakul. Empty seats as far as Karakul are also available on the Pakistan bus on a standby basis, though you may be asked to show a travel permit. Another option is to hire a Land Cruiser or minibus from Kashgar, do a trek with the Kashgar Mountaineering Association, who can also arrange stays in a Kyrgyz house or yurt, or a Tajik home in Tashkurghan. CITS offers a Karakul day trip from Kashgar by Land Cruiser for US$58 to US$132 per person depending on the size of the group.

Karakul to Tashkurghan

From the high ground west of Muztagh Ata, called the **Subash plateau**, the highway comes within about 10 km of Tajikistan, and several jeep tracks run that way. At the turn of the century this area was still in dispute, never having been properly mapped. Two to three hours south of Karakul is a police checkpost at **Kekyor**. From there, across the marshy **Tagh Arma basin**, it's about 1½ hours to Tashkurghan. Settlements from Tagh Arma to the border are mainly Tajik.

Tashkurghan

This is the administrative centre of the Tashkurghan Tajik Autonomous County, stretching from Muztagh Ata to the border, and home to most of China's 20,000 Tajiks. By bus in either direction between Kashgar and Sust, you'll probably have to spend the night here, so make the best of it.

In Uyghur *tash kurghan* means stone fortress. The ruins of a mud-brick fort still stand on the edge of town, and although this one is estimated to be about 600 years old, local lore says Tashkurghan has been a citadel for over 2300 years. The Chinese Buddhist pilgrim Hsuan Tsang wrote about the fortress in the 7th century, when it was the farthest frontier outpost of the Tang Dynasty.

There's only one street, one km long. A small bazar is on a side street 400 metres down from the main road. A department store and post office are at the other end of town.

Customs & Immigration Just south of Tashkurghan is the huge Chinese customs and immigration post. Buses arrive in Tashkurghan late and leave early the following morning, although customs may not open until 10.30 or 11 am. The bank by the customs post is the only place you can swap RMB for rupees; it's only open on weekdays, though there may be 'unofficial' moneychangers around too.

Fort The massive, crumbling fort is at the north-east corner of town, on the only hill in the Tashkurghan river's flood plain. Most of its multi-layered walls and battlements are still intact. Development around the fort makes it hard to reach – the easiest way is from the far end of town and up the fort's east side.

Places to Stay The bus will probably dump you at the filthy *Jiaotong Binguan* (Transport Hotel), with plain quads for US$2 per bed and doubles at US$7 per bed. Groups go to the *Pamir Hotel*, where a bed and two meals is about US$20. Individuals might also have some luck at a government resthouse called *Shi Ping Gongsi Lüshe*, which has cheap four-bed rooms. There's no English sign but it's in a courtyard behind a pair of restaurants west of the Pamir Hotel.

Places to Eat Food is an overpriced misery here. At the Pamir Hotel, set Chinese meals are about US$2, but if there are no groups about they may have nothing at all. The restaurant at the Jiaotong binguan's restaurant is just adequate. Two cafés with questionable hygiene and predatory prices are halfway down the main street. In the morning the bazar has hot bread, melons and some vegetables.

In 1987-88 hepatitis was epidemic in southern Xinjiang. This has now been brought under control, but Tashkurghan may still be one of the easiest places on the KKH to catch a stomach infection.

Getting There & Away A public bus runs between Kashgar and Tashkurghan daily except Sunday. A bus also takes passengers from Sust on to Kashgar the next morning, for about US$7 plus a few *yuan* per big bag. A local entrepreneur apparently sells tickets to Kashgar by the bank at the customs post; they're snapped up by Pakistan traders, and you may have to use your elbows to get one for yourself.

Tashkurghan to the Khunjerab Pass
This level stretch along the Tashkurghan river is grand and picturesque in fine weather. About 1½ hours south of Tashkurghan is **Dabdar**, the largest permanent Tajik settlement along the road. South

of Dabdar, the road passes the mouth of an enormous opening westward into the Pamir – the **Mintaka valley**, once a major Silk Road branch and historically one of the main routes to Hunza and on to Kashmir. Two hours from Tashkurghan is **Pirali**, the former Chinese customs post. South of here the Pamir gradually becomes the Karakoram.

THE KHUNJERAB PASS
At 4730 metres, the road over the Khunjerab pass (Chinese: Hongqilapu) is said to be the highest public highway in the world. *Khunjerab* is Tajik for 'Blood valley'. Nobody is sure where the name came from, although the area swarmed with bandits stalking caravans between Kashgar and Kashmir until the 1890s.

The alpine region between Pirali and the Pakistan security post at Dih is the only habitat of the rare, big-horned Marco Polo sheep, of which there are now only a few hundred in the world. The pass is also home to ibexes, Himalayan marmots, brown bears, foxes and, according to some, snow leopards. You may also see herds of shaggy wild yaks or domesticated dzu, a cross between a yak and a cow.

Both Pakistan and China have set aside nature reserves here. The Chinese established the 15,000 sq km Tashkurghan nature reserve (the road is within it from about Tashkurghan to the border) in 1984. On the Pakistan side, in a 20 km by 100 km strip along the border called the Karakoram national park. Huntinghere has been banned and grazing restricted since 1975, though surveys and enforcement are currently underfunded.

The pass itself is long and flat. A few km before the top is what must be China's loneliest security post, but save your tears. Recent letters tell of a scam by soldiers here: they flag you down, offer what appears to be complimentary tea or coffee, and afterwards demand US$5 per cup. One group of travellers was detained for three hours by soldiers who threatened to confiscate passports, cancel exit stamps and send them back to Kashgar if they didn't pay up. At the summit is a plaque commemorating the 1982 opening of the pass, and a Pakistan security post where cheerful guards will give you free tea and sympathy.

Scattered down the Pakistan side are deserted concrete buildings – hostels for Chinese KKH workers, built in the late 1960s. The walls of the lower valley are 'black, crumbling rock' (this is how the Uyghur words *'kara koram'* translate) and the river cuts through deep beds of gravel, the residue of repeated mud and rock slides.

About 50 km below the top (35 km from Sust) is the Pakistan security post of **Dih**. If you're coming from China you'll get a warm welcome. It's an hour from Dih to Sust, through some of the narrowest gorges on the KKH. Below the tributary valleys of Misgar and Chapursan, whose streams rise near the Afghan border, the Khunjerab river becomes the Hunza river.

GOJAL

The region known locally as Gojal ('go-JAAL') extends for about 60 km from Sust to where the Hunza river turns west. This is the only river that cuts across the high spine of the Karakoram, and it does so in Gojal. As a result the High Karakoram is more accessible here than anywhere else. At Passu and Gulmit several major glaciers nearly reach the highway.

Mountains with razor-edge summits drop sheer to the river, and the wind drives up the valley even on sunny days. The river picks its way among great fans of alluvium brought down by the smaller streams; most villages are built on these fertile deposits.

Gojal is usually described as 'upper Hunza'. Like the people of Hunza proper, Gojalis are Ismaili Muslims and were loyal subjects of the Mir of Hunza, but they're Tajik-speakers. They're probably the most warm-hearted people on the KKH, with easy greetings and hospitality for both men and women.

Sust

Although mainly a customs and immigration post, Sust, at 3100 metres, also has long

Wild Yaks are now reduced in numbers; they graze on grass and require much water.

walks, grand scenery, and even a hot spring. You can also visit the Khunjerab pass from here as a day trip. If you're leaving Pakistan it's almost essential to stay at Sust the night before.

Orientation & Information Customs, immigration, bank, post office, telephone exchange, a few shops and some hotels are clustered near the gate, and more hotels are up the road in the direction of Pakistan. The Pakistan Tourism Development Corporation (PTDC) and Northern Areas Transport Company (NATCO) offices are also near the gate. Customs and immigration will eventually move to a new site about one km upstream.

Customs & Immigration Sust is probably the most casual border post in Pakistan. But it must be a rough posting – the isolation from Pakistan and the proximity to all those foreigners, especially women, has clearly knocked a few moral screws loose, so stay awake.

Baggage inspection for foreigners usually consists of: 'What's in there?…OK'. Most visitors arriving without Pakistan visas get a three-week transit visa, which can be extended in Islamabad. If you stay in Pakistan more than 30 days you're supposed to register; most large towns, including Gilgit, have a foreigners' registration office, usually part of the police office.

If you're China-bound, remember that China does not issue visas of any kind at the border.

Hot Spring Six km upstream from Sust, rock piles mark a steep path to the river, where there are several shallow pools near the bank. You must leave your passport with immigration. You can hire a Suzuki pick-up (northern Pakistan's most common short-haul transport) for the round-trip. 'Hot spring' is *theen kook* in Wakhi, and *garam chashma* in Urdu.

Upper Village Heading uphill near the Mountain Refuge Hotel, turn left and continue for 400 metres, then turn right and follow the path through fields to upper Sust village and Sust Nala (a *nala* is a tributary canyon). The compact houses and walled fields, the poplars and fruit orchards, and the dramatic canyon are very different from the scene along the road.

Khudabad Across the Hunza river is Khudabad village and the narrow Khudabad Nala. A bridge spans the river 1.5 km upstream of Sust. A walk to the village and back takes an hour.

Places to Stay The *Mountain Refuge Hotel* is your best bet, with cheap dorm beds, doubles with attached toilet and cold shower for $US5, and good food. For similar prices you can also choose from several noisy inns near customs, with dreary food, no privacy and lots of cheerful Pakistanis.

The *Khunjerab View Hotel* beyond the Mountain Refuge, and the *Tourist Lodge* beside customs, have similar facilities, plus overpriced doubles with hot showers. The group-oriented *Dreamland Hotel* has cheaper doubles with hot showers, but it's two km down the road in the Pakistan direction. Most hotels will let you pitch a tent and

use their toilets and water for a fraction of the room cost, but keep in mind that most open space near the road is used as a toilet too!

Places to Eat The *Mountain Refuge Hotel* has sit-down Hunza-style dinners – rice, noodle soup, meat and vegetables – for Y45, normally for hotel guests only. They also serve western-style breakfasts. The *Tourist Lodge* has a buffet when groups are staying. Most hotels have basic Pakistan road food: gosht (curried mutton), dhal (lentils), chapatti (flat bread) and tea.

Getting There & Away The Northern Areas Transport Company (NATCO) runs buses and 4WD Land Cruisers on the six to seven hour trip to Tashkurghan, and the Pakistan Tourism Development Corporation (PTDC) runs its own smart minibuses. The per-person price to Tashkurghan is US$24. All minibuses, buses and Land Cruisers leave in the morning. Before June or after September there may not be buses daily. The best views are from the right side of the bus. It's a good idea to carry a day's water and snacks. From Tashkurghan a Chinese bus takes you to Kashgar the next morning.

In the other direction, a clapped-out NATCO bus leaves early every morning for Gilgit, taking four to five hours and stopping everywhere en route. In summer there are also private vans, leaving even earlier. Passu is six to seven hours away on foot.

Sust to Passu

As the valley widens near Passu the highway crosses a makeshift girder bridge over the **Batura glacier** stream. The glacier itself nearly reaches the road. This is one of the larger glaciers of the Karakoram, extending 60 km back into the cluster of 6000 to 7000 metre peaks called the Batura Muztagh. It advances and retreats from year to year. In 1976 it ground up the original Chinese bridge, which was then replaced by the permanently temporary girder bridge.

East of the bridge is the yawning **Shimshal valley**, once one of the remotest places in the old state of Hunza. It was from upper Shimshal, even as recently as the last century, that Hunza raiders plundered caravans heading to Kashmir. A 45 km road now heads up to Shimshal village at the valley's head.

Ten minutes from the bridge, at the north end of Passu, is a windy plain full of broken-down buildings. From 1968 until 1979 this was a camp for Chinese KKH workers. Now it's a mostly deserted Pakistan army post.

Places to Stay About seven km south of Sust near Morkhun is the *Greenland Hotel*, which has doubles with hot showers. At Khaibar, the *Khaibar Inn* has tea, light food and a few rooms.

Passu

Sitting between the black Batura glacier and the white Passu glacier, this is the place to stop if you like to walk. Passu, at 2400 metres, is the base for many dramatic day hikes and longer treks (ask your hotel-wallah about them). The 'cathedral' ridge across the river from Passu is called Tupopdan (Wakhi for 'hot rock', because in winter its slopes shed the snow quickly).

The village is below the Passu Inn, where the buses usually stop. Buses will also drop you 1½ km south at the Shisper Hotel, or 800 metres north at the Batura Inn, on the edge of the old road-camp.

Places to Stay & Eat The *Batura Inn, Passu Inn, Passu Guesthouse* and *Shisper Hotel* all have cheap dorms (all but the Batura Inn's are in traditional Gojal style (with a raised sleeping area surrounding a stove), doubles for around US$4, and good food. The spartan *Batura Inn* is the best value, mainly because of owner Izatullah Beg's plentiful, delicious meals at about US$1 a throw, and his psychedelic 'rumour books' are full of crazy, spaced-out notes and sketches as well as good (and bad) advice about the area. The Passu Inn and Passu Guesthouse also have more comfortable doubles for around US$10.

Gulmit

Gulmit ('GOOL-mit'), traditional second home of the mirs of Hunza, is the closest thing to a town in Gojal. It's very picturesque in spring and early summer when the fruit trees bloom.

Places to Stay & Eat The *Tourist Cottage* on the highway has a cheap traditional-style dorm, plus clean doubles with shared toilet for about US$8, and it's a good place for information on local trips. The friendly *Village Hotel*, up the road by the polo ground, has a few quiet doubles with shared toilet for similar rates, and more-expensive but good-value doubles in an old Gojal-style building. The nearby *Marco Polo Inn* (☎ 7) has evening videos and expensive doubles. Back down on the highway, the *Silk Route Lodge* and *Horse Shoe Motel* are priced for tour groups.

Every hotel has a dining room, and by request the *Tourist Cottage* serves Gojal-style whole-wheat bread and home-made apricot jam at breakfast, and (for a price) traditional Hunza and Gojal dishes at dinner.

HUNZA & NAGAR

For pure natural beauty, the Hunza valley is the centre-piece of the KKH. In spring everything is green shoots and white blossoms in endless tiers, and autumn is a riot of yellow poplars, reddening orchards and maize drying on rooftops. Above are broad brown mountain sides and, higher yet, the snowy peaks. Snaking across the slopes are Hunza's hallmark: the precision-made stone channels on which its life depends. Carrying water from canyons to fields and orchards as much as eight km away, they have transformed a dry valley with few horizontal surfaces into a breadbasket.

Added to this is a kind of mythology about Hunza's isolation and purity, spawned by James Hilton's 1933 novel *Lost Horizon*, nourished in films about the lost kingdom of Shangri-la, and fostered in the 1970s by media stories of extraordinary health and longevity. The KKH itself has put an end to Hunza's isolation, and while the Garden of

Eden image ignores a rather bloody and disreputable history, this hardly alters its appeal.

'Hunza' is commonly (and inaccurately) used in reference to the entire broad valley below Baltit. Two former princely states, Hunza and Nagar ('NAH-gr'), with a shared language and shared ancestry, face one another across the valley. Hunza, including its one-time satellite, Gojal, extends north and north-east to the Chinese border. The smaller but more populous Nagar occupies the entire south side of the valley and some of the north side near Chalt, and includes 7790 metre Rakaposhi.

Baltit & Karimabad

Baltit has always been the capital of Hunza. It consists mostly of Baltit Fort at the mouth of yawning Ultar Nala, and a compact village at its feet. The fort was the royal palace until the 1940s, when sounder quarters were built below. Karimabad is just a latter-day extension of Baltit with hotels, cafés and a bazar.

Orientation From the KKH, a link road climbs two km up from Ganesh to Karimabad bazar, and another weaves up the valley from west of Aliabad. A branch of the road from Ganesh goes round to Altit village, and another is being cut down to the KKH at Garelt, west of Ganesh. A link road also descends from the Karimabad bazar to Altit, and a track near the Rainbow Hotel leads up to Baltit.

New Hunza Tourist Hotel and Altit's Kisar Inn run free jeep shuttles up from Ganesh. Other jeeps lurking at Ganesh may ask US$5 or more per person, but prices quickly collapse to about US$1.

Information The post office is near the New Hunza Tourist Hotel. Change money at the National Bank of Pakistan. The tiny Hunza Book Centre has some works on local history and culture; there are also some books at the Hilltop Hotel's souvenir shop. There is a small hospital on the road from Ganesh.

Baltit Fort Tibetan-style Baltit Fort, on a throne-like ridge in front of Ultar Nala, was built in its original form 600 to 800 years ago. In about 1900, balconies and interior comforts were added. It was the royal residence until the 1940s, and the mir held his councils on the roof. The fort was near collapse when restoration was begun in the 1980s by a joint British-Pakistani team. It's temporarily closed to the public.

Altit Fort The small fort at Altit, with its carved lintels and window-frames, is older than Baltit's. In front is an apricot orchard, and behind is a vertical 300 metre drop to the Hunza river. It's a three km walk down from Karimabad and across the Ultar stream. An alternative route is via Mominabad. Fort is *gela* ('geh-LAH') in Burushaski.

Channel Walks It's amazing how many irrigation channels come out of a single canyon, and how far they go. A three or four hour walk along the main channels from Ultar Nala is a good way to see Hunza. Try to avoid the more delicate side-channels.

Climb past the polo ground, bearing left beside the channel. The path goes down the valley all the way to Hyderabad Nala. There, scramble down the stream-bed to the link road. Turning back to Karimabad, you can soon drop to another channel that goes all the way back, and go right on around Karimabad to the channel's headworks behind Baltit Fort. There are two more channels above these, and at least two on the other side of the nala.

Melishkar & Duikar These are side-by-side summer villages 300 metres above Altit; Melishkar is said to be Hunza's highest village. The five or six hour round-trip on foot includes a hard, dry climb past gravity-defying terraced fields, offering huge views. Just before reaching Altit's polo ground from Karimabad, branch left for the trail up.

Ultar Nala & Ultar Glacier A climb to the Ultar icefall will give you an appreciation for how vertical things are here. It's a strenuous day trip, or the sort of thing you might want

Baltit & Karimabad

To Hyderabad Nala
To Ultar Glacier

Continued on Inset (Same Scale)

To Hyderabad Nala

Hunza Lodge

Channel

Shops

Handicraft Shops

House

Fort

Baltit

Boys' High School

Polo Ground

Handicraft Shop

Silver Jubilee Hotel

Link Road to Aliabad & KKH

Hunza Book Centre

Rainbow Hotel

Karim Hotel

Continued From Main Map

Post Office

Channel

Channel

Path

Ultar Restaurant

To Altit

Amjad Soup Corner

Aqueduct

Hilltop Hotel

Park Hotel

Karakurum Hotel

Bazar

New Hunza Tourist Hotel

Cemetery

Gate

Rakaposhi View Hotel

Karimabad

Rakaposhi View Hotel

Mir's House

Serena Lodge (proposed)

National Bank of Pakistan

Karimabad Hotel

Hunza Inn

Mountain View Hotel

Hunza Inn

Hospital

Telephone Exchange

To Mominabad & Altit

To KKH at Gareit

To KKH at Ganesh

Baltit & Karimabad

0   50   100 m

to spend longer on. Some people hire a local guide – useful but not necessary.

Enter Ultar Nala from the top of Baltit village and follow a sometimes indistinct trail up the steep moraines. Three to four hours up at the foot of the rumbling icefall is a meadow in an amphitheatre of peaks, including Ultar peak (7388 metres). Until it was scaled in September 1991 by a British team, this was one of the world's highest unclimbed mountains.

Shepherds drive flocks up to the meadow and live in the stone huts all summer. You should ask before camping near their animals. With tea, salt, sugar, cigarettes or matches you might bargain with them for fresh milk *(mamu)*, yoghurt *(dumanu-mamu)*, buttermilk *(diltar)* or cheese *(burus)*.

West, and up from the huts, is a 4500 metre ridge called Hon with incredible views across to Nagar and Rakaposhi – but it takes up to four hours more and probably shouldn't be attempted unless you're staying the night. The ridge is not a technical climb but does require great care.

On the return trip, high water channels look like good trails but they aren't, because they leave you with some dangerous descents, and may pose a rockfall hazard below. If you must use a channel, walk *in* it if you can, so as not to damage it.

Carry water; the glacier's thrashing stream can be hard to approach, and there is no water at Hon. Take extra layers, even on a hot day, against the icy wind off the glacier. Rockfall hazard is high after prolonged rain, high winds or a thaw. In July and August, thunderstorms may roll through.

Places to Stay Among hotels with cheap dorm beds are the *New Hunza Tourist Hotel*, *Karim* and *Silver Jubilee*. These and the *Hunza Lodge*, *Karimabad Hotel*, *Rainbow Hotel* and Altit's friendly *Kisar Inn* also have doubles with toilet in the range of US$4 to US$10, negotiable in the off-season. The *Karim* and *Hunza Lodge* have sunny roofs with a view.

Hotels with cleaner, more comfortable doubles at around US$10 to US$20 include the *Karakurum*, *Park* and group-oriented *Hilltop*. At the upper end are the mir's own *Rakaposhi View Hotel*, with valley views and some rooms with hot showers, and the *Mountain View Hotel*. The concrete megalith opposite the bank will eventually be a four-star *Serena Lodge*.

Places to Eat Hunza food is closer to western food than anything else on the KKH. Typical items are potatoes, rice, daudoh (a noodle soup with vegetables, thickened with egg and whole-wheat flour) and phitti (thick whole-wheat bread). Oil and spices are used sparingly. Milk products include dumanu-mamu and diltar. Kurut is a sour, hard cheese made by boiling and drying diltar.

Most of the Northern Areas' dried fruit comes from here, and dried Hunza apricots are found in bazars all over Asia. There are at least 22 varieties of apricots. Wholesalers sort their apricots on the floor so you should soak them in boiling water to reduce the risk of illness.

Early autumn produce includes peaches, plums, apples, grapes, cherries and walnuts. A great travel snack is dried mulberries. If you're China-bound, Karimabad is the last good place to stock up for the trip.

Despite Muslim prohibition, some people carry on pre-Muslim traditions by brewing a rough grape wine called mel and a potent mulberry firewater called arak. Both are sometimes called 'Hunza water'.

The *New Hunza Tourist Hotel* serves a bargain Hunza-style meal for its guests. Food at the *Park Hotel* is good too. Most other hotels serve up something, usually dreary chicken curry, dhal and boiled potatoes. The best café in the bazar is *Ultar Restaurant*, with meat and vegetables, chips and tasty soup, and Cokes chilled in the stream. *Amjad Soup Corner* serves peppery chicken soup and is a meeting place for local adults, kids and most of the flies in the village.

If you don't like the look of Karimabad's murky water (due to minute flakes of mica), fill your bottle at a safe-to-drink-from clear spring 15 minutes beyond Baltit village on the Ultar trail, just past the channel head-works.

Getting There & Away Minibuses and Ford wagons leave for Gilgit from near Hunza Lodge in the morning, from about 6 am; in summer there are at least three daily. An alternative is to catch the Sust-Gilgit bus at Ganesh.

The cheapest way to Sust is taking whatever you can get at Ganesh, on the Gilgit-Sust bus. From Karimabad you could hire a jeep or van through your hotel.

GILGIT

Gilgit (at 1500 metres) is the hub of the KKH, with services, information, transport and relative luxury. It swarms with travellers, trekkers and climbers from May to October. The scenery is austere and brown, except for spring blossoms and autumn colours, but many nearby glacier-fed valleys above 2000 metres harbour pine and juniper forests and luxuriant meadows.

This is administrative headquarters for Pakistan's 70,000 sq km Northern Areas. For the Pakistan government it's a ticklish place, bordering India, China and Afghanistan, and a stone's throw from Tajikistan. The town is of interest mainly for its people and an eclectic, lively bazar.

Gilgit wakes up early, to muezzins in scores of mosques, calling the faithful to dawn prayers. Except for a few cafés and barbershops, the bazar is dark soon after sunset. There are very few local women on the streets. Foreign women are usually patronised or ignored, but there are stories of low-level sexual harassment, eg in passenger Suzukis after dark.

On the cards is an extension of the airport runway, which will allow jets to land and make the region more accessible for more of the year. Gilgit is on the way to becoming a city, though its infrastructure can't keep up – public services aren't multiplying as fast as hotels, and electricity and water are unreliable and vulnerable to heavy weather.

History

Gilgit, like Kashgar, was a colonial outpost during the Great Game well into the 20th century. A succession of British political agents managed by grace or guile to stay in charge in the wider area called the Gilgit Agency. A local militia, the Gilgit Scouts, was raised; its members dressed in the militia's own tartan.

In the 1930s and 1940s demands mounted both for Indian independence and for a separate Muslim homeland. Britain agreed to split the Raj into two separate countries, a Muslim-majority Pakistan and a Hindu-majority India. An awkward problem was the hundreds of princely states with direct allegiance to Britain, who theoretically stood to regain their original sovereignty. Of these the Muslim state of Kashmir, within which the present Northern Areas lay, was the biggest hot-potato of all; its Hindu maharajah, Hari Singh, stalled, hoping for his own independence.

As the 14 August 1947 date for the end of the empire came and went, Gilgit held its breath. Abruptly, on 26 October, the maharajah fled to Delhi, acceded to India and asked for military help. Within days a pro-Pakistan mob collected in Gilgit from neighbouring valleys, and the Kashmiri governor called the Bunji garrison, south of Gilgit, for help. Alas for him, among the reinforcements was Colonel Mirza Hassan Khan, banished to the Northern Areas for earlier conspiring to seize Kashmir for Pakistan. Meanwhile Major Mohammed Babar Khan of the Gilgit Scouts and several fellow-officers had been hatching their own rebellion. On 1 November Babar Khan arrested the governor and the rebels asked to join Pakistan.

Within a few days the Scouts, and Muslim soldiers of the Kashmiri army, joined an already ongoing war with India. In January 1949 this ended with a United Nations cease-fire. Pakistan was given temporary control over what is now the Northern Areas, plus a slice of western Kashmir. India got Ladakh and the Kashmir valley. The cease-fire line across Kashmir became the de facto border.

WESTERN XINJIANG & KKH

Gilgit

31

To Dainyor & KKH

See Inset

Yadgar Chowk

Shahrah-i-Quaid-i-Azam (Quaid-Azam Road)

To Jutial & KKH

Babar Road

30
29

Chinar Bagh Link Road

28
27
26

Chinar Bagh

32

Airport Road

Airport Chowk

33
34
35
36
37

Abdul Rab Nishtar Road

College Road

Gilgit River

24

25

JSR Plaza

39
38

Shaheed-i-Millat Road

23
22
21
20
19
18
17
16
15
14
13
12
11
10
9
8
7
6
5
4
3
2
1

Cinema Bazar

NLI Barracks

Hunza Chowk

Jamat Khana Bazar

Kashmir Bazar

Saddar Bazar

Gami Bagh

River View Road

Rajah Bazar

Bank Road

Sabzi Mandi

Polo Ground

Punial Road

To Kargah

Old Polo Ground

40

41
42
43

44
45

46

To Barmas

Hospital Road

Bank

Shahrah-i-Quaid-i-Azam (Quaid-Azam Road)

To Bazar

Yadgar Chowk

47

48

49

50

To Jutial & Serena Lodge

To Jutial & KKH

Jutial Road

Shaheed-i-Millat Road

Same Scale as Main Map

0   200   400 m

Memories of the uprising are still alive in Gilgit, and it's not 14 August but 1 November that Gilgit celebrates as Independence Day, with spontaneous music and dancing, and a week-long polo tournament.

Orientation

Gilgit is on the south bank of the Gilgit river, 10 km west of the KKH via the cantonment at Jutial (these tidy military sectors are a colonial holdover in large towns of India and Pakistan). A back road also comes from the KKH at Dainyor village, via bridges over the Hunza and Gilgit rivers.

The bazar is essentially a single two km street full of shops. South-west up Bank Rd are government offices, and further up are several villages, the biggest of which is Barmas. The airport is east of the bazar.

Gilgit is growing east toward Jutial along Quaid-i-Azam Rd. When the airport runway is extended west, traffic from the KKH to the bazar will be deflected down Shaheed-i-Millat Rd and/or east around the airport to River View Rd.

Many larger streets have two names, one common and one official. These include (official name in parentheses) Jamat Khana Bazar (Sir Aga Khan Rd), Bank Rd (Khazana Rd), Hospital Rd (Alama Mohammed Iqbal Rd) and Jutial Rd (Quaid-i-Azam Rd or Shahrah-i-Quaid-i-Azam).

Information

Tourist Offices The Pakistan Tourism Development Corporation (PTDC; ☎ 2562), at the Chinar Inn on Babar Rd, has Northern Areas brochures and can help with bookings and tours.

PTDC and the Aga Khan Rural Support Program have established a 'Village Guest House' homestay programme, in which tourists can book comfortable rooms and good meals in private homes around the Gilgit and

PLACES TO STAY		OTHER	
11	Kashgar Inn	1	Imamla Mosque
12	Mt Balore Motel	4	Jama Mosque
13	Madina Guesthouse	5	Police Post & Foreigners' Registration
17	Skyways Hotel		
19	JSR Hotel	6	Allied Bank
26	PTDC Chinar Inn	7	Habib Bank
27	Hunza Inn	8	Post Office
28	Chinese Lodge	9	Moti Mosque
29	Golden Peak Inn Camping	10	Mohammad Book Stall
30	Hunza Tourist House	14	Mashabrum Tours Bus Yard
33	Park Hotel	18	Cinema
40	New Lahore Hotel	20	PIA Booking Office
47	Golden Peak Inn	21	Pamir Tours
49	North Inn	23	General Bus Stand
50	Tourist Cottage	24	Uprising Memorial
		25	Town Hall
PLACES TO EAT		31	Airport Terminal
		34	Hunza Handicrafts
2	Yoghurt Stall	35	Mountain Movers
3	Turkistan Restaurant	36	Walji's Adventure Pakistan
15	Madina Cafe	37	Xama Shop
16	Pathan Hotel	38	Hunza-Gojal Transport
22	Baig's Restaurant	39	Natco Bus Yard
32	New Tabaq Restaurant	41	National Bank
		42	Library
		43	Gilgit Book Centre
		44	District Hospital
		45	Telephone Exchange
		46	Women's Hospital
		48	Police Headquarters

Hunza valleys; several travellers have written enthusiastically about it. Typical rates for a double with full board are about US$7.

Money The National Bank is off Bank Rd; Habib and Allied banks are in Saddar Bazar. Opening hours are Monday to Thursday from 9 am to 1 pm , and Sunday from 9 to 11 am.

US$ and pound Sterling travellers' cheques or cash are the most acceptable. At a pinch, some merchants will change US$ cash.

Post & Communications The post office is in Saddar Bazar. Opening hours are Saturday through Wednesday from 8 am to 2 pm. A window at the front sells stamps. Poste restante at the rear is also the place to get outgoing mail franked while you wait (to avoid the risk of stamp theft).

You can make overseas calls and send telegrams from the 24 hour telephone exchange in upper Hospital Rd. Some hotels can place calls for you at a higher rate. Gilgit has international direct-dialling (IDD); its telephone code is 0572. The Serena Lodge (fax 2525) will send and accept faxes.

Travel Agencies You don't need a guide unless you're trekking, though the surrounding area is full of remote valleys where hikes are easier with a locally known person who speaks some English. Agencies have multiplied like rabbits. Old ones like Mohammad Book Stall (now also called Adventure Centre) in Jamat Khana Bazar (☎ 2409), and Pamir Tours in JSR Plaza (☎ 3939), use local guides and can accommodate low-budget customers. Guides for up-scale outfits like Walji's Adventure Pakistan on Airport Rd (☎ 3848) are reliable and speak English well but don't always know local valleys.

Many hotel wallahs are quite knowledgeable about the surrounding valleys. Latif Anwar of the Golden Peak Inn on Quaid-i-Azam Rd has his own agency, Golden Peak Tours (☎ 3685). The Hunza Inn on Abdul Rab Nishtar Rd has good trekking information, guides and transport services.

Some agencies and hotels also rent equipment (though sleeping bags are scarce). Hunza Handicrafts, by the Park Hotel, occasionally has sleeping mats, stoves, clothing and climbing gear for rent or sale.

Bookshops The Northern Areas' best known shop is Mohammad Book Stall (☎ 2409) in Jamat Khana Bazar, with hard-to-find books on the region plus postcards and newspapers. Near the library is the Gilgit Book Centre, specialising in Northern Areas literature. Hunza Handicrafts, by the Park Hotel, has books among the curios and camping gear. The bookshop at the Serena Lodge is said to have a good selection of trekking maps.

Hospitals The district hospital is on upper Hospital Rd. Nearby is a women's hospital, with female doctors. Foreign women can go to either, though the district hospital apparently has more specialists.

Places to Stay

Bottom-end best bets are the cheap dorm beds at *Tourist Cottage, Golden Peak Inn, Hunza Inn, Chinese Lodge* and *Madina Guesthouse*. Tourist Cottage (☎ 2376), three km out on Quaid-i-Azam Rd, also has doubles with shower for about US$3, a garden and good cheap dinners (see the Places to Eat section).

Madina Guesthouse by the NLI barracks, with tea on arrival, basic doubles with shower for about US$5 and good food, is a popular place; but word is that they will be moving to a new site closer to the river. Other good bottom-end options (with rooms for about US$2 to US$4 per bed, and gardens) are the Golden Peak Inn (☎ 3538) on Quaid-i-Azam Rd and the Hunza Inn (☎ 2814) on Abdul Rab Nishtar Rd. In the same range are the Chinese Lodge on Chinar Bagh Link Rd, the noisy *Kashgar Inn* on Cinema Bazar and *New Lahore Hotel* (☎ 3327) on lower Hospital Rd.

In the middle range with more comfortable rooms (about US$5 to US$10 per bed) are the Hunza Inn again; the *Mt Balore Motel*

(☎ 2709), in a quiet garden behind a wall right in the middle of town; *Skyways Hotel* and *JSR Hotel* (☎ 3971) at JSR Plaza; and the huge *Park Hotel* (☎ 2379) on Airport Rd. At the top of the range but good value are the well-run *Hunza Tourist House* (☎ 2338, 3788) on Babar Rd, and *North Inn* (☎ 2887) on Quaid-i-Azam Rd.

PTDC's *Chinar Inn* (☎ 2562) on Abdul Rab Nishtar Rd has mid-range rooms for top-end prices. In Jutial, the posh *Serena Lodge* (☎ 2330, 2331) may not be the place for budget travellers to stay but, with free videos, all-you-can-eat buffet dinners and a free shuttle bus, it might be a good place to visit.

Places to Eat

Hygiene can be problematic if you have to eat with your fingers or scraps of chapatti, but even the lowliest place has a washstand, and something on the menu that's steaming hot. A bigger risk is drinking tap water from communal tumblers.

Vegetarians can get by, but meatless fare tends to be dreary. Some hotels will stir something up by request, especially if you bring the ingredients.

Cafés & Snacks Gilgit's most visible old eatery is the *Pathan Hotel* in Cinema Bazar, its back room full of men tucking into chapli kebabs (mutton-burgers) and other Pathan favourites. Highly recommended is half a braised chicken (karahi murgi). Friendly *Madina Cafe* in Cinema Bazar has Pakistani and western items. Beside the alley into the Mashabrum Tours bus yard is a nameless café offering only karahi gosht – mutton braised with vegetables, served in its own pan (and thus very hygienic).

Hotels Madina Guesthouse and Tourist Cottage cook their guests good communal dinners for about US$1.50. Hunza Tourist House has good but pricey Pakistani and Chinese dishes. The JSR Hotel and Park Hotel both have clean restaurants with ho-hum food. Serena Lodge has expensive all-you-can-eat buffets on Monday, Wednesday and Friday, but the food is first class.

Restaurants Opposite JSR Plaza is *Baig's Restaurant* – gloomy but clean, with good Pakistani dishes. The *New Tabaq Restaurant* on Chinar Bagh Link Rd has meaty Pakistani and Chinese dishes. In the vegetable market by Jama mosque is the *Turkistan Restaurant*, a cavernous medium-clean local hang-out which serves greasy food.

Self-Catering The stands on Airport Rd sell fruit and vegetables, especially in the evening. A vegetable market (sabzi mandi) is along the west side of Jama mosque. Apricot season is July and early August. The best dried apricots are in the small general stores. Apples, pomegranates, walnuts and Gilgit's own peaches appear in autumn.

Fresh nan is sold right out of the tandoor ovens in the sabzi mandi and elsewhere, but it disappears soon after 7 am. You can find yoghurt (dahi) in a stall at the back of the sabzi mandi. Numerous general stores have sweets, jam, cornflakes, long-life milk and tinned processed cheese.

Entertainment

The Serena Lodge screens western videos for free on most evenings at 5.30 and 8.30 pm, and provides a free shuttle service (see Getting Around).

Things to Buy

A Northern Areas bargain is the coarse, durable wool (patti or pattu) of Hunza and Nagar. Handicraft shops around Hunza Chowk have hats, waistcoats and embroidered cloaks called choghas, though some are of cheap, machine-woven wool and some shopkeepers will tell you anything. Good hand-made wool is thick and tight with an uneven grain. Brown and white are best, as colours fade quickly. Try the smaller shops of Jamat Khana Bazar, Rajah Bazar, Bank Rd and Punial Rd.

The Xama shop in Airport Rd has a great collection of old jewellery, rugs and flint-locks. A few curios and antiques are among the books at Mohammad Book Stall in Jamat Khana Bazar and at Hunza Handicrafts on Airport Rd.

Getting There & Away

Air The PIA booking office is in JSR Plaza in Cinema Bazar. The spectacular daily flights over the mountains to Islamabad and Skardu are very weather-dependent, so all bookings are on a standby basis. Confirm by leaving your ticket at PIA by 12.30 pm on the day before you're scheduled to go. At 2 pm they give it back and tell you the check-in time. The decision to fly is only made next morning. From Gilgit, a left-side seat on the 1¼ hour Islamabad flight looks out at Nanga Parbat. You may have to book ahead a month or more in summer.

An upcoming 600 metre runway extension will allow jets to land here even in cloudy weather.

Bus, Wagon & Van Long-distance operators are NATCO and Hunza-Gojal Transport on Airport Rd, Mashabrum Tours in Cinema Bazar, Sargin Travel at the JSR Hotel and Hamid Travel at the Skyways Hotel. The general bus stand, up a link road from JSR Plaza, has buses and wagons for Hunza-Nagar, but much regional transport tends to start where people from outlying towns have shops – eg Jamat Khana Bazar for Hunza and lower Bank Rd for Nagar. There is talk of a future NATCO station at Jutial.

To Rawalpindi This takes 14 to 17 hours. Mashabrum's comfortable small buses depart at 11 am, 3.30 and 7 pm. Sargin and Hamid Travel also have vans. NATCO's clunkers go at 4 and 9 am, and 1, 6 and 9 pm, with a 50% student discount on all except the 9 am 'deluxe' run. These times may vary with the season. Buy tickets the day before if possible.

To Sust A NATCO bus goes to Sust at 8 am; the trip takes four to five hours. Hunza-Gojal Transport also runs several vans to Sust and others to intermediate points. In the mornings, wagons go directly from Jamat Khana

Bazar to Karimabad, and from lower Bank Rd to Nagar.

Getting Around

Passenger Suzukis leave from near the post office and travel through the bazar to Jutial (Serena Lodge); others go to Dainyor. They can be flagged down anywhere, though they don't run much after dark. They're a few rupees. To signal a stop while you're riding, stomp on the floor. Suzukis also run west from Punial Rd.

Serena Lodge runs a free pick-up and return service from Hunza Chowk at 6.20 pm, near Hunza Inn at 6.30 and near the Park Hotel at 6.45, and up to the Serena. It heads back at 9 and 10.45 pm. It's not restricted to the Serena's overnight guests.

Jeep Rental For jeep rental see the agencies listed under Travel Agencies, or Mountain Movers or the Xama shop in Airport Rd, or your hotel-wallah. It's worth shopping around.

Bicycles Bikes can be hired by the hour (sometimes plus a security deposit) from shops near Hunza Chowk and Yadgar Chowk, from the Hunza Inn and elsewhere.

AROUND GILGIT
Kargah Buddha & Kargah Nala

A large standing Buddha carved on a cliff-face in Kargah Nala, west of Gilgit, may date from the 7th century. From Punial Rd catch a Suzuki toward Baseen and get off at Kargah (or it's a five km hike). Ten minutes' walk up the left side of Kargah Nala is a gully called Shuko Gah (*gah* means tributary valley in Shina), and the Buddha is high above this gully. On up Shuko Gah is Napur village, the ruins of a monastery and stupa, and a cave where Buddhist birch-bark texts (now called the Gilgit Manuscripts) were found in the 1930s. Cave is *kor* in Shina, and *gufa* in Urdu.

A return option with good valley views is to continue on this high path to Barmas village, and then back down into Gilgit; this takes about two hours.

Jutial Nala

The Gilgit valley is actually rather grand, but it's impossible to appreciate it from town. A fairly easy hike from Jutial along a high water channel gives a fine panorama of the valley, plus Rakaposhi and other peaks.

Take a Jutial Suzuki from Saddar Bazar to the end of the line, below Serena Lodge. Half a km uphill past the Serena, turn right and then left up the nala. Climb till you see a stream going off to the right – the headworks of the water channel. At Barmas village, near some water tanks, descend on Hospital Rd back into Gilgit. From the Serena to the bazar takes under two hours. A variation is to climb into Jutial Nala; it's two hours up to pine forests and excellent Rakaposhi views.

If there have been more than a few hours of rain in recent days, *stay away*, as the hillsides are very prone to rockslides.

Language Guide

Central Asia is a multilingual area, and so this chapter includes words and phrases from 10 different languages which you may find useful. The official languages of the former Soviet Central Asian countries are Kazak, Kyrgyz, Tajik, Turkmen and Uzbek, but Russian is still the language of government and academia (rather like English in India). Therefore the one language most useful for a visitor is still Russian, which most adults understand since it used to be everyone's second language studied in school. A few words of the local language will nonetheless give a disproportionate return in goodwill. At home, educated people normally speak a mishmash of Russian and their native tongue.

If you can read Russian Cyrillic characters, you already know most of every Central Asian Cyrillic-based alphabet too. Knowing how to count in local languages will allow you to listen in on discussions of prices in the markets. In public it is now often worthwhile letting non-Russians know in advance that you're not Russian, either by saying so or by starting out in English.

The largest portion of this language section is devoted to Russian. Useful words and phrases in Tajik, Uzbek, Kazak, Kyrgyz and Turkmen are also given in the table on page 523. There are also tables of the Cyrillic letters you may encounter in street signs and maps.

We also include smaller phrase lists for Mandarin Chinese (the most useful tongue in Xinjiang) and Uyghur (also Xinjiang) as well as Urdu, Wakhi, Burushaski and Shina (Pakistan), the languages of the Karakoram Highway. As a result, this is probably the most multilingual travel guidebook ever!

USEFUL BOOKS

Look out for Lonely Planet's *Central Asian phrasebook* due to be published in December 1996. Some marginally useful, locally produced phrasebooks are available here and there, eg the English-Russian-Kazak *Welcome to Kazakhstan Phrasebook*, which will help you confidently assert: 'Alma-Ata's vast concrete clad landing field lands up to 3000 passengers a day' and even 'We would gladly go to Mangyshlak'. For the serious student, Russian Information Services (within the USA and Canada ☎(800) 639-4301, fax (802) 223-6105), 89 Main St, Suite 2, Montpelier, VT 05602, USA, offers *Colloquial Uzbek* and *Colloquial Kazakh* audio cassettes.

RUSSIAN

Russian has no 'a' or 'the'. The verb 'to be' commonly drops out of simple sentences – eg 'I am an American' (male) is я – американец *(ya uh-mi-ri-KAHN-yits)*. Russians also don't normally use the verb 'to have'. Instead they use the preposition у, which means 'at' or 'by', with a special form of the pronoun: eg 'I have' is у меня *(u min-YA)*, literally 'by me (is)'.

Questions

The easiest way to turn a statement into a question is just to say it with a rising tone and a questioning look, or follow it with a quizzical *da?* – eg 'is this Moscow?', это Москва, да? *(EH-ta mahsk-VA, da?)*.

Negation

A sentence is made negative by putting не before its main word, eg 'this is not Moscow', это не Москва *(EH-ta nye mahsk-VA)*.

Essentials

Two words you're sure to use during your travels are Здравствуйте *('ZDRAST-vooy-tyeh')*, the universal 'hello' (but if you say it a second time in one day to the same person, they'll think you forgot you already saw them!), and Пожалуйста *('pa-ZHAHL-stuh')*, the multipurpose word for 'please' (commonly included in all polite requests), 'you're welcome', 'pardon me', 'after you' and more.

Russian Cyrillic Letters

Letter	Transliteration	Pronunciation
А, а	*a*	like the 'a' in 'father' (if in a stressed syllable) like the 'a' in 'about' (if in an unstressed syllable)
Б, б	*b*	like the 'b' in 'but'
В, в	*v*	like the 'v' in 'van'
Г, г	*g*	like the 'g' in 'god'
Д, д	*d*	like the 'd' in 'dog'
Е, е	*e**	like the 'ye' in 'yet' (if in a stressed syllable) like the 'yi' in 'yin' (if in an unstressed syllable)
Ё, ё**	*yo*	like the 'yo' in 'yore'
Ж, ж	*zh*	like the 's' in 'measure'
З, з	*z*	like the 'z' in 'zoo'
И, и	*i*	like the 'ee' in 'meet'
Й, й	*y*	like the 'y' in 'boy'
К, к	*k*	like the 'k' in 'kind'
Л, л	*l*	like the 'l' in 'lamp'
М, м	*m*	like the 'm' in 'mad'
Н, н	*n*	like the 'n' in 'not'
О, о	*o*	like the 'o' in 'more' (if in a stessed syllable) like the 'a' in 'hard' (if in an unstressed syllable)
П, п	*p*	like the 'p' in 'pig'
Р, р	*r*	like the 'r' in 'rub' (but rolled)
С, с	*s*	like the 's' in 'sing'
Т, т	*t*	like the 't' in 'ten'
У, у	*u*	like the 'oo' in 'fool'
Ф, ф	*f*	like the 'f' in 'fan'
Х, х	*kh*	like the 'ch' in 'Bach'
Ц, ц	*ts*	like the 'ts' in 'bits'
Ч, ч	*ch*	like the 'ch' in 'chin'
Ш, ш	*sh*	like the 'sh' in 'shop'
Щ, щ	*shch*	like the 'sh ch' in 'fresh chips'
ъ	(no symbol)	('hard sign'; see below)
Ы, ы	*y*	like the 'i' in 'ill'
ь	(no symbol)	('soft sign'; see below)
Э, э	*e*	like the 'e' in 'end'
Ю, ю	*yu*	like the 'u' in 'use'
Я, я	*ya*	like the 'ya' in 'yard' (if in a stressed syllable) like the 'ye' in 'yearn' (if in an unstressed syllable)

* The Cyrillic letter Е, е is transliterated *Ye, ye* when at the beginning of a word in Russian
** The Cyrillic letter Ё, ё is often printed without dots in Russian
Two letters have no sound but only modify others. A consonant followed by the 'soft sign' ь is spoken with the tongue flat against the palate, as if followed by the faint beginnings of a '*y*'. The rare 'hard sign' ъ after a consonant inserts a slight pause before the next vowel.

Greetings & Civilities
Hello.
 ZDRAST-vooy-tyeh Здравствуйте.
Goodbye.
 das-fi-DA-nya До свидания.
How are you?
 kak dyi-LAH Как дела?
I am well.
 kha-ra-SHOH хорошо
Yes/No.
 da/nyet Да/Нет.
Thank you (very much).
 spuh-SEE-ba Спасибо (большое).
 (bal-SHOY-uh)
What's your name?
 kahk vahs Как вас зовут?
 za-VOOT
My name is...
 min-YA za-VOOT Меня зовут...

Where are you from?
 aht-KUH-dah vi? Откуда вы?
Australia
 uf-STRAH-li-uh Австралия
Canada
 ka-NA-duh Канада
France
 FRAHN-tsi-yuh Франция
Germany
 gehr-MAH-ni-yuh Германия
Ireland
 eer-LAHN-di-yuh Ирландия
New Zealand
 NOH-vuh-yuh Новая Зеландия
 zyeh-LAHN-di-yuh
the UK (Great Britain)
 vi-LEE-ka-bri- Великобритания
 TA-ni-uh
USA, America
 seh sheh ah, США, Америка
 uh-MYEH-ri-kuh

good/OK
 kha-ra-SHOH хорошо
bad
 PLOH-kha плохо

Language Difficulties
I don't speak Russian.
 ya nye ga-var-YU pa-RU-ski
 Я не говорю по-русски.

I don't understand.
 ya nye pah-ni-MAH-yu
 Я не понимаю.
Do you speak English?
 vih ga-var-EE-tyeh pa-an-GLEE-ski
 Вы говорите по-английски?
Could you write it down, please?
 zuh-pi-SHEE-tyeh, pa-ZHAHL-stuh
 Запишите, пожалуйста.

Transport & Travel
Where is...?
 gdyeh Где...?
airport
 ah-EH-ra-port аэропорт
bus
 uf-TOH-boos автобус
railway station
 zhi-LYEZ-nuh железно
 da-ROHZH-ni дорожный
 vahg-ZAHL (ж. д.) вокзал
train
 PO-yest поезд

When does it leave?
 kug-DA aht-li-TA-yit
 Когда отлетает?
What town is this?
 kuh-KOY EH-tut GOR-ut
 Какой этот город?

hotel
 gus-TEE-nit-suh гостиница
square/plaza
 PLOH-shchut площадь (пл.)
street
 OO-leet-suh улица (ул.)
toilet
 tu-ah-LYET туалет

Food
restaurant
 ri-sta-RAHN ресторан
café
 ka-FYEH кафе
canteen
 sta-LO-vuh-yuh столовая
bill
 schyot счёт
bread
 khlep хлеб

rice
  rees   рис
water
  va-DAH   вода
boiled water
  ki-pya-TOHK   кипяток
tea
  chai   чай
meat
  MYA-suh   мясо
I can't eat meat.
  ya ni yem myis-NOH-va
  Я не ем мясного.

Money & Shopping
How much is it?
  SKOL-ka STO-eet   Сколько стоит?
Do you have...?
  u VAHS   У вас...?

money
  DYEN-gi   деньги
currency exchange
  ahb-MYEHN   обмен валюты
  vahl-YU-tuh
shop
  muh-guh-ZYIN   магазин
bookshop
  KNEEZH-ni   книжный магазин
  muh-guh-ZYIN
market
  RIH-nuk   рынок
pharmacy
  up-TYEK-a   аптека

Numbers
How many?
  SKOL-ka   Сколько?
zero
  nohl   ноль
one
  ah-DYIN   один
two
  dva   два
three
  tree   три
four
  chi-TIR-yeh   четыре
five
  pyaht   пять

six
  shest   шесть
seven
  syem   семь
eight
  VO-syim   восемь
nine
  DYEV-yut   девять
10
  DYES-yut   десять
20
  DVAHT-sut   двадцать
30
  TREET-sut   тридцать
40
  SO-ruk   сорок
50
  pi-dis-YAHT   пятьдесят
60
  shiz-dis-YAHT   шестьдесят
70
  SYEM-dis-yit   семьдесят
80
  VO-sim-dis-yit   восемьдесят
90
  di-vyi-NOH-sta   девяносто
100
  stoh   сто
1000
  TIH-suh-chuh   тысяча

Time, Days & Dates
Dates are given as day-month-year, with the month usually in Roman numerals. Days of the week are often represented by numbers in timetables; Monday is 1.

when?
  kahg-DA   когда?
today
  si-VOHD-nyuh   сегодня
yesterday
  fchi-RA   вчера
tomorrow
  ZAHF-truh   завтра

Monday
  pa-ni-DEL-nik   понедельник
Tuesday
  FTOR-nik   вторник

Wednesday	
sri-DA	среда
Thursday	
chit-VERK	четверг
Friday	
PYAT-nit-suh	пятница
Saturday	
su-BOHT-uh	суббота
Sunday	
vas-kri-SEN-yuh	воскресенье

Emergencies

I need a doctor.	
mnyeh NU-zhin vrahch	Мне нужен врач.
hospital	
BOHL-nit-suh	больница
police	
mi-LEET-si-yuh	милиция
Fire!	
pa-ZHAR	Пожар!
Help!	
na POH-mushch or	На помощь! or
pa-ma-GEET-yeh	Помогите!
Thief!	
vor	Вор!

KAZAK

Kazak is a Turkic language. Since 1940 it has been written in a 42-letter version of the Cyrillic alphabet. Most of the alphabet is identical to Russian Cyrillic, however there are a few different letters, shown in the table below. Kazakstan has no plans to go over to Roman script in the near future.

At least as many people in Kazakstan speak Russian as Kazak. Political tension over language issues has been rather neatly sidestepped by making Kazak the official state language, but permitting the majority language in local regions to be used in written government business there, and giving Russian national language status as 'language of inter-ethnic communication'.

Russian is the first language for some urban Kazaks as well as the large Russian minority who form about 35% of the population. Many Kazaks speak Russian well, even when Kazak is their first language. Only in some small Kazak towns and villages are you likely to have to look at all to find someone who speaks Russian. On the other hand, very few Russians speak Kazak.

Few people speak English or other western languages, but many of those who do tend to work in the tourist industry or with foreigners, so you'll very likely run into some of them, especially in Almaty.

Street signs are sometimes in Kazak, sometimes in Russian, sometimes in both. In this book we use the language you're most likely to come across in each town.

KYRGYZ

Kyrgyz is a Turkic language which has also been transliterated using a Cyrillic script since the early 1940s. Many of the letters are the same as the Russian Cyrillic script, with a few exceptions shown in the Kyrgyz Cyrillic Letters table on the next page.

Kazak Cyrillic Letters		
Letter	**Transliteration**	**Pronunciation**
Ә, ә	*a*	like the 'a' in 'man'
Ғ, ғ	*gh*	like the 'gh' in 'ugh'
Қ, қ	*q*	guttural 'k' like the 'q' in 'Iraq'
Ө, ө	*ö*	like the 'eu' in 'bleu'
Ұ, ұ	*u*	like the 'u' in 'full'
Ү, ү	*ü*	like the 'oo' in 'fool'
I, i	*i*	like the 'i' in 'ill'
Ң, ң	*n*	like the 'ng' in 'sing'
h, h	*h*	like the 'h' in 'hat'

Kyrgyz Cyrillic Letters		
Letter	Transliteration	Pronunciation
Ж, ж	j	like the 'j' in 'jail'
И, и	i	like the 'i' in 'bit'
Ң, ң	ng	like the 'ng' in 'sing'
О, о	o	like the 'o' in 'wrong'
Ө, ө	ö	like the 'eu' in 'bleu'
Ү, ү	ü	like the 'ew' in 'few'

Along with neighbouring Uzbekistan and Turkmenistan, Kyrgyzstan is in the process of changing over to a modified Roman alphabet. While international Roman letters have already been adopted for vehicle number plates, Kyrgyzstan is the slowest of these three countries in implementing the change from Cyrillic to Roman letters.

TAJIK

Tajik, the state language of Tajikistan since 1989, belongs to the south-west Iranian group of languages and is closely related to Farsi. This sets it apart from all the other Central Asian languages which are Turkic in origin.

In Dushanbe most people speak Tajik and Russian. Uzbek is also spoken by a significant number of the population.

There is constant mention of Russian being in decline, but we didn't find this to be the case. In the whole of our travels we never met a single person who didn't speak Russian – just as we almost never met a single person who spoke English.

Tajik was formerly written in a modified Arabic script and then in Roman, but since 1940 a modified Cyrillic script has been used. The letters which are different from the Russian Cyrillic script are listed in the Tajik Cyrillic Letters table below.

Under the short-lived IRP-led government there was an attempt to re-introduce the Arabic alphabet. A few shop signs appeared in it (some of which can still be seen) but they were completely incomprehensible to the majority of the population. There is now talk of switching to a Roman alphabet, but this is unlikely to happen because, linguistically, it would take Tajiks out of the sphere of their greatest benefactors, the Russians.

TURKMEN

Turkmen, the state language of Turkmenistan since 1990, has been described as '800-year old Turkish'. It belongs to the south-western group of Turkic languages together with the Turkish spoken in Turkey and Azerbaijan. In Turkmenistan virtually everyone speaks Russian and Turkmen (except for Russians who just speak Russian). Very few people speak English,

Tajik Cyrillic Letters		
Letter	Transliteration	Pronunciation
Ғ, ғ	gh	like the 'gh' in 'ugh'
Й, й	ee	*like the 'ee' in 'fee'*
Қ, қ	q	like the 'k' in 'keen'
Ӯ, ӯ	ö	like the 'eu' in 'bleu'
Х, х	kh	like the 'h' in 'hat'
Ҷ, ҷ	j	like 'j' in 'jig'

Turkmen Cyrillic Letters

Letter	Transliteration	Pronunciation
Г, г	g	like a Parisian rolled 'r', except at the beginning of a word where it is a hard 'g' as in 'get'
Х, х	h	like the 'h' in 'hat'
Ә, ә	a	like the 'a' in 'cinema'
Ж, ж	j	like 'j' in 'jump'
Ң, ң	n	soft 'n' hardly sounded
Ө, ө	ö	like the 'eu' in 'bleu'
Ү, ү	ü	like the 'ew' in 'few'

Turkmen Roman Alphabet

Aa	Bb	Çç	Dd	Ee
Ää	Ff	Gg	Hh	Ii
Jj	Ɉ̗	Kk	Ll	Mm
Nn	Ññ	Oo	Öö	Pp
Rr	Ss	Şç	Tt	Uu
Üü	Ww	Yy	Ÿÿ	Zz

usually only those in the tourist industry and some university students.

There's been a significant infiltration of Russian words and phrases into Turkmen, especially with the vocabulary which has arisen this century (words to do with science and technology particularly). Native-tongue Turkmen conversation is punctuated with Russian, to the extent that sentences will begin in Turkmen, then slip into Russian midway through. Turkmen seems a less complex language than either Kazak or Uzbek.

Three different scripts have been used to transliterate Turkmen; Arabic, Roman and Cyrillic. Arabic was the first, though little Turkmen was ever written in it (there's a popular style of calligraphy, often used on monuments, in which Cyrillic script is rendered in such a way that it almost resembles Arabic script). A modified Turkish Roman alphabet was introduced in 1940. The Turkmen Cyrillic is identical to its Russian progenitor but with the addition of five supplementary characters and two sound modifications shown in the table opposite. From 1 January 1996, theoretically, Turkmen Cyrillic will be replaced by a newly created, modified Turkmen Roman alphabet. Posters like that shown opposite are widespread, but few people know this script yet.

UZBEK

Uzbekistan has three major languages – Uzbek, Russian and Tajik. Uzbek is a Turkic language and is the official language of Uzbekistan, and with 15 million speakers it is the most widely spoken of the non-Slavic languages of the former Soviet Union. Uzbekistan has been the most publicly anti-Russian of the Central Asian countries, virtually eliminating the language from public view in things like street signs and transport timetables, in favour of written Uzbek, which will often drive you to distraction unless you happen to understand Uzbek. The US vice-consul in Tashkent figured it would be the year 2000 before most urban people were accustomed to the Uzbek names for everything, and perhaps longer in Tajik-speaking Samarkand and Bukhara.

Uzbek was written in Roman letters from 1918 to 1941. Since then it has used a modified Cyrillic script, which differs from the Russian script by only a few letters which are included in the table below.

Uzbekistan (like Kyrgyzstan and Turkmenistan) is gradually changing over to a Roman script in order to align itself more closely with Turkey, and gain better access to western markets.

MANDARIN CHINESE

Mandarin (or *putonghua*, 'people's speech') is China's official language, the dialect of Beijing and the language of bureaucrats. Basic spoken Mandarin is surprisingly easy: no conjugations, no declensions, word order like English – just string them together. The hard parts are tones and pronunciation. A given sound has many meanings depending on its tone. However with common phrases you will probably be understood even if you get the tones wrong. Syllables aren't stressed strongly. Mainland China's official Romanised

Uzbek Cyrillic Letters		
Letter	**Transliteration**	**Pronunciation**
Г, ғ	gh	like the 'gh' in 'ugh'
Ж, ж	j	like the 'j' in 'jail'
И, и	i	like the 'i' in 'bit'
К, қ	q	guttural 'k' like the 'q' in 'Iraq'
О, о	o	like the 'o' in 'wrong'
Ӯ, ӯ	u	like the 'oo' in 'book'
Х, х	kh	like the 'ch' in 'Bach'
Х, х	h	like the 'h' in 'hat'

'alphabet' of Chinese sounds is called Pinyin. It's very streamlined, but the sounds aren't always self-evident. The letters that don't sound quite like English are as follows:

Consonants

q (flat 'ch'); x (flat 'sh'); zh ('j'); z ('dz'); c ('ts'); r (tongue rolled back, almost 'z').

Vowels

a ('ah'); er ('ar', American pronunciation); ui ('oi' or 'wei'); iu ('yoh'); ao ('ow' as in 'now'); ou ('ow' as in 'low'); e ('uh') after consonants; ian ('yen'); ong ('oong'); u ('oo', or sometimes like 'ü': say 'ee' with your mouth rounded as if to say 'oo').

Useful Words & Phrases

Hello.	ni hao
Goodbye.	zaijian
Thank you.	xie xie
Where is (the toilet)?	(cesuo) zai na li?
How much is it ?	duo-shao qian?
Do you speak English?	ni shuo yingyü ma?
I can't speak Mandarin.	wo bu hui shuo putonghua
I don't understand.	wo ting bu dong
Do you understand?	ni dong ma?
bicycle	zixingche
bus (station)	qiche (zhan)
airport	feiji chang

train (station)	huoche (zhan)
I'm sick.	wo shengbingle
hospital	yiyuan
police	jingsha
Fire!	huozai!
Help!	jiuming a!
Thief!	xiaotou!

1	yi
2	er
3	san
4	si (sih)
5	wu
6	liu (lyoh)
7	qi (chee)
8	ba
9	jiu (jyoh)
10	shi (shr)

UYGHUR, URDU & THE LANGUAGES OF THE KARAKORAM HIGHWAY

Uyghur is spoken all over Xinjiang and in parts of Kyrgyzstan and Uzbekistan. In China, written Uyghur uses an Arabic script, although for a time children were taught a Romanised alphabet. Urdu is the national language of Pakistan. It sounds much like Hindi, the speech of north India, but is written in a modified Arabic script. Wakhi, a dialect of Tajik or Persian, is spoken in Gojal. Burushaski is the language of Hunza, and most of Nagar, and Shina is the speech of lower Nagar and Gilgit.

Uyghur, Urdu & the Languages of the Karakoram Highway

English	Uyghur	Urdu	Wakhi	Burushaski	Shina
Peace be with you.	asalam aleykum	asalam aleykum	asalam aleykum	asalam aleykum	asalam aleykum
Goodbye.	khayr kosh	khuda hafiz	khudar hafiz	khuda hafiz	khuda hafiz
How much?	neech pul?	kitna rupia?	tsumar?	besan gash bila?	–
Where is ...?	...khayerdeh?	... keddar heh?	...komar thei?	–	–
Thank you.	rakhmat	shukria	shukria	shukria	shukria
Yes/No.	owa/jyok	ha/nai	–	ju/baya	awah/neh
I don't understand.	bil mei men	me nahin samajta	majeh neh disht	o dayalam	mei hir nawato
Excuse me.	kechur siz	mafki-ji	–	–	–

Languages of Central Asia

English	Tajik	Uzbek	Kazak	Kyrgyz	Turkmen
Peace be with you.	assalom u aleykum	asalom u alaykhum	asalam aleykum	salam aleykum	salam aleykum
Hello.	salom	salom	salamatsyz ba?	salam	salam
Goodbye.	khayr naboshad	hayr	qosh-sau bolyngdar	jakshy kalyngydzar	sagh bol
Thank you	rakhmat/ teshakkur	rakhmat	rakhmet	rakhmat	tangyr
Yes/ No.	kha/ ne	kha/ yuk	ia/ zhoq	ova/ jok	howa/ yok
How are you?	naghzmi shumo?	qanday siz?	khal zhagh-dayyngyz qalay	jakshysüzbü?	–
I am well.	mannaghz	–	zhaqsy	jakshy	–
Do you speak English?	anglisi meydonet?	inglizcha bila sizmi?	aghylshynsa bilesiz be?	siz angliyscha süylöy süzbü?	–
I don't understand.	man manefakhmam	–	tusinbeymin	men tüshümböy jatamyn	men dushenamok
police	militsia	militsia	militsia	militsia	militsia
doctor	duhtur	tabib	dariger	doktur	lukman
hospital	bemorhona/ kasalhona	kasalhona	aurukhana	oruukana	keselkhana
bus station	istgoh	avtobeket	avtobus vokzal	avtobiket	durolha
train station	istgoh rohi ohan	temir yul vokzali	temir zhol vokzal	temir jol vokzal	vokzal
airport	furudgoh	tayyorgokh	aeroport	aeroport	aeroport
toilet	khojat'hona	hojat'hona	azhetkhana	darakana	hajat'hana
friend	doost	urmoq/doost	dos	dos	dost
good	khub/naghz	yakhshi	zhaqsy	jakshy	yakhsheh
bad	ganda	yomon	zhaman	jaman	ervet
Where is...?	... khujo ast?	... qayerda?	... qayda?	... kayda?	... niredeh?
How much?	chand pul?	qancha?, or nichpul?	qansha?	kancha?	nyacheh?
hotel	mekhmon'hona	mehmon'hona	qonaq uy/ meymankhana	meymankana	mikmankhana
restaurant	restoran	restoran	restoran	restoran	restoran
tea	choy	choy	shay	chay	chay
expensive	qimmat	qimmat	qymbat	kymbat	gummut
bread	non	non	nan	nan	churek
boiled water	obi jush	qaynatilgan suv	qaynaghan su	ysyk suu	gaina d'lan su
rice	birinj	guruch	kurish	kürüch	tui
meat	gusht	gusht	yet	et	et
1, 2	yak, du	bir, ikki	bir, yeki	bir, eki	bir, ikeh
3, 4	seh, chor	uch, turt	ush, tört	üch, tört	uch, durt
5, 6	panj, shish	besh, olti	bes, alty	besh, alty	besh, alty
7, 8	khaft, khasht	etti, sakkiz	zheti, segiz	jety, segiz	yedi, sekiz
9, 10	nukh, dakh	tuqqiz, un	toghyz, on	toguz, on	dokuz, on
100	sad	yuz	zhus	jüz	yuz
1000	khazor	ming	myng	ming	mun
Monday	dushanbe	dushanba	duysenbi	düshömbü	dushanbe
Tuesday	seshanbe	seyshanba	seysenbi	seyshembi	seshenbe
Wednesday	chorshanbe	chorshanba	sarsenbi	sharshembi,	charshanbe,
Thursday	panjanbe	payshanba	beysenbi	beishembi	penshenbe
Friday	juma	juma	zhuma	juma	anna
Saturday	shanbe	shanba	senbi	ishembi	shenbe
Sunday	yakshanbe	yakshanba	zheksenbi	jekshembi	yekshanbe

Glossary

ABBREVIATIONS
R – Russian
T – all the Turkic languages
A – Arabic

administrator – general word for chief or manager
aeroport – airport (R)
aerovokzal – airport bus station (R)
ak kalpak – felt hat worn by Kyrgyz men
aksakal – revered elder (Uzbek)
alakiz – Kyrgyz felt rug with coloured panels pressed on
alangy – public square (Kazak)
Ali Majlis – Uzbek Supreme Assembly
alpinistskiy lager – see *alplager*
alplager – mountaineer's camp (R) (also *alpinistsky lager*)
apparatchik – bureaucrat
arenda – literally 'lease' or 'rent', referring usually to buses or other vehicles which make a trip only if there are enough passengers (R)
ASSR – Autonomous Soviet Socialist Republic (R)
Aul Kazak – Kazak nomadic encampment
avtobiket – bus station (T)
avtobus – bus (R)
avtostantsia – bus stop or bus stand (R)
ayanty – public square (Kyrgyz)
ayollar hammomi – women's baths (Uzbek)
azan – the call to prayer; roughly translates as 'God most great. There is no God but Allah. Muhammad is God's messenger. Come to prayer, come to security. God is most great'. (A)

banya – public bath (R)
basmachi – literally 'bandits', the Russian term for Muslim guerilla fighters who resisted the Bolshevik takeover in Central Asia (R)
bazar – open market (R)
bifshteks – ground beefsteak (R)
biznesmen – businessmen (R)
biznes tsentr – business centre (R)

bolshoy rynok – 'big-farmer's market' (R)
bolnitza – hospital (R)
bufet – snack bar selling cheap cold meats, boiled eggs, salads, breads, pastries etc (R)
bulvar – boulevard (R)
buzkashi – traditional polo-like game played with a headless goat carcass rather than a ball (also *kökpar, kozlodranie*)
byuro puteshestviy i exkursiy – excursion bureau

caravanserai – a travellers' inn
chaban – cowboy (Kyrgyz, Kazak)
chay – tea
chaykhana (Kyrgyz) – tea-house; has various transliterations, eg chaykhana in Turkmen, choyhona in Uzbek and Tajik, shaykhana in Kazak
CIS – Commonwealth of Independent States, the loose political and economic alliance of most former member republics of the USSR (except the Baltic states); sometimes called NIS, for newly independent states
chowkidar – caretaker (Urdu)
chorsu – market arcade (T)
choy (Uzbek & Tajik) – see *chay*
choyhona – see *chaykhana*

dacha – a holiday bungalow, usually in the countryside just outside a town
dangghyly – avenue (Kazak)
darvish – a Sufi ascetic
darya – river (T)
dezhurnaya – 'floor-lady', the woman attendant on duty on each floor of a Soviet-era or Soviet-style state hotel; it literally means 'on duty' (R)
dom – building (R)
dom otdykha – rest home (R)
dopy (doppe) – black, four-sided skullcap embroidered in white and worn by Uzbek men (Uzbek)
drevniy gorod – ancient city (R)
duban – province or oblast (Kyrgyz)

erkakli hammomi – men's baths (Uzbek)

GAI – traffic police (R)
gastronom – speciality food shop (R)
ghanch – carved and painted plaster (T)
glasnost – literally 'openness'; the free expression aspect of the Gorbachev reforms (R)
glavpochtamt – main post office (R)
gorod – town (R)
gosposhlina – state transport duty tax
gosudarstvenny pvirodny park – national park
Great Game – the geopolitical 'Cold War' of territorial expansion between the Russian and British empires in the 19th and early 20th centurie in Central Asia
gril-bar – grill bar serving roast chicken and other meats (R)
guligans – hooligans (R)
gulyash – goulash (R)
GUM – gosudarstvennyy universalnyy magazine or state department store

Hadith – collected acts and sayings of the Prophet Muhammad
Hajj – the pilgrimage to Mecca, one of the 'five pillars of Islam' (to be made at least once during one's lifetime by devout Muslims) (A)
hammomi – baths
hammomi kunjak – common baths (Uzbek)
hammomi numur – private bath (Uzbek)
hanako – (Uzbek) see *khanaka*
hauz – an artificial pool (T)
hazrat – honorific title meaning 'majesty' or 'holy' (A)
Hegira – flight of Muhammad and his followers to Medina in 622 AD (A)
hiyoboni – a boulevard (Uzbek)
hokimyat – mayor's office (Uzbek)

IRP – Islamic Renaissance Party, a grouping of radical activists dedicated to the formation of Islamic rule in Central Asia
Ismaili – a branch of Shia Islam
izor – striped trousers worn underneath kurta

jailoo – summer pastures (Kyrgyz)

Jami mosque – a large (congregational) mosque
jeiran – Persian gazelle
Juma mosque – a mosque for Friday prayers

kalon – great (Tajik)
kassa – cashier or box office (R)
kesh-kumay – traditional game in which a man chases a woman on horseback and tries to kiss her, or gets chased and whipped if he fails (Kyrgyz)
khanaka – a Sufi contemplation hall and hostel for wandering ascetics; the room of an Eshon (Sufi leader) in which he and other Sufis perform their *zikr*
kino, kinoteatr – cinema (R)
kiosk economy – small-time dealers buying goods and reselling them at a higher price
köchösü – street (Kyrgyz)
kökpar – see *buzkashi*
kolkhoz – collective farm (R)
kommerchesky – private enterprise
komnaty otdykha – rest rooms (R)
kontrolno propusknoy punkt – permit station (R)
kösheshi – street (Kazak, Karakalpak)
koshma – multicoloured felt mats (Kazak)
kozlodranie – see *buzkashi*
kupeynyy – 2nd class or sleeping carriage on trains (R)
kurta – long, coloured dress worn by Tajik women
krytyy rynok – covered market (R)
kuchasi – street (Uzbek)

laghman – Central Asian noodles or noodle dish

mahalla – an urban neighbourhood (Uzbek)
majolica – earthenware tiles with baked enamel finish
manty – small stuffed dumplings (T)
markaz – centre (T)
marshrutnoe – marshrut is Russian for 'route'; a marshrutnoe taxi is a small bus or van that follows a fixed route but stops on demand to take on or let off passengers, with fares depending on distance travelled; a *marshrutnyy avtobus* is a larger bus that does

the same; a short term for either one is *marshrutka*

maydoni – public square (Uzbek)

medressa – an Islamic academy or seminary (A)

mikrorayon – micro region (R)

militsia – police (Russian and all Central Asian languages)

muezzin – the man who calls the Muslim faithful to prayer (A)

mufti – Islamic spiritual leader

mullah – an Islamic cleric

Naqshband – the most influential of many Sufi secret associations in central Asia

Nauroz – (Urdu) see *Navrus*

Nauryz – (Kazak) see *Navrus*

Navrus – 'New Days', the main Islamic spring festival; has various regional transliterations

Norruz – (Kyrgyz) see *Navrus*

Novruz – (Turkmen) see *Navrus*

oblast – province or region (R)

oblys – province or region (Kazak)

otdel exkursii – excursion office

OVIR – Otdel Vis I Registratsii, Office of Visas & Regulations (R)

panjara – a trellis of wood, stone or ghanch (T)

paranjeh, paranji – the practice of veiling Muslim women

perestroyka – literally 'restructuring'; Gorbachev's efforts to revive the economy

petrol hookers – roadside fuel dealers who buy fuel in Russian and undersell local distribution outlets

pishtak – entrance portals

platskartnyy – hard sleeper

ploshchad – square (R)

plov, pulau – a rice dish with meat, carrots or other additions (traditionally prepared by men for special celebrations)

pochta – post office (R)

pochta bulima – main post office (Uzbek)

propusk – permit (R)

prospekt – avenue (R, T)

provodnik (m), provodnitsa (f) – attendant on long-distance train

qala – fortress (Uzbek)

qyz-quu – (Kazak) see *kesh-kumay*

Quran or Koran – Islam's holiest book, the collected revelations of God to the Prophet Muhammad

remont – repair service, or under repair (R)

rumol – head scarf worn with kurta

rynok – market

salam aleykhum – traditional Muslim greeting, meaning 'peace be with you'.

samovar – urn used for heating water for tea, often found on trains

savdo dukoni – commercial shops

sharq – east (Tajik)

shashlyk – meat roasted on skewers over hot coals

shay – (Kazak) see *chay*

Shia or Shi'ite – one of the two main branches of Islam

shishbesh – game like backgammon (Tajik)

shosse – highway (R)

shyrdak – felt rug with coloured panels sewn on (Kyrgyz)

skibaza – ski base (R)

skotovod – see *chaban*

sozanda – folk music sung by women accompanied by percussion instruments such as tablas, bells and castanets

SSR – Soviet Socialist Republic

stolovaya – canteen/cafeteria (R)

Sufi – the mystical tradition in Islam

suzani, suzana or suzane – bright Uzbek silk embroidery on cotton cloth (Uzbek)

talon – coupon (R)

tebbetey – round fur-trimmed hat worn by Kyrgyz men

telpek – sheepskin hat worn by Turkmen males

tim – an arcade, eg in a market (T)

Transoxiana – a historical term for the region between the Amu-Darya and Syr-Darya rivers

TsUM – Tsentralnyy universalnyy magazin or central department store

turbaza (turistskaya baza) – holiday camp typically with spartan cabins, plain food, sports, video hall and bar; usually only open in summer (R)

ulak-tartysh – (Kyrgyz) see *buzkashi*
ulama – class of religious scholars or intellectuals (A)
ulitsa – street (R)
univermag – universalnyy magazin or department store (R)

viloyat – province (Uzbek)

ylag oyyny – see *buzkashi*
yurt – the traditional nomadic 'house', a collapsible cylindrical wood framework covered with felt (T)

zakat – obligatory alms tax, one of the Five Pillars of Islam (A)
zakaznik – nature reserve
zakuski – appetisers (R)
zapovednik – nature reserve (R)
zikr – recitation or contemplation of the names of God, recitation of sacred writings, one part of traditional Sufi practice (A)

Index

Acknowledgements

John King I once imagined I could write a book about Central Asia without much help. This project has brought me down to earth hard, and I am heavily indebted to many people for keeping it together, saving my neck, and in the end considerably raising the calibre of the book.

My greatest thanks go to my first-rate co-authors, John Noble and Andrew Humphreys, for their work in some of the more trying corners of Asia. Andrew made it look easy in Turkmenistan and Tajikistan, although it certainly wasn't. John surveyed some of the region's bleakest scenes, did extra research in Moscow, and got me out of trouble more than once with his keen reviewer's eye.

We in turn are indebted to several people who helped us write the introductory sections and, thanks to their own expertise and enthusiasm, did it better than we could have. Dan Prior, renegade Manas-head and author-publisher of his own guidebook to Bishkek (where he lives), wrote the History, Geography, People & Population, and Flora & Fauna sections, and the Manas aside in the Kyrgyzstan chapter. Thanks also to him for Bishkek tips and an amazing day of ibex-watching in the Kyrgyz Alatau, and to him and Laurie for hospitality and continuing friendship.

Serge Oumow wrote much of the wide-ranging Environment section, researched by him and Shivaun Scanlan in the course of volunteer work in Kyrgyzstan. Serge and Shivaun also provided good company, translation help and space in their Bishkek flat. Chefs Glenn Mack and Asele Surina turned their professional eye to Central Asian cuisine in the Food section. (Glenn knows what he is talking about, having cooked in restaurant kitchens in Tashkent.) Bruno de Cordier ably drafted the Government, Economy and Education sections.

Professor Philip Micklin was generous with expert information and comments for the section on the Aral Sea. John Glenn, graduate student in international politics, shared experiences and excellent notes from his Central Asia research and travels. Thanks to John Stonham of USAID in Almaty for sharing all he knows about that city.

Visually this book owes much to the beautiful woodcuts of the Manas legend cycle by Bishkek artist Theodor Herzen – one on the title page and one on pages 357.

For their incredible patience in the face of my repeated failures to deliver anything on time, and for forging everything into a handsome book, I am extremely grateful to our co-conspirators in Melbourne – senior editor Jane Fitzpatrick, book editors Katie Cody, Anne Mulvaney, Rowan McKinnon and Brigitte Barta, and designers and cartographors Tamsin Wilson, Ann Jeffree, Jacqui Saunders, Chris Love, Anthony Phelan and Matt King. Sally Steward and Nicola Daly created the fine Language section,

and Katie Cody prepared the Climate section. Thanks also to the industrious folks in the readers letters department, who kept us snowed under with readers' feedback. For timely research on US airfares and travel agencies, thanks to Greg Mills and Ann Neet of LP's Oakland office.

On the road I was helped at every turn by people with no other motive than generosity, and several of them are now friends too. Victor Tsoy provided information, encouragement and insight into life in Tashkent; thanks also to him, Irina, Marina and Yura for making me feel like a member of the family. Valentin, Galina and Yulia Derevyanko, and grandma Lena, offered extraordinary help and hospitality in Karakol, and named their pet yak after me. *Qatta rakhmat* to Egitaly Usmanov, Assistant Manager of Ferghana Valley Uzbektourism, poet, cook, host and unofficial ambassador of Uzbek culture. My best to Jay Cooper of Counterpart Consortium in Bishkek, and to Lena and Ilona, for happy travels and evenings at home. And for showing me Uzbek hospitality in its purest form, thanks to Kadirjon Mirzaboboev of Arslanbob.

I am also indebted to many Peace Corps volunteers for hospitality and enthusiastic help – especially to Jack Hillmeyer for good times in Naryn and information on his travels. Thanks to Mark Hannafin for photos, and to him and Ken Peavler, Larry Held, Thomas Fricke, Michelle Haugh, Andrea Steege and Megan Castle for help and hospitality.

The big-hearted crew at Center Interbilim in Bishkek – Asiya Sasykbaeva, Almash Naizabekova, Elmira Temirbekova and Emil Sultanbaev – always had ready smiles and the answers to a thousand questions; thanks also to Aygul Usubalieva for Kyrgyz language help. Others who extended true Central Asian hospitality were John and Fiona Addleton in Almaty, Davlat and Bahadur Negmadjanov in Samarkand (and thanks to Davlat for Tajik language help), and Mubinjon Tadjiev in Bukhara. Gairat Sharahmatov cheerfully showed me Tashkent's lesser-known attractions, and provided Uzbek language help. Thanks to Talant Samsaliev and his sturdy van for explorations between Bishkek and the Torugart pass, and to Zulifiya Tursun for hiding money at a strategic moment and for help in Ürümqi.

Consular folks who came to my aid include Shawn Dorman, vice-consul at the US Embassy in Bishkek (for many travel tips and, with Shawn MacKenzie, good hospitality), Martha Patterson and Zarrina Muhammadieva at the US Embassy in Dushanbe (for Tajik language help), and George Kent, vice-consul at the US Embassy in Tashkent. Cheers also to Dan O'Grady, Uzbekistan desk officer at the State Department in Washington.

I am very grateful to Scott Wayne and the World Tourism Organisation in Madrid, and to Uzbektourism in Tashkent, for their generous invitation to a conference on Silk Road tourism in 1994, and to the

WTO's Deborah Luhrmann for her able and unsung work keeping all of us happy.

Several people in the region's much-maligned state tourism offices rose above the call of duty, including Lilian Palatkina, Director of Tours & Excursions at Tashkent's Hotel Uzbekistan; Noila Kozijonova of Uzbektourism in Bukhara; Raisana Ainikenova, Akyen Boshkoyeva and Upel Jyrgalbekova at Kyrgyzintourist in Bishkek; and Xu Ling and Akbar Abdirahman of the Kashgar Mountaineering Association. Mr Zang Bing is head and shoulders above the rest at CITS in Ürümqi. Thanks to Akbar Jigitov, Director of the Kyrgyz State Committee of Tourism and Sport, and to the Committee's much-needed consultant, Max Haberstroh.

Staff at private agencies who bent over backwards for me include Rahul Brijnath and Nick Lunt at Steppes East in Swindon (UK), Mark Lawrence of Intourist Travel in London, Igor Salikhov and Ines Adalova of Asia Travel International in Samarkand, Dr Zhenya Krylova of Sayokh Extrem in Tashkent and Raisa Gareyeva of Salom in Bukhara.

Thanks also to Yuri Morgachev of the Karakol Tourism Association for his enthuiasm; to Darika Jusaeva at MFM in Karakol for translations; to Jumakan Mambetova, director of the Karakol regional museum, for help with documents on Nikolai Przhevalsky; to Stuart Christy of Arguments & Facts International for his *Atlas of Russia & the Post-Soviet Republics*; to James Strachan and Georgina Crofton for a fine picture show; to David St Vincent for Iran information; to Lorel Donaghey of Counterpart Consortium in Tashkent for her networking skills; and to Nick Selby for Getting Around information.

Finally, and most importantly, love and gratitude to two people who didn't see enough of me during this project – my wife Julia and son Kit.

John Noble I received so much enthusiastic help from so many people for my portions of this book that it's impossible to thank everyone adequately. Above all, thankyou to Jonathan Addleton for extremely generous hospitality and unstinting help with information and communications; to John Stonham for a warm welcome in Almaty and major help with information on that city, the Kazak language and Kazak carpets; to the US Peace Corps in Kazakstan for their enthusiastic help in so many ways – especially to Paul Burnore and David Buchanan for responding so keenly to my initial approaches, and to Chris Chatterton, Steven Ibelli and Jack Davis for hospitality and help in their cities, but also to Joel Benjamin, Phillip Chabot, Tracy Chambers, Davia, Jennifer David, Nanette Ellen, Douglas Francomano, Erik Giles, Keri Harrington, Marge Hatheway, Laura Johnson, John Manning, Michelle Ostrander, Joe Perry, John Silver, Liz Solly, Marla Swanson, John Thiele, Renee Vendetti, Carl Wagner and Eric White; and to Uzbektourism and to Scott Wayne and Deborah

Luhrman of the World Tourism Organisation for providing me with a wonderful introduction to Uzbekistan.

Thanks also go to Marat Bigaliev, Zhanat Suleymenov and co for their help in Semey; Alan Johnston for hospitality and access to his bookshelves; Professor Philip Micklin for generous help with Aral Sea info; to Michael Kliks and co for a great meal, videos and more; to Yegor and Alex (not their real names) for making Leninsk a friendlier place; to Dan Prior and John Glenn for invaluable historical and cultural information; to Uzbektourism in Nukus for their enthusiastic help; and to Fiona Addleton, Richard Andrews, Dr Goulhara Beekmukhamedova of the BBC, David Brian, Susan Forsyth, Ford Hart, Steve Lopez, Karlygash Makatova, Kevin McCabe, Jacek Micuta (for translations from Polish), Jan Passoff, Colin Richardson, Martin Taylor of the Kazakstan-UK Centre, Kazbek Valiev, and Nikolai Vernyaev for help in Shymkent; to all readers of *USSR* who wrote in with Central Asia tips; to the production team in Melbourne, and to Lonely Planet's London office for passing on yet more faxes; to Andrew Humphreys, again an impeccable co-author; and, far from least, to John King for his patience and being once again great to work with.

Andrew Humphreys Many thanks to Jim Pitts whose spare bed and beer created a welcome place of refuge in Ashghabat, and to other Central Asian Peace Corps volunteers, particularly Lowell Lander (Ashghabat), Irving Jones (Qarshi) and Dan Lamken (Charjou). Thanks to US Embassy staffer Lewis Elbinger whose intervention prevented me from being ejected from Turkmenistan before I'd even begun, and to Vladimir Volovik for filling me in on the bits that remained out of bounds. At the US Embassy I'm indebted to Martha Patterson, not least for the string of good and generous people she led me on to, including IRC's Rob Andrew and Whitney Stein of Save the Children. Back in England I was grateful for the input of Brian Aldiss and Yusef Azemoun. Most of all, my love and gratitude goes to Gädi Farfour, who was with me all the time.

More Thanks

It's clear from the preceding acknowledgements that we owe a special debt to a broad network of US Peace Corps volunteers across Central Asia. They are in many ways the perfect information source: enthusiastic, usually fond of their temporary homes, integrated into local life, speaking the language, and happy to offer a shot of Western-style hospitality along with abundant 'inside' information and advice. In fact this book's information on several cities in Kazakstan is based largely on data provided by 'PCVs', and Lonely Planet especially thanks the Peace Corps in Kazakstan for its enthusiastic help.

We also received an amazing amount of helpful

mail from fellow travellers. Tim Clairs (Australia) distinguished himself with excellent, Lonely Planet-quality notes. Others who made valuable contributions are:

Jens Baier (Germany), Zia Ullah Baig (Pakistan), Roger Beaud (Switzerland), Paul Bello (USA), Christy Bennett (USA), Geoff Bennett (UK), Marc Berman (USA), Elizabeth Blentzer (UK), David Bowers (Australia), Lyn Bowers (Australia), David Brian (Hong Kong), Georgina Brown (UK), Michel & Yasmine Cerutti (Switzerland), Juliet Chamberlin (UK), John & Kim Chesarek (USA), Geoff Cox (UK), Elsa Dalmasso (UK), James Doscher (USA), Karen Eberle (USA), Maud Ejdeholt (Sweden), Mark Elliot (USA), Rosemary Faulkner (USA), Ferdinand Fellinger (Austria), Pierre Flener (Luxemburg), Katrin Flohrs (Germany), Piotr Gaszynski (Poland), Paul Geldhof (Belgium), Mary Gijsen (Oman), Kate Glover (Australia), Liam Guilar (Australia), Robert Hanes (USA), Rob Harper (UK), Jane Hepburn (UK), Jonathan Hibbs (UK), Peter Holdforth (UK), Margaret Jepson (UK), Wil Klass (USA), Robert Kleinberg (USA), Agnieszka Kottonik (Poland), Kathleen Kuehnast (USA), Paul Lamarque (France), Piet Lambregts (Oman), John Mackle (UK), Calum Macleod (Hong Kong), N H K Mallet (UK), Anna Maspero (Italy), Kevin McCabe (Netherlands), Andrew McDonald (Australia), Philip McGurk (UK), Bernie Mendes (USA), Henriette Meyer (Germany), Claus Michelfelder (Germany), Steve Miles (UK), Tara Miller (UAE), Dennis Moors (Belgium), Ana Mulder (Netherlands), Carolyn Orcutt (USA), Andy & Sue Parrott (UK), Edward Pearson (UK), Dale Peers (UK), Michael & Oliver Power (UK), Marion Rimmer (Australia), Simon Robins (UK), Jean Robinson (UK), Jean Robinson (UK), Sebastian Roques (France), Gideon Rosenbaum (Israel), Adam Sebire (Australia), Howard Sethin (UK), John & Rita Sevcik (USA), Daphne Smith (UK), Peter Spurrier (UK), Mark Stachiew (Canada), John Steedman (UK), Frank Techel (Switzerland), Wim van Ginkel (Netherlands), Els van Kuijk (Netherlands), David Vanes (UK), George von der Muhll (USA), Hilary Walker (Australia) and Gérard Zaadzki (France).

We learned much from, and about, the Internet too. Among helpful Internet correspondents were John Clark (USA) for our story about Hoja Nasruddin, and William Dirks (USA), Marianne Ruth Kamp (USA), Jean-Louis Peyle (France), John Schoeberlein-Engel (USA), David Tyson (USA) and Russel Zanca (USA).

LONELY PLANET JOURNEYS

JOURNEYS is a unique collection of travellers' tales – published by the company that understands travel better than anyone else. It is a series for anyone who has ever experienced – or dreamed of – the magical moment when they encountered a strange culture or saw a place for the first time. They are tales to read while you're planning a trip, while you're on the road or while you're in an armchair, in front of a fire.

JOURNEYS books will catch the spirit of a place, illuminate a culture, recount a crazy adventure, or introduce a fascinating way of life. They will always entertain, and always enrich the experience of travel.

ISLANDS IN THE CLOUDS
Travels in the Highlands of New Guinea
Isabella Tree

This is the fascinating account of a journey to the remote and beautiful Highlands of Papua New Guinea and Irian Jaya. The author travels with a PNG Highlander who introduces her to his intriguing and complex world. *Islands in the Clouds* is a thoughtful, moving book, full of insights into a region that is rarely noticed by the rest of the world.

'One of the most accomplished travel writers to appear on the horizon for many years . . . the dialogue is brilliant' – Eric Newby

LOST JAPAN
Alex Kerr

Lost Japan draws on the author's personal experiences of Japan over a period of 30 years. Alex Kerr takes his readers on a backstage tour: friendships with Kabuki actors, buying and selling art, studying calligraphy, exploring rarely visited temples and shrines . . . The Japanese edition of this book was awarded the 1994 Shincho Gakugei Literature Prize for the best work of non-fiction.

'This deeply personal witness to Japan's wilful loss of its traditional culture is at the same time an immensely valuable evaluation of just what that culture was'
– Donald Richie of the Japan Times

THE GATES OF DAMASCUS
Lieve Joris
Translated by Sam Garrett

This best-selling book is a beautifully drawn portrait of day-to-day life in modern Syria. Through her intimate contact with local people, Lieve Joris draws us into the fascinating world that lies behind the gates of Damascus.

'A brilliant book . . . Not since Naguib Mahfouz has the everyday life of the modern Arab world been so intimately described' – William Dalrymple

SEAN & DAVID'S LONG DRIVE
Sean Condon

Sean and David are young townies who have rarely strayed beyond city limits. One day, for no good reason, they set out to discover their homeland, and what follows is a wildly entertaining adventure that covers half of Australia. Sean Condon has written a hilarious, offbeat road book that mixes sharp insights with deadpan humour and outright lies.

'Funny, pithy, kitsch and surreal . . . This book will do for Australia what Chernobyl did for Kiev, but hey you'll laugh as the stereotypes go boom' – Andrew Tuck, Time Out

PLANET TALK

Lonely Planet's FREE quarterly newsletter

We love hearing from you and think you'd like to hear from us.

When...is the right time to see reindeer in Finland?
Where...can you hear the best palm-wine music in Ghana?
How...do you get from Asunción to Areguá by steam train?
What...is the best way to see India?

For the answer to these and many other questions read PLANET TALK.

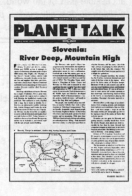

Every issue is packed with up-to-date travel news and advice including:

* a letter from Lonely Planet co-founders Tony and Maureen Wheeler
* go behind the scenes on the road with a Lonely Planet author
* feature article on an important and topical travel issue
* a selection of recent letters from travellers
* details on forthcoming Lonely Planet promotions
* complete list of Lonely Planet products

To join our mailing list contact any Lonely Planet office.

Also available: Lonely Planet T-shirts. 100% heavyweight cotton..

LONELY PLANET ONLINE

Get the latest travel information before you leave or while you're on the road

Whether you've just begun planning your next trip, or you're chasing down specific info on currency regulations or visa requirements, check out the Lonely Planet World Wide Web site for up-to-the-minute travel information.

As well as travel profiles of your favourite destinations (including interactive maps and full-colour photos), you'll find current reports from our army of researchers and other travellers, updates on health and visas, travel advisories, and the ecological and political issues you need to be aware of as you travel.

There's an online travellers' forum (the Thorn Tree) where you can share your experiences of life on the road, meet travel companions and ask other travellers for their recommendations and advice. We also have plenty of links to other Web sites useful to independent travellers.

With tens of thousands of visitors a month, the Lonely Planet Web site is one of the most popular on the Internet and has won a number of awards including GNN's Best of the Net travel award.

http://www.lonelyplanet.com

LONELY PLANET PRODUCTS

Lonely Planet is known worldwide for publishing practical, reliable and no-nonsense travel information in our guides and on our web site. The Lonely Planet list covers just about every accessible part of the world. Currently there are eight series: *travel guides*, *shoestring guides*, *walking guides*, *city guides*, *phrasebooks*, *audio packs*, *travel atlases* and *Journeys* – a unique collection of travellers' tales.

EUROPE

Austria • Baltic States & Kaliningrad • Baltic States phrasebook • Britain • Central Europe on a shoestring • Central Europe phrasebook • Czech & Slovak Republics • Dublin city guide • Eastern Europe on a shoestring • Eastern Europe phrasebook • Finland • France • Greece • Greek phrasebook • Hungary • Iceland, Greenland & the Faroe Islands • Ireland • Italy • Mediterranean Europe on a shoestring • Mediterranean Europe phrasebook • Poland • Prague city guide • Russia, Ukraine & Belarus • Russian phrasebook • Scandinavian & Baltic Europe on a shoestring • Scandinavian Europe phrasebook • Slovenia • St Petersburg city guide • Switzerland • Trekking in Greece • Trekking in Spain • Vienna city guide • Walking in Switzerland • Western Europe on a shoestring • Western Europe phrasebook

NORTH AMERICA & MEXICO

Alaska • Backpacking in Alaska • California & Nevada • Canada • Hawaii • Honolulu city guide • Los Angeles city guide • Pacific Northwest USA • Rocky Mountain States • San Francisco city guide • Southwest USA • USA phrasebook

CENTRAL AMERICA & THE CARIBBEAN

Baja California • Central America on a shoestring • Costa Rica • Eastern Caribbean • Guatemala, Belize & Yucatán: La Ruta Maya • Mexico

SOUTH AMERICA

Argentina, Uruguay & Paraguay • Bolivia • Brazil • Brazilian phrasebook • Buenos Aires city guide • Chile & Easter Island • Colombia • Ecuador & the Galápagos Islands • Latin American Spanish phrasebook • Peru • Quechua phrasebook • Rio de Janeiro city guide • South America on a shoestring • Trekking in the Patagonian Andes • Venezuela

ALSO AVAILABLE:

Travel with Children • Traveller's Tales

AFRICA

Arabic (Moroccan) phrasebook • Africa on a shoestring • Cape Town city guide • Central Africa • East Africa • Egypt & the Sudan • Ethiopian (Amharic) phrasebook • Kenya • Morocco • North Africa • South Africa, Lesotho & Swaziland • Swahili phrasebook • Trekking in East Africa • West Africa • Zimbabwe, Botswana & Namibia • Zimbabwe, Botswana & Namibia travel atlas

MAIL ORDER

Lonely Planet products are distributed worldwide. They are also available by mail order from Lonely Planet, so if you have difficulty finding a title please write to us. North American and South American residents should write to Embarcadero West, 155 Filbert St, Suite 251, Oakland CA 94607, USA; European and African residents should write to 10 Barley Mow Passage, Chiswick, London W4 4PH; and residents of other countries to PO Box 617, Hawthorn, Victoria 3122, Australia.

NORTH-EAST ASIA

Beijing city guide • Cantonese phrasebook • China • Hong Kong, Macau & Canton • Japan • Japanese phrasebook • Japanese audio pack • Korea • Korean phrasebook • Mandarin phrasebook • Mongolia • Mongolian phrasebook • North-East Asia on a shoestring • Seoul city guide • Taiwan • Tibet • Tibet phrasebook • Tokyo city guide

Travel Literature: Lost Japan

INDIAN SUBCONTINENT

Bengali phrasebook • Bangladesh • Delhi city guide • Hindi/Urdu phrasebook • India • India & Bangladesh travel atlas • Karakoram Highway • Kashmir, Ladakh & Zanskar • Nepal • Nepali phrasebook • Pakistan • Sri Lanka • Sri Lanka phrasebook • Trekking in the Indian Himalaya • Trekking in the Nepal Himalaya

SOUTH-EAST ASIA

Bali & Lombok • Bangkok city guide • Burmese phrasebook • Cambodia • Ho Chi Minh city guide • Indonesia • Indonesian phrasebook • Indonesian audio pack • Jakarta city guide • Java • Laos • Lao phrasebook • Malaysia, Singapore & Brunei • Myanmar (Burma) • Philippines • Pilipino phrasebook • Singapore city guide • South-East Asia on a shoestring • Thailand • Thailand travel atlas • Thai phrasebook • Thai audio pack • Thai Hill Tribes phrasebook • Vietnam • Vietnamese phrasebook • Vietnam travel atlas

AUSTRALIA & THE PACIFIC

Australia • Australian phrasebook • Bushwalking in Australia• Bushwalking in Papua New Guinea • Fiji • Fijian phrasebook • Islands of Australia's Great Barrier Reef • Melbourne city guide • Micronesia • New Caledonia • New South Wales & the ACT • New Zealand • Outback Australia • Papua New Guinea • Papua New Guinea phrasebook • Queensland • Rarotonga & the Cook Islands • Samoa • Solomon Islands • Sydney city guide • Tahiti & French Polynesia • Tonga • Tramping in New Zealand • Vanuatu • Victoria • Western Australia

Travel Literature: Islands in the Clouds • Sean & David's Long Drive

MIDDLE EAST & CENTRAL ASIA

Arab Gulf States • Arabic (Egyptian) phrasebook • Central Asia • Iran • Israel • Jordan & Syria • Middle East • Turkey • Turkish phrasebook • Trekking in Turkey • Yemen

Travel Literature: The Gates of Damascus

ISLANDS OF THE INDIAN OCEAN

Madagascar & Comoros • Maldives & Islands of the East Indian Ocean • Mauritius, Réunion & Seychelles

THE LONELY PLANET STORY

Lonely Planet published its first book in 1973 in response to the numerous 'How did you do it?' questions Maureen and Tony Wheeler were asked after driving, bussing, hitching, sailing and railing their way from England to Australia.

Written at a kitchen table and hand collated, trimmed and stapled, *Across Asia on the Cheap* became an instant local bestseller, inspiring thoughts of another book.

Eighteen months in South-East Asia resulted in their second guide, *South-East Asia on a shoestring*, which they put together in a backstreet Chinese hotel in Singapore in 1975. The 'yellow bible', as it quickly became known to backpackers around the world, soon became *the* guide to the region. It has sold well over half a million copies and is now in its 8th edition, still retaining its familiar yellow cover.

Today there are over 180 titles, including travel guides, walking guides, language kits & phrasebooks, travel atlases and travel literature. The company is one of the largest travel publishers in the world. Although Lonely Planet initially specialised in guides to Asia, we now cover most regions of the world, including the Pacific, North America, South America, Africa, the Middle East and Europe.

The emphasis continues to be on travel for independent travellers. Tony and Maureen still travel for several months of each year and play an active part in the writing, updating and quality control of Lonely Planet's guides.

They have been joined by over 70 authors and 170 staff at our offices in Melbourne (Australia), Oakland (USA), London (UK) and Paris (France). Travellers themselves also make a valuable contribution to the guides through the feedback we receive in thousands of letters each year.

The people at Lonely Planet strongly believe that travellers can make a positive contribution to the countries they visit, both through their appreciation of the countries' culture, wildlife and natural features, and through the money they spend. In addition, the company makes a direct contribution to the countries and regions it covers. Since 1986 a percentage of the income from each book has been donated to ventures such as famine relief in Africa; aid projects in India; agricultural projects in Central America; Greenpeace's efforts to halt French nuclear testing in the Pacific; and Amnesty International.

Lonely Planet's basic travel philosophy is summed up in Tony Wheeler's comment, 'Don't worry about whether your trip will work out. Just go!'

LONELY PLANET PUBLICATIONS

Australia
PO Box 617, Hawthorn 3122, Victoria
tel: (03) 9819 1877 fax: (03) 9819 6459
e-mail: talk2us@lonelyplanet.com.au

USA
Embarcadero West, 155 Filbert St, Suite 251,
Oakland, CA 94607
tel: (510) 893 8555 TOLL FREE: 800 275-8555
fax: (510) 893 8563
e-mail: info@lonelyplanet.com

UK
10 Barley Mow Passage, Chiswick,
London W4 4PH
tel: (0181) 742 3161 fax: (0181) 742 2772
e-mail: 100413.3551@compuserve.com

France:
71 bis rue du Cardinal Lemoine, 75005 Paris
tel: 1 44 32 06 20 fax: 1 46 34 72 55
e-mail: 100560.415@compuserve.com

World Wide Web: http://www.lonelyplanet.com